CALENDAR OF KENT COUNTY DELAWARE PROBATE RECORDS
1680 - 1800

Compiled by
Leon deValinger, Jr.
State Archivist

Southern Historical Press, Inc.
Greenville, South Carolina

This volume was reproduced from
An 1944 edition located in the
Publisher's private Library
Greenville, South Carolina

All rights reserved. No part of this publication may be reproduced,
stored in a retrieval system, transmitted in any form, posted
on to the web in any form or by any means without
the prior written permission of the publisher.

Please direct all correspondence and orders to:

www.southernhistoricalpress.com
or
SOUTHERN HISTORICAL PRESS, Inc.
PO BOX 1267
375 West Broad Street
Greenville, SC   29601
southernhistoricalpress@gmail.com

Originally published: Dover, Delaware, 1944
Copyright 1944
ISBN #0-89308-309-7
All rights Reserved.
Printed in the United States of America

PREFACE

Those seeking social, economic, or genealogical data of Kent County will not find a richer source than its probate records. Knowing that the territory within the confines of the State of Delaware was ruled by the Swedes 1638-1655, the Dutch 1655-1664, the Duke of York 1664-1682, and the Penn Proprietors 1682-1776, one naturally questions why this volume begins with 1680 rather than an earlier date of the Swedish or Dutch regimes. The Swedish and Dutch settlers were subject to practically the same laws that were in effect in the homeland. In accordance with the legal procedure of that time wills could be made orally or in writing. In either case the will was made before a notary or some similar public judicial officer. As public recording of the wills was not required the notaries retained among their own papers the few wills that were made with the result that these records have since become scattered or lost. With the acquisition of the Delaware territory by the Duke of York the system did not change noticeably because the laws governing this territory were not published until 1676. There were still no probate records of this county as it was not separated from the jurisdiction of the Whorekill Court and created as St. Jones County until 1680. With the establishment of a separate county public records were ordered kept with the result that recorded probate records begin at this time. The transition from the government of the Duke of York to William Penn in 1682 brought a change of name from St. Jones to Kent County and better laws and regulations for recording probate records.

It should be borne in mind that the volume is a calendar and does not attempt to give a complete abstract of the wills and administration accounts. The calendar was selected as the form for publishing this material as it serves as a guide to the records available and supplies most of the information generally requested. It is recognized that a complete abstract would have enhanced the value of this work but it would also have curtailed considerably the period of years that could have been included within the scope of this volume.

All of the original probate records in the Hall of Records have been compared with the recorded copies in the Kent County Court House in an effort to obtain as complete and accurate a record as possible. When both the original record and the recorded copy are extant the Register of Wills liber and folio are cited as well as the Archives volume and page on which the original document is mounted.

All of the probate records are arranged in chronological order by the probate date of the wills and by the date of granting letters of administration in the case of intestate estates. By this means a fairly accurate estimate may be obtained of the death date of each decedent. In the absence of the date of probate or granting letters of administration, the date when the will was made or the settlement date of the administration account is used.

Only in proper names has the orthography been preserved. When more than one spelling of a name occurs, as it frequently does, or when an interpretation has been supplied the alternate spelling and the added information appears in brackets.

It should be remembered that the Gregorian Calendar was not adopted in Delaware and the other English colonies in America until 1752. Under the old Augustine Calendar the year began on March 25th and December was the tenth rather than the twelfth month. Thus a date appearing in the text as 1682/83 will indicate that the year 1682 is nearly terminated and that 1683 is approaching. Furthermore, the difference between the Augustine and Gregorian Calendars will explain why some probate records would appear to be probated before they were made. Dates recorded in the Quaker method of dating have been transposed to conform with either the Augustine or the Gregorian Calendars. For example, 12th of 10th month 1682 has been changed to December 12, 1682 according to the Augustine or Old Style Calendar.

Even more confusing to research workers than the calendar changes are the relationships contained in some of these early probate records. Frequently, step-father or step-mother is intended when the record states father-in-law or mother-in-law. In other instances the step-parents will be designated as father or mother. There are also instances when the word cousin is used instead of nephew and niece. The compiler has not attempted to interpret such inconsistencies but has presented them as they appear in the document.

The word "copy" in parentheses following the word "Will" indicates that the document in the files at the Hall of Records is not the original record. The original document being missing the hiatus has been filled with a contemporary manuscript, typed, or photostat copy. Unless thus indicated the probate record in the custody of the Public Archives Commission is the original document.

There are some wills in which the foreign residence of the testator causes the reader to wonder why such a probate record was included with those of Kent County. These foreign wills were recorded in this county either to show what disposition was made of the non-resident's property within the county or because he may have made a deathbed will while visiting here. A notable example of a foreign will is that of John Penn, The American, who as everyone knows did not die in Kent County, Delaware. Nevertheless, his will was probated here August 13, 1747, after being probated in England nearly a year earlier, because of his property in this county.

In the compilation of this text with its multiplicity of details every effort has been made to achieve accuracy. To this end much time has been spent in checking and rechecking. Despite these precautions there are undoubtedly some discrepancies that have been overlooked. We can only ask our readers to be understanding if such errors do occur.

Finally it should be pointed out that this volume could not have been produced if it had not been for the wholehearted support of the Public Archives Commissioners and the careful work of Mrs. Wallace Hufnal, Misses Naomi C. Urian, Elsie Bloth, Virginia E. Shaw, Mrs. Evelyn S. Griffin and Mrs. Priscilla W. Fleming in the preparation of this text for publication.

LEON DEVALINGER, JR.
State Archivist

Dover, Delaware
1944

ABBREVIATIONS

acct.	account
Admin.	Administration
Adm'r	Administrator
Adm'x	Administratrix
Arch.	Archives
bro.	brother
c.	circa
C. T. A.	Con Testamento Annexo (with the will attached)
dau.	daughter
D. B. N.	De Bonis Non (of the goods or property not yet administered upon)
dec'd	deceased
Exec'r	Executor
Exec'x	Executrix
Hd.	Hundred
Jr.	Junior
K. Co.	Kent County
N. C. Co.	New Castle County
n. d.	no date
nunc.	nuncupative
Penna. Hist. Soc.	Pennsylvania Historical Society
Phila.	Philadelphia
Prob.	Probate
Reg. of Wills	Register of Wills
Sic.	Indicates a literal quotation
Sr.	Senior
vol.	volume
Wits.	Witnesses

Dawson, John. Will (nunc.) Made Dec. 21, 1680. St. Jones Hd. Heir: John Hillyard. Exec'r, John Hillyard. Adm'r, John Hill. Arch. vol. A13, page 195. Reg. of Wills, Liber A, folio 1.

Rawlings, John. Admin. of, to John Richardson. Sept. 21/22, 1681. Reg. of Wills, Liber A, folio 1.

Jones, Joseph. Will (copy). Made June 22, 1674. Heirs: negroes Sherry & Freegift Wansey; William Berry; William Winsmore; John Copeland; William Courtne; bro. Thomas Jones; children of Thomas Jones; mentions Francis Jones. Exec'r, negro Shery Wansey. Wits. Peter Bawcomb, George G. Bailey. Prob. June 15, 1682. Arch. vol. A27, page 232. Reg. of Wills, Liber A, folio 1.

Starker, Andrew. Merchant. Admin. of, to William Darnall. Sept. 18, 1683. Penna. Hist. Soc. Papers, vol. AM. 2013, page 5.

Cabley, John. Will (copy). Made Nov. 9, 1683. Mother Creek. Heirs: Caleb Curtis, Ann Curtis, Winlock Curtis, Elizabeth Curtis, John Curtis. [No exec'r]. Wits., Ann Carter, Cornelis Collton. [No probate.] Penna. Hist. Soc. Papers, vol. AM. 2013, page 16.

Park, Edward. Admin. of, to Alse Park. Dec. 20, 1683. Penna. Hist. Soc. Papers, vol. AM. 2013, page 9.

Griffen, Joseph. (dec'd, Dec. 4, 1682). Admin. of, to Elizabeth & John Brinkloe. Dec. 20, 1683. Penna. Hist. Soc. Papers, vol. AM. 2013, page 10.

Williams, Edward. Admin. of, to John Richardson. Dec. 20, 1683. Penna. Hist. Soc. Papers, vol. AM. 2013, page 10.

Batha, Tempest. Admin. of, to John Richardson. June 17, 1684. Penna. Hist. Soc. Papers, vol. AM. 2013, page 15.

Warner, Edmond. Admin. of, to wife and William Burry. Jones River. June, 1684 and Dec. 19, 1684. Penna. Hist. Soc. Papers, vol. AM. 2013, pages 19 and 25.

Whitwell, Francis. Admin. of, to William Southerby & William Burry. Aug. 20, 1684. Penna. Hist. Soc. Papers, vol. AM. 2013, page 20.

Hillyard, John. Will. Made Aug. 14, 1684. Heirs: wife, Mary; sons, John, Thomas, Oliver, Charles; daughter, Mary. Exec'rs, wife Mary and son John. Wits., Jno. Bradshaw, Evin Jones, William Ellingsworth, John Walker. Prob. Oct. 9, 1684. Arch. vol. A24, pages 39-40. Reg. of Wills, Liber G, folios 25-26. Penna. Hist. Soc. Papers, vol. AM. 2013, pages 21-23.

Welley, James. Admin. of, to Mary Welley & Richard Mitchell. Dec. 17, 1684. Penna. Hist. Soc. Papers, vol. AM. 2013, page 24.

Walker, Richard. Admin. of, to Anna Walker, widow. Dec. 17, 1684. Penna. Hist. Soc. Papers, vol. AM. 2013, page 35.

Glover, John. Admin. of, to Alse Glover, wife. Dec. 17, 1684. Penna. Hist. Soc. Papers, vol. AM. 2013, page 36.

Leavith, Richard. Admin. of, to Mary, wife. June 16, 1685. Penna. Hist. Soc. Papers, vol. AM. 2013, page 158.

Parvis, Robert. Will. Made Jan. 8, 1684. Heirs: sons, Robert and Jadwin; child unnamed; children of sisters Juda & Catterine Parvis; wife, Sirelly. Exec'x, wife. Trustees: William Santhers, Richard Mitchell, William Burry, Samuel Burrberry. Wits., Richard Ratliff, Samuel Mott, Benony Biship. Prob. July 10, 1685. Penna. Hist. Soc. Papers, vol. AM. 2013, pages 40-41. Note:—Mentions Robert Parvis the uncle of William and Robert Parvis father of William as eldest son of the testator. Robert Parvis the uncle of William is since deceased.

Parvis, Robert. Admin. of, to John Jadwin, relative. July 10, 1685. Penna. Hist. Soc. Papers, vol. AM. 2013, page 44. Arch. vol. A39, page 100.

Mitchall, Richard. High Sheriff & Deputy Surveyor. (wife Mary). Admin. of, to John Edmondson & William Dixson. Oct. 20, 1685. Penna. Hist. Soc. Papers, vol. AM. 2013, page 52.

Bowcomb, Peter. Admin. of, to George Marton & Ruth Bowcomb, wife. Oct. 20, 1685. Penna. Hist. Soc. Papers, vol. AM. 2013, page 53.

Mansur, John. Admin. of, to Richard Willson. Dec. 16, 1685. Penna. Hist. Soc. Papers, vol. AM. 2013, page 59.

Groves, Joseph. Admin. of, to Nicholas Bartlott & George Forbig. April 20, 1686. Penna. Hist. Soc. Papers, vol. AM. 2013, page 60.

Rogers, John. Admin. of, to Elizabeth Rogers, wife. April 20, 1686. Penna. Hist. Soc. Papers, vol. AM. 2013, page 61.

Bedwell, Robert. Admin. of, to Susannah Bedwell, widow. June 14, 1686. Penna. Hist. Soc. Papers, vol. AM. 2013, page 66.

Winsmore, William. Son of Thomas of Worcester, & grandson of Thos. Winsmore. Will (copy). Made May 8, 1686. Heirs: dau. Mary; sons-in-law Abell & Mathew Wilson; dau.-in-law Rebeckah Wilson; wife Elizabeth; son William. Exec'rs, wife & son William. Wits., Art[hur Meston], William Berry, John Evens. Prob. June 15, 1686. Penna. Hist. Soc. Papers, vol. AM. 2013, pages 67-68. Arch. vol. 56, page 46. Reg. of Wills, Liber C., folio 88.

Green, William. Admin. of, to Thomas Ehler. June 15, 1686. Penna. Hist. Soc. Papers, vol. AM. 2013, page 62.

Gibbon, Edmond. Will (copy). Made Feb. 21, 1685/6. Heirs: bro. Francis; Edmond, son of bro., George Gibbon; sisters, Ann, Martha; kin woman, Elizabeth Ladwell; bro. George; bro-in-law, Thomas Stratton & wife. Exec'rs, Francis Gibbon, Thomas Stratton, George Gibbon, John Edmondson, James Newell. Wits., James Smith, Nicholas Northway, Edmond Kout [Kont]. Prob. Sept. 10, 1686. Penna. Hist. Soc. Papers, vol. AM. 2013, pages 70-72.

Webb, Isack. Admin. of, to Mary Webb, widow. March 15, 1687. Penna. Hist. Soc. Papers, vol. AM. 2013, page 77.

Foster, Richard. Will (copy). Made Aug. 8, 1687. Heir: son John. Exec'r, son John. Wits., Thomas Groves, John Chant. Prob. Oct. 19, 1689. Penna. Hist. Soc. Papers, vol. AM. 2013, pages 105-106.

Bartlet, Nicklos. Admin. of, to Sarah Bartlet, widow. Feb. 12, 1689. Penna. Hist. Soc. Papers, vol. AM. 2013, page 112.

Forby, James. Admin. of, to Varner [Varier] Cannon. June 10, 1690. Penna. Hist. Soc. Papers, vol. AM. 2013, page 114.

Longpre, Cloude. Will (copy). Made Aug. 22, 1688. Heirs: wife Ruth; father-in-law, John Tingle; sons, John & Cloude; and one child not named. Wits., Walter Jones, Thomas Hillyard, John Hillyard. Prob. Sept. 10, 1690. Penna. Hist. Soc. Papers, vol. AM. 2013, page 129.

Longpre, Cloude. Admin. of, to Robert Palmetory. Sept. 10, 1690. Penna. Hist. Soc. Papers, vol. AM. 2013, page 128.

Tingle, John. Admin. of, to Johana, wife. Oct. 10, 1690. Penna. Hist. Soc. Papers, vol. AM. 2013, page 115.

Groves, Thomas. Will. Made Feb. 1, 1690. Dover River. Heir: friend, John Newall. Exec'r, John Newall. Wits., John Price, Stephens Simons, Francis Rennolds. [No prob.] Penna. Hist. Soc. Papers, vol. AM. 2013, page 134.

Harwar, William. Admin. of, to Susana Harwar, wife. June 9, 1691. Penna. Hist. Soc. Papers, vol. AM. 2013, page 130.

Reynolds, John. Will. Made Jan. 8, 1690. Fox Hall. Heirs: wife, [Waddey, named in Admin. Acct.]; sons John, Thomas, William, Joseph; dau. Waddey. Exec'x, wife. Wits., John Snooke, Henry Paremaine. Prob. Dec. 8, 1691. Arch. vol. A43, page 101. Reg. of Wills, Liber A, folio 7.

Whitehall, William. Admin. of, to Mark Manlove. Aug. 25, 1692. Reg. of Wills, Liber A, folio 3.

Mott, Samuel. Admin. of, to Sarah Mott, widow. Sept. 14, 1692. Reg. of Wills, Liber A, folio 3.

Toltwood, Henry. Son of Henry Toltwood in Hay Market near Charing Cross, London, England. Will. Made Sept. 23, 1692. Pesscattoway Co., in New England. Heirs: friend Ezekiel Needham, Sr.; bro. John Toltwood; sisters Grace, Jane & Elizabeth Toltwood; father Henry Toltwood. Exec'r, Ezekiel Needham, Sr. Wits., Thomas Stretton, Thomas Bedwell, Adam Latham. Prob. Oct. 17, 1692. Arch vol. A50, page 169. Reg. of Wills, Liber A, folio 4. Note:—Will mentions uncle John Stagge, dec'd, of Bedfordberry and aunt Martha Stagge.

Price, John. Admin. of, to Anna Price, widow. Oct. 22, 1692. Reg. of Wills, Liber A, folio 4.

Hall, Robert. Admin. of, to Elizabeth Hall, widow. Dec. 24, 1692. Reg. of Wills, Liber A, folios 4-5.

Morgan, David. Will (copy). Made Jan. 15, 1692. Heirs: wife, Phebe; dau. Phebe; sons David, John, Mathew. Exec'x, wife Phebe. Wits., Thomas Everitt, William Morton, John Shepherd. Prob. Feb. 12, 1692. Arch. vol. A36, page 130. Reg. of Wills, Liber A, folio 5.

Love, Andrew. Admin. of, to Elizabeth Love, widow. March 9, 1692/3. Reg. of Wills, Liber A, folio 6.

Palmatary, Robert. Will (copy). Made ...20, 1692. Heirs: wife, Joanna; sons, Robert & John; daus. Eleanor & Susanna. Wits., Jeffry Thomson, John Bradshaw. No probate. Arch. vol. A38, page 205. Reg. of Wills, Liber A, folio 3.

Emary, Arthur. Will (copy). Made July 11, 1693. Heirs: eldest son Arthur Emary; youngest son Arthur Emary. Exec'r, eldest son Arthur. Wits., John Hilliard, David Straughen, El. Straughen, Geo. Martin. Prob. Aug. 5, 1693. Arch. vol. A16, page 176. Reg. of Wills, Liber A, folio 6.

Porter, Robert. Will (copy). Made Dec. 26, 1692. Heirs: wife Elizabeth; two sons unnamed. Wits., Jacob Smith, John Smith. Prob. Jan. 26, 1693. Arch. vol. A40, page 202. Reg. of Wills, Liber A, folio 5.

Cannon, Ann. Widow of Christopher Stanley. Will (copy). Made Feb. 19, 1693/4. Duck Creek Hundred. Heirs: sons Moses Cannon, Christopher, & John Stanley. Exec'r, son, Christopher Stanley. Wits., Robert French, Peter Bourdet, John Brown, Christopher Stanley. Prob. March 14, 1693/4. Arch. vol. A7, page 197. Reg. of Wills, Liber A, folio 2.

Bishop, Sarah. Admin. of, to Owen Garvey, next of kin. Aug. 26, 1694. Reg. of Wills, Liber A, folio 7.

Berry, William. Admin. of, to Naomy Berry, widow. Talbot Co., Md. Sept. 14, 1694. Reg. of Wills, Liber A, folio 9.

Waddle, Thomas. Admin. of, to Evan Davis & Helen Davis, widow of Thomas Waddle. Oct. 9, 1694. Reg. of Wills, Liber A, folio 9.

Manlove, William. Will (copy). Made Sept. 16, 1694. Heirs: wife, Alce; sons Mark, William, Samuel; daus. Hannah, Mary, Elizabeth; bros. John, Mark & George. Exec'rs, wife Alice & son Mark. Trustees, bros. Mark & George. Wits., George Robisson, Richard Curtis. Prob. Oct. 10, 1694. Arch. vol. A33, page 131. Reg. of Wills, Liber A, folio 8.

Hartnell, Nicholas. Will (copy). Made Nov. 13, 1694. Duck Creek. Heirs: dau. Prudence; wife's children, Elizabeth & Samuel; bros. Richard Willson, Samson Allen. Exec'rs, Richard Willson & Samson Allen. Wits., John Bradshaw, John Hilliard, John Craven. Prob. Nov. 20, 1694. Arch. vol. A22, page 204. Reg. of Wills, Liber A, folio 8.

Peterson, Thomas. Admin. of, to John Richardson. Dec. 1, 1694. Reg. of Wills, Liber A, folio 10.

Simpkins, Michael. Admin. of, to John Richardson. Dec. 1, 1694. Reg. of Wills, Liber A, folio 10.

Jesop, Jesper. Will (copy). Made July 25, 1694. Heir: William, son of John Burton, Sr. Exec'r, John Burton, Sr. Wits., John Brinckloe, John Lane, Arthur Meston. Prob. Dec. 13, 1694. Arch. vol. A27, page 5. Reg. of Wills, Liber A, folio 9.

Launcelot, James. Admin. of, to John Hilliard. Jan. 1, 1694. Reg. of Wills, Liber A, folio 10.

Stevens, Henry. Planter. Will (copy). Made Dec. 7, 1694. Dover River. Heirs: wife Catherine; children unnamed. Exec'x, wife Catherine. Wits., Evan Davids, John Smith, Timothy Thorold. Prob. Jan. 7, 1694. Arch. vol. A48, page 216. Reg. of Wills, Liber A, folio 15.

Stone, Basil. Admin. of, to William Gupton, who married Catherine, the widow. Jan. 10, 1694/5. Reg. of Wills, Liber A, folio 10.

Cullen, Cornelius. Admin. of, to John Dubrois. Feb. 12, 1694/5. Reg. of Wills, Liber A, folio 10.

Shurly, Roger. Will (copy). Made Dec. 7, 1694. Heirs: wife Elizabeth; sons, John, Richard; daus. Naomi, Elizabeth, Mary. Exec'rs, wife Elizabeth & son John. Wits., John Robinson, Stephen Simons, Sarah Miller, Elizabeth Newell. Prob. Feb. 12, 1694/5. Arch. vol. A46, page 42. Reg. of Wills, Liber A, folio 13.

Manlove, George. Will (copy). Made Nov. 7, 1694. Heirs: wife Ann; son Jonathan; daus. Ann, Tabitha, Elizabeth; bros. Mark, Luke; John Walton. Wits., John Mulrony, John Walker. Prob. Feb. 12, 1694/5. Arch. vol. A33, page 91. Reg. of Wills, Liber A, folio 14.

Manlove, Mark. Will (copy). Made Nov. 24, 1694. Mispillion Creek Hd. Heirs: wife Elizabeth; sons, Mathew, Mark; daus., Rachel, Elizabeth, Rebecca, Sarah, Hannah Hillyard; son-in-law John Hillyard; bro. John Manlove; Henry Spencer. Exec'rs, wife Elizabeth & son Mathew. Wits., Alce Manlove, Mark Manlove, Jr., Richard Curtis, James Howell. Prob. Feb. 20, 1694/5. Arch. vol. A32, page 36. Reg. of Wills, Liber A, folio 13.

Courtney, John. Planter. Will (copy). Made Dec. 9, 1694. Dover River. Heirs: wife, Mary; sons, George, John, Nathaniel, Daniel & Thomas; dau. Joshean Courtney. Exec'x, Mary Courtney. Wits., William Perry, William Thomas, Robert French. Prob. Feb. 28, 1694/5. Arch. vol. A-11, page 64. Reg. of Wills, Liber A, folio 20.

Martin, George. Admin. of, to Ursilla Martin, widow. March 12, 1694/5. Reg. of Wills, Liber A, folio 11.

Jones, Daniel. Will (copy). Made Aug. 21, 1694. Jones Creek. Heirs: wife, Mary; son Daniel; dau. Sarah; son-in-law William Rodney. Exec'rs, wife Mary & son Daniel. Wits., John Clayton, Joseph Osburne, Arthur Meston. Prob. March 21, 1694/5. Arch. vol. A27, pages 150-151. Reg. of Wills, Liber A, folio 11.

Louder, Edward. Admin. of, to Peter Bourdet. July 17, 1695. Reg. of Wills, Liber A, folio 15.

Everett, Mark. Admin. of, to John Richardson. Oct. 9, 1695. Mentions, widow, Lydia Everett. Reg. of Wills, Liber A, folio 16.

Barns, John. Admin. of, to Daniel Pegg of Phila. Oct. 20, 1695. Reg. of Wills, Liber A, folio 17.

Brown [Browne], Daniel. Will (copy). Made Sept. 17, 1695. Heirs: Mary Draper; dau-in-law, Mary Thompson; wife Susannah; son Daniel; son-in-law William Thompson. Exec'rs, William Thompson, wife Susannah & son Daniel. Wits., William Rodney, Richard Willson, John Betts, Simon Hirons, Wm. Morton, John Hillyard. Prob. Oct. 30, 1695. Arch. vol. A6, page 35. Reg. of Wills, Liber A, folio 16.

Curtis, Richard. Will (copy). Made May 20, 1695. Mispillion Creek Hd. Heirs: Jehu Curtis; Winlock, son of Jehu Curtis; sister-in-law Elizabeth Jones; Nathaniel Hun; Samuel Low; son, Samuel Curtis; dau. Elizabeth Curtis; James Howell; John Arriskin; father-in-law John Curtis. Exec'rs, John Curtis & James Howell. Wits., Robert French, Samuel Atkins, Priscilla Curtis. Prob. Dec. 14, 1695. Arch. vol. A12, page 163. Reg. of Wills, Liber A, folio 17.

Maxwell, James. Admin. of, to wife Alce & Robert French. Dec. 20, 1695. Reg. of Wills, Liber B, folio 37.

Hewthat, Thomas. Will (copy). Made Nov. 29, 1695. Heirs: daus. Priscilla Edmunds [Edmonds], Ann Needham, Elliner Robisson, Mellesent Bedwell; grandchildren not named; son Ralph Hewthat; son-in-law Robert Edmunds. Exec'rs, son-in-law Robert Edmunds, Alexander Grans, schoolmaster. Wits., Henry Bedwell, Isaac Baker. Prob. Dec. 24, 1695. Arch. vol. A23, page 196. Reg. of Wills, Liber A, folio 20.

Skidmore, Thomas. Admin. of, to Mary Skidmore, widow. Jan. 6, 1695/6. Reg. of Wills, Liber A, folio 18.

Martin, George. Admin. of, to Ursula Martin. June 9, 1696. Reg. of Wills, Liber B, folio 31.

Hill, Samuel. Admin. of, to Isaac Hill, bro. Sept. 8, 1696. Reg. of Wills, Liber A, folio 18.

Baker, Isaac. Admin. of, to John Dubrois. Feb. 16, 1696/7. Mentions widow, Elizabeth Baker. Reg. of Wills, Liber A, folio 18.

Higgins, Francis. Admin. of, to Peter Bourdet. March 2, 1696/7. Reg. of Wills, Liber A, folio 19.

Nichols, Robert. Admin. of, to Mary Nichols, widow. March 6, 1696/7. Reg. of Wills, Liber A, folio 19.

Clayton, James. Admin. of, to Mary Clayton & Thomas Bedwell. March 13, 1696/7. Reg. of Wills, Liber A, folio 19.

Bradshaw, Thomas. Admin. of, to Robert French. April 7, 1697. Reg. of Wills, Liber A, folio 19.

Elder, Thomas. Admin. of, to Robert French, April 17, 1697. Reg. of Wills, Liber A, folio 21.

Chant, John. Admin. of, to Elizabeth Chant, widow. July 3, 1697. Reg. of Wills, Liber A, folios 21-22.

Davids, Evan. Admin. of, to John Richardson. Aug. 11, 1697. Reg. of Wills, Liber A, folio 22.

Willson, John. Will (copy). Made Feb. 19, 1696. Duck Creek. Heirs: wife Mary; dau. Susanna; three daus. unnamed; Simon Hirons. Exec'x, wife Mary. Wits., Thomas Bradshaw, William Morton. Prob. Dec. 10, 1697. Arch. vol. A55, page 213. Reg. of Wills, Liber B, folio 31.

Chance, Elizabeth. Widow. Will (copy). Made Dec. 16, 1697. Little Creek. Heirs: sons Robert & Laurence Porter. Exec'rs, sons Robert & Laurence Porter. Wits., George Clifford, Timothy Carrow, Elizabeth Clifford. Prob. Dec. 31, 1697. Arch. vol. A8, page 151. Reg. of Wills, Liber A, folio 23.

Betts, John. Will (copy). Made Nov. 16, 1697. Heirs: children of William Freeman; Elizabeth, wife of William Freeman; heirs of Richard & Sarah Williams; heirs of Edward & Mary Killingsworth; George Robisson; heirs of John Robisson; wife's dau. Susanna Stacie; wife's dau. Jane Stacie; wife's granddau. Mary Burbary, dau. of Samuel Burbary; bro. Edward Betts; wife Mary; William Rodeney, Jr. Exec'rs, Mary Betts & William Rodeney, Jr. Wits., Mathew Bryan, Elizabeth Miller, Susanna Miller. Prob. Jan. 3, 1697/8. Arch. vol. A4, page 35. Reg. of Wills, Liber A, folio 22.

Parry, William. Admin. of, to John Mahon. Feb. 1, 1697/8. Reg. of Wills, Liber A, folio 23.

Edmondson, John. Merchant. Will (copy). Made Oct. 9, 1697. Tredhaven Creek, Talbot Co., Md. Heirs: sons, James, William, Thomas, Samuel, John, dec'd; dau. Elizabeth Stevens; grandson, Edmondson Stevens; Emanuel Jenkinson; Philip Morgan; Abraham Morman; Abraham Morgan, Jr.; Elizabeth Morgan; wife Sarah Edmondson; heirs of Catherine Brook; William Sackwell; Robert Smith. Exec'rs, Sarah, James, William, Thomas Edmondson. Wits., John Nedells, Fran. Perkins, William Harris, Michal Mackenny. Prob. March 2, 1697/8. Arch. vol. A16, page 47. Reg. of Wills, Liber B, folio 34.

Nichols, William. Will (copy). Made Jan. 13, 1696/7. Heirs: son William; granddaus. Dinah Mohon, Mary Nichols; grandson Jeremiah Nichols; son-in-law John Mohon; grandson William Nichols (son of Robert). Exec'r, William Nichols. Wits., Gartre Lober the elder, Mary Nichols the elder, Margaret Lober, Richard Busby. Prob. March 6, 1697. Arch. vol. A37, page 228. Reg. of Wills, Liber A, folios 20-21.

Busby, Richard. Admin. of, to Thomas Bedwell. March 8, 1697/8. Reg. of Wills, Liber B, folio 26.

Reynolds, Thomas. Admin. of, to Anna Reynolds, widow. March 9, 1697/8. Reg. of Wills, Liber A, folio 23.

Jones, Walter. Admin. of, to Evan Jones. March 9, 1697/8. Mentions widow, Elinor Jones. Reg. of Wills, Liber A, folio 23.

Howell, John. Admin. of, to Griffith Jones. March 9, 1697/8. Reg. of Wills, Liber A, folio 24.

Dwyer, Thomas. Admin. of, to Mary Dwyer, widow. March 9, 1697/8. Reg. of Wills, Liber A, folio 24.

Chant, John. Admin. of, to John Foster, next of kin. March 22, 1697/8. Reg. of Wills, Liber A, folio 24.

Clifford, Thomas. Will (not signed). Made March 26, 1698. Little Creek. Heirs: sons Thomas & John; wife Elizabeth; daus. Elizabeth & Mary; bro. George. Exec'x, wife Elizabeth. [No witnesses.] [No probate.] Reg. of Wills, Liber A, folio 25.

Word, Patrick. Will (copy). Made Jan. 16, 1697. Duck Creek. Heirs: granddaus. Honor Kelly, Margaret Kelly, Judity Dwyer (dau. of Mary); sons-in-law John Kelly & Thomas Dwyer; dau. Sarah Kelly, wife of John Kelly; dau. Mary Dwyer. Exec'r, John Kelly. Wits., James Fitzjarrell, Simon Hirons, Jr., William Annand. Prob. April 12, 1698. Arch. vol. A56, pages 135-136. Reg. of Wills, Liber A, folios 24-25. Note:—Order from the Commissioners to John Kelley respecting Tobias Tunissen and wife, Mary (dau. of Patrick Word). Dec. 13, 1698. Reg. of Wills, Liber B, folio 32.

Flowers, Thomas. Admin. of, to son John Flowers. April 15, 1698. Reg. of Wills, Liber B, folio 26.

Loper, Peter. Will (copy). Made April 2, 1698. Heirs: wife Gartre; son Michael; daus. Mary Nichols (widow of William), Margaret Paradee, Gartre Loper, Agnes Smith. Exec'x, wife Gartre. Wits., Thomas Bedwell, William Nichols, Daniel Hudson. Prob. May 2, 1698. Arch. vol. A31, page 136. Reg. of Wills, Liber B, folio 27.

Curtis, John. Gentleman. Will (copy). Made April 22, 1698. St. Jones Hd. Heirs: wife unnamed; son Caleb; daus. Elizabeth & Ruth; grandson Jehu Curtis; Samuel Low. Exec'rs, Caleb Curtis & Priscilla Curtis (from Admin. Acct.). Wits., Richard Jackson, Michael Donoho, Jno. Foster. Prob. May 3, 1698. Arch. vol. A12, page 159. Reg. of Wills, Liber B, folios 26 & 32.

Bedwell, Henry. Will (copy). Made May 3, 1698. Heirs: wife Sarah; dau. Sarah; John Robisson; child unnamed. Exec'x, wife Sarah. Wits., Robert Bedwell, Adam Fisher, Anthony Jones. Prob. June 14, 1698. Arch. vol. A3, page 141. Reg. of Wills, Liber B, folio 28.

Tomson, Urbanus. Carpenter. Will (copy). Made March 23, 1697. Heirs: wife Mary; children unnamed. Adm'x, wife Mary. Wits., William Freeman, Henry Hoskins, Elliner Jones. Prob. June 15, 1698. Arch. vol. A50, page 229. Reg. of Wills, Liber B, folio 29.

Smith, Maurice, Sr. Will (copy). Made March 9, 1695/6. Heirs: wife Bethia; sons John, Solomon, & Maurice, Jr.; daus. Mary Clayton, Martha, Alce, Elizabeth Smith. Exec'x, wife Bethia. Wits., Jacob Smith, John Clayton, John Evans, William Rodeney, James Clayton. Prob. June 25, 1698. Arch. vol. A47, page 123. Reg. of Wills, Liber B, folio 30.

Mills, John. Will (copy). Made May 24, 1698. Heirs: wife Mary; dau. unnamed; 2 sons unnamed. Exec'x, wife Mary. Wits., Thomas Collins, John Mulruny. Prob. June 30, 1698. Arch. vol. A35, page 133. Reg. of Wills, Liber B, folio 30.

Bourdet, Peter. Will. Made Nov. 7, 1698. Heirs: father Stephen Bourdet; bro. Samuel; children of brother. Exec'r, bro. Samuel. [No wits.] Prob. Dec. 5, 1698 (in New York, Nov. 29, 1698). Reg. of Wills, Liber B, folio 32.

Curtis, Richard. Admin. of, to John Curtis, dec'd, James Howell and William Brinckloe. Jan. 2, 1698/9. Reg. of Wills, Liber B, folio 32.

Bishop, Thomas. Will (copy). Made July 23, 1699. Heirs: John Jones; Adam Latham; George Morgan; John Groves (son of Mary Shaw). Exec'r, George Morgan. Wits., Thomas Bedwell, Tarrasias Catrep. Prob. Aug. 18, 1699. Arch. vol. A4, page 70. Reg. of Wills, Liber B, folio 33.

Thomson, Walter. Will (copy). Made July 22, 1697. Heir: wife Alice. Exec'x, wife Alice. Wits., John Godfrey, James Wood, Henry Flower. Prob. Feb. 20, 1699. Arch. vol. A50, page 228. Reg. of Wills, Liber B, folios 35-36.

Ohagitha, Dennish. Admin. of, to Margaret Ohagitha. Feb. 20, 1699. Reg. of Wills, Liber B, folio 36.

Rogers, Thomas. Admin. of, to Robert French. Aug. 16, 1700. Reg. of Wills, Liber B, folio 36.

Atthow, Thomas. Admin. of, to William Rodeney. Aug. 16, 1700. Reg. of Wills, Liber B, folio 36.

Griffen, William. Admin. of, to Isaac Freeland. Oct. 14, 1700. Reg. of Wills, Liber B, folio 37.

Kairone, Timothy. Will (copy). Made Oct. 28, 1700. Heirs: Thomas & John Clifford, children of the widow Clifford. Exec'rs, John & Thomas Clifford. Guardians, William Winsmore, Dennish Dyer. Wits., Robert Porter, Dennish Dyer, John French. Prob. Nov. 16, 1700. Arch. vol. A28, page 80. Reg. of Wills, Liber B, folios 37 & 41.

Dun, John. Admin. of, to Margaret Dun. Nov. 21, 1700. Reg. of Wills, Liber B, folio 37.

Sharp, George. Will (copy). Made Nov. 20, 1700. Heirs: dau. Elizabeth Sharp; dau.-in-law Catron Fline; bro. Thomas Sharp. Exec'r, bro. Thomas Sharp. Wits., Lewis Owen, Joseph England, Robert Draughton, James Wythe. Prob. Dec. 16, 1700. Arch. vol. A45, page 186. Reg. of Wills, Liber B, folio 38.

Wilson, Richard. Will (copy). Made Dec. 17, 1700. Heirs: daus. Elizabeth & Mary Wilson; son Robert Wilson, in England; wife's son Lodiwick Hall. Exec'rs, friends Simon Irons, William Morton, William Rodeney. Wits., Simon Hirons, Abraham Fields, John French. Prob. Jan. 7, 1700. Arch. vol. A55, page 243. Reg. of Wills, Liber B, folios 38-39.

Dunn, Margaret. Admin. of, to John Dun. Jan. 13, 1700. Reg. of Wills, Liber B, folio 39.

Reynolds, Francis. Admin. of, to William Clark. Jan. 13, 1700. Reg. of Wills, Liber B, folio 39.

Lewkins, Nathaniel. Mariner. Will (copy). Made Feb. 7, 1700. Heirs: Elizabeth Wilson, widow of Richard Wilson; James Coutts, merchant; William Rodney; Samual Rowland; Margaret Listen; George Oldfield. Exec'x, Elizabeth Wilson. Wits., John Edinfield, John Walker. Prob. Feb. 15, 1700. Arch. vol. A30, page 165. Reg. of Wills, Liber B, folio 40.

Kelly, John. Admin. of, to Sarah Kelly. March 10, 1700. Reg. of Wills, Liber B, folios 40-41.

Wilson, Hugh. Merchant—in Old England. Will (copy). Made March 11, 1700. Heirs: mother Ann Wilson; bro. John; sisters Mary & Alice Wilson, of England; Esther Freeland, widow of William Freeland. Exec'rs, William Morton, Henry Molleston, Joseph Booth, Joseph Willcox. Wits., Simon Hirons, John Clayton, John French. Prob. April 15, 1700 [sic.]. Arch. vol. A55, page 208. Reg. of Wills, Liber B, folio 41.

Redman, Thomas. Will (copy). Made Oct. 5, 169-. Heirs: William & Edward Starkey. Exec'r, Edward Starkey. Wits., John E. Lisenbey, Edmond Gready, William Starkey. Prob. May 10, 1701. Arch. vol. A42, page 182. Reg. of Wills, Liber B, folio 42.

Everett, George. Admin. of, to Agnes Everett. May 12, 1701. Reg. of Wills, Liber B, folio 42.

Dun, John. Admin. of, to Robert French. May 20, 1701. Reg. of Wills, Liber B, folio 42.

Greeves, Mathew. Admin. of, to Eleanor Greeves. June 10, 1701. Reg. of Wills, Liber B, folio 43.

Whitehart, Richard. Will (copy). Made Oct. 11, 1701. Duck Creek. Heirs: wife Elizabeth; children unnamed. Exec'x, wife Elizabeth. Wits., Henry Hoskins, Sarah Kelly, Mary Tobias. Prob. Nov. 7, 1701. Arch. vol. A54, page 186. Reg. of Wills, Liber B, folio 44.

Groenendick, Peter. Admin. of, to Daniel England. Nov. 24, 1701. Reg. of Wills, Liber B, folio 43.

Fitz Jarrell, Edward. Admin. of, to William Wilson. Nov. 24, 1701. Reg. of Wills, Liber B, folio 43.

Walmsley, John. Admin. of, to Mary Walmsley. Jan. 30, 1701. Reg. of Wills, Liber B, folio 43.

Mathews, Samuel. Admin. of, to Thomas Skidmore. Feb. 4, 1701. Reg. of Wills, Liber B, folio 43.

Mulroney, John. Admin. of, to Elizabeth Mulroney. April 27, 1702. Reg. of Wills, Liber B, folio 44.

Hoskins, Henry. Will (copy). Made May 20, 1702. Heir: wife Rachel. Exec'x, wife Rachel. Wits., Evan Jones, Elizabeth Whitehart, Richard Whitehart, John Bradshaw. Prob. Nov. 2, 1702. Arch. vol. A25, page 38. Reg. of Wills, Liber B, folio 44.

Ditton, John. Admin. of, to Benjamin Dabbs. Dec. 8, 1702. Reg. of Wills, Liber B, folio 44.

Hart, George. Will (copy). Made Nov. 21, 1702. Heirs: wife Naomi; sons George, John, Henry. Exec'rs, wife Naomi & William Rodney. Wits., John Nelson, William Williams, William Annand. Prob. Dec. 10, 1702. Arch. vol. A22, page 190. Reg. of Wills, Liber B, folios 45-46.

Mulrony, Elizabeth. Widow of John Mulrony. Will (copy). Made Nov. 15, 1702. Heirs: mother Ann Williams; daus. Ann, Elizabeth, Jane; sons John & William. Wits., Mary Mills, Sarah Robinson, John Walker. Prob. Dec. 19, 1702. Arch. vol. A37, page 71. Reg. of Wills, Liber B, folio 45.

Mulrony, John. Admin. of, to Matthew Manlove & Mark Manlove. Dec. 23, 1702. Mentions wife Elizabeth. Reg. of Wills, Liber B, folios 44-45.

Turner, Richard. Admin. of, to John Elliot. Feb. 10, 1702/3. Reg. of Wills, Liber B, folio 46.

Curtis, Caleb. Admin. of, to Cornelia Curtis. March 20, 1702. Reg. of Wills, Liber B, folio 46.

Hawkey, Ursilla. Wife of Wm. Hawkey, formerly wife of George Martin, nee Collinner. Will (copy). Made March 17, 1702. Heirs: sons Samuel Hawkey, Josiah Martin & George Martin; daus. Ruth Hawkey & Elizabeth Martin; Evan Jones; Elizabeth Jones, wife of Evan Jones. Exec'rs, Evan Jones, Elizabeth Jones. Wits., John Bradshaw, Jonas Greenwood, Elizabeth Morris. Prob. May 12, 1703. Arch. vol. A23, page 9. Reg. of Wills, Liber B, folio 47.

Starkey, Edward. Will (copy). Made April 3, 1703. Heirs: wife Anna; sons William, Edward, John; daus. Rebecca, Elizabeth, Ann, Mary. Exec'x, wife Anna. Wits., Thomas Bedwell, Mary Porter, Robert Porter. Prob. May 12, 1703. Arch. vol. A48, page 162. Reg. of Wills, Liber B, folios 47-48.

Jones, Griffith. Gentleman. Will (copy). Made May 2, 1703. Heirs: wife Elizabeth; dau. Elizabeth; sons Griffith & Thomas; Elizabeth Baldridge, dau. of Adam Baldridge. Exec'r, William Rodney. Wits., Adam Baldridge, Joseph Daves, William Tong. Prob. May 24, 1703. Arch. vol. A27, page 180. Reg. of Wills, Liber B, folio 48.

Newton, Henry. Admin. of, to Mary Newton. June 15, 1703. Reg. of Wills, Liber B, folio 49.

McKenny, Edmund. Planter. Will (nunc. copy). Made June 12, 1703. Heirs: sisters Patience & Elizabeth; bro. Edward. Exec'rs, John Bowman, Jacob Emerson. Wits., Daniel Brown, Marget Emerson, Mary Newton, Richard Pearce. Prob. June 19, 1703. Arch. vol. A32, page 212. Reg. of Wills, Liber B, folio 49.

Mills, Mary. Widow. Admin. of, to Owen Garvey. June 19, 1703. Reg. of Wills, Liber B, folio 49.

Clifford, Thomas. Will (copy). Made July 2, 1703. Heirs: Elizabeth, Mary & Parnell Clifford; bro. John Clifford. Exec'rs, John Clayton, John Evans. Wits., William Morton, William Winsmore. Prob. July 12, 1703. Arch. vol. A9, page 139. Reg. of Wills, Liber B, folio 49.

Freeman, William. Admin. of, to Elizabeth Freeman. Nov. 29, 1703. Reg. of Wills, Liber B, folio 50.

Richardson, John, Sr. Will (copy). Made Oct. 12, 1703. Little Creek. Heirs: wife Mary; grandsons John Richardson, Daniel Brady; Benjamin Brady; Richard Levick; John Levick; Thomas Rodney; William Rodney; children of George & Jude Roes. Exec'x, wife Mary. Wits., William Morton, Jesper Harwood, Mary Slaughter. Prob. Jan. 3, 1703. Arch. vol. A43, page 164. Reg. of Wills, Liber B, folio 50.

Flowers, John. Admin. of, to Elizabeth Flowers. Aug. 28, 1704. Reg. of Wills, Liber B, folios 50-51.

Morton, William. Admin. of, to Catherine Morton. Oct. 21, 1704. Reg. of Wills, Liber B, folio 51.

Wilson, William. Admin. of, to Ann Wilson. Nov. 1, 1704. Reg. of Wills, Liber B, folio 51.

Morton, William. Will (copy). Made Jan. 12, 1700. Heirs: Samuel Berry; John French; Robert Porter; Esther Freeland, widow of Wm. Freeland; John Richardson, son of my wife, late dec'd; William Hirons, son of Simon & Piercey Hirons; Margaret Hirons, dau. of Simon & Piercey Hirons; Simon Hirons, Sr.; Thomas O'Horrell, servant. Exec'rs, Samuel Berry, John French, Simon Hirons, Sr., Robert Porter. Wits., John Evins, William Winsmore, Mathew Wilson. Prob. Nov. 14, 1704 (Phila. prob. April 11, 1705). Arch. vol. A37, page 63. Reg. of Wills, Liber B, folios 51-52.

Wilson, Abel. Admin. of, to William Winsmore. May 17, 1705. Reg. of Wills, Liber B, folio 52.

Wilson, Mathew. Will (copy). Made April 22, 1705. Heirs: sons William, Mathew; wife Garteret. Exec'x, Garteret Wilson. Wits., Thomas Bedwell, Thomas Harbutt, Adam Latham. Prob. May 21, 1705. Arch. vol. A55, page 239. Reg. of Wills, Liber B, folio 52.

Wilson, William. Admin. of, to John Clayton & Ann Wilson. Aug. 29, 1705. Reg. of Wills, Liber B, folio 53.

Wilson, Ann. Admin. of, to Thomas Bedwell. Sept. 30, 1705. Reg. of Wills, Liber B, folio 53.

Ashberry, Joseph. Will (copy). Made Aug. 30, 170—. Heirs: wife Elenor; son Joseph. Exec'x, wife Elenor. Wits., Thomas Bedwell, Thomas Colman, John Hudson. Prob. Nov. 16, 1705. Arch. vol. A2, page 10. Reg. of Wills, Liber B, folio 53.

Freeman, William. Admin. of, to William Freeman & Stephen Simons. Jan. 8, 1705/6. Reg. of Wills, Liber B, folio 54.

Portess, Deborah. Widow of John. Will (copy). Made Jan. 12, 1705. Colony of Virginia. Heirs: two sons & three daus. unnamed; husband John. Exec'rs, Simon Hirons, Sr., Pierces Hirons. Wits., Jonas Greenwood, Thomas Wilson, Sr., Henrietta Maria Conly. Prob. Feb. 13, 1705. Arch. vol. A40, page 207. Reg. of Wills, Liber B, folio 54.

Chance, Alexander. Admin. of, to Joanna Chance. April 6, 1706. Reg. of Wills, Liber B, folio 55.

Howell, James. Admin. of, to Thomas Bedwell & Edward Parnell. May 18, 1706. Reg. of Wills, Liber B, folio 55.

Permain, Henry. Will (copy). Made Oct. 10, 1706. Heirs: wife and children not named. Adm'x, Wade Permain. Wits., Benjamin Gumly, John Gumly, Phillip Denny. Prob. Dec. 5, 1706. Arch. vol. A39, page 234. Reg. of Wills, Liber B, folio 56.

Emerson, Jacob. Will (copy). Made Nov. 22, 1706. Heirs: wife Margret; sons John & Jacob; dau. Ellenar. Adm'x, wife. Wits., Nicholas Nixon, William Starkey, Nathaniel Marston. Prob. Dec. 16, 1706. Arch. vol. A16, page 132. Reg. of Wills, Liber B, folio 57.

Hirons, Simon, Sr. Will (copy). Made Oct. 12, 1706. Heirs: sons Francis, Simon, Robert, William, & John; wife Percess; dau. Margaret; Sarah Rodney, dau. of Capt. Wm. & Sarah Rodney; Anna Bedwell, dau. of Thomas & Milicent Bedwell; Samuel Berry, son-in-law; John Portess, son of John & Deborah Portess; Silvanus Portess, son of John & Deborah Portess. Exec'x, wife Percess. Wits., James Moore, Timothy Hanson, Joshua Clayton, Stephen Paradee. Prob. Dec. 16, 1706. Arch. vol. A24, page 97. Reg. of Wills, Liber B, folio 56.

Edmonds, Robert. Will (copy). Made Nov. 26, 1706. Murtherkill. Heirs: wife Anne; sons James, John, Robert; daus. Sarah Edmonds, Mary Clifton. Exec'x, wife Anne. Wits., William Annand, William Nickols, Nicholas Nixon. Prob. Dec. 17, 1706. Arch. vol. A16, page 38. Reg. of Wills, Liber B, folio 55.

Biles, John. Will (nunc. copy). Made Jan. 20, 1705. Heirs: wife and child not named. Exec'r, Stephens Simons. Wits., Owen Garvey, Elizabeth Newell, Mary Fisher. Prob. Jan. 25, 1706. Arch. vol. A4, page 50. Reg. of Wills, Liber B, folio 57.

Burton, John. Admin. of, to Isabella Burton & John Burton. March 18, 1706. Reg. of Wills, Liber B, folio 54.

Peterson, Thomas. Admin. of, to Mary Richardson, adm'x in lieu of John Richardson, dec'd. Sept. 17, 1707. Reg. of Wills, Liber B, folio 57.

Low, Samuel. Will (copy). Made Aug. 19, 1707. Heirs: Thomas Bedwell, creditor; Mary Brinckloe, dau. of William Brinckloe; James Whit; William Brinckloe, son of Wm. Brinckloe; Elizabeth Curtis, dau. of Richard Curtis; sisters Sarah & Mary Low; bro. Joseph Low. Exec'r, Joseph Low. Wits., Wm. Brinckloe, Elizabeth Brinckloe, Moses Harris. Prob. Sept. 23, 1707. Arch. vol. A31, page 92. Reg. of Wills, Liber B, folio 58.

Thorrold, Timothy. Admin. of, to Mary, wife. Oct. 28, 1707. Reg. of Wills, Liber B, folio 59.

Walker, John. Will (copy). Made Nov. 2, 1707. Heirs: dau. Mary; sons John & Daniel; Elizabeth Coal. Exec'rs, John, Daniel & Mary Walker. Guardians, Mark Manlove, Nathaniel Hunn & Edmond Needham. Wits., Abraham Skidmore, Zachariah Goeforth, John Robisson. Prob. Nov. 13, 1707. Arch. vol. A52, page 185. Reg. of Wills, Liber B, folio 59.

Whitehart, William. Admin. of, to Richard Whitehart. Feb. 5, 1707. Reg. of Wills, Liber B, folio 60.

Hogben, Elizabeth. Will (copy). Made March 10, 1703/4. Heirs: John Edmonds, Adam Fisher. Exec'r, Adam Fisher. Wits., Samuel Brooks, Richard Shurley, Richard Williams. Prob. March 9, 1707/8. Arch. vol. A24, page 166. Reg. of Wills, Liber B, folio 60.

Pennington, Henry. Will (nunc. copy). Made March 27, 1708. Heirs: Elenor Sipple; Offee Garrit; Elizabeth Newell, dau. of John & Mary Newell. Adm'r, John Newell. Wits., Thomas Skidmore, John Brown. Prob. March 31, 1708. Arch. vol. A39, page 217. Reg. of Wills, Liber B, folio 60.

Banks, John. Admin. of, to Anne Edmonds. April 9, 1708. Reg. of Wills, Liber B, folio 61.

Anderson, Frank. Admin. of, to Edward Burrows. April 6, 1708. Reg. of Wills, Liber B, folio 61.

Brown, John. Admin. of, to Elizabeth Brown. April 19, 1708. Reg. of Wills, Liber B, folio 61.

Ellitt, Thomas. Will (copy). Made Dec. 2, 1707. Little Duck Creek Hd. Heirs: wife Susannah; children not named or designated. Exec'x, Susannah. Trustees, Thomas Sharp & Evan Jones. Wits., Absolam Cuff, Thomas Sharp. Prob. April 20, 1708. Arch. vol. A16, page 114. Reg. of Wills, Liber B, folio 61.

Skidmore, Joseph. Will (copy). Made April 26, 1708. Heirs: dau. Susannah; son Joseph; wife Rebecca; bro. Thomas. Exec'x, wife Rebecca. Wits., Thomas Bedwell, John Newell, Roger Burgis. Prob. May 12, 1708. Arch. vol. A46, page 197. Reg. of Wills, Liber B, folio 62.

Brady, Benjamin. Admin. of, to Mary Brady. Aug. 30, 1708. Reg. of Wills, Liber B, folio 62.

Rodeney, William. Will (copy). Made May 1, 1708. Heirs: sons William, Thomas, John, Anthony, George & Caesar; dau. Sarah; mother Rachel; sisters Rachel, Elizabeth; wife Sarah; orphans of Richard Willson. Exec'x, wife Sarah. Wits., Elizabeth Annand, William Annand. Prob. Oct. 4, 1708. Arch. vol. A44, pages 96-98. Reg. of Wills, Liber B, folios 63-64.

Robisson, John. Will (copy). Made July 28, 1708. Heirs: wife Elinor; daus. Anna Richeson & Mary Robisson. Exec'x, wife Elinor. Wits., John Dubrois, John Edmonds, Elizabeth Dubrois, Tabitha Edmonds. Prob. Oct. 8, 1708. Arch. vol. A44, page 58. Reg. of Wills, Liber B, folio 65.

Rea, John. Will (copy). Made Oct. 4, 1708. Heirs: Mary Dunahoe [Dunnahoe], wife of my friend Michael Dunahoe; friends Thomas Crofford, Mary Betts, William Steel, Daniel Mahon, Mary Miller, Benjamin White. Exec'r, Benjamin White. Wits., William Steel, Robert Miller, Frances Steel. Prob. Oct. 13, 1708. Arch. vol. A42, page 169. Reg. of Wills, Liber B, folio 66.

Freeman, William. Admin. of, to Stephen Simons & wife Sarah Simons. Oct. 20, 1708. Reg. of Wills, Liber B, folio 65.

Molleston, Henry. Will (copy). Made Oct. 17, 1708. Heirs: wife Anne; son Henry; daus. Grace, Sarah, Mary Fisher, wife of Adam Fisher. Exec'x, wife Anne. Wits., John Wheeler, Robert Betts, Ann Williams, Mark Manlove. Prob. Nov. 12, 1708. Arch. vol. A35, page 203. Reg. of Wills, Liber B, folio 67.

Dyer, Dennish. Admin. of, to Anne Dyer & John Clayton. Dec. 7, 1708. Reg. of Wills, Liber B, folio 66.

Walker, John. Will (copy). Made Oct. 27, 1708. Heirs: wife Margret; Elizabeth Willson, dau. of Richard Willson & dau.-in-law of Vincent Emerson; Vincent Emerson; servant, Easther Hillyard; William Annand. Exec'rs, Easther Hillyard, Vincent Emerson. Wits., Abraham Taylor, Weakman Sippen, Elizabeth Sippen. Prob. Dec. 17, 1708. Arch. vol. A52, page 186. Reg. of Wills, Liber B, folio 69.

Updegrove, Herman. Will (copy). Made Sept. 13, 1708. Heirs: wife Deborah; children unnamed. Exec'x, wife Deborah. Wits., Derick Keys [Keyser] younger, Reynear Williams, Mark Manlove. Prob. Dec. 18, 1708. Arch. vol. A51, page 198. Reg. of Wills, Liber B, folio 67.

Tobias, Tunis. Will (copy). Made Dec. 12, 1708. Heir: wife Mary. Exec'x, wife Mary. Wits., James Jackson, John Chancy, Edward Murphy. Prob. Dec. 28, 1708. Arch. vol. A50, page 166. Reg. of Wills, Liber B, folio 68.

Simons, Stephen. Will (copy). Made Dec. 29, 1708. Heirs: wife Sarah; daus. Elizabeth, Mary & Susannah; sons William & Stephen; Randall Donawan; Adam Fisher. Exec'x, wife Sarah. Trustees, Adam Fisher, Randall Donafan, Daniel Mahon. Wits., John Tounzend, Thomas York, Edward Burrows. Prob. Jan. 4, 1708/9. Arch. vol. A46, page 55. Reg. of Wills, Liber B, folios 68-69.

Freeman, William. Carpenter. Will (copy). Made Dec. 1, 1708. Duck Creek Hd. Heirs: Michael Mason; son William; daus. Elizabeth & Mary; wife Mary. Exec'x, wife Mary. Trustee John Foster, uncle. Wits., Elizabeth Whithart, Mary Mason, Samuel Glew. Prob. Jan. 4, 1708/9. Arch. vol. A18, page 133. Reg. of Wills, Liber 8, folio 72.

Ohorrill, Thomas. Will (copy). Made Dec. 11, 1708. Heir: wife Mary. Exec'x, wife Mary. Wits., John Scott, Edward Murphy, John Chancy. Prob. Jan. 10, 1708. Arch. vol. A38, page 116. Reg. of Wills, Liber B, folio 70.

Nickolson, John. Will (copy). Made Dec. 29, 1708. Heir: wife Elizabeth. Exec'x, wife Elizabeth. Wits., John Clayton, John Evens, James Moir. Prob. Jan. 12, 1708. Arch. vol. A38, page 5. Reg. of Wills, Liber B, folio 71.

Register, William. Admin. of, to John Register. Jan. 15, 1708. Reg. of Wills, Liber B, folio 70.

Whithart, John. Will (copy). Made 1708. Heirs: bros. Richard, Samuel, James; sisters, Elizabeth, Mary; friend, Elizabeth Smith. Exec'r, Richard Whithart. Wits., Philemon Emerson, Thomas Ohorrill. Prob. Jan. 18, 1708/9. Arch. vol. A54, page 185. Reg. of Wills, Liber B, folio 72.

Mathewson, Andrew. Admin. of, to Thomas French. Jan. 19, 1708. Reg. of Wills, Liber B, folio 71.

Evans, John. Admin. of, to Martha Evans. Jan. 25, 1708. Reg. of Wills, Liber B, folio 73.

Stevenson, Henry. Admin. of, to James Fitzgerald and Cathrine his wife. Jan. 31, 1708. Reg. of Wills, Liber B, folio 73.

Burton, John. Admin. of, to Elizabeth Glover, wife of Richard. Feb. 2, 1708. Reg. of Wills, Liber B, folio 73.

Swan, Richard. Admin. of, to Elizabeth Swan. Feb. 5, 1708. Reg. of Wills, Liber B, folio 74.

Hall, John, Sr. Weaver. Will (copy). Made Jan. 7, 1708. Heirs: sons John, Jacob; Mary Tyler; Ann Young; Isaac Hall; wife Mary; daus. Ann & Mary. Exec'x, wife Mary. Wits., James Fitzgerald, George Hart, James Gordon. Prob. Feb. 5, 1708/9. Arch. vol. A21, page 90. Reg. of Wills, Liber B, folio 74.

Ellitt, John. Will (copy). Made Dec. 28, 1708. Duck Creek Hd. Heirs: wife Rebecca; daus. Margret, Rebecca, Angelico. Exec'x, Rebecca, wife. Wits., John Dawson, Charles Pedrick, John Bradsaw. Prob. Feb. 8, 1708/9. Arch. vol. A16, page 112. Reg. of Wills, Liber B, folio 73.

Dabbs, Benjamin. Yeoman. Will (copy). Made Feb. 10, 1708/9. Murtherkill Hd. Heirs: daus. Catherine, Easther & Elizabeth. Exec'r, Daniel Rutty. Wits., Rich. Jackson, William Trippett, Francis Allen. Prob. Feb. 18, 1708/9. Arch. vol. A12, page 173. Reg. of Wills, Liber B, folio 75.

Edmonds, John. Will (copy). Made Jan. 11, 1708/9. Heirs: son John; wife Margret. Exec'x, wife Margret. Wits., James Whyte, James Anderson. Prob. Feb. 28, 1708/9. Arch. vol. A16, page 34. Reg. of Wills, Liber B, folio 75.

Green, William. Yeoman. Will (copy). Made Jan. 15, 1708/9. Duck Creek. Heirs: wife Mercy; dau. Mercy; sons John & Thomas. Exec'x, wife. Wits., William Wells, Elizabeth Bride, John Waters. Prob. March 7, 1708/9. Arch. vol. A20, page 123. Reg. of Wills, Liber B, folio 76.

Jones, Gabriel. Will (copy). Made July 24, 1695. Heirs: son John; wife Margret; 2 orphan sons of Christopher Jackson. Exec'x, wife Margret. Wits., Thomas Hodgkins, Abraham Jarratt. Prob. March 19, 1708/9. Arch. vol. A27, page 176. Reg. of Wills, Liber B, folio 76.

Dawson, Richard. Will (copy). Made Jan. 9, 1708. Heirs: sons Robert, Richard, John; daus. Joanna, Elizabeth; wife Elenor. Exec'x, wife Elenor. Wits., Robert Draughton, Walter Johnson, Susanna Johnson. Prob. March 29, 1709. Arch. vol. A13, page 109. Reg. of Wills, Liber B, folio 77.

Sherrer, William. Will (copy). Made Jan. 24, 1705. Heirs: sons William, Robert; wife Mary; dau. Mary; Robert Draughton. Exec'x, wife. Wits., Henry Molleston, John Clayton, Thomas Bedwell. Prob. April 5, 1709. Arch. vol. A45, page 236. Reg. of Wills, Liber B, folio 77.

Molleston, John. Admin. of, to Helenor Molleston. April 5, 1709. Reg. of Wills, Liber B, folio 78.

Black, John. Admin. of, to Suies Duies. April 5, 1709. Reg. of Wills, Liber B, folio 78.

Nickolls, William. Admin. of, to Hannah Nickolls. April 5, 1709. Reg. of Wills, Liber B, folio 78.

Hall, John, Jr. Admin. of, to Jean Hall. April 5, 1709. Reg. of Wills, Liber B, folio 78.

Luff, Hugh. Will (copy). Made Jan. 7, 1709. Heirs: wife Sarah; daus. Sarah, Hannah; son Nathaniel; one other child. Exec'rs, Nathaniel Hunn, John Bowers. Wits., Charles Auston, Zacaria Goforth, Anne Burgess. Prob. April 16, 1709. Arch. vol. A31, page 223. Reg. of Wills, Liber B, folio 79.

Shepherd, John. Admin. of, to Sarah Shepherd. May 10, 1709. Reg. of Wills, Liber C, folio 79.

Ellitt, Susanna. Will (copy). Made March 16, 1709. Little Duck Creek Hd. Heirs: sons Thomas, Isaac, John; daus. Mary & Joanna. Exec'rs, Absalom Cuff & John Piggott. Guardian, James Steel. Wits., Francis Hirons, John Huff. Prob. May 25, 1709. Arch. vol. A16, page 113. Reg. of Wills, Liber C, folio 80.

Whyte, James. Will (copy). Made Sept. 18, 1709. Dover River. Heirs: son James; Daniel Smith, friend; wife not named. Exec'r, Daniel Smith. Wits., Jean Courtney, Elizabeth Hiken, Isaac Lenoir. Prob. Sept. 23, 1709. Arch. vol. A54, page 215. Reg. of Wills, Liber C, folio 80.

Shepherd, John. Admin. of, to Sarah Rodeney, wife of Wm. Rodeney. Oct. 4, 1709. Reg. of Wills, Liber C, folio 82.

White, Benjamin. Will (nunc. copy). Made Oct. 7, 1709. Heirs: mother-in-law, Mary Betts; son not named. Exec'r, Thomas Skidmore. Wits., William Steel, Walter Hamilton, Francis Steel, Robert Miller. Prob. Oct. 11, 1709. Arch. vol. A54, page 101. Reg. of Wills, Liber C, folio 81.

Steel, William. Admin. of, to Frances Steel. Oct. 29, 1709. Reg. of Wills, Liber 7, folio 82.

Burrows, Edward. Admin. of, to Sarah Burrows. Nov. 8, 1709. Reg. of Wills, Liber C, folio 81.

Steel, William. Admin. of, to Arthur Steel & Robert Miller. Dec. 13, 1709. Reg. of Wills, Liber C, folio 81.

Williams, Reynear. Will (copy). Made Dec. 12, 1709. Heirs: sons Reynear, William Aaron; wife Susanna; daus. Gerthy Nangisell, Susannah Manlove, Cathrine, Mary. Exec'r, son Reynear. Wits., Mark Manlove, Archibald Douglas, Lewis Aways. Prob. Dec. 20, 1709. Arch. vol. A55, page 137. Reg. of Wills, Liber C, folio 82.

Gumley, Benjamin. Yeoman. Will (copy). Made Sept. 16, 1709. Duck Creek. Heirs: sons John, James, William, Edward, Benjamin; daus. Rachel, Susanna, Ruth; Edward Burrows. Exec'rs, Absalom Cuff, son, Benjamin. Trustees, Joseph England, James Steel, Timothy Hanson, William Horn. Wits., Francis Wettswood, Thomas Dugdale, Absalom Cuff. Prob. Jan. 2, 1709/10. Arch. vol. A21, page 52. Reg. of Wills, Liber C, folios 83-84.

Manlove, Luke. Will (copy). Made Dec. 29, 1708. Heirs: sons Luke, William, George, John, Joseph; daus. Anne & Mary. Exec'rs, sons Luke & William. Trustees, Joseph Booth & Mark Manlove. Wits., William Simson, Rachel Manlove, Mark Manlove. Prob. Jan. 5, 1709/10. Arch. vol. A32, page 31. Reg. of Wills, Liber C, folios 84-85.

Betts, Mary. Will (copy). Made Dec. 5, 1709. Murther Creek. Heirs: grandsons Benjamin White, Thomas, Robert & William Winsmore; Elizabeth Crawford; sister Elizabeth Brinckloe; Samuel Burberry; John Brinckloe; Anne, dau. of George Robisson. Exec'rs, John Brinckloe, Arthur Meston, Stephen Nowell. Wits., Samuel Burberry, Walter Hamilton, James Miller. Prob. Jan. 30, 1709/10. Arch. vol. A4, pages 36 & 37. Reg. of Wills, Liber C, folios 85-86.

King, Richard. Admin. of, to John Pound. May 5, 1710. Reg. of Wills, Liber C, folio 86.

Cooke, Margaret. Will (copy). Made Dec. 23, 1712. Phila. Heirs: dau. Sarah; sons Joseph, John & Benjamin; granddaus. Mary Cooke, Catherine Vaughan, Margaret Morris; John Cadwalader. Exec'r, son John. Wits., Hugh Cordry, Richard Wood, Deborah Cordry. Prob. Jan. 24, 1712. Arch. vol. A10, page 130. Reg. of Wills, Liber G, folios 24-25. Reg. of Wills, Phila., Book O, 326.

Annand, William. Will (copy). Made Dec. 26, 1714. Heirs: wife Elizabeth; Andrew & James Hambleton, sons of Andrew Hambleton. Exec'x, wife Elizabeth. Trustee, Andrew Hambleton of Chester River. Wits., Vincent Emerson, James Maxwell, Josiah Martin, John Crowy. Prob. April 23, 1715. Arch. vol. A1, page 219. Reg. of Wills, Liber L, folio 42.

Coe, John. Will (copy). Made April 24, 1717. Heirs: sons William, John, Thomas; daus. Sarah, Patience; bro. William Coe; sons-in-laws Samuel, Isaac, & Cornelius Willbanks; servant Grace Lodge. Exec'r, bro. William Coe. Wits., John Jackson, Elizabeth Jackson, James Steele. Prob. June 4, 1717. Arch. vol. A9, page 182. Reg. of Wills, Liber K, folio 189.

Smith, Jacob. Admin. of, to John Morgan. April 22, 1718. Reg. of Wills, Liber D, folio 4.

Bowman, John. Will (copy). Made July 1, 1716. Heirs: sons Henary, John, Thomas & William; wife Patience. Exec'x, wife Patience. Wits., William Brinkle, Nathaniel Bowman, James Bowman, Edward Macinnee. Prob. June 23, 1718. Arch. vol. A5, page 45. Reg. of Wills, Liber D, folio 3.

Rock, Patrick. Admin. of, to Phillip Kearney & Rowland FitzGerald. July 17, 1718. Reg. of Wills, Liber D, folio 4.

Hunn, Nathaniel. Admin. of, to Ellinor Hunn. Aug. 25, 1718. Reg. of Wills, Liber D, folio 5.

MacNett, John. Admin. of, to Mary Smith. Oct. 17, 1718. Reg. of Wills, Liber D, folio 5.

Clayton, John. Admin. of, to Mary Clayton. Jan. 5, 1718. Reg. of Wills, Liber D, folio 6.

Wallis, James. Bristol, England. Admin. of, to John Bradshaw. Feb. 10, 1718. Reg. of Wills, Liber D, folio 38.

Crosley [Crosly], Richard. Bristol, England. Admin. of, to John Bradshaw. Feb. 10, 1718. Reg. of Wills, Liber D, folio 39.

Jones, Charles. Bristol, England. Admin. of, to John Bradshaw. Feb. 10, 1718. Reg. of Wills, Liber D, folio 39.

Taylor, Thomas. Bristol, England. Admin. of, to John Bradshaw. Feb. 10, 1718. Arch. vol. A48, page 6. Reg. of Wills, Liber D, folios 39-40.

Lenton, Nathaniel. Will (copy). Made Jan. 2, 1718. Heirs: daus. Ellinor, Mary, Rebecca; wife, Mary. Exec'x, wife Mary. Wits., Michael Lowbar, Arthur Brooks, Ann Nickols. Prob. Feb. 12, 1718. Arch. vol. A30, page 16. Reg. of Wills, Liber D, folio 6.

Alley, John. Will (copy). Made Feb. 19, 1718. Heirs: sons Peter, Abraham, Johanus [Johanns]; daus. Hannah, Mary, Elizabeth, Rachell, Jane Vanwinkle (wife of Simon Vanwinkle), Susannah (wife of John Vangasco); son Jacob; sons-in-law Simeon Vanwinkle & John Vangasco. Exec'rs, sons Peter, Abraham & Johanns. Wits., John Hillyard, Isabell Smith, John Bradshaw, Sr. Prob. March 16, 1718. Arch. vol. A1, page 98. Reg. of Wills, Liber D, folios 7-8.

Hendry, David. Admin. of, [no adm'r]. ...1718. Arch. vol. A23, page 128.

Jones, Charles. Admin. of, to John Bradshaw. March 25, 1719. Reg. of Wills, Liber D, folio 9.

Smith, David. Will (copy). Made April 2, 1719. Heir: William Rodeny. Exec'r, William Rodeny. Wits., Adam Fisher, Jerimiah Nickerson, Joseph Nickerson. Prob. May 13, 1719. Arch. vol. A47, page 18. Reg. of Wills, Liber D, folio 9.

Donn, Thomas. Admin. of, to George Martin. Aug. 20, 1719. Reg. of Wills, Liber D, folio 11.

Glover, Richard. Will (copy). Made Dec. 25, 1719. Heirs: daus. Mary & Elizabeth; son John. Exec'rs, sons John Glover & John Stevens. Wits., James Dean, John Maram. Prob. Jan. 13, 1719. Arch. vol. A-19, page 70. Reg. of Wills, Liber D, folios 11-12 & 17.

Willson, William. Admin. of, to Elizabeth Wilson. Jan. 18, 1719. Reg. of Wills, Liber D, folio 12.

Tilton, Mary. Admin. of, to John Tilton. Jan. 20, 1719. Reg. of Wills, Liber D, folio 13.

Smith, John. Admin. of, to John Lowden. Feb. 3, 1719. Reg. of Wills, Liber D, folio 13.

Smith, John. Will (copy—not signed). Made Jan. 27, 1719. Salsbury. Heirs: John Lowden, Joseph Lewden, Josiah Lowden, bros.-in-law. Exec'r, John Cook. [No prob.] Arch. vol. A47, page 70. Reg. of Wills, Liber D, folio 13.

Cook, John. Admin. of, to Mary Cook. Feb. 27, 1719. Reg. of Wills, Liber D, folio 14.

Vessey, Robert. Will (copy). Made Jan. 22, 1719/20. Heirs: bro. John; cousin Solomon Vessey. Exec'r, Solomon Vessey. Wits., John Pryor, Thomas Hackett. Prob. Feb. 27, 1719. Arch. vol. A52, page 33. Reg. of Wills, Liber D, folio 15.

Ellis, Thomas. Will (copy). Made Feb. 1, 1719. Heir: wife Rachell. Exec'x, wife Rachell. Wits., Michael Richman, John Price, John Cooke. Prob. Feb. 27, 1719. Arch. vol. A16, page 111. Reg. of Wills, Liber D, folio 15.

Register, William. Admin. of, to John Register. March 5, 1719. Reg. of Wills, Liber D, folio 16.

Mathews, Hugh. Admin. of, to Elizabeth Mathews. March 10, 1719. Reg. of Wills, Liber D, folio 16.

Hubbert, Robert. Admin. of, to William Morgan. March 12, 1719. Reg. of Wills, Liber D, folio 17.

Pugh, David. Admin. of, to John Powell. June 2, 1719. Reg. of Wills, Liber D, folio 19.

Downham, Thomas. Will (copy). Made Sept. 15, 1719. Heirs: sons Thomas, Richard; dau. Elenor; wife Agnes; four daughters not named. Exec'x, wife. Wits., Thomas Skidmore, Daniel Money. Prob. Nov. 3, 1719. Arch. vol. A14, page 234. Reg. of Wills, Liber D, folio 2.

Gascoin, John. Admin. of, to Sarah Gascoin. April 4, 1720. Reg. of Wills, Liber D, folios 17-18.

Clayton, Joshua. Admin. of, to Abraham Brooks. May 17, 1720. Reg. of Wills, Liber D, folio 18.

Rodeney, Anthony. Admin. of, to Daniel Rodeney. May 7, 1720. Reg. of Wills, Liber D, folio 19.

Hayes, Elizabeth. Will (copy, nunc.). Made May 18, 1720. Heir: Richard Richardson, landlord. Exec'r, Richard Richardson. Wits., Ann Clifford, Rachel Herbert. Prob. May 21, 1720. Arch. vol. A23, page 64. Reg. of Wills, Liber D, folio 18.

Pugh, Ann. Will (copy). Made Nov. 24, 1719. Heirs: sons John Pugh, David, Samuel, Jonathan, & Joseph Powell; daus. Ann Pugh & Christian Powell. Exec'rs, bro. John Howard, bro.-in-law William Powell, son John Powell. Wits., John Scot, Arthur Alsston, John Mifflin. Prob. June 2, 1720. Arch. vol. A41, page 198. Reg. of Wills, Liber D, folio 10.

Manlove, Mark. Farmer. Will (copy). Made May 7, 1720. Heirs: wife Mary; dau. Sarah Manlove. Exec'rs, wife Mary, bro. Mathew. Wits., Charles Maring, William Mucklegeare. Prob. June 18, 1720. Arch. vol. A32, page 37. Reg. of Wills, Liber D, folio 20.

Lewis, Lancellot. Will (copy, nunc.). Made July 24, 1720. Duck Creek. Heirs: sons Lancellot & John; daus. Martha, Elizabeth, & Mary, wife of Alexander Humphries. Wits., John Foster, James Tire, William Fortescue. Prob. July 25, 1720. Arch. vol. A30, page 107. Reg. of Wills, Liber D, folio 21.

Smith, Daniel. Admin. of, to William Rodeny. Aug. 2, 1720. Reg. of Wills, Liber D, folio 21.

Toas, Daniel. Admin. of, to John Hudson. Aug. 25, 1720. Reg. of Wills, Liber D, folio 22.

Black, John. Admin. of, to Jonathan Manlove. Aug. 25, 1720. Reg. of Wills, Liber D, folio 23.

Kelly, William. Admin. of, to James Jackson. Sept. 2, 1720. Reg. of Wills, Liber D, folio 24.

Ellitt, John. Planter. Will (copy). Made Nov. 7, 1720. Little Creek Hd. Heirs: bros. Thomas, Isaac; Rachell Alston; Samuel Freeman. Exec'r, bro. Thomas. Wits., Samuel Freeman, Gabriel Latchen. Prob. Sept. 13, 1720. Arch. vol. A16, page 98. Reg. of Wills, Liber D, folios 28-29.

Letort, Ann. Admin. of, to James Letort. Sept. 19, 1720. Reg. of Wills, Liber D, folio 29.

Fields, Abraham. Admin. of, to Elizabeth Fields. Sept. 23, 1720. Reg. of Wills, Liber D, folio 24.

Dean, James. Will (copy). Made Nov. 25, 1720. Heirs: wife Mary; dau. unnamed. Exec'x, wife. Wits., Thomas Winsmore, Jno. McDowell, William Morgan. Prob. Sept. 26, 1720. Arch. vol. A13, page 135. Reg. of Wills, Liber D, folios 30-31.

Coe, William. Will (copy). Made Sept. 12, 1720. Heirs: niece Sarah Coe, nephew, Thomas Coe, children of bro. John; wife Alice Coe. Exec'x, wife Alice. Wits., John Bowers, William Rodeney, Ruth Rodeney. Prob. Sept. 30, 1720. Arch. vol. A9, page 184. Reg. of Wills, Liber D, folios 24-25.

Freeman, Samuel. Will (copy). Made Dec. 3, 1720. Heirs: sons Samuel & Joseph; daus. Mary & Elizabeth. Exec'r, John Foster. Wits., John Hall, Richard Smith, Miles Mason. Prob. Sept. 30, 1720. (Codicil mentions wife Elizabeth as exec'x). Arch. vol. A18, page 131. Reg. of Wills, Liber D, folio 31.

Lester, ... [part of a will]. Heirs: son George; daus. Ann & Mary. Reg. of Wills, Liber D, folio 25.

Hargrove, Stephen. Admin. of, to George Hargrove. Oct. 27, 1720. Reg. of Wills, Liber D, folio 26.

Cook, Arthur. Will (copy, nunc.). Made Oct. 30, 1720. Heirs: wife Elizabeth; bro. John; child of James Morry. Wits., Jno. Hillyard, Michael Richmond, John Cook, Rachell Ellis. Prob. Nov. 2, 1720. Arch. vol. A10, page 107. Reg. of Wills, Liber D, folio 26.

Hillyard, John. Admin. of, to Griffith Jones & Jonathan Sturgis. Nov. 21, 1720. Reg. of Wills, Liber D, folio 27.

Pepper, Richard. Admin. of, to John Hall. Nov. 29, 1720. Reg. of Wills, Liber D, folio 27.

Mifflin, John. Will (copy). Made ..., 1720. Heirs: sons Benjamin, John; servant Samuel Greenwood; friend Timothy Hanson; bros. & sisters not named; Israel Pemberton; Clymon Plomstead. Exec'rs, Israel Pemberton & Clymon Plomstead. Wits., Samuel Greenwood, Richard Smith, Rachell Hillyard. Prob. Dec. 9, 1720. Arch. vol. A35, page 8. Reg. of Wills, Liber D, folios 27-28.

Allen, James. Tailor. Admin. of, to Samuell Gorden. Dec. 23, 1720. Reg. of Wills, Liber D, folio 30.

Dickenson, Walter. Admin. of, to Samuel Dickenson. Dec. 23, 1720. Reg. of Wills, Liber D, folio 30.

Green, George. Will (copy). Made Dec. 29, 1720. Heirs: sons Thomas, George, John. Exec'rs, wife Rachel, son George, son-in-law John Welles. Wits., John Hall, Christian Vannay, James Potter. Arch. vol. A20, page 66. Reg. of Wills, Liber D, folio 36.

Edinfield, John. Tailor. Will (copy). Made Dec. 2, 1720. Dover Hd. Heirs: wife Rebecca; sons John, Jonas, Thomas; daus. Elinor Edinfield & Ann Harte. Exec'x, Rebecca, wife. Trustees, Thomas French & John Bland. Wits., Thomas Winsmore, Christopher Corkram, John Bland. Prob. Jan. 7, 1720. Arch. vol. A16, page 14. Reg. of Wills, Liber D, folio 32.

Howard, Samuel. Will (copy, nunc.). Made Jan. 10, 1720. Heirs: dau. Mary; child of dau. Mary; bros. William & Jno.; wife not named. Exec'x, wife. Wits., William Coleson, Samuel Willson, Johanah Willson. Arch. vol. A25, page 54. Reg. of Wills, Liber D, folio 40.

Cook, Arthur. Will (copy). Made Sept. 30, 1699. Phila. Heirs: sons John, Thomas, Joseph, Benjamin; daus. Sarah, Pricilla; five children of son John; wife not named. Exec'x, wife. Wits., Griffith Jones, Jane Jones, William Preston. Prob. Jan. 17, 1720. Arch. vol. A10, page 106. Reg. of Wills, Liber G, folio 16. Note:—Original in Register's Book N, page 413, Phila.

Williams, William. Merchant. Will (copy). Made Jan. 19, 1720/21. Mispillion Hd. Heirs: dau. Susannah Pecker; sisters Susanna Manlove (wife of Mathew Manlove) & Gartrude Dingeesly. Exec'r, Mathew Manlove. Wits., Henry Hall, Robert Betts, Thomas May, Jr. [No prob.] Arch. vol. A55, page 172. Reg. of Wills, Liber D, folio 35.

Marim, Charles. Carpenter. Will (copy). Made Dec. 14, 1720. Heirs: wife Frances; bro. John; daus. Mary & Temmima; one child unnamed. Exec'rs, wife Frances, bro. John. Wits., Sarah Spencer, Mary Spencer, Thomas Esgate. Prob. Jan. 21, 1720. Arch. vol. A33, page 172. Reg. of Wills, Liber D, folio 33.

Fortus, Tobias. Cordwainer. Admin. of, to John Barns. Jan. 21, 1720. Reg. of Wills, Liber D, folio 34.

Tuilly, Robert. Admin. of, to John Rodulphus Bundelyn. Jan. 23, 1720. Reg. of Wills, Liber D, folio 34.

Green, George. Yeoman. Admin. of, to Rachel Green. Feb. 6, 1720. Reg. of Wills, Liber D, folio 35.

Hawkey, William. Will (copy). Made Jan. 26, 1720. Duck Creek. Heir: wife Hannah. Exec'x, wife Hannah. Wits., Evan Jones, Charles Hillyard, William Rush, George Martin, Nicholas Greenaway. Prob. Feb. 15, 1720. Arch. vol. A23, page 10. Reg. of Wills, Liber D, folio 36.

Jones, Griffith. Will (copy). Made Feb. 23, 1720/21. Dover Hd. Heirs: wife Frances; sons Griffith & Thomas; dau. Elizabeth. Exec'rs, wife Frances, James Gorden, Thomas Crawford, George Nowell.. Wits., Philip Morgan, John Mallcoon, John Rachlege. Prob. March 1, 1720/21. Arch. vol. A27, page 181. Reg. of Wills, Liber D, folio 37.

Dean, Mary. Widow of James. Admin. of, to Robert Gordon. March 10, 1720/21. Reg. of Wills, Liber D, folio 40.

Perrie, Thomas. Blacksmith. Admin. of, to Elinor Perrie. March 15, 1720. Reg. of Wills, Liber D, folio 37.

LaMott, Charles. Planter. Admin. of, to John Barnes. March 18, 1720. Reg. of Wills, Liber D, folio 38.

Manlove, Jonathan. Farmer. Will (copy). Made March 3, 1721. Heirs: daus. Mary, Ann; sister Sarah Molleston; wife Hannah; cousins Tabitha & Mary Williams; bros. Henry Molestone, Joseph Spencer; sister Tabitha's children. Exec'rs, wife Hannah, father-in-law Samuel Spencer. Wits., Mathew Manlove, Henry Hall, Luke Manlove. Prob. April 3, 1721. Arch. vol. A33, page 111. Reg. of Wills, Liber D, folio 41.

Jackson, James. Will (copy). Made March 13, 1721. Heirs: bro. Michael Mason; friend Samuel Glen; son James; Rebecca & Rachel Glen, daus. of Samuel Glen; Mathew & Richard Mason, sons of Michael. Exec'rs, Michael Mason, Isaac Snow. Wits., John Stiles, Thomas Leatherbury. Prob. April 5, 1721. Arch. vol. A26, pages 2-3. Reg. of Wills, Liber D, folio 42.

Crippen, John. Will (copy). Made March 1, 1720/21. Heirs: sons John & Thomas; wife Elizabeth. Exec'x, wife Elizabeth. Wits., William Haller, John Tomelin, William Manlove. Prob. April 11, 1721. Arch. vol. A11, page 226. Reg. of Wills, Liber D, folios 42-43.

Shurley, Richard. Admin. of, to John Willson & Thomas Crawford. April 12, 1721. Arch. vol. A46, pages 39-41. Reg. of Wills, Liber D, folio 50.

Emerson, Vincent. Gentleman. Will (copy). Made June 4, 1720. Heirs: Elizabeth Hall, dau. of John & Anna Hall; dau. Sarah. Exec'rs, dau. Sarah & John Hall. Wits., Barbery Queling, Morgan Bedwell, Elioner Bedwell, John Hall. Prob. April 15, 1721. Arch. vol. A16, page 172. Reg. of Wills, Liber D, folio 43.

Gilbert, Prissila. Widow. Will (copy). Made Jan. 22, 1719/20. Heirs: daus. Sarah Bowman, Prissila Walton & Ruth Rodney; son John Bowers; grandsons Nathaniel Hunn & Nathaniel Luff; granddau. Penelop Rodney, dau. of William & Ruth Rodney; Thomas Bowman, son of Nathaniel Bowman. Exec'rs, son John Bowers & son-in-law Nathaniel Bowman. Wits., Jonathan Manlove, Hannah Manlove. Prob. May 10, 1721. Arch. vol. A19, page 28. Reg. of Wills, Liber D, folio 44.

Sturges, Jonathan. Will (copy). Made April 23, 1721. Heir: wife Elizabeth. Exec'x, Elizabeth, wife. Wits., Robert Cuming, Barbury Smith, William Birkett. Prob. May 11, 1721. Arch. vol. A49, page 108. Reg. of Wills, Liber D, folio 45.

Wells, John. Will (copy). Made April 1, 1721. Heirs: wife Rachel; dau. Rachel; sons James & John. Exec'x, wife Rachel. Trustees, Thomas Wells, Hugh Durborow. Wits., John Hall, James Potter, William Maxwell. Prob. May 11, 1721. Arch. vol. A53, page 231. Reg. of Wills, Liber D, folio 46.

Winsmore, Thomas. Admin. of, to Samuel Berry. June 27, 1721. Reg. of Wills, Liber D, folio 47.

Cuff, Aboslom. Admin. of, to Charles Hillyard. Nov. 6, 1721. Reg. of Wills, Liber D, folio 47.

Brinckloe, John. Captain. Will (copy). Made May 10, 1720. Dover Hd. Heirs: friend Thomas Crawford; Evis, Mary, Letetia, Elizabeth, daus. of Thomas Crawford; cousin Peter Brinckloe; wife Elizabeth Brinckloe. Exec'rs, wife & Thomas Crawford. Wits., Charles Hillyard, John Plessenton. Prob. Dec. 8, 1721. Arch. vol. A5, page 221. Reg. of Wills, Liber D, folios 47-49.

Pain, Fletcher. Admin. of, to Ann Mitchell & Hugh Durborow. Dec. 15, 1721. Reg. of Wills, Liber D, folio 49.

Gumley, Benjamin. Admin. of, to James Gumley. Feb. 15, 1721. Reg. of Wills, Liber D, folio 50.

Jones, Evan. Will (copy). Made Dec. 28, 1720. Heirs: George Martin; Philip Denney; Susannah Greenwood; Josiah Martain; children of James Davis & Mathias Greenwood; Elizabeth Pain, wife of John; Elizabeth Pain, dau. of John; Mary Davis; Mary Reece, wife of David; Franci Taylor, son of Thomas; Josiah Martin; Isable & Robert Smith, wife and son of Richard Smith. Exec'rs, George Martin & Philip Denney. Wits., Charles Hillyard, Richard Smith, John Alee, John Tilton. Prob. March 21, 1721. Arch. vol. A27, pages 170-171. Reg. of Wills, Liber D, folio 51.

Kearny, Philip. Admin. of, to Rebecca Kearney, widow. April 7, 1722. Arch. vol. A28, page 88. Reg. of Wills, Liber D, folio 57.

Brinckle, William. Will (copy). Made April 1, 1722. Heirs: sons William, Winnlock [Winlock], & John Brinckle & John Curtis; daus. Elizabeth, Mariam [Miriam], & Sarah Brinckle & Mary Curtis; wife Elizabeth. Exec'rs, wife Elizabeth, son-in-law Jehu Curtis. Wits., Andrew Freasure, William Mulroney, Hannah Freasure. Prob. May 8, 1722. Arch. vol. A5, page 217. Reg. of Wills, Liber D, folios 52-54.

Hudson, Richard. Admin. of, to Thomas Skidmore. May 16, 1722. Reg. of Wills, Liber D, folio 54.

Wheeler, William. Planter. Admin. of, to Mary Wheeler. June 13, 1722. Reg. of Wills, Liber D, folio 62.

Ewins, Abraham. Admin. of, to Charles Hyliard. July 3, 1722. Reg. of Wills, Liber D, folio 57.

Nugent [Newgent], Christopher. Will (copy, nunc.). Made May 11, 1722. Heirs: mother Elizabeth; sister Eadith, widow of James Adams. Wits., Robert Hodgson, Robert Wilson. Prob. July 10, 1722. Arch. vol. A37, page 204. Reg. of Wills, Liber D, folios 57-58.

Ellis, Benjamin. Yeoman. Admin. of, to Andrew Caldwell. July 27, 1722. Reg. of Wills, Liber D, folio 58.

Jones, Frances. Admin. of, to James McDowell. July 31, 1722. Reg. of Wills, Liber D, folio 59.

Trood, Henry. Tanner. Admin. of, to John Bland. Aug. 6, 1722. Reg. of Wills, Liber D, folio 62.

Ellis, Benjamin. Carpenter. Will (copy). Made Oct. 26, 1721. Kent Co., Md. Heirs: sister Jane, wife of William Burroughs; dau. Ann. Exec'r, bro. Williams. Wits., George Mifflin, Joseph Tabor, Charles Osborne. Prob. Aug. 14, 1722. Arch. vol. A16, page 105. Reg. of Wills, Liber D, folios 54-55.

Webb, Robert. Will (copy). Made Jan. 8, 1708. Heir: wife Sarah. Exec'x, wife Sarah. Wits., Elizabeth Goodin, Daniel Goodin, Will Annand. Prob. Oct. 8, 1722. Arch. vol. A53, page 211. Reg. of Wills, Liber D, folio 59.

Willson, William. Planter. Will (copy). Made Sept. 4, 1717. Heirs: son Robert; wife Agnis; my other children; grandson William Armstrong. Exec'x, wife. Wits., Samuel Willson, Robert Willson, Francis Alexander. Prob. Oct. 27, 1722. Arch. vol. A56, page 22. Reg. of Wills, Liber D, folio 56. Probate wits., Andrew Caldwell, Jonah Willson, Margaret Caldwell.

Carleton, Edward. Admin. of, to John Harrison. Nov. 15, 1722. Reg. of Wills, Liber D, folio 55.

Bowden, Ezekiel. Planter. Admin. of, to Frances Bowden. Dec. 12, 1722. Reg. of Wills, Liber D, folio 60.

Foster, John. Yeoman. Will (copy). Made March 30, 1722. Phila. Heirs: wife Anne; son-in-law William Manlove; children of Thomas & Mary Davis; Ruth Steell, dau. of James Steell; Mary, William, & Joseph, children of William & Elizabeth Rush. Exec'x, wife. Wits., Samuel Harriott, William Parsons, William Rush. Prob. Jan. 31, 1722. Arch. vol. A18, page 43. Reg. of Wills, Liber D, folio 60.

Howard, Samuel. Yeoman. Admin. of, to William Morriss. Feb. 1, 1722. Reg. of Wills, Liber D, folio 60.

Sim, Margaret. Salisbury. Admin. of, to Robert Elliott. Feb. 5, 1722. Reg. of Wills, Liber D, folio 61.

Morgan, George. Admin. of, to William Morgan. Feb. 5, 1722. Reg. of Wills, Liber D, folio 62.

Brincklow, Elizabeth. Widow. Will. Made Dec. 9, 1721. Dover Hd. Heirs: great-grandchildren, Elizabeth, Mary, Evis, Letitia Crawford, children of Thomas & Elizabeth Crawford; grandson-in-law Thomas Crawford. Exec'r, grandson-in-law Thomas Crawford. Wits., Else Mahan, Charles Hyliard, Ann Gream. Prob. Sept. 28, 1723. Arch. vol. A5, page 179. Reg. of Wills, Liber D, folios 62-63.

Wilson, Richard. Merchant. Will (copy). Made Sept. 6, 1723. Heir: wife Letitia. Exec'x, wife Letitia. Wits., John Lindsay, Edward Jennings, Thomas Ward. Prob. Sept. 27, 1723. Arch. vol. A55, page 242. Reg. of Wills, Liber D, folio 63.

Hutton, John. Merchant. Admin. of, to Timothy Hudson. Oct. 26, 1723. Reg. of Wills, Liber D, folio 64.

Powell, John. Yeoman. Admin. of, to Andrew Caldwell. Nov. 16, 1723. Reg. of Wills, Liber D, folio 64.

Wheeler, John. Yeoman. Admin. of, to Joshua Wheeler. Nov. 27, 1723. Reg. of Wills, Liber D, folio 64.

Garve, Owen. Will (copy). Made Dec. 2, 1723. Heirs: sons Owen, Mathew, John, Silvester; daus. Mary & Elizabeth; wife Mary. Exec'x, wife Mary. Wits., Joshua Wheeler, Elizabeth Wheeler, William Manlove. Prob. Jan. 6, 1723. Arch. vol. A18, page 227. Reg. of Wills, Liber D, folio 65.

Donaldson, Charles. Yeoman. Admin. of, to Alexander Donaldson. March 27, 1724. Reg. of Wills, Liber D, folio 65.

Black, James. Planter. Admin. of, to Jane Black. July 15, 1724. Reg. of Wills, Liber D, folio 66.

Donavan [Dunnavan], Randall. Will (copy). Made Sept. 21, 1724. Heirs: sons Daniel & Randall; daus. Mary, Johannah, Sussanah; wife not named. Exec'rs, wife & friends Cornelius Sullivant, John Hart. Wits., Daniel Rodeney, Christopher Cockrum, Susannah Cockrum, Jean Nowell. Prob. Oct. 10, 1724. Arch. vol. A14, page 171. Reg. of Wills, Liber D, folio 66.

Nickeson [Nickerson], Jeremiah. Will (copy). Made Oct. 9, 1724. Dover Hd. Heirs: sons Joshua, Joseph; daus. Lidey, Persella, Mary, Richameg; grandsons, Nehemiah & Jeremiah Nickerson; wife not named. Exec'rs, wife & son Joshua. Wits., John Mayrom, Daniel Griffith, Daniel Rodeney. Prob. Oct. 31, 1724. Arch. vol. A37, page 231. Reg. of Wills, Liber D, folio 67.

Vaughan, Elizabeth. Widow. Admin. of, to John McDowell. Dec. 22, 1724. Reg. of Wills, Liber D, folio 67.

Nock, Thomas. Yeoman. Will (copy). Made Oct. 26, 1724. Heirs: wife Sarah; sons Ezekiell, Daniel & Thomas; daus. Patience, Ann, Sarah. Exec'x, wife. Trustees, Joseph Booth, Sr., Daniel Needham, Jabez Jenkins. Wits., William Rodeney, Jabez Jenkins, George Medcalfe, Benjamin Shurmer. Prob. Jan. 4, 1724. Arch. vol. A38, page 34. Reg. of Wills, Liber D, folio 68.

Carr, Robert. Will (copy). Made Dec. 11, 1724. Heirs: Mary Carr; Jeremiah Coventon; Neamiagh Powell; Elizabeth Christian; step-son Samuel Axell; Joseph Ashton; wife Prudence. Exec'rs, wife, Joseph Ashton. Wits., John Cowgill, Samuel Tomlinson, Isaac Snow. Prob. Jan. 7, 1724. Arch. vol. A7, page 240. Reg. of Wills, Liber D, folio 68.

Clayton, John. Yeoman. Admin. of, to Moses Freeman. Jan. 27, 1724. Reg. of Wills, Liber D, folio 69.

Hirons, Robert. Admin. of, to Mary Hirons. Feb. 5, 1724. Reg. of Wills, Liber D, folio 69.

Gooding, Daniel. Yeoman. Admin. of, to Elizabeth Gooding. Feb. 22, 1724. Reg. of Wills, Liber D, folio 69.

Fisher, Adam. Will (copy). Made March 29, 1725. Heirs: sons John, Adams, Joseph, Molliston, Isaac; daus. Mary, Susannah, Sarah; wife Mary. Exec'x, wife. Wits., John Newell, John Sipple, Abraham Morriss. Prob. May 18, 1725. Arch. vol. A17, page 113. Reg. of Wills, Liber F, folio 3.

Brown, Daniel. Admin. of, to Elizabeth Brown. June 4, 1725. Reg. of Wills, Liber F, folio 3.

Marten, Charles. Will (copy). Made Sept. 14, 1724. Heirs: sons Nathaniel & John; daus. Jane & Mary; wife Elizabeth. Exec'x, wife Elizabeth. Wits., William Morriss, Philip Brady, John Clampet. Prob. June 7, 1725. Arch. vol. A33, page 204. Reg. of Wills, Liber F, folio 4.

Whitehead, Isaiah. Carpenter. Admin. of, to Thomas Skidmore. Aug. 25, 1725. Reg. of Wills, Liber F, folio 5.

Berry, Edward. Will (copy). Made Sept. 3, 1725. Heirs: Edward Buck, son of John Buck; wife Elizabeth. Exec'x, wife Elizabeth. Wits., Mark Manlove, Joseph Booth, Jr., Rachel Manlove. Prob. Oct. 1, 1725. Arch. vol. A4, page 2. Reg. of Wills, Liber F, folio 7.

Bamton, John. Merchant. Admin. of, to Abraham Vannoy. Oct. 15, 1725. Reg. of Wills, Liber F, folio 5.

Mackedo, James. Weaver. Admin. of, to William Mackedo [Macadow]. Nov. 12, 1725. Reg. of Wills, Liber F, folio 5.

Adams, Thomas. Will (copy, nunc.). Heir: W. Housman. Exec'r, W. Housman. Wits., Ephriam Emerson, Mary Emerson. Prob. Dec. 3, 1725. Arch. vol. A1, page 12. Reg. of Wills, Liber F, folio 10.

Hammitt, Elizabeth. Wife of John Hammitt. Will (copy). Made Oct. 31, 1725. Heirs: sons Winlock & John Brinkle; daus. Mary Curtis, wife of Jehu Curtis, Elizabeth Clark, wife of John, Jr., Miriam & Sarah Brinkle. Exec'rs, sons John & Winlock Brinkle. Trustees, bros.-in-law John & Peter Brinkle. Wits., Elizabeth Brinkle, Hannah Masten, Curtis Brinkle. Prob. Dec. 8, 1725. Arch. vol. A21, page 189. Reg. of Wills, Liber F, folio 6.

Brinkle, Margarett. Widow. Admin. of, to Peter Brinkle. Dec. 14, 1725. Reg. of Wills, Liber F, folio 8.

Parvis, Richard. Yeoman. Admin. of, to Hugh Perry. Dec. 14, 1725. Reg. of Wills, Liber F, folio 9.

Manlove, William. Will (copy). Made April 13, 1724. Heirs: son Hezekiah; bro. Luke; wife Susannah. Exec'rs, wife Susannah & bro. Luke. Wits., William Manlove (carpenter), Joseph Manlove, Isaac Marratt. Prob. Dec. 15, 1725. Arch. vol. A33, page 132. Reg. of Wills, Liber F, folio 8.

Pain, John. Yeoman. Admin. of, to Elizabeth Pain. Dec. 21, 1725. Reg. of Wills, Liber F, folio 9.

Hillyard, John. Will (copy). Made Jan. 13, 1725. Heirs: sons Benjamin, Thomas; grandsons John, Oliver & Solomon; Rachel, dau. of Phillip Denny; Thomas Green. Exec'r, Thomas Green. Wits., John Peal, William Branigan, William Morphey. Prob. Jan. 26, 1725. Arch. vol. A24, page 41. Reg. of Wills, Liber F, folio 11.

Whitaker, Moses. Will (copy). Made ...1724. Heir: wife Anna. Exec'x, wife Anna. Wits., Caleb Hunn, John Tumblin, Michael Lowber, Abraham Morris. Prob. Feb. 10, 1725. Arch. vol. A54, page 96. Reg. of Wills, Liber F, folio 1.

Barns, John. Farmer. Will (copy). Made Feb. 14, 1725/6. Heirs: daus. Mary, Rebecca, Ann; son John; wife Eliner. Exec'x, wife. Wits., Uriah Collins, Charles Roberts, Robert Betts. Prob. March 9, 1725. Arch. vol. A2, page 217. Reg. of Wills, Liber F, folios 11-12.

Morphee, Nicholas. Will (copy). Made ... 16, 1723. Heirs: sons Samuel, David, William, Thomas; daus. Hannah, Rachel, Johannah, Rebecca; wife Mary. Exec'rs, son Samuel & wife. Wits., John Reece, Solomon Vessey, Richard Empson. Prob. March 20, 1725. Arch. vol. A36, page 182. Reg. of Wills, Liber F, folio 2.

Greenway, Nicholas. Merchant. Admin. of, to Elizabeth Greenway. June 4, 1726. Reg. of Wills, Liber F, folio 12.

Morgan, John. Yeoman. Admin. of, to Elizabeth Morgan. June 5, 1726. Reg. of Wills, Liber F, folio 12.

Morgan, Richard. Yeoman. Admin. of, to Daniel Hudson. June 10, 1726. Reg. of Wills, Liber F, folio 13.

Barker, James. Yeoman. Admin. of, to Thomas Barker. July 14, 1726. Reg. of Wills, Liber F, folio 14.

Ward, Thomas. Gentleman. Admin. of, to Mary Ward. July 30, 1726. Reg. of Wills, Liber F, folio 13.

Consela, Thomas. Laborer. Admin. of, to Joanna Consela. Aug. 6, 1726. Reg. of Wills, Liber F, folio 14.

Barrett, Humphrey. Will (copy). Made Aug. 11, 1726. Heirs: wife Pheby; sons Humphrey & William; two unnamed sons. Exec'x, wife. Trustee, David Morgan, bro.-in-law. Wits., Robert Howard, Mitchell Downs, David Morgan. Prob. Aug. 24, 1726. Arch. vol. A3, page 1. Reg. of Wills, Liber F, folio 14.

Hall, Henry. Admin. of, to Mary Hall. Aug. 29, 1726. Reg. of Wills, Liber F, folio 15.

Lackey, Alexander. Yeoman. Admin. of, to Mark Smith. Oct. 4, 1726. Reg. of Wills, Liber F, folio 15.

Cook, Mary. Widow. Will (copy). Made July 10, 1726. Duck Creek. Heirs: sons Robert & Michall; dau. Rachel Martin; dau.-in-law Hannah Cook. Exec'rs, sons Robert & Michall. Wits., John McKebb, Richard Empson, & Dorethy Empson. Prob. Oct. 20, 1726. Arch. vol. A10, page 123. Reg. of Wills, Liber F, folio 16.

Hall, Clary. Will (copy). Made Oct. 4, 1726. Duck Creek. Heirs: sons Jonas & John Greenwood; daus. Mary & Elizabeth Greenwood. Exec'r, son Robert Palmeterra. Wits., James Morris, Thomas Taylor, Susannah Taylor. Prob. Nov. 22, 1726. Arch. vol. A21, page 84. Reg. of Wills, Liber F, folio 17.

Worrall, James. Will (copy). Made Nov. 23, 1726. Duck Creek. Heirs: bro. Joseph; wife Mary; daus. Mary & Martha; son James. Exec'rs, wife Mary, Andrew Peterson, John Tilton. Wits., Josiah Little, Thomas Little, Henry Hodge, Benjamin Paskell. Prob. Dec. 8, 1726. Arch. vol. A56, page 139. Reg. of Wills, Liber F, folios 17-18.

Hawkey, William. Yeoman. Will (copy). Made Dec. 16, 1726. Duck Creek. Heirs: wife Elizabeth; George Martin; Josiah Martin; Elizabeth Hillyard; Elizabeth Strawhen; John Tilton, Jr.; Joseph Tilton; Mary Tilton; Martha Hawkey; grandson William Hawkey; dau.-in-law Martha Hawkey. Exec'rs, friends John Tilton, Simon Vanwinkle. Wits., George Mills, Robert Horyer, John Walvin. Prob. Dec. 28, 1726. Arch. vol. A23, pages 11-12. Reg. of Wills, Liber F, folios 18-19.

Cramer, William. Son of Thomas Cramer & grandson of William. Will (copy). Made Dec. 20, 1726. Heirs: mother Deborah Pennington; William Rodney; wife Susannah. Exec'x, wife Susannah. Wits., Edward Williams, Thomas Downham, George Brown, Elizabeth Skidmore. Prob. Dec. 31, 1726. Arch. vol. A11, pages 203-204. Reg. of Wills, Liber F, folios 19-20. Note:—Arch. vol. A11, page 204 shows Susanah Downham as exec'x.

Thomas, John. Tailor. Admin. of, to Thomas Jenckens. Jan. 20, 1726. Reg. of Wills, Liber F, folio 20.

Clifford, John. Yeoman. Will (copy). Made Dec. 9, 1726. Little Creek Hd. Heirs: son-in-law William Dyer; wife Ann; son Thomas. Exec'x, wife. Trustee, Daniel Needham. Wits., Richard Richardson, Thomas Slater, Agnes Slater. Prob. March 20, 1726. Arch. vol. A9, page 138. Reg. of Wills, Liber F, folio 22.

Allee, John. Will (copy). Made Nov. 20, 1726. Heirs: wife Gartrude; bros. Peter, Jacob; sisters Jane VanWinkle, Susannah Long, Ann Hawkins, Mary Allee, Elizabeth Allee, Rachell Allee; cousin John Allee. Exec'rs, wife and Jacob Allee, Simon VanWinkle. Wits., James Morris, Rebecka More, John Tilton. Prob. March 22, 1726. Arch. vol. A1, page 59. Reg. of Wills, Liber F, folio 21.

Vangasco, John. Yeoman. Admin. of, to Edward Long. March 22, 1726. Reg. of Wills, Liber F, folio 23.

French, Thomas. Yeoman. Will (copy). Made June 13, 1722. Dover Hd. Heirs: wife Susannah; daus. Christian, Katrain, Mary, Elizabeth. Exec'x, wife. Trustee, Robert Gordon. Wits., Samuel Strong, Elizabeth Hammond. [Prob. n. d. c. 1726.] Arch. vol. A18, page 137. Reg. of Wills, Liber F, folio 23.

Sumption, Anthony. Laborer. Admin. of, to Mitchell Down. March 25, 1727. Reg. of Wills, Liber F, folio 24.

Lenton, Mary. Widow. Will (copy). Made March 6, 1726/7. Heirs: son William Mokolls; Thomas Horsman; Isaac Opdegrof; Peter Graham; dau. Mary Lenton. Exec'x, dau. Mary Lenton. Wits., Michael Lowber, Daniel Reynolds, Grace Lowber. Prob. March 28, 1727. Arch. vol. A30, page 15. Reg. of Wills, Liber F, folio 24.

Walker, Richard. Yeoman. Admin. of, to Mary Walker, widow. April 5, 1727. Reg. of Wills, Liber F, folio 25.

Johnston, William. Yeoman. Admin. of, to Ann Johnston. April 5, 1727. Reg. of Wills, Liber F, folio 28.

White, Benjamin. Planter. Will (copy). Made April 8, 1727. Mispillion Hd. Heirs: wife Jamima; Benjamin, son of William & Hannah Broun; Mathew Manlove, Jr., Robert Windsmore; George Nawell. Exec'x, wife. Wits., John Robinson, Jo. McMillen, Mathew Manlove. Prob. April 8, 1727. Arch. vol. A54, page 102. Reg. of Wills, Liber F, folio 28.

Grier, George. Yeoman. Will (copy). Made March 2, 1726. Heirs: wife Mary; sons Mark, George, John. Exec'r, son Mark. Wits., Mark Smith, Elizabeth Smith. Prob. April 9, 1727. Arch. vol. A20, page 164. Reg. of Wills, Liber F, folio 25.

Morgan, Elizabeth. Will (copy). Made Oct. 3, 1726. Heirs: daus. Mary Donavan [Dunavan], Johanna Donavan, Susannah Donavan; sons Daniel & Randoll Donavan; friend Daniel Rodney. Exec'r, Daniel Rodney. Wits., Rebecca Edenfield, John Wilson. Prob. April 19, 1727. Arch. vol. A36, page 138. Reg. of Wills, Liber F, folio 26.

Sullyvan, Cornelius. Will (copy). Made Sept. 13, 1725. Heirs: wife Margery; sons Cornelius & William; son-in-law Stephen Simons; Susannah Sipple; Breget Moore. Exec'x, wife. Wits., Abraham Morris, Mary Fisher. Prob. April 19, 1727. Arch. vol. A49, page 115. Reg. of Wills, Liber F, folio 27.

Mahon, John. Admin. of, to John Housman. June 9, 1727. Reg. of Wills, Liber F, folio 29.

FitzGarreld, James. Will (copy). Made May 29, 1727. Heirs: sons John, James, Robert; dau. Susannah; wife Sarah; one unnamed child; Miriam Morgan; Keziah Stephens; Sarah Hirons. Exec'rs, wife & friends John Morgan, Daniel Rodney. Wits., John Stephens, John Wilson, Elizabeth Stephens. Prob. June 12, 1727. Arch. vol. A17, page 157. Reg. of Wills, Liber G, folios 2-3.

Brooks, James. (Affirmation relating to making of his will of 1713). Heirs: sons John, Arthur, Benjamin, James, Jr., Moses; daus. Elinor, Mary. Exec'r, Arthur Brooks. Wits., Michall Lowber, Unity Lowber, Mary Lenton. Prob. June 26, 1727. Arch. vol. A6, page 7. Reg. of Wills, Liber F, folio 29.

Hall, John. Admin. of, to Daniel Rodney. July 20, 1727. Reg. of Wills, Liber F, folios 29-30.

Molony, Loholen. Will (copy). Made June 11, 1727. Heirs: son James; wife not named. Exec'x, wife. Wits., John Clampit, Magdalon Thislewood. Prob. July 29, 1727. Arch. vol. A35, page 229. Reg. of Wills, Liber G, folio 3.

James, George. Yeoman. Admin. of, to Caterine James. Aug. 5, 1727. Reg. of Wills, Liber F, folio 30.

Finley, John. Laborer. Admin. of, to Thomas Barker. Aug. 14, 1727. Reg. of Wills, Liber F, folio 30.

Hoy, Richard. Admin. of, to John Hall. Oct. 28, 1727. Reg. of Wills, Liber F, folio 31.

Baily, Elias. Yeoman. Admin. of, to Sarah Baily. Nov. 7, 1727. Reg. of Wills, Liber F, folio 33.

Boak, Benjamin. Yeoman. Admin. of, to Joan Boak. Nov. 16, 1727. Reg. of Wills, Liber F, folios 33-34.

Morgan, Joshua. Will (copy). Made Oct. 28, 1727. Heirs: sons Joseph & Evan Bradbury Morgan; wife Elizabeth. Exec'r, son Even B. Morgan. Wit., William Addams. Prob. Nov. 16, 1727. Arch. vol. A36, page 158. Reg. of Wills, Liber F, folio 31.

Manlove, Joseph. Will (copy). Made April 10, 1727. Heirs: cousin Mary Nicholds, dau. of Wm. & Ann Nicholds; bros. Luke Manlove, Thomas Skidmore. Exec'r., bro. George Manlove. Wits., Stephen Simons, Adam Fisher. Prob. Nov. 29, 1727. Arch. vol. A32, page 30. Reg. of Wills, Liber F, folios 32, 33 & 26.

Wilson, Robert. Will (copy). Made Nov. 26, 1727. Heirs: sons William & Samuel; daus. Mary, Agnes, Johannah, Margaret; bro. Samuel; wife Elizabeth. Exec'x, wife. Wits., George Biodwell, Agness Wilson, Samuel Wilson, Jean Caldwell, Johannah Wilson. Prob. Dec. 29, 1727. Arch. vol. A56, page 1. Reg. of Wills, Liber F, folio 32.

Paradee, Stephen. Will (copy). Made ... 11, 1727. Heirs: sons Stephen, Jr., John, Benjamin; daus. Susannah, Agnes & Elizabeth Paradee & Sarah Fitzgarrel; wife Margaret. Exec'x, wife Margaret. Wits., Thomas Harbutt, John Sturgis, Abraham Morris. Prob. Jan. 2, 1727. Arch. vol. A38, pages 241-242. Reg. of Wills, Liber G, folio 1.

Slater, John. Will (copy). Made July 18, 1726. Heirs: sons John & Thomas; daus. Agness, Katrine Buckmaster; wife Mary. Exec'x, wife Mary. Wits., Samuel Berry, Sarah Berry. Prob. Jan. 12, 1727. Arch. vol. A46, page 218. Reg. of Wills, Liber G, folio 2.

Boak, Joan. Widow. Admin. of, to Anthony Wilkinson. Jan. 22, 1727. Reg. of Wills, Liber G, folio 15.

Ellett, Thomas. Will (copy). Made Dec. 26, 1727. Heirs: wife Elizabeth; dau. Martha. Exec'x, wife. Wits., Thomas Allston, Arthur Allston, John Pounds, Isaac Snow. Prob. Jan. 29, 1727. Arch. vol. A16, page 92. Reg. of Wills, Liber G, folio 4.

Betts, Robert. Planter. Will (copy). Made March 27, 1726. Mispillion Hd. Heirs: sons John & William; dau. Elizabeth; Mark, Jr. & Matthew, Jr., children of Mark & Matthew Manlove. Exec'r, bro.-in-law Matthew Manlove. Guardians, William Molleston, Tobitha Williams. Wits., John Ashley, Robert Cuming, William Barnabey. Prob. Feb. 15, 1727. Arch. vol. A4, pages 38 & 39. Reg. of Wills, Liber G, folios 5-6.

Hudson, Daniel. Will (copy). Made Jan. 6, 1727. Heirs: wife Margaret; sons Daniel, Alexander, Arnold, Absolom; daus. Sarah, Alce [Alee], Susannah, Elenor, Margaret, Ann. Exec'x, wife. Wits., Robert Cuming, Thomas Berry, Mark Manlove. Prob. Feb. 14, 1727. Arch. vol. A25, pages 101-102. Reg. of Wills, Liber G, folio 6.

Rees, David. Will (copy). Made Feb. 12, 1727/8. Heirs: bro. Evan; sisters Hester & Martha; wife Mary. Exec'rs, wife Mary and bro. Evan. Wits., Samuel Smith, Thomas Green, Samuel Pounds. Prob. Feb. 20, 1727. Arch. vol. A42, page 232. Reg. of Wills, Liber G, folio 7.

Dowglass, Archabald. Yeoman. Admin. of, to William Molleston. Feb. 29, 1727. Reg. of Wills, Liber G, folios 7-8.

Smith, Daniel. Laborer. Admin. of, to James Gordon. March 16, 1727. Arch. vol. A47, page 12. Reg. of Wills, Liber G, folio 8.

Barnsley, Thomas. Blacksmith. Will (copy). Made Feb. 12, 1727/8. Duck Creek. Heirs: eldest child of Richard Barnsley (in Ireland); sons-in-law Jonathan & Nehemiah Ogdon. Exec'rs, Richard Empson, John Holliday. Wits., Joseph England, Mary Green, Solomon Vessey. Prob. March 5, 1727. Arch. vol. A2, page 235. Reg. of Wills, Liber G, folios 8-9.

Hillyard, William. Will (copy). Made March 6, 1727. Heirs: Tamer, dau. of bro. John Hillyard; wife Elizabeth. Exec'x, wife Elizabeth. Wits., Elizabeth Cockrell, Mary Walker, Isaac Snow. Prob. March 16, 1727. Arch. vol. A24, page 50. Reg. of Wills, Liber F, folio 21.

Ruluf, Deborah. Admin. of, to Isaac Uptigrave. March 23, 1727. Reg. of Wills, Liber G, folio 9.

Cale, John. Yeoman. Will (copy). Made March 27, 1728. Heirs: Esther Dales; bro. Solomon; two children not named. Exec'rs, bro. Solomon & William Rodney. Wits., Cathern O'Heren, Robert Bevil, Robert Cuming. Prob. April 2, 1728. Arch. vol. A9, pages 199-200. Reg. of Wills, Liber G, folio 10.

Brinckle, Peter. Admin. of, to Elizabeth & Curtis Brinckle. April 15, 1728. Reg. of Wills, Liber G, folio 10.

Watkins, Samuel. Admin. of, to Anne Watkins. April 19, 1728. Reg. of Wills, Liber G, folio 11.

Rees, John. Will (copy). Made Nov. 10, 1727/28. Duck Creek. Heirs: son-in-law Michall Richman; grandsons John Richman & Evan Richman; granddaus. Temperance Richman & Elener Hootten; daus. Jane Marshall, Hannah Hootten, Martha Rees, Esther Rees; wife Elener; son Evan. Exec'rs, wife Elener & son Evan. Wits., Richard Empson, William Strickland, Catharing Strickland. Prob. April 20, 1728. Arch. vol. A43, page 17. Reg. of Wills, Liber G, folios 11-12.

Machan, John. Yeoman. Will (copy). Made June 10/24, 1727. Heirs: grandsons Thomas & Theodorus Park, & John, son of Thomas & Sarah Park; granddaus. Charity & Cecilia Park; dau. Sarah Park & dau. wife of Patrick Downs. Exec'r, grandson John Parks. Wits., Robert Potts, William Rodney, Susannah Tarrant, Thomas Tarrant. Prob. April 23, 1728. Arch. vol. A33, pages 55-56. Reg. of Wills, Liber G, folios 12-13.

Freeland, James. Yeoman. Admin. of, to Hannah Freeland. May 27, 1728. Reg. of Wills, Liber G, folio 13.

Philips, John. Admin. of, to John Newell. June 1, 1728. Reg. of Wills, Liber G, folio 14.

Joyce, Henry. Merchant. Admin. of, to William Rodney. June 11, 1728. Reg. of Wills, Liber G, folio 14.

Westbury, Thomas. Carpenter. Admin. of, to Mary Westbury. June 17, 1728. Reg. of Wills, Liber G, folio 14.

Ellis, Rachell. Widow. Admin. of, to Richard Empson. Aug. 29, 1728. Reg. of Wills, Liber G, folio 15.

Sallindine, William. Admin. of, to John Bell. Sept. 3, 1728. Reg. of Wills, Liber G, folio 16.

Dyer, William. Will (copy). Made Oct. 19, 1728. Heirs: bro. Thomas Clifford; cousins John Clayton, Hannah Levick & children of Elizabeth Booth; Isaac Booth; John Pound. Exec'rs, bro. Thomas Clifford & Isaac Booth. Wits., Philip Denny, Isaac Snow. Prob. Nov. 19, 1728. Arch. vol. A15, pages 230-231. Reg. of Wills, Liber G, folios 16-17.

Bowman, Peter Peterson. Will. Made Oct. 3, 1728. Heirs: wife Jane; cousin John Holliday. Exec'rs, wife & cousin. Wits., John Green, Phineas Greenwood, Robert Hootten. Prob. Dec. 23, 1728. Arch. vol. A40, page 34. Reg. of Wills, Liber G, folios 17-18.

Whitham, Joshua. Will. Made Dec. 17, 1728. Heir: friend Joshua Clayton. Exec'r, friend Joshua Clayton. Wits., Richard Brock, Samuel Williams. Prob. Dec. 23, 1728. Arch. vol. A54, page 214. Reg. of Wills, Liber G, folio 18 & Liber H, folio 66.

Coe, William. Admin. of, to William Walton. Jan. 2, 1728. Reg. of Wills, Liber G, folios 18-19.

House, Thomas. Laborer. Admin. of, to Honour House. Jan. 2, 1728. Reg. of Wills, Liber G, folios 20-21.

Payn, Samuel. Admin. of, to Ann Mitchell. Jan. 17, 1728. Reg. of Wills, Liber G, folio 21.

Newell, William. Will. Made Jan. 9, 1728/9. Heirs: sons Samuel, Joseph; wife Mary. Exec'x, wife. Wits., John Newell, Benjamin Barger, Joseph Barger. Prob. Feb. 3, 1728. Arch. vol. A37, page 198. Reg. of Wills, Liber G, folio 19.

Denis, Frederick. Will. Made Dec. 10, 1728. Heirs: wife Elenor; children unnamed. Exec'x, wife. Wits., Thomas Nixon, Hugh Durborrow, Jr. Prob. Feb. 5, 1728. Arch. vol. A14, page 10. Reg. of Wills, Liber G, folio 20. Note:—Bro. Thomas Denis mentioned.

Skidmore, Thomas. Will. Made Feb. 10, 1728. Heirs: nephew Thomas Skidmore, son of bro. Samuel Skidmore of Long Island; wife unnamed. Exec'r, Thomas Skidmore. Wits., John Wheelor, Robert Merydith, Mary Baxter. [No prob.] Arch. vol. A46, page 202.

Whitman, Samuel. Will. Made Feb. 13, 1727. Heirs: sons Samuel, Jonathan; daus. Phebe, Elizabeth. Exec'r, son Samuel. Wits., Richard Whitehart, Elizabeth Freeman, Isaac Snow. Prob. Feb. 25, 1728. Arch. vol. A54, page 208. Reg. of Wills, Liber G, folio 22.

Pusy, Caleb. Admin. of, to Thomas Crawford & Isabel Pusy. March 6, 1728. Reg. of Wills, Liber G, folios 21-22.

Chance, John. Planter. Will. Made March 1, 1728/9. Heirs: sons Joseph, John & Alexander; daus. Elizabeth Hosier & Honor Chance. Exec'rs, son Alexander & bro. William. Wits., John Sauls, Elizabeth Hosier. Prob. March 20, 1728. Arch. vol. A8, page 152. Reg. of Wills, Liber G, folio 27. Note:—Refers to "two eldest sons" and "two little girls."

Empson, Richard. Yeoman. Admin. of, to Dorothy & Thomas Empson. April 14, 1729. Arch. vol. A16, page 200. Reg. of Wills, Liber G, folio 23.

McHan, John. Admin. of, to James Maxwell. April 19, 1729. Arch. vol. A32, page 200. Reg. of Wills, Liber H, folios 111-112.

Cockrell, Elizabeth. Will (nunc.). Made April 24, 1729. Little Creek Hd. Heir: mother Elizabeth Sim. Exec'x, mother Elizabeth Sim. Wits., Arthur Alston, Elizabeth Smith. Prob. April 28, 1729. Arch. vol. A9, page 181. Reg. of Wills, Liber G, folios 23 & 25. Note:—Reg. of Wills, Liber G, folio 25 shows Edward Marshall as adm'r.

Reynalls, John, Sr. Farmer. Will. Made Jan. 26, 1727/28. Heirs: wife Elizabeth; sons Daniel, George, Robert & John; daus. Sara, Elizabeth & Marey. Exec'x, wife Elizabeth. Trustees, Archaball McK. Cook, John Gordon. Wits., Archaball McK. Cook, John Gordon, Edward Jenings. Prob. May 2, 1729. Arch. vol. A43, page 102. Reg. of Wills, Liber G, folios 23-24, & Liber H, folio 61.

Pickerell, William. Admin. of, to Dina Pickerell. May 15, 1729. Arch. vol. A40, page 63. Reg. of Wills, Liber G, folio 25.

Cockrell, Elizabeth. Admin. of, to Edward Marshall. May 20, 1729. Reg. of Wills, Liber G, folio 25 & Liber H, folios 106-107.

Greenaway, Nicholas. Admin. of, to Hugh Durborow & Elizabeth, his wife, late wife of Nicholas Greenaway. June 3, 1729. Arch. vol. A20, page 145.

McCook, Archibald. Admin. of, to Lelius McCook & James McCordie. Aug. 30, 1729. Reg. of Wills, Liber G, folio 29 & Liber H, folio 111.

Martin, George. Will. Made July 21, 1729. Duck Creek. Heirs: son George; wife Rachel; bro. Josiah Martin; David French; one child unnamed. Exec'rs, wife Rachel & William Collins. Trustees, Charles Hillyard, John Hall, & George Newell. Wits., Philip Denny, Alexander McKenzie, John Tilton. Prob. Sept. 1, 1729. Arch. vol. A33, pages 205-206. Reg. of Wills, Liber G, folios 27-28. Note:—Arch. vol. A33, page 206 shows that Rachel Martin later married ... Tybout.

Lackey, Gustavus. Admin. of, to Mary & Henry Lackey. Sept. 1, 1729. Reg. of Wills, Liber G, folio 29 & Liber H, folios 110-111.

Killingsworth, John. Will. Made Sept. 2, 1729. Heirs: sons Edward, George, John & Nathaniel; daus. Mary & Elizabeth; wife Sarah. Exec'x, wife Sarah. Trustees, Caleb Hunn, Nathaniel Luff. Wits., John Robbisson, Henry Harmson, Margaret Lorrence. Prob. Oct. 1, 1729. Arch. vol. A28, page 223. Reg. of Wills, Liber G, folios 29-30 & Liber H, folios 54-55.

Redman, Jane. Widow. Admin. of, to Joseph Barger. Oct. 8, 1729. Reg. of Wills, Liber G, folio 31.

Jones, John. Admin. of, to John Reynalls. Oct. 8, 1729. Reg. of Wills, Liber G, folio 31.

Samuels, John. Admin. of, to Thomas Crippen. Oct. 16, 1729. Reg. of Wills, Liber G, folio 32.

McCool, Gabriel. Admin. of, to James McCool. Oct. 22, 1729. Reg. of Wills, Liber G, folio 32.

Hogg, James. Admin. of, to Johannah Hogg. Dec. 12, 1729. Arch. vol. A24, page 167. Reg. of Wills, Liber G, folios 32-33.

McGoon, James. Laborer. Admin. of, to George & Susannah Fleman. Dec. 15, 1729. Reg. of Wills, Liber G, folios 32-33.

Williams, Samuel. Will (nunc.). Made Dec. 10, 1729. Heir: wife Mary. Exec'x, wife. Wits., Mark Manlove, John Housman, John Hall. Prob. Dec. 16, 1729. Arch. vol. A55, page 152. Reg. of Wills, Liber H, folio 64.

Bell, John. Innholder. Made Oct. 15, 1729. Dover. Heirs: son John; dau. Mary; wife Margaret. Exec'x, wife Margaret. Wits., Jno. Rees, John Register, David Rees. Prob. Dec. 17, 1729. Arch. vol. A3, page 172. Reg. of Wills, Liber G, folios 33-34.

Williams, Griffeth. Admin. of, to Elizabeth Williams. Dec. 20, 1729. Reg. of Wills, Liber H, folio 4.

Townsend, John. Admin. of, to Lydia Townsend. Dec. 24, 1729. Reg. of Wills, Liber H, folio 4.

Lackey, Mary. Spinister. Admin. of, to Richard James. Jan. 5, 1729. Reg. of Wills, Liber H, folio 3.

Rees, Martha. Will (nunc.). Made Jan. 9, 1729. Heirs: mother Elinor; bro. Evan; sisters Hannah Wootten, Jane Marshall, Hester Owens. Wits., Katherine Strictland. Prob. Jan. 9, 1729. Arch. vol. A43, page 24. Reg. of Wills, Liber G, folio 34 & Liber H, folio 66.

McCool, Gabriel. Weaver. Admin. of, to James McCool. Jan. 23, 1729. Reg. of Wills, Liber H, folio 99.

Phillips, John. Yeoman. Admin. of, to John Newell. Feb. 6, 1729. Arch. vol. A40, page 39. Reg. of Wills, Liber G, folios 34-35.

Nowell, Sarah. Wife of George Nowell. Will. Made Dec. 25, 1729. Heir: son Daniel Rodney. Exec'r, son Daniel Rodney. Wits., John Wilson, Sr., James White. Prob. Feb. 11, 1729. Arch. vol. A38, page 60. Reg. of Wills, Liber H, folio 2.

Clark, John. Yeoman. Will. Made Nov. 29, 1727. Heirs: sons William & John; daus. Sarah, Elizabeth & Susannah Winsmore; wife Katherine; Mary & Elias Williams. Exec'rs, wife Katherine & son John. Wits., John Hamnitt, Luke Manlove, James Taylor. Prob. Feb. 11, 1729. Arch. vol. A9, pages 2-3. Reg. of Wills, Liber G, folios 35-36 & Liber H, folios 74-75.

Young, Thomas. Yeoman. Admin. of, to Elisha Snow. Feb. 20, 1729. Reg. of Wills, Liber H. folio 3.

Pussey, Caleb. Admin. of, to Thomas Crawford & Isabella Pussey. March 6, 1729. Reg. of Wills, Liber H, folio 106.

Horsman, Thomas. Planter. Admin. of, to Waiteman Sipple. March 17, 1729. Reg. of Wills, Liber H, folio 4.

Williams, James. Will. Made Feb. 16, 1729. Heirs: sons James & John; dau. Ledey. Exec'r, John Clark. Wits., Luke Manlove, Thomas Jestor, Katherine Clark. Prob. March 23, 1729. Arch. vol. A55, pages 79 & 89. Reg. of Wills, Liber H, folio 7.

Samuels, John. Admin. of, to Sarah O'Neal. March 26, 1730. Reg. of Wills, Liber H, folio 5.

Nickerson, Joseph. Will. Made March 18, 1729. Heirs: Joseph Barger; wife Mary. Exec'r, wife. Trustee, bro. Joshua Nickerson. Wits., Stephen Paradee, John Wilson, Joseph Barger. Prob. April 11, 1730. Arch. vol. A37, page 233. Reg. of Wills, Liber H, folio 76. Note:—Jeremiah Nickerson is mentioned as the father.

Wheeler, John. Planter. Admin. of, to Thomas Skidmore, Jr. April 13, 1730. Reg. of Wills, Liber H, folio 5.

Smith, Samuel. Yeoman. Will. Made April 1, 1730. Heirs: wife Judith; sons Samuel & Daniel; other children unnamed. Exec'x, wife Judith. Wits., William Farson [Hanson], Elizabeth Offley, Samuel Reagh. Prob. April 18, 1730. Arch. vol. A47, pages 159-160. Reg. of Wills, Liber G, folios 36-37. Note:—Arch. vol. A47, page 160 shows Judith Smith later married John Chickens.

Harminson, John. Carpenter. Will. Made Aug. 22, 1727. Heir: wife Elizabeth. Exec'x, wife Elizabeth. Wits., Thomas Barker, John Killingsworth, Francis White. Prob. May 13, 1730. Arch. vol. A22, page 40. Reg. of Wills, Liber H, folio 1.

Fisher, Joseph. Yeoman. Admin. of, to John Fisher. May 15, 1730. Reg. of Wills, Liber H, folio 12.

Southard, Benjamin. Admin. of, to Abraham Allee. May 20, 1730. Arch. vol. A48, page 56. Reg. of Wills, Liber H, folio 6.

Manlove, William. Admin. of, to Elizabeth Manlove. June 5, 1730. Arch. vol. A33, page 133. Reg. of Wills, Liber H, folio 6.

Cook, Robert. Admin. of, to John Hall. June 6, 1730. Reg. of Wills, Liber H, folio 107.

Richardson, Mary. Widow. Will. Made Nov. 26, 1730. Little Creek. Heirs: son Richard Levick; grandsons Richard, William & Robert Levick; granddau. Sarah Levick; grandson John's two children. Exec'r, grandson Richard Levick. Wits., Patrick Douns, Petar Coodrat, John Rees. Prob. Oct. 11, 1730. Arch. vol. A43, page 165. Reg. of Wills, Liber H, folio 11.

Hillyard, Charles, Jr. Will. Made Oct. 17, 1730. Heirs: wife Elizabeth; son unnamed; bro. John. Exec'rs, wife Elizabeth & father Charles Hillyard, Sr. Wits., William Collins, Hannah Hutt, James McMillan. Prob. Nov. 15, 1730. Arch. vol. A24, page 51. Reg. of Wills, Liber H, folio 9.

Barger, Joseph. Merchant. Will. Made Oct. 25, 1730. Heirs: wife Mary; sons Thomas, John, Joseph. Exec'rs, wife Mary & friend John Bowers. Wits., Israel Pemberton, John Trapnell, Benjamin Barger, John Cadwalader. Prob. Nov. 17, 1730. Arch. vol. A2, page 158. Reg. of Wills, Liber H, folio 7.

Pound, Samuel. Mariner. Will. Made April 3, 1723. Duck Creek. Heirs: son James; dau. Hannah. Exec'rs, friends Charles Hillyard, Thomas Green. Trustee, son James. Wits., William Birkett, Charles Hillyard. Prob. Nov. 30, 1730. Arch. vol. A41, page 23. Reg. of Wills, Liber H, folio 8.

Levick, John. Yeoman. Will. Made Nov. 3, 1730. Little Creek. Heirs: wife Hannah; sons Clayton, John. Exec'x, wife Hannah. Wits., Jonathan Giffin, John Rees, Mary Tryall, Sarah Morgan. Prob. Dec. 1, 1730. Arch. vol. A30, page 32. Reg. of Wills, Liber H, folio 10.

Nowell, George. Will. Made March 2, 1730. Heirs: Sarah Cook, dau. of Thomas Cook; wife Margaret; dau.-in-law Mary Bell; son-in-law John Bell. Exec'x, wife Margaret. Wits., Mark Manlove, Benjamin Shurmer, Samuel Chew, of Maidstone. Prob. Feb. 18, 1730. Arch. vol. A37, page 186. Reg. of Wills, Liber H, folio 13.

Garve, Owen. Will. Made Dec. 13, 1729. Heir: bro. John. Exec'r, bro. John. Wits., John Harmison, Nathaniel Tomlin, Henry Harmison, John Wheeler. Prob. March 17, 1730. Arch. vol. A18, page 230. Reg. of Wills, Liber H, folios 1-2.

Fisher, Joseph. Yeoman. Will. Made Nov. 26, 1730. Heirs: bros. Molleston Fisher, Isaac Fisher; mother unnamed. Exec'x, mother. Wits., Ann Reynalds, Caleb Molloy, James McMillin. Prob. March 19, 1730. Arch. vol. A17, page 136. Reg. of Wills, Liber H, folios 12, 69-70.

Whitehart, Elizabeth. Will (nunc.). Made March 18, 1730. Heirs: sons John Horsted, Benjamin Whitehart, & James Whitehart; dau. Mary Whitehart. Exec'rs, Richard Whitehart & Arthur Allstone. Trustees, Thomas Allstone, Richard Whitehart, Arthur Allstone. Wits., Hannah Harwood, Rachel Hillyard. Prob. March 18, 1730. Arch. vol. A54, page 181. Reg. of Wills, Liber H, folios 13 & 66.

Whitehart, James. Admin. of, to Richard Whitehart & Arthur Allstone. March 20, 1730. Arch. vol. A54, page 182. Reg. of Wills, Liber H, folio 14.

Phillips, Hannah. Widow. Admin. of, to Thomas Berry. April 24, 1731. Reg. of Wills, Liber H, folios 19-20.

Glew [Glue], Samuel. Will. Made Feb. 10, 1725. Heirs: wife, former wife of Edward Berry; daus. Rachel, Elizabeth, & Rebecca; sons-in-law Samuel Manlove, Nicholas Powell. Exec'rs, dau. Rachel & Samuel Manlove. Wits., Lancelot Lewis, Edward Nickolls, Nickolas Greenaway. Prob. April 30, 1731. Arch. vol. A19, pages 67 & 71. Reg. of Wills, Liber H, folio 14. Note:—Arch. vol. A19, page 71 shows William Hazzard and wife Rachel as exec'rs.

Robisson, William. Admin. of, to Susanah Robisson. May 1, 1731. Reg. of Wills, Liber H, folios 18-19.

Moore, Henry. Will. Made April 3, 1721. Duck Creek. Heirs: wife Rebecca; dau. Mary; sons unnamed. Exec'x, wife Rebecca. Wits., John Bradshaw, Jethro Thomson. Prob. May 1, 1731. Arch. vol. A36, pages 18-19. Reg. of Wills, Liber H, folios 15, 11-12.

Richardson, Richard. Will (copy). Made Dec. 10, 1730. Little Creek & Phila. Heirs: daus. Mary Watters, Miriam & Ann Richardson; sons Richard & John; wife Ann; children of sister-in-law Mary Booth; bro.-in-law Joseph Booth. Exec'rs, wife Ann & Joseph Booth. Wits., Thomas Empson, John Holliday, Lewis Howell, James Steel. Prob. May 12, 1731. Arch. vol. A43, pages 166-167. Reg. of Wills, Liber H, folios 15-17.

Nicholds, Samuel. Admin. of, to Jane Nicholds. May 12, 1731. Reg. of Wills, Liber H, folio 18.

Colter, James. Admin. of, to Margory Colter. May 12, 1731. Arch. vol. A11, page 49. Reg. of Wills, Liber H, folio 18.

Ridley, Isaac. Will. Made March 30, 1731. Heirs: son Samuel; daus. Sarah, Hannah, Mansuell, Rebecca & Rachel; wife Mary. Exec'x, wife. Wits., Job Bunting, George Williams, Jacob Bragg. Prob. May 26, 1731. Arch. vol. A43, page 216. Reg. of Wills, Liber H, folio 17.

Brooks, Samuel. Planter. Will. Made May 17, 1731. Murderkill Hd. Heir: son Samuel. Exec'r, John Newton. Wits., Edward Ratledge, Urselly Ratledge, Edward Jenings. Prob. June 15, 1731. Arch. vol. A6, pages 14-15. Reg. of Wills, Liber H, folio 19.

Cowgill, John. Admin. of, to Rachel Cowgill. Sept. 2, 1731. Reg. of Wills, Liber H, folio 20.

Morris, John. Will (copy). Made Nov. 5, 1731. Heirs: bro. William; Elizabeth Payn. Exec'r, bro. William. Wits., Christopher Norrington, Edward Jones, Benjamin David. Prob. Nov. 23, 1731. Arch. vol. A36, page 225. Reg. of Wills, Liber H, folios 22 & 47.

Jackson, Christopher. Admin. of, to Bredget Jackson. Dec. 10, 1731. Arch. vol. A25, page 238. Reg. of Wills, Liber H, folio 24.

Adams, James. Planter. Admin. of, to Richard James. Dec. 22, 1731. Reg. of Wills, Liber H, folio 24.

Sharp, Thomas. Yeoman. Will (copy). Made Nov. 18, 1729. Duck Creek. Heirs: Andrew Hamilton; Henry Hodge; James Steel; mother-in-law Hannah Harwood; bro.-in-law Thomas Harwood; Johanna, wife of William Morphey; sisters-in-law Martha, Rachel & Mary Harwood; Elisha Snow; Elizabeth, wife of Jonathan Bacon; Thomas and Arthur Alston; Samuel Whitehart; Thomas Walker; Elizabeth, wife of James Whitehart; Rebecca, wife of John Greenwood; wife Sarah. Exec'rs, wife Sarah and friend Andrew Hamilton. Wits., Abraham Spicer, Stephen Potts, Francis Sherrard. Prob. Jan. 1, 1731. Arch. vol. A45, page 190. Reg. of Wills, Liber H, folio 21.

French, Charles. Will. Made Dec. 9, 1731. Jones Creek. Heir: wife Mary. Exec'x, wife Mary. Wits., Abraham Barber, Joseph Basker. Prob. Jan. 20, 1731. Arch. vol. A18, page 135. Reg. of Wills, Liber H, folios 22-23.

Hogg, Joanna. Widow. Will. Made Jan. 11, 1731. Salsbury. Heirs: sons John, George; daus. Elizabeth, Susannah, Rebeckah. Exec'rs, bro. Joseph Gregory, William Farson. Wits., Charles King, Hestear Parker, John Flintham, Jr. Prob. Feb. 10, 1731. Arch. vol. A24, page 168. Reg. of Wills, Liber H, folio 25.

Butcher, Robert. Yeoman. Will. Made July 26, 1722. Little Creek. Heirs: son Robert; Phillis Asco; wife Susannah; son-in-law Richard Pulling. Exec'r, son Robert. Wits., Sarah Lowder, Ann Tilton, John Tilton. Prob. Feb. 14, 1731. Arch. vol. A7, page 10. Reg. of Wills, Liber H, folios 23-24.

Huestead, Samuel. Admin. of, to Timothy Hanson & Edward Hart. March 2, 1731. Reg. of Wills, Liber H, folio 108.

Heath, Thomas. Yeoman. Admin. of, to Mary Heath. March 9, 1731. Reg. of Wills, Liber H, folio 25.

Hedger [Hidgar], William. Admin. of, to Abraham Wynkoop. March 28, 1732. Arch. vol. A24, page 116. Reg. of Wills, Liber H, folios 101-102.

Mackadow [McAdow], William. Will. Made Jan. 17, 1731. Heirs: daus. Margery, Ann, Margaret; cousins John & James McAdow, sons of Moses; wife Jane. Exec'x, wife. Wits., Mark Manlove, Mark Smith, John Fleming. Prob. April 5, 1732. Arch. vol. A32, pages 51-52. Reg. of Wills, Liber H, folio 26.

McCahan, Daniel. Will. Made April 15, 1732. Murtherkill. Heirs: sons John, Daniel; wife Elenor; Thomas Steel, son of Thomas Steel. Exec'r, friend Mark Smith. Wits., Thomas Berry, Margrit Berry, Hugh Durborow, Jr. Prob. May 17, 1732. Arch. vol. A32, page 88. Reg. of Wills, Liber H, folios 58-59.

Mason, Michael. Will. Made April 5, 1732. Heirs: wife Mary; son William; daus. Rachel Mason & Lurana Lucod; son-in-law Robert Willson. Exec'x, wife Mary. Wits., Philip Jones, Nathaniel Roach, Isaac Snow. Prob. June 3, 1732. Arch. vol. A34, pages 3-4. Reg. of Wills, Liber H, folio 27.

Freeman, Moses. Farmer. Will. Made June 2, 1732. Heirs: sons Moses, Ezekiall; daus. Mary, Penellope; friend Joseph Ambras. Exec'rs, wife Hannah & friend Joseph Powell. Wits., William Obyle, Catharine Ambras and Richard Cooper. Prob. July 13, 1732. Arch. vol. A18, page 127. Reg. of Wills, Liber H, folio 33.

Wells, Thomas. Yeoman. Will (copy). Made Jan. 24, 1731. Heirs: wife Ann; sons Thomas, John, James, George, Henry, Williams; daus. Patience, Ann. Exec'x, wife. Trustees, sons John & Thomas. Wits., Mark Manlove, David Rees, Ambrose Carrall. Prob. Sept. 10, 1732. Arch. vol. A54, pages 1-2. Reg. of Wills, Liber H, folios 27-28. Note:—Arch. vol. A54, page 2 shows Philip Fields as adm'r.

Thomas, David. Farmer. Will. Made Aug. 2, 1732. Little Creek. Heirs: son Solomon; Thomas Evans, Minister of Welsh Tract in N. C. Co.; wife Eleanor. Exec'x, wife. Wits., Rees Lewis, Joshua David, Joshua Evans. Prob. Sept. 16, 1732. Arch. vol. A50, page 51. Reg. of Wills, Liber H, folio 29.

Eldridge, Robert. Admin. of, to Thomas Eldridge. Oct. 5, 1732. Reg. of Wills, Liber H, folios 32-33.

Rodeney, William. Admin. of, to Ruth Rodeney. Oct. 19, 1732. Reg. of Wills, Liber H, folios 32 & 46.

Hall, John. Will. Made Oct. 31, 1732. Heirs: wife Letitia; daus. Hannah, Elinor, & Letitia Hall & Elizabeth Smith; sons John & Robert. Exec'x, wife. Trustees, Andrew Hamilton, David French, Timothy Hanson, William Tell, David Rees. Wits., Timothy Hanson, David Rees, Charles Tuthell. Prob. Nov. 16, 1732. Arch. vol. A21, pages 91 & 110. Reg. of Wills, Liber H, folios 30-31.

Wilson [Willson], John. Will. Made Nov. 16, 1732. Heirs: wife Anne; bro.-in-law George Lester; bro. Robert Wilson. Exec'r, friend John Hartt. Wits., Isaac Freland, William Condon. Prob. Nov. 21, 1732. Arch. vol. A55, pages 214-215. Reg. of Wills, Liber H, folio 30.

Booth, Joseph. Admin. of, to John Reynolds. Nov. 28, 1732. Reg. of Wills, Liber H, folio 109.

James, Daniel. Yeoman. Admin. of, to Elizabeth James. Dec. 9, 1732. Reg. of Wills, Liber H, folio 34.

Crawford, Thomas. Admin. of, to Katharine Crawford. Dec. 12, 1732. Arch. vol. A11, pages 218-219. Reg. of Wills, Liber H, folio 34. Note:—Arch. vol. A11, page 218 shows that Katharine Crawford later married Walter Dickinson.

Ridley, Mary. Admin. of, to Andrew Caldwell. Dec. 19, 1732. Reg. of Wills, Liber H, folio 112.

Hillyard, John. Will. Made Dec. 3, 1732. Heirs: dau. Elizabeth; cousins Charles Hillyard, Lurana Green & Mary Williams. Exec'rs, father Charles Hillyard & Thomas Green. Wits., John Tilton, Abraham Gullett, Michael Ruwark. Prob. Dec. 19, 1732. Arch. vol. A24, pages 37 & 38. Reg. of Wills, Liber H, folio 37.

Mitchell, Ann. Widow. Will. Made July 24, 1731. Dover Hd. Heirs: son Daniel; daus. Comfort Mitchel, Susannah Tire; grandson Thomas Tire; granddau. Ann Chance. Exec'rs, son Daniel & dau. Comfort Mitchell. Wits., Miles Goforth, Hugh Durborow, Jr. Prob. Dec. 20, 1732. Arch. vol. A35, page 167. Reg. of Wills, Liber H, folios 56-57.

Amos, Henry. Will. Made Aug. 15, 1732. Heirs: sons Henry, George; daus. Sarah, Tamer, Elizabeth; wife Catherine. Exec'x, wife. Wits., Isaac Freeland, John Wilson, Jr. Prob. Dec. 20, 1732. Arch. vol. A1, page 127. Reg. of Wills, Liber H, folio 41.

Harper, William. Will. Made Dec. 22, 1732. Heirs: daus. Susannah, Christian; sons John, James, Thomas, William. Exec'r, George Brown. Trustees, Mark Manlove, George Brown. Wits., Mark Manlove, Richard James, Daniel Griffen. Prob. Feb. 14, 17——. Arch. vol. A22, pages 78-79. Reg. of Wills, Liber H, folio 62.

Manlove, Ephriam. Will (copy). Made Nov. 29, 1732. Heirs: wife Sarah; sons Abner, Obediah; bro. Matthew Manlove. Exec'r, Matthew Manlove. Trustee, Matthew Manlove. Wits., Matthew Huse, Elizabeth Manlove. Prob. Dec. 23, 1732. Arch. vol. A33, page 90. Reg. of Wills, Liber H, folios 57-58.

Wood, Robert. Ship Carpenter. Will. Made Dec. 6, 1732. Little Creek Hd. Heirs: dau. Elizabeth; sons Robert & Jonathan; grandson John Worthenton; friend David Bush. Exec'rs, dau. Elizabeth & William Flud. Wits., John Small, David Bush. Prob. Dec. 23, 1732. Arch. vol. A56, page 93. Reg. of Wills, Liber H, folio 36.

Campling, Edward. Admin. of, to Pemberton Broun. Dec. 26, 1732. Reg. of Wills, Liber H, folio 105.

Richardson, Anna. Will (nunc.). Made Oct. 22, 1732. Little Creek. Heirs: four youngest children unnamed; dau. Mary Waters. Exec'r, Joseph Booth, bro.-in-law. Wits., Timothy Hanson, Susanah Hanson. Prob. Dec. 28, 1732. Arch. vol. A43, pages 160-161. Reg. of Wills, Liber H, folios 64 & 103. Note:—These names are mentioned with no relationship shown:—Mariam, Richard, John and Anna Richardson.

Hudson, Thomas. Admin. of, to John Housman. Dec. 29, 1732. Reg. of Wills, Liber H, folios 34 & 114.

Marim, John. Will. Made Nov. 24, 1732. Heirs: sons Thomas, John, Charles; wife Mary. Exec'rs, wife Mary and son Thomas. Wits., Thomas Irons [Hirons], Reece Price, James White, Marten Linch. Prob. Jan. 5, 1732. Arch. vol. A33, page 181. Reg. of Wills, Liber H, folio 40.

Haylor [Haytor], William. Admin. of, to David Haylor [Haytor]. Jan. 8, 1732. Reg. of Wills, Liber H, folio 33.

Edmunds, John. Will. Made Nov. 25, 1732. Heirs: sons Robert, John, James, Joseph; daus. Mary, Tabitha, Elizabeth; wife Elizabeth. Exec'rs, wife Elizabeth and friend Waitman Sipple, Sr. Wits., Mary Booth, Isaac Uptgrove, Jas. McMillan. Prob. Jan. 9, 1732. Arch. vol. A16, page 35. Reg. of Wills, Liber H, folio 72.

Thorel, Mary. Widow. Will. Made Aug. 26, 1732. Murderkill. Heirs: sons Joseph & John Rash; grandsons Samuel & Joseph Rash; granddaus. Elizabeth, Mary, Elinor & Sarah Rash; dau.-in-law Ann, wife of John Rash. Exec'r, son John. Wits., Elenor Pender, Eve Pender, John Glenn. Codicil:— son Walter Pardue [Pardee]; dau. Mary Bedshould; grandson Samuel Howell. Prob. Jan. 10, 1732. Arch. vol. A50, page 122. Reg. of Wills, Liber H, folios 35-36. Note:—James Howell and my dau. Elizabeth are parents of Samuel Howell.

Hart, Henry. Admin. of, to Mary Hart. Jan. 10, 1732. Reg. of Wills, Liber H, folios 93-94.

Wells, Thomas, Jr. Admin. of, to Susannah Wells. Jan. 13, 1732. Reg. of Wills, Liber H, folios 97-98.

Thorpe, Hannah. Will (copy). Made Dec. 14, 1732. Heirs: dau. Elizabeth Hall; sons Samuel Thorpe, Mark Thorpe. Exec'r, son Mark. Wits., Cinth. Rawlings, John Lane, Mary Rawlings. Prob. Jan. 15, 1732. Arch. vol. A50, page 128. Reg. of Wills, Liber H, folio 35.

Richardson, Thomas. Will. Made Dec. 13, 1732. Heirs: wife, Jean; sons unnamed. Exec'rs, Edmond Listen and wife Jean. Wits., David Marshall, John Turner, John Cherry. Prob. Jan. 18, 1732. Arch. vol. A43, page 171. Reg. of Wills, Liber H, folio 59.

Clark, Catheren. Widow. Will. Made Dec. 21, 1732. Heirs: son William; daus. Sarah & Elizabeth Clark, Alce Williams; Tobias Furches. Exec'rs, Tobias Furches and Alce Williams. Wits., John Robbison, John Bowman, Luke Manlove. Prob. Jan. 22, 1732. Arch. vol. A8, pages 220-221. Reg. of Wills, Liber H, folio 39.

Tumlin, Judah. Admin. of, to Ephraim Tumlin. Jan. 24, 1732. Reg. of Wills, Liber H, folio 105.

Voshall, Peter. Admin. of, to Susanah Voshell. Jan. 24, 1732. Arch. vol. A52, page 141. Reg. of Wills, Liber H, folio 113.

Jones, Lewis. Admin. of, to Phillip Jones. Feb. 2, 1732. Reg. of Wills, Liber H, folios 102-103.

Whitehart, Richard. Admin. of, to Grace Whitehart. Feb. 2, 1732. Reg. of Wills, Liber H, folio 100.

Jenkins, Jabez. Admin. of, to Sarah Jenkins. Feb. 12, 1732. Reg. of Wills, Liber H, folio 101.

Leckey [Lakey], Henry. Cordwainer. Will. Made Dec. 22, 1732. Heirs: dau. Margaret; son Robert; wife Mary. Exec'rs, wife Mary & bro.-in-law George Black. Wits., Robert Killen, Robert Lecky, Hugh Lecky. Codicil:—nephew John Lecky, son of bro. Gustavus; niece Rebecca Lecky, dau. of bro. Gustavus. Wits., Robert Lecky, Jane Black, William Boggs. Prob. Feb. 15, 1732. Arch. vol. A29, pages 92-93. Reg. of Wills, Liber H, folio 46.

Latham, Adam. Will. Made Dec. 18, 1732. Heirs: wife Elizabeth; son Absolem. Exec'x, wife. Wits., Richard Hill, Elizabeth Latham. Prob. Feb. 17, 1732. Arch. vol. A29, pages 124-125. Reg. of Wills, Liber H, folio 78. Note:—Arch. vol. A29, page 125 mentions Elizabeth, John, Catherine & Peter ..., Mary Latham; also father-in-law, William Wilson.

Cherry, John. Cordwainer. Will. Made Feb. 19, 1732/33. Heirs: sons James, William; dau. Jane; wife Susannah. Exec'rs, wife Susannah & John Holliday. Wits., John Turner, William Flintham, Charles King. Prob. ... 173—. Arch. vol. A8, page 159. Reg. of Wills, Liber H, folios 50-51.

Dawson, John. Will (copy). Made Aug. 21, 1732. Heirs: son John; dau. Mary; grandsons John & Robert; son Robert. Exec'r, son Robert. Wits., Isaac Snow, James Owen, William Fusse. Prob. Feb. 19, 1732. Arch. vol. A13, page 101. Reg. of Wills, Liber H, folio 38.

Cook, Andrew. Admin. of, to Mary Cook. Feb. 24, 1732. Arch. vol. A10, page 105.

Leckey, Hugh. Will. Made Feb. 23, 1732. Heirs: bro. Robert; cousins Andrew Leckey & Jean Jonston; sister Meary Leckey. Wits., H. Smith, Chen Steel. Exec'r, Andrew Leckey. Prob. March 1, 1732. Arch. vol. A29, page 226. Reg. of Wills, Liber H, folio 79.

Wilson, Thomas. Admin. of, to John Anderson. March 3, 1732. Reg. of Wills, Liber H, folio 101.

Hairgrove, George. Admin. of, to Hannah Hairgrove. March 15, 1732. Reg. of Wills, Liber H, folio 99.

Brook, Arthur. Admin. of, to Isabell Brook. March 16, 1732. Arch. vol. A6, page 2. Reg. of Wills, Liber H, folio 97.

Renolds [Renelds], Elizabeth. Memo. of will (copy). Made March 15, 1732. Heirs: son Robert; two daus. not named; cousin Elizabeth Gordon. Exec'rs, John Gordon & William Greer. Wits., James McMillan, Benjamin Johnson, John Harper. Prob. March 17, 1732. Arch. vol. A43, pages 94-95. Reg. of Wills, Liber H, folio 56.

Jones, Enoch. Admin. of, to John Jones. March 24, 1732. Arch. vol. A27, page 164. Reg. of Wills, Liber H, folio 113.

Thomson, John. Admin. of, to Henry Chambers. March 28, 1733. Reg. of Wills, Liber H, folio 98.

Shaw, Joshua. Will. Made March 19, 1732/3. Heirs: children Samuel, William, Ephriam, Mary, Prudence, Agness; wife not named. Exec'rs, John Craige, Samuel Shaw. Wits., John Craige, James Craige, Prudence Shaw, Martha Shaw. Prob. April 4, 1733. Arch. vol. A45, pages 200-201. Reg. of Wills, Liber H, folio 51.

Chambers, John. Admin. of, to Ann & Henry Chambers. April 7, 1733. Arch. vol. A8, page 141. Reg. of Wills, Liber H, folio 96. Note:—Arch. vol. A8, page 141 mentions heirs: James, Henry, Esther & Mary Chambers; also shows that Ann Chambers later married James Gray.

Hawkins, Thomas. Admin. of, to Jacob Allee. April 17, 1733. Arch. vol. A23, page 37. Reg. of Wills, Liber H, folios 96-97.

Stevens, John. Will. Made April 5, 1733. Heirs: wife Elizabeth; son John; daus. Catharine, Mary Ann, Elizabeth. Trustees, cousin Thomas Irons; bro. Stevan Paradee. Exec'x, wife Elizabeth. Wits., Mary Paradee, Thomas Wilson [Williams], Jean Francois. Prob. April 30, 1733. Arch. vol. A48, pages 230 & 227. Reg. of Wills, Liber H, folio 66. Note:—Arch. vol. A48, page 227 shows John Butler & wife Elizabeth as exec'rs.

Frazier, James. Admin. of, to Elizabeth Frazier. April 30, 1733. Arch. vol. A18, page 92. Reg. of Wills, Liber H, folio 104.

Wells, George. Yeoman. Admin. of, to Agnes Wells & Thomas Tarrent. May 1, 1733. Arch. vol. A53, page 229. Reg. of Wills, Liber H, folio 49.

Furby, Benjamin. Admin. of, to Susannah Furby. May 9, 1733. Arch. vol. A18, page 147. Reg. of Wills, Liber H, folios 105-106.

Thistlewood, William. Admin. of, to Garthry Thistlewood and Peter Lowber. May 10, 1733. Reg. of Wills, Liber H, folio 38.

Hooker, Samuel. Yeoman. Admin. of, to Mary Hooker. May 12, 1753. Arch. vol. A24, page 242. Reg. of Wills, Liber H, folios 95-96.

Brinklee, Elizabeth. Admin. of, to Caesar Rodney. May 31, 1733. Reg. of Wills, Liber H, folios 107-108.

Broun, John. Will. Made April 13, 1733. Heirs: wife Jean; Thomas Lockerman, son of John Lockerman. Exec'x, wife Jean. Wits., William Trippet, Mark Grier. Prob. June 12, 1733. Arch. vol. A6, page 49. Reg. of Wills, Liber H, folio 68.

Leach, David. Admin. of, to Mary Leach. June 13, 1733. Reg. of Wills, Liber H, folio 95.

Newton, George. Yeoman. Will. Made Feb. 3, 1732/3. Heirs: wife Alace [Allace]; 4 sons unnamed. Exec'x, wife. Wits., Peter Graham, James Moore. Prob. June 16, 1733. Arch. vol. A37, pages 217-218. Reg. of Wills, Liber H, folio 70.

Green, Mercy. Admin. of, to Thomas Green. June 22, 1733. Reg. of Wills, Liber H, folio 110.

Gormley, James. Admin. of, to John Cockran. July 3, 1733. Reg. of Wills, Liber H, folio 98.

Rowland, Thomas. Admin. of, to Robert Rowland. Aug. 22, 1733. Arch. vol. A44, page 175. Reg. of Wills, Liber H, folio 109.

Griffith, Eynon. Farmer. Will. Made Aug. 18, 1733. Duck Creek. Heirs: sons William & David Eynon; daus. Mary, Catherine, Elizabeth Eynon; wife Margaret. Exec'x, wife Margaret. Wits., Rees Lewis, John David, Joshua Evans. Prob. Sept. 10, 1733. Arch. vol. A20, page 240. Reg. of Wills, Liber H, folio 50.

Brock, Richard. Admin. of, to Abigail Brock. Sept. 29, 1733. Reg. of Wills, Liber H, folios 103-104.

Clark, Jonathan. Yeoman. Will. Made Oct. 30, 1733. Heirs: sons Joseph, Jonathan; dau. Temperance; grandson John; son-in-law Moses Freeman. Exec'x, wife Elizabeth. Wits., Maskel Clark, William Hazard, Jno. Talbutt. Prob. Nov. 13, 1733. Arch. vol. A9, page 38. Reg. of Wills, Liber H, folio 71.

Jones, Evan. Will. Made Oct. 27, 1733. Heirs: son Evan; wife Hannah. Exec'rs, wife Hannah & bro. David Rees. Trustees, Samuel Spencer, Mark Manlove. Wits., Thomas Tarrant, Abraham Morris, James McMillan, Jane Williams. Prob. Nov. 27, 1733. Arch. vol. A27, pages 172-175. Reg. of Wills, Liber H, folio 41. Note:—shows that Hannah Jones later married John David.

Bucher [Butcher], Robert. Yeoman. Will. Made Nov. 14, 1733. Heirs: wife Sarah; sons Moses, Benjamin, Robert, Conselah & Thomas. Exec'x, wife. Wits., William Morgan, John Clayton, Grace Morgan. Prob. Dec. 6, 1733. Arch. vol. A7, page 11. Reg. of Wills, Liber H, folio 77.

Halbert, Thomas. Will (nunc.). Heirs: David Rees; wife unnamed (she having deserted him). Exec'r, David Rees. Wit., Isabel French. Prob. Dec. 11, 1733. Arch. vol. A21, page 75. Reg. of Wills, Liber H, folio 80.

Watson, John. Turner. Will. Made Dec. 11, 1733. Heirs: sister Margit Watson; cousin Tabitha Watson. Exec'x, Tabitha Watson. Wits., Samuel Barratt, Jonathan Griffin, Lear Gaskins. Prob. ... 173—. Arch. vol. A53, page 179. Reg. of Wills, Liber H, folio 48.

Wells, John. Admin. of, to James Brooks and Anna, his wife. Jan. 20, 1733. Arch. vol. A53, page 232. Reg. of Wills, Liber H, folio 86.

Jones, John. Will. Made Nov. 10, 1733. Heirs: wife Jane; daus. Margrit Jones; wife's three children Mary, Hester & John David. Exec'rs, wife Jane & bro. Evan Jones. Wits., Ann Davis, Catharine Eynon, William Williams. Prob. Jan. 28, 1733. Arch. vol. A27, pages 214-215. Reg. of Wills, Liber H, folios 44-45. Note:—Arch. vol. A27, page 215 shows David Bowing and wife Jane [Jean] as exec'rs.

Robinson, James. Mariner. Will. Made Jan. 22, 1733. Duck Creek. Heirs: John Tilton, Jr.; Presley Raymond; Martha Harwood; Rebecca Steel; Alice King; friend Richard Watson. Exec'r, friend Richard Watson. Wits., Elias King, Elizabeth Hosier, John Tilton. Prob. Jan. 30, 1733. Arch. vol. A44, pages 45-46. Reg. of Wills, Liber H, folio 45.

Lues, John. Will. Made Dec. 29, 1733. Heirs: wife Phebee; daus. Kosiah, Elizabeth. Exec'rs, wife Phebee & Alexander Humphries. Wits., Wm. Talfray, Lanselot Lues, Thomas Green. Prob. Feb. 7, 1733. Arch. vol. A30, page 94. Reg. of Wills, Liber H, folio 44.

Whitman, Samuel. Will. Made April 26, 1733. Heirs: sisters Elizabeth Whitman & Phebe Lewis; wife Elizabeth; bro. Jonathan; son-in-law Joseph Freeman; son Samuel. Exec'x, wife. Wits., James Justice, Hugh Rowland, Isaac Snow. Prob. Feb. 7, 1733. Arch. vol. A54, pages 209-211. Reg. of Wills, Liber H, folio 73. Note:—Arch. vol. A54, page 211 shows that Elizabeth Whitman, widow of Samuel, married John Craig and later married Richard James; that Elizabeth, the sister, married Thomas Green; and Phebe Lewis married Jonathan Griffin.

Darson [Dorson], Richard. Admin. of, to Joyce Darson. Feb. 16, 1733. Reg. of Wills, Liber H, folios 86-87.

Levick, Richard. Yeoman. Admin. of, to Honour Levick and Richard Levick. Feb. 21, 1733. Reg. of Wills, Liber H, folio 94.

Brooks, Benjamin. Yeoman. Will. Made Feb. 3, 1733. Heirs: Rache Brooks; Arter Brooks; Mary Brooks, dau. of Arther Brooks, dec'd; Joshuway Brown's four children; John Brooks, Jr.; wife Jeane. Exec'rs, wife & friend George Wilson. Wits., Daniel Nock, Patience Wilson, Sarah Jenkins. Prob. Feb. 27, 1733. Arch. vol. A6, page 4. Reg. of Wills, Liber H, folios 75-76.

Grewell [Greuwell], John. Will. Made Jan. 23, 1733/4. Heirs: wife Mary; sons Jacob, Abraham, John, Peter. Exec'x, wife. Wits., Stockley Sturgis, William Shockley, Robert Mafell. Prob. March 5, 1733. Arch. vol. A20, page 146. Reg. of Wills, Liber H, folio 63.

Donovan, Daniel. Admin. of, to Esther Donovan. March 6, 1733. Reg. of Wills, Liber H, folio 114.

Voshall, Susannah. Admin. of, to Miles Goforth. March 15, 1733. Arch. vol. A52, page 141. Reg. of Wills, Liber H, folio 83.

Cook, William. Admin. of, to Mary Grewell. March 15, 1733. Reg. of Wills, Liber H, folio 108.

Robbison, George. Will. Made Aug. 15, 1730. Heirs: children of son William, dec'd; sons George, Daniel, John, Samuel; wife Mary; son-in-law John Bland; daus. Ann Bland & Charity Brinkly; son-in-law John Brinkly; grandsons Lawrence, son of George, & William, son of John. Exec'r, son Samuel. Wits., George Nowell, Robert Cumming, Daniel Rodney, Robert Hodgson, John Maysom, Train Hodgson. Prob. March 16, 1733. Arch. vol. A44, page 40. Reg. of Wills, Liber H, folios 67-68.

Pindor, Alexander. Will. Made Feb. 23, 1733. Heirs: wife Elenor; daus. Elizabeth, Eve; son George; Ciziah ...; Jemima ...; Elizabeth Bowman. Exec'x, wife. Wits., John Rash, Comfort Jackson, John Gleen [Glenn]. Prob. March 23, 1733. Arch. vol. A40, page 85. Reg. of Wills, Liber H, folio 42.

Worrall, James. Admin. of, to Mary Heath. March 19, 1734. Arch. vol. A56, page 140.

Shockley, William. Admin. of, to Sarah Shockley. March 24, 1733. Reg. of Wills, Liber H, folio 102.

Flood, William. Admin. of, to Elizabeth Flood, spinster. March 24, 1733. Reg. of Wills, Liber H, folio 112.

Reynolds, George. Admin. of, to Daniel Reynolds. April 8, 1734. Reg. of Wills, Liber H, folio 104.

Nys, Johannis [Niss, John D.]. Silversmith. Will. Made Feb. 26, 1733. Heirs: wife not named; dau. Letitia Hall. Exec'x, dau. Letitia Hall. Wits., Mary Irons, James McMillan. Prob. April 8, 1734. Arch. vol. A38, page 6. Reg. of Wills, Liber H, folio 48.

Walton, William. Gentleman. Will. Made April 5, 1734. Heirs: sons William, John, George; daus. Elizabeth, Mary; sister Sarah Gordon. Exec'x, sister Alse Roads. Wits., William Fisher, John Walker, George Gordon. Prob. April 18, 1734. Arch. vol. A53, pages 77-78. Reg. of Wills, Liber H, folios 43-44.

Watkins, Peter. Admin. of, to John Holyday. April 27, 1734. Reg. of Wills, Liber H, folio 100.

Levick, Richard. Admin. of, to Patience Levick. May 9, 1734. Reg. of Wills, Liber H, folio 110.

Register, John. Carpenter. Will. Made April 22, 1734. Heirs: dau. Mary Clark; wife Sarah; son John; grandson John Clark. Exec'rs, wife Sarah & son John. Wits., Elinor Pindor (widow), Elizabeth Bowman, John Glenn. Prob. May 20, 1734. Arch. vol. A43, page 61. Reg. of Wills, Liber H, folio 52.

Stanton [Stenton], Jonathan. Ship-carpenter. Will. Made March 8, 1733. Heirs: son Whittington; wife Elenor; bro. Steven; nephews William Stanton & John Stanton, sons of Steven; bro.-in-law John King; sister Jane Stanton. Exec'rs, wife, bro. William Barry and Robert King. Wits., Thomas Dixon, Nicholas Horton. Prob. May 21, 1734. Arch. vol. A48, page 152. Reg. of Wills, Liber H, folios 59-60.

Bermingham [Birmingham], John. Will (copy). Made ... 1732. Heirs: wife Veronica; sister Catherine; daus. Esther, Mary. Exec'rs, David French, bro. Richard. (Original will lost and early Recorder's records do not show dates or witnesses' signatures.). Arch. vol. A4, page 59 & Arch. vol. A3, page 245. Reg. of Wills, Liber H, folios 54 & 60.

Manlove, Samuel. Yeoman. Will. Made Sept. 13, 1731. Dover Hd. Heir: wife Elizabeth. Exec'rs, wife & bro. Mark Manlove. Wits., Katherine Roberts, Rachel Glue, Hugh Durborough, Jr. Prob. May 24, 1734. Arch. vol. A33, page 119. Reg. of Wills, Liber H, folio 53.

McKracken, Daniel. Admin. of, to Mark Smith. May 24, 1734. Arch. vol. A33, page 59.

Russel, George. Will. Made May 25, 1734. Heirs: sons George, Ebenezer; dau. Elizabeth. Exec'r, Robert Maxwell. Wits., John Glenn, Daniel Ginley, Sarah Shockley. Prob. June 3, 1734. Arch. vol. A44, page 181. Reg. of Wills, Liber H, folios 63-64.

Gooding, Daniel. Admin. of, to Hannah Gooding. June 12, 1734. Reg. of Wills, Liber H, folio 83.

McMillan, James. Will. Made June 11, 1734. Heirs: mother Elizabeth McMillan; bro. William; sister Jane McMillan. Exec'r, friend William Collins. Wits., Benjamin Shurmer, Richard Chibb, Charles Tuthell. Codicil, Rachel Collins. Prob. June 18, 1734. Arch. vol. A32, page 239. Reg. of Wills, Liber H, folio 79.

Dighton [Dithan], Richard. Cooper. Admin. of, to Abraham Wynkoop. Sept. 16, 1734. Arch. vol. A14, page 141. Reg. of Wills, Liber H, folio 80.

Cook, Thomas. Admin. of, to Caesar Rodney. Sept. 21, 1734. Mentions heir Sarah Cook, dau. Reg. of Wills, Liber H, folio 81.

Goforth, George. Will. Made Sept. 13, 1734. Jones Hd. Heirs: father Miles Goforth; wife Tamer Goforth. Exec'r, friend John Reynils. Wits., Thomas Wilson, John Marim, John Wilson. Prob. Oct. 10, 1734. Arch. vol. A19, page 90. Reg. of Wills, Liber H, folio 82.

Barratt, Phoebe. Will. Made Oct. 15, 1734. Heirs: sons George, Mathew, John, Moses; daus. Phebe & Mary Barratt & Elizabeth Broun; sons Humprey & William. Exec'rs, son William & dau. Mary. Wits., George Green, Rachel Hoy, Thomas Green. Prob. Oct. 21, 1734. Arch. vol. A3, pages 21-22. Reg. of Wills, Liber H, folio 81. Memorandum to the will of Phoebe Barratt shows David Morgan as a trustee.

Marshall, George. Yeoman. Admin. of, to Mary Marshall. Nov. 1, 1734. Reg. of Wills, Liber H, folio 84.

Gallaway, Richard. Admin. of, to Samuel Gallaway. Nov. 28, 1734. Reg. of Wills, Liber H, folio 84.

Sherwood, James. Bricklayer. Admin. of, to Jonathan Raymond. Dec. 10, 1734. Reg. of Wills, Liber H, folio 85.

McKee, Thomas. Yeoman. Admin. of, to Marjory McKee, widow, and Robert Edmonds. Dec. 19, 1734. Arch. vol. A32, page 210. Reg. of Wills, Liber H, folio 85.

Goforth, Elizabeth. Will. Made Dec. 2, 1734. Heirs: sons John & Daniel Brown; dau. Ann Brown. Exec'r, husband. Wits., Anthony Rawlings, Samuel Throp, Ann Throp. Prob. Jan. 7, 1734. Arch. vol. A19, page 89. Reg. of Wills, Liber H, folio 86.

Empson, Cornelius. Will. Made Jan. 30, 1734. Heirs: wife Mary; son Richard; dau. Margett. Exec'rs, wife Mary, bro. Thomas Empson, father-in-law James Morris. Wits., Nicholas Ridgly, Evan Rees, Michael Richmond. Prob. Feb. 13, 1734. Arch. vol. A16, page 194. Reg. of Wills, Liber H, folio 89.

Clinton, Christopher. Admin. of, to John Holliday. Feb. 14, 1734. Reg. of Wills, Liber H, folio 88.

Jennings, Edward. Admin. of, to David French. March 14, 1734. Reg. of Wills, Liber H, folio 91.

Craig, James. Admin. of, to Elizabeth Craig, widow, & David Craig. March 17, 1734/35. Reg. of Wills, Liber H, folio 87.

Connell, William. Admin. of, to David Marshall. March 18, 1734/5. Reg. of Wills, Liber H, folio 88.

Griffith, Margaret. Widow. Will (copy). Made Jan. 10, 1734/5. Duck Creek. Heirs: son-in-law Joshua Evans; sons David & William Eynon; daus. Catharine & Elizabeth Eynon. Exec'rs, Thomas Evans, son William Eynon & Joshua Evans. Wits., Griffith John, David Lewis, James Lewis. Prob. March 18, 1734/5. Arch. vol. A20, pages 245-246. Reg. of Wills, Liber H, folio 90.

Nixon, Nicholas. Admin. of, to Elizabeth Nixon. April 4, 1735. Arch. vol. A38, page 13. Reg. of Wills, Liber H, folio 91. Note:—Later administered by Thomas Nixon, Sept. 15, 1736.

Levick, Richard, Sr. Admin. of, to William Levick & Jonathan Griffin. April 6, 1735. Reg. of Wills, Liber H, folio 115.

Anderton [Anderson], Edward. Yeoman. Admin. of, to Mary Anderton. April 7, 1735. Arch. vol. A1, page 156. Reg. of Wills, Liber H, folio 92.

Cuming, Robert. Will. Made Nov. 20, 1734. Heirs: wife Violet; son Robert; wards Delictum & Lumino Cuming (alias Newman). Exec'r, Delictum Cuming. Wits., Ebenezar Wicks, Sarah Shurmer, William Shurmer. Prob. April 7, 1735. Arch. vol. A12, pages 132-133. Reg. of Wills, Liber H, folio 92.

Rawlings, John. Yeoman. Admin. of, to Anthony Rawlings. April 5 & 14, 1735. Reg. of Wills, Liber H, folio 93.

Manlove, Matthew. Will. Made May 17, 1735. Born Jan. 29, 1679. Heirs: wife Susannah; daus. Jemima Moleston, Mary Brinckle (wife of Curtis Brinckle), Susannah, Miriam, Tabitha, Elizabeth Manlove; sons Matthew, Jonathan; grandsons Abner & Obediah Manlove. Exec'r, son Matthew. Wits., Nathaniel Bowman, John Clark, Anthony Woodward. Prob. July 18, 1735. Arch. vol. A32, pages 42-43. Reg. of Wills, Liber H, folios 115-117.

David, Joshua. Yeoman. Admin. of, to Ann David. July 25, 1735. Arch. vol. A12, pages 228-229. Reg. of Wills, Liber H, folio 117. Note:—Arch. vol. A12, page 228 shows that Ann David later married John Johnson; also page 229 mentions a dau. Sarah David.

Thomas, Eleoner. Admin. of, to Solomon Thomas. July 25, 1735. Arch. vol. A50, page 52. Reg. of Wills, Liber H, folio 118.

McDowell, John. Ship-master. Will (copy). Made March 27, 1735. Heirs: Presbyterian Meeting House at Dover; Episcopal Church at Dover; half-bro. Robert McDowell; Arthur, son of William Morgan; Lydia Jones; uncle John McDowell; bro. James; sister Eleanor Nisbet; two half-sisters unnamed. Exec'rs, Hugh Campbell, James Espy, Robert McDowell, Mark Greer, Robert Rowland, bro.-in-law. Wits., Stephen Mott, Andrew Blyth, Magdalon Campbell, Augustus Delabastie. Prob. Sept. 9, 1735. Arch. vol. A32, page 170. Reg. of Wills, Liber H, folios 121-122.

Ridley, Mary. Widow. Admin. of, to William Parker. Jan. 13, 1735. Arch. vol. A43, page 240. Reg. of Wills, Liber H, folios 94-95.

Courtney, Thomas. Will (nunc.). Made Jan. 19, 1735. Heirs: son John; daus. Letitia, Mary. Exec'r, Alexander Donaldson. Wits., Eneas Machon, Hugh McDowell. Prob. Jan. 20, 1735. Arch. vol. A11, page 65. Reg. of Wills, Liber H, folios 141-142.

Grier, Mark. Will. Made Dec. 21, 1735. Heirs: mother Mary Robison, alias Grier, widow; bros. David & George Grier; sisters, Elizabeth Grier, Isabell Rowland. Exec'x, mother. Wits., Mark Smith, Robert Rowland, Ann Smith. Prob. May 13, 1736. Arch. vol. A20, pages 174 & 178. Reg. of Wills, Liber H, folio 139.

Knight, William. Admin. of, to John Knight. May 21, 1736. Reg. of Wills, Liber H, folio 144.

Reynals, Daniel. Yeoman. Will. Made May 4, 1736. Heirs: sons John, Miyckel; dau. Susanah; wife Grace. Exec'x, wife. Wits., Hugh Marydith, John Thomas, William Thompson, Margaret Males. Prob. June 14, 1736. Arch. vol. A43, page 91. Reg. of Wills, Liber H, folio 147.

Jenings, Edward. Yeoman. Admin. of, to Timothy Hanson. June 30, 1736. Reg. of Wills, Liber H, folio 128.

Goforth, Zachariah. Admin. of, to Zachariah Goforth, Jr. Aug. 3, 1736. Arch. vol. A19, page 104. Reg. of Wills, Liber H, folio 128.

Deart, William. Shallopman. Admin. of, to Jonathan Raymond. Oct. 30, 1736. Reg. of Wills, Liber H, folio 129.

Long, Edward. Admin. of, to Jennet Long. Nov. 11, 1736. Reg. of Wills, Liber H, folio 131. Note:—Arch. vol. A31, page 56 shows Jean Long, widow.

Evans, David. Admin. of, to John Evans. Nov. 11, 1736. Reg. of Wills, Liber H, folio 136.

McDowell, Hugh. Admin. of, to John Townsend. Nov. 12, 1736. Reg. of Wills, Liber H, folio 133.

Caldwell, William. Admin. of, to William Gooding. Nov. 16, 1736. Reg. of Wills, Liber H, folio 134.

Grier, David. Admin. of, to Katherine Grier. Nov. 26, 1736. Arch. vol. A20, pages 162-163. Reg. of Wills, Liber H, folio 119.

Simons, Stephen. Admin. of, to Susannah Simons. Dec. 1, 1736. Reg. of Wills, Liber H, folio 131. Note:—Later administered by Susannah Simons, George Goforth & wife Susana, Arch. vol. A46, page 56.

David, John. Blacksmith. Admin. of, to sons Jenkins & Joseph David. Dec. 1, 1736. Arch. vol. A12, page 221. Reg. of Wills, Liber H, folio 134.

Wilson, Thomas. Admin. of, to Isaac Booth. Dec. 4, 1736. Reg. of Wills, Liber H, folio 136.

White, William. Yeoman. Admin. of, to John Pleasonton. Dec. 18, 1736. Reg. of Wills, Liber H, folio 127.

Booth, Joseph. Will (nunc.). Made Jan. 4, 1736. Murderkill. Heirs: wife Mary; sons Thomas, John, Joseph; daus. Eleanor, Anna, Frances. Exec'rs, wife Mary & Mark Manlove. Wits., Miriam Richardson, William Fisher. Prob. Jan. 8, 1736. Arch. vol. A4, page 232. Reg. of Wills, Liber H, folios 119-120. Note:—Arch. vol. A4, page 236 shows that Mary Booth later married George Morgan.

McDonal, John. Yeoman. Admin. of, to James McDonal. Jan. 10, 1736. Reg. of Wills, Liber H, folio 127.

Alstone, Arthur. Admin. of, to Frances Alstone. Jan. 11, 1736. Reg. of Wills, Liber H, folio 133.

Green, William. Will (nunc.). Made Jan. 26, 1736. Heir: Alice Rhoades, mother of Wm. Walker. Wits., William Fisher, William Walker. Prob. Jan. 28, 1736. Arch. vol. A20, page 124. Reg. of Wills, Liber I, folio 55.

Ashborn [Ashburn], Martain. Tailor. Admin. of, to Catherine Ashborn. March 8, 1736. Reg. of Wills, Liber H, folio 130. Note:—Arch. vol. A2, page 11, shows later admin. by William Phillips & Cathrine, his wife; also mentions sons Richard and Martin Ashburn.

Flowers, Thomas. Admin. of, to Elizabeth Flowers. March 10, 1736. Reg. of Wills, Liber H, folio 135.

Dixon, Thomas. Yeoman. Will. Made Dec. 8, 1736. Heir: wife Ann. Exec'x, wife Ann. Wits., Charles Hirons, James Wells, Thomas Green. Prob. March 19, 1736. Arch. vol. A14, page 147. Reg. of Wills, Liber H, folios 124-125.

Morgan, David. Yeoman. Admin. of, to Katharine Morgan. March 28, 1737. Reg. of Wills, Liber H, folio 129.

Gray, John. Yeoman. Will. Made Dec. 23, 1732. Heirs: wife Sarah; son William. Exec'x, wife Sarah. Wits., Peter Coudrat, Peter Grahame, Arthur McDannel. Prob. April 16, 1737. Arch. vol. A20, page 21.

Molleston, William. Will. Made 1736. Heirs: wife Ann; sons William, Jonathan; daus. Mary, Ann, Sara Molleston & Elizabeth Skidmore; grandson John Skidmore; granddau. Mary Skidmore. Exec'rs, wife Ann & son William. Wits., Tabitha Williams, Mary Manlove, William Manlove. Prob. June 2, 1737. Arch. vol. A35, page 220. Reg. of Wills, Liber H, folios 142-143.

Boog, John. Admin. of, to William Boog. Aug. 11, 1737. Arch. vol. A4, page 174. Reg. of Wills, Liber H, folio 130.

Rees, Evan. Farmer. Will. Made July 18, 1737. Duck Creek. Heirs: daus. Eleanor, Mary; son David; son-in-law George Griffith; granddau. Esther Rees; son Richard. Exec'r, son Richard. Trustee, son Richard. Wits., John Jones, James Howell, Joshua Evans. Prob. Aug. 24, 1737. Arch. vol. A42, page 241. Reg. of Wills, Liber H, folio 140.

Wilkins, Mary. Admin. of, to Edward Beaman. Aug. 27, 1737. Reg. of Wills, Liber H, folio 132.

Fleming, Isabella. Admin. of, to Robert Fleming. Sept. 5, 1737. Reg. of Wills, Liber H, folio 135.

Richmond [Richman], Michael. Admin. of, to Martha Richmond. Nov. 10, 1737. Arch. vol. A43, pages 175-176. Reg. of Wills, Liber H, folio 132. Note:—Arch. vol. A43, page 176 mentions heirs Mary & Ann Richman.

David, Lewis. Farmer. Will. Made Aug. 27, 1937. Duck Creek. Heirs: wife Rebecca; granddau. Sarah David; dau. Rachel; son John; step-son Thomas Jones; Rees Lewis. Exec'x, wife. Guardian, son John. Wits., David Bowen, Robert Fleming, Joshua Evans. Prob. Nov. 10, 1737. Arch. vol. A12, pages 232-233. Reg. of Wills, Liber H, folio 126.

Train, Roger. Will. Made Nov. 9, 1736. Heirs: wife Mary; sons Hammelton, James; daus. Sarah and four younger ones unnamed. Exec'x, wife. Wits., William Greer, John Glenn, Samuel Robbisson. Prob. Nov. 24, 1737. Arch. vol. A51, page 62. Reg. of Wills, Liber H, folio 124.

Miller, John. Millwright. Admin. of, to Thomas Tarrant. Nov. 24, 1737. Reg. of Wills, Liber H, folio 137.

Hunn, Caleb. Admin. of, to Ruth Hunn. Dec. 13, 1737. Arch. vol. A25, page 131. Reg. of Wills, Liber H, folios 138-139.

Shurmer, Benjamin. Admin. of, to Sarah Shurmer. Dec. 16, 1737. Reg. of Wills, Liber H, folios 137-138.

Grier, John. Admin. of, to John Grier & Robert Patton. Dec. 22, 1737. Arch. vol. A20, page 165. Reg. of Wills, Liber H, folio 138.

Jones, Thomas. Admin. of, to Margaret Jones & John Stephens. Dec. 30, 1737. Arch. vol. A28, pages 25-26. Reg. of Wills, Liber H, folio 144.

Finley, Nehemiah. Admin. of, to Thomas Cripen [Crippen]. Jan. 21, 1737. Reg. of Wills, Liber H, folio 145.

Mason, Mary. Admin. of, to William Mason & John Hirons [Irons]. Feb. 1, 1737. Arch. vol. A34, page 2. Reg. of Wills, Liber H, folio 145.

Shurmer, Sarah. Widow. Admin. of, to William Shurmer & Nicholas Lockerman. Feb. 11, 1737. Reg. of Wills, Liber H, folio 146.

Covington, Samuel. Somerset Co. Admin. of, to Thomas Dixon & wife Anne. March 2, 1737. Arch. vol. A11, page 67.

Shurmer, Benjamin. Admin. of, to Nicholas Lockerman, son-in-law. March 9, 1737. Arch. vol. A46, pages 43-44. Reg. of Wills, Liber H, folios 146-147.

Wattkins, John. Admin. of, to Edward Beman. c. 1737. Arch. vol. A53, page 162.

Trippet, John. Will. Made Feb. 17, 1738. Heirs: sons John, Waitman & Gove; dau. Prinelopey; cousin Sarah Trippet; wife Ellse. Exec'rs, wife & bro. John Sipple. Wits., Mark Smith, Christopher Sipple. Prob. March 7, 1738. Arch. vol. A51, page 79. Reg. of Wills, Liber H, folio 149.

Anderson, Thomas. Will. Made Dec. 19, 1734. Heirs: sons James, Burthoremies, John; 3 daus. unnamed; wife Elizabeth. Exec'x, wife Elizabeth. Wits., John Sipple, Mark Smith. Prob. March 31, 1738. Arch. vol. A8, page 80 & Arch. vol. A1, page 209. Reg. of Wills, Liber H, folio 148.

Cleaves [Clives], Benjamin. Admin. of, to John Chicken. April 14, 1738. Arch. vol. A9, page 135. Reg. of Wills, Liber H, folios 147-148.

Rutty, Daniel. Yeoman. Will (copy). Made Jan. 1, 1735. Heir: wife Elizabeth. Exec'x, wife. Wits., Robert Patton, John Jackson, William Fisher. Prob. April 18, 1738. Arch. vol. A44, page 214. Reg. of Wills, Liber H, folios 149-150.

Colehale, William. Planter. Admin. of, to Uphra Colehale. July 1738. Arch. vol. A9, page 251. Reg. of Wills, Liber H, folio 150.

Woddle, David. Admin. of, to Charles Hylliard. July 14, 1738. Reg. of Wills, Liber H, folio 151.

Clubb, Richard. Doctor. Admin. of, to Thomas Tarrant. July 16, 1738. Arch. vol. A9, page 170. Reg. of Wills, Liber H, folio 152.

Pusley, Thomas. Planter. Admin. of, to Daniel Pusley. July 25, 1738. Reg. of Wills, Liber H, folio 151.

Green, John. Admin. of, to Rachel Green. Aug. 10, 1738. Reg. of Wills, Liber H, folio 26. Note:—Arch. vol. A20, page 76 shows sons Thomas, Robert, and Henry Green.

Flintham, Benjamin. Admin. of, to William Flintham. Sept. 5, 1738. Reg. of Wills, Liber H, folio 152.

Craig, John. Duck Creek. Admin. of, to Elizabeth Craig. Oct. 6, 1738. Reg. of Wills, Liber H, folio 153. Note:—Arch. vol. A11, page 166 shows Richard James & Elizabeth, his wife, adm'rs.

Clay, John. Admin. of, to Mark Smith. Oct. 9, 1738. Reg. of Wills, Liber H, folio 153.

Snow, John. Will. Made Oct. 9, 1738. Heirs: wife Hannah; son David. Exec'r, bro. Isaac. Wits., Elisha Snow, Abraham Cockrill, Thomas Harrad. Prob. Oct. 14, 1738. Arch. vol. A48, pages 12-13. Reg. of Wills, Liber I, folio 1.

Parke, Sarah. Will. Made Sept. 19, 1738. Heirs: sons Thomas, Theadore, Hugh; Ann, dau. of Thomas Tarrant; Rev. Arthur Ussher. Exec'r, friend Thomas Tarrant. Wits., Arthur Ussher, Mary Tuthill, Charles Tuthill. Prob. Oct. 19, 1738. Arch. vol. A39, pages 19-21. Reg. of Wills, Liber I, folio 4. Note:—Arch. vol. A39, pages 20-21 show this account later administered, D. B. N., by Robert Willcocks & Rev. Arthur Ussher.

Muncy, Francis. Will. Made Oct. 26, 1738. Heirs: wife Abigail; sons John, Thomas, Nathaniel, Samuel; grandson Francis, son of Samuel & Mary; dau. Belliharen. Exec'x, wife. Wits., Thomas Thomas, Hannah Thomas, John Flaharty. Prob. Nov. 11, 1738. Arch. vol. A37, page 74. Reg. of Wills, Liber I, folio 3.

Patton, Eliner. Will. Made April 29, 1732. Heirs: sons Robert, Thomas; dau. Sarah Fleming; grandau. Mary Fleming; son-in-law John Fleming. Exec'r, son Robert. Wits., Robert Lecky, Robert Fleming, David Barnhill. Prob. Dec. 11, 1738. Arch. vol. A39, page 135. Reg. of Wills, Liber I, folio 2.

Grier, Catharine. Will (nunc.). Made Dec. 9, 1738. Heirs: sons John, David; dau. Mary. Trustees, Robert Rowland, Elizabeth Grier, Mary Robisson. Wits., John Crawford, Daniel McKell, John Hathorn, Margt. McKnell. Prob. Dec. 11, 1738. Arch. vol. A20, page 161. Reg. of Wills, Liber I, folio 4. Note:—The three trustees are a bro.-in-law, sister-in-law, and mother-in-law, respectively.

McKemmy, Alexander. Admin. of, to Joseph Worrell. Dec. 19, 1738. Reg. of Wills, Liber H, folio 154.

Barns, John. Yeoman. Will. Made Dec. 5, 1738. Heir: son William. Exec'r, Phillip Fields. Trustee, Phillip Fields. Wits., Timothy Hanson, Sr., Timothy Hanson, Jr., William McKenny. Prob. Jan. 3, 1738. Arch. vol. A2, page 218. Reg. of Wills, Liber I, folio 5.

Hall, Letitia. Widow of John Hall. Will. Made Dec. 4, 1738. Heirs: sons John, Robert; dau. Letitia; sister Mary Tuthill; dau.-in-law Hannah Ballock [Bellach]. Exec'rs, friends, Andrew Hamilton of Phila., Thomas Noxon of New Castle Co., Jonathan Raymond of Kent Co. Wits., Simon Hirons, Ellinor Cole, Chas. Tuthill. Prob. Jan. 17, 1738. Arch. vol.

A21, pages 107-109. Reg. of Wills, Liber I, folio 5. Note:—Arch. vol. A21, page 108 shows that John Gooding & wife Sarah later administered the account.

Maxwell, William. Admin. of, to Alexander Donaldson. Jan. 27, 1738. Reg. of Wills, Liber H, folio 154.

Vance, James. Will. Made Jan. 23, 1738. Heirs: cousins Hannah Killpatrick (wife of John Killpatrick), George Vance, Charles Vance, Alexander Vance; half-bro. Charles Stewart; Rev. John Hones; uncle Alexander Vance; Patrick & Elizabeth Vance, children of sister Mary Vance. Exec'rs, friends James Gorrell, Robert Rowland. Wits., Alex. Farquhar, Benjamin Ogle, George Grier. Prob. Feb. 1, 1738. Arch. vol. A51, pages 218-224. Reg. of Wills, Liber I, folios 6-7.

Herresle, William. Merchant. Admin. of, to Joseph Lowns. Feb. 12, 1738. Reg. of Wills, Liber H, folio 155.

Farquhar, Alexander. Merchant. Will. Made Feb. 27, 1738. Heirs: wife Mary; dau. Isabel; sons George, Alexander, William. Exec'rs, wife & James Gorrell. Wits., Robert Jameson, Isabel Rowland, Mary Casi. Prob. March 14, 1738. Arch. vol. A17, pages 17-25. Reg. of Wills, Liber I, folio 8. Note:—Arch. vol. A17, page 23 shows that Mary Farquhar later married James Gorrell.

Donaldson, Alexander. Will. Made Feb. 3, 1738/9. Heirs: wife unnamed; cousin's husband John Townsend; cousins Mary & Letitia Courtney; friend Peter Goodrat; cousins Alexander Tumblin & Charles Townsend son of John; children of John Townsend; John Townsend, son of John. Exec'rs, wife, James Gordon, Sr., Peter Goodratt. Wits., James Gordon, Sr., James Gordon, Jr. Prob. March 14, 1738. Arch. vol. A14, page 160. Reg. of Wills, Liber I, folios 12-13.

Townsend, John. Admin. of, to Mary Townsend. April 18, 1739. Arch. vol. A51, page 20. Reg. of Wills, Liber H, folio 155.

Maxwell, William. Admin. of, to Thomas Skidmore, Jr. April 26, 1739. Arch. vol. A34, page 103. Reg. of Wills, Liber I, folios 11-12.

Vance, Alexander. Admin. of, to Mary Vance. April 30, 1739. Reg. of Wills, Liber I, folio 26.

Downham, John. Laborer. Admin. of, to James Gorrell. June 19, 1739. Reg. of Wills, Liber I, folio 27.

Craige, Moses. Admin. of, to Sarah Craige. June 22, 1739. Arch. vol. A11, page 185. Reg. of Wills, Liber I, folio 27. Note:— Arch. vol. A11, page 185 shows that this account was later settled by Alexander & Hugh Craige; also mentions children Moses, Thomas, Margaret & Elizabeth Craige.

Robisson, George. Will. Made June 14, 1739. Heirs: wife Hannah; sons George, Lawrence, Jereboam; daus. Sarah, Hannah. Exec'x, wife Hannah. Wits., James Jackson, Mary Hart, Daniel Robisson. Prob. July 4, 1739. Arch. vol. A44, pages 41-42. Reg. of Wills, Liber I, folios 9-10. Note:— Arch. vol. A44, page 42 shows that Hannah Robisson later married George Hart.

Parvis, William. Admin. of, to Betty Parvis. July 14, 1739. Reg. of Wills, Liber H, folio 156.

Richmond [Richman], Martha. Wife of Michael Richman. Admin. of, to John Tilton. July 31, 1739. Arch. vol. A43, page 173. Reg. of Wills, Liber H, folio 157.

Martain, James. Admin. of, to Samuel Smith. Oct. 15, 1739. Reg. of Wills, Liber H, folio 157.

Conselah, Thomas. Planter. Will. Made Sept. 26, 1739. Heirs: grandson, William; daus. Sarah Butcher, Elizabeth Francisco, Mary Conselah. Exec'x, dau. Mary. Wits., William Skinner, James Trail. Prob. Oct. 20, 1739. Arch. vol. A10, page 101. Reg. of Wills, Liber I, folio 11.

Wild, Robert. Admin. of, to Ruth Wild. Oct. 25, 1739. Reg. of Wills, Liber H, folio 158.

Rositor, John. Will. Made Jan. 2, 1739. Heirs: son William; wife Elizabeth. Exec'x, wife Elizabeth. Wits., Samuel Bready, Robert Fleming. Prob. Jan. 21, 1739. Arch. vol. A44, page 132. Reg. of Wills, Liber I, folio 13.

Newell, John. Will. Made Jan. 16, 1739/40. Heirs: sons William, John, Thomas; dau. Elizabeth; grandson James Clayton; granddau. Ruth Betts; wife Mary. Exec'x, wife Mary. Wits., James Clayton, John Hall, Rebecca Welsh. Prob. Feb. 4, 1739. Arch. vol. A37, page 190. Reg. of Wills, Liber I, folio 14.

Craige, Sarah. Will (nunc.). Made Feb. 13, 1739. Heirs: bros.-in-law Hugh & Alexander Craige; daus. Elizabeth & Margaret Craige; two children unnamed; Agnes Craige, wife of Hugh. Wits., Abraham Jackson, Margaret Jackson. Prob. Feb. 16, 1739. Arch. vol. A11, page 193.

Craige, Sarah. Widow. Admin. of, to Hugh Craige & Alexander Craige. Feb. 25, 1739. Reg. of Wills, Liber I, folio 64. Note:—Arch. vol. A11, page 185, shows sons Thomas, Moses; daus. Margaret, Elizabeth.

Evan, Joshua. Yeoman. Will. Made Feb. 21, 1739. "Lewyn Celyn" Duck Creek. Heirs: Margaret David, dau. of James; Rees Lewis; Rev. Thomas Evans of Welsh Tract in New Castle Co.; John Lewis; Jenkin David; John David, son of John David Morgan; Thomas David, son of John David Morgan; sister-in-law Catharine, wife of Joseph David; bro.-in-law David Einon; servant maid; children of Philip Evan & John Evan; mother Geveullian Evan. Exec'rs, mother & cousin John David. Wits., John Johnson, Ann Johnson, Jno. David. Prob. March 1, 1939. Arch. vol. A16, pages 225-226. Reg. of Wills, Liber I, folio 15.

Prior [Pryor], John. Yeoman. Admin. of, to Hannah Prior ... 1740. Reg. of Wills, Liber I, folio 12. Note:—Arch. vol. A41, page 190 shows sons John & Joseph, and widow Hannah.

Clifton, Absolom. Will (copy). Made April 4, 1739. Heirs: bros. William, Ephraim, John; sister Mary Townsin. Exec'r, bro. Ephraim. Wits., Ebenezer Manlove, John Knight, Sarah Wakup [Wacob]. Prob. April 8, 1740. Arch. vol. A9, page 145. Reg. of Wills, Liber I, folio 17.

Whithart, Samuel. Farmer. Will. Made Feb. 27, 1939/40. Little Creek. Heirs: sons James, Samuel, Solomon; dau. Saraha Snow; wife Sarah. Exec'rs, wife & son Samuel. Wits., William Flintham, Joseph Freeman. Prob. April 8, 1740. Arch. vol. A54, page 187. Reg. of Wills, Liber I, folio 20.

Irons, Timothy. Will. Made March 10, 1739/40. Heirs: sons John, Thomas, Timothy, Henry, Owen; daus. Catherine, Mary, Sarah, Meriam; wife Catherine. Exec'x, wife. Wits., Isaac Freeland, George Gordon, James Gordon. Prob. April 9, 1740. Arch. vol. A25, page 228. Reg. of Wills, Liber I, folio 18.

McKinley [McGinnely], Daniel. Laborer. Admin. of, to James Gorrell, merchant. April 23, 1740. Arch. vol. A32, page 191. Reg. of Wills, Liber I, folios 30-31.

Brinckle, Hester. Gentlewoman. Will. Made Jan. 19, 1739/40. Heirs: daus. Elizabeth Durborow, Hannah Fisher; sons John, Thomas, Daniel & Benjamin. Exec'r, son John. Wits., Daniel Brinckle, Susannah Brinckle, Isaac King. Prob. May 3, 1740. Arch. vol. A5, page 170. Reg. of Wills, Liber I, folio 19.

Curtis, John. Laborer. Admin. of, to Sarah Curtis. May 16, 1740. Reg. of Wills, Liber I, folio 32.

Crispin, Joseph. Tailor. Will. Made May 7, 1740. Heirs: son Silas; dau. Elizabeth; Samuel Barratt; Benjamin Barratt, Jr.; Jonathan Barratt. Exec'r, Ralph Needham. Trustee, Mary Barratt, aunt to Elizabeth. Wits., Peter Watson, Mary Hill, Timothy Hanson, Jr. Prob. May 24, 1740. Arch. vol. A11, pages 230-232. Reg. of Wills, Liber I, folios 16-17.

Francis, John. Admin. of, to Ann Francis. June 4, 1740. Reg. of Wills, Liber I, folio 32. Note:—Arch. vol. A18, page 77 shows a later admin. by Peter Watson & wife Ann, widow of John Francis.

Wild, Joshua. Admin. of, to Ruth Wild. June 16, 1740. Reg. of Wills, Liber H, folio 156. Note:—Arch. vol. A55, page 16 mentions eldest son, John Wild.

Manlove, Luke. Farmer. Will. Made May 27, 1740. Heirs: son William; dau. Sarah; one child unnamed; wife [in guardian acct. named Tabitha]; Nathaniel Hunn. Exec'rs, wife and Nathaniel Hunn. Wits., John Hammitt, Henry Molliston. Prob. June 30, 1740. Arch. vol. A32, pages 32-33. Reg. of Wills, Liber I, folio 19.

McCellen, Thomas. Will (nunc.). Made July 30, 1740. Heir: mother unnamed. Exec'r, John Gordon. Wit., Isabella Craige. Prob. Aug. 1, 1740. Arch. vol. A32, page 131. Reg. of Wills, Liber I, folio 20.

Finney, William. Will. Made July 19, 1740. Heirs: wife Ann; sons William, James, Daniel; daus. Patience, Alce; Stephen Black. Exec'x, wife Ann. Wits., John Hunter, Phillip Beady, Joseph Powell, William Trippett. Prob. Aug. 13, 1740. Arch. vol. A17, page 109. Reg. of Wills, Liber I, folio 21.

Gordon, James. Will. Made Aug. 18, 1740. Heirs: sons James, Griffith, George, David, Joshua, Robert; daus. Latitia, Mary. Exec'r, son Robert. Wits., Thomas Irons, John Parry, Timothy Irons. Prob. Aug. 18, 1740. Arch. vol. A19, pages 153-154. Reg. of Wills, Liber I, folios 46 & 139. Note:—Arch. vol. A19, page 154 shows James Gorrell as adm'r D. B. N.

Robbinson, William. Planter. Will. Made Oct. 29, 1739. Heirs: sons Thomas, William; daus. Mary McGrow, Mary Bensin, Margarett, Ann, Catharine Robbinson; wife Catharine. Exec'x, wife Catharine. Wits., John Feaston, Henry Harriss, Mary Harriss. Prob. Aug. 21, 1740. Arch. vol. A44, page 88. Reg. of Wills, Liber I, folio 22.

Cook, John. Admin. of, to Hannah Cook. Aug. 28, 1740. Arch. vol. A10, page 120. Reg. of Wills, Liber I, folios 32-33.

Tarrant, Thomas. Will. Made Aug. 28, 1740. Heirs: wife Mary; Robert Willcocks; daus. Susannah, Mary; sons Thomas, Manlove. Exec'rs, wife Mary & Robert Willcocks. Wits., Simon Hirons, David Giffing, Charles Tuthill. Prob. Sept. 22, 1740. Arch. vol. A39, pages 20-21, Arch. vol. A49, pages 156-161. Reg. of Wills, Liber I, folios 22-23. Note:—Arch. vol. A49, page 157 shows dau. Susannah married Lawrence Robbisson; page 161 shows wife Mary, the exec'x, married Arthur Ussher.

Twillin, Joshua. Laborer. Admin. of, to William Willson. Sept. 29, 1740. Reg. of Wills, Liber I, folio 28.

Flaharty, John. Admin. of, to Sarah Billiter. Oct. 1, 1740. Reg. of Wills, Liber I, folio 28.

Beauvett, Peter. Laborer. Admin. of, to Hannah Beauvett. Nov. 11, 1740. Reg. of Wills, Liber I, folio 29.

Molleston, Ann. Widow. Will. Made Oct. 11, 1740. Heirs: sons William, Jonathan; daus. Sarah & Ann Molleston, Elizabeth Skidmore, Mary Bryers; grandson John Molleston. Exec'r, William Molleston. Wits., John Robbisson, Rayneer Williams, Henry Molleston. Prob. Nov. 13, 1740. Arch. vol. A35, pages 201-202. Reg. of Wills, Liber I, folios 23-24.

Marrett, Zachariah. Laborer. Admin. of, to Nathaniel Luff. Dec. 2, 1740. Arch. vol. A33, page 198. Reg. of Wills, Liber I, folio 29.

Carter, Robert. Yeoman. Will. Made Nov. 18, 1740. Dover Hd. Heirs: sons Thomas, William; wife Jane; dau. Margarett. Exec'rs, wife Jane & friend James Carbin. Wits., James Gray, Patrick McDonogh, John David. Prob. Dec. 16, 1740. Arch. vol. A8, pages 38-39. Reg. of Wills, Liber I, folios 74-75. Note:—Arch. vol. A8, page 39 shows that Jane Carter later married James Carbin.

Betts, William. Laborer. Admin. of, to Elizabeth Betts. Dec. 29, 1740. Reg. of Wills, Liber I, folio 33. Note:—Arch. vol. A4, pages 40-41 shows a later admin. by John Caton, Jr., and Elizabeth Caton, his wife, mentioning son William & dau. Ruth Betts.

Bowman, Nathaniel. Will (copy). Made Nov. 16, 1740. Mispillion Hd. Heirs: wife Sarah; son Thomas; grandson Henry Bowman. Exec'r, son Thomas. Wits., Matthew Manlove, Isaac King, Nathaniel Luff. Prob. Dec. 31, 1740. Arch. vol. A5, page 79. Reg. of Wills, Liber I, folio 24.

Hamnitt, John. Farmer. Will. Made Dec. 18, 1740. Heirs: dau.-in-law Sarah Brinckle; housekeeper Catherine Owen. Exec'rs, Sarah Brinkle & Catherine Owen. Wits., William Shurley, Harman Burkeloe, Spencer Cole. Prob. Dec. 31, 1740. Arch. vol. A21, page 190. Reg. of Wills, Liber I, folio 25.

Fisher, William. Mariner. Admin. of, to Thomas Skidmore, Jr. Jan. 23, 1740. Reg. of Wills, Liber I, folio 30.

Hutcheson [Hutchinson], William. Admin. of, to James Paul Heath & Hugh Matthews. Feb. 11, 1740. Arch. vol. A25, page 202. Reg. of Wills, Liber I, folio 31.

Hirons, Francis. Admin. of, to William Hirons. Feb. 17, 1740. Arch. vol. A24, page 92. Reg. of Wills, Liber I, folio 30.

Manlove, Susannah. Will. Made Jan. 15, 1740. Heirs: daus. Jemima Moleston, Mary Brinckle, Miriam Bowman, Elizabeth Loper, Tabitha Manlove, Susannah Needham; sons Matthew, Jonathan. Exec'r, son Matthew. Wits., Reynear Williams, Nathaniel Hunn, Mary Hunn. Prob. Feb. 21, 1740. Arch. vol. A33, page 124. Reg. of Wills, Liber I, folio 34.

Hughes, David. Laborer. Admin. of, to John Harding. March 18, 1740. Arch. vol. A25, page 119. Reg. of Wills, Liber I, folios 27-28.

Cape, Joseph. Laborer. Admin. of, to William Shurmer. April 7, 1741. Arch. vol. A7, page 199. Reg. of Wills, Liber I, folio 34.

Chicken, John. Will. Made Feb. 24, 1740/1. Heirs: wife Judith; daus. unnamed; son John. Exec'x, wife. Wits., William Hammons, Michael Ofley, Elenor West. Prob. April 15, 1741. Arch. vol. A8, pages 166-167. Reg. of Wills, Liber I, folio 35.

Collins, William. Admin. of, to Rachel Collins. April 15, 1741. Reg. of Wills, Liber I, folio 55.

McCleland, Thomas. Admin. of, to John Gordon. May 26, 1741. Arch. vol. A32, page 106.

Lee, Richard. Admin. of, to Elizabeth Lee. June 3, 1741. Arch. vol. A29, pages 235-236. Reg. of Wills, Liber I, folio 56. Note:—Arch. vol. A29, page 236 mentions heirs Richard and William, dec'd; page 235 shows that Elizabeth Lee later married Andrew Patton.

Boyer, Daniel. Will. Made c. 1741. Heirs: sons James, Daniel; wife Elinor. Exec'x, wife. Wits., Nicholas Ridgely, Peter Calloway, David Lewis. Prob. June 5, 1741. Arch. vol. A5, pages 51-52. Reg. of Wills, Liber I, folio 36. Note:—Arch. vol. A5, page 52 shows later administered by Elioner Bready and husband Absolom Bready; five children not named.

Merchant, William. Admin. of, to Rachel Merchant. June 11, 1741. Reg. of Wills, Liber I, folio 57.

Sorath, William. Admin. of, to Thomas Skidmore, Jr. July 1, 1741. Reg. of Wills, Liber I, folio 57.

McMillan, William. Will. Made July 14, 1741. Heirs: sister Jane McMillan; bro. James; William Rowen; James Morris, Jr. Exec'r, friend James Morris. Wits., William Rowen, Margrett Morris. Prob. July 17, 1741. Arch. vol. A32, page 240. Reg. of Wills, Liber I, folio 37.

Bradey, Samuel. Admin. of, to Mary Bradey. Aug. 1, 1741. Reg. of Wills, Liber I, folio 56.

Brinckle, Thomas. Planter. Will. Made July 23, 1741. Murderkill. Heirs: wife Mary; dau. Hester; bros. John, Daniel, Benjamin; Alexander Bryer. Exec'x, wife. Wits., John Brinckle, Jr., Ann Brinckle, John Newton. Prob. Aug. 6, 1741. Arch. vol. A5, page 216. Reg. of Wills, Liber I, folio 38. Note:—Grandfather Tilton is mentioned in the will.

Diton, Margaret. Admin. of, to Joshua Diton. Aug. 14, 1741. Reg. of Wills, Liber I, folios 56-57.

Tuthill, Charles. Admin. of, to Mary Tuthill. Sept. 18, 1741. Arch. vol. A51, page 183. Reg. of Wills, Liber I, folio 58.

Whitaker [Whitacre], Anna. Will. Made Aug. 30, 1741. Heirs: grandson Caleb Hunn's four children Mary, Hannah, Ruth, Pricilla Hunn; grandsons Nathaniel Hunn, Waitman Sipple, Jr.; great-grandson Caleb Sipple. Exec'r, grandson Waitman Sipple, Jr. Wits., George Morgan, Benjamin Warren, James Dickson. Prob. Oct. 1, 1741. Arch. vol. A54, page 75. Reg. of Wills, Liber I, folios 54-55.

James, Evan. Admin. of, to Gwenlian James. Nov. 12, 1741. Arch. vol. A26, page 86. Reg. of Wills, Liber I, folio 58.

Brooks, Matthew. Will. Made Oct. 31, 1741. St. Jones Hd. Heirs: sons Jonathan, John, Thomas Evans; dau. Mary Green; son-in-law George Green. Exec'r, son Jonathan. Wits., John Clayton, Ebinezer Cowgill. Prob. Nov. 17, 1741. Arch. vol. A6, page 13. Reg. of Wills, Liber I, folio 54.

Cain, Owen. Yeoman. Will (called Codicil). Made Dec. 6. 1741. Heirs: sons Menasses, Owen; wife unnamed. Exec'x, wife. Wits., Peter Lowber, John Cain, Thomas Thomas. Prob. Dec. 9, 1741. Arch. vol. A7, page 78. Reg. of Wills, Liber I, folio 126.

Craige, George. Admin. of, to Isabella Craige. Dec. 15, 1741. Reg. of Wills, Liber I, folios 58-59. Note:—Arch. vol. A11, page 153 shows Ebenezer, Mary, Jane Craig as heirs.

Craige, James. Admin. of, to Prudence Craige. Dec. 15, 1741. Reg. of Wills, Liber I, folio 59. Note:—Arch. vol. A11, page 160 shows three sons, Samuel, John, James Craige.

Whitside, John. Trader & Shallopman. Will. Made Nov. 6, 1741. Heirs: eldest bro. William; other bros. & sisters unnamed. Exec'r, friend John Tilton. Wits., Jno. David, David Rees, George Wilson. Prob. Jan. 6, 1741. Arch. vol. A54, pages 201-203. Reg. of Wills, Liber I, folio 44.

Evan, Gwenllian. Will. Made Jan. 4, 1741. Duck Creek. Heirs: niece Elizabeth Jones; nephew William Edward; sister Alls David; Elizabeth Marick; friends John Lewis, Rees Levin; nephew John Edward, son of sister Eliz.; cousin James Edward. Exec'r, James Edward. Wits., Jenkin David, Owen David, Rees Lewis. Prob. Jan. 11, 1741. Arch. vol. A16, page 222. Reg. of Wills, Liber I, folios 40-41.

Maning, John. Will. Made Jan. 4, 1741/2. Heirs: friend William Wilson; wife Rachel. Exec'r, friend William Wilson. Wits., James Gilespy, William Morgan, Anna Jackson. Prob. Jan. 17, 1741. Arch. vol. A33, page 79. Reg. of Wills, Liber I, folios 42-43.

Coe, Mary. Will (copy, nunc.). [N. d.]. Murtherkill Hd. Heir: mother Alice Roads. Wits., Elizabeth Jackson, Jennet Boggs. Prob. Jan. 22, 1741. Arch. vol. A9, page 183. Reg. of Wills, Liber I, folio 55.

McCludy, James. Admin. of, to Thomas Dawson. Jan. 30, 1741. Arch. vol. A32, page 107.

Quilling, Thomas. Admin. of, to Barbary Quilling, widow. Feb. 13, 1741. Reg. of Wills, Liber I, folio 59. Note:—Arch. vol. A42, page 6 shows sons Teague, Alexander, Joseph; daus. Sarah, Lydia, Elizabeth Quilling; Benjamin, son of Thomas Quilling, Jr., dec'd.

Bowman, Sarah. Will. Made Sept. 14, 1741. Mispillion Hd. Heirs: sons Nathaniel Luff, Thomas Bowman; daus. Hannah Robisson, Sarah Clark; grandau. Ann Clark; grandson Henry Bowman. Exec'r, son Nathaniel Luff. Wits., John Brickle, Sarah Jester, Precillar Tharp. Prob. Feb. 25, 1741. Arch. vol. A5, page 86. Reg. of Wills, Liber I, folio 42.

Steel, James. Will (copy). Made Dec. 31, 1741. Philadelphia. Heirs: wife Martha; daus. Mary Hillyard, Rebecca Steel, Elizabeth Shute (wife of William), Ann Renshaw (wife of Richard), Ruth Thompson, Martha Pennington; sons-in-law William Shute, Richard Renshaw, Thomas Pennington;

grandchildren Rebecca, Martha, Elizabeth Shuite, children of William & Elizabeth; James Thompson; James Sanders; Rebecca Sanders; James & Martha Pennington; James, Henry, Elizabeth & Hanah Steel; Daniel Hammond, wife's half-bro.; John Hammond, son of Dan'l; Samuel Powel, Jr.; Lynford Lardner. Exec'rs, sons-in-law Charles Hillyard, Richard Renshaw, daus. Mary Hillyard, Rebecca Steel. Wits., Septimus Robisson, Isaac Jones. Prob. March 5, 1741. Arch. vol. A48, pages 199-200. Reg. of Wills, Liber I, folios 38-40.

Hallans, Jehosaphat. Admin. of, to Samuel Robbisson. March 6, 1741. Reg. of Wills, Liber I, folios 59-60.

Jones, William. Admin. of, to Catherine Jones, wife. March 13, 1741. Arch. vol. A28, page 28. Reg. of Wills, Liber I, folios 33-34.

McKlue, James. Admin. of, to Thomas Dawson. March 13, 1741. Reg. of Wills, Liber I, folio 60.

Stout, Benjamin. Laborer. Admin. of, to Elizabeth Stout. March 16, 1741. Arch. vol. A49, page 34. Reg. of Wills, Liber I, folio 31.

Willcocks, John. Carpenter. Will. Made March 20, 1741. Heirs: son James; dau. Mary. Exec'r, friend John Tilton. Wits., Alexander Montgomerrie, Jno. Tilton, Jr. Prob. April 1, 1742. Arch. vol. A55, pages 56-57. Reg. of Wills, Liber I, folio 41.

Moore, Richard. Tanner. Will. Made March 25, 1743 [sic.]. Heir: friend William Miller. Exec'r, William Miller. Wits., Joseph McMechon, James Alford, Mathew Dounloup. Prob. April 6, 1742. Arch. vol. A36, pages 81-82. Reg. of Wills, Liber I, folios 51-52.

Moore, Richard. Admin. of, to William Miller. April 6, 1742. Arch. vol. A36, page 82. Reg. of Wills, Liber I, folio 60.

Richardson, Richard. Admin. of, to George Morgan & wife Mary, late Mary Booth. D. B. N. April 9, 1742. Arch. vol. A43, page 168.

Billiter, Sarah. Will. Made April 18, 1742. Heirs: sons John, Thomas, Daniel & Joab; dau. Johanna. Trustees, Evan Lewis, William Wheelar. Wits., Thos. Thomas, Hannah Thomas, Thomas Lewes. Prob. April 30, 1742. Arch. vol. A4, page 53. Reg. of Wills, Liber I, folio 44.

Middleton, George. Will. Made June 14, 1740. Heirs: sons George, John; dau. Tabitha Basebridge; sons-in-law Samuel Horseman, Thomas Horseman; dau.-in-law Mary Horseman; wife Elenor. Exec'x, wife. Wits., Margaret Berry, Elizabeth White, Stephen Paradee. Prob. May 17, 1742. Arch. vol. A34, page 236. Reg. of Wills, Liber I, folio 45.

Caldwell, James. Admin. of, to John Johnson. May 27, 1742. Reg. of Wills, Liber I, folios 61 & 71.

Banning, Richard. Murtherkill Hd. Admin. of, to Hester Banning. May 28, 1742. Reg. of Wills, Liber I, folio 61. Note: —Arch. vol. A2, page 102 shows Matthew Jarrett and his wife Easther as admin'rs, dated Feb. 26, 1744.

Gordon, John. Will. Made June 1, 1742. Heirs: wife Elizabeth; sons Robert, John, Seth, James; cousin Samuel Gordon; daus. Sarah, Margarett, Elizabeth, Nanne; cousins Elizabeth & Martha Gordon. Exec'x, wife. Wits., Samuel Robinson, Richard Darling, Hanna Robinson. Prob. June 11, 1742. Arch. vol. A19, pages 161-162. Reg. of Wills, Liber I, folio 47.

Coombs, James. Admin. of, to Jonathan Raymond. June 17, 1742. Reg. of Wills, Liber I, folios 61-62.

Harper, William. Admin. of, to William Harper. July 14, 1742. Reg. of Wills, Liber I, folio 62.

McNatt, John. Admin. of, to Elizabeth McNatt. July 14, 1742. Arch. vol. A33, page 13. Reg. of Wills, Liber I, folio 71.

Foster, James. Admin. of, to Jacob Duhadway. July 24, 1742. Arch. vol. A18, page 41. Reg. of Wills, Liber I, folios 71-72.

Reynalds, John. Will (nunc.). Made Aug. 16, 1742. Duck Creek. Heirs: children unnamed. Exec'r, John Dawson. Trustee, John Dawson. Wits., James Vaughan, Thomas Jones. Prob. Aug. 18, 1742. Arch. vol. A43, pages 103-104. Reg. of Wills, Liber I, folio 48.

McAlexander, John. Admin. of, to Robert Jameson. Aug. 20, 1742. Reg. of Wills, Liber I, folio 62.

Delap, Robert. Admin. of, to Allen Delap. Oct. 4, 1742. Reg. of Wills, Liber I, folios 62-63.

Ford, David. Admin. of, to Rachel Ford, widow. Oct. 20, 1742. Reg. of Wills, Liber I, folio 105. Note:—Arch. vol. A17, page 225 shows sons William, David, Thomas, John, Benjamin; daus. Ann, Elizabeth, Frances.

Gray, Robert. Admin. of, to Mary Gray. Oct. 21, 1742. Reg. of Wills, Liber I, folio 63. Note:—Arch. vol. A20, page 33 shows this account later administered by Allen Gray, Feb. 25, 1746.

Jacquet, Johannes. Admin. of, to Richard Jacquett. Nov. 12, 1742. Reg. of Wills, Liber I, folio 63.

Flintham, Falk. Admin. of, to Charles Hyliard. Dec. 5, 1742. Reg. of Wills, Liber I, folios 64-65.

Hirons, Simon. Will. Made Dec. 21, 1742. Heirs: sons Mark, Luke, Matthew, William, Simon; daus. Rebecca Hirons, Hannah Hamer, Abigall Fropp; wife Mary. Exec'rs, wife Mary, son William, Joseph Dowding. Wits., Grace Leatherberry, Jonathan Griffin, Jonathan Leatherberry. Prob. Jan. 6, 1742. Arch. vol. A24, pages 98-99, 103, 105. Reg. of Wills, Liber I, folios 49-50.

Hutchenson, Ann. Will. Made Dec. 24, 1742. Heirs: sister Martha Steel, Mary Freeman; cousins Mary & Ruth Sullivan, Mary Hillyard; Joseph Freeman; two brothers' sons unnamed; Grace Leatherberry. Exec'rs, friends Charles Hillyard, John Tilton. Wits., Thomas Freeman, Samuel Johnson. Prob. Jan. 12, 1742. Arch. vol. A25, pages 195-196. Reg. of Wills, Liber I, folio 49.

Bradley, Josiah. Admin. of, to Henry Bradley. Jan. 20, 1742. Arch. vol. A5, page 115. Reg. of Wills, Liber I, folio 72. Note:—Arch. vol. A5, page 115 shows that this account was later administered by Margaret Bradley, adm'x of Henry Bradley.

Swift, William. Will. Made Sept. 3, 1742. Queen Ann's Co., Md. Heirs: wife Mary; sons John & Richard; bros. Thomas Swift & William Eubank; daus. Elizabeth & Neomy Swift. Exec'rs, father-in-law John Sipple & bro.-in-law William Sipple. Wits., James Horsley, Thomas Swift, Emanuel Swift, Prob. Feb. 25, 1742. Arch. vol. A49, pages 137-138. Reg. of Wills, Liber K, folios 17-18.

Kearny, Michael. Will (copy). Made March 12, 1740/41. Perth Amboy, Middlesex Co., N. J. Heirs: sons Philip & Michael; daus. Isabella Kearny, Mary Vanhorne, Sarah Kearny, Euphamia Annabella Kearny, Graham Kearny. Exec'rs, daus. Isabella Kearny, Mary Vanhorne, Sarah Kearny. Wits., John Miln, Elizabeth Stogdell, Patrick Devlin. Prob. March 9, 1742. Arch. vol. A28, page 87. Reg. of Wills, Liber K, folios 19-20.

Brinett, Paul. Will. Made Aug. 3, 1733. Heirs: son-in-law John LueColly; wife Mary. Exec'rs, wife Mary & Phillip Bivan. Wits., Caesar Rodeney, Henry Shaw. Prob. March 22, 1742. Arch. vol. A5, page 231. Reg. of Wills, Liber I, folio 51.

Mason, Isaac. Will. Made March 3, 1742/3. Heirs: sons Jacob, Elias; wife Ruth; rest of children unnamed. Exec'x, wife Ruth. Wits., Wm. Johnston, Wm. Manlove, Henry Bradley. Prob. March 26, 1743. Arch. vol. A33, pages 230-231. Note: —Later administered by John Clark and his wife Ruth, widow of Isaac Mason.

Deweese, Lewis. Admin. of, to William Deweese. April 5, 1743. Arch. vol. A14, page 47. Reg. of Wills, Liber I, folio 65.

Manlove, Matthew. Will. Made April 16, 1743. Heirs: wife Mary; son George; daus. Mary, Elizabeth, Susanna, Sarah; bro. Jonathan. Exec'x, wife. Wits., John Brinckle, John Clark, Isaac King. Prob. May 6, 1743. Arch. vol. A32, pages 44-46. Reg. of Wills, Liber I, folio 53. Note:—page 44 mentions Daniel Needham and wife Mary Manlove; page 45 mentions father Matthew Manlove, dec'd; page 46 shows that Mary Manlove was wife of Phillip Reasin; mentions Benjamin Reasin, son of Phillip.

Cowgle, Ebenezer. Admin. of, to Elizabeth Cowgle. May 7, 1743. Reg. of Wills, Liber I, folio 65.

Sapp, Henry. Will. Made May 2, 1743. Heirs: sons Henry, James, Benjamin, John, Edward; daus. Johannah Bradley, Anne Thistlewood, Elizabeth Sapp; wife Anne. Exec'rs, wife Anne, son John. Wits., Curtis Evans, John Williams, William Brannock. Prob. May 11, 1743. Arch. vol. A44, page 228. Reg. of Wills, Liber I, folio 52.

Newnam [Newman], Edward. Admin. of, to Mary Newnam. May 13, 1743. Arch. vol. A37, page 206. Reg. of Wills, Liber I, folio 66.

Mullin, James. Admin. of, to Joseph Nixon. May 16, 1743. Reg. of Wills, Liber I, folio 72.

Tybout, James. Admin. of, to Rachel Tybout. May 19, 1743. Reg. of Wills, Liber I, folio 73.

Jameson, Robert. Minister. Will. Made June 9, 1743. Heirs: wife Sarah; sister Janet Graham; father John Jameson; nephews John & Robert Graham; Dr. James Jackson of Dover; Elizabeth Jackson, wife of Dr. Jas. Jackson. Exec'rs, wife Sarah & Dr. James Jackson. Wits., John Cahoon, Moses Rankin, Isabella Farquhar. Prob. July 15, 1743. Arch. vol. A26, pages 98-99. Reg. of Wills, Liber I, folios 65-66.

Berry, Samuel. Will. Made Sept. 15, 1742. Little Creek Hd. Heirs: wife Sarah; son-in-law Josiah Gascoine; son Daniel; daus. Percis Heirons, Sarah Wade, Margarett Craige; granddau. Elizabeth Heirons. Exec'rs, wife Sarah & son Daniel. Wits., Thomas Cockron, Alex. McKenny, John David. Prob. Aug. 27, 1743. Arch. vol. A4, pages 12-13. Reg. of Wills, Liber I, folio 67.

Clark, Thomas. Admin. of, to George Reynix (next of kin), & Joseph Caldwell. Sept. 28, 1743. Reg. of Wills, Liber I, folio 73.

Moran, Andrew. Admin. of, to Jane Moran. Sept. 30, 1743. Reg. of Wills, Liber I, folios 73-74. Note:—Arch. vol. A36, page 126 shows Jane Moran later married Francis Keith.

Jackson, John. Laborer. Will. Made Oct. 27, 1742. Heirs: wife Betty; sons William, John. Wits., John Craige, Margrett Jackson. Prob. Oct. 1, 1743. Arch. vol. A26, page 5. Reg. of Wills, Liber I, folio 74.

Barr, Adam. Admin. of, to Jacob Sorinsee. Oct. 1, 1743. Reg. of Wills, Liber I, folio 77.

Greer, John. Will. Made July 16, 1743. Heirs: wife Margaret; sons John, Mark; daus. Elizabeth, Rachel. Exec'x, wife Margaret. Wits., Robert Patton, Ezekiel Tomson, John Hunter. Prob. Nov. 9, 1743. Arch. vol. A20, pages 166-168. Reg. of Wills, Liber I, folio 75.

Brinckle, Elizabeth. Will. Made April 9, 1741. Heirs: sons Curtis, Peter, Richard, Daniel, William; dau. Elizabeth. Exec'r, son Richard. Wits., John Brinckle, Ruth Brinkle, Susanna Brinkle. Prob. Nov. 9, 1743. Arch. vol. A5, pages 165-166. Reg. of Wills, Liber I, folio 129. Note:—Admin. acct. Arch. vol. A5, page 166 shows dau. Elizabeth married Herman Vanburkeeloe; mentions her father Peter Brinckle.

Hawkins, Allen. Admin. of, to Elinor Hawkins. Nov. 10, 1743. Arch. vol. A23, page 13. Reg. of Wills, Liber I, folio 77.

Randle, Thomas. Admin. of, to Elizabeth Ann Randle. Nov. 16, 1743. Arch. vol. A42, page 30. Reg. of Wills, Liber I, folio 64.

Hillyard, Charles. Will. Made Dec. 27, 1739. Heirs: wife Mary; daus. Lauran Green, Mary Williams, Martha Hillyard; son-in-law Thomas Green; seven children of Thomas Green unnamed; granddau. Elizabeth Hillyard; grandson Charles Hillyard; sons Charles & Steel Hillyard. Exec'x, wife. Wits., Joseph McMechon, Benjamin Jones. Prob. Dec. 6, 1743. Arch. vol. A24, page 24. Reg. of Wills, Liber I, folio 68.

Drumond, James. Admin. of, to Margrett Drumond. Dec. 12, 1743. Reg. of Wills, Liber I, folio 78. Note:—Arch. vol. A15, pages 88-89 show Margrett Drumond later married Gilbert Burns.

Glenn, Robert. Admin. of, to Mary Glenn. Dec. 15, 1743. Reg. of Wills, Liber I, folio 78.

Harper, Thomas. Admin. of, to Elizabeth Harper. Dec. 21, 1743. Reg. of Wills, Liber I, folios 78-79. Note:—Arch. vol. A22, page 74 shows a later admin. by Thomas Summers & Elizabeth, his wife, late Elizabeth Harper.

Donalson, Joshan. Will. Made Jan. 2, 1741/2. Heirs: nieces Mary & Letitia Courtney; nephew John Courtney; cousins Alexander Tumlin, John Courtney, Mary Courtney, Letitia Courtney, Charles & Mary Tounsin (children of John Tounsin), Eneas Mohan. Exec'rs, Joshua Nickalson, Peter Goodrat. Wits., Thomas Randoll, Elizabeth Randoll, Alexander Mohan. Prob. Jan. 23, 1743. Arch. vol. A14, pages 161 & 165. Reg. of Wills, Liber I, folio 69.

Draper, Alexander. Will. Made Dec. 30, 1743. Heirs: son Whittington Draper; wife Elizabeth; daus. Neomy, Easther; bro. Joseph Draper. Exec'x, wife. Wits., William Jackson, William Roads, Abraham Morris. Prob. Feb. 3, 1743. Arch. vol. A15, pages 23-27. Reg. of Wills, Liber I, folio 70. Note:— Later administered by John Faries and his wife Elizabeth Faries.

Morgan, David. Yeoman. Will. Made April 13, 1732. Little Creek. Heirs: wife Sarah; son David; daus. Phebe, Mary; son Matthew. Exec'x, wife. Wits., John Rees, Ralph Needham, John Cowgill. Prob. Feb. 18, 1743. Arch. vol. A36, pages 131-132. Reg. of Wills, Liber H, folios 31-32.

Howell, John. Will. Made Feb. 22, 1743. Duck Creek. Heirs: sons James & Thomas. Exec'rs, Robert Palmeter, John Vangasco. Wits., John Hawkins, Abraham Johnson, William Birkett. Prob. March 13, 1743. Arch. vol. A25, pages 67-68. Reg. of Wills, Liber I, folio 76.

Trail, James. Yeoman. Will. Made Feb. 22, 1743/4. Heirs: wife Rachel; children unnamed. Exec'x, wife. Wits., Samuel McCall, Darby Carty, Henry Stevens. Prob. April 1, 1744. Arch. vol. A51, pages 51-52. Reg. of Wills, Liber I, folios 79-80. Note:—Later administered by Powell Behen [Bahew] and Rachel, his wife.

Smith, Solomon. Will. Made May 17, 1738. Heir: wife Elizabeth. Exec'x, wife. Wits., Isaac Snow, David Morgan, Joseph Stafford. Prob. April 5, 1744. Arch. vol. A47, page 173. Reg. of Wills, Liber I, folio 76.

Giffin, Jonathan. Admin. of, to Phebe Giffin Wells. April 11, 1744. Arch. vol. A20, page 212. Reg. of Wills, Liber I, folio 79.

Bradley, Henry. Admin. of, to Margaret Bradley, mother. April 12, 1744. Arch. vol. A5, page 115. Reg. of Wills, Liber I, folios 82-83.

Jones, Catherine. Little Creek Hd. Admin. of, to John Jones, son. April 12, 1744. Arch. vol. A27, page 234. Reg. of Wills, Liber I, folios 83-84.

Jones, Samuel. Admin. of, to Phebe Jones. April 28, 1744. Reg. of Wills, Liber I, folio 79. Note:—Arch. vol. A28, page 18 shows a later admin. by James Morgan and Phebe his wife.

O'Neal, Conn. Admin. of, to David White. May 14, 1744. Reg. of Wills, Liber I, folio 84.

Snowden, Isaac. Admin. of, to David Morgan. May 19, 1744. Reg. of Wills, Liber I, folios 84-85.

McCall, Alexander. Laborer. Will. Made April 13, 1744. Heir: bro.-in-law Peter Quid-Rale. Exec'r, bro.-in-law. Wits., Thomas Nixon, William Phillips, Thadoras Park. Prob. May 25, 1744. Arch. vol. A32, page 92. Reg. of Wills, Liber I, folio 82.

Caton, John, Sr. Will. Made Feb. 17, 1743. Heirs: wife Agnas; sons Thomas, John, Jr., Benjamin, Robert; daus. Margrett, Sarah, Betty, Ester, Jennett; granddau. Susannah Caten. Exec'rs, wife, sons John & Benjamin. Wits., Samuel Robinson, Robert Hodgson, James Train. Prob. June 4, 1744. Arch. vol. A8, page 75. Reg. of Wills, Liber I, folios 80-81.

Cockran, Christopher. Admin. of, to Agnus Cockran. July 4, 1744. Reg. of Wills, Liber I, folio 85.

Burns, James. Admin. of, to Patrick McDonagh. July 19, 1744. Reg. of Wills, Liber I, folio 85.

Chew, Samuel. Doctor. Admin. of, to Mary Chew. July 30, 1744. Reg. of Wills, Liber I, folio 86.

Dillon, Richard. Will. Made Aug. 30, 1737. Heir: friend Thomas Skidmore. Exec'r, friend Thomas Skidmore. Wits., Waitman Sipple, William Spencer, Edward Williams. Prob. Aug. 16, 1744. Arch. vol. A14, page 140. Reg. of Wills, Liber I, folios 86-87.

Jackson, James. Admin. of, to Elizabeth Jackson. Aug. 30, 1744. Reg. of Wills, Liber I, folio 86.

Denney, Phillep. Will. Made July 26, 1741. Heirs: daus. Susanal, Anne; grandson Phillip Denney; Phillip Hylliard, son of Thomas Hylliard; granddau. Mary Gradon; wife unnamed. Exec'rs, sons Christopher & Evan. Trustee, son Phillip. Wits., Robert Smith, Edward Smith, Richard Smith. Prob. Oct. 1, 1744. Arch. vol. A13, pages 234-236. Reg. of Wills, Liber I, folios 87-88.

Cahoon, Marmeduke. Will. Made Sept. 24, 1744. Heirs: bros. Samuel, William, Thomas; cousin Elizabeth, dau. of William Cahoon; cousin Mary, dau. of Wm. Cahoon; cousin John, son of Wm. Cahoon. Exec'rs, bros. William & Thomas. Wits., Henry Hammond, William Long. Prob. Oct. 1, 1744. Arch. vol. A7, page 37. Reg. of Wills, Liber I, folio 88.

Maxwell, Robert. Will. Made June 12, 1744. Heirs: sons William, Robert, Moses, Thomas, James, Adam, Mark; daus. Elce, Sarah; George & Ebenesor Russell, sons of George Russell, dec'd. Exec'rs, sons Robert & Moses. Wits., John Talbutt, James Maxwell, Jr. Prob. Oct. 20, 1744. Arch. vol. A34, pages 92-95. Reg. of Wills, Liber I, folio 88.

Greenwood, Jonathan. Admin. of, to Ann Greenwood. Oct. 25, 1744. Arch. vol. A20, page 153. Reg. of Wills, Liber I, folio 93. Note:—Arch. vol. A20, page 153 mentions heirs, Joseph, William, Mary Ann Greenwood, & widow Ann Greenwood.

McKenny, Edward. Admin. of, to Nathaniel Luff. Nov. 5, 1744. Reg. of Wills, Liber I, folio 94.

Johnson, Benjamin. Admin. of, to Mary Johnson. Nov. 7, 1744. Reg. of Wills, Liber I, folio 93.

Snow, Joshua. Admin. of, to Elisha Snow, father. Nov. 9, 1744. Reg. of Wills, Liber I, folios 93-94. Note:—Arch. vol. A48, page 23 mentions bros. Elisha, James, Jesse, Silas, & John Snow.

Booth, Joseph. Will. Made Dec. 10, 1732. Heirs: son Joseph; grandson Thomas Booth. Exec'r, son Joseph. Wits., Mark Manlove, Abraham Wynkoop, John Morice, William Servant. Codicil. Dec. 11, 1732. Wits., Mark Manlove, Isaac Mason. Prob. Nov. 12, 1744. Arch. vol. A4, page 231. Reg. of Wills, Liber H, folio 65.

Lewis, Rees. Yeoman. Will. Made Oct. 15, 1744. Duck Creek. Heirs: wife Mary; sons John, David, James, Rees, Daniel, Mark; grandson Joell Lewis, son of James. Exec'rs, wife Mary & sons Rees, Daniel. Wits., Lewis Williams, Jenkin David, John David. Prob. Nov. 14, 1744. Arch. vol. A30, page 121. Reg. of Wills, Liber I, folios 88-89.

Williams, Thomas. Will. Made Nov. 4, 1744. Heirs: sons Thomas, Charles, Owen; daus. Rachel, Grace; wife Mary; servant William Cane. Exec'rs, wife & friend Thomas Clark. Wits., Rees Lewis, William Blackiston, John Holliday. Prob. Nov. 15, 1744. Arch. vol. A55, pages 165-168. Reg. of Wills, Liber I, folio 89 & Liber K, folio 58. Note:—Charles Hillyard is the father of Mary. Arch. vol. A55, page 167 shows Mary the widow later married Joseph Powell.

Williams, Reinear. Admin. of, to Nathaniel Hunn, Richard Brinkloe, John Brinkloe, Elias Samples. Nov. 17, 1744. Reg. of Wills, Liber I, folio 92.

Newel, Thomas. Admin. of, to bros. William & John Newel. Nov. 18, 1744. Reg. of Wills, Liber I, folio 105.

Correy, John. Will. Made Nov. 6, 1744. Duck Creek. Heirs: sons Samuel, John, Charles; wife Mary; daus. Ann & Mary; son Molleston. Exec'x, wife. Trustees, son Samuel & Henry Garson. Wits., William Farson, James Howell, Morris Howell. Prob. Nov. 20, 1744. Arch. vol. A10, page 252 & vol. A11, page 13. Reg. of Wills, Liber I, folio 90.

Smith, Nightingale. Admin. of, to wife Isabella Smith. Nov. 20, 1744. Reg. of Wills, Liber I, folio 95. Note:—Arch. vol. A47, page 129 shows two sons John and Joseph Nightingell Smith.

Trippet, William. Will (copy). Made Nov. 10, 1744. Heirs: wife Margret; Arnold Hudson; Joseph Morris. Exec'x, wife. Wits., Philip Bready, Matthew Lowber, Solomon Bready. Prob. Nov. 26, 1744. Arch. vol. A51, page 83. Reg. of Wills, Liber I, folio 90.

Gray, Mary. Admin. of, to son Allen Gray. Nov. 27, 1744. Reg. of Wills, Liber I, folio 94.

Rowland, Hugh. Admin. of, to Samuel Whitehart & James Snow. Nov. 27, 1744. Arch. vol. A44, page 160. Reg. of Wills, Liber I, folio 96.

Brown, Pemborton. Will. Made Nov. 4, 1744. Mispillion Hd. Heirs: son Daniel; daus. Mary & Elizabeth; wife Elizabeth; bro. Daniel. Exec'rs, wife & bro. Daniel. Wits., George Brown, Kezia Wheeler, George Goforth. Prob. Dec. 4, 1744. Arch. vol. A6, pages 86-87. Reg. of Wills, Liber I, folio 97. Note:—will mentions bro. John Brown; estate later administered by Daniel Brown, Thomas Carlisle and Elizabeth, his wife.

Amit [Amyatt], John. Cordwainer. Will. Made Nov. 20, 1744. Duck Creek. Heir: wife Jane. Exec'x, wife. Wits., Thomas Cahoon, Abraham Fields. Prob. Dec. 8, 1744. Arch. vol. A1, page 137. Reg. of Wills, Liber I, folio 98.

Orry, Richard. Will. Made Nov. 2, 1744. Duck Creek. Heirs: bro. William (in England); wife & children of bro. William. Exec'rs, friends James Hyatt, Wm. Hammans. Wits., Henry Jaffray, Samuel Correy, Joseph Hales. Prob. Dec. 12, 1744. Arch. vol. A38, pages 133 & 135. Reg. of Wills, Liber I, folios 96-97.

Hoy, Rachel. Admin. of, to James Wells, son. Dec. 15, 1744. Arch. vol. A25, page 85. Reg. of Wills, Liber I, folio 107. Note:—Arch. vol. A25, page 85 mentions an heir, William Hoy.

Hillyard, Oliver. Admin. of, to David Onion. Dec. 18, 1744. Reg. of Wills, Liber I, folios 95-96.

Gleen, Merey [Glenn, Mary]. Will. Made Dec. 12, 1744. Heirs: sons John, Thomas; daus. Merey, Ketren, Sarah McCeabe, Margret; grandson James McCeabe. Exec'rs, Matthew Steel, James Moore. Wits., William Green, Alexander McCeabe. Prob. Dec. 20, 1744. Arch. vol. A-19, page 68. Reg. of Wills, Liber I, folio 98.

Frazer, Joseph. Will. Made Dec. 5, 1744. Murderkill Hd. Heirs: bro. John Gray; aunt Isabella Craige. Exec'rs, bro. John Gray, aunt Isabella Craige. Wits., Mary Gray, James Alexander. Prob. Dec. 21, 1744. Arch. vol. A18, page 101. Reg. of Wills, Liber I, folio 99.

Pierce, Robert. Admin. of, to wife Elizabeth Pierce. Dec. 24, 1744. Reg. of Wills, Liber I, folio 95.

Dowling, John. Will (copy). Made Dec. 27, 1744. Heir: wife Mary. Exec'x, wife Mary. Wits., John Chambers, Mary Anderton. Prob. Dec. 28, 1744. Arch. vol. A14, page 216. Reg. of Wills, Liber I, folio 99.

Stevens, Henry. Yeoman. Will. Made Dec. 13, 1744. Little Creek Hd. Heirs: wife Hannah; sons-in-law Clayton Levick, John Levick; daus. Mary, Elizabeth; sons Henry, Daniel. Exec'rs, wife Hannah & cousin Thomas Irons. Wits., Samuel McCall, Darby Carty, Benjamin Barret, Jr. Prob. Jan. 2, 1744. Arch. vol. A48, pages 217-218. Reg. of Wills, Liber I, folio 100. Note:—Later administered by Thomas Irons and widow Hannah, who later intermarried with Thomas Irons.

Williams, Jean. Widow. Will. Made April 11, 1744. Heirs: bros. Thomas Reese, Lewes Reese; nephew David Reese; Lewes son of John & Hannah David; Joshua, bro. of Lewes David; John David. Exec'r, John David. Wits., Arthur McDannel, Elizabeth Misick [Mireck], Samuel McCall. Prob. Jan. 2, 1744. Arch. vol. A55, pages 92-93. Reg. of Wills, Liber I, folio 101.

Dwoolf, Edward. Admin. of, to Sarah Dwoolf, widow. Jan. 11, 1744. Arch. vol. A15, page 213. Reg. of Wills, Liber I, folios 108-109.

Lewis, David. Yeoman. Will. Made Dec. 19, 1744. Heirs: wife Susannah; heirs of Thomas Noxon; children unnamed. Exec'x, wife. Wits., Abraham Morris, Matthew Lowber, John Dowling. Prob. Jan. 12, 1744. Arch. vol. A30, pages 66, 67, 149. Reg. of Wills, Liber I, folios 101-102.

Alsop, Benjamin. Admin. of, to Elizabeth Alsop, widow. Jan. 12, 1744. Reg. of Wills, Liber I, folio 106. Note:—Arch. vol. A1, page 105 shows heirs, sons William & John; dau. Elizabeth.

Townsend, John. Admin. of, to Magdalene Townsend, widow. Jan. 12, 1744. Reg. of Wills, Liber I, folio 106.

Heyburn, Henry. Admin. of, to William Glenn. Jan. 19, 1744. Reg. of Wills, Liber I, folio 107.

Truitt, Henry. Admin. of, to Keys Truitt, widow. Jan. 19, 1744. Arch. vol. A51, page 103. Reg. of Wills, Liber I, folios 107-108.

Rodney, Daniel. Admin. of, to wife Margaret Rodney. Jan. 25, 1744. Arch. vol. A44, page 92. Reg. of Wills, Liber I, folio 96. Note:—Arch. vol. A44, page 92 mentions John Bell, Jr., and his father's legacy.

Berry, Thomas. Admin. of, to Waitman Sipple. Feb. 4, 1744. Reg. of Wills, Liber I, folio 108.

Skidmore, Thomas. Yeoman. Will. Made June 27, 1744. Heirs: daus. Sarah & Margrett Coningham; nephew Nathaniel Muncy; sister Abegall Muncy; nephews Thomas Skidmore (son of nephew Thomas Skidmore), William Skidmore (son of Thomas), John Skidmore, Samuel Skidmore (sons of nephew Thomas). Exec'r, nephew Thomas Skidmore. Trustee, John Newell. Wits., John Brown, James Clayton, Jr., Elizabeth Handley. Prob. Feb. 14, 1744. Arch. vol. A46, page 203. Reg. of Wills, Liber I, folio 103.

Morgan, William. Will. Made Feb. 16, 1744. Jones' Hd. Heirs: sons Arthur, George; wife Grace; daus. Grace, Elizabeth. Exec'rs, wife & son George. Trustees, James Maxwell, Dr. Cornelius Lynch. Wits., James Maxwell, Winifred Lynch, Cornelius Lynch. Prob. Feb. 16, 1744. Arch. vol. A36, page 175. Reg. of Wills, Liber I, folio 102.

Wharton, Rixom. Admin. of, to Isaiah Wharton, bro. Feb. 26, 1744. Arch. vol. A54, page 50. Reg. of Wills, Liber I, folio 108.

Wrath, William. Admin. of, to Thomas Skidmore. Feb. 27, 1744. Arch. vol. A56, page 144.

Leckey, Andrew. Inn Holder. Will. Made March 6, 1744. Heirs: wife Esther; daus. Jane, Mary, Isabella; son Isaac. Exec'rs, wife Esther & son-in-law Thomas Parke. Wits., Thomas Green, Timothy Cummins, Thomas Metcalf. Prob. March 14, 1744. Arch. vol. A29, page 222. Reg. of Wills, Liber I, folios 111-112.

Hall, Mary. Will. Made March 9, 1744/5. Heirs: sons Thomas Hemmons, John Hemmons, Henry Hall; daus. Marteriot Mariner (wife of Thomas Mariner), Mary Marriner (wife of William Marriner). Exec'rs, sons John Hemmons & Henry Hall. Wits., John Brinkle, John Treppet, Joseph Jester. Prob. March 22, 1744. Arch. vol. A21, pages 111-112. Reg. of Wills, Liber I, folios 103-104.

Gordon, Robert. Admin. of, to Griffith Gordon, bro. April 13, 1745. Arch. vol. A19, page 171. Reg. of Wills, Liber I, folios 148-149.

Smith, John. Will. Made April 23, 1745. Heirs: son John Smith; daus. Mary, Sarah, & Ester Smith; sister, Ann Manlove. Exec'r, Mark Manlove, bro.-in-law. Wits., Joshua Wheelor, Sarah Smith & Elizabeth Wheelor. [No prob.] Arch. vol. A47, page 71.

York, Thomas. Admin. of, to Thomas Skidmore. May 4, 1745. Reg. of Wills, Liber I, folio 109.

McDonough, Patrick. Admin. of, to Margery McDonough, widow. May 14, 1745. Reg. of Wills, Liber I, folio 109.

Forster [Foster], Mathew. Will. Made April 23, 1745. Heirs: children John, Thomas, Sidna; wife Jane; bro. James Foster. Exec'rs, wife Jane & son John. Wits., James Ellis, William Ellis, Thomas Slater. Prob. May 15, 1745. Arch. vol. A18, pages 33 & 47. Reg. of Wills, Liber I, folio 112. Note:—Arch. vol. A18, page 33 shows Jane later married William Wright.

Emerson, Wilson. Admin. of, to Sarah Emerson, widow. May 16, 1745. Arch. vol. A16, page 175. Reg. of Wills, Liber I, folio 110.

Mills, John. Admin. of, to Hannah Mills, widow. May 28, 1745. Arch. vol. A35, page 132. Reg. of Wills, Liber I, folio 110.

Leatherbury, Thomas. Will. Made Feb. 24, 1742/3. Heirs: sons Charles, John, William, Jonathan, Abell; dau. Mary; wife unnamed. Exec'rs, sons Charles & John. Wits., Jonathan Giffin, Mathew Parker, Thomas Parker. Prob. May 28, 1745. Arch. vol. A29, pages 213-214. Reg. of Wills, Liber I, folios 104-105.

Briar, Alexander. Admin. of, to Mary Briar, widow. May 29, 1745. Reg. of Wills, Liber I, folios 110-111.

Rodeney, Caesar. Admin. of, to Elizabeth Rodeney, widow. June 8, 1745. Reg. of Wills, Liber I, folio 111.

Cole, Elizabeth. Wife of Wm. Cole of Talbot Co. Will (nunc.). Made June 11, 1745. Heirs: sons Thomas & Joseph; daus. Mary, Susannah, Miriam, Sarah. Wits., Waitman Sipple, Lydia Sipple, Joseph Dowding. Prob. June 15, 1745. Arch. vol. A9, page 197. Reg. of Wills, Liber I, folio 106.

Thompson [Tomson], William. Admin. of, to James Gorrel. July 20, 1745. Arch. vol. A50, page 119. Reg. of Wills, Liber I, folio 111.

Bird, William. Admin. of, to Sarah Bird, widow. Aug. 14, 1745. Reg. of Wills, Liber I, folio 113.

Morris, Frederick. Admin. of, to bro. Rev. Theophilus Morris. Sept. 12, 1745. Arch. vol. A37, page 33. Reg. of Wills, Liber I, folio 114.

Slater, Thomas. Admin. of, to Esther Maxwell, late wife of Robert Maxwell, dec'd, former wife of said Thomas Slater. Sept. 12, 1745. Reg. of Wills, Liber I, folios 114-115.

Humphrys, Alexander. Yeoman. Will. Made April 22, 1744. Heirs: sons Alexander, Jr., John, Williams; daus. Margaret, Alce, Sarah. Exec'r, son John. Trustee, Thomas Green. Wits., Phebe Giffin, Elizabeth Green, Thomas Green. Prob. Sept. 18, 1745. Arch. vol. A25, page 128. Reg. of Wills, Liber I, folio 115.

Morris, Rev. Theophilus. Admin. of, to Robert Willcocks. Sept. 23, 1745. Arch. vol. A37, page 33. Reg. of Wills, Liber I, folio 114.

Williams, Reynear. Yeoman. Will. Made Dec. 5, 1743. Mispillion Hd. Heirs: daus. Mary Hunn, Tabitha Brinckle, Susannah Brinckle, Elizabeth Williams; sons Aaron, Reynear. Exec'r, son Aaron. Wits., Thomas Davis, Lewes Davis, Ralph Basnet. Prob. Oct. 9, 1745. Arch. vol. A55, page 138. Reg. of Wills, Liber I, folio 125.

Hill, Elizabeth. Admin. of, to Jonathan Sturgess & Stokeley Sturgess. Oct. 12, 1745. Reg. of Wills, Liber I, folio 113.

Henderson, Alexander. Admin. of, to Prudence Craige. Nov. 9, 1745. Arch. vol. A23, page 118. Reg. of Wills, Liber I, folios 115-116.

Bradshaw, John. Admin. of, to Sinah Bradshaw, widow. Nov. 18, 1745. Arch. vol. A5, page 126. Reg. of Wills, Liber I, folio 116.

Newell, Joseph. Admin. of, to John Bowers. Nov. 21, 1745. Arch. vol. A37, page 192. Reg. of Wills, Liber I, folio 116.

Rash, Joseph. Yeoman. Will. Made Nov. 17, 1745. Heirs: sons John, Ambrose, Joseph; daus. Sarah, Patience, Grace; wife Sarah; Jemyma Kersey. Exec'rs, sons Ambrose & Joseph. Wits., Owen Sena, John Clayton, Jr. Prob. Dec. 14, 1745. Arch. vol. A42, pages 41-42. Reg. of Wills, Liber I, folio 117. Note:—Arch. vol. A42, page 42 shows this estate later administered, D. B. N., by John Rash, Robert Wilson & wife Sarah.

Miller, William. Will. Made Nov. 18, 1745. Heir: friend Joseph Miller. Exec'r, Joseph Miller. Wits., Peter Allen, Jane Boggs, Patrick Mackey. Prob. Dec. 14, 1745. Arch. vol. A35, pages 120-121. Reg. of Wills, Liber I, folio 118.

Reynolds, John. Admin. of, to Catherine Reynolds, widow. Dec. 17, 1745. Reg. of Wills, Liber I, folios 116-117. Note:—Arch. vol. A43, page 105 shows a joint acct. to Samuel Galloway & Catherine Reynolds, Feb. 24, 1747.

Parsons, John. Will. Made April 21, 1744. Heirs: wife unnamed; Rebecca Wood; John Wood, son of Rebecca. Exec'x, Rebecca Wood. Wits., Mary Winterton, Ralph Winterton, Rachel Larence. Prob. Jan. 18, 1745. Arch. vol. A39, page 81. Reg. of Wills, Liber I, folio 119.

Tompson, Jethro. Will (copy). Made Dec. 30, 1745. Heirs: bros. John, Robert, James, Joseph; sister Doritha Swallo; Agnis Loatman. Exec'r, bro. John. Wits., Daniel Robinson, Henry Wonsor, James Morris. Prob. Jan. 18, 1745. Arch. vol. A50, page 226. Reg. of Wills, Liber I, folios 119-120.

Jenkins, Sarah. Widow. Will (copy). Made Jan. 13, 1745/6. Heirs: sons Ezekiel Nox, Daniel Nox, Thomas Nox, Jabez Jenkins; granddaus. Rachel & Sarah (daus. of James Willson), Mary Willson (dau. of George), Anne Willson (dau. of George). Exec'rs, Ezekiel & Daniel Nox. Appraisers, John Holliday, James Gorrell. Wits., Peter Galloway, Samuel Robinson, James Gorrell. Prob. Feb. 3, 1745. Arch. vol. A26, page 240. Reg. of Wills, Liber I, folios 120-121. Note:—Will mentions second husband Jabez Jenkins, dec'd.

Worrell, Joseph. Admin. of, to Mary Worrell, widow. Feb. 5, 1745. Reg. of Wills, Liber I, folio 117. Note:—Arch. vol. A56, pages 141-142 show Mary later married John Spruance.

Jordan, Andrew. Admin. of, to Margarett Jordan. March 13, 1745. Reg. of Wills, Liber I, folio 121. Note:—Arch. vol. A28, page 41 shows Margarett later married John McClehenny.

Fisher, Isaac. Admin. of, to Mary Lightly. April 1, 1746. Arch. vol. A56, page 228. Reg. of Wills, Liber I, folios 121-122.

Lowber, Michael. Will (copy). Made Jan. 2, 1744. Heirs: daus. Unity (wife of John Emerson), Susannah Lewis; sons Michael, Peter, Matthew, Isaac; daus. Garty Muncy, Margarett Manlove, Agnes Walker; wife Rachel; grandchildren of dau. Grace Brown; grandsons Michael (son of Peter Lowber), John & Michael Reynalds, Michael Emerson (son of Unity & John Emerson), granddau. Susannah Reynalds. Exec'rs, wife Rachel & son Peter. Wits., Isabella Brooks, Arthur Brooks, Mary Brooks, now Mary Jackson. Prob. April 7, 1746. Arch. vol. A31, pages 172-174. Reg. of Wills, Liber I, folios 122-123.

Price, John. Will. Made April 5, 1746. Heirs: son Joseph; wife Mary; grandson Joseph Price. Exec'x, wife Mary. Wits., Thomas Skidmore, Sarah Severson, Mary Shiver [Shiner]. Prob. April 14, 1746. Arch. vol. A41, pages 142-143. Reg. of Wills, Liber I, folios 123-124. Note:—Arch. vol. A41, page 143 shows Mary first married Daniel Casey, then John Price and finally John Clark.

Cummins, Timothy. Admin. of, to Agnes Cummins, widow. April 17, 1746. Reg. of Wills, Liber I, folios 122 & 139. Note:—Arch. vol. A12, pages 139-145 shows a son Daniel and dau. Hannah Cummins; also that Agness later married John David.

Collins, William. Admin. of, to George Martin, D. B. N. May 27, 1746. Arch. vol. A10, pages 30-31. Reg. of Wills, Liber I, folio 135. Note:—Arch. vol. A10, page 30 shows the estate unadministered by James Tybout & wife Rachel.

Tybout, James. Admin. of, to George Martin, D. B. N. May 27, 1746. Arch. vol. A10, pages 30-31 & vol. A51, pages 185-187. Reg. of Wills, Liber I, folio 135.

Tybout, Rachel. Admin. of, to George Martin. May 27, 1746. Arch. vol. A10, pages 30-31 & vol. A51, pages 185-187. Reg. of Wills, Liber I, folios 135-136.

Emmett, John. Admin. of, to Jane Redeford, alias Emett. May 28, 1746. Arch. vol. A16, page 177.

Cuming, Robert. Doctor. Admin. of, to Robert Cuming. May 29, 1746. Arch. vol. A12, page 136.

Conner, Samuel. Admin. of, to Sarah Conner. May 30, 1746. Reg. of Wills, Liber I, folios 132-133.

Hutton, Robert. Carpenter. Will. Made Oct. 21, 1745. Duck Creek. Heirs: wife Eleaner; orphans Daniel Burkelow, Mary Boardman; John, son of Evan Reece. Exec'rs, wife Eleaner & John Snow. Wits., Thomas Ford, Rachel Simmons, Samuel White. Prob. June 19, 1746. Arch. vol. A25, page 206. Reg. of Wills, Liber I, folios 126-127.

Thomas, Thomas. Will (copy). Made Feb. 13, 1745/6. Heirs: wife Hannah; sons John, Thomas, William, James; daus. Abigal, Hannah, Ruth, Sarah, Susannah Wilson. Exec'x, wife Hannah. Wits., Thomas Muncy, Unity Thiselwood, Nathaniel Muncy. Prob. June 19, 1746. Arch. vol. A50, page 68. Reg. of Wills, Liber I, folio 127.

Dushane, Charles. Admin. of, to Mary Dushane, widow. June 25, 1746. Arch. vol. A15, page 198. Reg. of Wills, Liber I, folio 133. Note:—Arch. vol. A15, page 198 shows that Mary Dushane later married Cornelius Carty.

Griffeth, Daniel. Will. Made June 23, 1746. Heirs: wife Mary; William Cardeen. Exec'rs, wife Mary & William Cardeen. Wits., Solomon Brady, Alexander Hudson, Philip Brady. Prob. June 26, 1746. Arch. vol. A20, page 239. Reg. of Wills, Liber I, folio 128.

Holliday, John. Admin. of, to Susanna Holliday, widow. July 8, 1746. Reg. of Wills, Liber I, folios 133-134. Note:—Arch. vol. A24, pages 197-198 shows that Susanna later married Joseph Hales.

Wilson, William. Admin. of, to Rachel Wilson. July 19, 1746. Reg. of Wills, Liber I, folio 134.

Fullerton, John. Admin. of, to Ann Fullerton. Aug. 14, 1746. Reg. of Wills, Liber I, folio 134. Note:—Arch. vol. A18, page 140 shows estate settled by John Purnell, adm'r, D. B. N.

Lott, Bartholomew. Admin. of, to Eleanor Lott. Oct. 25, 1746. Reg. of Wills, Liber I, folio 140. Note:—Arch. vol. A31, page 90 shows Eleanor, the widow, later married Alexander McFarland.

Tilton, John. Admin. of, to Elizabeth Tilton, widow. Oct. 30, 1746. Reg. of Wills, Liber I, folio 140. Note:—Arch. vol. A50, page 146 shows Elizabeth, the widow, later married Samuel Galloway.

Kearle, Thomas. Admin. of, to Abraham Wynkoop. Oct. 31, 1746. Reg. of Wills, Liber I, folio 141.

Skidmore, Thomas. Admin. of, to Elizabeth Skidmore, widow. Nov. 17, 1746. Reg. of Wills, Liber I, folio 141. Note:—Arch. vol. A46, pages 204-206 shows Elizabeth, the widow, later married Daniel Robison; mentions children, John, Thomas, Samuel, & William Skidmore.

Brown, Thomas. Admin. of, to Grace Brown. Nov. 21, 1746. Reg. of Wills, Liber I, folio 142. Note:—Arch. vol. A6, page 92 shows Grace married Anthony Pandergrass; also mentions daus. Agnis & Rachel Brown.

Gray, Robert. Admin. of, to Allen Gray, son, D. B. N. Nov. 27, 1746. Reg. of Wills, Liber I, folio 136.

Rhodes, Alice. Widow. Will. Made March 3, 1745. Heirs: sons John Walker, William Walker, sons of first husband John Walker, dec'd; dau. Alice Rhodes & son William Rhodes, children of dec'd husband John Rhodes; dau. Elizabeth Boyer. Exec'r, son William Walker. Wits., Joseph Dowding, Elizabeth Dowding, George Walton. Prob. Jan. 7, 1746. Arch. vol. A43, page 131. Reg. of Wills, Liber I, folios 131-132.

Allston, Thomas. Will. Made Dec. 13, 1746. Heirs: sons Iseral, Randell, Arture; wife Seara; daus. Ester Reese, Seara Keth. Exec'rs, wife Seara & son Iseral. Wits., William Reese, Alexander McFarland. Prob. Jan. 19, 1746. Arch. vol. A1, page 120. Reg. of Wills, Liber I, folios 129-130.

Lucas, Mason. Admin. of, to Robert Wilson. Feb. 3, 1746. Arch. vol. A31, page 196. Reg. of Wills, Liber I, folio 142.

Smith, Samuel. Admin. of, to Elizabeth Smith, widow. Feb. 11, 1746. Arch. vol. A47, page 161. Reg. of Wills, Liber I, folio 143.

Swallow, Joshua. Admin. of, to Dorothy Swallow, widow. Feb. 14, 1746. Reg. of Wills, Liber I, folio 143.

Hall, John. Admin. of, to Robert Ballach, D. B. N. Feb. 14, 1746. Arch. vol. A21, page 110. Reg. of Wills, Liber I, folio 161.

Stevens, Daniel. Farmer. Will. Made Feb. 10, 1746. Heirs: wife Letitia; son James; dau. Mary. Exec'x, wife Letitia. Wits., Caesar Rodeney, Ebenezer Manlove, John Smith. Prob. Feb. 17, 1746. Arch. vol. A48, page 212. Reg. of Wills, Liber I, folio 130.

Hirons, Simon. Admin. of, to Pearcee Hirons, widow. Feb. 20, 1746. Arch. vol. A24, page 104. Reg. of Wills, Liber I, folio 144.

Hannah, Thomas. Admin. of, to William Master. Feb. 23, 1746. Arch. vol. A21, page 204. Reg. of Wills, Liber I, folio 145.

Raymond, Jonathan. Admin. of, to Sarah Raymond. Feb. 24, 1746. Reg. of Wills, Liber I, folio 145. Note:—Arch. vol. A42, pages 150-151, dated 1758, shows Sarah married John Gooding.

Kirkley, William. Admin. of, to John Kirkley, son. Feb. 25, 1746. Arch. vol. A29, page 53. Reg. of Wills, Liber I, folio 146.

Hill, Thomas. Admin. of, to William Jacobs. March 2, 1746. Arch. vol. A24, page 17. Reg. of Wills, Liber I, folio 146.

Watson, William. Will. Made Feb. 1, 1746. Heirs: sons William, Benony, Francis, Solomon; daus. Maryam, Rebacka, Elizabeth; wife Rebacka. Exec'x, wife Rebacka. Wits., Thomas Parke, Timothy Griffen, Samuel Bostick. Prob. March 6, 1746. Arch. vol. A53, pages 187-188. Reg. of Wills, Liber I, folio 138. Note:—Arch. vol. A53, page 188 shows Rebecca later married William Smith.

Hawkins, William. Admin. of, to Phebee Hawkins. March 11, 1746. Reg. of Wills, Liber I, folio 147.

Hallans [Hallands], Jehosaphat. Admin. of, to Spencer Cole. March 12, 1746. Arch. vol. A24, page 188. Reg. of Wills, Liber I, folio 147.

Kearsey, Daniel. Admin. of, to Mary Kearsey. March 18, 1746. Reg. of Wills, Liber I, folios 147-148.

Pearson, William. Admin. of, to Mary Pearson. March 20, 1746. Arch. vol. A39, page 182. Reg. of Wills, Liber I, folio 148. Note:—Arch. vol. A39, page 182 mentions heir, Elizabeth Pearson.

Chew, Samuel. Admin. of, to Benjamin Chew, son, D. B. N. April 3, 1747. Arch. vol. A8, pages 163-165. Reg. of Wills, Liber I, folios 136-137.

Chew, Mary. Admin. of, to Benjamin Chew, son. April 3, 1747. Arch. vol. A8, pages 161-165. Reg. of Wills, Liber I, folio 137.

Gordon, Lettisha. Will. Made March 29, 1747. Heirs: sister Mary Gordon; bros. David & Joshua Gordon. Exec'r, Griffith Gordon. Wits., Mary Johnson, Thomas Murfey, William Shurmer. Prob. April 11, 1747. Arch. vol. A19, page 170. Reg. of Wills, Liber I, folios 137-138.

Prior, Jacob. Admin. of, to James Gorrell. April 30, 1747. Reg. of Wills, Liber I, folio 166.

Clifford, Thomas. Yeoman. Will. Made April 7, 1747. Heirs: wife Esther; sons John, Peter; daus. Anne, Mary, Martha, Elizabeth, Esther. Exec'x, wife. Trustees, father Peter Coudrat & friend Thomas Irons. Wits., John Coudrat, Hannah Irons, Samuel McCally. Prob. May 9, 1747. Arch. vol. A9, pages 140-142. Reg. of Wills, Liber I, folios 149-150. Note:—Arch. vol. A9, page 141 shows Esther later married Wilson Buckmaster.

Emerson, Emanuel. Admin. of, to Rebecca Emerson, widow. May 9, 1747. Arch. vol. A16, page 122.

Johnson, John. Planter. Will. Made Feb. 6, 1746. Heirs; daus. Elizabeth, Rachel, Marget, Feebe; sons James, John, Samuel, William; wife Marget. Exec'x, wife Marget. Wits., Isaac Freeland, Jeremiah Morris. Prob. May 13, 1747. Arch. vol. A27, pages 75-76. Reg. of Wills, Liber I, folio 165.

Booth, Joseph. Admin. of, to John Booth. May 14, 1747. Reg. of Wills, Liber I, folio 176.

Bouden, William. Admin. of, to Ezekiel Bouden. May 23, 1747. Reg. of Wills, Liber I, folio 162.

Cole, William. Admin. of, to Susanna Cole, widow. May 26, 1747. Reg. of Wills, Liber I, folio 162.

Candey, Robert. Admin. of, to Deborah Candey, widow. May 27, 1747. Reg. of Wills, Liber I, folios 162-163.

Poultney, Francis. Duck Creek Hd. Admin. of, to David Marshal. May 27, 1747. Arch. vol. A41, page 22.

Vanbuskirk, John. Admin. of, to Lawrence Vanbuskirk. July 20, 1747. Reg. of Wills, Liber I, folio 163.

White, Robert. Admin. of, to Sarah White. July 24, 1747. Arch. vol. A54, page 146. Reg. of Wills, Liber I, folio 149.

Penn, John. Will (copy). Made Oct. 24, 1746. Hitcham, Bucks (Buckingham) County, England. Heirs: sister Margaret Freame; bros. Thomas, Richard; nephews John & Richard (sons of bro. Richard), William Penn (Cork, Ireland); nieces Hannah (dau. of bro. Richard), Philadelphia Hannah Freame; grand-nephews Robert Edward Fell (son of Gulielma Maria Fell), Springett (son of William Penn, of Cork); grand-nieces Christiana Gulielma (dau. of William Penn, of Cork), Mary Margaretta Fell, Gulielma Maria Frances Fell (daus. of Gulielma Maria Fell); servants John Travels, Thomas Penn, Hannah Roberts; friends Thomas Hyam & David Barclay (London merchants), William Vigor, Joseph Freame, Lascelles Metcalfe; Jane, wife of Henry Aldridge (White Waltham, Berks County). American exec'rs, bros. Richard & Thomas Penn. English exec'rs, William Vigor (merchant), Joseph Freame (banker), Lascelles Metcalft (Esquire). Wits., John Cormell, Ferd John Paris, Robert Gwyn. English prob. Nov. 12, 1746. Kent. Co. prob. Aug. 13, 1747. Arch. vol. A39, pages 185-197. Reg. of Wills, Liber I, folios 150-160. Note:—Will mentions grandfather Thomas Callowhill.

Glenn, Robert. Admin. of, to James Moor, D. B. N. Aug. 21, 1747. Reg. of Wills, Liber I, folio 164. Note:—Arch. vol. A19, page 69, mentions wife, Mary; sons Thomas & John; daus. Mary, Sarah, Catherine, Margaret.

Richardson, Stephen. Admin. of, to John Richardson. Sept. 1, 1747. Arch. vol. A43, page 170. Reg. of Wills, Liber I, folio 164.

Tomblin, John. Admin. of, to Hannah Tomblin, widow. Nov. 3, 1747. Reg. of Wills, Liber I, folios 166-167. Note:—Arch. vol. A50, pages 172-173 show Hannah, the widow, married John Cowgill and later married Robert Hall; also shows sons Joseph & John Tomblin; dau. Susannah, who married James Piper.

Wells, John. Admin. of, to Phebe Wells, widow. Nov. 5, 1747. Arch. vol. A53, page 233. Reg. of Wills, Liber I, folios 167-168.

Knox, John. Admin. of, to John Hunter, Esq. Nov. 5, 1747. Reg. of Wills, Liber I, folios 202-203.

Morris, James. Will. Made July 13, 1744. Heirs: wife Margaret; son James; daus. Phebe Morris, Mary Jones, wife of Benjamin Jones; Benjamin Jones; granddau. Margaret Empson; grandson Richard Empson. Exec'r, son James. Wits., Thomas James, Thomas Green, Michael Cook. Prob. Nov. 7, 1747. Arch. vol. A36, page 211. Reg. of Wills, Liber I, folios 172-173.

Vanderford, Thomas. Admin. of, to wife Jane Vanderford. Nov. 7, 1747. Reg. of Wills, Liber I, folio 175. Note:—Arch. vol. A51, page 227 shows Jane later married Absolem Tims; also shows son George & daus. Mary and Elinoer Vanderford.

Bowen, Solomon. Admin. of, to Hannah Bowen, widow. Nov. 17, 1747. Reg. of Wills, Liber I, folio 167.

Cahoon, James. Will (nunc). Made Nov. 18, 1747. Koniwagojigg, Lankaster Co. but at the house of James Carbin, Kent Co., Del. Heir: James Carbine. Wits., John Barnat, Sarah Murray. Prob. Nov. 24, 1747. Arch. vol. A7, page 32. Reg. of Wills, Liber I, folio 175.

Willson, Jonathan. Admin. of, to Thomasin [Tamsen] Willson, widow. Dec. 4, 1747. Reg. of Wills, Liber I, folio 190. Note:—Arch. vol. A55, page 232 shows Samuel Smith & Tamsen, his wife are adm'rs.

Stone, James. Admin. of, to Katherine [Catherine] Stone, widow. Dec. 7, 1747. Arch. vol. A49, page 27. Reg. of Wills, Liber I, folios 168-169.

Stephenson, Robert. Admin. of, to Agnes Stephenson, widow. Dec. 8, 1747. Reg. of Wills, Liber I, folio 169.

Morgan, David. Admin. of, to Elizabeth Morgan, widow. Dec. 12, 1747. Reg. of Wills, Liber I, folio 170. Note:—Arch. vol. A36, pages 133-135 shows Elizabeth later married Joseph Freeman.

Bishop, John. Admin. of, to Comfort Bishop, widow. Dec. 15, 1747. Reg. of Wills, Liber I, folios 169-170.

Prior [Pryor], Hannah. Admin. of, to William Farsons. Dec. 16, 1747. Arch. vol. A41, page 189. Reg. of Wills, Liber I, folios 170-171.

Edingfield, Jonas. Admin. of, to Tabitha Edingfield, widow. Dec. 21, 1747. Reg. of Wills, Liber I, folio 171.

Potter, James. Yeoman. Aug. 4, 1747. Murtherkill Hd. Heirs: wife Mary; sons Parismus, James; daus. Sarah, Rachel, Dorothy Jones (wife of Benjamin Jones), Mary Moor (wife of Samuel Moor). Exec'rs, wife Mary & son James. Wits., John Hardin, John Miller, Edmond Hardin. Prob. Dec. 21, 1747. Arch. vol. A41, pages 3-4. Reg. of Wills, Liber I, folio 174.

Walker, John. Admin. of, to John Walker. Dec. 30, 1747. Reg. of Wills, Liber I, folios 190-191.

Miller, Joseph. Will. Made Jan. 1, 1747. Heirs: sons David, Andrew, Abraham, Samuel. Exec'rs, friends Ebenezer Hathorn, Joseph Dowding. Wits., Robert Cuming, Thomas Downham, Susan Downham. Prob. Jan. 6, 1747. Arch. vol. A35, pages 92-94. Reg. of Wills, Liber I, folio 176.

Cunningham, Andrew. Admin. of, to Mary Cunningham, widow. Jan. 7, 1747. Arch. vol. A10, page 60. Reg. of Wills, Liber I, folio 191. Note:—Arch. vol. A10, page 60 shows this acct. later administered by Dennis Driscal & wife Mary.

Moore, Thomas. Admin. of, to William Downs. Jan. 8, 1747. Reg. of Wills, Liber I, folio 197.

Marrett, Mark. Farmer. Will. Made April 15, 1746. Heirs: dau. Elizabeth Lecount; cousins John (son of Hezekiah Marrett), Mary (dau. of Hezekiah Marrett), Mark (son of John Marrett); children of Elizabeth Lecount; child of John Marrett. Exec'r, John Marrett. Wits., Thomas Graham, John Marrett, Sr., Samuel Crabtree. Prob. Jan. 15, 1747. Arch. vol. A33, page 197. Reg. of Wills, Liber I, folio 179.

Robinson [Robisson], Samuel. Yeoman. Will. Made June 21, 1747. Heirs: wife Hannah; sons Daniel, Samuel, Asa; daus. Miriam, Hannah; nephew Samuel, son of bro. Daniel; bro. Daniel. Exec'x, wife Hannah. Wits., Thomas Clark, James Gorrell, Peter Lowber. Prob. Jan. 20, 1747. Arch. vol. A44, pages 84-85. Reg. of Wills, Liber I, folios 177-178. Note:— Will mentions George Robinson as the father; settlement of estate completed by Mathew Lowber & Hannah, his wife.

McKell, Elizabeth. Will (nunc.). Made Jan. 20, 1747. Murtherkill Hd. Heirs: bro.-in-law Richard Rannals; Esther, dau. of William & Rose Kearney. Exec'rs, Richard Rannals. Wits., Robert Patton, William Kearney. Prob. Jan. 22, 1747. Arch. vol. A32, pages 209 & 211. Reg. of Wills, Liber I, folio 180.

Taylor, William. Admin. of, to John Taylor, Sr. Feb. 1, 1747. Arch. vol. A49, page 223. Reg. of Wills, Liber I, folios 196-197.

Davis, John. Planter. Will. Made Jan. 9, 1747. Heirs: son John; daus. Rachel, Rebekah, Mary, Sarah; wife Mary. Exec'x, wife Mary. Wits., John Hatfield, Thomas Smith, Joshua Merydith. Prob. Feb. 10, 1747. Arch. vol. A13, page 18. Reg. of Wills, Liber I, folios 180-181.

Anderson, John. Admin. of, to George Goforth. Feb. 18, 1747. Arch. vol. A1, page 181. Reg. of Wills, Liber I, folio 200.

Howell, Morris. Will. Made Feb. 8, 1747. Heirs: wife Elennor; daus. Lydia, Sarah; son James. Exec'rs, friends Daniel Nock, Mathew Griffen. Wits., James Howill, Richard Rees, Henry Farson. Prob. Feb. 24, 1747. Arch. vol. A25, pages 74-75. Reg. of Wills, Liber I, folios 181-182.

Morgan, John David. Yeoman. Will. Made Dec. 26, 1747. Duck Creek. Heirs: wife Gwenllyan; son John David, Jr. Exec'rs, wife Gwenllyan & son John. Wits., James William, James James, John Lewis. Prob. Feb. 24, 1747. Arch. vol. A36, page 155. Reg. of Wills, Liber I, folio 182.

Whiteside, Peter. Admin. of, to Arthur Whiteside & Richard Patterson. Feb. 24, 1747. Reg. of Wills, Liber I, folios 197-198.

Finlay, Joseph. Will. Made July 29, 1746. Heirs: William & Thomas Barker, sons of Thomas & Jannat Barker; Sarah, Phebe, Mary (sisters of William Barker). Exec'r, William Barker. Wits., William Barker, Sarah Barker, Phebe Barker. Prob. Feb. 26, 1747. Arch. vol. A17, pages 107-108. Reg. of Wills, Liber I, folio 183.

Hart, George. Admin. of, to George Robisson. Feb. 26, 1747. Arch. vol. A22, pages 191-192. Reg. of Wills, Liber I, folio 198.

Morris, William. Yeoman. Will. Made Feb. 12, 1747/8. Duck Creek. Heirs: son William; dau. Hannah. Exec'rs, son William, sister Mary Tracy. Wits., John Denney, David Murphey, John Joy. Prob. March 1, 1747. Arch. vol. A37, page 38. Reg. of Wills, Liber I, folio 184.

Uptegrave, Rachel. Admin. of, to Joseph Uptegrave. March 4, 1747. Reg. of Wills, Liber I, folio 186.

Coudrat, Daniel. Will. Made Feb. 2, 1747. Heirs: wife Elizabeth; sons Daniel, Mark; dau. Martha. Exec'x, wife Elizabeth. Trustees, father & father-in-law ... Bardon. Wits., James Small, Thomas Billeter, Robert Maxwell. Prob. March 5, 1747. Arch. vol. A-11, pages 38-39. Reg. of Wills, Liber I, folio 185. Note:—Arch. vol. A-11, page 39 shows that Elizabeth Coudrat later married ... Hinseley.

Goodwin, Samuel. Admin. of, to Sarah Goodwin, widow. March 5, 1747. Reg. of Wills, Liber I, folios 186-187. Note:—Arch. vol. A19, page 144 shows the widow Sarah later married William Maxwell; mentions dau. Elizabeth & son Samuel Goodwin.

Rehue [Reyhoe], Powell. Admin. of, to Rachel Reyhoe. March 5, 1747. Arch. vol. A43, page 68. Reg. of Wills, Liber I, folio 187. Note:—Arch. vol. A43, page 68 shows that Rachel Rehue later married William Levick.

O'Callaghan, Benjamin. Admin. of, to Mark Smith. March 7, 1747. Reg. of Wills, Liber I, folios 187-188.

Loatman [Lootman], John. Admin. of, to Esther & Jeremiah Lootman. March 12, 1747. Arch. vol. A30, page 201. Reg. of Wills, Liber I, folio 188.

Coudrat, Peter. Yeoman. Will. Made Feb. 28, 1747. Heirs: wife Frances; sons John, Peter; children of daus. Hestor Clefford & Mary Harper; children of son Daniel Coudrat, dec'd. Exec'rs, wife Frances & son John. Wits., David White, William Jackson, John Clayton, Jr. Prob. March 14, 1747. Arch. vol. A-11, page 47. Reg. of Wills, Liber I, folio 189.

Wesbury, William. Son of Thomas Westbery. Will (nunc.). Made March 17, 1747. Murtherkill Hd. Heirs: sister-in-law Mary Cumings, dau. of Patrick Cumings; mother Mary Cumings; bro. Daniel, son of Patrick Cumings; father-in-law Patrick Cumings. Exec'r, Patrick Cumings. Wits., Abraham Jackson, Margrat Jacson. Prob. March 21, 1747. Arch. vol. A54, page 32. Reg. of Wills, Liber I, folios 191-192.

Cain, Danael. Will. Made Dec. 27, 1747. Heirs: cousin Franssus Cain; wife Elener; Dennes Cain; son Thomas; dau. Ann. Exec'r, Peter Lowber. Trustee, Peter Lowber. Wits., Peter Coudrat, Thomas Billiter, William Jackson. Prob. March 28, 1748. Arch. vol. A7, page 50 & vol. A30, page 207. Reg. of Wills, Liber I, folio 192.

Joy, Edward. Admin. of, to Jane Joy & John Joy. March 28, 1748. Reg. of Wills, Liber I, folios 199-200. Note:—Arch. vol. A28, page 52 shows sons, John & Josiah; dau. Ann Joy.

Robbisson, John. Yeoman. Will. Made March 5, 1747. Heirs: sons Jonathan, William; daus. Elizabeth, Mary, Sarah; Mary, dau. of Mary Cammell; bro. Daniel. Exec'rs, son William & bro. Daniel Robbisson. Wits., Spencer Cole, William Masten, Elias Scott. Prob. April 4, 1748. Arch. vol. A44, pages 59-61. Reg. of Wills, Liber I, folios 193-194. Note:— Arch. vol. A44, page 61 mentions daus. Mary Hudgason & Elizabeth Gildersleeve; page 60 shows John Marim & Mary, his wife, as the adm'rs of William Robisson.

Stevens, Daniel. Admin. of, to Elizabeth Rodeney, D. B. N. April 4, 1748. Reg. of Wills, Liber I, folios 200-201.

Stevens, Letitia. Widow. Admin. of, to Elizabeth Rodeney. April 4, 1748. Reg. of Wills, Liber I, folio 201.

Furchas, Tobias. Farmer. Will. Made March 6, 1747. Mispillion Hd. Heirs: wife Mary; children unnamed. Exec'rs, wife & John Caten. Wits., Nathaniel Hunn, Thomas Bowman, Jr., Spencer Cole. Prob. April 4, 1748. Arch. vol. A18, pages 188-189. Reg. of Wills, Liber I, folios 194-195. Note:—Arch. vol. A18, page 189 shows Stephen Lewes & his wife Mary as exec'rs.

Hudson, Robert. Will. Made March 15, 1747/8. Heirs: sons Elisha & John; one child unnamed; wife Mary. Exec'rs, wife Mary & friend John Brinckle. Wits., Alice Manlove, Adam Capatrick, Daniel Hudson. Prob. April 4, 1748. Arch. vol. A25, pages 110-111. Reg. of Wills, Liber I, folios 195-196.

Burkeloo, Harman. Yeoman. Will. Made April 8, 1748. Heirs: daus. Margaret, Elizabeth; wife Elizabeth. Exec'x, wife Elizabeth. Wits., William Sherley, Richard Brinkle, Michael Casey. Prob. April 8, 1748. Arch. vol. A6, page 200. Reg. of Wills, Liber I, folios 214-215.

Redman, Joshua. Admin. of, to Esther Redman, widow. April 8, 1748. Reg. of Wills, Liber I, folio 202.

McWhorty, Andrew. Chapman. Will. Made April 3, 1748. New Castle County. Heir: bro. John McWhorty. Exec'r, bro. John. Wits., John Food, Alexander Leith. Prob. April 11, 1748. Arch. vol. A33, page 40. Reg. of Wills, Liber I, folio 204.

Rutter, Philip. Admin. of, to Amy Rutter. April 12, 1748. Reg. of Wills, Liber I, folio 203. Note:—Arch. vol. A44, page 213 shows Amy, the widow, later married Mark Pickford, Feb. 27, 1750.

Howell, Jenkin. Admin. of, to Margaret Howell, widow. April 12, 1748. Reg. of Wills, Liber I, folios 203-204.

Grewell [Gruwell], Mary. Will (nunc.). Made March 27, 1748. Little Creek Hd. Heirs: daus. Mary Grewel, Elizabeth Grewel; son Jacob Grewel. Exec'r, son Jacob. Wits., John Wade, Mary Collins. Prob. April 13, 1748. Arch. vol. A21, page 28. Reg. of Wills, Liber I, folios 215-216.

Cunningham, John. Admin. of, to Robert Patton. April 15, 1748. Reg. of Wills, Liber I, folio 205. Arch. vol. A12, page 149.

Legg, James. Admin. of, to Elizabeth Patton. April 18, 1748. Reg. of Wills, Liber I, folios 205-206.

Manin, John. Admin. of, to Patience Manin. April 19, 1748. Reg. of Wills, Liber I, folio 206.

Dawson, John. Admin. of, to Thomas Dawson, bro. April 23, 1748. Reg. of Wills, Liber I, folios 206-207.

Curtis, William. Admin. of, to Mary Curtis, widow. April 23, 1748. Reg. of Wills, Liber I, folio 207. Note:—Arch. vol. A12, page 167 mentions son John Curtis; also Mary Oleger as adm'x.

Dowding, Joseph. Admin. of, to Elizabeth Dowding, widow. April 23, 1748. Arch. vol. A14, page 246. Reg. of Wills, Liber I, folios 207-208. Note:—Arch. vol. A14, page 246 shows that Elizabeth Dowding later married John Faries.

Greer [Greir], William. Will (nunc.). Made 1748. Little Creek Hd. Heirs: son William Greer; daus. Ann Delap, Rebeckah Greer, Agnis Delap. Exec'r, James Edwards. Wits., George Lewis & Joseph David. Prob. April 23, 1748. Arch. vol. A20, pages 181-183. Reg. of Wills, Liber I, folios 216-217.

Moore, James. Admin. of, to Jane Moore, widow. April 28, 1748. Arch. vol. A36, page 31. Reg. of Wills, Liber I, folio 208.

Cook, Mickale [Michael]. Will. Made April 15, 1748. Duck Creek Hd. Heirs: sons John & Michael; dau. Marget. Exec'r, George Martin. Trustee, George Martin. Wits., William Strickland, Thomas James, Rachel Strickland. Prob. April 29, 1748. Arch. vol. A10, pages 131-132. Reg. of Wills, Liber I, folio 217.

Jackson, William. Will. Made March 23, 1746/7. Heirs: sons Richard, James, Thomas, Joseph, William; grandson Caleb, son of Thomas Jackson. Exec'r, son James. Wits., James Small, James Bedwell, Jas. Howell, Jr. Prob. April 30, 1748. Arch. vol. A26, pages 55-56. Reg. of Wills, Liber I, folios 218-219.

Throp [Thorp], Mark. Will. Made May 2, 1748. Heirs: wife [Abigail, from admin. bond]; son Samuel; dau. Hanna; bro. Samuel. Exec'x, wife Abigail. Wits., John Waller, Somerset Donoho, Joseph Parsons. Prob. May 11, 1748. Arch. vol. A50, page 129. Reg. of Wills, Liber I, folio 219.

Throp, Samuel. Will (copy). Made May 13, 1748. Heirs: wife [Ann, from admin. acct.]; dau. Elizabeth. Exec'rs, wife & Jonathan Manlove. Wits., John Waller, Abigal Throp, Ann Arpin. Prob. May 11, 1748 [sic.]. Arch. vol. A50, pages 130-131. Reg. of Wills, Liber I, folio 220.

Wheeler, Joshua. Admin. of, to Elizabeth Wheeler, widow. May 11, 1748. Reg. of Wills, Liber I, folios 208-209. Note:— Arch. vol. A54, page 64 shows sons Samuel, Joshua, Whinlock; daus. Elizabeth, Mary Ann, Miriam Wheeler.

Clark, Wenlock. Admin. of, to Sarah Clark, widow. May 11, 1748. Arch. vol. A9, page 97. Reg. of Wills, Liber I, folio 209. Note:—Arch. vol. A9, page 97 mentions children, Elizabeth & Susan Clark; also shows Samuel Wheeler & wife Sarah as adm'rs.

Daws, William. Admin. of, to Mary Daws, widow. May 11, 1748. Reg. of Wills, Liber I, folio 209.

Fleming, Samuel. Admin. of, to Archibald Fleming, bro. May 11, 1748. Reg. of Wills, Liber I, folio 210.

Vanwye, Jacob. Admin. of, to Thomas Elliot. May 13, 1748. Reg. of Wills, Liber I, folio 210.

Morgan, William. Yeoman. Will. Made March 31, 1748. Dover Hd. Heirs: wife Grace; son George; daus. Elizabeth Rowan (wife of William Rowan), Grace Morgan; grandsons William Morgan (son of Arthur & Sarah Morgan), George Nickerson (son of Joshua & Veranica Nickerson), William Rowan (son of William, the elder, & Elizabeth Rowan); granddau. Veranica Nickerson, dau. of Joshua Nickerson; cousin George Morgan (of Murtherkill Hd.). Exec'rs, wife Grace & son George. Wits., William Ware, Mary Ware, Jno. David. Prob. May 14, 1748. Arch. vol. A36, page 176. Reg. of Wills, Liber I, folios 213-214.

Lester, George. Will. Made April 6, 1748. Dover Hd. Heirs: sisters Mary Ware, Anna Roads; bros.-in-law Jonathan Pleasanton, David Pleasanton; nephew Johnny Ware. Exec'r, bro.-in-law William Ware. Wits., Benjamin Chew, Grace Morgan, Anna Morgan. Prob. May 14, 1748. Arch. vol. A30, page 17. Reg. of Wills, Liber I, folio 221.

Barnet, John. Farmer. Will. Made May 11, 1748. Heirs: bros. Moses, Samuel, Hugh, Andrew; Richard McKinstrey & wife Gean. Exec'r, Andrew Barnet. Wits., David Neal, Andrew Neal, Jean McKinstrey. Prob. May 17, 1748. Arch. vol. A2, page 196. Reg. of Wills, Liber I, folio 222.

Uptegrave, Rachel. Admin. of, to William Uptegrave, D. B. N. May 18, 1748. Arch. vol. A51, page 201. Reg. of Wills, Liber I, folio 211.

Uptegrave, Joseph. Admin. of, to William Uptegrave. May 18, 1748. Arch. vol. A51, page 200. Reg. of Wills, Liber I, folio 211.

McCarady [McCardell], James. Admin. of, to Isaiah Wharton. May 19, 1748. Arch. vol. A32, page 96. Reg. of Wills, Liber I, folio 212.

Hendricham [Hendrickam], Moses. Will. Made May 11, 1748. Heirs: wife Marget; sons John, Moses; dau. Mary; sister Keitren. Exec'x, wife Marget. Wits., Nicholas Lockerman, William Rees, John Ross. Prob. May 21, 1748. Arch. vol. A23, pages 131-132. Reg. of Wills, Liber I, folios 222-223. Note:—Arch. vol. A23, page 132 shows Margaret later married Thomas Murphey.

Winterton, Ralph. Admin. of, to Mary Winterton, widow. May 24, 1748. Reg. of Wills, Liber I, folio 212. Note:—Arch. vol. A56, pages 49-50 shows Mary, the widow, later married John Wade, ante Aug. 30, 1750.

Whithart [Whitehart], James. Weaver. Will. Made May 18, 1748. Heirs: friend Nancy Winterton; Arthur Duncan. Exec'x, Nancy Winterton. Wits., William Sherwin, Matthew Taylor, Edward Norman. Prob. May 24, 1748. Arch. vol. A54, page 184. Reg. of Wills, Liber I, folios 223-224.

Whithart, Samuel. Planter. Will. Made May 9, 1748. Little Creek Hd. Heirs: wife Sarah; son Powell. Exec'x, wife Sarah. Wits., James Whithart, Edward Norman, Elizabeth Morgan. Prob. May 24, 1748. Arch. vol. A54, page 188. Reg. of Wills, Liber I, folio 224.

Wootten, Robert. Admin. of, to Eleanor Wootten. May 25, 1748. Arch. vol. A56, page 126.

Morris, Frederick. Admin. of, to Robert Wilcocks, D. B. N. May 25, 1748. Reg. of Wills, Liber I, folio 213.

Willson, John, Sr. Will. Made April 16, 1748. Heirs: wife unnamed; sons Thomas, William; dau. Elizabeth. Exec'r, son Thomas. Wits., Stephen Paradee, Caesar Rodney, Thomas Horseman. Prob. June 3, 1748. Arch. vol. A55, page 216. Reg. of Wills, Liber I, folio 225.

Manlove, William, Jr. Will. Made May 1, 1748. Heirs: wife Elizabeth; daus. Mary, Elizabeth. Exec'rs, wife Elizabeth, friends Joseph Mason, William Walton. Wits., George Walton, John Brown, James Freeland. Prob. June 3, 1748. Arch. vol. A33, pages 134-136. Reg. of Wills, Liber I, folio 226. Note:—Arch. vol. A33, page 135 shows Elizabeth, the widow, later married Jacob Warrington.

Jackson, William. Admin. of, to Thomas Jackson, D. B. N. June 5, 1748. Reg. of Wills, Liber I, folio 227.

Jackson, James. Admin. of, to bro. Thomas Jackson, D. B. N. June 5, 1748. Reg. of Wills, Liber I, folio 227.

Taylor, James. Admin. of, to Elizabeth Taylor, widow. June 9, 1748. Arch. vol. A48, page 5. Reg. of Wills, Liber I, folio 228.

Butler, Edmond. Admin. of, to Mary Butler, widow. June 10, 1748. Reg. of Wills, Liber I, folios 228-229. Note:—Arch. vol. A7, page 13 shows Mary, the widow, later married Robert Brooks, ante June 24, 1750.

Emerson, Jacob. Admin. of, to Jerusa Emerson, widow. June 11, 1748. Arch. vol. A16, page 133. Reg. of Wills, Liber I, folio 229.

Bellach, Robert. Admin. of, to Jennett Bellach, widow. June 21, 1748. Arch. vol. A3, pages 206-207. Reg. of Wills, Liber I, folios 229-230. Note:—Arch. vol. A3, page 206 mentions children, John, James & Ann Bellach, son-in-law Robert Graham; also shows Thomas Irons & wife Jennett as adm'rs.

Smith, John. Admin. of, to Isabella Smith, widow. June 28, 1748. Arch. vol. A47, page 72. Reg. of Wills, Liber I, folio 230.

Burns, Gilbart. Will. Made May 3, 1748. Duck Creek. Heirs: John Joy; Josiah Joy; Anne Joy; Thomas Scot, son of John Scott of New Castle; oldest son of Thomas Dawson. Exec'rs, Benjamin Chew, gentleman, John Joy. Wits., Samuel Exell, William Morris, Joseph Joy. Prob. July 6, 1748. Arch. vol. A6, page 202. Reg. of Wills, Liber I, folios 226-227.

Meredith, Job. Admin. of, to Robert Meredith. July 7, 1748. Arch. vol. A34, page 175. Reg. of Wills, Liber I, folios 230-231.

Sisco, Thomas. Admin. of, to Patience Sisco, widow. July 16, 1748. Reg. of Wills, Liber I, folio 231.

David, Evan. Admin. of, to Ann David, widow. July 16, 1748. Reg. of Wills, Liber I, folio 232.

Hall, John. Admin. of, to John Hall & James Smith, D. B. N. July 22, 1748. Reg. of Wills, Liber I, folios 232-233. Arch. vol. A21, page 92.

Thomas, Daniel. Admin. of, to Grace Thomas, widow. Aug. 10, 1748. Reg. of Wills, Liber I, folio 233.

Catts, Stephen. Admin. of, to Penelope Catts, widow. Aug. 10, 1748. Arch. vol. A8, page 96. Reg. of Wills, Liber I, folios 233-234.

Clayton, Jonathan. Admin. of, to Abraham Vanhoy & wife Susanna Vanhoy. Aug. 23, 1748. Arch. vol. A9, page 120. Reg. of Wills, Liber I, folio 234.

Willson, John, Jr. Admin. of, to William Hyrons. Aug. 23, 1748. Arch. vol. A55, page 217. Reg. of Wills, Liber I, folios 234-235.

Gray, James. Will. Made July 15, 1748. Heirs: wife Margaret; dau. Margaret Pasley; son Petter Gray. Exec'rs, Robert Willcocks, & Margaret Gray. Wits., John Rees, Alexander McFarland. Prob. Sept. 10, 1748. Arch. vol. A20, page 16. Reg. of Wills, Liber I, folio 244.

Benson, Thomas. Mariner. Will (nunc.). Made Sept. 14, 1748. Heirs: mother unnamed; father unnamed; Mally Fox (of Cross-Gill); bros. John Benson, William Fox; 3 sisters at home unnamed; own 4 sisters unnamed; sister Dorothy; nephews Thomas & Christopher Benson; an aunt (at Gosforth) unnamed; uncle & aunt (at Saint Bees) unnamed; 2 orphans of Robert Stephenson (at Whitehaven); children of bro. William Fox unnamed; friends Joseph Waite, Capt. John Thompson, Mrs. Patience Wilson, George Wilson, Thomas Benson, Jr. (at Egremond); pall-bearers, Samuel Bowman, Philip Walker, John Benson, James Fox, Thomas Harrison, Capt. John Wyly. Exec'r, Samuel Bowman. Wits., Thomas Harrison, Jr. (of Whitehaven, Cumberland Co., England), George Wilson. Prob. Sept. 21, 1748. Arch. vol. A3, page 244. Reg. of Wills, Liber I, folios 245-246.

Brinkle, William. Admin. of, to bros. Peter, Richard, Daniel Brinkle & sister Elizabeth VanBurkelo. Oct. 1, 1748. Arch. vol. A5, page 218. Reg. of Wills, Liber I, folios 238-239.

Evans [Evens], Curtis. Will. Copy. Made July 21, 1748. Heirs: wife Margaret; daus. Elizabeth King, Mary & Barthulay Evens; son Edmond. Exec'rs, wife Margaret & friend William Newell. Wits., Ezekiel Thomson, William Carden, Pheabe Andrea [Arderea]. Prob. Oct. 5, 1748. Arch. vol. A16, pages 214-216. Reg. of Wills, Liber I, folios 243-244.

Orr, James. Admin. of, to bro. William Orr. Oct. 12, 1748. Reg. of Wills, Liber I, folio 239.

Bready, Solomon. Admin. of, to Sarah Bready, widow. Oct. 12, 1748. Reg. of Wills, Liber I, folio 239.

Needles, William. Admin. of, to Hannah Needles, widow. Oct. 18, 1748. Reg. of Wills, Liber I, folio 240. Note:—Arch. vol. A37, page 175 shows Hannah, the widow, later married William Harris, ante Feb. 27, 1750.

Hart, John, Jr. Will. Made Dec. 12, 1748. Heirs: sisters Mary Spring, Sabrough Hart; Elizabeth Jarrell. Exec'r, friend John Stephens. Wits., George Robbisson, Larrance [Laurence] Robbisson. Prob. Oct. 21, 1748. Arch. vol. A22, pages 195-197. Reg. of Wills, Liber I, folio 258.

Cockran, Christopher. Admin. of, to bro. John Cockran. Oct. 24, 1748. Reg. of Wills, Liber I, folio 240.

Pennington, William. Admin. of, to John Pennington & Thomas Smith. Oct. 25, 1748. Arch. vol. A39, pages 225-227. Reg. of Wills, Liber I, folios 240-241.

Ware, William. Admin. of, to Mary Ware, widow. Oct. 25, 1748. Arch. vol. A53, page 110. Reg. of Wills, Liber I, folio 241.

Carter, William, Jr. Admin. of, to Mary Carter, widow. Oct. 26, 1748. Arch. vol. A8, page 43. Reg. of Wills, Liber I, folio 241.

Fullerton, John. Admin. of, to John Purnel & Walter Purnel, D. B. N. Oct. 26, 1748. Reg. of Wills, Liber I, folio 242. Note:—Arch. vol. A18, pages 141-142 shows daus. Elizabeth, Catherine, Mary, Ann; sons Thomas, William & John.

Fullerton, Ann. Admin. of, to John Purnel & Walton Purnel. Oct. 26, 1748. Arch. vol. A18, pages 141-142. Reg. of Wills, Liber I, folios 242-243. Note:—Arch. vol. A18, page 142 mentions, Thomas, Elizabeth, Catherine, William, Ann Fullerton; page 141 mentions, John, Thomas, William, Mary, Elizabeth, Catherine & Ann Fullerton, children of John & Ann Fullerton, dec'd.

Paradee, John. Will. Made Oct. 24, 1748. Heirs: sons John & David; daus. Mary & Elizabeth. Exec'rs, bro. Stephen Paradee & Joshua Nickerson. Wits., Peter Pursel, William Manson, Dad [David] Rees. Prob. Oct. 29, 1748. Arch. vol. A38, pages 236-238. Reg. of Wills, Liber I, folio 235. Note:—Arch. vol. A30, page 60 shows dau. Mary married George Gordon.

Rutter, John. Will (nunc.). Made Oct. 3, 1748. Little Creek Hd. Heirs: wife Jane; son John. Exec'r, Francis Keeth (landlord). Wits., Robert Arthurs, Patrick Coyle. Prob. Oct. 31, 1748. Arch. vol. A44, pages 210-211. Reg. of Wills, Liber I, folios 244-245.

Pleasanton, Jonathan. Yeoman. Will. Made Oct. 8, 1748. Dover Hd. Heirs: son Jonathan; dau. Elizabeth; bros. John & David; Elizabeth Rodeney, Jr. Exec'rs, John Pleasonton, Sr., father & John Pleasonton, Jr., bro. Wits., Richard Wells, Caesar Rodeney, William Clark. Prob. Nov. 1, 1748. Arch. vol. A40, pages 123, 127-128. Reg. of Wills, Liber I, folio 236.

Whitehead, Joseph. Admin. of, to Stokely Sturgess. Nov. 1, 1748. Reg. of Wills, Liber I, folio 242.

Euin [Ewing], James. Admin. of, to Maty Euing, widow. Nov. 1, 1748. Reg. of Wills, Liber I, folio 243.

Smith, John. Yeoman. Will. Made Oct. 26, 1748. Heirs: wife Katherine; daus. Sarah, Susannah; one child unnamed; bros. in Europe unnamed; bro. Thomas Smith. Exec'r, wife Katherine. Wits., John Irons, Dad [David] Rees, Evis Rees. Prob. Nov. 10, 1748. Arch. vol. A47, pages 73-74. Reg. of Wills, Liber I, folios 236-237. Note:—Arch. vol. A47, page 73 shows that Katherine Smith married Andrew Lackey ante May 30, 1751.

Hawkins, John. Will. Made Oct. 30, 1748. Duck Creek. Heirs: wife unnamed; sons John, Thomas, Arnal, Abraham; dau. Susanner; other daus. unnamed. Exec'x, Hannah Hawkins, widow (from admin. acct. in Court House). Wits., Robert Palmatre, Thomas Hawkins, Robert Lowber. Prob. Nov. 23, 1748. Arch. vol. A23, page 26. Reg. of Wills, Liber I, folio 246.

Palmatary, Robert. Will. Made Nov. 9, 1748. Heirs: wife Elizabeth; sons John, Robert, Allen; daus. Grace, Elizabeth, Susannah Tompson & husband John Tompson. Exec'r, friend James Morris. Wits., Phebe Morris, William Hirons, John Hawkins. Prob. Nov. 23, 1748. Arch. vol. A38, pages 206-207. Reg. of Wills, Liber I, folio 247.

Ketch, James. Will (nunc.). Made Nov. 22, 1748. Murtherkill Hd. Heir: son-in-law William Sylavan. Exec'r, son-in-law William Sylivan. Wits., William Chiltman, Caleb Furbee. Prob. Nov. 26, 1748. Arch. vol. A28, pages 158 & 83. Reg. of Wills, Liber I, folio 247. Note:—Arch. vol. A28, page 83 shows that this acct. was later administered by John Newell and then by Andrew Caldwell.

Rash, Ambrose. Yeoman. Will (copy). Made Oct. 26, 1748. Heirs: mother Sarah Rash; sisters Grace & Patience Rash & Sarah Forkem; bro. John Rash; bro.-in-law John Forkem. Exec'rs, mother Sarah Rash & bro. John Rash. Wits., William Fryer, William Jackson, John Clayton, Jr. Prob. Nov. 26, 1748. Arch. vol. A42, page 33. Reg. of Wills, Liber I, folios 248-249.

Tilton, John. Admin. of, to Comfort Tilton, widow. Nov. 29, 1748. Reg. of Wills, Liber I, folio 248. Note:—Arch. vol. A50, pages 147-148 show Comfort, the widow, later married Jacob Stout; also show a son John Tilton, Jr.

Hart, George, Sr. Will. Made Feb. 6, 1747. Heirs: wife Anne; sons John, Aron, Elijah, Thomas, George; daus. Alloner, Anne Barber, Sarah, Ruth Jarrel, Mary Gordon. Exec'x, wife Anne. Wits., John Hart, Abraham Barber, George Gordon. Prob. Dec. 1, 1748. Arch. vol. A22, page 193. Reg. of Wills, Liber I, folio 249.

Sympson [Simpson], William. Admin. of, to Margarett Simpson, widow. Dec. 15, 1748. Arch. vol. A46, page 81. Reg. of Wills, Liber I, folio 250.

Moore, John. Will. Made Jan. 23, 1747. Duck Creek. Heirs: wife Mary; sons John & Samuel; other children not named. Exec'x, wife Mary. Trustees, bro. William Moore & Henery Farson. Wits., William White, Constantine Oneill, Daniel Brein. Prob. Dec. 27, 1748. Arch. vol. A36, pages 48-50. Reg. of Wills, Liber I, folios 260-261. Note:—Arch. vol. A36, page 49, shows Mary, the widow, later married John Hamilton; also shows daus. Jane & Mary Moore.

Brown, John. Yeoman. Will. Made Jan. 5, 1748/9. Murderkill Hd. Heirs: wife Eliz.; son John; daus. Rachel, Elizabeth, Mary, Susanah. Exec'r, wife Eliz. Wits., John Newell, Zachariah Goforth, Daniel Brinckle. Prob. Jan. 14, 1748. Arch. vol. A6, page 50. Reg. of Wills, Liber I, folio 260.

Little, Mary. Will. Made Jan. 6, 1748. Heirs: daus. Susannah Edmonds, Sarah Morgan, Mary Walker; grandson Addam Fisher; granddaus. Mary Fisher, Eliner Booth, dau. of Sarah Fisher; children of John & Mary Walker; Molliston Fisher; Robert & Susannah Edmonds. Exec'rs, friends John Walker & John Fisher. Wits., William Newell, John Waller, William Silliven. Prob. Jan. 14, 1748. Arch. vol. A30, pages 196-197. Reg. of Wills, Liber I, folio 261.

Turley, William. Admin. of, to Benjamin Warren. Jan. 16, 1748. Reg. of Wills, Liber K, folio 2.

Morgan, James. Admin. of, to Phebee Morgan, widow. Jan. 21, 1748. Reg. of Wills, Liber I, folio 250. Note:—Arch. vol. A36, page 152, shows Phebe, the widow, later married Isaac Turner.

Bluett, Thomas. Will. Made July 30, 1748. Dover. Heirs: wife Eleanor; dau. Martha. Exec'x, wife Eleanor. Wits., Nicholas Ridgely, Peter Galloway, Robert Willcocks. Prob. Feb. 3, 1748. Arch. vol A4, pages 149 & 154. Reg. of Wills, Liber K, folio 1.

Snow, Isaac. Admin. of, to Alice Snow, widow. Feb. 15, 1748. Arch. vol. A47, page 241. Reg. of Wills, Liber I, folio 251.

Hering, James. Admin. of, to Eleanor Hering, widow. Feb. 15, 1748. Reg. of Wills, Liber I, folio 251.

Maxfeald, James. Will. Made Jan. 21, 1748. Duck Creek. Heirs: wife Hannah; son James; daus. Mary, Jean, Hannah; one child unnamed. Exec'rs, wife Hannah & friend Daniel Nock. Wits., Mathew Steel, Samuel Griffeth, William Pope. Prob. Feb. 15, 1748. Arch. vol. A34, pages 74-76. Reg. of Wills, Liber I, folio 262.

Dowell, Phillip. Will. Made Jan. 11, 1748. Heirs: William Fryar & Elizabeth, his wife. Exec'r, William Fryar. Wits., John Clayton, Jr., Robert Wilson. Prob. Feb. 15, 1748. Arch. vol. A14, page 215. Reg. of Wills, Liber I, folio 262.

Morey, Thomas. Admin. of, to William Downs. Feb. 28, 1748. Arch. vol. A37, page 34.

Newell, William. Yeoman. Will (copy). Made Feb. 20, 1748/9. Heirs: wife Sarah; daus. Sarah, Louisa, Mary, Elizabeth & Rachel; bro. Jno. Newell. Exec'rs, wife & bro. Jno. Wits., Zachariah Goforth, Sylvester Tompson, James Clayton. Prob. March 4, 1748. Arch. vol. A37, pages 199-201. Reg. of Wills, Liber I, folios 258-259. Note:—Arch. vol. A37, page 200, shows Sarah, the widow, later married Thomas Coe; will mentions bro. Thomas, dec'd.

Brinckle, John, Sr. Will. Made Jan. 31, 1748/9. Heirs: wife Ruth; daus. Hannah Fisher, Elis Durborow; sons John, Daniel & Benjamin; grandson Joseph Brinckle; granddau. Hester Brinckle. Exec'rs, sons John & Benjamin. Wits., Jno. Brinckle, Curtis Brinckle, Sarah Brinckle. Prob. March 4, 1748. Arch. vol. A5, pages 171-172. Reg. of Wills, Liber I, folio 263.

Olliett, Mary. Admin. of, to William & George Griffin. March 9, 1748. Reg. of Wills, Liber I, folio 252.

Galloway, Richard. Will. Made March 3, 1748. Heirs: sisters Susannah & Mary Galloway; bro.-in-law Samuel Johns; bro. Joseph Galloway. Exec'rs, bro.-in-law Samuel Johns & bro. Joseph Galloway. Wits., Robert Willcocks, Benj. Chew, Theodore Parke. Prob. March 11, 1748. Arch. vol. A18, page 205. Reg. of Wills, Liber I, folio 264.

Currey [Correy], John. Will. Made Jan. 23, 1748. Duck Creek. Heirs: wife Mary; bros. Charles & Molleston; sisters Ann & Mary. Exec'x, wife Mary. Wits., William Jacobs, Hugh Stone, Henery Farson. Prob. March 14, 1748. Arch. vol. A-11, page 14. Reg. of Wills, Liber I, folio 265. Note:—Will mentions mother Mary Correy.

Howell, James. Will. Made Jan. 2, 1748. Duck Creek. Heirs: wife Mary; dau. Lydia Griffin; granddau. Mary Howell, dau. of son Philip Howell; son Phillip; 3 children of son Morris Howell. Exec'rs, wife Mary & friend Henery Farson. Wits., John Jones, David Rees, Mary Rees. Prob. March 14, 1748. Arch. vol. A25, page 63. Reg. of Wills, Liber I, folio 265.

David, James. Admin. of, to Katherine David, widow. March 16, 1748. Reg. of Wills, Liber I, folio 253.

Brown, Daniel. Will. Made March 6, 1748/9. Mispillin Hd. Heirs: wife Elizabeth; son Steven; daus. Susannah & Elizabeth; Charles Dickinson; cousin Daniel Brown. Exec'x, wife Elizabeth. Wits., Charles Dickinson, Luke Manlove, Grace Dickinson. Prob. March 18, 1748. Arch. vol. A6, page 36. Reg. of Wills, Liber I, folio 266. Note:—Arch. vol. A6, page 34 shows the widow later married William Freasure.

Lyndsey, David. Admin. of, to Priscilla Peterson (nearest of kin). March 27, 1749. Arch. vol. A30, page 172. Reg. of Wills, Liber I, folios 253-254.

David, Sarah. Will (nunc.). Made March 26, 1749. Duck Creek. Heirs: Samuel Johnson, son of father-in-law Jno. Johnson; Edward Johnson, son of John Johnson; Thomas Owen, son of James Owen. Wits., Ann Smith, Daniel Dawley, William Cross. Prob. March 28, 1749. Arch. vol. A12, pages 237-238. Reg. of Wills, Liber I, folio 268. Note:—Will mentions father Joshua David, dec'd & grandfather Lewis David, dec'd.

Kersie, James. Admin. of, to Jemima Kersie, widow. April 15, 1749. Arch. vol. A28, page 163. Reg. of Wills, Liber I, folio 253.

Walker, Robert. Admin. of, to Mary Walker, widow. April 15, 1749. Reg. of Wills, Liber I, folio 254.

Woodley, Edward. Admin. of, to Daniel Robbisson. April 22, 1749. Reg. of Wills, Liber I, folio 255.

Benson, John. Admin. of, to Elizabeth Benson, widow. April 24, 1749. Reg. of Wills, Liber I, folio 254.

Smith, Mark. Will. Made 1749. Heirs: wife unnamed; sons Mark & Ewin; daus. Elizabeth, Martha, Jean & Mary; grandsons Isaac Leckey, Jacob Smith, Isaac Smith; granddau. Margret White. Exec'r, son Mark. Wits., John Sipple, William Berry, James Berry. Prob. April 26, 1749. Arch. vol. A47, pages 110-111. Reg. of Wills, Liber I, folio 267.

Collee, John Lewee [Coller, John Lewis]. Admin. of, to Mary Lewee Collee, widow. May 2, 1749. Reg. of Wills, Liber I, folio 255.

Killingsworth, George. Admin. of, to Rachel Killingsworth, widow. May 6, 1749. Reg. of Wills, Liber I, folios 255-256.

Dyer, John. Admin. of, to Elizabeth Dyer, widow. May 10, 1749. Reg. of Wills, Liber I, folio 256. Note:—Arch. vol. A15, page 222 shows Elizabeth, the widow, later married Richard Collings ante Nov. 26, 1751.

Robbisson, William. Tavernkeeper. Will. Made April 27, 1749. Mispillion. Heirs: wife Mary; bro. Jonathan; sister Sarah. Exec'x, wife Mary. Wits., Nathaniel Luff, John Newell, Spencer Cole. Prob. May 11, 1749. Arch. vol. A44, page 89. Reg. of Wills, Liber I, folio 268.

McLane [McCleane], Selena. Will (nunc.). Made May 27, 1749. Heirs: Priscilla Peterson; Mary Wills, wife of Hugh Wills. Exec'x, Priscilla Peterson. Wits., Mary Hillyard, Mary Wills. Prob. May 30, 1749. Arch. vol. A32, page 238. Reg. of Wills, Liber I, folio 267.

Thompson, Thomas. Admin. of, to William Darling (nearest of kin). June 2, 1749. Reg. of Wills, Liber I, folio 256.

Hunter, John. Admin. of, to Robert Bohannon (near of kin) & John Craige. June 5, 1749. Reg. of Wills, Liber I, folio 269. Note:—Arch. vol. A25, pages 171-175 mentions dau. Mary & son Samuel Hunter.

Benson, Daniel. Admin. of, to Mary Benson, widow. June 10, 1749. Reg. of Wills, Liber I, folio 257.

Manlove, Absolom. Admin. of, to Margaret Manlove, widow. July 13, 1749. Reg. of Wills, Liber I, folio 257. Note:—Arch. vol. A33, page 80 shows children, Mark, Absolom, Matthew & Rachel Manlove; also the widow Margaret later married Alexander Craige ante May 30, 1751.

Walker, Samuel. Admin. of, to Mary Walker, widow. July 24, 1749. Arch. vol. A52, page 198. Reg. of Wills, Liber I, folios 257-258 & Liber K, folio 2.

Bryers, Alexander. Admin. of, to Mary Padmore. Aug. 8, 1749. Arch. vol. A6, page 113. Note:—Arch. vol. A6, page 113 shows Mary Padmore, late Mary Bryers, wife of John Padmore; also mentions children Ann & Elizabeth Bryers & one child dec'd.

King, Isaac. Will. Made June 15, 1749. Heirs: wife Anne; sons Isaac, Valentine, Jacob, James, Peter; daus. Mary Dewais, Susanna, Anne, Sarah, Eliz.; grandson Peter King. Exec'rs, wife Ann & son Isaac. Wits., John Brinckle, Jno. Jordan, Adam Capatrick. Prob. Aug. 10, 1749. Arch. vol. A29, page 24. Reg. of Wills, Liber K, folio 10.

Gibbs, John. Admin. of, to Francis Keeth. Aug. 11, 1749. Reg. of Wills, Liber I, folios 269-270.

Poillion, John. Admin. of, to Hannah Poillion. Aug. 23, 1749. Arch. vol. A40, page 148. Note:—Arch. vol. A40, page 148 mentions children, Sarah & Hannah Poillion.

Summers, Thomas. Planter. Will. Made Aug. 20, 1749. Heirs: wife Rosanna; sons Thomas, John, William, Joseph. Exec'rs, wife & son Thomas. Wits., Robert Killen, Alexander Whitely, Priscilla Ward. Prob. Sept. 9, 1749. Arch. vol. A49, pages 120-121. Reg. of Wills, Liber K, folio 1.

Butcher, Moses. Admin. of, to bro. Robert Butcher, the second. Sept. 12, 1749. Reg. of Wills, Liber K, folios 2-3.

Harper, John. Will. Made Sept. 24, 1749. Heirs: wife Mary; sons Mark, John, Peter; dau. Frances. Exec'x, wife Mary. Wits., William Boyls, Frances Codrat, John Clayton, Jr. Prob. Oct. 18, 1749. Arch. vol. A22, page 51. Reg. of Wills, Liber K, folios 10-11.

Phillips, William. Yeoman. Will. Made June 9, 1749. Heirs: wife Katherine; daus. Ann, Katherine, & Mary Forster; granddau. Mary Grant. Exec'x, wife. Wits., Edmond Badger, Robert Willcocks, David Rees. Prob. Oct. 25, 1749. Arch. vol. A40, pages 40-41. Reg. of Wills, Liber K, folio 11.

Syddle, James. Will (nunc.). Made Nov. 6, 1749. Duck Creek. Heirs: Mary Heath; Martha Wilmore, wife of Lambert Wilmore & dau. of Mary Heath. Wits., John Wilson, John Cahoon, Mary Cahoon, Jr. Prob. Nov. 7, 1749. Arch. vol. A49, page 141. Reg. of Wills, Liber K, folios 16-17. Note:— memorandum to nunc. will mentions: Lambert Wilmore & his wife Martha; Mary Worrel, dau. of Joseph Worral, dec'd.; John Spruance, father-in-law of Mary Worrel; Spruance married widow of Joseph Worrel. Testified Jan. 15, 1749. Reg. of Wills, Liber K, folio 17.

Paswater, Jonas. Admin. of, to James Darling. Nov. 9, 1749. Reg. of Wills, Liber K, folio 43.

Falconer, John. Admin. of, to Elizabeth Falconar, widow. Nov. 12, 1749. Reg. of Wills, Liber K, folio 3.

Poition, Ann. Admin. of, to Joseph Carman, bro. Nov. 13, 1749. Reg. of Wills, Liber K, folio 3.

McClammy, Oney. Admin. of, to William Docktree. Nov. 16, 1749. Reg. of Wills, Liber K, folio 5.

Correy, Charles. Will. Made Nov. 6, 1749. Duck Creek. Heirs: bros. Moleston & Samuel Correy; mother Mary Jacobs; sisters Ann & Mary Correy. Exec'r, friend Henry Farson. Wits., William Farson, John Lewis, Mary Person. Prob. Nov. 16, 1749. Arch. vols. A-11, page 12 & A12, page 151. Reg. of Wills, Liber K, folio 14.

Rees, William. Planter. Will. Made Nov. 9, 1749. Heirs: wife Elizabeth; sons David, William, Jonathan; daus. Sarah, Margaret; bros. John & Thomas. Exec'rs, wife Elizabeth, John Rees, & Phillip Lewis. Wits., Randel Blackshare, James Edwards, Edward Norman. Codicil Hannah Rees; mentions Sarah Alston, grandmother of dau. Sarah Rees. Prob. Nov. 16, 1749. Arch. vol. A43, pages 40-43. Reg. of Wills, Liber K, folios 12-13. Note:—Arch. vol. A43, page 42 shows Elizabeth married Timothy Hirons.

Bradley, Josiah. Admin. of, to Josiah & William Bradley. Nov. 28, 1749. Arch. vol. A5, page 114.

Cowgle, Thomas. Admin. of, to Sarah Cowgle, widow. Dec. 7, 1749. Arch. vol. A-11, page 119. Reg. of Wills, Liber K, folio 4. Note:—Arch. vol. A-11, page 119 shows Ezekiel Cowgill, adm'r, D. B. N.

Hudson, Alexander. Admin. of, to Isabella Hudson, widow. Jan. 2, 1749. Reg. of Wills, Liber K, folio 4.

Eghmont [Egmount-Edgemont], Cornelius. Will. Made Jan. 14, 1748. Heirs: sons Christopher, Batholomew, Ezekiel, Laurence; daus. Elener Lott, Febee Hoye; grandson Cornelius Lott; granddaus. Nancy & Mary Lott. Exec'r, son Christopher. Wits., Thomas Crain, Alexander McFarland. Prob. Jan. 5, 1749. Arch. vol. A16, pages 11 & 84. Reg. of Wills, Liber K, folios 13-14, 20-21.

Manlove, Mark. Will. Made March 16, 1747. Heirs: sons Absolam, Ezenezer, William, Mark, & Gideon; grandsons Nathan (son of Mark Manlove), Matthew (son of Absolam Manlove), Mark, son of Ebenezer Manlove, William, son of William; granddaus. Eunice (dau. of Mark Manlove), Kesiah Wheler, Margaret Manlove, Mary, Hannah, Ruth, & Priscilla Hunn, daus. of Ruth Hunn, dec'd. Exec'rs, sons Absolam, Ebenezer & Mark. Wits., Samuel Bussee, Samuel Bussee, Jr., George Brown, Mary Bussee. Prob. Jan. 8, 1749. Arch. vol. A32, page 38. Reg. of Wills, Liber K, folios 18-19.

Hilliard, Thomas. Admin. of, to Rebecca Hilliard, widow. Jan. 15, 1749. Reg. of Wills, Liber K, folios 4-5.

Butler, Peter. Admin. of, to William Cahoon. Jan. 15, 1749. Arch. vol. A7, page 17. Reg. of Wills, Liber K, folio 36.

Potter, Mary. Widow of James Potter. Will (nunc.). Made Jan. 20, 1749. Murtherkill. Heirs: daus. Dorothy (wife of Benjamin Jones) & Sarah Potter; son James. Exec'r, son James. Wits., John Hardin, Sarah Hardin. Prob. Jan. 23, 1749. Arch. vol. A41, page 15. Reg. of Wills, Liber K, folio 15.

Hoye, William. Admin. of, to Phebee Hoye, widow. Jan. 25, 1749. Arch. vol. A25, page 86. Reg. of Wills, Liber K, folios 5-6.

Cuming, Robert. Admin. of, to Patrick Cuming (nearest of kin). Feb. 1, 1749. Reg. of Wills, Liber I, folio 251.

Nock, Daniel. Will. Made Dec. 6, 1749. Duck Creek. Heirs: wife Barthia; sons Thomas, Daniel; dau. Ann; other child or children unnamed. Exec'x, wife Barthia. Trustees, bro. Ezekiel Nock, Thomas Nock & Henry Farson. Wits., William Farson, Richard Johns, John Woodall. Prob. Feb. 14, 1749. Arch. vol. A38, pages 18-19. Reg. of Wills, Liber K, folios 15-16. Note:—Arch. vol. A38, page 19 shows Elizabeth Pearson as dau. of William and Mary Pearson.

Reese, David. Admin. of, to Avis [Evis] Reese, widow. Feb. 15, 1749. Arch. vol. A42, pages 235-236. Reg. of Wills, Liber K, folio 6. Note:—Arch. vol. A42, page 235 mentions heir, Crawford Reese; also shows that Avis Reese later married George Robisson.

Hollet, Mary. Duck Creek Hd. Admin. of, to George & William Griffin. Feb. 27, 1749. Arch. vol. A24, page 190.

Oakford, John. Admin. of, to Griffith Thomas. Feb. 28, 1749. Reg. of Wills, Liber K, folios 6-7. Note:—Arch. vol. A38, page 106 shows dau. Susannah Oakford.

Smith, Henry. Blacksmith. Will. Made May 11, 1749. Murderkill Hd. Heirs: wife Mary Ann; son David; grandson Henry Smith. Exec'x, wife Mary Ann. Wits., Patrick Cummins, Thomas Pratt, George Stephenson. Prob. Feb. 28, 1749. Reg. of Wills, Liber K, folio 20.

Arnett, James. Admin. of, to Elizabeth Arnett, widow, & Preston Berry. March 2, 1749. Arch. vol. A1, page 238. Reg. of Wills, Liber K, folio 7.

Mills, George. Admin. of, to Sarah Mills, widow. March 14, 1749. Arch. vol. A35, page 130. Reg. of Wills, Liber K, folio 7.

Russell, William. Admin. of, to Grace Russel, widow. March 16, 1749. Reg. of Wills, Liber K, folios 7-8.

Mullen, Ann. Admin. of, to bro. Robert Mullen. March 24, 1749. Reg. of Wills, Liber K, folio 8.

Paten, Andrew. Admin. of, to Elizabeth Paten, widow. March 26, 1749. Reg. of Wills, Liber I, folio 199.

Bardon, Mark. Will. Made Dec. 15, 1750. Heirs: grandsons Daniel & Mark Coudrat, sons of Daniel Coudrat, dec'd; daus. Sarah Maxwell, Presemene Brian (wife of John Brian), Elizabeth Armitage (wife of Daniel Coudrat, dec'd). Exec'rs, sons-in-law John Bryan & Joseph Powell. Wits., Robert Wilson, David Pugh, Mary Ann Willson. Prob. March 26, 1750. Arch. vol. A2, pages 156-157. Reg. of Wills, Liber K, folios 32 & 115.

Graydon, John. Duck Creek Hd. Admin. of, to Mary Graydon, widow. March 28, 1750. Arch. vol. A20, pages 43-44. Reg. of Wills, Liber K, folio 9. Note:—Arch. vol. A20, page 43 shows that Mary Graydon later married John Foster; page 44 mentions heirs, Alexander, John, William & Mary Graydon; also shows that Mary Foster later married John Ashford.

Mott, Adam. Admin. of, to widow Elizabeth & son Richbell Mott. March 29, 1750. Arch. vol. A37, pages 64-65. Reg. of Wills, Liber K, folios 6 & 8.

Lang, James. Admin. of, to William Hunt. April 16, 1750. Reg. of Wills, Liber K, folios 9-10.

Burrough [Burrows], Giles. Admin. of, to Alice Burrough, widow. April 16, 1750. Arch. vol. A6, page 211. Reg. of Wills, Liber K, folio 19.

Mackpeters [McPeters], James. Will. Made March 10, 1749/50. Heirs: wife unnamed; daus. Mary, Jane, Sarah; son John. Exec'rs, wife & friend Jacob Allee. Wits., John Wood, David FitzRandolph. Prob. May 1, 1750. Arch. vol. A33, page 32. Reg. of Wills, Liber K, folio 21.

York, Thomas. Admin. of, to Daniel Robisson, D. B. N. May 9, 1750. Reg. of Wills, Liber K, folio 23.

Evans, David. Admin. of, to Elizabeth Evans, widow. May 9, 1750. Reg. of Wills, Liber K, folio 26. Note:—Arch. vol. A16, page 217 shows Daniel & Zachariah & daus. Rachel David, Mary Oborn, Deborah Evans.

Smith, Elizabeth. Admin. of, to Mark Smith, bro. May 22, 1750. Reg. of Wills, Liber K, folios 26-27.

Richmond, Ann. Dau. of Michael Richmond. Admin. of, to Comfort Tilton. May 24, 1750. Arch. vol. A43, page 174.

Throp, Abigal. Will. Made May 22, 1750. Heirs: son Samuel; George Mackee. Exec'r, George Mackee. Trustee, George Mackee. Wits., Moses Nicholls, Thomas Brown, Martha Brown. Prob. June 13, 1750. Arch. vol. A50, page 127. Reg. of Wills, Liber K, folio 22.

Hunn, John. Will. Made May 26, 1750. Heirs: wife Tabitha; mother Elinor Maxwell; sons David, John, Caleb; dau. Susanna. Exec'x, wife Tabitha. Wits., Benjamin Chew, Richard Johns, Isaiah Wharton. Prob. June 21, 1750. Arch. vol. A25, pages 142-143. Reg. of Wills, Liber K, folio 23. Note:—Arch. vol. A25, page 143 shows Tabitha, the widow, later married Silas Crispin.

Greenhood, William. Admin. of, to Joseph Greenhood. July 16, 1750. Arch. vol. A20, page 134. Reg. of Wills, Liber K, folio 27.

Williams, Lewis. Admin. of, to Slayter Bouchell, of Cecil Co., Md. July 30, 1750. Reg. of Wills, Liber K, folio 87.

Cowgill, Sarah. Widow. Will. Made July 15, 1750. Heirs: sons Ezekiel & Thomas; daus. Sarah, Ellen, Rachel & Jane Smyth. Exec'rs, son Ezekiel & son-in-law Daniel Smith. Wits., Clayton Levick, William Snow, Samuel McCall. Prob. Aug. 16, 1750. Arch. vol. A-11, page 116. Reg. of Wills, Liber K, folio 22.

Reese, David. Will (nunc.). Made Aug. 23, 1750. Duck Creek Hd. Heirs: bro. Richard; sister Eleanor Howell; bro.-in-law John Griffin. Wits., Patrick Maddin, Mary Jacobs. Prob. Aug. 28, 1750. Arch. vol. A42, page 233. Reg. of Wills, Liber K, folio 30.

David, Benjamin. Admin. of, to James Brown & wife Margaret, late Margaret David. Aug. 29, 1750. Arch. vol. A12, page 209.

Reese, David. Admin. of, to Mary Reese, widow & her father Alexander Chance. 1750. Reg. of Wills, Liber K, folio 30. Note:—Arch. vol. A42, page 234, shows Mary, the widow, later married Moses Alford; also shows the following legatees: John & Mary Griffin, Daniel & Elanore David, Richard and Mary Reese.

Tyndle, William. Will (nunc.). Made Aug. 28, 1750. Heir: father-in-law Luke Manlove. Exec'r, Luke Manlove. Wits., Gove Trippett, Luke Manlove. Prob. Aug. 31, 1750. Arch. vol. A51, page 190. Reg. of Wills, Liber K, folio 25.

Hoalston, Thomas. Admin. of, to Jacob Warrington. Sept. 17, 1750. Arch. vol. A24, page 238. Reg. of Wills, Liber K, folio 27.

Parker, Thomas. Will (copy). Made March 24, 1749. Heirs: daus. Susannah Bruce, Sarah, Naomi Hill; sons Mathew, Thomas, John, William. Exec'rs, son Thomas & bro. Anderson Parker. Wits., John Parker, Sr., Leah Parker, Betty Nelson. Prob. Sept. 25, 1750. Arch. vol. A39, pages 44-45. Reg. of Wills, Liber K, folios 20-21.

Martin, William. Duck Creek. Admin. of, to Richard & Ann Wooderson. Oct. 2, 1750. Reg. of Wills, Liber K, folios 43-44. Note:—Arch. vol. A33, page 211 shows Jean Martin as a dau.

Sap, William. Bachelor. Will. Made Nov. 1, 1750. Duck Creek. Heirs: bro. Isaac Sap; mother Rachell Brown; sister Esther Sap. Exec'r, friend John Willson. Wits., Daniel Smith, Mary Heath, John Lewis. Prob. Oct. 10, 1750. Arch. vol. A44, pages 237-238. Reg. of Wills, Liber K, folio 31.

Walker [Wolker], Jean. Will. Made Jan. 6, 1749/50. Heirs: grandsons John & Robert Walker; children of son Robert Walker; children of son Samuel Walker; Mary, widow of Robert Walker. Exec'rs, friend James White & Joseph Mason. Wits., William Manlove, Thomas Ellet, Joseph Lain. Prob. Oct. 17, 1750. Arch. vol. A52, pages 181-184. Reg. of Wills, Liber K, folio 24. Note:—Arch. vol. A52, page 182 mentions heirs, Ann, Jane, & Robert Walker; also shows that this account was later administered, D. B. N. by Charles Mason.

Miller, John. Farmer. Will. Made April 15, 1749. Murtherkill Hd. Heirs: wife Dorithy; sons Henry, Chilion, John, Cunrod, Adam, Peter; dau. Susanna Quilling. Exec'rs, wife & sons John & Cunrod. Wits., John Hardin, Parismus Potter, Martin Hardin. Prob. Oct. 20, 1750. Arch. vol. A35, page 77. Reg. of Wills, Liber K, folio 25.

Warren, Thomas. Admin. of, to Jacob Vanwinkle. Oct. 26, 1750. Reg. of Wills, Liber K, folio 37.

Berry, William. Admin. of, to Sarah Berry, widow. Nov. 13, 1750. Arch. vol. A4, page 14. Reg. of Wills, Liber K, folio 9. Note:—Arch. vol. A4, page 14 shows that Sarah Berry later married John Virdin.

Underwood, Joshua. Admin. of, to Sarah Underwood. Nov. 27, 1750. Arch. vol. A51, page 192. Reg. of Wills, Liber K, folio 28.

Evans, Thomas. Admin. of, to Simon Hirons. Nov. 29, 1750. Arch. vol. A16, page 229.

Fransisco, Thomas. Admin. of, to Patience Fransisco. Nov. 29, 1750. Arch. vol. A18, page 89.

Mason, William. Admin. of, to Lurania Mason, widow. Dec. 15, 1750. Arch. vol. A34, pages 11-12. Reg. of Wills, Liber K, folio 27. Note:—Arch. vol. A34, page 11 mentions heirs, Carman & William Mason & Mary Robinson, wife of George Robinson; also shows that Lurania Mason later married James Start.

Ellis, Jeffray. Admin. of, to Martha Ellis, widow. Dec. 24, 1750. Reg. of Wills, Liber K, folio 28.

Warren, Thomas. Admin. of, to Simon Van Winkle. Dec. 28, 1750. Arch. vol. A53, page 151. Reg. of Wills, Liber K, folio 28.

Richee, Samuel. Admin. of, to Rebecca Richee, widow. 1750. Arch. vol. A43, page 172. Reg. of Wills, Liber K, folio 29.

Beswick, William. Admin. of, to Eleanor Beswick, widow. Jan. 15, 1750. Reg. of Wills, Liber K, folio 5. Note:—Arch. vol. A4, page 17 shows Eleanor, the widow, later married Thomas Lawful.

Evans, Margaret. Admin. of, to John Meekins. Jan. 17, 1750. Arch. vol. A16, page 227. Reg. of Wills, Liber K, folio 29.

Green, William. Admin. of, to Thomas Green, bro. Jan. 23, 1750. Reg. of Wills, Liber K, folios 29-30.

Anderson, John. Admin. of, to Joyce Anderson, widow, & James Anderson. Jan. 25, 1750. Arch. vol. A1, page 182. Reg. of Wills, Liber K, folio 29.

Smith, Thomas. Will (nunc.). Made Jan. 26, 1750. Murtherkill Hd. Heirs: wife unnamed; son John; dau. Martha; bros. John, Daniel, & Ralph. Wits., Elenor Cane, Rachel Meredie, John Monsie, Robert Meredie, Jr., Joshua Meredie. Prob. Feb. 5, 1750. Arch. vol. A47, page 176. Reg. of Wills, Liber K, folio 26.

Evens, Edmond. Will. Made Jan. 23, 1750/51. Heirs: nephew Peter King, eldest sister's son; cousin Thomas Meekings, son of Aunt Mary & Uncle John. Exec'r, uncle John Meekings. Wits., Ich[a]bod Warner, Thomas Cox, John Bostick. Prob. Feb. 6, 1750. Arch. vol. A16, page 218. Reg. of Wills, Liber K, folios 31-32. Note:—Will mentions parents Curtis & Margreat Evens, dec'd & sister Barthulay, dec'd.

Swallow, George. Farmer. Will. Made Feb. 7, 1749/50. Heirs: wife Johana; sons Silvenus, George, John. Exec'rs, wife Johana & John Snow. Wits., Sarah Alston, Mary Sterling, James Sterling. Prob. Feb. 13, 1750. Arch. vol. A49, page 132. Reg. of Wills, Liber K, folios 30-31.

Summers [Somers], Rosannah. Admin. of, to Thomas Summers [Somers]. March 3, 1751. Arch. vol. A49, page 119. Reg. of Wills, Liber K, folio 30.

Woodle, Joseph. Duck Creek. Admin. of, to Mary Woodle, widow. March 13, 1750. Arch. vol. A56, pages 106-108. Reg. of Wills, Liber K, folios 34-35. Note:—Arch. vol. A56, page 106 shows that Mary Woodle, widow, later married Matthew Hutchisson; also page 108 mentions heirs, Joseph Woodle & Elizabeth Woodle, wife of Thomas Wallace.

Severson, John. Admin. of, to Mercy Severson, widow. March 14, 1750. Reg. of Wills, Liber K, folio 35.

Haynes, John. Will. Made March 1, 1750. Heirs: sons John, Daniel, Samuel & Joseph Ranaday Haynes; dau. Mary; wife Rachel. Exec'x, wife Rachel. Wits., William Manlove, Josiah Bradly, Mary Bradly. Prob. March 28, 1751. Arch. vol. A23, page 72. Reg. of Wills, Liber K, folio 33.

Griscomb, Tobias. Carpenter. Will (nunc.). Made March 18, 1751. Heir: dau. in Phila. unnamed. Exec'r, Thomas Nixon. Wits., Dr. Richard Wells, John Boggs. Prob. March 29, 1751. Arch. vol. A21, pages 12-13. Reg. of Wills, Liber K, folio 33.

Brion [Bryan], John. Admin. of, to Presemene Brion, widow. March 29, 1751. Reg. of Wills, Liber K, folio 35. Note:— Arch. vol. A6, page 107 shows Presemene, the widow, later married John Ryon; also shows a son John & a dau. Prisimina Bryan.

Booth, John. Will. Made March 8, 1750. Heirs: wife Mary; son Waightman. Exec'x, wife. Wits., Waitman Sipple, Daniel Robison, Mary Jones. Prob. March 30, 1751. Arch. vol. A4, page 215. Reg. of Wills, Liber K, folio 34.

Roach, Nathaniel. Admin. of, to John Roach, son. April 5, 1751. Reg. of Wills, Liber K, folio 37. Note:—Arch. vol. A44, page 18 shows a son Nathaniel Roach.

Nixon, Joseph. Admin. of, to bro. Thomas Nixon. April 6, 1751. Reg. of Wills, Liber K, folio 36.

Caldwell, Andrew. Admin. of, to son Andrew Caldwell. April 8, 1751. Reg. of Wills, Liber K, folio 35.

Craige, Andrew. Admin. of, to Henritta Craige, widow. April 15, 1751. Reg. of Wills, Liber K, folio 36.

Storey, James. Admin. of, to Mary Storey, widow. May 15, 1751. Reg. of Wills, Liber K, folio 37.

Hawkins, Eleanor. Will. Made May 4, 1751. Heirs: sons Allen & Thomas; daus. Mary & Grace; Mary Snow, dau. of Wm. Snow; son-in-law Joseph Thomson. Exec'r, Elisha Snow, Jr. Wits., Benjamin Allbery, James Snow. Prob. May 15, 1751. Arch. vol. A23, pages 22-23. Reg. of Wills, Liber K, folio 38.

Williams, Aaron. Will. Made March 6, 1750/51. Heirs: wife Sarah; son Renear; bro. Renear; dau. Hester. Exec'x, wife Sarah. Wits., John Brincklee, Jonathan Molleston, Elliner Annett. Prob. May 22, 1751. Arch. vol. A55, pages 65-66. Reg. of Wills, Liber K, folio 39. Note:—Arch. vol. A55, page 66 shows Sarah, the widow, married a Draper; vol. 1, page 28 of the Marriage Records gives the name Nehemiah Draper.

Smith, Elizabeth. Will. Made April 6, 1751. Heirs: daus. Martha, Mary Ewing, Jane Jacobs; son Mark; grandson Robert Ewing; granddaus. Mary Lackey, dau. of Andrew & Esther Lackey, Margaret White, Elizabeth Smyth. Exec'x, dau. Martha. Wits., John Miller, Robert Buchannan, William Silliven. Prob. May 27, 1751. Arch. vol. A47, page 32. Reg. of Wills, Liber K, folio 39.

Benston, Daniel. Admin. of, to Mary Benston. May 28, 1751. Arch. vol. A3, page 234.

Benston, John. Admin. of, to Elizabeth Benston. May 28, 1751. Arch. vol. A3, page 238.

Stanton, Stephen. Little Creek Hd. Admin. of, to Elizabeth Stanton, widow. June 1, 1751. Arch. vol. A48, pages 154-155. Reg. of Wills, Liber K, folio 44.

KirkPatrick, David. Admin. of, to Thomas Park. June 10, 1751. Reg. of Wills, Liber K, folios 37-38.

Maxwell, Robert. Admin. of, to Nicholas Ridgely. June 10, 1751. Reg. of Wills, Liber K, folio 38.

Barratt, Benjamin. Tailor. Will. Made May 9, 1751. Little Creek. Heirs: sons Benjamin & Jonathan; grandson Silas Crispin; granddau. Martha Neal. Exec'r, son Benjamin. Wits., Mary Smith, Miles Francis, Timothy Hanson. Prob. June 11, 1751. Arch. vol. A2, page 241. Reg. of Wills, Liber K, folio 40.

Brady, Absolom. Admin. of, to Eleanor Bradey, widow, & bro. Phillip Brady. July 13, 1751. Reg. of Wills, Liber K, folio 44.

Hunter, John. Farmer. Will (copy). Made July 30, 1751. Whiteland, County of Chester. Heirs: wife Ann; sons James & John; daus. Hannah, Margaret, Elizabeth, Ann, Mary. Exec'rs, wife Ann & bros. William & James. Wits., Andrew Buchannan, William Hudson & Malachi Jones. Arch. vol. A25, page 175.

Fleming, Archibald. Admin. of, to Elizabeth Fleming, widow. Aug. 13, 1751. Reg. of Wills, Liber K, folios 44-45.

Lockwood, Armwell. Admin. of, to Mary Lockwood, widow. Aug. 29, 1751. Arch. vol. A30, page 213. Reg. of Wills, Liber K, folio 45.

Wallace, David. Will (copy). Made April 19, 1751. Heirs: wife Barbara; sons Matthew, Solomon, William, Benjamin, Reuben, Joshua, Josiah; daus. Deborah Williams, Hannah Caldwell, Rhoda; granddau. Sarah Wallace. Exec'rs, wife & son Reuben. Wits., Joseph Howell, George Meoller, John Brinkle. Prob. Aug. 31, 1751. Arch. vol. A52, pages 223-224. Reg. of Wills, Liber K, folios 40-41. Note:—Arch. vol. A52, page 224, shows James Caldwell as the husband of Hannah Caldwell.

Anderson, Jacob. Merchant. Will. Made Sept. 23, 1751. Worcester Co., Md. Heirs: bro. Isaac Anderson; sister Catherine Sherrad; nephew Jacob, son of my bro. Abraham Anderson. Exec'rs for estate in or near Maryland—Robert Burton, son of William Burton, & Joseph Carter. Exec'rs for estate in the Jersey's—bro. Isaac Anderson, Joseph Decoe & Samuel Johnson. Wits., Nicholas Powell, Rebecca Powell, his wife, Edward Norman, William Hazard. Prob. Sept. 27, 1751. Arch. vol. A1, page 171. Reg. of Wills, Liber K, folio 41.

Moor, Henry. Will. Made Oct. 5, 1751. New Castle Co. Heirs: sons Henry, Robert, John; wife Elizabeth; 4 daus. unnamed. Exec'rs, wife & John Draughton. Wits., Henaritta Moor, Jacob Allee, Thomas Cahoon. Prob. Oct. 14, 1751. Arch. vol. A36, pages 22-23. Reg. of Wills, Liber K, folio 42. Note:— Arch. vol. A36, page 23 shows Elizabeth, the widow, married Isaac Sap; also shows Elizabeth and Rachel Moore are daus.

Draughton, Robert. Duck Creek Hd. Admin. of, to bro. John. Oct. 14, 1751. Arch. vol. A15, page 82. Reg. of Wills, Liber K, folio 45.

Griffing [Griffin], George. Blacksmith. Will. Made Sept. 10, 1751. Heir: wife Rebekah. Exec'r, wife & bros. William & Mathew Griffin. Wits., Peter Stoutt, Lydia Griffing. Prob. Oct. 15, 1751. Arch. vol. A20, pages 197-199. Reg. of Wills, Liber K, folio 42. Note:—Arch. vol. A20, page 199 shows Rebecca married Peter Stoutt; page 198 shows she later married Jabez Jenkins.

Melvin, Edmund. Mispillion Hd. Admin. of, to Ann Melvin, widow. Oct. 21, 1751. Arch. vol. A34, page 140. Reg. of Wills, Liber K, folios 45-46.

McAllister, Archibald. Admin. of, to John Murray Nov. 28, 1751. Arch. vol. A32, page 53. Reg. of Wills, Liber K, folio 46.

Gregorie, Jeremiah. Will (nunc.). Made Dec. 8, 1751. Mispillion Hd. Heirs: wife (Mary from admin. bond); wife's two sons Randle & Joseph Powell; dau. in New Castle unnamed. Wits., Joseph Parsons, Margarett Nickerson. Prob. Dec. 10, 1751. Arch. vol. A20, page 184. Reg. of Wills, Liber K, folios 47-48.

Smith, Thomas. Yeoman. Will. Made Nov. 8, 1749. Heirs: Thomas Penington, son of William Penington; Couteler Pennington, dau. of William Penington. Exec'rs, Nicholas Ridgely, Esq., & John Housman, Esq. Wits., Noah Gildersleeve, Richbell Mott, Jos. Carman. Prob. Dec. 25, 1751. Arch. vol. A47, page 177. Reg. of Wills, Liber K, folio 47.

Smith, Thomas. Dover Hd. Admin. of, to Daniel Fawsitt, nearest of kin. Dec. 25, 1751. Arch. vol. A47, page 178. Reg. of Wills, Liber K, folio 47.

Gorrell, James. Will. Made Oct. 16, 1751. Heirs: wife Ruth; son James; dau. Sarah; nephews James, son of bro. Wm. Gorrell, dec'd, & Robert, son of bro. John Gorrell. Exec'rs, friends John Vining, Esq., & Wm. Killen. Wits., Nicholas Ridgely, Andrew Caldwell, John Wright. Prob. Jan. 1, 1752. Arch. vol. A19, pages 192-193. Reg. of Wills, Liber K, folio 49.

Farthing, Samuel. Duck Creek. Admin. of, to Phebe, widow. Jan. 6, 1752. Reg. of Wills, Liber K, folio 46.

David, Rebecca. Duck Creek. Admin. of, to Benjamin Jones, son. Jan. 14, 1752. Reg. of Wills, Liber K, folio 47.

Vanwinkle, Simon. Will. Made Dec. 17, 1748. Heirs: wife Jane; sons Jacob, John, Simon; dau. Susannah Talbort; grandson Simon Draughton. Exec'x, wife Jane. Wits., Wm. Cahoon, Mary Cahoon, John Cahoon. Prob. Jan. 23, 1752. Arch. vol. A52, pages 24-26. Reg. of Wills, Liber K, folios 50-51.

Dickinson, Sarah. Duck Creek. Admin. of, to William Green. Jan. 28, 1752. Reg. of Wills, Liber K, folio 54.

Goforth, Zachariah. Will. Made Sept. 2, 1748. Heirs: wife Mary; sons Zachariah & John; daus. Mary, Ann, Elizabeth. Exec'x, wife Mary. Wits., Wm. Newell, Sarah Newell, James Wilson. Prob. Feb. 2, 1752. Arch. vol. A19, pages 105 & 109. Reg. of Wills, Liber K, folios 49-50. Note:—Sarah Newell, wife of William Newell, later married Thomas Coe.

Snow, Elisha, Sr. Yeoman. Will. Made Jan. 15, 1744. Duck Creek. Heirs: sons Elisha, James, Jesse; wife Elizabeth. Exec'x, wife Elizabeth. Wits., William Snow, Abraham Fields. Prob. Feb. 8, 1752. Arch. vol. A47, page 238. Reg. of Wills, Liber K, folios 53-54.

Jones, Griffith. Duck Creek. Admin. of, to James Morris. Feb. 12, 1752. Arch. vol. A27, page 179. Reg. of Wills, Liber K, folio 54.

Draper, Lawrence. Will. Made Feb. 13, 1752. Heirs: sons James, Digbe, Jacob Dryer & David Draper; dau. Hannah. Exec'r, friend John Draughton. Wits., William Sherard, Daniel FitzRandolph. Trustee, bro.-in-law Lewis Cloather. Prob. Feb. 21, 1752. Arch. vol. A15, pages 52 & 81. Reg. of Wills, Liber K, folio 51.

Sipple, Christopher. Will. Made Dec. 7, 1751. Heirs: wife unnamed; sons Christopher, Raymond, Silva; daus. Mary, Elizabeth, Alice & Priscilla Sipple & Sarah Goforth & Mary Ann Jenkins; granddau. Mary Jenkins. Exec'rs, wife, bro. John Sipple & friend Mark Manlove. Wits., John Emerson, William Gray, Unity Emerson. Prob. Feb. 24, 1752. Arch. vol. A46, pages 110-115. Reg. of Wills, Liber K, folio 52. Note:— Arch. vol. A46, page 115 shows Mary, the widow, later married Ezekiel Cowgill.

Empson, Cornelius. Merchant. Will. Made Dec. 21, 1751. Heirs: daus. Hannah & Sarah Empson, Elizabeth Battle; sons Cornelius, William & Charles. Exec'rs, dau. Hannah, son-in-law French Battle. Trustee, friend Benjamin Chew. Wits., Benjamin Chew, Thomas Alford, William Smyth. Prob. Feb. 25, 1752. Arch. vol. A16, pages 195-198. Reg. of Wills, Liber K, folio 53.

Styles, John. Duck Creek. Admin. of, to Martha Stiles, widow. Feb. 27, 1752. Reg. of Wills, Liber K, folio 55.

Weldon, Joseph. Little Creek Hd. Admin. of, to Ann Weldon, widow. March 2, 1752. Arch. vol. A53, page 225. Reg. of Wills, Liber K, folio 55.

Needham, Ralph. Admin. of, to Phebee Needham, widow. March 7, 1752. Arch. vol. A37, pages 156-157. Reg. of Wills, Liber K, folio 55.

Marim, Thomas. Dover Hd. Admin. of, to Charles Marim, bro. March 10, 1752. Reg. of Wills, Liber K, folio 56.

Snow, Mary. Duck Creek. Admin. of, to Elizabeth Snow. March 16, 1752. Reg. of Wills, Liber K, folio 56.

Galloway, Peter. Admin. of, to widow Elizabeth, son Joseph & son-in-law Samuel Johns. March 16, 1752. Reg. of Wills, Liber K, folio 56.

Durborow, John. Murtherkill. Admin. of, to Elizabeth, widow. March 31, 1752. Reg. of Wills, Liber K, folio 57. Note:— Arch. vol. A15, page 163 shows that Elizabeth Durborow later married Levy Blunt; also mentions children Mary, Sarah, John & Luke Durborow.

Hirons, Charles. Will. Made April 5, 1752. Heirs: sons Charles, John; wife Mary. Exec'rs, wife Mary & Stokely Sturgis. Wits., Daniel Shanen, John Swaney, James Small. Prob. April 11, 1752. Arch. vol. A24, pages 89-91. Reg. of Wills, Liber K, folio 58. Note:—Arch. vol. A24, page 91 shows Daniel Brinkley, exec'r of Mary Ann Hirons, dec'd.

Jones, David. Little Creek. Admin. of, to John David. April 31, 1752. Arch. vol. A27, page 154. Reg. of Wills, Liber K, folio 57.

Hathorne, Ebenezer. Merchant. Will (unsigned). Made 1749. Heirs: son William; daus. Elizabeth, Mary, Ann, Ruth; bro. Joseph Hathorn of Salem in New England. Exec'r, [John Vandike, from admin. acct.]. Wits., Andrew Vandike, Thomas Clark, Mark Manlove, Zakariah Goforth, Bridget Cannon, Mary Gray, John Gray. Prob. May 6, 1752. Arch. vol. A23, pages 51-54 & vol. A22, page 247. Reg of Wills, Liber K, folio 59. Note:—Arch. vol. A23, pages 51-54 show John McCutchin as the husband of dau. Elizabeth; also mentions Grace Peterson, John Jones, Jacob Peterson, John Vandike, Jr., Elizabeth McCutchin, Francis McCutchin.

Marsh, John. Admin. of, to Robert Hall. May 7, 1752. Reg. of Wills, Liber K, folio 57.

Jaffray, Henry. Doctor. Will. Made March 22, 1752. Heirs: wife Rebecca; dau. Sarah; friend Benjamin Chew. Exec'x, wife Rebecca. Trustee, friend Benj. Chew. Wits., Jacob Jones, Thomas Green, Charles Green. Prob. May 25, 1752. Arch. vol. A26, page 83. Reg. of Wills, Liber K, folios 59-60.

Jacobs, William. Yeoman. Will. Made Nov. 27, 1750. Duck Creek. Heirs: wife Mary; sister Elizabeth Jacobs; half-sister unnamed; two sisters' children unnamed. Exec'x, wife Mary. Wits., Daniel Evans, John Lewis, Mary Person. Prob. June 6, 1752. Arch. vol. A26, page 67. Reg. of Wills, Liber K, folio 67.

Bassill, Robert. Will. Made June 30, 1752. Heirs: mother unnamed; wife Susanna; Jacob Stout. Exec'rs, wife Susanna & Jacob Stout. Wits., John Allee, Thomas Parker, James Small. Prob. July 6, 1752. Arch. vol. A3, page 51. Reg. of Wills, Liber K, folio 78.

Hirons, Mary Ann. Will. Made June 29, 1752. Heirs: eldest son John; other children unnamed. Exec'rs, Daniel Brinckle of Little Creek Hd., Stokley Sturgis. Guardian, Daniel Brinckle, of other children unnamed. Wits., Mary Jones, Catherine Rannels, James Small. Prob. July 28, 1752. Arch. vol. A24, page 96. Reg. of Wills, Liber K, folio 81. Note:— Will mentions husband, Charles Hirons, dec'd.

Cowgill [Cowgle], John. Little Creek Hd. Admin. of, to Hannah Cowgill, widow. July 29, 1752. Reg. of Wills, Liber K, folios 60-61. Note:—Arch. vol. A11, page 96 shows Hannah, the widow, later married Robert Hall; also mentions dau. Lydia Cowgill.

Beswick, George. Millwright. Will. Made Aug. 1, 1752. Dover. Heirs: bros. John & Robert Beswick. Exec'r, father-in-law Vincent Lockerman. Wits., John Miller, William Killen. Prob. Aug. 4, 1752. Arch. vol. A4, page 24. Reg. of Wills, Liber K, folio 79.

Man, Samuel. Will. Made July 17, 1752. Heirs: sisters Agness, Isable Hudson, Rachel Wilson, Annalana Man, Abigail Man; niece Marget Hudson, dau. of sister Isable; nephew Samuel Kelly, son of sister Anipil. Exec'rs, sister, Rachel Wilson & Hugh Craige. Wits., Ephraim Shaw, Elizabeth Craige, Leah Craige. Prob. Aug. 12, 1752. Arch. vol. A33, pages 74-76. Reg. of Wills, Liber K, folios 78-79. Note:—Arch. vol. A33, page 75 shows Rachel Wilson later married Francis Murrey.

Walton, William. Will. Made July 25, 1752. Heirs: wife Hannah; son John. Exec'x, wife. Wits., Caleb Luff, Mary Gordon, Mary Cummins. Prob. Aug. 12, 1752. Arch. vol. A53, page 79. Reg. of Wills, Liber K, folio 79.

Fraser, William. Mispillion. Admin. of, to Catherine Phillips. Aug. 17, 1752. Reg. of Wills, Liber K, folio 61.

Pratt, Thomas. Yeoman. Will. Made April 15, 1734. Murtherkill. Heirs: wife Dinah; son George. Exec'x, wife Dinah. Wits., Andrew Caldwell, William Chance, Ann Pines, Diana Pickrell. Prob. Aug. 24, 1752. Arch. vol. A41, pages 134-135. Reg. of Wills, Liber K, folio 79.

Hall, Absolom. Mispillion. Admin. of, to Nathaniel Luff. Aug. 30, 1752. Reg. of Wills, Liber K, folio 61.

Ward, Joseph. Duck Creek. Admin. of, to Eleanor Ward, widow. Sept. 9, 1752. Reg. of Wills, Liber K, folios 63-64. Note:— Arch. vol. A53, page 94 mentions William & Joseph Ward, minors.

Middleton, Ellenor. Little Creek. Admin. of, to Samuel Horseman, son. Oct. 6, 1752. Reg. of Wills, Liber K, folio 62.

Maxwell, James Jr. Joiner. Will. Made Oct. 2, 1752. Heirs: daus. Elizabeth Maxwell, Anna Helford, Ann Darling (dau. of my wife); bro. Robert. Exec'r, bro. Robert. Trustee, Henry Upprithart. Wits., Samuel Robisson, John Taylor, Jr., Mathew Claghorn. Prob. Oct. 11, 1752. Arch. vol. A34, pages 80-84. Reg. of Wills, Liber K, folio 80.

Gallaway, Peter. Admin. of, to Elizabeth Gallaway, widow, & Samuel Johns, son-in-law. Oct. 19, 1752. Reg. of Wills, Liber K, folio 66.

Wills, Hugh. Farmer. Will. Made Oct. 11, 1752. Duck Creek. Heirs: bro. John Wills; Elizabeth Donaven. Exec'rs, Elizabeth Donaven & Silvester Luck. Wits., Richard Rutherford, Margaret Holland. Prob. Nov. 1, 1752. Arch. vol. A55, pages 195-196. Reg. of Wills, Liber K, folio 80.

Taylor, John, Sr. Yeoman. Will. Made Oct. 25, 1752. Heirs: son John; Rachel Taylor, dau. of William Taylor; Halburt & Thomas Taylor, sons of John Taylor, Jr. Exec'r, William Wells. Wits., Robert Mullin, Sarah Pounds, William Shurmer. Prob. Nov. 2, 1752. Arch. vol. A49, page 193. Reg. of Wills, Liber K, folios 80-81.

French, Charles. Duck Creek. Admin. of, to Roger Pugh. Nov. 16, 1752. Arch. vol. A18, page 136. Reg. of Wills, Liber K, folio 62.

Carpenter, John. Admin. of, to Mary Carpenter, widow. Dec. 7, 1752. Arch. vol. A7, page 231. Reg. of Wills, Liber K, folio 63. Note:—Arch. vol. A7, page 231 shows William Carpenter exec'r of Mary Carpenter.

Keith, Francis. Will (copy). Made May 4, 1752. Duck Creek. Heirs: wife Jane; nephews John, James & Thomas, sons of bro. James Keith; bro. James Keith; Martha Moaran, dau. of wife Jane. Exec'rs, wife Jane & bro. James. Wits., Mary

Grimes, John Lennan, Henry Farson. Prob. Dec. 13, 1752. Arch. vol. A28, pages 89-90. Reg. of Wills, Liber K, folio 82. Note:—Arch. vol. A28, page 90 shows Andrew Moran & dau. Elizabeth; Elizabeth Moran married Daniel McDavit and later married Francis Keith.

Matthews, Charles. Innholder. Will. Made Nov. 18, 1752. Dover. Heirs: wife Mary Anne; daus. Elizabeth & Mary Matthews. Exec'x, wife Mary Anne. Wits., John Faries, Catherine Forckham, Thomas Alford. Prob. Dec. 15, 1752. Arch. vol. A34, pages 64-65. Reg. of Wills, Liber K, folio 82. Note:— Arch. vol. A34, page 65 shows Mary Ann later married George Pender.

Sipple, John. Will. Made Oct. 30, 1752. Heirs: wife Prudence; sons Martinus, Nathaniel, Uriah, John, William; daus. Rachel, Sarah, Joanna; Sarah Millally. Exec'rs, wife Prudence, sons William & John. Wits., Mark Smith, John Clother, James Berry. Prob. Dec. 16, 1752. Arch. vol. A46, pages 141-142. Reg. of Wills, Liber K, folio 82.

Booth, John, Sr. Will. Made Dec. 9, 1752. Heir: wife Mary. Exec'x, wife Mary. Wits., Richard Morris, Mary Bartlet. Prob. Jan. 3, 1753. Arch. vol. A4, pages 216-217. Reg. of Wills, Liber K, folio 83. Note:—Arch. vol. A4, page 217 shows Mary, the widow, later married Andrew Caldwell.

Henry, John. Duck Creek. Admin. of, to Rebecca Henry, widow. Feb. 6, 1753. Reg. of Wills, Liber K, folio 63.

Hutton, Elliner. Spinster. Will. Made Jan. 4, 1753. Heirs: son Ebenezer Jones; nieces Elliner Oens & Mary Borriss. Exec'r, son Ebenezer. Wits., Frances Baxter, Joseph Hallyday, James Hyatt, Mary Carpenter. Prob. March 10, 1753. Arch. vol. A25, page 202. Reg. of Wills, Liber K, folio 83.

Greenwood, Jonas. Admin. of, to John Greenwood. March 21, 1753. Arch. vol. A20, page 152.

Bradey, Phillip. Admin. of, to Margarett Bradey, widow. March 26, 1753. Arch. vol. A5, page 127. Reg. of Wills, Liber K, folio 64.

Doney, John. Farmer. Will. Made Dec. 16, 1749. Duck Creek. Heirs: wife Hannah; sons Peter & James. Exec'x, wife Hannah. Wits., George Martin, Eliz. Martin, Philip Denne. Prob. April 2, 1753. Arch. vol. A14, page 177. Reg. of Wills, Liber K, folios 83-84.

Exall [Excell], Samuel. Duck Creek. Admin. of, to Presley Raymond. April 4, 1753. Arch. vol. A16, page 236. Reg. of Wills, Liber K, folio 64.

Clary, John. Will. Made March 14, 1753. Heirs: wife [Jane, from admin. acct.]; daus. Mary & Rebecca. Exec'rs, wife & Robert Willcocks. Wits., Christian Tanner, James Byrne, William Shurmer. Prob. April 14, 1753. Arch. vol. A9, pages 100-103. Reg. of Wills, Liber K, folio 84. Note:—Arch. vol. A9, page 101 shows Jane, the widow, later married James Byrne.

Stiles, John. Admin. of, to Mary Stiles. May 23, 1753. Arch. vol. A49, page 23.

Johnson, Mary. Dover. Admin. of, to Robert Hall & John Bell. July 30, 1753. Reg. of Wills, Liber K, folio 65.

Park, Frances. Dau. of Joseph Booth, dec'd. Admin. of, to Theodore Park, husband, D. B. N. Aug. 7, 1753. Reg. of Wills, Liber K, folio 68.

Macey, Thomas. Duck Creek. Admin. of, to Mary Macey, widow. Aug. 18, 1753. Reg. of Wills, Liber K, folio 65.

Delap, Allen. Will. Made July 12, 1753. Heirs: wife Sarah; sons Allen, William, John, Matthew, James, Peter; daus. Mary Steele & Sarah Delap. Exec'x, wife. Wits., Thomas Dawson, David Anderson, John Clayton, Jr. Prob. Aug. 25, 1753. Arch. vol. A13, page 178. Reg. of Wills, Liber K, folios 89-90.

Deweese, Samuel. Mispillion. Admin. of, to Mary Deweese, widow. Sept. 11, 1753. Reg. of Wills, Liber K, folios 65-66.

Barns, William. Will. Made Nov. 5, 1751. Heirs: wife unnamed; four youngest daus.; daus. Elizabeth Folkner, Catherine Barns; sons William, John, Stephen, Abraham Folkner. Exec'rs, two youngest sons. Wits., Peter Allee, Thomas Weston. Prob. Sept. 18, 1753. Arch. vol. A2, pages 230-231. Reg. of Wills, Liber K, folio 85.

Strickland, William. Will. Made Nov. 19, 1753. Heirs: wife Rachel; daus. Rachel, Mary Corbet, Rebecca Truax; grandchildren William Strickland Corbet & Isaac Corbet. Exec'rs, wife Rachel & Jacob Corbet. Wits., Andrew Peterson, Sarah Peterson, Elizabeth Due. Codicil, son-in-law Charles Hudson. Wits., Paul Alfree, Thomas Slater. Prob. Oct. 10, 1753. Arch. vol. A49, pages 87-88. Reg. of Wills, Liber K, folio 86. Note:—Arch. vol. A49, page 88 shows Rachel, the widow, later married Thomas Cahoon.

Howell, James. Farmer. Will. Made Oct. 8, 1753. Heirs: wife Ruth; sons Samuel, James, Joseph, David, Thomas; dau. Hannah. Exec'rs, Evan Lewis & John Caton. Wits., Samuel Morris, Edward Henry, John Talbot. Prob. Oct. 16, 1753. Arch. vol. A25, pages 64-65. Reg. of Wills, Liber K, folios 85-86.

Maxwell, William. Will. Made Oct. 8, 1753. Heir: wife Sarah. Exec'x, wife Sarah. Wits., Elizabeth Armitage, Alice Maxwell, John Clayton, Jr. Prob. Oct. 16, 1753. Arch. vol. A34, page 104. Reg. of Wills, Liber K, folio 87.

Delap, Sarah. Widow of Allen Delap. Will. Made Nov. 8, 1753. Heir: dau. Sarah Delap. Exec'rs, sons John & Matthew Delap. Wits., Thomas Tagart, James Clayton, Robert Teat. Prob. Nov. 27, 1753. Arch. vol. A13, page 182. Reg. of Wills, Liber K, folio 90.

Pleasanton, John. Yeoman. Will. Made Dec. 8, 1753. Dover Hd. Heirs: wife Mary; sons John, Charles, George & David; granddau. Elizabeth Field; grandson Jonathan Pleasanton. Exec'r, son David. Wits., Ebenezer Manlove, William Shurmer, Abraham Barber. Prob. Dec. 15, 1753. Arch. vol. A40, pages 108-110. Reg. of Wills, Liber K, folio 88. Note:— Will mentions wife's dau. Easter; Arch. vol. A40, page 109 shows Mary Maxwell & Thos. Brinckle as parents of Hester Brinckle, dec'd.

Jester, Thomas. Will. Made Feb. 2, 1753. Heirs: daus. Barbara, Elizabeth & Sarah Jester, Ann Mann, Esther Winsmore; sons Thomas, Joshua, Daniel, Joseph, Jonathan, Jacob, Abraham, Isaac, Richard & John Jester; heirs of dau. Mary Jester. Exec'r, son John Jester. Wits., Jno. Brinckle, Grace Russell & Joseph Russell. [No prob.]. Arch. vol. A27, page 49.

Dawson, Thomas. Will. Made Dec. 17, 1753. Heirs: wife Margaret; son Richard; dau. Sarah. Exec'x, wife. Wits., Matthew Lowber, Henry Camel, Robert Smith. Prob. Jan. 12, 1754. Arch. vol. A13, pages 115-116. Reg. of Wills, Liber K, folios 87-88. Note:—Arch. vol. A13, page 116 shows Margaret, the widow, later married Benjamin Parson.

Brown, James. Will. Made Jan. 4, 1755. Duck Creek. Heirs: wife Margret; son-in-law Joshua David. Exec'rs, wife Margret & her son-in-law John Carror. Wits., Theophilus Lyson, William West, Henry Farson. Prob. Feb. 13, 1754/5. Arch. vol. A6, page 47. Reg. of Wills, Liber K, folio 102.

Darling, James. Will. Made Sept. 5, 1753. Duck Creek. Heirs: sons William, James & Richard; dau. Sarah. Exec'rs, sons William & James. Wits., Richard Darling, Daniel Evans. Prob. Feb. 14, 1754. Arch. vol. A12, page 188. Reg. of Wills, Liber K, folio 89.

Johnson, John. Will. Made Jan. 3, 1754. Heirs: wife Mary; sons George, James, David; daus. Jane (wife of Samuel Nicholas, Jr.) & Mary; son-in-law Samuel Nicholas. Exec'x, wife Mary. Wits., John Clayton, Mark Smith, James Clayton. Prob. Feb. 14, 1754. Arch. vol. A27, page 77. Reg. of Wills, Liber K, folio 92.

Allen, Charles. Will. Made Feb. 23, 1754. Heirs: wife Patience; dau. Patience. Exec'x, wife Patience. Wits., William Shurmer, William Clark, Matthew Boogs. Prob. March 11, 1754. Arch. vol. A1, page 79. Reg. of Wills, Liber K, folio 93.

Craige, Isabella. Widow. Will. Made Feb. 11, 1754. Heirs: daus. Jane Craige & Mary Walker; granddau. Isabella Walker. Exec'rs, dau. Jane Craige & son-in-law William Walker. Wits., Samuel Harris, John Caten, John Chambers. Prob. March 21, 1754. Arch. vol. A11, page 156. Reg. of Wills, Liber K, folio 91.

Gorrell, Ruth. Widow. Will. Made Dec. 6, 1753. Heirs: dau. Sarah; niece Ann Warfield; nephews Elisha Warfield, Benjamin & Nicholas Vining; son-in-law James Gorrell; father Nicholas Ridgely, Esq.; bro. Charles Greenberry Ridgely; sisters Sarah & Elizabeth Ridgely. Exec'rs, father & bro. John Vining. Guardian, Benjamin Chew. Wits., Richard

Wells, Mary Vining, Mary Rue. Codicil—Feb. 25, 1754. Wits., Mary Vining, Richard Wells, Mary Rue. Prob. April 8, 1754. Arch. vol. A19, page 194. Reg. of Wills, Liber K, folio 92.

McCabe, James. Will (nunc.). Made May 8, 1754. Heirs: Mary Diskel; Sara Cunickem, dau. of Mary Diskel. Wits., Francis Meredith, Thomas Ellis, Sarah Cusins, Marget Darling. Arch. vol. A32, page 87.

Horseman, Samuel. Admin. of, to Mary Horseman. May 29, 1754. Arch. vol. A25, page 37.

Morgan, Brian. Will. Made June 6, 1754. Heirs: sons James & Patrick Morgan. Exec'rs, Patrick McVay, Francis Maryday. Wits., Peter Stoutt, David Leech. Arch. vol. A36, page 128.

Brooks, James. Will. Made July 16, 1754. Heirs: wife Annah; dau. Rachel; son Daniel; Benjamin Brooks; mother unnamed. Exec'rs, John Brooks & Vincent Lockerman. Wits., Emanuel Stoutt, David Giffing. Prob. July 22, 1754. Arch. vol. A6, pages 8-9. Reg. of Wills, Liber K, folio 95.

Fleming, Robert. Will. Made April 20, 1751. Heirs: wife Aliss; dau. Fillis [Phillis]; Margarett Barnhill, dau. of David Barnhill; Martha & Hester Fleming, daus. of George Fleming; Robert, son of Alexander Fleming; David, son of John Fleming; Elizabeth, dau. of William Fleming; Hannah, dau. of James Fleming; bro.-in-law David Barnhill; bros. & sisters unnamed. Exec'r, David Barnhill. Wits., Daniel Robisson, Elizabeth Robisson, Sarah Robisson (later Sarah Warren). Prob. Aug. 11, 1754. Arch. vol. A17, pages 196-197. Reg. of Wills, Liber K, folio 94.

Tilton, Joseph. Will. Made Feb. 8, 1754. Heirs: wife Rachel; daus. Ann, Rachel, Sarah. Exec'rs, wife Rachel & James Morris. Wits., Thomas Tilton, Mary Webb, Nathaniel Wells. Prob. Aug. 14, 1754. Arch. vol. A50, pages 149-150. Reg. of Wills, Liber K, folio 93. Note:—Arch. vol. A50, page 150 shows Rachel, the widow, later married Richard Hoff.

Carpenter, Mary. Widow. Will. Made June 26, 1754. Heirs: son Richard; daus. Eliz. & Mary Carpenter, Sarah Upton; granddau. Elizabeth Upton, dau. of Moses Upton. Exec'r, cousin William Carpenter. Wits., Isaac England, Ebenezer Jones, Mary Rush. Prob. Aug. 17, 1754. Arch. vol. A7, pages 231-233. Reg. of Wills, Liber K, folios 93-94.

Deweese, Samuel. Admin. of, to Rachel Deweese. Aug. 29, 1754. Arch. vol. A14, page 51.

Brinckle, Esther [Hester]. Dau. of Thomas, dec'd. Will. Made Sept. 17, 1754. Heirs: sister Mary Campbell; mother Mary Plesonton. Exec'x, mother. Prob. Oct. 10, 1754. Wits., Stephen Paradee, Nimrod Maxwell, Annah Maxwell. Arch. vol. A5, pages 167-168. Reg. of Wills, Liber G, appendix 5. Note:—The first unwitnessed will is recorded in Arch. vol. A5, page 168 & Reg. of Wills, Liber K, folio 136.

Hanson, Timothy. Yeoman. Will. Made July 31, 1754. Little Creek Hd. Heirs: sons Timothy, Samuel, Thomas; daus. Mary & Elizabeth Hanson & Rebecca Train, wife of James Train; children of dau. Susanna Course; children of dau. Barbara. Exec'r, son Thomas. Wits., Eliz. Jenkins, Ann Chicken, Hugh Shannon. Prob. Oct. 14, 1754. Arch. vol. A21, page 218. Reg. of Wills, Liber K, folios 95-96.

Brinckle, Daniel. Will. Made Sept. 28, 1754. Little Creek Hd. Heirs: wife Kesiah; bros. Curtis, Peter, Richard; Ezekiel, Peter & Susanna, children of bro. Richard; sister Elizabeth Davis; cousins, Phebe Bessex [Beswick], William Brinckle, Peter Brinckle, Margaret Vanburkeloe & Mary Bessex [Beswick]. Exec'x, wife Kesiah. Wits., Robert Hall, Mark Hirons, John Brinckle. Prob. Nov. 4, 1754. Arch. vol. A5, pages 163-164. Reg. of Wills, Liber K, folio 97. Note:— Arch. vol. A5, page 164 shows Kesiah, the widow, later married Isaac Carty; also shows John Hirons as a child of Charles Hirons. Will mentions mother Elizabeth Brinckle, dec'd.

Housman, John. Esq. Will. Made March 7, 1754. Heirs: friends John Miller, William Killin, Benjamin Chew. Exec'r, Benjamin Chew. Wits., Thomas Alford, Thomas Parke, Richard Wells. Prob. Nov. 12, 1754. Arch. vol. A25, page 41. Reg. of Wills, Liber K, folio 98.

Stewart, John (alias Hester Releigh). Plasterer. Admin. of, to William Wells, innholder. Nov. 19, 1754. Reg. of Wills, Liber K, folio 104.

Hales, Joseph. Will. Made June 27, 1754. Duck Creek. Heirs: nephew Joseph Nock, son of sister Barthia; cousin Thomas Hill; sisters Martha Clark, Barthia Nock, Rachel Liston; son-in-law Richard Holliday; Joseph Jenkins, son of Jabez;

friend William Hammans; Robert Holliday, Hannah Jenkins, Susanna Hammans, Richard Holliday, Mary Holliday, Joseph Holliday, children of late wife. Exec'rs, son-in-law Rob. Holliday, Thomas Hammans. Wits., William Farson, Roger Pugh, Jane Farson. Prob. Nov. 21, 1754. Arch. vol. A21, pages 76-77. Reg. of Wills, Liber K, folios 98-99.

Driskle, Dennis. Will. Made Nov. 15, 1754. Duck Creek. Heirs: wife Mary; dau. Susanna; son Joseph. Exec'x, wife Mary. Wits., Daniel Evans, Isaac Hurlock, William Darling. Prob. Nov. 23, 1754. Arch. vol. A15, page 87. Reg. of Wills, Liber K, folio 99.

Smith, Henry. Will (copy). Made Nov. 12, 1754. Heirs: bro. James; rest of bros., sisters & mother unnamed. Exec'r, bro. James. Wits., William Wheeler, Mary Skinner. Prob. Dec. 3, 1754. Arch. vol. A47, page 45. Reg. of Wills, Liber K, folio 100.

Jones, David. Admin. of, to Timothy Irons, D. B. N. Dec. 11, 1754. Arch. vol. A27, page 154. Reg. of Wills, Liber K, folios 103-104.

Jones, Griffith. Minister. Admin. of, to Jeanet Jones & John Jones. Dec. 11, 1754. Reg. of Wills, Liber K, folio 104.

Green, Thomas. Will. Made May 5, 1753. Dover. Heirs: wife Elizabeth; youngest dau. of bro. George Green. Exec'x, wife Elizabeth. Wits., Sarah Johnson, Samuel Johnson, Robert Willcocks. Prob. Jan. 1, 1755. Arch. vol. A20, pages 113-114. Reg. of Wills, Liber K, folios 100-101.

James, Nathaniel. Mariner. Admin. of, to James James, yeoman. Jan. 12, 1756. Arch. vol. A26, pages 92-94. Reg. of Wills, Liber K, folio 126.

Smith, Henry. Will. Made April 19, 1754. Heirs: wife Mary Ann; son David; dau. Rachel. Exec'x, wife Mary Ann. Wits., Patrick Cumings, Daniel Cumings, Mary Cumings. Prob. Jan. 25, 1755. Arch. vol. A47, pages 46-47. Reg. of Wills, Liber K, folio 101.

Clark, John. Farmer. Admin. of, to Elizabeth Clark, widow. Jan. 25, 1755. Reg. of Wills, Liber K, folios 104-105. Note:— Arch. vol. A9, pages 4-5 shows Elizabeth, the widow, later married Peter Lowber.

Freeman, Joseph. Farmer. Admin. of, to Elizabeth Freeman, widow. Feb. 4, 1755. Reg. of Wills, Liber K, folio 105. Note: —Arch. vol. A18, pages 123-124 show Elizabeth, the widow, later married Philip McKean [McCain]; also show dau. Sarah & sons Samuel, Charles & Joseph Freeman.

Ridgely, Nicholas. Will. Made Feb. 15, 1755. Heirs: wife Mary; son Charles Greenberry Ridgely; daus. Sarah & Elizabeth Ridgely; grandchildren Benjamin & Nicholas Vining & Sarah Gorrell; dau.-in-law Mary Vining; granddau. Ann Warfield; grandsons Elisha, Nicholas, Benjamin & Joshua Warfield, children of dau. Rebecca Warfield. Exec'rs, wife & son Charles. Wits., Benjamin Chew, Richard Wells, Henry Bickerton. Prob. March 3, 1755. Arch. vol. A43, pages 226, 228-232. Reg. of Wills, Liber K, folio 103.

Chaimbers, Harry. Admin. of, to James Gray, cordwainer. March 10, 1755. Reg. of Wills, Liber K, folio 105.

Train, Mary. Will (copy). Made Dec. 23, 1754. Heirs: daus. Easter & Bersheba Train. Exec'rs, daus. Easter & Bersheba. Wits., Samuel Johns, John Bush, Elizabeth Mackinley. Codicil, sons Hamilton & James Train; daus. Sarah Johnson & Mary Caldwell, wife of Joseph Caldwell. Prob. March 21, 1755. Arch. vol. A51, page 61. Reg. of Wills, Liber K, folio 107.

Durborow, Hugh. Admin. of, to Elizabeth Durborow, widow, & son Daniel. March 24, 1755. Arch. vol. A15, pages 162, 164-165. Reg. of Wills, Liber K, folio 108.

Boyle, William. Admin. of, to Eve Boyle, widow, & John Clayton, Jr. March 26, 1755. Arch. vol. A5, page 71. Reg. of Wills, Liber K, folios 108-109.

Coffy, Hugh. Admin. of, to Simon Vanwinckle. April 4, 1755. Reg. of Wills, Liber K, folio 109. Note:—Arch. vol. A9, page 185 shows this acct. later administered by John Rees who married Lurania, widow of Simon Vanwinckle.

Scot, James. Admin. of, to Frances Scot, widow. April 5, 1755. Reg. of Wills, Liber K, folios 109-110.

Fitzsimons, Thomas. Admin. of, to Shockley Fitzsimons & Elisha Morris. April 7, 1755. Arch. vol. A17, page 161. Reg. of Wills, Liber K, folio 110.

Hammans, William. Will. Made June 4, 1755. Duck Creek (town of Salisbury). Heirs: wife Mary; son Thomas Hammans; daus. Mary Smedly, Martha Yarnall, Sarah Pugh; grandsons William Smedly, William Yarnall, William Pugh. Exec'r, son Thomas. Wits., David Offley, Ebenezer Jones, Thomas Brown. Prob. April 15, 1755. Arch. vol. A21, page 188. Reg. of Wills, Liber K, folios 110-111.

Watson, Thomas. Admin. of, to Margaret Watson, widow. April 18, 1755. Reg. of Wills, Liber K, folios 111-112.

Hillyard, Martha. Spinster. Admin. of, to Charles Hillyard. May 3, 1755. Reg. of Wills, Liber K, folio 112.

Mason, Abraham. Will. Made May 1, 1754. Heirs: wife Jean; sons Abraham & Isaac. Exec'r, friend Edward Dill. Wits., James White, John Brown, William Carter. Prob. May 14, 1755. Arch. vol. A33, page 220. Reg. of Wills, Liber K, folios 112-113.

Greenlee, John. Admin. of, to Priscilla Greenlee, widow. May 27, 1755. Reg. of Wills, Liber K, folio 113.

Marim, John. Will. Made May 19, 1755. Heirs: wife Mary; daus. Ruhamah, Mary, Elizabeth; bro. Charles Marim; father-in-law Nathaniel Luff. Exec'x, wife Mary. Wits., John Brinckle, Wm. Revell, Elizabeth Haines. Prob. June 6, 1755. Arch. vol. A33, pages 182-183. Reg. of Wills, Liber K, folios 113-114. Note:—Arch. vol. A33, page 183 shows John Skidmore married the widow.

Rash, Samuel. Yeoman. Will (nunc.). Made June 14, 1755. Heirs: sons Henry, John; dau. Mary. Wits., Benjamin Forkham, bro. Joseph Rash, sister Anna Rash. Prob. June 18, 1755. Arch. vol. A42, pages 72-73. Reg. of Wills, Liber K, folio 115.

Rash, Samuel. Yeoman. Admin. of, to Anna Rash, widow. June 23, 1755. Reg. of Wills, Liber K, folios 114-115.

Offley, David. Will (nunc.). Made July 19, 1755. Duck Creek. Heir: wife unnamed. Wits., Charles Green, Mary Hammans. Prob. Aug. 2, 1755. Arch. vol. A38, pages 107-108. Reg. of Wills, Liber K, folio 119. Note:—Arch. vol. A38, page 108 shows Mercy, the widow, later married Howell Buckingham.

McKeney, John. Will. Made June 5, 1755. Heirs: cousins Samuel Tom, William Tom, John McNeal, Elizabeth Campbell, James McDaniel. Exec'r, James McDaniel. Wits., Thomas Clark, John Ladden, Margaret Ladden. Prob. Aug. 13, 1755. Arch. vol. A32, page 213. Reg. of Wills, Liber K, folio 115.

Manlove, Luke. Will. Made April 10, 1755. Heirs: wife Alce; son Emanuel; daus. Elizabeth Frashar, Mary Pratt, Grace Dickenson; granddau. Sarah Moleston. Exec'x, wife Alce. Wits., Jonathan Manlove, Wateman Treppett, Mary Davis. Prob. Aug. 15, 1755. Arch. vol. A32, pages 34-35. Reg. of Wills, Liber K, folio 118.

Clark, Maschall. Farmer. Will. Made June 16, 1755. Heirs: wife Elizabeth; dau. Ruama; sons Nehemiah, Hezekiah, Joshua, Race, David & Benjamin Clark. Exec'rs, wife Elizabeth, son Nehemiah. Wits., Stephen Durborow, Rachel Freeman. Prob. Aug. 20, 1755. Arch. vol. A9, pages 53 & 55. Reg. of Wills, Liber K, folio 116.

West, Thomas. Yeoman. Admin. of, to Mary West, widow. Aug. 21, 1755. Arch. vol. A54, page 30. Reg. of Wills, Liber K, folio 120.

Morgan, George. Will. Made Aug. 12, 1755. Heirs: wife Martha; sons Jacob, Robert, George; daus. Elizabeth, Hannah, Mary, Grace; son-in-law John Boyd, son of John Boyd, dec'd. Exec'rs, wife Martha & bro. John Clayton, Esq. Wits., Mark Smith, James Clayton, Robert Buchanan. Prob. Aug. 27, 1755. Arch. vol. A36, pages 145-148. Reg. of Wills, Liber K, folio 117.

Maxwell, James. Yeoman. Admin. of, to Elinor Maxwell, widow. Sept. 10, 1755. Arch. vol. A34, page 83. Reg. of Wills, Liber K, folio 121.

Rowan, William. Laborer. Admin. of, to Elizabeth Rowan, widow. Oct. 1, 1755. Reg. of Wills, Liber K, folio 120.

Morgan, Martha. Widow. Admin. of, to John Clayton. Nov. 14, 1755. Arch. vol. A36, pages 160-161. Reg. of Wills, Liber K, folio 121.

Dunn, Joseph. Admin. of, to William & David McIlvaine, merchants. Nov. 14, 1755. Arch. vol. A15, pages 117-118. Reg. of Wills, Liber K, folio 125.

Wallace, Barbara. Will. Made Oct. 19, 1754. Heirs: sons Matthew, Solomon, William, Benjamin, Ruben, Josiah, Joshua; daus. Deborah Williams, Hannah Caldwell. Exec'r, son Joshua. Wits., Richard Lockwood, Mary Horn, William Wallace. Prob. Nov. 21, 1755. Arch. vol. A52, pages 210-211. Reg. of Wills, Liber K, folio 122.

Wood, John. Yeoman. Admin. of, to Joseph Wood, yeoman. Nov. 25, 1755. Arch. vol. A56, page 68. Reg. of Wills, Liber K, folios 122-123.

Hudson, Daniel. Admin. of, to Mary Hudson, widow, & Joshua Brown. Dec. 16, 1755. Arch. vol. A25, page 103. Reg. of Wills, Liber K, folio 123.

Emmerson, John. Will. Made Feb. 26, 1755. Heirs: wife Unity; sons Govey, Michael, Jonathan, Vincent. Exec'rs, wife Unity & son Jonathan. Wits., Waitman Sipple, Mark Manlove, Matthew Jarrard. Prob. Jan. 10, 1756. Arch. vol. A16, page 138. Reg. of Wills, Liber K, folios 124-125.

Martin, George. Admin. of, to Elizabeth Martin, widow, & Thomas Collins. Jan. 12, 1756. Arch. vol. A33, pages 207-208. Reg. of Wills, Liber K, folios 123-124. Note:—Arch. vol. A24, page 25 shows this acct. later administered by Mary Raymond, adm'x of Charles Hillyard, who with his wife Elizabeth and Thomas Collins was adm'r of the estate of George Martin.

James, Nathaniel. Mariner. Admin. of, to James James, yeoman. Jan. 12, 1756. Arch. vol. A26, pages 92-94. Reg. of Wills, Liber K, folio 126.

Shaw, William. Yeoman. Admin. of, to Ephriam Shaw, yeoman. Jan. 17, 1756. Arch. vol. A45, page 218. Reg. of Wills, Liber K, folio 126.

Smith, Benjamin. Admin. of, to Mary Smith, widow. Feb. 11, 1756. Reg. of Wills, Liber K, folio 127.

Maddin, Patrick. Admin. of, to Elizabeth Maddin, widow. Feb. 16, 1756. Reg. of Wills, Liber K, folio 127.

Cole, Spencer. Practioner. Will. Made Jan. 23, 1756. Heirs: wife Sary; son Spencer; daus. unnamed. Exec'x, wife Sary. Wits., William Shirley, John Furchos, John Tucker, Jr. Prob. Feb .23, 1756. Arch. vol. A9, pages 211-212. Reg. of Wills, Liber K, folios 127-128 & Liber L, folio 5. Note:—Arch. vol. A9, page 212 shows Reynear Williams, adm'r, D. B. N.

Edenfield, William. Admin. of, to Ann Edenfield, widow. Feb. 24, 1756. Reg. of Wills, Liber K, folios 128-129.

Moore, James. Admin. of, to Mary Moore, widow. Feb. 25, 1756. Reg. of Wills, Liber K, folio 129. Note:—Arch. vol. A36, pages 32-33 show Mary, the widow, later married Fretwell Wright; also show children, Ruth, Martha, Thomas.

Booth, Thomas. Admin. of, to Andrew Caldwell. Feb. 25, 1756. Reg. of Wills, Liber K, folios 129-130.

Vanwinckle, Simon. Will. Made Dec. 18, 1755. Duck Creek. Heirs: wife Lureaney; son Simon; dau. Lureaney; other children unnamed; mother Gean Vanwinckle. Exec'rs, wife & friend David Clark. Trustees, bro.-in-law William Grieer, friend William Killen. Wits., John Vanwinckle, John Vangasken, Patrick Martin. Prob. Feb. 27, 1756. Arch. vol. A52, pages 25, 27-28. Reg. of Wills, Liber K, folio 131. Note:— Arch. vol. A52, pages 27-28 show Lurania, the widow, later married John Rees.

Cummins, Robert. Admin. of, to Patrick Cummins. March 3, 1756. Arch. vol. A12, pages 134-135.

James, James. Yeoman. Admin. of, to James Edwards, yeoman. March 3, 1756. Arch. vol. A26, page 90. Reg. of Wills, Liber K, folio 130.

James, Nathaniel. Admin. of, to James Edwards, yeoman. March 3, 1756. Arch. vol. A26, pages 92-94. Reg. of Wills, Liber K, folios 130-131.

Nickerson, Joshua. Yeoman. Will. Made March 8, 1756. Dover Hd. Heirs: sons John, George; dau. Ruhamah Marim, wife of Charles Marim; grandson John Marim, son of Charles & Ruhamah Marim; granddau. Elizabeth Marim, dau. of Charles & Ruhamah Marim. Exec'rs, Charles Marim &

George Nickerson. Trustee, Andrew Doz. Wits., James Carben, Daniel Lewis, John Paradee, John Cockram. Prob. March 17, 1756. Arch. vol. A37, page 239. Reg. of Wills, Liber K, folios 132-133.

Sudrey, John. Yeoman. Admin. of, to John Clayton, Esq. April 7, 1756. Arch. vol. A49, page 114. Reg. of Wills, Liber K, folio 132.

Tomlin, Nathaniel. Carpenter. Will. Made Jan. 27, 1755. Heirs: wife Mary; sons Covel, Jacob, Isaac, Nathaniel; daus. Mary, Margaret, Neomy. Exec'x, wife Mary. Wits., Mark Manlove, Jacob Gray, John Tucker, Jr. Prob. April 10, 1756. Arch. vol. A50, page 178. Reg. of Wills, Liber K, folio 134.

Jones, Benjamin. Yeoman. Admin. of, to Margaret Jones, widow. April 22, 1756. Arch. vol. A27, page 134. Reg. of Wills, Liber K, folio 135.

Barnet, Thomas. Admin. of, to Thomas Littleton, yeoman. May 7, 1756. Arch. vol. A2, page 210. Reg. of Wills, Liber K, folios 135-136.

Brinckle, Hester [Esther]. Will. Made Sept. 13, 1754. Heirs: sister Mary Campbell; mother Mary Pleasenton. Exec'x, mother Mary Pleasenton. Wits., Stephen Paradee, Nimrod Maxwell, Anna Maxwell. Prob. Oct. 10, 1756. Arch. vol. A5, pages 167-169. Reg. of Wills, Liber K, folio 136. Note:— Will mentions father Thomas Brinckle, dec'd; Arch. vol. A5, page 169 shows Mary Maxwell, nee Pleasanton, as exec'x.

Wilson, William. Yeoman. Will. Made April 29, 1756. Heirs: wife Ann; sons William, John, George, Peter, Jacob; dau. Jean Hopkens, Abigail, Rechel, Ruth & Sarah Wilson. Exec'x, wife Ann. Wits., Thomas Muncy, James Wilson, Richard Vinson. Prob. June 5, 1756. Arch. vol. A56, page 23. Reg. of Wills, Liber K, folios 137-138.

Perkins, Thomas. Yeoman. Admin. of, to Elizabeth Perkins, widow. June 10, 1756. Reg. of Wills, Liber K, folio 137.

McKenny, Eleazer. Yeoman. Admin. of, to Amos McKenny, yeoman. June 18, 1756. Reg. of Wills, Liber K, folio 138.

Barnet, Samuel. Yeoman. Admin. of, to Elizabeth Barnet, widow. June 21, 1756. Reg. of Wills, Liber K, folios 138-139. Note: —Arch. vol. A2, pages 207-208 show Elizabeth later married Patrick Williams.

Potter, Parismus. Will. Made June 20, 1756. Murtherkill Hd. Heirs: wife Eleanor; son James; other children unnamed. Exec'x, wife Eleanor. Wits., Sarah Potter, Martin Hardin. Prob. July 24, 1756. Arch. vol. A41, page 16. Reg. of Wills, Liber K, folio 140.

Dunlap, Matthew. Admin. of, to Peter Dunlap, yeoman. July 30, 1756. Arch. vol. A13, page 181. Reg. of Wills, Liber K, folio 139.

Dunlap, Allen. Admin. of, to Peter Dunlap. July 30, 1756. Arch. vol. A13, page 179. Reg. of Wills, Liber K, folio 139.

Potter, James. Yeoman. Will. Made Oct. 31, 1754. Murderkill Hd. Heirs: wife Ann; bro. Parismus; sisters Sarah & Rechel. Exec'rs, wife Ann & Thomas Hardin. Wits., Edmund Hardin, Sarah Hardin, Susanna Gano. Prob. July 31, 1756. Arch. vol. A41, pages 5-6. Reg. of Wills, Liber K, folios 140-141.

Hackney, John. Will. Made . . . 1756. Heirs: sons Joseph; daus. Vebey, Cattorn, Rosener; wife unnamed. Exec'rs, son Joseph & wife. Wits., Allen Melvill, John Reed, Thomas Wietet. Prob. Aug. 11, 1756. Arch. vol. A21, page 59. Reg. of Wills, Liber K, folio 141.

Mahanna, John. Yeoman. Admin. of, to Mary Mahanna, widow. Aug. 19, 1756. Reg. of Wills, Liber K, folio 142. Note:— Arch. vol. A33, page 70 mentions heirs, Sarah, Mary, Benjamin, Elizabeth, John, William, Sophia & Eleanor Mahanna, Henrietta Smith & Mariah Munt.

Wallace, Joshua. Yeoman. Admin. of, to Reuben Wallace. Aug. 28, 1756. Arch. vol. A53, page 1. Reg. of Wills, Liber K, folio 142.

Mant, Honour. Spinster. Admin. of, to Mary Mant. Sept. 13, 1756. Reg. of Wills, Liber K, folio 143.

Rees, Margaret. Admin. of, to David Rees, yeoman. Sept. 13, 1756. Reg. of Wills, Liber K, folios 143-144. Note:—Arch. vol. A43, page 23 shows the following names, William, David, Hannah & Jonathan Rees.

Medcalf [Metcalf], John. Will. Made Sept. 16, 1756. Dover Hd. Heirs: wife Mary; children unnamed. Exec'rs, wife Mary & Nicholas Loockerman. Wits., Hugh Torbert, Maurice McBride, Richard Butler. Prob. Sept. 21, 1756. Arch. vol. A34, page 235. Reg. of Wills, Liber K, folio 144.

Howell, Joseph. Will. Made Aug. 13, 1756. Murderkill Hd. Heirs: wife Priscilla; sons James & Sabrit; daus. Sarah, Priscilla, Comfort & Mary Manwaring. Exec'x, wife Priscilla. Wits., William Manlove, Chilion Miller, Wren Forkham. Prob. Sept. 28, 1756. Arch. vol. A25, pages 69-70. Reg. of Wills, Liber K, folio 145.

Annet, Robert. Yeoman. Admin. of, to Penelope Annet, widow. Oct. 8, 1756. Reg. of Wills, Liber K, folio 145. Note:—Arch. vol. A1, pages 220-221 show Penelope, the widow, later married Robert Caton; also mentions Gove Annett, Penelopy Annett & Mary McDaniel, wife of James McDaniel.

Uptegrove, William. Will. Made Sept. 1, 1756. Mispillion Hd. Heirs: wife Sary; daus. Mary & Sary; cousins Sary & Elizabeth Uptegrove. Exec'rs, wife Sary & bro. John Uptegrove. Wits., Henry Hermoson, William Daus, Samuel Merydith. Prob. Oct. 11, 1756. Arch. vol. A51, pages 202-203. Reg. of Wills, Liber K, folios 145-146. Note:—Arch. vol. A51, page 203 shows Sarah, the widow, later married Robert Clifton.

Jones, Philip. Admin. of, to William Leatherbury. Oct. 11, 1756. Reg. of Wills, Liber K, folio 147.

Doney, Peter. Yeoman. Admin. of, to Rachael Doney, widow. Oct. 15, 1756. Reg. of Wills, Liber K, folio 146.

Swancey, Barbara. Will. Made Sept. 14, 1756. Heirs: daus. Margaret Gragg, Elinor Ellet, Barbara Reed, Lydia Sturgen, Ann Ellet; son Francis Ferguson. Exec'r, son Francis Fargeson. Wits., Thomas Clark, Archibald Cary, Thomas Smother. Prob. Oct. 19, 1756. Arch. vol. A49, pages 135-136. Reg. of Wills, Liber K, folio 147.

Wilson, George. Will. Made Aug. 31, 1756. Heirs: wife unnamed; sons Derdin, William, George; daus. Ann Hunn, Mary Hunn, Margaret Wilson. Exec'x, wife. Appraisers, Govey & Jonathan Emmerson. Wits., Ezekiel Nock, Jabez Jenkins. Codicil names sons-in-law Jonathan & Renear Hunn as alternate exec'rs. Wits., Thomas Nock. Made Sept. 1, 1756. Prob. Oct. 23, 1756. Arch. vol. A55, pages 203-204. Reg. of Wills, Liber K, folio 148. Note:—Arch. vol. A55, page 204 shows Patience married Daniel Robisson.

Murray, Bryan. Will. Made Oct. 14, 1756. Little Creek Hd. Heirs: wife unnamed; son Henry; daus. Elizabeth & Modlin. Exec'rs, wife & son Henry. Wits., James Carben, John Barns. Prob. Nov. 6, 1756. Arch. vol. A37, pages 112-113. Reg. of wills, Liber K, folios 148-149. Note:—Arch. vol. A37, page 113 shows Ann Murray as surviving exec'x; also mentions Maudlin, Perry & Alexander Holland.

Murray, Henry. A minor. Admin. of, to Ann Murray, mother, widow. Nov. 6, 1756. Arch. vol. A37, page 114. Reg. of Wills, Liber K, folio 149.

Silliven [Sullivan], William. Yeoman. Will. Made Nov. 4, 1756. Heirs: friends Caleb Sipple & John Newell. Exec'r, John Newell. Wits., Isaac Smith, Robert Bedwell, Margret Smith. Prob. Nov. 10, 1756. Arch. vol. A46, page 46 & vol. A49, pages 145-146. Reg. of Wills, Liber K, folio 150.

Giles, James. Yeoman. Admin. of, to Thomas Nixon, merchant. Nov. 13, 1756. Reg. of Wills, Liber K, folios 150-151.

England, Isaac. Carpenter. Will. Made July 13, 1756. Heirs: wife Ann; sons Isaac, Jacob, David, James; daus. Ann, Mary, Martha. Exec'x, wife Ann. Wits., William Seeds, Sarah Seeds, Mark Moran. Prob. Nov. 18, 1756. Arch. vol. A16, page 201. Reg. of Wills, Liber K, folios 143 & 151.

Robinson, Jeroboam. Admin. of, to John Gilbert and wife Elizabeth, late Elizabeth Robinson. Nov. 24, 1756. Arch. vol. A44, pages 56-57.

Bennet, Elinor. Admin. of, to John Clayton, Esq. Dec. 3, 1756. Reg. of Wills, Liber K, folio 152.

Smith, William. Yeoman. Admin. of, to Rebecca Smith, widow, & William Watson. Dec. 6, 1756. Arch. vol. A47, pages 192-194. Reg. of Wills, Liber K, folios 152-153.

Jordan, John. Yeoman. Admin. of, to Beatrice Jordan, widow. Dec. 15, 1756. Arch. vol. A28, page 45. Reg. of Wills, Liber K, folio 153.

Clampit, Ezekiel. Will. Made Nov. 15, 1756. Heirs: wife Elizabeth; dau. Nancy; nephew John Clampit, son of William Clampit. Exec'rs, wife Elizabeth & bro. William Clampit. Wits., Thomas Clark, Henry Clampit, Ebenezer Clampit. Prob. Dec. 23, 1756. Arch. vol. A8, pages 200-201. Reg. of Wills, Liber K, folio 153. Note:—Arch. vol. A8, page 201 shows Elizabeth, the widow, later married Francis Murray.

Needham, Daniel. Yeoman. Admin. of, to Susannah Needham, widow. Dec. 28, 1756. Arch. vol. A37, page 142. Reg. of Wills, Liber K, folio 154.

Vannette [Venetta], James. Admin. of, to Elizabeth Vannetta, widow. Jan. 8, 1757. Arch. vol. A52, page 7. Reg. of Wills, Liber K, folios 154-155.

Lewis, David. Yeoman. Admin. of, to Rachel Lewis & John Lewis. Jan. 10, 1757. Reg. of Wills, Liber K, folio 155.

Greenwood, Fennes [Phenice]. Will. Made Oct. 28, 1756. Heirs: daus. Sarah & Rachael; grandsons Abel & Jeremiah Rees; bro. John Greenwood; Jonas Greenwood; Elizabeth .Buck. Exec'rs, daus. Sarah & Rachel. Wits., Alexander McFarland, James Gilespy. Prob. Jan. 27, 1757. Arch. vol. A20, page 158. Reg. of Wills, Liber K, folios 155-156.

Rees, Jeremiah. Will. Made Dec. 12, 1756. Little Creek Hd. Heirs: wife unnamed; son Abel; four daus. unnamed; bros. Thomas & John Rees; niece Hannah Rees. Exec'rs, son Abel & bro. Thomas. Wits., Thomas Murphy, Catherine David, John Lewis. Prob. Jan. 31, 1757. Arch. vol. A43, pages 1-3. Reg. of Wills, Liber K, folio 156.

Hinds, William. Yeoman. Admin. of, to John Hinds, yeoman. Feb. 9, 1757. Reg. of Wills, Liber K, folio 157.

Hinds, Mary. Widow. Admin. of, to John Hinds, yeoman. Feb. 9, 1757. Reg. of Wills, Liber K, folio 157.

Reily, Hugh. Laborer. Admin. of, to Samuel McCall, practitioner. Feb. 10, 1757. Arch. vol. A43, page 69. Reg. of Wills, Liber K, folios 157-158.

Allen, John. Yeoman. Admin. of, to Sarah Allen, widow. Feb. 10, 1757. Arch. vol. A1, page 81. Reg. of Wills, Liber K, folio 158.

Jackson, Richard. Yeoman. Admin. of, to Elizabeth Jackson & Margaret Wallace. Feb. 15, 1757. Reg. of Wills, Liber K, folio 158. Note:—Arch. vol. A26, pages 29-31 show John Voshall & wife Elizabeth & Richard Lockwood & wife Margaret as adm'rs; also mention Moses, Ezekiel & Esther Jackson & George Horn.

Wright, Margaret. Will. Made Jan. 19, 1757. Duck Creek. Heirs: sons Philip Denny, Christopher Denny, Evan Denny, John Denny, Joseph Denny; daus. Rebecca Hillyard, Mary Foster; dau.-in-law Sarah Denny; grandson James Pearson. Exec'rs, sons Joseph & Christopher Denny. Trustee, son Joseph Denny. Wits., Benjamin Jones, Jacobus Hawkins, Philip Hillyard. Prob. Feb. 16, 1757. Arch. vol. A56, page 157. Reg. of Wills, Liber K, folios 158-159. Note:—Will mentions dau. Susannah, dec'd.

Blackshear, Randal. Yeoman. Admin. of, to Ebe Blackshear, widow. Feb. 21, 1757. Arch. vol. A4, page 98. Reg. of Wills, Liber K, folio 159.

Wright, William. Farmer. Will. Made April 16, 1752. Heirs: wife Margaret; dau. Catherine Draughton; sons-in-law John & Thomas Foster, John Draughton; grandsons John & Wright Draughton. Exec'r, son-in-law John Draughton. Wits., James Morris, Elizabeth Talbert, William Morris, Jr. Prob. Feb. 23, 1757. Arch. vol. A56, pages 160-161. Reg. of Wills, Liber K, folio 160.

David, John. Admin. of, to James Hunter and wife Mary, late Mary David. Feb. 24, 1757. Arch. vol. A12, pages 222-223 & 230. Note:—Arch. vol. A12, page 230 mentions Joshua David & his guardian, Robert Willcocks.

Johnson, Samuel. Admin. of, to Stephen Durborow and wife Sarah, late Sarah Johnson. Feb. 24, 1757. Arch. vol. A27, pages 103-104.

Rash, Samuel. Admin. of, to James Clayton. Feb. 24, 1757. Arch. vol. A42, page 74.

Snow, John. Yeoman. Admin. of, to Sarah Snow, widow. March 31, 1757. Arch. vol. A48, page 14. Reg. of Wills, Liber K, folios 160-161.

Denny, Philip. Yeoman. Admin. of, to Margaret Denny, widow. April 19, 1757. Reg. of Wills, Liber K, folio 161. Note:— Arch. vol. A13, page 237 shows Margaret, widow, later married Philemon Owens.

Gray, Jacob. Will. Made April 6, 1757. Heirs: wife Rachael; sons John & William; daus. Rodah & Elizabeth. Exec'rs, wife Rachael & bro. Andrew Gray. Wits., Mark Manlove, Robert Buchannan, Moses Nicolls, Jr. Prob. April 22, 1757. Arch. vol. A20, pages 14-15. Reg. of Wills, Liber K, folio 161.

Becket, William. Will. Made Jan. 31, 1757. Heirs: wife Comfort; sons Nathan, William; daus. Comfort, Sarah, Mary; Mary Concelor. Exec'rs, wife Comfort & Nicholas Powell. Wits., Immanuel Stout, Nehemiah Handzer, Frederick Hine. Prob. May 7, 1757. Arch. vol. A3, pages 130-131. Reg. of Wills, Liber K, folio 162.

Bartlet, Samuel. Yeoman. Admin. of, to Rachael Bartlet, widow. May 12, 1757. Reg. of Wills, Liber K, folio 163. Note:— Arch. vol. A3, page 40 shows Jonathan & Rachel Bartlett as heirs.

Coffey, Hugh. Admin. of, to John Rees and wife Lurania Rees. May 26, 1757. Arch. vol. A9, page 185. Note:—Lurania was the wife of Simon Vanwinckle before she married John Rees.

Marshall, David. Duck Creek Hd. Admin. of, to Hugh Neill. May 27, 1757. Arch. vol. A33, pages 202-203.

Jester, Richard. Yeoman. Admin. of, to William Jester. May 31, 1757. Arch. vol. A27, page 47. Reg. of Wills, Liber K, folio 163.

Jackson, Abraham. Yeoman. Admin. of, to John Vining. May 31, 1757. Reg. of Wills, Liber K, folio 164.

Purdon, Andrew. Yeoman. Admin. of, to Martha Purdon, widow. June 8, 1757. Arch. vol. A41, page 204. Reg. of Wills, Liber K, folio 164.

Cuming (alias Newman), Lumino. Will. Made May 5, 1757. Heirs: mother unnamed; bro. Delictum; nephew Robart Cumin, son of Delictum. Exec'x, mother. Wits., William Wilson, Ann Wilson, Cettey Whitely. Prob. June 23, 1757. Arch. vol. A12, page 130. Reg. of Wills, Liber K, folios 164-165.

Cuming, Lumino. Admin. of, to Margaret Newman. June 23, 1757. Reg. of Wills, Liber K, folio 165.

Lloyd, Samuel. Will. Made Sept. 23, 1750. Heir: wife Elizabeth. Exec'x, wife. Wits., Edward Best, William Sherry, Thomas Slater. Prob. Sept. 3, 1757. Arch. vol. A30, page 198. Reg. of Wills, Liber K, folio 165.

Hirons, William. Will. Made Aug. 13, 1757. Duck Creek. Heirs: son John; dau. Grace. Exec'rs, John Draughton & James Morris. Wits., Arnold Hawkins, Margaret Doney, Samuel McCall. Prob. Sept. 12, 1757. Arch. vol. A24, pages 106-108. Reg. of Wills, Liber K, folio 166.

Hillyard, Charles. Gentleman. Admin. of, to Mary Raymond, widow. Sept. 12, 1757. Reg. of Wills, Liber K, folio 166.

Tompson, Jethro. Yeoman. Admin. of, to John & Robert Tompson. Sept. 16, 1757. Reg. of Wills, Liber K, folios 167 & 175. Note:—Arch. vol. A50, page 90 shows a son Jethro.

Willson, Robert. Will. Made Sept. 10, 1757. Heirs: wife Sarah; son Robert; dau. Anne; son-in-law Robert Bedwell. Exec'rs, son Robert & son-in-law Robert Bedwell. Wits., William Manlove, Jr., Nathan Williams, Sarah Forcum. Prob. Oct. 4, 1757. Arch. vol. A56, page 2. Reg. of Wills, Liber K, folio 167.

Bisbin, John. Yeoman. Will (copy, nunc.). Made ... 1757. Heirs: William & James Darling; wife unnamed. Wits., Richard Darling, Judith Bell. Prob. Oct. 7, 1757. Arch. vol. A4, page 60. Reg. of Wills, Liber K, folios 168-170.

Howell, Mary. Widow. Admin. of, to Mathew Griffith, yeoman. Oct. 11, 1757. Reg. of Wills, Liber K, folio 168. Note:—Arch. vol. A25, page 71 shows heirs, Morris, Sarah, Phillip & James Howell, Lydia Griffin.

Dill, Edward. Yeoman. Admin. of, to Mary Dill, widow. Oct. 25, 1757. Arch. vol. A14, page 90. Reg. of Wills, Liber K, folio 168.

Maffet, John. Planter. Will. Made ... 1757. Jones' Hd. Heirs: wife Janet; sons John, William, James, Robert; daus. Susannah, Rachael & Mary, wife of John Martain. Exec'rs, wife Janet & son John. Wits., John Hardin, William Maffet, Thomas Hardin. Prob. Oct. 25, 1757. Arch. vol. A35, page 189. Reg. of Wills, Liber K, folio 169.

Sap, Isaac. Yeoman. Admin. of, to Elizabeth Sap, widow. Nov. 2, 1757. Arch. vol. A44, page 230. Reg. of Wills, Liber K, folio 170.

Hillyard, Steel. Yeoman. Admin. of, to Mary Raymond, widow. Nov. 10, 1757. Reg. of Wills, Liber K, folio 170.

Rakes, Nicholas. Yeoman. Admin. of, to Fenwick Fisher, yeoman. Nov. 22, 1757. Arch. vol. A42, page 16. Reg. of Wills, Liber K, folio 171.

Jones, John. Yeoman. Admin. of, to Mary Jones, widow. Nov. 23, 1757. Arch. vol. A27, page 216. Reg. of Wills, Liber K, folio 171.

Simpson, William. Yeoman. Will. Made Nov. 13, 1757. Heirs: wife Urcilla [Urcella]; son Moses; daus. Jean, Elizabeth, Jamima. Exec'rs, wife Urcilla & son Moses. Wits., Robert Killen, John Stuerd, Ann Stuerd. Prob. Dec. 10, 1757. Arch. vol. A46, pages 82-84. Reg. of Wills, Liber K, folio 171.

Allen, John. Yeoman. Admin. of, to John Hamilton, yeoman, D. B. N. Dec. 17, 1757. Arch. vol. A1, pages 81-82. Reg. of Wills, Liber K, folio 172. Note:—Arch. vol. A1, page 82 shows estate unanministered by Sarah Allen, widow, & mentions Rachel, Hugh & John Allen as heirs; John Hamilton, adm'r, D. B. N., later died and his wife Mary became adm'x of this estate.

Allen, Sarah. Spinster. Admin. of, to William Clark & John Hamilton, yeoman. Dec. 17, 1757. Arch. vol. A1, page 94. Reg. of Wills, Liber K, folio 172.

Isgate, Philip. Laborer. Admin. of, to Philip Perrimore, yeoman. Dec. 19, 1757. Reg. of Wills, Liber K, folios 172-173.

Keeth, James. Yeoman. Will. Made Sept. 22, 1757. Little Creek Hd. Heirs: wife Sarah; sons Thomas, James, John, Francis; daus. Miriam, Sarah, Jane, Hannah. Exec'rs, wife Sarah & sons Thomas, James, John. Wits., Hugh McEllroy, Edward Norman, John Rutter. Prob. Dec. 24, 1757. Arch. vol. A28, pages 92-93. Reg. of Wills, Liber K, folio 173.

Hunter, James. Merchant. Admin. of, to Mary Hunter & Robert Bell. Dec. 28, 1757. Reg. of Wills, Liber K, folios 173-174.

Hendrickson, John. Yeoman. Admin. of, to Even Denny & John Sprunce. Jan. 2, 1758. Arch. vol. A23, page 142. Reg. of Wills, Liber K, folio 174.

Tepen [Tippen], Thomas. Will. Made Oct. 8, 1758. Heirs: wife Lidea; sons Thomas, Richard; daus. Ann, Sarah. Exec'x, wife Lidea. Wits., Stokely Sturgis, John Coudrat. Prob. Jan. 3, 1759. Arch. vol. A50, page 163. Reg. of Wills, Liber K, folios 195-196.

McKnitt, James. Yeoman. Will. Made July 3, 1753. Heirs: wife Cattern; daus. Esebele Fleming, Mary Cocks; son James. Exec'r, son James. Wits., Robert Killen, Archibald Fleming, Elizabeth Fleming. Prob. Jan. 19, 1758. Arch. vol. A32, page 223. Reg. of Wills, Liber K, folio 174.

Corker, Dennis. Yeoman. Admin. of, to Mary Corker, widow. Jan. 24, 1758. Reg. of Wills, Liber K, folio 175. Note:— Arch. vol. A11, page 1 shows Mary, the widow, later married Moses Beard; mentions dau. Rachel Corker.

Pearson, John. Yeoman. Admin. of, to Elizabeth Pearson, widow. Feb. 2, 1758. Arch. vol. A39, page 170. Reg. of Wills, Liber K, folios 175-176.

Malony, Joseph. Yeoman. Admin. of, to Sarah Malony, widow. Feb. 10, 1758. Arch. vol. A33, page 72. Reg. of Wills, Liber K, folio 176.

Kenderdine, John. Yeoman. Admin. of, to Benoni Watson & Benjamin Caten, yeoman. Feb. 8, 1758. Arch. vol. A29, pages 19-20. Reg. of Wills, Liber K, folio 176.

Rose, Ephriam. Yeoman. Admin. of, to Jeremiah Loatman, yeoman. Feb. 15, 1758. Arch. vol. A44, page 133. Reg. of Wills, Liber K, folios 176-177.

Alberry [Norberry], Benjamin. Farmer. Admin. of, to James Snow, yeoman. Feb. 15, 1758. Arch. vol. A38, page 42. Reg. of Wills, Liber K, folio 177.

Shirly, William. Yeoman. Admin. of, to Keziah Shirly, his wife. Feb. 15, 1758. Reg. of Wills, Liber K, folio 177. Note:— Arch. vol. A45, pages 245-246 show Keziah later married Benjamin Reason.

Johns, Samuel. Esq. Admin. of, to Elizabeth Johns, widow. Feb. 27, 1758. Reg. of Wills, Liber K, folios 177-178. Note:— Arch. vol. A27, pages 61-62 show Elizabeth, the widow, later married Charles Hillyard; mention daus. Elizabeth & Nancy; Nancy married Richard Holliday.

Rees, David. Admin. of, to Abel & Thomas Rees, D. B. N. March 1, 1758. Arch. vol. A42, page 237.

Samples, Elias. Planter. Admin. of, to Mary Samples & Reynear Williams, yeoman. March 9, 1758. Reg. of Wills, Liber K, folio 178. Note:—Arch. vol. A44, page 223 shows Mary, the widow, later married Zadok Crapper.

Maxwell, Elinor. Admin. of, to Nimrod Maxwell, planter. March 14, 1758. Reg. of Wills, Liber K, folio 178.

Enloe, Thomas. Mariner. Admin. of, to Richbell Mott, planter. March 17, 1758. Arch. vol. A25, page 214. Reg. of Wills, Liber K, folios 178-179.

Reynolds, Robert. Laborer. Admin. of, to Rachael Reynolds, widow. March 21, 1758. Arch. vol. A43, page 116. Reg. of Wills, Liber K, folio 179.

Hoy, Phebe. Admin. of, to James Tybout, gentleman. March 27, 1758. Arch. vol. A28, page 244. Reg. of Wills, Liber K, folio 179.

Davison, Thomas. Yeoman. Admin. of, to Margaret Davison, widow. April 1, 1758. Reg. of Wills, Liber K, folio 179.

Wilmore, Thomas. Yeoman. Admin. of, to Mary Wilmore & Hugh Talbot. April 7, 1758. Reg. of Wills, Liber K, folio 180.

Blackiston, William. Planter. Admin. of, to John Pleasentine. April 19, 1758. Arch. vol. A4, pages 139-140. Reg. of Wills, Liber K, folio 180.

Raymond, Mary. Widow. Will. Made March 28, 1758. Heirs: son James; grandson Joseph Hillyard, son of dau. Martha Hillyard; nephew James Steel; Rebecca Hood & Martha Renshaw, daus. of Wm. & Elizabeth Shute. Exec'rs, friends James Morris, Robert Holladay. Trustee, Abraham Allee, Sr. Wits., John Gooding, William Collins, Silvester Luck. Prob. April 27, 1758. Arch. vol. A42, page 156. Reg. of Wills, Liber K, folios 180-181. Note:—Will mentions sister Rebecca Steel & father James Steel, dec'd, of Phila.

Underwood, Richard, Sr. Will. Made July 27, 1757. Heirs: wife Mary; son Richard, Jr.; daus. Mary McNatt (wife of Wm. McNatt) & Miram Morice (wife of Edward Maurice [Morice]); grandsons Richard & Joshua Underwood, sons of Joshua, dec'd, & Abraham & Joshua Underwood, sons of Richard, Jr. Exec'x, wife Mary. Wits., Thomas Clark, Sarah Clark, Benjamin Clark. Prob. May 1, 1758. Arch. vol. A51, page 195. Reg. of Wills, Liber K, folios 181-182.

Dixon, Thomas. Yeoman. Admin. of, to John Clayton. May 8, 1758. Reg. of Wills, Liber K, folio 182.

Martin, Mary. Wife of Patrick Martin. Admin. of, to Charles Ridgely, practitoner. May 9, 1758. Reg. of Wills, Liber K, folio 182.

Thompson [Tompson], Joseph. Will (copy). Made April 18, 1758. Heirs: wife Rachel; sons Joseph, Jeffery. Exec'x, wife Rachel. Wits., William Sappington, Daniel Macy, John Dawson. Prob. May 10, 1758. Arch. vol. A50, page 227. Reg. of Wills, Liber K, folios 182-183.

Jackson, Moses. Planter. Admin. of, to Margaret Jackson, widow. May 22, 1758. Reg. of Wills, Liber K, folio 183.

Tobin, Cornelius. Admin. of, to John Gooding. May 24, 1758. Reg. of Wills, Liber K, folio 183.

Dunlap, John. Yeoman. Admin. of, to Peter Dunlap, planter. May 24, 1758. Reg. of Wills, Liber K, folio 184.

Barns, William. Admin. of, to John & Stephen Barns. May 26, 1758. Arch. vol. A2, page 231. Note:—Mentions Ann Barns, William Barns; Culbarth Green & Priscilla Green, his wife; Joseph Massy & Rebecca Massy, his wife; Nathan Massy & Sarah Massy, his wife.

Raymond, Presley. Yeoman. Admin. of, to James Morris, planter. May 26, 1758. Reg. of Wills, Liber K, folios 164 & 184. Note:—Arch. vol. A42, page 164 shows acct. unadministered by Mary Raymond, the widow.

Perrymore, Philip. Planter. Admin. of, to Susannah Price & Thomas Clark. June 12, 1758. Reg. of Wills, Liber K, folios 184-185.

Blunt, Levy. Yeoman. Admin. of, to Daniel Durborow, gentleman. June 13, 1758. Reg. of Wills, Liber K, folio 185.

Rees, David. Laborer. Admin. of, to Caesar Rodney. June 13, 1758. Reg. of Wills, Liber K, folio 185.

Henry, Edward. Yeoman. Admin. of, to Martha Henry, widow. Aug. 2, 1758. Arch. vol. A23, page 148. Reg. of Wills, Liber K, folios 185-186.

Moore, John. Will. Made June 26, 1758. Duck Creek Hd. Heirs: wife Jean; son Peter. Exec'rs, wife Jean & bro. Samuel Moor. Wits., James Houstown, John Hamilton. Prob. Aug. 5, 1758. Arch. vol. A36, pages 51-53. Reg. of Wills, Liber K, folio 186. Note:—Arch. vol. A36, page 53 shows Jane, the widow, later married Jonas Edingfield; mentions dau. Mary Moor.

Hillyard, Charles. Gentleman. Admin. of, to James Morris, planter. Aug. 11, 1758. Reg. of Wills, Liber K, folio 186.

Brown, John. Admin. of, to Ann Brown & Daniel Robisson. Aug. 23, 1758. Arch. vol. A6, pages 51-52.

Cole, Sarah. Widow of Spencer Cole. Will. Made July 5, 1758. Heirs: son Spencer; daus. Penelope, Sarah, Mary, Ameli. Exec'r, bro. John Brinckle. Wits., Curtis Brinckle, William Abbitt, Elizabeth Murphy. Prob. Aug. 24, 1758. Arch. vol. A9, pages 207-208. Reg. of Wills, Liber K, folio 187. Note:— Will mentions father-in-law John Hamnitt, dec'd. Arch. vol. A9, page 208 shows Reynear Williams as adm'r.

Hammans, Thomas. Will. Made July 22, 1758. Duck Creek. Heirs: wife Susannah; son William; mother-in-law Mary Hammans; Neomy Potter. Exec'x, wife. Wits., Samuel McCall, Jabez Jenkins, Robert Holliday. Prob. Sept. 11, 1758. Arch. vol. A21, page 187. Reg. of Wills, Liber K, folio 187.

Munt, Mary. Will. Made July 7, 1758. Heirs: son Robert; daus. Elener, Abigal, Charity; dau.-in-law Mary Ann Munt; grand-dau. Julania Munt. Exec'r, son Robert. Wits., James Manson, Sarah Manson, George Gordon. Codicil, dau.-in-law Mary Ann Munt, wife of Robert Munt. Prob. Sept. 14, 1758. Arch. vol. A37, pages 79-81. Reg. of Wills, Liber K, folios 188-189.

Byndelin, John Rudolphus. Will (copy). Made Aug. 13, 1758. Heir: friend Samuel Beauenes Turner. Exec'r, Samuel Beauenes Turner. Wits., William Fleming, Jr., David Hilford, George Fleming, the younger. Prob. Oct. 2, 1758. Arch. vol. A4, page 201. Reg. of Wills, Liber K, folio 188.

Smith, John. Will. Made Sept. 23, 1758. Heirs: wife Rebecca; daus. Elinor Jons, Sarah McNatt, Mary, Rebecca, Elizabeth & Louisea Smith; sons Robert, John & William. Exec'x, wife Rebecca. Wits., Robert Smith, James Anderson, Jeremiah Morris. Prob. Oct. 28, 1758. Arch. vol. A47, pages 75-77. Reg. of Wills, Liber K, folio 190.

Skinner, William. Admin. of, to Esther Skinner, widow. Nov. 10, 1758. Reg. of Wills, Liber K, folio 190.

McDevett, James. Peddler. Will. Made Oct. 18, 1758. Duck Creek. Heirs: bro. Daniel; cousin Margaret Moran. Exec'r, bro. Daniel. Wits., Abraham Hawkins, Thomas Runnels, Malachi Roan. Prob. Nov. 14, 1758. Arch. vol. A32, pages 161-162. Reg. of Wills, Liber K, folio 191.

Jester, Thomas. Will. Made Feb. 1, 1758. Heirs: wife Catherine; sons Thomas, Arnall, Elias; daus. Mary, Sarah, Annice. Exec'x, wife Catherine. Wits., John Brinckle, Curtis Brinckle, John Veech. Prob. Nov. 15, 1758. Arch. vol. A27, page 50. Reg. of Wills, Liber K, folios 191-192.

Murray, Ann. Will. Made Aug. 23, 1758. Heirs: daus. Elizabeth Green, Maudlin Perry; Alexander Holland. Exec'r, Alexander Holland. Wits., Henry Bickerton, Daniel Perry, Jane Cockran. Prob. Nov. 16, 1758. Arch. vol. A37, page 111. Reg. of Wills, Liber K, folio 192.

Whitehead, Isaiah. Yeoman. Admin. of, to Sophia Whitehead, widow. Nov. 20, 1758. Arch. vol. A54, page 192. Reg. of Wills, Liber K, folio 193.

Townsend, Gabriel. Yeoman. Admin. of, to Andrew Townsen, yeoman. Nov. 25, 1758. Reg. of Wills, Liber K, folio 193.

Conolly, Thomas. Yeoman. Admin. of, to Ann Conolly, widow. Dec. 4, 1758. Arch. vol. A10, page 68. Reg. of Wills, Liber K, folios 193-194.

Gillespie, James. Yeoman. Admin. of, to George Crow, watchmaker. Dec. 9, 1758. Arch. vol. A19, page 55. Reg. of Wills, Liber K, folio 194.

Garvey, John. Yeoman. Admin. of, to Sarah & Owen Garvey. Dec. 19, 1758. Arch. vol. A18, page 228. Reg. of Wills, Liber K, folio 194.

Hawkins, Jacob. Yeoman. Will. Made May 27, 1758. Heir: bro. William. Exec'r, bro. William. Wits., William Wells, Edward Gibbs, William Shurmer. Prob. Dec. 20, 1758. Arch. vol. A23, page 24. Reg. of Wills, Liber K, folio 194.

Langrell, George. Planter. Will. Made Dec. 15, 1756. Heirs: wife Rebeckah; James Langrell; William Langril, Sr.; Alce Smith; Sarah Morrett. Exec'r, bro. William. Wits., James Anderson, James Rawley, Rice Willace [Willis]. Prob. Jan. 1, 1759. Arch. vol. A29, page 122. Reg. of Wills, Liber K, folio 195.

Dawson, Richard. Will. Made April 25, 1758. Heir: friend Thomas Nixon. Exec'r, Thomas Nixon. Wits., William Smyth, Vincent Loockerman, John Pryor. Prob. Jan. 5, 1759. Arch. vol. A13, page 110. Reg. of Wills, Liber K, folio 196.

Jester, Daniel. Yeoman. Admin. of, to Elizabeth Jester, widow. Jan. 19, 1759. Reg. of Wills, Liber K, folios 196-197.

Gordon, Robert. Will. Made Dec. 20, 1758. Heirs: wife Filles [Philis]; sons John & Robert; bros. James & Seath; nephew James Darling. Exec'x, wife Filles. Wits., Jane Caldwell, Martha Henry, Mary Morgan. Prob. Feb. 15, 1759. Arch. vol. A19, pages 172-174. Reg. of Wills, Liber K, folio 197. Note:—Arch. vol. A19, page 173 shows Philis, the widow, later married William Merydith.

Shankmire, Peter. Yeoman. Admin. of, to Robert Hall, yeoman. Feb. 20, 1759. Reg. of Wills, Liber K, folios 197-198.

Darling, William. Will. Made Jan. 3, 1759. Duck Creek. Heirs: wife Elizabeth; son Gorden; daus. Margret & Ann; sister Sarah; bros. James & Richard. Exec'rs, wife Elizabeth & bro. James. Wits., Lau. Walsh, James Gordon. Prob. Feb. 23, 1759. Arch. vol. A12, pages 194-195. Reg. of Wills, Liber K, folio 198. Note:—Arch. vol. A12, page 195 shows Elizabeth, the widow, later married John Speer.

Hall, John, Sr. Admin. of, to James Smith, D. B. N. Feb. 27, 1759. Arch. vol. A21, page 94.

Ewing, James. Yeoman. Admin. of, to Daniel Finney. March 2, 1759. Reg. of Wills, Liber K, folios 198-199. Note:— Arch. vol. A16, pages 233-234 show Mary Ewing married Daniel Finney; mentions children, Robert, Frances, Elizabeth Ewing.

Payne [Pain], Thomas. Yeoman. Admin. of, to Levin Adams & William Gray. March 12, 1759. Arch. vol. A38, page 184. Reg. of Wills, Liber K, folio 199.

Downham, Thomas. Yeoman. Will. Made March 8, 1759. Heirs: wife Mary Ann; sons Joseph, John, Thomas; daus. Sarah Pickren, Eleanor Vanatta, Annis Downham; son-in-law Thomas Cramer. Exec'x, wife Mary Ann. Wits., John Newell, William Merydith, Joseph Alford. Prob. March 23,

1759. Arch. vol. A14, pages 235-236. Reg. of Wills, Liber K, folios 199-200. Note:—Arch. vol. A14, page 236 shows Mary, the widow, later married Joseph Alford; mentions heirs, Samuel Vanata & James Pickerran.

Stinson, Jean [Jane]. Widow. Admin. of, to John Spruance, planter. April 2, 1759. Arch. vol. A49, page 24. Reg. of Wills, Liber K, folio 200.

Marshall, Edward. Planter. Admin. of, to Ann Marshall, widow, & John Newell, yeoman. April 4, 1759. Reg. of Wills, Liber K, folio 200.

McCain, Philip. Will. Made March 29, 1759. Little Creek. Heirs: wife Elizabeth; friend John Morgan. Exec'x, wife Elizabeth. Wits., Jacob Stout, Solomon Whithart, Martin Hardin. Prob. April 12, 1759. Arch. vol. A32, pages 89-91. Reg. of Wills, Liber K, folio 201. Note:—Arch. vol. A32, page 90 shows Elizabeth Crumeen later as adm'x; Charles & Joseph Freeman, children of Joseph Freeman; George, James & Isaiah Morgan, children of David Morgan.

Robinson, John. Will. Made March 19, 1759. Heirs: wife Sarah; dau. Rachel; sons Charles & John; bros. Jorden & Andrew. Exec'rs, wife Sarah, bro. Jorden & James Morris. Wits., Daniel McDavitt, Marcy Holston, Sarah Wells. Prob. April 13, 1759. Arch. vol. A44, pages 62-63. Reg. of Wills, Liber K, folio 201. Note:—Arch. vol. A44, page 63 shows Sarah Frazar as one of the adm'rs.

Barker, Thomas. Will. Made April 14, 1759. Heirs: sons William & Thomas; daus. Jean [Jane], Sarah Hall, Phebe Melven. Exec'rs, sons William & Thomas. Wits., Thomas Clark, John Williams, John Stradlin. Prob. April 25, 1759. Arch. vol. A2, page 176. Reg. of Wills, Liber K, folio 202.

McMurry, William. Yeoman. Admin. of, to John McMurry, yeoman. May 8, 1759. Reg. of Wills, Liber K, folios 202-203.

Clayton, John, Sr. Yeoman. Will. Made Dec. 24, 1754. Heirs: wife Grace; sons James & John; dau. Sarah Caldwell; granddau. Sarah Caldwell; grandson John Caldwell. Exec'r, son James. Wits., Elizabeth Armitage, James Egnew, Robert Teat. Prob. May 9, 1759. Arch. vol. A9, page 112. Reg. of Wills, Liber K, folio 203.

Numbers, James. Yeoman. Admin. of, to Rebecca Numbers, widow. May 10, 1759. Reg. of Wills, Liber K, folio 204. Note:— Arch. vol. A38, page 69 shows Rebecca, the widow, later married Abraham Cheffins.

Williams, James. Yeoman. Queen Ann's Co., Md. Admin. of, to Mary Williams, widow. May 24, 1759. Reg. of Wills, Liber K, folio 204.

Barns, Stephen. Gentleman. Admin. of, to John Barns, gentleman. May 24, 1759. Arch. vol. A2, pages 226-227. Reg. of Wills, Liber K, folio 205.

Maugridge, Joseph. Planter. Admin. of, to Owen Wheeler, yeoman. May 24, 1759. Arch. vol. A34, page 72. Reg. of Wills, Liber K, folio 205.

McKenney, Eleazer. Admin. of, to Amos McKenney. May 24, 1759. Arch. vol. A32, page 215.

Fleming, George [Goove]. Yeoman. Will. Made Feb. 21, 1758. Mispillion. Heirs: wife Elizabeth; sons Samuel, George; daus. Martha & Esther. Exec'rs, wife Elizabeth & friend Archibald Fleming. Wits., Robert Killen, Robert King, William Killen. Prob. May 25, 1759. Arch. vol. A17, pages 177-178. Reg. of Wills, Liber K, folio 205.

Slaughter, John. Shoemaker. Admin. of, to Mary Slaughter, widow. May 25, 1759. Reg. of Wills, Liber K, folio 206.

Edenfield, John. Planter. Admin. of, to Persis Edenfield, widow. May 29, 1759. Arch. vol. A16, page 15. Reg. of Wills, Liber K, folio 206.

Tomlinson, James. Yeoman. Admin. of, to Rhoda Tomlinson, widow. June 15, 1759. Reg. of Wills, Liber K, folio 207. Note:— Arch. vol. A50, pages 192-193 mentions Rhoda Peterkin as adm'x; also mentions heirs, Mary Holston (wife of Purnal Holston), Sophia Candy (wife of William Candy) & Cary Tomlinson.

Brown, Phillip. Tailor. Admin. of, to Daniel Newnam, yeoman. June 18, 1759. Reg. of Wills, Liber K, folio 207.

Morris, Cornelius. Planter. Admin. of, to Jeremiah Morris, yeoman. June 23, 1759. Arch. vol. A36, page 196. Reg. of Wills, Liber K, folio 207.

Johnson, James. Yeoman. Admin. of, to Mary Johnson, widow. July 14, 1759. Reg. of Wills, Liber K, folio 208. Note:— Arch. vol. A27, page 66 shows Mary, the widow, later married Elisha Stafford.

Barns, Ann. Will. Made Sept. 13, 1758. Little Creek. Heirs: sons William, John, Stephen; daus. Elizabeth Faulkner, Sarah Barns, Prisiler Green, Rebecca Massy, Jane & Cathrine Barns; granddaus. Prisiler & Sarah Faulkner; grandson Gilbert Faulkner. Exec'r, son Stephen. Wits., Robert Blackshere, Thomas Murphy. Prob. July 30, 1759. Arch. vol. A2, pages 213-214. Reg. of Wills, Liber K, folio 208.

Henderson, Andrew. Yeoman. Admin. of, to William Scantlin, innholder. Aug. 1, 1759. Arch. vol. A23, page 119. Reg. of Wills, Liber K, folio 209.

Wilcot, Josias. Will. Made Feb. 18, 1759. Heirs: wife Anne; son Joseph; daus. Charity, Anne, Martha. Exec'x, wife Anne. Wits., James White, William Kendel. Prob. Aug. 15, 1759. Arch. vol. A54, page 230. Reg. of Wills, Liber K, folio 209.

Roan, Malachi. Will. Made July 25, 1759. Duck Creek. Heirs: Jane McDevet, dau. of Daniel McDevet; William Farson, son of Henry Farson; Roger Magee (in Ireland); bros. & sisters unnamed. Exec'r, friend Daniel McDevet. Wits., Mary Farson, Martha Turner, Henry Farson. Prob. Aug. 16, 1759. Arch. vol. A44, pages 19-20. Reg. of Wills, Liber K, folio 210.

Parke, Theodore. Infant. Admin. of, to Hugh Parke, hatter. Aug. 17, 1759. Reg. of Wills, Liber K, folios 210-211.

Betts (alias McSparren), Ruth. Admin. of, to John McSparran, merchant. Aug. 17, 1759. Reg. of Wills, Liber K, folio 211.

Ussher, Mary. Will. Made Dec. 19, 1750. Dover Hd. Heirs: sons John Ussher, Manlove Tarrant; dau. Hannah Ussher. Exec'r, bro. Laurence Robisson. Trustee, bro. Laurence Robisson. Wits., Joshua Nickerson, Charles Marim, Hannah Hart. Prob. Aug. 29, 1759. Arch. vol. A51, page 209. Reg. of Wills, Liber K, folio 211.

McDavett, Daniel. Yeoman. Will. Made Feb. 27, 1759. Duck Creek. Heirs: dau. Jane; Margaret Moran; Christopher Wan. Exec'rs, Jacob Allee, Sr., & James McMullan, merchant. Trustee, mother-in-law Jane Keith. Wits., Peter McGlew, John Mason, Patrick Moron. Prob. Aug. 29, 1759. Arch. vol. A32, pages 158-160, 162. Reg. of Wills, Liber K, folio 212. Note:—Arch. vol. A32, pages 159-160 show Jane [Jean] later married Thomas Alston; Margaret Moran later married Thomas Murphy.

Brinckle, Richard. Admin. of, to Tabitha Brinckle & Andrew Gray. Sept. 5, 1759. Arch. vol. A5, page 203. Note:— Shows that Tabitha, the widow, later married Andrew Gray.

Roanny, Peter. Laborer. Admin. of, to Samuel Robisson, yeoman. Sept. 19, 1759. Arch. vol. A44, page 21. Reg. of Wills, Liber K, folio 213.

Vandervour, George. Farmer. Will. Made Feb. 22, 1758. Heirs: wife Elionor; sons John, Hollingworth, Mathew, George; daus. Eleoner, Esther, Rachel. Exec'x, wife Elionor. Wits., Richard Newnam, Thomas Russell. Prob. Oct. 14, 1759. Arch. vol. A51, page 229. Reg. of Wills, Liber K, folio 213.

Hodgson [Hudgson], Joseph. Will. Made Oct. 24, 1759. Heirs: sons Jonathan, John; daus. Sarah, Mary; uncle Andrew Caldwell. Exec'r, bro. Robert Hodgson, Jr. Trustee, mother Train Hodgson. Wits., John Skidmore, Elizabeth Faries, Elizabeth Tayler. Prob. Nov. 2, 1759. Arch. vol. A24, pages 122-126. Reg. of Wills, Liber K, folio 214.

Anderson, James. Farmer. Admin. of, to John Anderson, yeoman. Nov. 15, 1759. Reg. of Wills, Liber K, folio 214.

Hendrickson, Hendrick. Will. Made July 19, 1759. Heirs: wife Sarah; cousin Sarah Trewax & her son Henry. Exec'rs, wife Sarah & James Morris. Wits., Thomas Hawkins, Sarah Palmatary, Allen Palmatary. Prob. Nov. 16, 1759. Arch. vol. A23, pages 134-135. Reg. of Wills, Liber K, folio 215.

Long, Timothy. Yeoman. Admin. of, to Sarah Long, widow. Nov. 16, 1759. Arch. vol. A31, pages 59-60. Reg. of Wills, Liber K, folio 215.

Newell, John. Will. Made Nov. 14, 1759. Heirs: sons Henry & William; daus. Tabitha Russell, Lydia, Hannah, Meriam Newell. Exec'r, Andrew Caldwell. Wits., Silvester Tomson, William Sipple, Durdin Wilson. Prob. Nov. 20, 1759. Arch. vol. A37, page 191. Reg. of Wills, Liber K, folio 216. Note:— Will mentions Mary Warren, grandmother.

Hillyard, Steel. Yeoman. Admin. of, to James Morris, gentleman. Nov. 29, 1759. Reg. of Wills, Liber K, folios 216-217.

Seeds, William. Yeoman. Admin. of, to Sarah Seeds, widow. Nov. 29, 1759. Reg. of Wills, Liber K, folio 217. Note:— Arch. vol. A45, page 122 shows Stokely Sturgis later administered for his wife.

Paradee, Stephen. Will. Made Nov. 29, 1759. Heirs: wife Lydia; dau. Mary; son Stephen; grandsons Daniel & Stephen Lewis; granddaus. Ruhamy, Hannah & Mary Lewis. Exec'rs, wife Lydia & son-in-law Daniel Lewis. Appraisers, James Clayton & Charles Marim. Wits., Charles Inglis, Richard Wells, James Sykes. Prob. Dec. 18, 1759. Arch. vol. A38, pages 243-244 & vol. A39, pages 1-2. Reg. of Wills, Liber K, folios 217-218. Note:—Arch. vol. A39, page 2 shows Jonathan Caldwell & wife Peggy, late Peggy Lewis, adm'rs, D. B. N.

French, Robert. Yeoman. Admin. of, to Benjamin Brown, bricklayer. Dec. 25, 1759. Reg. of Wills, Liber K, folio 218.

Mann, William, Sr. Yeoman. Admin. of, to William Mann, Jr., yeoman. Jan. 24, 1760. Reg. of Wills, Liber K, folio 219.

Caffee, William. Yeoman. Admin. of, to Mary Caffee, widow. Jan. 26, 1760. Reg. of Wills, Liber K, folios 218-219.

Skidmore, Mary. Will (nunc.). Made Jan. 24, 1760. Heirs: husband John Skidmore; bro. John Luff. Wits., Benjamin Howring, Ruhamey Mearham, Nathaniel Luff. Prob. Feb. 4, 1760. Arch. vol. A46, page 198. Reg. of Wills, Liber K, folio 224.

Leech [Leach], David. Yeoman. Admin. of, to Mary Leech, widow. Feb. 6, 1760. Reg. of Wills, Liber K, folio 219. Note:—Arch. vol. A29, page 204 shows Mary, the widow, later married Immanuel Stout.

Bell, Robert. Will. Made Nov. 7, 1759. Heirs: bros. John, Thomas, Henry Bell & James Sykes; sister Lucy Bell; mother Mary Hunter. Exec'r, bro. James Sykes. Wits., Richard Mott, William Clark. Prob. Feb. 11, 1760. Arch. vol. A3, page 184. Reg. of Wills, Liber K, folio 220.

Rees, Even. Farmer. Will. Made Oct. 31, 1759. Duck Creek. Heirs: wife Mary; sons Edward, Robert, William, John; dau. Sarah; granddau. Sarah Rees, dau. of son John; son of dau. Sarah; Theophilus Lyson, son of my wife. Exec'r, wife Mary & sons Edward, Robert, William. Wits., Finwick Fisher, Thomas Brown, Susanna Hammans, Mary Fisher. Prob. Feb. 12, 1760. Arch. vol. A42, page 242. Reg. of Wills, Liber K, folios 220-221.

McDivet, James. Admin. of, to James McMullan & Jacob Allee, D. B. N. Feb. 14, 1760. Reg. of Wills, Liber K, folio 221.

Roan, Malachi. Admin. of, to James McMullan & Jacob Alle, Sr., D. B. N. Feb. 14, 1760. Arch. vol. A44, page 20. Reg. of Wills, Liber K, folio 222.

Dewees, Hezekiah. Yeoman. Admin. of, to Mary Dewees, widow. Feb. 14, 1760. Reg. of Wills, Liber K, folio 222. Note:— Arch. vol. A14, page 44 shows children, Elizabeth, Mary, Isaac, Ezekiel & Joseph Dewees.

Nickerson, George. Farmer. Will. Made Dec. 22, 1759. Heirs: bro. John; sister Ruhamy Marim; cousins John & Elizabeth Marim, children of Charles & Ruhamy Marim; bro.-in-law Charles Marim. Exec'r, bro. John & bro.-in-law Charles Marim. Wits., James Sykes, John Maxwell, George Stevens. Prob. Feb. 14, 1760. Arch. vol. A37, page 229. Reg. of Wills, Liber K, folios 222-223.

Ganoe, Lewis. Admin. of, to Ann Ganoe & Daniel Ganoe. Feb. 14, 1760. Arch. vol. A18, page 210. Reg. of Wills, Liber K, folio 223.

Hirons, William. Yeoman. Admin. of, to William Leatherbury, yeoman. Feb. 27, 1760. Reg. of Wills, Liber K, folios 223-224.

Hall, John, Sr. Admin. of, to James Smith, D. B. N. Feb. 27, 1759. Arch. vol. A21, page 94.

Luff, Nathaniel, Sr. Gentleman. Will. Made Feb. 3, 1760. Heirs: wife Deborah; sons Caleb, Nathaniel, John; daus. Hannah Paradee, Deborth Pleasanton. Exec'rs, sons Caleb & Nathaniel. Wits., Samuel Merydith, Sarah Maston, Thomas Clark. Prob. Feb. 27, 1760. Arch. vol. A31, pages 229-238. Reg. of Wills, Liber K, folio 225. Note:—Arch. vol. A31, page 235 shows John Paradee as husband of Hannah; David Pleasanton as husband of Deborah; Deborah later married Stephen Lewis. Page 236 shows Deborah, the widow, later married Jonathan Manlove. Page 238 shows Philip Reason [Rasin] only son of Sarah had heirs, Jemiah Ford, Robert Meeks & Joseph Rasin.

Bradly, William. Yeoman. Admin. of, to Margrett Bradly, widow. March 5, 1760. Reg. of Wills, Liber K, folio 226. Note:— Arch. vol. A5, page 123 shows Margaret as the wife of William Revell.

McFarland, Alexander. Farmer. Will. Made March 17, 1760. Heirs: wife unnamed; sons John, William, Samuel; dau. Jean. Exec'rs, wife & son William. Wits., Cornelius Lott, Rachel Mathews, William Dodd. Prob. April 4, 1760. Arch. vol. A32, pages 180-181. Reg. of Wills, Liber K, folio 226.

Manson, James, Jr. Yeoman. Admin. of, to James Manson, Sr., yeoman. April 24, 1760. Reg. of Wills, Liber K, folio 227.

Skidmore, Thomas. Gentleman. Admin. of, to Daniel Robisson, gentleman. April 26, 1760. Reg. of Wills, Liber K, folio 228.

Russell, Ebenezer. Yeoman. May 6, 1760. Admin. of, to Tabitha Russell, widow. Reg. of Wills, Liber K, folio 227.

Durborow, Stephen. Cordwainer. Admin. of, to Sarah Durborow, widow. May 7, 1760. Reg. of Wills, Liber K, folio 227.

Underhay, Jacob. Yeoman. Admin. of, to Heneritha Underhay, widow. May 14, 1760. Reg. of Wills, Liber K, folio 228.

Brooks, John. Will. Made April 28, 1760. Heirs: wife Martha; son Benjamin; daus. Charity, Rebecca, Esther, Ann, Mary; mother unnamed. Exec'rs, wife Martha, son Benjamin & Nicholas Lockerman. Wits., Andrew Lackey, Fredrick Hines, Rebecca Mitchell. Prob. May 21, 1760. Arch. vol. A6, page 10. Reg. of Wills, Liber K, folio 228.

Maxwell, Mary. Wife of Nimrod Maxwell. Admin. of, to Nimrod Maxwell. May 27, 1760. Reg. of Wills, Liber K, folio 229.

Carter, William. Will. Made May 24, 1760. Heirs: Elizabeth Carter; William Carter, Jr.; Jane & Sarah Carter, daus. of William Carter; Mearrim, Rachel & Nyca Brown, daus. of Thos. Brown; daus. Jane Brown, Comfort Powel & Ann Donneho. Wits., John Tucker & Thomas Brown. Prob. May 31, 1760. Arch. vol. A8, page 44.

Carter, William. Yeoman. Admin. of, to Leah Carter, widow. May 31, 1760. Reg. of Wills, Liber K, folios 229-230. Note:— Arch. vol. A8, page 45 shows heirs, Jonathan, William, Rachel, Eve, Elizabeth & Sarah Carter.

Henderson, Andrew. Yeoman. Admin. of, to John Henderson. June 4, 1760. Reg. of Wills, Liber K, folio 232.

Chance, John. Yeoman. Admin. of, to Alexander Chance, yeoman. June 6, 1760. Reg. of Wills, Liber K, folio 232. Note:— Arch. vol. A8, page 153 mentions dau. Prudence Chance; Alexander Chance & John Turner as joint adm'rs.

Barret, Benjamin. Yeoman. Admin. of, to Silas Crispen, yeoman. June 30, 1760. Reg. of Wills, Liber K, folio 233. Note:— Arch. vol. A2, page 241 shows Joseph Barratt as sole heir.

Miller, Robert. Miller. Admin. of, to Elizabeth Miller. July 10, 1760. Reg. of Wills, Liber K, folio 233.

Torbert, Hugh. Tanner. Will. Made Dec. 28, 1757. St. Jones' Hd. Heirs: wife Susannah; sons John, Peter & Simon; daus. Susannah, Jane & Margarett; bros. & sisters unnamed. Exec'rs, wife Susannah & son John. Wits., John Hardin, Alexander McFarland, William Shurmer. Prob. July 21, 1760. Arch. vol. A50, pages 232-233. Reg. of Wills, Liber K, folios 233-234.

Dickinson, Samuel. Gentleman. Will. Made Dec. 11, 1759. Heirs: wife Mary; sons Henry, John & Philemon; dau. Elizabeth Goldsborrough; son-in-law Charles Goldsborrough; grandsons Samuel Dickinson & Charles Goldsborrough; granddaus. Mary, Elizabeth & Joanna Dickinson. Exec'rs, wife Mary, sons John & Philemon. Wits., Walter Dickinson,

Thomas Willson, William Killen, Margaret Jones. Prob. July 26, 1760. Arch. vol. A14, page 63. Reg. of Wills, Liber K, folios 230-231. Note:—Will mentions grandfather Walter Dickinson, dec'd.

Caine, Rachael. Widow. Admin. of, to Manasses Caine. July 26, 1760. Reg. of Wills, Liber K, folio 234.

Cain, Rachel. Widow. Will. Made May 27, 1760. Heirs: sons Manasses, Oen & James Cain. Wits., Moses Freeman, Elizabeth Swells, Elizabeth Bryan. Prob. July 26, 1760. Arch. vol. A7, page 79.

Bowman, Miriam. Will. Made Aug. 12, 1756. Heir: son Henry. Exec'r, husband Thomas Bowman. Wits., Jonathan Manlove, Miriam Bowman. Prob. Aug. 13, 1760. Arch. vol. A5, page 50. Reg. of Wills, Liber K, folio 235.

Carbin, James. Yeoman. Admin. of, to Jane Carbin, widow, & Wm. Carter. Aug. 13, 1760. Arch. vol. A7, pages 201-202. Reg. of Wills, Liber K, folio 235.

Manlove, Emanuel [Amanuel]. Will. Made June 11, 1760. Heirs: bros. Waitman & Govey Trippet; sisters Mary Pratt & Penelope Caton; niece Sary Molleston, wife of Henry Molleston, Jr.; mother Alce Manlove; Sary & William Trippet, children of bro. John Trippet; friend William Smith. Exec'rs, bro. Waitman Trippet & friend Robert Caton. Wits., Samuel Merydith, Ailse Annet, James Corkeran. Prob. Aug. 19, 1760. Arch. vol. A33, pages 86-87. Reg. of Wills, Liber K, folio 236.

Howell, Sabrit. Yeoman. Admin. of, to Rhody Howell, widow. Aug. 25, 1760. Reg. of Wills, Liber K, folio 236.

McSparron, John. Will (copy). Made Aug. 15, 1760. Phila. Heirs: child unnamed; bros. Archibald, Joseph. Exec'r, bro. Archibald. Wits., Sara Brudey, William Murray. Prob. Aug. 25, 1760. Arch. vol. A33, page 33. Reg. of Wills, Liber K, folio 239.

Rees, Thomas. Will. Made Aug. 6, 1760. Little Creek Hd. Heirs: son Nathan; dau. Sarah; nephews Able Rees, John Reese (son of bro. John Rees); Mary Tolly [Jolly]. Exec'r, bro. John Rees. Wits., John Barns, Samuel Roach, Joseph Currey. Prob. Aug. 27, 1760. Arch. vol. A43, pages 33-36. Reg. of Wills, Liber K, folio 237.

Murphey, William. Yeoman. Admin. of, to Sarah Murphey, widow. Aug. 29, 1760. Reg. of Wills, Liber K, folios 237-238.

Morgan, Elizabeth. Spinster. Admin. of, to John Clayton, Esq. Sept. 9, 1760. Reg. of Wills, Liber K, folio 238. Note:— Arch. vol. A36, pages 139-140 mention mother Martha Morgan.

McDaniel, James. Admin. of, to Mary McDaniel, widow. Sept. 10, 1760. Reg. of Wills, Liber K, folio 238.

Hall, John. Will. Made Jan. 23, 1758. Heirs: sons William, Thomas, Isaac; daus. Mary Goforth, Isable Clark & Anne Manlove, wife of Mark Manlove; grandsons John Smith, son of dau. Sarah, dec'd, & Benjamin Spencer, son of dau. Elizabeth; Sarah Richards & Esther Steel, sisters of grandson John Smith. Exec'r, son Isaac. Wits., John Brinckle, Daniel Jestor, Arthur Steel. Prob. Oct. 2, 1760. Arch. vol. A21, page 93. Reg. of Wills, Liber K, folio 239.

Dunning, Samuel. Will. Made Aug. 31, 1754. Heirs: wife Tamar; sons Thomas, Samuel, John, William; daus. Mary, Martha. Exec'rs, wife Tamar & son Thomas. Wits., Joseph Powell, William Powell, Mary Powell. Prob. Oct. 2, 1760. Arch. vol. A15, pages 134-135. Reg. of Wills, Liber K, folio 240.

Linnon [Linnin], John. Will. Made Aug. 13, 1760. Duck Creek. Heirs: wife Grace; sons John & Arthur. Exec'x, wife Grace. Trustee, friend James McMullan. Wits., William Creighton, John Rees. Prob. Oct. 9, 1760. Arch. vol. A30, page 173. Reg. of Wills, Liber K, folios 240-241. Note:—Will mentions father-in-law Thomas Green.

Murphy, Sarah. Widow. Will. Made Oct. 7, 1760. Little Creek Hd. Heirs: daus. Sarah & Rebecca; son Benjamin. Exec'r, bro. Paradee Courtney. Wits., Sarah Paradee, Mary Stewart, Daniel Smith. Prob. Oct. 11, 1760. Arch. vol. A37, page 103. Reg. of Wills, Liber K, folios 241-242. Note:—Will mentions husband William Murphy, dec'd.

Murphy, William. Yeoman. Admin. of, to Thomas Harwood, yeoman. Oct. 13, 1760. Reg. of Wills, Liber K, folio 242.

McCombs, Grace. Widow. Admin. of, to Bartholomew McCombs, yeoman. Oct. 15, 1760. Arch. vol. A32, page 138. Reg. of Wills, Liber K, folios 242-243. Note:—Arch. vol. A32, page 138 shows that Grace McCombs was exec'x of James McCombs.

Manwaring, Richard. Yeoman. Admin. of, to John Hill, yeoman. Oct. 17, 1760. Arch. vol. A33, page 165. Reg. of Wills, Liber K, folio 243.

Gooding, John. Esq. Will. Made Oct. 5, 1760. Duck Creek. Heirs: wife Sarah; son John; daus. Rebecca Fowler & Gertrude Floyd; grandchildren William & Susannah Gooding. Exec'rs, wife Sarah, Samuel Floyd, Archibald Fowler. Wits., Abraham Allee, John Smithers, Silvester Luck. Prob. Oct. 24, 1760. Arch. vol. A19, page 130. Reg. of Wills, Liber K, folio 244.

Crumeen, Thomas. Yeoman. Admin. of, to Elizabeth Crumeen, widow. Nov. 8, 1760. Arch. vol. A12, pages 32-33. Reg. of Wills, Liber K, folio 245.

Molleston, Jemima. Wife of Henry Molleston. Will. Made Aug. 20, 1760. Heirs: sons John, Jonathan, Henry & William; dau. Jemima Brinckle, wife of John Brinckle. Exec'rs, sons John & Henry. Wits., Elizabeth Faries, G. Russell, Mark Manlove. Prob. Nov. 11, 1760. Arch. vol. A35, pages 211-212. Reg. of Wills, Liber K, folios 245-246.

Rork, William. Yeoman. Admin. of, to Milicent Rork. Nov. 12, 1760. Arch. vol. A29, page 89. Reg. of Wills, Liber K, folio 246.

Lucas, Thomas. Admin. of, to Robert Garreld, yeoman. Nov. 13, 1760. Reg. of Wills, Liber K, folio 246.

Houstown, James. Yeoman. Admin. of, to Hannah Houstown, widow. Nov. 14, 1760. Reg. of Wills, Liber K, folio 246. Note:—Arch. vol. A25, page 45 shows Hannah, the widow, later married William Cleaver.

Allston, Israel. Will. Made Nov. 5, 1760. Little Creek. Heirs: wife Sarah; sons Thomas, Abner, Joab [Job], Joshua, Israel, John; daus. Elizabeth, Sarah. Exec'x, wife. Wits., Randall Allston, John Roach, Edward Norman. Codicil, bros. Randall & Arthur Allston. Prob. Nov. 22, 1760. Arch. vol. A1, pages 106-108. Reg. of Wills, Liber K, folio 247. Note:— Arch. vol. A1, page 107 shows Sarah, the widow, later married Benjamin Hughbanks [Eubanks].

Jones, Philip. Farmer. Will. Made July 21, 1760. Heirs: child of Cathrine Thornton; bros. Lewis & Evan Jones; Cathrine Thornton; Thomas Jones. Exec'r, friend Jacob Stout. Wits., John Humpris, John Buris. Prob. Nov. 24, 1760. Arch. vol. A28, pages 5-7. Reg. of Wills, Liber K, folios 247-248.

Webb, John. Will. Made Oct. 29, 1760. Heirs: wife Ann; daus. Elizabeth & Sarah; sons Caleb & Daniel. Exec'rs, wife Ann & John Caton, Esq. Wits., Stephen Lewis, James Howell, Thomas Cain. Prob. Dec. 1, 1760. Arch. vol. A53, pages 203-205. Reg. of Wills, Liber L, folios 195, 204-205. Note:— Arch. vol. A53, page 205 shows that Ann Webb married James Howell.

Jubart, Andrew. Yeoman. Will. Made Jan. 16, 1760. Redlion Hd., N. C. Co. Heirs: wife Sarah; son Peter; daus. Sarah & Mary. Exec'rs, friends Jerome Dushane & Ardian Laforge, yeoman. Wits., John Dodd, James Watt, William Robinson. Prob. Dec. 12, 1760. Arch. vol. A28, page 67. Reg. of Wills, Liber K, folio 244.

Gray, John. Yeoman. Admin. of, to James Gray, yeoman. Dec. 22, 1760. Arch. vol. A20, page 22. Reg. of Wills, Liber K, folio 249.

Reynalls, Henry. Will. Made Dec. 15, 1760. Heirs: wife Sarah; sons Ephriam & Richard; dau. Elizabeth Williams, wife of Ezekiel Williams; dau.-in-law Mary Reynalls, wife of son Ephriam; son-in-law Ezekiel Williams; grandsons John Reynalls (son of Ephriam & Mary Reynalls) & Thomas Williams (son of Ezekiel & Elizabeth Williams). Exec'rs, wife Sarah & son Richard. Wits., Thomas Clark, John Brown, Jonathan Cottingham. Prob. Dec. 23, 1760. Arch. vol. A43, pages 98-100. Reg. of Wills, Liber K, folio 249. Note:—Arch. vol. A43, page 99 shows heirs, Rachel Turner, Milliset Bourke, Lurania Darbe.

Smith, Sarah. Widow. Will. Made Oct. 31, 1760. Heirs: sons Samuel Jois & Joseph Smith; grandsons Samuel Jois, son of Samuel, & John Smith, son of Nightingal Smith; grandchildren John Smith, Sarah Richards, Esther Start [Hart], children of son John Smith; dau.-in-law Isabel Clark. Exec'rs, grandson John Smith & dau.-in-law Isabel Clark. Wits., Mark Manlove, Neal Daus. Prob. Dec. 23, 1760. Arch. vol. A47, page 168. Reg. of Wills, Liber K, folio 250.

Robinson, Asa. Admin. of, to Daniel Robinson, Jr., saddler. Dec. 24, 1760. Arch. vol. A44, page 33. Reg. of Wills, Liber K, folios 250-251.

Dill, William. Planter. Will. Made Nov. 2, 1760. Heirs: wife Mary; sons & daus. unnamed. Exec'x, wife. Wits., John Dill, Mary Dill. Prob. Dec. 27, 1760. Arch. vol. A14, pages 122-123. Reg. of Wills, Liber K, folio 251.

Butcher, John. Yeoman. Admin. of, to Sarah Butcher, widow. Dec. 29, 1760. Reg. of Wills, Liber K, folio 248. Note:— Arch. vol. A7, page 8 shows Sarah, the widow, later married Thomas Murphey.

Tool, Charles. Yeoman. Admin. of, to Hannah Tool, widow. Dec. 29, 1760. Arch. vol. A50, page 230. Reg. of Wills, Liber K, folios 248-249.

Rash, John. Will. Made Oct. 13, 1757. Heirs: sons Joseph, James, William; daus. Elizabeth Swails, Mary Downham (wife of Thomas Downham), Sarah Smith (wife of David Smith), Hannah Forkham (wife of Renn Forkham). Exec'rs, son James & Joseph Powell. Wits., William Powell, John Millaway, John Powell. Prob. Jan. 3, 1761. Arch. vol. A42, pages 38-39. Reg. of Wills, Liber K, folio 251.

Hillyard, Charles. Tailor. Admin. of, to Eleanor Hillyard, widow. Jan. 8, 1761. Reg. of Wills, Liber K, folio 252.

Jemison, Jenett. Widow. Will. Made Aug. 28, 1759. Duck Creek. Heirs: sons Andrew, Joseph, Joshua, Thomas, Alexander; daus. Rebecca Hull, Ann Hutson; Jenett Jemison, dau. of Alexander Jemison. Exec'r, son Andrew. Wits., Sam. Smith, Hugh McEllroy, Rebecca Tolan. Prob. Jan. 9, 1761. Arch. vol. A26, page 200. Reg. of Wills, Liber K, folio 252.

Few, Daniel. Yeoman. Admin. of, to Esther Few. Jan. 10, 1761. Arch. vol. A16, page 246. Reg. of Wills, Liber K, folio 253.

Rose, James. Yeoman. Admin. of, to Mary Rose, widow. Jan. 14, 1761. Reg. of Wills, Liber K, folio 253.

Moore, Jane [Jean]. Will. Made April 26, 1756. Heirs: sons John & James; John Miller; daus. Mary Miller, Jane [Jean] Moore. Exec'rs, son John & John Miller. Wits., Augustain Voshall, John Tomson, Benjamin Jones. Prob. Jan. 15, 1761. Arch. vol. A36, page 47. Reg. of Wills, Liber K, folios 253-254.

Clayton, Joshua. Will. Made Sept. 2, 1760. Little Creek Hd. Heirs: wife Sarah; grandsons John, Henry, Thomas, Ezekiel &Clayton Cowgill; granddaus. Eunice Ozbun, Sarah Hand, Elenor Cowgill, Rachel Grewell, Sarah Register, Elizabeth Neal, Jean Smith & Lydia Durborow. Exec'rs, friend Timothy Hanson & grandson-in-law Jonathan Ozbun. Wits., Mary Manlove, Elizabeth Manlove, Sarah Needham. Prob. Jan. 26, 1761. Arch. vol. A9, pages 121-122. Reg. of Wills, Liber K, folios 254-255. Note:—Will mentions dau. Sarah Cowgill, dec'd.

Peterson, Andrew. Will. Made Jan. 3, 1761. Heirs: wife Sarah; sons Andrew & Israel; dau. Mary. Exec'x, wife Sarah. Wits., Jacob Corbet, William Strickland Corbet, Elizabeth Green. Prob. Jan. 29, 1761. Arch. vol. A40, pages 16-18. Reg. of Wills, Liber K, folio 255. Note:—Arch. vol. A40, page 17 shows Sarah, the widow, later married Isaac Carty.

Sherrad, William. Yeoman. Admin. of, to Hannah Sherrad, widow. Jan. 29, 1761. Reg. of Wills, Liber K, folio 256.

Crippen, William, Sr. Yeoman. Admin. of, to William Crippen, Jr. Feb. 3, 1761. Arch. vol. A11, page 229. Reg. of Wills, Liber K, folio 256.

Snow, John. Yeoman. Will. Made Dec. 29, 1760. Duck Creek. Heirs: sister Phebe Snow; bro. Silas Snow. Exec'rs, bro. Silas & Silvester Luck. Wits., Thomas Malone, Mary Malone. Prob. Feb. 11, 1761. Arch. vol. A48, page 15. Reg. of Wills, Liber K, folio 256.

Deweese, William. Will. Made Dec. 11, 1760. Heirs: wife Sarah; daus. Mary, Sarah, Nancy & Rachel; sons John, William, Matthew, Elijah, Daniel. Exec'rs, wife Sarah & bro. Cornelius Deweese. Wits., Samuel Merydith, Rachel Bartlett,

Mary Dewese. Prob. Feb. 11, 1761. Arch. vol. A14, pages 55-58. Reg. of Wills, Liber K, folio 257. Note:—Will shows Sarah, the widow, later married Thomas Bowman.

McClement, Andrew. Yeoman. Admin. of, to Agness McClement, widow. Feb. 26, 1761. Reg. of Wills, Liber K, folio 258. Note:—Arch. vol. A32, page 103 shows that Agnes McClement later married Alexandrew McLeheney.

Brown, Ann. Admin. of, to Jonathan Molleston, yeoman. March 4, 1761. Arch. vol. A6, page 16. Reg. of Wills, Liber K, folio 258.

Pratt, Dinah. Widow. Admin. of, to George Pratt, yeoman. March 11, 1761. Arch. vol. A41, page 64. Reg. of Wills, Liber K, folios 258-259.

Martin, Patrick. Gentleman. Admin. of, to John Clayton, Esq. March 14, 1761. Arch. vol. A33, page 210. Reg. of Wills, Liber K, folio 259.

Smith, Mark. Gentleman. Admin. of, to Elizabeth Smith, widow, and Henry Peterson. March 14, 1761. Reg. of Wills, Liber K, folio 259.

Thomson, Martha. Will. Made Feb. 7, 1761. Duck Creek. Heir: bro. Moses Thomson. Exec'r, bro. Moses. Wits., Mary Person, Mary Best. Prob. March 14, 1761. Arch. vol. A50, page 100. Reg. of Wills, Liber K, folio 261.

Wallace, Thomas. Yeoman. Admin. of, to Ruth Wallace widow. March 21, 1761. Reg. of Wills, Liber K, folios 259-260.

Manlove, William. Will. Made Aug. 16, 1760. Mispillion. Heirs: wife Alse; daus. Mary Mason & Sarah Masten; son-in-law Joseph Mason; granddaus. Sarah Mason (dau. of Joseph & Mary Mason), Mary & Elizabeth Manlove; grandson William Masten, Jr. Exec'r, Joseph Mason. Wits., Elias Mason, Isaac Codery, Samuel Burrows. Prob. March 24, 1761. Arch. vol. A33, pages 137-139. Reg. of Wills, Liber K, folio 260.

Brown, James. Admin. of, to Elizabeth Brown, widow. March 28, 1761. Arch. vol. A6, page 253. Reg. of Wills, Liber K, folio 262.

Irons, Timothy. Admin. of, to Elizabeth Irons, widow. April 6, 1761. Arch. vol. A25, page 229. Reg. of Wills, Liber K, folio 261.

Cavender, Jane. Admin. of, to Sarah Connor, spinster. April 17, 1761. Reg. of Wills, Liber K, folio 262.

Clayton, James. Gentleman. Admin. of, to John Clayton, Esq. May 20, 1761. Arch. vol. A9, pages 110-111. Reg. of Wills, Liber K, folio 262.

Spring, Jesper. Yeoman. Admin. of, to Mary Spring, widow. May 27, 1761. Reg. of Wills, Liber K, folio 263.

David, Lewis. A minor. Admin. of, to Robert Willcocks. May 29, 1761. Arch. vol. A12, pages 234-235.

Galloway, Richard. Admin. of, to Lydia Galloway, widow. June 8, 1761. Reg. of Wills, Liber K, folio 263. Note:—Arch. vol. A18, pages 206-207 show Lydia, the widow, later married Peter Goforth; also mention Henrietta Smith, Elizabeth, Samuel & Joseph Galloway.

Maxwell, William. Yeoman. Will. Made March 6, 1761. Little Creek Hd. Heirs: wife Jane [Jean]; sons William, James, Samuel; daus. Mary, Sarah, Lydia, Elizabeth. Exec'x, wife Jane [Jean]. Trustee, friend Henry Stevens. Wits., William Levick, Clayton Levick, Mark Hirons. Prob. June 13, 1761. Arch. vol. A34, page 105. Reg. of Wills, Liber K, folio 264.

Alford, Mary. Widow. Admin. of, to Richard Wells, Esq. June 17, 1761. Reg. of Wills, Liber K, folio 263.

Alford, Mary. Will. Made Aug. 23, 1759. Heirs: son Moses; grandchildren Mary & Thomas, children of son Moses Alford. Wits., George Willson, James Willson. Prob. June 17, 1761. Arch. vol. A1, page 28. Reg. of Wills, Liber K, folios 263-264.

Loatman, Jeremiah. Admin. of, to Agnuss Loatman. June 18, 1761. Reg. of Wills, Liber K, folio 264. Note:—Arch. vol. A30, page 200 shows Agness, the widow, later married William Sappington.

Lennard, John. Admin. of, to Charles Green, yeoman. June 29, 1761. Reg. of Wills, Liber K, folio 264.

Lennard, Grace. Widow. Admin. of, to Charles Green, yeoman. June 29, 1761. Reg. of Wills, Liber K, folio 265.

Drew, William. Yeoman. Admin. of, to Thomas Nixon, merchant. June 30, 1761. Reg. of Wills, Liber K, folio 265.

Lewis, Daniel. Will. Made June 22, 1761. Dover Hd. Heirs: wife Peggy; sons Daniel & Stephen; dau. Elizabeth. Exec'rs, wife Peggy & son Stephen. Wits., Caesar Rodney, Charles Marim, Wilson Buck[master]. Prob. July 22, 1761. Arch. vol. A30, pages 59-62. Reg. of Wills, Liber K, folio 265. Note:—Arch. vol. A30, page 61 shows Daniel Lewis a relative of Stephen Paradee; also mentions Geo. Gordon & wife Mary, dau. of John Parradee; page 59 shows Margaret, the widow, later married Jonathan Caldwell.

Beard, Ann. Admin. of, to Moses Beard, yeoman. July 28, 1761. Reg. of Wills, Liber K, folio 266.

Barns, Ann. Admin. of, to John Blackshear & Jane, his wife. Aug. 13, 1761. Reg. of Wills, Liber K, folio 266.

Gold [Gould], Thomas. Admin. of, to Sarah Gold [Gould], widow. Aug. 15, 1761. Reg. of Wills, Liber K, folio 266. Note:— Arch. vol. A19, page 128 mentions heirs, Sarah & Thomas Gold.

Brinckle, Richard. Admin. of, to Andrew Gray, D. B. N. Aug. 27, 1761. Arch. vol. A5, page 204.

Peasley, John. Yeoman. Admin. of, to Margaret Peasley, widow. Sept. 5, 1761. Arch. vol. A39, page 183. Reg. of Wills, Liber K, folio 267.

Pope, William. Yeoman. Admin. of, to Catharine Pope, widow. Sept. 8, 1761. Reg. of Wills, Liber K, folio 267. Note:—Arch. vol. A4, pages 186-187 show heirs, Mary, Susanna, Charles, William, Sarah & Rachel Pope; also shows Catherine, the widow, later married Charles Stuart.

Smith, James. Yeoman. Admin. of, to Henerettha Smith, widow. Oct. 14, 1761. Arch. vol. A47, pages 60-62. Reg. of Wills, Liber K, folio 267.

Brooks, Jonathan. Laborer. Admin. of, to John Evans, laborer. Oct. 15, 1761. Reg. of Wills, Liber K, folio 268.

Brooks, Martha. Widow. Admin. of, to John Hamilton. Oct. 28, 1761. Arch. vol. A6, page 12. Reg. of Wills, Liber K, folio 268.

Holegeros, Mary. Widow. Admin. of, to William Crippen, yeoman. Nov. 12, 1761. Reg. of Wills, Liber K, folios 268-269.

Trippet, Daniel. Yeoman. Admin. of, to Ann Trippett. Nov. 26, 1761. Arch. vol. A51, page 74. Reg. of Wills, Liber K, folio 269.

Taylor, Ann. Widow. Admin. of, to Ruben Taylor, laborer. Nov. 28, 1761. Reg. of Wills, Liber K, folio 269.

Revell, William. Yeoman. Admin. of, to Anthony Rawlings. Nov. 30, 1761. Reg. of Wills, Liber K, folios 269-270.

Sapp, Ann. Widow. Admin. of, to Henry Sapp & Benjamin Sapp. Dec. 12, 1761. Arch. vol. A44, page 226. Reg. of Wills, Liber K, folio 270.

Ridgely, Mary. Admin. of, to Charles Ridgely, Esq. Dec. 21, 1761. Arch. vol. A43, page 227. Reg. of Wills, Liber K, folio 270.

Wyatt, Thomas. Yeoman. Admin. of, to Mary Ann Wyatt, widow, & William Morris, son of Mary. Jan. 5, 1762. Reg. of Wills, Liber K, folio 271. Note:—Arch. vol. A56, page 175 shows Thomas as youngest of nine children.

Alford, Thomas. Yeoman. Admin. of, to Richard Wells, Esq. Jan. 6, 1762. Arch. vol. A1, page 247. Reg. of Wills, Liber K, folio 271.

Wells, William. Innholder. Admin. of, to Elizabeth Wells, widow. Jan. 6, 1762. Arch. vol. A54, pages 4-6. Reg. of Wills, Liber K, folio 272.

Reddick, Robert, Sr. Will. Made Dec. 11, 1761. Heirs: wife unnamed; sons Cornelius, James, John, Robert, William, Benjamin; daus. Mary & Rachel. Exec'rs, wife & son Cornelius. Wits., Hugh Maguire, John Rees, John Carrow. Prob. Jan.

8, 1762. Arch. vol. A42, pages 177-178. Reg. of Wills, Liber K, folio 272. Note:—Arch. vol. A42, page 178 shows Catharine Reddick as exec'x.

Bibbin, John. Hatter. Admin. of, to Jane Bibbin, widow. Jan. 12, 1762. Arch. vol. A4, page 45. Reg. of Wills, Liber K, folio 273.

Bibbin, John. Will (nunc.). Made Jan. 8, 1762. Heir: wife Jean [Jane]. Wits., Rachel Bohannan, Samuel McCall, William Conikin. Prob. Jan. 16, 1762. Arch. vol. A4, page 45. Reg. of Wills, Liber K, folio 273.

Durborow, Elizabeth. Widow of Hugh Durborow. Will. Made Dec. 18, 1761. Murtherkill. Heirs: sons Daniel, Benjamin, David Durborow & John Greenaway; daus. Mary Durborow, Elizabeth Roe (wife of James Roe), Hannah Moor (wife of James Moor), Esther McCombs (wife of Bartholomew McCombs), Sarah Miller [Mitter] (wife of Camel Miller [Mitter]). Exec'r, son Benjamin. Wits., John Barns, John Parker. Prob. Jan. 16, 1762. Arch. vol. A15, page 161. Reg. of Wills, Liber K, folio 274.

Parker, Sarah. Widow. Admin. of, to William Parker, yeoman. Jan. 20, 1762. Reg. of Wills, Liber K, folios 274-275.

McKemmey, John. Yeoman. Admin. of, to Andrew Caldwell, Esq. Feb. 1, 1762. Reg. of Wills, Liber K, folio 275.

Sipple, Caleb. Yeoman. Admin. of, to Sarah Sipple, widow. Feb. 10, 1762. Reg. of Wills, Liber K, folio 275. Note:—Arch. vol. A46, pages 87-89 show Sarah, the widow, later married David Lewis; also mention children Nancy, John, Caleb, Mary, Thomas, Elizabeth & Garret.

Sipple, Waitman. Will. Made Jan. 27, 1762. Heirs: wife Mary; sons Waitman, Jonathan & Elijah; daus. Anna Furbee & Meriam Barrett; children of son Caleb. Exec'rs, sons Waitman & Jonathan. Wits., Daniel Robisson, Silvester Tomson, Henry Whitacur. Prob. Feb. 11, 1762. Arch. vol. A46, pages 174-176. Reg. of Wills, Liber K, folio 276.

Campbell, James. Schoolmaster. Admin. of, to Wilson Buckmaster. Feb. 12, 1762. Reg. of Wills, Liber K, folios 275-276.

Jones, James. Yeoman. Admin. of, to Mary Jones, widow. Feb. 23, 1762. Reg. of Wills, Liber K, folio 277. Note:—Arch. vol. A27, page 200 shows Mary, the widow, later married Emanuel Stout.

Molleston, Henry. Will. Made Dec. 21, 1761. Heirs: sons Henry, Jonathan, William; dau. Jemimah Brinckle; granddau. Mary Molleston, dau. of son Henry; grandson Henry Molleston, son of son Henry; Eleanor Hall. Exec'r, son Henry. Wits., Daniel Robisson, William Manlove, Elizabeth Miller. Prob. Feb. 23, 1762. Arch. vol. A35, pages 204-205. Reg. of Wills, Liber K, folio 280.

Skidmore, John. Practitioner. Admin. of, to Samuel Skidmore. Feb. 24, 1762. Arch. vol. A46, pages 194-196. Reg. of Wills, Liber K, folio 277.

Lockwood, Armwell. Admin. of, to John Purdon & wife Mary, late Mary Lockwood. Feb. 25, 1762. Arch. vol. A30, page 214. Note:—Mentions heirs, Nehemiah, Mary & Israel Holland Lockwood.

Hoy, Pheebe. Admin. of, to Thomas Parke. Feb. 26, 1762. Reg. of Wills, Liber K, folios 277-278.

West, David, Jr. Yeoman. Admin. of, to Rebecca West, widow. March 2, 1762. Reg. of Wills, Liber K, folio 278. Note:— Arch. vol. A54, page 10 shows Rebecca, the widow, later married Simon Vanwinckle.

Asbee, Eleanor. Widow. Will. Made Nov. 24, 1761. Heirs: son John Asbee; daus. Esther, Sofiah & Henrietta Mariah Asbee. Wits., Ruth Clark & Thomas Clark. Prob. March 4, 1762. Arch. vol. A2, page 9.

Alle, Jacob, Jr. Yeoman. Admin. of, to John Alle, gentleman. March 16, 1762. Reg. of Wills, Liber K, folio 278.

Merydith, Job. Admin. of, to Jonathan Hunn, yeoman. March 17, 1762. Reg. of Wills, Liber K, folios 278-279.

Savage, John. Yeoman. Admin. of, to Thomas Nixon, merchant. March 20, 1762. Reg. of Wills, Liber K, folio 279.

Garvey, Owen. Yeoman. Admin. of, to Sarah Garvey & John Garvey. March 24, 1762. Arch. vol. A18, page 229. Reg. of Wills, Liber K, folio 279.

Fitzgerald, Robert. Yeoman. Admin. of, to Elizabeth Fitzgerald, widow. April 14, 1762. Reg. of Wills, Liber K, folio 281. Note:—Arch. vol. A17, page 160 shows Elizabeth, the widow, later married John Vandeford.

Hanson, Timothy. Yeoman. Admin. of, to Elizabeth Hanson, widow. May 9, 1762. Reg. of Wills, Liber K, folio 281.

Carty, Sarah. Will. Made March 9, 1762. Duck Creek. Heirs: children unnamed; husband Isaac Carty. Exec'r, husband. Trustee, husband Isaac Carty. Wits., Edward Knott, Thomas Brown. Prob. May 12, 1762. Arch. vol. A8, page 56. Reg. of Wills, Liber K, folios 281-282.

Anderson, James. Will. Made April 3, 1761. Heirs: wife Elizabeth; sons James, Jr., William, Ezekiel, Elijah & Major; daus. Elizabeth Killingsworth (wife of Nathaniel Killingsworth), Rebecca McNatt (wife of Richard McNatt), Mary & Ann Anderson. Exec'x, wife Elizabeth. Wits., Thomas Clark, Rebecca Smith, Robert Smith. Prob. May 13, 1762. Arch. vol. A1, pages 172-173. Reg. of Wills, Liber K, folio 282.

Farson, William. Admin. of, to Jane Farson & Henry Farsons. May 13, 1762. Reg. of Wills, Liber K, folio 283.

Howell, Priscilla. Admin. of, to James Howell, Sr., yeoman. May 14, 1762. Reg. of Wills, Liber K, folio 283.

Powell, Nicholas. Will. Made April 9, 1762. Little Creek. Heirs: wife Mary; grandson Powell Whitehart; children of Thomas Jones; children of John Clark; Esther, dau. of William Siddin. Exec'rs, wife Mary & grandson Powell Whitehart. Wits., John Torbert, Daniel Newnam, William Corse. Prob. May 24, 1762. Arch. vol. A41, pages 43-44. Reg. of Wills, Liber K, folio 284. Note:—Arch. vol. A41, page 44 shows Mary, the widow, later married William Wilson.

Bowman, Henry. Yeoman. Admin. of, to Mary Bowman & Thomas Bowman. June 1, 1762. Reg. of Wills, Liber K, folio 284. Note:—Arch. vol. A5, pages 41-42 show Mary, the widow, later married Robert Minors; also Nathaniel Bowman, a son.

Burrows, John. Yeoman. Admin. of, to William Burrows. June 2, 1762. Arch. vol. A6, page 215. Reg. of Wills, Liber K, folio 285.

Mott, Richbell. Yeoman. Little Creek Hd. Admin. of, to Mathew Manlove & Sarah Manlove. June 10, 1762. Arch. vol. A37, pages 67-68. Reg. of Wills, Liber K, folio 285.

Whitehart, Solomon. Yeoman. Admin. of, to Grace Whitehart. June 14, 1762. Arch. vol. A54, page 191. Reg. of Wills, Liber K, folios 285-286.

Rawlings, Anthony. Trader. Admin. of, to Sarah Rawlings & Reynear Williams. June 23, 1762. Reg. of Wills, Liber K, folio 286. Note:—Arch. vol. A42, page 134 shows this acct. was later administered by Sarah Adams & Reynear Williams.

Revell, William. Yeoman. Admin. of, to Sarah Rawlings & Reynear Williams. June 23, 1762. Reg. of Wills, Liber K, folio 286.

Peerson, Moses. Yeoman. Admin. of, to Christopher Denny, yeoman. July 19, 1762. Reg. of Wills, Liber K, folio 287.

Frazer, Alexander. Will. [n. d.]. Heirs: son William; wife Sarah; bro. Andrew. Exec'x, wife Sarah. Wits., Thomas Ross, John Rees, Larania Rees. Prob. July 20, 1762. Arch. vol. A18, page 90. Reg. of Wills, Liber K, folio 287.

Hunn, Reynear. Farmer. Will (copy). Made July 29, 1762. Heirs: father Nathaniel Hunn; bro. Jonathan; nephew Nathaniel, son of bro. Jonathan; niece Mary, dau. of bro. Jonathan; sister Sarah Hunn; Skidmore Wilson, son of William Wilson. Exec'rs, father Nathaniel & bro. Jonathan. Wits., Nathan Adams, John Plesenton, Joice Lynch. Prob. Aug. 11, 1762. Arch. vol. A25, page 170. Reg. of Wills, Liber K, folio 288.

Blacks, Samuel. Yeoman. Admin. of, to Catherine Blacks. Aug. 11, 1762. Reg. of Wills, Liber K, folio 289.

Frazier, William. Yeoman. Mispillion. Admin. of, to Rhoda Frazier, widow. Aug. 25, 1762. Reg. of Wills, Liber K, folio 289. Note:—Arch. vol. A18, pages 102-104 show Rhoda, the widow, later married Thomas Peterkin; also William & Elizabeth as children of William; Edward Carey married Susannah Frazier, heir of William Frazier.

McDonnel [McDonald], James. Admin. of, to Mary McDonnel. Aug. 25, 1762. Arch. vol. A32, page 163. Note:—Mentions heirs, Sarah, Mary and Alexander McDonald.

Carl, Thomas. Admin. of, to Abraham Wynkoop. Aug. 26, 1762. Arch. vol. A7, page 216.

Mills, Sarah. Admin. of, to Elizabeth Boyer. Aug. 31, 1762. Reg. of Wills, Liber K, folios 289-290.

Gascoigne, Mary. Admin. of, to Govey Emmerson, yeoman. Sept. 6, 1762. Reg. of Wills, Liber K, folio 290.

Warren, Benjamin. Will. Made July 3, 1762. Murtherkill Hd. Heirs: wife Mary; son Benjamin; grandsons Benjamin & John Warren; granddaus. Miriam & Lydia Newell. Exec'rs, son Benjamin & wife Mary. Wits., Daniel Robisson, John Dunning, Mary Feagins. Prob. Sept. 21, 1762. Arch. vol. A53, page 127. Reg. of Wills, Liber K, folios 290-291.

Plummer, Moses. Cordwainer. Admin. of to, Mary Plummer, widow. Sept. 23, 1762. Arch. vol. A40, page 144. Reg. of Wills, Liber K, folio 291.

Wallace, Mathew. Will. Made Aug. 21, 1762. Heirs: wife Agnes; sons Thomas, David; daus. Barbary Rash, Barsheba & Jenet Wallace; granddau. Agnes Rash. Exec'x, wife Agnes. Wits., James Hussey, Elizabeth Wallace, Deborah Williams. Prob. Sept. 25, 1762. Arch. vol. A53, page 5. Reg. of Wills, Liber K, folios 291-292.

Ruall, James. Yeoman. Admin. of, to Elenor Ruall. Sept. 30, 1762. Arch. vol. A44, page 177. Reg. of Wills, Liber K, folio 292.

Ross, Andrew. Yeoman. Admin. of, to William Ross, yeoman. Oct. 4, 1762. Reg. of Wills, Liber K, folios 292-293.

Brown, Joshua. Yeoman. Admin. of, to William & John Brown. Oct. 13, 1762. Arch. vol. A6, pages 70-71. Reg. of Wills, Liber K, folio 293. Note:—Arch. vol. A6, page 70 mentions heirs, John, William, Benjamin & James Brown, Elizabeth Anderson, Mary Wallace, Sarah Berry.

Hudson, Daniel. Yeoman. Admin. of, to Mary Hudson, widow. Oct. 19, 1762. Reg. of Wills, Liber K, folio 293.

White, William. Admin. of, to Sarah White. Nov. 1, 1762. Arch. vol. A54, pages 170-171. Reg. of Wills, Liber K, folios 293-294.

Montgomery, Alexander. Merchant. Admin. of, to George Monroe. Nov. 4, 1762. Reg. of Wills, Liber K, folio 301.

Hawkins, Thomas. Yeoman. Admin. of, to Arnald Hawkins & John Hawkins. Nov. 10, 1762. Arch. vol. A23, page 38. Reg. of Wills, Liber K, folio 294.

Galloway, Daniel. Will. Made Oct. 30, 1762. Murderkill Hd. Heirs: sisters Elizabeth Galloway & Henneritt Smith; bro. Samuel Galloway; Joseph Pearson; Joseph Galloway; James Smith, Jr. Exec'r, William Fryer. Wits., Benjamin Wynn, Thomas Hardin. Prob. Nov. 10, 1762. Arch. vol. A18, page 204. Reg. of Wills, Liber K, folio 294.

Harrington, James. Yeoman. Admin. of, to Elizabeth Harrington, widow. Nov. 10, 1762. Arch. vol. A22, page 115. Reg. of Wills, Liber K, folio 295.

Whithart [Whitehart], Sarah. Widow. Will. Made Oct. 11, 1762. Little Creek Hd. Heirs: grandsons Samuel, John, Allen, Solomon & Powell Whitehart; granddaus. Sarah & Mary Whitehart. Exec'x, dau. Grace Whitehart. Wits., Elizabeth Cremine, Silvester Luck, Thomas Alberry. Prob. Nov. 11, 1762. Arch. vol. A54, page 189. Reg. of Wills, Liber K, folios 300-301. Note:—Will mentions sons Solomon & Samuel, dec'd.

Allen, John. Cordwainer. Duck Creek Hd. Admin. of, to Thomas Wilson, yeoman. Nov. 12, 1762. Reg. of Wills, Liber K, folio 295. Note:—Arch. vol. A1, page 83 shows John Dickinson, as adm'r, D. B. N.; also mentions a son John Allen, Jr., with guardians John & William Johnson.

Jones, Benjamin. Will. Made Oct. 25, 1762. Heirs: wife Barbara; sons James, Nicholas, Stanford, Benjamin; daus. Lydia Parvin, Jerusha Williams, Elizabeth Salley, Mary Vanderford, Ann Rash, Dorithy Willis, Sarah Thomas & Levice Jones. Exec'r, son Benjamin. Wits., William Wheeler, Mary Hall. Prob. Nov. 13, 1762. Arch. vol. A27, pages 135-136. Reg. of Wills, Liber K, folios 295-296.

Gordon, Griffith. Will. Made Sept. 27, 1762. Heirs: wife Sarah; daus. Elizabeth, Letitia, Sarah; sons John & Coe. Exec'rs, wife Sarah, dau. Elizabeth & son John. Appraisers, Caesar Rodney & James Sykes. Wits., James Sykes, Ebenezer Manlove, Caesar Rodney. Prob. Nov. 13, 1762. Arch. vol. A19, pages 150-152. Reg. of Wills, Liber K, folios 296-297.

Kelly, William. Laborer. Admin. of, to Vincent Loockerman, merchant. Nov. 17, 1762. Arch. vol. A28, page 110. Reg. of Wills, Liber K, folio 297.

Wheeler, Samuel. Yeoman. Admin. of, to Sarah Wheeler, widow. Nov. 24, 1762. Reg. of Wills, Liber K, folio 298. Note:— Arch. vol. A54, page 67 shows Sarah, the widow, later married Andrew Gray.

Rogers, Roger. Schoolmaster. Will. Made March 1, 1761. Whitemarsh Forrest. Heirs: son John; housekeeper Martha Kitts [Kins]. Exec'x, Martha Kitts. Wits., John Baynard, William Baynard, Anthony Wise. Prob. Nov. 27, 1762. Arch. vol. A44, page 128. Reg. of Wills, Liber K, folio 298.

Penny, John. Will. Made Nov. 21, 1762. Murtherkill Hd. Heir: wife Susannah. Exec'x, wife Susannah. Wits., Richard Hooper, John Larkin, Thomas Hardin. Prob. Dec. 6, 1762. Arch. vol. A39, page 229. Reg. of Wills, Liber K, folios 298-299.

Miller, Dorathy. Will. Made...1761. Heirs: dau. Susannah Quilling; granddau. Mary Quilling; sons Henry, Peter, Adam, Chillen, John & Conrad Miller. Exec'rs, sons Adam & Chillen Miller. Wits., John Wood, Joseph Quilling. Prob. Dec. 7, 1762. Arch. vol. A35, page 74. Reg. of Wills, Liber K, folio 299. Note:—Will mentions Clement Quilling.

Larkins, John. Laborer. Admin. of, to James Colgun, trader. Dec. 17, 1762. Reg. of Wills, Liber K, folio 300.

Tomlin [Tumblin], Joseph. Cabinetmaker. Admin. of, to James Piper, trader. Jan. 11, 1763. Arch. vol. A50, page 177. Reg. of Wills, Liber K, folios 301-302.

Toogood [Twogood], James. Farmer. Will. Made Dec. 29, 1762. Heir: friend and housekeeper Elizabeth Buirch. Exec'x, Elizabeth Buirch. Wits., Robert Teat, Timothy Roberts. Prob. Jan. 14, 1763. Arch. vol. A51, page 184. Reg. of Wills, Liber K, folio 302.

Hewes, Isabel. Widow. Will. Made June 13, 1757. Little Creek Hd. Heirs: dau. Sarah; son John; son-in-law John Durham. Exec'x, dau. Sarah. Wits., Mary Barton, Sarah Harris, Edward Norman. Prob. Jan. 19, 1763. Arch. vol. A23, pages 194-195. Reg. of Wills, Liber K, folios 302-303. Note:— Arch. vol. A23, page 195 shows Sarah later married James Dean.

Tompson, John. Yeoman. Admin. of, to Ruth Tompson, widow. Jan. 21, 1763. Arch. vol. A50, pages 92-94. Reg. of Wills, Liber K, folio 303.

Peterson, Adam. Will (copy). Made Jan. 23, 1763. St. Georges Hd., N. C. Co. Heirs: wife Veronica Peterson; cousins Richard & Lydia Cantwell. Exec'x, wife Veronica. Wits., Robert Moody, James Lattomus, A. Belveal. [No prob.]. Arch. vol. A40, page 15.

Adams, William. Yeoman. Admin. of, to Nathan Adams. Jan. 29, 1763. Arch. vol. A1, page 10. Reg. of Wills, Liber K, folios 303-304.

Wells, John. Yeoman. Admin. of, to Stockly Sturgis. Feb. 8, 1763. Arch. vol. A53, page 234. Reg. of Wills, Liber K, folio 304.

Hardin, Thomas. Yeoman. Admin. of, to Hannah Hardin, widow. Feb. 9, 1763. Reg. of Wills, Liber K, folio 304. Note:—Arch. vol. A24, page 24 shows that Hannah Hardin married Clayton Levick.

Fisher, John. Yeoman. Admin. of, to Hannah Fisher, widow. Feb. 9, 1763. Reg. of Wills, Liber K, folios 304-305.

Benson, Jonathan. Yeoman. Admin. of, to Mary Benson. Feb. 9, 1763. Arch. vol. A3, page 241. Reg. of Wills, Liber K, folio 305.

Snow, Elisha. Farmer. Will. Made Feb. 16, 1761. Heirs: son Anthony; daus. Elizabeth Brown & Mary Snow. Exec'r, son Anthony. Wits., Benjamin Snow, Richard Tobin. Prob. Feb. 9, 1763. Arch. vol. A47, page 239. Reg. of Wills, Liber K, folio 305.

Greenwood, John. Will. Made Dec. 31, 1762. Little Creek Hd. Heir: cousin Richard Holliday. Exec'r, cousin Richard Holliday. Wits., Daniel Smith, Sarah Frazar, Robert Holliday. Prob. Feb. 9, 1763. Arch. vol. A20, page 150. Reg. of Wills, Liber K, folio 306.

Copner, Cornelius. Admin. of, to Catherine Copner. Feb. 11, 1763. Reg. of Wills, Liber K, folios 306-307.

Morgan, George. Admin. of, to John Clayton. Feb. 23, 1763. Arch. vol. A36, pages 146-148. Note:—Arch. vol. A36, page 148 mentions widow Martha Morgan.

Delap, Allen. Will. Made Dec. 24, 1762. Heirs: bros. William & Peter. Exec'r, bro. William. Wits., John Chalsant, Paul Jaquat, Thomas Edmunds, Mary Steel. Prob. Feb. 26, 1763. Arch. vol. A13, page 180. Reg. of Wills, Liber K, folio 307.

Caldwell, Joseph. Yeoman. Admin. of, to Mary Caldwell, widow. March 10, 1763. Arch. vol. A7, pages 119-120. Reg. of Wills, Liber K, folios 307-308.

Sherwood, Hannah. Will. Made Nov. 15, 1762. Duck Creek. Heirs: granddaus. Hannah Owens, Mary & Elizabeth Sherwood (daus. of son William); son-in-law Ishmael Owens. Exec'rs, son William & son-in-law Ishmael Owens. Wits., John Dawson, Edward Litman. Prob. March 12, 1763. Arch. vol. A45, page 240. Reg. of Wills, Liber K, folio 308.

McBride, William. Yeoman. Admin. of, to Margaret McBride, widow. March 25, 1763. Arch. vol. A32, page 86. Reg. of Wills, Liber K, folio 309.

Newnan, Richard. Yeoman. Admin. of, to Daniel Newnan, Sr., yeoman. April 1, 1763. Reg. of Wills, Liber K, folios 308-309.

Clampett, John, Jr. Yeoman. Admin. of, to Ebenezer & Moses Clampet. April 8, 1763. Arch. vol. A8, page 205. Reg. of Wills, Liber K, folio 309.

Floyd, Thomas. Yeoman. Admin. of, to Elizabeth Floyd, widow, & Letitia Lee. May 7, 1763. Arch. vol. A17, page 210. Reg. of Wills, Liber K, folios 309-310.

Wilson, Thomas. Will. Made April 4, 1763. Dover Hd. Heirs: wife Elizabeth; son John; dau. Sarah; bro. William; James Stevens. Exec'rs, wife Elizabeth & friend John Dickinson. Wits., Ebenezer Manlove, Caesar Rodney, Philn. Dickinson, William Rodney. Prob. May 10, 1763. Arch. vol. A56, pages 19-20. Reg. of Wills, Liber K, folio 310.

Carman, Joseph, Sr. Carpenter. Admin. of, to Joseph Carman, Jr. May 11, 1763. Reg. of Wills, Liber K, folio 311.

Wallace, Josiah. Will. Made April 22, 1763. Heirs: housekeeper Easther Knott; bro. Benjamin; cousin Josiah Wallace, son of Benjamin; Nancy Knott, dau. of Easther Knott. Exec'rs, Easther Knott & bro. Benjamin Wallace. Wits., Jabez Jenkins, James Gordon. Prob. May 12, 1763. Arch. vol. A52, pages 240-244. Reg. of Wills, Liber K, folio 311.

Lewis, Susannah. Will. Made March 20, 1763. Heirs: sons Bowers, Michael, Caleb & Benjamin Furbey, Daniel, David, Joseph & Stephen Lewis; dau. Elizabeth Boyer. Exec'r, son Michael Furbey. Trustees, friends John Caton, Daniel Robisson. Wits., Daniel Robisson, Hanahretta Anderton, Febey Pecue. Prob. May 18, 1763. Arch. vol. A30, pages 147-148. Reg. of Wills, Liber K, folio 312. Note:—Arch. vol. A30, page 148 shows James Boyer & Mary Furbee, adm'rs, D. B. N.

Brinckle, John. Yeoman. Will. Made July 30, 1762. Little Creek Hd. Heirs: wife Ann; sons John & Joseph. Exec'r, son John. Wits., Peter Brinckle, Robert Hall, William Brinckle. Prob. June 7, 1763. Arch. vol. A5, page 173. Reg. of Wills, Liber K, folios 312-313.

Gildersleeves, Noah. Yeoman. Admin. of, to Elizabeth Gildersleeves. June 14, 1763. Arch. vol. A19, page 54. Reg. of Wills, Liber K, folio 313.

Gooding, Sarah. Gentlewoman. Will. Made July 23, 1763. Duck Creed Hd. Heirs: sons John & Jonathan Raymond; daus. Rachel Raymond, Sarah Alston. Exec'rs, sons John & Jonathan, John Jones. Wits., Abraham Allee, Mary Steel, Thomas Tilton. Prob. Aug. 10, 1763. Arch. vol. A19, pages 132-133. Reg. of Wills, Liber K, folios 313-314.

Davis, Thomas. Yeoman. Admin. of, to Eliner Davis. Aug. 18, 1763. Reg. of Wills, Liber K, folio 314. Note:—Arch. vol. A13, page 67 shows Elinor Purtle was adm'x.

Severson, John. Will. Made April 2, 1761. Duck Creek Hd. Heirs: wife Sarah; sons Simon & James; daus. Sarah Palmatary, Mary, Ann & Rachel Severson. Exec'x, wife Sarah. Wits., James Morris, William David, Elizabeth David. Prob. Aug. 24, 1763. Arch. vol. A45, pages 145-146. Reg. of Wills, Liber K, folios 314-315.

Willson, James. Admin. of, to Nancy Willson, widow. Sept. 9, 1763. Reg. of Wills, Liber K, folio 315.

Connolly, William. Yeoman. Admin. of, to Sarah Connolly, widow. Sept. 17, 1763. Arch. vol. A10, page 69. Reg. of Wills, Liber K, folio 316.

Collins, William. Yeoman. Admin. of, to Elizabeth Collins, widow, & Robert Blackshere. Sept. 21, 1763. Arch. vol. A10, pages 32-34. Reg. of Wills, Liber K, folio 316. Note:—Arch. vol. A10, page 32 shows Elizabeth, the widow, later married John Raymond; page 34 shows Sarah & William Collins as heirs.

Clampitt, John. Yeoman. Admin. of, to Judith Clampitt, widow, & William Clampitt. Oct. 24, 1763. Reg. of Wills, Liber K, folio 317.

Thompson, Silvester. Yeoman. Admin. of, to John Thompson. Oct. 26, 1763. Arch. vol. A50, pages 113-116. Reg. of Wills, Liber K, folio 317. Note:—Arch. vol. A50, p. 113 shows heirs, Elizabeth, Esther, Celia, Jonathan & John Thompson, Frances (wife of John Firches) & Miriam (wife of James King).

Rees, Ephriam. Weaver. Admin. of, to John Forster. Oct. 29, 1763. Reg. of Wills, Liber K, folios 317-318. Note:—Arch. vol. A42, page 240 shows Mary Foster, widow of John Foster, later administered.

Dawson, Isaac. Farmer. Will. Made Oct. 22, 1763. Heirs: Ann [wife]; dau. Esther Vinsen, wife of Jesse Vinsen; sons John, Thomas, Isaac, Daniel, Joshua; heir of son Richard. Exec'rs, wife [Ann] & son Isaac. Wits., John Walker, Susannah Morris, William Maston. Prob. Nov. 9, 1763. Arch. vol. A13, pages 96-98. Reg. of Wills, Liber K, folio 318. Note:—Arch. vol. A13, page 97 shows Ann Walker as an exec'x.

Crumpton, John, the elder. Yeoman. Admin. of, to John Crumpton. Nov. 10, 1763. Reg. of Wills, Liber K, folio 319.

Walton, George. Yeoman. Admin. of, to David Peterkin. Nov. 10, 1763. Arch. vol. A53, pages 52-53. Reg. of Wills, Liber K, folio 319.

Buckley, James. Yeoman. Admin. of, to Mary Buckley, widow. Nov. 10, 1763. Arch. vol. A6, page 134. Reg. of Wills, Liber K, folios 319-320.

Sharpless, Joseph. Yeoman. Admin. of, to Joseph Vaughan. Nov. 11, 1763. Arch. vol. A45, page 192. Reg. of Wills, Liber K, folio 320.

Nichols, Edward, Sr. Yeoman. Admin. of, to Edward Nichols, Jr. Nov. 11, 1763. Arch. vol. A37, page 221. Reg. of Wills, Liber K, folios 320-321.

Brown, Daniel. Will (nunc.). Made Oct. 18, 1763. Murtherkill Hd. Heir: cousin Stephen Brown. Wits., Zachariah Goforth, Mary Long, Sarah Goforth. Prob. Nov. 20, 1763. Arch. vol. A6, pages 37-38. Reg. of Wills, Liber K, folios 329-330.

McIlhenney, Alexander. Yeoman. Admin. of, to Agnes McIlhenney, widow. Nov. 23, 1763. Arch. vol. A32, pages 218-219. Reg. of Wills, Liber K, folio 321.

Brinckle, Esther. Admin. of, to Nimrod Maxwell, D. B. N. Nov. 24, 1763. Arch. vol. A5, page 169.

Willson, Elisabeth. Widow. Admin. of, to Caesar Rodney. Nov. 28, 1763. Reg. of Wills, Liber K, folio 321.

Jones, Barbary. Will. Made Nov. 21, 1763. Heirs: sons George Howard, John Benet, John Gould Howard; dau. Mary Quilling; son-in-law Benjamin Jones. Exec'r, son-in-law Benjamin Jones. Wits., Benjamin Jones, Jr., John Robearts, Susanah Steelman. Prob. Dec. 7, 1763. Arch. vol. A27, page 133. Reg. of Wills, Liber K, folios 321-322.

Craige, Hugh. Will. Made Oct. 31, 1763. Heirs: wife Annaleny; sons Moses, James, John, Samuel; daus. Sarah, Neiome, Isabel & Nanne Craige, Leah Shaw (wife of Ephraham). Exec'x, wife Annaleny. Wits., Joseph Powell, Samuel Craige, John Craige. Prob. Dec. 12, 1763. Arch. vol. A11, pages 154-155. Reg. of Wills, Liber K, folio 322.

Reynolds, Catharine. Widow. Admin. of, to George Amos. Dec. 13, 1763. Reg. of Wills, Liber K, folio 323.

Clark, Thomas. Will. Made Nov. 20, 1763. Heirs: wife [Sarah, from admin. acct.]; sons John & Benjamin; daus. Ann McKnatt, Priscilla Henderson, Sarah Finchwait, Elizabeth Herrington, Ruth Tharp. Exec'rs, wife Sarah & sons John & Benjamin. Wits., James Finchwait, John Harrington, David Hilford. Prob. Dec. 13, 1763. Arch. vol. A9, pages 82-84. Reg. of Wills, Liber K, folios 326-327.

Badger, Edmund. Cordwainer. Will. Made Dec. 14, 1763. Dover. Heirs: wife Letitia; sons Eleazor, Edmund; Society of Quakers (Little Creek). Exec'r, Samuel McCall, practitioner. Wits., Richard Wells, Thomas Skillington, James Maning. Prob. Dec. 15, 1763. Arch. vol. A2, pages 46-47. Reg. of Wills, Liber K, folios 327-328.

Wilds, John. Will (nunc.). Made Dec. 3, 1763. Heirs: sister Mary Wilds; Hannah Maxfield; Cathrien Jones. Exec'r, Thomas Murphy. Wits., John Hays, Moses Craige. Prob. Dec. 19, 1763. Arch. vol. A55, pages 6-7. Reg. of Wills, Liber K, folio 328.

Gordon, Seth. Admin. of, to Thomas Craige. Dec. 26, 1763. Reg. of Wills, Liber K, folio 330.

Shurmer, William.. Admin. of, to Sarah Shurmer, widow. Dec. 26, 1764. Reg. of Wills, Liber K, folio 330.

White, Andrew. Farmer. Will. Made July 7, 1763. Heirs: son James; grandsons Robert & James (sons of James White), Andrew McClemings (son of dau. Jane), Gilbert White (son of James), Andrew Patten (son of Isabell Patten); granddaus. Elizabeth White (dau. of son Robert), Margaret Munsey (dau. of Isabell Patten), Mary Patten (dau. of Isabell Patten), Molly White (dau. of James). Exec'rs, James White & Isabell Patten. Wits., Robert Terrell Purtee, William Bowin, Burton Allcock. Prob. Dec. 29, 1763. Arch. vol. A54, pages 99-100. Reg. of Wills, Liber K, folios 330-331.

Arthur, Robert. Will. Made Dec. 8, 1763. Little Creek Hd. Heirs: wife Hanah; daus. Margaret Smith, Ann Arthur; grandson Robert Smith; son William. Exec'x, wife Hanah. Wits., James Edwards, John Johnson, John Lewis. Prob. Dec. 31, 1763. Arch. vol. A2, pages 1-3. Reg. of Wills, Liber K, folios 331-332. Note:—Arch. vol. A2, page 2 shows Hannah, the widow, later married Thomas Cahoon.

Crumpton, John. Will. Made Sept. 14, 1763. Heirs: wife Elizabeth; daus. Elizabeth Crumpton, Mary New, Sarah Tumbleston, Rachel Williams; sons John & Thomas. Exec'rs, wife Elizabeth & son Thomas. Wits., John Masten, Marmeduke Morgan, John Newman. Prob. Jan. 2, 1764. Arch. vol. A12, page 34. Reg. of Wills, Liber K, folios 332-333.

Train, James. Admin. of, to Hambleton Train & Jabez Jenkins. Jan. 4, 1764. Arch. vol. A51, pages 55-57. Reg. of Wills, Liber K, folio 333.

Moor, Abraham. Will. Made Dec. 8, 1763. Little Creek Hd. Heirs: wife Martha; daus. Elizabeth Moor, Mary Long, Rebecca Horn; son Abraham. Exec'x, wife Martha. Wits., William Corse, Jordan Robinson, William Reynolds. Prob. Jan. 7, 1764. Arch. vol. A35, pages 238-239. Reg. of Wills, Liber K, folios 333-334.

Rodney, Daniel. Admin. of, to Meriam Rodney, widow. Jan. 18, 1764. Arch. vol. A44, page 93. Reg. of Wills, Liber K, folio 334.

Robisson, Daniel. Will. Made Jan. 10, 1764. Heirs: wife Patience (former wife of George Willson, dec'd); sons Joseph, Samuel; dau. Elizabeth Hudson, wife of William Hudson; granddaus. Hannah, Elizabeth & Sarah Manlove, daus. of William Manlove; grandson George Manlove; son-in-law William Manlove. Exec'r, son Samuel. Wits., Samuel Skidmore, James Edmunds, John Hinds. Codicil, wife's son George Willson. Prob. Jan. 28, 1764. Arch. vol. A44, pages 36-39. Reg. of Wills, Liber K, folios 335-336.

Brannock, Thomas. Admin. of, to Samuel Robisson. Jan. 31, 1764. Reg. of Wills, Liber K, folios 336-337.

Keith, John. Admin. of, to Joshua Hardis [Ardis]. Feb. 4, 1764. Arch. vol. A28, page 100. Reg. of Wills, Liber K, folio 337.

Hall, John. Admin. of, to Sarah Hall, widow. Feb. 8, 1764. Reg. of Wills, Liber K, folio 337. Note:—Arch. vol. A21, page 95 shows Sarah, the widow, later married John Brown.

Walker, William. Admin. of, to William Walker, N. C. Co. Feb. 9, 1764. Arch. vol. A52, page 200. Reg. of Wills, Liber K, folio 338.

Fullerton, John. Admin. of, to Benjamin Warren. Feb. 11, 1764. Arch. A18, page 139. Reg. of Wills, Liber K, folio 338.

Jester, Jonathan. Admin. of, to Mary Jester, widow. Feb. 15, 1764. Reg. of Wills, Liber K, folios 338-339. Note:—Arch. vol. A28, page 241 shows that Robert Maxwell & wife Marah later administered on the acct.

Blacksare [Blacksheare], Ebenezer. Admin. of, to Susannah Blacksare. Feb. 29, 1764. Reg. of Wills, Liber K, folio 339. Note:—Arch. vol. A4, page 80 shows Suanah later married William Greer.

Stout, Peter. Admin. of, to Rebecca Stout, widow. March 10, 1764. Reg. of Wills, Liber K, folio 342. Note:—Arch. vol. A49, page 45 shows Rebecca, the widow, later married Jabez Jenkins.

Farqueher, George. Admin. of, to Hannah Farqueher. March 19, 1764. Reg. of Wills, Liber K, folios 399-340. Note:— Arch. vol. A17, pages 26-27 show Hannah later married Zebedee Triger.

Foster, John. Admin. of, to Mary Foster & William Graydon. April 4, 1764. Reg. of Wills, Liber K, folio 340. Note:— Arch. vol. A18, pages 44-46 show Mary, the widow, later married John Ashford.

Chrispin, Sylas. Admin. of, to Tabitha Chrispin, widow. April 14, 1764. Reg. of Wills, Liber K, folio 341. Note:—Arch. vol. A11, pages 233-235 show children, Mary, Tabitha, Elizabeth & Sarah Crispen.

Kelly, John. Farmer. Will. Made March 14, 1764. Murderkill Hd. Heirs: son Enock; son-in-law Samuel Goodwin; dau.-in-law Elizabeth Goodwin. Exec'r, friend William Wallace, Sr. Trustee, Charles Ridgly. Wits., Mark Harper, Daniel

Coudret, Joshua Wallace. Prob. April 24, 1764. Arch. vol. A28, pages 99, 106-108. Reg. of Wills, Liber K, folio 342. Note:—Arch. vol. A28, page 106 shows William Wallace, dec'd, & Catherine, his wife, adm'rs.

Cain, Francis. Will. Made Dec. 26, 1763. Heirs: sons John, Dennes, Daniel, Francis; dau. Elizabeth Skinner; grandsons Francis & Daniel Cain, sons of son Dennes. Exec'r, son Francis. Wits., Michael Lowber, Ezebell Dagnell. Prob. April 30, 1764. Arch. vol. A7, pages 61-62. Reg. of Wills, Liber K, folios 340-341.

Story, Peter. Will. Made Feb. 14, 1762. Duck Creek. Heirs: wife Penelope; dau. Penelope. Exec'rs, wife Penelope & Rowland Parry. Wits., Robert Wild, John Gorsuch, Judah Pugh. Prob. April 30, 1764. Arch. vol. A49, pages 30-32. Reg. of Wills, Liber K, folio 343. Note:—Arch. vol. A49, page 31 shows Penelope, the widow, later married William Mulett.

Creighton, Thomas. Admin. of, to Mary Creighton, widow. May 9, 1764. Arch. vol. A11, page 223. Reg. of Wills, Liber K, folio 343.

Grewell, John. Admin. of, to Jonathan Grewell. May 10, 1764. Reg. of Wills, Liber K, folio 344.

Inloe, Thomas. Admin. of, to Mathew Manlove. May 11, 1764. Arch. vol. A25, page 214. Reg. of Wills, Liber K, folio 344.

Ross, John. Admin. of, to John Parker and wife Elizabeth, late Elizabeth Ross. May 24, 1764. Arch. vol. A44, pages 137-138, 140-141. Note:—Arch. vol. A44, page 140 shows that Margaret Ross later married William Wallace; page 141 mentions dau. Margaret Ross & son William Ross.

Brinckley, Benjamin. Admin. of, to Bettey Brinckley, widow. June 8, 1764. Arch. vol. A5, pages 154-156. Reg. of Wills, Liber K, folios 344-345. Note:—Arch. vol. A5, page 154 shows that Betty Brinckle later married George Monro; also mentions heirs, Mary, William, Benjamin & Joseph Brincklee & Leah Brinckley, wife of Joshua Cottman.

Haynes [Hanes], Daniel. Admin. of, to Peter Brinckley. June 19, 1764. Arch. vol. A23, page 71. Reg. of Wills, Liber K, folio 345.

Stratton, Thomas. Admin. of, to Jacob Stratton. July 24, 1764. Arch. vol. A49, page 83. Reg. of Wills, Liber K, folios 345-346.

Wann, Christopher. Admin. of, to Sarah Snow, widow. July 24, 1764. Arch. vol. A53, page 86. Reg. of Wills, Liber K, folio 346.

Cowgill, Clayton. Admin. of, to Martha Cowgill. Aug. 2, 1764. Reg. of Wills, Liber K, folio 346.

Pickering, James. Admin. of, to Solomon Wallace. Aug. 17, 1764. Arch. vol. A40, pages 45-46. Reg. of Wills, Liber K, folio 347.

Newell [Nowell], John. Admin. of, to Andrew Caldwell. Aug. 30, 1764. Arch. vol. A38, page 54. Note:—Shows that John Newell was guardian to Ruth Betts, wife of John McSparran, & Rachel Newell, wife of Henry Sapp; also mentions Henry & William Newell.

Brinckle, John. Will (unsigned). Made Sept. 25, 1764. Heirs: wife unnamed; nephew Spencer Cole; nieces Sarah, Mary & Emilia Cole; Penelope Williams; Brinckle Adams; John Molleston; Reynear Williams; Joseph Nicholls. Exec'rs, wife and Reynear Williams. Wits., John Haslet, Curtis Brinckle, Sarah Brinckle. [No prob.]. Arch. vol. A5, pages 174-176. Reg. of Wills, Liber K, folios 1-2.

Barnet, Moses. Admin. of, to Andrew Barnet & Hugh Sutor. Oct. 2, 1764. Arch. vol. A2, pages 193 & 199. Reg. of Wills, Liber K, folio 347. Note:—Arch. vol. A2, page 199 mentions children, Sarah, Elizabeth & Moses Barnet.

Horn, Robert. Admin. of, to Sarah Horn. Oct. 5, 1764. Reg. of Wills, Liber K, folio 348.

Busby [Busban], James. Admin. of, to Samuel Griffith. Oct. 6, 1764. Arch. vol. A7, page 2. Reg. of Wills, Liber K, folio 348.

Brinckle, John. Esq. Admin. of, to Jemima Brinckle, widow. Oct. 8, 1764. Reg. of Wills, Liber K, folios 348-349. Note:— Arch. vol. A5, pages 177-181 show Jemima, the widow, later married John Haslet.

Curry, James. Admin. of, to Thomas Cahoon. Nov. 1, 1764. Arch. vol. A12, page 152. Reg. of Wills, Liber K, folio 349.

Spry, John [Joseph]. Admin. of, to Edward Gibbs. Nov. 13, 1764. Arch. vol. A48, page 124. Reg. of Wills, Liber K, folios 349-350.

Lassey, James. Will. Made Oct. 10, 1764. Heirs: wife Mary; daus. Mary Griffin, Rebecca & Nansey Lassey. Exec'x, wife Mary. Wits., James White, William Pegg, Joseph Parsons. Prob. Nov. 28, 1764. Arch. vol. A29, page 123. Reg. of Wills, Liber K, folio 350.

Hilford, Mathew. Will. Made Feb. 15, 1763. Heirs: wife Ann; sons Thomas & David; daus. Susannah Truit (wife of Hezekiah Truit), Martha, Ann, Jane, Ester, Mary & Rachel Hilford. Exec'rs, wife Ann & son Thomas. Wits., Thomas Clark, John Stuard, Moses Stuard. Prob. Nov. 28, 1764. Arch. vol. A23, pages 227-229. Reg. of Wills, Liber K, folio 351.

Copner, Cornelius. Admin. of, to Curtis Brinckle. Nov. 29, 1764. Reg. of Wills, Liber K, folio 352. Note:—Arch. vol. A10, page 234 shows Catherine Copner, widow.

Cowgill, Martha. Admin. of, to Henry Cowgill. Dec. 4, 1764. Arch. vol. A11, page 111. Reg. of Wills, Liber K, folio 352.

Cowgill, Clayton. Admin. of, to Henry Cowgill. Dec. 4, 1764. Arch. vol. A11, page 83. Reg. of Wills, Liber K, folio 353.

Shepard, Samuel. Admin. of, to Diana Shepard, widow. Dec. 7, 1764. Reg. of Wills, Liber K, folio 353. Note:—Arch. vol. A45, page 232 shows Dinah, the widow, later married Zebulon Casey.

Tucker, John. Admin. of, to Jessey Tucker. Dec. 18, 1764. Reg. of Wills, Liber L, folio 2.

Morris, Absolem. Admin. of, to Mathew Jarrard. Dec. 27, 1764. Arch. vol. A36, pages 184-185. Reg. of Wills, Liber K, folio 354.

McGure, Elizabeth. Admin. of, to Hugh McGuyre [McGure], nearest of kin. Feb. 1, 1765. Reg. of Wills, Liber L, folio 2.

Bedwell, Robert. Admin. of, to Margaret Bedwell, widow. Feb. 6, 1765. Reg. of Wills, Liber L, folio 2.

Bohannan, Robert. Admin. of, to Ann Bohannan & Robert Killen. Feb. 13, 1765. Reg. of Wills, Liber L, folio 2. Note:—Arch. vol. A6, pages 115-116 show Ann, the widow, later married John Carpenter.

Wharton, Augustus. Admin. of, to Susannah Wharton, widow. Feb. 15, 1765. Reg. of Wills, Liber L, folio 2. Note:—Arch. vol. A54, page 42 shows Susanna, the widow, later married David Pell.

Ross, Samuel. Will. Made Jan. 17, 1765. Heirs: wife Jane; children unnamed. Exec'x, wife Jane. Wits., George Pratt, John Brice. Prob. Feb. 18, 1765. Arch. vol. A44, pages 146-147. Reg. of Wills, Liber L, folio 5.

Irons, Elizabeth. Will. Made March 4, 1765. Little Creek Hd. Heirs: sons Jonathan Rees, Timothy & William Irons. Exec'r, Thomas Irons, Esq. Wits., Robert Blackshear, Mary Jolly. Prob. March 6, 1765. Arch. vol. A25, pages 215-216. Reg. of Wills, Liber L, folio 4.

Melvin, Ann. Admin. of, to Edward [Edmond] Melvin. March 12, 1765. Arch. vol. A34, page 135. Reg. of Wills, Liber L, folios 2-3.

Steel, Henry. Admin. of, to Mary Steel, widow. March 14, 1765. Reg. of Wills, Liber L, folio 3.

Underhay, Heneritte. Admin. of, to John Dicheus. March 18, 1765. Arch. vol. A51, page 191. Reg. of Wills, Liber L, folio 3.

Keith, James. Admin. of, to Thomas Keith. March 19, 1765. Arch. vol. A28, page 94. Reg. of Wills, Liber L, folio 3.

Hannah, David. Admin. of, to Elizabeth Hannah, widow. March 29, 1765. Reg. of Wills, Liber L, folio 3. Note:—Arch. vol. A21, page 203 shows Elizabeth, the widow, later married Christopher Ratlage.

Brinckle, Peter. Will. Made Jan. 10, 1764. Little Creek Hd. Heirs: wife Mary; sons William, Jesse, Peter; dau. Mary. Exec'rs, wife Mary & son William. Wits., John Keeth, John Hamilton, Thomas Freeman. Prob. March 30, 1765. Arch. vol. A5, pages 193-200. Reg. of Wills, Liber L, folios 4-5. Note:—Arch. vol. A5, page 194 shows Mary, the widow, later married Aaron Hart.

Mason, John. Admin. of, to Elizabeth Mason, widow, & Jacob Stout. April 1, 1765. Reg. of Wills, Liber L, folio 5.

David, William. Admin. of, to Elizabeth David, widow. April 4, 1765. Reg. of Wills, Liber L, folio 5. Note:—Arch. vol. A12, page 239 shows Elizabeth, the widow, later married Thomas Macey.

Carter, William. Will. Made March 16, 1765. St. Jones' Hd. Heirs: bro. James Carbine; mother [Jane, in admin. acct.]; sisters Margret, Jane, Sarah & Mary Carbine. Exec'rs, mother & Thomas Murphey Smith. Wits., David Hanna, Benjamin Quillen, Edward Norman. Prob. April 5, 1765. Arch. vol. A8, pages 46-48. Reg. of Wills, Liber L, folios 7-8.

Richards, Henry. Admin. of, to Elizabeth Richards, widow. April 22, 1765. Arch. vol. A43, page 151. Reg. of Wills, Liber L, folio 3.

McGear, Michael. Admin. of, to Martha McGear, widow. May 4, 1765. Arch. vol. A32, page 187. Reg. of Wills, Liber L, folio 3.

Furbee, Michael. Yeoman. Will. Made April 9, 1765. Heirs: wife Mary; son Benjamin; daus. Mary & Nancy; a child unnamed. Exec'rs, wife Mary & friend James Boyer. Wits., Caleb Furbee, Stephen Lewis, Alexander Craige. Prob. May 15, 1765. Arch. vol. A18, pages 166-169. Reg. of Wills, Liber L, folio 6. Note:—Will mentions Susannah Lewis as mother of Michael; Arch. vol. A18, page 169 shows Mary, the widow, later married Arthur Wheatley and mentions Michael Furbee as a son.

Henry, John. Admin. of, to Jane Henry, widow. May 22, 1765. Arch. vol. A23, page 154. Reg. of Wills, Liber L, folio 3.

Keith, Jane. Admin. of, to Randol Alstone & Thomas Murphey. May 22, 1765. Arch. vol. A28, page 98. Reg. of Wills, Liber L, folio 3.

Gordon, Robert. Admin. of, to William Meridith. May 23, 1765. Reg. of Wills, Liber L, folio 3. Note:—Arch. vol. A19, pages 173-174 show Phylis, the widow, later married William Merydith; also mention sons John & Robert Gordon.

Turner, Martin. Admin. of, to Mary Turner, widow. May 29, 1765. Reg. of Wills, Liber L, folio 3.

Underwood, Richard. Minor. Admin. of, to Sarah, Benjamin & John Clark, D. B. N. (in right of Thomas Clark, guardian of Richard Underwood). May 29, 1765. Arch. vol. A51, page 196.

Simpson, Moses. Admin. of, to Mary Simpson, widow, & Joseph Parsons. June 13, 1765. Reg. of Wills, Liber L, folio 5. Note:—Arch. vol. A46, pages 67-68 show Mary, the widow, later married Thomas Shockley.

Stanton, John. Admin. of, to Mary Stanton, widow. June 18, 1765. Reg. of Wills, Liber L. folio 6. Note:—Arch. vol. A48, pages 149-151 show Mary, the widow, later married James Calhoon.

Manlove, George. Admin. of, to Ebenezar Manlove, next of kin. July 18, 1765. Reg. of Wills, Liber L, folio 6.

Holston, Benjamin. Will. Made May 8, 1765. Heirs: wife Esther; son Elijah; daus. Mary, Nancy. Exec'rs, wife Esther & bro.-in-law Belitha Laws. Wits., Jeremiah Morris, Joseph Fleming, Sr., Joshua Laws. Prob. July 19, 1765. Arch. vol. A24, pages 233-234. Reg. of Wills, Liber L, folios 5-6.

Sharp, Adam. Will. Made May 17, 1765. Heirs: sons Stogdon, Nehemiah, John, Edward. Exec'r, John Draughton. Wits., John Draughton, Jr., John Dawson. Prob. July 27, 1765. Arch. vol. A45, pages 182-183. Reg. of Wills, Liber L, folio 7.

Train, Esther. Admin. of, to Sarah Durborow, next of kin. July 30, 1765. Reg. of Wills, Liber L, folio 7.

Pearson, Aaron. Admin. of, to Sarah Pearson, widow. Aug. 20, 1765. Reg. of Wills, Liber L, folio 7.

Fullerton, William. Admin. of, to Isaac Killen, next of kin. Oct. 2, 1765. Arch. vol. A18, page 143. Reg. of Wills, Liber L, folio 8.

Hirons, Simon. Admin. of, to Letitia Hirons, widow. Oct. 12, 1765. Arch. vol. A24, page 100. Reg. of Wills, Liber L, folio 8.

McKlehaten, Patrick. Admin. of, to Allen Aiken. Oct. 16, 1765. Arch. vol. A32, page 199. Reg. of Wills, Liber L, folio 8.

Boggs, John. Admin. of, to Matthew Boggs, next of kin. Oct. 18, 1765. Reg. of Wills, Liber L, folio 8. Note:—Arch. vol. A4, page 175 shows a minor son John Boggs, Jr.

Rees, Abel. Admin. of, to Rebecca Rees & James Snow. Oct. 30, 1765. Arch. vol. A42, pages 230-231. Reg. of Wills, Liber L, folio 9. Note:—Arch. vol. A42, page 230 shows Rebecca Rees, the widow, later married John Moore.

Pugh, Roger. Yeoman. Will. Made March 16, 1764. Duck Creek Hd. Heirs: wife Sarah; sons Gideon, William, Roger; daus. Sarah, Mary, Susannah. Exec'rs, sons Gideon & William. Wits., John Farmer, Michal Dyal, Finwick Fisher. Prob. Oct. 31, 1765. Arch. vol. A41, pages 199-201. Reg. of Wills, Liber L, folio 9.

David, Joshua. Will. Made Oct. 15, 1765. Heir: mother Mary Hunter. Exec'x, mother Mary Hunter. Wits., John Lock, Thomas Tufft, Thomas Russell, John Bell. Prob. Nov. 9, 1765. Arch. vol. A12, page 231. Reg. of Wills, Liber L, folio 10.

Bennet, John. Will (nunc.). Made Dec. 24, 1765. Heir: wife Sarah. Wits., James Manson, Mary Bucknel. Prob. Jan. 22, 1766. Arch. vol. A3, pages 215-216. Reg. of Wills, Liber L, folio 9.

Snow, James. Will. Made Dec. 4, 1762. Little Creek Hd. Heirs: wife unnamed; child unnamed; sons Joseph & James; daus. Rebecca Rees, Sarah & Nancy Snow. Exec'rs, son Joseph & son-in-law Abel Rees. Wits., John Toy, Thomas Gould, Marcy

Holston. Prob. Jan. 22, 1766. Arch. vol. A48, pages 2-4. Reg. of Wills, Liber L, folio 10. Note:—Arch. vol. A48, page 4 shows widow Margaret Snow; son John Snow, minor; Sarah Snow married John Wood, & Rebecca later married John Moor, Jr.

Hill, Susannah. Will. Made Feb. 27, 1766. Heirs: sons William, George Hill; daus. Martha Hill & Sarah Hudson. Exec'x, dau. Sarah Hudson. Wits., Elizabeth Sap, Walter Reed, Lawrence Hobson. Prob. March 31, 1766. Arch. vol. A24, page 16. Reg. of Wills, Liber L, folio 14.

Wynkoop, Esther. Will (unsigned). Made April 22, 1766. Heirs: bros. Benjamin Wynkoop, John Vining, Abraham & James Wynkoop; sisters Pheebe Vining, Mary Ridgely; niece Mary Vining; nephew John Vining; mother Mary Wynkoop; cousin Elizabeth Fisher; bro.-in-law Charles Ridgely; godson Stephen Sykes; Miss Sarah Ridgely; Christ Church in Dover. Exec'r, bro. Benjamin Wynkoop. Wits., Esther Fisher, Sarah Ridgely. Prob. April 28, 1766. Arch. vol. A56, pages 180-181. Reg. of Wills, Liber L, folios 13-14.

Arrowsmith, Thomas. Admin. of, to Mary Arrowsmith, widow. May 13, 1766. Reg. of Wills, Liber L, folio 11. Note:—Arch. vol. A1, pages 240-242 show that Mary, the widow, later married John Meekins; also children Derander, Mirende, William, Henry & Edmond Arrowsmith.

Hamilton, John. Admin. of, to Mary Hamilton, widow, & son John, Jr. May 14, 1766. Arch. vol. A2, page 161. Reg. of Wills, Liber L, folio 11.

Lyson, Theophilus. Admin. of, to Edward Rees. May 15, 1766. Arch. vol. A32, page 29. Reg. of Wills, Liber L, folio 20.

Robinson, George. Admin. of, to Mary Robinson, widow. May 15, 1766. Reg. of Wills, Liber L, folio 11. Note:—Arch. vol. A44, pages 43-44 shows that Mary, the widow, later married Thomas Bell.

Manlove, George. Farmer. Will. Made May 10, 1766. Little Creek Hd. Heirs: sons Matthew, John & Tredwell; grandson George Manlove, son of Matthew; daus. Mary Manlove, Sarah Emerson (wife of Govey Emerson). Exec'rs, sons Matthew & John. Trustee, James Sykes, Esq. Wits., Clayton

Levick, Mary Hunter, John Molleston. Prob. May 20, 1766. Arch. vol. A33, pages 92-94. Reg. of Wills, Liber L, folios 11-12. Note:—Arch. vol. A33, page 92 shows that dau. Mary Manlove married John Clayton.

Molleston, William. Admin. of, to John Clark, Esq., next of kin. May 21, 1766. Reg. of Wills, Liber L, folio 12.

Allee, Abraham, Jr. Admin. of, to Sarah Allee, widow. May 21, 1766. Reg. of Wills, Liber L, folio 21.

Anderson, James. Admin. of, to Elizabeth Anderson, widow. June 18, 1766. Reg. of Wills, Liber L, folio 12.

Green, Thomas, Sr. Will. Made May 14, 1766. Duck Creek Hd. Heirs: sons Charles, James, Thomas, John, William; daus. Mercy Buckingham, Luranah Rees. Exec'rs, sons James & William. Wits., Thomas Brown, Elizabeth Devenport, Owen Matthews. Prob. June 21, 1766. Arch. vol. A20, pages 115-117. Reg. of Wills, Liber L, folio 22.

Johnson, Robert. Blacksmith. Will (copy, nunc.). Made May 30, 1766. Dover. Heir: mother unnamed. Wits., Samuel McCall, John Pryor. Prob. June 25, 1766. Arch. vol. A27, page 102. Reg. of Wills, Liber L, folio 12. Note:—Admin. was granted to his mother, Sarah Durborow.

Bowers, John. Will. Made Aug. 13, 1765. Murderkill Hd. Heirs: wife Rachel; son John; daus. Elizabeth Corse, Mary Lowber, Ruth Bowers. Exec'rs, wife Rachel & friends Samuel Hanson & Thomas Hanson. Wits., John Gray, Prudence Gray, Agness McElhenny. Prob. June 25, 1766. Arch. vol. A5, pages 27-28. Reg. of Wills, Liber L, folios 12-13.

Fleming, William, Sr. Will. Made Feb. 27, 1765. Heirs: wife Martha; sons George, Robert, Isaac; dau. Mary Bradley; children of son Isaac. Exec'rs, son Robert & wife Martha. Wits., Archibald Fleming, William Fleming, Jr., Joseph Fleming. Prob. July 1, 1766. Arch. vol. A17, pages 206-207. Reg. of Wills, Liber L, folio 13.

Gray, Andrew. Admin. of, to Sarah Gray, widow. July 5, 1766. Arch. vol. A20, page 7. Reg. of Wills, Liber L, folio 13.

Crawford, David. Admin. of, to William Manson, D. B. N. July 13, 1766. Reg. of Wills, Liber L, folio 16.

Barber, Abraham. Admin. of, to Ann Barber, widow. July 19, 1766. Arch. vol. A2, pages 110-111. Reg. of Wills, Liber L, folio 14. Note:—Arch. vol. A2, page 110 shows that Ann Barber married John Ware; page 111 mentions heirs, John, Abraham, Francis, Ann & Joseph Barber, & Persilla Walker, wife of John Walker.

Greenaway, John. Admin. of, to Mary Greenaway, widow. July 23, 1766. Arch. vol. A20, pages 143-144. Reg. of Wills, Liber L, folio 14. Note:—Arch. vol. A20, page 143 shows that Mary Greenway, the widow, married William Ringold.

Ashford, John, Sr. Yeoman. Will. Made June 15, 1766. Heirs: wife Mary; sons Perygran, John, William, James; daus. Mary, Catharine. Exec'rs, wife Mary & son John. Wits., William Griffen, Jr., Benjamin Hudson, Mary Pope. Prob. Aug. 2, 1766. Arch. vol. A2, pages 12-13. Reg. of Wills, Liber L, folio 15.

Jenkins, Enoch. Admin. of, to John Jenkins, & John Haze. Aug. 13, 1766. Arch. vol. A26, pages 206-207. Reg. of Wills, Liber L, folio 15. Note:—Arch. vol. A26, page 207 shows Martha Hayse, widow of John Hayse, later administered on the acct.

Cammell [Campbell], James. Admin. of, to Elizabeth Cammell [Campbell], widow. Aug. 13, 1766. Arch. vol. A7, page 183. Reg. of Wills, Liber L, folio 15.

Brown, Margret. Admin. of, to Charles David, next of kin. Aug. 14, 1766. Arch. vol. A6, page 76. Reg. of Wills, Liber L, folio 15.

Smith, Mark, Jr. Admin. of, to Isaac Smith, next of kin. Aug. 16, 1766. Reg. of Wills, Liber L, folio 15.

Jacobs, William. Planter. Will. Made Feb. 28, 1763. Heirs: wife Rebecca; sons Abraham, Speakman, Bosman & William Jacobs; dau. Sarah Downham; Sarah, dau. of wife. Exec'x, wife Rebecca. Wits., Samuel Bussee, Leven Gibson. Prob. Aug. 25, 1766. Arch. vol. A26, page 79. Reg. of Wills, Liber L, folio 16.

Gray, Sarah. Widow. Will. Made Aug. 7, 1766. Heirs; sons Samuel, Molleston & Joshua Wheeler & William Gray; daus. Mary McSparron, Elizabeth Carry, Sarah Wheeler. Exec'r, bro.-in-law John Clark. Wits., William Cats, Joseph Chadwick, Elizabeth Miller. Prob. Sept. 1, 1766. Arch. vol. A20, page 34. Reg. of Wills, Liber L, folio 17.

Hull, Daniel. Admin. of, to Rebecca Hull, widow. Oct. 13, 1766. Arch. vol. A25, page 122. Reg. of Wills, Liber L, folio 16. Note:—Dau. Ann Hull is mentioned.

Denny, Evan. Admin. of, to Isabella Denny, widow. Oct. 13, 1766. Arch. vol. A13, pages 200-204. Reg. of Wills, Liber L, folio 16. Note:—Arch. vol. A13, page 200 shows that Isabella Denny later married Joseph Pierce; also mentions heirs, Evan, Joseph & Elizabeth Denny.

Allee, Jacob. Yeoman. Will. Made Sept. 16, 1766. Heirs: wife unnamed; son John, Jr.; dau. Rebecca Killen, wife of William Killen; granddaus. Elizabeth & Mary, daus. of William & Rebecca Killen. Exec'r, son John, Jr. Wits., Abraham Allee, Jonathan Allee, Thomas Wild. Prob. Oct. 13, 1766. Arch. vol. A1, pages 57-58. Reg. of Wills, Liber L, folios 19-20.

Akin [Ecan], Allen. Admin. of, to John Shaw. Oct. 15, 1766. Arch. vol. A1, page 246. Reg. of Wills, Liber L, folio 21.

Parke, Thomas. Admin. of, to Ann Parke. Nov. 4, 1766. Arch. vol. A39, pages 27-29. Reg. of Wills, Liber L, folios 21 & 48.

Fisher, Hannah. Admin. of, to Samuel Smith, next of kin. Nov. 8, 1766. Arch. vol. A17, pages 125-127. Reg. of Wills, Liber L, folio 16.

McKleway [McElvain], Francis. Admin. of, to Edward Knot. Nov. 12, 1766. Arch. vol. A32, page 178. Reg. of Wills, Liber L, folio 17.

Craige, John. Yeoman. Will. Made April 14, 1766. Heirs: wife Agnes; son Thomas; daus. Mary (wife of William Watson), Prudence (wife of Andrew Neal), Ezabel, Ann, Margret & Elizabeth Craige. Exec'x, wife Agnes. Wits., John Arnett, Edward Gibbs, John Newman. Prob. Nov. 12, 1766. Arch. vol. A11, pages 167-169. Reg. of Wills, Liber L, folio 18.

West, William. Admin. of, to Sarah West, widow. Nov. 14, 1766. Arch. vol. A54, page 31. Reg. of Wills, Liber L, folio 17.

Dean, Thomas. Admin. of, to Mary Dean, widow. Nov. 18, 1766. Arch. vol. A13, page 142. Reg. of Wills, Liber L, folio 17.

Clayton, Sarah. Admin. of, to Jonathan Ozburn, next of kin. Nov. 19, 1766. Arch. vol. A9, page 124. Reg. of Wills, Liber L, folio 18.

Tilton, Sarah. Admin. of, to Richard Hoff & James Wallace, next of kin. Nov. 19, 1766. Reg. of Wills, Liber L, folio 21.

Hull, David. Admin. of, to James Hull, bro. Dec. 7, 1766. Arch. vol. A25, pages 123-124. Reg. of Wills, Liber L, folio 18.

Smith, James. Admin. of, to Robert Hall, next of kin. Dec. 12, 1766. Arch. vol. A47, pages 61-62. Reg. of Wills, Liber L, folio 23. Note:—Arch. vol. A47, page 62 shows that Jerusha Hall later administered, D. B. N.; also mentions heirs, Mary & James Smith, Jr.

Sapington, William. Admin. of, to Agnes Sapington, widow, & Samuel Whitman. Dec. 16, 1766. Arch. vol. A44, page 241. Reg. of Wills, Liber L, folio 20.

Mott, Richard. Admin. of, to Jerusha Mott, widow. Dec. 17, 1766. Arch. vol. A37, page 66. Reg. of Wills, Liber L, folio 21.

Adams, Leven. Yeoman. Will. Made Nov. 18, 1766. Heirs: son Brinckle; nephew Nathan Adams. Exec'r, Nathan Adams. Wits., George Manlove, William Brown, Miriam Mitten. Prob. Dec. 24, 1766. Arch. vol. A1, pages 3 & 9. Reg. of Wills, Liber L, folios 18-19.

Smith, Martha. Will. Made Nov. 11, 1766. Heirs: cousins Mary Rush, Margret White, Elizabeth Smith, Cecilea Simmons, Isaac & Jacob Smith (sons of Mark Smith, dec'd); Rev. John Miller. Exec'r, John Caton, Esq. Wits., Richard Butler, Mary Ashburn, Ann Richardson. Prob. Dec. 24, 1766. Arch. vol. A47, pages 113-114. Reg. of Wills, Liber L, folio 23.

Price, Joseph, Jr. Admin. of, to William Price, eldest bro. Dec. 26, 1766. Arch. vol. A41, pages 149-150. Reg. of Wills, Liber L, folio 18.

Gray, William, Sr. Admin. of, to William Gray, Jr. Jan. 7, 1767. Reg. of Wills, Liber L, folio 25. Note:—Arch. vol. A20, page 35 shows heirs, son William, Jr.; daus. Sarah & Hannah Gray; heirs of dau. Ruth Gray.

David, Joshua. Admin. of, to Tabitha David, widow. Jan. 8, 1767. Reg. of Wills, Liber L, folio 21.

Fortner, Samuel. Admin. of, to James May. Jan. 10, 1767. Reg. of Wills, Liber L, folio 20.

Barns, John. Will. Made Jan. 6, 1767. Little Creek Hd. Heirs: sons John, William & Stephen; dau. Percilla; Robert Blackshear; Elizabeth Rowe; John Vining. Exec'rs, friends William Killen & John Caton. Wits., Richard Smith, Thomas Steward, Sarah Upton, John Lomax, Edward Holiday, Martha Queilling. Codicil, Caesar & Elizabeth Rowe, children of James Rowe. Prob. Jan. 10, 1767. Arch. vol. A2, pages 219, 221-222. Reg. of Wills, Liber L, folios 23-24.

Falkner, John. Admin. of, to Thomas Sherriff. Jan. 16, 1767. Arch. vol. A17, page 91. Reg. of Wills, Liber L, folio 20.

Killingsworth, Josiah. Admin. of, to Caleb Furbee. Jan. 29, 1767. Arch. vol. A28, page 224. Reg. of Wills, Liber L, folio 21.

Blackshear, Eve. Will. Made June 16, 1762. Little Creek Hd. Heirs: sons Robert, Morgan, George, John, Ezenezar; daus. Mary Liston, Elizabeth Collins; granddau. Eve Liston. Exec'r, son George. Wits., Ruth Green, John Lewis. Prob. Feb. 3, 1767. Arch. vol. A4, page 81. Reg. of Wills, Liber L, folio 20.

Hill, Thomas. Admin. of, to Elizabeth Hill, widow. Feb. 10, 1767. Arch. vol. A24, page 18. Reg. of Wills, Liber L, folio 21.

New, Robert. Admin. of, to Mary New, widow. Feb. 11, 1767. Reg. of Wills, Liber L, folio 21.

Skidmore, Thomas. Admin. of, to Thomas Skidmore & Samuel Skidmore. Feb. 12, 1767. Reg. of Wills, Liber L, folio 25.

Blackshare, John. Admin. of, to Jane [Jean] Blackshare & Morgan Blackshare. Feb. 13, 1767. Arch. vol. A4, pages 85-86. Reg. of Wills, Liber L, folio 21. Note:—Acct. mentions children Ann & Sarah Blackshare.

Wilson, John. Will. Made Jan. 30, 1767. Duck Creek Hd. Heirs: wife Martha; sons Jesse, Thomas, Samuel, Jonathan, David. Exec'rs, wife Martha & son Samuel. Wits., Peter Booth, William Wilson, Daniel Smith. Prob. Feb. 13, 1767. Arch. vol. A55, pages 218-221. Reg. of Wills, Liber L, folio 26.

Holling, Abraham. Admin. of, to Daniel James. Feb. 21, 1767. Arch. vol. A24, page 222. Reg. of Wills, Liber L, folio 21.

Frazier, Elizabeth. Widow. Will. Made Aug. 28, 1765. Heirs: son Samuel Willson; daus. Agnes (wife of Joseph Pop), Elizabeth (wife of John Millis), Mary (wife of Benjamin Jones). Exec'r, son-in-law Benjamin Jones. Wits., Joseph Powell, Richard Downham, Mary Gordon. Prob. Feb. 23, 1767. Arch. vol. A18, page 91. Reg. of Wills, Liber L, folio 29.

Clemmons, Thomas. Admin. of, to Sarah Clemmons, widow. Feb. 26, 1767. Reg. of Wills, Liber L, folio 22.

Rowe, James. Admin. of, to Elizabeth Rowe, widow. Feb. 26, 1767. Arch. vol. A44, pages 112-114. Reg. of Wills, Liber L, folio 22. Note:—Arch. vol. A44, page 112 mentions children, Hugh, Caesar, Brinckle & Elizabeth Rowe, & Mary Stevens (nee Rowe).

Barns, Stephen. Admin. of, to Curthbert Green, D. B. N. Feb. 30, 1767. Arch. vol. A2, page 228. Reg. of Wills, Liber L, folio 23.

Cockran, Agnes. Admin. of, to Daniel Cockran, next of kin. March 9, 1767. Reg. of Wills, Liber L, folio 24.

New, Mary. Admin. of, to John Crumpton, next of kin. March 13, 1767. Arch. vol. A37, page 182. Reg. of Wills, Liber L, folio 25.

New, Robert. Admin. of, to John Crumpton, D. B. N. March 30, 1767. Arch. vol. A37, page 183. Reg. of Wills, Liber L, folio 25.

Vanderford, Thomas. Admin. of, to Charles Vanderford, next of kin. April 7, 1767. Arch. vol. A51, page 228. Reg. of Wills, Liber L, folio 24.

Nicholas, Samuel. Admin. of, to Jane Nicholas, widow. April 8, 1767. Reg. of Wills, Liber L, folio 25. Note:—Arch. vol. A37, pages 222-223 show that Jane Nicholas, the widow, later married Ebenezar Clampit & later Benjamin Sparks; also show sons Samuel, David & John.

Brinckle, Curtis. Farmer. Will. Made March 21, 1767. Heirs: wife Sarah; dau. Phebe Bessix, wife of John; cousins William Brinckle (son of Peter), Ezekiel Brinckle, Brinckle Davis, George Manlove (son of Matthew) ; Robert Hamilton, tenant. Exec'x, wife Sarah. Wits., John Haslet, John Molleston, Joshua Jester. Prob. April 8, 1767. Arch. vol. A5, pages 159-162. Reg. of Wills, Liber L, folio 28. Note:—Arch. vol. A5, page 160 shows that Sarah Brinckle later married George Ogle.

Guy, Andrew. Admin. of, to Elizabeth Guy, widow. April 10, 1767. Arch. vol. A21, page 53. Reg. of Wills, Liber L, folio 25.

Griffin, Owen. Admin. of, to Susannah Griffin, widow. April 13, 1767. Arch. vol. A20, pages 218-219. Reg. of Wills, Liber L, folio 25. Note:—This acct. was later administered by Henry Killen and Susanna, his wife.

Pratt, George. Farmer. Will. Made March 30, 1767. Heirs: wife Mary; sons Nathan, Luke, George, Frederick; daus. Esther Taylor, Ann, Dinah, Mary & Ruth Pratt. Exec'x, wife Mary. Wits., George Sexton, Leven Gibson, Esther Jarrard. Prob. April 15, 1767. Arch. vol. A41, pages 82-85. Reg. of Wills, Liber L, folios 26-27.

Albany, John. Admin. of, to Rachel Albany, widow, & Joseph Snow. April 18, 1767. Arch. vol. A1, page 18. Reg. of Wills, Liber L, folio 26.

Williams, James. Admin. of, to Mary Williams & John Williams. April 21, 1767. Reg. of Wills, Liber L, folio 25. Note:—Arch. vol. A55, page 80 shows that Mary Williams later married Henry Wells; also mentions son John Williams.

Barnet, John. Admin. of, to Mary Barnet, widow. April 29, 1767. Arch. vol. A2, page 197. Reg. of Wills, Liber L, folio 25.

Moor, Martha. Widow. Will. Made Feb. 28, 1767. Little Creek Hd. Heir: son Abraham. Exec'r, friend William Corse. Trustee, friend William Corse. Wits., Thomas Cirmichael, Thomas Shaw, William Shaw. Prob. May 4, 1767. Arch. vol. A36, pages 70-72. Reg. of Wills, Liber L, folio 27.

Robinson, Joseph. Admin. of, to Sarah Robinson, widow. May 13, 1767. Arch. vol. A44, page 74. Reg. of Wills, Liber L, folio 25.

Cowgill, Thomas. Admin. of, to Benjamin Dawson. May 14, 1767. Arch. vol. A11, page 120. Reg. of Wills, Liber L, folio 26.

Cary [Cairy], Bowin. Will. Made May 2, 1767. Heirs: wife Elizabeth; dau. Ann; William Gray, son of Andrew Gray; bro. Thomas Cary, ship-carpenter. Exec'x, wife Elizabeth. Wits., John Haslet, Thomas Peterkin, Rhoda Peterkin. Prob. May 14, 1767. Arch. vol. A7, pages 214 & 241. Reg. of Wills, Liber L, folios 28-29. Note:—Arch. vol. A7, page 214 shows that Elizabeth Cary later married David Peterkin, Jr.; page 241 mentions a dau. Mary Cary born after the testator's death.

Wells, Richard. Esq. Will. Made March 11, 1767. Heirs: Catherine Buckmaster; John Wells Buckmaster, James Wells Buckmaster, Mary Well Buckmaster, Sarah Wells Buckmaster, children of Catherine Buckmaster. Exec'x, Catherine Buckmaster. Wits., Lewis David, Daniel Smith. Prob. May 20, 1767. Arch. vol. A53, pages 241-244. Reg. of Wills, Liber L, folios 29-30. Note:—Arch. vol. A53, pages 243-244 show son Thomas Wells, minor.

Dunning, John. Admin. of, to Mary Dunning, widow. May 22, 1767. Arch. vol. A15, page 127. Reg. of Wills, Liber L, folio 30.

Allford, Thomas. Admin. of, to Ann Park. May 22, 1767. Reg. of Wills, Liber L, folio 30.

Ruttherford, William. Admin. of, to John Robinson, next of kin. May 26, 1767. Arch. vol. A44, page 152. Reg. of Wills, Liber L, folio 30.

Parke, Theodore. Admin. of, to Thomas Parke. May 27, 1767. Arch. vol. A39, pages 25-26.

Bowden, Ezekiel. Will. Made June 12, 1761. Little Creek Hd. Heirs: wife Ruth; John Albany. Exec'x, wife Ruth. Wits., Samuel Moore, Eleanor Carny, John Lewis. Prob. July 20, 1767. Arch. vol. A5, pages 14-15. Reg. of Wills, Liber L, folio 30. Note:—Arch. vol. A5, page 15 shows adm'x, Ruth Creighton, formerly Bowden.

Bostick, James. Admin. of, to Mary Bostick, widow. July 20, 1768. Arch. vol. A4, page 260. Reg. of Wills, Liber L, folio 31.

Bohannan, Robert. Yeoman. Will. Made July 14, 1767. Murtherkill Hd. Heirs: son Robert, Jr.; daus. Rachel & Mary Bohannan, Elizabeth Henry (wife of Robert Henry), Isabella Mannering, Anne Reese; grandson William Mannering; granddau. Mary Reese. Exec'rs, son Robert, Jr., & dau. Rachel. Wits., Sarah McCall, George McCall, Samuel McCall. Prob. July 21, 1767. Arch. vol. A4, pages 188-190. Reg. of Wills, Liber L, folios 31-32. Note:—Arch. vol. A4, page 189 shows Rachel, wife of Mathew Boggs; page 190 shows Mathew Boggs adm'r with Robert Bohannan.

Purden, John. Will. Made May 18, 1767. Heirs: wife Mary; sons John, Andrew, Joseph; daus. Catherine, Jean [Jane], Sarah. Exec'rs, sons John & Andrew. Wits., John Caton, William Merydith. Prob. July 24, 1767. Arch. vol. A41, page 219. Reg. of Wills, Liber L, folios 32-33.

Thompson, Joseph. Admin. of, to John Vangaskin. July 28, 1767. Reg. of Wills, Liber L, folio 33.

Hodgson, Robert, Sr. Will (copy). Made Jan. 11, 1765. Heirs: sons Robert, William, David; daus. Mary Catlin, Margarett Prichard. Exec'rs, bro.-in-law Andrew Caldwell & son Robert. Wits., Preston Berry, Jane Caldwell, Ann Reynolds, David Caldwell. Prob. Aug. 12, 1767. Arch. vol. A24, pages 129-131. Reg. of Wills, Liber L, folios 33-34.

Ryon, John. Cooper. Admin. of, to Hugh Parke. Aug. 14, 1767. Arch. vol. A44, page 219. Reg. of Wills, Liber L, folio 34.

Ebtharp, Thomas. Yeoman. Will. Made Sept. 1, 1766. Duck Creek Hd. Heirs: wife Elizabeth; nephew John Tilton; stepsons Peter & John Numbers; Robert Wood; Anne Anderson. Exec'rs, wife Elizabeth & step-son John Numbers. Wits.,

Nathaniel Wild, Mary Wilds, Samuel McCall. Prob. Aug. 15, 1767. Arch. vol. A15, pages 239-240. Reg. of Wills, Liber L, folios 34-35.

Lacy, James. Admin. of, to Mary Lacy. Aug. 26, 1767. Arch. vol. A29, page 94.

Fleming, Alexander. Will. Made Sept. 3, 1767. Heirs: wife Ezebell; sons James, Mathew, Joseph, Robert & Archibald; dau. Catren Fleming. Exec'x, wife Ezebell. Wits., Robert Killen, William Fleming, Arch'd. Currey. [No prob.]. Arch. vol. A17, page 166.

Jacobs, Abraham. Admin. of, to Elizabeth Jacobs, widow. Sept. 6, 1767. Arch. vol. A26, page 63. Reg. of Wills, Liber L, folio 35.

Bradley, Josiah. Will. Made Aug. 18, 1767. Heirs: wife Mary; sons William, Jesse, Isaac, Nathan, Josiahs; daus. Ann Plowman (wife of John Plowman), Elizabeth & Mary Bradley. Exec'rs, son William & wife Mary. Wits., William Hazzard, Thomas Carrey, Jr., Robert Fleming. Prob. Sept. 7, 1767. Arch. vol. A5, pages 116-119. Reg. of Wills, Liber L, folios 35-36. Note:—Arch. vol. A5, pages 117-118 show Mary Bradley, widow, married Azeael Spencer; page 117 shows dau. Elizabeth, wife of Laurence Riley; page 118 shows Benj. Granger & wife Margaret Bradley, dau. of Wm. Bradley.

Smith, Thomas. Admin. of, to William Skinner & wife Elizabeth, late Elizabeth Smith. Sept. 10, 1767. Arch. vol. A47, pages 179-180.

Stradley, John. Admin. of, to Mary Ann Clarrothan. Sept. 19, 1767. Arch. vol. A49, page 65. Reg. of Wills, Liber L, folio 36.

Smith, Joseph. Will. Made March 9, 1761. Heirs: wife Mary; sons Henry & James; dau. Mary. Exec'x, wife Mary. Wits., William Wheeler, Solomon Hobbs. Prob. Sept. 30, 1767. Arch. vol. A47, pages 100-101. Reg. of Wills, Liber L, folios 36-37.

Ruth, John. Admin. of, to William Levick. Oct. 5, 1767. Reg. of Wills, Liber L, folio 37.

Merydith, Robert. Will. Made April 1, 1767. Heirs: wife Rachel; son Job. Exec'r, son Job. Wits., John Caton, Thomas Moor, Wheelor Merydith. Prob. Oct. 7, 1767. Arch. vol. A34, pages 226, 208-210. Reg. of Wills, Liber L, folio 37.

Levick, Clayton. Admin. of, to Henry Stevens, next of kin. Nov. 5, 1767. Arch. vol. A30, pages 23-26. Reg. of Wills, Liber L, folio 38. Note:—Arch. vol. A30, page 23 shows children, William, John, Robert, Hannah, Catherine & Lydia.

Massey, Nathan. Admin. of, to Sarah Massey, widow. Nov. 7, 1767. Arch. vol. A34, pages 19-20. Reg. of Wills, Liber L, folio 38. Note:—Arch. vol. A34, page 20 shows children, John, Nathan & Elizabeth.

Meridith, John. Admin. of, to Sophia Merideth, widow. Nov. 11, 1767. Arch. vol. A34, page 196. Reg. of Wills, Liber L, folio 38.

Whitacre, William. Admin. of, to Mary Whitacre, widow. Nov. 11, 1767. Arch. vol. A54, page 97. Reg. of Wills, Liber L, folio 38.

Wells, Thomas. Admin. of, to Sarah Wells & Henry Farsons. Nov. 11, 1767. Arch. vol. A54, page 3. Reg. of Wills, Liber L, folio 38.

Consiglio, Jean. Wife of Francis Consiglio. Will. Made Sept. 12, 1765. Heir: friend Dr. Charles Ridgely. Exec'r, friend Dr. Charles Ridgely. Wits., Timothy Jenkins, Ann Jakes, Sarah Gray. Prob. Nov. 13, 1767. Arch. vol. A10, page 102. Reg. of Wills, Liber L, folios 42-43. Note:—Shows Jean Consiglio was formerly the wife of John Bibbin.

Freeman, Joseph. Admin. of, to Elizabeth Curmean, late Elizabeth Freeman. Nov. 25, 1767. Arch. vol. A18, page 125.

Merchant, William. Admin. of, to Thomas Bowman, Sr. Dec. 16, 1767. Arch. vol. A34, page 174. Reg. of Wills, Liber L, folio 38.

Wallace, William, Sr. Admin. of, to Catherine Wallace, widow. Dec. 17, 1767. Arch. vol. A52, pages 220-222. Reg. of Wills, Liber L, folio 38. Note:—Arch. vol. A6, page 108 shows that William Wallace was guardian of John Ryan & this acct. was later administered by widow Catharine Wallace.

Miller, Rebecca. Admin. of, to Hannah Miller & Hester Miller, next of kin. Dec. 23, 1767. Arch. vol. A35, page 113. Reg. of Wills, Liber L, folio 38.

Cleave, Joseph. Admin. of, to Elijah Morris. Dec. 24, 1767. Arch. vol. A9, page 126. Reg. of Wills, Liber L, folio 38.

Thomas, George. Admin. of, to John Thomas, next of kin. Dec. 26, 1767. Reg. of Wills, Liber L, folio 38.

Venables, Purkins. Admin. of, to Catherine Venables, widow. Dec. 26, 1767. Reg. of Wills, Liber L, folios 38-39. Note:— Arch. vol. A52, page 31 shows children, Catherine, Mary, Martha & Elener.

Parker, John. Admin. of, to Thomas Nixon. Dec. 28, 1767. Reg. of Wills, Liber L, folio 39.

Freeman, Charles. Admin. of, to George Morgan, next of kin. Jan. 7, 1768. Reg. of Wills, Liber L, folio 39.

Dickinson [Dickerson], William. Admin. of, to Sarah Dickinson, widow. Jan. 8, 1768. Arch. vol. A14, pages 65-67. Reg. of Wills, Liber L, folio 39. Note:—Arch. vol. A14, page 67 shows Sarah Dickinson married Stephen Lewis; page 65 mentions children, John, William, Elizabeth & Anne.

Harper, John. Admin. of to Agnes Harper, widow. Jan. 8, 1768. Reg. of Wills, Liber L, folio 39.

Jackson, William. Farmer. Murderkill Hd. Admin. of, to David Anderson, next of kin. Jan. 9, 1768. Arch. vol. A26, pages 57-58. Reg. of Wills, Liber L, folios 39-42.

Chadwick, Thomas. Admin. of, to Mary Chadwick, widow. Jan. 11, 1768. Reg. of Wills, Liber L, folio 39. Note:—Arch. vol. A8, page 132 shows children, Hannah & Mary.

Speer [Sphear], John. Admin. of, to Elizabeth Speer, widow. Jan. 19, 1768. Arch. vol. A48, page 79. Reg. of Wills, Liber L, folio 39.

Craige, Thomas. Admin. of, to Nancy Craige, widow. Jan. 20, 1768. Reg. of Wills, Liber L, folio 39. Note:—Arch. vol. A11, page 170 shows this acct. later administered by Edward & Nanny Stradly.

Watts, John. Admin. of, to Ann Watts, widow. Jan. 21, 1768. Reg. of Wills, Liber L, folio 40. Note:—Arch. vol. A53, page 189 shows Rhodes Clark & wife Anne as adm'rs.

Few, Esther. Admin. of, to Robert Finney, next of kin. Feb. 3, 1768. Arch. vol. A16, page 247. Reg. of Wills, Liber L, folio 40.

Parker, William. Admin. of, to Elizabeth Parker, widow. Feb. 6, 1768. Reg. of Wills, Liber L, folio 40.

Hander [Hansor], William. Will. Made Aug. 28, 1756. Heirs: wife Mary; sons Cornelius, William, Jonathan, Nehemiah; dau. Noumy. Exec'rs, son Cornelius & wife Mary. Wits., John Darling, Esther Darling, Hannah French. Prob. Feb. 5, 1768. Arch. vol. A21, page 221. Reg. of Wills, Liber L, folio 40.

Bostick, William. Admin. of, to Margaret Bostick, widow. Feb. 11, 1768. Reg. of Wills, Liber L, folio 40.

Hairgrove, Stephen. Murderkill Hd. Admin. of, to Ann Hairgrove, widow. Feb. 15, 1768. Arch. vol. A21, pages 69-70. Reg. of Wills, Liber L, folio 40. Note:—Arch. vol. A21, page 69 mentions heirs, Mary, George Anne, Katherine & Thomas Hairgrove; page 70 shows that Ann Hairgrove, widow, later married Edmond Baily.

Wells, John. Admin. of, to Thomas Parker. Feb. 25, 1768. Arch. vol. A53, page 235.

Cahoon, William. Admin. of, to Eleanor Cahoon, widow. Feb. 25, 1768. Reg. of Wills, Liber L, folio 40.

Bostick, Abraham. Admin. of, to Shadrach Bostick, next of kin. March 5, 1768. Arch. vol. A4, page 252. Reg. of Wills, Liber L, folio 40.

Commings [Cuming], Delectum. Admin. of, to Rachel Commings, widow. March 7, 1768. Reg. of Wills, Liber L, folio 43.

Chadwick, James. Will. Made Jan. 2, 1768. Heirs: daus. Mary Summers (wife of John) & Jane Chadwick; sons John, Joseph, David & Jonathan; dau.-in-law Mary Chadwick; grandsons Thomas, Samuel & James Chadick. Exec'r, Benjamin Clark.

Wits., John Ryon, John Harrington, Susanna Chadwick. Prob. March 8, 1768. Arch. vol. A8, pages 129-130. Reg. of Wills, Liber L, folios 41-42.

Ross, William. Admin. of, to Hugh Parke. March 10, 1768. Reg. of Wills, Liber L, folio 43.

Blackshear, Thomas. Will. Made Feb. 15, 1768. Heirs: son Thomas; daus. Letitia Moore, Elizabeth Reynalds. Isabell Bullick, Mariam Reynalds, Lucretia Whitely, Ann & Sarah Blackshear. Exec'r, son Thomas. Wits., Thomas Ratledge, James Harden, Samuel Robisson. Prob. March 12, 1768. Arch. vol. A4, page 111. Reg. of Wills, Liber L, folio 41.

Hazell, Isaac. Will. Made Feb. 10, 1768. Duck Creek Hd. Heirs: wife Barthia; nephew George Hill; George Hazell; Joseph Nock; Mary Nock; Isaac Curry; Jonathan Hazell; Moses Shelly; Thomas Nock, Jr.; Thomas Nock, son of Thomas Nock, Jr. Exec'x, wife Barthia. Wits., Molleston Correy, Andrew Jamison, Mary Farsons, Jr. Prob. March 22, 1768. Arch. vol. A23, pages 88-91. Reg. of Wills, Liber L, folio 43.

Harmison, Henry. Admin. of, to Sabrah Harmison, widow. March 29, 1768. Arch. vol. A22, page 38. Reg. of Wills, Liber L, folio 43.

David, Owen. Admin. of, to Benjamin Wallace. April 12, 1768. Arch. vol. A12, page 236. Reg. of Wills, Liber L, folio 43. Note:—Wife Mary is mentioned.

Train, Esther. Admin. of, to David Johnson, next of kin, D. B. N. April 16, 1768. Reg. of Wills, Liber L, folio 43.

Johnson, Robert. Admin. of, to David Johnson, next of kin, D. B. N. April 16, 1768. Reg. of Wills, Liber L, folio 43.

Durborow, Sarah. Admin. of, to David Johnson, next of kin. April 16, 1768. Reg. of Wills, Liber L, folio 43.

Craige, Moses. Will. Made March 26, 1768. Heirs: bros. James, John & Samuel; mother-in-law unnamed; Eaphream Shaw. Exec'r, Alexander Craige. Wits., James Wilson, William Wilson, John Anderton. Prob. April 25, 1768. Arch. vol. A11, pages 186-188. Reg. of Wills, Liber L. folios 43-44. Note:—Arch. vol. A11, page 188 mentions Annalena Craige & children.

Southard, Benjamin. Admin. of, to Thomas Buckmaster. April 25, 1768. Arch. vol. A48, page 57. Reg. of Wills, Liber L, folio 44.

Hadabuck, Jacob. Admin. of, to Dolla Hadabuck, widow. April 28, 1768. Arch. vol. A22, page 248 & vol. A21, pages 60-63. Reg. of Wills, Liber L, folio 44. Note:—Arch. vol. A21, page 61 shows that Dolly [Dorothy] Haddabuck married Benjamin Jones, Jr.; page 60 shows that Dolly [Hadabuck] Jones later married Andrew Jenkins; vol. A22, page 248 mentions children, Warwick, Abraham, Isaac Hattabaugh, & Elizabeth Hurlock.

Smith, John. Will. Made April 7, 1768. Heirs: mother Rebekah Smith; bro. William. Exec'x, mother Rebekah Smith. Wits., Elisha Morriss, Isaac Jones, Jehu Staton. Prob. May 13, 1768. Arch. vol. A47, page 78. Reg. of Wills, Liber L, folios 44-45.

Train, Hamilton. Admin. of, to Alice Train & James Train, next of kin. May 19, 1768. Arch. vol. A51, pages 53-54. Reg. of Wills, Liber L, folio 45.

Akles, John. Admin. of, to Sarah Akles, widow. May 21, 1768. Reg. of Wills, Liber L, folio 45.

Fisher, John. Admin. of, to Samuel Smith, D. B. N. May 26, 1768. Arch. vol. A17, pages 124, 132-133. Reg. of Wills, Liber L, folio 45.

Falkner, Samuel. Admin. of, to James May. May 26, 1768. Arch. vol. A17, page 93.

Smith, Henry. Admin. of, to Joseph Alford. May 27, 1768. Arch. vol. A47, page 48.

Allee, Abraham, Jr. Admin. of, to Christopher Denney, next of kin. May 27, 1768. Arch. vol. A1, pages 48-49. Reg. of Wills, Liber L, folio 45. Note:—Arch. vol. A1, page 49 shows children, Isaac, Abraham, Jacob & Mary Allee.

Pemberton, John. Admin. of, to Sarah Pemberton, widow. May 30, 1768. Arch. vol. A39, page 184. Reg. of Wills, Liber L, folio 45.

Buckmaster, Willson. Admin. of, to Esther Buckmaster, widow. May 31, 1768. Reg. of Wills, Liber L, folio 45.

Barns, William. Admin. of, to William Killen & John Katon, D. B. N. June 15, 1768. Arch. vol. A2, page 232.

Hardin, John. Admin. of, to Ann Hardin, widow. June 18, 1768. Arch. vol. A22, page 17. Reg. of Wills, Liber L, folio 45.

Heyse, John. Will. Made June 9, 1768. Duck Creek. Heirs: wife Martha; dau. Ann; sons Benjamin, Robert & John. Exec'x, wife Martha. Trustee, friend Samuel Griffith. Wits., Teresa Milstead, Thomas Carmichael, John Lewis. Prob. July 27, 1768. Arch. vol. A23, pages 66-70. Reg. of Wills, Liber L, folios 45-46. Note:—Arch. vol. A23, page 69 shows that Martha Heyse later married . . . Shaw.

Callahan, Edward. Admin. of, to Rebeccah Callahan, widow. Aug. 11, 1768. Reg. of Wills, Liber L, folio 46.

Dickson, Richard. Admin. of, to Sarah Dickson, widow. Aug. 24, 1768. Arch. vol. A14, page 62. Reg. of Wills, Liber L, folio 46.

Bloom, Peter. Admin. of, to Mary Bloom, widow. Aug. 29, 1768. Arch. vol. A4, pages 152-153. Reg. of Wills, Liber L, folio 46. Note:—Arch. vol. A4, page 153 mentions children, Peter, Jr., & Eve Bloom; also shows that Mary Bloom married Thomas Myers.

McGeah, Hugh. Farmer. Will. Made Aug. 17, 1768. Little Creek Hd. Heirs: wife Elizabeth; daus. Mary & Sarah; sons Hugh & Michael; children of bro. Michael unnamed. Exec'x, wife Elizabeth. Guardian, friend Samuel Hanson. Wits., Thomas Irons, Timothy Jenkins, James Sykes. Prob. Aug. 30, 1768. Arch. vol. A32, pages 183-185. Reg. of Wills, Liber L, folio 47. Note:—Arch. vol. A32, page 184 shows Elizabeth as wife of William Owens.

Swallow, George. Admin. of, to Silvanus Swallow, next of kin. Sept. 2, 1768. Arch. vol. A49, page 133. Reg. of Wills, Liber L, folio 47.

Burrows, Thomas. Will. Made Aug. 26, 1768. Heirs: wife Elizabeth; daus. Elizabeth Underling, Mary Perry; sons William, Lemuel, Thomas. Exec'x, wife Elizabeth. Wits., Elizabeth Roe, Francis Stevens, Benjamin Goodwin. Prob. Sept. 3, 1768. Arch. vol. A6, pages 203 & 219. Reg. of Wills, Liber L, folios 47-48.

Stevens, John. Admin. of, to Ann Parke. Sept. 7, 1768. Reg. of Wills, Liber L, folio 48.

Hart, Henry. Admin. of, to Tamer Hart, widow. Sept. 13, 1768. Arch. vol. A22, page 194. Reg. of Wills, Liber L, folio 48.

Bullet, Mary. Admin. of, to Thomas Meyer, next of kin. Oct. 14, 1768. Reg. of Wills, Liber L, folio 48. Note:—Arch. vol A6, page 181 mentions daus. Margaret [Peggy] & Mary [Polly].

Loatman, Benjamin. Admin. of, to Jonathan Allee. Nov. 9, 1768. Arch. vol. A30, page 199. Reg. of Wills, Liber L, folio 48.

Davis, William. Admin. of, to Rachel Davis, widow. Nov. 9, 1768. Arch. vol. A13, page 78. Reg. of Wills, Liber L, folio 48.

Parke, Thomas. Admin. of, to Cecilia Parke, next of kin, D. B. N. Nov. 12, 1768. Arch. vol. A39, pages 27-29. Reg. of Wills, Liber L, folios 48 & 21. Note:—Arch. vol. A39, page 27 shows that Cecillia Parke later married Bertles Shee.

Parke, Ann. Admin. of, to Cecilia Parke, next of kin. Nov. 12, 1768. Arch. vol. A39, pages 6-7. Reg. of Wills, Liber L, folio 49. Note:—Arch. vol. A39, page 6 shows that Cecilia Parke later married Bertles Shee.

Meridith, Robert. Admin. of, to Nathan Adams. Nov. 24, 1768. Reg. of Wills, Liber L, folio 49.

Jerrard, Matthew, Sr. Will. Made Oct. 14, 1768. Heirs: wife Esther; sons Matthew, Jr., James & Wilson; daus. Mary Cox, Ruth Clark, Nancy Hutcheson, Prudence Purden. Exec'r, son Matthew, Jr. Wits., Samuel Lisle, Ann Brady, William Harper. Prob. Nov. 25, 1768. Arch. vol. A26, pages 107-109. Reg. of Wills, Liber L, folio 49. Note:—Arch. vol. A26, page 108 shows granddaus. Tamer & Rachel Dunning; also shows Thomas Cox and wife Mary & Benjamin Clark & wife Ruth.

Shaw, Thomas. Admin. of, to Martha Shaw, widow. Dec. 3, 1768. Arch. vol. A45, pages 215-217. Reg. of Wills, Liber L, folio 50. Note:—Arch. vol. A45, page 217 shows that Martha Shaw was formerly the wife of John Hayes.

Numbers, Peter. Admin. of, to Mary Numbers, widow. Dec. 13, 1768. Arch. vol. A38, pages 90-94. Reg. of Wills, Liber L, folio 50. Note:—Arch. vol. A38, page 92 shows that Mary Numbers later married Nicholas Lynch; also shows children, John, Sarah, Mary, Susanna & Peter Numbers.

Start, James. Admin. of, to Lurana Start, widow. Dec. 13, 1768. Reg. of Wills, Liber L, folio 50. Note:—Arch. vol. A48, page 176 shows that Lurana Start married John Wheelton; also shows children, James, Jerusha, Joseph, Esther & Elijah Start.

Hansor, William. Admin. of, to Sarah Hansor & John Durham. Dec. 16, 1768. Arch. vol. A21, pages 205 & 227. Reg. of Wills, Liber L, folios 39-40. Note:—Arch. vol. A21, page 205 mentions heirs, Cornelius, Naomi, Rhoda, Rachel & Sarah Handzor.

Hirons, Luke. Admin. of, to Elizabeth Hirons, widow. Jan. 2, 1769. Arch. vol. A24, pages 94-95. Reg. of Wills, Liber L, folio 50. Note:—Arch. vol. A24, page 94 shows heirs, Phebe & Keziah Hirons.

Stewart, John. Admin. of, to James Brown. Jan. 2, 1769. Arch. vol. A49, page 4. Reg. of Wills, Liber L, folio 50.

Robinson, Lawrance. Admin. of, to Susannah Robinson, widow. Jan. 3, 1769. Arch. vol. A44, page 79. Reg. of Wills, Liber L, folio 50.

Brown, Benjamin, Sr. Will. Made July 16, 1767. Heirs: wife [Meriam, from admin. acct.]; sons John, Benjamin, Jonathan; daus. Rebecca Smith, Rachel, Mary, Miriam, Susanah & Sealy Brown; Ann Bostick; Elezebarth Howell. Exec'x, wife Meriam. Wits., Joshua Nickerson, John McKow, Elesibeath Nickerson. Prob. Jan. 6, 1769. Arch. vol. A6, pages 20-22. Reg. of Wills, Liber L, folios 50-51. Note:—Arch. vol. A6, page 22 shows that Meriam Brown married Mark Maxwell.

Darling, James. Farmer. Will. Made Dec. 9, 1768. Duck Creek. Heirs: wife Mary; sons William & James; other children unnamed. Exec'x, wife Mary. Wits., Richard Burrows, William Burrows, John McDanield. Prob. Jan. 7, 1769. Arch. vol. A12, pages 189-190. Reg. of Wills, Liber L, folio 51.

Richards, Elizabeth. Admin. of, to William Richards, next of kin. Jan. 9, 1769. Reg. of Wills, Liber L, folio 51.

Manson, William. Admin. of, to Mary Manson, widow. Jan. 10, 1769. Reg. of Wills, Liber L, folio 51.

Hardin, Thomas. Admin. of, to Henry Stevens, D. B. N. Jan. 12, 1769. Arch. vol. A22, page 23. Reg. of Wills, Liber L, folio 52.

Molleston, Jonathan, Sr. Yeoman. Will (copy). Made Dec. 26, 1768. Mispillion Hd. Heirs: wife Elizabeth; sons William, Jonathan; daus. Mary & Elizabeth. Exec'x, wife Elizabeth. Wits., Reynear Williams, Penelope Williams, Amelia Brinkle. Prob. Jan. 18, 1769. Arch. vol. A35, pages 213-214. Reg. of Wills, Liber L, folio 52.

Rash, James. Will. Made Jan. 16, 1769. Heirs: bro. Joseph; sister Hannah Forcom. Exec'r, Renatus Forcom. Wits., James Caldwell, Vinsant Vandeford, Michey Rash. Prob. Jan. 28, 1769. Arch. vol. A42, page 36. Reg. of Wills, Liber L, folios 52-53.

Parker, Sarah. Admin. of, to Christopher Denny, next of kin, D. B. N. Jan. 30, 1769. Arch. vol. A39, page 43. Reg. of Wills, Liber L, folio 53.

Ralph, Edward. Admin. of, to Sarah Ralph, widow. Feb. 3, 1769. Arch. vol. A42, page 17. Reg. of Wills, Liber L, folio 53.

Hall, David. Admin. of, to Mary Hall, widow. Feb. 6, 1769. Arch. vol. A21, page 85. Reg. of Wills, Liber L, folio 53.

Needham, Phebee. Admin. of, to Ezekiel Needham, son. Feb. 14, 1769. Reg. of Wills, Liber L, folio 53.

Catts, William. Admin. of, to John Catts, next of kin. Feb. 14, 1769. Reg. of Wills, Liber L, folio 53.

Chamnis, John. Admin. of, to William Chamnis, next of kin. Feb. 15, 1769. Reg. of Wills, Liber L, folio 53.

Dickenson, Walter. Admin. of, to Sarah Dickenson, next of kin. Feb. 18, 1769. Reg. of Wills, Liber L, folio 54. Note:—Arch. vol. A14, page 64 shows that Sarah Dickenson married Stephen Lewis.

Walker, William. Admin. of, to Agnes Walker, widow. Feb. 23, 1769. Arch. vol. A52, page 201. Reg. of Wills, Liber L, folio 54.

Allee, John, Jr. Admin. of, to William Killen, Esq., next of kin. March 6, 1769. Reg. of Wills, Liber L, folio 54.

Slaught, John. Duck Creek Hd. Admin. of, to John Slaught, next of kin. March 7, 1769. Arch. vol. A46, page 220. Reg. of Wills, Liber L, folio 54.

Williams, John. Admin. of, to Jacob Warrington. March 9, 1769. Arch. vol. A55, page 94. Reg. of Wills, Liber L, folio 54.

Downing, Ezekiel. Will. Made Jan. 21, 1765. Duck Creek Hd. Heirs: sons Joseph, Benjamin & William; Sarah Nelson. Exec'r, Thomas Collins. Wits., Susannah Bayard, Elizabeth Nelson. Prob. March 13, 1769. Arch. vol. A14, pages 243-245. Reg. of Wills, Liber L, folios 54-55.

Ralph, Edward. Admin. of, to John Carpenter & Elijah Berry, D. B. N. March 17, 1769. Arch. vol. A42, page 17. Reg. of Wills, Liber L, folio 55.

Ralph, Sarah. Admin. of, to John Carpenter & Elijah Berry. March 17, 1769. Arch. vol. A42, page 18. Reg. of Wills, Liber L, folio 55.

Smith, Daniel. Admin. of, to Jane Smith, widow. March 20, 1769. Arch. vol. A47, page 13. Reg. of Wills, Liber L, folio 55.

Griffin, Samuel. Admin. of, to Martha Griffin, widow. March 20, 1769. Arch. vol. A20, pages 220-223. Reg. of Wills, Liber L, folio 56. Note:—Arch. vol. A20, page 220 shows heirs, Owen Griffin, John Patterson & wife Rachel, Joseph Meredith & wife Elizabeth, Samuel & Isaac Griffith.

Stanton, Elizabeth. Will. Made March 1, 1769. Little Creek. Heirs: daus. Sara Miller, Ann Smith, Elizabeth Irons; sons Mathais & Jonathan; granddau. Sara Stanton; Mary Cahoon (alias Stanton). Exec'r, son-in-law Conrad Miller. Wits., James Jones, John Russel. Prob. March 21, 1769. Arch. vol. A48, pages 147-148. Reg. of Wills, Liber L, folios 55-56.

Virden, John, Sr. Will. Made Feb. 25, 1769. Heirs: wife Ellinor; dau. Ealce; sons John, William, Absolom, Isaac, Daniel; grandson James Read. Exec'rs, wife Ellinor & son William. Wits., John Caton, William Hughey. Prob. March 27, 1769. Arch. vol. A52, pages 90-93. Reg. of Wills, Liber L, folios 56-57. Note:—Arch. vol. A52, page 91 shows that Ealce Virden married John Kilpatrick.

Calloway, Peter. Will. Made Dec. 18, 1768. Heirs: wife Elizabeth; sons James, Joseph, Peter, Thomas; daus. Susanna Carter, Elizabeth Williams (wife of Thomas Williams), Ratchel & Sarah Calloway. Exec'r, son Peter. Wits., Robert Killen, Archibald Curry, Richard Williams. Prob. March 28, 1769. Arch. vol. A7, pages 154-155. Reg. of Wills, Liber L, folios 80-81.

Russell, Joseph. Will. Made March 12, 1769. Heirs: mother unnamed; bros. Henry & William; Susanna Morris. Exec'x, [Grace Russell, from admin. acct.]. Wits., Thomas Bowman, Elijah Wood. Prob. March 29, 1769. Arch. vol. A44, page 183. Reg. of Wills, Liber L, folio 57.

Greenwood, Maryann. Admin. of, to Joseph Greenwood, next of kin. March 29, 1769. Reg. of Wills, Liber L, folio 57.

Stevens, John. Admin. of, to Cecelia Parker, D. B. N. March 30, 1769. Reg. of Wills, Liber L, folio 57.

Brown, John. Admin. of, to Sarah Brown, widow. March 30, 1769. Reg. of Wills, Liber L, folio 57. Note:—Arch. vol. A6, page 53 shows that Sarah Brown married John Morris.

Hirons, Mark. Admin. of, to Sarah Hirons, widow. April 3, 1769. Reg. of Wills, Liber L, folio 57.

Hines, John. Admin. of, to Mary Hines, widow. April 3, 1769. Arch. vol. A24, page 52. Reg. of Wills, Liber L, folio 58.

Hawkins, Thomas. Admin. of, to Doraty Hawkins, widow. April 7, 1769. Reg. of Wills, Liber L, folio 59.

Mulett, William. Yeoman. Will. Made March 21, 1769. Duck Creek Hd. Heirs: wife Penelope; wife's dau. Penelope Story. Exec'x, wife Penelope. Wits., Thomas Brown, John Walraven, John Cremean. Prob. May 10, 1769. Arch. vol. A37, page 70. Reg. of Wills, Liber L, folio 59.

Willy, John. Will. Made March 25, 1769. Heirs: wife [Alce, from admin. acct.]; sons Levin, Gabril, Zadok; daus. unnamed. Exec'x, wife. Wits., Zadok Crapper, Presilla Davis. Prob. May 10, 1769. Arch. vol. A55, pages 62-63. Reg. of Wills, Liber L, folio 60.

Lewis, Thomas. Will. Made May 13, 1769. Duck Creek Hd. Heirs: wife Mary; cousin Hannah Morris, wife of Thomas Morris; Thomas Jones & Elizabeth Jones, children of David Jones; Dr. John Lewes. Exec'rs, wife Mary & friend Robert Blacksheare. Wits., James Moore, Richard Meradith. Prob. May 23, 1769. Arch. vol. A30, pages 150-152. Reg. of Wills, Liber L, folio 60.

Boardman, Robert. Admin. of, to Ebenezar Manlove, D. B. N. May 25, 1769. Reg. of Wills, Liber L, folio 61.

Ridley, Isaac. Admin. of, to Ebenezar Manlove, D. B. N. May 25, 1769. Reg. of Wills, Liber L, folio 61.

Killam, Isaac. Admin. of, to Catharin Killam, widow. May 30, 1769. Arch. vol. A28, pages 208-209. Reg. of Wills, Liber L, folio 61.

Rees, John. Will. Made March 15, 1769. Little Creek Hd. Heirs: wife Esther; sons John, Jeremiah, Thomas, David; daus. Mary Griffith, Lydia Chance, Sarah Rees. Exec'rs, wife Esther & son John. Wits., Levi Dungan, Thomas Murphy, John Russel. Prob. June 4, 1769. Arch. vol. A43, pages 18-20. Reg. of Wills, Liber L, folios 58-59.

Green, William. Admin. of, to Hannah Green & William Jordan. June 20, 1769. Arch. vol. A20, page 132. Reg. of Wills, Liber L, folio 61.

Muckeleheney, Agnes. Widow. Will. Made June 15, 1769. Heirs: daus. Mary Jesops, Agnes Muckeleheney & Jane Tolbert; sons Robert, William & James McClemons; bro. John Gray; Andrew Scott. Exec'r, bro. John Gray. Wits., Jabez Jenkins,

Thomas Nock, John Craige. Prob. June 23, 1769. Arch. vol. A37, page 82 & vol. A32, pages 176-177. Reg. of Wills, Liber L, folio 61. Note:—Arch. vol. A32, page 176 mentions heir, Agnis Meridith; shows estate later settled by Elizabeth Gray, widow of John.

Greenwood, Jonathan. Admin. of, to Joseph Greenwood, next of kin. June 23, 1769. Arch. vol. A20, page 154. Reg. of Wills, Liber L, folio 62.

Whitehead, Joseph. Admin. of, to Cornilious Chapman. June 26, 1769. Reg. of Wills, Liber L, folio 62.

Parke, Hugh. Will. Made July 15, 1769. Dover. Heirs: wife Elizabeth; son Thomas. Exec'x, wife Elizabeth. Wits., William Rodney, Crawford Rees. Prob. July 22, 1769. Arch. vol. A39, pages 8-11. Reg. of Wills, Liber L, folio 62. Note:— Arch. vol. A39, page 9 shows that Elizabeth Parke married John Carson.

Berry, James. Yeoman. Will. Made July 18, 1769. Murderkill Hd. Heirs: dau. Nancy; sons William, John, Benjamin, Elijah, Joseph; bro. Elijah Berry. Exec'rs, friends John & William Brown. Trustees, friends John & William Brown. Wits., Daniel James, William Snow, Lydia Jackson. Prob. July 22, 1769. Arch. vol. A4, pages 4-6. Reg. of Wills, Liber L, folios 62-63.

White, Sarah. Admin. of, to John White, next of kin. July 28, 1769. Arch. vol. A54, page 155. Reg. of Wills, Liber L, folio 63.

Cottingham, Thomas. Admin. of, to Ansley & Jonathan Cottingham. July 29, 1769. Arch. vol. A11, page 34. Reg. of Wills, Liber L, folio 63.

Griffin, Samuel. Tavernkeeper. Admin. of, to Jane Griffin & William Cahoon, Jr. Aug. 9, 1769. Arch. vol. A20, pages 224-225. Reg. of Wills, Liber L, folio 63.

Caton, John. Will. Made May 28, 1765. Heirs: wife Elizabeth; bro. Benjamin; sisters Esther Pearce & Jenat Chaplin; stepson William Betts; nephews James Caton (son of bro. Benjamin), John & Sampson Williamson. Exec'x, wife Elizabeth. Wits., William Thomas, Periscilla Walker. Codicil—

Wit., Charles Ridgely. Prob. Aug. 19, 1769. Arch. vol. A8, pages 74 & 84. Reg. of Wills, Liber L, folios 63-64. Note:— Arch. vol. A8, page 84 shows Elizabeth as wife of William Carpenter.

Lewis, Mary. Admin. of, to Ebenezar Clampitt. Sept. 4, 1769. Reg. of Wills, Liber L, folio 65. Note:—Arch. vol. A30, page 117 shows that Jane Clampitt married Benjamin Sparks.

Maxwell, Jean. Admin. of, to Sarah Hirons. Oct. 7, 1769. Reg. of Wills, Liber L, folio 65.

Furman, William. Admin. of, to Michal Doyl. Oct. 10, 1769. Reg. of Wills, Liber L, folio 65.

Manson, William. Admin. of, to Andrew Lackey, D. B. N. Oct. 12, 1769. Arch. vol. A33, page 164. Reg. of Wills, Liber L, folio 65.

Manson, Mary. Admin. of, to Andrew Lackey. Oct. 12, 1769. Arch. vol. A33, page 163. Reg. of Wills, Liber L, folio 65.

Craige, John. Admin. of, to Ann Craige, next of kin, D. B. N. Oct. 31, 1769. Arch. vol. A11, page 168. Reg. of Wills, Liber L, folio 65.

Lewis, Philip. Will. Made Oct. 17, 1769. Little Creek Hd. Heirs: wife Mary; son Philip. Exec'x, wife Mary. Wits., Richard Smith, John Evans, Thomas Murphey, Jr. Prob. Nov. 1, 1769. Arch. vol. A30, pages 118-120. Reg. of Wills, Liber L, folios 65-66.

Maxwell, Robert. Will. Made Sept. 20, 1769. Heirs: sons David, James, Bedwell; daus. Joannah & Mellesent. Exec'rs, friends Edward Gibbs, William Meredith. Trustee, William Meredith. Wits., Daniel Virdin, Oliver Crawford, Elizabeth Virdin. Codicil, dau. Elizabeth. Prob. Nov. 4, 1769. Arch. vol. A34, pages 96-98. Reg. of Wills, Liber L, folios 66-67.

Jackson, Elizabeth. Widow of John Jackson. Admin. of, to John Jackson. Nov. 18, 1769. Arch. vol. A25, pages 248-249. Reg. of Wills, Liber L, folio 67.

Morgan, George. Admin. of, to Elizabeth Morgan, widow. Nov. 21, 1769. Reg. of Wills, Liber L, folio 67. Note:—Arch. vol. A36, page 149 shows that Elizabeth married William Owens.

Clampitt, Ebenezar. Admin. of, to Jean Clampitt, widow. Nov. 22, 1769. Arch. vol. A8, pages 202-203. Reg. of Wills, Liber L, folio 67. Note:—Arch. vol. A8, page 203 shows that Jean [Jane] Clampitt married Benjamin Sparks.

Lewis, Mary. Admin. of, to Jean Clampit, next of kin, D. B. N. Nov. 22, 1769. Reg. of Wills, Liber L, folio 67.

McFarlen, John. Admin. of, to Prudence McFarlen, widow. Nov. 22, 1769. Reg. of Wills, Liber L, folio 67. Note:—Arch. vol. A32, page 182 shows that Prudence McFarland married John Massey.

Crawford, David. Admin. of, to Andrew Lackey, D. B. N. Nov. 30, 1769. Arch. vol. A11, page 215. Reg. of Wills, Liber L, folio 67.

Cockran, Mary. Admin. of, to John Middleton, next of kin. Dec. 1, 1769. Reg. of Wills, Liber L, folio 67.

Manlove, Absalom. Shallopman. Will. Made Nov. 26, 1769. Heirs: bro.-in-law John Williams, son of John Williams; Thomas Cockrum. Exec'r, bro.-in-law John Williams. Wits., Mary Hunn, Richard Furbush, Rachel Bullen. Prob. Dec. 1, 1769. Arch. vol. A33, page 81. Reg. of Wills, Liber L, folios 67-68.

Lewis, John. Will. Made Nov. 26, 1769. Heirs: sons Rees, Mark & Amram. Exec'r, friend John Russel. Trustee, friend John Russel. Wits., James Lewis, Timothy Russel, Hugh Russel. Prob. Dec. 4, 1769. Arch. vol. A30, page 95. Reg. of Wills, Liber L, folio 68.

King, Isaac. Admin. of, to Martha King, widow. Dec. 5, 1769. Arch. vol. A29, pages 25-26. Reg. of Wills, Liber L, folio 68. Note:—Arch. vol. A29, page 26 shows that Martha King married Jacob Morgan.

Brinckle, Southby. Admin. of, to Emily Brinckle, widow, & Reynear Williams. Dec. 9, 1769. Arch. vol. A5, pages 212-215. Reg. of Wills, Liber L, folio 68. Note:—Arch. vol. A5, page 212 shows heirs, bros. William & Joseph Brinckle; Elizabeth Brinckle, dau. of Benjamin Brinckle; page 213 shows that Amelia Brinckle married John Revell; page 215 mentions a son Southey Brinckle.

Wynn, Benjamin. Admin. of, to Elizabeth Wynn, widow. Dec. 15, 1769. Arch. vol. A56, pages 182-184. Reg. of Wills, Liber L, folio 68. Note:—Arch. vol. A56, pages 183-184 mention heirs, Benjamin, Joseph, Simon, Mary, Isaac, Elizabeth & John Wynn.

Brinckle, John. Admin. of, to John Brinckle, next of kin. Dec. 19, 1769. Arch. vol. A5, pages 183-186. Reg. of Wills, Liber L, folio 68.

Griffin, Timothy. Admin. of, to William Clark. Dec. 19, 1769. Reg. of Wills, Liber L, folio 68.

Brown, Benjamin. Admin. of, to Elizabeth Brown, widow. Dec. 22, 1769. Arch. vol. A6, pages 23-24. Reg. of Wills, Liber L, folio 69.

Lumm, Samuel. Admin. of, to Samuel Ball. Dec. 23, 1769. Reg. of Wills, Liber L, folio 69.

Sundergill, Phillip. Admin. of, to Joshua Sundergill, next of kin. Dec. 27, 1769. Arch. vol. A49, page 125. Reg. of Wills, Liber L, folio 69.

Hussey, James. Admin. of, to Roger Barrett. Dec. 27, 1769. Reg. of Wills, Liber L, folio 69.

Shelley, Moses. Admin. of, to John Shelley of Md., next of kin. Dec. 28, 1769. Arch. vol. A45, page 226. Reg. of Wills, Liber L, folio 69.

Calloway, James. Admin. of, to Phebee Calloway, widow, and Joseph Marrett. Dec. 29, 1769. Arch. vol. A7, pages 145-147. Reg. of Wills, Liber L, folio 69. Note:—Arch. vol. A7, page 146 shows that Phebe Calloway married Richard Brinckle.

Williams, John. Admin. of, to Mary Williams, widow. Dec. 29, 1769. Arch. vol. A55, pages 95-96. Reg. of Wills, Liber L, folio 69. Note:—Arch. vol. A55, page 95 shows heirs, Elizabeth Ward, Tabitha, John & Thomas Williams, Joseph & Peter Calloway, James Sapp & William Wyatt.

Steel, Henry. Admin. of, to James Raymond, next of kin, D. B. N. Jan. 6, 1770. Arch. vol. A48, pages 197-198. Reg. of Wills, Liber L, folio 85.

Steel, Mary. Admin. of, to James Raymond, next of kin. Jan. 6, 1770. Reg. of Wills, Liber L, folio 85.

Vanderford, John. Admin. of, to Elizabeth Vanderford, widow. Jan. 6, 1770. Reg. of Wills, Liber L, folio 69.

Hellings, Jacob. Admin. of, to Mary Hellings, widow. Jan. 17, 1770. Reg. of Wills, Liber L, folio 69.

Sleighter, George. Admin. of, to Henry Moore. Jan. 22, 1770. Reg. of Wills, Liber L, folio 69.

Willson, William, Sr. Admin. of, to Ann Willson, widow. Jan. 22, 1770. Arch. vol. A56, page 24. Reg. of Wills, Liber L, folio 69.

Melvin, Edmond. Admin. of, to Phebee Melvin, widow. Jan. 23, 1770. Arch. vol. A34, pages 141-142. Reg. of Wills, Liber L, folio 70.

Bostick, John. Admin. of, to Margarett Bostick, widow. Jan. 23, 1770. Arch. vol. A4, page 264. Reg. of Wills, Liber L, folio 70.

Smith, William. Merchant. Will. Made Jan. 19, 1770. Heirs: William Carpenter; Zachariah Goforth; John Dill; Nance Wiles. Exec'rs, William Carpenter & Zachariah Goforth. Wits., Benjamin Dill, Thomas Davis, Henry Simmons, Jr. Prob. Feb. 2, 1770. Arch. vol. A47, page 195. Reg. of Wills, Liber L, folio 70.

Carpenter, John. Admin. of, to Hannah Carpenter, widow. Feb. 5, 1770. Reg. of Wills, Liber L, folio 70. Note:—Arch. vol. A7, page 232 shows that Hannah Carpenter married Benjamin Silvester.

Hall, Robert. Yeoman. Will. Made Jan. 16, 1770. Little Creek. Heirs: wife Jerucy; sons John & Robert; sister Letitia Bell. Exec'x, wife Jerucy. Wits., John Frazer, William Cook, Thomas Parry. Prob. Feb. 10, 1770. Arch. vol. A21, pages 117-118. Reg. of Wills, Liber L, folios 70-71.

Booth, Peter. Farmer. Will. Made Jan. 29, 1770. Duck Creek. Heirs: wife Sarah; son Isaac; dau. Tamer; children of wife's sister, Sarah & Mary Stuart. Exec'x, wife Sarah. Wits., Cuthbart Green, Thomas Wilson, Thomas Brown. Prob. Feb. 13, 1770. Arch. vol. A4, pages 246-248. Reg. of Wills, Liber L, folio 71. Note:—Arch. vol. A4, page 248 shows that Sarah Booth married . . . Hillyard; also shows Tamer Booth as wife of John Steward.

Jacobs, William. Admin. of, to William Jacobs, next of kin. Feb. 14, 1770. Reg. of Wills, Liber L, folio 71.

Smith, Rebecca. Will. Made Feb. 4, 1770. Heirs: daus. Sarah McNitt (wife of Joseph McNitt), Mary, Rebecca, Elizabeth & Levice Smith; sons Robert & William Smith. Exec'rs, son William & Elijah Anderson. Wits., Robert Killen, Archibald Currey, Ratchel Owtwell. Prob. Feb. 14, 1770. Arch. vol. A47, pages 143-145. Reg. of Wills, Liber L, folios 71-72.

Knight, William. Admin. of, to Mary Knight, widow. Feb. 23, 1770. Reg. of Wills, Liber L, folio 72.

Cahoon, Thomas. Will. Made Sept. 12, 1768. Duck Creek. Heirs: wife Rachel; wife's dau. Rachel Strickland; bro. William Cahoon; nephews Mark & Charles, sons of bro. William Cahoon; Thomas Cahoon. Exec'x, wife Rachel. Wits., Lawrance Hobson, Peter Mannee, Rachel Strickland. Prob. March 1, 1770. Arch. vol. A7, pages 42-43. Reg. of Wills, Liber L, folio 72. Note:—Arch. vol. A7, page 43 shows that Rachel Cahoon married . . . Eglin.

Blundell, James. Yeoman. Will. Made Feb. 1, 1770. Little Creek. Heirs: wife Susannah; bro. Jonathan Ozbun; son James; daus. Sarah & Susannah; other bros. and sisters unnamed; Friends Meeting House. Exec'x, wife Susannah. Wits., Govey Emmerson, John Cowgill, Thomas Parry. Prob. March 3, 1770. Arch. vol. A4, pages 155-156. Reg. of Wills, Liber L, folio 73. Note:—Arch. vol. A4, page 156 shows Jonathan & Edmond Needham as sons of Susannah Blundell.

Morris, Aaron. Admin. of, to Daniel Morris, next of kin. March 3, 1770. Arch. vol. A36, page 183. Reg. of Wills, Liber L, folio 73.

Williams, Richard. Admin. of, to Rachel Williams, widow. March 5, 1770. Reg. of Wills, Liber I, folio 73. Note:—Arch. vol. A55, page 151 shows that Rachel Williams married William Cardeen.

Barns, John, Jr. Admin. of, to Jonathan Rees, next of kin. March 26, 1770. Reg. of Wills, Liber L, folio 73.

Edmunds, James. Will. Made Feb. 13, 1770. Heirs: son John; cousin Henry Newell. Exec'r, Phillip Barratt. Wits., Waitman Sipple, Jr.; George Wilson, John Mileway. Prob. March 28, 1770. Arch. vol. A16, pages 31-33. Reg. of Wills, Liber L, folio 74.

Turner, Samuel. Will. Made Nov. 21, 1769. Heirs: wife Sarah; daus. Joyce & Lear; sons Elias, Jehu, Henry & Samuel Beavens Turner. Exec'rs, wife Sarah & son Jehu. Wits., Susener Murphy, Jeremiah Morris, Jeremiah Morris, Jr. Prob. March 30, 1770. Arch. vol. A51, pages 178-180. Reg. of Wills, Liber L, folio 74.

Lober [Lowber], Peter, Jr. Admin. of, to Mary Lober, widow. March 30, 1770. Arch. vol. A31, pages 137-138. Reg. of Wills, Liber L, folios 74-75. Note:—Arch. vol. A31, page 138 shows that Mary Lober married Thomas Davis.

McKnown [McKaune], John. Admin. of, to Robert McGarmant. April 2, 1770. Arch. vol. A32, page 214. Reg. of Wills, Liber L, folio 75.

Smith, William. Will. Made Feb. 7, 1770. Heirs: wife Elizabeth; son Samuel; daus. Nancey & Tishey. Exec'rs, wife Elizabeth & friend Daniel Virdin. Wits., Absalom Virdin, Sarah Virdin, Elizabeth Brown. Prob. April 3, 1770. Arch. vol. A47, pages 196-197. Reg. of Wills, Liber L, folio 75.

Stuart [Steward], Hugh. Yeoman. Will. Made Feb. 17, 1770. Motherkill Hd. Heirs: sons Moses, Andrew; sister Rose Skott; Elizabeth Lemon. Exec'r, William Gray. Wits., William Hughey, Elizabeth Lemon. Prob. April 9, 1770. Arch. vol. A48, pages 241-243. Reg. of Wills, Liber L, folios 75-76.

Manlove, John. Will. Made Feb. 23, 1770. Little Creek. Heirs: wife Margett; dau. Susannah; a child unnamed; nephew John Manlove, son of bro. Matthew. Exec'rs, wife Margett & bro. Matthew Manlove. Wits., Mary Manlove, Joseph Galloway, Govey Emmerson. Prob. April 11, 1770. Arch. vol. A33, pages 101-102. Reg. of Wills, Liber L, folio 76. Note:—Arch. vol. A33, page 102 shows that Margett Manlove married Ezekiel Hales.

Giffen, David. Admin. of, to William Cook. April 23, 1770. Arch. vol. A20, page 195. Reg. of Wills, Liber L, folio 76.

Sumers, John. Will. Made April 2, 1770. Heirs: wife Mary; sons Thomas, Nathan, Nathaniel, David, James, John; daus. Mary, Sarah, Nicy, Sely, Nanney, Bety. Exec'rs, wife Mary & son Thomas. Wits., Thomas Peterkin, Solomon Brady, Sophia Tomlinson. Prob. April 23, 1770. Arch. vol. A49, pages 116-117. Reg. of Wills, Liber L, folios 76-77.

Vandike, Thomas. Will. Made April 9, 1770. Duck Creek. Heirs: mother Ann Vandyke; bro. James; Elizabeth & Daniel Vandyke. Exec'r, bro. James. Wits., Samuel Scott, Isaac Carty. Prob. April 24, 1770. Arch. vol. A51, page 237. Reg. of Wills, Liber L, folio 77.

Downs, William. Yeoman. Will. Made Feb. 18, 1770. Heirs: sons Hezekiah & Levin. Exec'rs, James White & Richard Dellenar. Wits., Robert Killen, William Tharp, Mark Killen. Prob. April 24, 1770. Arch. vol. A15, pages 21-22. Reg. of Wills, Liber L, folios 77-78.

Pugh, Roger. Admin. of, to Mary Pugh, widow, D. B. N. May 8, 1770. Reg. of Wills, Liber L, folio 78.

Willson, Martha. Duck Creek Hd. Admin. of, to Jonathan Willson, next of kin. May 9, 1770. Arch. vol. A55, page 238. Reg. of Wills, Liber L, folio 78.

Freeman, Charles. Admin. of, to Samuel Freeman, next of kin, D. B. N. May 9, 1770. Arch. vol. A18, pages 115-116. Reg. of Wills, Liber L, folio 78.

Hodgson, William. Will. Made April 4, 1770. Mispillion Hd. Heirs: wife Nancey; son Joseph; daus. Esther & Train; bro. David. Exec'r, bro. David. Wits., Daniel Smith, Seth Catlen,

James Bostick. Prob. May 11, 1770. Arch. vol. A24, pages 137-142 & 127. Reg. of Wills, Liber L, folio 78. Note:— Arch. vol. A24, page 142 shows that Nancy married Andrew Saxton; page 140 shows Nancy as wife of William Brown.

Wallace, Agnis. Widow of Matthew. Will. Made April 16, 1770. Murtherkill Hd. Heirs: dau. Jennet Wallace; sons Thomas & David; son-in-law James Lukons; grandchildren Agnis, John & Mirim Rash, children of dau. Barbre. Exec'r, son Thomas. Wits., James Caldwell, Stephen Lewis, Mary Lee. Prob. May 14, 1770. Arch. vol. A52, page 168. Reg. of Wills, Liber L, folio 79.

Wyatt, Maryan. Admin. of, to William Morris, next of kin. May 18, 1770. Reg. of Wills, Liber L, folio 79.

Biship, Samuel. Admin. of, to George Biship, next of kin. May 21, 1770. Reg. of Wills, Liber L, folio 79.

Rees, Sarah. Admin. of, to Esther & John Rees, D. B. N. May 23, 1770. Arch. vol. A43, page 32.

Rees, Jane. Admin. of, to Daniel Wright Newman. May 25, 1770. Arch. vol. A42, pages 243-244.

Skidmore, Thomas. Admin. of, to Esther Skidmore, widow, & John Banning. May 25, 1770. Reg. of Wills, Liber L, folio 79.

Collins, William. Admin. of, to John White, next of kin. May 26, 1770. Arch. vol. A10, page 35. Reg. of Wills, Liber L, folio 79.

Pleasonton, John. Admin. of, to Sarah Pleasonton, widow. May 26, 1770. Arch. vol. A40, pages 105-107. Reg. of Wills, Liber L, folio 79. Note:—Arch. vol. A40, page 105 show heirs, John, David, Elizabeth, Letitia & Rachel; page 106 shows that Elizabeth Pleasonton married Daniel Thomas.

Moore, Samuel. Admin. of, to Mary Hamilton, next of kin. June 9, 1770. Reg. of Wills, Liber L, folio 79.

Humphris, John. Admin. of, to Susanna Humphris, widow. June 27, 1770. Reg. of Wills, Liber L, folio 79.

Parke, John. Admin. of, to Bertles Shee & wife Cecilia. July 16, 1770. Arch. vol. A39, pages 15-17.

Crockett, John. Admin. of, to Margarett Crockett, widow. July 18, 1770. Arch. vol. A11, pages 243-244. Reg. of Wills, Liber L, folio 79. Note:—Arch. vol. A11, page 243 shows heirs, Margarett, Mary & Elizabeth Crockett.

Hill, Elizabeth. Will. Made Jan. 15, 1770. Duck Creek. Heirs: daus. Sarah Sawyer, Susanna Hill, Mary Denny; sons Thomas, Joseph, Robert, John, Jacob; grandson Thomas Foster. Exec'rs, sons Thomas & Joseph. Wits., Thomas Wild, Elizabeth Wild, Lawrence Hobson. Prob. July 21, 1770. Arch. vol. A23, pages 235-236. Reg. of Wills, Liber L, folio 80.

Morgan, Jacob. Son of George. Admin. of, to John Clayton. July 25, 1770. Arch. vol. A36, page 150. Note:—Mentions a sister Elizabeth and bro. George.

Morgan, Robert. Son of George. Admin. of, to John Clayton. July 25, 1770. Arch. vol. A36, page 164. Note:—Mentions a sister Elizabeth and bro. George.

Whitacre, Mary. Admin. of, to Jacob Morgan, next of kin. July 26, 1770. Reg. of Wills, Liber L, folio 81.

Evans, Zachariah. Admin. of, to Deborah Thomas, next of kin, & Enoch Jones. Aug. 1, 1770. Reg. of Wills, Liber L, folio 81. Note:—Arch. vol. A16, page 230 shows Deborah as wife of James Dickinson.

Morton, James. Tailor. Will. Made July 21, 1770. Murtherkill Hd. Heirs: mother unnamed; father James McCullough (of Broad Island, Ireland); sisters Mary Neelson (wife of Alexander Neelson of Broad Island, Ireland), Agnes (widow, of Broad Island, Ireland), Elizabeth (lives with mother & father, James McCullough of Broad Island, Ireland), Margaret Fairess (wife of James Fairess of Learn Town, Ireland); cousin John Lyle (of near Mill-Town or White Clay Creek, N. C. Co.). Exec'r, Dr. Samuel McCall. Wits., William Hynman, Thomas Elliott, George McCall. Prob. Aug. 9, 1770. Arch. vol. A37, pages 57-58. Reg. of Wills, Liber L, folios 81-82.

Harper, John. Admin. of, to William White. Aug. 15, 1770. Arch. vol. A22, pages 52-53. Reg. of Wills, Liber L, folio 82.

Wheelar, Elizabeth. Widow. Will. Made Aug. 11, 1770. Heirs: son Winlock Wheelar; daus. Mary Ann Long, Elizabeth Chadwick; granddaus. Penelope Catts & Sarah Wheelar; Samuel Wheelar, son of Samuel, dec'd. Exec'rs, son Winlock & Joseph Chadwick. Wits., Benjamin Benston, Elizabeth Benston, David Peterkin, Jr. Prob. Aug. 16, 1770. Arch. vol. A54, page 63. Reg. of Wills, Liber L, folio 82.

Allee, Abraham, Sr. Gentleman. Will. Made May 8, 1770. Duck Creek. Heirs: wife Mary; sons John & Jonathan; daus. Mary Carpenter, Sabrah Tilton; son-in-law Thomas Tilton; grandsons Abraham Allee (son of Jonathan), Abraham Allee (son of John); grandchildren of dau. Mary Carpenter by her first husband, Henry Rothwell; grandchildren Isaac, Abraham, Jacob & Mary, children of son Abraham Allee, dec'd. Exec'rs, sons John & Jonathan & son-in-law Thomas Tilton. Wits., James Tilton, John V^{n}Gaskin, Jr., John Hawkins, Jr. Prob. Aug. 20, 1770. Arch. vol. A1, pages 50-53. Reg. of Wills, Liber L, folio 83.

Brooks, Arthur. Will. Made July 16, 1770. Heirs: wife Johanah; sons Arthur & Isaac. Exec'x, wife Johanah. Wits., Daniel Billiter, Bridget Freeman, Iddy Crane. Prob. Aug. 23, 1770. Arch. vol. A6, page 3. Reg. of Wills, Liber L, folios 83-84.

Flemming, Alexander. Admin. of, to Isabel Fleming & Robert Fleming. Aug. 30, 1770. Arch. vol. A17, page 167. Reg. of Wills, Liber L, folio 86.

Barns, John. Minor. Admin. of, to George Blackshare, guardian. Sept. 1, 1770. Arch. vol. A2, page 220.

Francis, Ellis. Will. Made March 3, 1770. Little Creek Hd. Heirs: friend Elizabeth Due; Robert Holliday; James Holliday, son of Robert. Exec'r, Robert Holliday. Wits., James Lewis, Joel Lewis, James Fortune. Prob. Sept. 17, 1770. Arch. vol. A18, pages 75-76. Reg. of Wills, Liber L, folio 84.

Haines, Rachel. Admin. of, to Major Henderson. Oct. 8, 1770. Arch. vol. A23, page 73. Note:—Mentions daus. Sarah, Ann & Leah Haines.

Hudson, John. Admin. of, to Benjamin Hudson, next of kin. Oct. 8, 1770. Reg. of Wills, Liber L, folio 84.

Davison, James. Admin. of, to Joseph Hill. Oct. 16, 1770. Arch. vol. A13, page 85. Reg. of Wills, Liber L, folio 84.

Sipple, Caleb, Jr. Admin. of, to Jonathan Sipple, next of kin. Oct. 29, 1770. Reg. of Wills, Liber L, folio 84.

Hillford, Ann. Mispillion Hd. Admin. of, to David Hillford, next of kin. Nov. 14, 1770. Arch. vol. A23, pages 221-222. Reg. of Wills, Liber L, folio 85.

Murphey, David. Admin. of, to Susannah Murphey, widow. Nov. 19, 1770. Reg. of Wills, Liber L, folio 85. Note:—Arch. vol. A37, page 85 shows that Susannah Murphey later married Thomas Herwood.

Vining, John. Will. Made Nov. 13, 1770. Heirs: wife Pheebe; dau. Mary; sons Benjamin, Nicholas, John. Exec'rs, friend Benjamin Chew of Phila., Attorney-at-law; bro. Charles Ridgely of Dover, doctor; Benjamin Wyncoop of Phila., merchant. Wits., Thomas Bond, Jonathan Elmer, Ann Nicholson. Prob. Nov. 22, 1770. Arch. vol. A52, pages 59-65. Reg. of Wills, Liber L, folios 86-87.

Bellach, John. Admin. of, to Stockley Sturgis. Nov. 27, 1770. Arch. vol. A3, pages 204-205. Reg. of Wills, Liber L, folio 86. Note:—Arch. vol. A3, page 205 mentions heirs, Mary Daugherty, née Bellach, & Hanah Rowan, née Bellach; also shows Wm. Levick later administered, D. B. N.

Smith, Henrietta. Admin. of, to Charles Hillyard. Nov. 28, 1770. Arch. vol. A47, page 44. Reg. of Wills, Liber L, folio 86.

Smith, James, Jr. Admin. of, to Charles Hillyard, next of kin, D. B. N. Nov. 28, 1770. Arch. vol. A47, page 60. Reg. of Wills, Liber L, folio 85.

Hill, Robert. Admin. of, to Thomas Hill, next of kin. Dec. 1, 1770. Reg. of Wills, Liber L, folio 86.

Richardson, Anne. Admin. of, to William Haslton, Sr. Dec. 11, 1770. Arch. vol. A43, page 159. Reg. of Wills, Liber I, folio 86.

Hayes, David. Admin. of, to Mary Hayes, widow. Dec. 20, 1770. Reg. of Wills, Liber L, folio 85.

Kent, Magdalen. Widow. Will. Made Aug. 26, 1770. Murtherkill Hd. Heirs: dau. Mary Caldwell; son Joseph. Exec'r, son Joseph. Wits., James Caldwell, Timothy Caldwell, Kesiah Pulle. Prob. Dec. 26, 1770. Arch. vol. A28, pages 143-144. Reg. of Wills, Liber L, folio 85.

Kent, Joseph. Admin. of, to James Caldwell, Jr., next of kin. Dec. 26, 1770. Arch. vol. A28, page 142. Reg. of Wills, Liber L, folio 85.

Nicolls, Joseph. Will (copy). Made Jan. 23, 1770. Heirs: wife Mary; children unnamed. Exec'x, wife Mary. Wits., Covil Tumlin, James Anderson, David Hillford. Prob. Dec. 31, 1770. Arch. vol. A37, pages 226-227. Reg. of Wills, Liber L, folio 87. Note:—Arch. vol. A37, page 226 shows that Mary Nicolls married Levin Charles.

Dill, Mary. Will. Made Oct. 10, 1770. Heirs: sons Benjamin, John; daus. Lydia, Hannah, Eliza Dill. Exec'r, son John. Wits., James Purden, John Fisher, Henry Simmons. Prob. Jan. 3, 1771. Arch. vol. A14, pages 103 & 106. Reg. of Wills, Liber L, folios 88-89.

Sipple, Christopher. Admin. of, to Ann Sipple, widow. Jan. 3, 1771. Arch. vol. A46, page 116. Reg. of Wills, Liber L, folio 89.

Shaw, Ephriam. Admin. of, to Leah Shaw, widow. Jan. 4, 1771. Arch. vol. A45, pages 195-196. Reg. of Wills, Liber L, folio 89. Note:—Arch. vol. A45, page 196 shows that Leah, the widow, later married Daniel Cain.

Streep, William. Admin. of, to Rachel Streep, widow. Jan. 9, 1771. Arch. vol. A49, page 86. Reg. of Wills, Liber L, folio 89.

Smalley, John. Admin. of, to Elizabeth Smalley, widow. Jan. 10, 1771. Arch. vol. A46, pages 243-244. Reg. of Wills, Liber L, folio 89. Note:—Arch. vol. A46, page 243 shows that Elizabeth Smalley married . . . Silver.

Brinckle, Daniel. Admin. of, to Isaac Carty. Jan. 14, 1771. Reg. of Wills, Liber L, folio 89.

Poulson, William. Yeoman. Formerly of Brandywine Hd., N. C. Co. Admin. of, to Jacob Derrickson. Jan. 15, 1771. Arch. vol. A41, page 21.

Killen, Mary. Admin. of, to Henry Killen, next of kin. Jan. 18, 1771. Reg. of Wills, Liber L, folio 89.

Killen, Robert, Esq. Will. Made Jan. 1, 1771. Heirs: wife Mary; sons Robert, William, Adam, Henry, John & Mark; grandchildren Polly, Betty & Sally Buckannon. Exec'r, son Henry. Wits., John Haslet, Archibald Fleming, Richard Dillaner. Prob. Jan. 18, 1771. Arch. vol. A28, pages 194-200. Reg. of Wills, Liber L, folios 87-88. Note:—Arch. vol. A28, page 197 mentions Margaret Fleming as an heir.

Bryan, John. Admin. of, to John Pryer. Jan. 19, 1771. Arch. vol. A6, page 109. Reg. of Wills, Liber L, folio 89.

Bowman, Thomas. Yeoman. Will. Made Jan. 15, 1771. Mispillion Hd. Heirs: wife Mary; sons Nathaniel & Thomas; daus. Elizabeth & Jemima Bowman, Miriam MacSparren, Susannah Fisher, Sary Panter; grandson Nathaniel Bowman; granddaus. Elizabeth & Margaret Fisher. Exec'rs, son Thomas & son-in-law Edward Fisher. Wits., Jonathan Manlove, Ebenezer Manlove, Susannah Manlove. Prob. Jan. 23, 1771. Arch. vol. A5, pages 87, 89-90. Reg. of Wills, Liber L, folio 90. Note:—Arch. vol. A5, page 90 shows Thomas Bowman as guardian of Nathaniel Bowman.

Elsberry, Benjamin. Admin. of, to Elizabeth Elsberry, widow. Feb. 5, 1771. Reg. of Wills, Liber L, folio 90. Note:—Arch. vol. A16, page 115 mentions heirs, Elizabeth, Frederick, Benjamin, Jacob & William Elsberry.

Handzor, Sarah. Admin. of, to John Durham, next of kin. Feb. 8, 1771. Arch. vol. A21, page 226. Reg. of Wills, Liber L, folio 90.

Freeman, Joseph. Admin. of, to Samuel Freeman, next of kin. Feb. 13, 1771. Reg. of Wills, Liber L, folio 91.

Roach, John. Admin. of, to Sarah Roach, widow, & Jacob Stout, Esq. Feb. 13, 1771. Reg. of Wills, Liber L, folio 91. Note:— Arch. vol. A44, page 15 shows that Sarah Roach later married . . . Blackshare.

Bedwell, James. Admin. of, to Robert Bedwell, next of kin. Feb. 15, 1771. Arch. vol. A3, page 142. Reg. of Wills, Liber L, folio 91.

Beauchamp, Marcy. Yeoman. Will. Made Jan. 21, 1771. Murderkill Hd. Heirs: wife Grace; sons Marcy, David, William, Isaac, John; daus. Rachold, Esther & Grace Beauchamp, Mary Thompson & Ann Walton. Exec'x, wife Grace. Wits., James Boyer, David Anderson, Elizabeth Anderson. Prob. Feb. 19, 1771. Arch. vol. A3, pages 118-119. Reg. of Wills, Liber L, folio 91.

Craige, James. Will. Made Feb. 18, 1771. Heirs: mother Anelena; sisters Leah Shaw, Isbel Craige, Nanny Craige; bros. John & Samuel; nephew James Shaw; cousins John Craige & James Craige; uncle Alexander Craige; Alexander Huston. Exec'r, cousin John Craige. Wits., Benjamin Jackson, Ann Craige. Prob. Feb. 27, 1771. Arch. vol. A11, pages 161-163. Reg. of Wills, Liber L, folios 94-95. Note:—Will mentions bro. Moses, dec'd.

Ebtharp, Elizabeth. Widow. Will. Made Dec. . . . 1767. Heirs: sons Peter & John Numbers; grandchildren Mary & William Numbers, children of John; other grandchildren unnamed. Exec'r, son John. Wits., Robert Wood, Ann Wood, Thomas Carmichael. Prob. March 1, 1771. Arch. vol. A15, pages 235 & 238. Reg. of Wills, Liber L, folios 91-92.

Denny, Phillip. Admin. of, to Phillip Denny & Francis Denny, D. B. N. March 1, 1771. Reg. of Wills, Liber L, folio 92.

Thomas, Daniel. Admin. of, to Elizabeth Thomas. March 1, 1771. Arch. vol. A50, page 43.

Mason, Elizabeth. Admin. of, to James Starling. March 2, 1770. Arch. vol. A33, page 229. Reg. of Wills, Liber L, folio 92.

Maxwell, James. Admin. of, to John Spruance and wife Hannah, late Hannah Maxwell. March 13, 1771. Arch. vol. A34, page 85. Note:—Mentions heirs, Hannah & Joan Maxwell & Mary Craige, wife of Moses Craige.

Loockerman, Nicholas. Farmer. Will. Made Oct. 31, 1765. Heirs: sons Vincent, Richard; dau.-in-law Susannah, wife of son Vincent; grandsons Vincent & Nicholas; niece Letitia Bell, wife of John Bell; Negroes Reuben & wife Nancy. Exec'rs, son Vincent & grandson Vincent Loockerman. Wits., James Sykes, Agnes Sykes, Lucy Bell. Codicil. Made March 5, 1771. Sarah Taylor. Wits., Thomas Rodney, Charles Ridgely. Prob. March 15, 1771. Arch. vol. A30, page 203. Reg. of Wills, Liber L, folios 92-93.

Jackson, John. Admin. of, to Warner Mifflin. March 15, 1771. Arch. vol. A26, page 6. Reg. of Wills, Liber L, folio 93.

Skidmore, Samuel. Will. Made Jan. 6, 1771. Heirs: wife Elizabeth; son Thomas Skidmore, son of Elizabeth Merony; dau. Mary Skidmore, dau. of Elizabeth Merony; cousins Dr. William Molleston, Pemberton Brown, Ann Clark, Ann Dill, Elizabeth Peterkin, Archibald McSparran (son of Joseph McSparran). Exec'x, wife Elizabeth. Trustee, Phillip Barratt. Wits., James Cary, Sarah Painter, George Painter. Prob. March 24, 1771. Arch. vol. A46, pages 199-201. Reg. of Wills, Liber L, folio 94.

Weldon, John. Weaver. Little Creek Hd. Admin. of, to Isaac Weldon, next of kin. March 26, 1771. Arch. vol. A53, page 223. Reg. of Wills, Liber L, folio 94.

Dunning, Thomas. Will. Made April 15, 1771. Heirs: wife Mary; sons James & Thomas; dau. Jerusha; Elizabeth & Abel Shelds. Exec'x, wife Mary. Appraisers, David Hilford & Benjamin Chipman. Wits., Benjamin Chipman, John Ironsides, William Dunning, Valentine Pegg. Prob. May 13, 1771. Arch. vol. A15, pages 140-141. Reg. of Wills, Liber L, folios 95-96. Note:—Arch. vol. A15, pages 140, 145-146 show Mary Dunning as wife of Francis Edmonson.

Duning, Samuel. Farmer. Will (copy). Made April 11, 1771. Murderkill Hd. Heirs: wife Mary; children unnamed. Wits., Benjamin Chipman, Mary Chipman, Job Maryday. Prob. May 13, 1771. Arch. vol. A15, pages 136-139. Reg. of Wills, Liber L, folio 96. Note:—Arch. vol. A15, page 137 mentions heirs, Tamer, Martha, John, Thomas & Samuel Dunning.

Rutter, John. Admin. of, to Mary Rutter, widow. May 15, 1771. Arch. vol. A44, page 212. Reg. of Wills, Liber L, folio 96.

Pugh, William. Admin. of, to Michael Offelly. May 15, 1771. Reg. of Wills, Liber L, folio 96.

Egland, John. Doctor. Admin. of, to Rachel Egland, widow. May 15, 1771. Reg. of Wills, Liber L, folio 96. Note:—Arch. vol. A16, page 83 mentions a son Richard Egland.

Raymond, Jonathan. Gentleman. Will. Made May 10, 1771. Duck Creek Hd. Heirs: sisters Sarah Alston, wife of Arthur & Rachel Tybout; niece Sarah Raymond, dau. of bro. John; cousin James Raymond; Edward McElroy. Exec'rs, Thomas Collins, Esq., & Thomas Tilton. Wits., Matthew Crozier, Thomas Keith, Rachel Crozier. Prob. May 16, 1771. Arch. vol. A42, pages 152-155. Reg. of Wills, Liber L, folios 96-97.

Hamilton, Alexander. Admin. of, to James Hamilton, next of kin. May 17, 1771. Arch. vol. A21, page 156. Reg. of Wills, Liber L, folio 97.

Potter, Enoch. Admin. of, to Mary Hammon & Richard Gooding, next of kin. May 21, 1771. Arch. vol. A41, page 2. Reg. of Wills, Liber L, folio 97.

Hendrick, Sarah. Admin. of, to Francis Denny, next of kin. May 28, 1771. Arch. vol. A23, page 130. Reg. of Wills, Liber L, folio 97.

Killen, Adam. Admin. of, to Polly Killen, widow. May 30, 1771. Arch. vol. A28, pages 175-177. Reg. of Wills, Liber L, folio 97. Note:—Arch. vol. A28, page 175 shows that Mary Killen married Joshua Laws; page 177 mentions heirs, Abel & Mary Killen.

Milvin, Ann. Admin. of, to Phebee Milvin, next of kin. May 31, 1771. Reg. of Wills, Liber L, folio 97.

Jessops, Mary. Admin. of, to Jacob Jessops, next of kin. May 31, 1771. Reg. of Wills, Liber L, folios 97-98.

Harris, William. Will. Made Aug. 25, 1770. Heirs: wife Hannah; son Abraham; Thomas & William Needles; Ann Crankfeald. Exec'x, wife Hannah. Wits., Edward Collins, Samuel Prevo, Rachel Prevo. Prob. June 29, 1771. Arch. vol. A22, pages 180-181. Reg. of Wills, Liber L, folio 98.

Hart, John. Admin. of, to Sarah Hart, widow. July 10, 1771. Arch. vol. A22, page 196. Reg. of Wills, Liber L, folio 98.

Rash, James. Admin. of, to Charles Ridgely, Esq., D. B. N. July 18, 1771. Arch. vol. A42, page 37. Reg. of Wills, Liber L, folio 98.

Dawson, Joshua. Admin. of, to John Walker. Aug. 13, 1771. Arch. vol. A13, page 106. Reg. of Wills, Liber L, folio 98.

Smith, Holliday. Will. Made Feb. 5, 1771. Dorchester Co., Md. Heirs: sons Holliday & Samuel Smith; daus. Martha, Elizabeth & Reachel Smith; wife Sarah. Exec'x, wife Sarah. Wits., Olive Smith, Eliab Vinson, Owen Cooper. Prob. Aug. 13, 1771. Arch. vol. A47, pages 50-52, 131. Reg. of Wills, Liber O, folios 139-140. Note:—Arch. vol. A47, page 52 mentions Elizabeth Hattabough; also shows acct. later settled by Holliday Smith, D. B. N., C. T. A.

Allee, John. Will. Made Aug. 8, 1771. Duck Creek Hd. Heirs: sons Abraham, Peter, John, Presley; dau. Mary. Exec'rs, sons Abraham, Peter, John. Wits., Immanuel Stout, William Cook, Thomas Parry. Prob. Aug. 14, 1771. Arch. vol. A1, pages 60-62. Reg. of Wills, Liber L, folios 98-99.

Dill, George. Admin. of, to William Manlove. Aug. 24, 1771. Arch. vol. A14, page 91. Reg. of Wills, Liber L, folio 99.

Creighton, William. Admin. of, to Ruth Creighton, widow. Aug. 27, 1771. Arch. vol. A11, pages 224-225. Reg. of Wills, Liber L, folio 99. Note:—Arch. vol. A11, page 225 shows that Ruth Creighton married David Gordon.

Holliday, Thomas. Admin. of, to John Holliday, next of kin. Aug. 28, 1771. Arch. vol. A24, page 217. Reg. of Wills, Liber L, folio 99.

Gordon, Robert. Admin. of, to William Hazel, next of kin. Aug. 29, 1771. Arch. vol. A19, pages 175-176. Reg. of Wills, Liber L, folio 99.

Gordon, Robert. Minor son of Robert. Admin. of, to James Gordon, guardian. Aug. 30, 1771. Arch. vol. A19, page 179. Note:—Mentions a bro. John Gordon.

Leyvick, William. Admin. of, to Henry Stevens, next of kin. Sept. 13, 1771. Arch. vol. A30, pages 42-44. Reg. of Wills, Liber L, folio 99. Note:—Arch. vol. A30, page 42 mentions heirs, Hannah, John, Catharine, Lydia & Robert Leyvick.

Murphey, Thomas. Admin. of, to Margrett Murphey, widow. Sept. 30, 1771. Arch. vol. A37, page 104. Reg. of Wills, Liber L, folio 100.

Sowder, Henry. Admin. of, to Sarah Sowder, widow. Oct. 4, 1771. Arch. vol. A48, pages 71-73. Reg. of Wills, Liber L, folio 100. Note:—Arch. vol. A48, page 71 mentions heirs, John, Margaret, Sarah, Mary & Henry Sowder; also page 73 shows that Sarah Sowder married Isiah Morgan.

Barns, Charlton. Will. Made May 5, 1771. Little Creek Hd. Heirs: wife Sarah; dau. Bridget Charlton Barns; sons John Letherberry Barns, Charlton Barns. Exec'x, wife Sarah. Wits., Henry Wilkensen, William Fowler. Prob. Oct. 9, 1771. Arch. vol. A2, pages 215-216. Reg. of Wills, Liber L, folio 100.

Green, John. Admin. of, to Elizabeth Green, widow. Nov. 13, 1771. Arch. vol. A20, page 77. Reg. of Wills, Liber L, folio 100.

Hays, Darby. Admin. of, to Samuel Robisson. Nov. 15, 1771. Arch. vol. A23, page 63. Reg. of Wills, Liber L, folio 100.

Burns, Anthony. Admin. of, to Frances Burns, widow. Nov. 15, 1771. Reg. of Wills, Liber L, folio 100.

Edingfield, John. Will. Made Oct. 22, 1771. St. Jones's Hd. Heirs: dau. Elizabeth Parke; grandsons Thomas Parke (son of Hugh & Elizabeth Parke) & John Clayton (son of James Clayton). Exec'x, dau. Elizabeth Parke. Wits., Richard Butler, Anake Lucas, John Irons, John Irons, Jr. [No. prob.]. Arch. vol. A16, page 16. Reg. of Wills, Liber L, folios 100-103.

Brown, George. Admin. of, to Christian Brown, widow. Nov. 19, 1771. Reg. of Wills, Liber L, folio 104.

Edingfield, John. Admin. of, to William Rodney & Ledia Rodney. Nov. 21, 1771. Arch. vol. A16, page 17. Reg. of Wills, Liber L, folio 103.

Seenea, Owen. Will. Made Oct. 16, 1771. Heirs: wife Martha; sons John, William, Owen, Bryan; daus. Elizabeth, Ann, Elenor, Martha Powell (wife of William Powell), Mary Bedwell (wife of Elijah Bedwell). Exec'rs, wife Martha & son Bryan. Wits., Thomas Bedwell, Jemima Beadwell, Maleston Maxwell. Prob. Nov. 22, 1771. Arch. vol. A45, pages 120-121. Reg. of Wills, Liber L, folio 103.

McNitt, James. Mispillion Hd. Admin. of, to Magdelin McNitt, widow. Nov. 26, 1771. Arch. vol. A32, page 224. Reg. of Wills, Liber L, folio 104.

Wells, Elizabeth. Admin. of, to Henry Wells, Sr., next of kin. Nov. 30, 1771. Reg. of Wills, Liber L, folio 104.

Raymond, John. Yeoman. Duck Creek Hd. Admin. of, to Elizabeth Raymond & Silas Snow. Dec. 14, 1771. Arch. vol. A42, pages 140-144. Reg. of Wills, Liber L, folio 104. Note:— Arch. vol. A42, page 144 mentions a dau. Sarah Raymond.

Wood, Joseph. Admin. of, to Christopher Cole, next of kin. Dec. 16, 1771. Reg. of Wills, Liber L, folio 104.

Beswick, John. Yeoman. Will. Made Nov. 15, 1771. Mispillion Hd. Heirs: wife Pheebe; sons Curtis, George, Vincent; daus. Sarah, Mary. Exec'rs, wife Pheebe & father Vincent Loockerman. Guardians, father Vincent Loockerman & bro. Vincent Loockerman, Jr. Wits., John Clark, John Haslet, Jonathan Dewees. Prob. Dec. 18, 1771. Arch. vol. A4, pages 27-28. Reg. of Wills, Liber L, folio 104. Note:—Arch. vol. A4, page 28 shows that Pheebe, the widow, later married Smith Farsett.

Boogs, Williams. Will. Made Nov. 25, 1771. Heirs: daus. Elizabeth Kearsey, Jean Murphy, Esther Boogs; sons John, Joseph & David. Exec'rs, dau. Esther. Wits., James Caldwell, John Meekins, Ann Darling. Prob. Dec. 21, 1771. Arch. vol. A4, page 184. Reg. of Wills, Liber L, folio 105.

Williams, Deborah. Admin. of, to Isaiah Williams, next of kin. Dec. 23, 1771. Reg. of Wills, Liber L, folio 105.

Cain, James. Admin. of, to William Thompson. Dec. 30, 1771. Reg. of Wills, Liber L, folio 105.

Wallace, Benjamin. Admin. of, to Rachel Wallace, widow. Jan. 8, 1772. Arch. vol. A52, pages 212-213. Reg. of Wills, Liber L, folio 105. Note:—Arch. vol. A52, page 212 mentions a son Benjamin Wallace.

Spence, John. Farmer. Mispillion Hd. Admin. of, to Mary Spence, widow. Jan. 10, 1772. Arch. vol. A48, page 88. Reg. of Wills, Liber L, folio 105.

McBride, Roger. Yeoman. Will. Made Nov. 27, 1771. Heirs: wife Elizabeth; daus. Elizabeth & Isabela; sons Samuel, John, William, James, Benjamin; granddau. Elizabeth Hendrey. Exec'rs, sons James & Benjamin. Wits., Thomas Wilson, James Nock, Thomas Porter. Prob. Jan. 14, 1772. Arch. vol. A32, page 78. Reg. of Wills, Liber L, folios 105-106.

Barratt, John. Admin. of, to John Brinckle. Jan. 22, 1772. Reg. of Wills, Liber L, folio 106.

Blackshare, George. Admin. of, to Deborah Blackshare, widow. Jan. 23, 1772. Arch. vol. A4, page 82. Reg. of Wills, Liber L, folio 106.

Mastin, William. Farmer. Mispillion Hd. Admin. of, to Sarah Mastin, widow. Jan. 23, 1772. Arch. vol. A34, page 55. Reg. of Wills, Liber L, folio 106.

Ford, William. Planter. Will. Made Aug. 5, 1771. Heirs: wife Mary; sons Thomas, William, Daniel; daus. Esther, Rebecca, Mary. Exec'rs, wife Mary & son Thomas. Wits., Solomon Hinesly, Rachel Corker, Paul Quenouaull. Prob. Jan. 25, 1772. Arch. vol. A17, pages 246-247. Reg. of Wills, Liber L, folios 106-107.

Macy, Thomas. Farmer. Will (copy). Made Jan. 21, 1772. Duck Creek. Heirs: wife Elizabeth; bro. Daniel; son Thomas; daus. Elizabeth & Sarah. Exec'rs, wife Elizabeth & bro. Daniel. Guardian, bro. Daniel Macy. Wits., Stephen Doney, Thomas Howell. Prob. Feb. 11, 1772. Arch. vol. A33, pages 52-53. Reg. of Wills, Liber L, folio 107.

Chicken, Martha. Admin. of, to John Chicken, next of kin. Feb. 12, 1772. Reg. of Wills, Liber L, folio 107.

Hawkins, Dohority [Dorothea]. Admin. of, to John Swallow, next of kin. Feb. 12, 1772. Arch. vol. A23, page 21. Reg. of Wills, Liber L, folios 107-108.

Clark, Sarah. Widow of Thomas Clark, Esq. Will. Made Oct. 6, 1766. Heirs: sons John & Benjamin; daus. Ann Brown, Sarah Finshwait, Prisalla Henderson, Elizabeth Harrington, Ruth Tharpthorn. Exec'rs, Jonathan Finsthwait, Major Henderson. Wits., James Finsthwait, John Harrington, Martha Harrington. Prob. Feb. 13, 1772. Arch. vol. A9, pages 73-74. Reg. of Wills, Liber L, folio 108.

Humphres, Susannah. Admin. of, to John Larwood. Feb. 14, 1772. Reg. of Wills, Liber L, folio 108.

Alston, Randal. Will. Made Nov. 5, 1771. Heirs: daus. Hannah, Elizabeth; sons Stephen, Andrew, Thomas; wife Martha. Exec'x, wife Martha. Guardian, bro. Arthur Alston of N. C. Co. Wits., Joseph Smith, Mary Smith, Silas Snow. Prob. Feb. 19, 1772. Arch. vol. A1, pages 116-117. Reg. of Wills, Liber L, folio 108. Note:—Arch. vol. A1, page 117 shows John Bennett & wife Martha as exec'rs.

Blackshare, Jane. Will. Made Feb. 11, 1772. Little Creek Hd. Heirs: daus. Sarah, Anne; sisters Sarah, Priscilla Green. Exec'r, friend Morgan Blackshare. Wits., James Jones, William Fowler. Prob. Feb. 22, 1772. Arch. vol. A4, pages 83-85. Reg. of Wills, Liber L, folio 109. Note:—Arch. vol. A4, page 83 shows dau. Sarah married John Grimes.

Long, William. Will (nunc.). Made Jan. 15, 1772. Heir: wife unnamed. Wits., Abraham Booth & John Crawford. Prob. Feb. 25, 1772. Arch. vol. A31, pages 61-62. Reg. of Wills, Liber L, folio 109. Note:—Arch. vol. A31, page 62 shows that admin. was granted to Margarett Long, widow, who later married Stephen Marcer.

Jones, Priscilla. Admin. of, to Jacob Jones, next of kin. Feb. 25, 1772. Reg. of Wills, Liber L, folio 109.

Craige, Agnes. Admin. of, to Ann Craige. Feb. 27, 1772. Arch. vol. A11, page 146.

Howell, James. Admin. of, to Susannah Howell, widow. Feb. 27, 1772. Reg. of Wills, Liber L, folio 109. Note:—Arch. vol. A25, page 66 shows that Susannah Howell married Richard Jackson.

Long, Jane. Will. Made Feb. 16, 1772. Heirs: dau. Mary Peterson; son-in-law Jonas Peterson; grandson William Long, son of son Edward. Exec'r, son-in-law Jonas Peterson. Wits., John Cole, Andrew Peterson, Thomas Cahoon. Prob. Feb. 27, 1772. Arch. vol. A31, page 57. Reg. of Wills, Liber L, folios 109-110.

Hunter, Mary. Admin. of, to John Bell, next of kin. Feb. 27, 1772. Reg. of Wills, Liber L, folio 110.

Cross, William. Admin. of, to John Cross, next of kin. March 4, 1772. Reg. of Wills, Liber L, folio 110.

Wallace, Reuben. Will. Made Dec. 11, 1771. Heirs: William, Joshua & Margret (children of Solomon & Margret Wallace); friend William Rhodes, Esq.; bro. Solomon Wallace. Exec'r, bro. Solomon Wallace. Wits., James Tilton, William Collins, John Rhodes. Prob. March 9, 1772. Arch. vol. A53, page 7. Reg. of Wills, Liber L, folio 110.

Cattlin, Robert. Admin. of, to Mary Cattlin, widow. March 9, 1772. Reg. of Wills, Liber L, folio 110.

West, Sarah. Admin. of, to Immanuel Stout. March 28, 1772. Reg. of Wills, Liber L, folio 110. Note:—Arch. vol. A54, page 29 mentions heirs, Sarah, Ann, Mary & Susannah West.

Torbert, Simon. Admin. of, to John Torbert & Peter Torbert. March 28, 1772. Reg. of Wills, Liber L, folio 110.

Hirons, Charles. Admin. of, to William Hirons. April 7, 1772. Reg. of Wills, Liber L, folio 111.

Robinson, John. Admin. of, to Mary Robinson, widow. April 10, 1772. Arch. vol. A44, page 64. Reg. of Wills, Liber L, folio 111.

Edengfield, Pearsis [Persis]. Admin. of, to Robert Hirons, next of kin. April 17, 1772. Reg. of Wills, Liber L, folio 111.

Green, James. Will. Made Feb. 3, 1769. Duck Creek Hd. Heirs: wife Mary; bros. William, John, Charles & Thomas Green; sisters Leurana Rees; Marcy Buckingham. Exec'rs, wife Mary & Molleston Carry. Wits., Elizabeth Devenport, Mary Vanvincle, Margarett Thomas. Prob. April 21, 1772. Arch. vol. A20, pages 69-70. Reg. of Wills, Liber L, folio 111. Note:—Arch. vol. A20, page 70 shows that Mary Green later married Jordan Robinson.

Viccory, John. Will. Made March 28, 1772. Mispillion Hd. Heirs: wife Elizabeth; sons John, Walter, Thomas, Ezekiah, Waitman; daus. Mary & Liddia. Exec'x, wife Elizabeth. Wits., Matthew Jarrard, Henry Sapp, Sarah Sapp. Prob. April 21, 1772. Arch. vol. A52, pages 36-38. Reg. of Wills, Liber L, folios 111-112. Note:—Arch. vol. A52, page 37 shows that Elizabeth Viccory married Solomon Townsend.

Warren, Benjamin. Yeoman. Murtherkill Hd. Admin. of, to Elizabeth Warren, widow. April 21, 1772. Arch. vol. A53, pages 128-129. Reg. of Wills, Liber L, folio 112.

Read [Reed], Walter. Admin. of, to Thomas Reed, next of kin. April 22, 1772. Reg. of Wills, Liber L, folio 112. Note:—Arch. vol. A42, page 223 mentions heirs, Ann, Susanna & Abraham Reed.

Cowdratt, Daniel. Farmer. Mispillion Hd. Admin. of, to Mary Cowdratt, widow. April 25, 1772. Arch. vol. A11, pages 40-46. Reg. of Wills, Liber L, folio 112. Note:—Arch. vol. A11, page 40 shows that Mary Cowdratt later married Samuel Goodwin; also mentions heirs, Joshua, Hillary & Bardon Cowdratt.

Hall, Oliver. Yeoman. Mispillion Hd. Admin. of, to John Hall, next of kin. May 1, 1772. Reg. of Wills, Liber L, folio 112. Note:—Arch. vol. A21, page 113 shows this acct. later settled by Richard Reynolds & James Hattfield.

Hall, William. Admin. of, to Lucy Hall, widow. May 1, 1772. Arch. vol. A21, pages 131-132. Reg. of Wills, Liber L, folio 112.

Snow, James. Admin. of, to Mary Snow, widow. May 2, 1772. Reg. of Wills, Liber L, folio 112. Note:—Arch. vol. A48, page 8 shows that Mary Snow married Francis Barber.

Cox, Thomas, Jr. Will. Made April 29, 1772. Mispillion Hd. Heirs: wife Esther; sons John, Edward, Matthew, Nathan, Jarrard & Thomas; daus. Barbara & Mary. Exec'r, bro. Daniel Cox. Wits., Thomas Sheriff, Joseph Greenwood, Thomas Jester. Prob. May 7, 1772. Arch. vol. A11, pages 142-143. Reg. of Wills, Liber L, folio 112.

Melvin, Phebee. Widow. Mispillion Hd. Admin. of, to Thomas Parker, next of kin. May 12, 1772. Arch. vol. A34, pages 165-166. Reg. of Wills, Liber L, folio 113. Note:—Arch. vol. A34, page 165 mentions heirs, Elizabeth, Jonathan, David, Meriam, John & Ann Melvin.

Chambers, William. Admin. of, to Mary Chambers, widow. May 14, 1772. Reg. of Wills, Liber L, folio 113.

Matthews, Isaac. Cooper. Mispillion Hd. Admin. of, to Jerusha Matthews, widow. May 14, 1772. Arch. vol. A34, page 66. Reg. of Wills, Liber L, folio 113.

McVay, Danis. Admin. of, to John Russell. May 19, 1772. Reg. of Wills, Liber L, folio 113.

Upthegrove, John. Admin. of, to Sarah Upthegrove, widow. May 28, 1772. Arch. vol. A51, page 199. Reg. of Wills, Liber L, folio 113.

Beaston, John. Admin. of, to Susanna Beaston, widow. May 29, 1772. Reg. of Wills, Liber L, folio 116.

Mileham, Samuel. Will. Made April 20, 1772. Mispillion Hd. Heirs: wife Mary Ann; sons Samuel, Massey, Walter; daus. Hannah, Elizabeth, Unity, Margaret, Catherine & Grace Mileham, & Sarah Stradly. Exec'rs, wife Mary Ann & friend Edward Gibbs. Wits., Matthew Jarrard, James Bostick, Edward Carter. Prob. May 29, 1772. Arch. vol. A35, pages 56-57. Reg. of Wills, Liber L, folio 113.

Sipple, Waitman, Sr. Will. Made Jan. 10, 1772. Heirs: wife Lidia; son Garret; daus. Susanna Killen (wife of Henry Killen), Mary Caldwell (wife of Andrew Caldwell); granddau. Elizabeth Griffin, dau. of Susanna by her late husband Owen Griffin; grandson John Hilliard, son of Charles Hilliard & dau. Ruth, dec'd; Waitman Booth; son-in-law Henry Killen. Exec'r, son Garret. Wits., Benjamin Chew, Edward Tilghman, Jr., Joseph Alford, Elisha Morriss, Edward Cole, James Taggert. Prob. May 30, 1772. Arch. vol. A46, page 177. Reg. of Wills, Liber L, folio 115.

Hill, John. Yeoman. Duck Creek Hd. Admin. of, to Thomas Hill and Joseph Hill, next of kin. June 2, 1772. Arch. vol. A23, pages 243-244. Reg. of Wills, Liber L, folio 114.

Chipman, Benjamin. Will. Made April 19, 1772. Heirs: wife Mary; daus. Susanna; sons Stephen & Benjamin. Exec'x, wife Mary. Wits., Patrick Crain, Peres Chipman, Reuben Sheild. Prob. June 23, 1772. Arch. vol. A8, page 182. Reg. of Wills, Liber L, folio 114.

Chipman, Stephen. Admin. of, to Agnes Chipman. June 23, 1772. Arch. vol. A8, page 189. Reg. of Wills, Liber L, folio 114.

Hall, Thomas. Will. Made May 22, 1772. Heirs: wife Rebecca; sons Asa, Nathan, Allen, Rynear & Jordan; daus. Perthena & Rebecca. Exec'x, wife Rebecca. Wits., James Harrington, Thomas Russum, Burtonwood Allcock. Prob. June 26, 1772. Arch. vol. A21, pages 125-126. Reg. of Wills, Liber L, folios 114-115.

Reddick, Benjamin. Admin. of, to William Reddick, next of kin. June 29, 1772. Arch. vol. A42, page 176. Reg. of Wills, Liber L, folio 115.

Davis, Moses. Will. Made May 13, 1772. Heir: son Abisha. Adm'x, wife Elizabeth. Wits., Jehu Davis, Caleb Davis, Caleb Tucker. Prob. June 29, 1772. Arch. vol. A13, pages 42-45. Reg. of Wills, Liber L, folio 115. Note:—Will mentions wife and other children unnamed. Arch. vol. A13, page 43 shows that Elizabeth Davis married Caleb Tucker; page 44 shows this acct. later administered by Jehu Davis; also mentions heirs, minor children Ann & Elizabeth Davis; page 45 mentions heirs, Abisha, Mary, Leah & Thomas Davis.

Walker, John. Will. Made Dec. 9, 1771. Heirs: wife Ann; sons William & John; daus. Ailse Frazier, Elizabeth Walker; grandson John King; granddau. Mary King. Exec'rs, wife Ann & son John. Wits., Samuel Meridith, Henry Molliston, Sarah Molliston. Prob. July 1, 1772. Arch. vol. A52, page 187. Reg. of Wills, Liber L, folio 116.

Cowdratt, John. Admin. of, to Esther Buckmaster, next of kin. July 7, 1772. Arch. vol. A11, page 45. Reg. of Wills, Liber L, folio 116.

Cowdratt, Peter. Admin. of, to Mary Cowdratt, next of kin. July 7, 1772. Arch. vol. A11, page 48. Reg. of Wills, Liber L, folio 117.

Lowber, Matthew, Sr. Will. Made June 8, 1772. Heirs: wife Hannah; sons Matthew, Jr., Peter & Jonathan; daus. Susanna, Elizabeth & Meriam; son-in-law William Virdin; granddau. Elizabeth Virdin, dau. of William; grandson Hugh Durborrow. Exec'r, son Peter. Wits., Richard Bassett, Jacob Duhadway, Sr., Daniel Duhadway. Prob. July 29, 1772. Arch. vol. A31, pages 123-126. Reg. of Wills, Liber L, folio 117. Note:—Arch. vol. A31, page 125 mentions a dau. Susanah Durbrow.

Collins, James. Admin. of, to Nelly Collins, widow. Aug. 12, 1772. Reg. of Wills, Liber L, folio 118.

Fults [Folts], Elizabeth. Will. Made Jan. 13, 1772. Heirs: friend Robert Holliday; cousin Sarah Watkins. Exec'r, friend Robert Holliday. Wits., Walter Bourke, William Jordan, Samuel West. Prob. Aug. 12, 1772. Arch. vol. A18, pages 144-145. Reg. of Wills, Liber L, folio 118.

Townsend, Charles. Will. Made May 28, 1772. Murderkill Hd. Heirs: wife Mary; sons Solomon, Epheraim, William, Charles; daus. Mary, Meriam, Sarah, Ansley, Rachel & Elizabeth. Exec'r, son Solomon. Wits., Zephaniah Harper, William Harper, Samuel Kelly. Prob. Aug. 12, 1772. Arch. vol. A51, pages 1-2. Reg. of Wills, Liber L, folios 118-119.

Underwood, Mary. Widow. Will. Made Oct. 13, 1762. Mispillion Hd. Heirs: sons John Marrett, Joseph Marrett, John Underwood, Richard Underwood; grandsons Joseph Marrett (son of Zachariah Marrett), Joshua Underwood & Abraham Underwood. Exec'rs, son Richard Underwood & friend Thomas Clark. Wits., Sarah Clark, Ann McNatt [Brown], Ruth Clark. Prob. Aug. 13, 1772. Arch. vol. A51, pages 193-194. Reg. of Wills, Liber L, folios 117-118.

Hall, Jonas. Admin. of, to Susanna Hall, widow. Aug. 19, 1772. Arch. vol. A21, page 106. Reg. of Wills, Liber L, folio 119.

Simmons, Elizabeth. Admin. of, to Solomon Simmons, Jr. Aug. 27, 1772. Reg. of Wills, Liber L, folio 119.

Emerson, Unity. Murderkill Hd. Admin. of, to Michael Emerson, next of kin. Aug. 27, 1772. Arch. vol. A16, pages 124-126. Reg. of Wills, Liber L, folio 119. Note:—Arch. vol. A16, page 124 shows heirs, Jonathan, Vincent & Michael Emerson; also mentions widow of Jonathan.

Russum, Peter. Will. Made Aug. 12, 1772. Heirs: wife Elizabeth; son Thomas; daus. Sarah & Elizabeth. Exec'rs, wife Elizabeth & friend John Furchas. Wits., Susannah Morris, Frances Furchas. Prob. Aug. 27, 1772. Arch. vol. A44, pages 192-193 & 196. Reg. of Wills, Liber L, folio 119. Note:—Arch. vol. A4, page 196 shows that Elizabeth Russum, widow, later married William Needles.

Allston, Thomas. Admin. of to Jane Allston, widow. Sept. 7, 1772. Arch. vol. A1, page 121. Reg. of Wills, Liber L, folio 120.

Stuart, Moses. Will. Made Aug. 21, 1772. Heirs: wife unnamed; sons John, Moses, Alexander, William, Daniel, Elias; daus. Elener, Mary, Sarah, Rachel, Ann. Exec'x, wife [Mary, from admin. acct.]. Wits., Zadok Crapper, Robert Smith, Mary Smith. Prob. Sept. 14, 1772. Arch. vol. A49, pages 9-10. Reg. of Wills, Liber L, folio 120.

Molleston, William. Admin. of, to Ailce Molleston, widow. Oct. 12, 1772. Reg. of Wills, Liber L, folio 120. Note:—Arch. vol. A35, page 221 shows that Ailce Molleston married Jacob Carmean.

Jacobs, Elizabeth. Admin. of, to James White. Oct. 12, 1772. Reg. of Wills, Liber L, folio 120.

Palmatree, John. Admin. of, to Margarett Palmatree & James Severson. Oct. 24, 1772. Reg. of Wills, Liber L, folio 120.

Manlove, Ebenezar. Admin. of, to Sarah Manlove & Asa Manlove. Nov. 2, 1772. Arch. vol. A33, pages 83-85. Reg. of Wills, Liber L, folio 120. Note:—Arch. vol. A33, page 83 mentions heirs, Mary Hall (wife of David), Ellis Fisher (wife of James), Thos. Manlove, Sara Coleman, Asa Manlove & Sarah, the widow.

Cole, Spencer. Admin. of, to Reynear Williams, next of kin. Nov. 12, 1772. Reg. of Wills, Liber L, folio 120.

Morris, Jeremiah. Will. Made April 12, 1764. Heirs: daus. Ann Pursele, Edelia Ions [Jons]; sons William, Elijah, Cornelius, Elisha, Eliphas. Exec'r, son Eliphas. Wits., Belitha Laws, Joshua Laws, Rachel Laws. Prob. Nov. 12, 1772. Arch. vol. A36, page 218. Reg. of Wills, Liber L, folio 121.

Catts, James. Admin. of, to Prudence Catts, widow. Nov. 16, 1772. Arch. vol. A8, pages 86-87. Reg. of Wills, Liber L, folio 121. Note:—Arch. vol. A8, page 86 shows that Prudence Catts married Bednego Wheelar.

Middleton, John. Admin. of, to John Banning. Nov. 28, 1772. Reg. of Wills, Liber L, folio 121.

Thompson, John. Admin. of, to Rachel Thompson, widow. Dec. 12, 1772. Reg. of Wills, Liber L, folio 121.

Candy, Cashenna. Admin. of, to Susanna & William Candy. Dec. 15, 1772. Reg. of Wills, Liber L, folio 121. Note:—Arch. vol. A7, page 187 shows that Susanna Candy married Edward Rich.

Vandeford [Vandevare], Matthew. Admin. of, to Unity Vandeford, widow. Dec. 15, 1772. Reg. of Wills, Liber L, folio 121. Note:—Arch. vol. A52, page 57 shows that Unity Vandevare later married Robert McClemings.

Vickery, Walter. Admin. of, to Walter Mileham, next of kin. Dec. 17, 1772. Arch. vol. A52, page 50. Reg. of Wills, Liber L, folio 121.

Dawson, Joshua. Admin. of, to Anne Walker & Isaac Dawson, D. B. N. Dec. 22, 1772. Arch. vol. A13, page 106. Reg. of Wills, Liber L, folio 122.

Sapp, Henry. Admin. of, to Sarah Sapp, widow. Dec. 23, 1772. Arch. vol. A44, page 229. Reg. of Wills, Liber L, folio 122.

Stuart, Charles. Admin. of, to Katharine Stuart, widow. Dec. 23, 1772. Arch. vol. A49, page 92. Reg. of Wills, Liber L, folio 122.

Wood, John, Sr. Farmer. Will. Made Dec. 21, 1772. Murderkiln Hd. Heirs: sons Elias, John, Enoch, William, Charles, George & Nicholas; daus. Mary Pierson, Rebekah Pierson & Sarah Wood. Exec'r, son Elias. Wits., William Reddick, Paul Quenonaul. Prob. Dec. 28, 1772. Arch. vol. A56, pages 67-72. Reg. of Wills, Liber L, folio 122.

Anderton, John. Yeoman. Will. Made Dec. 22, 1772. Murderkill Hd. Heirs: daus. Susannah, Ruth, Ealce & Miriam, Mary Daugherty, Elizabeth Potter. Exec'r, son-in-law John Smith. Wits., Benjamin Smith, Robert McClyment, Alexander Huston. Prob. Dec. 28, 1772. Arch. vol. A1, pages 216-218. Reg. of Wills, Liber L, folios 122-123.

Jester, William. Yeoman. Will. Made Dec. 15, 1772. Mispillion Hd. Heirs: sons Richard & William; daus. Rachel Tompson, Elenor & Nance Jester. Exec'rs, sons Richard & William. Wits., John Barns, Joshua Willis, Joshua Morris. Prob. Jan. 4, 1773. Arch. vol. A27, pages 52-53. Reg. of Wills, Liber L, folios 123-124.

Taylor, James. Admin. of, to Luke Hardin. Jan. 4, 1773. Reg. of Wills, Liber L, folio 124.

Fitzgerrald, James. Farmer. Mispillion Hd. Admin. of, to Elizabeth Fitzgerrald, widow. Jan. 4, 1773. Arch. vol. A17, pages 158-159. Reg. of Wills, Liber L, folio 124. Note:—Arch. vol. A17, page 159 mentions heirs, Marmaduke, James, Rachel & Mary Fitzgerrald & Priscilla Craner.

Goodfellow, Joseph. Will. Made Nov. 29, 1772. Heirs: wife Margret; six children unnamed. Exec'rs, wife Margret & friend Warner Mifflin. Wits., James Nock, Stephen Millis, Samuel Goodwin. Prob. Jan. 9, 1773. Arch. vol. A19, pages 134-135. Reg. of Wills, Liber L, folio 124.

Houston, Benjamin. Admin. of, to Luke Davis & wife Esther, late Esther Houston. Jan. 12, 1773. Arch. vol. A25, page 42. Note:—Mentions heirs, Elijah, Nancy & Mary Houston.

Irons, Timothy. Admin. of, to James Bellach, next of kin. Jan. 13, 1773. Reg. of Wills, Liber L, folio 124.

Ford, John. Will. Made Dec. 4, 1772. Heirs: wife Mary; sons James, John, Isaac, Thomas, Jesay, William, Robart, Edward, Richard; daus. Elizabeth Haziel, Rachel, Ann, Mary & Barshby Ford. Exec'x, wife Mary. Wits., Samuel West, Hugh Spear, William Darling. Prob. Jan. 16, 1773. Arch. vol. A17, page 236. Reg. of Wills, Liber L, folios 124-125.

Staton, Jehu. Will. Made Dec. 25, 1772. Heirs: wife Mary; nephews James Staton Collings (son of sister Rebeccah Collings), Jehu Nowells (son of sister Sarah Nowells). Exec'rs, wife Mary & bro. Nehemiah Staton. Wits., Elisha Morris, William Anderson, Joseph Lester. Prob. Jan. 16, 1773. Arch. vol. A48, page 186. Reg. of Wills, Liber L, folio 125.

Smith, William. Farmer. Mispillion Hd. Admin. of, to Joseph McKnatt, next of kin. Jan. 21, 1773. Arch. vol. A47, pages 198-199. Reg. of Wills, Liber L, folio 125.

New, William. Yeoman. Mispillion Hd. Admin. of, to Elijah Berry. Jan. 22, 1773. Arch. vol. A37, page 184. Reg. of Wills, Liber L, folio 125.

Quilling, John. Chairmaker. Little Creek Hd. Admin. of, to Sarah Quilling & James Cummins. Jan. 26, 1773. Arch. vol. A42, page 3. Reg. of Wills, Liber L, folio 125.

Killingsworth, Nathaniel. Will. Made Jan. 20, 1773. Heirs: sons Anderson & John; daus. Ann, Mary, Sarah, Rebecca, Elizabeth & Febe. Exec'r, friend William Anderson. Wits., Jehu Jester, Francis Jester, Martin Pegg. Prob. Jan. 26, 1773. Arch. vol. A28, pages 225-227. Reg. of Wills, Liber L, folio 126.

Hillyard, Joseph. Minor. Admin. of, to James Raymond, next of kin. Jan. 26, 1773. Reg. of Wills, Liber L, folio 126.

Knotts, Esther. Admin. of, to Edward Knotts, next of kin. Jan. 27, 1773. Reg. of Wills, Liber L, folio 126.

Greenwood, Joseph. Admin. of, to Sarah Greenwood, widow. Feb. 3, 1773. Arch. vol. A20, pages 155-156. Reg. of Wills, Liber L, folio 126.

Boggs, Matthew. House-carpenter. Will. Made Dec. 22, 1772. Murtherkill Hd. Heirs: nephew John Boggs, Jr., son of bro. John Boggs, dec'd; cousin John Boggs, son of William Boggs. Exec'r, John Boggs, cordwainer. Wits., Samuel McCall, Sarah McCall, Jr., John Brickell. Prob. Feb. 6, 1773. Arch. vol. A4, pages 182-183. Reg. of Wills, Liber L, folios 126-127.

Addams, Joshua. Admin. of, to Nathan Addams, next of kin. Feb. 10, 1773. Reg. of Wills, Liber L, folio 127.

Mannship, George. Admin. of, to Sarah Mannship, widow. Feb. 10, 1773. Reg. of Wills, Liber L, folio 127.

Millaway, Joseph. Admin. of, to William Potter, next of kin. Feb. 12, 1773. Reg. of Wills, Liber L, folio 127.

Milloway, Ann. Admin. of, to Annsley White, next of kin. Feb. 17, 1773. Reg. of Wills, Liber L, folio 127.

Milloway, John. Admin. of, to Annsley White, next of kin. Feb. 17, 1773. Arch. vol. A35, page 131. Reg. of Wills, Liber L, folio 127.

Brown, John. Admin. of, to John Morris, next of kin, D. B. N. Feb. 22, 1773. Reg. of Wills, Liber L, folio 127. Note:—Arch. vol. A6, pages 53 & 56 mention heirs John & Thomas Brown; also shows that John Malris married Sarah Brown.

Maxfield, William. Admin. of, to John Draughton, Sr. Feb. 23, 1773. Reg. of Wills, Liber L, folios 127-128.

Story, Francis. Yeoman. Mispillion Hd. Admin. of, to Ruth Story, widow. Feb. 24, 1773. Reg. of Wills, Liber L, folio 127. Note:—Arch. vol. A49, page 29 shows that Ruth Story married James Thompson.

Underwood, Richard. Admin. of, to Prisilla Underwood, widow. Feb. 25, 1773. Reg. of Wills, Liber L, folio 128.

Bowman, John. Admin. of, to Rachel Bowman, widow. Feb. 25, 1773. Arch. vol. A5, page 47. Reg. of Wills, Liber L, folio 128.

Palmer, John. Admin. of, to Alexander Palmer, next of kin. Feb. 27, 1773. Reg. of Wills, Liber L, folio 128.

Saxton, Andrew. Admin. of, to Nancy Saxton, widow. Feb. 27, 1773. Arch. vol. A45, pages 39-40. Reg. of Wills, Liber L, folio 128. Note:—Arch. vol. A45, page 39 shows that Nancy, the widow, later married William Brown; page 40 mentions an heir, Prudence Saxton.

King, James. Yeoman. Mispillion Hd. Admin. of, to Mariam King, widow, & John Furchas. March 3, 1773. Arch. vol. A29, page 29. Reg. of Wills, Liber L, folio 128.

Irons [Hirons], Simon. Admin. of, to John Bell, D. B. N. March 4, 1773. Reg. of Wills, Liber L, folio 128. Note:—Arch. vol. A24, page 101 mentions a dau. Perce Irons.

Brown, Christian. Admin. of, to William Brown, next of kin. March 12, 1773. Arch. vol. A6, page 33. Reg. of Wills, Liber L, folio 128.

Brown, George. Admin. of, to William Brown, next of kin, D. B. N. March 12, 1773. Arch. vol. A6, page 43. Reg. of Wills, Liber L, folio 128.

Hardin, John. Farmer. Will. Made Jan. 17, 1773. Heirs: grandchildren Ruth & John Hardin (children of Thomas & Hannah Hardin, both dec'd), Edmond Hardin, Sr. (son of Edmond & Martha Hardin. Exec'rs, grandson Edmond Hardin, Sr., & Richard Lockwood. Guardian, Richard Lockwood. Wits., Thomas Nixon, Joseph Buckingham, Paul Quenouault, Sarah Buckingham. Prob. March 12, 1773. Arch. vol. A22, pages 18-20. Reg. of Wills, Liber L, folios 128-129.

Morris, Richard. Admin. of, to Rebecca Morris, widow, & Thomas Morris. March 25, 1773. Arch. vol. A37, page 1. Reg. of Wills, Liber L, folio 129.

Doherty, Morgan. Shoemaker. Murderkill Hd. Admin. of, to Mary Doherty, widow. March 27, 1773. Arch. vol. A14, pages 179-180. Reg. of Wills, Liber L, folio 129. Note:— Arch. vol. A14, page 180 shows that Mary Doherty married . . . Fowler & mentions children, Benjamin, Charles, John Doherty.

Ringgold, William. Admin. of, to Mary Ringgold, widow. March 30, 1773. Reg. of Wills, Liber L, folio 110.

Stewart, James. Admin. of, to Rachel Stewart, widow. April 2, 1773. Reg. of Wills, Liber L, folio 129. Note:—Arch. vol. A49, page 97 shows that Rachel Stewart married Solomon Mumford.

Anderson, Elijah. Admin. of, to Sarah Anderson, widow. April 3, 1773. Reg. of Wills, Liber L, folio 130.

Lewis, Joseph. Admin. of, to Ruth Lewis, widow. April 3, 1773. Arch. vol. A30, pages 103-104. Reg. of Wills, Liber L, folio 130.

Howren, Benjamin. Admin. of, to Mary Howren, widow. April 7, 1773. Reg. of Wills, Liber L, folio 130.

Mellogue, Samuel. Admin. of, to Mary Mellogue, widow. April 8, 1773. Reg. of Wills, Liber L, folio 130. Note:—Arch. vol. A35, page 135 shows this acct. later administered by Mary Cummins.

Thompson, Robert. Admin. of, to Elizabeth Thompson, widow. April 8, 1773. Reg. of Wills, Liber L, folio 130.

Freeman, William. Admin. of to William Gray. April 9, 1773. Arch. vol. A18, page 134. Reg. of Wills, Liber L, folio 129.

West, David. Yeoman. Will. Made Nov. 26, 1770. Duck Creek Hd. Heirs: sons Joseph & Benjamin; daus. Ann Surencey & Mary Varnan. Exec'rs, sons Joseph & Benjamin. Wits., Samuel West, Mary Smith. Prob. April 21, 1773. Arch. vol. A54, pages 11-13. Reg. of Wills, Liber L, folio 130.

Hill, Thomas. Yeoman. Duck Creek Hd. Admin. of, to Joseph Hill, next of kin. April 21, 1773. Arch. vol. A24, page 19. Reg. of Wills, Liber L, folio 130.

Holliday, John. Admin. of, to James Moore. April 21, 1773. Reg. of Wills, Liber L, folio 131.

Dunning, Martha. Will. Made March 23, 1773. Heirs: sister Mary Dunning; cousin Deborah Gaskins. Exec'x, sister Mary Dunning. Wits., John Edmondson, John Morris, Patrick Crain. Prob. April 21, 1773. Arch. vol. A15, pages 128-129. Reg. of Wills, Liber L, folio 131.

Greer, Susannah. Admin. of, to Norman Blackshare. April 21, 1773. Arch. vol. A20, page 180. Reg. of Wills, Liber L, folio 131.

Jones, Benjamin, Jr. Yeoman. Murderkill Hd. Admin. of, to Dolly Jones, widow. April 22, 1773. Arch. vol. A27, pages 137-139. Reg. of Wills, Liber L, folio 131. Note:—Arch. vol. A27, page 138 shows that Dolly Jones married Andrew Jenkins.

King, Elianer. Admin. of, to John Craige, next of kin. April 22, 1773. Arch. vol. A29, page 23. Reg. of Wills, Liber L, folio 131.

Fleming, Joseph. Blacksmith. Mispillion Hd. Admin. of, to Rachel Fleming, widow. April 22, 1773. Reg. of Wills, Liber L, folio 131. Note:—Arch. vol. A17, page 182 shows that Rachel Fleming married Robert McGonigel.

Miller, Joseph. Blacksmith. Little Creek Hd. Admin. of, to Margret Miller, widow. April 26, 1773. Arch. vol. A35, pages 95-97. Reg. of Wills, Liber L, folio 131. Note:—Arch. vol. A35, page 97 shows that Margret Miller married John Levick; also mentions a dau. Lydia Miller.

Humphries, Alexander. Admin. of, to Elizabeth Humphries, widow. April 28, 1773. Reg. of Wills, Liber L, folio 131. Note:—Arch. vol. A25, page 129 shows that Elizabeth Humphries married Vincent Manlove.

Burns, Darias. Admin. of, to Rebecca Burns, widow. May 6, 1773. Reg. of Wills, Liber L, folio 131. Note:—Arch. vol. A6, page 201 shows that Rebecca Burns married Bryan Holland.

Parker, Thomas. Yeoman. Will. Made April 7, 1773. Little Creek Hd. Heirs: wife Sarah; sons Thomas & William; a child unnamed; bro. John Parker; children of bro. William. Exec'rs, wife Sarah & friend Jacob Stout. Guardian, Jacob Stout. Wits., Immanuel Stout, Christopher Denny, Thomas Parry. Prob. May 12, 1773. Arch. vol. A39, pages 46-47. Reg. of Wills, Liber L, folio 132. Note:—Arch. vol. A39, page 47 shows that Sarah Parker married Isaiah Wharton, Jr.

Cattlin [Catlin], Robert. Admin. of, to George Ogle, D. B. N. May 12, 1773. Arch. vol. A8, page 80. Reg. of Wills, Liber L, folio 132.

Cattlin [Catlin], Mary. Admin. of, to George Ogle, D. B. N. May 12, 1773. Arch. vol. A8, page 78. Reg. of Wills, Liber L, folio 132.

Campbel, Edward. Admin. of, to Charles Hillyard. May 12, 1773. Arch. vol. A7, page 181. Reg. of Wills, Liber L, folio 133.

Moore, Samuel. Farmer. Will. Made May 1, 1773. Heirs: wife Margaret; sons Joseph, Samuel & David; daus. Susanna Smith, Sarah Hales, Mary, Elizabeth & Ann Moore. Exec'rs, wife Margaret & son David. Wits., Benjamin Goodwin, James Moore, Paul Quenounault. Prob. May 13, 1773. Arch. vol. A36, pages 86-87. Reg. of Wills, Liber L, folios 132-133.

Dicus, John. Will. Made April 20, 1773. Duck Creek Hd. Heirs: wife Julan; sons William, Samuel, John; daus. Sarah, Mary & Henrity. Exec'x, wife Julan. Wits., Samuel Griffith, Hugh Speer, Thomas Knock. Prob. May 20, 1773. Arch. vol. A14, pages 69-70. Reg. of Wills, Liber L, folios 133-134.

Goodwin, Benjamin. Admin. of, to Jane Goodwin, widow. May 20, 1773. Arch. vol. A19, page 136. Reg. of Wills, Liber L, folio 134.

Morris, John. Admin. of, to Daniel Morris, next of kin. May 20, 1773. Reg. of Wills, Liber L, folio 134.

Emmerson, Govey. Yeoman. Will. Made March 5, 1773. Little Creek Hd. Heirs: sons Jacob, Govey, Manlove & Jonathan. Exec'rs, sons Jacob & Govey. Guardians, friends Samuel Hanson, Sr., Ezekiel Cowgill, John Cowgill, Warner Mifflin, Garret Sipple. Wits., Samuel Hanson, Sr., Ezekiel Cowgill, Thomas Parry. Prob. May 21, 1773. Arch. vol. A16, pages 127-129. Reg. of Wills, Liber L, folios 133-134. Note:—Will mentions father John Emerson, dec'd.

Allee, Peter. Yeoman. Will. Made May 17, 1773. Duck Creek Hd. Heirs: bros. Presley, Abraham & John Allee; sister Mary Allee; Frances Cooper. Exec'rs, Abraham & John Allee. Wits., John Dawson, George Harris, Lucey Cooper. Prob. May 24, 1773. Arch. vol. A1, pages 69-72. Reg. of Wills, Liber L, folios 133-136. Note:—Arch. vol. A1, page 72 mentions a sister Mary Vanwinckle.

Forkum, Renatus. Admin. of, to William Rash, next of kin. May 25, 1773. Arch. vol. A17, page 221. Reg. of Wills, Liber L, folio 136.

Forkum, Hannah. Admin. of, to William Rash, next of kin. May 25, 1773. Reg. of Wills, Liber L, folio 136.

Spence, John. Admin. of, to James Spence, next of kin. May 25, 1773. Reg. of Wills, Liber L, folio 136.

Christopher, Thomas. Mispillion Hd. Admin. of, to Richard Reynolds & wife Ruth, late Ruth Christopher. May 26, 1773. Arch. vol. A8, pages 197-199. Note:—Arch. vol. A8, page 197 mentions heirs, Sarah, John, Elizabeth, Ruth, Thomas, Annsly, William & James Christopher.

Spence, Mary. Widow. Mispillion Hd. Admin. of, to James Spence, next of kin. May 26, 1773. Arch. vol. A48, pages 89-90. Reg. of Wills, Liber L, folio 136.

Hudson, Daniel. Admin. of, to Ebenezer Manlove. May 27, 1773. Arch. vol. A25, page 104. Note:—Mentions heirs, John, Sarah & Mary Hudson.

Hill, Robert. Admin. of, to Joseph Hill, next of kin, D. B. N. May 27, 1773. Arch. vol. A24, page 11. Reg. of Wills, Liber L, folio 130.

Snipe, William. Will. Made May 9, 1773. Heirs: wife Rachel; dau. Nancy; son Joseph. Exec'rs, wife Rachel & Matthew Hendrey. Wits., John Miller, William Drew, Samuel Brees. Prob. May 29, 1773. Arch. vol. A47, pages 230-231. Reg. of Wills, Liber L, folios 136-137. Note:—Arch. vol. A47, page 231 shows that Rachel Snipe married John Miller.

Maddox, Alexander. Yeoman. Mispillion Hd. Admin. of, to Jemima Maddox, widow. May 29, 1773. Arch. vol. A33, page 64. Reg. of Wills, Liber L, folio 137.

Baily, Thomas. Yeoman. Little Creek Hd. Admin. of, to Mary Baily, widow. June 4, 1773. Arch. vol. A2, page 76. Reg. of Wills, Liber L, folio 137.

Whittington, John. Admin. of, to Elizabeth Whittington, widow. June 4, 1773. Reg. of Wills, Liber L, folio 137.

Elliott, Obediah. Yeoman. Duck Creek Hd. Admin. of, to Elizabeth Elliott, widow. June 11, 1773. Arch. vol. A16, page 99. Reg. of Wills, Liber L, folio 137.

Berry, Joseph. Blacksmith. Murtherkill Hd. Admin. of, to Unity Berry, widow. June 12, 1773. Arch. vol. A4, pages 7-8. Reg. of Wills, Liber L, folio 137. Note:—Arch. vol. A4, page 8 shows that Unity Berry later married John Gilder.

Robinson, Rachel. Admin. of, to Richard Smith, Esq., next of kin. June 15, 1773. Reg. of Wills, Liber L, folio 137.

Downham, Richard. Will. Made Sept. 4, 1771. Heirs: daus. Ruth, Mary Beauchamp (wife of John Beauchamp), Sarah, Elizabeth, Rachel; sons Isaac & Richard. Exec'rs, son Isaac & bro.-in-law William Powell. Wits., Elias Townsend, Dorothy Jones, Joseph Downham. Prob. June 18, 1773. Arch. vol. A14, pages 227-229. Reg. of Wills, Liber L, folios 137-138.

Hall, David. Admin. of, to Thomas Skillington, D. B. N. June 23, 1773. Arch. vol. A21, page 85. Reg. of Wills, Liber L, folio 138.

Leyvick, John. Yeoman. Dover Hd. Admin. of, to Susannah Howell & William Howell, next of kin. June 29, 1773. Arch. vol. A30, pages 33-35. Reg. of Wills, Liber L, folio 138. Note:—Arch. vol. A30, page 34 shows that Susannah Howell later married . . . Jackson.

Rattledge, John. Farmer. Will. Made May 6, 1773. Heirs: wife Mary; sons John, Thomas, James, Moses & William; daus. Elizabeth Buckler, Ruth, Jemmimah. Exec'x, wife Mary. Wits., Benjamin Caton, Miriam Caton, Archable [Archibald] Jackson. Prob. July 26, 1773. Arch. vol. A42, pages 96-97. Reg. of Wills, Liber L, folios 138-139. Note:—Arch. vol. A42, page 97 shows that Mary Rattledge married Jeremiah Calhoon.

Jenkins, Jabez. Will (copy). Made June 26, 1773. Heirs: wife Rebecca; dau. Hannah; sons Joseph, Jabez, Thomas, John. Exec'rs, kinsman Warner Mifflin, friend Charles Ridgely. Wits., Ezekiel Nock, Timothy Jenkins, Thomas Nock. Prob. July 27, 1773. Arch. vol. A26, page 217. Reg. of Wills, Liber L, folio 139.

Studham, John. Ship-carpenter. Will. Made July 26, 1773. Little Creek Hd. Heir: John McKey. Exec'r, John McKey. Wits., James Sykes, Phillip McGaogey. Prob. Aug. 12, 1773. Arch. vol. A49, page 107. Reg. of Wills, Liber L, folio 139.

Anderson, John. Admin. of, to Elizabeth Anderson, widow. Aug. 14, 1773. Reg. of Wills, Liber L, folio 140.

White, John. Admin. of, to Judith White, widow. Aug. 14, 1773. Arch. vol. A54, pages 117-118. Reg. of Wills, Liber L, folio 140.

David, James. Bachelor. Will. Made April 16, 1770. Duck Creek Hd. Heirs: sister Rachel Elbourn; nephew James Elbourn, son of sister Rachel; bro. John David; niece Mary David, dau. of bro. John. Exec'r, bro. John David. Wits., Benjamin Jones, Richard Morris, Mary Jones. Prob. Aug. 24, 1773. Arch. vol. A12, page 220. Reg. of Wills, Liber L, folio 140.

Lockwood, John. Admin. of, to Charles Pope. Aug. 25, 1773. Reg. of Wills, Liber L, folio 140.

Byrne, Anthony. Admin. of, to Fanny Esgate. Aug. 25, 1773. Arch. vol. A7, page 18.

Marratt, Isaac. Will. Made Jan. 25, 1754. Heirs: daus. Anne & Sarah Marratt, Rachel Stafford, Elizabeth Hudson, Mary Kimmy; granddau. Sarah Stafford. Exec'xes, daus. Anne & Sarah Marratt, Rachel Stafford. Wits., Mark Manlove, Ann Manlove, Ruth Manlove. Prob. Aug. 25, 1773. Arch. vol. A33, page 193. Reg. of Wills, Liber L, folio 140.

Taylor, Francis. Admin. of, to John Reynolds. Sept. 8, 1773. Reg. of Wills, Liber L, folio 140.

Wiley, John. Yeoman. Admin. of, to Vincent Loockerman, Sr. Sept. 9, 1773. Arch. vol. A55, page 64. Reg. of Wills, Liber L, folio 141.

Gardner, James. Gentleman. Will. Made May 31, 1773. Heirs: daus. Martha Rees, wife of William Rees, Nancy McMullan; grandsons James, Francis & William Gardner McMullan (children of James & dau. Nancy); son-in-law James McMullan; kinsmen James & William McCulloch, of North Carolina; James Gardner, son of kinsman John; Trustees of Newark Academy; Jennet Crompton, wife of Watkins Crompton of Wilmington; Rev. John McCannon, of White Clay Creek Hundred; friend George Reed, Esq., & three sons; friends William Killen, Robert McCai (of Connecochoque in Cumberland Co.). Exec'rs, George Reed, Esq. & William Killen. Wits., James Tilton, Peter Stout. Codicil, Aug. 2, 1773. Samuel Gardner, son of kinsman John; kinswoman Margaret Carr, the elder. Wits., Ezekiel Needham, John Darrach. Prob. Sept. 10, 1773. Arch. vol. A18, pages 214-215. Reg. of Wills, Liber L, folios 140-141.

Jones, Jacob. Admin. of, to Penelope Holt Jones, widow. Sept. 22, 1773. Reg. of Wills, Liber L, folio 141. Note:—Arch. vol. A27, page 195 mentions son Jacob Jones, minor.

Williamson, Jacob. Admin. of, to William Manlove. Sept. 22, 1773. Reg. of Wills, Liber L, folio 141.

Crozier, Matthew. Yeoman. Duck Creek Hd. Admin. of, to Rachel Crozier, widow. Sept. 27, 1773. Arch. vol. A12, pages 26-31. Reg. of Wills, Liber L, folio 141. Note:—Arch. vol. A12, page 29 shows that Rachel married Thomas Parry; page 27 mentions heirs, Mary Robinson (née Crozier), wife of Charles; Sarah Besswicik (née Crozier), wife of Robert; Rhoda, Matthew & Robert Crozier; page 26 shows this acct. later administered by William Cahoon & James Starling.

Hamilton, Mary. Will. Made March 19, 1773. Heirs: dau. Mary Brinckle, wife of William; grandchildren Peter Moore & Mary Moore, children of John Moore; grandsons Curtis & Joseph Brinckle, sons of William Brinckle; Robert Hamilton. Exec'r, Robert Hamilton. Wits., Ann Harris, John Ham. Prob. Oct. 2, 1773. Arch. vol. A21, page 165. Reg. of Wills, Liber L, folios 141-142.

Reynalls, John. Farmer. Will. Made Sept. 21, 1773. Heirs: wife Elizabeth; John Reynalls, son of Michell Reynalls. Exec'x, wife Elizabeth. Wits., William Betts, Elizabeth Betts. Prob. Oct. 7, 1773. Arch. vol. A43, pages 106-107. Reg. of Wills, Liber L, folio 142. Note:—Arch. vol. A43, page 107 shows that Elizabeth Reynalls married James White.

Taylor, Francis. Admin. of, to Elizabeth Reynolds, D. B. N. Oct. 7, 1773. Reg. of Wills, Liber L, folio 142. Note:—Arch. vol. A49, page 179 shows that Elizabeth Reynolds, widow of John Reynalls, married James White.

Dill, Edward. Admin. of, to William Dill, next of kin, D. B. N. Oct. 11, 1773. Reg. of Wills, Liber L, folio 142.

Stanton, Matthias. Admin. of, to Richard Smith, Esq., next of kin. Oct. 25, 1773. Reg. of Wills, Liber L, folio 142.

Denny, Philip. Admin. of, to Elizabeth Denny, widow. Oct. 26, 1773. Reg. of Wills, Liber L, folio 143. Note:—Arch. vol. A13, page 238 shows that Elizabeth Denny married James Cockrel.

Hudson, Enoch. Admin. of, to Alexander Hudson, next of kin. Oct. 27, 1773. Reg. of Wills, Liber L, folio 143.

Barker, William. Admin. of, to Jean Barker, next of kin. Nov. 1, 1773. Reg. of Wills, Liber L, folio 143.

Warrington, Jacob. Yeoman. Mispillion Hd. Admin. of, to Elizabeth Warrington, widow. Nov. 11, 1773. Arch. vol. A53, pages 158-159. Reg. of Wills, Liber L, folio 143. Note:— Arch. vol. A53, page 158 shows heirs, Sarah, Patience, Rachel, Esther & Comfort Warrington.

Ozbun, Jonathan. Yeoman. Will. Made Aug. 24, 1773. Little Creek Hd. Heirs: wife Eunice; son Jonathan; daus. Eunice & Tabitha Ozbun, Elizabeth Cowgill, Mary Alstone; son-in-law Israel Alstone. Exec'x, wife Eunice. Guardian, Robert Holliday. Wits., Robert Regester, Elizabeth Stevens, Thomas Parry. Prob. Nov. 11, 1773. Arch. vol. A38, pages 166-167. Reg. of Wills, Liber L, folio 143. Note:—Will mentions grandfather Joshua Clayton, dec'd.

Painter, George. Scribner. Town of Dover. Admin. of, to Edward Fisher. Nov. 12, 1773. Arch. vol. A38, pages 194-195. Reg. of Wills, Liber L, folio 144.

Meredith, Wheelor. Admin. of, to Susannah Meredith, widow. Nov. 15, 1773. Reg. of Wills, Liber L, folio 144. Note:— Arch. vol. A34, page 220 shows that Susannah Meredith married John Lambert.

Leatherberry, William. Yeoman. Will. Made Oct. 18, 1773. Little Creek Hd. Heirs: wife Sarah; sons William & Thomas; dau. Mary; cousin Thomas Leatherberry, son of bro. Charles; three children of sister Mary Miers. Exec'rs, wife Sarah, John Brinckle. Wits., Christopher Deney, John McGear, James Aaron. Prob. Nov. 17, 1773. Arch. vol. A29, pages 220-221. Reg. of Wills, Liber L, folio 144.

Williams, Deborah. Admin. of, to John Bannin, D. B. N. Nov. 18, 1773. Reg. of Wills, Liber L, folio 144.

Williams, Isaiah. Admin. of, to John Banning. Nov. 18, 1773. Reg. of Wills, Liber L, folio 144.

Ellett, Thomas. Farmer. Will. Made Oct. 17, 1773. Heirs: sons Isaac, Jacob, Edward; dau. Mary; Thomas Ellett. Exec'rs, sons Isaac & Jacob. Wits., Thomas Cordray, Matthew Cox, Daniel Bartlett. Prob. Nov. 19, 1773. Arch. vol. A16, page 104. Reg. of Wills, Liber L, folios 144-145.

Snow, John. Admin. of, to Sarah Snow. Nov. 26, 1773. Arch. vol. A48, page 16. Note:—Mentions heirs, Isaac, Lydia & John Snow.

Nock, Ezekiel. Will. Made Oct. 28, 1773. Heirs: sons Thomas, Joseph, Daniel; daus. Ann Griffin, Mary Nock; grandchildren Jabez, Daniel & Sarah Griffin, John & Thomas Brown. Exec'r, son Thomas. Wits., Thomas Nock, James Nock, Joseph Jenkins. Prob. Nov. 30, 1773. Arch. vol. A38, pages 22-24 & 27. Reg. of Wills, Liber L, folio 145.

Bowen, William. Will. Made Oct. 30, 1773. Heirs: wife Susannah; sons John, Joseph, William, James; dau. Rachel; other three daus. unnamed. Exec'rs, wife Susannah & son William. Wits., James Harrington, Robert White, Elias Stuart. Prob. Dec. 2, 1773. Arch. vol. A5, pages 22-23 & 46. Reg. of Wills, Liber L, folio 146. Note:—Arch. vol. A5, page 23 shows daus. Catherine, Susanna & Mary Bowen.

Griffin, Matthew. Farmer. Will. Made Nov. 21, 1773. Duck Creek Hd. Heirs: wife Lydia; sons Samuel, Matthew, David, Ebenezer, William; daus. Lydia & Elizabeth. Exec'rs, wife Lydia & son David. Wits., Thomas Brown, Enock Jones, William Griffin, miller. Prob. Dec. 8, 1773. Arch. vol. A20, pages 216-217. Reg. of Wills, Liber L, folios 146-147.

Carmon, Rachel. Admin. of, to William Griffin, miller. Dec. 8, 1773. Reg. of Wills, Liber L, folio 147.

Gray, Anne. Widow. Murderkill Hd. Admin. of, to Andrew Lackey, next of kin. Dec. 9, 1773. Arch. vol. A20, page 8. Reg. of Wills, Liber L, folio 147.

Brown, Elizabeth. Admin. of, to Daniel Virdin, Absalom Virdin & Levin Gibson, next of kin. Dec. 11, 1773. Reg. of Wills, Liber L, folio 147. Note:—Arch. vol. A6, page 42 shows acct. later administered by Joseph Jackson & wife Elizabeth, late Elizabeth Virden & Sarah Virden.

Kimmey, William. Yeoman. Will. Made Nov. 21, 1773. Heirs: wife unnamed; sons William, Solomon, Robert, Charles, Levin & Thomas; daus. Ealender Benson Kimmy, Nancy Addams Kimmy, Sarah Causey, Rachel Correy, Dianna Causey. Exec'rs, wife & son William. Wits., Robert Brodie, Joseph Lister, Levin Benson. Prob. Dec. 14, 1773. Arch. vol. A29, pages 15 & 18. Reg. of Wills, Liber L, folio 147.

Start, Martha. Admin. of, to Benjamin Start, next of kin. Dec. 20, 1773. Arch. vol. A48, page 184. Reg. of Wills, Liber L, folio 147.

Manlove, Matthew. Farmer. Will. Made Dec. 13, 1773. Heirs: sister Margret Craige; bro. Mark Manlove; nephew Matthew Manlove, son of bro. Mark. Exec'r, bro. Mark Manlove. Wits., Jonathan Sipple, James Reed, Silvanus Swallow. Prob. Dec. 23, 1773. Arch. vol. A32, page 47. Reg. of Wills, Liber L, folios 147-148.

Manship, George. Admin. of, to Powel Cox & Solomon Wallace, D. B. N. Dec. 24, 1773. Arch. vol. A33, page 162. Reg. of Wills, Liber L, folio 148.

Manship, Sarah. Murderkill Hd. Admin. of, to Powel Cox & Solomon Wallace. Dec. 24, 1773. Arch. vol. A33, page 161. Reg. of Wills, Liber L, folio 148.

Leatherberry, Sarah. Admin. of, to John Brinckle. Dec. 24, 1773. Arch. vol. A29, page 212. Reg. of Wills, Liber L, folio 148.

Buckingham, Joseph. Admin. of, to Sarah Buckingham, widow. Dec. 31, 1773. Arch. vol. A6, page 131. Reg. of Wills, Liber L, folio 148.

Pugh, Sarah. Admin. of, to Joseph Smith, next of kin. Jan. 3, 1774. Reg. of Wills, Liber L, folio 148.

Graydon, Alexander. Admin. of, to Rebecca Graydon, widow. Jan. 3, 1774. Reg. of Wills, Liber L, folio 148. Note:—Arch. vol. A20, page 42 shows that Rebecca Graydon married Josiah Hitchens.

Griffith, Samuel. Will. Made Dec. 20, 1773. Heirs: wife Jean; daus. Mary & Rachel Griffith, Esther Morris; sons John, Solomon, Hyllard, Nathan, James, Samuel, Isaac. Exec'x, wife Jean. Wits., Mathias Maston, Solomon Clark, John Minner. Prob. Jan. 4, 1774. Arch. vol. A21, page 3 & vol. A20, page 226. Reg. of Wills, Liber L, folios 148-149.

Morris, William. Yeoman. Murderkill Hd. Admin. of, to Priscilla Morris, widow. Jan. 12, 1774. Arch. vol. A37, page 39. Reg. of Wills, Liber L, folio 149.

Ringgold, Thomas. Admin. of, to John Ringgold, next of kin. Jan. 13, 1774. Arch. vol. A44, page 14. Reg. of Wills, Liber L, folio 149.

Brown, Joseph. Admin. of, to Joseph Brown, next of kin. Jan. 18, 1774. Arch. vol. A6, page 67. Reg. of Wills, Liber L, folio 149.

Trippett, Caleb. Admin. of, to Mary Trippett, widow. Jan. 19, 1774. Reg. of Wills, Liber L, folio 149.

Cox, Isaac. Chaisemaker. Admin. of, to Robert McGarment. Jan. 19, 1774. Arch. vol. A11, page 133. Reg. of Wills, Liber L, folio 149.

McCombs, Bartholemew. Dover Hd. Admin. of, to Esther McCombs, widow. Jan. 20, 1774. Arch. vol. A32, pages 133-134. Reg. of Wills, Liber L, folio 149.

Bell, Thomas. Dover Hd. Admin. of, to Mary Bell, widow. Jan. 20, 1774. Arch. vol. A3, page 188. Reg. of Wills, Liber L, folio 149.

Freeman, Moses, Jr. Admin. of, to Lydia Freeman, widow. Jan. 21, 1774. Arch. vol. A18, pages 128-129. Reg. of Wills, Liber L, folio 149. Note:—Arch. vol. A18, page 128 shows heirs, Abraham, Isaac & Jacob Freeman; page 129 shows that Lydia Freeman married . . . Fitzgerald.

Amor [Amour], John. Admin. of, to Susanna Amor & John Amor. Jan. 21, 1774. Arch. vol. A1, page 129. Reg. of Wills, Liber L, folio 149.

Boggs, Matthew. Admin. of, to David Boggs, next of kin, D. B. N. Jan. 25, 1774. Arch. vol. A4, page 183. Reg. of Wills, Liber L, folio 149.

Boggs, John. Tanner. Murderkill Hd. Admin. of, to David Boggs, next of kin. Jan. 25, 1774. Arch. vol. A4, pages 176-177. Reg. of Wills, Liber L, folio 149.

Allen, Joseph. Yeoman. Mispillian Hd. Admin. of, to Elizabeth Allen, widow. Appraisers, James Anderson, Ezekiel Anderson. Jan. 26, 1774. Arch. vol. A1, pages 87-89. Reg. of Wills, Liber L, folio 150. Note:—Arch. vol. A1, page 87 shows that Elizabeth Allen married Benjamin Morris; page 89 shows heirs, Henrietta, Andrew, Margaret, John, Joseph & Jacob Allen.

Trigar, Zebedee. Will. Made Jan. 20, 1774. Heirs: wife Hannah Trigar; a child of dau. Hannah unnamed; daus.-in-law Ann & Mary Forker; son-in-law Samuel Forker. Exec'x, wife Hannah. Wits., Edward Fisher, John Crompton, William Anderson. Prob. Jan. 27, 1774. Arch. vol. A51, pages 69-73. Reg. of Wills, Liber L, folio 150. Note:—Arch. vol. A51, page 73 shows that Hannah Trigar married David Thornton; page 71 mentions a son James Trigar.

Tharp, Isaac. Will (rejected). Made Feb. 2, 1774. Heirs: wife Peggy; dau. Nancy Tharp; sons David & John; four youngest children unnamed. Exec'rs, sons David & John. Wits., Charlotta, Richard & Sarah Dallinar. [No prob.]. Arch. vol. A49, page 237.

Johnson, John. Yeoman. Will. Made Aug. 24, 1761. Murderkill Hd. Heirs: wife Jean; sons John, Robert, William, James, Thomas, Samuel; daus. Margaret, Agnes, Elizabeth, Mary. Exec'rs, wife Jean & John Hamilton. Wits., David White, John Chambers, Stephen Hairgrove. Prob. Feb. 9, 1774. Arch. vol. A27, pages 78-79. Reg. of Wills, Liber L, folio 150.

Williams, John. Admin. of, to Evan Lewis & Arnald Hudson. Feb. 9, 1774. Reg. of Wills, Liber L, folio 151.

Catts, John. Yeoman. Mispillion Hd. Admin. of, to Mary Catts, widow. Feb. 23, 1774. Arch. vol. A8, pages 93-94. Reg. of Wills, Liber L, folio 151.

Catts, William. Admin. of, to Mary Catts, next of kin, D. B. N. Feb. 23, 1774. Arch. vol. A8, page 105. Reg. of Wills, Liber L, folio 151.

Arrowsmith, Thomas. Admin. of, to Reynear Williams, D. B. N. Feb. 24, 1774. Arch. vol. A1, pages 243-245. Reg. of Wills, Liber L, folio 151. Note:—Arch. vol. A1, page 243 shows Avary Draper as joint adm'r.

Richards, Mary. Admin. of, to William Richards. Feb. 24, 1774. Arch. vol. A43, page 154.

Brown, James. Farmer. Murderkill Hd. Admin. of, to Jonathan Clampitt, next of kin. Feb. 28, 1774. Arch. vol. A6, page 48. Reg. of Wills, Liber L, folio 151.

Anderson, Elizabeth. Admin. of, to James Anderson, next of kin. March 8, 1774. Arch. vol. A1, page 158. Reg. of Wills, Liber L, folio 151.

Melchop, George. Will (copy, nunc.). Made Feb. 9, 1774. Heirs: sister Sarah Melechop; wife & two children unnamed. Exec'rs, wife, John Dill & Warner Mifflin. Wits., John Tomlin, Celah Tomlin, Charles Ross, John Dill. Prob. March 12, 1774. Arch. vol. A34, page 129. Reg. of Wills, Liber L, folio 151. Note:—Admin. acct. shows Sarah Melechop as adm'x.

Melowchop, George. Admin. of, to Sarah Melowchop, John Dill & Timothy Caldwell. March 12, 1774. Arch. vol. A34, page 130 & vol. A35, pages 61-62. Reg. of Wills, Liber L, folio 151. Note:—Arch. vol. A35, page 61 mentions James Mellochop, a minor.

King, Ann. Will. Made July 30, 1773. Heirs: son Vallantine; Elizabeth Betts. Exec'r, son Vallantine. Wits., Patrick Crain, William Meredith, William Meredith, Jr. Prob. March 19, 1774. Arch. vol. A29, page 22. Reg. of Wills, Liber L, folios 151-152.

Pleasanton, David. Will. Made March 28, 1774. Dover Hd. Heirs: wife Deborah; dau. Sarah; sons Nathaniel, John, David, Caleb. Exec'rs, wife Deborah & William Rodney. Commissioners, Caleb Luff, John Williams, James Sykes, Esq., William Rodney, Samuel Hanson. Wits., James Stevens, Jonathan Pleasanton, Benjamin Nixon. Prob. April 5, 1774. Arch. vol. A40, pages 94-99. Reg. of Wills, Liber L, folio 152. Note:—Arch. vol. A40, page 96 shows that Deborah Pleasanton married Stephen Lewis.

Grewell, Peter. Admin. of, to George & Sarah Richards. April 6, 1774. Reg. of Wills, Liber L, folio 152.

Register, Jeremiah. Will. Made March 26, 1774. Murderkill Hd. Heirs: wife Elezebeth; daus. Rachel Crawford (wife of Oliver Crawford), Leaer Cummins; sons John, Isaac, Robert, Jeremiah, Francis, Elija. Exec'rs, sons Robert & Jeremiah. Wits., William Dunning, Nimrod Maxwell, Coe Gordon. Prob. April 11, 1774. Arch. vol. A43, pages 57-58. Reg. of Wills, Liber L, folio 152.

Pickeral, William. Admin. of, to Mary Pickerel, widow. April 12, 1774. Reg. of Wills, Liber L, folio 153.

Irons, Titus. Admin. of, to George McCall. April 14, 1774. Reg. of Wills, Liber L, folio 153.

Hattfield, John, Sr. Yeoman. Mispillion Hd. Admin. of, to John Hattfield, next of kin. May 10, 1774. Arch. vol. A22, page 233. Reg. of Wills, Liber L, folio 153.

Harmon, Daniel. Admin. of, to Elizabeth Harmon, widow. May 10, 1774. Reg. of Wills, Liber L, folio 153. Note:—Arch. vol. A22, page 31 shows that Elizabeth Harmon married Joseph Latern.

Cahoon, William. Yeoman. Will. Made Aug. 5, 1771. Duck Creek Hd. Heirs: wife Mary; sons Thomas, Charles, William & Mark; daus. Elizabeth, Rachel, Jean & Nancy; grandson John Edwards. Exec'rs, sons Thomas, Charles, William, Mark. Wits., James Edwards, James Raymond, Allen McLeane, Jr. Prob. May 11, 1774. Arch. vol. A7, pages 45-46. Reg. of Wills, Liber L, folio 153.

Wheelor, Owen. Admin. of, to Anne Wheelor, widow. May 11, 1774. Arch. vol. A54, page 66. Reg. of Wills, Liber L, folio 153.

Hylands, Meriam. Admin. of, to Thomas Muncy, next of kin. May 11, 1774. Arch. vol. A25, page 209. Reg. of Wills, Liber L, folio 153.

Holliday, Richard. Admin. of, to Anne Holliday, widow. May 17, 1774. Reg. of Wills, Liber L, folio 153. Note:—Arch. vol. A24, page 204 shows that Anne Holliday married Isaiah Rowland.

Beakham, Francis. Yeoman. Will. Made March 23, 1774. Heirs: wife Mary; sisters Elizabeth Pearson, Jean Ryley, Rachel Boming, Ann Bags; heirs of sister Mary Caffy. Exec'rs, wife Mary & Vallentine Pegg. Wits., Ezekiel Anderson, James Anderson, Joseph Standley. Prob. May 21, 1774. Arch. vol. A3, page 90. Reg. of Wills, Liber L, folios 153-154.

Murphey, Esther. Admin. of, to Thomas Murphey. May 24, 1774. Reg. of Wills, Liber L, folio 154.

Johnson, Jean. Widow. Murtherkill Hd. Admin. of, to John Johnson & William Johnson, next of kin. May 24, 1774. Arch. vol. A27, page 74. Reg. of Wills, Liber L, folio 154.

Johnson, John, the elder. Murtherkill Hd. Admin. of, to John & William Johnson, next of kin, D. B. N. May 24, 1774. Reg. of Wills, Liber L, folio 154. Note:—Arch. vol. A27, page 79 mentions John Allen, son of John Allen.

Willson, Thomas. Admin. of, to Mary Willson, widow. May 25, 1774. Reg. of Wills, Liber L, folio 154. Note:—Arch. vol. A56, page 21 shows that Mary Willson married Noah Hickman.

Draper, Sarah. Admin. of, to Elizabeth Draper, next of kin. May 25, 1774. Arch. vol. A15, pages 62-63. Reg. of Wills, Liber L, folio 154. Note:—Arch. vol. A15, page 63 shows that Elizabeth Draper married Thomas Bowman.

Houston, Elijah. Minor son of Benjamin. Admin. of, to Bolitha Laws. May 26, 1774. Arch. vol. A25, page 42.

Reynolds, Samuel. Admin. of, to Rachel Reynolds, widow. May 28, 1774. Reg. of Wills, Liber L, folio 154.

Kimmey, Charles. Will. Made Dec. 14, 1771. Heirs: wife Mary; bros. Thomas, Levin, Solomon. Exec'x, wife Mary. Wits., Arnold Hudson, Elizabeth Lecount, Sarah Greenwood. Prob. June 6, 1774. Arch. vol. A28, page 233. Reg. of Wills, Liber L, folio 154.

Oliver, Reuben. Admin. of, to Esther Oliver, widow. June 10, 1774. Reg. of Wills, Liber L, folio 154. Note:—Arch. vol. A38, page 130 shows that Esther Oliver married George Lychum.

Watkins, Peter. Admin. of, to Mary Watkins, widow. June 18, 1774. Reg. of Wills, Liber L, folio 155.

Wood, John. Admin. of, to Sarah Wood & Joseph Snow. June 21, 1774. Arch. vol. A56, pages 73-74. Reg. of Wills, Liber L, folio 155. Note:—Arch. vol. A56, page 73 shows that Sarah Wood married James Vandyke.

Hunn, David. Yeoman. Will. Made June 24, 1774. Little Creek Hd. Heirs: wife Mary; bro. Caleb Hunn; mother Tabitha Crispin. Exec'rs, wife Mary & bro. Caleb Hunn. Wits., Hannah Wilbank, Mary Clifford, James Chattin. Prob. July 2, 1774. Arch. vol. A25, page 132. Reg. of Wills, Liber L, folio 155.

Brown, John. Will. Made March 19, 1772. Heirs: grandson Henry Runnolds; daus. Sarah Bowing, Ann Duhadway, Elizabeth & Christanny Brown; sons Caleb, John, Solomon & William Brown. Exec'r, son William. Wits., Jacob Duhadway, Thomas Benet, John Ingram. Prob. July 20, 1774. Arch. vol. A6, page 54. Reg. of Wills, Liber L, folio 155.

Brannock, William. Will. Made Aug. 4, 1774. Mispillion Hd. Heirs: wife Ailce; son William; daus. Elizabeth Brannock, Mary Abbet, Rachel Wilkinson. Exec'rs, wife Ailce & friend John Cox, son of Thomas. Wits., Aron Wieyatt, William Wieyatt, Richard North. Prob. Aug. 9, 1774. Arch. vol. A5, pages 149-150. Reg. of Wills, Liber L, folio 156.

Edwards, James. Will. Made June 17, 1774. Duck Creek Hd. Heirs: sons John & Joshua. Exec'r, Joshua Edwards. Guardian, William Cahoon. Wits., Andrew Jamison, Joseph Jamison, Daniel David, Jr. Prob. Aug. 11, 1774. Arch. vol. A16, page 73. Reg. of Wills, Liber L, folio 156.

Hall, Robert. Yeoman. Little Creek Hd. Admin. of, to Thomas Cahoon, D. B. N. Aug. 11, 1774. Arch. vol. A21, pages 119-120. Reg. of Wills, Liber L, folio 156.

Robinson, Mary. Will. Made Aug. 9, 1774. Duck Creek Hd. Heirs: sons Robert & James; daus. Sarah Cole, Mary Robinson. Exec'r, William Truax. Guardian, Elizabeth Severson. Wits., William Shervan, Joseph Robinson. Prob. Aug. 16, 1774. Arch. vol. A44, page 82. Reg. of Wills, Liber L, folio 156.

Hamer, John. Will. Made March 4, 1774. Queen Anns Co., Md. Heirs: sister Sarah Smith; children of sister Sarah Smith; children of sister Ann Little; godson of John Hamer Wright. Exec'rs, nephews John Smith & Lazarus Little. Wits., Richard Smith, Howell Buckingham. Prob. Aug. 17, 1774. Arch. vol. A21, page 155. Reg. of Wills, Liber L, folios 156-157.

Griffin, Samuel. Yeoman. Mispillion Hd. Admin. of, to Jean Griffin. Aug. 25, 1774. Arch. vol. A20, page 226. Note:— Arch. vol. A20, page 226 mentions heirs, Solomon, Nathan, Henry, Hillyard, John & James Griffin, & Esther Morris, wife of James Morris.

Richardson, Richard. Admin. of, to Andrew Butler & wife Elizabeth. Aug. 25, 1774. Arch. vol. A43, page 169.

Dill, Edward. Admin. of, to Elijah Dill, next of kin. Aug. 30, 1774. Reg. of Wills, Liber L, folio 157.

Draighton, John, the younger. Yeoman. Duck Creek Hd. Admin. of, to John Draighton, the elder. Sept. 12, 1774. Arch. vol. A15, pages 75-76. Reg. of Wills, Liber L, folio 157. Note:— Arch. vol. A15, page 76 mentions a son Edmond Draighton.

Menshall, Samuel. Admin. of, to Jean Menshall & Isaac Menshall. Sept. 17, 1774. Reg. of Wills, Liber L, folio 157.

Boyd, John. Admin. of, to Thomas Rodney. Oct. 15, 1774. Arch. vol. A5, page 72. Reg. of Wills, Liber L, folio 157.

Catts, Vincent. Admin. of, to Elizabeth Catts, widow. Oct. 18, 1774. Arch. vol. A8, page 101. Reg. of Wills, Liber L, folio 157.

Saunders, Robert. Admin. of, to Smith Fasset. Oct. 19, 1774. Reg. of Wills, Liber L, folio 157.

Jackson, Richard. Admin. of, to Susanna Jackson & William Howell. Oct. 20, 1774. Arch. vol. A26, page 32. Reg. of Wills, Liber L, folio 157.

Webster, John. Admin. of, to Catherine Webster, widow. Oct. 27, 1774. Reg. of Wills, Liber L, folio 157.

Glann, Thomas. Admin. of, to James Hutchingson. Nov. 9, 1774. Reg. of Wills, Liber L, folio 157.

Wheeler, William. Shoemaker. Will. Made Oct. 28, 1774. Heirs: wife Elizabeth; sons William, Joseph, Jesse. Exec'r, friend Joseph Alford. Wits., Pierce Jones, Thomas Downham, Mary Cane. Prob. Nov. 9, 1774. Arch. vol. A54, pages 68, 71-72. Reg. of Wills, Liber L, folios 157-158.

Parkason, Thomas. Will. Made Feb. 25, 1773. Cecil Co., Md. Heir: bro. Christopher. Exec'r, bro. Christopher. Wit., Michael Ruley. Prob. Nov. 9, 1774. Arch. vol. A39, page 68. Reg. of Wills, Liber L, folio 158.

Caldwell, Andrew, Esq. Admin. of, to James Sykes, Esq. Nov. 14, 1774. Arch. vol. A7, page 99. Reg. of Wills, Liber L, folio 158.

Melven, John. Admin. of, to Mary Milven, widow. Nov. 23, 1774. Arch. vol. A34, pages 151-152. Reg. of Wills, Liber L, folio 158. Note:—Arch. vol. A34, page 151 shows that Mary Melvin married Govey Clampitt; also mentions heirs, James, Hilda & Sarah Melvin.

Melven, Edmond. Yeoman. Mispillion Hd. Admin. of, to Thomas Barker, next of kin. Nov. 23, 1774. Arch. vol. A34, page 141. Reg. of Wills, Liber L, folio 158.

Hampton, David. Admin. of, to Ruth Hampton, widow. Nov. 23, 1774. Reg. of Wills, Liber L, folio 158.

Stratton, Jacob. Admin. of, to Isaac Stratton, next of kin. Nov. 23, 1774. Reg. of Wills, Liber L, folio 158.

Champbell [Campbell], Sarah. Admin. of, to Archibald Fleming. Nov. 24, 1774. Reg. of Wills, Liber L, folio 158.

Robinson, Samuel. Merchant. Will (copy). Made Nov. 14, 1774. Phila. Heirs: bro. Daniel Robinson; nephews Samuel Barret (son of Roger Barret), Samuel, Thomas & John Robinson (sons of Daniel), Samuel Forker (son of George Forker); sisters Hannah Trigger, Miriam Barret, Penelope Irons (eldest dau. of Penelope Irons); nieces Jane Barret (dau. of Miriam) & Ann Robinson (dau. of Daniel); Moses Freeman, Mary Freeman (wife of Moses Freeman). Exec'r, bro. Daniel. Wits., John Sims, Nehemiah Allen, James VanDyke. Prob. Nov. 28, 1774. Arch. vol. A44, page 86. Reg. of Wills, Liber L, folio 167.

Hawkens, John. Farmer. Will. Made Aug. 15, 1774. Duck Creek Hd. Heirs: wife Jean; bro. William; nephews John & Jacob Hawkens, sons of bro. William. Exec'rs, wife Jean & bro. William. Wits., Moses Thompson, Joseph Robinson, Allen Palmetree. Prob. Dec. 8, 1774. Arch. vol. A23, pages 27-29. Reg. of Wills, Liber L, folio 158. Note:—Arch. vol. A23, page 28 shows that Jean Hawkens married James Lewis.

Sipple, Mary. Widow. Will. Made Aug. 26, 1767. Heirs: sons Waitman, Elijah, Jonathan; daus. Ann Furbee, Miriam Barratt; John, Caleb, Garratt, Thomas, Mary & Elizabeth Sipple & Nancy Mott (children of son Caleb). Exec'rs, sons Jonathan & Elijah. Wits., Andrew Butler, John Williams, Ann Richardson. Prob. Dec. 8, 1774. Arch. vol. A46, page 152. Reg. of Wills, Liber L, folio 159.

Hillford, David. Yeoman. Mispillion Hd. Admin. of, to Sarah Hillford, widow. Dec. 19, 1774. Arch. vol. A23, pages 223-224. Reg. of Wills, Liber L, folio 159.

Hillford, Ann. Admin. of, to Thomas Hillford, next of kin, D. B. N. Dec. 19, 1774. Arch. vol. A23, page 222. Reg. of Wills, Liber L, folio 159.

Slocom, Benjamin. Yeoman. Murderkill Hd. Admin. of, to Joseph Slocom, next of kin. Dec. 20, 1774. Arch. vol. A46, pages 236-237. Reg. of Wills, Liber L, folio 159. Note:—Arch. vol. A46, page 237 mentions heirs, Ann Downam (wife of Thomas Downam), Thomas Green, Mary, Elizabeth, John & Joseph Slocom, . . . Marcollester.

Walker, William. Yeoman. Will. Made Nov. . . . 1774. Mispillion Hd. Heirs: wife Susanna; sons John & William; daus. Mary & Ailse Walker. Exec'rs, wife Susanna & friend Henry Molleston. Wits., Samuel Meredith, Winlock Hall, Abraham Griffith. Prob. Dec. 21, 1774. Arch. vol. A52, pages 202-203. Reg. of Wills, Liber L, folio 159. Note:—Will mentions father John Walker, dec'd.

Beauchamp, John. Admin. of, to Grace Beauchamp, widow. Dec. 31, 1774. Reg. of Wills, Liber L, folio 160.

Evan, David. [C. 1775]. Duck Creek Hd. Admin. of, to Joshua Evan. Arch. vol. A16, page 220.

Simpson, John. Yeoman. Will. Made March 17, 1772. Heirs: sons Robert, John; dau. Mary. Exec'r, son John. Wits., David Hilford, Samuel Smith, John Richards. Prob. Jan. 4, 1775. Arch. vol. A46, page 63. Reg. of Wills, Liber L, folio 160.

Bohannon [Buckhannan], Robert. Admin. of, to Lydia Bohannon, widow. Jan. 12, 1775. Reg. of Wills, Liber L, folio 160. Note:—Arch. vol. A6, page 117 shows that Lydia Bohannon married . . . Lewis.

Barber, Abraham. Admin. of, to Rachel Barber, widow. Jan. 16, 1775. Arch. vol. A2, pages 112-113. Reg. of Wills, Liber L, folio 160. Note:—Arch. vol. A2, page 112 shows that Rachel Barber married Peter Miller; page 113 mentions heirs, Priscilla, Francis, Joseph, Robert, Jonathan & Ann Barber.

Steelman, John. Admin. of, to Daniel Morris. Jan. 17, 1775. Arch. vol. A48, page 211. Reg. of Wills, Liber L, folio 160.

Vanhoy, Abraham. Admin. of, to Abraham Vanhoy, the younger. Jan. 20, 1775. Arch. vol. A52, page 3. Reg. of Wills, Liber L, folio 160.

Lowder, Ralph. Admin. of, to James Thompson. Jan. 25, 1775. Reg. of Wills, Liber L, folio 160.

Sipple, William. Admin. of, to William Sipple, the younger. Jan. 26, 1775. Reg. of Wills, Liber L, folio 160.

Dixon, Sarah. Widow. Little Creek Hd. Admin. of, to William Dixon, next of kin. Jan. 28, 1775. Arch. vol. A14, page 146. Reg. of Wills, Liber L, folio 161.

Blundel, Susanna. Admin. of, to Ezekiel Needham & Jonathan Needham. Jan. 30, 1775. Arch. vol. A4, page 168. Reg. of Wills, Liber L, folio 161.

Fields, John. Duck Creek Hd. Admin. of, to Rachel Fields, widow. Jan. 31, 1775. Arch. vol. A17, pages 99-106. Reg. of Wills, Liber L, folio 161. Note:—Arch. vol. A17, page 100 shows that Rachel Fields married Jacob Jones; page 102 shows that Rachel later married Solomon Barnet; pages 99 & 106 mentions heirs, Mary, Ann, Sarah, John Fields & Elizabeth Harris, wife of George Harris.

Messex [Mezicks], Julien. Admin. of, to Jonathan Pleasonton. Feb. 10, 1775. Arch. vol. A34, page 230. Reg. of Wills, Liber L, folio 161.

Pratt, Mary. Widow. Will. Made May 20, 1774. Murderkill Hd. Heirs: sons Nathan, Luke, Frederick, George; daus. Ann Reed, Dinah Clampitt, Mary Pratt; granddau. Mary Taylor. Exec'r, son Nathan. Wits., Patrick Crain, John Pegg, Sarah Pratt. Prob. Feb. 11, 1775. Arch. vol. A41, pages 120-123. Reg. of Wills, Liber L, folios 161 & 230.

Manlove, Sarah. Admin. of, to Asa Manlove, next of kin. Feb. 11, 1775. Arch. vol. A33, page 121. Reg. of Wills, Liber L, folio 161.

Darling, John. Admin. of, to Richard Burris, next of kin. Feb. 20, 1775. Reg. of Wills, Liber L, folio 161.

Cullen, John. Admin. of, to Hannah Cullen & Thomas Sheriff. Feb. 27, 1775. Reg. of Wills, Liber L, folio 161. Note:— Arch. vol. A12, page 88 shows that Hannah Cullen married Rhodes Clarke.

Furbee, Benjamin. Murderkill Hd. Admin. of, to Sarah Furbee, widow. Feb. 28, 1775. Arch. vol. A18, page 149. Reg. of Wills, Liber L, folio 161.

Porter, William. Admin. of, to Sarah Porter, widow. March 2, 1775. Arch. vol. A40, pages 205 & 209. Reg. of Wills, Liber L, folio 161. Note:—Arch. vol. A40, page 205 shows that Sarah Porter married Edmund Baily.

Morgan, Marmaduke. Weaver. Will. Made July 1, 1772. Mispillion Hd. Heirs: wife Sarah; dau. Mary; sons Jonathan, John, Evan, William, Thomas, James. Exec'rs, wife Sarah & son Thomas. Wits., William Stanford, Elijah Morris, Boas Morris. Prob. March 2, 1775. Arch. vol. A36, page 159. Reg. of Wills, Liber L, folio 161.

Crapper, Zadok. Admin. of, to Mary Crapper, widow. March 6, 1775. Arch. vol. A11, pages 210-212. Reg. of Wills, Liber L, folio 162. Note:—Arch. vol. A11, page 212 mentions a dau. Sarah Caldwell, wife of Timothy Caldwell; also shows that Mary Crapper later married James Johnson, Sr.

Molleston, Jonathan. Yeoman. Mispillion Hd. Admin. of, to Elizabeth Molleston, widow. March 8, 1775. Arch. vol. A35, pages 214-217. Reg. of Wills, Liber L, folio 162. Note:— Arch. vol. A35, page 216 shows that Elizabeth Molleston married John Sipple.

Darling, William. Admin. of, to Anne Darling, widow. March 12, 1775. Reg. of Wills, Liber L, folio 162.

Pickerell, Youell. Admin. of, to William Pickerell, next of kin. March 20, 1775. Arch. vol. A40, page 62. Reg. of Wills, Liber L, folio 162.

Caldwell, Andrew. Will. Made Oct. 5, 1774. Heirs: wife Mary; son David; dau. Jean Gray; grandsons Andrew Gray, Andrew Reynolds (son of dau. Ann Reynolds), William Reynolds; granddau. Jean Reynolds. Exec'r, William Gray, merchant. Wits., Thomas Buckmaster, Samuel Smith, Ruth Smith. Prob. April 8, 1775. Arch. vol. A7, pages 87-99 & A20, page 39. Reg. of Wills, Liber L, folios 162-166.

Craige, Analena. Widow. Will. Made Jan. 3, 1775. Murderkill Hd. Heirs: son Samuel; daus. Isabel & Nanny Craige. Exec'rs, nephew James Craige & dau. Isabel. Wits., Alexander Craige, Benjamin McBride, Anne Craige. Prob. April 5, 1775. Arch. vol. A11, pages 149-151. Reg. of Wills, Liber L, folio 168. Note:—Will mentions son Moses, dec'd.

Gilder, Reubin. Will. Made March 17, 1775. Heirs: sons Henry, John, Reubin; daus. Ann Adkison, Elizabeth Gilder. Exec'rs, sons Henry, John. Wits., William Peirce, Train Caldwell, Charles Emory. Prob. April 5, 1775. Arch. vol. A19, page 38. Reg. of Wills, Liber L, folio 168.

Greenwood, Robert. Carpenter. Will. Made April 5, 1775. Heirs: wife Mary; dau. Sarah; James Hagon; Elizabeth Hagon; Rachel Greenwood; friend John Gray, blacksmith. Exec'r, John Gray. Wits., Solomon Wallace, Coe Gordon. Prob. April 24, 1775. Arch. vol. A20, page 159. Reg. of Wills, Liber L, folios 168-169.

Steward [Stewart], Thomas. Will. Made April 10, 1775. Little Creek Hd. Heirs: wife Mary; dau. Sarah; sister Jane Steward; children of dec'd bro. Charles; nephews Henry & John Steward. Exec'x, wife Mary. Wits., Richard Smith, Hugh Sutter, James Raymond. Prob. April 23, 1775. Arch. vol. A49, page 11. Reg. of Wills, Liber L, folio 169.

Greenwood, Robert. Admin. of, to William Manlove. April 24, 1775. Arch. vol. A20, page 160. Reg. of Wills, Liber L, folio 169.

Miers, Thomas. Admin. of, to John Banning. May 8, 1775. Reg. of Wills, Liber L, folio 169.

Trippet, Govey. Admin. of, to Rachael Trippet. May 16, 1775. Arch. vol. A51, pages 76-78. Reg. of Wills, Liber L, folio 169. Note:—Arch. vol. A51, page 76 mentions heirs, Jonathan, John, Mary & Alice Trippet; page 77 shows that Rachel Trippet married Elisha West.

Humphries, William. Yeoman. Little Creek Hd. Admin. of, to Martha Humphries, widow. May 19, 1775. Arch. vol. A25, page 130. Reg. of Wills, Liber L, folio 170.

Miller, Killen. Admin. of, to Mary Miller, widow. May 19, 1775. Reg. of Wills, Liber L, folio 170.

Hunn, Caleb. Admin. of, to Susannah Lewis, next of kin. June 3, 1775. Reg. of Wills, Liber L, folio 170.

Lewis, Stephen. Admin. of, to Susannah Lewis, widow, & Jonathan Pleasontine. June 3, 1775. Reg. of Wills, Liber L, folio 170. Note:—Arch. vol. A30, page 141 shows that Susannah Lewis married John Brady.

Edwards, John. Admin. of, to Andrew Edwards & Philemon Dill. June 5, 1775. Arch. vol. A16, page 75. Reg. of Wills, Liber L, folio 170.

Jones, Lewis. Admin. of, to Catharine Jones, widow, & Elija Chance. July 1, 1775. Reg. of Wills, Liber L, folio 170. Note:—Arch. vol. A27, page 244 shows that Catherine Jones married John Martin.

Cullen, Jonathan. Will. Made June 16, 1775. Mispillion Hd. Heirs: wife Nancy; bros. George & Elias; nephews John & Charles Cullen, sons of bro. George; Mary Crapper, Jr., dau. of Zadoc Crapper, Esq. Exec'rs, wife Nancy & wife's father Benjamin Rasin. Wits., John Haslet, Solomon Davis, John Taylor. Prob. July 12, 1775. Arch. vol. A12, pages 89-91. Reg. of Wills, Liber L, folio 170. Note:—Arch. vol. A12, page 90 shows that Nancy Cullen married John Taylor.

Smith, Joseph. Yeoman. Will. Made March 1, 1772. Duck Creek Hd. Heirs: wife Mary; son Charles; daus. Elizabeth Stevenson, Sophiah Craigh, Mary Smith; John Matthews, orphan. Exec'rs, wife Mary & son Charles. Wits., Thomas Tilton, Silas Snow. Prob. July 17, 1775. Arch. vol. A47, page 102. Reg. of Wills, Liber L, folios 170-171.

Crumpton, John. Mispillion Hd. Admin. of, to Mary Crumpton & Curtis Crumpton. July 17, 1775. Arch. vol. A12, pages 35-36. Reg. of Wills, Liber L, folio 171.

Allee, Jonathan. Admin. of, to Sarah Allee, widow. July 17, 1775. Arch. vol. A1, pages 65-66. Reg. of Wills, Liber L, folio 171. Note:—Arch. vol. A1, page 66 mentions heirs, Elizabeth, Ann & Abraham Allee & Mary Liston, Sarah Conner.

Buckingham, Howell. Will. Made Dec. 16, 1774. Little Creek Hd. Heirs: son Isaac; sister Elizabeth Price; granddau. Barbary Buckingham; niece Margret Price, dau. of sister Elizabeth Price. Exec'r, son Isaac. Wits., Cuthbert Green, Samuel Reah, Daniel Cummins. Prob. July 22, 1775. Arch. vol. A6, pages 124-127. Reg. of Wills, Liber L, folio 171. Note:— Arch. vol. A6, page 126 shows the acct. later settled by Margaret Lamb, late Margaret Buckingham; also shows Barbary Buckingham as wife of John Numbers.

Jackson, William. Admin. of, to Ruth Jackson, widow. Aug. 9, 1775. Arch. vol. A26, pages 59-60. Reg. of Wills, Liber L, folio 171. Note:—Arch. vol. A26, page 60 shows that Ruth Jackson married Samuel Wheelor; also mentions heirs, Thomas, Joseph, William, Ruth, Caleb, Jonathan, Mary, Susannah & James Jackson & Elizabeth Warran.

Munt, Robert. Admin. of, to Mary Munt, widow. Aug. 9, 1775. Reg. of Wills, Liber L, folio 171.

Parkeson, Christopher. Admin. of, to Sarah Parkeson, widow. Aug. 10, 1775. Reg. of Wills, Liber L, folio 171.

Parkerson, Thomas. Admin. of, to Sarah Parkerson, D. B. N. Aug. 10, 1775. Reg. of Wills, Liber L, folio 172.

Beaucham, Robert. Yeoman. Will. Made April 3, 1772. Heirs: wife Hester; sons Jessy, John, Conston, Stephen, Levy; dau. Grace Handy, wife of William Handy. Exec'rs, wife Hester & son Coston. Wits., Jonathan Emerson, Benjamin Chipman & Henry Clampitt. Prob. Aug. 18, 1775. Arch. vol. A3, pages 126-127. Reg. of Wills, Liber L, folio 172.

West, Benjamin. Will. Made April 18, 1775. Duck Creek Hd. Heirs: bro. Joseph; sisters Ann & Mary; niece Jamima Sorency; nephew David West, son of Joseph. Exec'r, bro. Joseph. Wits., Daniel David, Thomas Hackett, Daniel David, Jr. Prob. Aug. 12, 1775. Arch. vol. A54, page 9. Reg. of Wills, Liber L, folio 172.

Snow, William, Jr. Duck Creek Hd. Admin. of, to Silas Snow, next of kin. Sept. 7, 1775. Arch. vol. A48, page 30. Reg. of Wills, Liber L, folio 172.

Whiteacre, Isaac. Farmer. Mispillion Hd. Admin. of, to Mary Ann Whiteacre, widow. Sept. 12, 1775. Reg. of Wills, Liber L, folio 172. Note:—Arch. vol. A54, page 82 shows that Mary Ann Whiteacre married John Furchase.

Wood, John, Jr. Admin. of, to Elizabeth Wood, widow. Sept. 12, 1775. Arch. vol. A56, pages 75-77. Reg. of Wills, Liber L, folio 172. Note:—Arch. vol. A56, page 76 shows that Elizabeth Wood married William Pearce; page 77 shows that Elizabeth Pearce later married Daniel Smith.

Hare, Lydia. Admin. of, to James Cummins, next of kin. Sept. 12, 1775. Arch. vol. A22, page 88. Reg. of Wills, Liber L, folio 173.

Duncan, John. Admin. of, to Elizabeth Duncan, widow. Sept. 13, 1775. Arch. vol. A15, pages 114-115. Reg. of Wills, Liber L, folio 173. Note:—Arch. vol. A15, page 114 mentions a son William Duncan.

Dawson, John. Admin. of, to Rachel Dawson, widow. Oct. 13, 1775. Reg. of Wills, Liber L, folio 173.

Chance, Elijah. Yeoman. Will. Made Oct. 10, 1775. Little Creek Hd. Heirs: wife Lydia; dau. Mary; bro. Alexander. Exec'r, friend Jacob Stout. Wits., Evan Jones, David Evans, John Matthews. Prob. Oct. 31, 1775. Arch. vol. A8, pages 147-150, 154. Reg. of Wills, Liber L, folio 173. Note:—Arch. vol. A8, page 148 shows that Lydia Chance married Amon Owen.

Loftis, John, Sr. Will. Made May 5, 1774. Murtherkill Hd. Heirs: wife Sarah; sons John, Joseph, Burton; daus. Rebeckah Dill, Sarah Clark, Anna Dill; Jemima Chance. Exec'r, son Burton. Wits., George Upton, Jr., John Burton Scully. Codicil, Absolam Clark & wife Sarah; John Clark, son of Absolam. Wits., John Burton Scully, William Douglass. Prob. Nov. 6, 1775. Arch. vol. A31, pages 50-52. Reg. of Wills, Liber L, folios 173-174.

Galloway, Joseph. Admin. of, to John Bell. Nov. 14, 1775. Reg. of Wills, Liber L, folio 174.

Peterkin, Thomas. Will. Made Oct. 10, 1775. Heirs: wife Rhoda; dau. Rhoda; heirs of John Peterkin & Comfort Curtes; nephews Thomas Black, Tobias Furches, Thomas Peterkin (son of bro. John). Exec'x, wife Rhoda. Wits., Izariah Richardson, Stephen Jarril, Mary Hilford. Prob. Nov. 15, 1775. Arch. vol. A40, pages 7-8 & 10. Reg. of Wills, Liber L, folios 174-175. Note:—Arch. vol. A40, page 8 shows this acct. later administered by Cary Tomlenson.

Scotton, James. Will. Made Sept. 30, 1775. Heirs: wife Ann; sons John & James; dau. Ann Rolf, Marah, Elisabeth & Araminta Scotton. Exec'r, John, son. Wits., John Scotten, Thomas Jackson, William Abbott. Prob. Nov. 15, 1775. Arch. vol. A45, pages 76-77. Reg. of Wills, Liber G, appendix 7.

Freeman, William. Admin. of, to Ann Freeman, widow. Nov. 18, 1775. Reg. of Wills, Liber L, folio 175.

Gibbs, Edward. Merchant. Will. Made Nov. 6, 1775. Murderkill Hd. Heirs: wife Mary; sons Benjamin, Joseph, John, Edward, Thomas; daus. Ann & Elizabeth; sister Margaret Hook. Exec'rs, wife Mary & son Benjamin. Wits., Selah Tomlin, George Wallace, John Tomlin. Prob. Nov. 20, 1775. Arch. vol. A19, pages 16-18. Reg. of Wills, Liber L, folio 175.

Meroney, William, Sr. Will. Made Jan. 20, 1775. Mispillion Hd. Heirs: wife Exsprance; son William; grandson Olauar Meroney; daus. Elizabeth Colweel, Mary Turley. Exec'x, wife. Wits., John Parsons, Mary Parsons, Elizabeth Crippen. Prob. Nov. 21, 1775. Arch. vol. A34, page 224. Reg. of Wills, Liber L, folios 175-176.

Wells, James, Sr. Admin. of, to James Wells, Jr., next of kin. Nov. 21, 1775. Arch. vol. A53, page 230. Reg. of Wills, Liber L, folio 176.

Numbers, John. Admin. of, to Mary Numbers, widow. Nov. 23, 1775. Arch. vol. A38, pages 78-80. Reg. of Wills, Liber L, folio 176.

Douglass, Adam. Admin. of, to James McMullan. Nov. 27, 1775. Reg. of Wills, Liber L, folio 176.

Morgan, Jacob. Yeoman. Murderkill Hd. Admin. of, to Martha Morgan, widow. Dec. 1, 1775. Arch. vol. A36, page 151. Reg. of Wills, Liber L, folio 176.

Smith, Denton. Admin. of, to Benjamin Smith & Arthur Whitely. Dec. 6, 1775. Reg. of Wills, Liber L, folio 176.

Meridith, Joshua. Yeoman. Murderkill Hd. Admin. of, to Ruth Meridith & Luff Meridith. Dec. 28, 1775. Arch. vol. A34, page 200. Reg. of Wills, Liber L, folio 176.

Hamilton, Robert. Admin. of, to Jacob Stout, Esq. Jan. 1, 1776. Arch. vol. A21, page 170. Reg. of Wills, Liber L, folio 176.

Vandyke, Daniel. Admin. of, to James Vandyke, next of kin. Jan. 5, 1776. Reg. of Wills, Liber L, folio 176.

Suitter, Hugh. Admin. of, to Sarah Barnet, next of kin. Jan. 9, 1776. Arch. vol. A49, page 126. Reg. of Wills, Liber L, folio 176.

Collings, Johnathan. Farmer. Will. Made Dec. 19, 1775. Heirs: wife Mary; sons Curtes, Richard, Alaxander; a child unnamed; dau. Betsay. Exec'x, wife Mary. Wits., Jehu Turner, Samuel Johnson, Isaac Cordery. Prob. Jan. 11, 1776. Arch. vol. A9, page 222 & vol. A10, page 6. Reg. of Wills, Liber L, folios 176-177. Note:—Arch. vol. A10, page 6 shows Mary Collins as wife of Isaac Coudery.

Matthews, Joseph. Admin. of, to John Gordon. Jan. 13, 1776. Reg. of Wills, Liber L, folio 177.

Carrow, John. Admin. of, to Elizabeth Carrow, widow. Jan. 20, 1776. Arch. vol. A7, page 243. Reg. of Wills, Liber L, folio 177.

Hamilton, Robert. Will (nunc.). Made Dec. 30, 1775. Heir: Negro man Naull be free. Wits., Matthew Montgomery, Mary Newnam, Benjamin Keys. Prob. Jan. 18, 1776. Arch. vol. A21, page 169. Reg. of Wills, Liber L, folio 179.

Powell, Joseph. Will. Made Nov. 20, 1774. Heirs: sons William, John; daus. Mary Maxwell (wife of Thomas), Ann Freeman (wife of William), Sarah Downham (wife of Joseph); children of dau. Mary Maxwell; child of dau. Hannah Downham, dec'd, wife of Richard Downham. Exec'rs, sons John & William. Wits., Alexander Winford, George Spencer, Benjamin Brown, Thomas Anderson. Codicil. Wits., John Beauchamp, Christopher Green. Prob. Feb. 19, 1776. Arch. vol. A41, pages 83-84. Reg. of Wills, Liber L, folio 177.

Price, Joseph. Will. Made Oct. 22, 1774. Heirs: son William; daus. Mary Jackson, Elizabeth Price. Exec'r, Philip Barratt. Trustee, Philip Barratt. Wits., Caleb Furbee, Moses Crankfeald, Sarah Killingsworth. Prob. Feb. 21, 1776. Arch. vol. A41, pages 151 & 153. Reg. of Wills, Liber L, folio 178.

Moore, John. Admin. of, to Ann Moore, widow. Feb. 23, 1776. Arch. vol. A42, page 231. Reg. of Wills, Liber L, folio 178.

Teat, Robert. Admin. of, to Rhoda Teat, widow. Feb. 24, 1776. Reg. of Wills, Liber L, folio 178.

Hyat, Mary. Will. Made Dec. 6, 1775. Heirs: sons George & David Johnston; dau. Mary Dunning; grandchildren Samuel, David, John Nichols (sons of Samuel Nichols). Exec'r, son-in-law William Dunning. Wits., Francis Many, Mary Many, Nancey Sipple. Prob. Feb. 26, 1776. Arch. vol. A25, page 207. Reg. of Wills, Liber L, folio 178.

Mastin, Sarah. Widow of William Mastin. Mispillion Hd. Admin. of, to William Mastin, next of kin. March 1, 1776. Arch. vol. A34, pages 48-51. Reg. of Wills, Liber L, folio 178. Note:—Arch. vol. A34, page 48 mentions heirs, William, John & David Mastin, Mary Green, Sarah Morris & Deborah Morris.

Mastin, William. Farmer. Mispillion Hd. Admin. of, to William Mastin, Jr., next of kin, D. B. N. March 1, 1776. Arch. vol. A34, pages 53-54 & 56. Reg. of Wills, Liber L, folio 179. Note:—Arch. vol. A34, page 53 mentions heirs, William, Deborah, John & David Mastin, Mary Green & Sarah Morris.

David, Lewis. Admin. of, to Elizabeth David, widow. March 26, 1776. Reg. of Wills, Liber L, folio 179.

Sapp, William. Admin. of, to Philip Hillyard, next of kin. March 27, 1776. Reg. of Wills, Liber L, folio 179.

Vangaskin, John, Sr. Admin. of, to Sarah Vangaskin & John Vangaskin, Jr. March 27, 1776. Reg. of Wills, Liber L, folio 179.

Soward, George. Yeoman. Will. Made March 10, 1776. Heirs: wife Elenor; sons Thomas & George; daus. Susannah Shahan, Sarah, Rebecca; granddaus. Sarah Swift, Elenor Thomas; grandsons George (son of son Thomas), George (son of son George). Exec'rs, wife Elenor, sons Thomas & George. Wits., Richard Lockwood, John Wilson, John Vandeford. Prob. March 27, 1776. Arch. vol. A45, page 151 & vol. A48, pages 59-60. Reg. of Wills, Liber L, folio 179.

Jester, Charles. Admin. of, to Joshua Jester, next of kin. April 11, 1776. Reg. of Wills, Liber L, folio 179.

Muncey, Levey. Admin. of, to Margaret Muncey & Armwell Lockwood. April 20, 1776. Arch. vol. A37, pages 75-76. Reg. of Wills, Liber L, folio 179. Note:—Arch. vol. A37 mentions heirs, Thomas, James, John, Levy, Isabella & Margaret Muncey, Mary Hatfield (wife of Levy Hatfield) & Gartery Shaw (wife of Hugh Shaw).

Dixon, William. Admin. of, to Michael Cary Aaron, next of kin. April 23, 1776. Arch. vol. A14, page 148. Reg. of Wills, Liber L, folio 180.

Dixon, Sarah. Admin. of, to Michael Cary Aaron, next of kin, D. B. N. May 15, 1776. Reg. of Wills, Liber L, folio 180.

Virdin, Daniel. Admin. of, to Elizabeth Virdin, widow. May 15, 1776. Arch. vol. A52, pages 83-86. Reg. of Wills, Liber L, folio 180. Note:—Arch. vol. A52, page 83 mentions heirs, Neomah, Sarah, Alexander & Eleanor Virdin; page 84 shows that Elizabeth Virdin married Joseph Jackson.

Oliver, Reubin. Admin. of, to Edward Fisher & John Furchase. May 29, 1776. Arch. vol. A38, page 129. Reg. of Wills, Liber L, folio 180.

Purden, James. Admin. of, to Mary Purden, widow. May 29, 1776. Arch. vol. A41, pages 214-218. Reg. of Wills, Liber L, folio 180. Note:—Arch. vol. A41, page 218 shows Mary Purden married James Gordon; page 214 shows she later married John Tumlin.

Meridith, Samuel. Admin. of, to Jacob Meridith, next of kin. June 6, 1776. Reg. of Wills, Liber L, folio 180.

Leby, Cadrup. Admin. of, to Levin Wainright. June 18, 1776. Reg. of Wills, Liber L, folio 180.

Derham, John, Jr. Admin. of, to John Derham, Sr. June 19, 1776. Reg. of Wills, Liber L, folio 180.

Holliday, William. Will. Made May 3, 1776. Duck Creek Hd. Heirs: bros. Benjamin, John; sisters Mary, Hannah & Rachel; nephew Samuel Watkins. Exec'r, Robert Watkins. Guardian, Robert Watkins, father of nephew Samuel. Wits., George Barkhurst, Joseph Barkhurst, Philip Cox, Thomas Watkins. Prob. June 29, 1776. Arch. vol. A24, pages 218-221. Reg. of Wills, Liber L, folio 180.

Sutton, John. Admin. of, to Jonathan Hunn, next of kin. Aug. 1, 1776. Reg. of Wills, Liber L, folio 180.

Primrose, John. Admin. of, to Jonathan Hunn, next of kin. Aug. 1, 1776. Arch. vol. A41, page 162. Reg. of Wills, Liber L, folio 181.

Murphy, John. Admin. of, to Mary Murphy, widow. Aug. 6, 1776. Reg. of Wills, Liber L, folio 181.

Numbers, Anne. Admin. of, to Michael Numbers, next of kin. Aug. 28, 1776. Reg. of Wills, Liber L, folio 181.

Pearce, Joseph. Admin. of, to William Pearce, next of kin. Sept. 18, 1776. Arch. vol. A39, pages 156-157. Reg. of Wills, Liber L, folio 181.

McKinstry, Richard. Admin. of, to Mary McKinstry, widow. Oct. 5, 1776. Arch. vol. A32, pages 216-217. Reg. of Wills, Liber L, folio 181.

Benn, James. Admin. of, to Sarah Benn & John Ralston. Oct. 7, 1776. Reg. of Wills, Liber L, folio 181.

Moore, John. Yeoman. Will. Made April 21, 1776. Duck Creek Hd. Heirs: wife Heneritta; daus. Angelica Raymond, Rachel Allee, Elizabeth Moore; son-in-law James Raymond. Exec'rs, wife Heneritta & son-in-law James Raymond. Wits., John Barratt, Jacob Hill. Prob. Oct. 12, 1776. Arch. vol. A36, pages 54-55 & 34-36. Reg. of Wills, Liber L, folio 181.

Knight, John. Will. [N. d.]. Heirs: sons Caesar & Daniel; heirs of dau. Elizabeth Ryan, dec'd; dau. Sarah Knight. Exec'r, son Caesar. Wits., John Boyd, George Stevans, John Vannoy. Prob. Oct. 14, 1776. Arch. vol. A29, page 61. Reg. of Wills, Liber L, folio 181.

Emerson, Michael. Admin. of, to Sarah Emerson, widow. Oct. 14, 1776. Reg. of Wills, Liber L, folio 182.

Tomlinson, Joseph. Yeoman. Will. Made June 7, 1776. Little Creek Hd. Heirs: sons John, Richard, Thomas; dau. Mary Parsons, wife of John Parsons; grandchildren Sophia Candy, Carry & Mary Tomlinson (children of son James, dec'd), Mary, Nathan, John, Isaac Meroney (children of dau. Rachel, dec'd). Exec'rs, sons John & Richard. Wits., James Sykes, Samuel Hanson, Jr., Abram Allee. Prob. Oct. 15, 1776. Arch. vol. A50, pages 203-204. Reg. of Wills, Liber L, folio 182.

Newell, William. Tailor. Will. Made Dec. 21, 1769. Murderkill Hd. Heirs: bro. Henry; sisters Miriam, Lyday; children of sister Hannah; sister Tabitha. Exec'rs, bro. Henry. Wits., John Mileway, Morgan Dugerty. Prob. Oct. 17, 1776. Arch. vol. A37, pages 202-203. Reg. of Wills, Liber L, folio 182.

Pearce, Isabella. Widow of Joseph Pearce, dec'd. Duck Creek Hd. Admin. of, to William Pearce, next of kin. Oct. 18, 1776. Arch. vol. A40, page 68. Reg. of Wills, Liber L, folio 183.

Howell, James. Admin. of, to Obedience Howell, widow. Oct. 22, 1776. Reg. of Wills, Liber L, folio 183.

Macknatt, William. Will. Made Nov. 14, 1775. Mispillion Hd. Heirs: wife Mary; sons Richard, William & Joseph; daus. Ruth, Sarah, Mary, Jean, Cathorin, Ann & Rachel; Major Macknatt, son of Richard. Exec'rs, wife Mary & William Macknatt. Wits., Samuel Graham, Solomon Griffith, Rachael Graham. Prob. Oct. 23, 1776. Arch. vol. A33, pages 23-24. Reg. of Wills, Liber L, folio 183.

Forster, Matthew. Will. Made Jan. 1, 1776. Duck Creek Hd. Heirs: wife Rebeccah; dau. Mary Forster; Elizabeth Ashford; mother unnamed. Exec'rs, wife Rebeccah & Isaac Carty. Wits., Samuel Wilson, James Vandyke, William Fields. Prob. Oct. 24, 1776. Arch. vol. A18, page 34. Reg. of Wills, Liber L, folio 183.

New, John. Yeoman. Murderkill Hd. Admin. of, to Joshua Dewees, next of kin. Oct. 25, 1776. Arch. vol. A37, page 181. Reg. of Wills, Liber L, folio 183.

Morris, William. Admin. of, to Thomas Morris & Eliphaz Morris, next of kin. Oct. 31, 1776. Reg. of Wills, Liber L, folio 184.

Kimmey, William. Will. Made July 14, 1776. Mispillion Hd. Heirs: wife Levicy; bro. Robert. Exec'x, wife Levicy. Wits., Major Anderson, Joshua Gullet, Solomon Kimmey. Prob. Nov. 5, 1776. Arch. vol. A29, pages 16-17. Reg. of Wills, Liber L, folio 184. Note:—Arch. vol. A29, page 17 shows that Levicy Kimmey married William Laws.

Allee, Mary. Widow of Abraham Allee, Sr. Will. Made Nov. 10, 1776. Duck Creek Hd. Heirs: grandsons John Tilton, Abraham Allee (son of Jonathan & Sarah Allee); grandchildren Ann Allee, Sarah, James, Rachel & Thomas Tilton (children of Thomas & Sabrah Tilton), Mary Liston, Sarah, Elizabeth & Ann Allee (children of Jonathan & Sarah Allee); son-in-law Thomas Tilton; son Janathan. Exec'r, son-in-law Thomas Tilton. Wits., James Raymond, Richard Hall. Prob. Nov. 20, 1776. Arch. vol. A1, page 68. Reg. of Wills, Liber L, folio 184.

Ebtharp, Elizabeth. Admin. of, to Mary Numbers, next of kin, D. B. N. Nov. 27, 1776. Arch. vol. A15, pages 236-237. Reg. of Wills, Liber L, folio 185. Note:—Arch. vol. A15, page 236 mentions heirs, Elizabeth, Michael, Jacob, John, Sarah, Mary & Susannah Numbers (children of Peter Numbers); James, Thomas & Joseph Numbers (children of James Numbers); Mary & William Numbers (children of John Numbers).

Hunn, Nathaniel. Will. Made Oct. 11, 1776. Heirs: son Jonathan; grandsons Skidmore Willson & Nathaniel Hunn. Exec'r, son Jonathan. Wits., Nathaniel Luff, Nathan Manlove, Edmond Bayly. Prob. Nov. 28, 1776. Arch. vol. A25, page 165. Reg. of Wills, Liber L, folio 193.

McCombs, Esther. Will. Made June 5, 1776. Heirs: dau. Elizabeth; sons John & Jonathan. Exec'r, bro. David Durborow. Guardians, sister Elizabeth Roe & bro. David Durborow. Wits., Daniel Durborow, Sary Quilling, Elizabeth Roe, Jr. Prob. Dec. 4, 1776. Arch. vol. A32, pages 135 & 137. Reg. of Wills, Liber L, folio 185. Note:—Will mentions dec'd father Hugh Durborow.

Morris, Joseph. Farmer. Mispillion Hd. Admin. of, to Phebe Morris, widow. Dec. 5, 1776. Arch. vol. A36, pages 222-223. Reg. of Wills, Liber L, folio 185.

Vanwinkle, Jacob. Admin. of, to Mary Vanwinkle, widow. Dec. 17, 1776. Reg. of Wills, Liber L, folio 185.

Ratledge, Thomas. Admin. of, to James Ratledge, next of kin. Dec. 19, 1776. Arch. vol. A42, page 109. Reg. of Wills, Liber L, folio 185.

Buckhannon, Robert. Murderkill Hd. Admin. of, to Jacob Stout, D. B. N. Dec. 19, 1776. Arch. vol. A6, pages 118-123. Reg. of Wills, Liber L, folio 185. Note:—Arch. vol. A6, page 121 mentions heirs, Mary, Nancy & Stout Buckhannon; page 118 shows that dau. Mary married . . . Murphy.

Lilly, Timothy. Admin. of, to Mary Lilly, widow, & Joseph Meeks. Dec. 21, 1776. Reg. of Wills, Liber L, folio 185. Note:—Arch. vol. A30, page 169 shows that Mary Lilly married Joseph Crafton.

Smith, William. Will. Made March 26, 1774. Heirs: wife Ann; son William; dau. Elizabeth. Exec'x, wife Ann. Wits., William Rea, James Smyth. Prob. Dec. 31, 1776. Arch. vol. A47, page 200. Reg. of Wills, Liber L, folios 185-186.

Chipman, Mary. Admin. of, to Susanna Libby & Reubin Shield, next of kin. Jan. 4, 1777. Reg. of Wills, Liber L, folio 186. Note:—Arch. vol. A8, page 188 shows that Susannah Libby later married Samuel Moore.

Reynolds, Richard. Farmer. Mispillion Hd. Admin. of, to Ruth Reynolds, widow. Jan. 29, 1777. Arch. vol. A43, pages 113-115. Reg. of Wills, Liber L, folio 186. Note:—Arch. vol. A43, page 114 mentions heirs, Henry & Eloner Reynolds.

Chrispen, Tabitha. Admin. of, to John Hunn, next of kin. Feb. 3, 1777. Reg. of Wills, Liber L, folio 186.

Thompson, Rachel. Admin. of, to Richard Jester & Richard McNatt. Feb. 10, 1777. Arch. vol. A50, page 105. Reg. of Wills, Liber L, folio 186.

Sundergill, Joshua. Admin. of, to Mary Sundergill, widow. Feb. 12, 1777. Arch. vol. A49, pages 123-124. Reg. of Wills, Liber L, folio 186. Note:—Arch. vol. A49, page 123 mentions heirs, Ann & Phebe Sundergill; page 124 shows that Mary Sundergill married Joseph Jamison.

Grimes, John. Admin. of, to Thomas Murphy. Feb. 13, 1777. Reg. of Wills, Liber L, folio 186.

White, Richard, the younger. Admin. of, to Rebecca White, widow. Feb. 15, 1777. Reg. of Wills, Liber L, folio 196.

Curry, William. Admin. of, to Mary Curry, widow. Feb. 28, 1777. Reg. of Wills, Liber L, folio 186.

Gardener, Mary. Admin. of, to William Rees. Feb. 28, 1777. Reg. of Wills, Liber L, folio 186.

Fields, James. Admin. of, to William Fields. March 4, 1777. Reg. of Wills, Liber L, folio 186.

Harrington, Gedion. Admin. of, to Nancy Harrington. March 4, 1777. Arch. vol. A22, page 95. Reg. of Wills, Liber L, folio 186.

Smith, Mary. Admin. of, to Charles Smith, next of kin. March 6, 1777. Arch. vol. A22, page 95. Reg. of Wills, Liber L, folio 186.

Haslet, John. Colonel. Will. Made Aug. 6, 1776. Mispillion Hd. Heirs: wife Jemima; sons Joseph & John; daus. Mary, Ann, Jemima. Exec'x, wife Jemima. Exec'r & guardian, friend William Killen, Esq. Wits., Vincent Loockerman, Robert McGarmant, Peter Torbert. Prob. March 6, 1777. Arch. vol. A22, pages 225-230. Reg. of Wills, Liber L, folios 186-187. Note:—Arch. vol. A22, page 226 shows that Ann Haslet married Major John Patten & Mary Haslet married . . . McGarment.

Watson, Pryor. Will. Made Feb. 6, 1777. Heirs: dau. Priscilla Watson; children of uncle John Pryor; John James & Hannah Irons. Exec'r, Nathaniel Nock. Wits., Daniel Cummins, George Cummins. Prob. March 8, 1777. Arch. vol. A53, pages 185-186. Reg. of Wills, Liber L, folio 187.

Stevans, George. Admin. of, Sarah Stevans, widow. March 10, 1777. Arch. vol. A48, page 214. Reg. of Wills, Liber L, folio 187.

Evans, David. Admin. of, to Jacob Stout, Esq. March 10, 1777. Arch. vol. A16, page 219. Reg. of Wills, Liber L, folio 187.

Brady, Jonathan. Admin. of, to Mary Ann Brady, widow. March 10, 1777. Arch. vol. A5, pages 133-134. Reg. of Wills, Liber L, folio 187.

Moor, Henniritta. Will. Made Nov. 24, 1776. Duck Creek Hd. Heirs: dau. Elizabeth; granddaus. Mary Raymond & Rebecca Moore. Exec'r, son-in-law James Raymond. Wits., Thomas Tilton, Enoch Miller. Prob. March 10, 1777. Arch. vol. A36, pages 20-21. Reg. of Wills, Liber L, folios 187-188.

Lewis, Richard. Will. Made Jan. 31, 1777. Heirs: wife Mary; sons Thomas, Henry; dau. Elizabeth. Exec'x, wife Mary. Wits., William Drew, John Seney. Prob. March 11, 1777. Arch. vol. A30, pages 124-127. Reg. of Wills, Liber L, folio 188. Note:—Arch. vol. A30, page 125 shows that Mary Lewis married Thomas Mansfield; page 126 mentions heirs, John & Richard Lewis.

Handy, William. Admin. of, to Grace Handy, widow. March 11, 1777. Reg. of Wills, Liber L, folio 188.

Felton, William. Admin. of, to Catharine Felton, widow. March 11, 1777. Reg. of Wills, Liber L, folio 188. Note:—Arch. vol. A17, page 119 mentions Catherine Felton later married . . . Shaw; also mentions heirs, Sarah, John, William & Robert Felton.

Miller, John, Jr. Doctor. Admin. of, to Benjamin Hazle. March 14, 1777. Arch. vol. A35, page 78. Reg. of Wills, Liber L, folio 188.

Haslet, Jemima. Widow of Col. John Haslet. Admin. of, to William Killen, Esq. March 14, 1777. Arch. vol. A22, pages 223-224. Reg. of Wills, Liber L, folio 188.

Dawson, Isaac. Admin. of, to Mary Dawson, widow. March 15, 1777. Arch. vol. A13, pages 99-100. Reg. of Wills, Liber L, folio 188. Note:—Arch. vol. A13, page 99 shows that Mary Dawson married Joseph Alford.

Lane, James. Admin. of, to John Lane, next of kin. March 23, 1777. Arch. vol. A29, page 115. Reg. of Wills, Liber L, folio 188.

Hutchison, James. Admin. of, to Mary Hutchison & William Hutchison. March 26, 1777. Arch. vol. A25, page 197. Reg. of Wills, Liber L, folio 189.

Bullock, Richard. Admin. of, to Mary Bullock, widow. March 28, 1777. Arch. vol. A6, pages 186-187. Reg. of Wills, Liber L, folio 189. Note:—Arch. vol. A6, page 186 mentions heirs, Thomas, Dorcus, Nancy & John Bullock; page 187 shows that Mary Bullock married Henry Fisher.

Jones, Jacob. Duck Creek Hd. Admin. of, to Rachael Jones & Robert Moore. March 28, 1777. Arch. vol. A27, pages 192-194. Reg. of Wills, Liber L, folio 189. Note:—Arch. vol. A27, page 192 mentions heirs, John, Jacob, James, Samuel, Enoch, Joseph & Millesant Jones & Martha Greenwood, wife of Joseph Greenwood; page 193 shows that Rachel Jones married Solomon Barnet.

Baker, William, Sr. Admin. of, to Sarah Baker, widow. April 2, 1777. Arch. vol. A2, page 84. Reg. of Wills, Liber L, folio 189.

Primrose, William. Admin. of, to Sarah Primrose, widow. April 4, 1777. Arch. vol. A41, pages 170-171. Reg. of Wills, Liber L, folio 189. Note:—Arch. vol. A41, page 170 mentions heirs, Thomas & Sarah Primrose; page 171 shows that Sarah Primrose married Samuel Pennywell.

Hawkins, William. Yeoman. Duck Creek Hd. Admin. of, to Thomas Hawkins, next of kin. April 7, 1777. Arch. vol. A23, pages 47-48. Reg. of Wills, Liber L, folio 189. Note:—Arch. vol. A23, page 47 mentions heirs, Moses, Elizabeth & Phebe Hawkins.

Craige, James. Laborer. Admin. of, to William Smith, next of kin. April 9, 1777. Reg. of Wills, Liber L, folio 189.

Robinson, Jordan. Admin. of, to Jean [Janet or Jennet] Parsons, next of kin. April 10, 1777. Arch. vol. A44, pages 70-73. Reg. of Wills, Liber L, folio 189.

Marker, Philip. Admin. of, to Mary Marker, widow. April 12, 1777. Arch. vol. A33, page 192. Reg. of Wills, Liber L, folio 189.

Colgan, John. Planter. Will. Made March 26, 1777. Heirs: wife unnamed; sons Richard, John, Edward, Isaac; daus. Mary, Elizabeth & Rachael. Exec'rs, son-in-law Matthew Norris & son Richard. Wits., David Angus, John Burrows, Benjamin Blackiston. Prob. April 24, 1777. Arch. vol. A9, page 220. Reg. of Wills, Liber L, folio 189.

Walker, John. Murderkill Hd. Admin. of, to Susanna Walker, widow. April 26, 1777. Arch. vol. A52, pages 188-191. Reg. of Wills, Liber L, folio 189. Note:—Arch. vol. A52, page 188 shows that Susanna Walker married William Johnson.

Barns, Thomas. Admin. of, to John Barns. April 28, 1777. Reg. of Wills, Liber L, folio 189.

Alexander, Richard. Admin. of, to Resdon Bishop. May 1, 1777. Reg. of Wills, Liber L, folio 190.

Howell, William. Farmer. Will. Made Sept. 29, 1775. St. Jones Hd. Heirs: sons John, Shadrach, William; daus. Anne Howell, Sarah & Reuhama. Exec'r, John Howell. Wits., Shadrack Bostick, Samuel French, George French. Prob. May 5, 1777. Arch. vol. A25, pages 82-84. Reg. of Wills, Liber L, folio 190.

Sipple, Silvey. Admin. of, to Daniel Cowgill, next of kin. May 9, 1777. Arch. vol. A46, page 160. Reg. of Wills, Liber L, folio 190.

Wallace, Solomon. Will. Made April 29, 1777. Heirs: wife Margaret; sons Reuben, Jonathan, William; daus. Elizabeth Clark, Ann Dixon, Mary Smith, Peggy Caldwell Gordon. Exec'x, wife Margaret. Wits., William Rhodes, Sarah Greenwood, Ann Brady. Prob. May 13, 1777. Arch. vol. A53, pages 10-13. Reg. of Wills, Liber L, folios 190-191. Note:— Arch. vol. A53, page 13 shows that Margaret Wallace married . . . Hendry.

Catts, William. Will. Made Dec. 23, 1776. Heirs: son unnamed. Exec'r, Joshua Nicholson. Wits., Thomas Peachey Coates, Thomas Hilford. Prob. May 13, 1777. Arch. vol. A8, page 104. Reg. of Wills, Liber L, folio 191.

Alexander, Richard. Admin. of, to Thomas Barnett, next of kin. May 15, 1777. Arch. vol. A1, page 22. Reg. of Wills, Liber L, folio 191.

Alexander, Margaret. Admin. of, to Thomas Barnett, next of kin. May 21, 1777. Arch. vol. A1, page 20. Reg. of Wills, Liber L, folio 191. Note:—Mentions an only child, Thomas Barnett.

Gildersleve, Elizabeth. Admin. of, to John Gildersleve, next of kin. May 30, 1777. Reg. of Wills, Liber L, folio 191.

Harminson, John. Will. Made May 9, 1777. Heirs: wife Sarah; sons Harmin, John & Isaac; dau. Ann. Exec'rs, wife Sarah & son Harmin. Wits., Jonathan Emerson, Edward Fisher, Hugh Fall. Prob. June 3, 1777. Arch. vol. A22, page 39. Reg. of Wills, Liber L, folios 191-192.

Brinckle, Joseph. Will. Made March 10, 1776. Heir: bro. William. Exec'r, bro. William. Wits., Reynear Williams, Thomas Right, Penelope Williams. Prob. June 17, 1777. Arch. vol. A5, page 191. Reg. of Wills, Liber L, folio 192.

Clampett, William. Admin. of, to Allice Clampett, widow. June 24, 1777. Reg. of Wills, Liber L, folio 192.

Neighbours, John. Admin. of, to Jonathan Neighbours, next of kin. July 19, 1777. Reg. of Wills, Liber L, folio 192.

Greenwood, Benjamin. Admin. of, to Elizabeth Greenwood, widow. July 30, 1777. Reg. of Wills, Liber L, folio 192.

Summers, William. Farmer. Will. Made June 25, 1777. Heirs: wife Elizabeth; children unnamed. Exec'rs, wife Elizabeth & son Major Summers. Wits., Samuel Kemp, John Morgan, Jonathan Finsthwait. Prob. Aug. 6, 1777. Arch. vol. A49, page 122. Reg. of Wills, Liber L, folios 192-193.

Lambert, John. Admin. of, to Susannah Lambert, widow. Aug. 13, 1777. Arch. vol. A29, pages 109-111. Reg. of Wills, Liber L, folio 193. Note:—Arch. vol. A29, page 110 mentions children as heirs, James, John, Levi & Sarah Lambert; and Henry Lambert, father.

Richardson, Azariah. Laborer. Mispillion Hd. Admin. of, to Elizabeth Richardson, widow. Aug. 13, 1777. Arch. vol. A43, page 162. Reg. of Wills, Liber L, folio 193.

Bennet, Andrew. Laborer. Will. Made July 27, 1777. Murderkill Hd. Heirs: wife [Sarah, from admin. acct.]; son John; other children unnamed. Exec'x, wife. Wits., Elias Wood, David Durborow, William Wilkenson. Prob. Aug. 18, 1777. Arch. vol. A3, pages 209-210. Reg. of Wills, Liber L, folio 193.

Rolph, William. Admin. of, to Richard Smith, Esq. Aug. 19, 1777. Arch. vol. A44, page 131. Reg. of Wills, Liber L, folio 193.

Cahoon, Mark. Gentleman. Will. Made Aug. 28, 1776. Duck Creek Hd. Heirs: sisters Elizabeth Elliott, Rachel Crosier, Jane Cahoon; niece Sarah, dau. of sister Jane. Exec'rs, bros. Thomas & Charles Cahoon. Wits., Thomas Cahoon, Hester Brown, Mary Brown. Prob. Aug. 28, 1777. Arch. vol. A7, page 36. Reg. of Wills, Liber L, folio 194.

Emerson, Philemon. Admin. of, to Miriam Emerson, next of kin. Sept. 29, 1777. Arch. vol. A16, pages 167-168. Reg. of Wills, Liber L, folio 194. Note:—Arch. vol. A16, page 167 shows Meriam Emerson as the wife of David Emerson.

Stradly, Dill. Admin. of, to Rebeccah Stradly, widow. Oct. 1, 1777. Arch. vol. A49, pages 59-61. Reg. of Wills, Liber L, folio 194. Note:—Arch. vol. A49, page 59 shows that Rebecca Stradly married Philemon Cubbage; page 60 mentions heirs, Shediru & Surepta Dill.

Williams, John, Sr. Will. Made Oct. 6, 1777. Heirs: daus. Ruth Sipple, Margaret, Sarah & Rachel; sons James & Absalom. Exec'rs, sons John & Caleb. Wits., Nathaniel Luff, Jr., Deborah Lewis, Caleb Luff. Prob. Oct. 22, 1777. Arch. vol. A55, pages 97-98. Reg. of Wills, Liber L, folio 194.

Steward, Catharine. Admin. of, to Mary Numbers, next of kin. Oct. 23, 1777. Reg. of Wills, Liber L, folio 194.

Nichols, Moses. Admin. of, to Ruth Nichols, widow. Nov. 5, 1777. Reg. of Wills, Liber L, folio 194.

Smith, Isaac. Admin. of, to Edmund Bealy, next of kin. Nov. 19, 1777. Reg. of Wills, Liber L, folio 194.

Manlove, Jonathan. Yeoman. Will. Made Jan. 5, 1770. Mispillion Hd. Heirs: wife Deborah; son Matthew; daus. Susanna, Mary, Sarah, Elizabeth & Jemima. Exec'r, son Matthew. Wits., Charles Ridgely, Edward Fisher. Prob. Nov. 20, 1777. Arch. vol. A33, pages 112-113. Reg. of Wills, Liber L, folios 195-196.

Pennell [Pennuel], William. Admin. of, to Mary Pennell, widow. Nov. 26, 1777. Arch. vol. A39, pages 230-232. Reg. of Wills, Liber L, folio 194. Note:—Arch. vol. A39, page 230 shows children, Samuel, Elijah, Hannah, David, Mary, Elizabeth & Lydia Pennell.

Craige, Alexander. Farmer. Will. Made Dec. 5, 1777. Murderkill Hd. Heirs: wife Isabel; dau. Susannah; grandson Alexander Hall; Alexander Hudson; James Willson. Exec'x, wife Isabel. Wits., John Craige, Thomas Perkins, Samuel Craige. Prob. Dec. 13, 1777. Arch. vol. A11, pages 145, 147-148. Reg. of Wills, Liber L, folio 196.

Quillen, Thomas. Admin. of, to Samuel Quillen. Dec. 14, 1777. Reg. of Wills, Liber L, folio 197.

Young, Wells. Admin. of, to Kesiah Young. Dec. 27, 1777. Reg. of Wills, Liber L, folio 197.

Manlove, Matthew. Yeoman. Will. Made April . . . 1775. Heirs: wife Sarah; children unnamed. Exec'r, wife Sarah. Wits., Samuel McCall, Thomas Rodney, John Comegys. Prob. Jan. 1, 1778. Arch. vol. A32, pages 48-50. Reg. of Wills, Liber L, folio 197. Note:—Ach. vol. A32, page 50 mentions heirs, George & Mott Manlove.

Bacon, Jacob. Admin. of, to Ann Bacon, widow. Jan. 5, 1778. Reg. of Wills, Liber L, folio 197.

Jarrard, Wilson. Admin. of, to William Brown. Jan. 19, 1778. Arch. vol. A26, page 112. Reg. of Wills, Liber L, folio 197.

Cardeen, William. Farmer. Will. Made Jan. 7, 1778. Mispillion Hd. Heirs: wife unnamed; son Daniel; daus. Sarah Bostick, Elizabeth Williams, Esther Sapp, Mary Artis, Prisilla Bendy, Mariam & Prudence. Exec'r, James Bostick. Wits., Samuel Kemp, Thomas Stradley, James Williams. Prob. Jan. 31, 1778. Arch. vol. A7, pages 209-211. Reg. of Wills, Liber L, folio 212. Note:—Arch. vol. A7, page 110 shows that wife was Rachel & married James Summers; also shows daus. Mary Artis [Arthurs], wife of Robert Arthurs; Priscilla Bendy [Banning], wife of Phinas Banning; Elizabeth Williams, wife of Ward Williams.

Hilliard, Rebecca. Widow. Will. Made Jan. 14, 1778. Duck Creek Hd. Heirs: son Thomas; grandson John Hilliard, son of Charles; granddaus. Rebecca Hilliard (dau. of Christopher), dau. of son John; Susanna, wife of Christopher; Sarah Noxton; Jeremiah Lee; Sarah Jones; Evan Denney, son of Evan, dec'd. Exec'r, [Thomas Hillyard, from admin acct.]. Wits., William Smith, Meriam Gill, Richard Lee. Prob. Feb. 23, 1778. Arch. vol. A24, page 44. Reg. of Wills, Liber L, folios 197-198.

Price, James. Admin. of, to Jean [Jane] Price. Feb. 25, 1778. Reg. of Wills, Liber L, folio 198.

Scott, John. Mariner. Will. Made Feb. 16, 1778. Town of Dover. Heirs: dau. Ann Martha Scott. Exec'rs, bro.-in-law William Carson of N. C. Co., tavernkeeper; friend Alexander Rutherford, of Dover. Guardians, William Carson & Alexander Rutherford. Wits., Samuel McCall, Robert McGermant, Thomas North. Prob. Feb. 27, 1778. Arch. vol. A45, page 65. Reg. of Wills, Liber L, folio 198.

White, William. Admin. of, to John Darrach. Feb. 28, 1778. Reg. of Wills, Liber L, folio 198.

Jarrard, James. Admin. of, to William Rhoads, Esq. March 2, 1778. Arch. vol. A26, page 105. Reg. of Wills, Liber L, folio 198.

Capron, Jarrard. Admin. of, to John Cole [Coole]. March 6, 1778. Reg. of Wills, Liber L, folio 198.

Blackshare, Robert. Admin. of, to Jean Blackshare & Morgan Blackshare. March 14, 1778. Arch. vol. A4, page 103. Reg. of Wills, Liber L, folio 199. Note:—Acct. shows that Jean [Jane] Blackshare married Michael Numbers.

Webb, Thomas. Will. Made March 8, 1778. Heir: wife Sarah. Exec'x, wife Sarah. Wits., William Kirkley, Henry Richardson, William Powell. Prob. March 18, 1778. Arch. vol. A53, page 214. Reg. of Wills, Liber L, folio 199.

Eustice, Charles. Admin. of, to Rachel Eustice, widow. March 24, 1778. Arch. vol. A16, page 213. Reg. of Wills, Liber L, folio 199.

Hunn, Mary. Widow. Will. Made July 31, 1777. Little Creek Hd. Heirs: sister Sarah Havalow; bro. William Millard; nieces Lydia Millard (dau. of dec'd bro. Joseph), Ann & Mary Millard (children of bro. Williams); mother unnamed. Exec'r, bro. William. Wits., Joseph Palmer, Jonathan Needham, John Brady. Prob. March 30, 1778. Arch. vol. A25, pages 163-164. Reg. of Wills, Liber L, folios 199-200.

Crockett, Jesse. Admin. of, to Jonathan Crockett & John Crockett. April 4, 1778. Arch. vol. A11, page 239. Reg. of Wills, Liber L, folio 200.

Baily, Edmond. Admin. of, to Arthur Whitely. April 15, 1778. Reg. of Wills, Liber L, folio 200.

Smith, Isaac. Admin. of, to Arthur Whitely, D. B. N. April 15, 1778. Reg. of Wills, Liber L, folio 200.

Brown, William. Will. Made April 18, 1778. Heirs: wife Rachel; sons Aaron, John & Benjamin; daus. Ruth Brown, Sarah Lowber (wife of Jonathan Lowber). Exec'rs, wife Rachel & son Aaron. Wits., John Brown, Benjamin Brown, Abel Shield, John Powell. Prob. May 15, 1778. Arch. vol. A6, pages 99 and 102-103. Reg. of Wills, Liber L, folio 200.

Brinckley, Mary. Admin. of, to Jesse Brinckley. May 19, 1778. Arch. vol. A5, page 192. Reg. of Wills, Liber L, folio 200.

Cummins, Robert. Admin. of, to Rachel Reynolds. May 28, 1778. Reg. of Wills, Liber L, folio 201.

Biddle, Augustine. Will. Made April 6, 1778. Mispillion Hd. Heirs: wife Ruth; son Jacob. Exec'x, wife Ruth. Wits., Edward Cox, Thomas Jester, John Hartshorn. Prob. June 18, 1778. Arch. vol. A4, pages 46-47. Reg. of Wills, Liber L, folio 201.

Mullet, Thomas. Yeoman. Will. Made Jan. 31, 1778. Little Creek Hd. Heir: wife Elizabeth. Exec'x, wife Elizabeth. Wits., Francis Barber, Joseph Barber. Prob. June 23, 1778. Arch. vol. A37, page 69. Reg. of Wills, Liber L, folio 201. Note:— Will mentions William Mullet, father.

Leatherberry, Thomas. A minor. Little Creek Hd. Admin. of, to John Goldsmith. June 26, 1778. Arch. vol. A29, pages 215-216 & 219. Reg. of Wills, Liber L, folio 202. Note:— Arch. vol. A29, page 219 shows William Leatherberry, adm'r, D. B. N., in right of John Goldsmith.

Steward [Stewart], James. Yeoman. Duck Creek Hd. Admin. of, to Mary Steward. July 19, 1778. Arch. vol. A49, page 1. Reg. of Wills, Liber L, folio 197.

Fisher, Molleston. Admin. of, to Adam Fisher & Daniel Fisher. July 20, 1778. Arch. vol. A17, page 138. Reg. of Wills, Liber L, folio 202.

Ogle, George. Admin. of, to Sarah Ogle. July 24, 1778. Arch. vol. A38, pages 109-110. Reg. of Wills, Liber L, folio 202. Note:—Arch. vol. A38, page 109 shows that Sarah Ogle married . . . Caldwell.

Jenkins, Timothy. Will. Made March 17, 1778. Little Creek Hd. Heirs: wife [Ellen, from admin. acct.]; eldest son Jabez; other children unnamed. Exec'rs, wife & son Jabez. Trustees, friends Samuel Hanson, Thomas Hanson, John Cowgill, William Wilson, Henry Cowgill & Israel Alston. Wits., Samuel Smith, Joseph Palmer, Susanna Cox. Prob. Aug. 12, 1778. Arch. vol. A26, pages 244-250. Reg. of Wills, Liber L, folio 202 & Liber N, folios 35-36. Note:—Arch. vol. A26, page 247 mentions heirs, Ellen, Jabez, Samuel & Sarah Jenkins & Elizabeth Ferguson, wife of John Ferguson.

Lewis, Joel. Will. Made Aug. 9, 1778. Duck Creek Hd. Heirs: sisters Rachel Lewis, Anne Palmatry, Sarah Lewis, Lydia Lewis. Exec'rs, father James Lewis & sister Rachel Lewis. Wits., Jess Watson, Enoch Lewis, Stephen Stanton. Prob. Aug. 14, 1778. Arch. vol. A30, pages 92-93. Reg. of Wills, Liber L, folio 202.

Fortner, James. Admin. of, to Anne Fortner. Aug. 17, 1778. Arch. vol. A13, page 37. Reg. of Wills, Liber L, folio 203. Note:—Acct. shows that Anne Fortner married Robert Irons [Hirons]; also mentions heirs, John, James, Rebecca & Ann Fortner.

Fortner, James. Admin. of, to Sarah Fortner. Aug. 17, 1778. Reg. of Wills, Liber L, folio 203.

McVay, James. Admin. of, to Elizabeth McVay. Aug. 18, 1778. Arch. vol. A33, pages 37-38. Reg. of Wills, Liber L, folio 203. Note:—Arch. vol. A33, page 37 shows that Elizabeth McVay married John Hogan.

Rash, Joseph. Farmer. Will. Made Sept. 27, 1774. Murderkill Hd. Heirs: wife Ann; daus. Mary, Elizabeth, Sarah & Ann; sons Samuel & Joseph. Exec'rs, dau. Mary & bro-in-law Joseph Alford. Wits., Joseph Boogs, Solomon Morris, William Powell. Codicil, July 21, 1778. Grandson John Nox, son of Samuel. Wits., Joseph Forcum, William Powell. Prob. Aug. 19, 1778. Arch. vol. A42, pages 42-47. Reg. of Wills, Liber L, folios 203-204. Note:—Arch. vol. A42, page 47 shows that admin. was granted to Ann Rash who later married William Mays.

Thomas, Jonathan. Admin. of, to Benjamin Thomas & Charles Pope. Aug. 25, 1778. Reg. of Wills, Liber L, folio 204.

Voshell, Obediah, Sr. Will. Made June 25, 1778. Murderkill Hd. Heirs: wife Elizabeth; sons John, Joseph & Obediah; daus. Elizabeth Jackson & Mary Thomson. Exec'rs, wife Elizabeth & son Obediah. Wits., William Manering, John Trippett, Jerusha Williams. Prob. Sept. 16, 1778. Arch. vol. A52, pages 137-138. Reg. of Wills, Liber L, folio 204.

Blackiston, George. Farmer. Will. Made Aug. 9, 1778. Duck Creek Hd. Heirs: wife Martha; sons Ebenezar & John; daus. Frances, Sarah, Prisilah. Exec'x, wife Martha. Wits., Samuel West, James Cheffins, Abraham Parsons. Prob. Oct. 1, 1778. Arch. vol. A4, pages 129-131. Reg. of Wills, Liber L, folios 205-206. Note:—Arch. vol. A4, page 130 shows that Martha Blackiston married James Berry.

Whitehart, Grace. Admin. of, to Samuel Whitehart & James Potter. Oct. 1, 1778. Arch. vol. A54, page 183. Reg. of Wills, Liber L, folio 206.

Williams, Eleanor. Admin. of, to Margaret Williams. Oct. 10, 1778. Reg. of Wills, Liber L, folio 206.

Zelefro, Joseph. Admin. of, to Elizabeth Zelefro. Oct. 19, 1778. Reg. of Wills, Liber L, folio 206.

Brown, Benjamin. Admin. of, to Darkus Brown. Nov. 6, 1778. Arch. vol. A6, pages 26-27. Reg. of Wills, Liber L, folio 206. Note:—Arch. vol. A6, page 27 mentions heirs, Mary, Ann, Elizabeth, Margaret, Charles & William Brown; page 26 shows the acct. later administered by Thomas Blackshore & wife Darcus.

Allee, Abraham, Jr. Yeoman. Will. Made Oct. 7, 1778. Duck Creek Hd. Heirs: wife Elizabeth; daus. Rebecca & Mary. Exec'rs, father-in-law Immanuel Stout, bro. John Allee & Thomas Tilton. Guardians, Immanuel Stout, Mary Stout, John Allee, Thomas Tilton. Wits., James Raymond, John Stinson. Prob. Nov. 10, 1778. Arch. vol. A1, pages 54-56. Reg. of Wills, Liber L, folio 207.

Allee, Presley. Will. Made Aug. 12, 1778. Duck Creek Hd. Heirs: wife Ann; son Thomas. Exec'rs, wife Ann & father-in-law Thomas Tilton. Wits., Edward McElroy, Solomon Barnet. Prob. Nov. 13, 1778. Arch. vol. A1, page 73. Reg. of Wills, Liber L, folio 208.

Evans, John. Admin. of, to Alce Evans. Nov. 13, 1778. Reg. of Wills, Liber L, folio 207.

Murry, Jean. Widow. Admin. of, to James McMullan. Nov. 13, 1778. Reg. of Wills, Liber L, folio 207.

Virdin, Absalom. Farmer. Will. Made Oct. 30, 1778. Mispillion Hd. Heirs: wife Sarah; son William; dau. Cintha. Exec'x, wife Sarah. Wits., Salley Brady, John Kilpatrick, John Bell. Prob. Nov. 13, 1778. Arch. vol. A52, pages 76-78. Reg. of Wills, Liber L, folio 206. Note:—Arch. vol. A52, page 78 shows that Sarah Virdin married William Gaskin.

Wilson, Anne. Widow. Murderkill Hd. Admin. of, to James Wilson & William Wilson. Nov. 14, 1778. Arch. vol. A55, page 197. Reg. of Wills, Liber L, folio 206.

Bryan, Timothy. Admin. of, to Martha Burrows. Nov. 26, 1778. Reg. of Wills, Liber L, folio 208.

Cullen, William. Admin. of, to Sarah Cullen. Dec. 2, 1778. Arch. vol. A12, pages 94-95. Reg. of Wills, Liber L, folio 208. Note:—Arch. vol. A12, page 94 mentions heirs, Ruth Tripitt (wife of William Trippett), John, William, Mary, James, Thomas, David, Nathan & Nathaniel Cullen; also shows that Sarah Cullen married William Thomson.

Jackson, John. Admin. of, to Anna Jackson. Jan. 12, 1779. Arch. vol. A26, page 7. Reg. of Wills, Liber L, folio 208.

Hart, Govey. Admin. of, to George Goforth, Sr. Jan. 13, 1779. Reg. of Wills, Liber L, folio 209.

Mason, Isaac. Will. Made Dec. 17, 1778. Mispillion Hd. Heirs: wife Catharine; sons John, Isaac & Daniel; daus. Persy Spencer & Susannah Crapper; five youngest daus. unnamed. Exec'x, wife Catharine. Wits., John Clark, Joshua Clark, Thomas Bowman. Prob. Jan. 13, 1779. Arch. vol. A33, pages 232-233. Reg. of Wills, Liber L, folios 208-209.

Chipman, Benjamin. Farmer. Murderkill Hd. Admin. of, to Samuel Moore & Reuben Shields, D. B. N. Feb. 17, 1779. Arch. vol. A8, pages 183-184. Reg. of Wills, Liber L, folio 209.

Rakes, Weston. Admin. of, to Thomas Nixon. Feb. 21, 1779. Reg. of Wills, Liber L, folio 209.

Leatherbery, Mary. Admin. of, to John Brinckle. Feb. 24, 1779. Arch. vol. A29, page 218.

Leatherbery, Thomas. Admin. of, to John Brinckle. Feb. 24, 1779. Arch. vol. A29, page 217.

Moore, John, Jr. Farmer. Duck Creek Hd. Admin. of, to Wheelor Pennington & wife Ann, the late Ann Moore. Feb. 24, 1779. Arch. vol. A36, pages 56-58.

Jump, Benjamin. Admin. of, to William Trippett. April 29, 1779. Reg. of Wills, Liber L, folio 209.

Molleston, Henry. Admin. of, to Sarah Molleston. May 3, 1779. Arch. vol. A35, pages 206-207. Reg. of Wills, Liber L, folio 209. Note:—Arch. vol. A35, page 206 mentions heirs, Henry Molleston & Mary Sipple.

Manning, James. Admin. of, to Avis Manning. May 4, 1779. Arch. vol. A33, page 78. Reg. of Wills, Liber L, folio 209. Note:—Admin. shows that Avis Manning married John White.

Wainwright, Levin. Farmer. Murderkill Hd. Admin. of, to Jane Wainwright. June 15, 1779. Arch. vol. A52, pages 156-159. Reg. of Wills, Liber L, folio 209. Note:—Arch. vol. A52, page 156 shows that Jane Wainwright later married Joseph Wright.

Hutchison, Matthew. Will (nunc.). June 3, 1779. Heirs: dau. of Joseph Woodles; Nancy Dikins; son John; wife unnamed. Wits., David Anderson & Elizabeth Anderson. Prob. June 19, 1779. Arch. vol. A25, page 200. Reg. of Wills, Liber L, folios 209-210.

Hutchison, Matthew. Admin. of, to Mary Hutchison & John Hutchison. June 19, 1779. Reg. of Wills, Liber L, folio 210.

Hart, Hannah. Admin. of, to Sarah Pemberton. July 27, 1779. Reg. of Wills, Liber L, folio 210.

Hardesty, William. Will. Made June 21, 1779. Heirs: wife Elizabeth; sons William & Thomas. Exec'x, wife Elizabeth. Wits., John Hoopkins, Thomas Smith, Sr., Thomas Smith. Prob. Aug. 9, 1779. Arch. vol. A22, page 10. Reg. of Wills, Liber L, folio 210.

Holmes, John. Mispillion Hd. Admin. of, to George Black. Aug. 10, 1779. Arch. vol. A24, page 232.

Dennum [Denman], Frederick. Will. Made July 5, 1779. Heirs: wife Ann; sons Arthur, John & Michael; dau. Nancy Griffin. Exec'rs, wife Ann & son Arthur. Wits., Waitman Goslen, John Pearce & Eliab Vinson. Prob. Aug. 11, 1779. Arch. vol. A15, pages 90 & 225. Reg. of Wills, Liber L, folios 210-211.

Spencer, William. Admin. of, to Elizabeth Spencer. Aug. 13, 1779. Reg. of Wills, Liber L, folio 211.

Wallace, William. Admin. of, to Hannah Wallace & Layton Jones. Aug. 27, 1779. Reg. of Wills, Liber L, folio 211.

Goforth, Zachariah. Yeoman. Will. Made Aug. 9, 1764. Heirs: wife Sarah; nephew Peter Goforth, son of bro. Thomas Goforth; William Reddett, son of William Reddett. Exec'rs, wife Sarah & Jonathan Emerson. Wits., Alexander Whiteley, Uriah Sipple, Mary Jenkins. Prob. Aug. 29, 1779. Arch. vol. A19, pages 106-108. Reg. of Wills, Liber L, folios 190 & 211.

Rich, William. Will. Made June 29, 1779. Heirs: wife Susanna; son William; daus. Mary, Rebecca, Ann & Elizabeth; one child unnamed; Benson Stanton. Exec'x, wife Susanna. Wits., Thomas White, Peter Rich, Gove Cox. Codicil, dated Aug. 29, 1779. Wits., William Whiteley, Allon Wilson, Peter Rich. Prob. Oct. 1, 1779. Arch. vol. A43, pages 144-147. Reg. of Wills, Liber L, folio 213. Note:—Arch. vol. A43, page 147 shows that Susanna Rich married Allen Wilson.

Jackson, David. Bricklayer. Murderkill Hd. Oct. 19, 1779. Admin. of, to Jonathan Jackson. Arch. vol. A25, page 240. Reg. of Wills, Liber L, folios 211-212.

Russell, William. Admin. of, to Elizabeth & Richard Banning. Oct. 27, 1779. Arch. vol. A44, pages 187 & 189. Reg. of Wills, Liber L, folio 212. Note:—Arch. vol. A44, page 187 shows that Elizabeth Banning married Abraham Smith; page 189 mentions heirs, Mary Godwin (the late Mary Russell), & widow Elizabeth Russell.

West, Joseph. Will. Made Oct. 3, 1779. Duck Creek Hd. Heirs: wife Sarrah; wife's son Bable French; dau. Hannerata; sons David, William & Joseph; bro. Benjamin West. Exec'x, wife Sarrah. Wits., Samuel West, Enoch Jones, Daniel David. Prob. Oct. 25, 1779. Arch. vol. A54, pages 23-24. Reg. of Wills, Liber L, folio 214. Note:—Arch. vol. A54, page 24 shows that Sarah West married Lemuel Cole.

Beard, John. Admin. of, to Mary Beard & Thomas Jones. Oct. 25, 1779. Reg. of Wills, Liber L, folio 213.

Davis, Thomas. Admin. of, to Andrew Lackey. Nov. 3, 1779. Arch. vol. A13, page 68. Reg. of Wills, Liber L, folio 213.

Wallace, Hannah. Widow of William Wallace, Sr. Admin. of, to Isaac Stratton. Nov. 9, 1779. Reg. of Wills, Liber L, folio 213. Note:—Arch. vol. A52, page 229 mentions heirs, David & Solomon Wallace.

Murphy, Margaret. Admin. of, to Jacob Stout, Esq. Nov. 23, 1779. Arch. vol. A37, page 99. Reg. of Wills, Liber L, folio 213.

Snow, Joseph. Duck Creek Hd. Admin. of, to Jean [Jane] Snow, Thomas Keith & Benjamin Stout. Nov. 23, 1779. Arch. vol. A48, pages 20-22. Reg. of Wills, Liber L, folio 213. Note:— Arch. vol. A48, page 21 shows that Jean Snow married James Smith; also mentions heirs, Ann & James Snow, Rebecca Denney (wife of Robert), Mary Downing (wife of Ezekiel), Lydia Farrow (wife of Joseph), Sarah Vanstavoren, the late Sarah Morgan (wife of William Vanstavoren).

Lewis, James. Admin. of, to Jean Lewis, widow. Dec. 16, 1799. Arch. vol. A30, page 86. Reg. of Wills, Liber L, folio 216.

Nixon, Thomas. Will. Made Nov. 18, 1779. Heirs: wife Ann; sons Thomas, Charles, Nicholas & Nixon; daus. Nancy Hazell, Letitia Coakley & Rachel Robinson; granddaus. Fedelia Rogerson, Nancy Vandyke, Nancy Robinson; grandson unnamed. Exec'rs, wife Ann & son Charles. Wits., Henry Forster, Daniel Freeman, Rachel Forster. Prob. Dec. 29, 1779. Arch. vol. A38, pages 14-15. Reg. of Wills, Liber L, folios 215-216. Note:—Will mentions dau. Elizabeth Vandyke, dec'd.

Potter, James. Will. Made Jan. 5, 1780. Little Creek Hd. Heirs: dau. Sarah; sisters Elenor Howard & Jean Patterson. Exec'r, friend Thomas Keith. Wits., Francis Keith, Allen Whiteheart, Ann Roland. Prob. Jan. 10, 1780. Arch. vol. A41, pages 7-8. Reg. of Wills, Liber L, folio 214.

Hamilton, James. Admin. of, to James Raymond. Jan. 10, 1780. Reg. of Wills, Liber L, folio 216.

Anderson, James. Admin. of, to James Sterling. Feb. 6, 1780. Reg. of Wills, Liber L, folio 270.

Sipple, Jonathan. Admin. of, to Ruth Sipple & Arthur Whiteley. Feb. 9, 1780. Arch. vol. A46, pages 148-149. Note:—Arch. vol. A46, page 149 shows that Ruth Sipple married Daniel Boyer.

Simpson, Thomas. Admin. of, to Jennette Simpson. Feb. 14, 1780. Reg. of Wills, Liber L, folio 216.

Stewart, Mary. Will. Made Feb. 12, 1780. Little Creek Hd. Heirs: dau. Sarah Barnet; granddaus. Jane & Mary Barnet. Exec'r, son-in-law Moses Barnet. Wits., James Raymond, William Harper. Prob. Feb. 23, 1780. Arch. vol. A49, pages

8 & 11a. Reg. of Wills, Liber L, folios 214-215. Note:—Arch. vol. A49, page 11a shows this acct. later administered by Elias Dale & wife Sarah, late Sarah Barnett, widow of Moses.

Hutchinson, William. Admin. of, to Mary & James Hutchinson. Feb. 26, 1780. Reg. of Wills, Liber L, folio 218.

Ervy, William. Admin. of, to William Watson. March 28, 1780. Reg. of Wills, Liber L, folio 216.

Edmondson, Francis. Admin. of, to Mary Edmondson. April 18, 1780. Arch. vol. A16, pages 44-46. Reg. of Wills, Liber L, folio 216. Note:—Arch. vol. A16, page 44 mentions heirs, Mary Roberts, née Edmondson, William, Samuel & Mark Greer Edmondson.

Watkins, John. Murderkill Hd. Admin. of, to Thomas Nixon. April 26, 1780. Arch. vol. A53, page 163. Reg. of Wills, Liber L, folio 216.

Concelio, William. Admin. of, to John Durrum [Durham]. May 1, 1780. Arch. vol. A10, page 100. Reg. of Wills, Liber L, folio 216.

Hamilton, Mary. Admin. of, to Jacob Stout, D. B. N. May 10, 1780. Arch. vol. A21, page 166. Reg. of Wills, Liber L, folio 217.

Voshall, Levi. Admin. of, to William Voshall. May 10, 1780. Reg. of Wills, Liber L, folios 216-217.

Bonine, Abel. Admin. of, to William Moleston. May 13, 1780. Reg. of Wills, Liber L, folio 217.

Dunkin [Duncan], Elizabeth. Admin. of, to Thomas Dean. May 17, 1780. Arch. vol. A15, page 113. Reg. of Wills, Liber L, folio 217.

Irons, John, Sr. Farmer. Will. Made Oct. 18, 1779. Dover Hd. Heirs: sons Henry & John; daus. Avis Manning & Naomy (dau. of first wife); grandchildren Timothy & Thomas Irons (children of son Thomas, dec'd), John, Thomas, Samuel & Lydia Wilson (children of Samuel Wilson & dau. Sarah, dec'd.). Exec'r, son Henry. Wits., James Sykes, Agnes Sykes, Grace Vandever. Prob. June 1, 1780. Arch. vol. A25, pages 217-218. Reg. of Wills, Liber L, folios 217-218.

Maxwell, William. Admin. of, to Naomy Maxwell. June 2, 1780. Arch. vol. A34, page 106. Reg. of Wills, Liber L, folio 218.

Hudson, Arnold. Admin. of, to Elizabeth Hudson. June 13, 1780. Reg. of Wills, Liber L, folio 218. Note:—Arch. vol. A25, page 100 shows that Elizabeth Hudson married Ferdenand Casson.

Kendal, Benjamin. Admin. of, to Joseph Kendal. July 3, 1780. Reg. of Wills, Liber L, folio 218.

Hirons, Simon, Jr. Admin. of, to John Bell, D. B. N. Aug. 15, 1780. Arch. vol. A24, page 102.

Williams, Sarah. Admin. of, to Arthur Culley. Aug. 15, 1780. Arch. vol. A55, page 154.

Tinch, Samuel. Admin. of, to Mary Tinch. Sept. 11, 1780. Reg. of Wills, Liber L, folio 218. Note:—Arch. vol. A50, page 155 shows that Mary Tinch married David Sullivan.

Caldwell, David. Will. Made Aug. 29, 1780. Heir: wife Elizabeth. Exec'x, wife. Wits., Phillip Barratt, Benjamin Bradley, James Parker. Prob. Sept. 15, 1780. Arch. vol. A7, pages 104-105. Reg. of Wills, Liber L, folio 218.

Johnson, John. Admin. of, to Elizabeth Johnson. . . . 1780. Reg. of Wills, Liber L, folio 219.

King, Alexandra. Admin. of, to Esther King. Oct. 6, 1780. Arch. vol. A29, page 30. Reg. of Wills, Liber L, folio 219.

Owen, William. Admin. of, to Elenor Owen. Oct. 11, 1780. Arch. vol. A38, pages 164-165. Reg. of Wills, Liber L, folio 219. Note:—Arch. vol. A38, page 164 mentions heirs, Mary, Matthew & Rachel Owen.

Downing, William. Admin. of, to Susanah Downing. Oct. 21, 1780. Arch. vol. A14, page 250. Reg. of Wills, Liber L, folio 219.

Owen, Owen. Admin. of, to Elizabeth Owen & John Ham. Nov. 7, 1780. Reg. of Wills, Liber L, folio 219. Note:—Arch. vol. A38, page 157 shows that Elizabeth Owen married William Sullivan.

Porter, William. Farmer. Will. Made July 4, 1780. St. Jones Hd. Heirs: sons Joseph & Benjamin; daus. Rebecca, Sarah, Tabitha, Elizabeth & Mary. Exec'rs, Robert Register & daus. Sarah & Tabitha Porter. Guardian, Robert Register. Wits., Joseph Taylor, Mark Maxwell. Prob. Nov. 10, 1780. Arch. vol. A40, pages 206-208 & 210-212. Reg. of Wills, Liber L, folios 219-220. Note:—Arch. vol. A40, page 211 shows that Sarah Porter married Charles Stuart & Tabitha Porter married Henry Stuart.

Hawkins, Arnold. Will. Made July 12, 1780. Duck Creek Hd. Heirs: wife Susanah; sons Arnold & Thomas; daus. Susanah & Elizabeth. Exec'rs, wife Susanah & sons Arnold & Thomas. Wits., Thos. Sherven, Jane Sidens, James Morris, Jr. Prob. Nov. 13, 1780. Arch. vol. A23, page 15. Reg. of Wills, Liber L, folios 220-221.

Herren, George. Admin. of, to Mary Herren. Nov. 15, 1780. Reg. of Wills, Liber L, folio 221.

Peterson, Andrew. Admin. of, to Esrael Peterson. Nov. 15, 1780. Reg. of Wills, Liber L, folio 221.

Russ, Robert. Admin. of, to Jane Russ & Edward Russ. Nov. 24, 1780. Reg. of Wills, Liber L, folio 221.

Cully, Arthur. Admin. of, to Alice Cully. Dec. 1, 1780. Reg. of Wills, Liber L, folio 221.

Ewbank, Benjamin. Will. Made Nov. 7, 1780. Heirs: wife Jane; dau. Sarah Barnes; one child unnamed; friend Benjamin Stout. Exec'r, wife Jane & Benjamin Stout. Wits., Elisha Snow, Elizabeth Snow, John Cook. Prob. Dec. 4, 1780. Arch. vol. A16, page 235. Reg. of Wills, Liber L, folios 221-222.

Collins, Edward. Farmer. Murderkill Hd. Admin. of, to Rebecca Collins & William Collins. Dec. 9, 1780. Arch. vol. A9, pages 231-235. Reg. of Wills, Liber L, folio 223. Note:—Arch. vol. A9, page 231 mentions heirs, Richard, Ann, Benjamin, Rebecca & Edward Collins, Sarah Crumpton (wife of John Crumpton), Armenta Yoe; page 233 shows that Rebecca Collins married Nathaniel Dyer.

Murphy, Elizabeth. Admin. of, to William Griffin. Dec. 16, 1780. Arch. vol. A37, page 86. Reg. of Wills, Liber L, folio 223.

Edwards, William. Admin. of, to Penelopy Edwards. Dec. 19, 1780. Reg. of Wills, Liber L, folio 223. Note:—Arch. vol. A16, page 82 shows that Penelopy Edwards married Thomas Shusane.

Houldson, John. Will. Made Nov. 28, 1780. Heirs: wife Mary; sons John, William, Elijah & Robert; daus. unnamed. Exec'rs, wife Mary & son Abraham. Wits., John Dill, Luke Pratt, Caleb Taylor. Prob. Dec. 21, 1780. Arch. vol. A25, page 39. Reg. of Wills, Liber L, folios 222-223.

Townsend, John. Will. Made May 22, 1777. Heirs: mother Febey Morris; bro. William Morris; sisters Elizabeth, Rachel & Mary . . . Exec'x, mother Febey Morris. Wits., Richard Brinkle, Febey Brinkle. Prob. Jan. 8, 1781. Arch. vol. A51, pages 21-22. Reg. of Wills, Liber L, folio 233.

Clark, Nehimiah. Dover Hd. Admin. of, to Ezekeal Clark. Jan. 13, 1781. Arch. vol. A9, page 61. Reg. of Wills, Liber L, folio 222.

Vangaskin, John, Jr. Admin. of, to John Slaught. Jan. 20, 1781. Arch. vol. A51, pages 241 & 243. Reg. of Wills, Liber L, folio 222.

Calaway, Thomas. Admin. of, to Elizabeth Calaway & Jacob Calaway. Jan. 20, 1781. Arch. vol. A7, pages 162-163. Reg. of Wills, Liber L, folio 222. Note:—Arch. vol. A7, page 162 mentions heirs, Jacob & John Calaway & Isabella Harmon.

Teague, Silba. Admin. of, to Sarah Teague. Feb. 3, 1781. Reg. of Wills, Liber L, folio 222.

Furbee, Bowers. Will. Made May 4, 1775. Heirs: wife Anna; sons Waitman, Caleb, Jonathan & John; daus. Mirriam Davis, Anna & Elizabeth Furbee; grandson Bowers Davis. Exec'x, wife Anna. Wits., Philip Barritt, Caleb Sipple, Elizabeth Sipple. Prob. Feb. 12, 1781. Arch. vol. A18, page 148. Reg. of Wills, Liber L, folios 223-224.

Jacobs, William. Admin. of, to Elizabeth Jacobs. Feb. 12, 1781. Reg. of Wills, Liber L, folio 222.

Dyer, Edward. Farmer. Murderkill Hd. Admin. of, to Mary Dyer. Feb. 16, 1781. Arch. vol. A15, pages 217-221. Reg. of Wills, Liber L, folio 224. Note:—Arch. vol. A15, page 219 mentions heirs, Elizabeth, Mary, Prudence, Edward & Nancy Dyer; page 217 shows that Mary Dyer married . . . Steel.

Fowler, William. Admin. of, to Mary Neel. Feb. 19, 1781. Arch. vol. A18, page 61. Reg. of Wills, Liber L, folio 225.

Davis, Elizabeth. Will. Made Aug. 4, 1773. Heirs: dau. Rachel Clarke; sons Joseph & James; granddaus. Sarah Davis & Elizabeth Clarke. Exec'rs, son James Davis & son-in-law Nehemiah Clarke. Wits., Jonathan Clarke, Lias Wood, Paul Quenouault. Prob. Feb. 20, 1781. Arch. vol. A12, page 244. Reg. of Wills, Liber G, Appendix 1.

Brown, John. Admin. of, to Elizabeth Brown. Feb. 21, 1781. Arch. vol. A6, page 55. Reg. of Wills, Liber L, folio 225.

Allee, Abraham. Admin. of, to Abraham Conner. Feb. 26, 1781. Reg. of Wills, Liber L, folio 225.

Vanwinkle, Jacob. Admin. of, to William Truax, D. B. N. Feb. 27, 1781. Arch. vol. A52, pages 17-19. Reg. of Wills, Liber L, folio 225. Note:—Arch. vol. A52, page 17 mentions heirs, Simon, John, William, Jonas, Benjamin, Susana, Mary & Ann Van Winkle.

Vanwinkle, Mary. Admin. of, to William Truax. Feb. 27, 1781. Arch. vol. A52, page 21. Reg. of Wills, Liber L, folio 225.

James, James. Will. Made Feb. 17, 1781. Duck Creek Hd. Heirs: wife Elizabeth; mother Sarah Jones; bro. Joshua David. Exec'x, wife Elizabeth. Wits., Thomas Roberts, William Hawkins, James Morris, Jr. Prob. March 9, 1781. Arch. vol. A26, page 91. Reg. of Wills, Liber L, folio 225.

North, Richard. Will. Made March 4, 1781. Heirs: wife Rachel; sons Thomas, John & Daniel; daus. Ann Wiat, Mary & Rachel North. Exec'x, wife Rachel. Guardian, son-in-law Thomas Wiat. Wits., Solothial Newman, Robert Loud, Elezabeth Newnam. Prob. March 16, 1781. Arch. vol. A38, page 48. Reg. of Wills, Liber L, folios 225-226.

Rodney, Margaret. Widow. Will. Made Oct. 20, 1773. Heir: grandson Nathaniel Luff. Exec'r, grandson Nathaniel Luff. Wits., Thomas Rodney, George McCall. Prob. March 23, 1781. Arch. vol. A44, pages 94-95. Reg. of Wills, Liber L, folio 226.

Torbert, Peter. Will. Made Feb. . . ., 1781. Murderkill Hd. Heirs: wife Jane; sons John & William; one child unnamed. Exec'rs, wife Jane & friend James McClemmons. Wits., Major Taylor, John Pryor, John Torbert. Prob. March 28, 1781. Arch. vol. A50, pages 236-237. Reg. of Wills, Liber L, folio 227.

Wells [Walls], Henry. Admin. of, to Sarah Wells & William Wells. April 5, 1781. Reg. of Wills, Liber L, folio 227.

Ware, John. Admin. of, to Ann Ware & Frances Barber. April 11, 1781. Arch. vol. A53, pages 102-104. Reg. of Wills, Liber L, folio 227. Note:—Arch. vol. A53, page 102 mentions bros. as heirs, William & David Ware.

Bullen, John. Carpenter. Will (copy). Made April 4, 1781. Town of Dover. Heirs: wife Rachel; son John, Jr.; daus. Rachel, Sarah, Ann & Elizabeth Bullen, Mary Wells; George Brown. Exec'x, wife Rachel. Wits., John Bell, Jr., John Dawson, Samuel McCall. Prob. April 17, 1781. Arch. vol. A6, page 178. Reg. of Wills, Liber L, folio 228.

Gordon, James. Yeoman. Will. Made Feb. 2, 1781. Mispillion Hd. Heirs: wife Mary; dau. Mary; nephew James Rogers; niece Mary Gordon, dau. of sister Charity Brady. Exec'x, wife Mary. Wits., John Tomlin, Caleb Sipple, Selah Tomlin. Prob. April 17, 1781. Arch. vol. A19, pages 155-160. Reg. of Wills, Liber L, folio 234. Note:—Arch. vol. A19, page 159 shows that Mary Gordon married John Tomlin.

Eades, Daniel. Admin. of, to Mary Eades. April 25, 1781. Reg. of Wills, Liber L, folio 228. Note:—Arch. vol. A15, page 233 shows this acct. later administered by Jesse Ford & wife Mary.

Stout, Immanuel. Admin. of, to Mary Stout. April 25, 1781. Arch. vol. A49, pages 39-41. Reg. of Wills, Liber L, folio 228. Note:—Arch. vol. A49, page 40 shows Jacob Stout, Jr., guardian of Rebecca Allee, dau. of Abraham Allee, dec'd.

Barber, Joseph. Will. Made April 20, 1781. Heirs: nephew Joseph Barber, son of bro. Francis; other nephews unnamed. Exec'r, bro. Francis. Wits., Ann Ware, William Ware, George Gorden. Prob. May 22, 1781. Arch. vol. A2, page 141. Reg. of Wills, Liber L, folios 228-229.

Porter, Thomas. Admin. of, to Ann Porter & Ebenezer Wilson. May 29, 1781. Arch. vol. A40, page 204. Reg. of Wills, Liber L, folio 229. Note:—Arch. vol. A40, page 204 shows that Ann Porter married William Hineman.

Black, Stephen. Admin. of, to Stephen Black. May 29, 1781. Reg. of Wills, Liber L, folio 229.

Duncan, John. Admin. of, to Henry Stephens, D. B. N. May 30, 1781. Arch. vol. A15, pages 114-115. Reg. of Wills, Liber L, folio 244. Note:—Arch. vol. A15, page 114 mentions a son William Duncan.

Runnels, Richard. Admin. of, to Ruth Runnels. May 30, 1781. Arch. vol. A44, page 180.

Wallace, William. Admin. of, to Layton Jones. May 31, 1781. Arch. vol. A53, pages 18 & 20-21. Note:—Arch. vol. A53, page 20 mentions heirs, Mary Jones, William David, Elizabeth & Solomon Wallace.

Pheady, Randolph. Admin. of, to Mary Pheady. June 11, 1781. Reg. of Wills, Liber L, folio 229.

Griffith, Martha. Will. Made May 14, 1777. Duck Creek Hd. Heirs: sons Samuel & Isaac; daus. Rachel Patterson & Elizabeth Mearadeth; granddau. Elizabeth Griffith. Exec'r, son Isaac. Wits., Rachel Wallace, Martha Wallace, Daniel Durborow. Prob. July 24, 1781. Arch. vol. A20, page 247. Reg. of Wills, Liber L, folio 235.

Ford, Mary. Will. Made July 14, 1781. Heirs: sons Daniel & Thomas; daus. Mary & Rebecah. Wits., Sarah Berry, Mary Perry, William Berry. Prob. July 25, 1781. Arch. vol. A17, page 237. Reg. of Wills, Liber L, folio 235.

Ford, Mary. Admin. of, to Daniel Ford. July 25, 1781. Arch. vol. A17, page 237. Reg. of Wills, Liber L, folio 229.

Willson, John. Will. Made June 28, 1781. Murderkill Hd. Heirs: wife Susannah; son Nathan; daus. Mary, Susannah, Hannah, Sarah, Ruth, Elizabeth, Rachel, Mariam, Margaret, Ann & Lutisi. Exec'rs, wife Susannah, son Nathan & William Green. Wits., Thomas Thomas, James Jones, William Thomas. Prob. July 30, 1781. Arch. vol. A55, pages 222-223. Reg. of Wills, Liber L, folio 236.

Adams, Nathan. Admin. of, to Sarah Adams. Aug. 2, 1781. Reg. of Wills, Liber L, folio 229.

Beauchamp, Grace. Will. Made Oct. 6, 1788. Heirs: sons John, Isaac, William, Marcy & David; daus. Mary Thompson, Ann Walton, Grace Broom, Rachel & Esther Smithers. Exec'rs, sons Marcy & David. Wits., Elizabeth Manlove, Sarah Manlove, William Manlove. Prob. Aug. 15, 1781. Arch. vol. A3, page 109. Reg. of Wills, Liber L, folios 236-237.

Bond, Joseph. Admin. of, to Benjamin Coombs. Aug. 16, 1781. Arch. vol. A4, page 200. Reg. of Wills, Liber L, folio 229.

Wilkison, James. Farmer. Will. Made July 21, 1781. Jones Hd. Heirs: sons Henry, James, Moses, Aaron & Thomas; daus. Mary Linnard, Rachel, Sarah, Lidia & Naoma Wilkison. Exec'r, son Thomas. Wits., Thomas Barnett, William Watts. Prob. Aug. 17, 1781. Arch. vol. A55, page 55. Reg. of Wills, Liber L, folio 237.

Caldwell, Jonathan. Yeoman. Will. Made Aug. 18, 1781. Murderkill Hd. Heirs: wife Margaret; bro. Timothy Caldwell; sister Esther Caldwell; nephews James, Timothy, John, Jabez & Jonathan Caldwell, sons of bro. Joseph; niece Mary Caldwell, dau. of Timothy; Elizabeth Bell, wife of Henry Bell; John Bell, son of Elizabeth Bell; Nathan Stevens, son of Henry & his late wife Ann Stevens. Exec'r, bro. Timothy. Wits., William Rhodes, Rebecca Ambros, Charles Ridgely. Prob. Sept. 11, 1781. Arch. vol. A4, pages 115-117. Reg. of Wills, Liber L, folios 237-238.

Edmonds, Alice. Admin. of, to Solamon Barwick. Sept. 11, 1781. Arch. vol. A16, page 30. Reg. of Wills, Liber L, folio 229.

Dorrell, James. Admin. of, to Mary Dorrell & Caleb Sipple. Sept. 17, 1781. Arch. vol. A14, page 198. Reg. of Wills, Liber L, folio 229.

Wright, Sarah. Admin. of, to Edyth McKee & John Bell. Oct. 2, 1781. Reg. of Wills, Liber L, folio 229.

Aron, William. Admin. of, to Sarah Aron. Oct. 11, 1781. Reg. of Wills, Liber L, folio 276.

Stuart, Sarah. Admin. of, to Thomas Stuart. Oct. 23, 1781. Arch. vol. A49, page 101. Reg. of Wills, Liber L, folio 229.

Stuart, Sarah. Will (nunc.). Made July 25, 1781. Duck Creek Hd. Heirs: sons Thomas & Solomon; dau. Mary; other children unnamed. Wits., John Stuart, Nehemiah Cloak. Prob. Oct. 23, 1781. Arch. vol. A49, page 101. Reg. of Wills, Liber L, folio 238.

Harrington, Henry. Will. Made June 23, 1781. Heirs: wife Susannah; sons Samuel & William; dau. Agnes. Exec'x, wife Susannah. Wits., James Boyer, William Ross, Rachold Scotten. Prob. Oct. 23, 1781. Arch. vol. A22, pages 96 & 99 & vol. A23, page 167. Note:—Arch. vol. A22, page 99 shows that Susannah Harrington later married Thomas Sipple.

Reed, James. Murderkill Hd. Admin. of, to Sarah Reed. Oct. 24, 1781. Arch. vol. A42, pages 171 & 193. Reg. of Wills, Liber L, folio 229. Note:—Arch. vol. A42, page 93 mentions heirs, Meriam, George & Charles Reed.

Jester, Joseph. Admin. of, to Esther Jester. Nov. 6, 1781. Arch. vol. A27, page 34. Reg. of Wills, Liber L, folio 230.

Marim, Charles. Farmer. Will. Made Oct. 29, 1781. Dover Hd. Heirs: wife Mariam; sons John & Charles; daus. Annaka Casson & Mary Marim. Exec'r, son John. Appraisers, William Rodney, Joshua Gordon & James Sykes. Wits., James Sykes, John Nickerson, Elizabeth Rowan. Arch. vol. A33, pages 173, 176-177. Reg. of Wills, Liber L, folio 245. Note:— Arch. vol. A33, page 176 shows that Annaka Casson is the wife of Miers Casson & Mary Marim married Stephen Paradee.

Simmons, Daniel. Murderkill Hd. Admin. of, to Mary Simmons. Nov. 14, 1781. Arch. vol. A46, page 50.

West, John. Will. Made Aug. 19, 1781. Heirs: wife Elizabeth; sons Thomas, John, Jr. & Ephraim. Exec'rs, sons Thomas & John, Jr. Wits., Charles Reading, Elisha West. Prob. Nov. 17, 1781. Arch. vol. A54, pages 17-19. Reg. of Wills, Liber L, folio 246.

North, William. Admin. of, to Luke Pratt. Nov. 23, 1781. Reg. of Wills, Liber L, folio 230.

Bird, Joseph. Will (nunc.). Made Nov. 24, 1781. Heir: wife Nancy. Wits., Elsberry Bert, Richard Parvis, Rachel Simmons. Prob. Nov. 26, 1781. Arch. vol. A4, page 57. Reg. of Wills, Liber M, folio 102.

Revel, William. Admin. of, to Sarah Adams, D. B. N. Nov. 28, 1781. Arch. vol. A43, pages 87-89. Note:—Arch. vol. A43, page 87 mentions heirs, John, Sarah [Adams], Elizabeth, dec'd, Mary & Sabre Revel; acct. shows that Sarah Adams was wife of Anthony Rawlins.

Hammon, William. Admin. of, to Joseph Holliday & John Holliday. Nov. 28, 1781. Reg. of Wills, Liber L, folio 230.

Arnet, John. Admin. of, to Rebeccah Arnet. Nov. 29, 1781. Reg. of Wills, Liber L, folio 230. Note:—Arch. vol. A1, page 239 shows that Rebeccah Arnet married James Rogers.

Millis, Thomas. Admin. of, to Stephen Millis. Nov. 30, 1781. Reg. of Wills, Liber L, folio 230.

Parmacy, Robert. Admin. of, to Rebecca Parmacy. Nov. 30, 1781. Reg. of Wills, Liber L, folio 230.

Cowgill, John, Jr. Admin. of, to Lydia Cowgill. Dec. 4, 1781. Reg. of Wills, Liber L, folio 230.

Needham, Benjamin. Yeoman. Will. Made Oct. 28, 1781. Heirs: wife Agathy; nephews Samuel Maxwell (son of sister Christini) & Daniel Needham (son of bro. Ezekiel). Exec'rs, wife Agathy & nephew Samuel Maxwell. Wits., Abraham Vanhoy, James Sklinton, Clayton Cowgill. Prob. Dec. 4, 1781. Arch. vol. A37, pages 138-141. Reg. of Wills, Liber L, folios 246-247. Note:—Arch. vol. A37, page 140 shows the acct. later settled by John Wiltbank who married Elizabeth Maxwell; page 141 mentions heirs, Sally Arrington & Elizabeth Maxwell, widow of S. Maxwell.

Quillen, Joseph. Admin. of, to Elizabeth Quillen. Dec. 11, 1781. Reg. of Wills, Liber L, folio 230.

Shaw, Richard. Will. Made Nov. 26, 1781. Heirs: wife Sarah; sisters Elizabeth Hudson & Sarah Shaw; bros. William & Edward; nephew Richard Shaw, son of bro. John Shaw, dec'd. Exec'x, wife Sarah. Wits., David Durborow, Hugh Roberts, Mary Ennals, James Oliver Cromwell. Prob. Dec. 12, 1781. Arch. vol. A45, page 209. Reg. of Wills, Liber L, folios 247-248.

Griffin, Ann. Will. Made May 22, 1781. Duck Creek Hd. Heirs: husband William; uncle Richard Darling; heirs of uncle James Darling; aunt Sarah Burrows. Exec'r, husband William Griffin. Wits., Ebenezer Griffin, Rachel Greenwood, Daniel David, Jr. Prob. Dec. 15, 1781. Arch. vol. A20, page 185. Reg. of Wills, Liber L, folio 248.

Park, John. Admin. of, to John Bell. Dec. 17, 1781. Reg. of Wills, Liber L, folio 230.

Bulger, Peter. Admin. of, to Robert McGarmant. Dec. 21, 1781. Arch. vol. A6, page 177. Reg. of Wills, Liber L, folio 230.

Rhodes, William. Esq. Will. Made Jan. 9, 1777. Heirs: wife Mary; three children unnamed; grandson William Gerrard. Exec'rs, son John Rhodes & friend John Banning, merchant. Wits., Francis Many, William Killin. Prob. Dec. 22, 1781. Arch. vol. A43, page 139. Reg. of Wills, Liber L, folios 248-249. Note:—William Rhodes made this will prior to entering the army.

Rhodes, John. Admin. of, to Mary Rhodes. Dec. 24, 1781. Reg. of Wills, Liber L, folio 230.

Bush, Abraham. Admin. of, to Jacob Emerson. Dec. 29, 1781. Reg. of Wills, Liber L, folio 230.

Godwin, Kimuel. Will. Made Aug. 25, 1781. Heirs: wife Mary; sister Rachel Fisher; nieces Mary Godwin (dau. of bro. Joseph), Prudence Price (dau. of sister Lanston); Thomas Cortly Story, son of Nancy Story; grandson William Adams Godwin; nephew Henry Godwin, son of bro. Prieston; son-in-law Thomas Ogle. Exec'x, wife Mary. Wits., Thomas Russum, Andrew Bowen, Jonathan Rowland. Prob. Dec. 29, 1781. Arch. vol. A19, page 82. Reg. of Wills, Liber L, folio 249.

Hilliard, Phillip. Yeoman. Will. [N. d.]. Duck Creek Hd. Heirs: wife [Sarah, from admin. acct.]; bros. Christopher, Thomas & John; nephew Thomas Hilliard, son of Christopher. Exec'rs, wife & bro. Christopher. Wits., Samuel Wilson, Evan Denny, Isaac Booth. Prob. Dec. 29, 1781. Arch. vol. A24, page 43. Reg. of Wills, Liber L, folio 250.

McCall, Samuel. Admin. of, to Sarah McCall & Clark McCall. Dec. 31, 1781. Arch. vol. A32, page 95. Reg. of Wills, Liber L, folio 230.

McEver, Timothy. Yeoman. Will. Made Oct. 27, 1781. Murderkill Hd. Heirs: wife Mary; sons James, Timothy & John. Exec'rs, wife Mary & son John. Wits., Simon W. Wilson & Joseph Rogers. Prob. Jan. 2, 1782. Arch. vol. A32, page 179. Reg. of Wills, Liber L, folio 233.

Cambel, Joseph. Will. Made Dec. 24, 1781. Heirs: sons William, Joseph & Jonathan; grandson James Sexton; daus. Margaret & Ruth; Alexander Cambel. Exec'r, son Jonathan. Wits., John Reed, Henry Wegens. Prob. Jan. 3, 1782. Arch. vol. A7, pages 179 & 184. Reg. of Wills, Liber L, folios 250-251.

Booth, Isaac. Admin. of, to John Stuart. Jan. 5, 1782. Arch. vol. A4, page 214. Reg. of Wills, Liber L, folio 230.

Manlove, Ann. Admin. of, to Mark Manlove. Jan. 5, 1782. Reg. of Wills, Liber L, folio 230.

Battle, French. Colonel. Town of Dover. Admin. of, to Elizabeth Battle. Arch. vol. A3, pages 64-66. Reg. of Wills, Liber L, folio 230.

Water, Thomas. Weaver. Will. Made Jan. 4, 1782. Little Creek Hd. Heir: friend Benjamin Stout. Exec'r, friend Benjamin Stout. Wits., James Wells, James Morgan. Prob. Jan. 16, 1782. Arch. vol. A53, page 160. Reg. of Wills, Liber L, folio 251.

Teague, Selby. Admin. of, to John Farmer, D. B. N. Jan. 17, 1782. Reg. of Wills, Liber L, folio 230.

Rasin, Benjamin. Will. Made Dec. 25, 1781. Heirs: wife Rachel; sons Phillip, George & Joseph; dau. Mary; one child unnamed. Exec'rs, wife Rachel & bro. George Manlove. Wits., William Truitt, Nathan Bowman. Prob. Jan. 17, 1782. Arch. vol. A42, pages 86-88. Reg. of Wills, Liber L, folio 251. Note:—Arch. vol. A42, page 88 shows that Rachel Rasin married William Burrows. Arch. vol. A42, page 87 shows that Rachel Burrows later married Charles Mason; also mentions an heir, James Rasin.

Molleston, Sarah. Widow of Henry Molleston. Will. Made Nov. 17, 1781. Heirs: son Henry; dau. Mary Sipple; father Luke Manlove; Ann & Elizabeth Molleston; Jammimah Haslett. Exec'r, son Henry. Wits., John Parsons, Winlock Hall, John Parson, Jr. Prob. Jan. 21, 1782. Arch. vol. A35, pages 218-219. Reg. of Wills, Liber L, folio 252.

Smith, Abigail. Will. Made May 28, 1781. Heirs: sons Edward, Thomas, William, Oliver; heirs of dau. Sarah Dawson; daus. Sophia Jump, Sabrah Harmon & Sabino Banning; son-in-law William Saulsbery; granddaus. Lydia Smith & Sabrah Smith; grandsons William Banning Smith & Thomas Smith. Exec'r, son Edward. Wits., Daniel Sherwood, High Sherwood. Prob. Jan. 21, 1782. Arch. vol. A46, page 245. Reg. of Wills, Liber L, folios 234-235.

Carpenter, John. Admin. of, to Jean Carpenter. Feb. 5, 1782. Reg. of Wills, Liber L, folio 230.

Hendrey, Matthew. Will. Made Jan. 31, 1782. Heirs: wife Margaret; children of dau. Elizabeth Moore; nephew Robert Hendrey, son of bro. Robert; nieces Miriam, Rachel, Elizabeth Hendrey (daus. of bro. Robert). Exec'r, bro. Robert Hendrey. Wits., Robert Merydith, Mary Wallace, Elizabeth Merydith. Prob. Feb. 6, 1782. Arch. vol. A23, pages 129 & 157. Reg. of Wills, Liber L, folios 252-253.

Stokely, Benjamin. Admin. of, to Susanah Stokely. Feb. 8, 1782. Reg. of Wills, Liber L, folio 231.

Brinckle, John. Admin. of, to Elizabeth Brinckle & John Marim. Feb. 8, 1782. Arch. vol. A5, pages 187-190. Reg. of Wills, Liber L, folio 230. Note:—Arch. vol. A5, page 190 shows that Elizabeth Brinckle married Isaiah Wharton.

Cook, Samuel. Admin. of, to Prisilla Cook. Feb. 15, 1782. Arch. vol. A10, pages 138-140. Reg. of Wills, Liber L, folio 231.

Durborow, David. Admin. of, to Rebeckah Durborow. Feb. 18, 1782. Arch. vol. A15, pages 159-160. Reg. of Wills, Liber L, folio 231.

Casson, John. Hatter. Will. Made Feb. 24, 1781. Town of Dover. Heirs: wife Elizabeth. Exec'x, wife Elizabeth. Wits., Joseph Pryor, Stephen Alston, Mark McCall. Prob. Feb. 21, 1782. Arch. vol. A8, pages 59-61. Reg. of Wills, Liber L, folios 253-254. Note:—Arch. vol. A8, page 60 shows that Elizabeth Casson married John Banning.

Jester, John. Admin. of, to Lucretia Jester. Feb. 22, 1782. Reg. of Wills, Liber L, folio 231. Note:—Arch. vol. A27, page 32 shows that Lucretia Jester married Roger Scully.

Stevens, Nathan. Admin. of, to John Chicken. Feb. 27, 1782. Arch. vol. A48, page 231. Reg. of Wills, Liber L, folio 231.

Jarrard, James. Admin. of, to Benjamin Coombs & William Merydith, D. B. N. March 9, 1782. Arch. vol. A26, page 106. Reg. of Wills, Liber L, folio 231.

Rhodes, John. Captain. Admin. of, to Nehemiah Tilton, D. B. N. March 9, 1782. Arch. vol. A43, pages 132-135. Reg. of Wills, Liber L, folio 231. Note:—Arch. vol. A43, page 132 mentions heirs, William Jarrard & Mary Rhodes; also mentions bro. James Rhodes, dec'd.

Rhodes, William, Esq. Colonel. Admin. of, to Nehemiah Tilton, D. B. N. March 9, 1782. Arch. vol. A43, page 140. Reg. of Wills, Liber L, folio 231.

Stuart, Mary. Admin. of, to Peter Lowber, Jr. March 9, 1782. Reg. of Wills, Liber L, folio 231.

Clark, John. Yeoman. Will. Made Dec. 15, 1781. Mispillion Hd. Heirs: sons William, John, Winlock & Clement; wife Ann; a child unnamed; daus. Elizabeth & Sarah Clark, Nancy Barrett (wife of Andrew Barrett). Exec'x, wife Ann. Wits., Sydenham Thorn, Finwick Fisher, Jr., Garrett Sipple. Prob. March 13, 1782. Arch. vol. A9, pages 6-10. Reg. of Wills, Liber L, folios 255-256. Note:—Arch. vol. A9, page 7 shows that Ann Clark married Nathaniel Luff, Sr.; page 9 mentions heirs, Elizabeth Truitt & Jonathan Clark.

Fraizier, John. Will. Made Feb. 19, 1782. Little Creek Hd. Heirs: wife Alice; sons John, William, James, George; daus. Mary Hanson, Rebeccah & Elizabeth. Exec'rs, wife Alice & son John. Guardian, son William. Wits., James McManus, James Smith, Samuel Maxfield. Prob. March 13, 1782. Arch. vol. A18, page 96. Reg. of Wills, Liber L, folios 256-257.

Lynch, William. Admin. of, to Sarah Lynch. March 15, 1782. Reg. of Wills, Liber L, folio 231.

Meridith, Ruth. Admin. of, to Luff Meridith. March 23, 1782. Reg. of Wills, Liber L, folio 231.

Robinson, John. Will. Made Sept. 15, 1781. Duck Creek Hd. Heirs: wife Mary; son-in-law Charles Conner. Exec'rs, wife Mary & son-in-law Charles Conner. Wits., John Allee, William Hawkins. Prob. March 25, 1782. Arch. vol. A44, page 65. Reg. of Wills, Liber L, folios 257-258.

Wood, Robert. Farmer. Will. Made April 17, 1781. Duck Creek Hd. Heirs: sons Joseph, Stephen, John, Robert & William; daus. Catherine, Sarah Numbers; granddau. Barbary Buckingham. Exec'rs, sons Joseph & John. Wits., Joseph Moore, Presly Spruance, Mark Lewis, Thomas Brown. Prob. March 27, 1782. Arch. vol. A56, pages 94-98. Reg. of Wills, Liber L, folios 258-259.

White, Robert. Admin. of, to Mary White. April 2, 1782. Arch. vol. A54, pages 147-152. Reg. of Wills, Liber L, folio 231. Note:—Arch. vol. A54, page 149 shows that Mary White married Nathan Lecompt; page 147 mentions heirs, Susannah, John, Elizabeth, James & Mary White.

Rhodes, Mary. Widow. Will. Made Feb. 19, 1782. Heirs: son Samuel; dau. Mary; grandson William Jarrard, son of dau. Alice; friend Trainy Collin. Exec'rs, dau. Mary & friend Nehemiah Tilton, Esq. Wits., Sarah Reed, Ann Brady, Ruthy Piper. Prob. April 5, 1782. Arch. vol. A43, pages 136-138. Reg. of Wills, Liber L, folio 259. Note:—Arch. vol. A43, page 138 shows that Mary Rhodes married William Carpenter.

Soden, James. Will. Made Feb. 20, 1782. Heirs: wife Amerity; sons William, Thomas, James & Dingley Grey Soden; daus. Lurany, Elizabeth, Mary & Vilater. Exec'x, wife Amerity. Wits., Soden Lister; Samuel Graham, John Cain. Prob. April 6, 1782. Arch. vol. A48, pages 31 & 38-39. Reg. of Wills, Liber L, folio 260. Note:—Arch. vol. A48, page 39 shows that Elizabeth Soden married . . . Fisher.

Younger, Thomas. Admin. of, to Prisilla Younger. April 8, 1782. Reg. of Wills, Liber L, folio 231.

Williams, Lewis. Duck Creek Hd. Admin. of, to Ruth Williams & Nathaniel Wild. April 17, 1782. Reg. of Wills, Liber L, folio 231. Note:—Arch. vol. A55, page 122 shows that Ruth Williams married Stephen Eynon; also mentions heirs, Levis and Edward Williams.

Axell, Sarah. Admin. of, to Samuel Axell. April 17, 1782. Reg. of Wills, Liber L, folio 231.

Downing, Joseph. Admin. of, to Perthina Downing & Benjamin Downing. April 25, 1782. Arch. vol. A14, pages 247-249. Reg. of Wills, Liber L, folio 231. Note:—Arch. vol. A14, page 248 shows that Perthina Downing married Joseph Hill, Jr.

Erb, Jacob. Laborer. Will. Made March 21, 1782. Little Creek Hd. Heirs: Mary Hart, wife of John Hart, Jr; Margaret Srowder. Exec'r, friend Jacob Stout. Wits., Robert Wood, John Srowders. Prob. April 27, 1782. Arch. vol. A16, page 209. Reg. of Wills, Liber L, folios 260-261.

Black, Stephen, Jr. Admin. of, to Mary Black. April 30, 1782. Reg. of Wills, Liber L, folio 231.

Black, Stephen. Admin. of, to Rebecah Black. April 30, 1782. Reg. of Wills, Liber L, folio 231.

Macey, Daniel. Will. Made March 9, 1782. Heirs: wife Mary; sons John, Thomas, Daniel, Henry; daus. Mary, Jean & Susannah; one child unnamed. Exec'rs, wife Mary & son John. Wits., Arnold Hawkins, Aron Dodd, John Joy. Prob. May 1, 1782. Arch. vol. A33, pages 43-44, 47 & 51. Reg. of Wills, Liber L, folio 262. Note:—Arch. vol. A33, pages 44, 47 & 51 show Francis Denny as guardian of Daniel, Jr., Jean, & Susannah Macey; also page 47 shows that Jean Macey married James Palmetry.

Ayler, William. Will. Made Feb. 19, 1782. Heir: wife Charity. Exec'x, wife Charity. Wits., John Patton, Thomas Needles, John Manning. Prob. May 7, 1782. Arch. vol. A2, page 34. Reg. of Wills, Liber L, folio 263.

Hollingsworth, Margaret. Admin. of, to Oliver Crawford. May 21, 1782. Reg. of Wills, Liber L, folio 231.

Wharton, Isaiah. Yeoman. Will. Made Aug. . . ., 1779. Heirs: wife Grace; sons Garrett & Isaiah; daus. Ann, Elizabeth Clayton & Susannah Pell; grandson Sipple Wharton, son of Isaiah; granddau. Mary Wharton, dau. of son Isaiah; son-in-law James Clayton. Exec'x, wife Grace. Wits., Richard Butler, Simon W. Wilson, Thomas North. Prob. May 23, 1782. Arch. vol. A54, page 43. Reg. of Wills, Liber L, folios 242-243.

Caldwell, Hannah. Admin. of, to Thomas Wallace. June 3, 1782. Arch. vol. A7, page 107. Reg. of Wills, Liber L, folio 231.

Durborow, Daniel. Farmer. Will. Made May 8, 1782. Little Creek Hd. Heirs: wife Rachel; son Hugh; daus. Lydia, Elizabeth Durborow, & Sarah Handerson; grandson Daniel Durborow, son of son Hugh. Exec'r, son Hugh. Guardian, son Hugh. Wits., Samuel Whitehart, George Legg, Thomas Albenny. Prob. June 3, 1782. Arch. vol. A15, pages 157-158. Reg. of Wills, Liber L, folios 263-264. Note:—Will mentions Benjamin Wallace, dec'd, grandfather of Daniel Durborow.

Lewis, James. Admin. of, to James David, D. B. N. June 5, 1782. Reg. of Wills, Liber L, folio 231.

Caldwell, James. Admin. of, to Joseph Caldwell, D. B. N. June 8, 1782. Arch. vol. A7, page 111. Reg. of Wills, Liber L, folio 232.

Corse, James. Admin. of, to William Corse. June 21, 1782. Reg. of Wills, Liber L, folio 232.

Snow, John. Minor son of James Snow. Admin. of, to James Vandike. June 22, 1782. Reg. of Wills, Liber L, folio 232. Note:—Arch. vol. A48, page 17 shows Thomas Keith as guardian.

Powell, John. Will. Made June 19, 1782. Heirs: wife Jane; son John; daus. Mary, Elizabeth & Sarah; one child unnamed. Exec'x, wife Jane. Trustees, Isaac Brown, Aron Brown, Thomas Blackshiar & Daniel Duhadaway. Wits., Benjamin McBride, John McBride, Angelo Bennet. Prob. June 22, 1782. Arch. vol. A41, pages 24-26. Reg. of Wills, Liber L, folios 264-265. Note:—Arch. vol. A41, page 25, shows that Jane Powel married Jacob Pierce; page 26 shows that Mary Powel married William Davis and also mentions a son William Powel.

Van Birculoe, John. Admin. of, to Peter Van Birculoe. July 9, 1782. Reg. of Wills, Liber L, folio 232.

Burrows, James. Admin. of, to William Watkins. July 10, 1782. Arch. vol. A6, page 212. Reg. of Wills, Liber L, folio 232.

Lynch, William. Admin. of, to Richard Turley, D. B. N. July 11, 1782. Arch. vol. A32, pages 27-28. Reg. of Wills, Liber L, folio 232. Note:—Arch. vol. A32, page 27 shows this acct. later administered by Sarah Nowland, the late Sarah Turley.

Irons, Henry. Admin. of, to John Faris. July 15, 1782. Reg. of Wills, Liber L, folio 232.

Eliott, Isaac. Admin. of, to Ruth Elliott. July 17, 1782. Reg. of Wills, Liber L, folio 232.

Burrows, William. Will. Made June 24, 1782. Heirs: wife Sarah; sons John, William, James & Richard; daus. Ester, Mary, Elizabeth & Margaret. Exec'rs, wife Sarah & William Seyers. Wits., Samuel West, William Reed. Prob. July 29, 1782. Arch. vol. A6, pages 220-222. Reg. of Wills, Liber L, folio 265. Note:—Arch. vol. A6, page 221 shows that Ester Burrows married . . . Sears & Mary Burrows married . . . Hogins.

Lynch, Sarah. Admin. of, to Richard Turley. July 30, 1782. Reg. of Wills, Liber L, folio 232.

Robinson, John. Admin. of, to Deborah Robinson. Aug. 1, 1782. Reg. of Wills, Liber L, folio 232.

Levick, William. Yeoman. Will. Made Jan. 6, 1780. Heirs: wife Rachel; son William; dau. Sarah Sturgis; granddau. Sarah Sturgis; grandsons William Hirons & Stockely Sturgis. Exec'r, son William. Wits., Abraham Vanhoy, Nicholas Vining, Robert Hirons. Prob. Aug. 2, 1782. Arch. vol. A30, page 45. Reg. of Wills, Liber L, folios 265-266.

Lee, Richard. Will. Made July 24, 1782. Duck Creek Hd. Heir: illegitimate son Jeremiah Lee, alias Jones, son of Sarah Jones. Exec'r, Jeremiah Lee. Wits., William Whiteal, Charles Doney, Charles Green. Prob. Aug. 6, 1782. Arch. vol. A29, page 237. Reg. of Wills, Liber L, folio 266.

Frazer, William. Admin. of, to Charles Robinson. Aug. 11, 1782. Reg. of Wills, Liber L, folio 232.

Latchum, Hester. Admin. of, to George Latchum. Aug. 15, 1782. Reg. of Wills, Liber L, folio 232.

Fowler, Benjamin. Admin. of, to Rachel Fowler. Aug. 16, 1782. Arch. vol. A18, pages 53-54. Reg. of Wills, Liber L, folio 232. Note:—Arch. vol. A18, page 53 shows that Rachel Fowler married . . . Barcus.

Gray, James. Admin. of, to Darcus Gray. Aug. 16, 1782. Arch. vol. A20, pages 18-19. Reg. of Wills, Liber L, folio 232. Note:—Arch. vol. A20, page 18 mentions heirs, Sarah & James Gray.

Fowler, Benjamin. Will (copy). Made Jan. 8, 1782. Heirs: wife unnamed; sons Benjamin & William Clark Fowler; daus. Rachel, Mary, Ann & Elizabeth. Guardians, Abraham Parsons & wife Martha Parsons. Wits., William Clark, Robert Fowler. Prob. Aug. 16, 1782. Arch. vol. A18, pages 52-54. Reg. of Wills, Liber L, folio 266. Note:—Arch. vol. A18, page 53 shows Rachel Barcus, née Fowler, as exec'x.

Ratlidge, John. Farmer. Will. Made Aug. 16, 1782. Heirs: son John; dau. Elizabeth; bro.-in-law John Truitt, son of John Truitt; Elizabeth Hudson, dau. of Major & Elizabeth Hudson. Exec'r, John Truitt. Wits., William King, Jemima Truitt, Sarah Ceny. [No prob.]. Arch. vol. A42, page 102.

Cain, Owen. Admin. of, to James Cain. Aug. 19, 1782. Reg. of Wills, Liber L, folio 232.

Jester, Joshua. Admin. of, to Thomas Primrose. Aug. 20, 1782. Arch. vol. A27, pages 35-37. Reg. of Wills, Liber L, folio 232. Note:—Arch. vol. A27, page 36 mentions heirs, Joshua Jester, Mary Godwin & Selah Fitzgarrald.

Neill, Hugh. Will (certified copy). Made May 3, 1781. Queen Anns Co., Md. Heirs: son William Charles Neill; daus. Henrietia Standley, Mary Neill; grandson William Standley, son of dau. Heneretia; John Wells Emory, son of Arthur, Jr.; Mrs. Ann Emory, wife of Arthur, Jr. Exec'rs, son of William Charles Neill, daus. Heneretia Standley & Mary Neill. Trustees, friends Thomas Wright & Arthur Emory, Jr. Wits., Robert Dawson, Edw. Thomas, William Dimond & Samuel Betton. Prob. Aug. 26, 1782. Arch. vol. A37, page 180. Reg. of Wills, Liber L, folios 266-267.

Wheeler, William. Admin. of, to Alice Wheeler. Aug. 28, 1782. Arch. vol. A54, pages 69-70. Reg. of Wills, Liber L, folio 266. Note:—Arch. vol. A54, pages 69-70 show that Alice Wheeler married John Gregg.

England, David. Admin. of, to Ester England. Aug. 28, 1782. Reg. of Wills, Liber L, folio 266.

Tomlinson, James. Admin. of, to Rhoda Peterkin. Aug. 28, 1782. Arch. vol. A50, page 192. Note:—Shows Sophia Tomlinson as the wife of William Candy, Mary Tomlinson as the wife of Purnal Holson & mentions Cary Tomlinson as an heir.

Stuart, Charles. Admin. of, to Mary Numbers, D. B. N. Aug. 29, 1782. Arch. vol. A49, pages 91 & 93. Note:—Mentions heirs, Catherine & Samuel Stuart.

Pierce, Joseph. Admin. of, to Margaret Freeland. Sept. 14, 1782. Arch. vol. A40, pages 75-77. Note:—Arch. vol. A40, page 75 mentions heirs, Joseph, William & Rachel Pierce.

Freeland, Emanuel. Admin. of, to Margaret Freeland. Sept. 14, 1782. Arch. vol. A18, page 112. Reg. of Wills, Liber L, folio 232. Note:—Arch. vol. A18, page 112 shows that Margaret Freeland later married . . . Dickinson.

Hubbard, Charles. Admin. of, to John Hopkins, D. B. N. Sept. 23, 1782. Arch. vol. A25, pages 88-90. Reg. of Wills, Liber L, folio 232. Note:—Arch. vol. A25, page 90 mentions heirs, Sarah, Daniel, Charles & James Hubbard.

Cox, Powell. Will (copy). Made Sept. 19, 1782. Talbot Co. Heirs: wife Sarah; dau. Sarah; sons Daniel, Nicholas & Edward. Exec'r, son Daniel. Wits., Robert Lloyd, Samuel Sharp, Daniel Powell Cox, Elizabeth Lloyd. Prob. Oct. 2, 1782. Arch. vol. A11, page 141. Reg. of Wills, Liber M, folio 4.

Game, Robert. Will. Made Sept. . . ., 1782. Murderkill Hd. Heirs: wife Elizabeth; wife's daus. Mary & Sarah Lanthorn. Exec'x, wife Elizabeth. Wits., William Wells, French Battle. Prob. Oct. 17, 1782. Arch. vol. A18, page 208. Reg. of Wills, Liber L, folios 267-268.

Murphey, Thomas. Admin. of, to Elizabeth Murphey. Oct. 21, 1782. Reg. of Wills, Liber L, folio 232.

Van Hazel, John. Admin. of, to Stacy Van Hazel. Oct. 23, 1782. Reg. of Wills, Liber L, folio 232.

Sapp, John. Admin. of, to Elizabeth Sapp. Nov. 4, 1782. Reg. of Wills, Liber L, folio 232.

Luff, Caleb. Admin. of, to Nathaniel Luff, Jr. Nov. 5, 1782. Arch. vol. A31, pages 205-209. Reg. of Wills, Liber L, folio 233.

Enloe, Ridgbal. Admin. of, to Elizabeth Enloe. Nov. 7, 1782. Reg. of Wills, Liber L, folio 233.

Hudson, Arnold. Admin. of, to Absolom Hudson. Nov. 18, 1782. Reg. of Wills, Liber L, folio 268.

Lewis, Daniel. Admin. of, to Henry Bell. Nov. 20, 1782. Reg. of Wills, Liber L, folio 268.

Lane, Gallant. Admin. of, to William Lane. Nov. 27, 1782. Arch. vol. A29, page 114. Reg. of Wills, Liber L, folio 268.

Cambel, William. Admin. of, to James Cambel. Nov. 27, 1782. Reg. of Wills, Liber L, folio 268.

Roley, James. Admin. of, to Charity Roley & Elijah Roley. Nov. 28, 1782. Reg. of Wills, Liber L, folio 268.

Snipe, Joseph. Son of William. Admin. of, to Robert Hendry, D. B. N. (in lieu of Matthew Hendry, guardian). Nov. 28, 1782. Arch. vol. A47, page 227.

Dill, Mary. Widow. Admin. of, to Elijah Dill & Nimrod Dill. Dec. 2, 1782. Arch. vol. A14, pages 104-105. Reg. of Wills, Liber L, folio 268. Note:—Arch. vol. A14, page 104 mentions heirs, William, Job, John, Edward, James, Elizabeth, Joseph, Solomon, Rebecca, Philemon & Sarah Dill (wife of Cornelius Shehorn).

Hanson, Joseph. Admin. of, to Emelia Hanson, widow. Dec. 5, 1782. Reg. of Wills, Liber L, folio 268.

Tanney, Jacob. Admin. of, to Lewis Tanney. Dec. 9, 1782. Reg. of Wills, Liber L, folio 268.

Cordery, Noble. Farmer. Admin. of, to Mary Cordery & Thomas Cordery. Arch. vol. A10, page 265. Reg. of Wills, Liber L, folio 268.

Wood, Robert, Jr. Admin. of, to Hannah Wood & Abraham Ayers. Dec. 10, 1782. Arch. vol. A45, page 99. Reg. of Wills, Liber L, folio 268.

Story, Marmaduke. Will. Made March 3, 1780. Heirs: wife Ann; son Marmaduke. Exec'x, wife Ann. Wits., Burton Faulkner, William Yeats. Prob. Dec. 13, 1782. Arch. vol. A49, page 33. Reg. of Wills, Liber L, folios 243-244.

Farson, Henry. Will. Made Dec. 3, 1782. Duck Creek Hd. Heirs: wife unnamed; sons David, William, John. Exec'rs, sons William, John & son-in-law Samuel Starr. Trustees, James Morris, Robert Holliday, Thomas Collins, Michael Offley & Isaac Griffin. Wits., John Chicken, William Johnston & Rebecca Hook. Prob. Dec. 19, 1782. Arch. vol. A17, page 56. Reg. of Wills, Liber M, folios 95-96.

Walker, Agnes. Admin. of, to Caleb Sipple. Dec. 20, 1782. Arch. vol. A52, page 169. Reg. of Wills, Liber L, folio 269.

Chance, Elijah. Admin. of, to Alexandria Chance. Jan. 3, 1783. Reg. of Wills, Liber L, folio 269.

Cross, John. Admin. of, to John Cross, Jr. Jan. 6, 1783. Reg. of Wills, Liber L, folio 269.

Smith, Benjamin. Admin. of, to Martha Smith & John Smith. Jan. 24, 1783. Reg. of Wills, Liber L, folio 269.

Moore, Joseph. Admin. of, to Christiana Moore, widow. Jan. 24, 1783. Reg. of Wills, Liber L, folio 269.

Thompson, John. Admin. of, to Hannah Thompson, widow. Jan. 24, 1783. Reg. of Wills, Liber L, folio 269.

Caldwell, John. Will. Made Oct. 18, 1781. Little Creek Hd. Heirs: wife Margaret; sons Timothy & John; dau. Hannah Amor, wife of John Amor. Exec'x, wife Margaret. Wits., Richard Smith, Andrew Mairs. Prob. Jan. 30, 1783. Arch. vol. A7, page 112. Reg. of Wills, Liber L, folio 270.

Hall, John. Yeoman. Will. Made Dec. 13, 1782. Heirs: wife Isbil; sons James & David; daus. Elenor, Sarah, Miriam, Elizabeth & Mary. Exec'rs, wife Isbil & son David. Prob. Jan. 31, 1783. Arch. vol. A21, page 96. Reg. of Wills, Liber L, folios 268-269.

Peterson, Jacob. Admin. of, to Peter Peterson. Feb. 6, 1783. Reg. of Wills, Liber L, folio 270.

Stuart, Daniel. Yeoman. Mispillion Hd. Admin. of, to Rachel Stuart, widow. Feb. 6, 1783. Arch. vol. A48, page 240. Reg. of Wills, Liber L, folio 270.

Whitman, Samuel. Will. Made May 15, 1776. Little Creek Hd. Heirs: wife Agnes; son Jonathan; dau. Savory; nephew Samuel Freeman; Sarah Watkins, wife of Peter Watkins; Thomas Parker; children of Elizabeth Irons. Exec'rs, wife Agnes & friend Silas Snow. Guardian, Silas Snow. Wits., Thomas Butcher, John Grey, Elizabeth Loatman. Prob. Feb. 10, 1783. Arch. vol. A54, pages 212-213. Reg. of Wills, Liber L, folios 270-271.

Benston, Elisha. Admin. of, to Nice Benston. Feb. 10, 1783. Arch. vol. A3, page 237. Reg. of Wills, Liber L, folio 271.

Butler, Andrew. Innkeeper. Town of Dover. Admin. of, to Elizabeth Butler & James Townsend. Feb. 14, 1783. Arch. vol. A7, page 12. Reg. of Wills, Liber L, folio 271.

Maxwell, John. Admin. of, to Ann Maxwell & William Maxwell. Feb. 17, 1783. Reg. of Wills, Liber L, folio 271.

Saunders, Paul. Admin. of, to Elizabeth Saunders. Feb. 26, 1783. Reg. of Wills, Liber L, folio 271. Note:—Arch. vol. A45, page 27 mentions heirs, Sarah, William, Clark & Abraham.

Williams, Thomas. Admin. of, to Mary Godwin, the late Mary Williams. Feb. 26, 1783. Arch. vol. A55, page 169. Note:— Mentions an heir, Nancy Story, wife of Marmaduke Story.

Freeman, Thomas. Admin. of, to Richard Kirklin. March 6, 1783. Reg. of Wills, Liber L, folio 271.

Luff, Caleb. Admin. of, to Ruben Wallace. March 19, 1783. Reg. of Wills, Liber L, folio 271. Note:—Arch. vol. A31, page 215 mentions heirs, John & Nathaniel Luff.

Knotts, Edward. Admin. of, to Ruben Wallace. March 19, 1783. Reg. of Wills, Liber L, folio 272.

McGear, Mary. Admin. of, to John Ferguson. March 24, 1783. Reg. of Wills, Liber L, folio 272.

Dill, Solomon. Admin. of, to Rachel Dill. March 25, 1783. Reg. of Wills, Liber L, folio 272.

Craner, Charles, Sr. Planter. Will. Made Aug. 6, 1781. Mispillion. Heirs: wife Elizabeth; daus. Lucresey Jester, Mary & Dorcas Craner; sons Charles, Thomas, Samuel & Moses. Exec'x, wife Elizabeth. Wits., Eliab Vinson, John Meredith, Elizabeth Vinson. Prob. April 19, 1783. Arch. vol. A11, pages 194-195. Reg. of Wills, Liber M, folio 6. Note:—Arch. vol. A11, page 195 shows that Elizabeth Craner married Leven Meredith.

Barrow, Samuel. Watchmaker. Will. Made March 31, 1783. Heir: friend Matthias Davis. Exec'r, [Matthias Davis, from admin. acct.]. Wits., Jehu Davis, Robert McGonigal, Isaac Minshall. Prob. April 19, 1783. Arch. vol. A3, pages 28-31. Reg. of Wills, Liber L, folios 272-273.

Meeks, Joseph. Will. Made March 4, 1783. Heirs: wife Sophia; daus. Araminta, Sophia & Ann; niece Melkiah Meeks, dau. of St. Leger Meeks. Exec'rs, wife Sophia & friend John Clayton, Esq. Guardian, Richard Bassett, attorney-at-law.

Wits., Joseph Pryor, Major Taylor & Nathaniel Smithers. Prob. April 23, 1783. Arch. vol. A34, pages 113-115. Reg. of Wills, Liber M, folio 5. Note:—Arch. vol. A34, page 114 shows that Sophia Meeks married James Marriner.

Denny, Christopher, Sr. Will. Made Feb. 26, 1783. Duck Creek Hd. Heirs: dau. Nancy Walker; sons William & Christopher; children of dau. Hester Deaton; children of dau. Nancy Walker; granddau. Elizabeth Deaton. Exec'rs, sons William & Christopher. Wits., Silas Snow, Thomas Wallace. Prob. April 26, 1783. Arch. vol. A13, page 194. Reg. of Wills, Liber M, folio 7.

Fleming, Isabel. Will. Made Feb. 17, 1783. Heirs: sons James, Matthew, Robert, Joseph & Archibald; dau. Cathran Mittan. Exec'r, son Archibald. Wits., William Hudson, Archibald Fleming, Jr., John Steward. Prob. April 26, 1783. Arch. vol. A17, page 181. Reg. of Wills, Liber M, folios 7-8.

Fleming, Archibald. Will. Mode April 1, 1783. Heirs: wife Easther; sons Samuel, George, Andrew & Alexander; daus. Sarah, Barbary & Isabel; granddaus. Elizabeth & Amilia Fleming, daus. of son Joseph. Exec'x, wife Easther. Wits., Richard Dallinar, William Hudson, Samuel Hudson. Prob. April 26, 1783. Arch. vol. A17, page 170. Reg. of Wills, Liber M, folio 8.

Laws, Bolitha. Will. Made Sept. 15, 1781. Heirs: wife Leah; sons Joshua, John, William, Outten, Major & Truston; daus. Charlote, Anne, Esther, Leah, Hesse Laws, Elizabeth Anderson & Sarah Manlove; grandsons Bolitha Anderson (son of Ezekiel & Elizabeth Anderson), Bolitha Laws (son of John), & William McGonagill; granddau. Ziporah Laws. Exec'rs, wife Leah & son Joshua. Wits., Nathan Fleming, Lyda Fleming, John Ralston. Prob. April 26, 1783. Arch. vol. A29, pages 139-141. Reg. of Wills, Liber M, folios 8-10.

Furchas, John. Will. Made Aug. 30, 1782. Heirs: wife Mary Ann; daus. Sarah, Mary & Miriam; sons John & Tobias. Exec'rs, wife Mary Ann & bro.-in-law Joshua Clarke. Wits., John Patten, William Betts. Prob. April 28, 1783. Arch. vol. A18, pages 182-186. Reg. of Wills, Liber M, folio 10. Note:— Will mentions step-father Stephen Lewis, dec'd.

Edmondson, Francis. Will. Made Jan. 2, 1775. Heirs: wife Rachel; dau. Mary; sons Mark Greer Edmondson, William & Samuel. Exec'x, wife Rachel. Wits., Sarah Edmondson, Rebeccah Edmondson, William Edmondson. Prob. April 29, 1783. Arch. vol. A16, page 43. Reg. of Wills, Liber M, folios 11-12.

Caldwell, James. Will. Made March 25, 1782. Heirs: wife Hannah; James Caldwell, son of Joseph & Joannah Caldwell; Janet Smith. Exec'x, wife Hannah. Wits., John Gordon, Jr., Margaret Hendry, Alice Kearn. Prob. April 30, 1783. Arch. vol. A7, page 109. Reg. of Wills, Liber L, folios 261-262.

Dunwidde, Samuel. Admin. of, to Mary Dunwidde. May 2, 1783. Arch. vol. A15, pages 149-150. Reg. of Wills, Liber M, folio 3. Note:—Arch. vol. A15, page 150 shows heirs, James, Mary, Samuel, John & Nancy Dunwidde.

Prichard [Prichett], Edward. Farmer. Mispillion Hd. Admin. of, to Sarah Prichard, widow. May 13, 1783. Arch. vol. A41, page 174. Reg. of Wills, Liber M, folio 4.

Aron, Michael Carey. Admin. of, to Isaac Jester & Jonathan Rowland, May 14, 1783. Reg. of Wills, Liber M, folio 13.

Eckels, Richard. Will. Made April 20, 1783. Heirs: wife Ann; sons John, Anthoney & Richard. Exec'x, wife Ann. Wits., Frances Yester, Major Anderson, Phillis Yester. Prob. May 14, 1783. Arch. vol. A16, pages 1-3. Reg. of Wills, Liber M, folios 12-13. Note:—Arch. vol. A16, page 2 mentions heirs, Esther, Julana, Jessey, Lydia & Hannah Eckels, & Sarah & Mary Jester.

Patton, Robert. Yeoman. Will. Made Jan. 29, 1776. Heirs: wife Mary; sons William, Andrew, John; daus. Margaret Patton & Mary David; grandson Robert Patton. Exec'rs, sons William & Andrew. Wits., John Gray, William Cockran, William Crouch. Prob. May 17, 1783. Arch. vol. A39, pages 143-145. Reg. of Wills, Liber M, folios 15-16. Note:—Arch. vol. A39, page 144 shows that Margaret Patton married ... Muncy.

Freeman, Miriam. Admin. of, to John Freeman. May 29, 1783. Reg. of Wills, Liber M, folio 13.

Dill, William. Admin. of, to John Dill. May 29, 1783. Arch. vol. A14, pages 124-125. Reg. of Wills, Liber M, folio 15.

Robertson, Mary. Admin. of, to William Truax. May 30, 1783. Arch. vol. A44, page 32.

Hanson, Thomas. Will. Made Jan. 25, 1783. Heirs: wife Mary; dau. Susannah Howell; bro. Samuel Hanson; heirs of bros. Timothy & Samuel Hanson; granddau. Mary Howell, dau. of Susannah; nephew John Conningham, son of sister Elizabeth Conningham; son-in-law Samuel Howell; Thomas Hanson Bellach, son of James Bellach; Thomas Hanson, son of nephew Samuel Hanson; Thomas Lamb, son of niece Susannah Lamb; Priscilla & Susanna Cox, daus. of niece Susanna Hunn; Ezekiel Cowgill. Exec'rs, wife Mary & son-in-law Samuel Howell. Wits., Jabez Jenkins, Thomas Jenkins & John Conner. Prob. June 3, 1783. Arch. vol. A21, page 217. Reg. of Wills, Liber M, folios 13-15.

Knotts, Edward. Admin. of, to Hannah Knotts. June 5, 1783. Reg. of Wills, Liber M, folio 15.

Smith, James. Admin. of, to Rebecca Smith. June 5, 1783. Arch. vol. A47, page 64. Reg. of Wills, Liber M, folio 15.

Nock, Thomas. Will. Made Feb. 26, 1782. Heirs: grandson Daniel Nock, Jr.; Eleanor Bostick; nephews Thomas Jenkins (son of bro. Jabez), & Daniel Nock (son of bro. Ezekiel). Exec'r, kinsman Joseph Jenkins. Wits., Joseph Nock, David Beauchamp, James Muncy, Samuel Morris. Codicil, Joseph Jenkins, Thomas Jenkins. Prob. June 10, 1783. Arch. vol. A38, page 35. Reg. of Wills, Liber L, folios 254-255.

Balton, James. Admin. of, to William Porter. June 12, 1783. Reg. of Wills, Liber M, folio 16.

Morris, Martha. Will. Made May 23, 1782. Heirs: daus. Elizabeth & Hannah. [No exec'rs.]. Wits., Michael Lowber, Daniel Lowber, Joshua Shaw. [No prob.]. Arch. vol. A37, page 37. Reg. of Wills, Liber L, folio 263. Recorded June 14, 1783.

Clark, Jonathan, the elder. Yeoman. Will. Made March 1, 1783. Dover Hd. Heirs: cousin Ezekiel Clark; Sarah & Mary Clark, daus. of Ezekiel Clark; James Ayler, carpenter. Exec'r, Ezekiel Clark. Wits., Charles Ridgely, Maskill Clark, John Aylor. Prob. June 17, 1783. Arch. vol. A9, pages 39-41. Reg. of Wills, Liber M, folios 16-17.

Macey, Mary. Admin. of, to John Macey, Jr. June 21, 1783. Reg. of Wills, Liber L, folio 273.

Gray, John. Will. Made May 2, 1783. Heirs: dau. Mary Dyer; son John; wife Elizabeth; dau.-in-law Nancy Broadaway; granddaus. Elizabeth, Mary, Prudence & Nancy Dyer. Exec'x, wife Elizabeth. Wits., Edward Callahan, Richard White, Michael Reynalls. Prob. June 23, 1783. Arch. vol. A20, page 23. Reg. of Wills, Liber M, folio 12.

Faris, Matthew. Admin. of, to Elenor Faris. June 26, 1783. Reg. of Wills, Liber L, folio 273.

Hall, Alexander. A minor. Murderkill Hd. Admin. of, to Thomas Buckmaster. June 26, 1783. Arch. vol. A21, pages 81-83. Reg. of Wills, Liber L, folio 273. Note:—Arch. vol. A21, page 81 mentions heirs, Unity Buckmaster, Margaret Hudson & Margaret Furbee.

Maxwell, William. Admin. of, to Joshua Gordon. July 10, 1783. Reg. of Wills, Liber L, folio 273.

Sullivan, David. Admin. of, to Samuel Freeman. July 12, 1783. Reg. of Wills, Liber L, folio 273.

Quenanault, Paul. Admin. of, to Sarah Quenanault & James Clark. Aug. 2, 1783. Reg. of Wills, Liber L, folio 273. Note: —Arch. vol. A42, page 7 mentions a son Thomas Quenanault.

Brinklee, Jesse. Admin. of, to Anthony Snow. Aug. 7, 1783. Reg. of Wills, Liber L, folio 274.

Griffin, William. Miller. Admin. of, to Ann Griffin. Aug. 12, 1783. Arch. vol. A20, page 233. Reg. of Wills, Liber L, folio 274.

Morgan, Daniel. Admin. of, to James Morgan. Aug. 12, 1783. Reg. of Wills, Liber L, folio 274.

Walton, John. Will. Made July 17, 1783. Murderkill Hd. Heirs: wife Ann; sons Beauchamp, Bagwell, William, Isaac, George & John; daus. Sarah, Rachel, Patience, Elizabeth & Esther; son-in-law John Hutchison. Exec'x, wife Ann. Wits., Mary Bauchamp, Esther Harrington, Nathaniel Smithers, Jr. Prob. Aug. 13, 1783. Arch. vol. A53, page 63. Reg. of Wills, Liber L, folios 274-275.

Minshall, Jane. Admin. of, to John Gordon. Aug. 14, 1783. Reg. of Wills, Liber L, folio 275.

Excel, Samuel. Will. Made July 11, 1783. Duck Creek Hd. Heirs: niece Mary McFarlin; cousin John Alee. Exec'r, cousin John Allee. Wits., Moses Morris, Elizabeth Dawson. Prob. Aug. 20, 1783. Arch. vol. A16, page 237. Reg. of Wills, Liber L, folio 275.

Thomson, James. Admin. of, to James Thomson, Jr. Aug. 21, 1783. Arch. vol. A50, pages 85-86. Reg. of Wills, Liber L, folio 275. Note:—Arch. vol. A50, pages 85-86 show Thomas Thomson as the adm'r of the unsettled accts. of James Thomson, Sr., & James Thomson, Jr.; also show that Thomas married Elizabeth, widow of James, Jr. The heirs are mentioned, James, Abraham & Mary Thomson.

David, John. Will. Made Aug. 11, 1783. Heirs: wife Anne; dau. Mary. Exec'r, James Severson. Wits., James Morris, Jr., John David, Sarah Severson. Prob. Aug. 26, 1783. Arch. vol. A12, pages 224 & 226. Reg. of Wills, Liber L, folios 275-276. Note:—Will mentions bro. James, dec'd.

Robinson, John. Admin. of, to Thomas Keith. Aug. 27, 1783. Reg. of Wills, Liber L, folio 276.

Furbee, Benjamin. Admin. of, to Michael Furbee. Aug. 28, 1783. Arch. vol. A18, page 150.

Hastings, Isaac. Admin. of, to John Whitely. Aug. 29, 1783. Arch. vol. A22, page 231.

Spencer, William. Admin. of, to Charles Everen & Jacob Hurlock. Sept. 11, 1783. Arch. vol. A48, page 107. Reg. of Wills, Liber L, folio 276.

Wallace, William. Admin. of, to Jonathan Clampit. Oct. 2, 1783. Reg. of Wills, Liber L, folio 276.

Gordon, David. Admin. of, to Joshua Gordon. Oct. 16, 1783. Arch. vol. A19, page 149. Reg. of Wills, Liber L, folio 276.

Neil, James. Admin. of, to William Neil. Oct. 18, 1783. Reg. of Wills, Liber L, folio 276.

Cooley, Daniel. Duck Creek. Admin. of, to Nathaniel Wilds. Oct. 23, 1783. Arch. vol. A10, page 143. Reg. of Wills, Liber L, folio 276.

Hull, James. Admin. of, to Mary Hull. Oct. 24, 1783. Arch. vol. A25, pages 125-126. Reg. of Wills, Liber L, folio 276.

Smith, John. Admin. of, to Sarah Smith. Oct. 24, 1783. Arch. vol. A47, pages 79-81. Reg. of Wills, Liber L, folio 276. Note:—Arch. vol. A47, page 81 shows that Sarah Smith married John Stow.

Hazell, Benjamin. Gentleman. Will. Made Sept. 11, 1783. Town of Dover. Heirs: wife Ann; son William; cousin George Hazel (son of Benjamin); nephew John Gordon; nieces Mary Gordon & Mary Corey (dau. of Molleston Corey); nephews Molleston Corey, Jr., & Charles Corey (sons of Molleston); Abraham Falkner (son of Gilbert Falkner). Exec'rs, wife Anne & bro.-in-law Charles Nixon. Wits., George McCall, William McClements, Benjamin Vining, Nicholas Ridgely. Prob. Oct. 27, 1783. Arch. vol. A23, pages 75-79. Reg. of Wills, Liber M, folios 2-3.

Newman, Mary. Admin. of, to James Wells, Sr. Nov. 10, 1783. Arch. vol. A37, page 212. Reg. of Wills, Liber M, folio 17.

Barrot, Roger. Admin. of, to Miriam Barrot. Nov. 13, 1783. Reg. of Wills, Liber M, folio 17. Note:—Arch. vol. A3, page 25 mentions heirs: Jane Jackson (wife of Alexander Jackson), Hannah Conner (wife of John), Letitia Anderson (wife of Clothier), and Samuel Barrot; also shows that Miriam Barrot married . . . Blackshere.

Killen, Mary. Widow of Robert Killen. Mispillion Hd. Admin. of, to Henry Killen. Nov. 26, 1783. Arch. vol. A28, page 192.

Vangaskin, John, Sr. Admin. of, to John Slaught, D. B. N. Nov. 28, 1783. Arch. vol. A51, pages 242-244.

Wheelor, William. Admin. of, to James Craig & James Jones. Nov. 28, 1783. Arch. vol. A54, pages 69-71. Reg. of Wills, Liber M, folio 17. Note:—Arch. vol. A54, page 69 shows heirs, Alice Wheelor (widow), daus. Sarah Wheelor & Mary Wheelor, dec'd; also shows Alice, the widow, married John Gregg, and Sarah married Thomas Cavendar.

Spruance, John. Admin. of, to Jean Spruance. Dec. 4, 1783. Reg. of Wills, Liber M, folio 17.

Vangaskin, Sarah. Admin. of, to Thomas Cutler. Dec. 4, 1783. Reg. of Wills, Liber M, folio 18.

McEver, Mary. Admin. of, to John McEver. Dec. 8, 1783. Reg. of Wills, Liber M, folio 17.

Richardson, John. Admin. of, to Elizabeth Butler & James Townsend. Dec. 8, 1783. Reg. of Wills, Liber M, folio 17.

Caffey, Ezekiel. Farmer. Will. Made Nov. 24, 1783. Mispillion Hd. Heirs: wife Maryan; mother Pinelepy Cats; nephew William Williams; Parey Bane & wife Sarah. Exec'x, wife Maryan. Wits., John Parker, Levin Willey. Prob. Dec. 18, 1783. Arch. vol. A7, pages 22-24. Reg. of Wills, Liber M, folio 18. Note:—Arch. vol. A7, page 23 shows that Maryan Caffey married Jacob Harrington.

Windle, William. Admin. of, to Ann Windle. Dec. 22, 1783. Reg. of Wills, Liber M, folio 18. Note:—Arch. vol. A56, page 36 mentions a son William Windle.

Cubbage, Thomas. Admin. of, to Anna Cubbage. Jan. 2, 1784. Arch. vol. A12, pages 54-56. Reg. of Wills, Liber M, folio 18. Note:—Arch. vol. A12, page 56 mentions heirs, John, Thomas, George & Phillimon Cubbage, Sarah Needles, Mary Dorhety, Elizabeth Conner & Susannah Harris.

Alford, Charity. Will. Made Sept. 24, 1781. Heirs: son Philip Samuel; daus. Sarah Alston, Elizabeth Casson. Exec'rs, John Casson & Richard Basset. Wits., John Pryor, John Taylor, Joseph Pryor. Prob. Jan. 7, 1784. Arch. vol. A1, page 24. Reg. of Wills, Liber M, folios 18-19.

Alford, Charity. Admin. of, to John Banning. Jan. 8, 1784. Reg. of Wills, Liber M, folios 19-20.

Foreman, Henry. Murderkill Hd. Admin. of, to Arthur Foreman. Jan. 13, 1784. Arch. vol. A18, page 28. Reg. of Wills, Liber M, folio 20.

Corse, George. Admin. of, to William Corse. Jan. 19, 1784. Arch. vol. A11, pages 19-21. Reg. of Wills, Liber M, folio 20. Note:—Arch. vol. A11, page 19 mentions heirs, John, William, Thomas, Hanson, Susannah Corse & Elizabeth Carbine, wife of James Carbine.

Harrington, Henry. Admin. of, to Thomas Sipple, D. B. N. Feb. 4, 1784. Arch. vol. A22, pages 97-101. Reg. of Wills, Liber L, folio 269. Note:—Arch. vol. A22, page 97 shows that Agnes Harrington married Peter Lowber; page 99 shows that Thomas Sipple married Susanah Harrington, widow of Henry.

Craig, James. Admin. of, to Sophia Craig. Feb. 11, 1784. Reg. of Wills, Liber L, folio 271.

Reed, James. Admin. of, to Sarah Reed. Feb. 12, 1784. Reg. of Wills, Liber M, folio 20. Note:—Arch. vol. A42, page 170 shows that Sarah Reed married John Coppage.

Templemen, Henry. Yeoman. Murderkill Hd. Admin. of, to Elizabeth Templemen & Oliver Crawford. Feb. 12, 1784. Reg. of Wills, Liber M, folio 20. Note:—Arch. vol. A49, page 233 shows that final settlement was made by Andrew Anderson & wife Rachel (widow of Oliver Crawford).

Betts, William. Admin. of, to Elizabeth Betts. Feb. 13, 1784. Arch. vol. A4, pages 42-44. Reg. of Wills, Liber M, folio 20. Note:—Arch. vol. A4, page 44 mentions heirs, Isaac, Elizabeth, Ann, Ruth & Susannah Betts; page 42 shows that Job Meredith married Elizabeth Betts.

Pennuel, William. Admin. of, to Smith Fosett, D. B. N. Feb. 14, 1784. Reg. of Wills, Liber M, folio 20.

Arnet, Thomas. Admin. of, to Sarah Arnet. Feb. 21, 1784. Reg. of Wills, Liber M, folio 20.

Moore, Samuel. Admin. of, to Mary Moore. Feb. 23, 1784. Arch. vol. A36, page 88. Reg. of Wills, Liber L, folio 271.

Skillington, Elijah. Admin. of, to Thomas Skillington. Feb. 24, 1784. Arch. vol. A46, page 209. Reg. of Wills, Liber M, folio 20.

Williams, John, Jr. Dover Hd. Admin. of, to John Gordon. March 5, 1784. Arch. vol. A55, page 99. Reg. of Wills, Liber M, folio 20.

Long, Samuel. Late soldier in Delaware regiment. Admin. of, to John Register & Benjamin Coombs. March 12, 1784. Reg. of Wills, Liber M, folio 20.

Sipple, Garrat. Admin. of, to Mary Dushane. March 17, 1784. Reg. of Wills, Liber M, folio 21.

Tucker, Zadock. Admin. of, to Levy Tucker. March 26, 1784. Reg. of Wills, Liber M, folio 21.

Steel, Joseph. Admin. of, to Mary Steel. March 26, 1784. Arch. vol. A48, pages 206-207. Reg. of Wills, Liber M, folio 21. Note:—Arch. vol. A48, page 206 mentions a son Joseph Steel.

McGarment, Robert. Admin. of, to Mary McGarment. April 10, 1784. Reg. of Wills, Liber M, folio 21.

Whaling, Phillip. Admin. of, to Thomas North. April 13, 1784. Reg. of Wills, Liber M, folio 21.

Register, Robert. Admin. of, to Ruth Register. April 19, 1784. Reg. of Wills, Liber M, folio 21.

Howard, Ann. Admin. of, to Mary Howard. April 21, 1784. Reg. of Wills, Liber M, folio 21.

Raly, Philip. Admin. of, to Robert Faral. April 24, 1784. Reg. of Wills, Liber M, folio 21.

Creighton, John. Admin. of, to Elizabeth Creighton. April 27, 1784. Arch. vol. A11, pages 220-222. Reg. of Wills, Liber M, folio 21. Note:—Arch. vol. A11, page 220 mentions heirs, Robert, David, John & Matthew Creighton; page 222 shows that Elizabeth married Joseph Melson.

Scotten, Thomas. Laborer. Murderkill Hd. Admin. of, to Eli Scotten. May 2, 1784. Arch. vol. A45, page 100. Reg. of Wills, Liber M, folio 21.

Morgan, Robert. Blacksmith. Mispillion Hd. Admin. of, to Nancy Morgan. May 11, 1784. Arch. vol. A36, pages 165-167. Reg. of Wills, Liber M, folio 21. Note:—Arch. vol. A36, page 167 shows that Nancy Morgan married John Gibbs; page 165 mentions heirs, George & Robert Morgan.

Metten, William. Yeoman. Mispillion Hd. Admin. of, to James Metten. May 12, 1784. Arch. vol. A35, pages 186-187. Reg. of Wills, Liber M, folio 21.

White, David. Admin. of, to John Darrach. May 22, 1784. Arch. vol. A54, page 103. Reg. of Wills, Liber M, folio 21.

Cahoon, Thomas. Admin. of, to Elizabeth Cahoon. May 24, 1784. Reg. of Wills, Liber M, folio 21.

Layton, Nichols. Admin. of, to Mary Layton. May 24, 1784. Reg. of Wills, Liber M, folio 21. Note:—Arch. vol. A29, page 200 shows that Mary Layton married James Ross.

Herring, George. Admin. of, to James Dill & wife Mary, late Mary Herring. May 28, 1784. Arch. vol. A23, pages 165-166. Note:—Mentions children Riche, Elizabeth, James, John & William Herring.

Robinson, John. Will. Made Oct. 5, 1783. Little Creek Hd. Heirs: aunt Jennet Parsons; Mary Parsons, dau. of aunt Jennet. Exec'x, aunt Jennet Parsons. Wits., John Reec, Jr., James Wells, Ar. Moore. Prob. May 28, 1784. Arch. vol. A44, page 66. Reg. of Wills, Liber M, folio 22.

Copes, Robert. Admin. of, to Susannah Copes. June 5, 1784. Arch. vol. A10, pages 232-233. Reg. of Wills, Liber M, folio 23.

Fleming, William. Will. Made May 3, 1784. Heirs: wife Ann; sons Boaz, Nathan, Bannia & Thomas; dau. Mary Fleming, wife of Mathew Fleming. Exec'rs, sons Boaz & Nathan Fleming. Wits., William Hudson, John Ralston, Sarah Talbott. Prob. June 7, 1784. Arch. vol. A17, pages 205 & 208.

Whalling, Phillip. Admin. of, to Margaret North. June 8, 1784. Reg. of Wills, Liber M, folio 23.

North, Thomas. Admin. of, to Margaret North. June 8, 1784. Arch. vol. A38, page 49. Reg. of Wills, Liber M, folio 23.

Hutchison, Ann. Admin. of, to William Hutchison. June 10, 1784. Reg. of Wills, Liber M, folio 23.

Bowen, Nathan. Admin. of, to Stephen Bowen. June 15, 1784. Reg. of Wills, Liber M, folio 23.

Hudson, Moses. Admin. of, to Penelope Hudson. June 15, 1784. Reg. of Wills, Liber M, folio 23.

Wilds, Abraham. Admin. of, to Mary Wilds. June 15, 1784. Reg. of Wills, Liber M, folio 23.

Wilkerson, James. Admin. of, to Adam Wilkerson. June 15, 1784. Reg. of Wills, Liber M, folio 23.

Holden, Frederick. Admin. of, to William Holden. June 16, 1784. Reg. of Wills, Liber M, folios 23-24.

McWilliam, Samuel. Admin. of, to George & Rachel Fitzjarrald. June 17, 1784. Reg. of Wills, Liber M, folio 24.

Rees, William. Admin. of, to Martha Rees & James M. Gardiner. June 17, 1784. Arch. vol. A43, pages 44-45. Reg. of Wills, Liber M, folio 24. Note:—Arch. vol. A43, page 45 shows that Martha Rees married Thomas Skillington.

Cain, Daniel. Admin. of, to Isaiah Latchem & John Smith. June 19, 1784. Arch. vol. A7, page 51. Reg. of Wills, Liber M, folio 24.

Emerson, Jonathan. Will. Made April 3, 1784. Heirs: wife Ruth; children unnamed; wife's father John Bowers. Exec'rs, wife & friends Ezekiel Cowgill, John Cowgill & Warner Mifflin. Wits., John Bowers, Govey Emerson, John Dickinson, Joseph Jenkins. Codicil, James Chipman, son of Stephen Chipman, dec'd. Prob. July 11, 1784. Arch. vol. A16, page 146. Reg. of Wills, Liber M, folios 24-25.

Sipple, William. Will. Made June 15, 1784. Heirs: wife Cattoran; bro. Boaz; sisters Leady Booth, Elizabeth Downs & Ruth Elot. Exec'x, wife [Catherine, from admin. acct.]. Wits., Saley Depray, John Depray. Prob. July 17, 1784. Arch. vol. A46, page 183. Reg. of Wills, Liber M, folios 25-26.

Jester, Richard. Admin. of, to Rebecca Jester. July 23, 1784. Reg. of Wills, Liber M, folio 26.

Drew, William. Admin. of, to Joseph Caldwell. July 23, 1784. Reg. of Wills, Liber L, folio 273.

Cullen, John. Admin. of, to William Thompson & Sarah, his wife. July 27, 1784. Reg. of Wills, Liber M, folio 26.

Irons, Mary. Admin. of, to Elizabeth Wynn. July 30, 1784. Reg. of Wills, Liber M, folio 26.

McDowell, Hugh. Admin. of, to Thomas Wilkins. July 30, 1784. Reg. of Wills, Liber M, folio 26.

Slaughter, John. Admin. of, Elizabeth Slaughter. July 30, 1784. Reg. of Wills, Liber M, folio 26.

McDowell, Hugh. Admin. of, to Hugh McDowell, Jr. Aug. 3, 1784. Reg. of Wills, Liber M, folio 26.

Roe, William. Admin. of, to Naomi Roe. Aug. 11, 1784. Reg. of Wills, Liber M, folio 27.

Corse, Susannah. Admin. of, to William Corse. Aug. 12, 1784. Arch. vol. A11, pages 25-26. Reg. of Wills, Liber M, folio 27. Note:—Arch. vol. A11, page 25 mentions heirs, John, William, Thomas & Hanson Corse & Elizabeth Carbine, wife of James Carbine.

Elliot, Isaac. Mispillion Hd. Admin. of, to Edward Elliot, D. B. N. Aug. 12, 1784. Arch. vol. A16, pages 95-97. Reg. of Wills, Liber M, folio 27. Note:—Arch. vol. A16, page 95 mentions heirs, Edward, Elizabeth, Susannah & Ruth Elliot.

Rodney, Caesar. (The Signer). Eldest son of Caesar Rodney, dec'd. Will. Made Jan. 20, 1784. Heirs: bros. William & Thomas; half-sister Sarah Wilson; half-bro. John Wilson; nephew Caesar Augustus Rodney; nieces Lavinia Rodney (dau. of bro. Thomas), Letitia Rodney (dau. of bro. William), Elizabeth Gordon (dau. of sister Mary, dec'd), Sarah Rodney (dau. of bro. Daniel); Caesar Rodney Wilson, son of half-sister Sarah Wilson; children of sister Mary Gordon; Wardens of Christ Church in Dover; George Read, Esq., & Finwick Fisher, merchant (both of N. C. Co.). Exec'r, bro. Thomas. Wits., Charles Ridgely, William Molleston, Edward Tilghman, Jr. Codicil, dated March 27, 1784. Wits., William Molleston & H. Matthews. Prob. Aug. 14, 1784. Arch. vol. A44, pages 246-247. Reg. of Wills, Liber L, folios 238-242.

Gordon, John, Jr. Admin. of, to William Molleston. Aug. 24, 1784. Reg. of Wills, Liber M, folio 27.

Morris, Richard. Admin. of, to Prudence Morris. Aug. 25, 1784. Reg. of Wills, Liber M, folio 27.

Emerson, Jonathan. Admin. of, to Ruth Emerson. Sept. 11, 1784. Arch. vol. A16, pages 147-154. Reg. of Wills, Liber M, folio 28. Note:—Mentions heirs, Rachel, John, Jacob & Govey Emerson; also shows that Ruth Emerson married Isaiah Rowland.

White, James. Will. Made Aug. 26, 1784. Heirs: sons Gilbert & James; grandsons James & William Carpenter, sons of William & Mary; granddaus. Elizabeth Carpenter (dau. of William & Mary), Nancy Barratt, & Elizabeth & Margaret White (daus. of Gilbert White); grandchildren, the children of Robert White, dec'd, & Mary White. Exec'r, son James. Wits., Benjamin Sparks, John Cox, Soden Lester. Prob. Sept. 11, 1784. Arch. vol. A54, pages 111-113. Reg. of Wills, Liber M, folios 27-38. Note:—Arch. vol. A54, page 113 mentions heirs, Mary, Susannah, John, James & Elizabeth White; pages 112-113 show that Major McNatt married the widow Mary White.

Manering, William. Admin. of, to Susannah Manering & Obadiah Voshall. Sept. 20, 1784. Reg. of Wills, Liber M, folio 28.

Peterkin, Rhoda. Will. Made March 9, 1784. Heirs: sons Cary Tomlinson & William Frayzer; daus. Sophia Candy, Mary Houston & Rhoda Houston; grandson James Houston. Exec'r, son Cary Tomlinson. Wits., George Manlove, William Laws. Prob. Sept. 25, 1784. Arch. vol. A40, pages 4-6. Reg. of Wills, Liber M, folios 28-29.

Ackroyd, John. Admin. of, to John Fields, John Hays & James Stevenson. Oct. 5, 1784. Arch. vol. A1, pages 4-6. Reg. of Wills, Liber M, folio 29.

Meres, Andrew. Admin. of, to Rebecca Meres. Oct. 6, 1784. Reg. of Wills, Liber M, folio 29.

Rowen, Henry. Admin. of, to Elizabeth Rowen. Oct. 9, 1784. Reg. of Wills, Liber M, folios 29-30.

Read, James. Cordwainer. Admin. of, to Sarah Read. Oct. 23, 1784. Arch. vol. A42, page 194. Reg. of Wills, Liber M, folio 30. Note:—Shows that Sarah Read married . . . Bostick & later married John Coppage.

Davis, Thomas. Admin. of, to Comfort Davis & Elijah Houston. Oct. 25, 1784. Arch. vol. A13, page 70. Reg. of Wills, Liber M, folio 30. Note:—Shows that Elizabeth, the widow of Elijah Houston, later married John Eckles; also shows Comfort, the widow of Thomas Davis, later married Levin Wilcuts.

Hart, Aron. Admin. of, to John Hart. Oct. 29, 1784. Reg. of Wills, Liber M, folio 30.

Nixon, Anne. Admin. of, to Charles Nixon. Nov. 4, 1784. Reg. of Wills, Liber M, folio 29.

Cullen, John. Admin. of, to James Johnson, D. B. N. Nov. 9, 1784. Reg. of Wills, Liber M, folio 30.

Entwesle, Edmund. Admin. of, to Mary Entwesle. Nov. 9, 1784. Arch. vol. A16, page 207. Reg. of Wills, Liber M, folio 30.

Alcock, John. Mispillion Hd. Admin. of, to Solomon Alcock, D. B. N. Nov. 12, 1784. Arch. vol. A1, page 19. Reg. of Wills, Liber M, folio 30.

McMullen, James. Will. Made March 22, 1782. Heirs: sons James, Francis, French & John; daus. Mary & Martha; Mrs. Martha Rees, wife of William Rees. Exec'rs, son James & Eleazer McComb. Wits., Samuel Wilson, William Rees, Mary Creighton. Prob. Nov. 12, 1784. Arch. vol. A33, page 1. Reg. of Wills, Liber M, folios 30-32. Note:—Will mentions grandfather of sons James & Francis, James Gardner, dec'd.

Mileham, Samuel. Admin. of, to Elizabeth Mileham. Nov. 12, 1784. Reg. of Wills, Liber M, folio 30.

Willey, Ailse. Widow. Will. Made Sept. 18, 1784. Heirs: sons Gabriel & Levin; daus. Eunucy Benston, Elizabeth Webb & Ann Postles; grandson James Benston, son of dau. Eunucy; granddaus. Selah Willey (dau. of son Levin), & Elizabeth Postles; Zadock Postles. Exec'rs, dau. Eunucy Benston & son-in-law Shadrick Postles. Wits., William Hazzard, Thomas Manlove, William Daniel. Prob. Nov. 18, 1784. Arch. vol. A55, pages 59-61. Reg. of Wills, Liber M, folios 32-33.

Morris, John. Murderkill Hd. Admin. of, to Thomas Johnson, D. B. N. Nov. 22, 1784. Reg. of Wills, Liber M, folio 33.

Kimmy, Mary. Admin. of, to Absolem Hudson. Nov. 23, 1784. Reg. of Wills, Liber M, folio 33.

Barratt, Philip. Will. Made May 18, 1783. Murtherkill Hd. Heirs: wife Meriam; sons Andrew, Caleb, Nathaniel, Philip & Elijah; daus. Mary Wilson (wife of George Wilson), Meriam & Lydia. Exec'rs, wife Meriam & son Andrew. Trustees, friends Thomas White, Richard Loockwood & Richard Bassett, Esquires. Wits., Richard Bassett, Samuel Dewees, Rachel Dewees. Prob. Nov. 23, 1784. Arch. vol. A3, pages 16-18. Reg. of Wills, Liber M, folios 33-35.

Rees, Robert. Admin. of, to Edward & Jane Rees. Nov. 25, 1784. Arch. vol. A43, page 26.

Hodgson, Train [Traney]. Dau. of William Hodgson. Admin. of, to William Brown. Nov. 24, 1784. Arch. vol. A24, pages 135-136. Note:—Arch. vol. A24, page 136 mentions bros. & sisters Joseph Hodgson, Prudence Sexton, Nancy & Matthew Brown.

Lynch, Henry. Admin. of, to William Lynch. Nov. 27, 1784. Reg. of Wills, Liber M, folio 35.

Watts, John. Admin. of, to Richard Brinckle & Thomas Morgan. Nov. 27, 1784. Reg. of Wills, Liber M, folio 35.

Lane, Timothy. Admin. of, to Priscilla Lane. Dec. 3, 1784. Arch. vol. A29, pages 120-121. Reg. of Wills, Liber M, folio 35. Note:—Arch. vol. A29, page 120 mentions heirs, Margaret, Prudy, Elizabeth, Thomas, James & Mathew Lane.

Maxwell, Samuel. Admin. of, to Elizabeth Maxwell. Dec. 4, 1784. Reg. of Wills, Liber M, folio 35. Note:—Arch. vol. A34, page 100 shows that Elizabeth Maxwell married John Wiltbank.

Tharp, Isaac, Sr. Admin. of, to Sarah Tharp. Dec. 4, 1784. Arch. vol. A49, pages 240-241. Reg. of Wills, Liber M, folio 35. Note:—Arch. vol. A49, page 240 mentions heirs, Isaac, John, James, Aron, David, Joseph, Daniel, Jeremiah & Nancy Tharp, Rachel Wilcuts (wife of Joseph Wilcuts), Susannah Hudson (wife of Robert Hudson).

Furniss, Robert. Admin. of, to Eleaner Furniss & George Martin. Dec. 8, 1784. Reg. of Wills, Liber M, folio 36.

Ardess, Robert. Admin. of, to William Course, Jr. Dec. 11, 1784. Reg. of Wills, Liber M, folio 36.

Smith, Thomas Peacock. Admin. of, to John Gordon, Esq. Dec. 11, 1784. Arch. vol. A47, page 182. Reg. of Wills, Liber M, folio 36.

Pool, Richard Curry. Admin. of, to Elizabeth Jordon. Dec. 16, 1784. Reg. of Wills, Liber M, folio 36.

Townsend, Mary. Murderkill Hd. Admin. of, to Solomon Townsend. Dec. 16, 1784. Arch. vol. A51, page 32. Reg. of Wills, Liber M, folio 36.

Trial, John. Admin. of, to Rachel Burch & George Wilson. Dec. 18, 1784. Reg. of Wills, Liber M, folio 36.

Green, Thomas, Jr. Admin. of, to John Green. Dec. 23, 1784. Arch. vol. A20, pages 118-119. Reg. of Wills, Liber M, folio 36.

Chance, Elijah. Admin. of, to Alexandria Chance. Jan. 3, 1785. Reg. of Wills, Liber L, folio 269.

Wallace, Mary. Murderkill Hd. Admin. of, to Joseph & John Wallace. Jan. 4, 1785. Arch. vol. A53, pages 3-4. Reg. of Wills, Liber M, folio 36. Note:—Arch. vol. A53, page 3 mentions heirs, Robert, William, Joseph & John Wallace.

Baker, William. Will. Made Dec. 8, 1784. Duck Creek Hd. Heir: mother Sarah Baker. Exec'x, mother Sarah Baker. Wits., Finwick Fisher, Samuel Starr & James Saunders. Prob. Jan. 10, 1785. Arch. vol. A2, page 85. Reg. of Wills, Liber M, folio 37.

Ellars, Carty. Will. Made Dec. 4, 1784. Duck Creek Hd. Heirs: wife Mary; sons Benjamin & John. Exec'x, wife Mary. Wits., Aquilla Attix, Isaac Carty, Mary Numbers. Prob. Jan. 11, 1785. Arch. vol. A16, page 91. Reg. of Wills, Liber M, folio 38.

Reynolds, Ruth. Will. Made Dec. 25, 1784. Heirs: sons William, James, & John Christopher; dau. Elizabeth Cordray; son-in-law Benjamin Dailey. Exec'r, son-in-law Thomas Cordray. Wits., Thomas Shepherd, Esther Shepherd. Prob. Jan. 11, 1785. Arch. vol. A43, page 119. Reg. of Wills, Liber M, folio 39.

Garland, Rose. Admin. of, to William Arthurs. Jan. 18, 1785. Reg. of Wills, Liber M, folio 39.

Goodfellow, Margaret. Admin. of, to William Moliston. Jan. 19, 1785. Reg. of Wills, Liber M, folio 94.

Virden, John. Admin. of, to Joseph Caldwell. Jan. 20, 1785. Reg. of Wills, Liber M, folios 39-40.

Gardner, James. Will. Made Dec. 11, 1784. Heirs: bros. Francis Gardner, French & John McMullan; sisters Mary & Martha McMullan; relative James McMullan; Capt. Edward Rees; William Clark, Esq.; friends Eleazer McComb, Esq., & Major John Patten. Exec'rs, Eleazer McComb, Esq., & Major John Patten. Wits., James Tilton, Robert Jamison, Eleazer McComb, Jr. Prob. Jan. 21, 1785. Arch. vol. A18, page 249. Reg. of Wills, Liber M, folios 39-42. Note:—Arch. vol. A18, page 249 mentions bro. Wm. Gardner McMullen, dec'd, and grandfather James Gardner, dec'd. Arch. vol. A18, page 214, the will of the grandfather James Gardner, states that Francis McMullan took the surname Gardner.

Barrow, Gilbert. Will. Made Aug. 15, 1781. Duck Creek Hd. Heirs: wife Mary; dau. Elizabeth; Samuel Price (of Talbot Co., Md.); Barrow Price, son of Samuel. Exec'rs, wife Mary & Silas Snow. Guardian, Silas Snow. Wits., John Stinson, Thomas Wallace. Prob. Jan. 25, 1785. Arch. vol. A3, pages 26-27. Reg. of Wills, Liber M, folios 42-43.

Duhadaway, Daniel. Admin. of, to Catherine Duhadaway. Jan. 25, 1785. Arch. vol. A15, pages 94-97. Reg. of Wills, Liber M, folio 42.

Vanburkalow, Peter. Admin. of, to Peter Vanburkalow & John Wheelton. Jan. 25, 1785. Arch. vol. A15, pages 94-97. Reg. of Wills, Liber M, folio 42.

Irons, Thomas. Will. Made Dec. 25, 1784. Heirs: wife Jennet; son-in-law Eleazer McComb; dau. Lydia McComb, wife of Eleazer; grandson Thomas Irons McComb; granddaus. Jennet & Elizabeth [McComb]; bro. Owen Irons; sister Sarah Shurmer. Exec'rs, Lydia & Eleazer McComb. Wits., James Tilton, Thomas Bellach, Francis McMullan. Prob. Jan. 26, 1785. Arch. vol. A25, page 225. Reg. of Wills, Liber M, folios 43-44.

Burrows, Jesse. Admin. of, to Esther Burrows. Feb. 7, 1785. Reg. of Wills, Liber M, folio 44.

Wyatt, John. Admin. of, to Henry Wigens. Feb. 12, 1785. Reg. of Wills, Liber M, folio 45.

Perry, Daniel. Will. [N. d.]. Heirs: mother Mary Perry; friend David Wallace. Exec'r, David Wallace. Wits., David Jones, Barsheba Tucker, Thomas Wallace. Prob. Feb. 15, 1785. Arch. vol. A39, page 235. Reg. of Wills, Liber M, folio 45.

Smith, Benjamin. Admin. of, to Mary Smith. Feb. 15, 1785. Reg. of Wills, Liber M, folio 46.

Pryor, John. Will. Made June 29, 1782. Heirs: wife Elizabeth; sons John, Jr., & Abraham; daus. Hannah Barns (widow of Wm. Barns, dec'd) & Elizabeth Lockerman (wife of Vincent, the elder); granddau. Elizabeth Lockerman; grandson John Pryor Barns. Exec'rs, wife Elizabeth & son John, Jr. Wits., William Killin, John Bell, Jr. Prob. Feb. 15, 1785. Arch. vol. A41, page 191. Reg. of Wills, Liber M, folios 46-48.

Derochbrune, Joseph. Admin. of, to Rachel Derochbrune. Feb. 16, 1785. Arch. vol. A14, pages 14-16. Reg. of Wills, Liber M, folio 48. Note:—Arch. vol. A14, page 15 shows that Rachel Derochbrune married William Wyatt; page 16 mentions children, Jacob & Charlotte Derochbrune.

Janney, Jacob. Duck Creek Hd. Admin. of, to Levi Janney. Feb. 18, 1875. Arch. vol. A26, page 103.

Albany, Thomas. Admin. of, to Joshua Albany. Feb. 21, 1785. Reg. of Wills, Liber M, folio 48.

Killin, Robert. Admin. of, to Mark Killin. March 1, 1785. Reg. of Wills, Liber M, folio 48.

Cahoon, Mary. Widow of William Cahoon. Will. Made April 6, 1783. Duck Creek Hd. Heirs: son Charles; daus. Elizabeth Elliott, Jane Cahoon & Rachel Perry; granddau. Elizabeth Cahoon, dau. of Charles; grandsons Mark Cahoon (son of Charles), John Cahoon (son of William), Mark Cahoon (son of Thomas). Exec'r, son Charles. Wits., John Wood, Joshua Edwards, Mary Harden. Prob. March 2, 1785. Arch. vol. A7, page 38. Reg. of Wills, Liber M, folios 48-49.

Garland, Abraham. Admin. of, to William Arthur. March 2, 1785. Reg. of Wills, Liber M, folio 49.

Reynolds, Richard. Admin. of, to William Brown. March 4, 1785. Reg. of Wills, Liber M, folio 49.

Jackson, Levi. Admin. of, to Jonathan Jackson. March 15, 1785. Reg. of Wills, Liber M, folio 50.

Burrows, Elijah. Admin. of, to Rebecca Burrows. March 18, 1785. Reg. of Wills, Liber M, folio 50.

Henry, William. Will (copy). Made May 8, 1783. Georgetown, K. Co., State of Maryland. Heirs: wife unnamed; a child unnamed; bro. James Henry; sisters Martha Fitzgerrald & Sarah Seaney; heirs of bro. Hugh Henry. Exec'r, bro. James. Wits., William Clark, John Wright, Thomas Browning. Prob. March 28, 1785. Arch. vol. A23, pages 161-163. Reg. of Wills, Liber M, folio 1.

Jackson, Elizabeth. Admin. of, to Daniel Jackson. March 31, 1785. Arch. vol. A26, page 1. Reg. of Wills, Liber M, folio 52.

Moore, David. Farmer. Will. Made March 12, 1785. Heirs: wife Elizabeth; sons Henry & David. Exec'x, wife Elizabeth. Wits., John Hogins, Joseph Vanpelt, William Burrows. Prob. March 31, 1785. Arch. vol. A36, pages 15-16. Reg. of Wills, Liber M, folio 51. Note:—Will mentions father Samuel Moore.

Warrington, Elizabeth. Widow of Jacob Warrington. Will. Made Feb. 14, 1784. Heirs: daus. Mary Beauchamp (wife of Isaac), Comfort Warrington, Sarah Oliver (wife of Joseph), Rachel Warrington, Esther Hairgrove (wife of George), Elizabeth Beachamp (wife of William); grandsons George, Joseph, William, Jacob, Thomas & James Killon. Exec'r, step-son Joseph Oliver. Wits., Jonathan Rowland, John Knight & Mary Godwin. Prob. March 31, 1785. Arch. vol. A53, pages 155-157. Reg. of Wills, Liber M, folios 50-51.

Timmans, Jesse. Soldier of the Delaware Regiment. Admin. of, to Matthew Hillford. April 2, 1785. Reg. of Wills, Liber M, folio 52. Note:—Arch. vol. A50, page 246 mentions his father George Timmons.

Hindley, Daniel. Admin. of, to Matthew Hillford. April 2, 1785. Reg. of Wills, Liber M, folio 52.

Meridith, Luff. Admin. of, to Mary Meridith. April 4, 1785. Reg. of Wills, Liber M, folio 52.

Treasurers, Richard. Admin. of, to Matthew Hillford. April 4, 1785. Reg. of Wills, Liber M, folio 52.

Draper, Avery. Admin. of, to Esther Draper & Cornelius Deweese. April 6, 1785. Arch. vol. A15, pages 30-31. Reg. of Wills, Liber M, folio 52. Note:—Arch. vol. A15, page 31 mentions heirs, Mary, Avery, Henry, John & Elizabeth Draper; also shows that Esther married Arthur Jester.

Sipple, Elijah. Admin. of, to Mary Sipple & Reynor Williams. April 6, 1785. Arch. vol. A46, pages 120-122, 125-126 & 128. Reg. of Wills, Liber M, folio 52.

Jones, Isaac, Sr. Admin. of, to Hannah Jones. April 7, 1785. Arch. vol. A27, pages 182-183. Reg. of Wills, Liber M, folio 52. Note:—Arch. vol. A27, page 183 mentions heirs, John, Zachariah, Isaac, Mary, Hezekiah, Elizabeth, Brown & Manlove Jones.

Kingham, Joshua. Soldier in the Delaware troops. Admin. of, to Mary Kingham & James Coakley. April 8, 1785. Arch. vol. A29, pages 38-39. Reg. of Wills, Liber M, folio 52. Note:— Arch. vol. A29, page 38 mentions heirs, Joshua & James Kingham.

Pratt, Luke. Admin. of, to Sarah Pratt. April 8, 1785. Arch. vol. A41, pages 118-119. Reg. of Wills, Liber M, folio 52. Note: —Arch. vol. A41, page 118 mentions heirs, Esther & Frederick Pratt.

Parsons, Jennet. Will. Made June 26, 1783. Little Creek Hd. Heirs: dau. Mary Parsons; cousins John Robinson, Jr., & William Vandyke. Exec'rs, dau. Mary Parsons & Samuel Wilson. Wits., Jean Wilson, Peter Haggans, Arthur Moore. Codicil, cousin Thomas Robinson. Wits., Susanna Briers, Catherine Batte, Arthur Moore. March 22, 1785. Prob. April 14, 1785. Arch. vol. A39, page 80. Reg. of Wills, Liber M, folios 53-54.

Robinson, Jordon. Admin. of, to Charles Robinson. April 14, 1785. Reg. of Wills, Liber M, folio 54.

Piper, John. Admin. of, to Leven Shaver. April 21, 1785. Reg. of Wills, Liber M, folio 54.

Davis, Matthias. Will. Made April 9, 1785. Heirs: sons Brinkley, John; daus. Susana & Sarah. Exec'r, son Brinkley. Wits., Nehemiah Cary, Nathaniel Summers & Charles Rock. Prob. April 22, 1785. Arch. vol. A13, pages 39-41. Reg. of Wills, Liber M, folio 119.

Lambden, George. Will. Made March 12, 1785. Heirs: sons George, John, Daniel & Matthew; daus. Mary, Nancy & Elizabeth. Exec'r, son John. Wits., Solomon Connor, Pearis Stradlin, Major Stradley. Prob. April 22, 1785. Arch. vol. A29, pages 103-104. Reg. of Wills, Liber M, folio 54.

Millan, William. Will (copy, nunc.). [N. d.]. Heirs: bro. Abraham Millan; heirs of bro. John Millan. Exec'r, bro. Abraham Millan. Wits., Isaac Carty & Charles Pope. Prob. April 26, 1785. Arch. vol. A35, page 60. Reg. of Wills, Liber M, folio 55.

Holliday, Richard. Admin. of, to Isaiah Rowland, D. B. N. May 13, 1785. Arch. vol. A2, pages 202-203 & 205-206. Reg. of Wills, Liber M, folio 55.

Wheatley [Whitely], Arthur. Admin. of, to Jacob Furby. May 18, 1785. Arch. vol. A54, page 197. Reg. of Wills, Liber M, folio 55.

Burrows, William. Admin. of, to Ebenezer Burrows. May 21, 1785. Reg. of Wills, Liber M, folio 55.

Blackiston, Benjamin. Admin. of, to Hannah Blackiston. May 25, 1785. Arch. vol. A4, pages 117-120. Reg. of Wills, Liber M, folio 55. Note:—Arch. vol. A4, page 120 mentions heirs, John, Benjamin, Sarah, Ann, Francis & Nicholas Blackiston; page 117 shows adm'rs Barnet Everson & wife Hannah.

Chance, Elijah. Admin. of, to John Ringold. May 27, 1785. Reg. of Wills, Liber M, folio 55.

Harper, Agnes. Widow. Will. Made Nov. 26, 1784. Little Creek Hd. Heirs: sons William, David & John; dau. Margaret Oyston; grandsons John Oyston, John & William Nash (sons of dau. Ann); grandchildren Ann Stanly, Margaret Redick & William Haley (children of dau. Jane, dec'd). Exec'rs, sons William & John. Wits., Rachel North, Francis Keeth, William Farson. Prob. May 27, 1785. Arch. vol. A22, pages 41-42. Reg. of Wills, Liber M, folios 56-57.

Jones, Sarah. Admin. of, to Daniel Jones. May 28, 1785. Arch. vol. A28, pages 19-20.

Reed, James. Admin. of, to Sarah Reed. May 28, 1785. Arch. vol. A42, page 193. Reg. of Wills, Liber M, folio 20.

Johnston, William. Carpenter. Will. Made Dec. 8, 1784. Duck Creek Hd. Heirs: wife Elizabeth; children unnamed. Exec'x, wife Elizabeth. Wits., William Farson, Andrew Jamison, William Graydon. Prob. June 1, 1785. Arch. vol. A27, page 124. Reg. of Wills, Liber M, folio 57.

Williams, Christopher. Admin. of, to Aramenta Williams. June 3, 1785. Arch. vol. A55, pages 70-71. Reg. of Wills, Liber M, folio 57. Note:—Arch. vol. A55, page 70 mentions heirs, John & Mary Williams; also shows that Aramenta married Jonathan Wallace.

Howell, Sarah. Minor dau. of Wm. Howell. Admin. of, to Elizabeth Howell. June 9, 1785. Arch. vol. A25, page 79. Reg. of Wills, Liber M, folios 57-58.

Howell, Elizabeth, Jr. Admin. of, to Elizabeth Howell. June 9, 1785. Reg. of Wills, Liber M, folio 57.

Howell, Ruhanna. Minor dau. of Wm. Howell. Admin. of, to Elizabeth Howell. June 9, 1785. Arch. vol. A25, page 76. Reg. of Wills, Liber M, folio 58.

Howell, William. A minor son of Wm. Howell. Admin. of, to Elizabeth Howell. June 9, 1785. Arch. vol. A25, page 81. Reg. of Wills, Liber M, folio 58.

Huston, Alexander. Will. Made Dec. 31, 1784. Murderkill Hd. Heirs: wife Ann; sons John & Samuel; dau. Ann; other children unnamed. Exec'rs, wife Ann & friends Peter Lowber, Peter Hardcastle. Wits., Elizabeth Hardcastle, Catherine Lowber, Patrick Crain. Prob. June 11, 1785. Arch. vol. A25, page 185. Reg. of Wills, Liber M, folios 58-59.

Lane, John. Admin. of, to Sarah Lane. June 24, 1785. Reg. of Wills, Liber M, folio 59.

Ogle, Thomas. Yeoman. Mispillion Hd. Admin. of, to Jehu David, Esq. June 30, 1785. Arch. vol. A38, pages 114-115. Reg. of Wills, Liber M, folio 59.

Lewis, William. Admin. of, to Elizabeth Lewis. July 1, 1785. Arch. vol. A30, page 162. Reg. of Wills, Liber M, folio 59.

Golt, Thomas. Will. Made Nov. 24, 1780. Heirs: wife Isabela; sons William, George & Thomas. Exec'r, friend John Morris. Wits., George Hairgrove, Robert McClement, Brian Connor. Prob. July 16, 1785. Arch. vol. A19, page 129. Reg. of Wills, Liber M, folio 60.

Rees, Martha. Admin. of, to Thomas Skillington. July 30, 1785. Reg. of Wills, Liber M, folio 60.

Rees, William. Admin. of, to Edward Rees, D. B. N. July 30, 1785. Reg. of Wills, Liber M, folio 60.

Gregg, Mark. Murderkill. Admin. of, to Rebecca Gregg. Aug. 11, 1785. Arch. vol. A20, pages 48-49. Reg. of Wills, Liber M, folio 61. Note:—Arch. vol. A20, page 48 mentions heirs, Samuel, Sarah, Rachel & Thomas Gregg.

Millis, John. Admin. of, to Philip Jones. Aug. 11, 1785. Arch. vol. A35, page 134. Reg. of Wills, Liber M, folio 61.

Heffernan, William. Admin. of, to Isaac Lowber. Aug. 12, 1785. Arch. vol. A23, page 117. Reg. of Wills, Liber M, folio 61.

Evans, William. Admin. of, to Charles Nixon. Aug. 18, 1785. Reg. of Wills, Liber M, folio 61.

Clayton, Thomas. Will. Made March 4, 1785. Heirs: wife Elizabeth; sons Charles & John; bros. Joshua & John. Exec'r, bro. John Clayton. Guardian, bro. John Clayton. Wits., James Wells, John Wild. Prob. Aug. 24, 1785. Arch. vol. A9, page 125. Reg. of Wills, Liber M, folio 61.

Sundergill, Lambert. Admin. of, to Mary Sundergill. Aug. 24, 1785. Reg. of Wills, Liber M, folio 61.

Rees, Robert. Admin. of, to Samuel Wilson. Aug. 26, 1785. Arch. vol. A43, page 27.

Forster, John. Yeoman. Duck Creek Hd. Admin. of, to Mary Ashford. Aug. 27, 1785. Arch. vol. A18, page 32. Note:— Admin. mentions sons David & Thomas Forster.

Knotts, William. Admin. of, to Sarah Pratt, D. B. N. Aug. 27, 1785. Arch. vol. A29, page 83.

Loockerman, Vincent, the elder. Gentleman. Will. Made March 9, 1784. Town of Dover. Heirs: wife Elizabeth; dau. Elizabeth; sons Nicholas & Vincent, Jr.; father-in-law John Pryor; Robert Beswick, grandson of my late wife Susanna, dec'd; Phillip Barret; Richard Basset; John Bell, Jr., of Dover, a hatter; Govert Haskins, son of Wm. Haskins, dec'd. Exec'r, son Vincent, Jr. Guardians, wife Elizabeth & bro.-in-law John Pryor, Jr. Wits., Benjamin Vining, Joseph Pryor, William Killen. Prob. Aug. 30, 1785. Arch. vol. A30, pages 208-211. Reg. of Wills, Liber M, folios 62-67.

Riley [Rieley], Laurence. Admin. of, to Elizabeth Rieley. Sept. 12, 1785. Arch. vol. A44, pages 6-7. Reg. of Wills, Liber M, folio 67. Note:—Arch. vol. A44, page 6 shows that Elizabeth Riley later married Levin Crapper.

Barns, William. Admin. of, to Alexander McClain. Sept. 20, 1785. Reg. of Wills, Liber M, folio 67.

Jester, William. Will. Made July 18, 1785. Mispillion Hd. Heirs: wife Delilah; sons David, Lenny, Elijah & William; daus. Delilah, Mahaly, Mary & Charlotte. Exec'x, wife Delilah. Wits., William Hudson, John Ralston & Esther Calloway. Prob. Oct. 1, 1785. Arch. vol. A27, pages 54-57. Reg. of Wills, Liber M, folios 67-68. Note:—Arch. vol. A27, page 55 shows that Delilah Jester married William Vaulx.

Clark, Charles. Admin. of, to Whitington Durham. Oct. 20, 1785. Reg. of Wills, Liber M, folio 68.

Townsend, James. Admin. of, to Ann Townsend. Oct. 25, 1785. Arch. vol. A51, page 9. Reg. of Wills, Liber M, folio 68.

Harper, James. Admin. of, to Elizabeth Harper. Oct. 27, 1785. Arch. vol. A22, pages 43-49. Reg. of Wills, Liber M, folio 68. Note:—Arch. vol. A22, page 48 shows that Elizabeth Harper married Major Bostick; page 47 mentions heirs, John, James, Pery & William Harper.

Saterfield, Nathaniel, Sr. Farmer. Will. Made Feb. 11, 1785. Heirs: wife unnamed; sons Aaron, Joseph & Nathaniel, Jr.; daus. Sarah Leverton, Sidney Nowell, Margaret Taylor & Mary Ann Kirk. Exec'rs, wife & son Nathaniel, Jr. Wits., Anthony Lane & Philip May Stephenson. Prob. Oct. 27, 1785. Arch. vol. A45, page 1. Reg. of Wills, Liber M, folios 68-69.

Sipple, Garret, Jr. Admin. of, to Caleb Sipple. Oct. 29, 1785. Arch. vol. A46, page 129. Reg. of Wills, Liber M, folio 69.

Clifton, Thomas. Farmer. Will. Made Oct. 29, 1783. Heirs: sons Richard, Thomas, Clemment, Ezekiel, Matthew, Shadrick, Daniel & Nathan; daus. Betty Burns, Ann Anderson, Mary Mills, Benitha Morgan, Phebee Cole; granddau. Seala Clifton; grandson Isaiah Clifton; housekeeper Mary Morgan. Exec'r, son Nathan. Wits., Daniel Morris, Sr., Robert Morris, Brinkley Morris, Mary Morris. Prob. Nov. 2, 1785. Arch. vol. A9, pages 154 & 158. Reg. of Wills, Liber M, folios 69-71.

Potter, Edmond. Admin. of, to William Parker. Nov. 7, 1785. Reg. of Wills, Liber M, folio 71.

Calwell, Elizabeth. Will. Made Oct. 23, 1785. Murderkill Neck. Heirs: son Thomas Skidmore; Thomas Sipple, son of Garret. Exec'r, friend Garret Sipple. Wits., John West, Mary Caldwell, Isabele Burrows. Prob. Nov. 10, 1785. Arch. vol. A7, pages 106 & 173. Reg. of Wills, Liber M, folios 71-72.

Potter, Edmond. Yeoman. Will. Made Feb. 26, 1785. Heirs: wife Mary; sons Edmond, John, Benjamin & Charles; daus. Absbeth Brinky [Elizabeth Brinkley], Sarah Scarborgh Griffen, Mary Parker. Exec'rs, wife Mary & son Edmond. Wits., Leven Willey, Richard Coverill. Prob. Nov. 14, 1785. Arch. vol. A41, page 1. Reg. of Wills, Liber M, folios 72-73.

Crawford, Oliver. Admin. of, to Rachel Crawford. Nov. 16, 1785. Reg. of Wills, Liber M, folio 73. Note:—Arch. vol. A11, pages 216-217 mention heirs, William Crawford & Elizabeth Hatfield; also show that Rachel Crawford married Andrew Anderson.

Bedlow, William. Admin. of, to Jerusha Bedlow. Nov. 17, 1785. Arch. vol. A3, pages 135-137. Reg. of Wills, Liber M, folio 73. Note:—Arch. vol. A3, page 136 shows that Jerusha Bedlow married Thomas Moore; page 137 mentions heirs, Ariminta & George Bedlow.

White, Stephen. Admin. of, to John White. Nov. 17, 1785. Reg. of Wills, Liber M, folio 73.

Goodwin, Aron. Admin. of, to Richard Smith, Esq. Nov. 19, 1785. Reg. of Wills, Liber M, folio 73.

Heath, Mary. Admin. of, to James Worrell. Nov. 23, 1785. Reg. of Wills, Liber M, folio 73.

Vining, Benjamin. Gentleman. Will. Made Nov. 14, 1785. Heirs: step-mother Phebe Vining; bros. Nicholas & John; sister Mary Vining; nephew John Vining, son of bro. Nicholas; nieces Elizabeth & Mary (dau. of bro. Nicholas); uncle Dr. Charles Ridgely. Exec'r, bro. John. Wits., William Killen, Nicholas Ridgely, William Killen, Jr. Prob. Nov. 29, 1785. Arch. vol. A52, page 58. Reg. of Wills, Liber M, folios 73-75.

Erickson, Johnson. Admin. of, to Leven Gibson. Nov. 30, 1785. Arch. vol. A16, page 211. Reg. of Wills, Liber M, folio 75.

Garland, John. Admin. of, to Cuthbert Cole & wife Rebecca, the late Rebecca Garland. Dec. 1, 1785. Arch. vol. A18, pages 217-218. Note:—Arch. vol. A18, page 217 mentions children, Christin, Abraham, Rosamond, John & Ebenezer Garland.

Rawley, James. Admin. of, to Elijah & Charity Rawley. Dec. 1, 1785. Arch. vol. A42, pages 130-132.

Ridgely, Charles. Will. Made Sept. 28, 1785. Town of Dover. Heirs: wife Ann; sons Nicholas, Charles, Abraham, Henry Moore, & George Wemys Ridgely; daus. Willimina, Mary & Ann Ridgely. Exec'rs, wife Ann & son Nicholas. Guardians, wife Ann & son Nicholas. Wits., John Clayton, James Clark & Robert Cook. Codicil, dated Nov. 20, 1785. Wits., John Chew, Thomas Wild, James Newnam. Prob. Dec. 5, 1785. Arch. vol. A43, page 222. Reg. of Wills, Liber M, folios 75-79. Note:—Will mentions father Nicholas Ridgely, dec'd.

Corse, William. Will. Made June 5, 1784. Little Creek Hd. Heirs: wife Ann; sons John, William, Thomas & Hanson; dau. Elizabeth Kirben, wife of James; grandsons Benjamin & John Corse, sons of William. Exec'rs, wife Ann, Stephen Mercer & John Hopson. Guardians, wife Ann & John Hopson. Wits., James Townsend, Ann Townsend, James Newnam. Codicil, dau. Susannah. Nov. 4, 1785. Exec'r, Richard Smith, Esq. Wits., Agatha Needham, Elizabeth Carrow, Catron McKay. Prob. Dec. 7, 1785. Arch. vol. A11, pages 30-33 & 61. Reg. of Wills, Liber M, folios 79-82. Note:—Arch. vol. A11, page 31 shows that Ann Corse married Benjamin Wells.

Boggs, Joseph. Admin. of, to Ruth Boggs & Robert Lewis. Dec. 9, 1785. Reg. of Wills, Liber M, folio 82.

Smith, Philip. Will. Made Nov. 22, 1785. Duck Creek Hd. Heirs: wife Sarah. Exec'x, wife Sarah. Wits., Joseph Howard, James Smith, Thomas Parry. Prob. Dec. 12, 1785. Arch. vol. A47, page 136. Reg. of Wills, Liber M, folios 82-83.

Caldwell, Timothy. Admin. of, to Sarah Caldwell. Dec. 13, 1785. Arch. vol. A7, pages 129-133. Reg. of Wills, Liber M, folio 83.

Fowler, George. Admin. of, to Mary Fowler. Dec. 13, 1785. Reg. of Wills, Liber M, folio 83.

Chambers, John. Will. Made Nov. 9, 1782. Heirs: wife Frank; sons John & Joseph Chambers; dau. Mary Craige; granddau. Polly Craige, dau. of son-in-law James Craige. Exec'rs, wife Frank & son John. Wits., Joseph Alford, Alefair Abbet, Jonathan Jackson. Prob. Dec. 14, 1785. Arch. vol. A8, pages 142-143. Reg. of Wills, Liber G, Appendix 3.

Windol, Thomas. Farmer. Will. Made Nov. 4, 1785. Heirs: sons William & Thomas; dau. Mary. Exec'r, son William. Wits., James Scotton, Joseph Beltch, Elizabeth Beltch. Prob. Dec. 14, 1785. Arch. vol. A56, page 35. Reg. of Wills, Liber M, folio 83.

Goforth, Sarah. Will. Made June 7, 1785. Heirs: Peter Goforth, son of Thomas; Sarah, Zachariah & Jonathan Murphey, children of Charles Murphey; Mary Murphey, wife of Charles; Elizabeth Sheridine; Zachariah & Sarah Goforth, children of George; William Redin, Charles Redin, Thomas, William & Rachel Glanding; Nancy Ricketts, wife of Thomas; Charles Murphey. Exec'r, Thomas Ricketts. Wits., William Richardson, Samuel Clampett, Tabithy Wilson. Prob. Dec. 16, 1785. Arch. vol. A19, pages 101-103. Reg. of Wills, Liber M, folios 84-85.

Walker, Robert. Admin. of, to Nancy Ann Walker. Dec. 16, 1785. Arch. vol. A52, pages 196-197. Reg. of Wills, Liber M, folio 85.

Draughton [Drayton], John. Admin. of, to Francis Barber & Peter Hawkins. Dec. 19, 1785. Arch. vol. A15, pages 77-80. Reg. of Wills, Liber M, folio 85. Note:—Arch. vol. A15, page 78 mentions heirs, Mary Hawkins, Mary Barber, William Drayton & heirs of Simon Drayton, John & Robert.

Furbee, Anna. Will. Made Nov. 14, 1785. Murderkill Hd. Heirs: sons Jonathan, Waitman & Caleb; daus. Meriam Davis, Anna Davis, & Elizabeth Dohorty. Exec'r, son Jonathan. Codicil. Wits., Thomas Ceary, Mary Roe, Selia Jester. Prob. Dec. 20, 1785. Arch. vol. A18, page 146. Reg. of Wills, Liber M, folios 85-86.

Tomlinson, Thomas. Yeoman. Will (copy). Made Dec. 2, 1784. Heirs: wife Sarah; sons Thomas, James, William & Joseph; daus. Mary Fraizer & Sarah Tomlinson. Exec'x, wife Sarah. Wits., John Parsons, Hezikiah Cullen, Mary Ann Cullen. Prob. Dec. 20, 1785. Arch. vol. A50, pages 223-224. Reg. of Wills, Liber M, folios 86-87.

Moffet, John. Will. Made Dec. 12, 1785. Dover Hd. Heirs: sons Robert, John, Archibald & William; daus. Mary, Sarah & Martha. Exec'r, son Robert. Wits., Richard Smith, Joseph Vanpelt, Joseph Fouracres. Prob. Dec. 22, 1785. Arch. vol. A35, page 190. Reg. of Wills, Liber M, folios 87-88.

Price, John. Admin. of, to Hannah Price. Dec. 23, 1785. Reg. of Wills, Liber M, folio 88.

Blackshere, Morgan. Admin. of, to Sarah Blackshere. Dec. 28, 1785. Arch. vol. A4, pages 93-94. Reg. of Wills, Liber M, folio 88. Note:—Arch. vol. A4, page 94 mentions heirs, John, Sarah, Deborah, Morgan & George Blackshare.

Cockerel, James. Admin. of, to Elizabeth Cockerel. Dec. 29, 1785. Reg. of Wills, Liber M, folio 89.

Handzar, Nehemiah. Will. Made Dec. 15, 1785. Heirs: wife Johanah; son Nehemiah; granddaus. Elizabeth & Jamima Handzar. Exec'rs, wife Johanah & friend Peter Miller, Sr. Wits., Daniel Billiter, Lewis Gano, Ruth Gano. Prob. Dec. 29, 1785. Arch. vol. A21, pages 200 & 224. Reg. of Wills, Liber M, folio 89.

Smith, Philip. Admin. of, to Robert Moore. Dec. 29, 1785. Reg. of Wills, Liber M, folio 88.

Edwards, John. Admin. of, to Sarah Edwards. Dec. 30, 1785. Reg. of Wills, Liber M, folio 90. Note:—Arch. vol. A16, page 74 shows that Sarah Edwards married John Conner.

Ford, Thomas. Admin. of, to John Dickinson. Dec. 30, 1785. Reg. of Wills, Liber M, folio 90.

Roberts, Thomas. Admin. of, to Annis Roberts. Dec. 31, 1785. Reg. of Wills, Liber M, folio 90.

Berry, Elijah. Blacksmith. Will. Made Nov. 29, 1785. Heir: wife Grace. Exec'r, friend John Clayton, Esq. Wits., William Berry, John Arthur, Elijah Berry, Jr. Prob. Jan. 2, 1786. Arch. vol. A4, page 3. Reg. of Wills, Liber M, folio 90.

Mason, Joseph, Sr. Will. Made April 27, 1785. Heirs: sons Jacob, Charles, Elias & Joseph; daus. Sarah Cullin & Mary Burroughs; granddaus. Pearcy & Sarah Cullin, Mary & Sarah Mason. Exec'rs, sons Jacob & Charles. Wits., Thomas Manlove, William Cullen, Caleb Davis. Prob. Jan. 4, 1786. Arch. vol. A34, page 1. Reg. of Wills. Liber M. folios 90-91.

Corse, George. Admin. of, to John Corse & William Corse, D. B. N. Jan. 7. 1786. Reg. of Wills. Liber M. folio 92.

Course, Susanna. Admin. of, to John Course & William Corse, D. B. N. Jan. 7. 1786. Reg. of Wills. Liber M. folio 91.

Stewart [Stuart], John. Admin. of, to Charles Stewart. Jan. 7, 1786. Reg. of Wills. Liber M. folio 92.

McGinnas, James. Admin. of, to Thomas Skillington. Jan. 17, 1786. Reg. of Wills, Liber M, folio 92.

Carpenter, William, Sr. Will. Made March 5, 1785. Heirs: wife Sarah; granddaus. Mary Hartshorn (dau. of John Dill) & Eamy Dill; children of dau. Martha Brown; grandsons William Carpenter (son of Samuel, dec'd) & Samuel Carpenter (son of William); dau. Martha Brown; son-in-law Thomas Brown. Exec'rs, wife Sarah & John Cook, Esq. Wits., Thomas Williams, Paris Griffith, James Lowry. Prob. Jan. 18, 1786. Arch. vol. A7, pages 236-239. Reg. of Wills, Liber M, folios 92-94. Note:—Arch. vol. A7, page 236 mentions wife's former husband, William Douglass; page 237 mentions heirs, Mary, Martha & Hannah Morgan, Sarah, William & Thomas Brown; page 239 shows George Walton & wife Amy, granddau. of Wm. Carpenter.

Jamison, Alexander. Admin. of, to Mary Jamison & Alexander Jamison. Jan. 25, 1786. Reg. of Wills, Liber M, folio 94.

Jenkins, Andrew. Admin. of, to Dolly Jenkins. Jan. 25, 1786. Arch. vol. A26, pages 201-202. Reg. of Wills, Liber M, folio 94.

Crumpton, Mary. Will (nunc.). Made Jan. 27, 1786. Heir: Negro woman Ambo to be free. [No exec'rs]. Wits., Sarah Canday, Ann Cullen. Prob. Jan. 30, 1786. Arch. vol. A12, page 42. Reg. of Wills, Liber M, folio 98.

Crocket, Margaret. Admin. of, to John Crocket. Feb. 6, 1786. Arch. vol. A12, pages 11-12. Reg. of Wills, Liber M, folio 95. Note:—Arch. vol. A12, page 11 mentions children, Samuel, Jonathan, John, Elenor, Margaret & Elizabeth Crockett & son-in-law William Paradee.

Owen, William. Will (nunc.). Made Feb. 5, 1786. Heirs: bros. Robert & Aman. Exec'rs, [bros. Robert & Aman, from admin. acct.]. Wits., William Numbers & William Chase. Prob. Feb. 7, 1786. Arch. vol. A38, page 163. Reg. of Wills, Liber M, folios 94-95.

White, John. Admin. of, to Isabella White. Feb. 8, 1786. Arch. vol. A54. page 119. Reg. of Wills, Liber M, folio 95.

White, Stephen. Admin. of, to Isabella White. Feb. 8, 1786, D. B. N. Arch. vol. A54, pages 164-165. Reg. of Wills, Liber M, folio 95. Note:—Arch. vol. A54, page 164 mentions heirs, Jacob, William & Isaac White, Sarah Smith (wife of John), William Needles (son of Rachel White), Mary King (wife of William), heirs of John White.

Harwood, Samuel. Admin. of, to Mary Harwood. Feb. 9, 1786. Reg. of Wills, Liber M, folio 95.

Henry, Robert. Admin. of, to Isaac Draper. Feb. 11, 1786. Arch. vol. A23. pages 159-160. Reg. of Wills, Liber M, folio 95.

Harmanson, Arman. Admin. of, to George Mitchell. Feb. 12, 1786. Arch. vol. A22, page 36. Reg. of Wills, Liber M, folio 97.

Morgan, William. Admin. of, to William Clampit. Feb. 13, 1786. Reg. of Wills, Liber M, folio 96.

Read, James. Admin. of, to John Kilpatrick. Feb. 13, 1786. Arch. vol. A42, pages 195-196. Reg. of Wills, Liber M, folio 96. Note:—Arch. vol. A42, page 195 mentions heirs, William, Isaac, John, Daniel & Absalom Virdin & Alce Kilpatrick.

Buckmaster, Esther [Hester]. Widow of Wilson Buckmaster. Will. Made Dec. 4, 1779. Little Creek Hd. Heirs: sons John Clifford, George & Wilson Buckmaster; heirs of daus. Ann Vanhoy (wife of John Vanhoy) & Elizabeth Owen (wife of William Owen). Exec'rs, sons George & Wilson Buckmaster. Wits., Sarah McCall, Sarah McClement, Elizabeth McCall. Prob. Feb. 15, 1786. Arch. vol. A6, page 135. Reg. of Wills, Liber M, folios 97-98.

Crumpton, Mary. Admin. of, to Curtis Crumpton. Feb. 15, 1786. Reg. of Wills, Liber M, folio 98.

Bratcher, Nathan. Planter. Will. Made Feb. 7, 1786. Heirs: wife Mary; dau. Sarah Atkins; Thomas Atkins; Henry Jones. Exec'x, wife Mary. Wits., James Herrington, David Booth, John Herrington. Prob. Feb. 16, 1786. Arch. vol. A5, page 151. Reg. of Wills, Liber M, folio 100.

Howel, Elizabeth. Will. Made Jan. 19, 1786. Heirs: daus. Mary & Ann. Exec'r, bro. Jonathan Brown. Guardian, bro. Jonathan Brown. Wits., Mark Maxwell, Susan Brown, Hosea Wilson. Prob. Feb. 16, 1786. Arch. vol. A25, pages 57-60. Reg. of Wills, Liber M, folio 101. Note:—Arch. vol. A25, page 58 mentions heirs, John Howell & Ann Milles.

Farmer, John. Admin. of, to Eleazer McComb. Feb. 29, 1786. Reg. of Wills, Liber M, folio 101.

Swallow, John. Admin. of, to Sarah Swallow. Feb. 29, 1786. Arch. vol. A49, page 134. Reg. of Wills, Liber M, folio 101. Note:—Admin. acct. shows Sarah Danes as adm'x.

Baynard, Thomas. Will. Made March 15, 1777. Heirs: wife Elizabeth; sons Henry, John, Thomas; sons-in-law John Anderton & Henry Ennals; daus. Rachel Turpen, Sarah & Nancy Baynard. Exec'r, son Henry. Wits., Thomas White, Edward White, Waitman Goslen. Prob. March 1, 1786. Arch. vol. A3, pages 84-86. Reg. of Wills, Liber M, folios 98-100. Note:—Arch. vol. A3, page 86 mentions heirs, Nancy Martin & Sarah Wheatly.

Dunning, William, Saddler. Will. Made Feb. 18, 1786. Town of Dover. Heirs: wife Rachel; sister Tamer Dunning. Exec'rs, wife Rachel & friend Stephen Alston. Wits., George Crow, Philip Samuel Alford, James Molan. Prob. March 2, 1786. Arch. vol. A15, pages 142 & 147. Reg. of Wills, Liber M, folio 102. Note:—Arch. vol. A15, page 142 shows that Rachel Dunning married Henry Runnals.

Virden, Eleanor. Admin. of, to William Virden. March 2, 1786. Arch. vol. A52, pages 88-89. Reg. of Wills, Liber M, folio 101. Note:—Arch. vol. A52, page 88 mentions heirs, John, Daniel, Absalom & Isaac Virden, Alce Kilpatrick (wife of John), Enock Jenkins & William Gaskin.

Falconer, James. Yeoman. Little Creek Hd. Admin. of, to Robert Hirons & wife Anne, late Ann Falconer. March 3, 1786. Arch. vol. A17, page 85.

Bird, Joseph. Admin. of, to Henry Smith. March 7, 1786. Arch. vol. A4, page 57. Reg. of Wills, Liber M, folio 103.

Stewart [Stuart], Jean. Admin. of to Moses Barnet. March 11, 1786. Arch. vol. A49, pages 2-3. Reg. of Wills, Liber M, folio 103. Note:—Arch. vol. A49, page 2 mentions heirs, Thomas & Charles Stuart; also shows Sarah Dale as widow of Moses Barnett.

Lewis, Evan, Sr. Will. Made Feb. 26, 1783. Murderkill Hd. Heirs: wife Sarah; sons Robert & Evan; daus. Ruth Boogs, Miriam Cranston & Elizabeth Newton; grandson David Lewis, son of Evan & Elizabeth; granddau. Lydia Lewis, dau. of Abraham & Lydia. Exec'r, son Robert. Wits., John Peirce, Hannah Peirce, Robert Wilson. Prob. March 13, 1786. Arch. vol. A30, page 78. Reg. of Wills, Liber M, folio 104.

Shepherd, Thomas. Admin. of, to Esther Shepherd. March 13, 1786. Reg. of Wills, Liber M, folio 103.

Walker, Ann. Will. Made March 7, 1786. Heir: son Daniel Dorson [Dawson]. Exec'r, son Daniel. Wits., John Parson, John King, Mary Alford. Prob. March 14, 1786. Arch. vol. A52, pages 172-174. Reg. of Wills, Liber M, folios 105-107.

Bartlett, Elijah. Admin. of, to Ann Bartlett & Simon Vanwinkle. March 27, 1786. Arch. vol. A3, pages 37-39. Reg. of Wills, Liber M, folio 119. Note:—Arch. vol. A3, page 37 shows that Ann Bartlett married Joseph Farrow; page 39 mentions heirs, Elijah, Henerietta & George Bartlett.

Henry, Matthew. Admin. of, to Archibald McSparron, D. B. N. March 28, 1786. Reg. of Wills, Liber M, folio 104.

Matthews, John. Admin. of, to Stephen Jarrell. March 29, 1786. Arch. vol. A34, page 68. Reg. of Wills, Liber M, folio 104.

Black, Thomas. Admin. of, to Ann Black. March 30, 1786. Reg. of Wills, Liber M, folios 104-105.

James, John. Admin. of, to Celicia James & Mark Maxwell. April 6, 1786. Reg. of Wills, Liber M, folio 107.

Fury, Peter. Shopkeeper. Murderkill Hd. Admin. of, to Simon W. Wilson. April 8, 1786. Arch. vol. A18, page 203. Reg. of Wills, Liber M, folio 107.

Lockwood, Richard. Yeoman. Will. Made March 14, 1786. Heirs: wife Margaret; sons Armwell, John, Caleb & David; daus. Sarah, Nancy, Merium, Rebekah, Elizabeth, Mary & Margaret. Exec'rs, wife Margaret & son John. Guardians, wife Margaret & son John. Wits., William Kirkley, Armwell Lockwood, Thomas Wallace. Prob. April 12, 1786. Arch. vol. A31, pages 4-5. Reg. of Wills, Liber M, folios 107-109. Note: —Arch. vol. A31, page 5 shows that Margaret Lockwood married Matthew Cox.

Welber, John. Admin. of, to Smith Farset. April 19, 1786. Reg. of Wills, Liber M, folio 109.

Meers [Mears], Rebeckah. Will. Made April 18, 1786. Duck Creek Hd. Heirs: son Andrew Meers; dau. Mary Meers. Exec'r, son James Numbers. Wits., Andrew Jamison, Joseph Numbers. Prob. April 24, 1786. Arch. vol. A34, pages 110-111 & 116. Reg. of Wills, Liber M, folio 110.

Shahan [Shehorn], David. Admin. of, to Levicee Shehorn. April 27, 1786. Arch. vol. A45, pages 154-155. Reg. of Wills, Liber M, folio 110. Note:—Arch. vol. A45, page 154 mentions heirs, John, David, George, Joshua & Louisa Shahan; also shows that Louisa Shahan later married Mathias Nowland.

Scotton, Nathan. Admin. of, to William Scotton. May 9, 1786. Reg. of Wills, Liber M, folio 110.

Winsmore, Robert. Admin. of, to Thomas Winsmore. May 9, 1786. Arch. vol. A56, page 41. Reg. of Wills, Liber M, folio 110.

Shepherd, Thomas. Admin. of, to Jonathan Rowland, D. B. N. May 15, 1786. Arch. vol. A45, pages 234-235. Reg. of Wills, Liber M, folio 110. Note:—Arch. vol. A45, page 235 shows that Polly Rowland married William Mifflin and was adm'x of Jonathan Rowland who was adm'r, D. B. N., of Thomas Shepherd.

Falconer, William. Admin. of, to Alexander Jackson. May 26, 1786. Arch. vol. A17, pages 95-96. Reg. of Wills, Liber M, folio 110. Note:—Arch. vol. A17, page 95 mentions heirs, wife Sarah, Elizabeth, Thomas, Andrew, William & Sophia Falconer.

Anderson, Elijah. Admin. of, to Daniel Thomas & wife Sarah. May 26, 1786. Arch. vol. A1, page 157.

Benson, Daniel. Admin. of, to Levin Benson. May 29, 1786. Reg. of Wills, Liber M, folios 110-111.

Fitz Jarrell, Eleazar. Will. Made April 6, 1786. Heirs: wife Sarah; daus. Ruth & Mary; sons John, James, Eleazer & Richard. Exec'x, wife Sarah. Wits., John Powell, Mark Powell, Elizabeth Downham, William Powell. Prob. June 1, 1786. Arch. vol. A17, page 150. Reg. of Wills, Liber M, folio 111. Note:—Will mentions father James FitzJarrel, dec'd.

Farson, William. Admin. of, to Susanna Farson. June 2, 1786. Arch. vol. A17, pages 83-84. Reg. of Wills, Liber M, folio 111. Note:—Arch. vol. A17, page 84 shows that Susanna Farson married Joseph Nock.

Leathem, James. Will. Made May 26, 1786. Heirs: wife Mary; son Robert; daus. Mary, Elizabeth & Ann. Exec'rs, Allen McLane, Esq., & John Cole. Wits., Roger Pugh, James Leathem, Jr., Hannah Mileham. Prob. June 10, 1786. Arch. vol. A29, pages 207-209. Reg. of Wills, Liber M, folios 111-112.

Cahoon, Thomas. Admin. of, to George Harris. June 12, 1786. Arch. vol. A7, page 44. Reg. of Wills, Liber M, folio 112.

Bennett, John. Farmer. Will. Made June 17, 1786. Murtherkill Hd. Heirs: wife Sarah; sons Benjamin & William. Exec'rs, wife Sarah & son William. Wits., Nehemiah Tilton, Robert Jamison, Nathaniel Smithers, Sr. Prob. June 21, 1786. Arch. vol. A3, pages 217-218. Reg. of Wills, Liber M, folios 112-113.

Wilcut, Joseph. Mispillion Hd. Admin. of, to Rachel Wilcut & Reuben Wilcut. June 21, 1786. Arch. vol. A54, pages 227-229. Reg. of Wills, Liber M, folio 112. Note:—Arch. vol. A54, page 229 mentions heirs, Josias, Martha, William, Levi. Joseph, Susannah, Sally, Polly, David & Nancy Wilcuts.

Hopkins, John. Planter. Will. Made June 18, 1785. Heirs: wife Jean; sons John, Robert, James & Zebulon; dau. Betty Gullett. Exec'r, son Zebulon. Wits., Eli Saulsbury, Thomas Smith, John Rolston. Prob. June 26, 1786. Arch. vol. A25, pages 11-12. Reg. of Wills, Liber M, folios 113-115.

Ayres, Abraham. Will. Made May 8, 1786. Heirs: sons James, Abraham & Simon; daus. Mary, Shealah & Susannah Ayres, Elizabeth Crabbin, Sarah Taylor & Hannah Wood. Exec'rs, sons Abraham, James & Simon. Wits., Michael Numbers, Robert Blackshare, Nicholas Lynch. Prob. July 18, 1786. Arch. vol. A2, pages 35-38. Reg. of Wills, Liber M, folios 113-114.

Brice, Benidict. Admin. of, to Mary Brice. Aug. 1, 1786. Reg. of Wills, Liber M, folio 115. Note:—Arch. vol. A5, page 152 shows that Mary Brice married James Cook.

Morris, James, the elder. Will. Made May 2, 1783. Duck Creek Hd. Heirs: son James; daus. Mary Griffin & Margaret Morris; Robert Holliday; Fenwick Fisher. Exec'r, son James. Wits., Robert Holliday, Thomas Tilton, Ezekiel Needham. Prob. Aug. 2, 1786. Arch. vol. A36, page 224. Reg. of Wills, Liber M, folios 115-117.

Vickory, Hezekiah. Mispillion Hd. Admin. of, to Mary Vickory. Aug. 9, 1786. Arch. vol. A52, page 34. Reg. of Wills, Liber M, folio 117.

Smith, John. Admin. of, to Richard Smith. Aug. 14, 1786. Reg. of Wills, Liber M, folio 117.

Durham, Daniel. Yeoman. Will. Made Dec. 7, 1779. Little Creek Hd. Heirs: wife Elennor; sons Benjamin, Daniel & Thomas; daus. Joanah, Hester, Rachel, Mary, Ellenor & Sarah. Exec'rs, wife Ellenor & son Benjamin. Wits., Thomas Keith, James Smith, James Wells. Prob. Aug. 17, 1786. Arch. vol. A15, pages 175, 178 & 180. Reg. of Wills, Liber M, folio 118.

Meredith, Levy. Admin. of, to William McClyment. Aug. 26, 1786. Reg. of Wills, Liber M, folio 127.

Caldwell, Jonathan. Admin. of, to John Caldwell, D. B. N. Aug. 30, 1786. Reg. of Wills, Liber M, folio 119.

Jester, Ezekiel. Minor son of Charles Jester. Admin. of, to Thomas Primrose. Sept. 2, 1786. Reg. of Wills, Liber M, folio 120. Note:—Arch. vol. A27, page 19 mentions a mother Sarah Jester & grandparents Ruth & Thomas Christopher.

Starr, Samuel. Admin. of, to Mary Starr. Sept. 2, 1786. Reg. of Wills, Liber M, folio 120.

Hughes, Jonathan. Admin. of, to John Wheeldon. Sept. 9, 1786. Reg. of Wills, Liber M, folio 120.

Lewis, Sarah. Admin. of, to Michael Cook. Oct. 12, 1786. Reg. of Wills, Liber M, folio 120.

Killen, Henry. Yeoman. Will. Made Sept. 20, 1786. Little Creek Hd. Heirs: wife Susanna; daus. Nancy, Mary, Ruth & Susanna. Exec'x, wife Susanna. Wits., James Tilton, Hester Vanstavern. Prob. Oct. 12, 1786. Arch. vol. A28, pages 180-183. Reg. of Wills, Liber M, folios 120-121. Note:—Arch. vol. A28, page 182 mentions heirs, Mary Killen, Nancy Hopkins, Ruth Dagman, Susannah George.

Caldwell, Margaret. Admin. of, to John Caldwell. Oct. 21, 1786. Reg. of Wills, Liber M, folio 121.

Parsons, Joseph. Will. Made March 23, 1785. Mispilling Hd. Heirs: wife Peggy; sister's children, Thomas, James & John Catts & Selea Volks. Exec'x, wife Peggy. Wits., David Young, Bersha Harrington, Rachel Johnston. Prob. Oct. 24, 1786. Arch. vol. A39, page 86. Reg. of Wills, Liber M, folio 121.

Wilson, James. Admin. of, to Elizabeth Wilson. Oct. 26, 1786. Arch. vol. A55, pages 210-212. Reg. of Wills, Liber M, folio 122. Note:—Arch. vol. A55, page 210 mentions heirs, William & Elizabeth Wilson.

David, John. Admin. of, to Lydia David. Oct. 28, 1786. Arch. vol. A12, pages 225 & 227. Reg. of Wills, Liber M, folio 122. Note:—Arch. vol. A12, page 227 shows that Lydia David married John Severson.

Tomlinson, Joseph. Admin. of, to Sarah Tomlinson. Nov. 1, 1786. Reg. of Wills, Liber M, folio 122.

McVay, Denis. Admin. of, to John McVay. Nov. 2, 1786. Reg. of Wills, Liber M, folio 122.

Bedwell, Ezekiel. Admin. of, to Agnes Bedwell. Nov. 11, 1786. Arch. vol. A3, pages 139-140. Reg. of Wills, Liber M, folio 122. Note:—Arch. vol. A3, page 140 mentions heirs, Preston, Elizabeth & Deboraugh Bedwell.

West, John. Will. Made Oct. 30, 1786. Heirs: bros. James & William West; sisters Elizabeth Dawson & Nancy Bell; son John West alias John Dewes (son of Rachel Dewes); dau. Elizabeth West alias Elizabeth Dewes (dau. of Rachel Dewes). Exec'x, friend Rachel Dewes. Wits., Daniel Dewes, Sarah Dewes, Joshiah Davis. Prob. Nov. 13, 1786. Arch. vol. A54, pages 20-21. Reg. of Wills, Liber M, folios 122-124.

Boyer, Richard. Admin. of, to Mary Boyer & Richard Keys. Nov. 16, 1786. Arch. vol. A5, page 62. Reg. of Wills, Liber M, folio 124.

Wilson, John. Captain—late of the Delaware Regiment. Tanner. Murderkill Hd. Admin. of, to Simon Wilmer Wilson. Nov. 23, 1786. Arch. vol. A55, pages 224-225. Reg. of Wills, Liber M, folio 124.

Berchine, Joseph. Admin. of, to Elizabeth Burchinal. Nov. 24, 1786. Reg. of Wills, Liber M, folio 124.

Byrem, James. Admin. of, to Nancy Harden. Nov. 25, 1786. Reg. of Wills, Liber M, folio 124.

Anderson, John. Admin. of, to Clother Anderson. Nov. 30, 1786. Arch. vol. A1, pages 183-184. Reg. of Wills, Liber M, folio 124.

Elliott, Ruth. Admin. of, to Edward Elliott. Nov. 30, 1786. Arch. vol. A16, pages 100-101.

Caldwell, Margaret. Admin. of, to Jonathan Pleasonton. Dec. 12, 1786. Reg. of Wills, Liber M, folio 124.

Maffett, Robert. Will. Made Dec. 3, 1786. Dover Hd. Heirs: bros. William, John & Archibald; sisters Martha & Mary; grandmother Gennit Maffet. Exec'r, friend Lawrence Hammond. Guardian, Lawrence Hammond. Wits., George Harris, Joseph Foreacres, Elizabeth Harris. Prob. Dec. 16, 1786. Arch. vol. A35, page 195. Reg. of Wills, Liber M, folios 124-125.

Pattison, Samuel. Admin. of, to Samuel Griffin. Dec. 26, 1786. Arch. vol. A39, pages 128-129. Reg. of Wills, Liber M, folio 125. Note:—Arch. vol. A39, page 128 shows the acct. later settled by Mary Griffin.

Lewis, Sarah. Admin. of, to Joshua Underwood. Dec. 27, 1786. Reg. of Wills, Liber M, folio 125.

Roe, Caesar. Will. Made Dec. 14, 1786. Duck Creek Hd. Heirs: wife Elizabeth; son Benjamin; a child unnamed. Exec'rs, wife Elizabeth & Isaac Griffin. Wits., Richard Smith, William Numbers, John McBride. Prob. Dec. 27, 1786. Arch. vol. A44, pages 107-108. Reg. of Wills, Liber M, folio 126. Note:—Arch. vol. A44, page 108 shows that Elizabeth Roe married Francis Meridith.

Ross, Levey. Admin. of, to Samuel Mileham. Dec. 27, 1786. Reg. of Wills, Liber M, folio 126.

Roberts, Thomas. Admin. of, to Richard Banning, D. B. N. Dec. 30, 1786. Arch. vol. A44, page 28. Reg. of Wills, Liber M, folio 127.

Hopkins, James. Admin. of, to Neomi Hopkins. Jan. 3, 1787. Arch. vol. A25, pages 7-9. Reg. of Wills, Liber M, folio 128. Note:—Arch. vol. A25, page 7 mentions heirs, Samuel, Sarah, Waitman, James, Elizabeth & William Hopkins; page 8 shows that Neomi Hopkins married John Staffard.

Merrick, Isaac. Admin. of, to Margaret Merrick. Jan. 6, 1787. Reg. of Wills, Liber M, folio 128.

Harrington, John. Farmer. Will. Made Sept. 5, 1786. Mispillion Hd. Heirs: wife Martha; sons Jacob, John, Isaac, William, Jonathan, Nathan, David & Aron; dau. Sarah; grandson James Harrington. Exec'rs, wife Martha & son Jacob. Wits., James Curry, Matthew Clarke, John Hamilton. Prob. Jan. 12, 1787. Arch. vol. A22, page 117 and vol. A23, page 169. Reg. of Wills, Liber M, folios 128-129.

Goodwin, Jane. Will. Made Oct. 28, 1783. Murtherkill Hd. Heirs: sons Moses & Aron; daus. Susannah & Mary Goodwin & Rachel Bourace. Exec'r, friend Joseph Van Pelt. Wits., George Van Pelt, Leah Harden, Sam. Smith. Prob. Jan. 13, 1787. Arch. vol. A19, pages 137-140. Reg. of Wills, Liber M, folio 158. Note:—Arch. vol. A19, page 139 shows that final settlement was made by Daniel Smith & wife Elizabeth, widow of Joseph Van Pelt.

Taylor, William. Admin. of, to John Taylor. Jan. 13, 1787. Reg. of Wills, Liber M, folio 129.

Maxwell, Mark. Will. Made Dec. 31, 1786. Heirs: wife Meriam; son-in-law Thomas Brown. Exec'rs, wife Meriam & friend John Gordon. Wits., William Hudson, Jonathan Brown. Prob. Jan. 15, 1787. Arch. vol. A34, pages 87-88. Reg. of Wills, Liber M, folio 129.

Craige, James. Farmer. Murderkill Hd. Admin. of, to Samuel Craige. Jan. 24, 1787. Arch. vol. A11, page 165. Reg. of Wills, Liber M, folio 130.

Culbreth, Jonathan. Admin. of, to Daniel Mifflin. Jan. 29, 1787. Reg. of Wills, Liber M, folio 130.

Smithers, John. Farmer. Will. Made May 30, 1786. Heirs: sons Joseph, William, David, John & Nathaniel; daus. Mary & Sarah Beauchamp, Rachel & Grace Smithers. Exec'rs, sons Nathaniel & John. Wits., Stephen Downs, Stephen Downs, Jr., Elizabeth Smithers. Prob. Jan. 29, 1787. Arch. vol. A47, pages 209-210. Reg. of Wills, Liber M, folios 130-131.

Windul, Jonathan. Admin. of, to Elizabeth Windul. Feb. 1, 1787. Reg. of Wills, Liber M, folio 131.

Furbush, Richard. Admin. of, to Ester Furbush. Feb. 2, 1787. Reg. of Wills, Liber M, folio 131.

Hawkins, William. Admin. of, to John & Jacob Hawkins. Feb. 6, 1787. Reg. of Wills, Liber M, folio 131.

Barton, Joseph. Admin. of, to Benjamin Bassett. Feb. 14, 1787. Arch. vol. A3, page 43. Reg. of Wills, Liber M, folio 131.

Brown, Benjamin. Will (nunc.). Made Jan. 31, 1787. Heir: bro. Thomas. Wits., John Faris, Susan Brown. Prob. Feb. 12, 1787. Arch. vol. A6, page 25. Reg. of Wills, Liber M, folio 131.

Brown, Benjamin. Admin. of, to Jonathan Brown. Feb. 14, 1787. Reg. of Wills, Liber M, folio 131.

Wood, John. Admin. of, to Polly Wood. Feb. 14, 1787. Reg. of Wills, Liber M, folio 131.

West, Joseph. Admin. of, to Enoch Jones. Feb. 16, 1787. Arch. vol. A54, pages 25-26. Reg. of Wills, Liber M, folio 132. Note:—This acct. was later administered by Lydia (widow of Enoch Jones) & Enoch Jones, Jr.

Woodley, Thomas. Admin. of, to Joseph Barker. Feb. 17, 1787. Arch. vol. A56, pages 115-116. Reg. of Wills, Liber M, folio 132.

Alee, John. Admin. of, to Rachel Alee & James Raymond. Feb. 27, 1787. Arch. vol. A1, pages 63-64. Reg. of Wills, Liber M, folio 132.

Virdin, Alexander. A minor son of Daniel Virdin, dec'd. Admin. of, to Joseph Jackson. Feb. 27, 1787. Arch. vol. A52, page 79. Reg. of Wills, Liber M, folio 132.

Virdin, Eleanor. A minor dau. of Daniel Virdin, dec'd. Admin. of, to Joseph Jackson. Feb. 27, 1787. Arch. vol. A52, page 89. Reg. of Wills, Liber M, folio 132.

Baynard, Elizabeth. Widow of Thomas Baynard. Will. Made Jan. 21, 1786. Heirs: sons Henry, Thomas & John; cousin Mary Fiddeman. Wits., Thomas White, Solomon Barwick, Edward Barwick. Prob. March 1, 1787. Arch. vol. A3, pages 77-78. Reg. of Wills, Liber M, folio 127.

Benston, Daniel. Admin. of, to Levin Benston. March 1, 1787. Arch. vol. A3, pages 235-236.

Bell, John. Will. Made Feb. 16, 1787. Little Creek Hd. Heirs: wife Mary; daus. Nancy, Margaret, Mary & Elizabeth. Exec'rs, wife Mary & bro. Henry Bell. Wits., John Edenfield, Daniel Holmes, Stephen Sykes. Prob. March 1, 1787. Arch. vol. A3, page 173. Reg. of Wills, Liber M, folios 132-133.

Holliday, Joseph. Admin. of, to Joshua Fisher, George Wilson & John Holliday. March 5, 1787. Reg. of Wills, Liber M, folio 132.

Joy, John. Will. Made Dec. 6, 1786. Duck Creek Hd. Heirs: two sons unnamed; dau. Jean. Wits., William Cahoon, Thomas Parke, Elias Wood, William Hill. Prob. March 13, 1787. Arch. vol. A28, page 56. Reg. of Wills, Liber M, folios 149-155. Note:—Recorder of Deeds Office, Liber Z, folios 130-132 mention heirs, sons Edward & William Joy, daus. Eleanor Joy & Rachel Denny (wife of Philip Denny) & father Edward Joy.

Wells, Lydia. Admin. of, to John Wells, March 13, 1787. Reg. of Wills, Liber M, folio 140.

Purden, John. Admin. of, to Andrew Purden. March 14, 1787. Reg. of Wills, Liber M, folio 140.

Ross, Nathan. Admin. of, to John Cox. March 14, 1787. Arch. vol. A44, pages 144-145. Reg. of Wills, Liber M, folio 140. Note:—Arch. vol. A44, page 144 mentions heirs, John, William, Nathan & Elizabeth Ross.

Strong, Benjamin. Admin. of, to William Brown. March 15, 1787. Reg. of Wills, Liber M, folio 133.

Deweese, Daniel. Admin. of, to Jerusha Deweese. March 22, 1787. Reg. of Wills, Liber M, folio 133.

Starling, James. Admin. of, to John Starling. March 23, 1787. Reg. of Wills, Liber M, folio 133.

Hudson, Samuel Robinson. Scrivener. Admin. of, to William Hudson. March 31, 1787. Arch. vol. A25, page 114. Reg. of Wills, Liber M, folio 133.

Hudson, Daniel. Mariner. Admin. of, to William Hudson. March 31, 1787. Reg. of Wills, Liber M, folio 133.

Huston, Charles. Cordwainer. Admin. of, to Jacob Lycan. April 6, 1787. Reg. of Wills, Liber M, folio 133.

Bostick, Robert. Admin. of, to Sarah Bostick. April 13, 1787. Arch. vol. A5, pages 2-4. Reg. of Wills, Liber M, folios 133-134. Note:—Arch. vol. A5, page 2 shows that Sarah Bostick, widow, married John Coppage; page 3 mentions heirs, Jacob & Sarah Bostick; page 4 shows that Sarah, the late Sarah Bostick, married Silvia Sipple.

Hammond, Lawrence. Will. Made April 7, 1787. Heirs: nephew James Lundergin; friend Thomas Jenkins; John & William Maffet, sons of John, dec'd. Exec'r, Thomas Jenkins. Guardian, Thomas Jenkins. Wits., Daniel Mifflin, Joseph Jenkins, Elizabeth Bostick. Prob. April 17, 1787. Arch. vol. A21, page 194. Reg. of Wills, Liber M, folio 134.

Hammond, Lawrence. Admin. of, to Jonathan Hunn. April 17, 1787. Arch. vol. A21, page 195. Reg. of Wills, Liber M, folio 134.

Edmondson, John. Will. Made Feb. 7, 1780. March 2, 1781. Heirs: wife unnamed; sons Joseph, John & Emanuel; dau. Elizabeth Fiddy. Exec'x, wife. Wits., John Smith, Sarah Smith. Prob. April 21, 1787. Arch. vol. A16, page 48. Reg. of Wills, Liber M, folios 134-135.

Killen, Susannah. Admin. of, to John Warren. April 21, 1787. Reg. of Wills, Liber M, folio 134.

Edmondson, John. Admin. of, to Thomas Edmondson. April 21, 1787. Arch. vol. A16, pages 49-51. Reg. of Wills, Liber M, folio 135.

Maffett, John. Admin. of, to John Voshall, Jr., D. B. N. April 24, 1787. Arch. vol. A35, pages 191-194. Reg. of Wills, Liber M, folio 135. Note:—Arch. vol. A35, page 194 mentions heirs, Robert, John & Mary Maffit, Sarah Voshall & Martha Muncey (wife of John Muncey).

Maffett, Robert. Admin. of, to John Voshall, Jr., D. B. N. April 24, 1787. Arch. vol. A35, pages 196-197. Reg. of Wills, Liber M, folio 135.

Killen, Henry. Admin. of, to John Warren, D. B. N. April 28, 1787. Reg. of Wills, Liber M, folio 135.

Tumblin, Covil. Will. Made April 15, 1787. Heirs: son John; wife Sarath; daus. Ann Garrel, Elizabeth Holden, Leah, Ruth & Rhodea Tumblin. Exec'x, [wife Sarah, from admin. acct.]. Wits., John Tucker, Stephen Jarrild, Jr., William Laws. Prob. April 28, 1787. Arch. vol. A51, page 136 & vol. A50, pages 170-171. Reg. of Wills, Liber M, folio 136. Note:— Arch. vol. A50, page 170 mentions a Levin Tomblin.

Loftis, Sarah. Widow of John Loftis. Will. Made Dec. 14, 1775. Heir: son John. Exec'r, son John. Wits., George Upton, John Dill, Sr. Codicil, April 7, 1781. Heir, son Joseph. Prob. April 28, 1787. Arch. vol. A31, page 55. Reg. of Wills, Liber M, folios 136-137.

Cole, Cuthbert. Admin. of, to Rebecca Cole. April 28, 1787. Arch. vol. A9, page 196. Reg. of Wills, Liber M, folio 137. Note:—Arch. vol. A9, page 196 shows that this acct. was later administered by Joseph David, D. B. N.

Harris, George. Dover Hd. Admin. of, to William Edwards. April 30, 1787. Arch. vol. A22, page 173. Reg. of Wills, Liber M, folio 137.

Curtis, John. Admin. of, to Comfort Curtis. May 4, 1787. Arch. vol. A12, pages 161-162. Reg. of Wills, Liber M, folio 137. Note:—Arch. vol. A12, page 161 mentions heirs, Elizabeth, William, Mary, Sarah & Thomas Curtis.

May, James. Admin. of, to Susanna May. May 4, 1787. Arch. vol. A34, page 107. Reg. of Wills, Liber M, folio 137.

Buckingham, Isaac. Farmer. Will. Made April 4, 1787. Little Creek Hd. Heirs: wife Margaret; sons Howell & Isaac; daus. Ann & Mary. Exec'rs, wife Margaret & Thomas Lamb. Wits., John Hill, James Jones, John Ward. Prob. May 19, 1787. Arch. vol. A6, pages 128-130. Reg. of Wills, Liber M, folios 140-141. Note:—Arch. vol. A6, page 129 shows that Margaret, the widow, later married . . . Lamb.

Sturgis, Stokely. Yeoman. Will. Made April 26, 1787. Little Creek Hd. Heirs: son Stokly; dau. Sarah; grandchildren unnamed. Exec'rs, son Stokly, Jacob Stout & William Levick. Wits., William Corse, Daniel Clifford, Lydia Cowgill. Prob. May 14, 1787. Arch. vol. A49, pages 109-110. Reg. of Wills, Liber M, folios 137-138.

Howard, Stephen. Will. Made April 27, 1787. Duck Creek Hd. Heirs: sister Mary; bro. John; niece Ann Keech, dau. of sister Rebikah Keech; nephew Jarman Keech, son of sister Rebikah Keech; Nathan Keech. Exec'r, Nathan Keech. Wits., William Irons, John McKenney, Daniel David, Jr. Prob. May 15, 1787. Arch. vol. A25, page 55. Reg. of Wills, Liber M, folios 138-139.

Peterkin, David. Will. Made April 9, 1787. Heirs: sons John & David; daus. Naomy Black, Comfort Curtis; granddau. Rhoda Peterkin, dau. of Thomas; grandsons David, George & John Walton & Tobias Furchas. Exec'r, grandson David Walton. Wits., Henry Molleston, John Killam, John Dill. Prob. May 4, 1787. Arch. vol. A39, pages 238-244. Reg. of Wills, Liber M, folios 139-140.

McDowell, Hugh. Admin. of, to Barsheba McDowell. May 24, 1787. Reg. of Wills, Liber M, folio 141.

Wood, Joseph. Admin. of, to Mary Wood. May 30, 1787. Arch. vol. A56, pages 91-92. Reg. of Wills, Liber M, folio 158. Note:—Arch. vol. A56, page 92 shows that Mary Wood later married Daniel Sherwood.

Vandevere, John. Admin. of, to Elizabeth Vandevere. May 31, 1787. Arch. vol. A51, page 230.

Walton, Bagwell. Admin. of, to Ruth Walton. May 31, 1787. Arch. vol. A53, pages 45-47. Reg. of Wills, Liber M, folio 141. Note:—Arch. vol. A53, page 45 shows that Ruth Walton later married John Smithers; also mentions heirs, John, Elizabeth & Mirrium Walton.

King, Robert. Will. Made Feb. 20, 1783. Mispillion Hd. Heirs: daus. Mary Johnson, Martha Fleming (wife of George Fleming); son John; grandson Robert King, son of Alexander King; Esther King, widow of Alexander King; granddaus. Mary & Elizabeth King, daus. of Alexander. Exec'r, son John. Wits., Samuel Fleming, John Ralston. Prob. June 5, 1787. Arch. vol. A29, pages 33-34. Reg. of Wills, Liber M, folios 142-143.

Jarrald, Stephen, Sr. Admin. of, to Lydia Jarrald & Stephen Jarrald, Jr. June 16, 1787. Arch. vol. A26, pages 155 & 168-169. Reg. of Wills, Liber M, folio 143. Note:—Arch. vol. A26, page 155 shows Mary Jarrald, wife of Stephen, Jr., as joint adm'x with Lydia Jarrald; page 169 shows that Lydia Jarrald later married . . . Brown and mentions heirs, Morris, James, Jonathan & Moses Jarrald.

Crammer, Thomas. Will. Made March 12, 1787. Heirs: wife Miriam; sons Skidmor, George, Jonathan & Thomas; daus. Mary Black, Margret & Lydia Crammer. Exec'rs, wife Miriam & son Thomas. Wits., Waitman Sipple, Henry Newell, George Wilson. Prob. June 22, 1787. Arch. vol. A11, pages 197-199. Reg. of Wills, Liber M, folios 143-144.

Dean, James. Will. Made June 2, 1787. Little Creek Hd. Heirs: wife Sarah; son Jesse; daus. Rebeckah, Keziah. Exec'rs, wife Sarah & son Jesse. Wits., Thomas Keith, John McEver, Moses McClan. Prob. June 26, 1787. Arch. vol. A13, pages 136-137. Reg. of Wills, Liber M, folios 144-145.

Caldwell, Mary. Widow. Will. Made Oct. 15, 1786. Heirs: sons Andrew, John, Robert, Train & James; dau. Esther; grandchildren unnamed (children of eldest son Train Caldwell). Exec'rs, sons John & Robert. Wits., Brady Morris, Janet Mair, Sary Johns. Prob. June 30, 1787. Arch. vol. A7, page 122. Reg. of Wills, Liber M, folios 145-146.

Ironside, John. Will. Made April 26, 1787. Heirs: dau. Margaret Ironside; other children unnamed. Exec'r, son-in-law Emanuel Morris. Wits., Duncan Smith, Robert McClyment, Richard Baning. Prob. July 9, 1787. Arch. vol. A25, pages 231-232. Reg. of Wills, Liber M, folio 145.

Neal, Jonathan. Admin. of, to Sarah Neal. July 28, 1787. Arch. vol. A37, pages 131-134. Reg. of Wills, Liber M, folio 147. Note:—Arch. vol. A37, page 131 mentions heirs, Anne, James, Sarah, Hannah, Mary, Jonathan, Ruth, Elizabeth, Samuel, Daniel & Francis Neal.

Wilson, Samuel. Farmer. Will. Made July 4, 1787. Duck Creek Hd. Heirs: wife Mary; sons John, Thomas, Samuel, Gustavus; daus. Ann & Lydia. Exec'x, wife Mary. Trustees, John Cook, John Stuart, Andrew Jamison. Wits., Robert Cook, John Cook, John Stewart. Prob. July 28, 1787. Arch. vol. A56, pages 10-13. Reg. of Wills, Liber M, folios 147-148.

Hill, Rachel. Wife of James Hill. Admin. of, to Joseph Denny. July 30, 1787. Reg. of Wills, Liber M, folio 147.

Thomas, Daniel. Admin. of, to Sarah Thomas. Aug. 8, 1787. Reg. of Wills, Liber M, folio 148.

Hazel, Barthia. Widow. Will. Made Dec. 29, 1784. Duck Creek Hd. Heirs: sons Joseph Nock; grandson Thomas Nock, son of son Thomas Nock; granddaus. Mary & Barthia Nock, daus. of son Thomas Nock. Exec'r, son Joseph Nock. Wits., John Brown, William Farson, Mary Smith. Prob. Aug. 13, 1787. Arch. vol. A23, page 74. Reg. of Wills, Liber M, folios 148-149.

Parry, Thomas. Admin. of, to Jacob Stout, Jr. Aug. 13, 1787. Reg. of Wills, Liber M, folio 148.

Clark, James, Jr. Admin. of, to Maskilin Clark. Aug. 17, 1787. Arch. vol. A8, page 239. Reg. of Wills, Liber M, folio 149.

Pratt, Nathan. Admin. of, to Ann Pratt. Aug. 31, 1787. Arch. vol. A41, pages 128-130. Reg. of Wills, Liber M, folio 158. Note:—Arch. vol. A41, page 128 mentions heirs, Nathan, Jonathan & Elizabeth Pratt; page 129 shows that Ann Pratt later married Philemon Cubbidge.

Green, Christopher. Admin. of, to James Green. Sept. 5, 1787. Reg. of Wills, Liber M, folio 155.

Holliday, John. Admin. of, to George Wilson, Joshua Fisher & James Holliday. Sept. 6, 1787. Reg. of Wills, Liber M, folio 155.

Wharton, Isaiah. Admin. of, to Joseph Driskill. Sept. 6, 1787. Reg. of Wills, Liber M, folio 155.

Winsmore, William. Will. Made Aug. 24, 1787. Mispillion Hd. Heirs: wife Rosen; sons Ely, Thomas, Vallentine; dau. Sarah. Exec'r, son Thomas. Wits., David Young, Edmund Bayly, William Thompson, Jr. Prob. Sept. 8, 1787. Arch. vol. A56, pages 47-48. Reg. of Wills, Liber M, folios 158-159.

Rodney, William. Son of Caesar Rodney (the youngest son of William Rodney). Will. Made Sept. 6, 1787. St. Jones' Hd. Heirs: dau. Letticia; niece Elizabeth Wilson, dau of sister Sarah Wilson; granddau. Elizabeth Frazer; nephews Caesar Rodney Wilson & Thomas Wilson, sons of sister Sarah Wilson; John Homestead; Sarah Edenfield. Exec'rs, dau. Letticia Rodney, Thomas Rodney, John Marim. Wits., William Molleston, Charles Ridgely, French Battell, Evan Thomas. Codicil. Prob. Sept. 13, 1787. Arch. vol. A44, pages 99-101. Reg. of Wills, Liber M, folios 155-157.

Jones, Benjamin. Yeoman. Will. Made April 7, 1783. Murderkill Hd. Heirs: wife Mary; sons Layton & Philip; grandsons Benjamin, Layton & Silas Jones. Exec'rs, wife Mary & sons Layton & Philip. Wits., William Thompson, William Lynch, Nicholas Vining. Prob. Sept. 25, 1787. Arch. vol. A27, pages 140-141. Reg. of Wills, Liber M, folios 159-160.

Casson, John. Admin. of, to John Baning & wife Elizabeth. Sept. 26, 1787. Arch. vol. A7, page 246.

Ross, Levi. Admin. of, to Thomas Viccory, D. B. N. Sept. 26, 1787. Arch. vol. A44, page 139. Reg. of Wills, Liber M, folio 160.

Baker, George. Admin. of, to Thomas Leathem. Oct. 1, 1787. Reg. of Wills, Liber M, folio 160.

Spruance, John. Will. Made May 11, 1787. Duck Creek Hd. Heirs: sons John & Presly; daus. Elizabeth David, Susannah Farsons & Jemima Griffin; grandchildren Henry, John, Mary, Presly, William & Jemima (children of son John Spruance); grandsons John & Daniel (sons of son Presly). Exec'r, son Presly. Wits., Robert Holiday, John Cowgill, Henry Cowgill. Prob. Oct. 13, 1787. Arch. vol. A48, page 111. Reg. of Wills, Liber M, folios 160-161.

Hutchinson, John. Admin. of, to Sarah Hutchinson. Oct. 15, 1787. Reg. of Wills, Liber M, folio 162.

Broadway, Ambrose. Admin. of, to Mary Broadway. Oct. 16, 1787. Arch. vol. A5, pages 232-233. Reg. of Wills, Liber M, folio 162. Note:—Arch. vol. A5, page 233 shows that Mary Broadway later married Israel Merrick.

Lockwood, Armwell, Jr. Yeoman. Will. Made June 27, 1787. Heirs: wife Lucretia; sons Richard Comerford & Thomas; dau. Elizabeth. Exec'rs, wife Lucretia & friend William Alliband. Guardian, William Alliband. Wits., William Kirkly, Mathew Cox, John Lockwood. Prob. Oct. 16, 1787. Arch. vol. A30, pages 215 & 219-220. Reg. of Wills, Liber M, folios 162-163. Note:—Arch. vol. A30, page 220 mentions a Richard Lockwood.

Emory, Thomas, Jr. Admin. of, to Mary Emory & Thomas Emory, Sr. Oct. 17, 1787. Arch. vol. A16, pages 189-192. Reg. of Wills, Liber M, folio 163. Note:—Arch. vol. A16, page 189 mentions heirs, Thomas & Tilly Emory & widow Mary Shankland.

Beard, Moses. Admin. of, to Mary Beard. Oct. 24, 1787. Reg. of Wills, Liber M, folio 163.

Flyn, John. Admin. of, to Ann Flynn. Nov. 5, 1787. Reg. of Wills, Liber M, folio 163. Note:—Arch. vol. A17, page 213 shows that Ann Flynn later married Elijah Stafford.

Emmerson, Michael. Admin. of, to Henry Simmons, D. B. N. Nov. 10, 1787. Reg. of Wills, Liber M, folio 163.

Knight, William. Admin. of, to Darcus Knight. Nov. 10, 1787. Reg. of Wills, Liber M, folio 163.

Errickson, Mathew. Bricklayer. Admin. of, to William Ross. Nov. 12, 1787. Arch. vol. A16, page 212. Reg. of Wills, Liber M, folio 163.

Freeman, Daniel. Admin. of, to Rebecca Freeman & John Freeman. Nov. 13, 1787. Reg. of Wills, Liber M, folio 163.

Baynard, Henry. Will. Made Feb. 7, 1787. Heirs: bros. John & Thomas; sister Sarah Whitely; housekeeper Elizabeth Casson. Exec'r, bro. John. Wits., Thomas White, Edward White, Jr., Elijah Morris, William Lane. Prob. Nov. 15, 1787. Arch. vol. A3, pages 79-80. Reg. of Wills, Liber M, folios 164-165.

McKnit, Magdalene. Widow. Will. Made Nov. 12, 1784. Heirs: sons James, John, Robert & William; dau. Betsy Black. Exec'rs, sons James & John. Wits., John King, Robert Fleming, Jr., Elizabeth Fleming. Prob. Nov. 15, 1787. Arch. vol. A32, pages 232-234. Reg. of Wills, Liber M, folios 163-164.

Baynard, Elizabeth. Admin. of, to John Baynard. Nov. 16, 1787. Reg. of Wills, Liber M, folio 165. Note:—Arch. vol. A3, page 78 mentions heirs, Henry Baynard & Mary Feddaman.

McGlaughlin, Henry. Admin. of, to John Watson. Nov. 21, 1787. Arch. vol. A32, page 193. Reg. of Wills, Liber M, folio 165.

Parkerson, Christopher. Admin. of, to William Kirkly, D. B. N. Nov. 29, 1787. Arch. vol. A39, page 66. Reg. of Wills, Liber M, folio 165. Note:—Arch. vol. A39, page 66 mentions a widow Sarah Parkerson.

Knotts, Jonathan. Will. Made Oct. 9, 1787. Heirs: son William; dau. Rebecka Hanes; grandson William Knotts, son of Nathaniel Knotts. Exec'r, son William. Wits., William Larwood, Richard Chaddack, Elizabeth Larwood. Prob. Dec. 6, 1787. Arch. vol. A29, page 79. Reg. of Wills, Liber M, folios 165-166.

Furbee, Benjamin. Admin. of, to Thomas Rickets. Dec. 11, 1787. Arch. vol. A18, pages 151-152. Reg. of Wills, Liber M, folio 166.

Darling, Richard. Admin. of, to Joshua Darling. Dec. 17, 1787. Reg. of Wills, Liber M, folio 166.

Bullen, John. Admin. of, to Hannah Bullen. Dec. 20, 1787. Arch. vol. A6, pages 179-180. Reg. of Wills, Liber M, folio 166. Note:—Arch. vol. A6, page 180 shows that Hannah Bullen later married James Barry.

Thompson, John. Admin. of, to Robert Thompson. Dec. 29, 1787. Reg. of Wills, Liber M, folio 166.

Gordon, Coe. Will. Made Nov. 16, 1787. Heirs: wife Sarah; son John; dau. Sidney; one child unnamed. Exec'rs, wife Sarah, bro. John Gordon, friends Ezekiel Cowgill, Manlove Emmerson. Wits., Dennis Shee, Stephen Millis, John Coombe. Prob. Jan. 1, 1788. Arch. vol. A19, page 145. Reg. of Wills, Liber M, folios 166-167.

Clow, China, Jr. Admin. of, to Stephen Attax & Henrietta Attax. Jan. 3, 1788. Reg. of Wills, Liber M, folio 166.

Sipple, Caleb. Admin. of, to Peter Lowber, Jr. Jan. 4, 1788. Arch. vol. A46, pages 93-94. Reg. of Wills, Liber M, folio 166.

Manlove, Sarah. Admin. of, to George Manlove. Jan. 18, 1788. Arch. vol. A33, pages 120 & 122. Reg. of Wills, Liber M, folio 167.

White, James. Admin. of, to Mary White. Jan. 21, 1788. Arch. vol. A54, page 112. Reg. of Wills, Liber M, folio 167.

Winsmore, Valentine. Admin. of, to Thomas Winsmore. Jan. 22, 1788. Arch. vol. A56, page 45. Reg. of Wills, Liber M, folio 167.

Taggart, James. Admin. of, to Sarah Taggart. Feb. 1, 1788. Reg. of Wills, Liber M, folio 167.

Truax, Benjamin. Admin. of, to Catharine Truax. Feb. 2, 1788. Reg. of Wills, Liber M, folio 167.

Wilcuts, Josiah. Admin. of, to Caleb Wilcuts. Feb. 4, 1788. Arch. vol. A54, pages 231-235. Reg. of Wills, Liber M, folio 167. Note:—Arch. vol. A54, pages 231-235 mention heirs: Susannah Godwin; Rachel, Joseph & Martha Wilcuts; Sarah, Mary & David Wilcuts (children of Joseph Wilcuts); William & Levi Wilcuts; David, Rachel & Daniel Tharp (children of Isaac Tharp); William, Martha, Levi, Joseph, Sarah, Mary, Nancy Wilcuts; Susanna Stark (wife of Philip Stark).

Cahoon, Thomas. Admin. of, to Mark Cahoon, D. B. N. Feb. 12, 1788. Reg. of Wills, Liber M, folio 167.

Cummings, Daniel, Jr. Admin. of, to George Cummings. Feb. 13, 1788. Reg. of Wills, Liber M, folio 167.

Cook, Michael. Admin. of, to John Cook. Feb. 16, 1788. Reg. of Wills, Liber M, folio 168.

Mumford, Solomon. Admin. of, to Rachel Mumford. Feb. 19, 1788. Arch. vol. A37, pages 72-73. Reg. of Wills, Liber M, folio 168. Note:—Arch. vol. A37, page 72 shows that Rachel Mumford later married William Sullivan.

Parker, Thomas. Admin. of, to Margaret Parker. Feb. 20, 1788. Arch. vol. A39, pages 48-49 & 51. Reg. of Wills, Liber M, folio 168. Note:—Arch. vol. A39, page 51 shows that the widow Margaret Parker later married George Kirkley; page 48 shows that Margaret Parker Kirkley married William Harper, Jr.; also page 48 mentions heirs, Peter, Thomas & Sarah Parker.

Cavender, William. Admin. of, to James Sykes, Jr. Feb. 25, 1788. Reg. of Wills, Liber M, folio 168.

Paradee, Hannah. Admin. of, to Stephen Paradee. Feb. 26, 1788. Reg. of Wills, Liber M, folio 168.

Lewis, **Daniel.** Admin. of, to Stephen Lewis, Jr. Feb. 28, 1788. Reg. of Wills, Liber M, folio 168.

Tibbit, **Mary.** Admin. of, to Samuel Tibbit. Feb. 28, 1788. Reg. of Wills, Liber M, folio 168.

Lewis, **Sarah.** Admin. of, to John Cook, D. B. N. March 1, 1788. Reg. of Wills, Liber M, folio 168.

Hazell, **Benjamin.** Admin. of, to Elizabeth Hazell. March 12, 1788. Reg. of Wills, Liber M, folio 168.

Burch, **Rachel.** Admin. of, to George Wilson. March 13, 1788. Reg. of Wills, Liber M, folio 168.

Steel, **James.** Admin. of, to James Morris. March 17, 1788. Arch. vol. A48, pages 201-202. Reg. of Wills, Liber M, folio 168.

Beauchamp, **John.** Farmer. Will. Made Feb. 10, 1788. Murderkill Hd. Heirs: wife Mary; daus. Rachel & Nancy; sons Risden, Isaac, John, Marcy & David. Exec'x, wife Mary. Trustees, bro. Marcy Beauchamp & Nathaniel Smithers, Jr. Wits., Thomas Nock, Philip Jones, James Lundergin. Prob. March 20, 1788. Arch. vol. A3, page 112. Reg. of Wills, Liber M, folios 168-169.

Purden, **Andrew.** Admin. of, to Prudence Purden. April 1, 1788. Arch. vol. A41, pages 205-207. Reg. of Wills, Liber M, folio 169. Note:—Arch. vol. A41, page 205 shows that Prudence Purden later married William Verden; also mentions heirs, Sarah, John, Elizabeth & Andrew Purden & Esther Pratt.

Burrows, **Ebenezer.** Admin. of, to Edward Burrows. April 10, 1788. Reg. of Wills, Liber M, folio 169.

Smith, **George.** Admin. of, to Elizabeth Smith. April 12, 1788. Reg. of Wills, Liber M, folio 169.

Tygart, **James.** Admin. of, to Thomas Pickering, D. B. N. April 15, 1788. Arch. vol. A51, pages 188-189. Reg. of Wills, Liber M, folio 169.

Pryor, **Joseph.** Admin. of, to John Pryor. April 19, 1788. Arch. vol. A41, pages 196-197. Reg. of Wills, Liber M, folio 170. Note:—Arch. vol. A41, page 196 mentions heirs, Abraham & John Pryor & Elizabeth Nixon, wife of Charles.

Lewis, Deborah. Will. Made April 21, 1788. Heirs: husband Stephen; sons Luff & Stephen Lewis, John Plesenton & David Pleasanton; daus. Sarah Laws & Deborah Lewis. Exec'r, husband Stephen. Wits., James Pemberton, Robert McKnitt, Elizabeth Rynet. [No prob.]. Arch. vol. A30, pages 72-73. Reg. of Wills, Liber G, Appendix 10. Note:—Arch. vol. A30, pages 72-73 show that this will was void and never probated; will mentions father Nathaniel Luff.

Griffith, Jean. Admin. of, to John Griffith. April 25, 1788. Reg. of Wills, Liber M, folio 170. Note:—Arch. vol. A20, page 243 mentions children, James & Mastin Morris, Isaac, Mary, Solomon, Nathan, James & Hillyard Griffith.

Lackey, Andrew. Yeoman. Will. Made March 8, 1787. Little Creek Hd. Heirs: wife Rachel; daus. Mary Wilson & Ann Wills; son Andrew; grandson Gustavus Wilson. Exec'rs, son Andrew & Samuel Wilson. Wits., Jno. Ham, Susanah Ham, Margaret Ham. Prob. April 28, 1788. Arch. vol. A29, pages 90-91. Reg. of Wills, Liber M, folios 169-170.

Snow, John. Admin. of, to Sarah Vandyke. May 1, 1788. Reg. of Wills, Liber M, folio 170.

Galt, Thomas. Admin. of, to Neomi Galt. May 13, 1788. Arch. vol. A19, page 199. Reg. of Wills, Liber M, folio 171.

Durham, John. Yeoman. Will. Made April 9, 1788. Little Creek Hd. Heirs: sons William, Isaiah & Whitenton; daus. Sarah Sisco, Letitia Lacount, Elizabeth & Hannah Conselar; children of son John Durham; Rebecca Durham; Clayton Durham. Exec'r, friend Robert Holiday. Wits., Thomas Keith, Mary Conselar, Eleanor Puckim. Prob. May 14, 1788. Arch. vol. A15, pages 189-193. Reg. of Wills, Liber M, folios 170-171. Note:—Arch. vol. A15, page 190 shows Thomas Conselar as husband of Elizabeth Conselar & Thos. Lacount as husband of Letitia.

Stewart, Moses. Admin. of, to Rachel Stewart. May 14, 1788. Reg. of Wills, Liber M, folio 171.

Kelson, George. Will. Made March 25, 1788. Heirs: wife Rebekah; Ann William Stewart, dau. of Charles Stewart; Charles Stewart. Exec'r, Charles Stewart. Wits., Abraham Parsons, William Burrows, Mary Burrows. Prob. May 15, 1788. Arch. vol. A28, page 117. Reg. of Wills, Liber M, folios 171-172.

Jarrad, William. Admin. of, to William Carpenter. May 24, 1788. Reg. of Wills, Liber M, folio 172.

Pleasonton, Nathaniel. Farmer. Will. Made April 17, 1788. Heirs: wife Margaret; children unnamed. Exec'x, wife Margaret. Wits., Nathaniel Luff, Jr., Edward White, William White, Sr. Prob. May 27, 1788. Arch. vol. A40, page 130.

Price, William, Jr. Admin. of, to Mary Price. May 27, 1788. Reg. of Wills, Liber M, folio 172.

Vanhoy, Abraham, Jr. Admin. of, to Sarah Vanhoy. May 28, 1788. Arch. vol. A52, page 3. Reg. of Wills, Liber M, folio 172.

Aaron, Michael McCary. Admin. of, to James Everett & wife Hannah, late Hannah Aaron. May 29, 1788. Arch. vol. A54, page 2. Note:—Acct. mentions heirs, Cary Aaron, Sarah Cary Aaron & Elizabeth Cary Aaron.

Benston, Levin. Admin. of, to John Rickards. May 29, 1788. Arch. vol. A3, page 242. Reg. of Wills, Liber M, folio 172.

White, William. Admin. of, to Isabella White. May 29, 1788. Arch. vol. A54, page 172. Note:—Acct. mentions heirs, William Needles, Sarah Smith (wife of John Smith), Mary King (wife of Wm. King), Stephen, Jacob & Isaac White.

Goodfellow, Ann. Admin. of, to John Bell, Jr. May 31, 1788. Reg. of Wills, Liber M, folio 172.

Goodfellow, James. Admin. of, to Nicholas Ridgely, Esq. May 31, 1788. Reg. of Wills, Liber M, folio 172.

Stoops, Sarah. Will. Made March 15, 1787. Heirs: bros. unnamed; Sarah Sterling, dau. of John Sterling. [No exec'rs]. Wits., John Howard, Hannah Blackiston, James Tigner. Prob. May 31, 1788. Arch. vol. A49, page 28. Reg. of Wills, Liber M, folio 172.

Cutler, Thomas. Admin. of, to Sarah Cutler, Charles Connor & Charles Doney. June 6, 1788. Arch. vol. A12, page 171. Reg. of Wills, Liber M, folio 173.

Pearson, Hannah. Admin. of, to James Pearson. June 7, 1788. Reg. of Wills, Liber M, folio 173.

Tully, Sarah. Admin. of, to Stephen Alston. June 7, 1788. Arch. vol. A51, pages 130-132. Reg. of Wills, Liber M, folio 173. Note:—Arch. vol. A51, page 130 shows that Sarah Tully was the widow of Arthur Alston.

Causey, Priscilla. Admin. of, to Daniel Dawson. June 9, 1788. Arch. vol. A8, page 115. Reg. of Wills, Liber M, folio 173.

Train, James. Admin. of, to Lydia Train. June 10, 1788. Reg. of Wills, Liber M, folio 173.

Brinckley, Richard. Mispillion Hd. Admin. of, to Phebe Brinckly. June 23, 1788. Arch. vol. A5, pages 206-209. Reg. of Wills, Liber M, folio 173.

Pleasonton, Nathaniel. Admin. of, to Margaret Pleasonton. June 27, 1788. Arch. vol. A40, pages 131-133. Reg. of Wills, Liber M, folio 173. Note:—Arch. vol. A40, pages 131-132 show that Margaret Pleasonton married Charles Nabb; also mentions heirs, Edward, Deborah & Nathaniel Pleasonton.

Laws, John. Admin. of, to Elizabeth Laws. July 2, 1788. Arch. vol. A29, pages 150-152. Reg. of Wills, Liber M, folio 173.

Stradly, Samuel. Admin. of, to Lucretia Stradly. July 17, 1788. Reg. of Wills, Liber M, folio 173. Note:—Arch. vol. A49, page 78 shows that Lucretia Stradly married Philip Sherwood.

Nowell, Henry. Admin. of, to Sarah Nowell. July 26, 1788. Reg. of Wills, Liber M, folio 173.

Wells, Richard. Admin. of, to David Wells & David Wallace. July 28, 1788. Reg. of Wills, Liber M, folio 173.

Conner, John. Admin. of, to Samuel Howell. Aug. 9, 1788. Arch. vol. A10, page 83. Reg. of Wills, Liber M, folio 173.

Peterson, Peter. (Negro). Admin. of, to Abraham Peterson (Negro). Aug. 9, 1788. Reg. of Wills, Liber M, folio 173.

Pratt, Mary. Admin. of, to Philemon Cubbidge, D. B. N. Aug. 26, 1788. Arch. vol. A41, pages 124-127. Reg. of Wills, Liber M, folio 173. Note:—Arch. vol. A71, pages 124-125 mention heirs, George & Frederick Pratt, heirs of sisters Esther Taylor, Ann Reed, Dinah Clampitt & bros. Nathan & Luke Pratt.

Brown, Stephen. Admin. of, to Catharine Brown. Aug. 28, 1788. Reg. of Wills, Liber M, folio 174.

Walton, Ann. Widow of John Walton. Will. Made Aug. 3, 1788. Murderkill Hd. Heirs: sons Isaac, William & Beauchamp; daus. Rachel, Esther & Patience. Exec'rs, bros. Isaac & Marcy Beauchamp. Guardians, bros. Isaac & Marcy Beauchamp. Wits., David Beauchamp, Nathaniel Smithers, Jr., Esther Smithers. Prob. Aug. 29, 1788. Arch. vol. A53, pages 40 & 42. Reg. of Wills, Liber M, folio 174.

Walton, John. Admin. of, to Isaac & Marcy Beauchamp, D. B. N. Aug. 29, 1788. Arch. vol. A53, pages 64-66. Reg. of Wills, Liber M, folio 174.

Pryor, Elizabeth. Widow of John Pryor. Will. Made June 29, 1788. Heirs: sons Abraham & John; dau. Elizabeth Nixon. Exec'r, son John. Wits., Nicholas Ridgely, Mathias Clifton, Joseph Hodgson. Prob. Sept. 1, 1788. Arch. vol. A41, pages 187-188. Reg. of Wills, Liber M, folios 174-175.

Ridgely, Charles, Jr. Admin. of, to Nicholas Ridgely. Sept. 25, 1788. Reg. of Wills, Liber M, folio 176.

Jester, Francis. Will. Made Oct. 28, 1781. Heirs: sons John, Emanuel, Francis, Jr., Jehu, Jesse, Lyes & Joshuaway; dau. Sarah; wife unnamed. Exec'r, son Emanuel. Wits., Major Anderson, Richard Eckels. Prob. Oct. 1, 1788. Arch. vol. A27, pages 20-23. Reg. of Wills, Liber M, folio 176.

Scotten, Thomas, Sr. Farmer. Will. Made Jan. 7, 1788. Heirs: wife Sarah; sons John, William & Thomas; daus. Rachel Scotten, Sarah Martin & Julea Baily; granddau. Minta Vickars. Exec'r, [Thomas Scotton, from admin. acct.]. Wits., Samuel Milbourn, James Birum, Edward Jones. Prob. Oct. 17, 1788. Arch. vol. A45, pages 98-99 & 101. Reg. of Wills, Liber M, folio 176.

McNatt, Richard. Admin. of, to Mary McNatt. Oct. 22, 1788. Arch. vol. A38, page 22. Reg. of Wills, Liber M, folio 177.

Burrows, Sarah. Admin. of, to John Burrows. Oct. 22, 1788. Reg. of Wills, Liber M, folio 177.

Torbet, John. Admin. of, to Rachel Torbet & Hugh Torbet. Oct. 25, 1788. Reg. of Wills, Liber M, folio 177.

Bradly [Brady], Benjamin. Admin. of, to Elizabeth Bradly & Joseph Bradly. Nov. 5, 1788. Reg. of Wills, Liber M, folio 177.

Wilson, George. Will. Made April 27, 1788. Heirs: sons George, Philip; daus. Patience, Ann, Peggy; friend Henry Newell. Exec'r, Henry Newell. Wits., Thomas Skidmore, David Boggs, Robert Haul [Hall]. Prob. Nov. 6, 1788. Arch. vol. A55, pages 205-206. Reg. of Wills, Liber M, folios 177-178.

Beauchamp, John. Admin. of, to Nathaniel Smithers & Marcy Beauchamp, D. B. N. Nov. 12, 1788. Arch. vol. A3, pages 113-114. Reg. of Wills, Liber M, folio 178.

Beauchamp, Mary. Widow of John Beauchamp. Will. Made July 3, 1788. Murderkill Hd. Heirs: sons Risdon, Isaac, Marcy, David & John; daus. Nancy & Rachel. Exec'rs, sons Marcy & David. Wits., Ann Walton, Esther Smithers, Nathaniel Smithers, Jr. Prob. Nov. 12, 1788. Arch. vol. A3, pages 122-123. Reg. of Wills, Liber M, folios 178-179. Note:— Will mentions father Richard Downham, dec'd.

Hatfield, John. Soldier in Delaware Regiment. Murderkill Hd. Admin. of, to Thomas Hatfield. Nov. 12, 1788. Arch. vol. A22, pages 234-235. Reg. of Wills, Liber M, folio 178. Note: —Arch. vol. A22, page 234 mentions heirs, James & Thomas Hatfield, Sarah Whitby & Anne Davis.

Howard, Joseph. Admin. of, to Mary Howard. Nov. 12, 1788. Reg. of Wills, Liber M, folio 178.

Ridge, William. Admin. of, to Samuel Griffin. Nov. 12, 1788. Reg. of Wills, Liber M, folio 178.

Shay, Dennis. Admin. of, to Elizabeth Shay. Nov. 12, 1788. Reg. of Wills, Liber M, folio 178.

Barns, John. Admin. of, to Rachel Barns. Nov. 13, 1788. Reg. of Wills, Liber M, folio 179.

Smith, William. Mispillion Hd. Admin. of, to Samuel Smith & Holiday Smith. Nov. 13, 1788. Arch. vol. A47, pages 201-202. Reg. of Wills, Liber M, folio 179.

Corse, William. Admin. of, to Rebecca Corse. Nov. 14, 1788. Reg. of Wills, Liber M, folio 179.

Saulsbury, William. Will. Made Oct. 13, 1788. Heirs: daus. Rebecca, Marget & Eliner; sons Gove, Thomas, William & Henry. Exec'x, dau. Rebecca. Wits., Thomas Dawson, Abraham Fisher, George Wilson. Prob. Nov. 25, 1788. Arch. vol. A45, pages 20-23. Reg. of Wills, Liber M, folio 179. Note:— Arch. vol. A45, page 21 shows that Rebecca Saulsbury married Gove Cox and later married Vincent Dowety; also mentions Margaret Wilson.

Sipple, Jonathan. Admin. of, to Daniel Boyer, D. B. N. Nov. 27, 1788. Reg. of Wills, Liber M, folio 180.

Smith, Robert, Sr. Will. Made April 22, 1785. Mispillion Hd. Heirs: sons Ebenezer & Samuel; daus. Jeamimah Morris, Elizabeth Kirkly & Alice Smith; grandson Jesse Smith. Exec'r, son Samuel. Wits., Robert McGonigall, Esais Rigs, Elizabeth Brown. Prob. Nov. 27, 1788. Arch. vol. A47, page 158. Reg. of Wills, Liber M, folios 180-181.

Dushane, Garrett. Tanner. Duck Creek Hd. Admin. of, to William Truax Marsh & wife Mary, the late Mary Dushane. Nov. 28, 1788. Arch. vol. A15, pages 199-202. Note:— Arch. vol. A15, page 200 mentions a Letitia Richardson, widow of John Richardson, who later married Robert Johnson.

Heritage, John. Admin. of, to Dolly Jenkins. Nov. 28, 1788. Reg. of Wills, Liber M, folio 180.

Denny, Joseph. Admin. of, to Evan Denny. Dec. 10, 1788. Arch. vol. A13, pages 228-230. Reg. of Wills, Liber M, folio 181. Note:—Arch. vol. A13, page 229 mentions heirs, Evan, Philip, Joseph & John Denny, Rebeccah Barnett, Margaret McClain & Mary Thompson.

North, Margaret. Admin. of, to Stephen Alston. Dec. 10, 1788. Arch. vol. A38, pages 46-47. Reg. of Wills, Liber M, folio 181.

Burt, Henry. Admin. of, to Elsebury Burt. Dec. 13, 1788. Reg. of Wills, Liber M, folio 181.

Moore, Robert. Admin. of, to Lydia Moore. Dec. 16, 1788. Arch. vol. A36, pages 83-84. Reg. of Wills, Liber M, folio 181. Note:—Arch. vol. A36, page 83 shows that Lydia Moore married ... Marce; also mentions heirs, Henry, James, John, Abraham, Robert & Joseph Moore.

Vandyke, James. Will. Made July 2, 1787. Duck Creek Hd. Heirs: wife Sarah; sons Nicholas, Thomas & John; dau. Rebecca. Exec'x, wife Sarah. Wits., Silas Snow, Ann Wood. Prob. Dec. 16, 1788. Arch. vol. A51, page 231. Reg. of Wills, Liber M, folio 181.

Vandyke, James. Admin. of, to Charles Carson. Dec. 16, 1788. Reg. of Wills, Liber M, folio 181.

Drayton, William. Admin. of, to James Morris. C. Dec. 22, 1788. Arch. vol. A15, page 83.

Ellis, Eleanor. Admin. of, to John Wilson. Dec. 27, 1788. Arch. vol. A16, pages 107-110. Reg. of Wills, Liber M, folio 182. Note:—Arch. vol. A16, page 107 mentions bros. & sisters, Thomas & Samuel Ellis, Elizabeth Clemons (widow of Edward), Sarah Wilson & Catherine Stewart.

Smith, James. Millwright. Will. Made Dec. 12, 1788. Heirs: wife Susanah; son James. Exec'x, wife Susanah. Wits., Benjamin Crooks, William Jones. Prob. Dec. 27, 1788. Arch. vol. A47, page 63. Reg. of Wills, Liber M, folio 182.

Millis, Ann. Admin. of, to James Millis. Dec. 29, 1788. Reg. of Wills, Liber M, folio 182.

Greenlee, Michael. Farmer. Will. Made Nov. 8, 1788. Murderkill Hd. Heirs: wife Esther; sons Samuel, John, James, Michael, David, William & Allen; daus. Mary Roggers, Elizabeth Griffin, Selia Callaway. Prob. Jan. 2, 1789. Arch. vol. A20, pages 138-140. Reg. of Wills, Liber M, folios 182-183.

Duyer, Joseph. Farmer. Will. Made Nov. 25, 1788. Heirs: wife Rosamond; dau. Harriet. Exec'x, wife Rosamond. Wits., Samuel Spencer Blackiston, Robert Watkins, James Snow. Prob. Jan. 6, 1789. Arch. vol. A15, pages 214-216. Reg. of Wills, Liber M, folio 183. Note:—Arch. vol. A15, page 215 shows that Rosamond Duyer married James Steen.

Smith, Samuel. Admin. of, to Mary Smith. Jan. 7, 1789. Arch. vol. A47, pages 162-163. Reg. of Wills, Liber M, folio 183. Note:—Arch. vol. A47, page 162 mentions children, George, Benjamin, Fisher, William, Ruth & John Revel Smith & Mary Bowman.

Barns, William. Admin. of, to Richard Smith, Esq. Jan. 8, 1789. Arch. vol. A2, page 233. Reg. of Wills, Liber M, folio 183.

Dunbar, Samuel. Admin. of, to John Coleman. Jan. 12, 1789. Reg. of Wills, Liber M, folio 184.

Gruwell, Eleazer. Admin. of, to John Srowders. Jan. 12, 1789. Arch. vol. A21, page 16. Reg. of Wills, Liber M, folio 183.

Brown, Aaron. Admin. of, to Hanah Brown. Jan. 15, 1789. Reg. of Wills, Liber M, folio 184.

Purdin, John. Admin. of, to William Verden, D. B. N. Jan. 23, 1789. Arch. vol. A41, page 221. Reg. of Wills, Liber M, folios 184-185.

Furbee, Jonathan. Admin. of, to Hesther Furbee. Jan. 24, 1789. Arch. vol. A18, page 162. Reg. of Wills, Liber M, folio 185.

Walton, David. Admin. of, to Nancy Walton. Jan. 24, 1789. Reg. of Wills, Liber M, folio 185.

Delap, Catharine. Admin. of, to Mary Southward. Feb. 6, 1789. Reg. of Wills, Liber M, folio 185.

Butler, Jane. Will. Made Oct. 20, 1788. Heirs: sisters Ann Polin & Margaret Struthers; heirs of sister Ann Polin; Mrs. Ann Ridgely; Elizabeth Read; Ann Ridgely, the younger; Henry Moore Ridgely; George Wemyss Ridgely. Exec'x, Ann Ridgely. Wits., Nicholas Ridgely, Daniel Cummings. Prob. Feb. 7, 1789. Arch. vol. A7, page 16. Reg. of Wills, Liber M, folio 185.

Clark, Ezekiel. Yeoman. Dover Hd. Admin. of, to Esther Clark. Feb. 11, 1789. Arch. vol. A8, page 229. Reg. of Wills, Liber M, folio 186.

Godwin, Ezekiel. Admin. of, to Eleanor Godwin. Feb. 11, 1789. Arch. vol. A19, pages 73-74. Reg. of Wills, Liber M, folio 186. Note:—Arch. vol. A19, page 73 mentions heirs, Daniel & Eleanor Godwin, Lydia Catlin (wife of Joseph) & Catharine Powell (wife of Zodak).

Clark, John. Admin. of, to Elizabeth Clark. Feb. 13, 1789. Arch. vol. A9, pages 11-12. Reg. of Wills, Liber M, folio 186. Note:—Arch. vol. A9, page 11 mentions heirs, Betsy, Caleb, Hugh, Susannah, Priscilla, Henry & Elizabeth Clark.

Crockett, John. Admin. of, to John & Jonathan Crockett. Feb. 25, 1789. Arch. vol. A11, pages 245-247. Note:—Arch. vol. A11, page 247 mentions heirs, Samuel, Jonathan, John, Elinor, Margarett & Elizabeth Crockett & William Parediee.

Mears, Andrew. Admin. of, to James Numbers, D. B. N. Feb. 25, 1789. Arch. vol. A34, pages 108-109. Reg. of Wills, Liber M, folio 186.

Patton, Mary. Will. Made July 22, 1787. Heirs: son Armwell Lockwood; dau. Mary Tumblin; granddaus. Sarah Purden, Mary Gordon, Sarah Lockwood. Exec'r, [Armwell Lockwood, from admin. acct.]. Wits., Mathew Coxe, Margaret Merick, Nancy Lockwood. Prob. Feb. 25, 1789. Arch. vol. A39, pages 139-141. Reg. of Wills, Liber M, folio 186.

Jackson, Nimrod. Admin. of, to Meriam Jackson. Feb. 26, 1789. Arch. vol. A26, pages 24-25. Reg. of Wills, Liber M, folio 186. Note:—Arch. vol. A26, page 24 mentions heirs, Mary, Samuel & Nimrod Jackson; also shows that Meriam Jackson married William Harper.

Brown, John. Admin. of, to Joshua Brown & Robert Caldwell. Feb. 28, 1789. Reg. of Wills, Liber M, folio 186.

Hazle, Mathew. Admin. of, to James Hazle. March 5, 1789. Reg. of Wills, Liber M, folio 187.

Bowman, Thomas, Sr. Will. Made June 21, 1787. Heirs: wife Sarah; sons Thomas & Nathan; dau. Mary Godwin; William Bowman; four children of Joshua & Elizabeth Dewes. Exec'x, wife Sarah. Wits., Benjamin Dill, Nathaniel Summers, Isaac Dewees. Prob. March 11, 1789. Arch. vol. A5, page 88. Reg. of Wills, Liber M, folio 187.

Benson, Nancy. Admin. of, to Levin Benson. March 19, 1789. Reg. of Wills, Liber M, folio 187.

Penal, John. Admin. of, to Elizabeth Pennell & John Brown. March 21, 1789. Reg. of Wills, Liber M, folio 187.

Skidmore, Thomas. Will. Made March 6, 1789. Heirs: wife Sally; a child unnamed. Exec'x, wife Sarah. Wits., Timothy Caldwell, John George, Joseph Alford. Prob. March 21, 1789. Arch. vol. A46, pages 207-208. Reg. of Wills, Liber M, folios 187-188.

Clark, James. Admin. of, to Mary Clark & Robert Clark. March 30, 1789. Arch. vol. A8, pages 240-241. Reg. of Wills, Liber M, folio 188. Note:—Arch. vol. A8, page 40 mentions heirs, Elenor, John, James, Jane & Robert Clark & Mary, wife of John Roberts.

Cullipher, Benjamin. Admin. of, to Thomas Foulke. April 3, 1789. Arch. vol. A12, pages 97 & 99. Reg. of Wills, Liber M, folio 188.

Warner, Mankin. Admin. of, to Thomas Foulke. April 3, 1789. Arch. vol. A53, page 123. Reg. of Wills, Liber M, folio 188.

Collins, Thomas. Will. Made Sept. 29, 1784. Duck Creek Hd. Heirs: son William; daus. Mary Barker (wife of Joseph), Elizabeth & Sarah Collins. Exec'r, friend John Cook. Guardian, Richard Bassett, Esq. Trustee, Edward Tilghman, Jr., Esq. Wits., George Wilson, Thomas Parke, Israel Peterson. Codicil, March 27, 1789. Heirs: son of Elizabeth Brown; Savannah & Blackswamp Churches in Mispillion Hd.; Benjamin Danens; John Offley; George Cummins; dau. Elizabeth Denny; granddaus. Elizabeth, Sarah, Mary & Susannah Barker (children of Mary Barker), Mary & Sarah Denny (daus. of Elizabeth Denny). Wits., John Offley, George Cummins. Prob. April 4, 1789. Arch. vol. A10, pages 21-24. Reg. of Wills, Liber M, folios 188-192.

Fleming, Elizabeth. Will. Made Aug. 27, 1787. Heirs: sons Samuel & George; dau. Esther King; grandchildren Nancy, Caleb & Anthony Cox (children of dau. Martha & John Cox, Sr.). Exec'rs, sons Samuel & George. Wits., John King, Robert Fleming, Susanna Gordon. Prob. April 11, 1789. Arch. vol. A17, pages 175-176. Reg. of Wills, Liber M, folio 192.

Houston, Elijah. Will. Made Sept. 29, 1788. Heirs: wife Elizabeth; dau. Eliza; mother Esther Davis. Exec'x, wife Elizabeth. Wits., James Finsthwait, Esais Riggs. Prob. April 25, 1789. Arch. vol. A25, pages 43-44. Reg. of Wills, Liber M, folios 192-193. Note:—Arch. vol. A25, page 44 shows that Elizabeth, the widow, married John Eckles & later married John Murphy; also, dau. Eliza married Nutter Marvel.

George, Rachel. Will. Made Jan. 18, 1789. Heirs: sons Daniel, Joseph, Thomas, John & James; daus. Rachel Downham, Sarah Wilson, Mary & Hannah George. Exec'r, son John. Wits., Joseph Alford, John Gildersleve, Mary Alford. Prob. April 28, 1789. Arch. vol. A19, pages 5-8. Reg. of Wills, Liber M, folios 193-194.

Clayton, Elizabeth. Admin. of, to Garret Wharton. May 1, 1789. Reg. of Wills, Liber M, folio 194.

Butler, Esther. Admin. of, to Thomas Parker. May 2, 1789. Reg. of Wills, Liber M, folio 194.

Hirons, Robert. Admin. of, to Ann Hirons. May 9, 1789. Reg. of Wills, Liber M, folio 194.

Darling, Robert. Admin. of, to Elizabeth Lewis. May 12, 1789. Arch. vol. A12, page 193. Reg. of Wills, Liber M, folio 194.

Watkins, Robert. Admin. of, to Rachel Watkins. May 12, 1789. Arch. vol. A53, pages 165-166. Reg. of Wills, Liber M, folio 194. Note:—Arch. vol. A53, page 166 mentions heirs, James, Samuel, Sarah, Robert, Christopher & Thomas Watkins; also shows that Rachel married Clayton Curwell.

Smith, Philip. Admin. of, to Lydia Moore, D. B. N. May 22, 1789. Arch. vol. A47, pages 137-138. Reg. of Wills, Liber M, folio 194.

Willoughby, Eleanor. Admin. of, to John Cross. May 22, 1789. Reg. of Wills, Liber M, folio 194.

Pryor, John. Admin. of, to Nicholas Ridgely, Esq. May 25, 1789. Arch. vol. A41, pages 194-195. Reg. of Wills, Liber M, folio 194.

Harmanson, Elizabeth. Admin. of, to George Mitchell. May 27, 1789. Arch. vol. A22, page 37. Note:—Mentions a son John Harmanson. An earlier acct. was settled in S. Co., May 11, 1787.

Read, James. Admin. of, to John Coppage & wife Sarah, late Sarah Read. May 29, 1789. Arch. vol. A42, page 170.

Farsons, Margaret. Admin. of, to Henry Farsons & Nancy Hook. May 30, 1789. Reg. of Wills, Liber M, folios 194-195.

Collins, George. Admin. of, to John Cook, Esq., D. B. N. June 13, 1789. Arch. vol. A9, page 243. Reg. of Wills, Liber M, folio 195.

Morris, Jesse. Admin. of, to William Barcus. June 13, 1789. Reg. of Wills, Liber M, folio 195.

Clayton, John Edmonds. Admin. of, to John Clayton, Esq. June 15, 1789. Reg. of Wills, Liber M, folio 195.

Gilder, Henry. Admin. of, to Susanah Gilder & James Miles. June 16, 1789. Arch. vol. A19, pages 29-33. Reg. of Wills, Liber M, folio 195. Note:—Arch. vol. A19, page 32 mentions a dau. Mary Gilder; page 33 shows that Susanah Gilder married Alexander Hamilton.

George, John. Admin. of, to John George, D. B. N. June 19, 1789. Arch. vol. A18, pages 245-246. Reg. of Wills, Liber M, folio 195. Note:—Arch. vol. A18, page 245 mentions heirs, Daniel & Hannah George; page 244 shows other heirs.

Jackson, Joseph. Farmer. Will. Made April 12, 1789. Heirs: sons Noah & John; daus. Nancy & Elizabeth. Exec'rs, son John & Alexander Jackson (son of Thomas). Wits., Jonathan Gildersleeve, Lydia Spencer, George Purvis. Prob. June 19, 1789. Arch. vol. A26, pages 12-17. Reg. of Wills, Liber M, folios 195-196. Note:—An earlier will made March 12, 1788 in Reg. of Wills, Liber G, Appendix 8 & Arch. vol. A26, page 13 shows wife Elizabeth & wits., William Patton, Aaron Brown & William Virden.

Kerney, Morris. Will. Made Dec. 30, 1788. Duck Creek Cross Roads. Heir: wife Lydia. Exec'x, wife Lydia. Wits., William Daily, Paty Corbet, Benoni Harris, Jurusha Morris. Prob. June 26, 1789. Arch. vol. A28, page 148. Reg. of Wills, Liber M, folio 196.

Jarrald, Stephen, Jr. Farmer. Mispillion Hd. Admin. of, to Mary [Polly] Jarrold. July 1, 1789. Arch. vol. A26, pages 170-171. Reg. of Wills, Liber M, folio 196. Note:—Arch. vol. A26, page 170 mentions Lydia Jarrald, mother of Stephen, Jr.; page 171 mentions a dau. Nancy Jarrald.

Stevens, Henry. Will. Made July 3, 1789. Little Creek Hd. Heirs: daus. Mary Fisher (wife of Thomas), Hannah Marim (wife of John) & Susannah Stevens; grandsons Henry Fisher (son of dau. Mary Fisher) & Henry Marim (son of dau. Hannah Marim); son-in-law John Marim; friend Susannah Wilson. Exec'rs, John Marim & dau. Susanah. Guardian, John Marim. Wits., Boaz Truit, John Pemberton, Nicholas Ridgely. Prob. July 8, 1789. Arch. vol. A48, pages 219-222. Reg. of Wills, Liber M, folios 196-198. Note:—Arch. vol. A48, page 222 mentions an heir, Susannah Pleasanton.

Sutton, Edward. Will. Made July 9, 1789. Murderkiln Hd. Heirs: father Edward Sutton; bros. James & William Sutton; sisters Catherine & Ann Sutton; half-sister Mary Hurlick; sister-in-law Mary Middlebrooks; John Wheeler. Exec'r, John Wheeler. Wits., Patrick Connolly, George Hicks, Mary Hicks. Prob. July 13, 1789. Arch. vol. A49, pages 127-129. Reg. of Wills, Liber M, folio 198.

Lewis, Thomas. Yeoman. Will (copy). Made May 23, 1789. Heirs: sons Joseph, Thomas & John; daus. Mary (Lewis) Manlove & Elizabeth (Lewis) Depoister; grandchildren John, Mary, Fowler & Lewes Simmons, & James Stuart; heirs of Richard Lewis, dec'd; heirs of William Lewis, dec'd. Exec'r, son John Lewis. Wits., John Lockwood, Sarah Kirk, Sarah Harbet. Prob. July 16, 1789. Arch. vol. A30, page 153. Reg. of Wills, Liber M, folios 199-200.

Emory, Thomas, Sr. Will. Made Jan. 8, 1789. Heirs: wife Deborah; sons Thomas, Arthur, John & William; daus. Tillah Emory, Ann Willoughby (wife of Solomon), Elizabeth Cook (wife of William), Deborah Frazer (wife of James), Sarah Sherwood (wife of Daniel); grandson Dickenson Emory. Exec'rs, wife Deborah & son Thomas. Wits., Mark Cooper, Sr., William Cooper, Mark Cooper. Prob. July 20, 1789. Arch. vol. A16, page 188. Reg. of Wills, Liber M, folios 200-201.

Hill, Rachel. Admin. of, to James Hill. July 21, 1789. Reg. of Wills, Liber M, folios 196-200. Note:—Admin. to Joseph Denny revoked & granted to James Hill.

Clark, Rachel. Admin. of, to Abraham Parsons. July 27, 1789. Reg. of Wills, Liber M, folio 201.

Chipman, Thomas. Will. Made July 8, 1789. Heirs: bros. Vincent, Andrew & Isaac Moore & James Chipman. Exec'r, father-in-law Isaac Moore. Wits., Patrick Crain [Crane], Sarah Middleton. Prob. July 28, 1789. Arch. vol. A8, page 191. Reg. of Wills, Liber M, folios 201-202.

Pemberton, Sarah. Admin. of, to John Pemberton. Aug. 5, 1789. Reg. of Wills, Liber M, folio 202.

Numbers, Sarah. Will. Made April 17, 1785. Heirs: sister Elizabeth Greenly; cousin Elizabeth Greenly; William, Elizabeth & Joshua (children of sister Elizabeth Greenly). Exec'r, bro.-in-law Robert Greenly. Wits., William Merydith, Sarah Merydith. Prob. Aug. 7, 1789. Arch. vol. A38, page 97. Reg. of Wills, Liber M, folio 202.

Peterkin, John. Admin. of, to Sarah Peterkin. Aug. 11, 1789. Reg. of Wills, Liber M, folio 202.

Hilyard, Charles. Admin. of, to Charles Hilyard, the younger. Aug. 14, 1789. Reg. of Wills, Liber M, folio 202.

Emmerson, Jacob. Admin. of, to Sarah Emmerson & Manlove Emmerson. Aug. 18, 1789. Arch. vol. A16, pages 134-136. Reg. of Wills, Liber M, folio 202.

Doany [Doney], James. Admin. of, to Sarah Doany. Aug. 26, 1789. Arch. vol. A14, page 176. Reg. of Wills, Liber M, folio 203.

Howard, Cornelius. Admin. of, to James Raymond, Esq. Aug. 26, 1789. Reg. of Wills, Liber M, folio 203.

Paradee, John. Admin. of, to Carman Mason & Stephen Paradee. Aug. 26, 1789. Reg. of Wills, Liber M, folio 203.

Montgomery, William. Admin. of, to Abner Dill. Sept. 1, 1789. Reg. of Wills, Liber M, folio 203.

Myers, Stephen. Admin. of, to William Myers. Sept. 3, 1789. Reg. of Wills, Liber M, folio 203.

Fowler, William. Admin. of, to James Carbine, D. B. N. Sept. 10, 1789. Reg. of Wills, Liber M, folio 203.

Howard, Mary. Admin. of, to Richard Mason. Sept. 19, 1789. Reg. of Wills, Liber M, folio 203.

Howard, Joseph. Admin. of, to Richard Mason, D. B. N. Sept. 19, 1789. Reg. of Wills, Liber M, folio 203.

Barcus, James. Admin. of, to Rachel Barcus. Oct. 1, 1789. Reg. of Wills, Liber M, folio 203.

Morris, James. Admin. of, to Esther Morris. Oct. 1, 1789. Arch. vol. A36, pages 212-213. Reg. of Wills, Liber M, folio 203. Note:—Arch. vol. A36, page 212 mentions heirs, Samuel, Lemuel, Selah, Rachel, Mary, Fannah & James Morris.

Craige, Isbel. Will. Made Sept. 8, 1789. Heirs: sons Alexander Hudson & Daniel . . .; granddau. Margret Hudson. Exec'r, Alexander Hudson. Wits., Jaramiah Whitehead, Thomas Perkins. Prob. Oct. 1, 1789. Arch. vol. A11, page 159. Reg. of Wills, Liber M, folios 203-204.

Evans, Thomas. Admin. of, to Samuel Evans. Oct. 6, 1789. Reg. of Wills, Liber M, folio 204.

Turly, Richard. Yeoman. Will. Made July 7, 1789. Little Creek Hd. Heirs: wife Sarah; daus. Jerusha & Mary; sons James, Richard & William. Exec'x, wife Sarah. Trustees, Richard Smith, John Clayton, Manlove Emmerson & Joshua Fisher. Wits., Joshua Fisher, Marget Studers, Alice Colley. Prob. Oct. 7, 1789. Arch. vol. A51, pages 146-150. Reg. of Wills, Liber M, folios 204-205. Note:—Arch. vol. A51, page 149 shows that Sarah Turly married Matthias Nowland.

Hawkins, John. Admin. of, to Mary Hawkins. Oct. 10, 1789. Arch. vol. A23, pages 30-31. Reg. of Wills, Liber M, folio 205. Note:—Arch. vol. A23, page 30 shows that Mary Hawkins married ... Thompson.

McSparon, Archibald. Admin. of, to Andrew Bunner. Oct. 21, 1789. Arch. vol. A33, page 34. Reg. of Wills, Liber M, folio 205.

Jones, Zachariah. Will. Made Sept. 25, 1789. Heirs: dau. Unity; granddau. Bersheba Jones; grandson Robert Jones. Exec'r, friend John Hopkins, Sr. Wits., Robert Hopkins, John Eckles, Anthony Eckles. Prob. Oct. 22, 1789. Arch. vol. A28, pages 38-40. Reg. of Wills, Liber M, folios 205-206.

Allee, Sarah. Will. Made April 3, 1789. Duck Creek Hd. Heirs: daus. Elizabeth Comegys, Ann Allee, Sarah Conner; son Abraham; granddau. Mary Conner. Exec'rs, bro. Dr. James Tilton & nephew James Morris. Wits., Lydia Tilton, Nehemiah Tilton. Prob. Oct. 26, 1789. Arch. vol. A1, pages 74-75. Reg. of Wills, Liber M, folio 206. Note:—Arch. vol. A1, page 75 mentions an heir, Ann Rasin.

Neal, Mary. Admin. of, to James Smith. Oct. 28, 1789. Reg. of Wills, Liber M, folio 206.

Clark, James. Admin. of, to Robert Clark. Oct. 31, 1789. Reg. of Wills, Liber M, folio 206. Note:—Mary Clark renounced her right.

Hutchinson, John. Admin. of, to James Hutchinson. Nov. 2, 1789. Reg. of Wills, Liber M, folio 207.

Jamison, Andrew. Admin. of, to Robert Jamison. Nov. 2, 1789. Reg. of Wills, Liber M, folio 207. Note:—Arch. vol. A26, page 95 mentions heirs, Robert, Thomas & Nancy Jamison.

Clampit, Jonathan. Admin. of, to Elijah Berry. Nov. 9, 1789. Reg. of Wills, Liber M, folio 207.

Tilton, Thomas. Will. Made Sept. 19, 1788. Duck Creek Hd. Heirs: wife Sabrah; sons James, Abraham & Thomas; dau. Rachel. Exec'rs, wife Sabrah & bro. Nehemiah Tilton. Wits., Sarah Allee, John Goldsmith, Joseph Tuckerman. Prob. Nov. 9, 1789. Arch. vol. A50, pages 153-154. Reg. of Wills, Liber M, folio 207.

Killingsworth, Rebecca. Admin. of, to Isaac Stratton. Nov. 11, 1789. Reg. of Wills, Liber M, folio 208.

Broadaway, Ambrose. Will (copy, nunc.). Made Nov. 5, 1789. Heirs: wife Rebecca. Exec'rs, wife Rebecca & bro. William Broadaway. Wits., John M. Gifford, John Harwood. Prob. Nov. 13, 1789. Arch. vol. A5, pages 234-236. Reg. of Wills, Liber M, folio 208. Note:—Arch. vol. A5, page 235 mentions heir, Mary Broadaway; page 236 shows that Rebecca Broadaway married William Moore.

Jester, Thomas. Admin. of, to Robert Hodgson. Nov. 13, 1789. Reg. of Wills, Liber M, folio 208.

Dickie, William. Admin. of, to John Hutchins. Nov. 14, 1789. Reg. of Wills, Liber M, folio 208.

Wharton, Garret. Admin. of, to William Warner. Nov. 14, 1789. Reg. of Wills, Liber M, folio 208.

Morgan, Daniel. Admin. of, to Daniel Clifford. Nov. 16, 1789. Reg. of Wills, Liber M, folio 208.

Black, John. Admin. of, to Elsbury Burt. Nov. 17, 1789. Arch. vol. A4, page 73. Reg. of Wills, Liber M, folio 208.

Boyce, Alexander. Admin. of, to Sarah Boyce. Nov. 17, 1789. Reg. of Wills, Liber M, folio 209.

Pryor, John. Admin. of, to Charles Nixon, D. B. N. Nov. 18, 1789. Reg. of Wills, Liber M, folio 209.

Broadaway, James. Admin. of, to Samuel Broadaway. Nov. 19, 1789. Arch. vol. A5, page 239. Reg. of Wills, Liber M, folio 209.

Hickey, Thomas. Yeoman. Will. Made Nov. 11, 1789. Little Creek Hd. Heirs: sons John & Benjamin; daus. Mary & Margaret. Exec'r, John Starling. Wits., John Hickey, William Drew. Prob. Nov. 21, 1789. Arch. vol. A23, page 205. Reg. of Wills, Liber M, folio 209.

Howell, Mary. Will (nunc.). Made Nov. 16, 1789. Heir: sister Ann Howell. [No exerc'rs]. Wits., William Brown, John Corker, Thomas Vandever. Prob. Nov. 21, 1789. Arch. vol. A25, page 72.

Numbers, Susannah. Admin. of, to John Numbers. Nov. 23, 1789. Reg. of Wills, Liber M, folio 209.

Clark, William. Admin. of, to James Frazer. Nov. 24, 1789. Arch. vol. A9, page 93. Reg. of Wills, Liber M, folio 209.

Venatta, Benjamin. Admin. of, to Thomas Venatta. Nov. 24, 1789. Arch. vol. A52, page 6. Reg. of Wills, Liber M, folio 209.

Collier, Henry. Admin. of, to James Collier. Nov. 24, 1789. Reg. of Wills, Liber M, folio 209.

Goslin, Samuel. Admin. of, to Anna Goslin. Nov. 24, 1789. Reg. of Wills, Liber M, folio 209.

Griffin, Lydia. Will. Made Oct. 13, 1787. Duck Creek Hd. Heirs: sons Samuel, David, Matthew, William & Ebenezer; dau. Elizabeth Roe; granddaus. Elizabeth Griffin (dau. of son William & Mary Wells. Exec'r, son Ebenezer. Wits., Enoch Jones, Henry Farsons, Daniel David, Jr. Prob. Nov. 24, 1789. Arch. vol. A20, page 213. Reg. of Wills, Liber M, folio 210.

Carter, Edward. Admin. of, to Mary Carter. Nov. 26, 1789. Arch. vol. A7, pages 251-253. Reg. of Wills, Liber M, folio 210. Note:—Arch. vol. A7, page 251 mentions heirs, Ruth, Mary, William, Edward, Rachel, John Whitacre & Edward Broadaway Carter & Sarah Bailey; page 253 shows that Mary, the widow, later married Joseph Dawson.

McClyment Robert. Admin. of, to Unity McClyment. Nov. 30, 1789. Arch. vol. A32, pages 121-122. Reg. of Wills, Liber M, folio 210. Note:—Arch. vol. A32, page 121 shows that Unity married Stephen Hairgrove; also mentions heirs, Robert & Elizabeth McClyment & Jane Dorrell (wife of James Dorrell).

Turner, Martin. Admin. of, to Lucretia Bishop. Nov. 30, 1789. Arch. vol. A51, page 177. Reg. of Wills, Liber M, folio 210.

Shaw, Samuel. Admin. of, to Thomas Price. Dec. 2, 1789. Arch. vol. A45, pages 210-211. Reg. of Wills, Liber M, folio 210. Note:—Arch. vol. A45, page 210 mentions heirs, Hugh & James Shaw, Thomas Price, Neoma Teat & heirs of William Shaw.

Shaw, William. Admin. of, to Thomas Price. Dec. 2, 1789. Arch. vol. A45, pages 219-220. Reg. of Wills, Liber M, folio 210. Note:—Arch. vol. A45, page 219 mentions heirs, Joshua & Elizabeth Shaw.

Craig, Samuel. Admin. of, to Elizabeth Craig. Dec. 3, 1789. Reg. of Wills, Liber M, folio 210.

Walston, John. Admin. of, to Rhoda Walston. Dec. 3, 1789. Arch. vol. A53, page 35. Reg. of Wills, Liber M, folio 211.

Burrows, John. Admin. of, to Susanah Burrows. Dec. 4, 1789. Reg. of Wills, Liber M, folio 211.

Smith, Jacob. Admin. of, to Mary Smith. Dec. 5, 1789. Reg. of Wills, Liber M, folio 211.

Shaw, Joshua. Will. Made Nov. 10, 1789. Murderkiln Hd. Heirs: bro. James Shaw; sister Naomy Shaw; nephew Joshua Shaw. Exec'r, bro. James. Wits., Armwell Lockwood, William Morris, Jr., Armwell Lockwood, Jr. Prob. Dec. 5, 1789. Arch. vol. A45, page 202. Reg. of Wills, Liber M, folio 211.

Venatta, Ruth. Admin. of, to John Harding. Dec. 7, 1789. Reg. of Wills, Liber M, folio 211.

Worth, Jonathan. Admin. of, to John Bell, Jr. Dec. 7, 1789. Arch. vol. A56, page 143. Reg. of Wills, Liber M, folio 211.

Black, Mary. Admin. of, to Thomas Crammer. Dec. 8, 1789. Arch. vol. A4, pages 75-76. Reg. of Wills, Liber M, folio 211.

Black, Stephen. Admin. of, to Thomas Crammer, D. B. N. Dec. 8, 1789. Arch. vol. A4, pages 77-79. Reg. of Wills, Liber M, folio 211. Note:—Arch. vol. A4, page 78 mentions a dau. Rebecca Sharp.

Wallace, William. Admin. of, to Elizabeth Wallace. Dec. 8, 1789. Arch. vol. A53, pages 19 & 22. Reg. of Wills, Liber M, folio 212.

Wrotten, William. Admin. of, to Henry Wroten & James Wroten. Dec. 8, 1789. Arch. vol. A56, pages 170-171. Reg. of Wills, Liber M, folio 211.

Numbers, Susanah. Admin. of, to Robert Smith, D. B. N. Dec. 10, 1789. Arch. vol. A38, page 98. Reg. of Wills, Liber M, folio 212.

FitzJarold, George. Yeoman. Mispillion Hd. Admin. of, to Celia FitzJarold & John FitzJarold. Dec. 12, 1789. Arch. vol. A17, page 154. Reg. of Wills, Liber M, foilo 212. Note:—Heirs mentioned are Sarah, George, Isaac & Ezekiel FitzJarrold.

Chittington, James. Admin. of, to Jane Chittington. Dec. 14, 1789. Arch. vol. A8, page 192. Reg. of Wills, Liber M, folio 212. Note:—Admin. shows that Jane Chittington married Thomas Parker.

Cornelius, George. Admin. of, to Margaret Cornelius. Dec. 15, 1789. Arch. vol. A11, pages 7-8. Reg. of Wills, Liber M, folio 212. Note:—Arch. vol. A11, page 7 mentions heirs, Ann & George Cornelius; page 8 shows that Margaret Cornelius later married Samuel Spear.

Numbers, Michael. Admin. of, to Jane Numbers & Randolph Blackshare. Dec. 15, 1789. Reg. of Wills, Liber M, folio 212.

White, Elizabeth. Admin. of, to William White. Dec. 15, 1789. Reg. of Wills, Liber M, folio 212.

Chambers, Joseph. Admin. of, to Rachel Chambers. Dec. 21, 1789. Reg. of Wills, Liber M, folio 212. Note:—Arch. vol. A8, page 145 shows that Rachel Chambers later married Joseph Laws.

Pryor, Joseph. Admin. of, to Charles Nixon, D. B. N. Dec. 21, 1789. Reg. of Wills, Liber M, folio 212.

Baily, John. Admin. of, to Elsbury Burt. Dec. 22, 1789. Arch. vol. A2, pages 61-62. Reg. of Wills, Liber M, folio 212. Note: —Arch. vol. A2, page 62 mentions heirs, widow Isabelle, Alice & James Baily.

Ogle, George. Admin. of, to George Truit, D. B. N. Dec. 23, 1789. Arch. vol. A38, pages 111-113. Reg. of Wills, Liber M, folio 213. Note:—Settlement made May 30, 1793.

Jones, Layton. Admin. of, to Peggy Jones & Jonathan Wallace. Dec. 26, 1789. Arch. vol. A27, pages 238-239. Reg. of Wills, Liber M, folio 213.

Jones, Mary. Admin. of, to Philip Jones. Dec. 28, 1789. Reg. of Wills, Liber M, folio 213.

Jarrold, Morris. Admin. of, to Anna Jarrold. Jan. 1, 1790. Arch. vol. A26, pages 165-166. Reg. of Wills, Liber M, folio 214. Note:—Arch. vol. A26, page 166 mentions heirs, Sarah, Mary & Margaret Jarrold; also shows that Anne Jarrold later married William Williams.

Scottin, John. Admin. of, to James Scottin. Jan. 1, 1790. Arch. vol. A45, page 92. Reg. of Wills, Liber M, folio 214.

Cook, John. Will. Made Oct. 27, 1789. Duck Creek Hd. Heirs: wife Elizabeth; sons Michael & Robert; daus. Margaret Peterson, Elizabeth Cloak, Sarah Clark; grandson John Cook; granddau. Sarah Cook. Exec'r, son Robert. Wits., George Cummins, William Denny, John Offley. Prob. Jan. 4, 1790. Arch. vol. A10, pages 121-122. Reg. of Wills, Liber M, folio 215.

Boyer, Littleton. Admin. of, to Sarah Boyer. Jan. 5, 1790. Arch. vol. A5, page 56. Reg. of Wills, Liber M, folio 216.

Goldsmith, Elizabeth. Widow of John Goldsmith. Will. Made Dec. 15, 1789. Heirs: sons John Goldsmith, Edward McElroy, John, James & Jonathan Green; granddau. Sarah Goldsmith; grandsons John & William Goldsmith; James Raymond; John & Jonathan Raymond (sons of James Raymond); Miss Jane Merrich. Exec'r, James Raymond, Esq. Trustees, James Raymond, Esq., Silas Snow & Mark McCall. Wits., Solomon Barnett, Robert Palmatary, Charles Doney. Prob. Jan. 7, 1790. Arch. vol. A19, pages 113-114. Reg. of Wills, Liber M, folios 218-220.

Jones, Enoch. Will. Made Dec. 27, 1789. Duck Creek Hd. Heirs: wife Lydia; sons Enoch & Abel; daus. Mary, Eleanor & Lydia. Exec'rs, wife Lydia & son Enoch. Wits., Charles Michel, Joshua Wilds, Daniel David, Jr. Prob. Jan. 7, 1790. Arch. vol. A27, pages 165-166. Reg. of Wills, Liber M, folio 216.

Numbers, John. Admin. of, to Barbara Numbers & James Numbers. Jan. 7, 1790. Arch. vol. A38, page 81. Reg. of Wills, Liber M, folio 216. Note:—Barbara Numbers is shown as the wife of William Numbers.

Woodcock, Elizabeth. Admin. of, to Anthony Woodcock. Jan. 7, 1790. Reg. of Wills, Liber M, folio 216.

Smith, George. Admin. of, to Harrington Sylvester, D. B. N. Jan. 8, 1790. Arch. vol. A47, page 37. Reg. of Wills, Liber M, folio 217.

Follis, Thomas. Little Creek Hd. Admin. of, to Martha Follis. Jan. 9, 1790. Arch. vol. A17, page 218. Reg. of Wills, Liber M, folio 217.

Jarold, Stephen. Admin. of, to Robert Jarold. Jan. 9, 1790. Reg. of Wills, Liber M, folio 217.

Doaney, Charles. Admin. of, to Elizabeth Doaney. Jan. 11, 1790. Reg. of Wills, Liber M, folio 217.

Cayton, Mary. Admin. of, to Ambrose Wright. Jan. 11, 1790. Arch. vol. A9, page 123. Reg. of Wills, Liber M, folio 217.

Flynn, John. Admin. of, to Mary Carter & Benjamin Brady, D. B. N. Jan. 11, 1790. Arch. vol. A17, pages 211-212. Reg. of Wills, Liber M, folio 217. Note:—Arch. vol. A17, page 211 mentions heirs, Sarah, Ann, Elizabeth, Mary, John, Edward & Rebecca Flynn.

Hobbs, Stephen. Admin. of, to George Gildersleave. Jan. 11, 1790. Arch. vol. A17, pages 211-212. Reg. of Wills, Liber M, folio 217.

Stafford, Elijah. Farmer. Murderkill Hd. Admin. of, to Mary Carter & Benjamin Brady. Jan. 11, 1790. Arch. vol. A48, pages 126-127.

Caldwell, Timothy. Admin. of, to John Coombe, D. B. N. Jan. 15, 1790. Arch. vol. A7, pages 127-128. Reg. of Wills, Liber M, folio 217.

Colgen, Jane. Admin. of, to William Flowers. Jan. 18, 1790. Reg. of Wills, Liber M, folio 217.

Irons, Mary. Will. Made Dec. 24, 1789. Little Creek Hd. Heirs: daus. Jane Irons & Elizabeth Souders. Exec'x, dau. Jane Irons. Wits., Samuel York, Joseph Irons, John Vanhoy, Mary Irons. Prob. Jan. 18, 1790. Arch. vol. A25, page 221. Reg. of Wills, Liber M, folio 221.

Curtis, Comfort. Admin. of, to George Walton. Jan. 25, 1790. Arch. vol. A12, pages 153-154. Reg. of Wills, Liber M, folio 217. Note:—Arch. vol. A12, page 154 mentions children, Elizabeth, William & Thomas Curtis, George Walton, Mary Williams (wife of Nathan Williams) & heirs of son David Walton; also shows Richard Cocker & wife Rachel.

Forkum, John. Admin. of, to Elizabeth Forkum. Jan. 26, 1790. Reg. of Wills, Liber M, folio 217.

Harding, John. Admin. of, to Leah Harding. Jan. 26, 1790. Reg. of Wills, Liber M, folio 217.

Gibbs, John. Admin. of, to Nancy Gibbs & Peter Lowber. Jan. 27, 1790. Reg. of Wills, Liber M, folio 217.

Wells, William. Admin. of, to Maria Wells & Stephen Alstone. Jan. 29, 1790. Arch. vol. A54, page 7. Reg. of Wills, Liber M, folio 217.

Venatta, Ruth. Admin. of, to Thomas Venatta, D. B. N. Jan. 30, 1790. Reg. of Wills, Liber M, folio 217.

Greenwood, John. Duck Creek Hd. Admin. of, to William Manwaring. Feb. 8, 1790. Arch. vol. A20, page 151. Reg. of Wills, Liber M, folio 221.

Evans, Zachariah. Admin. of, to Francis Meredith, D. B. N. Feb. 9, 1790. Reg. of Wills, Liber M, folio 221.

Pratt, Charity. Admin. of, to George Gilpin. Feb. 9, 1790. Reg. of Wills, Liber M, folio 221.

Starr, Samuel. Admin. of, to George Gilpin. Feb. 9, 1790. Arch. vol. A48, pages 170-171. Reg. of Wills, Liber M, folio 221.

Brooks, John. Admin. of, to Nicholas Brooks. Feb. 10, 1790. Reg. of Wills, Liber M, folio 221.

Hawkins, Jacob. Admin. of, to Peter Hawkins. Feb. 10, 1790. Arch. vol. A23, page 25. Reg. of Wills, Liber M, folio 221.

Hawkins, William. Admin. of, to Peter Hawkins, D. B. N. Feb. 10, 1790. Reg. of Wills, Liber M, folio 221.

Jenkins, Joseph. Will. Made Feb. 24, 1788. Heirs: bros. Jabez & Thomas; niece Hanah Alston; Joseph Jenkins. Exec'rs, bros. Jabez & Thomas. Wits., Thomas Lee, John Deal, Debbe Mifflin. Prob. Feb. 11, 1790. Arch. vol. A26, page 228. Reg. of Wills, Liber M, folio 222.

Lewis, Elizabeth. Admin. of, to James Lewis & John Lewis. Feb. 12, 1790. Arch. vol. A30, pages 74-75. Reg. of Wills, Liber M, folio 223. Note:—Arch. vol. A30, page 75 mentions heirs, Sarah, Robert, Joseph, Thomas, William, John & James Lewis.

Runnels, John. Admin. of, to Katharine Runnels. Feb. 12, 1790. Reg. of Wills, Liber M, folio 222.

Thomas, William. Yeoman. Will. Made Feb. 2, 1790. Heir: wife Rebecca. Exec'x, wife Rebecca. Wits., Armwell Lockwood, Susanah Willson, Thomas Soward. Prob. Feb. 12, 1790. Arch. vol. A50, pages 70-72. Reg. of Wills, Liber M, folio 22. Note:—Arch. vol. A50, page 71 shows that Rebecca Thomas married James Harrington.

Caldwell, Robert. Admin. of, to Andrew Caldwell. Feb. 17, 1790. Reg. of Wills, Liber M, folio 222.

Boggs, Joseph. Murderkill Hd. Admin. of, to Robert Lewis. Feb. 24, 1790. Arch. vol. A4, page 178.

Reed, James. Admin. of, to John Coppage, D. B. N., & Sarah Coppage, late Sarah Bostick. Feb. 24, 1790. Arch. vol. A42, page 194.

Winford, Alexander. Will. Made Jan. 13, 1790. Heirs: wife Margret; sons William, John, Joseph, Alexander, Benjamin & Jonathan; daus. Elizabeth West & Rebecca, Mary & Margret Winford. Exec'x, wife Margret. Wits., Sorden Lister, Arthur Hill, Jacob Bostick. Prob. Feb. 24, 1790. Arch. vol. A56, pages 37-38. Reg. of Wills, Liber M, folio 223.

Blandon, George. Will (nunc.). [N. d.]. Heirs: son Charles Blandon; orphan James Sapp; Charles & Joshua Blandon, sons of Charles. Exec'rs, [Hezikah Cullen & Joshua Dewees, from admin. acct.]. Wits., Thomas Tumlinson, Joshua Dewees, Hezikah Cullen. Prob. Feb. 25, 1790. Arch. vol. A4, page 148. Reg. of Wills, Liber M, folio 223.

Palmatry, Robert. Admin. of, to Tamzy Palmatry. Feb. 25, 1790. Arch. vol. A38, page 208. Reg. of Wills, Liber M, folio 223.

Morris, Daniel. Admin. of, to Phoeby Morris. Feb. 25, 1790. Reg. of Wills, Liber M, folio 223.

Leckey, Andrew. Admin. of, to Mary Wilson. Feb. 26, 1790. Reg. of Wills, Liber M, folios 223-224.

Reynalds, William. Admin. of, to Sarah Reynolds. Feb. 26, 1790. Arch. vol. A43, pages 129-130. Reg. of Wills, Liber M, folio 224. Note:—Arch. vol. A43, page 129 mentions heirs, James, William, Eleaner, Nancy, Stephen & Joanna Reynolds.

Smith, Richard. Esq. Will. Made Dec. 11, 1789. St. Jones or Dover Hd. Heirs: wife Sarah; sons Stephen, Cesar, Richard, Robert, Edward, William & James; daus. Harriett, Ann & Sarah; granddau. Ann Goodwin; Joseph Harper; John Wiltbank. Exec'rs, Nicholas Ridgely & Joshua Fisher, Esquires. Wits., Ezekial Needham, Edward Miller. Codicil, Jan. 12, 1790. Wits., Ann Skillington, Sarah Blackshire. Prob. Feb. 26, 1790. Arch. vol. A47, pages 146-147. Reg. of Wills, Liber M, folios 224-227. Note:—Reg. of Wills, Liber M, folio 251 shows Sarah, the widow, renounced her right.

Corse, James. Admin. of, to John Corse. Feb. 27, 1790. Reg. of Wills, Liber M, folio 224.

Pearce, William. Admin. of, to Elizabeth Pearce. March 1, 1790. Arch. vol. A39, page 160. Reg. of Wills, Liber M, folio 227.

Pearson, Robert. Admin. of, to Baxter Pearson, William Harper & Peter Brinckle. March 1, 1790. Arch. vol. A40, page 84 & vol. A39, page 179. Reg. of Wills, Liber M, folio 228. Note:—Arch. vol. A40, page 84 mentions a Robert Pierson; also mentions Rebecca Morgan, otherwise Baxter Pierson.

Saxton, Prudence. Admin. of, to Joseph Hodson. March 1, 1790. Reg. of Wills, Liber M, folios 227-228.

Callaway, Peter. Will. Made Feb. 1, 1790. Heirs: wife Sarah; sons William, Lammas, Curtis & John; daus. Sarah, Theaner & Suly. Exec'rs, wife Sarah & son William. Wits., Jenifer Taylor, John Harrington, Aaron Herrington. Prob. March 8, 1790. Arch. vol. A7, pages 156-159. Reg. of Wills, Liber M, folio 228.

Gregg, Rebecca. Admin. of, to John Culbreath. March 12, 1790. Reg. of Wills, Liber M, folio 229.

Mair, Janet. Will. Made March 9, 1790. Heirs: Sarah Holly; Moody Meekins; William Meridith, Sr.; Hugh McFarsons. Exec'r, Hugh McFarsons. Wits., John Gilder, Philip Jones, Nancy Bullock, Moody Meekins. Prob. March 12, 1790. Arch. vol. A33, page 71. Reg. of Wills, Liber M, folios 228-229.

Shoemaker, John. Admin. of, to Mary Shoemaker. March 15, 1790. Reg. of Wills, Liber M, folio 229.

Barns, Ezekiel. Admin. of, to John Barns, Sr. March 16, 1790. Reg. of Wills, Liber M, folio 229.

Wallace, David. Yeoman. Will. Made March 3, 1790. Heirs: wife Frances & friend James Berry. Guardian, bro. Thomas Wallace. Wits., John Lockwood, Joseph Wallace, Andrew Murphy, Mary Shannon. Codicil, March 4, 1790. Prob. March 16, 1790. Arch. vol. A52, pages 225-228. Reg. of Wills, Liber M, folios 230-231.

Treppett, Watman. Will. Made Nov. 12, 1789. Heirs: daus. Alce, Nancy; dau.-in-law Elizabeth; sons William & Govey; son-in-law Samuel Jump. Exec'r, son Govey. Wits., Elias Jester, Thomas Clark, Elizabeth Clark. Prob. March 17, 1790. Arch. vol. A51, pages 80-82. Reg. of Wills, Liber M, folio 229. Note:—Arch. vol. A51, page 81 mentions a dau. Ailce Carmean.

Jenkins, Sarah. A minor dau. of Eleanor Jenkins & Timothy Jenkins, dec'd. Admin. of, to Elen [Eleanor] Jenkins. March 19, 1790. Arch. vol. A26, pages 241-243. Reg. of Wills, Liber M, folio 229. Note:—Arch. vol. A26, page 241 mentions bros. Jabez & Samuel Jenkins.

Jarold, James. Admin. of, to Martha Jarold. March 20, 1790. Arch. vol. A26, pages 161-162. Reg. of Wills, Liber M, folio 231.

Harding, Nancy. Admin. of, to James Harding. March 22, 1790. Reg. of Wills, Liber M, folio 231.

Wiatt, Boaz. Admin. of, to Elizabeth Wiatt. March 22, 1790. Reg. of Wills, Liber M, folio 231. Note:—Arch. vol. A54, page 216 shows that Elizabeth Wiatt married Philliman Cubbage; also mentions minor children Sarah & Charlotte Wiatt.

Gano, John. Admin. of, to Lewis Gano. March 22, 1790. Reg. of Wills, Liber M, folio 231.

Caldwell, Andrew. Admin. of, to John Caldwell, D. B. N. March 23, 1790. Reg. of Wills, Liber M, folio 231.

Caldwell, Robert. Admin. of, to John Caldwell, D. B. N. March 23, 1790. Reg. of Wills, Liber M, folio 231.

Griffin, David. Admin. of, to Jemima Griffin. March 23, 1790. Reg. of Wills, Liber M, folio 231. Note:—Arch. vol. A20, page 196 shows that Jemima Griffin later married David Rees.

Hurlick, William. Admin. of, to Elizabeth Hurlick. March 24, 1790. Reg. of Wills, Liber M, folio 231.

Jenkins, Dorothy. Will. Made Feb. 21, 1790. Heirs: sons Isaac & Abraham Hatabough; dau. Elizabeth Hurlock; two daus.-in-law unnamed. Exec'r, son Abraham Hatabough. Wits., William Virdin, John Virdin, Edward Coxe. Prob. March 24, 1790. Arch. vol. A26, page 203. Reg. of Wills, Liber M, folio 232.

Boyer, James. Gentleman. Will. Made Feb. 4, 1790. Murderkiln Hd. Heirs: sons Caleb & Charles; grandsons James Boyer (son of Charles), Francis A. Boyer (son of Caleb). Exec'r, son Caleb. Wits., William Johnson, John Nock, Huldah Milvin. Prob. March 25, 1790. Arch. vol. A5, pages 53-54. Reg. of Wills, Liber M, folio 234.

Dill, James. Admin. of, to Mary Dill. March 27, 1790. Reg. of Wills, Liber M, folio 234.

Hairgrove, Sarah. Admin. of, to George Hairgrove. March 30, 1790. Arch. vol. A21, page 65. Reg. of Wills, Liber M, folio 234.

Cheffins, James. Yeoman. Will. Made March 16, 1790. Duck Creek Hd. Heirs: wife Margret; sons James, Enoch & Benjamin; dau. Sarah. Exec'r, son James. Guardian, son James. Wits., William Cheffins, George Smith, Ebenezer Blackiston. Prob. April 3, 1790. Arch. vol. A8, pages 173-174. Reg. of Wills, Liber M, folio 234. Note:—Arch. vol. A8, page 195 mentions heirs, Sarah Blackshear, formerly Sarah Chevins [Cheffins], & Randall Blackshear.

Blackshare, Thomas. Will. Made Feb. 18, 1790. Murderkill Hd. Heirs: wife Miriam; sisters Isabel McGregory, Meriam Reynalds (wife of Michiel Reynalds); nephews Ezekiel Bullock, Stephen & Hursley Nedles (sons of William & Ann Nedles), Robert, Hursley, Thomas, Edward, Ezekiel & Absolem Knotts (sons of Absolem & Sarah Knotts); nieces Sarah & Leucrecia Nedles (daus. of William & Ann Nedles); tenant Lemual Parvis; Mary McBride (wife of Robert McBride); daus.-in-law Elizabeth & Margret Brown; son-in-law Charles Brown; Joshua Brown (son of James Brown, dec'd); dau. of John Peterson by first wife; Negroes Sue, Mez, Ruben (son of Mez), Tony & Jacob. Exec'rs, wife Meriam & Ezekiel Bullock. Wits., Richard Cooper, George Truitt, Joseph Sneeps, William Pennawell. Prob. April 5, 1790. Arch. vol. A4, pages 112-116 & 143. Reg. of Wills, Liber M, folios 234-236.

Bullock, Ezekiel. Admin. of, to Nancy Bullock. April 5, 1790. Reg. of Wills, Liber M, folio 237. Note:—Arch. vol. A6, page 182 shows Ann Bullock as the wife of Robert Spear.

Wells, Mary. Admin. of, to George McCall. April 5, 1790. Arch. vol. A53, page 237. Reg. of Wills, Liber M, folio 237.

Caldwell, James. Admin. of, to John Caldwell. April 9, 1790. Reg. of Wills, Liber M, folio 237.

Hirons, Joseph. Farmer. Will. Made March 11, 1790. Little Creek Hd. Heirs: wife Mary; sister Leah; bros. Simon, William, Mark & Robert. Exec'x, wife Mary. Wits., Timothy Sweany, Jane Hirons, Sarah Birch, Samuel York. Prob. April 9, 1790. Arch. vol. A24, page 93. Reg. of Wills, Liber M, folio 237.

Lily, John. Admin. of, to Elizabeth Lilly. April 12, 1790. Reg. of Wills, Liber M, folio 237.

Hilyard, Elizabeth. Admin. of, to Warner Mifflin & Abraham Readgrave. April 12, 1790. Reg. of Wills, Liber M, folio 237.

Numbers, James. Admin. of, to Sarah Numbers. April 13, 1790. Arch. vol. A38, pages 70-71. Reg. of Wills, Liber M, folio 237. Note:—Arch. vol. A38, page 70 mentions heirs, James Numbers & Rebeccah Wood, wife of Enoch Wood.

Greenwood, Thomas. Admin. of, to Joseph Taylor. April 17, 1790. Reg. of Wills, Liber M, folio 237.

Foreman, Robert. Admin. of, to Edmund Bayly. April 17, 1790. Arch. vol. A18, page 30. Reg. of Wills, Liber M, folio 237.

Brodie, Robert. Will. Made March 2, 1790. Heirs: wife [Christian, from admin. acct.]; sons Robert, William & Thomas. Exec'x, wife. Wits., Thomas Smith, David Smith, William Smith. Prob. April 21, 1790. Arch. vol. A5, page 248. Reg. of Wills, Liber M, folio 238.

Roe, Elizabeth. Widow. Will. Made July 27, 1789. Murderkill Hd. Heirs: sons Hugh, Brinkle & Caesar, dec'd; dau. Elizabeth Corse, wife of John Corse; grandson Benjamin Roe, son of Caesar Roe, dec'd; granddaus. Elizabeth Durborow Stevens (dau. of John & Mary Stevens), Lidia Roe (dau. of Caesar Roe, dec'd), Elizabeth Roe (dau. of son Hugh). Exec'r, son Brinkle. Wits., Sarah Craig, Priscilla Stanton, Thomas Nixon. Prob. April 22, 1790. Arch. vol. A44, page 109. Reg. of Wills, Liber M, folios 238-239. Note:—Will mentions father Hugh Durborow, dec'd.

Darnall, William. Admin. of, to William Flowers. April 22, 1790. Arch. vol. A12, page 198. Reg. of Wills, Liber M, folio 239.

Foreacre, Isaac. Admin. of, to John Foreacre & Daniel Jones. April 24, 1790. Reg. of Wills, Liber M, folio 239.

Rowland, Jonathan. Admin. of, to Mary Rowland. April 24, 1790. Reg. of Wills, Liber M, folio 239.

Craig, Sophia. Admin. of, to John Ham. April 26, 1790. Reg. of Wills, Liber M, folio 239.

Conner, Dennis. Admin. of, to John Conner. April 26, 1790. Arch. vol. A10, page 78. Reg. of Wills, Liber M, folio 240.

Wiatt, William, Sr. Will. Made April 2, 1790. Mispillion Hd. Heirs: sons Thomas, William, Moses, Aaron, Furbush & John; daus. Judah Newman, Edeliah Griffith & Margit Griffith; grandsons Lamuel & Thomas Wiatt. Exec'r, son Thomas. Wits., Ester Wilkenson, Thomas Wilkenson, Thomas Wilkenson, Jr., Thomas Wilkenson, Sr. Prob. April 27, 1790. Arch. vol. A54, pages 219-221. Reg. of Wills, Liber M, folio 240.

Train, Timothy. Admin. of, to Joseph Nock. May 10, 1790. Reg. of Wills, Liber M, folio 240.

Lockerman, Vincent. Admin. of, to Mary Lockerman, Edward Miller & Joseph Miller. May 11, 1790. Arch. vol. A30, pages 242-244. Reg. of Wills, Liber M, folio 240.

Kelly, Thomas. Farmer. Will. Made March 25, 1776. Heirs: wife Rebecca; son James; daus. Margaret, Elizabeth & Mary. Exec'x, wife Rebecca. Wits., John Dill, William Dill, John Gibson. Prob. May 11, 1790. Arch. vol. A28, page 109. Reg. of Wills, Liber M, folios 244-245.

Wilkinson, William. Admin. of, to William Wilkinson & James Jones. May 14, 1790. Arch. vol. A55, page 53. Reg. of Wills, Liber M, folio 241.

Lockerman, Vincent. Admin. of, to Charles Nixon, D. B. N. May 14, 1790. Reg. of Wills, Liber M, folio 241.

Harwood, John. Will. Made April 29, 1790. Duck Creek Hd. Heirs: wife Margaret; sons Thomas & Jasper; daus. Elizabeth & Margret; bro. Jasper Harwood. Exec'rs, wife Margaret & bro. Jasper. Wits., Philip Alexander, Thomas Hawkins. Prob. May 14, 1790. Arch. vol. A22, pages 214 & 216-218. Reg. of Wills, Liber M, folios 241-242. Note:—Arch. vol. A22, page 217 mentions an Elizabeth Oneil; page 216 shows that Margaret Harwood later married John Truax & Grace, wife of Jasper, married Joshua Wilds.

Slator, Jonathan. Admin. of, to Rachel Slator. May 15, 1790. Reg. of Wills, Liber M, folio 242.

Parsons, Abraham. Farmer. Duck Creek Hd. Admin. of, to Rachel Parson. May 21, 1790. Arch. vol. A39, page 69. Reg. of Wills, Liber M, folio 242.

Young, Preston. Admin. of, to Charles Nixon. May 24, 1790. Reg. of Wills, Liber M, folios 242-243.

Downing, Benjamin. Admin. of, to Mary Downing. May 25, 1790. Reg. of Wills, Liber M, folio 243.

Davis, John. Farmer. Will. Made May 11, 1790. Murtherkill Hd. Heirs: wife unnamed; sons Thomas, Isaac, John, James & Ezekiel; daus. Sarah Smith, Rebecca & Nancy Davis. Exec'r, son Thomas. Wits., William Morris, John Smith, William White. Prob. May 26, 1790. Arch. vol. A13, pages 19-25. Reg. of Wills, Liber M, folio 243. Note:—Arch. vol. A13, page 20 mentions Elizabeth Davis as widow; also shows Sarah Smith as wife of Richard Smith; Nancy Davis married James Smith.

Truitt, William. Yeoman. Will. Made May 3, 1790. Mispillion Hd. Heirs: wife Martha; son George; dau. Liddiah Tompson. Exec'r, son George. Wits., Nathaniel Luff, Caleb Davis, Catherine Runneralds. Prob. May 26, 1790. Arch. vol. A51, pages 121-125. Reg. of Wills, Liber M, folios 243-244. Note: —Arch vol. A51, page 122 shows Liddiah Tompson as wife of Cary Tompson.

Jarrold, Stephen, the elder. Mispillion Hd. Admin. of, to Lydia Broun, late Lydia Jarrold. May 26, 1790. Arch. vol. A26, pages 168-169. Note:—Arch. vol. A26, page 169 mentions heirs, Stephen, Morris, James, Jonathan & Moses Jarrold.

Townshend, William. A minor. Admin. of, to Mary Listor, D. B. N. May 27, 1790. Arch. vol. A51, page 48.

Havoloe, Luke. Admin. of, to Zadoc Heavalo. May 27, 1790. Arch. vol. A23, page 178.

Snipe, Joseph. Admin. of, to Jonathan Hunn. May 31, 1790. Arch. vol. A47, pages 226 & 228. Reg. of Wills, Liber M, folio 244.

Gillow, Alexander. Admin. of, to James Darling. June 2, 1790. Reg. of Wills, Liber M, folio 245.

Reynalds, Eleanor. Admin. of, to John Bowan. June 7, 1790. Reg. of Wills, Liber M, folio 245.

Scotton, Nathan. Admin. of, to Abraham Booth, D. B. N. June 16, 1790. Reg. of Wills, Liber M, folio 245.

Brown, Joseph. Admin. of, to Lydia Brown, widow. June 17, 1790. Arch. vol. A6, pages 68-69. Reg. of Wills, Liber M, folio 245. Note:—Arch. vol. A6, page 68 mentions heirs, William Brown, Sarah & Thomas Welbore; also shows Lydia Brown, widow, later married John Brown.

Burrows, Nehemiah. Admin. of, to Elizabeth Burrows. June 17, 1790. Reg. of Wills, Liber M, folio 245.

Kemp, Henry. Mispillion Hd. Admin. of, to Mary Kemp. June 18, 1790. Arch. vol. A28, page 119. Reg. of Wills, Liber M, folio 246. Note:—Mary Kemp later married Elias Turner.

McVay, John. Admin. of, to Elizabeth McVay. June 19, 1790. Reg. of Wills, Liber M, folio 246.

Greenwood, Margaret. Little Creek Hd. Admin. of, to William Harper. June 22, 1790. Arch. vol. A20, page 157. Reg. of Wills, Liber M, folio 246.

Truitt, Martha. Will. Made May 31, 1790. Heirs: son William Runnels; daus. Rebecca Bowman, Leah Jester, Catren Runnels. Exec'r, son-in-law Nathan Bowman. Wits., David Peterkin, Hester Milven, Elizth Wheelar. Codicil, Leady Thompson. Prob. June 27, 1790. Arch. vol. A51, pages 105-108. Reg. of Wills, Liber M, folio 245. Note:—Will mentions husband William Truett, dec'd.

Mercer, Stephen. Admin. of, to Margaret Mercer. June 29, 1790. Reg. of Wills, Liber M, folio 246.

Barnet, Solomon. Admin. of, to John Ham. June 29, 1790. Arch. vol. A2, page 209. Reg. of Wills, Liber M, folio 246.

Parsons, Martha. Admin. of, to Rachel Parsons. July 2, 1790. Reg. of Wills, Liber M, folio 246.

Barnet, John. Admin. of, to John Ham. July 10, 1790. Arch. vol. A2, page 198. Reg. of Wills, Liber M, folio 246.

Busse, Samuel. Will. Made June 12, 1790. Heirs: wife Susanah; granddaus. Lydia Bennet & Mahale McCarty. Exec'r, friend Jacob Furbee. Wits., Caleb Furbee, Jacob Furbee, Rebeccah Bennett. Prob. July 14, 1790. Arch. vol. A7, pages 6-7. Reg. of Wills, Liber M, folio 246.

Dickie, William. Admin. of, to John Hutchins, D. B. N. July 14, 1790. Reg. of Wills, Liber M, folio 246.

Standley, Richard. Admin. of, to Joseph Barker. July 15, 1790. Reg. of Wills, Liber M, folio 247.

Mansfield, Thomas. Yeoman. Murderkill Hd. Admin. of, to Mary Mansfield. July 15, 1790. Arch. vol. A33, page 160. Reg. of Wills, Liber M, folio 247.

Gregg, Rebecca. Admin. of, to William Smith, D. B. N. July 19, 1790. Arch. vol. A20, page 50. Reg. of Wills, Liber M, folio 247.

Blackshare, Sarah. Will. Made June 19, 1790. Little Creek Hd. Heirs: daus. Sarah & Deborah. Exec'r, bro. John Roach. Wits., John Pearce, Risdon Bishop, Jr., John Calwell. Prob. July 24, 1790. Arch. vol. A4, page 106. Reg. of Wills, Liber M, folio 247.

Patton, Ann. Admin. of, to John Patton. July 27, 1790. Reg. of Wills, Liber M, folio 247.

Culbreath, John. Admin. of, to Rebecca Culbreath & William Culbreath. July 28, 1790. Reg. of Wills, Liber M, folio 248.

Scotton, John. Will. Made May 9, 1790. Heirs: wife Sarah; bros. William & Thomas; sisters Julea Baley, Rachel Mumford & Sarah Martin; nephew John Scotton; Minty Vickers; Mealy Scotton. Exec'r, bro. William. Wits., Charles Rickitts, Nickles Dudly, Jesse Jones. Prob. July 31, 1790. Arch. vol. A45, pages 89-91. Reg. of Wills, Liber M, folio 248.

Scurlog, John. Town of Dover. Admin. of, to James Smith, merchant. Aug. 9, 1790. Arch. vol. A45, page 111. Reg. of Wills, Liber M, folio 249.

Brown, John. Schoolmaster. Admin. of, to Jabez Jenkins. Aug. 12, 1790. Arch. vol. A6, page 57. Reg. of Wills, Liber M, folio 250.

Pleasenton, Letitia. Admin. of, to Sarah Thomas. Aug. 13, 1790. Reg. of Wills, Liber M, folio 250.

Pleasenton, David. Admin. of, to Sarah Thomas. Aug. 13, 1790. Reg. of Wills, Liber M, folio 250.

Pleasenton, Rachel. Admin. of, to Sarah Thomas. Aug. 13, 1790. Reg. of Wills, Liber M, folio 250.

Stradly, Thomas. Admin. of, to Zadock Stradly. Aug. 16, 1790. Arch. vol. A49, pages 80-82. Reg. of Wills, Liber M, folio 250. Note:—Arch. vol. A49, page 80 mentions heirs, Sarah, Thomas, Isaiah, Zedock & Sarah Stradly, Rachel Sapp & Cealy Conner.

Martin, Richard. (Mulatto). Admin. of, to Dr. James Sykes. Aug. 20, 1790. Reg. of Wills, Liber M, folio 250.

Wells, John. Admin. of, to Sarah Wells. Aug. 24, 1790. Reg. of Wills, Liber M, folio 250. Note:—Arch. vol. A53, page 236 shows that Sarah Wells married William Wood; also mentions a minor dau. Mary Wells.

Blackshare, Morgan. Farmer. Little Creek Hd. Admin. of, to Randal Blackshare, D. B. N. Aug. 25, 1790. Arch. vol. A41, page 95. Reg. of Wills, Liber M, folio 250.

Morris, Absolem. Admin. of, to William Morris, Jr. Aug. 25, 1790. Reg. of Wills, Liber M, folio 250.

Shepard, Easter [Hester]. Will. Made May 8, 1786. Mispillion Hd. Heirs: daus. Betsy & Rubey. Exec'r, bro. Jonathan Rowland. Wits., George Manlove, Isaac Minshall, Jacob Callaway. Prob. Aug. 26, 1790. Arch. vol. A45, page 229. Reg. of Wills, Liber M, folios 250-251.

Sheppard, Esther. Admin. of, to Polly Rowland, D. B. N. Aug. 26, 1790. Arch. vol. A45, page 230.

Sunders, Jacob. (Negro). Admin. of, to Hugh Durborrow. Aug. 26, 1790. Reg. of Wills, Liber M, folio 251.

Brandal, George. Admin. of, to Joshua Dewees. Aug. 27, 1790. Arch. vol. A5, pages 146-147.

Cummins, Sarah. Admin. of, to George Cummins. Aug. 27, 1790. Reg. of Wills, Liber M, folio 251.

Shepherd, Thomas. Admin. of, to David Rowland, D. B. N. Aug. 27, 1790. Arch. vol. A45, page 233. Reg. of Wills, Liber M, folio 251.

Furbee, Joseph. Admin. of, to Thomas Brown. Aug. 31, 1790. Arch. vol. A18, page 163. Reg. of Wills, Liber M, folio 251.

Lynch, Edmund. Will. Made Nov. 8, 1788. Duck Creek Hd. Heirs: wife Mary; dau. Martha Numbers, wife of Thomas Numbers; grandsons Edmond Lynch (son of my son Edmond), Edmund & Benjamin Numbers (sons of dau. Martha & Thomas Numbers), Edmond Lynch (son of my son Nicholas); granddaus. Selener & Mary Lynch (daus. of son Nicholas). Exec'rs, son-in-law Thomas Numbers & grandson Edmund Lynch (son of Nicholas Lynch). Wits., Richard Smith, Robert Smith. Prob. Aug. 31, 1790. Arch. vol. A32, pages 20-21. Reg. of Wills, Liber M, folios 251-252.

Askins, William. Admin. of, to Mary Askins. Sept. 13, 1790. Reg. of Wills, Liber M, folio 253. Note:—Arch. vol. A2, page 19 shows David Davis and wife Mary as joint adm'rs.

Starr, Mary. Admin. of, to George Griffin. Sept. 20, 1790. Reg. of Wills, Liber M, folio 253.

Irons, Sarah. Late Sarah Covey. Admin. of, to William Irons. Sept. 24, 1790. Reg. of Wills, Liber M, folio 253.

Hutchenson, Margaret. Admin. of, to James Hutchenson. Oct. 1, 1790. Reg. of Wills, Liber M, folio 253.

Hutchenson, Mary. Admin. of, to James Hutchenson. Oct. 1, 1790. Reg. of Wills, Liber M, folio 253.

Harwood, John. Will (nunc.). Made Sept. 26, 1790. Heirs: sister Teresia Harwood; bro. Peter Harwood; Thomas Merydith. Exec'r, Peter Harwood. Wits., Thomas Moore, George Moore. Prob. Oct. 2, 1790. Arch. vol. A22, page 215. Reg. of Wills, Liber M, folio 253.

Manlove, Mott. Yeoman. Will. Made Sept. 29, 1790. Town of Dover. Heirs: dau. Elizabeth Manlove; bro. George Manlove. Exec'r, John Clayton, Esq. Wits., Nicholas Ridgely, Stephen Alston, William Howell. Prob. Oct. 12, 1790. Arch. vol. A33, page 115. Reg. of Wills, Liber M, folios 253-254.

Downs, William. Admin. of, to Rachel Downs. Oct. 12, 1790. Reg. of Wills, Liber M, folio 254.

Jones, William. Admin. of, to Rachel Jones. Oct. 19, 1790. Arch. vol. A28, page 29. Reg. of Wills, Liber M, folio 254.

Williams, William. Admin. of, to Easter Williams. Oct. 20, 1790. Reg. of Wills, Liber M, folio 254.

Ware, Ann. Widow. Will. Made Oct. 1, 1786. Dover Hd. Heirs: dau. Ann Ware; son Francis Barber; grandson John Walker; granddaus. Ann & Prescilla Ware & Ann Barber; John Barber. Exec'r, son Francis Barber. Wits., John Hawkins, James David, Rachel Bossick. Prob. Oct. 22, 1790. Arch. vol. A53, page 101. Reg. of Wills, Liber M, folios 254-255.

Moleston, William. Physician. Will. Made Sept. 26, 1790. Town of Dover. Heirs: wife Elizabeth Ann; nearest relations. Exec'rs, wife Elizabeth Ann, John Gordon, Esq., & Henry Moleston. Wits., Richard Bassett, John Vining, John White. Prob. Oct. 29, 1790. Arch. vol. A35, page 222. Reg. of Wills, Liber M, folios 255-256.

Cowgill, John. Admin. of, to Mary Cowgill & Clayton Cowgill. Oct. 30, 1790. Arch. vol. A11, page 97. Reg. of Wills, Liber M, folio 256.

Dyer, John. Will. Made Oct. 29, 1790. Heirs: wife Catran; son James; dau. Martha. Exec'rs, wife Catran & Joab Dyer. Guardian, Joab Dyer. Wits., Job Meridith, Jacob Duhadway. Prob. Nov. 5, 1790. Arch. vol. A15, pages 223-224. Reg. of Wills, Liber M, folio 256. Note:—Arch. vol. A15, page 224 shows that Catharine Dyer married Jeremiah Burchinal.

Cummins, James. Admin. of, to Lydia Cummins. Nov. 8, 1790. Reg. of Wills, Liber M, folio 257.

Register, Robert. Admin. of, to Thomas Corse. Nov. 9, 1790. Reg. of Wills, Liber M, folio 257.

Hilford, Thomas. Will. Made Aug. 17, 1784. Heirs: wife Elizabeth; sons David, Robert, Zadock & Boaz; daus. Martha, Elizabeth & Mary. Exec'r, [Robert Hilford, from admin. acct.]. Wits., Gilbert White, Mark Killen, Benjamin Simpson. Prob. Nov. 9, 1790. Arch. vol. A23, pages 232-234. Reg. of Wills, Liber M, folio 257. Note: Arch. vol. A23, page 233 mentions heirs, Martha Fenchwait (wife of Jonathan Fenchwait) & Elizabeth Clark (wife of Henry Clark).

Bostick, Moses. Will. Made Sept. 25, 1790. Heirs: sister Susannah Gording; father Thomas Bostick. Exec'x, sister Susannah Gording. Wits., Vincent Dehorty, Samuel Harrington. Prob. Nov. 11, 1790. Arch. vol. A4, pages 267-268. Reg. of Wills, Liber M, folio 258. Note:—Arch. vol. A4, page 268 shows that Susannah Gording married . . . Eccles.

Dixon, Robert. Admin. of, to Ann Dixon & John Green. Nov. 12, 1790. Arch. vol. A14, page 145. Reg. of Wills, Liber M, folio 258.

Marim, Meriam. Widow of Charles Marim. Will. Made Nov. 11, 1790. Little Creek Hd. Heirs: dau. Nancy King; son Charles. Exec'x, dau. Nancy King. Wits., John Marim, John Edenfield, Cornelius Vanstavoren. Prob. Nov. 20, 1790. Arch. vol. A33, page 190. Reg. of Wills, Liber M, folio 258.

Parsons, Michael. Admin. of, to Ann Parsons. Nov. 24, 1790. Arch. vol. A39, pages 90-91. Reg. of Wills, Liber M, folio 259. Note:—Arch. vol. A39, page 90 mentions an heir, Mary Parsons; also shows that Ann Parsons later married Benjamin Smith.

Graham, John. Admin. of, to Thomas Murphy. Nov. 24, 1790. Arch. vol. A19, pages 288-229.

Broadway, William. Farmer. Caroline Co., Md. Admin. of, to Robert Broadway. Nov. 25, 1790. Arch. vol. A5, pages 246-247. Note:—Arch. vol. A5, page 246 mentions heirs, Robert, Isaac, Elizabeth, Ambrose, Nancy, Abner, Sarah & Samuel Broadway.

Jervis, Caleb. Will. Made Nov. 16, 1789. Heirs: sons Joseph, Caleb & Daniel; daus. Alce Townsend & Mary Jervis. Exec'rs, son Caleb Jervis & Ezekiel Anderson, Esq. Wits., Isaiah Stradley, Androson Androson, Solomon Lofland. Prob. Nov. 25, 1790. Arch. vol. A27, page 4. Reg. of Wills, Liber M, folio 233.

Carty, Isaac. Will. Made Nov. 14, 1789. Heirs: wife Ann; sons John, Samuel & David. Exec'rs, wife Ann & Nicholas Ridgely. Guardian, wife Ann. Wits., Risdon Bishop, Robert Smith. Prob. Nov. 27, 1790. Arch. vol. A8, pages 49-54. Reg. of Wills, Liber M, folios 240-241. Note:—Arch. vol. A8, pages 50-52 show this acct. later administered by John Darrach.

Rash, John, Sr. Farmer. Will. Made July 1, 1782. Murderkill Hd. Heirs: sons Daniel, Andrew, Martin & Joseph; daus. Sarah Shelton, Mary, Easter, Ann, Letitia, Ansley & Patience Rash. Exec'r, son Andrew. Wits., Laurence Hammond, Richard Mason, Agness Mason. Prob. Nov. 30, 1790. Arch. vol. A42, page 40. Reg. of Wills, Liber M, folio 259.

Horn, George. Admin. of, to Keziah Horn. Nov. 30, 1790. Reg. of Wills, Liber M, folio 260.

Quillen, Elizabeth. Admin. of, to James Jones. Dec. 4, 1790. Reg. of Wills, Liber M, folio 260.

Caldwell, Robert. Admin. of, to Robert Lewis. Dec. 13, 1790. Reg. of Wills, Liber M, folio 260.

Caldwell, Andrew. Admin. of, to Robert Lewis. Dec. 13, 1790. Reg. of Wills, Liber M, folio 260.

Mason, Carman. Admin. of, to Deborough Mason. Dec. 20, 1790. Arch. vol. A33, pages 221-222. Reg. of Wills, Liber M, folio 260. Note:—Arch. vol. A33, page 221 mentions heirs, John, Hannah, Carman, Caleb, William & David Mason; also shows that Deborough Mason later married . . . Manlove.

Simpson, John. Admin. of, to Moses Barnet. Dec. 22, 1790. Reg. of Wills, Liber M, folio 260.

Caldwell, Sarah. Will. Made Jan. 20, 1786. Mispillion Hd. Heirs: cousin George Truit. Exec'r, George Truit. Wits., Warner Mifflin, Daniel Mifflin, Jr., Joseph Nock, Jr. Prob. Dec. 23, 1790. Arch. vol. A7, page 125. Reg. of Wills, Liber M, folios 212-213.

Newcomb, John. Admin. of, to Mary Newcomb. Dec. 27, 1790. Reg. of Wills, Liber M, folio 260.

Mifflin, Walker. Admin. of, to Sarah Mifflin. Dec. 28, 1790. Arch. vol. A35, page 21. Reg. of Wills, Liber M, folio 260.

Wilkinson, Isabella. Admin. of, to Moses Wilkinson. Dec. 29, 1790. Arch. vol. A55, page 45. Reg. of Wills, Liber M, folio 260.

Tarr, Azariah. Admin. of, to Abner Barker. Dec. 29, 1790. Arch. vol. A49, page 155. Reg. of Wills, Liber M, folio 260.

Voshal, James. Will. Made Feb. 11, 1789. Heirs: dau. Mary Rash; son Obediah Voshel; granddau. Lutisey Rash, dau. of my dau. Mary Rash; grandchildren (heirs of Agnis Price) & (heirs of dau. Sarah Bennet). Exec'r, Moses Jackson. Wits., John Caton, Abraham Parnel, John Wheeler. Prob. Dec. 29, 1790. Arch. vol. A52, page 126. Reg. of Wills, Liber M, folio 213.

Crooks, Benjamin. Will. Made Dec. 15, 1790. Murderkill Hd. Heirs: wife Ann. Exec'x, wife Ann. Wits., Elizabeth Vining, John White. Prob. Dec. 30, 1790. Arch. vol. A12, pages 19-20. Reg. of Wills, Liber M, folios 260-261.

Hargrove, George. Yeoman. Will. Made June 10, 1786. Heirs: wife Sarah; sons John, George & Stephen. Exec'x, wife Sarah. Wits., Richard Banning, Charles Boyer, James Boyer. Prob. Dec. 31, 1790. Arch. vol. A22, page 30. Reg. of Wills, Liber M, folio 214.

Miller, Peter, Jr. Admin. of, to Peter Miller. Jan. 7, 1791. Reg. of Wills, Liber M, folio 261.

Goldsmith, John. Admin. of, to William Leatherberry. Jan. 10, 1791. Arch. vol. A19, pages 115-117. Reg. of Wills, Liber M, folio 261.

Brown, William. Merchant. Will. Made Oct. 15, 1790. Town of Dover. Heirs: sons Matthew & William; dau. Nancy. Exec'rs, John Brown, Esq., & John Banning, Esq. Wits., Joseph Nock, Jr., Joseph Hale, Stephen Alston. Prob. Jan. 13, 1791. Arch. vol. A6, page 98. Reg. of Wills, Liber M, folios 261-262.

Kearney, Dyer. Esq. Admin. of, to Nicholas Hammond. Jan. 15, 1791. Arch. vol. A28, page 86. Reg. of Wills, Liber M, folio 262.

Thompson, Jacob. Admin. of, to Rachel Thompson. Jan. 22, 1791. Reg. of Wills, Liber M, folio 262. Note:—Arch. vol. A50, page 84 shows that Rachel Thompson married James Lewis.

Coppage, John. Will. Made Dec. 13, 1790. Heirs: wife Sarah; daus. Elizabeth Callaway, Mary Bostick, Nancy & Martha Coppage; granddau. Martha Callaway; dau.-in-law Mary Reed. Exec'x, wife Sarah. Wits., William Listor, William Reed, Sorden Listor. Prob. Jan. 25, 1791. Arch. vol. A10, pages 235-239. Reg. of Wills, Liber M, folio 263. Note:— Arch. vol. A10, page 236 shows that Sarah, the widow, married Sylvia Sipple; page 237 mentions Jacob & John Bostwick.

Jester, Sarah. Admin. of, to Thomas Primrose. Jan. 27, 1791. Reg. of Wills, Liber M, folio 263.

McPherson, Hugh. Admin. of, to Robert Hodgson. Jan. 27, 1791. Reg. of Wills, Liber M, folio 262.

Craig, Isabella. Admin. of, to Thomas Perkins. Jan. 31, 1791. Arch. vol. A11, pages 157-158. Reg. of Wills, Liber M, folio 263. Note:—Arch. vol. A11, page 157 mentions heirs, Daniel, Alexander, Margaret & Alexander Hudson.

Hudson, Alexander. Will. Made March 8, 1789. Heirs: wife Ruth; mother unnamed; daus. Elizabeth & Marget. Exec'r, Thomas Perkins. Wits., John Bossick, Maurice Brady, Jemimah Whitehead. Prob. Jan. 31, 1791. Arch. vol. A25, pages 94-99. Reg. of Wills, Liber M, folios 263-264. Note:— Arch. vol. A25, page 95 mentions heirs, Margaret Boyer, Elizabeth & William Hudson; page 96 shows Thos. Buckmaster married Unity, dau. of Alexander Craige, & Waitman Furbee married Margaret, dau. of Alexander Craige.

Irons, John. Admin. of, to Henry Irons. Feb. 4, 1791. Reg. of Wills, Liber M, folio 264.

Wheeler, Lemuel. Murderkill Hd. Admin. of, to Ruth Wheeler. Feb. 4, 1791. Arch. vol. A54, page 65. Reg. of Wills, Liber M, folio 267.

Pleasenton, Jonathan. Admin. of, to Ruhama Pleasenton. Feb. 12, 1791. Arch. vol. A40, page 126. Reg. of Wills, Liber M, folio 264.

Williams, Jacob. Admin. of, to Presley Spruance. Feb. 15, 1791. Reg. of Wills, Liber M, folios 264-265.

Lundergin, James. Admin. of, to John Lambden. Feb. 15, 1791. Reg. of Wills, Liber M, folio 265.

Roe, Samuel. Will. Made Jan. 20, 1791. Little Creek Hd. Heirs: wife Isabella; son Samuel; daus. Maria & Nancy. Exec'rs, George Truitt, George Cummins. Wits., William Denny, Elizabeth Town, Sarah Miller. Prob. Feb. 16, 1791. Arch. vol. A44, pages 116-119. Reg. of Wills, Liber M, folio 265.

Revel, John. Will. Made Jan. 14, 1791. Heirs: wife [Amelia, from admin. acct.]; sons John, William & James; daus. Sarah, Mary & Elizabeth. Exec'rs, wife & William Adams. Wits., Benjamin Yoe, Smith Farset, Sother Brinkle. Prob. Feb. 18, 1791. Arch. vol. A43, pages 79, 82-83 & 86. Reg. of Wills, Liber M, folios 265-266.

Banning, John. Admin. of, to Elizabeth Banning. Feb. 23, 1791. Arch. vol. A2, pages 94-95. Reg. of Wills, Liber M, folio 266. Note:—Arch. vol. A2, page 94 shows that Elizabeth Baning later married William McKee.

Lyle, John. Admin. of, to John Stuart. Feb. 25, 1791. Arch. vol. A32, page 19. Reg. of Wills, Liber M, folio 266.

Deweese, Cornelius. Yeoman. Will. Made March 1, 1786. Heirs: sons Cornelius, David & Jonathan; daus. Esther Draper, Sarah Munsey. Exec'rs, sons David & Cornelius. Wits., Joshua Deweese, Nathan Bowman, James Hendrickson. Prob. March 2, 1791. Arch. vol. A14, pages 29-30. Reg. of Wills, Liber M, folios 266-267.

Clothier, John. Admin. of, to Sarah Clothier. March 5, 1791. Reg. of Wills, Liber M, folio 267.

Anderson, James. Will. Made Feb. 9, 1791. Mispillion Hd. Heirs: wife Ann; sons John, James, Isaac, Daniel, Elijah, Major & Eli; dau. Ann Callay. Exec'rs, wife Ann & sons James & Daniel. Wits., Abraham Kimme, Unisey Cain, Ezekiel Anderson. Prob. March 7, 1791. Arch. vol. A1, pages 174 & 176. Reg. of Wills, Liber M, folios 267-268.

Crippen, John. Will. Made Feb. 23, 1791. Heirs: wife Rachel; son James; grandson John Harrington; William Harrington (father of John); Silvester Tatman. Exec'rs, wife Rachel & son James. Wits., William Bradley, Charles Mason, Benjamin Yoe. Prob. March 14, 1791. Arch. vol. A11, page 227. Reg. of Wills, Liber M, folios 268-269.

Scronders, James. Admin. of, to Thomas Venatta. March 19, 1791. Reg. of Wills, Liber M, folio 269.

Wilson, Joseph. Admin. of, to James Miles. March 22, 1791. Reg. of Wills, Liber M, folio 269.

Smith, John. Admin. of, to Sarah Smith. March 22, 1791. Arch. vol. A47, pages 82-83. Reg. of Wills, Liber M, folio 269. Note:—Arch. vol. A47, page 82 mentions heirs, Sarah, Thomas, John, William & Daniel Smith & Martha Hutchins.

Walton, David. Admin. of, to Elias Shockley. March 23, 1791. Arch. vol. A53, pages 49-51. Reg. of Wills, Liber M, folio 269. Note:—Arch. vol. A53, page 49 mentions heirs, David & Rachel Walton.

Walton, Nancy. Will. Made March 11, 1791. Village of Milford. Heirs: son David; dau. Rachel. Exec'r, friend Elias Shockley. Trustees, Samuel Pacely & wife Rachel. Wits., Joseph Oliver, Thomas Winsmore, Benjamin Yoe. Prob. March 23, 1791. Arch. vol. A53, pages 76, 41 & 43-44. Reg. of Wills, Liber M, folio 269.

Maxwell, Nimrod. Will. Made June 17, 1790. Murderkill Hd. Heirs: wife Elizabeth; sons Edmonson & Nimrod; dau. Sarah Gordon. Exec'r, son Edmonson. Guardian, son Edmonson. Wits., Martha Edmondson, Joshua Edmondson, Evan Thomas. Prob. March 24, 1791. Arch. vol. A34, pages 89-90. Reg. of Wills, Liber M, folios 270-271.

Banning, Phineas. Admin. of, to Phebe Banning & Richard Banning. March 29, 1791. Arch. vol. A2, pages 99-101. Reg. of Wills, Liber M, folio 271. Note:—Arch. vol. A2, page 99 mentions heirs, Esther, Elizabeth, Gartery, Nathaniel & Priscilla Banning.

Russell, Henry. Admin. of, to Thomas Bowman. March 29, 1791. Arch. vol. A44, page 182. Reg. of Wills, Liber M, folio 271.

Russell, William. Admin. of, to Thomas Bowman. March 29, 1791. Arch. vol. A44, page 188. Reg. of Wills, Liber M, folio 271.

Downing, Ann. Minor dau. of Joseph Downing. Admin. of, to Thomas Murphey & wife Mary, late Mary Downing. March 30, 1791. Arch. vol. A14, page 238.

Reynolds, John. Admin. of, to Catharine Dyer, late Catharine Reynolds, widow of John Dyer. March 31, 1791. Arch. vol. A43, page 108.

Jones, Eleanor. Will. Made Oct. 2, 1790. Duck Creek Hd. Heirs: bros. Abel & Enoch; sisters Lydia & Mary Jones; niece Lydia Spruance, dau. of my sister Mary Spruance; other children of Mary Spruance unnamed; Hannah Greenwood. Exec'r, bro. Enoch. Wits., James Davis, Joshua Owens, Daniel David, Jr. Prob. March 31, 1791. Arch. vol. A27, page 161. Reg. of Wills, Liber M, folio 271.

Hall, Winlock. Farmer. Will. Made Feb. 25, 1791. Mispillion Hd. Heirs: wife [Mary, from admin. acct.]; sons William, Winlock & John; daus. Mary, Nancy, Salley. Exec'x, wife Mary. Wits., Isaac Lowber, John Walker, James Fisher. Prob. April 4, 1791. Arch. vol. A21, pages 135-140. Reg. of Wills, Liber M, folio 272. Note:—Arch. vol. A21, page 140 shows Tomlinson Parsons, who married Mary Hall, widow of Winlock.

Carmean, Jacob. Admin. of, to Alice Carmean. April 7, 1791. Arch. vol. A7, pages 223-224. Reg. of Wills, Liber M, folio 272. Note:—Arch. vol. A7, page 223 mentions heirs, Sarah Farcett & husband Smith Farcett & Mary Bowman & husband Curtis Bowman.

Smith, Solomon. Will. Made March 25, 1785. Heirs: wife Violet; sons George & Solomon; dau. Martha. Exec'rs, son George & Holoday Smith. Wits., William Cheffins, Susannah Ozbeen, Elizabeth Ozbeen. Prob. April 7, 1791. Arch. vol. A47, pages 174-175. Reg. of Wills, Liber M, folio 273.

Caldwell, Robert. Admin. of, to Esther Lewis & George Truitt. April 11, 1791. Reg. of Wills, Liber M, folio 272. Note:— Arch. vol. A7, page 124 shows that Mary Caldwell, dec'd, is mother of Robert.

Caldwell, John. Admin. of, to Esther Caldwell & George Truitt, D. B. N. April 11, 1791. Arch. vol. A7, page 114. Reg. of Wills, Liber M, folio 273.

Lewis, Robert. Admin. of, to Esther Lewis & George Truitt. April 11, 1791. Arch. vol. A30, pages 128-130. Reg. of Wills, Liber M, folio 273. Note:—Arch. vol. A30, page 130 mentions heirs, Mary & Robert Lewis; also shows that Esther Lewis married . . . Morgan.

Caldwell, Andrew. Admin. of, to Esther Lewis & George Truitt, D. B. N. April 11, 1791. Arch. vol. A7, page 100. Reg. of Wills, Liber M, folio 273.

Whitehart, Solomon. Will. Made Nov. 2, 1789. Little Creek Hd. Heirs: nephew Solomon Whitehart, son of Samuel Whitehart; niece Sarah Potter, dau. of James Potter; Hugh Durborow. Exec'r, Hugh Durborow. Wits., Timothy Burch, John Hickey, Lucretia Bishop. Prob. April 18, 1791. Arch. vol. A54, page 190. Reg. of Wills, Liber M, folio 274.

Hanson, Mary. Admin. of, to Samuel Howell. April 22, 1791. Arch. vol. A21, page 208. Reg. of Wills, Liber M, folio 274.

Lowber, Catharine. Admin. of, to Peter Lowber. May 1, 1791. Reg. of Wills, Liber M, folio 274.

Headon, Edward. Admin. of, to William Jordan. May 9, 1791. Reg. of Wills, Liber M, folio 274.

Hodgson, Robert. Admin. of, to Joseph Hodgson & George Truitt, Esq. May 10, 1791. Arch. vol. A24, pages 128, 132-134. Reg. of Wills, Liber M, folio 274. Note:—Arch. vol. A24, page 132 shows heirs, Margaret Pritchett, Robert Pritchard, Mary Catlen (wife of Joseph Catlen), Joseph, Jonathan & William Hodgson & Caleb Jackson.

Emory, Thomas. Will. Made April 28, 1791. Heirs: sons Giddion & John; wife Sarah; grandson Thomas Emory, son of Thomas, dec'd; granddau. Latilly Emory, dau. of son Thomas, dec'd. Exec'rs, sons Giddion & John. Wits., John Brinckle, Samuel Gordon. Prob. May 16, 1791. Arch. vol. A16, page 193. Reg. of Wills, Liber M, folios 274-275.

Buckley, Arnold. Admin. of, to Ann Buckley. May 18, 1791. Arch. vol. A6, pages 132-133. Reg. of Wills, Liber M, folio 275. Note:—Arch. vol. A6, page 132 shows that Ann Buckley is the wife of Philip Perkins; page 133 mention heirs, Elizabeth & Joseph Buckley.

David, Joseph, Sr. Admin. of, to Joseph David. May 18, 1791. Reg. of Wills, Liber M, folio 275.

Caldwell, Mary. Admin. of, to Easther Lewis & George Truitt, D. B. N. May 24, 1791. Arch. vol. A7, page 123.

Appleton, Robert. Admin. of, to Allen McLane & Edward Martin. May 31, 1791. Arch. vol. A1, pages 228-229. Reg. of Wills, Liber M, folio 275.

Snow, Isaac. Admin. of, to Benjamin Jones. June 1, 1791. Reg. of Wills, Liber M, folio 275.

Mason, Catharine. Admin. of, to John Mason. June 6, 1791. Arch. vol. A33, page 223. Reg. of Wills, Liber M, folio 276.

Irons, Mark. Admin. of, to Mary Irons. June 7, 1791. Reg. of Wills, Liber M, folio 276.

Foreacre, Joseph. Admin. of, to Elizabeth Foreacre. June 8, 1791. Arch. vol. A18, page 8. Reg. of Wills, Liber M, folio 276.

Turly, William. Admin. of, to Henry Bell. June 20, 1791. Arch. vol. A51, pages 151-155. Reg. of Wills, Liber M, folio 276. Note:—Arch. vol. A51, page 151 mentions bros. & sisters, James, Richard & Jerusha Turly & Mary Vanburcaloe.

Brooks, Nicholas. Admin. of, to Edith & Ann Brooks. July 5, 1791. Arch. vol. A6, page 11. Reg. of Wills, Liber M, folio 276.

Slay, George. Will. Made May 27, 1791. Motherkill Hd. Heirs: bro. Edward Slay; sisters Esther Slay & Mary Newsom. Exec'r, cousin Daniel Ford. Wits., Elizabeth Young, Rachel Wilkinson, Thomas Ford. Prob. July 5, 1791. Arch. vol. A46, page 233. Reg. of Wills, Liber M, folio 276.

Brooks, John. Admin. of, to Edith Brooks & Ann Brooks, D. B. N. July 18, 1791. Arch. vol. A6, page 11. Reg. of Wills, Liber M, folio 277.

Brown, Elizabeth. Admin. of, to Thomas Taylor. July 18, 1791. Reg. of Wills, Liber M, folio 277.

West, Joseph. Admin. of, to David West, D. B. N. July 19, 1791. Reg. of Wills, Liber M, folio 277.

Bell, John. Admin. of, to John Bell. July 24, 1791. Reg. of Wills, Liber M, folio 277.

Rowan, George. Admin. of, to Ruhamath Rowan & George Nickerson. July 25, 1791. Arch. vol. A44, page 155. Reg. of Wills, Liber M, folio 277.

Taylor, Benjamin. Admin. of, to Joseph Taylor. July 25, 1791. Reg. of Wills, Liber M, folio 277.

Caldwell, Mary. Admin. of, to Waitman Booth. Aug. 8, 1791. Reg. of Wills, Liber M, folio 277.

Fisher, Joshua. Attorney at law. Will. Made July 16, 1791. Town of Dover. Heirs: mother unnamed; father Fenwic Fisher; bro. James Fisher; sister Susannah Fisher; nephew William Fisher Corbit; Nicholas Ridgely; Elizabeth Garnet, the younger; Richard Bassett. Exec'rs, father Fenwic Fisher, friends George Wilson & Nicholas Ridgely. Wits., George McCall, William Guy. Prob. Aug. 8, 1791. Arch. vol. A17, page 137. Reg. of Wills, Liber M, folio 278.

Caldwell, John. Will. Made June 8, 1790. Heirs: nephew James Caldwell (son of bro. Train); sister Esther Lewis. Exec'r, bro.-in-law Robert Lewis. Wits., Warner Mifflin, Timothy Caldwell, Sarah Smith. Prob. Aug. 10, 1791. Arch. vol. A7, page 113. Reg. of Wills, Liber M, folio 249. Note:—Will mentions mother Mary Caldwell, dec'd, and bros. Andrew & Robert, dec'd.

Ware, William. Admin. of, to William Ware, Jr. Aug. 10, 1791. Reg. of Wills, Liber M, folio 278.

Green, James. Admin. of, to Sarah Green. Aug. 10, 1791. Reg. of Wills, Liber M, folio 278.

Fisher, Edward. Will. Made July 23, 1791. Heirs: sons Jabez, Fenwick, Edward, Thomas; daus. Elizabeth Luff & Margret Barrett; grandson Edward Luff. Exec'rs, sons Thomas & Edward. Wits., Thomas Bowman, Martha Griffith. Prob. Aug. 12, 1791. Arch. vol. A17, pages 114-115. Reg. of Wills, Liber M, folios 278-279.

Power, Abraham. Will. Made June 23, 1791. Heirs: bro. Archable Hanner; sisters Margaret & Hanah Power. Exec'r, bro. Archable Hanner. Wits., Isaac Hasel, Elizabeth Sears, Sarah Hasel. Prob. Aug. 12, 1791. Arch. vol. A41, page 52. Reg. of Wills, Liber N, folio 1.

Jordan, Isabella. Widow. Will. Made Aug. 10, 1791. Town of Dover. Heirs: nieces Esther McComb & Mary Simmonds; Isabella McComb. Exec'rs, John McComb & Mary Simmonds. Wits., Alecy Freeman, Sarah Wilson, Simon W. Wilson. Prob. Aug. 13, 1791. Arch. vol. A28, page 42. Reg. of Wills, Liber N, folio 2.

Clift, Joseph. Will (nunc.). Made Aug. 10, 1791. St. Jones' Hd. Heirs: friend Ruth Dean; Betsy, William & Joseph Knight (children of Dorcus Knight); Henry Shaw. Exec'x, Ruth Dean. Wits., Dr. James Sykes, Ruth Dean. Prob. Aug. 15, 1791. Arch. vol. A9, pages 143-144. Reg. of Wills, Liber N, folio 1.

Bileter, Daniel. Will. Made July 22, 1791. Dover Hd. Heirs: wife Sarah; son Samuel; daus. Nancy, Mahala, Elizabeth & Lydia. Exec'rs, wife Sarah & friend Joseph Taylor. Wits., Lewis Gano, John Maddock, Moses Person. Prob. Aug. 18, 1791. Arch. vol. A4, pages 51-52. Reg. of Wills, Liber N, folios 1-2.

Slaughter, Jonathan. Admin. of, to Rachel Slaughter. Aug. 24, 1791. Arch. vol. A46, page 223.

Doaney, Charles. Admin. of, to Benjamin Jones & wife Elizabeth. Aug. 24, 1791. Arch. vol. A14, page 173.

Blackshare, Morgan. Admin. of, to John Roach, D. B. N. Aug. 25, 1791. Arch. vol. A4, page 96.

Morris, Sarah. Will (copy). Made March 2, 1791. Heirs: son John; bro. William Morris. Exec'r, son John. Wits., John Jester, William Taylor. Prob. Aug. 26, 1791. Arch. vol. A37, page 14. Reg. of Wills, Liber N, folios 2-3.

Miller, John. Clerk. Will. Made May 15, 1790. Heirs: sons Samuel & James; other children unnamed. Exec'rs, sons Edward & Joseph Miller. Wits., Hugh Torbert, Rachel Torbert, Isaac Torbert. Prob. Aug. 27, 1791. Arch. vol. A35, pages 79 & 86-87. Reg. of Wills, Liber N, folio 3. Note:—Arch. vol. A35, page 87 mentions heirs, Edward & Joseph Miller, Elizabeth Miller, Elizabeth McLain & Mary Patten.

Richardson, John. Admin. of, to Joseph Miller. Aug. 29, 1791. Reg. of Wills, Liber N, folio 4.

Parvis, William, Jr. Admin. of, to Samuel Chapman. Sept. 1, 1791. Arch. vol. A39, page 101. Reg. of Wills, Liber N, folio 4.

Williams, Ward. Admin. of, to Richard Williams. Sept. 6, 1791. Arch. vol. A55, page 171. Reg. of Wills, Liber N, folio 4.

Carvil, Isaac. Admin. of, to Patrick McCalaster. Sept. 7, 1791. Arch. vol. A8, page 57. Reg. of Wills, Liber N, folio 4.

Graham, Andrew. Will (copy, nunc.). Made June 22, 1791. Heirs: William Sares; Risden Bishop, Jr. Exec'r, [Risdon Bishop, from admin. acct.]. Wit., Risdon Bishop, Sr. Prob. Sept. 22, 1791. Arch. vol. A19, page 200. Reg. of Wills, Liber N, folio 4.

Spear, John. Admin. of, to Samuel Spear. Sept. 26, 1791. Reg. of Wills, Liber N, folio 4.

Leathim, Mary. Admin. of, to Robert Leathim. Oct. 1, 1791. Reg. of Wills, Liber N, folio 4.

Anderson, William. Admin. of, to Reuben Anderson & Harmon Anderson. Oct. 1, 1791. Arch. vol. A1, pages 210-212. Reg. of Wills, Liber N, folio 4. Note:—Arch. vol. A1, page 212 mentions heirs, Gilbert, Reuben, Harmon, William, Matthias, Curtis & James Anderson & Eliza Masten, wife of John Masten.

Griffin, Ann. Admin. of, to Jabez Griffin, D. B. N. Oct. 5, 1791. Arch. vol. A20, pages 186-187. Reg. of Wills, Liber N, folio 4. Note:—Arch. vol. A20, page 186 mentions heirs, Jabez, William, Daniel, Ezekiel, Barthia & Charles Griffin & Sarah Chivens, wife of James Chivens.

Griffin, William. Admin. of, to Jabez Griffin, D. B. N. Oct. 5, 1791. Arch. vol. A20, pages 232 & 234-235. Reg. of Wills, Liber N, folio 4. Note:—Arch. vol. A20, page 232 mentions heirs, Jabez, William, Daniel, Ezekiel, Barthia & Charles Griffin & Sarah Chiffins.

Jackson, Thomas. Will. Made June 12, 1790. Murderkiln Hd. Heirs: wife Susanah; sons Thomas & Alexander; daus. Eleanor Downham, Comfort Jarold & Polly Jackson; Kezia, the eldest child of son Alexander; eldest child of dau. Eleanor; eldest child of dau. Comfort. Exec'x, wife Susanah. Wits., Thomas Lockwood, Lemuel Wheeler, Sarah Bradly. Prob. Oct. 19, 1791. Arch. vol. A26, pages 39-41. Reg. of Wills, Liber N, folio 5. Note:—Arch. vol. A26, page 40 mentions other heirs, Thomas Jarold & Keziah Downham.

Minner, Peter. Admin. of, to Elizabeth Minner. Oct. 24, 1791. Reg. of Wills, Liber N, folio 5.

Franscisco, John. Admin. of, to Charles Francisco. Oct. 24, 1791. Reg. of Wills, Liber N, folio 5.

Morris, John. Carpenter. Mispillion Hd. Admin. of, to James Bowen. Oct. 27, 1791. Arch. vol. A36, pages 219-221. Reg. of Wills, Liber N, folio 5. Note:—Arch. vol. A36, page 221 mentions heirs, half-sisters Rebecca Bright, Lurana Madden (wife of Elisha Madden) & Catherine Conner (widow of Thomas Conner).

Rich, Edward. Will. Made May 20, 1791. Heir: son Stephen. Exec'r, son Stephen. Wits., Richard Cooper, Elijah Dawson. Prob. Oct. 27, 1791. Arch. vol. A43, page 142. Reg. of Wills, Liber N, folio 6.

Forcum, John. Admin. of, to Joshua Forcum. Oct. 29, 1791. Reg. of Wills, Liber N, folio 6.

David, Daniel, Sr. Will. Made April 18, 1791. Duck Creek Hd. Heirs: son Daniel; dau. Rachel Darling; grandsons John Spruance & John Darling, son of dau. Rachel; granddaus. Eleanor Darling & Nancy David. Exec'r, son Daniel. Wits., John Farson, Mathew Griffin, William Ford. Prob. Nov. 14, 1791. Arch. vol. A12, page 211. Reg. of Wills, Liber N, folio 6.

Barns, Sarah. Will. Made July 29, 1791. Little Creek Hd. Heirs: sons John & Chaltron; grandson Warner Barns; granddau. Sally Barns. Exec'r, son Chaltron. Wits., Paul Sprague, Thomas Ratlidge. Prob. Nov. 15, 1791. Arch. vol. A2, pages 224-225. Reg. of Wills, Liber N, folio 7.

Ross, William. Admin. of, to James Ross. Nov. 17, 1791. Reg. of Wills, Liber N, folio 7.

Gaskins, William. Admin. of, to Sarah Gaskins. Nov. 23, 1791. Reg. of Wills, Liber N, folio 7.

Gordon, John. Esq. Will. Made Nov. 20, 1791. Town of Dover. Heirs: wife Hanah; Sarah Garner, dau. of Rebecca Garner; William K. Boyer; James Mellichops, son of sister Sarah; Mary Coomb, dau. of Benjamin Coomb, Esq.; Sidney Gordon, dau. of bro. Coe Gordon; Rebecca Garner; John Coomb, son of Benjamin Coomb, Esq.; John Gordon, son of bro. Coe Gordon; John Clayton; Geo. Cummins. Exec'rs, John Clayton & George Cummins, Esquires. Wits., James Tilton, Edward Miller. Prob. Nov. 29, 1791. Arch. vol. A19, pages 163-165. Reg. of Wills, Liber N, folios 8-9.

Pennell, John. Admin. of, to Thomas Jenkins & wife Elizabeth, late Elizabeth Pennell. Nov. 29, 1791. Arch. vol. A39, pages 197-199. Note:—Arch. vol. A39, page 198 mentions heirs, Thomas & Joseph Pennell, Mary Rogers, Rebecca Wells, Nancy Coomb & Abigal Templeman.

Virden, William. Will. Made Feb. 24, 1791. Heirs: wife Prudence; sons John, Peter, Matthew, William & Daniel; daus. Mary Verden, Elizabeth Purdin, Susanah Dyer, Unity Lockwood & Jemima Pratt. Exec'rs, wife Prudence & son John. Wits., Richard Cooper, John Gilder. Codicil. Prob. Nov. 30, 1791. Arch. vol. A52, pages 105-108. Reg. of Wills, Liber N, folios 7-8. Note:—Arch. vol. A52, page 106 shows Joseph Purdin as husband of Elizabeth, Thomas Lockwood as husband of Unity & Frederick Pratt as husband of Jemima Pratt.

Comerford, Peter. Admin. of, to Thomas Comerford. Dec. 2, 1791. Reg. of Wills, Liber N, folio 10.

Rasin, Philip. Will. Made Feb. 11, 1777. Heirs: sisters Sarah Rasin & Ann Rasin. Exec'r, [Jeremiah Ford, from admin. acct.]. Wits., Joseph Raisin, George Raisin, Mary Raisin. Prob. Dec. 6, 1791. Arch. vol. A42, page 92. Reg. of Wills, Liber N, folio 48.

Needles, Thomas. Farmer. Will. Made Oct. 28, 1790. Heirs: wife Sarah; son William; daus. Mary & Nancy Clymer & Sarah Dehorty. Exec'x, wife Sarah. Wits., Edward Callahan, Margaret Callahan, Esther Callahan. Codicil, Nov. 18, 1791. Wits., Edward Callahan, Edward Thrawley. Prob. Dec. 10, 1791. Arch. vol. A37, pages 170 & 173. Reg. of Wills, Liber N, folio 10. Note:—Reg. of Wills, Liber N, folio 121 shows heirs in later admin, D. B. N.

Coleman, James. Will. Made Dec. 6, 1791. Murderkill Hd. Heirs: wife Sarah; Thomas Sipple. Exec'rs, wife Sarah & Thomas Sipple. Wits., Elizabeth Vining, Hanah Garrett, Thomas Sipple. Prob. Dec. 15, 1791. Arch. vol. A9, pages 215-216. Reg. of Wills, Liber N, folios 10-11.

Runnells [Reynolds], Joseph. Will (copy, nunc.). Made Dec. 3, 1791. Heirs: Robert Runnels; sister Araminty Manning. Exec'r, Robert Runnels. Wits., James McMulland, John Jarvice. Prob. Dec. 20, 1791. Arch. vol. A44, page 179. Reg. of Wills, Liber N, folio 11.

Hane, Abraham. Will. Made April 23, 1789. Heir: wife Sarah. Exec'x, wife Sarah. Wits., Charles Green, Israel Peterson, Allen Palmatary. Prob. Dec. 20, 1791. Arch. vol. A21, page 201. Reg. of Wills, Liber N, folio 11.

Minner, Stephen. Admin. of, to Sarah Minner & Thomas Minner. Jan. 4, 1792. Arch. vol. A35, pages 155-157. Reg. of Wills, Liber N, folio 12. Note:—Arch. vol. A35, page 155 mentions heirs, Sarah, Thomas, Stephen, Jesse, Elijah, John & Mary Minner, Dennis Conner, Scinty Wyat (wife of Noah Wyat) & Sealy Morris (wife of Lemuel Morris).

Wilson, John. Blacksmith. Admin. of, to Eleanor Wilson. Jan. 5, 1792. Arch. vol. A55, page 226. Reg. of Wills, Liber N, folio 12.

Tomlin, John. Admin. of, to Mary Tomlin & Thomas Foulke. Jan. 12, 1792. Arch. vol. A50, pages 174-176. Reg. of Wills, Liber N, folio 12.

Bishop, Risden. Will. Made July 27, 1790. Heirs: dau. Ann Elizabeth Evans, wife of Dr. Thomas Evans; sons Risden & Rees. Exec'rs, son Risden & son-in-law Dr. Thomas Evans. Guardian, Thomas Evans. Wits., Thomas Rodney, Jacob McCasley, Mary Kelly. Prob. Jan. 27, 1792. Arch. vol. A4, page 63. Reg. of Wills, Liber N, folio 12.

Bowen, John. Will. Made Dec. 10, 1791. Heirs: wife Sarah; sons John, Joseph & Jeremiah Brown Bowen; daus. Sarah & Elizabeth. Exec'x, wife Sarah. Wits., James Bowen, Caleb Wilcut, Solomon Bowen. Prob. Jan. 30, 1792. Arch. vol. A5, pages 18 & 34. Reg. of Wills, Liber N, folios 12-13.

Barnet, Moses. Will (copy nunc.). Made Jan. 21, 1792. Little Creek Hd. Heirs: dau. Jean Barnett; other children unnamed. Exec'r, [Sarah Barnett, from admin. acct.]. Wits., William Arthur, John Deel. Prob. Feb. 4, 1792. Arch. vol. A2, pages 200-201. Reg. of Wills, Liber N, folio 13. Note:— Arch. vol. A2, page 201 shows the acct. later settled by Sarah Dale, late Sarah Barnett.

Scotten, Richard. Will. Made Jan. 10, 1792. Heirs: sons Eli & Richard; daus. Teeny, Sarah & Tabitha Scotten & Mary Thomas. Exec'r, [Richard Scotten, from admin. acct.]. Wits., John Moore, H. Layton, Samuel Milbourn, Jr. Prob. Feb. 4, 1792. Arch. vol. A45, page 96. Reg. of Wills, Liber N, folios 13-14.

Dewees, Rachel. Admin. of, to Samuel Dewees. Feb. 7, 1792. Arch. vol. A14, pages 49-50. Reg. of Wills, Liber N, folio 13. Note:—Arch. vol. A14, page 49 mentions heirs, John & Elizabeth Dewees.

Dill, John. Esq. Admin. of, to Letitia Dill & Henry Molleston. Feb. 8, 1792. Arch. vol. A14, pages 93-100. Reg. of Wills, Liber N, folio 13. Note:—Arch. vol. A14, page 93 mentions heirs, Zepporah, Hester & Andrew Dill, Sarah White (wife of Samuel White), Anna Walton & Mary Walker.

Davis, Thomas. Will. Made Jan. 8, 1792. Heirs: wife Sarah; sons John, William, Lewis & Thomas; daus. Mary Glass, Rachel Crumpton, Sarah, Elizabeth & Anner Davis. Exec'rs, wife Sarah & her bro. Abner Dill. Wits., Joseph Oliver, Thomas Winsmore, Benjamin Yoe. Prob. Feb. 14, 1792. Arch. vol. A13, page 69. Reg. of Wills, Liber N, folio 14.

Williams, Benjamin. Admin. of, to David Wilson. Feb. 15, 1792. Reg. of Wills, Liber N, folios 21-22.

Reese, Jeremiah, Jr. Will. Made Feb. 9, 1792. Little Creek Hd. Heirs: sister Rebecca Starling; aunt Jean Wilson; James & Mary Starling, children of John Starling; James, Aaron & Ann Wood, children of John Wood, dec'd; Mary Snow, alias Wallace (dau. of Elizabeth Wallace, spinster). Exec'r, bro.-in-law John Starling. Wits., Robert Denny, Presley Raymond. Prob. Feb. 16, 1792. Arch. vol. A43, pages 7-9. Reg. of Wills, Liber N, folios 14-15.

Edwards, Joshua. Admin. of, to Charles Pope. Feb. 17, 1792. Arch. vol. A16, page 77. Reg. of Wills, Liber N, folio 15.

Bradford, Isaac. Admin. of, to Pearcy Bradford & Samuel Powell. Feb. 17, 1792. Arch. vol. A5, pages 103-108. Reg. of Wills, Liber N, folio 15. Note:—Arch. vol. A5, page 103 mentions heirs, Kendal, Thomas & Mary Bradford.

Pell, David. Admin. of, to Susanah Pell. Feb. 17, 1792. Reg. of Wills, Liber N, folio 15.

Bedwell, Agness. Admin. of, to Preston Bedwell. Feb. 27, 1792. Arch. vol. A3, page 138. Reg. of Wills, Liber N, folio 15.

Williams, John. Admin. of, to Mary Williams. Feb. 29, 1792. Arch. vol. A55, page 100. Note:—Mentions heirs, James Williams & Amah Sapp (née Williams), wife of Jacob Sapp.

Draper, William. Admin. of, to Ann Draper. March 19, 1792. Arch. vol. A15, pages 68-71. Reg. of Wills, Liber N, folio 15. Note:—Arch. vol. A15, page 68 mentions heirs, Ann, Unicey, Nehemiah, John, Samuel, William, Nancy, Catharine & Lemuel Draper & Elizabeth Moore.

Mullen [Mutton], William. Admin. of, to Hanah Mullen. March 23, 1792. Reg. of Wills, Liber N, folio 15.

Butcher, Jacob. Admin. of, to George Frazer. March 23, 1792. Reg. of Wills, Liber N, folio 15.

Attax, Aquilla. Farmer. Will. Made March 15, 1792. Duck Creek Hd. Heirs: sons Aquilla, Stephen & Thomas; dau. Sarah Attax; Betsy Alford, dau. of Aaron Alford; grandson Charles Attax, son of my son John, dec'd. Exec'rs, sons Aquilla & Stephen. Wits., John Ringold, James Scotton, Simon Ayres. Prob. March 27, 1792. Arch. vol. A2, pages 20-23. Reg. of Wills, Liber N, folio 16.

Morris, Jeremiah. Admin. of, to Jemima Morris. March 27, 1792. Reg. of Wills, Liber N, folio 16.

Skinner, William. Will. Made March 27, 1792. Heirs: wife Rebecca; sons John, Thomas, Daniel, Stephen; daus. Nelly & Betsey Skinner; dau.-in-law Mary Cole. [No prob.]. Wits., Martenus Sipple & John Cole. Arch. vol. A46, page 216.

Mason, Jacob. Mispillion Hd. Admin. of, to Sarah Mason. March 28, 1792. Arch. vol. A33, pages 236-237. Reg. of Wills, Liber N, folio 16. Note:—Arch. vol. A33, page 236 mentions a minor son Isaac Mason, dec'd; page 237 shows that Sarah Mason married Morgan Williams.

Morris, John. Duck Creek Neck. Admin. of, to Patrick Conner. April 9, 1792. Reg. of Wills, Liber N, folio 18.

Jones, James. Tanner. Will. Made March 14, 1792. Heirs: wife Mary; child unnamed; bro. David Jones; sister Ann Dulin. Exec'rs, wife Mary & William Thomas. Wits., John Simmons, Thomas Shulcock, James Smith. Prob. April 10, 1792. Arch. vol. A27, page 201. Reg. of Wills, Liber N, folio 18.

Godwin, Nahor. Will. Made Feb. 24, 1791. Heirs: wife Frances; sons Thomas, John, William, James, Peter & Nahor. Exec'x, wife Frances. Wits., Jenifer Taylor, Major Bostick, Joseph Godwin. Prob. April 11, 1792. Arch. vol. A19, pages 85-86. Reg. of Wills, Liber N, folio 18.

Sykes, James. Will. Made April 2, 1792. Heirs: wife Agnes; sons James, Stephen, George & Nathaniel; daus. Mary Whethered, Ann, Lucy Matilda & Harriott Sykes. Exec'rs, wife Agnes & son James. Guardians, wife Agnes & son James. Wits., Nicholas Ridgely, James Wakeman. Prob. April 16, 1792. Arch. vol. A49, page 142. Reg. of Wills, Liber N, folios 16-17.

Maree, John. Admin. of, to Lydia Maree. April 24, 1792. Arch. vol. A33, pages 168-169. Reg. of Wills, Liber N, folio 19. Note:—Arch. vol. A33, page 168 mentions heirs, Lydia, Reubin, John, Isaac & Mary Maree.

Berry, Charles. Admin. of, to William Berry. April 30, 1792. Reg. of Wills, Liber N, folio 19.

Nicolls, Vincent. Admin. of, to Susanah Nicolls. May 12, 1792. Reg. of Wills, Liber N, folio 19.

Harwood, Thomas. Admin. of, to Jasper Harwood. May 14, 1792. Reg. of Wills, Liber N, folio 19.

Finsthwait, Thomas. Admin. of, to Hanah Finsthwait. May 15, 1792. Arch. vol. A10, pages 255-256. Reg. of Wills, Liber N, folio 19. Note:—Admin. shows Hannah Finsthwait as Hannah Pierce.

Snow, Isaac. Admin. of, to Elizabeth Jones. May 15, 1792. Arch. vol. A47, pages 242-245. Reg. of Wills, Liber N, folio 19. Note:—Arch. vol. A47, page 242 mentions heirs, Clayton, Silas & Isaac Snow; also shows that Elizabeth Jones married James Robinson; page 245 mentions Rachel Snow as the wife of Isaac Snow.

Jones, Benjamin. Duck Creek Hd. Admin. of, to Elizabeth Jones. May 15, 1792. Reg. of Wills, Liber N, folio 19. Note:—Arch. vol. A27, page 142 shows Elizabeth Jones as the wife of James Robinson.

Cole [Coole], Rebecca. Admin. of, to Ebenezer Cloke. May 21, 1792. Reg. of Wills, Liber N, folio 19.

Molleston, William. Esq. Admin. of, to Robert Clark, Esq., D. B. N. May 23, 1792. Arch. vol. A35, page 225. Reg. of Wills, Liber N, folio 19.

Bostwick, Sarah. Admin. of, to Jacob Bostwick. May 28, 1792. Reg. of Wills, Liber N, folio 19.

Tinch, Samuel. Admin. of, to Mary Sullivan. May 29, 1792. Reg. of Wills, Liber N, folio 19.

Jacobs, Speakman. Admin. of, to William Jacobs. June 1, 1792. Arch. vol. A26, pages 77-78. Reg. of Wills, Liber N, folio 19. Note:—Arch. vol. A26, page 77 mentions heirs, Leah, Abraham & William Jacobs.

Clifford, Daniel. Admin. of, to Lydia Clifford & John Vanloden. June 5, 1792. Reg. of Wills, Liber N, folio 19.

Irons, Henry. Admin. of, to Anica Irons. June 5, 1792. Reg. of Wills, Liber N, folio 19.

Hopkins, John. Will. Made March 5, 1787. Mispillion Hd. Heirs: wife Mary; sons John, Robert & Henry; daus. Comfort, Mary, Jean, Sarah, Nancy, Amelia & Ora. Exec'rs, wife Mary & son Robert. Wits., Zebulon Hopkins, Zachariah Jones, Jr., John Ralston. Prob. June 7, 1792. Arch. vol. A25, pages 13-16. Reg. of Wills, Liber N, folio 20.

Pattison [Patterson], John. Will. Made May 1, 1792. Duck Creek Hd. Heirs: wife Rachel; sons John, Thomas, George, Isaac & William; dau. Betsey Wallace, wife of Josiah Wallace; grandson Samuel Wallace, son of dau. Betsey Wallace; other children of dau. Betsey unnamed. Exec'rs, wife Rachel & son George. Wits., John Ringold, Martha Ashford, Enoch Wood. Prob. June 7, 1792. Arch. vol. A39, pages 109-110 & 124-126. Reg. of Wills, Liber N, folios 25-26.

Cloak [Cloke], Ebenezer. Admin. of, to Elizabeth Cloke. June 13, 1792. Reg. of Wills, Liber N, folio 20.

Humphrys, George. Admin. of, to Martha Follis. July 13, 1792. Reg. of Wills, Liber N, folio 21.

Jones, Stanford. Will. Made March 26, 1788. Heirs: wife Esther; son John; daus. Elener, Nancy, Jerusa Jones & Meriah Skiner. Exec'rs, dau. Elener & Thomas Skiner. Wits., James Jones, John Preston, Daniel Cox. Prob. July 14, 1792. Arch. vol. A28, pages 23-24. Reg. of Wills, Liber N, folio 21.

Morgan, James. Admin. of, to David Young. June 16, 1792. Reg. of Wills, Liber N, folios 20-21.

Smith, James. Tanner. Will. Made April 26, 1792. Dorchester Co., Md. Heirs: aunt Mary Smith; Nancy Scoggins; James & William Rea, children of Peter Rea of Cambridge, Md.; mulatto boys Dick & George; John Hall, hatter, of Dover. Exec'r, Peter Rea. Wits., George Ward, Charles McQuire, Peregrin Beaston. Prob. July 27, 1792. Arch. vol. A47, page 65. Reg. of Wills, Liber N, folio 23.

Jones, Standford, Jr. Admin. of, to John Jones. July 28, 1792. Reg. of Wills, Liber N, folio 21.

Skulley [Scully], John Burton. Farmer. Will. Made March 16, 1792. Heirs: daus. Sarah Dill, Triphener Conner, Mary Dill, Lydia Oldfield; grandsons Burton & Solomon Dill (sons of dau. Sarah), Burton Conner (son of dau. Triphener); granddau. Minty [Conner]; Solomon Conner. Exec'r, son-in-law John Green. Wits., John Billing, William Dill, Henry Carter. Prob. Aug. 3, 1792. Arch. vol. A45, pages 107 & 110. Reg. of Wills, Liber N, folios 24-25.

Woodrop, Daniel. Admin. of, to George Hinds. Aug. 4, 1792. Arch. vol. A56, page 118. Reg. of Wills, Liber N, folio 27.

Snow, John. Admin. of, to John Starling, D. B. N. Aug. 21, 1792. Reg. of Wills, Liber N, folio 26.

Anderson, James. Will. Made April 2, 1792. Heirs: sons Andrew & William; John Anderson; George Anderson; daus. Rachel & Anor; Esther Anderson. Exec'r, son Andrew. Wits., Mathew Clark, Daniel Jarvis, Caleb Jarvis. Prob. Aug. 22, 1792. Arch. vol. A1, pages 175, 177 & 180. Reg. of Wills, Liber N, folio 26.

Parke, Thomas. Admin. of, to Jane Parke. Aug. 23, 1792. Arch. vol. A39, pages 30-35. Reg. of Wills, Liber N, folio 26. Note: —Arch. vol. A39, page 30 mentions heirs, Thomas, Ann, Susan, Samuel, Joshua & Robert Parke.

Wyatt, William. Admin. of, to Thomas Wyatt. Aug. 29, 1792. Arch. vol. A56, page 179.

Jones, Layton. Admin. of, to Peter Lister & wife Peggy, widow of Layton Jones. Aug. 31, 1792. Arch. vol. A27, page 237.

Wallace, William. Admin. of, to Peter Lister & wife Margaret, late Margaret Jones, the widow of Layton Jones. Aug. 31, 1792. Arch. vol. A53, page 17. Note:—Admin. mentions heirs, Mary Jones, William, Elizabeth (Elizabeth McVay), David & Solomon Wallace.

Garnett, Elizabeth. Admin. of, to William Garnett. Sept. 1, 1792. Arch. vol. A18, pages 223-225. Reg. of Wills, Liber N, folio 27.

Anderson, Jacob. Admin. of, to Joseph Anderson. Sept. 5, 1792. Reg. of Wills, Liber N, folio 27.

Robeson, Edward. Admin. of, to Noah Hickman. Sept. 6, 1792. Reg. of Wills, Liber N, folio 27.

Forcum, Joshua. Admin. of, to Mary Forcum. Sept. 13, 1792. Reg. of Wills, Liber N, folio 27.

Hamilton, John, Jr. Admin. of, to John Hamilton, Sr. Sept. 29, 1792. Reg. of Wills, Liber N, folio 27.

Thompson, William. Mispillion Hd. Admin. of, to William Thompson. Oct. 2, 1792. Reg. of Wills, Liber N, folio 27.

Cole, Rebecca. Duck Creek Hd. Admin. of, to William Arthurs. Oct. 4, 1792. Reg. of Wills, Liber N, folio 27.

McSparron, Archibald. Admin. of, to Stephen Alston. Oct. 9, 1792. Reg. of Wills, Liber N, folios 27 & 33.

Mannering, William. Farmer. Will. Made Sept. 26, 1792. Duck Creek Hd. Heirs: bro. Peter Mannering; sons Nathan Greenwood, William & John Mannering. Exec'r, Eben Blackiston, Sr. Wits., Benjamin Hazel, John West & Esther Griffin. Prob. Oct. 12, 1792. Arch. vol. A33, pages 149-151. Reg. of Wills, Liber N, folios 27-28.

McLane, Moses. Admin. of, to Margaret McLane. Oct. 17, 1792. Reg. of Wills, Liber N, folio 28.

Entwezle, Mary. Gentlewoman. Will. Made Dec. 27, 1790. Murderkill Hd. Heirs: son William Durbrow; daus. Elizabeth & Mary Entwezle. Exec'r, son William Durbrow. Wits., Benjamin Smith, William Potter, John Ward. Prob. Oct. 19, 1792. Arch. vol. A16, page 208. Reg. of Wills, Liber N, folios 28-29.

Owens, Amon. Admin. of, to Robert Owens. Oct. 20, 1792. Arch. vol. A38, page 139. Reg. of Wills, Liber N, folio 29.

Reed, John, Sr. Will. Made Oct. 7, 1792. Heirs: wife Ann; daus. Ann Hutson & Sarah Dill; sons Thomas, John, James, William & Ebenezer. Exec'r, Ebenezer Reed. Wits., John Cubbidge, John Grigg, Absalom Stradley, Jr. Prob. Oct. 22, 1792. Arch. vol. A42, page 201. Reg. of Wills, Liber N, folio 29.

Savin, William. Will. Made May 19, 1792. Duck Creek Hd. Heirs: half-bro. George William Smith; bros. Perigrin & Joshua Savin; nephew Perigrin Biddle; daus. Mary Savin (alias Bostick) & Ann Savin (alias Bostick), daus of Rachel Bostick, spinster; sons John & James Savin (alias Bostick), sons of Rachel Bostick, spinster. Exec'r, bro. Perigrin Savin. Wits., Silas Snow, Wheeler Pennington, Moses Thompson. Prob. Oct. 29, 1792. Arch. vol. A45, page 32. Reg. of Wills, Liber N, folio 30.

Johnson, Samuel. Will. Made Sept. 29, 1792. Heirs: wife Mary Ann; sons William, Nathan, Purnal & James; daus. Elizabeth Davis (wife of Nathan Davis), Sarah, Mary, Priscilla, Nancy & Phebe Johnson. Exec'rs, wife Mary Ann & son William. Wits., Beniah Fleming, Samuel Fleming, John Collings. Prob. Oct. 29, 1792. Arch. vol. A27, pages 105-107. Reg. of Wills, Liber N, folio 31.

McBride, Morris. Farmer. Will. Made Oct. 17, 1792. Murderkiln Hd. Heirs: wife Ann; children of first wife (Agness Johnson), John, Robert, Samuel & James McBride & Jane Pearce; William Powell, son of John Powell; dau. Elizabeth McBride; Mary Morris, dau. of wife Ann. Exec'rs, wife Ann & friend Richard Banning. Wits., Caleb Boyer, George Hairgrove, Mary Russell. Prob. Nov. 2, 1792. Arch. vol. A32, pages 70-73. Reg. of Wills, Liber N, folio 32. Note:—Arch. vol. A32, page 71 shows that Ann McBride later married John Cloak.

Sprague, Paul. Admin. of, to Allen McLane, Esq. Nov. 3, 1792. Arch. vol. A48, page 109. Reg. of Wills, Liber N, folio 32.

Battell, French. Admin. of, to John Battell, D. B. N. Nov. 12, 1792. Reg. of Wills, Liber N, folio 32.

Battell, Elizabeth. Admin. of, to John Battell. Nov. 12, 1792. Reg. of Wills, Liber N, folios 32-33.

Watkins, Thomas. Admin. of, to Ann Watkins. Nov. 14, 1792. Arch. vol. A53, pages 172-173. Reg. of Wills, Liber N, folio 33. Note:—Arch. vol. A53, page 172 mentions heirs, William, Mary, Ann, Elizabeth & Thomas Watkins.

Cowgill, Ezekiel. Admin. of, to Daniel Cowgill. Nov. 28, 1792. Reg. of Wills, Liber N, folio 33.

Worknott, Alexander. Admin. of, to Mary Worknott. Dec. 8, 1792. Arch. vol. A56, pages 137-138. Reg. of Wills, Liber N, folio 33. Note:—Arch vol. A56, page 137 shows that Mary Worknott later married Gideon Emory; also mentions an heir, Martin Worknott.

Staten, Hillard. Admin. of, to Nathaniel Hunn. Dec. 13, 1792. Arch. vol. A48, page 185. Reg. of Wills, Liber N, folio 33.

Hunn, Jonathan. Will. Made May 24, 1792. Heirs: wife unnamed; daus. Mary & Patience; sons Ezekiel, John, Nathaniel & Jonathan; grandson Jonathan Jenkins. Exec'rs, sons Ezekiel, Nathaniel & Jonathan. Wits., James Sykes, William Maffett, Amely Henry. Prob. Dec. 18, 1792. Arch. vol. A25, pages 144-148 & 150-152. Reg. of Wills, Liber N, folios 34-35. Note:—Arch. vol. A25, page 145 shows Mary Hunn as the wife of Caleb Bickham & Patience Hunn as the wife of Jabez Jenkins; pages 146 & 148 mentions a Susanna Hunn.

Tippitt, Samuel. Admin. of, to Charles Pope. Dec. 20, 1792. Reg. of Wills, Liber N, folio 33.

Morgan, David. Admin. of, to Sarah Morgan. Jan. 1, 1793. Reg. of Wills, Liber N, folio 35. Note:—Arch. vol. A36, page 136 mentions heirs, Lydia Buckhannion, John & David Morgan; also shows that Sarah Morgan later married William Vanstaverin.

Blackshare, Robert. Farmer. Duck Creek Hd. Admin. of, to Dr. James Snow. Jan. 1, 1793. Arch. vol. A4, pages 104-105. Reg. of Wills, Liber N, folio 37.

Raymond, Presly. Admin. of, to James Raymond. Jan. 8, 1793. Arch. vol. A42, pages 166 & 168. Reg. of Wills, Liber N, folio 37. Note:—Arch. vol. A42, page 168 mentions Henry, Jacob, Joseph & John Raymond, Mary Collins (wife of William) & Angelica Parson (wife of Joseph).

Raymond, Mary (formerly Mary Snow). Deposition. Jan. 14, 1793. Heirs: father Silas Snow; sister Phebe Snow. Wits., James Raymond, Elizabeth Snow. Arch. vol. A42, page 167.

Chipman, Stephen. Admin. of, to Elizabeth Chipman. Jan. 23, 1793. Reg. of Wills, Liber N, folio 37.

Heald, Joseph. Will. Made July 17, 1791. Heirs: son Rich; dau. Synthia; wife unnamed. Exec'rs, son Rich & Nicholas Ridgely, Esq. Wits., Wm. Whiteley, Thomas Berry, John Muncy. Prob. Jan. 24, 1793. Arch. vol. A23, page 113. Reg. of Wills, Liber N, folios 37-38.

Vanloden, John. Admin. of, to Sarah Vanloden. Feb. 1, 1793. Reg. of Wills, Liber N, folio 38. Note:—Arch. vol. A52, page 5 mentions heirs, Lydia, Thomas & Sarah Vanloden; also shows that Sarah Vanloden later married . . . Neal.

Conner, Abraham. Admin. of, to Sarah Conner, who later married Henry Hoffecker. Feb. 1, 1793. Arch. vol. A10, pages 70-71. Reg. of Wills, Liber N, folio 38. Note:—Arch. vol. A10, page 70 mentions heirs, widow Sarah Hoffecker, late Conner, Mary Snow (wife of Clayton), Abraham, John & Patrick Conner & Elizabeth Hackett, late Conner.

Hirons, Mary. Admin. of, to Samuel Vanburkelo. Feb. 14, 1793. Reg. of Wills, Liber N, folio 38.

White, William. Admin. of, to Deborah White. Feb. 16, 1793. Reg. of Wills, Liber N, folio 38.

Broxon, John. Admin. of, to John Broxon, the younger. Feb. 25, 1793. Arch. vol. A6, page 59. Reg. of Wills, Liber N, folio 38.

Smith, Charles. Admin. of, to Mary Smith. Feb. 25, 1793. Reg. of Wills, Liber N, folio 38.

McCoomb, John. Admin. of, to Esther McCoomb & William Harper. Feb. 26, 1793. Arch. vol. A32, pages 139-141. Reg. of Wills, Liber N, folio 39. Note:—Arch. vol. A32, page 139 mentions that Esther McCoomb, the widow, later married William Pennuel.

Walker, John. Duck Creek Hd. Admin. of, to Andrew Barratt. Feb. 27, 1793. Reg. of Wills, Liber N, folio 39.

Boice, Alexander. Admin. of, to John & Sarah Bostwick. Feb. 27, 1793. Arch. vol. A4, page 191.

Forbes, Richard. Admin. of, to Nalce Jones & wife Esther (late Esther Forbes). May 28, 1793. Arch. vol. A17, page 219.

Gregg, Rebecca. Admin. of, to William Culbreath, D. B. N. Feb. 28, 1793. Arch. vol. A20, page 51.

Ware, William, the younger. Admin. of, to John Ware. March 1, 1793. Arch. vol. A53, pages 120-122. Reg. of Wills, Liber N, folio 39. Note:—Arch. vol. A53, page 120 mentions heirs, John, Nancy & Elizabeth Ware, Lydia Tygart, Mary Pearson & Cally Fulcian.

Gordon, Coe. Admin. of, to Daniel Cowgill, D. B. N. March 1, 1793. Arch. vol. A19, pages 146 & 148.

Chipley, James. Admin. of, to Jane Chipley & George Baily. March 6, 1793. Arch. vol. A8, page 181. Reg. of Wills, Liber N, folio 39.

Miller, Conrod. Yeoman. Will. Made Dec. 9, 1791. Murderkill Hd. Heirs: wife Sarah; sons Conrod, John & Stephen; daus. Susanah Miller (wife of John Miller), Mary Goodwin (wife of Moses), Elizabeth Pierce (wife of William Pierce) & Martha Miller. Exec'x, wife Sarah. Wits., Peter Miller, William McClyment, Thomas Nixon. Prob. March 6, 1793. Arch. vol. A35, page 64. Reg. of Wills, Liber N, folios 39-40.

Gray, James. Will. Made Feb. 8, 1793. Heirs: mother Darcus Gray; Franses Boon & heirs. Exec'x, mother Darcus Gray. Wits., Samuel Blackiston, Richard Beck, Benjamin Blackiston. Prob. March 8, 1793. Arch. vol. A20, page 17. Reg. of Wills, Liber N, folio 40.

Gray, Darcus. Will (nunc.). Made Feb. 20, 1793. Duck Creek Hd. Heirs: cousin Frances Boon; Amelia Marsh; William Morris, bro. of Frances Boon. Exec'x, Frances Boon. Wits., Abraham King, Elizabeth King. Prob. March 8, 1793. Arch. vol. A20, page 11. Reg. of Wills, Liber N, folio 40.

Ayres, James. Admin. of, to Simon Ayres. March 13, 1793. Reg. of Wills, Liber N, folio 40.

Johnson, John. Admin. of, to William Johnson & James Johnson. March 14, 1793. Arch. vol. A27, pages 80-81. Reg. of Wills, Liber N, folio 41. Note:—Arch. vol. A27, page 80 mentions heirs, widow Mary Johnson, William, John, Henry, Jonathan & James Johnson, Elizabeth Draper, Mary & Esther Dill, Ruth Slaughter & Rachel Needles.

Thorne, Sydenham. Clergyman. Will. Made Feb. 12, 1793. Milford. Heirs: wife Betty; bro. Robert Thorne; nephew Peter Caverly, son of sister Ann; Richard (Miller) Clark. Exec'rs, wife Betty & nephew Peter Caverly. Wits., William Adams, Isaiah James, Miers Fisher. Prob. March 15, 1793. Arch. vol. A50, page 126. Reg. of Wills, Liber N, folio 41.

McElroy, Allen. Admin. of, to Edward McElroy. March 16, 1793. Reg. of Wills, Liber N, folio 41.

Wharton, William. Admin. of, to Elizabeth Wharton. March 18, 1793. Reg. of Wills, Liber N, folio 41.

Robinson, John. Admin. of, to Purnel Loffland. March 18, 1793. Reg. of Wills, Liber N, folio 41.

Barcus, Rachel. Will. Made March 6, 1793. Heirs: son Benjamin Fowlar; daus. Rachel, Mary, Ann & Elizabeth Fowlar; Rachel Parsons. Exec'rs, daus. Rachel & Mary. Wits., Richard Beck, Benjamin Blackiston, Rachel Parsons. Prob. March 22, 1793. Arch. vol. A2, pages 154-155. Reg. of Wills, Liber N, folios 41-42. Note:—Arch. vol. A2, page 154 shows that Rachel Fowlar later married John Clark.

Bennett, Sarah. Will. Made Oct. 1, 1792. Heirs: sons James, Benjamin, Anglo, John & William; dau. Elizabeth Holloway; Backstar Brinkly. Exec'r, son James. Wits., Lewis Gano, John Maddock, Meriam Maddock. Prob. March 23, 1793. Arch. vol. A3, page 225. Reg. of Wills, Liber N, folio 42.

Pickeral, Littleton. Admin. of, to Joseph Truitt. March 25, 1793. Arch. vol. A40, page 64. Reg. of Wills, Liber N, folio 43. Note:—Testation shows a sister Abigail Jewell, wife of William Jewell. Wit., Elizabeth Harmon.

Garland, John. Admin. of, to William Arthurs. March 26, 1793. Reg. of Wills, Liber N, folio 41.

Thompson, John. Mispilion Hd. Admin. of, to Caleb Chance. March 26, 1793. Arch. vol. A50, page 95. Reg. of Wills, Liber N, folio 43.

Pattison [Patterson], Rachel. Will. Made Feb. 21, 1793. Duck Creek Hd. Heirs: sons John, Thomas, George, Isaac & William; dau. Betsy Wallace, wife of Josias Wallace; sister Elizabeth Meredith; grandson Samuel Wallace, son of dau. Betsy & Josias Wallace. Exec'r, son George. Wits., John Ringold, Enoch Wood, Mary Pattison. Prob. March 26, 1793. Arch. vol. A39, pages 113-114 & 127. Reg. of Wills, Liber N, folios 43-44.

McCoy, Andrew. Admin. of, to Alexander McCoy. April 1, 1793. Arch. vol. A32, pages 143-144. Reg. of Wills, Liber N, folio 44. Note:—Arch. vol. A32, page 143 mentions heirs, Margaret & Andrew McCoy.

Morris, Susana. Will. Made May 29, 1789. Heirs: sisters Comfort Nichels, Hanah Macknat (wife of William Macknat), Deborah Jester (wife of Samuel Jester), Sarah Merine, Lyday Masten (wife of Hezekiah Masten); bros. Daniel, Masten, Nathaniel, Hezekiah & John Morris; Nathaniel Luff, Jr.; John Merine. Exec'r, Hezekiah Masten. Wits., Mathias Masten, Sr., Mathias Masten, Jr., Alexander Clarke. Prob. April 8, 1793. Arch. vol. A37, pages 26-30. Reg. of Wills, Liber N, folio 44 & Liber O, folio 264.

Dill, John. Farmer. Will. Made Jan. 2, 1793. Heirs: sons Thomas & William; grandson John Dill. Exec'r, son Thomas. Wits., Samuel Conner, Solomon Conner, Henry Carter. Prob. April 17, 1793. Arch. vol. A14, page 92. Reg. of Wills, Liber N, folio 45.

Lord, Henry. Admin. of, to William Wyatt. April 23, 1793. Reg. of Wills, Liber N, folio 45.

Stradly, Paris. Admin. of, to Rebecca Stradly. May 2, 1793. Arch. vol. A49, page 77. Reg. of Wills, Liber N, folio 45.

Birk, Charles. Will. Made April 21, 1793. Heirs: wife Rachel; cousin John Freeman. Exec'x, wife Rachel. Wits., Peter Degman, Benjamin Wynn. Prob. May 7, 1793. Arch. vol. A4, page 58. Reg. of Wills, Liber N, folios 45-46.

Lister, William. Will. Made April 19, 1793. Heirs: wife [Ann, from admin. acct.]; sons Levi, Peter, William, Sworden; sons-in-law Levin Jump & Ace Freeman; grandson Joseph Dwiggins; granddau. Ann Quinley. Exec'rs, wife Ann & son William. Wits., William Charles Neill, Henry Wrench, John Bartlett. Prob. May 17, 1793. Arch. vol. A30, pages 190 & 178-179. Reg. of Wills, Liber N, folio 46.

Martin, James. Admin. of, to William Frazer. May 18, 1793. Reg. of Wills, Liber N, folio 47. Note:—Arch. vol. A33, page 209 mentions heirs, Nancy Lafferty (wife of James), Rachel Craig & heirs of John Craig.

Bell, John. Will. Made April 30, 1793. Town of Dover. Heirs: wife Nancy; son John Hall Bell; dau. Sally Bell. Exec'rs, wife Nancy & friend William K. Boyer. Wits., Nathaniel Luff, Jr., Jacob Furbee, Armwell Lockwood, Jr. Prob. May 18, 1793. Arch. vol. A3, pages 176-177. Reg. of Wills, Liber N, folio 47.

Cain, Othaniel. Admin. of, to Christian Cain. May 24, 1793. Arch. vol. A7, pages 75-77. Reg. of Wills, Liber N, folio 48. Note:—Arch. vol. A7, page 75 shows that Christian Cain later married ... Kinnamon; also mentions heirs, Mary & Eli Cain.

Ogle, George. Admin. of, to George Truitt, D. B. N. May 30, 1793. Arch. vol. A38, pages 111-113. Reg. of Wills, Liber M, folio 213.

Lecky, Andrew, the elder. Farmer. Dover Hd. Admin. of, to William Harper. May 30, 1793. Arch. vol. A29, pages 223-225. Note:—Arch. vol. A29, page 224 mention heirs, Mary Wilson, Andrew Lecky & Ann Wills.

Jordan, Isabella. Widow. Town of Dover. Admin. of, to Esther McComb, D. B. N. May 31, 1793. Arch. vol. A28, page 43. Note:—Esther McComb named adm'x in lieu of John McComb, exec'r, of Little Hd., blacksmith.

Jordan, Isabella. Widow. Town of Dover. Admin. of, to Noah Smith & wife Mary, late Mary Simons, D. B. N. May 31, 1793. Arch. vol. A28, page 44.

Graham, William. Yeoman. Will. Made May 16, 1793. Duck Creek Hd. Heirs: two children unnamed. Exec'r, James Lafferty. Wits., Daniel Cummings, Elizabeth Peers, Nehemiah Cloak. Prob. May 31, 1793. Arch. vol. A20, pages 3-5. Reg. of Wills, Liber N, folio 48. Note:—Arch. vol. A20, page 4 mentions heirs, Sarah & Nancy Graham.

Corker, John, Sr. Admin. of, to Richard Corker. June 3, 1793. Arch. vol. A11, page 2. Reg. of Wills, Liber N, folio 48.

Pattison, John. Admin. of, to Thomas Pattison. July 9, 1793. Reg. of Wills, Liber N, folio 48.

Pattison, Isaac. Admin. of, to Thomas Pattison. July 9, 1793. Reg. of Wills, Liber N, folio 48.

Curwell, Clayton. Admin. of, to John Hurt. July 15, 1793. Reg. of Wills, Liber N, folio 49.

Watkins, Robert. Admin. of, to James Scotten, D. B. N. July 15, 1793. Arch. vol. A53, pages 164 & 167-171. Reg. of Wills, Liber N, folio 49. Note:—Arch. vol. A53, page 164 mentions heirs, Rachel Curwell (late Rachel Watkins, widow), Samuel, James, Sarah, Robert, Christopher & Thomas Watkins.

Spencer, John. Admin. of, to Azail Spencer. July 19, 1793. Reg. of Wills, Liber N, folio 49.

Chicken, John. Admin. of, to John Chicken & Daniel Chicken. July 22, 1793. Arch. vol. A8, page 168. Reg. of Wills, Liber N, folio 49.

David, Charles. Will (nunc.). Made July 2, 1793. Duck Creek Hd. Heirs: dau. Jemima; other children unnamed. Exec'r, John David. Wits., James Morris, Susannah Wheeldon, Mary Anderson. Prob. July 26, 1793. Arch. vol. A12, page 210. Reg. of Wills, Liber N, folio 49.

Wells, William. Admin. of, to Benjamin Farrow. July 31, 1793. Reg. of Wills, Liber N, folio 49.

Wells, Mary. Spinster. Will. Made July 20, 1793. Heirs: daus. Rachel, Mary, Nancy, Marthew, Rody & Rebeckey Wells & Sarah Shehorn; sons Richard & David. Exec'rs, son David & Josiah Wallace. Wits., Wm. Allaband, Josiah Wallace, David Wells, Mary Wells, Jr. Prob. Aug. 2, 1793. Arch. vol. A53, pages 239-240. Reg. of Wills, Liber N, folio 49.

McSparron, Meriam. Will. Made June 15, 1793. Caroline Co., Md. Heirs: grandson John Boon, son of Thomas Boon; Meriam & John Crumpton, children of sister Jemimah Crumpton. Exec'r, John Pleasonton. Wits., John Ralston, Esq., John Williams. Prob. Aug. 13, 1793. Arch. vol. A33, pages 34-36. Reg. of Wills, Liber N, folios 49-50.

Ozburn, Eunice. Widow. Little Creek Hd. Admin. of, to Henry Cowgil. Aug. 14, 1793. Arch. vol. A38, page 168. Reg. of Wills, Liber N, folio 50.

Catlin, Joseph. Admin. of, to Lydia Catlin & George Truitt, Esq. Aug. 14, 1793. Arch. vol. A8, pages 76-77. Reg. of Wills, Liber N, folio 50. Note:—Arch. vol. A8, page 76 mentions heirs, John, Robert & Mary Catlin & Sarah Godwin; also shows that Lydia Catlin married . . . Jones.

Morris, Samuel, Jr. Admin. of, to James Whitaker. Aug. 14, 1793. Arch. vol. A37, page 5. Reg. of Wills, Liber N, folio 50.

Coley, Daniel. Admin. of, to Ebenezer Blackiston. Aug. 14, 1793. Arch. vol. A9, pages 218-219. Reg. of Wills, Liber N, folio 50.

Forcum, John, Sr. Admin. of, to Mary Forcum, D. B. N. Aug. 29, 1793. Arch. vol. A17, page 220.

Turner, Samuel Bevans. Will. Made Feb. 22, 1793. Mispillion Hd. Heirs: wife Jean Huet Turner; sons Benjamin, Samuel, George, Jesse & Elias; daus. Polly & Levicy Turner, Nicy Fisher & Sally Langrel; grandsons Samuel Turner (son of Levin, dec'd) & Levin Turner (son of Elias); granddau. Polly Fisher. Exec'rs, wife Jean Huet Turner & son Samuel. Wits., Robert McGonigal, Jehu Turner, Jesse Turner. Prob. Aug. 31, 1793. Arch. vol. A51, pages 179 & 181-182. Reg. of Wills, Liber N, folios 50-51.

Murphy, Andrew. Admin. of, to Simon Vanwinkle. Sept. 6, 1793. Arch. vol. A37, page 83. Reg. of Wills, Liber N, folio 52.

Butler, Elizabeth. Will. Made Aug. 13, 1793. Town of Dover. Heirs: dau. Ann Townsend; grandson Charles Townsend; granddaus. Elizabeth & Ann R. Townsend. Exec'x, dau. Ann Townsend. Wits., Andrew Barratt, William Guy. Prob. Sept. 12, 1793. Arch. vol. A7, page 14. Reg. of Wills, Liber N, folio 54.

Nock, Daniel. Will. Made Aug. 26, 1793. Duck Creek Hd. Heirs: bro. Joseph Nock; sister Mary Smith, wife of Joseph Smith; niece Susana Berry, dau. of sister Susana Berry; nephew Thomas Brown, son of sister Sarah Brown. Exec'r, bro. Joseph Nock. Wits., George Cummins, Israel Peterson, Robert Patterson. Prob. Sept. 14, 1793. Arch. vol. A38, page 20 & A29, page 68. Reg. of Wills, Liber N, folio 52. Note:—Arch. vol. A29, page 68 mentions an heir, Sarah Berry.

Howel, William. Admin. of, to Hanah Garrett. Sept. 17, 1793. Reg. of Wills, Liber N, folio 52.

Jones, David. Admin. of, to Mary Alford & William Guy. Sept. 18, 1793. Arch. vol. A27, page 155. Reg. of Wills, Liber N, folio 52.

Morris, William, Jr. Admin. of, to William Morris. Sept. 21, 1793. Arch. vol. A37, page 40. Reg. of Wills, Liber N, folio 52.

Williams, Reynear. Will. Made Aug. 10, 1793. Heirs: wife Penelope; sons Aaron, John, Reynear & Spencer; dau. Sarah Hill, wife of Nathan Hill. Exec'rs, wife Penelope & sons Aaron & John. Wits., Sarah Peterkin, John Hudson, John Ralston. Prob. Sept. 24, 1793. Arch. vol. A55, page 139. Reg. of Wills, Liber N, folio 53.

Edmondson, Thomas. Will. Made Sept. 11, 1793. Heirs: wife Sophia; son John; daus. Sophia Edmondson, Margaret Lee. Exec'rs, wife Sophia & son John. Wits., Thomas Jenkins, William Edmondson. Prob. Sept. 26, 1793. Arch. vol. A16, pages 62-63. Reg. of Wills, Liber N, folio 54. Note:—Will in Archives is fragmentary.

Virden, Peter. Admin. of, to Peter Lowber. Sept. 30, 1793. Arch. vol. A52, pages 101-102. Reg. of Wills, Liber N, folio 55. Note:—Arch. vol. A52, page 101 mentions heirs, Samuel Virden & Elizabeth Young, wife of Robert Young.

Johnson, William. Surveyor. Admin. of, to Nathan Johnson. Oct. 1, 1793. Arch. vol. A27, pages 114-116. Reg. of Wills, Liber N, folio 55. Note:—Arch. vol. A27, page 114 mentions heirs, Nathan, James, Purnell, Priscilla, Nancy & Phebe Johnson & sisters Elizabeth Davis, Sally Brown & Polly Willey (wife of Wm. Willey).

Jordan, William. Will. Made Sept. 24, 1793. Duck Creek [Hd.] Cross Roads. Heirs: wife Rachel; sister Elizabeth Jordan; Elizabeth Spearman, dau. of Simon Vanwinkle; William Green, son of Charles; two sons of Arthur & Hannah Boardly; William Boardly, son of Stephen; Thomas Boardly, son of William; negro Ephraim. Exec'x, wife Rachel. Wits., Benjamin Farrow, Simon Vanwinkle, Charles Green. Prob. Oct. 7, 1793. Arch. vol. A28, pages 48-49. Reg. of Wills, Liber N, folios 55-56.

Manwaring, Elizabeth. Admin. of, to Peter Manwaring. Oct. 7, 1793. Reg. of Wills, Liber N, folio 56.

Ware, William. Pilot. Dover Hd. Admin. of, to Joseph Tygart, D. B. N. Oct. 8, 1793. Arch. vol. A53, page 113. Reg. of Wills, Liber N, folio 56.

Knock, Joseph. Farmer. Duck Creek Hd. Admin. of, to Susannah Knock & Daniel Knock. Oct. 15, 1793. Arch. vol. A29, pages 80-81. Reg. of Wills, Liber N, folio 56.

Meredith, Job. Admin. of, to Lydia Meredith. Oct. 17, 1793. Arch. vol. A34, pages 192-193. Reg. of Wills, Liber N, folio 56. Note:—Arch. vol. A34, page 192 mentions heirs, Lydia, Davis, Peter, Job, Obedi, Henry, Stephen, James, David, Abner & Benjamin Meredith, Rachel Keys (wife of Jno.) & Elizabeth Cooper (wife of Absolum).

Needham, Agatha. Widow. Will. Made Oct. 7, 1793. Little Creek Hd. Heirs: sons Cornelius, Nicholas & William Vanstavern; dau. Elizabeth Wilbank; granddaus. Ann Vanstavern (dau. of Cornelius) & Sarah Maxfield (dau. of Elizabeth Wilbank); grandson Thomas Vantavern (son of Nicholas). Exec'rs, Cornelius & William Vanstavern & Elizabeth Wilbank. Wits., Daniel Cowgill, Clayton Cowgill, Sarah Cowgill. Prob. Oct. 18, 1793. Arch. vol. A37, pages 136-137. Reg. of Wills, Liber N, folio 57.

Anderson, Ezekiel. Will. Made Sept. 11, 1793. Mispillion Hd. Heirs: wife Eliza; children unnamed. Exec'rs, wife Eliza, bro. Major Anderson & Stephen Alston. Wits., Bartholomew Melvin, Hosea Hamilton, Mary Gauslin. Prob. Oct. 22, 1793. Arch. vol. A1, pages 160-162. Reg. of Wills, Liber N, folios 57-58. Note:—Arch. vol. A1, page 161 shows Dr. Wm. McKee, who intermarried with Elizabeth Banning (widow of late John Banning, Esq.).

Taylor, Joseph. Will. Made Sept. 11, 1791. Heirs: daus. Mary, Alice, Sarah, Margaret & Elizabeth; sons Samuel & Charles; grandchildren Elizabeth, Sarah & John, children of son Benjamin Taylor, dec'd. Exec'rs, daus. Mary & Alice. Wits., James Tilton, Charles Hillyard. Prob. Oct. 23, 1793. Arch. vol. A49, pages 206-209. Reg. of Wills, Liber N, folios 58-59. Note:—Dau.-in-law Mary Taylor, widow of son Benjamin, dec'd, is mentioned.

Snow, Silas. Will. Made Oct. 22, 1793. Heirs: sons George, Silas & Joseph Snow, John Snow, alias Jones (son of Susannah Jones, spinster) & James Snow, alias Wallace (son of Elizabeth Wallace, spinster); dau. Phebe Snow. Exec'rs, sons John & James. Wits., James Raymond, Amelia Whaley. Prob. Nov. 6, 1793. Arch. vol. A48, pages 26-29. Reg. of Wills, Liber N, folio 59.

Coxe, John, Jr. Admin. of, to Alice Coxe. Nov. 7, 1793. Reg. of Wills, Liber N, folios 59-60.

Eynon, Stephen. Admin. of, to Ruth Eynon. Nov. 8, 1793. Arch. vol. A16, page 241. Reg. of Wills, Liber N, folio 60.

Miller, Conrad. Blacksmith. Murderkill Hd. Admin. of, to John Miller, son of Henry. Nov. 12, 1793. Arch. vol. A35, pages 65-66. Reg. of Wills, Liber N, folio 60.

Sipple, Martinus. Will. Made Sept. 3, 1793. Duck Creek. Heirs: Rebecca Sipple; friend John Cole; Sarah Sipple. Exec'r, friend John Cole. Wits., James Henry, John Edwards, Samuel Staats. Prob. Nov. 12, 1793. Arch. vol. A46, page 151. Reg. of Wills, Liber N, folio 60.

Miller, Sarah. Widow. Will. Made July 19, 1793. Murtherkill Hd. Heirs: sons Stephen & John Miller; daus. Elizabeth Pierce, Susannah Miller, Mary Goodwin & Martha Miller; grandson John Wood. Exec'r, son John. Wits., Richard Taylor, Abraham Taylor, Thomas Nixon. Prob. Nov. 12, 1793. Arch. vol. A35, page 115. Reg. of Wills, Liber N, folios 60-61.

Smith, Joseph. Blacksmith. Admin. of, to Mary Smith. Nov. 14, 1793. Reg. of Wills, Liber N, folio 61.

White, John. Will. Made Nov. 10, 1793. Town of Dover. Heir: wife Avis. Exec'x, wife Avis. Wits., Stephen Alston, Joseph Harper, Hetty Harper. Prob. Nov. 16, 1793. Arch. vol. A54, pages 120-121. Reg. of Wills, Liber N, folio 61.

Lee, Thomas. Merchant. Will. Made Sept. 8, 1791. Camden, Murderkill Hd. Heirs: wife Margaret; one child unnamed; Sarah Edmondson. Exec'rs, wife Margaret & father-in-law Thomas Edmondson. Wits., Thomas Jenkins, Samuel Howell. Prob. Nov. 22, 1793. Arch. vol. A29, pages 238-241 & vol. A30, pages 1-2. Reg. of Wills, Liber N, folio 62. Note:— Arch. vol. A30, page 2 mentions Margaret Williams (late Margaret Lee), Thomas Lee & Sarah Edmondson.

Walters, William. Admin. of, to Ann Walters. Nov. 23, 1793. Reg. of Wills, Liber N, folio 62.

Smith, Nathaniel. Admin. of to Elsbury Burtt. Nov. 26, 1793. Arch. vol. A47, pages 124-125. Reg. of Wills, Liber N, folio 62. Note:—Arch. vol. A47, page 124 mentions heirs, Mary, Elizabeth, Nancy & Sarah Smith; also shows the acct. later settled by Hadden Smith, D. B. N., C. T. A.

Barber, Francis. Admin. of, to Joseph Barber. Nov. 26, 1793. Reg. of Wills, Liber N, folio 62.

Cloud, John, Sr. Planter. Will. Made Nov. 9, 1793. Heirs: wife Sarah; sons James, John & William; daus. Rachel, Elizabeth, Sarah & Martha. Exec'r, son William. Wits., Jacob Hurlock, Samuel Sharine, Richard Beck. Prob. Nov. 30, 1793. Arch. vol. A9, pages 165-167. Reg. of Wills, Liber N, folio 63. Note:—Arch. vol. A9, page 166 shows Martha Hazel as the wife of Benjamin Hazel.

McCall, Mark. Surveyor. Admin. of, to George McCall. Dec. 2, 1793. Reg. of Wills, Liber N, folio 63.

Goodfellow, Sarah. Admin. of, to George McCall, Esq. Dec. 3, 1793. Reg. of Wills, Liber N, folio 63.

Vincent, Daniel. Admin. of, to Margaret Vincent. Dec. 3, 1793. Reg. of Wills, Liber N, folio 63. Note:—Arch. vol. A52, page 52, mentions heirs, Margarett, Isaac & Cornelia Vincent & Elizabeth Cahall.

Ware, William, Sr. Admin. of, to John Ware, D. B. N. Dec. 5, 1793. Arch. vol. A53, pages 111 & 116-119. Note:—Arch. vol. A53, page 111 mentions heirs, John, Nancy & Betsy Ware, Lydia Tygart, Mary Pearson & Sally Fulcin.

Townsend, Jeremiah. Admin. of, to McKimmey Smack. Dec. 10, 1793. Arch. vol. A51, pages 12-14. Reg. of Wills, Liber N, folios 63-64. Note:—Arch. vol. A51, page 12 mentions heirs, Brickhus, Ebe, Eli, William, Sarah & Nancy Townsend & Polly Stevens (wife of John Stevens).

Cook, Michael. Admin. of, to Robert Kernohan, D. B. N. Dec. 10, 1793. Reg. of Wills, Liber N, folios 56-57.

Steward, Thomas. Admin. of, to Sarah Steward. Dec. 10, 1793. Reg. of Wills, Liber N, folio 64.

Hindsley, Ambrose. Admin. of, to Ann Hindsley. Dec. 13, 1793. Arch. vol. A24, pages 62-64. Reg. of Wills, Liber N, folio 64. Note:—Arch. vol. A24, page 62 mentions heirs, Daniel, Patience, Amos, John, Garrett, Nathan, Hannah, James & Mary Hindsley (alias Scotton); also shows that Anne Hindsley, widow, married George Temple.

Pierce, William. Will. Made Dec. 1, 1793. Heirs: wife Elizabeth; dau. Nancy; John Wood, son of my wife by her former husband. Exec'x, wife Elizabeth. Wits., Jonathan McNatt, George Vanpelt. Prob. Dec. 13, 1793. Arch. vol. A39, pages 158-159 & 161. Reg. of Wills, Liber N, folio 64. Note:—Arch. vol. A39, page 159 shows that Elizabeth Pierce married Joseph Vanpelt & later married Daniel Smith.

Kelly, William. Admin. of, to Rosannah Kelly. Dec. 19, 1793. Arch. vol. A28, pages 111-112. Reg. of Wills, Liber N, folio 64.

Melvin, Solomon. Will. Made Nov. 28, 1793. Heirs: wife [Alifair, from admin. acct.]; dau. Mary; sons George & John; eight younger children unnamed. Exec'x, wife. Wits., Sorden Lister, Andrew Anderson, David Melvin. Prob. Dec. 24, 1793. Arch. vol. A34, pages 168-171. Reg. of Wills, Liber N, folios 64-65. Note:—Arch. vol. A34, page 169 shows that Alifair [Allefare] Melvin married Thomas Barker; also mentions heirs, Joshua, Noble, Brummel, James, Prudence, Rhoda & Aron Melvin & Elinor Ginings.

Dawson, Benjamin. Hatter. Will. Made Sept. 26, 1788. Duck Creek Hd. Heirs: wife unnamed; sons Solomon, Benjamin, William, Isaac & James; daus. Susannah . . . & Deborah Dawson; Sarah Cox, dau. of Susannah. Exec'rs, sons Solomon, William & Isaac. Wits., Thomas Parke, James Morris, Daniel Smith. Prob. Dec. 26, 1793. Arch. vol. A13, page 92. Reg. of Wills, Liber N, folio 65.

Durham, Whittington. Admin. of, to James Morris. Dec. 26, 1793. Arch. vol. A14, page 18. Reg. of Wills, Liber N, folio 66.

Quinault, Sarah. Admin. of, to Elijah Barratt. Dec. 31, 1793. Arch. vol. A42, pages 8-9. Reg. of Wills, Liber N, folio 66.

Caldwell, Sarah. Admin. of, to John Caldwell. Jan. 2, 1794. Reg. of Wills, Liber N, folio 68.

Money, John. Admin. of, to Ann Money. Jan. 8, 1794. Arch. vol. A35, page 230. Reg. of Wills, Liber N, folio 68.

Bellach, James. Esq. Will. Made Jan. 9, 1793. Little Creek Hd. Heirs: wife Elizabeth; sons Thomas Hanson Bellach & John Bellach; dau. Ann. Exec'rs, wife, son Thomas Hanson Bellach, John Patten, Esq. Appraisers, Manlove Emerson & John Patten. Guardians, wife Elizabeth, son Thomas Hanson Bellach, John Patten, Esq. Wits., John Darrach, Nicholas Ridgely. Codicil, same date as will & same heirs. Another codicil dated Oct. 28, 1793 shows exec'x, wife Elizabeth; trustee, John Patten, Esq.; wits., James Sykes, Joseph Miller. Prob. Jan. 8, 1794. Arch. vol. A3, page 201. Reg. of Wills, Liber N, folios 68-72.

Savin, William. Admin. of, to Mary Taylor, D. B. N. Jan. 8, 1794. Arch. vol. A45, page 33.

Bellach, Thomas Hanson. Admin. of, to Elizabeth Bellach. Jan. 9, 1794. Reg. of Wills, Liber N, folio 73.

Nicolls, Susannah. Admin. of, to John Marim. Jan. 13, 1794. Reg. of Wills, Liber N, folio 73.

Mason, Richard. Tailor. Will. Made Jan. 8, 1794. Heirs: sons Thomas & Joseph. Exec'r, Matthew Cox. Guardians, William Kirkly, Matthew Cox. Wits., Wm. Allaband, John Lockwood, David Smith. Prob. Jan. 16, 1794. Arch. vol. A34, pages 5-8. Reg. of Wills, Liber N, folio 74.

Jackson, John. Admin. of, to George Jackson. Jan. 18, 1794. Reg. of Wills, Liber N, folio 74.

Garland, John Chevins. Yeoman. Duck Creek Hd. Admin. of, to Christian Arthur, D. B. N. Jan. 20, 1794. Arch. vol. A18, page 219. Reg. of Wills, Liber N, folio 75.

White, Richard. Will. Made Feb. 27, 1792. Murtherkill Hd. Heirs: sons William & Thomas White; daus. Martha & Lydia White, Sarah & Mary Hatfield, Rachel & Elizabeth Craige. Exec'r, son William. Wits., Thomas Davis, Isaac Davis & James Davis. Prob. Jan. 20, 1794. Arch. vol. A54, pages 140-143. Reg. of Wills, Liber N, folio 75. Note:—Arch. vol. A54, page 141 mentions a Lydia Knotts (late White).

Arthur, William. Admin. of, to Joseph David. Jan. 28, 1794. Reg. of Wills, Liber N, folio 76.

Cole, Rebecca. Widow of Cuthbert Cole. Duck Creek Hd. Admin. of, to Joseph David, D. B. N. Jan. 28, 1794. Reg. of Wills, Liber N, folio 76. Note:—Arch. vol. A9, page 206 mentions a dau. Elizabeth Cole, dec'd.

Jarrad, Mathew. Yeoman. Mispillion Hd. Admin. of, to Benjamin Clark & wife Ruth. Jan. 31, 1794. Arch. vol. A26, page 111. Reg. of Wills, Liber N, folio 76.

Pearce, John. Admin. of, to William Sears. Feb. 3, 1794. Reg. of Wills, Liber N, folio 76.

Spencer, Isaiah. Admin. of, to Mary Spencer. Feb. 6, 1794. Reg. of Wills, Liber N, folio 76.

Barker, Mary. Admin. of, to Joseph Barker. Feb. 13, 1794. Reg. of Wills, Liber N, folio 77.

Alexander, Philip. Admin. of, to John Jamison. Feb. 17, 1794. Reg. of Wills, Liber N, folio 77. Note:—Arch. vol. A1, page 21 mentions heirs, David & Rachel Alexander & Susannah Alexander, minor, dec'd.

Dehorty, John. Will. Made Jan. 21, 1794. Heirs: wife Prudence; son John; daus. Peggy Travers, Mary Dehorty. Exec'x, wife Prudence. Trustees, friends John White, Peter Rich, Solomon Beswick, Thomas Berry, William Whitely. Wits., Wm. Whitely, John Thomas, Richard Words. Prob. Feb. 19, 1794. Arch. vol. A13, page 156. Reg. of Wills, Liber N, folio 78. Note:—Mary Dehorty later married . . . Graham; Matthew Travers was husband of Peggy Travers.

Mason, Elias. Admin. of, to Joseph Mason. Feb. 21, 1794. Arch. vol. A33, pages 226-228. Reg. of Wills, Liber N, folio 79. Note:—Arch. vol. A33, page 226 mentions heirs, Sarah, Joseph, Elias & Elizabeth Mason.

Jackson, Henry. Admin. of, to Patrick Corran. Feb. 21, 1794. Reg. of Wills, Liber N, folio 79.

Harper, William. Farmer. Murderkill Hd. Admin. of, to Joseph Harper, farmer. Feb. 28, 1794. Arch. vol. A22, pages 80 & 82. Reg. of Wills, Liber N, folio 79.

Morris, William. Admin. of, to John Morris. Feb. 28, 1794. Reg. of Wills, Liber N, folio 79.

Numbers, Jane. Will (nunc.). Made Feb. . . ., 1794. Heir: Negro woman Tish. Exec'r, [Randal Blackshere, from admin. acct.]. Wits., Randal Blackshere, Benjamin Denny, William Deshin. Prob. March 1, 1794. Arch. vol. A38, page 72. Reg. of Wills, Liber N, folio 79.

Battell, John French. Admin. of, to James Battell. March 10, 1794. Arch. vol. A3, page 71. Reg. of Wills, Liber N, folio 80.

Battell, Elizabeth. Admin. of, to James Battell, D. B. N. March 10, 1794. Arch. vol. A3, pages 62-63. Reg. of Wills, Liber N, folio 80.

Marley, Abraham. Admin. of, to Michael Bryan. March 10, 1794. Reg. of Wills, Liber N, folio 80.

Battell, French. Admin. of, to James Battell, D. B. N. March 10, 1794. Arch. vol. A3, pages 67-70. Reg. of Wills, Liber N, folio 80. Note:—Arch. vol. A3, page 70 mentions heirs, John F., French, James & Cornelius Battell.

Nicoson, Abraham. Miller. Admin. of, to William Nicoson. March 11, 1794. Reg. of Wills, Liber N, folio 80.

Longfellow, John. Farmer. Will. Made Feb. 8, 1794. Heirs: wife Rosannah; dau. Elizabeth . . .; Jonathan . . ., son of dau. Elizabeth. Exec'x, wife Rosannah. Wits., Henry Carter, James Greenlee. Prob. March 18, 1794. Arch. vol. A31, page 66. Reg. of Wills, Liber N, folio 81.

Wilcuts, David. Minor. Admin. of, to Rachel Wilcuts, guardian. March 19, 1794. Reg. of Wills, Liber N, folio 82.

Belch, Joseph. Yeoman. Duck Creek Hd. Admin. of, to Elizabeth Belch. March 19, 1794. Arch. vol. A3, pages 165-167. Reg. of Wills, Liber N, folio 82. Note:—Arch. vol. A3, page 167 mentions heirs, Joseph, Nathan & Elizabeth Belch, Sarah Calgan, Elizabeth Larwood & Ann Walls.

Blundell, Sarah. Admin. of, to Jonathan Needham, guardian. March 28, 1794. Reg. of Wills, Liber N, folio 82.

Morris, Susannah (formerly Blundell). Admin. of, to Jonathan Needham, guardian. March 28, 1794. Reg. of Wills, Liber N, folio 82.

Hathorne [Harthorne], Ebenezer. Admin. of, to John McCutchin, D. B. N. April 4, 1794. Reg. of Wills, Liber N, folio 82.

Fultz, Elizabeth. Admin. of, to Robert Holliday. April 4, 1794. Reg. of Wills, Liber N, folio 82.

Emerson, Govey. Admin. of, to Manlove Emerson, D. B. N. May 5, 1794. Reg. of Wills, Liber N, folio 82.

Morgan, Thomas. House carpenter. Mispillion Hd. Admin. of, to Elishua Morgan. April 7, 1794. Arch. vol. A36, pages 171-174. Reg. of Wills, Liber N, folio 82. Note:—Arch. vol. A36, pages 171-172 mention heirs, widow Elishua Morgan, Sarah Hilford, Mary Crockett, James, Elizabeth, John, Thomas, Evan & Nancy Morgan.

Talbot, Sarah. Admin. of, to Elishua Morgan. April 7, 1794. Reg. of Wills, Liber N, folio 83.

Davis, Robert. Will. Made Sept. 19, 1786. Mispillion Hd. Heirs: wife Susannah; sons Robert, Mathias, John, William, Nathan & Thomas; granddaus. Mahalah Clifton & Susannah Davis, dau. of son John; grandson Joseph Davis. Exec'rs, wife Susannah & son Thomas. Wits., John Ralston, Abel Killen, Henry Edgin. Prob. April 8, 1794. Arch. vol. A13, page 55. Reg. of Wills, Liber N, folios 83-84.

Waters, William. Admin. of, to Ann Waters. April 9, 1794. Arch. vol. A53, page 161. Reg. of Wills, Liber N, folio 84.

Goforth, George, the elder. Cordwainer. Murderkill Hd. Admin. of, to William Guy. April 11, 1794. Arch. vol. A19, page 91. Reg. of Wills, Liber N, folio 84.

Carter, Daniel. Admin. of, to Thomas Jenkins & Ezekiel Barratt. April 14, 1794. Reg. of Wills, Liber N, folio 84.

Hodgson, Train. Admin. of, to Joseph Hodgson. April 15, 1794. Reg. of Wills, Liber N, folio 84.

Bedwell, Thomas. Will. Made Feb. 23, 1794. Heirs: wife Jemima; sons Thomas, George, James, Preston & Caleb; daus. Sarah Bedwell & Elizabeth Stant; granddau. Easter Stant, dau. of Elizabeth Stant. Exec'rs, wife Jemimah & dau. Sarah Bedwell. Wits., Severson Brown, William Rash & William Powell. Prob. April 17, 1794. Arch. vol. A3, pages 157-158. Reg. of Wills, Liber N, folios 84-85.

Masten, Gilbert. Minor. Mispillion Hd. Admin. of, to Robert Hopkins. April 26, 1794. Arch. vol. A34, page 24. Reg. of Wills, Liber N, folio 85.

Magair, Mary. Admin. of, to John Ferguson. April 29, 1794. Arch. vol. A33, page 67.

Burchinal, Joseph. Admin. of, to Jeremiah Jarrell & wife Elizabeth (late Elizabeth Burchinal). April 29, 1794. Arch. vol. A6, pages 195-198. Note:—Arch. vol. A6, pages 195-196 mention heirs, John, Hannah, Jeremiah, Rebecca, Joseph & Sarah Burchinal & Elizabeth Jarrell.

Harmon, Thomas. Yeoman. Mispillion Hd. Admin. of, to Elizabeth Harmon, widow. May 10, 1794. Arch. vol. A22, page 35. Reg. of Wills, Liber N, folio 86.

Hazell, George. Admin. of, to Benjamin Hazell, next of kin. May 10, 1794. Arch. vol. A23, pages 84-85. Reg. of Wills, Liber N, folio 86.

Miller, John. Son of Chillion. Yeoman. Dover Hd. Admin. of, to Mary Miller & Peter Miller, Jr. May 21, 1794. Arch. vol. A35, pages 80-82 & 85. Reg. of Wills, Liber N, folio 86. Note:—Arch. vol. A35, page 80 mentions heirs, bros. Killen, Peter Jr., & William Miller; sister Dohertha Barber, wife of John Barber; Mary Quillen, wife of John Quillen; nephew Wm. Maffett, son of sister Sarah Maffett, dec'd, (wife of John Maffett, dec'd).

George, Joseph. Admin. of, to Patience George, widow. June 4, 1794. Arch. vol. A19, pages 1-2. Reg. of Wills, Liber N, folio 86. Note:—Arch. vol. A19, page 2 mentions heirs, Rachel Saxton, Margarett, Mary, Newel & John George.

Jones, Ann. Admin. of, to Jacob Jones. June 6, 1794. Reg. of Wills, Liber N, folio 86.

Barber, Joseph. Admin. of, to William McClyment, D. B. N. June 7, 1794. Arch. vol. A2, pages 142-145. Reg. of Wills, Liber N, folio 86. Note:—Arch. vol. A2, page 145 mentions heirs, Sarah Muselmon & Rachel Barber.

Barber, Francis. Admin. of, to William McClyment, D. B. N. June 7, 1794. Arch. vol. A2, pages 123-127. Reg. of Wills, Liber N, folio 86. Note:—Arch. vol. A2, page 127 mentions heirs, Ann Ward (wife of George Ward) & Joseph Barber.

Barns, James. Admin. of, to Nicholas Vandyke. June 13, 1794. Reg. of Wills, Liber N, folio 86.

Parker, John. Mispillion Hd. Admin. of, to Leah Parker & John Houston. June 17, 1794. Reg. of Wills, Liber N, folio 86.

Freeman, William. Admin. of, to Thomas Taylor. June 20, 1794. Reg. of Wills, Liber N, folio 86.

Wilson, Thomas Rodney. Admin. of, to Simon Wilmer Wilson. June 25, 1794. Reg. of Wills, Liber N, folio 86.

Gaskins, William, the younger. Admin. of, to Sarah Gaskins. July 19, 1794. Reg. of Wills, Liber N, folio 86.

White, William. Jones' Hd. Admin. of, to Anna White (widow of Charles White), next of kin. July 25, 1794. Arch. vol. A54, page 174. Reg. of Wills, Liber N, folio 86.

Smith, Robert. Admin. of, to Mary Smith. July 30, 1794. Reg. of Wills, Liber N, folio 110.

Alston, Israel. Admin. of, to Mary Alston & Jonathan Alston. Aug. 5, 1794. Arch. vol. A1, pages 109-110. Reg. of Wills, Liber N, folio 110. Note:—Arch. vol. A1, page 109 mentions heirs, Mary, Sarah, Jonathan, Elizabeth, Asbun, Israel, Unice & Susan Alston & Mary Sharpless.

Lister, William. Will. Made July 26, 1794. Murderkill Hd. Heirs: mother Ann Lister; bro. Levi Lister; sister Mary Quinnally; niece Elizabeth Freeman, dau. of sister Alecy Freeman. Exec'r, bro. Levi. Wits., Joseph Harper, Timothy Lister. Prob. Aug. 18, 1794. Arch. vol. A30, pages 191-192. Reg. of Wills, Liber N, folios 110-111.

Anderson, James. Innkeeper. Murderkill Hd. Admin. of, to Elizabeth Anderson. Aug. 18, 1794. Arch. vol. A1, page 178.

White, William. Admin. of, to George Ward, D. B. N. Aug. 28, 1794. Arch. vol. A54, page 176.

Wize, John Fredrick. Baker. Will. Made Aug. 8, 1794. Duck Creek Hd. Heirs: wife Mary; son-in-law John Lackey; Nancy Standly. Exec'x, wife Mary. Wits., Robert Jamison, Samuel Powell. Prob. Aug. 28, 1794. Arch. vol. A56, page 51. Reg. of Wills, Liber N, folio 111.

Brinckle, Richard. Farmer. Mispillion Hd. Admin. of, to Joseph Huzza, D. B. N. Sept. 2, 1794. Arch. vol. A5, page 205. Reg. of Wills, Liber N, folio 111. Note:—This acct. was unadministered by widow Phebe Brinckley.

Start, Elijah. Admin. of, to Mary Start. Sept. 12, 1794. Arch. vol. A48, pages 172-175. Reg. of Wills, Liber N, folio 111. Note:—Arch. vol. A48, page 172 mentions heirs, Jerusha, Elisha, James & Elizabeth Start; also shows that Mary Start married Levin Clifton.

Snipe, Joseph. Admin. of, to Jonathan Hunn, next of kin. Sept. 16, 1794. Arch. vol. A47, page 229. Reg. of Wills, Liber N, folio 111.

Whitaker, Henry. Will. Made Jan. 22, 1793. Heirs: wife Elizabeth; son James Whitaker; daus. Elizabeth Cox, Lydia, Dorcas & Susannah Meredith; grandsons Jacob Bostick, John, William & Edward Carter & Jacob Meredith; granddaus. Mary Beetle, Elizabeth Pindergrass, Sarah, Ruth & Mary Carter; twins of granddau. Sarah Bostick. Exec'r, son James. Wits., John Cox, Sr., Samuel Kemp, Elizabeth Kemp. Prob. Sept. 25, 1794. Arch. vol. A54, pages 76-77. Reg. of Wills, Liber N, folio 112.

Downham, Isaac. Admin. of, to Eleanor Downham & Elias Jarrald. Sept. 26, 1794. Arch. vol. A14, pages 220-221. Reg. of Wills, Liber N, folio 112. Note:—Arch. vol. A14, page 220 mentions heirs, James, Nancy, Richard, Elizabeth, Sarah, Ruth, Keziah & Mary Downham.

Skewes, James. Admin. of, to John Stewart. Oct. 4, 1794. Reg. of Wills, Liber N, folio 112.

Stewart, Charles. Admin. of, to John Stewart. Oct. 4, 1794. Arch. vol. A48, page 239 & vol. A49, page 94. Reg. of Wills, Liber N, folio 112. Note:—Arch. vol. A48, page 239 shows the acct. later settled by Benjamin Chiffins; also mentions heirs, William Stewart and Rachel Ricketts, wife of Jonathan; a Charles Stewart is shown as the father of Charles Stewart.

Searmon, Joseph. Admin. of, to Elias Shockley. Nov. 3, 1794. Reg. of Wills, Liber N, folio 89.

Rees, Thomas. Duck Creek Hd. Admin. of, to John Rees. Nov. 17, 1794. Arch. vol. A43, page 37. Reg. of Wills, Liber N, folio 88.

Young, David. Blacksmith. Will. Made Aug. 8, 1794. Mispillion Hd. Heirs: wife Clear; son William; daus. Mary, Nancy & Elizabeth Young. Exec'x, wife Clear. Wits., Thomas Joyce, William Thompson, James Kelly. Prob. Nov. 18, 1794. Arch. vol. A56, pages 201-204. Reg. of Wills, Liber N, folio 87. Note:—Arch. vol. A56, page 202 shows that Clear Young, widow, married Nathan Bowman & Nancy Young married Mathew Coverdill.

Tomlinson, Sarah. Will. Made July 25, 1794. Heirs: sons Thomas, James, William & Joseph; daus. Sarah Tomlinson & Mary Frazar; nephew Nehemiah Davis, son of sister Mary Holston. Exec'r, son Thomas. Wits., William Walker, John Parsons,

Ed. Tomlinson. Prob. Nov. 18, 1794. Arch. vol. A50, pages 219-222. Reg. of Wills, Liber N, folios 87-88. Note:—Arch. vol. A50, page 222 shows Sarah Raison as the wife of Philip Raison.

Cain, John. Farmer. Admin. of, to Triphana Cain. Nov. 18, 1794. Arch. vol. A7, pages 68-69. Reg. of Wills, Liber N, folio 88. Note:—Arch. vol. A7, page 68 mentions heirs, Margaret Cain (wife of Thomas Wiatt), Susanna Cain (wife of Elijah Anderson), Lydia Cain (wife of Elijah Sapp), Hastey, Tilda, Ruben & Triphana Cain; page 69 mentions children, Major & John Cane.

Goforth, Peter. Admin. of, to Lydia Goforth & John Goforth. Nov. 18, 1794. Arch. vol. A18, pages 99-100. Reg. of Wills, Liber N, folio 88.

Pratt, Fredirec. Admin. of, to George Pratt & Jemima Pratt. Nov. 18, 1794. Arch. vol. A41, pages 77-78. Reg. of Wills, Liber N, folio 88. Note:—Arch. vol. A41, page 77 shows that Jemima Pratt, widow, later married Thomas Berry; also mentions daus. Polly & Esther Pratt.

Wilson, Nathan. Admin. of, to Margaret Wilson & William Green. Nov. 18, 1794. Arch. vol. A55, page 240. Reg. of Wills, Liber N, folio 88.

Starling, John. Admin. of, to Rebecah Starling & Jacob Stout, Jr. Nov. 18, 1794. Arch. vol. A48, pages 163-165. Reg. of Wills, Liber N, folio 88. Note:—Arch. vol. A48, page 163 shows that Rebecah Starling married Robert Hill; also mentions heirs, Mary & James Starling.

Moore, Margaret. Admin. of, to James Sutten. Nov. 18, 1794. Arch. vol. A36, pages 68-69. Reg. of Wills, Liber N, folio 89. Note:—Arch. vol. A36, page 68 mentions heirs, Elizabeth Sutten (wife of James Sutten), heirs of David Young, Mary Hindsley (wife of Solomon Hindsley) & Anne Hoofacre (wife of Henry Hoofacre).

Hilyard, John. Admin. of, to Joseph Farrow. Dec. 2, 1794. Reg. of Wills, Liber N, folio 89.

Killen, Mark. Admin. of, to Esther Killen. Dec. 3, 1794. Reg. of Wills, Liber N, folio 89.

Noel, Edward. Admin. of, to Sidney Noel. Dec. 3, 1794. Reg. of Wills, Liber N, folio 89.

Skiner, William. Admin. of, to Rebecca Skiner. Dec. 4, 1794. Reg. of Wills, Liber N, folio 89.

Lowber, Peter, Sr. Will. Made April 2, 1794. Murderkill Hd. Heirs: son Daniel; daus. Catharine Duhadaway & Eunity Gilder; granddau. Catharine Cooper (dau. of Peter Lowber, dec'd); grandsons Benjamin, Peter & John Catron (sons of Benjamin Catron, Esq., dec'd), Jacob Duhadaway (son of Catharine), Peter Lowber (son of Daniel), John Lowber (son of Mathew, dec'd); dau.-in-law Mary Lowber (wife of Daniel); son-in-law John Gilder; John & Sarah Hatfield (children of Wm. Hatfield); William & Peter Berry (sons of Eunity Gilder). Exec'r, son Daniel. Wits., William Skinner, James Shaw, Joseph Flood. Prob. Dec. 4, 1794. Arch. vol. A31, pages 139-142. Reg. of Wills, Liber N, folios 90-93.

Manwaring, Richard. Will. Made Feb. 9, 1793. Heirs: wife Susanah; sons Charles, Thomas & Richard; daus. Hannah Street, Sarah Guessford, Margaret Emory, Ann Davis & Elizabeth Davis. Exec'rs, wife Susannah & friend William Green. Wits., Thomas Jackson, Robert Pippen, William Powell. Prob. Dec. 5, 1794. Arch. vol. A33, pages 166 & 145-147. Reg. of Wills, Liber N, folios 89-90.

Mansfield, Edward. Admin. of, to James Sykes. Dec. 5, 1794. Reg. of Wills, Liber N, folio 95.

Smith, Daniel, Sr. Farmer. Will. Made Aug. 12, 1794. Mispillion Hd. Heirs: wife Mary; sons Thomas, William, Ralph & Daniel, Jr.; daus. Mary, Anna & Martha; granddau. Esther Barker; grandson William Bostick. Exec'rs, wife Mary & son Thomas. Wits., Thomas Williams, Daniel Cardeen & James Williams. Prob. Dec. 9, 1794. Arch. vol. A47, pages 14-16. Reg. of Wills, Liber N, folios 93-94. Note:—Arch. vol. A47, page 15 shows Martha Herrington as the wife of Isaac Herrington, Anna White as the wife of William White, & Esther Barker as the wife of Thomas Barker.

Draper, Lemuel. Admin. of, to Ann Draper. Dec. 10, 1794. Arch. vol. A15, pages 60-61. Reg. of Wills, Liber N, folio 95. Note:—Arch. vol. A15, page 60 mentions heirs, Unica, Nehemiah, John, William, Nancy, Samuel [Lemuel], Kattran & Eliza Draper.

Harrington, Samuel. Admin. of, to Thomas Sipple, guardian. Dec. 10, 1794. Reg. of Wills, Liber N, folio 95.

Lowber, Peter. Admin. of, to Daniel Lowber. Dec. 11, 1794. Reg. of Wills, Liber N, folio 95.

Ennalls, Joseph. Will. Made May 19, 1793. Heirs: son Granbey Brookes; daus. Rachel, Linda & Delia Brookes. Exec'r, son Granbey. Wits., Thomas White, Leavin Smith, John Morgan. Prob. Dec. 16, 1794. Arch. vol. A16, page 117. Reg. of Wills, Liber N, folios 94-95.

Vickery, Thomas. Admin. of, to John Vickery. Dec. 17, 1794. Arch. vol. A52, pages 43-45. Reg. of Wills, Liber N, folio 96. Note:—Arch. vol. A52, page 43 shows that Thomas Vickery married Elizabeth Mileham.

Anderson, Elizabeth. Widow. Murderkill. Admin. of, to Garey Leverton. Dec. 27, 1794. Arch. vol. A1, page 159. Reg. of Wills, Liber N, folio 96.

Massey, Joshua. Admin. of, to Feby Massey. Dec. 29, 1794. Reg. of Wills, Liber N, folio 96. Note:—Arch. vol. A34, page 18 shows that Pheby Massey later married . . . Johnston.

Whitel, William. Will (copy). Made Dec. 26, 1794. Heirs: sister Catharine McGinnis (wife of Daniel McGinnis); Lucrecia Needles; Uscelia Needles; Hannah Davis; Thomas, Daniel & Hugh Mullen (sons of sister Catharine McGinnis). Exec'r, friend Abraham Redgrave. Wits., Wm. McKenney, James Lenox, Elizabeth Berryman. Prob. Jan. 3, 1795. Arch. vol. A54, pages 178 & 204. Reg. of Wills, Liber N, folio 98.

Fisher, John. Admin. of, to Sarah Fisher & William Fisher. Jan. 3, 1795. Arch. vol. A56, page 231. Reg. of Wills, Liber N, folio 96.

Townsend, William. Admin. of, to Charles Townsend. Jan. 7, 1795. Arch. vol. A51, page 47. Reg. of Wills, Liber N, folio 96.

Lewis, William. Yeoman. Duck Creek Hd. Admin. of, to Robert Denney. Jan. 7, 1795. Arch. vol. A30, pages 163-164. Reg. of Wills, Liber N, folio 97.

Durborough, Rebecca. Admin. of, to John Ringold. Jan. 7, 1795. Arch. vol. A15, pages 172-173. Reg. of Wills, Liber N, folio 97.

Cooper, George, Sr. Will. Made July 31, 1787. Heirs: wife [Elizabeth, from admin. acct.]; sons John & George, Jr.; dau. Deborah Cubbage. Exec'rs, wife & son John. Wits., Vinson Pinkine, Thomas Emory, Thomas Emory, Arter Emory. Prob. Jan. 7, 1795. Arch. vol. A10, pages 187-189. Reg. of Wills, Liber N, folios 106-107. Note:—Arch. vol. A10, page 189 shows Deborah Cubbage as the wife of George Cubbage; page 188 shows that Elizabeth Cooper, widow, was previously the widow of Philemon Cubbage.

Hardcastle, Peter. Will. Made Feb. 1, 1794. Murderkill Hd. Heirs: wife Elizabeth; nephew Philip Hardcastle; Charlott Hinson. Exec'rs, wife Elizabeth & friend Andrew Barratt. Wits., William Gray, Elizabeth Gray. Prob. Jan. 8, 1795. Arch. vol. A21, pages 231 & 233. Reg. of Wills, Liber N, folio 99.

Latcham, Joshua. Mispillion. Admin. of, to Cornelia Latcham. Jan. 8, 1795. Arch. vol. A29, page 129. Note:—Reg. of Wills, Liber N, folio 97 shows this name as Joseph Latchamp.

Bostick, James. Admin. of, to Sarah Bostick & Major Bostick. Jan. 8, 1795. Arch. vol. A4, pages 261-262. Reg. of Wills, Liber N, folio 97. Note:—Arch. vol. A4, page 262 mentions heirs, Sarah Bostick (widow), Jean, Priscilla, John, Lydia, Sarah, James & Major Bostick, Jacob Bostick (son of Noah, dec'd) & Ezekiah Vickory, son of Elizabeth, dec'd, (wife of John Vickory).

Barratt, Roger. Admin. of, to Meriam Blackshere, née Barratt. Jan. 8, 1795. Reg. of Wills, Liber N, folio 97.

Hanson, Samuel. Will. Made Jan. 5, 1791. Dover Hd. Heirs: wife Sarah; sons Timothy & Samuel; dau. Susannah Hunn (wife of Jonathan Hunn & widow of Isaac Cox, dec'd); grandsons James Cox, Samuel & Thomas Hanson (sons of son Timothy), Timothy Hanson (son of Samuel Hanson); dau.-in-law Lydia Hanson (wife of Samuel). Exec'rs, wife Sarah & friends James Bellach & Nicholas Ridgely. Wits., George Dixon, Jestinh Needham. Codicil, same date. Wit., Absolum Stradley. Another codicil, March 24, 1794. Exec'r, Daniel Cowgill. Wits., Jos. Miller & Edw. Miller. Prob. Jan. 9, 1795. Arch. vol. A21, pages 210-213. Reg. of Wills, Liber N, folios 99-102.

Maxwell, Ann. Will. Made Oct. 28, 1794. Duck Creek Hd. Heir: dau. Priscilla. Exec'x, dau. Priscilla. Wits., Edward Rees, Catherine Brooks, Robert Rees. Prob. Jan. 9, 1795. Arch. vol. A34, pages 77-78. Reg. of Wills, Liber N, folio 103. Note:—Arch. vol. A34, page 78 shows Priscilla as the wife of Robert Rees.

Gordon, Joshua. Will. Made Dec. 27, 1794. St. Jones' Hd. Heirs: son Samuel; daus. Sarah Gordon & Elizabeth Brinckly (wife of Dr. John Brinckly); Andrew Barratt; Nicholas Ridgely. Exec'rs, Andrew Barratt & Nicholas Ridgely. Guardians, Andrew Barratt & Nicholas Ridgely. Wits., Benjamin Coombe, Jr., Samuel Coombe. Codicil, same date, mentions dau. Sarah Pleasonton. Exec'rs, friend Andrew Barratt & son Samuel. Prob. Jan. 10, 1795. Arch. vol. A19, pages 166-167 & 169. Reg. of Wills, Liber N, folios 103-105.

Anderson, Andrew. Admin. of, to Rachel Anderson. Jan. 10, 1795. Reg. of Wills, Liber N, folio 97.

Beauchamp, Isaac. Admin. of, to Nathaniel Smithers, guardian. Jan. 15, 1795. Reg. of Wills, Liber N, folio 107.

Alston, Thomas. Will. Made Nov. 18, 1794. Heirs: uncle Joab Alston; bro. Daniel Rees; Israel & Jonathan Wilson (sons of William Wilson); Jonathan Alston (son of Israel). Exec'r, uncle Joab Alston. Wits., John Lamb, Rosa Lamb, Thomas Maslin, Jr. Prob. Jan. 15, 1795. Arch. vol. A1, pages 124-125. Reg. of Wills, Liber N, folio 119.

Beauchamp, Marcy. Admin. of, to Nathaniel Smithers, guardian. Jan. 15, 1795. Reg. of Wills, Liber N, folio 107.

Beauchamp, John. Admin. of, to Marcy Beauchamp, guardian. Jan. 15, 1795. Reg. of Wills, Liber N, folio 107.

Beauchamp, David. Admin. of, to Marcy Beauchamp, guardian. Jan. 15, 1795. Reg. of Wills, Liber N, folios 107-108.

Wilcuts, Caleb. Admin. of, to Nancy Wilcuts. Jan. 31, 1795. Arch. vol. A54, page 226. Reg. of Wills, Liber N, folio 108.

Many, Francis. Admin. of, to John Vining, Esq. Feb. 3, 1795. Reg. of Wills, Liber N, folio 108.

Sapp, James. Admin. of, to Rebeckah Sapp. Feb. 4, 1795. Arch. vol. A44, pages 231-232. Reg. of Wills, Liber N, folio 108. Note:—Arch. vol. A44, page 231 mentions heirs, widow Rebecca & children James, Luke, Unity, Peter & Arminta Sapp.

Alleband, Thomas. Admin. of, to William Alleband. Feb. 4, 1795. Arch. vol. A1, page 41. Reg. of Wills, Liber N, folio 108.

Griffin, Samuel. Will. Made Jan. 9, 1795. Duck Creek Hd. Heirs: wife Mary; sons John, Thomas & Isaac; daus. Ann, Esther & Mary. Exec'rs, wife Mary & son John. Wits., James Jones, Joseph Meridith. Prob. Feb. 4, 1795. Arch. vol. A20, pages 227-229 & vol. A21, pages 4-5. Reg. of Wills, Liber N, folios 108-109.

Thomas, Sarah. Will. [N. d.]. Heirs: son Daniel; bros. & sisters unnamed. Exec'r, friend Thomas Pickering. Wits., John Buck, Thomas Weyott, Thomas Pickering. Prob. Feb. 4, 1795. Arch. vol. A50, pages 66-67. Reg. of Wills, Liber N, folio 109.

Curtis, John. Admin. of, to George Walton, D. B. N. Feb. 4, 1795. Reg. of Wills, Liber N, folio 110. Note:—Arch. vol. A12, page 160 mentions heirs, widow Comfort Curtis & children Elizabeth, William, Sarah & Thomas Curtis & Mary Williams (wife of Nathan Williams).

Mileham, Samuel. Farmer. Mispillion Hd. Admin. of, to John Vickery, D. B. N. Feb. 4, 1795. Arch. vol. A35, pages 58-59. Reg. of Wills, Liber N, folio 110. Note:—Arch. vol. A35, page 59 mentions Elizabeth Vickery, the late Elizabeth Mileham (wife of Thomas Vickery).

Minors, Robert. Will. Made July 1, 1791. Heirs: wife Mary; son Robert; daus. Ann & Love; two daus. unnamed; granddau. Priscilla Beswick. Exec'x, wife Mary. Wits., William Brinckle, Sarah Demes, Isaac Templin. Prob. Feb. 4, 1795. Arch. vol. A35, pages 161-162 & 166. Reg. of Wills, Liber N, folio 110. Note:—Arch. vol. A35, page 162 mentions heirs, Sally Hill, Lovey Polk & Nancy & Polly Beswick.

McGifford, John. Admin. of, to George Crammer. Feb. 5, 1795. Arch. vol. A32, pages 188-189. Reg. of Wills, Liber N, folio 110. Note:—Arch. vol. A32, page 188 mentions heirs, widow Mary McGifford & dau. Catherine Crammer.

Keith, Thomas. Little Creek Hd. Admin. of, to Ann Keith, widow, & Andrew Naudine. Feb. 5, 1795. Arch. vol. A28, pages 102 & 104. Reg. of Wills, Liber N, folio 110. Note:—Arch. vol. A28, page 104 mentions Sarah Knotts, the late Sarah Potter (wife of William Knotts).

Taylor, John. Mispillion Hd. Admin. of, to Nancy Taylor. Feb. 5, 1795. Arch. vol. A49, pages 201-202. Reg. of Wills, Liber N, folio 110. Note:—Arch. vol. A49, page 201 mentions heirs, Keziah, John, Elizabeth & Benjamin Taylor, Mary Masten (wife of John Masten), Nancy Quigley (wife of James Quigley) & Nancy Parsons (wife of Tumlinson Parsons).

Reed, James. Admin. of, to Mary Ann Reed, widow. Feb. 11, 1795. Reg. of Wills, Liber N, folio 110.

Roach, John. Yeoman. Little Creek Hd. Admin. of, to Joseph David & James Jones. March 3, 1795. Arch. vol. A44, pages 16-17. Reg. of Wills, Liber N, folio 113.

Alston, Stephen. Town of Dover. Admin. of, to Sarah Alston, widow. March 4, 1795. Arch. vol. A1, pages 118-119. Reg. of Wills, Liber N, folio 113.

Edenfield, John. Admin. of, to Rachel Edenfield, widow. March 5, 1795. Arch. vol. A16, pages 18 & 21. Reg. of Wills, Liber N, folio 113. Note:—Arch. vol. A16, page 18 shows that Rachel Edenfield married Jonathan McNatt.

Lewis, David. Farmer. Will. Made Jan. 27, 1795. Murderkill Hd. Heirs: wife Sarah; son-in-law John Sipple; Garratt & Sarah Sipple, children of son-in-law John Sipple; Elizabeth, Nancy, Caleb & James (children of son-in-law Thomas Sipple); nephew Jacob Lewis, son of bro. Daniel; Nathaniel Smithers; John Mott, son of Seaman Mott; Sampson (Negro). Exec'rs, wife Sarah & son-in-law Thomas Sipple. Wits., David Beauchamp, Patience Walton, Marcy Smithers. Prob. March 5, 1795. Arch. vol. A30, pages 68-71. Reg. of Wills, Liber N, folios 113-114. Note:—Arch. vol. A30, page 70 shows that Nancy Sipple married John Spencer.

Pearce, Jacob. Admin. of, to William Pearce, Jr., next of kin. March 5, 1795. Arch. vol. A39, page 152. Reg. of Wills, Liber N, folio 114.

Fleming, Robert. Will. Made June 9, 1794. Heirs: wife Margaret; sons James & Jacob; daus. Elizabeth & Nancy. Exec'rs, sons James & Jacob. Wits., John King, Robert King, Thomas Cordray. Prob. March 9, 1795. Arch. vol. A17, pages 198-200. Reg. of Wills, Liber N, folios 113-114.

Jump, Levin. Admin. of, to Nancy Jump, widow. March 10, 1795. Arch. vol. A28, pages 71-74. Reg. of Wills, Liber N, folio 115. Note:—Arch. vol. A28, page 73 mentions heirs, Sarah & William Jump, Elizabeth Bryant & Margarett Latchamp; also shows Nancy Jump as wife of Robert Hilford.

Dixon, Andrew. Yeoman. Will (nunc.). Made Feb. 22, 1795. Duck Creek Hd. Heirs: Thomas Reed; Phebe . . . Exec'r, Thomas Reed. Wits., George Hinds & James Pearson. Prob. March 10, 1795. Arch. vol. A14, page 142. Reg. of Wills, Liber N, folio 115.

White, Thomas. Will. [N. d.]. Heirs: wife Margaret; son Samuel; daus. Anna White, Sarah Cook & Margaret Nutter Polk. Exec'rs, wife Margaret & son Samuel. Wits., Samuel White, Jr., Thomas Eagle, Edw. White. Prob. March 11, 1795. Arch. vol. A54, pages 166-167. Reg. of Wills, Liber N, folios 115-117.

Pierce, Jean. Admin. of, to Samuel McBride, next of kin. March 16, 1795. Arch. vol. A40, pages 71-72. Reg. of Wills, Liber N, folio 117. Note:—Arch. vol. A40, page 71 mentions Jane Pierce (late Jane Powell) & William Powell (minor son of John Powell); also shows Jean Pierce as one of the daus. of Morris McBride.

Irons, Mark. Admin. of, to Purnal Lofland, D. B. N. March 21, 1795. Arch. vol. A25, pages 219-220. Reg. of Wills, Liber N, folio 117. Note:—Arch. vol. A25, page 219 mentions heirs, Timothy & Susannah Irons.

Calloway, Sarah. Widow of Peter Callaway. Mispillion Hd. Admin. of, to John Calloway & William Calloway. March 21, 1795. Arch. vol. A7, pages 160-161. Reg. of Wills, Liber N, folio 117. Note:—Arch. vol. A7, page 160 mentions heirs, John, William, Sula, Lammy, Sarah, Taner & Curtis Calloway.

Soper, Robert. Admin. of, to Elizabeth Soper, widow, D. B. N. March 23, 1795. Arch. vol. A48, page 32. Reg. of Wills, Liber N, folio 117.

Ayres, Simon. Farmer. Duck Creek Hd. Admin. of, to Mary Ayres, widow. March 24, 1795. Arch. vol. A2, pages 42-44. Reg. of Wills, Liber N, folio 117. Note:—Arch. vol. A2, page 43 mentions heirs, James & William Ayres; page 42 shows Susannah Ayres as wife of Daniel Ford.

Dillen, Nehemiah. Admin. of, to Elizabeth Dillen, widow. March 26, 1795. Reg. of Wills, Liber N, folio 117.

Butcher, Selah. Admin. of, to Thomas Butcher, next of kin. March 26, 1795. Reg. of Wills, Liber N, folio 117.

Holliday, Samuel. Will. Made June 4, 1794. Duck Creek Hd. Heirs: sister Susannah Blackiston (wife of Ebenezer Blackiston); half-bro. Joseph Rowland; Susannah Redgrave (dau. of Abraham Redgrave & wife Ann); Elizer Blackiston (dau. of Ebenezer Blackiston & wife Susannah); Cato Crosby; Elizabeth Benn; Mary & Elizabeth Ruth. Exec'rs, Ebenezer Blackiston, Jr., & Abraham Redgrave. Wits., Benj. Benn, John Cole, Moses Tennant. Prob. March 26, 1795. Arch. vol. A24, pages 209 & 212-216. Reg. of Wills, Liber N, folios 117-118.

Whitacre, Elizabeth. Admin. of, to Jonathan Meredith, next of kin. March 30, 1795. Reg. of Wills, Liber N, folio 118.

Pleasanton, David. A minor. Admin. of, to John Pleasonton, D. B. N. March 31, 1795. Reg. of Wills, Liber N, folio 118.

Pleasonton, Letitia. A minor. Admin. of, to John Pleasonton, D. B. N. March 31, 1795. Reg. of Wills, Liber N, folio 118.

Pleasonton, Rachel. A minor. Admin. of, to John Pleasonton, D. B. N. March 31, 1795. Reg. of Wills, Liber N, folio 118.

Bowman, William. Farmer. Will. Made March 6, 1795. Mispillion Hd. Heirs: wife Mary; sons Henry, William & John; daus. Ann, Amelia & Priscilla Bowman, Sarah New, Patience Dewees & Mary Meridith. Exec'rs, wife Mary & son William. Wits., William Adams, Nathan Bowman, Mary Jester. Prob. March 31, 1795. Arch. vol. A5, pages 96-99. Reg. of Wills, Liber N, folios 118-119.

Gordon, Coe. Admin. of, to Jabez Caldwell, D. B. N. April 3, 1795. Reg. of Wills, Liber N, folio 119. Note:—This admin. was granted to Jabez Caldwell in right of his wife Sidney, dau. of Sarah Gordon, the late exec'x of Coe Gordon.

Coulter, William. Admin. of, to Nancy Coulter, widow. April 6, 1795. Arch. vol. A11, page 249. Reg. of Wills, Liber N, folio 119.

Pearson, Mary. Admin. of, to John Denny. April 9, 1795. Arch. vol. A39, page 175. Reg. of Wills, Liber N, folio 120.

Farlow, John. Yeoman. Will. Made Feb. 18, 1795. Duck Creek Hd. Heirs: wife Sarah; sons Daniel, Jesse, William, John, George & Elijah Tindall Farlow; daus. Leah & Sarah. Exec'rs, wife Sarah & son Jesse. Wits., James Stevenson, John Cahoon. Prob. April 9, 1795. Arch. vol. A17, pages 7-9. Reg. of Wills, Liber N, folio 120.

Meredith, Joseph. Admin. of, to William Meredith, next of kin. April 14, 1795. Reg. of Wills, Liber N, folio 121.

Needles, Thomas. Admin. of, to William Needles, next of kin, D. B. N. April 27, 1795. Reg. of Wills, Liber N, folio 121. Note:—Arch. vol. A37, pages 171-172 mention heirs, George, John, Anna, Philemon, Hannah, Cubbage, Andrew & William Needles, Mary & Nancy Clymer & Sarah Dehorty (wife of Absolam Dehorty) & Sarah Needles (widow).

Needles, Sarah. Widow. Admin. of, to George Needles, next of kin. April 27, 1795. Arch. vol. A37, pages 167-169. Reg. of Wills, Liber N, folio 121. Note:—Arch. vol. A37, page 167 mentions heirs, Mary & Nancy Clammer, Sarah Dehorty, George, John, Anna, Philemon, Hannah, Cubbage & Andrew Needles.

Stout, Jacob, Sr. Yeoman. Will. Made March 2, 1795. Little Creek Hd. Heir: son Benjamin. Exec'r, son Benjamin. Wits., Risdon Bishop, James Tilton, Jr., Nicholas Clark. Prob. April 30, 1795. Arch. vol. A49, page 44. Reg. of Wills, Liber N, folio 121.

Vansant, Jean. Admin. of, to John Turner & wife Rachel. March 4, 1795. Reg. of Wills, Liber N, folio 121.

Ayres, James. Admin. of, to William Taylor, D. B. N. May 5, 1795. Reg. of Wills, Liber N, folio 121.

Carman, James. Admin. of, to Elias Shockley. May 6, 1794. Arch. vol. A7, page 222. Reg. of Wills, Liber N, folio 121.

Ayres, James. Admin. of, to Mary Ayres, D. B. N., (in lieu of Simon Ayres). May 10, 1795. Arch. vol. A2, page 39.

Crockett, Jonathan. Admin. of, to Sarah Crockett, widow. May 11, 1795. Arch. vol. A12, page 6. Reg. of Wills, Liber N, folio 121. Note:—Sarah Crockett later married William Numbers.

Jump, Solomon. Admin. of, to Sarah Jump, widow. May 15, 1795. Reg. of Wills, Liber N, folio 121. Note:—Arch. vol. A28, page 76 mentions heirs, Mary Keets (wife of William), John, Isaac & William Jump; heirs of Benjamin & Elijah Jump & Nancy Sheppard; also shows that Sarah Jump married Curtis Marker.

Clemens, Edward. Will. Made April 2, 1795. Duck Creek Hd. Heirs: wife Elizabeth; son Thomas; daus. Mary, Elizabeth & Catherine; mother unnamed. Exec'x, wife Elizabeth. Wits., Mary Hillerd, Mary Wilson, John Stewart. Prob. May 15, 1795. Arch. vol. A9, pages 128-130. Reg. of Wills, Liber N, folio 122. Note:—Arch. vol. A9, page 130 shows that Elizabeth, widow, later married John Hill.

Willoughby [Willoby], Job. Admin. of, to Asa Willoughby [Willoby], next of kin. May 18, 1795. Arch. vol. A55, page 187. Reg. of Wills, Liber N, folio 122.

Caldwell, Train. Admin. of, to Warner Mifflin. May 25, 1795. Arch. vol. A7, page 135. Reg. of Wills, Liber N, folio 122.

Meredith, William. Captain. Admin. of, to Edmond Hopkins. May 26, 1795. Arch. vol. A34, pages 222-223. Reg. of Wills, Liber N, folio 122.

Stedham, Thomas. Farmer. Murderkill. Admin. of, to Anne Stedham, widow. June 8, 1795. Arch. vol. A48, pages 193-194. Reg. of Wills, Liber N, folio 122. Note:—Arch. vol. A48, page 193 mentions heirs, children Emory, Anne, Polly, Charles & George Stedham & widow Anne Stedham.

Lewis, Sarah. Widow of David Lewis. Will. Made March 16, 1795. Murderkill Hd. Heirs: sons John, Caleb & Thomas Sipple; daus. Elizabeth Edmonds & Mary Dehorty; granddau. Mary Edmonds; Nancy Hudson (dau. of Anthony Boyer's wife). Exec'r, son Thomas. Wits., Isaac Harrington, Sarah Jester & Nathaniel Smithers. Prob. June 8, 1795. Arch. vol. A30, pages 138-140. Reg. of Wills, Liber N, folio 122.

Hutchins, Thomas. Admin. of, to Martha Hutchins, widow. June 11, 1795. Reg. of Wills, Liber N, folio 123. Note:—Arch. vol. A25, page 194 mentions George Gildersleeve as adm'r.

Davis, Susannah. Widow. Admin. of, to Matthias Davis, next of kin. June 13, 1795. Arch. vol. A13, pages 65-66. Reg. of Wills, Liber N, folio 123. Note:—Arch. vol. A13, page 65 mentions heirs, Thomas, Nathan, William, John, Mathias & Robert Davis & Mary Clifton (wife of Thomas Clifton).

Shahan [Shehorn], David, Sr. Admin. of, to Susanna Shehorn, widow. June 15, 1795. Arch. vol. A45, pages 156-157. Reg. of Wills, Liber N, folio 123. Note:—Arch. vol. A45, page 157 mentions heirs, John, Jonathan, Joshua, Eleanor & heirs of David Shahan, Jr.; Sidney Wallace, wife of James Wallace; Mary Moore, wife of George Moore.

Esteel, William. Admin. of, to Mary Esteel, widow. June 17, 1795. Reg. of Wills, Liber N, folio 123.

Smith, Thomas. Will. Made April 5, 1795. Heirs: wife Mary; sons Thomas, William & David Melvil Smith; dau. Frances Wroten; heirs of daus. Mary Ross, Ann Layton & Sarah Dawson, all dec'd. Exec'x, wife Mary. Wits., Olive Jump, Thomas Saulsbury, Nancy Brown. Prob. June 17, 1795. Arch. vol. A47, page 181. Reg. of Wills, Liber N, folios 123-124.

Burrows, James. Farmer. Duck Creek Hd. Admin. of, to Naomi Burrows, widow. June 18, 1795. Arch. vol. A6, pages 213-214. Reg. of Wills, Liber N, folio 123. Note:—Arch. vol. A6, page 214 shows that Naomi Burrows married George Kearsey; also mentions a son William Burrows.

Smith, Daniel. Admin. of, to Eleanor Jenkins. June 19, 1795. Reg. of Wills, Liber N, folio 124.

Smith, Daniel. Renunciation of Ezekiel Smith. June 19, 1795. Reg. of Wills, Liber N, folio 124.

Lemar, Henry. Admin. of, to Eleanor Lemar, widow, & George Soward. June 20, 1795. Arch. vol. A30, page 12. Reg. of Wills, Liber N, folio 124.

Hartshorne, John. Will. Made June 10, 1795. Heirs: wife [Mary, from admin. acct.]; son George. Exec'r, George Walton. Wits., Edward Miller, John Patten, Levi Lister. Codicil, June 11, 1795. Prob. July 8, 1795. Arch. vol. A22, pages 208-210. Reg. of Wills, Liber N, folios 124-125. Note:—Arch. vol. A22, page 210 shows that Mary Hartshorne, the widow, later married Daniel Walker.

Rolinson, Samuel. Admin. of, to Alexander Hamilton. July 13, 1795. Reg. of Wills, Liber N, folio 125.

Potter, John. Admin. of, to Henry Potter. July 20, 1795. Reg. of Wills, Liber N, folio 125.

Cain, Francis. Yeoman. Will. Made June 2, 1795. Murderkill Hd. Heirs: wife Mary; granddau. Annastaticy Plummer; daus. Miriam Plummer & Sarah Cain; wife's niece Ann Chance (wife of Aaron Chance & dau. of Sarah Cook, dec'd). Exec'rs, wife Mary & Matthias Clifton. Wits., Samuel Craig, Samuel Willoughby, William Smith. Prob. July 21, 1795. Arch. vol. A7, pages 63-65. Reg. of Wills, Liber N, folios 125-126.

Meredith, Jacob. Yeoman. Duck Creek Hd. Admin. of, to Martha Meredith. July 27, 1795. Arch. vol. A34, pages 188-189. Reg. of Wills, Liber N, folio 126. Note:—Arch. vol. A34, page 189 shows that Martha Meredith later married Nathan Bradley; also mentions heirs, Mary & Lydia Meredith.

Greer, John, Jr. Admin. of, to Mark Greer. July 28, 1795. Arch. vol. A20, pages 170-171. Reg. of Wills, Liber N, folio 126. Note:—Arch. vol. A20, page 170 mentions heirs, Mark Greer, Sarah Maxwell & Mary & Rachel Chambers.

Lowber, Mathew. Admin. of, to Peter Lowber. July 30, 1795. Arch. vol. A31, pages 127-128. Reg. of Wills, Liber M, folio 126. Note:—Arch. vol. A31, page 127 mentions heirs, William & Peter Lowber, Agnis Jackson (wife of Jonathan Jackson) & Elizabeth Jackson (wife of . . . Jackson).

Pleasonton, Deborah. Minor dau. of Nathaniel. Admin. of, to . . .C. Aug. 1, 1795. Arch. vol. A40, page 104.

Derham, Thomas. Admin. of, to Thomas Hughes. Aug. 10, 1795. Arch. vol. A15, page 195. Reg. of Wills, Liber N, folio 126. Note:—Arch. vol. A14, page 17 mentions heirs, Mary, Jemima, Sarah, Whittenton & Thomas Derram. Arch. vol. A15, page 195 shows that Thomas Hughes married Mary Derham.

Cary, John. Admin. of, to Rachel Cary. Aug. 10, 1795. Arch. vol. A7, page 215. Reg. of Wills, Liber N, folio 126.

Lockwood, Armwell, Jr. Tax collector. Murderkill Hd. Admin. of, to Armwell Lockwood, Sr. Aug. 11, 1795. Arch. vol. A30, pages 216-218. Reg. of Wills, Liber N, folio 126. Note:— Arch. vol. A30, page 216 mentions heirs, Thomas, Isaac, Levy, John, Unity, Gartery & Margarett Lockwood & Mary Lewis.

Sipple, Elijah. Admin. of, to John Wood, D. B. N. Aug. 11, 1795. Arch. vol. A46, pages 124 & 127. Reg. of Wills, Liber N, folio 126.

Anderson, Joseph. Admin. of, to Mary Griffith. Aug. 19, 1795. Reg. of Wills, Liber N, folio 126.

Bishop, Reese. Will. Made May 20, 1795. Heirs: bro. Risdon Bishop; unborn son of bro. Philip Lewis & wife Dorcus. Exec'r, bro. Risdon Bishop. Wits., John Fisher, John Ham, Jr. Prob. Aug. 20, 1795. Arch. vol. A4, page 62. Reg. of Wills, Liber N, folios 126-127.

Amous, James. Admin. of, to Elizabeth Amous. Aug. 21, 1795. Reg. of Wills, Liber N, folio 127.

Gray, David. Admin. of, to George Moore. Aug. 24, 1795. Arch. vol. A20, page 12. Reg. of Wills, Liber N, folio 127.

Blackiston, John. Admin. of, to Priscilla Blackiston. Aug. 25, 1795. Arch. vol. A4, page 132. Reg. of Wills, Liber N, folio 127.

York, Samuel. Captain. Admin. of, to Tabitha York. Aug. 28, 1795. Arch. vol. A56, page 222. Reg. of Wills, Liber N, folio 127.

Boon, Thomas. Yeoman. Murderkill Hd. Admin. of, to Peter Chance. Aug. 29, 1795. Arch. vol. A4, pages 212-213. Reg. of Wills, Liber N, folio 127. Note:—Arch. vol. A4, page 213 mentions heirs, Ann (widow), Sarah & Samuel Boon, Margaret Melvin, Esther Fairfield, Elizabeth Falconer (wife of William Falconer) & Rebecca Chance (wife of Peter Chance).

Vincent, James. Admin. of, to Mary Vincent & Isaac Vincent. Aug. 31, 1795. Reg. of Wills, Liber N, folio 127.

Rees, Jeremiah. Admin. of, to Jacob Stout, D. B. N. Sept. 2, 1795. Arch. vol. A43, pages 10-12. Reg. of Wills, Liber N, folio 128. Note:—Arch. vol. A43, page 12 mentions Rebecca Snow, the late Rebecca Starling; page 11 mentions Robert Hill who intermarried with Rebecca Starling; page 11 also mentions a Mary Starling.

Hickey, Thomas. Admin. of, to Jacob Stout, D. B. N. Sept. 2, 1795. Arch. vol. A23, pages 206-207. Reg. of Wills, Liber N, folio 128. Note:—Arch. vol. A23, page 206 mentions a son Benjamin Hickey, dec'd; page 207 mentions Rebeccah Snow, late Rebecca Starling.

Jester, Isaac. Blacksmith. Mispillion Hd. Admin. of, to Charles Jester. Sept. 14, 1795. Arch. vol. A27, pages 24-25. Reg. of Wills, Liber N, folio 128.

Stuart [Stewart], John. Admin. of, to Ruth Stewart & Hilla Druman Stayton. Sept. 16, 1795. Arch. vol. A49, pages 99-100. Reg. of Wills, Liber N, folio 128. Note:—Arch. vol. A49, page 99 mentions heirs, Ann Records, heirs of Jane Marratt, heirs of Lavica Griffith (Unicy & Nancy Griffin).

Vinson, Bathsheba [Vincent, Barsheba]. Admin. of, to Eliab Vinson. Sept. 18, 1795. Arch. vol. A52, page 69. Reg. of Wills, Liber N, folio 128.

Empson, Hannah. Will. Made Aug. 22, 1794. Town of Dover. Heirs: nephew Cornelius Battell; mulatto girl, Selah. Exec'r, nephew Cornelius Battell. Wits., Joseph Harper, Nancy Wrench. Prob. Sept. 21, 1795. Arch. vol. A16, page 199. Reg. of Wills, Liber N, folio 128.

Pemberton, James. Admin. of, to John Pemberton. Sept. 28, 1795. Reg. of Wills, Liber N, folio 128.

Bostick, Noah. Admin. of, to Margaret Bostick. Sept. 30, 1795. Reg. of Wills, Liber N, folio 128. Note:—Arch. vol. A4, page 269 shows that Margaret Bostick married Thomas Wiatt.

Morris, Jemimah. Admin. of, to Elias Winsmore. Oct. 6, 1795. Reg. of Wills, Liber N, folio 128.

Wroten, Sabre. Widow. Will. Made Sept. 10, 1795. Mispillian Hd. Heirs: dau. Ann Adams; sons Henry & James; grandson Henry Adams (Wroten). Exec'r, son Henry Wroten. Wits., Vincent Dehorty, Mary Hobkins, Mary Dehorty. Prob. Oct. 7, 1795. Arch. vol. A56, page 172. Reg. of Wills, Liber N, folios 128-129.

Watts, William. Admin. of, to William Watts. Oct. 12, 1795. Arch. vol. A53, page 190. Reg. of Wills, Liber N, folio 129.

Perry, George. Admin. of, to Eleanor Perry. Oct. 16, 1795. Reg. of Wills, Liber N, folio 129. Note:—Arch. vol. A39, page 236 shows that Eleanor Perry married ... Saxton.

Fisher, Sarah. Admin. of, to William Fisher. Oct. 16, 1795. Reg. of Wills, Liber N, folio 129.

Marratt, Joseph. Will. Made Oct. 25, 1793. Heirs: sons John & Samuel Marratt; daus. Martha Jones & Easter Ann Molonix; housekeeper Elinor Russel; Tamer Welch; Selathial Jones; grandchildren (children of Jacob Harrington, Pheby Brinckly & Rachel Ryan), all unnamed. Exec'rs, son Samuel Marratt & Selathial Jones. Wits., Richard Dallinar, Nathan Harrington, Sarah Howard. Prob. Oct. 21, 1795. Arch. vol. A33, pages 194-196. Reg. of Wills, Liber N, folios 129-130.

Cahoon, William. Will. [N. d.]. Heirs: wife Lydia; sons Samuel, William & John; daus. Ann Leatherbury, Mary & Sary Cahoon. Exec'rs, sons Samuel & John. Wits., Robert Jamison, Benjamin Simpson, William Robertson. Prob. Oct. 23, 1795. Arch. vol. A7, pages 47-49. Reg. of Wills, Liber N, folio 130.

Whiteart [Whitehart], Henry. Admin. of, to Jenny Whiteart. Oct. 23, 1795. Reg. of Wills, Liber N, folio 131.

Russum, Peter. Admin. of, to Sarah Russum. Oct. 24, 1795. Arch. vol. A44, pages 194-195. Reg. of Wills, Liber N, folio 131. Note:—Arch. vol. A44, page 194 shows that Sarah Russum married Samuel Brumly.

Davis, Joshua. Admin. of, to John Petigrew. Oct. 28, 1795. Arch. vol. A13, page 31. Reg. of Wills, Liber N, folio 131.

Bowman, John. Admin. of, to William Bowman & Mary Bowman. Oct. 28, 1795. Arch. vol. A5, pages 48-49. Reg. of Wills, Liber N, folio 131. Note:—Arch. vol. A5, page 48 mentions heirs, Rebeccah & Sally Bowman; also shows that Mary Bowman, widow, later married Isaac Jester.

White, Edward. Will. Made March 16, 1795. Heirs: sons John, William, Baynard, Thomas & Edward; grandsons Edward & Nathaniel Pleasenton. Exec'rs, sons William & Thomas. Wits., John Baynard, Samuel White, Thomas Eagle. Prob. Oct. 28, 1795. Arch. vol. A54, pages 104-106. Reg. of Wills, Liber N, folios 131-133.

Craig, John. Farmer. Will. Made Feb. 4, 1794. Heirs: wife Mary; sons Samuel, John & James; daus. Franky, Bathshaba & Mary Craig. Exec'x, wife Mary. Wits., Newell Beauchamp, Sarah Downham. Prob. Oct. 29, 1795. Arch. vol. A11, pages 171-175. Reg. of Wills, Liber N, folio 133. Note:—Arch. vol. A11, page 172 mentions Bathsheba Wallace.

Jackson, Ezekiel. Admin. of, to Elizabeth Jackson. Nov. 4, 1795. Reg. of Wills, Liber N, folios 133-134.

Vincent, James. Admin. of, to Eliab Vinson. Nov. 4, 1795. Arch. vol. A52, page 73. Reg. of Wills, Liber N, folio 134.

Bowen, William. Admin. of, to Elizabeth Bowen. Nov. 4, 1795. Arch. vol. A5, pages 24-25. Reg. of Wills, Liber N, folio 135. Note:—Arch. vol. A5, page 24 mentions heirs, widow Elizabeth, Sarah, Mary, Susannah, James & William Bowen.

Mitten, James, Sr. Admin. of, to James Mitten. Nov. 7, 1795. Arch. vol. A35, pages 180-181. Reg. of Wills, Liber N, folio 134. Note:—Arch. vol. A35, page 180 mentions heirs, James & Mary Mitten, Hester Gore, Jemima Sheridan & heirs of William Mitten (John & James Mitten).

Massey, Hannah. Widow. Duck Creek Hd. Admin. of, to Rachel Parsons. Nov. 10, 1795. Arch. vol. A34, page 17. Reg. of Wills, Liber N, folio 134.

Goodin, Samuel. Admin. of, to Hillary Coudratt. Nov. 10, 1795. Arch. vol. A19, page 131. Reg. of Wills, Liber N, folio 134.

Dickinson, John. Admin. of, to Margaret Dickinson. Nov. 20, 1795. Reg. of Wills, Liber N, folio 134.

Sipple, John. Will. Made Feb. 12, 1788. Muspillion Hd. Heirs: son Zadock; daus. Susannah Sipple & Delilah Harper; heirs of son Caleb; heirs of dau. Ann; granddau. Elizabeth West; John Virgin; Joseph Harper. Exec'r, son Zadock. Wits., Mathias Masten, Sr., William Masten, Mathias Masten, Jr. Prob. Nov. 24, 1795. Arch. vol. A46, page 143. Reg. of Wills, Liber N, folios 134-135.

Manliff, Mathew. Admin. of, to George Manliff, D. B. N. Nov. 30, 1795. Reg. of Wills, Liber N, folio 134.

Dawson, Elijah. Admin. of, to Catharine Dawson. Dec. 2, 1795. Reg. of Wills, Liber N, folio 134.

Kimmy, Solomon. Admin. of, to Mary & Charles Kimmy. Dec. 3, 1795. Arch. vol. A29, page 11. Reg. of Wills, Liber N, folio 134.

Draper, Isaac. Admin. of, to John Clarke. Dec. 7, 1795. Arch. vol. A15, pages 46-47. Reg. of Wills, Liber N, folio 135.

Anderson, James. Innkeeper. Murderkill Hd. Admin. of, to John Brown, farmer, of Murderkill Hd. Arch. vol. A1, page 179. Reg. of Wills, Liber N, folio 135. Note:—Acct. unadministered by Elizabeth Anderson, widow, now dec'd.

Cook, Michael. Admin. of, to Robert Cook, D. B. N. Dec. 9, 1795. Arch. vol. A10, pages 133-134. Reg. of Wills, Liber M, folio 135. Note:—Arch. vol. A10, page 133 shows that Margaret, widow of Michael, later married Robert Kernohan.

White, Gilbert. Will. Made Nov. 9, 1795. Heirs: wife Sarah; son George; daus. Elizabeth Rickets, Peggy, Mary, Ann, Pheby, Sarah, Esther & Henrietta White. Exec'x, wife Sarah. Wits., Richard Dallinar, Nathan LeCompt, John White. Prob. Dec. 9, 1795. Arch. vol. A54, pages 108-109. Reg. of Wills, Liber N, folio 135. Note:—Will mentions grandfather Andrew White, dec'd, & first wife Rebecca Bradly.

Clarke, John. Admin. of, to Rebecca Clark. Dec. 10, 1795. Reg. of Wills, Liber N, folio 135.

Miller, James. Admin. of, to Edward Miller. Dec. 10, 1795. Reg. of Wills, Liber N, folio 137.

Stevenson, George. Admin. of, to Joseph Miller. Dec. 10, 1795. Reg. of Wills, Liber N, folio 137.

Gorden, Samuel. Admin. of, to John Brinckly. Dec. 11, 1795. Arch. vol. A19, pages 181-184. Reg. of Wills, Liber N, folio 136. Note:—Arch. vol. A19, page 181 mentions heirs, Elizabeth Brinckle & Mary Pleasonton.

Nixon, Thomas. Doctor. Admin. of, to Benoni Harris. Dec. 13, 1795. Arch. vol. A38, page 16. Reg. of Wills, Liber N, folio 136.

Godwin, Francis. Admin. of, to Thomas Godwin. Dec. 13, 1795. Reg. of Wills, Liber N, folio 136.

Bellach, Elizabeth. Widow of James Bellach. Will. Made Aug. 8, 1795. Little Creek Hd. Heirs: dau. Ann; son John. Exec'r, John Patten, Esq. Wits., Sarah Hanson, Joseph Miller. Prob. Dec. 13, 1795. Arch. vol. A3, page 197. Reg. of Wills, Liber N, folio 136.

Tumlinson, Cary. Yeoman. Will. Made Nov. 18, 1795. Heirs: bro. William Frazar; sisters Rhoday Houston, Sophia Canday (wife of Purnel) & Mary Houston; bro.-in-law William Canday; Thomas Canday (son of William); James Houston. Exec'r, bro.-in-law William Canday. Wits., John Parsons, Sr., Nancy Taylor, Magdalen Stuart. Prob. Dec. 21, 1795. Arch. vol. A51, pages 139-143. Reg. of Wills, Liber N, folios 136-137.

Brown, John. Will. Made Dec. 3, 1795. Heirs: wife Rachel; sons Joshua, John, Samuel & William; daus. Sarah, Ann & Mary. Exec'r, [John, from admin. acct.]. Wits., Henry Miller, Sarah Kirk, Levin Bell. Prob. Dec. 24, 1795. Arch. vol. A6, pages 58-59. Reg. of Wills, Liber N, folio 137.

Downs, James. Admin. of, to Elizabeth Downs. Dec. 30, 1795. Arch. vol. A15, pages 11-12. Reg. of Wills, Liber N, folio 138. Note:—Arch. vol. A15, page 12 shows that Elizabeth Downs married . . . Vanpelt; page 11 shows that Elizabeth Downs Vanpelt married Daniel Smith.

Bellach, James. Admin. of, to Daniel Cowgill, D. B. N. Dec. 30, 1795. Arch. vol. A3, pages 202-203. Reg. of Wills, Liber N, folio 137. Note:—Arch. vol. A3, page 203 mentions heirs, John, Ann & Elizabeth Bellach.

Meridith, Joseph. Admin. of, to Samuel Meridith. Jan. 4, 1796. Arch. vol. A34, pages 197-199. Reg. of Wills, Liber N, folio 138. Note:—Arch. vol. A34, page 199 mentions heirs, Samuel & Jacob Meridith, Martha Anguish, Elizabeth Ford & Ann Hartshorn.

Vansant, William. Admin. of, to Margaret Vansant. Jan. 4, 1796. Reg. of Wills, Liber N, folio 137.

Keith, Francis. Admin. of, to Elizabeth Keith. Jan. 5, 1796. Reg. of Wills, Liber N, folio 160. Note:—Arch. vol. A28, page 91 mentions heirs, Sarah, Francis & John Keith; also shows that Elizabeth Keith married . . . Standley.

Soward, Eleanor. Admin. of, to Thomas Soward & George Soward. Jan. 5, 1796. Arch. vol. A48, page 58. Reg. of Wills, Liber N, folio 160.

Virdin, John. Admin. of, to Sarah Virdin. Jan. 5, 1796. Arch. vol. A52, pages 94-95. Reg. of Wills, Liber N, folio 160. Note:—Arch. vol. A52, page 94 mentions heirs, Andrew & Elizabeth Virdin; also shows that Sarah Virdin married Thomas Green.

Bowman, Nathaniel. Admin. of, to Charles Draper. Jan. 7, 1796. Arch. vol. A5, pages 80-83. Reg. of Wills, Liber N, folio 137.

Bright, Jonathan. Admin. of, to Smith Faucet. Jan. 7, 1796. Reg. of Wills, Liber N, folio 138.

Hamilton, John. Yeoman. Murderkill Hd. Admin. of, to Jonathan Hamilton. Jan. 7, 1796. Arch. vol. A21, page 162. Reg. of Wills, Liber N, folio 138.

Meridith, Joseph. Admin. of, to Mary Meridith. Jan. 12, 1796. Reg. of Wills, Liber N, folio 137.

Draper, Whittington. Admin. of, to William K. Boyer. Jan. 12, 179... Reg. of Wills, Liber N, folio 138.

Lecount, Thomas. Yeoman. Duck Creek Hd. Admin. of, to William Lecount. Jan. 12, 1796. Arch. vol. A29, page 232. Reg. of Wills, Liber N, folio 138.

Harwood, Jasper. Will. Made Dec. 11, 1795. Heirs: wife Grace; Thomas, Elebth & Margaret Harwood (heirs of John Harwood, dec'd); Thomas Shirven (sister's son). Exec'x, wife Grace. Wits., James Davis, Moses Tompson, Jr., Peter Hawkins. Prob. Jan. 13, 179... Arch. vol. A22, page 212. Reg. of Wills, Liber N, folio 138.

McGonigal, Robert. Will. Made Nov. 17, 1795. Mispillion Hd. Heirs: wife Hessy [Esther]; sons George, David & Joshua; dau. Anna. Exec'x, wife Hessy. Wits., Isaac Davis, Caleb Cox, Warrin Burrows. Prob. Jan. 13, 1796. Arch. vol. A32, pages 196-198. Reg. of Wills, Liber N, folios 138-139. Note:—Arch. vol. A32, page 197 shows that Esther McGonigal married Jestus Lowry.

Hudson, John. Will. Made Dec. 27, 1795. Heirs: sons John, William & Ebenezer; daus. Lydia, Mary, Marget & Senty. Exec'r, Ebenezer Reed. Wits., George Reed, Thomas Dehorty, Dorah Stradley. Prob. Jan. 13, 1796. Arch. vol. A25, page 105. Reg. of Wills, Liber N, folio 139.

Clark, Joshua. Farmer. Will. Made Jan. 9, 1796. Mispillion Hd. Heirs: sons Thomas, Joshua; daus. Penelopy, Mary, Nancy & Charlotey Clark; dau.-in-law Rebecca Clark; grandchildren Sarah & Major Clark. Exec'rs, son Thomas, John Clark (son of John Clark, Esq.). Wits., George Manlove, Risdon Beauchamp. Prob. Jan. 13, 1796. Arch. vol. A9, pages 44-46. Reg. of Wills, Liber N, folios 139-140.

Taylor, Leurenah. Admin. of, to John Lemar. Jan. 18, 1796. Arch. vol. A49, pages 210-212. Reg. of Wills, Liber N, folio 140. Note:—Arch. vol. A49, page 210 mentions heirs, Major, Henry, Margarett & Thomas Taylor.

Vanwinkle, Jonas. Yeoman. Duck Creek Hd. Admin. of, to James Robinson, Sr. Jan. 19, 1796. Arch. vol. A52, page 20. Reg. of Wills, Liber N, folio 140.

Hunn, Nathaniel. Admin. of, to Ann Hunn & Ezekel Hunn. Jan. 21, 1796. Arch. vol. A25, pages 166-169. Reg. of Wills, Liber N, folio 141. Note:—Arch. vol. A25, page 167 mentions heirs, widow Ann Hunn, Ann Mifflin (wife of Samuel Mifflin) & Elizabeth Norris (wife of John Norris).

Crankfield, Nancy. Widow of Moses Crankfield. Murderkill Hd. Admin. of, to Moses Crankfield. Jan. 25, 1796. Arch. vol. A11, pages 208-209. Reg. of Wills, Liber N, folio 141. Note:—Arch. vol. A11, page 208 mentions heirs, Joseph, John, Nancy, Rachel, Lydia & Moses Crankfield, Polly Summers (wife of Zael Summers) & Elizabeth Meredith.

Murphy, Charles. Admin. of, to Jenkins Murphy & Charles Murphy. Jan. 26, 1796. Arch. vol. A37, page 84. Reg. of Wills, Liber N, folio 141.

Hawkins, Simon. Admin. of, to Peter Hawkins. Feb. 2, 1796. Arch. vol. A23, page 36. Reg. of Wills, Liber N, folio 141.

Hawkins, William. Admin. of, to Peter Hawkins. Feb. 2, 1796. Reg. of Wills, Liber N, folio 141.

Laws, John M. Admin. of, to Eleshe Laws. Feb. 4, 1796. Arch. vol. A29, pages 153-155. Reg. of Wills, Liber N, folio 141. Note:—Arch. vol. A29, page 153 shows that Eleshe Laws married Caleb Sipple.

Green, John. Admin. of, to James Raymond. Feb. 4, 1796. Arch. vol. A20, page 79. Reg. of Wills, Liber N, folio 141.

Hinsley, Amos, Sr. Yeoman. Will. Made Jan. 18, 1796. Murderkill Hd. Heirs: wife Pations; sons James, John, Amos & Daniel; daus. Meriam Scotton, Hannah & Pations Hinsley. Exec'rs, sons John & Amos. Wits., William Thomas, Daniel Cox, Jonathan Elbert. Prob. Feb. 4, 1796. Arch. vol. A24, pages 53 & 57-58. Reg. of Wills, Liber N, folio 141.

Hill, William. Shallopman. Will. Made Feb. 2, 1794. Duck Creek Hd. Heirs: wife Hester; daus. Elizabeth & Rebecca Hill; bro. Crosedill Hill (of township of Bristol, Penna.); sister Agnes January. Exec'rs, wife Hester & John Dusha. Wits., Edward Joy, George Cummins. Prob. Feb. 4, 1796. Arch. vol. A24, pages 21-23. Reg. of Wills, Liber N, folios 141-142.

Cardeen, Daniel. Will. Made Dec. 12, 1795. Mispillion Hd. Heirs: wife Deborah; sons William & John; daus. Elizabeth & Ruth. Exec'x, wife Deborah. Wits., William Masten, James Williams, Mathias Maston. Prob. Feb. 9, 1796. Arch. vol. A7, pages 204, 212-213. Reg. of Wills, Liber N, folio 140. Note:—Arch. vol. A7, page 212 mentions Sarah Willoughby.

Meridith, Nathan. Yeoman. Murderkill Hd. Admin. of, to Elizabeth Meridith. Feb. 12, 1796. Arch. vol. A34, pages 205-206. Reg. of Wills, Liber N, folio 142. Note:—Arch. vol. A34, page 205 shows that Elizabeth Meridith married . . . Hazeltine; also mentions Samuel Meredith.

Hattabaugh, Warwick. Admin. of, to Mary Hattabaugh. Feb. 16, 1796. Reg. of Wills, Liber N, folio 143.

Lowber, Daniel. Will (nunc.). Made Feb. 4, 1796. Heirs: wife Mary; sons William & Peter. Exec'x, wife Mary. Wits., John Wheeler, Rebecca Skiner, Deborah Meridith. Prob. Feb. 18, 1796. Arch. vol. A31, pages 98-100. Reg. of Wills, Liber N, folio 142.

Williams, James. Admin. of, to Miriam Williams. Feb. 22, 1796. Arch. vol. A55, pages 83-84. Reg. of Wills, Liber N, folio 143. Note:—Arch. vol. A55, page 83 mentions heirs, Elizabeth, John, George & Susannah Williams.

Jones, Daniel. Will. Made Jan. 24, 1796. Heirs: wife Lettisha; sons Enoch, Daniel, Jonathan & Lody; dau. Letty. Exec'rs, wife Lettisha & son Enoch. Wits., H. Layton, Elizabeth Bedwell. Prob. Feb. 23, 1796. Arch. vol. A27, pages 152-153. Reg. of Wills, Liber N, folio 143.

Owens, Ishmael. Admin. of, to Joshua Owens. Feb. 23, 1796. Arch. vol. A38, page 153. Reg. of Wills, Liber N, folio 143.

Morgan, William. Will. Made Jan. 5, 1796. Heir: wife Hester. Exec'x, wife Hester. Wits., Thomas Jenkins, Jabez Jenkins, Benjamin Brady. Prob. Feb. 29, 1796. Arch. vol. A36, pages 177-178. Reg. of Wills, Liber N, folios 145-146.

Ridgaway, Zedekiah. Admin. of, to Daniel Godwin. March 7, 1796. Arch. vol. A43, page 239. Reg. of Wills, Liber N, folio 144.

Clifton, Thomas. Yeoman. Mispillion. Admin. of, to Sarah Clifton & Smith Fauset. March 7, 1796. Arch. vol. A9, pages 157 & 162. Reg. of Wills, Liber N, folio 144. Note:—Arch. vol. A9, page 162 mentions heirs, Daniel, Mary, Perthenca, Nathaniel, Sarah, John, Benitha, Ann, Thomas, Levica & James Clifton.

Dicus, William. Admin. of, to Samuel Dicus. March 10, 1796. Arch. vol. A14, pages 72-74. Reg. of Wills, Liber N, folio 144.

Saxton, George. Admin. of, to Vincent Catts. March 13, 1796. Arch. vol. A45, page 43. Reg. of Wills, Liber N, folio 144.

Stevens, Daniel. Will. Made Feb. 17, 1792. Little Creek Hd. Heirs: wife Mary; adopted son John Stevens (son of wife Mary). Trustees of Poor of Kent County. Exec'x, wife Mary. Wits., James Calley, Timothy Swaeny, Robert Clark. Prob. March 14, 1796. Arch. vol. A48, page 213. Reg. of Wills, Liber N, folio 143.

Townsend, Stephen. Admin. of, to Sally Townsend. March 16, 1796. Reg. of Wills, Liber N, folio 144. Note:—Arch. vol. A51, page 44 shows that Sally Townsend later married Noah Spencer.

Mileham, Harmon. Minor son of Samuel. Admin. of, to John Vickery. March 23, 1796. Arch. vol. A35, page 52. Reg. of Wills, Liber N, folio 144.

Green, Jonathan. Will (nunc.). Made March 9, 1796. Heir: wife Penelope. Wits., James Raymond, Esq., & John Raymond. Prob. March 23, 1796. Arch. vol. A20, pages 71 & 81. Reg. of Wills, Liber N, folio 144. Note:—Admin. granted to James Raymond, Arch. vol. A20, page 81. Penelope Green renounced her rights.

Snow, John. Admin. of, to James Snow, D. B. N. March 24, 1796. Reg. of Wills, Liber N, folio 144.

Meridith, Jonathan. Admin. of, to Vincent Catts. March 24, 1796. Reg. of Wills, Liber N, folio 144.

Stant, Charles. Admin. of, to Joseph Stant. March 25, 1796. Arch. vol. A48, page 135. Reg. of Wills, Liber N, folio 145.

Herington, John. Admin. of, to Sarah Herington. March 25, 1796. Arch. vol. A22, pages 118-119 & vol. A23, page 170. Reg. of Wills, Liber N, folio 45. Note:—Arch. vol. A22, page 118 mentions heirs, Sarah, Asa, Mathew, John, Hannah, Sarah, Mary, Barbara, Abner & Benjamin Harrington & Ruth Sipple.

Jarrad, Mathew. Admin. of, to Thomas & Matthew Clark. March 25, 1796. Arch. vol. A26, pages 110-111. Reg. of Wills, Liber N, folio 145. Note:—Arch. vol. A26, page 111 mentions heirs, (heirs of Rachel Dunning), Mary Cox, Ruth Clark, Nancy Brown & Prudence Purden.

Owens, Sarah. Admin. of, to Zadock Hilford. March 25, 1796. Arch. vol. A38, pages 161-162. Reg. of Wills, Liber N, folio 145. Note:—Arch. vol. A38, page 161 mentions heirs, William, Samuel & John Owens, Nancy Downs; also mentions heirs of Elizabeth Hilford (Elizabeth Dorman, David, Boz, Robert & Martha Hilford, wife of Jonathan Finsthwait).

Clark, Benjamin. Will. Made Jan. 25, 1796. Heirs: wife unnamed; sons Thomas & Matthew; dau. Sarah Harrington, wife of John. Exec'rs, sons Thomas & Matthew. Wits., James Catts, Prudence Catts, Nancy Laws Shaver. Prob. March 25, 1796. Arch. vol. A8, pages 216-219. Reg. of Wills, Liber N, folio 145.

Mitchell, Thomas. Admin. of, to Elizabeth Mitchell. April 7, 1796. Reg. of Wills, Liber N, folio 146.

Carter, Samuel. Admin. of, to Mary Carter. April 7, 1796. Arch. vol. A8, page 40. Reg. of Wills, Liber N, folio 146.

Lewis, Thomas. Admin. of, to Mary Lewis. April 7, 1796. Arch. vol. A30, pages 154-155. Reg. of Wills, Liber N, folio 146. Note:—Arch. vol. A30, page 155 mentions an only child David Lewis; also shows that Mary Lewis married ... Colier.

Ashford, Mary. Admin. of, to John Graydon. April 16, 1796. Arch. vol. A2, pages 15-18. Reg. of Wills, Liber N, folio 146. Note:—Arch. vol. A2, pages 17-18 show the acct. later settled by Benj. Boggs, who married Jane Graden (adm'x of John Graden); page 18 mentions heirs: John, Joseph, Marrium, Elizabeth & James Graden (heirs of William Graden); Mary Foster, heir of Matthew Foster; Alexander & James Graden (heirs of Alexander Graden); Mary Merrett, heir of Elizabeth Graden.

Eckles, John. Admin. of, to Elizabeth Eckles. April 18, 1796. Arch. vol. A15, pages 247-249. Reg. of Wills, Liber N, folio 146. Note:—Arch. vol. A15, page 247 mentions heirs, James & Benjamin Eckles; also shows that Elizabeth Eckles married John Murphy.

Eckles, Ann. Widow of Richard Eckles. Admin. of, to Anthony Eckles. April 18, 1796. Arch. vol. A15, pages 241-244. Reg. of Wills, Liber N, folio 146. Note:—Arch. vol. A15, page 241 mentions heirs, Jesse, Julana, Lydia, John, Richard & Anthony Eckles, Sarah & Mary Jester, Anny & Esther Taylor.

Jester, Sarah. Admin. of, to Emanuel Jester. April 18, 1796. Arch. vol. A27, page 48. Reg. of Wills, Liber N, folio 146.

Jenkins, Samuel. Admin. of, to Jabez Jenkins. April 18, 1796. Arch. vol. A26, page 239. Reg. of Wills, Liber N, folio 146.

Eckles, Richard. Will. Made March 17, 1796. Heirs: sister Lidea Jester; bro. Jessy Eckles; other bros. & sisters unnamed. Exec'r, John Eckles. Wits., Zachariah Pritchett, Roger Scully, Ezekiel Anderson. Prob. April 18, 1796. Arch. vol. A16, page 4. Reg. of Wills, Liber N, folio 146.

Forsyth, Alexander. Admin. of, to Major Anderson. April 19, 1796. Arch. vol. A18, page 35. Reg. of Wills, Liber N, folio 146.

Brown, Joshua. Admin. of, to Thomas Williams. April 19, 1796. Arch. vol. A6, page 72. Reg. of Wills, Liber N, folio 147.

Hopkins, Hampton. Admin. of, to Nancy Hopkins. April 20, 1796. Reg. of Wills, Liber N, folio 147.

Foreacre, Isaac. Admin. of, to Letitia Jones & Enoch Jones, D. B. N. April 21, 1796. Arch. vol. A18, pages 1-2. Note:— Arch. vol. A18, page 1 mentions heirs, John, Robert, Isaac, Joseph, Marcer, James & William Foreacre.

Whitehead, Lemuel. Admin. of, to Jacob Whitehead. April 22, 1796. Arch. vol. A54, page 196. Reg. of Wills, Liber N, folio 147.

Plowman, Josiah. Admin. of, to Jonathan Manlove. April 25, 1796. Arch. vol. A40, pages 141-142. Reg. of Wills, Liber N, folio 147.

Meredith, Martha. Dau. of Solomon Smith. Admin. of, to Samuel Meredith. April 26, 1796. Arch. vol. A34, page 204. Reg. of Wills, Liber N, folio 147.

Polk, Daniel, Esq. Admin. of, to Margaret N. Polk. May 1, 1796. Reg. of Wills, Liber N, folio 147.

Cain, Thomas. Admin. of, to William Purden. May 2, 1796. Reg. of Wills, Liber N, folio 147.

Craige, James. Tailor. Dover Hd. Admin. of, to Samuel Craige. May 2, 1796. Arch. vol. A11, page 164. Note:—A dau. Mary Craige is mentioned.

Amos, Elizabeth. Admin. of, to Outten Laws. May 2, 1796. Reg. of Wills, Liber N, folio 147. Note:—Arch. vol. A1, page 130 mentions George Amous, son of James Amous.

Gore, William. Will. Made March 21, 1796. Heirs: wife Mary Ann; son Richard. [No exec'r]. Wits., James Gibbeson, William Manlove. Prob. May 3, 1796. Arch. vol. A19, page 191. Reg. of Wills, Liber N, folio 147.

Stedham, Ann. Widow of Thomas Stedham. Murderkill Hd. Admin. of, to John Day & Joshua Temple. May . . ., 1796. Arch. vol. A48, page 191 & vol. A49, pages 13-15. Note:— Arch. vol. A49, page 15 mentions heirs, Emory, Ann, Mary, George & Charles Stedham.

Clark, Jane. Will. Made March 25, 1796. Heirs: mother Mary Clark; bros. John & Robert Clark. Exec'x, mother Mary Clark. Wits., Elizabeth Banning, Robert Clark. Prob. May 3, 1796. Arch. vol. A8, pages 247-248. Reg. of Wills, Liber N, folio 148. Note:—Will mentions sister Elenor, dec'd, father James Clark, dec'd, & bro. David Clark, dec'd.

Pendigrist, Patrick. Admin. of, to Rachel Pendigrist. May 6, 1796. Arch. vol. A41, pages 137-138. Reg. of Wills, Liber N, folio 148. Note:—Arch. vol. A41, page 138 mentions heirs, Catharine, Elizabeth, Hugh & Mary Pendegrest.

Brice, Benedict. Admin. of, to Richard Kenneard. May 6, 1796. Arch. vol. A5, page 153. Reg. of Wills, Liber N, folio 148.

Furbee, Caleb. Admin. of, to Sarah Furbee. May 9, 1796. Arch. vol. A18, pages 153-154. Reg. of Wills, Liber N, folio 148. Note:—Arch. vol. A18, page 153 mentions Jacob Furby.

Lowber, Peter. Farmer. Murderkill Hd. Admin. of, to Mary Lowber. May 9, 1796, D. B. N. Arch. vol. A31, pages 143-144. Reg. of Wills, Liber N, folio 148. Note:—Arch. vol. A31, page 143 mentions heirs, Daniel & Peter Lowber, Catherine Duhadaway, Peter, Benjamin & John Caton, Sarah Vanburkeloe & Unity Gilder, wife of John Gilder.

Voshall, Obadiah. Farmer. Will. Made April 21, 1796. Heirs: wife Hannah; sons Titus, Owen & James; dau. Nancy. Exec'rs, wife Hannah & son Titus. Wits., Mary Bell, Isaac Kent, Benoni Harris. Codicil, son Daniel. Prob. May 9, 1796. Arch. vol. A52, pages 139-140. Reg. of Wills, Liber N, folio 147.

Taylor, Francis. Admin. of, to Elizabeth Taylor. May 11, 1796. Reg. of Wills, Liber N, folio 148.

Farlow, William. Farmer. Murderkill Hd. Admin. of, to Mary Farlow. May 13, 1796. Arch. vol. A17, pages 14-15. Reg. of Wills, Liber N, folio 148. Note:—Arch. vol. A17, page 14 mentions children, Polly, Samuel, George, Turner, John, William, Archibald & Abigal Farlow.

Darling, James. Admin. of, to Rachel Darling. May 13, 1796. Arch. vol. A12, pages 191-192. Reg. of Wills, Liber N, folio 148. Note:—Arch. vol. A12, page 191 mentions heirs, John, James, Daniel, Mary, Lydia & Ellinor Darling.

Pratt, George. Admin. of, to Thomas Pratt & Jacob Calloway. May 31, 1796. Arch. vol. A41, pages 86-88. Reg. of Wills, Liber N, folio 150. Note:—Arch. vol. A41, page 86 mentions heirs, Thomas, George, John, Ruth, Henry & William Pratt; page 87 mentions Mary & Ester Pratt (minor daus. of Frederick Pratt, dec'd).

Berry, Benjamin. Admin. of, to William Berry. June 1, 1796. Arch. vol. A4, page 1. Reg. of Wills, Liber N, folio 148.

Mifflin, Mathew. Admin. of, to Andesiah Mifflin. June 1, 1796. Reg. of Wills, Liber N, folio 148.

King, John. Admin. of, to Barbara King, widow. June 1, 1796. Arch. vol. A29, page 31. Reg. of Wills, Liber N, folio 150.

Jarral, John. Admin. of, to Elizabeth Jarrel, widow, & Robert Jarrel. June 3, 1796. Arch. vol. A26, pages 130-131. Reg. of Wills, Liber N, folio 150. Note:—Arch. vol. A26, page 130 mentions heirs, widow Elizabeth Jarral, Free Born, John Wesley & Susannah Fleming Jarral.

Wade, William. Admin. of, to Elizabeth Wade, widow. June 3, 1796. Reg. of Wills, Liber N, folio 150.

Ward, John. Admin. of, to William Ward & James Ward. June 9, 1796. Reg. of Wills, Liber N, folio 150.

Lathem, Robert. Admin. of, to Mary Lathem, widow. June 9, 1796. Arch. vol. A29, pages 210-211 & 135. Reg. of Wills, Liber N, folio 150. Note:—Arch. vol. A29, page 210 shows that Mary Lathem later married Thomas Hartup; page 211 mentions children, Polly, Rhoady & Catharine Leathem.

Fitzjarrald, Eleazer. Admin. of, to Richard Manwaring, D. B. N. June 13, 1796. Arch. vol. A17, pages 151-152. Reg. of Wills, Liber N, folio 150. Note:—Arch. vol. A17, page 152 shows that the heirs called themselves Jarrel, namely, Ruth, Mary, John, Eleazer & Richard Jarrel.

Shane, Mary. Admin. of, to Edward Shane. June 14, 1796. Arch. vol. A45, pages 167-171. Reg. of Wills, Liber N, folio 151. Note:—Arch. vol. A45, page 168 mentions heirs, Edward, James, Thomas & Benjamin Shane & Phebe Shane (wife of John Hill).

Sullivan, Mary. Admin. of, to Henry Truax. June 14, 1796. Reg. of Wills, Liber N, folio 151.

Macy, Thomas. Admin. of, to Nancy Macy. June 14, 1796. Reg. of Wills, Liber N, folio 151.

Frazier, William. Admin. of, to Mary Frazier. June 17, 1796. Arch. vol. A18, pages 106-108. Reg. of Wills, Liber N, folio 151. Note:—Arch. vol. A18, page 106 mentions heirs, Cary & Sarah Frazier; also shows that Mary Frazier married Thomas Sipple.

Moore, Thomas. Admin. of, to Sarah Moore. June 17, 1796. Reg. of Wills, Liber N, folio 151.

Nixon, Charles. Admin. of, to Elizabeth Nixon, widow. June 25, 1796. Arch. vol. A38, pages 8-10. Reg. of Wills, Liber N, folio 151.

Jacobs, Bozman. Admin. of, to James Jacobs. July 6, 1796. Arch. vol. A26, pages 65-66. Reg. of Wills, Liber N, folio 157. Note:—Arch. vol. A26, page 66 mentions heirs, James, Nancy, Bozman, Elizabeth, Molton & Jonathan Jacobs.

Murphy, William. Admin. of, to Sarah Murphy, widow. July 11, 1796. Arch. vol. A37, pages 105-106. Reg. of Wills, Liber N, folio 149. Note:—Arch. vol. A37, page 105 mentions minor children, William, Samuel & John Murphy.

Clark, Robert. Attorney at law. Will. Made July 5, 1796. Town of Dover. Heirs: bro. John Clark; friends Miss Hannah Britton (dau. of Thomas Britton, Esq.), Mrs. Catherine Batson, Mrs. Maria Vining, Miss Araminta Meeks, John Fisher, Esq., Major Elijah Barratt, John W. Batson, Esq., William K. Boyer, Samuel White, Esq. Exec'r, friend Andrew Barratt, Esq.' Wits., Edward Miller, Matthew Lowber, Thomas Huston. Prob. July 12, 1796. Arch. vol. A9, pages 67-69. Reg. of Wills, Liber N, folios 149-150.

Macey [Massy], John. Admin. of, to John Massy, eldest son of John, dec'd. July 13, 1796. Arch. vol. A33, pages 48-49. Reg. of Wills, Liber N, folio 149. Note:—Arch. vol. A33, pages 48-49 show the acct. administered by John Anderson; page 48 mentions heirs, John & Jonathan Macey.

Laws, William. Will. Made Aug. 14, 1794. Mispillion Hd. Heirs: sons John May Laws, Lodowick, Elijah, Clemon & George Laws; dau. Lydia Houston; grandson William Laws (son of Lodowick Laws); granddau. Elizabeth Houston (dau of Robert Houston & wife Lydia); Negroes Morear, Pero. Exec'r, son Lodowick. Commissioners, James Harris, Isaac David, Lodowick Laws. Wits., Isaac Davis, Mary Davis, James Thistlewood. Prob. July 13, 1796. Arch. vol. A29, pages 175-179. Reg. of Wills, Liber N, folios 149-150 & 181.

Nixon, Abraham. Admin. of, to William Nixon. July 19, 1796. Arch. vol. A38, page 7.

Carman, Joseph. Admin. of, to Elias Shockley. July 26, 1796. Arch. vol. A7, page 225.

Downing, Benjamin. Admin. of, to Mary Murphy, wife of Thomas Murphy. July 26, 1796. Arch. vol. A14, pages 239-240. Note:—Arch. vol. A14, page 239 mentions heirs, Mary Roaf, Elizabeth Denny, Joseph, Nicy, John & Benjamin Downing.

Eagle, Thomas. Admin. of, to Thomas Berry. July 27, 1796. Reg. of Wills, Liber N, folio 148.

White, William. Farmer. Dover Hd. Admin. of, to George Ward & wife Ann, the late Ann White, D. B. N. Aug. 4, 1796. Arch. vol. A54, pages 173 & 175. Note:—Arch. vol. A54, page 173 mentions heirs, children of bro. Charles White, dec'd, & heirs of sister Ann White, wife of William Graham, both dec'd.

Stevens, John. Admin. of, to Robert Hall. Aug. 4, 1796. Reg. of Wills, Liber N, folio 148. Note:—Arch. vol. A48, page 229 mentions heirs, George & William Stevens.

Herrington, Martha. Widow. Will. Made Nov. 17, 1795. Mispillion Hd. Heirs: dau. Sarah Howard; sons Jacob, John, Isaac, William, Nathan, David, Aaron & Jonathan; heirs of Mary Ann Graham; grandsons William & John Marratt, James Herrington. Exec'r, son Nathan. Wits., Matthew Clark, William Calloway, Elijah Minner. Prob. Aug. 15, 1796. Arch. vol. A23, pages 172-173. Reg. of Wills, Liber N, folio 152.

Gullett, George. Will. Made May 14, 1796. Heirs: daus. Nancy Smith, Margaret Clifton; sons John & George; grandson Isaac Jester; other children unnamed. Exec'rs, sons John & George. Wits., Thomas Buckner, Aylett Buckner, Stephen Huddleston. Prob. Aug. 17, 1796. Arch. vol. A21, pages 37-38. Reg. of Wills, Liber N, folios 156-157. Note:—Arch. vol. A21, page 38 mentions heirs, Waitman, Samuel, George, Lydia & John Gullett, Nancy Hambleton, Margaret Clifton, Elizabeth Aydelott & Mary Pearson.

Birch, George. Admin. of, to Nancy Birch. Aug. 23, 1796. Reg. of Wills, Liber N, folio 152.

Ferguson, John. Admin. of, to Sarah Ferguson, widow, & Daniel Ferguson. Aug. 29, 1796. Reg. of Wills, Liber N, folio 152.

Pearson, Joseph. Admin. of, to Sarah Pearson. Aug. 30, 1796. Reg. of Wills, Liber N, folio 153. Note:—Arch. vol. A39, page 172 shows that Sarah Pearson later married Lewis Gano.

Pearson, Elias. Admin. of, to Sarah Pearson, widow. Aug. 30, 1796. Arch. vol. A39, pages 168-169. Reg. of Wills, Liber N, folio 153. Note:—Arch. vol. A39, page 168 mentions a minor son Joseph Pearson; also shows that Sarah Pearson married Lewis Gano.

Thomas, Daniel. Will. Made July 23, 1796. Heirs: wife Mary Ann; nephew Daniel Thomas, son of bro. James Thomas. Exec'x, wife Mary Ann. Wits., Olive Jump, Salathiel Jones, William Anderson. Prob. Aug. 31, 1796. Arch. vol. A50, pages 44-46. Reg. of Wills, Liber N, folio 154. Note:—Arch. vol. A50, page 45 shows that Mary Ann Thomas, widow, married John Anderson.

Summers, Nathaniel. Admin. of, to Peter Lowber, Jr. Sept. 9, 1796. Arch. vol. A49, page 118. Reg. of Wills, Liber N, folio 153 .

Wilcutts, Levin. Admin. of, to Elizabeth Wilcuts, widow. Sept. 12, 1796. Arch. vol. A54, pages 236-238. Reg. of Wills, Liber N, folio 153. Note:—Arch. vol. A54, page 236 mentions an heir, Josiah Wilcuts; also shows that Elizabeth Wilcuts married Levy Lister.

Beauchamp, Nancy. Admin. of, to John Buck. Sept. 13, 1796. Reg. of Wills, Liber N, folio 151.

Vandiver, Thomas. Admin. of, to Elizabeth Vandiver & William Bostick. Sept. 16, 1796. Reg. of Wills, Liber N, folio 153.

Doughurty, Daniel. Admin. of, to Mary Daughurty, widow. Sept. 23, 1796. Reg. of Wills, Liber N, folio 153.

Jessop, William. Admin. of, to William Lowber. Sept. 25, 1796. Reg. of Wills, Liber N, folio 151. Note:—Arch. vol. A27, page 6 mentions an heir, Unice Jessop.

Wilson, Susannah. Admin. of, to William Green. Oct. 4, 1796. Arch. vol. A56, pages 15-16. Reg. of Wills, Liber N, folio 151. Note:—Arch. vol. A56, page 15 mentions heirs, Mary & Hannah Soward, Susannah Green, Sarah Hindsley, Eliza Young, Ruth Bodaway, Merryum Pollins, Nancy Burchinal, Letitia Shaw.

Shea, Elizabeth. Admin. of, to John Brady. Oct. 4, 1796. Reg. of Wills, Liber N, folio 151.

Carey, William. Admin. of, to Bowen Carey. Oct. 6, 1796. Reg. of Wills, Liber N, folio 151.

Polk, Daniel. Admin. of, to Samuel White, Esq., D. B. N. Oct. 7, 1796. Arch. vol. A40, pages 149-153 & 155-156. Reg. of Wills, Liber N, folio 152. Note:—Arch. vol. A40, pages 150-151 mention heirs, Elizabeth Clayton (wife of James L. Clayton), John, Margaret, Anna, Maria, Daniel & Samuel White Polk.

Hilford, Matthew. Admin. of, to John Simpson, D. B. N. Oct. 7, 1796. Reg. of Wills, Liber N, folio 152.

Jackson, Ebenezer. Admin. of, to Ann Jackson, widow. Oct. 11, 1796. Arch. vol. A25, page 244. Reg. of Wills, Liber N, folio 152.

Jones, John. Admin. of, to Triphana Jones, widow. Oct. 11, 1796. Arch. vol. A27, pages 217-221 & 223. Reg. of Wills, Liber N, folio 152. Note:—Arch. vol. A27, page 220 mentions heirs, Isaac, John, Charles, Asa, Zachariah & Waitman Jones.

Robinson, Samuel. Admin. of, to Alexander Hamilton. Oct. 12, 1796. Arch. vol. A44, page 87.

McCoomb, Jonathan. Admin. of, to William Pennewell. Oct. 17, 1796. Reg. of Wills, Liber N, folio 153.

Edmondson, John. Admin. of, to Lydia Edmondson, widow, & John Miller. Oct. 17, 1796. Arch. vol. A16, pages 52-58. Reg. of Wills, Liber N, folio 153. Note:—Arch. vol. A16, page 58 mentions heirs, Elizabeth & Margarett Edmondson; also shows that Lydia Edmondson married Isaac Taylor.

Edmondson, Thomas. Admin. of, to Lydia Edmondson & John Miller, D. B. N. Oct. 17, 1796. Arch. vol. A16, pages 64-65. Reg. of Wills, Liber N, folio 153. Note:—Arch. vol. A16, page 64 mentions heirs, John Edmondson, Margaret Lua, Sophia Register (late Edmondson).

Blackiston, Samuel. Admin. of, to Frances Blackiston, widow, & Benjamin Blackiston. Oct. 21, 1796. Reg. of Wills, Liber N, folio 153.

Smith, Robert. Admin. of, to William Smith. Oct. 24, 1796. Reg. of Wills, Liber N, folio 153.

Keys, William. Admin. of, to Mary Keys, widow. Oct. 24, 1796. Arch. vol. A28, pages 169-170. Reg. of Wills, Liber N, folio 153. Note:—Arch. vol. A28, page 170 mentions heirs, Mary, Elizabeth, Pricilla, Ann & William Keys; also shows that Mary Keys, widow, married Timothy Lister.

Greenly, Michael. Yeoman. Murderkill Hd. Admin. of, to Daniel Reynalds, D. B. N. Oct. 25, 1796. Arch. vol. A20, page 141. Reg. of Wills, Liber N, folio 153.

Stapleford, Sarah. Will. Made Oct. 12, 1796. Heirs: sons William, Robert, John & Bruff; dau. Henney Brown; granddau. Lilley Brown. Exec'r, Perry Prittaman. Wits., Thomas Shockley, Rachel Prettyman. Prob. Oct. 26, 1796. Arch. vol. A48, pages 157-159. Reg. of Wills, Liber N, folio 154.

Wilcuts, Josiah. Admin. of, to Levy Wilcuts, D. B. N. Oct. 26, 1796. Arch. vol. A54, pages 234-235. Reg. of Wills, Liber N, folio 154. Note:—Arch. vol. A54, page 234 mentions heirs, Nancy, Mary, Sarah, Joseph, Levi, Martha & William Wilcuts & Susannah Stark, wife of Philip Stark.

Nock, Joseph. Admin. of, to Susannah & Daniel Nock. Oct. 26, 1796. Arch. vol. A38, page 28.

Longfellow, John. Admin. of, to John Potts. Oct. 26, 1796. Arch. vol. A31, page 67. Reg. of Wills, Liber N, folio 154.

Lowber, William. Admin. of, to Letitia Lowber, widow. Oct. 31, 1796. Reg. of Wills, Liber N, folio 154. Note:—Arch. vol. A31, page 171 mentions heirs, Sarah & Susannah Lowber; also shows that Letitia Lowber later married James Shaw.

Hurlock, Jacob. Will. Made July 27, 1796. Heirs: wife Lewcresey; sons Ebenezer, Jacob, John, Samuel; daus. Elizabeth, Ann, Mary, Sarah, Rachel, Martha. Exec'x, wife Lewcresey. Wits., William Clouds, Solomon Smith, Richard Beck. Prob. Nov. 2, 1796. Arch. vol. A25, pages 180-183. Reg. of Wills, Liber N, folio 155. Note:—Arch. vol. A25, page 181 shows that Lucrecia Hurlock married Samuel Green.

Harper, John. Will (nunc.). Made Oct. 20, 1796. Heirs: wife Jean; son Nathaniel. Exec'rs, [Jean & William Harper, from admin. acct.]. Wits., Edward Joy, William Harper, Evan Denny. Prob. Nov. 3, 1796. Arch. vol. A22, pages 55-59. Reg. of Wills, Liber N, folios 154-155.

Cox, William Clark. Admin. of, to Daniel Cox. Nov. 10, 1796. Arch. vol. A11, page 144. Reg. of Wills, Liber N, folio 156.

Snow, James. Admin. of, to Rebecca Snow, widow. Nov. 11, 1796. Arch. vol. A48, pages 9-11. Reg. of Wills, Liber N, folio 156. Note:—Arch. vol. A48, page 11 shows that Rebecca, the widow, later married Robert Hill; page 10 shows that Levi Haughay was her third husband; page 9 mentions an heir, John Snow.

Stradly, Absalom. Farmer. Mispillion Hd. Admin. of, to Darcus Stradly. Nov. 16, 1796. Arch. vol. A49, pages 48-49. Reg. of Wills, Liber N, folio 156. Note:—Arch. vol. A49, page 48 mentions children, Darcus, Anne, Margaret, Absolom, Zebulon & Caleb Stradly & widow Darcus Stradly.

Grewell, John, Sr. Will. Made Feb. 26, 1795. Murderkill Hd. Heirs: wife Elizabeth; sons Jacob & John; Elizabeth Longfellow, née Badger; Jonathan Badger. Exec'x, wife Elizabeth. Wits., Sally Broadaway, Barsheba Craig, William Skinner. Prob. Nov. 16, 1796. Arch. vol. A21, page 23. Reg. of Wills, Liber N, folio 156.

Chicken, John. Admin. of, to Daniel Chicken. Nov. 25, 1796. Reg. of Wills, Liber N, folio 157.

Robinson, John H. Admin. of, to Joseph Nock. Nov. 25, 1796. Arch. vol. A44, page 67. Reg. of Wills, Liber N, folio 157.

Coleman, Sarah. Widow. Will. Made Oct. 28, 1796. Town of Dover. Heirs: nephews David Manlove & Robinson Manlove (sons of bro. Asa Manlove); nieces Sarah Manlove (dau. of bro. Asa), Rachel, Ruth & Lydia Fisher (daus. of sister Alce Fisher); Methodist Episcopal Church of Dover; Anne Crooks, widow of Benj. Crooks of Dover; Sarah Bell, widow of John Bell, Sr., of Dover; Nancy Bell, widow of John Bell, Jr., of Dover; Sarah Alston, widow of Stephen Alston of Dover. Exec'r, James Sykes. Wits., Joseph Hale, Nicholas Ridgely. Prob. Nov. 25, 1796. Arch. vol. A9, page 217. Reg. of Wills, Liber N, folio 157.

Hairgrove, George. Admin. of, to George Hairgrove, D. B. N. Nov. 30, 1796. Arch. vol. A21, pages 64 & 67. Reg. of Wills, Liber N, folio 157.

Morris, Joshua. Admin. of, to John Reed. Dec. 7, 1796. Reg. of Wills, Liber N, folio 157.

Cummins, Daniel. Admin. of, to Elizabeth Cummins & Polly Cummins. Dec. 14, 1796. Reg. of Wills, Liber N, folios 157-158.

Polk, Margaret N. Will (nunc.). Made Sept. 22, 1796. Village of Milford. Heirs: sister Sarah Cook; children Ann, Samuel, Meriah, Peggy & John. Exec'r, Samuel White. Wits., Sally Cook & Anna White. Prob. Dec. 14, 1796. Arch. vol. A40, pages 161-166. Reg. of Wills, Liber N, folios 151-152.

Harper, Joseph. Admin. of, to Nancy Harper, widow. Dec. 14, 1796. Arch. vol. A22, pages 68-69. Reg. of Wills, Liber N, folio 158. Note:—Arch. vol. A22, page 68 mentions heirs, William, Caleb, Susannah, John & Rebeccah Harper.

Mors [Morris], Elizabeth. Widow of John Gray. Will. Made April 12, 1796. Murderkill Hd. Heirs: sons John Gray, Samuel, Abner & Robert Broadaway; daus. Sarah Hynson, Ann Badger, Elizabeth Meredith; grandchildren Ambrose Broadaway & Samuel Broadaway (children of Isaac Broadaway), Mary Broadaway (dau. of Ambrose Broadaway). Exec'r, son Samuel Broadaway. Wits., Joseph Flood, Sarah Meridith, Elizabeth Cooper. Prob. Dec. 14, 1796. Arch. vol. A36, pages 203-204. Reg. of Wills, Liber N, folio 158.

Coombe, John. Admin. of, to Benjamin Coombe & Samuel Coombe. Dec. 15, 1796. Arch. vol. A10, page 154. Reg. of Wills, Liber N, folio 158.

Gray, John. Blacksmith. Murderkill Hd. Admin. of, to Samuel Broadaway, D. B. N. Dec. 17, 1796. Arch. vol. A20, pages 24-25. Reg. of Wills, Liber N, folio 158. Note:—Arch. vol. A20, page 24 shows that Elizabeth Gray later married a Morris; page 25 shows Thomas Denny & wife Jean (dau. of Agnes McHoney) & Joshua Meredith & wife Agness (dau. of Agnes McHoney).

Buck, James. Admin. of, to Joseph Lewis. Dec. 18, 1796. Arch. vol. A6, page 114. Reg. of Wills, Liber N, folio 158.

Scales, William. Admin. of, to Mariam Scales. Dec. 25, 1796. Reg. of Wills, Liber N, folio 159.

Laws, Major. Admin. of, to Nancy Laws & Joseph Aydelott. Dec. 31, 1796. Arch. vol. A29, pages 166-168. Reg. of Wills, Liber N, folio 159.

Gray, William. Will. Made Nov. 1, 1796. Heirs: sons Andrew Gray; dau. Elizabeth Gray. Exec'rs, son Andrew & friend William Berry, Esq. Wits., Jacob Stout, James Craig, George Reed. Prob. Jan. 3, 1797. Arch. vol. A20, pages 36-38. Reg. of Wills, Liber N, folios 159-160. Note:—Will mentions heir, Negro Drummer.

Perkins, Thomas. Yeoman. Will. Made Dec. 29, 1796. Heirs: Church Wardens of Episcopal Church of Milford (Jehu Davis, William Sorden); Hester Howring; Hetty Smack (dau. of McKemmy Smack); William Russom; William Hutson, son of Alexander Hutson. Exec'rs, John Gildersleve & Elijah Barratt. Wits., Nathaniel Knotts, Edward Callahan, Samuel Willoughby. Prob. Jan. 5, 1797. Arch. vol. A39, page 233 & vol. A41, page 227. Reg. of Wills, Liber N, folio 160.

Greer, John. Will. Made Oct. 13, 1796. Heirs: wife Mary; son Mark; daus. Rachel Chambers, Sarah Maxwell & Mary Chambers. Exec'rs, wife Mary & son Mark. Wits., Henry Carter, William Meredith, James Stuard. Prob. Jan. 9, 1797. Arch. vol. A20, pages 172-173. Reg. of Wills, Liber N, folio 161.

Fields, Marian. Admin. of, to Francis Register. Jan. 9, 1797. Reg. of Wills, Liber N, folio 161.

Dempsy, James. Admin. of, to Nancy Dempsy. Jan. 10, 1797. Reg. of Wills, Liber N, folio 161.

Dicus, Sarah. Will. Made Nov. 22, 1796. Duck Creek Hd. Heirs: son Benoni Dicus; sister Anna Dicus. Exec'r, Enoch Jones. Wits., Samuel Dicus, Rachel Woodell, James Jones. Prob. Jan. 10, 1797. Arch. vol. A14, page 71. Reg. of Wills, Liber N, folio 162. Note:—Will mentions bro. William Dicus, dec'd.

Hardcastle, Elizabeth. Admin. of, to John Warren & Samuel Warren. Jan. 14, 1797. Arch. vol. A21, pages 228-229. Reg. of Wills, Liber N, folio 162. Note:—Arch. vol. A21, page 229 mentions heirs, John, Benjamin, Zipporah & Samuel Warren, Elizabeth Jones & Mary Peterson (alias Wheatley).

Teppins, Thomas. Will. Made Dec. 23, 1796. Heirs: dau. Elizabeth; sons Thomas & John. Wits., Nancy Teppins, Liddy Bennet, George Buckmaster. Prob. Jan. 14, 1797. Arch. vol. A50, pages 164-165. Reg. of Wills, Liber N, folio 162. Note: —Arch. vol. A50, page 165 shows that the admin. was granted to George Buckmaster; also mentions Elizabeth Collins as an heir.

Wilcuts, Nancy. Will. Made Oct. 20, 1796. Heir: son George. Exec'r, Ferdinan Casson. Wits., Sarah Gaskins, Cynthea Verdin, Rebeca McNatt. Prob. Jan. 16, 1797. Arch. vol. A54, pages 239-240. Reg. of Wills, Liber N, folio 162.

Weaver, John. Will. Made Dec. 15, 1796. Heirs: daus. Sarah & Elizabeth Weaver; son William. Exec'r, Charles Heath. Wits., Martha Ann Heath, Ann York. Prob. Jan. 16, 1797. Arch. vol. A53, page 201. Reg. of Wills, Liber N, folio 163.

Duhadway, Catharine. Will (copy). Made Sept. 14, 1796. Somerset Co., Md. Heirs: son Jacob; granddaus. Katharine Duhadway, Betsy Betts; grandsons Daniel & John Rennolds; son-in-law Isaac Betts. Exec'r, son-in-law Isaac Betts. Wits., John H. Adams, Henry Craig. Prob. Jan. 17, 1797. Arch. vol. A15, page 105. Reg. of Wills, Liber N, folio 165.

Wallace, James. Admin. of, to Richard Taylor & Brinckle Roe. Jan. 18, 1797. Reg. of Wills, Liber N, folio 163. Note:— Arch. vol. A52, page 230 shows that this acct. was later settled by John Clark, Esq.

Venoi, Sarah. Admin. of, to John Venoi. Jan. 19, 1797. Reg. of Wills, Liber N, folio 163.

Lampden, John. Admin. of, to Sarah Lampden. Jan. 19, 1797. Reg. of Wills, Liber N, folio 163.

Turner, Jehu. Will. Made May 10, 1796. Mispillion Hd. Heirs: sons Charles, Jesse, William & Reuben; daus. Unicy Turner & Elizabeth Fleming (wife of Beniah Fleming); grandsons Tilmon Turner & Jehu Fleming. Exec'rs, sons Jesse & Reuben. Wits., Caleb Cox, Benja. Turner, James Johnson. Prob. Jan. 26, 1797. Arch. vol. A51, pages 167-169. Reg. of Wills, Liber N, folios 163-164.

Clark, Gideon. Admin. of, to Obidienu Clark. Jan. 25, 1797. Reg. of Wills, Liber N, folio 164. Note:—Arch. vol. A8, page 235 shows that the widow married John Fowler.

Viccory, Waitman. Admin. of, to Mary Viccory. Jan. 26, 1797. Arch. vol. A52, pages 46-47. Reg. of Wills, Liber N, folio 164. Note:—Arch. vol. A52, page 46 mentions heirs, Thomas & Solomon Viccory; also shows that Mary Viccory later married Samuel Harrington.

Truitt, Zadock. Admin. of, to Rebecca Truitt. Jan. 30, 1797. Reg. of Wills, Liber N, folio 164. Note:—Arch. vol. A51, page 126 shows that Rebecca Truitt later married Benjamin Wells.

Wallace, Benjamin. Admin. of, to James Wallace. Feb. 1, 1797. Reg. of Wills, Liber N, folio 164.

Williams, James. Admin. of, to Rachel Williams. Feb. 1, 1797. Arch. vol. A55, pages 81-82. Reg. of Wills, Liber N, folio 164. Note:—Arch. vol. A55, page 81 shows that Rachel later married Peter Taylor.

Harwood, Mary. Will. Made Jan. 24, 1797. Heirs: son James Harwood; dau. Trace Loftis, wife of Gedion Loftis; granddau. Polly Smith, dau. of Thomas Smith. Exec'rs, son James & Matthias Clifton. Wits., John Emmory, Elizabeth Vinn, Ruben Warren. Prob. Feb. 1, 1797. Arch. vol. A22, page 219. Reg. of Wills, Liber N, folio 164.

Harwood, Samuel. Admin. of, to James Harwood, D. B. N. Feb. 1, 1797. Reg. of Wills, Liber N, folio 164.

Tomblinson, Richard. Admin. of, to Richard Tomblinson. Feb. 1, 1797. Arch. vol. A50, pages 211-214. Reg. of Wills, Liber N, folio 165. Note:—Arch. vol. A50, page 211 mentions heirs, John, Sophia, Betsy, Auston, Lewis, Richard, Polly, Sally & Thomas Tomblinson & widow Elizabeth Tomblinson.

Hargadine, William. Admin. of, to William Allaband. Feb. 1, 1797. Arch. vol. A22, page 29. Reg. of Wills, Liber N, folio 165.

Wilkerson, Henry. Admin. of, to Moses Wilkerson. Feb. 2, 1797. Arch. vol. A55, page 43. Reg. of Wills, Liber N, folio 165.

Betheards, William G. Admin. of, to Elizabeth Beatheards. Feb. 3, 1797. Reg. of Wills, Liber N, folio 165.

Lane, Anthony. Admin. of, to Lydia Lane. Feb. 7, 1797. Arch. vol. A29, pages 112-113. Reg. of Wills, Liber N, folio 165. Note:—Arch. vol. A29, page 113 mentions a dau. Maryum Lane; also shows that Lydia Lane married Jessy Jester.

Vannatta, Samuel. Will. Made Oct. 4, 1792. Heirs: son Thomas Vannatta; granddau. Elenor Vannatta. Exec'r, son Thomas. Wits., John Wheelton, John Fisher. Codicil, Jan. 22, 1797, names an heir, Elizabeth Chippy. Wits., Thomas Crammer & Thomas Downham. Prob. Feb. 8, 1797. Arch. vol. A52, page 8. Reg. of Wills, Liber N, folios 165-166.

Stuart, George. Admin. of, to William Hall. Feb. 8, 1797. Arch. vol. A49, pages 95-96. Reg. of Wills, Liber N, folio 166. Note:—Arch. vol. A49, page 95 mentions heirs, George & Magdaline Stuart, Polly Wood & Elizabeth Hall.

McBride, Robert. Farmer. Murderkill Hd. Admin. of, to Mary McBride & Samuel McBride. Feb. 11, 1797. Arch. vol. A32, pages 74-77. Reg. of Wills, Liber N, folio 166. Note:—Arch. vol. A32, page 74 mentions heirs, William, Nancy, Mary, Unity & Robert McBride; pages 75-76 show that Charles Brown later administered portion of Mary McBride, dec'd.

White, Margaret. Dau. of Gilbert White, dec'd. Admin. of, to Major McNatt. Feb. 16, 1797. Arch. vol. A54, page 135. Reg. of Wills, Liber N, folio 166.

White, Mary. Dau. of Gilbert White, dec'd. Admin. of, to Major McNatt. Feb. 16, 1797. Arch. vol. A54, page 138. Reg. of Wills, Liber N, folio 166.

Ayler, James. Will. Made March 28, 1795. Dover Hd. Heirs: wife Sarah; Elizabeth Ayler; Charlotte Clark, dau. of Ezekiel & Easter Clark. Exec'x, wife Sarah. Wits., Maskilne Clark, Elizabeth Clark, Easter Clark. Prob. Feb. 16, 1797. Arch. vol. A2, page 33. Reg. of Wills, Liber N, folio 166.

Burns, William. Admin. of, to Jane Burns. Feb. 16, 1797. Arch. vol. A6, pages 204-205. Reg. of Wills, Liber N, folio 166. Note:—Arch. vol. A6, page 205 mentions heirs, Mary & Fanny Burns; also shows that Jane Burns married Joseph Foreacres.

Morris, William. Will. Made Jan. 31, 1797. Murderkill Hd. Heirs: sons Thomas & Daniel; daus. Elizabeth Alford, Hannah Davis, Mary Lowber (widow) & Margaret Cole (widow of Edward); granddaus. Letticia Broadaway, Margaret & Susannah Morris; grandson William Morris, son of Wm. Morris; Nancy Burchnal, former wife of Wm. Morris, dec'd. Exec'rs, son-in-law William Alford, son Thomas Morris. Wits., John Wheeler, John Lockwood, Alexander Saxton. Prob. Feb. 16, 1797. Arch. vol. A37, pages 41 & 44-49. Reg. of Wills, Liber N, folio 167.

Gore, Thomas. Admin. of, to George Gore. Feb. 19, 1797. Reg. of Wills, Liber N, folio 167. Note:—Arch. vol. A19, page 190 mentions heirs, James, Jonathan, Mehala, Selah, Rebecca, John & George Gore.

Strong, Samuel. Admin. of, to Benjamin Wells. Feb. 19, 1797. Arch. vol. A49, page 89. Reg. of Wills, Liber N, folio 167.

Beckworth, William. Admin. of, to Joshua Laws. Feb. 21, 1797. Arch. vol. A6, pages 174-175 & Arch. vol. A3, pages 132-133. Reg. of Wills, Liber N, folio 168. Note:—Arch. vol. A3, page 133 mentions heirs, widow Rhoda, Nancy & Sally Beckworth.

Cain, Francis. Admin. of, to Rachel Cain. Feb. 21, 1797. Arch. vol. A7, pages 66-67. Reg. of Wills, Liber N, folio 168. Note:—Arch. vol. A7, page 66 mentions heirs, Daniel & Sarah Cain & Ellinor Howard; also shows that Rachel Cain later married Walter Conner.

Walston, William. Admin. of, to Rachel Walston. Feb. 22, 1797. Reg. of Wills, Liber N, folio 168.

Heald, Rich. Will. Made Feb. 1, 1797. Heirs: wife Patients; bro. Joab Heald; sister Sinthy Heald; William Pain; William Bishop; Elizabeth Wilson. Exec'rs, wife Patients & Edward Callahan. Wits., James Shaw, William Shaw. Prob. Feb. 22, 1797. Arch. vol. A23, pages 114-115. Reg. of Wills, Liber N, folio 168. Note:—Arch. vol. A23, page 115 shows that Patients Heald married Robert Broadaway.

Hill, Joseph. Admin. of, to Robert Hill & Joseph Hill. Feb. 23, 1797. Arch. vol. A24, pages 3-5. Reg. of Wills, Liber N, folio 168.

Green, John. Admin. of, to Nancy Green. Feb. 26, 1797. Arch. vol. A20, page 78. Reg. of Wills, Liber N, folio 168.

Clark, Henry. Admin. of, to Elizabeth Clark. Feb. 26, 1797. Arch. vol. A8, pages 236-237. Reg. of Wills, Liber N, folio 168. Note:—Arch. vol. A8, page 236 mentions heirs, Mary Clark & Henrietta Clark (wife of Zadok Crapper Clark); page 237 shows that Elizabeth Clark, widow, married George Dorman.

Lovegrove, James. Admin. of, to Gennett Lovegrove. Feb. 26, 1797. Reg. of Wills, Liber N, folio 168.

Farrow, Ebenezar. Cordwainer. Duck Creek Hd. Admin. of, to Robert Kernohan. March 1, 1797. Arch. vol. A17, page 30. Reg. of Wills, Liber N, folio 169.

Smally, John, Sr. Admin. of, to John Jester. March 2, 1797. Reg. of Wills, Liber N, folio 169.

Downham, James. Son of Isaac Downham, dec'd. Admin. of, to Elias Jarrel. March 3, 1797. Arch. vol. A14, page 222. Reg. of Wills, Liber N, folio 169.

Johnson, William. Admin. of, to James Johnson & Thomas Johnson. March 4, 1797. Arch. vol. A27, page 121. Reg. of Wills, Liber N, folio 169.

Jennings, John. Admin. of, to George Jennings. March 6, 1797. Arch. vol. A27, page 2 & vol. A18, page 234. Reg. of Wills, Liber N, folio 169.

Cacey, Elijah Foreman. Son of Dorcas Foreman. Will. Made Jan. 9, 1797. Heirs: cousins Henry Rochester, James Cacey (son of uncle Othoniel Cacey, dec'd), Samuel Cacey (son of uncle John Cacey), Elizabeth & Bewly Harris (daus. of Benoni Harris). Exec'r, Benoni Harris. Wits., Jos. Harper, Thomas Proctor, David C. Lee. Prob. March 6, 1797. Arch. vol. A7, pages 19-20. Reg. of Wills, Liber N, folio 169. Note:—Arch. vol. A7, page 20 shows Beauly Harris as the wife of John Buckhannon.

Mifflin, Andesiah. Admin. of, to Benjamin Brinckly. March 14, 1797. Arch. vol. A34, page 241 & vol. A35, page 18. Reg. of Wills, Liber N, folio 169. Note:—Arch. vol. A35, page 18 mentions heirs, James, Mary, Martha, Sarah, Andasiah & Esther Mifflin & Ellinor Brincklee.

Mifflin, Mathew. Admin. of, to Benjamin Brinckly. March 14, 1797. Arch. vol. A34, page 239 & vol. A35, page 18. Reg. of Wills, Liber N, folio 169. Note:—Arch. vol. A35, page 18 mentions heirs, James, Mary, Martha, Sarah, Andasiah & Esther Mifflin & Ellinor Brincklee.

Loftis, John. Admin. of, to Barbary Loftis. March 14, 1797. Arch. vol. A31, pages 53-54. Reg. of Wills, Liber N, folio 169. Note:—Arch. vol. A31, page 54 mentions heirs, Josh, Burton & Barbary Loftis, Jamima Chance, Ann Dill, Sarah Clark & Rebecca Loftis (late Dill).

Tumblin, Sarah. Will. Made March 2, 1797. Caroline Co., Md. Heirs: daus. Leare, Elizabeth & Anney. [No exec'rs]. Wits., Priscilla Swan, May Swan, Edwd. Swan. Prob. March 16, 1797. Arch. vol. A51, page 135. Reg. of Wills, Liber N, folio 173.

Wells, Benjamin. Blacksmith. Will. Made Dec. 12, 1796. Little Creek Hd. Heirs: son Benjamin, Jr.; dau.-in-law Rachel Wells (wife of son Daniel, dec'd); grandchildren, Daniel & Hannah Wells (children of son Daniel), Arthur Wells (son of William), Allen, William, Thomas, John & Elizabeth Gray (children of dau. Ann Gray). Exec'r, son Benjamin. Wits., Allen McLane, Rachel Wells, Rebecca McLane. Prob. March 20, 1797. Arch. vol. A53, pages 226-228. Reg. of Wills, Liber N, folio 170.

Bradly, Nathan. Admin. of, to Martha Bradly. March 20, 1797. Reg. of Wills, Liber N, folio 170.

Baily, Edmund, the elder. Admin. of, to Rachel Baily. March 27, 1797. Arch. vol. A2, pages 52-53. Reg. of Wills, Liber N, folio 170. Note:—Arch. vol. A2, page 53 mentions heirs, widow Rachel, Mary, Robert, Edward, Edmund & Rachel Bailey, Hannah Hynson (wife of Nathaniel), Sally Joyce (wife of Thomas) & Elizabeth Cullen (wife of Hezekiah Cullen); also shows estate later administered by Edmund Bailey, D. B. N.

Postles, Acilia [Selah]. Admin. of, to Samuel Brumley. March 28, 1797. Arch. vol. A40, page 221. Reg. of Wills, Liber N, folio 170.

Crathers, William. Admin. of, to Ann Cratis. March 31, 1797. Arch. vol. A11, page 214. Reg. of Wills, Liber N, folio 170.

White, John. Admin. of, to Alexander White. March 31, 1797. Arch. vol. A54, pages 122-123. Reg. of Wills, Liber N, folio 170. Note:—Arch. vol. A54, page 123 mentions Mary White, dau. of William White.

With, William. Will. Made March 30, 1797. Heirs: dau. Mary; son William. Exec'r, Francis Register. Wits., Nathan Cullin, Joseph Dixon. Prob. April 3, 1797. Arch. vol. A56, page 55. Reg. of Wills, Liber N, folio 171.

Johnson, William. Will. Made Feb. 22, 1796. Mispillion Hd. Heirs: wife Mary; sons Samuel, James, John & William; daus. Charlotty & Margaret. Exec'rs, wife Mary & son Samuel. Wits., Samuel Fleming, Purnel Johnson, James Johnson. Prob. April 3, 1797. Arch. vol. A27, pages 117-119. Reg. of Wills, Liber N, folio 171.

Durborough, Hugh. Admin. of, to Amy Durborough. April 4, 1797. Reg. of Wills, Liber N, folio 171.

Jack (negro of David Williams). Admin. of, to Morgan Williams. April 4, 1797. Reg. of Wills, Liber N, folio 171.

Robinson [Robertson], Caleb. Mispillion Hd. Admin. of, to William M. Satterfield. April 10, 1797. Arch. vol. A44, pages 34-35. Reg. of Wills, Liber N, folio 172. Note:—Arch. vol. A44, page 34 mentions heirs, Anny & Sarah Robertson.

Gray, John. Admin. of, to Susan Gray. April 10, 1797. Arch. vol. A20, pages 26-27. Reg. of Wills, Liber N, folio 172. Note:—Arch. vol. A20, page 26 mentions children, Mary, Thomas & James Gray; also shows the acct. later settled by John Draper & wife Susannah.

Bell, Nancy. Will. Made March 20, 1797. Town of Dover. Heirs: dau. Sarah Bell; son John Bell; friend Sarah Bell; Nancy West; William K. Boyer; William & Mary Boyer (children of Wm. K. Boyer). Exec'r, William K. Boyer. Wits., Peggy Boyer, Phebe Merdith, James Sykes. Prob. April 13, 1797. Arch. vol. A3, page 182. Reg. of Wills, Liber N, folio 172.

Hambleton [Hamilton], James. Admin. of, to Betty Hamilton [Hambleton]. April 15, 1797. Arch. vol. A21, pages 153-154. Reg. of Wills, Liber N, folio 172. Note:—Arch. vol. A21, page 153 mentions heirs, Anna, James, Major, Selathiel, Rhoda & Betsy Hambleton, Sally & Mary Ann Spencer, Rebecca McNitt.

Lee, Jeremiah. Admin. of, to Charles Pope, Esq. April 17, 1797. Reg. of Wills, Liber N, folio 172.

Homes, David. Admin. of, to to Daniel Homes. April 27, 1797. Reg. of Wills, Liber N, folio 172.

Pryor, John, the elder. Admin. of, to Elizabeth Nixon, D. B. N. May 2, 1797. Arch. vol. A41, pages 192-193. Reg. of Wills, Liber N, folios 172-173.

Smith, Noah. Admin. of, to Sarah Smith & William Bostick. May 5, 1797. Arch. vol. A47, page 130. Reg. of Wills, Liber N, folio 173.

Downham, Mary. Admin. of, to Ezekel Downham. May 5, 1797. Reg. of Wills, Liber N, folio 173.

Tumblin, Sarah. Admin. of, to John Houston. May 18, 1797. Reg. of Wills, Liber N, folio 173.

Barns, Stephen. Admin. of, to Joseph Harper. May 19, 1797. Reg. of Wills, Liber N, folio 173.

Parker, William. Will. Made April 30, 1797. Town of Dover. Heirs: Ann Quinlin, dau. of Mary Quinlin; bro. Anderson Parker; half-bro. Isaiah Wharton. Exec'rs, friends Daniel Cowgill & Jonathan Needham. Wits., Asa Freeman, James Schee, Joseph Hale. Prob. May 20, 1797. Arch. vol. A39, pages 61-62. Reg. of Wills, Liber N, folios 173-174.

Rees, Mary. Admin. of, to Edward Rees. May 23, 1797. Reg. of Wills, Liber N, folio 174.

Wilson, William. Admin. of, to Skidmore Wilson. May 23, 1797. Arch. vol. A56, page 25. Reg. of Wills, Liber N, folio 174.

Jarrell, Jeremiah. Admin. of, to Hart Jarrell & Elias Jarrell. May 26, 1797. Arch. vol. A26, pages 129 & 164. Reg. of Wills, Liber N, folio 174.

White, Isabella. Admin. of, to Alexander White. May 31, 1797. Reg. of Wills, Liber N, folio 174. Note:—Arch. vol. A54, page 110 mentions Isaac & William White.

Johnston, John. Admin. of, to Margaret Johnston. June 2, 1797. Arch. vol. A27, pages 82-83. Reg. of Wills, Liber N, folio 174. Note:—Arch. vol. A27, page 82 mentions heirs, Margaret, Robert, John & Isaac Johnston.

Price, Joseph. Admin. of, to Samuel Price. June 2, 1797. Arch. vol. A41, page 154. Reg. of Wills, Liber N, folio 174.

Hatfield, William. Yeoman. Will. Made July 25, 1795. Heirs: wife Mary; sons Levi, William, Jonathan, Levin, Wheatly, Nathan & Owen; daus. Betsy, Mary & Sary. Exec'rs, wife Mary & son Levi. Wits., Thomas Davis, John Hatfield, William Hatfield. Prob. June 5, 1797. Arch. vol. A22, pages 243 & 246. Reg. of Wills, Liber N, folios 174-175.

Smith, Jacob. Miller. Admin. of, to Joseph Harper. June 5, 1797. Reg. of Wills, Liber N, folio 175.

Smith, John. Minor son of John. Admin. of, to Joseph Harper. June 5, 1797. Reg. of Wills, Liber N, folio 175.

Smith, Mary. Minor dau. of John. Admin. of, to Joseph Harper. June 5, 1797. Reg. of Wills, Liber N, folio 175.

Harper, Thomas, Sr. Will. Made Sept. 30, 1791. Murderkill Hd. Heirs: wife Elizabeth; sons Thomas & William; daus. Ann, Susanah & Mary Harper, Elizabeth Hollingsworth (wife of John). Exec'x, wife Elizabeth. Wits., Richard Cooper, Job Meredith, Jr., Daniel Reynolds. Prob. June 6, 1797. Arch. vol. A22, pages 75-77. Reg. of Wills, Liber N, folios 175-176.

Killen, Abel. Admin. of, to Elizabeth Killen & Isaac Davis. June 12, 1797. Arch. vol. A28, pages 173-174. Reg. of Wills, Liber N, folio 176. Note:—Arch. vol. A28, page 174 mentions heirs, William & Assenith Killen, Sally Short (wife of Edward Short), Polly Hinson (wife of Matthew Hinson) & Elizabeth Hammond (wife of Isaac Hammond).

Cahoon, Jean. Will. Made Jan. 16, 1787. Duck Creek Hd. Heirs: dau. Sarah; bro. Charles Cahoon. Exec'r, bro. Charles Cahoon. Wits., Joseph Elliott, James Peterson, William Jordan. Prob. June 12, 1797. Arch. vol. A7, page 33. Reg. of Wills, Liber N, folio 176.

Cox, Gove. Will. Made Feb. 28, 1796. Heirs: wife Rebeckah; nephew Gove Cox (son of bro. Charles Cox). Exec'rs, wife Rebekah & William Whitely of Caroline Co. Wits., Olive Jump, George Turner, Thomas Smith. Prob. June 13, 1797. Arch. vol. A11, pages 130-131. Reg. of Wills, Liber N, folio 177. Note:—Arch. vol. A11, page 131 shows that Rebekah Cox married Vincent Dehorty.

Gullett, John. Will. Made Feb. 12, 1791. Heirs: wife Betty; sons John, George, James, Ezekiel, Daniel & Solomon; daus. Nancy Pritchett, Betty & Rachel Gullett. Exec'rs, wife Betty & son John. Wits., Olive Jump, Christopher Jump, Anna Thomas. Prob. June 13, 1797. Arch. vol. A21, pages 39 & 42-43. Reg. of Wills, Liber N, folios 177-178.

Cummins, Daniel. Yeoman. Will. Made June 8, 1797. Duck Creek Hd. Heirs: wife Mary; sons Timothy, George, John, David; daus. Sibbey & Nancy; grandson Daniel Cummins Lockwood. Exec'rs, sons Timothy, George, John. Wits., James McDowel, Daniel McDowel. Prob. June 21, 1797. Arch. vol. A12, pages 98 & 100-103. Reg. of Wills, Liber N, folio 178 & Liber P, folio 166. Note:—Arch. vol. A12, page 102 mentions Francis Cummins.

Tubman, Aninias. Admin. of, to Ann Tubman. July 5, 1797. Arch. vol. A51, pages 127-128. Reg. of Wills, Liber N, folio 179. Note:—Arch. vol. A51, page 127 mentions heirs, widow Ann, Elizabeth, John, Susannah, Sylvenus & Jereboam Tubman.

Carlton, Richard. Admin. of, to Margaret Carlton. July 6, 1797. Reg. of Wills, Liber N, folio 179.

Murphy, John. Admin. of, to Comfort Murphy & Levin Murphy. July 24, 1797. Arch. vol. A37, pages 94-95. Reg. of Wills, Liber N, folio 179. Note:—Arch. vol. A37, page 94 mentions heirs, William, Jonathan, Daniel, John, Elijah & Levin Murphy, Elizabeth Taylor & Ruth McNatt.

Durham, William. Admin. of, to Mary Durham. July 27, 1797. Arch. vol. A15, pages 196-197 & vol. A14, pages 19-20. Reg. of Wills, Liber N, folio 179. Note:—Arch. vol. A15, page 196 mentions heirs, Ibba & Benjamin Durham; Arch. vol. A14, page 19 mentions heirs, Mary, William, Benjamin & Isabella Derram, Elizabeth Dean (wife of John), Mary Hughs, Deborough Colt & Susannah Hansor.

Nixon, Thomas, the elder. Admin. of, to Letitia Coakley, D. B. N. Aug. 1, 1797. Reg. of Wills, Liber N, folio 179.

Mason, William. Admin. of, to Ann Mason & Matthew Cox. Aug. 9, 1797. Arch. vol. A34, pages 13-14. Reg. of Wills, Liber N, folio 179. Note:—Arch. vol. A34, page 13 mentions heirs, William, Elizabeth, Samuel & Richard W. Mason; also shows that Ann Mason later married Joshua Melvin.

Lecompte, Nathan. Will. Made July 20, 1797. Heirs: wife unnamed; three children unnamed. Exec'r, Charles Lacompte. Wits., Richard Dallinar, Martha Wilcut, Polly Wilcut. Prob. Aug. 10, 1797. Arch. vol. A29, pages 228-231. Reg. of Wills, Liber N, folios 179-180. Note:—Arch. vol. A29, page 230 mentions Leah Lewis (late Leah Lecount), exec'x of Charles Lecount; page 231 mentions heirs, Charles, Nancy & Precilla Lecompte.

Cullen, Hezekiah. Will. Made Nov. 1, 1787. Heirs: wife Mary Ann; sons Henry, George & Hezekiah; daus. Elizabeth, Sarah & Anne; grandson Charles Brandel. Exec'x, wife Mary Ann. Wits., Thomas Tumlinson, Rhoda Davis, Lodawick Laws. Prob. Aug. 14, 1797. Arch. vol. A12, page 78. Reg. of Wills, Liber N, folio 180.

Severson, James. Admin. of, to Elizabeth Severson. Aug. 25, 1797. Arch. vol. A45, pages 143-144. Reg. of Wills, Liber N, folio 180. Note:—Arch. vol. A45, page 143 mentions heirs, Elizabeth, John & Robert Severson, Susannah Truax, Sarah Green, Mary Phillips & heirs of James Severson.

Burch, George. Admin. of, to Ann Burch. Aug. 29, 1797. Arch. vol. A6, pages 190-191. Note:—Arch. vol. A6, page 190 shows this acct. later administered by Bassett Furguson; also mentions a minor dau. Sarah Burch (wife of John Mitchell); Ann Burch married a Ferguson & later married a Joyce.

Venoi, Abraham. Admin. of, to Rachel Venoi & John Caton, D. B. N. Sept. 20, 1797. Reg. of Wills, Liber N, folio 181.

Scully, John Burton. Admin. of, to Nancy Green, D. B. N. Sept. 26, 1797. Arch. vol. A45, pages 108-109. Note:—Arch. vol. A45, page 108 mentions heirs, Sarah & Mary Dill, Triphener Conner (wife of Soloman Conner), Lydia Oldfield, Minty Conner, Solomon Conner & Nancy Green.

Jarrell, Hart. Will. Made Sept. 3, 1797. Heirs: wife Sarah; son Jeremiah; daus. Mary, Ruth & Ann; one child unnamed. Exec'r, bro. Elias Jarrall. Guardian, bro. Elias Jarrall. Wits., John Lockwood, John Powell. Prob. Sept. 27, 1797. Arch. vol. A26, pages 122-124 & 160. Reg. of Wills, Liber N, folio 182. Note:—Arch. vol. A26, page 123 mentions a Hannah Jarrell as an heir.

Manlove, Asa. Admin. of, to John Clayton, Esq. Sept. 27, 1797. Reg. of Wills, Liber N, folio 182.

Frazor, William. Admin. of, to James McClyments. Oct. 6, 1797. Arch. vol. A18, page 109. Reg. of Wills, Liber N, folio 182.

Masten, John. Will. Made Jan. 18, 1791. Mispillion Hd. Heirs: wife Sarah; sons Matthias, William & Hezekiah; daus. Hannah Jeans (widow of Isaac Jeans), Mary Morris, Elizabeth Griffith, Deborah Cardeen, Sarah Layton; grandchildren (heirs of son John, dec'd); granddaus. Mary Luff & Deborah Luff (daus. of Caleb Luff). Exec'rs, wife Sarah & son William. Wits., Matthew Jarrard, Solomon Townsend, Elizabeth Townsend. Prob. Oct. 10, 1797. Arch. vol. A34, pages 30-32. Reg. of Wills, Liber N, folio 183. Note:—Arch. vol. A34, page 32 mentions heirs, John Masten, Hannah Jones, Ruth Luff, Rebecca Thomas, John & Gilbert Masten; also mentions heirs of Mathias Masten (Rachel, Sarah, Hannah, Philip & Mary Masten).

Blackstone, John. Admin. of, to Sarah Blackstone & George Blackstone. Oct. 16, 1797. Reg. of Wills, Liber N, folio 183.

Burrows, Elizabeth. Admin. of, to William Burrows. Oct. 18, 1797. Arch. vol. A6, pages 207-208. Reg. of Wills, Liber N, folio 183. Note:—Arch. vol. A6, page 207 mentions heirs, Margaret, Richard & William Burrows, Esther Sears & children of John & James Burrows & Mary Hogins.

Rench, James. Admin. of, to Frances Rench. Nov. 3, 1797. Arch. vol. A43, page 70. Reg. of Wills, Liber N, folio 184.

Buckingham, Isaac. Admin. of, to Elizabeth Buckingham. Nov. 3, 1797. Reg. of Wills, Liber N, folio 184.

Cole, Edward. Admin. of, to Matilda Cole. Nov. 3, 1797. Reg. of Wills, Liber N, folio 184.

Caton, Benjamin. Admin. of, to Mary Caton. Nov. 7, 1797. Arch. vol. A8, pages 82-83. Reg. of Wills, Liber N, folio 184. Note:—Arch. vol. A8, page 83 mentions heirs, John, Merrium & Margaret Caton; also shows that Mary Caton later married George Crammer.

Tindall, Elizabeth. Widow of John. Will (nunc.). Made Oct. 16, 1797. Heirs: sons Purnell Tindall & Isaac Purnell; Hannah Tindall. Exec'r, son John. Wits., Hannah Tindall, Jesse Tindall. Prob. Nov. 7, 1797. Arch. vol. A50, page 156. Reg. of Wills, Liber N, folio 184.

Driskill, Capt. Joseph. Admin. of, to James Berry. Oct. 10, 1797. Arch. vol. A15, page 86. Reg. of Wills, Liber N, folio 184.

Barratt, Nathaniel. Yeoman. Will. Made Oct. 21, 1797. Heirs: bro. Philip Barratt; Elijah Barratt; sisters Miriam & Lydia Barratt; mother Miriam White. Exec'r, bro. Elijah Barratt. Wits., Samuel Dewees, James Neall, Jonathan Neall. Prob. Nov. 13, 1797. Arch. vol. A3, pages 13-14. Reg. of Wills, Liber N, folios 184-185. Note:—Arch. vol. A3, page 14 mentions Lydia Barratt (wife of Mathew Patton) & Meriam Barratt (wife of John Martindell); also mentions father Phillip Barratt, dec'd.

Stedham, Thomas. Admin. of, to Joshua Temple & John Day. Nov. 14, 1797. Arch. vol. A49, pages 21-22. Reg. of Wills, Liber N, folio 185.

Hutchinson, Mary. Admin. of, to Thomas Woodal. Nov. 16, 1797. Reg. of Wills, Liber N, folio 185.

Sipple, John. Admin. of, to Priscilla Sipple. Nov. 20, 1797. Arch. vol. A46, pages 144-147. Reg. of Wills, Liber N, folio 185.

Fleming, Samuel. Admin. of, to Joseph Fleming. Nov. 28, 1797. Reg. of Wills, Liber N, folio 185. Note:—Arch. vol. A17, page 202 mentions heirs, Joseph, Robert, Mary & Mahala Fleming.

Tilton, Sabrah. Widow of Thomas Tilton. Will. Made Feb. 27, 1796. Heirs: sons James, Abraham & Thomas; daus. Sarah Allee (wife of Abraham Allee), Nancy Steel (widow of James Steel); son-in-law Abraham Allee. Exec'r, son James. Wits., Benjamin Stout, William Gould. Prob. Nov. 28, 1797. Arch. vol. A50, pages 151-152. Reg. of Wills, Liber N, folios 186-187.

Cahoon, Lydia. Admin. of, to John Cahoon. Nov. 29, 1797. Reg. of Wills, Liber N, folio 186.

Quilling, John. Farmer. Will. Made Nov. 12, 1797. Murderkill Hd. Heirs: son Joseph; daus. Martha & Priscilla. Exec'r, Perry Boon. Wits., Nathl. Smithers, James Wooters, Mary Smithers. Prob. Nov. 30, 1797. Arch. vol. A41, pages 239-240 & vol. A42, page 4. Reg. of Wills, Liber N, folios 185-186.

Shane, James. Admin. of, to Edward Shane. Dec. 1, 1797. Arch. vol. A45, pages 164-166. Reg. of Wills, Liber N, folio 187. Note:—Arch. vol. A45, page 164 mentions heirs, Edward, Thomas & Benjamin Shane & Phebe Hill.

Bostick, Sarah. Widow of James Bostick. Will. Made Feb. 29, 1796. Mispillion Hd. Heirs: sons Major, James & John Bostick; daus. Liday, Sarah, Jean & Prussillah Bostick, heirs of dau. Elizabeth; heirs of Noah Bostick. Exec'r, son Major. Wits., William Masten, John Masten, Mathias Masten. Prob. Dec. 3, 1797. Arch. vol. A5, pages 5-7. Reg. of Wills, Liber N, folio 159. Note:—Arch. vol. A5, page 6 shows that Prusillah Bostick married Nathan Mills.

Pearson, John. Admin. of, to Smith Farsett. Dec. 4, 1797. Reg. of Wills, Liber N, folio 187.

Ward, John. Admin. of, to James Jones, D. B. N. Dec. 6, 1797. Reg. of Wills, Liber N, folio 187.

Manlove, Mark. Admin. of, to James Lafferty. Dec. 9, 1797. Arch. vol. A32, pages 39-41. Reg. of Wills, Liber N, folio 187.

Owens, Robert. Admin. of, to Dr. Robert Jamison. Dec. 13, 1797. Arch. vol. A38, pages 158-159. Reg. of Wills, Liber N, folio 187. Note:—Arch. vol. A38, page 158 mentions heirs, Ellinor, Ammon, Owen & Elizabeth Owens, Sarah, Leah, Jane & William Irons & . . . Barns, half-bro.

Spence, Patrick. Will. Made Nov. 19, 1795. Mispillion Hd. Heirs: wife Mary; sons John, Pierce & Patrick; daus. Martha & Sarah. Exec'rs, wife Mary & John Spence. Wits., Vincent Dehorty, William Layton. Prob. Dec. 14, 1797. Arch. vol. A48, pages 91-92. Reg. of Wills, Liber N, folios 187-188.

Manlove, Tredwell. Admin. of, to George Cummins, Esq. Dec. 18, 1797. Arch. vol. A33, pages 125-126. Reg. of Wills, Liber N, folio 188.

Smith, Stephen. Admin. of, to Rachel & William Smith. Dec. 18, 1797. Reg. of Wills, Liber N, folio 188.

Woodell, Mary. Will. Made July 23, 1796. Duck Creek Hd. Heirs: son Edward Clemons; John Woodell; George Clemons alias George Farmer. Exec'r, Ezekiel Smith. Wits., Mary Wilson, Lydia Train, Jane Nock. Prob. Dec. 19, 1797. Arch. vol. A56, page 109. Reg. of Wills, Liber N, folios 188-189.

White, Benjamin. Admin. of, to Thomas Brown. Dec. 23, 1797. Reg. of Wills, Liber N, folio 189.

Glackan, Patrick. Will (nunc.). Made Dec. 8, 1797. Heir: Mrs. Aydelott, wife of Joseph Aydelott. Wits., John Collins, John Davis. Prob. Dec. 26, 1797. Arch. vol. A19, page 60. Reg. of Wills, Liber N, folio 189.

Glackan, Patrick. Admin. of, to Joseph Aydelott. Dec. 26, 1797. Arch. vol. A19, page 61. Reg. of Wills, Liber N, folio 189.

Meredith, William. Admin. of, to Margaret Meredith. Dec. 28, 1797. Arch. vol. A34, page 221. Reg. of Wills, Liber N, folio 189.

Start, James. Admin. of, to Moses Thomas & Benjamin Thomas. Dec. 29, 1797. Arch. vol. A48, pages 177-178. Reg. of Wills, Liber N, folio 189. Note:—Arch. vol. A48, page 177 shows the acct. settled by John Goldsmith, D. B. N.; also mentions heirs, Elijah & Mary Start.

Moore, Thomas. Admin. of, to William Knotts & Aquila Attix. Jan. 2, 1798. Arch. vol. A36, pages 100-101 & 104. Reg. of Wills, Liber N, folio 190. Note:—Arch. vol. A36, page 104 mentions heirs, John, Samuel & Isaac Moore.

Semans, Gilbert. Will. Made Dec. 12, 1797. N. C. Co. Heirs: dau. Jane; William, Thomas, Stephen Semans & Hannah Browning (children of bro. Thomas Semans); children of sister Elizabeth [Owins], bros. William & Lambert Semans, unnamed. Exec'rs, bro. William, James Raymond & John Cole. Wits., Charles Nabb, John Palmatary, Henry Onail. Prob. Jan. 2, 1798. Arch. vol. A45, pages 126-127 & vol. A46, pages 51-52. Reg. of Wills, Liber N, folio 190.

Goforth, John. Will. Made Dec. 21, 1797. Heirs: wife Mary; son James; daus. Hessey & Nancy; one child unnamed. Exec'x, wife Mary. Wits., Sorden Lister, Thomas Minner, Meredith Bostick. Prob. Jan. 3, 1798. Arch. vol. A19, pages 92-96. Reg. of Wills, Liber N, folios 190-191. Note:—Arch. vol. A19, page 93 shows that Mary Goforth later married John Johnson; also mentions heirs, James Goforth, Kitty Willabaugh, Ann Satterfield & Jule Ann Goforth; page 94 mentions John Halston & wife Lydia Goforth.

Moore, Sarah. Admin. of, to William Knotts & Aquila Attix. Jan. 3, 1798. Reg. of Wills, Liber N, folio 191.

Moore, Sarah. Admin. of, to George Clow, D. B. N. Jan. 8, 1798. Arch. vol. A36, pages 91-96. Reg. of Wills, Liber N, folio 191. Note:—Arch. vol. A36, page 96 mentions heirs, Frances Barcus (wife of William Barcus), Elisha, Abner & Sidney Burrows, Rebecca Clow (wife of George Clow).

Burrows, William. Farmer. Will. Made Dec. 17, 1797. Mispilion Hd. Heirs: sons Boaz, Benjamin, Jonathan, John & William; wife [Rachel, from admin. acct.]. Exec'rs, wife & bro. Benjamin. Wits., William Clark, William Adams, Morgan Williams. Prob. Jan. 9, 1798. Arch. vol. A6, pages 223-228. Reg. of Wills, Liber N, folios 191-192. Note:—Arch. vol. A6, page 227 shows that Rachel Burrows, widow, later married Charles Mason.

Boggs, Joseph. Admin. of, to Hester Morgan, the late Hester Lewis, & George Truitt, D. B. N. Jan. 9, 1798. Arch. vol. A4, pages 179-180. Note:—Arch. vol. A4, page 180 mentions the heirs, Lewis, Elizabeth & Miriam Boggs, minor children.

Stratten, Thomas. Admin. of, to William Moore. Jan. 13, 1798. Reg. of Wills, Liber N, folio 192. Note:—Arch. vol. A49, page 84 shows the acct. later settled by Isaac Moore, D. B. N.

Lee, Richard. Admin. of, to Charles Pope, D. B. N. Jan. 13, 1798. Reg. of Wills, Liber N, folio 192.

Godwin, Eleanor. Admin. of, to Daniel Godwin. Jan. 17, 1798. Arch. vol. A19, page 72. Reg. of Wills, Liber N, folio 192.

Wharton, Sipple. Admin. of, to Ann Wharton. Jan. 16, 1798. Reg. of Wills, Liber N, folio 192.

Clark, John. Admin. of, to Thomas Primrose. Jan. 16, 1798. Arch. vol. A9, pages 14-17. Reg. of Wills, Liber N, folio 193. Note:—Arch. vol. A9, page 16 mentions heirs, Sarah & Major Clark; also shows that Thomas Primrose married Rebecca Clark.

Thompson, Jethro. Admin. of, to Mary Thompson. Jan. 16, 1798. Arch. vol. A50, page 91. Reg. of Wills, Liber N, folio 193.

Thomas, William. Will. Made March 29, 1796. Heirs: sons Philip, Wesley, Daniel, John; wife Miriam; daus. Unity, Susannah & Miriam Thomas, Mary Milburn, Elizabeth Bright. Exec'rs, wife Miriam & son Philip. Wits., Matthew Coxe, James Smith, Mary Rash. Prob. Jan. 20, 1798. Arch. vol. A50, pages 73-77. Reg. of Wills, Liber N, folios 193-194.

Headen, Edward. Admin. of, to Rachel Jordon, D. B. N. Jan. 20, 1798. Arch. vol. A23, page 112.

Tindall, John. Will. Made Nov. 22, 1798. Heirs: bros. Isaac & Purnel; sister Hannah. Exec'r, bro. Jesse. Wits., Thomas Brown, Richard Jefferson. Prob. Jan. 21, 1798. Arch. vol. A50, pages 161-162. Reg. of Wills, Liber G, appendix 11.

Jordan, William. Admin. of, to Charles Green, D. B. N. Jan. 29, 1798. Arch. vol. A28, page 50.

Walls, John Milborn. Schoolmaster. Will. Made Dec. 26, 1797. Heirs: nieces Elizabeth Greenwood, Ann Boyer & Elenor Boyer. Exec'r, James Greenwood. Wits., John Day, Samuel Milborn, Mary Milborn. Prob. Feb. 5, 1798. Arch. vol. A53, pages 28-30. Reg. of Wills, Liber N, folios 194-195. Note:— Arch. vol. A53, page 29 mentions heirs, James, Ellinor Boyer & Ann Boyer (wife of Perrigrine) & Elizabeth Greenwood.

Herrington, Nathan. Admin. of, to Mary [Margaret] Herrington & Aaron Herrington. Feb. 5, 1798. Reg. of Wills, Liber N, folio 195.

Fransisco, Charles. Will. Made Jan. 20, 1798. Little Creek Neck. Heirs: sister Lydia Fransisco; niece Elizabeth Fransisco, dau. of Lydia. Exec'x, Lydia Fransisco. Wits., Cornelius Vanstavoren, Robert Hopkins. Prob. Feb. 9, 1798. Arch. vol. A18, pages 78-80. Reg. of Wills, Liber N, folios 195-196. Note:—Arch. vol. A18, pages 79-80 show that Elizabeth Fransisco settled the acct., D. B. N., in right of Lydia Fransisco.

Boyer, William K. Admin. of, to John Clayton, Esq. Feb. 9, 1798. Reg. of Wills, Liber N, folio 196. Note:—Arch. vol. A5, page 64 shows the acct. later settled by James Clayton, D. B. N.

Sipple, Thomas. Will (unsigned). [N. d.]. Dover Hd. Heirs: wife Ann; dau. Eliza Tatnall Sipple; sisters Lydia Boon & Elizabeth Hardcastle; Thomas Sipple Hillyard; William (Miller) Talley. Exec'rs, Garret Sipple & Joseph Tatnall, Jr. Wits., John Fisher, Timothy Hanson. Prob. Feb. 16, 1798. Arch. vol. A46, pages 164-166. Reg. of Wills, Liber N, folios 196-197. Note:—Arch. vol. A46, page 165 shows that Ann, the widow, later married John Bellach.

Walton, George. Admin. of, to Sarah Hutchinson & Charles Boyer. Feb. 19, 1798. Arch. vol. A53, pages 54-55. Reg. of Wills, Liber N, folio 197.

Bowen, Sarah. Admin. of, to Solomon Bowen & William Wilcuts. Feb. 22, 1798. Arch. vol. A5, pages 20 & 35. Reg. of Wills, Liber N, folio 197. Note:—The heirs are mentioned, Elizabeth, Joseph, John, Sarah & Jeremiah Bowing.

Bowen, John. Admin. of, to William Wilcuts. Feb. 22, 1798. Arch. vol. A5, pages 19 & 32-33. Reg. of Wills, Liber N, folio 197. Note:—The heirs are mentioned, Elizabeth, Joseph, John, Sarah & Jeremiah B. Bowen.

Baning, James. Admin. of, to Joseph Harrison. Feb. 24, 1798. Reg. of Wills, Liber N, folio 197.

Edmondson, John. Admin. of, to Samuel Edmondson. Feb. 26, 1798. Reg. of Wills, Liber N, folios 197-198.

Warren, Zipporah. Dau. of Elizabeth Hardcastle. Admin. of, to John Warren. March 5, 1798. Reg. of Wills, Liber N, folio 198. Note:—Arch. vol. A53, page 153 mentions heirs, John & Samuel Warren, Elizabeth Jones, Mary Wheatly & heirs of Benjamin Warren.

Stuart, James. Admin. of, to George Manliff & wife Mary, late Mary Stuart. March 8, 1798. Arch. vol. A49, page 98. Note: —Acct. mentions heirs, Thomas, James & Charles Stuart.

David, Daniel. Admin. of, to Ann David. March 13, 1798. Arch. vol. A12, pages 212-218. Reg. of Wills, Liber N, folio 198. Note:—Arch. vol. A12, page 212 mentions heirs, Elinor Chicken, Mary Grewell, Daniel, Nancy, Henry & Lydia David; also shows that Ann David married William Ford.

Farsons, Henry. Admin. of, to John Farsons. March 13, 1798. Arch. vol. A17, pages 57-61. Reg. of Wills, Liber N, folio 199. Note:—Arch. vol. A17, page 60 mentions heirs, Rachel Knock (wife of Daniel) & Presley Spruance II; page 61 shows Rebecca Farsons, adm'x, D. B. N.

Milvin, David. Son of Edmond Milvin. Admin. of, to William Tharp. March 13, 1798. Reg. of Wills, Liber N, folio 199. Note:—Arch. vol. A34, page 137 mentions John Milvin, son of Edmond.

Roe, Thomas. Admin. of, to Matilda Roe. March 19, 1798. Arch. vol. A44, pages 120-121. Reg. of Wills, Liber N, folio 199. Note:—Arch. vol. A44, page 120 mentions heirs, Rebecca, William, Mary, Ann, Jane & Sarah Roe; also shows that Matilda Roe later married John Kilpatrick.

Griffen, John. Admin. of, to David Reese. March 19, 1798. Arch. vol. A20, pages 205 & 244. Reg. of Wills, Liber N, folio 199.

Spruance, Henry. Admin. of, to Rebecca Spruance. March 19, 1798. Reg. of Wills, Liber N, folio 199. Note:—Arch. vol. A48, page 110 shows that Rebecca Spruance married Thomas Hawkins; also mentions an heir, Henry Spruance.

Grewell, Margaret. Admin. of, to Jacob Grewell. March 22, 1798. Reg. of Wills, Liber N, folio 200.

McCall, George, Esq. Admin. of, to Elizabeth McCall. March 30, 1798. Reg. of Wills, Liber N, folio 200.

Wallace, Sarah. Admin. of, to James Wallace. April 2, 1798. Reg. of Wills, Liber N, folio 200. Note:—Arch. vol. A53, page 9 mentions heirs, James, Benjamin, Carbine & Margarett Wallace.

Rowen, John. Admin. of, to Sarah Rowen. April 3, 1798. Arch. vol. A44, pages 156-157. Reg. of Wills, Liber N, folios 200-201. Note:—Arch. vol. A44, page 157 mentions a son James Rowen.

Durborough, David. Admin. of, to John Durborough, D. B. N. April 11, 1798. Reg. of Wills, Liber N, folio 201.

Reynolds, Robert. Will. Made July 17, 1796. Murderkill Hd. Heirs: mother Miriam Reynolds; bro. Thomas; Daniel, Michael & George Reynolds; children of sister Leticia; children of John Reynolds. Exec'r, bro. Thomas. Wits., Joshua Beauchamp, Jacob Gruwell, Absalom Knotts. Prob. April 21, 1798. Arch. vol. A43, pages 117-118. Reg. of Wills, Liber O, folios 215-216.

Catlin, Polly [Mary]. Admin. of, to Zadok Powel. April 25, 1798. Arch. vol. A8, page 79. Reg. of Wills, Liber N, folio 202.

Jones, James. Admin. of, to Thomas Marim & Thomas Phillip, D. B. N. April 26, 1798. Arch. vol. A27, pages 202-203. Note:—Arch. vol. A27, page 203 shows that Mary Jones, exec'x of James Jones, later married Samuel Milburn.

Stradley, Caleb. Admin. of, to Margaret Stradley. April 26, 1798. Arch. vol. A49, pages 53-54. Reg. of Wills, Liber N, folio 202. Note:—Arch. vol. A49, page 54 mentions heirs, Absolum, Caleb & Theodore Stradley, Nancy Anderson, Rebeccah Trippit, Margaret & Nimrod Smithers; page 53 mentions a Jonathan Meridith, grandson of Henry Whitacre.

Vincent, Jethro. Admin. of, to Elizabeth Vincent. May 7, 1798. Reg. of Wills, Liber N, folio 202.

Dillen, Nehemiah. Admin. of, to Richard Cole. May 8, 1798. Arch. vol. A14, pages 138-139. Reg. of Wills, Liber N, folio 202. Note:—Arch. vol. A14, page 138 shows that Richard Cole married Elizabeth Dillen; also mentions heirs, James & Sarah Dillen.

Jackson, Eben. Admin. of, to Jonathan Melvin. May 10, 1798. Arch. vol. A25, page 245. Reg. of Wills, Liber N, folios 202-203.

Harrington, Martha. Admin. of, to Aron Harrington. May 12, 1798. Arch. vol. A22, pages 125-127. Reg. of Wills, Liber N, folio 203. Note:—Acct. mentions heirs, sons Jacob, John, Isaac, William, Nathan, David, Aaron & Jonathan Harrington & dau. Sarah Howard (wife of John); also mentions grandsons William & John Marratt & James Harrington, heirs of Mary Graham, Elizabeth (wife of Zadok Haveloe), Martha (wife of John Tumblin) & John Graham.

Smith, Mary. Admin. of, to Josiah Revel. May 12, 1798. Arch. vol. A47, pages 115-116. Reg. of Wills, Liber N, folio 203. Note:—Arch. vol. A47, page 115 mentions an heir, Ruth Smith.

Mileham, Maryann. Admin. of, to Francis Register. May 12, 1798. Arch. vol. A35, page 55.

Corker, John, Jr. Admin. of, to Richard Corker. May 15, 1798. Arch. vol. A11, page 3. Reg. of Wills, Liber N, folio 203.

Foreakers, Samuel. Admin. of, to James David. May 15, 1798. Arch. vol. A18, page 18. Reg. of Wills, Liber N, folio 203.

Ham, John. Farmer. Will. Made Dec. 5, 1796. Heirs: wife Susannah; sons Dr. John, Charles, Alexander & Benjamin; daus. Margaret Stout, Ann, Susannah, Mary & Lurania Ham; grandsons Thomas & James Stout (sons of dau. Margaret Stout & husband Benjamin Stout). Exec'rs, son John & nephew Phillip Lewis. Trustees, Col. Thomas Rodney, Dr. John Laws, John Fisher, Esq. Wits., Caesar A. Rodney, Ken. Smack, John Fisher. Prob. May 16, 1798. Arch. vol. A21, pages 151 & 178-183. Reg. of Wills, Liber N, folios 203-207. Note:—Arch. vol. A21, page 179 mentions Ann Keith; page 182 mentions other heirs, Susan Hukill & James Stant (children of dau. Margaret Stant), daus. Ann Keith, Susan [Susannah] Pollin, Mary Barnet (wife of Thomas) & Lurania Knotts (wife of Benjamin).

With, Aner. Admin. of, to Asa Willoughby. May 17, 1798. Reg. of Wills, Liber N, folio 207.

Jones, Esther. Admin. of, to John Skinner. May 17, 1798. Arch. vol. A27, pages 168-169. Reg. of Wills, Liber N, folio 207. Note:—Arch. vol. A27, page 169 mentions heirs, Eleanor Smith (née Jones), Neley Price (née Jones) & Jerusha Jones.

Poor, Henry. Will. Made May 23, 1798. Heirs: wife Jane; dau. Fanny; son Thomas. Exec'rs, wife Jane & dau. Fanny. Wits., John Day, Sary Mandrell, Thomas Downey. Prob. June 5, 1798. Arch. vol. A40, pages 176-178. Reg. of Wills, Liber N, folios 207-208. Note:—Arch. vol. A40, page 177 shows that Jane Poor later married Samuel Lisby.

Thompson, James. Admin. of, to Elizabeth Thompson. June 13, 1798. Arch. vol. A50, pages 88-89. Reg. of Wills, Liber N, folio 208. Note:—Arch. vol. A50, page 88 mentions heirs, Phebe, Sarah & Susannah Thompson; also shows that Elizabeth Thompson, widow, later married Thomas Thompson.

Kinnamon [Keneam], Ambros. Admin. of, to Christian Kinnamon [Keneam]. June 20, 1798. Arch. vol. A29, pages 40-41. Reg. of Wills, Liber N, folio 208. Note:—Arch. vol. A29, page 41 mentions heirs, Samuel & Thomas Kinnamon; also shows that Christian Kinnamon later married Edward Porter.

Beauchamp, David. Will. Made May 22, 1798. Dover Hd. Heirs: son Nathaniel; bro. Marcy Beauchamp. Exec'r, bro. Marcy. Guardian, bro. Marcy. Wits., Patience Smithers, John Smithers, Nathaniel Smithers. Prob. June 20, 1798. Arch. vol. A3, pages 107-108. Reg. of Wills, Liber N, folios 208-209.

McGifford, Mary. Widow. Will. Made Nov. 14, 1797. Heirs: bro. Joshua Meridith; friend Gidion Ferrel. Exec'r, bro. Joshua Meridith. Wits., Job Meridith, Geo. Cranmer, Abigale Herrik. Prob. July 7, 1798. Arch. vol. A32, page 190. Reg. of Wills, Liber N, folios 209-210.

Molleston, William. Admin. of, to John Clark, Esq. July 16, 1798. Arch. vol. A35, page 226. Reg. of Wills, Liber N, folio 210.

Hendrickson, Jecobus. Will. Made Jan. 23, 1796. Heirs: wife Elenor; sons James, Henry, Samuel & John; dau. Majer Hilman. Exec'rs, wife Elenor & son Samuel. Wits., Cornelius Deweese, Edward Fisher. Prob. July 24, 1798. Arch. vol. A23, pages 139-141. Reg. of Wills, Liber N, folios 199-200.

Heazel, James. Farmer. Will. Made Nov. 20, 1797. Heirs: wife Sarah; sons James, Matthew, Hugh & Ezekel; daus. Rachel, Elizabeth, Martha, Susannah & Sarah. Exec'rs, son James & dau. Elizabeth. Wits., Thomas Lamb, Howel Buckingham, Ann Buckingham. Prob. July 30, 1798. Arch. vol. A23, pages 96-98. Reg. of Wills, Liber N, folios 201-202. Note:— Arch. vol. A23, page 97 shows that Elizabeth Heazel married James Scotten & Susanna Heazel married Jno. McDonald.

Hudson, Margaret. Admin. of, to Jacob Biddle. July 31, 1798. Reg. of Wills, Liber N, folio 210.

Lockerman, Susan H. Late Susan H. Stoops. Admin. of, to James Stoops. Aug. 2, 1798. Reg. of Wills, Liber N, folio 210.

Hawkins, William. Admin. of, to Mary Hawkins. Aug. 13, 1798. Reg. of Wills, Liber N, folio 210. Note:—Arch. vol. A23, page 49 shows that Benjamin Smith married Mary David (late Mary Hawkins, widow & adm'x of Wm. Hawkins).

Thompson, Sarah. Admin. of, to John Houston. Aug. 20, 1798. Arch. vol. A50, pages 110-111. Reg. of Wills, Liber N, folios 210-211.

Loftis, Burton, Sr. Yeoman. Will. Made July 13, 1798. Heirs: wife Mary; sons William, Burton & Gideon; daus. Mary Purnell (wife of Hinson Purnell), Nancy Jarrell (wife of John Jarrell), Rebecca Meridith (wife of Robert Meredith) & Elizabeth Loftis; Mathias Clifton. Exec'rs, sons William & Burton. Wits., Samuel Craige, Matthias Clifton, Peter Harwood. Prob. Aug. 20, 1798. Arch. vol. A31, pages 46-49. Reg. of Wills, Liber N, folios 211-212. Note:—Arch. vol. A31, page 48 mentions an Elizabeth Williams.

Tumblin, Ruth. Admin. of, to William Williams. Aug. 20, 1798. Reg. of Wills, Liber N, folio 212.

Day, John. Farmer. Will. Made March 4, 1796. Heirs: wife Mary; son Mathias; daus. Ariminta, Rebecka & Mary Day. Exec'x, wife Mary. Wits., Joshua Tempel, Jno. Hutchins, Samuel Milborn, Nathan Herington. Prob. Aug. 20, 1798. Arch. vol. A13, pages 117-122. Reg. of Wills, Liber N, folios 212-214.

Sipple, Sylvia. Admin. of, to Sarah Sipple. Aug. 23, 1798. Arch. vol. A46, pages 161-163. Reg. of Wills, Liber N, folio 214.

Conner, John. Admin. of, to Anna Conner. Aug. 29, 1798. Arch. vol. A10, page 84. Reg. of Wills, Liber N, folio 214.

Henderson, John. Doctor. Admin. of, to John Pettigrew. Sept. 7, 1798. Reg. of Wills, Liber N, folio 214.

Maxwell, Bedwell. Admin. of, to Sarah Maxwell, widow. Oct. 1, 1798. Arch. vol. A34, page 79. Reg. of Wills, Liber N, folio 215.

Crumpton, John. Will. Made Aug. 31, 1798. Heirs: mother Elizabeth Crumpton; daus. Mary & Rachel Crumpton. Exec'r, James Crumpton. Wits., John Brown, Stephen Lewis, Ann Roberson. Prob. Oct. 2, 1798. Arch. vol. A12, pages 37-40. Reg. of Wills, Liber N, folio 215.

Parker, Thomas, Jr. Admin. of, to Thomas Parker, Sr. Oct. 4, 1798. Arch. vol. A39, pages 52-54. Reg. of Wills, Liber N, folio 215. Note:—Arch. vol. A39, page 52 mentions heirs, Elizabeth, William & Mary Parker.

Robinson, Joseph. Will. Made Aug. 10, 1798. Duck Creek Hd. Heirs: wife Elizabeth; sons George, John, William; daus. Deborah, Rebecca, Martha. Exec'rs, wife Elizabeth & son William. Wits., James Morris, Jr., A. Allee, Jr., James Morris. Prob. Oct. 9, 1798. Arch. vol. A44, pages 75-78. Reg. of Wills, Liber N, folios 215-216. Note:—Arch. vol. A44, page 76 mentions heirs, James, Daniel & Lydia Robinson & Margaret Foreacres; also shows that Elizabeth Robinson married Ostend Tomlinson.

Miller, Joseph, Esq. Admin. of, to John Patten, Esq. Oct. 16, 1798. Arch. vol. A35, pages 98-102. Reg. of Wills, Liber N, folio 216. Note:—Arch. vol. A35, pages 98-99 & 101-102 mention John Fisher as adm'r, D. B. N.; page 100 mentions John M. Clayton as adm'r, D. B. N.

Truax, Hennery H. Will. Made Sept. 29, 1798. Duck Creek Hd. Heirs: son Hennery H. Truax; daus. Sary & Elizabeth Truax; bro. Isack Truax. Exec'r, bro. Isack. Wits., Peter Hawkins, John Anderson. Prob. Oct. 19, 1798. Arch. vol. A51, pages 86-89. Reg. of Wills, Liber N, folios 216-217.

Rogers, Edward. Admin. of, to Mary Rogers, widow. Oct. 20, 1798. Arch. vol. A44, pages 124-125. Reg. of Wills, Liber N, folio 217. Note:—Arch. vol. A44, page 124 mentions heirs, Sarah, Maria & John E. Rogers; also shows that Stephen Townsend married Mary McCulloch, late Mary Rogers.

Wiggins, Charles. Will. Made Oct. 9, 1797. Duck Creek Hd. Heirs: Deborah Sparks, wife of Lambert Sparks; Elizabeth Holliday, wife of Benjamin Holliday; Joseph Moore; Sarah Foreacres; Robert Wiggins. Exec'rs, Sarah & Samuel Foreacres & Robert Wiggins. Wits., Thomas Pattison, John Stewart, George Cummins. Prob. Oct. 23, 1798. Arch. vol. A54, pages 222-223. Reg. of Wills, Liber N, folio 217.

Harper, John. Admin. of, to Major Bostick. Oct. 24, 1798. Arch. vol. A22, pages 52 & 54. Reg. of Wills, Liber N, folio 217.

Campbell, Joseph. Admin. of, to Alexander Saxton. Nov. 5, 1798. Reg. of Wills, Liber N, folio 217.

Wallace, Carbin. Admin. of, to James Wallace. Nov. 5, 1798. Reg. of Wills, Liber N, folios 217-218.

Jarrel, Robert. Admin. of, to Comfort Jarrell, widow. Nov. 5, 1798. Arch. vol. A26, pages 152-153. Reg. of Wills, Liber N, folio 218. Note:—Arch. vol. A26, page 153 shows that Comfort Jarrell later married Jonathan Gildersleve.

Robertson, Alexander. Gentleman. Will. Made Oct. 17, 1798. Caroline Co., Md. Heirs: Nathaniel Smithers; Susannah Smithers, sister of my late wife Elizabeth; Nathaniel Smithers, son of Nathaniel; sister-in-law Katharine Smithers; son John; Sally Smithers; children of sisters Margaret Emory (wife of Arthur) & Amelia Taylor (wife of Nathaniel). Exec'rs, Nathaniel & Katharine Smithers. Guardian, Dr. Elijah Barratt. Wits., Samuel Culbreth, William Smithers, Samuel Ross. Prob. Nov. 6, 1798. Arch. vol. A44, pages 29-30. Reg. of Wills, Liber N, folios 218-219.

Hadabough, Abraham. Admin. of, to Samuel White, merchant. Nov. 9, 1798. Reg. of Wills, Liber N, folio 218.

Pierce, John. Admin. of, to Hannah Finstrait (alias Vinstreet) late Hannah Pierce. Nov. 12, 1798. Arch. vol. A40, pages 73-74. Note:—Arch. vol. A40, page 73 mentions heirs, Jacob & Mary Pierce.

Wilson, Hosea. Admin. of, to James Sykes, Esq. Nov. 13, 1798. Reg. of Wills, Liber N, folio 218.

Whaley, John. Will. Made Oct. 13, 1798. Heirs: wife Elizabeth; sons William, Nathan, David, John, Levy, Daniel & James; daus. Nancy & Henrietta Massey Whaley. Exec'rs, wife Elizabeth & Salathael Jones. Wits., Mathew Jones, Mary Jones, William White. Prob. Nov. 20, 1798. Arch. vol. A54, pages 35-38. Reg. of Wills, Liber N, folio 219.

Dobson, Edward. Admin. of, to Jonathan Hunn. Nov. 23, 1798. Reg. of Wills, Liber N, folio 220.

Jester, James. Admin. of, to Levi Jester. Nov. 27, 1798. Arch. vol. A27, pages 27-29. Reg. of Wills, Liber N, folio 220. Note:—Arch. vol. A27, page 29 mentions heirs, James, Thomas & Elizabeth Jester & widow Sarah Jester.

Vinson, Jethro. Admin. of, to Thomas C. Allen. Nov. 27, 1798. Arch. vol. A52, pages 55-56. Reg. of Wills, Liber N, folio 220.

Coppage, Peter. Negro. Admin. of, to James Henry, Esq. Nov. 28, 1798. Reg. of Wills, Liber N, folio 220.

Gordon, Coe. Admin. of, to John Caldwell, D. B. N. Nov. 29, 1798. Arch. vol. A19, page 147. Note:—This acct. shows that John Caldwell married Sarah, widow of Coe Gordon.

Dixon, Charles. Admin. of, to George Dixon. Dec. 1, 1798. Reg. of Wills, Liber N, folio 220.

Caldwell, Timothy. Admin. of, to Benjamin Coombe & Samuel Coombe. Dec. 1, 1798. Reg. of Wills, Liber N, folio 220.

Amous, James. Admin. of, to Outten Laws, D. B. N. Dec. 3, 1798. Arch. vol. A1, pages 131-133. Reg. of Wills, Liber N, folio 220. Note:—Arch. vol. A1, page 132 mentions heirs, Elizabeth & George Amous.

Eckles, Richard. Admin. of, to Anthony Eckles, D. B. N. Dec. 4, 1798. Arch. vol. A16, pages 5-7. Note:—Arch. vol. A16, page 7 mentions sister Lydia & bro. Jesse Eckles.

Wright, William. Admin. of, to Edmond Pettit. Dec. 5, 1798. Reg. of Wills, Liber N, folio 220. Note:—Arch. vol. A56, page 162 shows that Rachel Pettit later settled the acct.; also mentions George Wright as guardian of the heirs of William Wright.

Bradley, William. Admin. of, to Mary Bradley & Josiah Bradley. Dec. 7, 1798. Arch. vol. A5, pages 124-125. Reg. of Wills, Liber N, folio 220. Note:—Arch. vol. A5, page 124 shows that Mary Bradley later married Levin Latcham.

Blackshare, Randal. Admin. of, to Sarah Blackshare. Dec. 7, 1798. Arch. vol. A4, pages 99-102. Reg. of Wills, Liber N, folio 220. Note:—Arch. vol. A4, page 99 shows that Sarah Blackshare later married John Gorman; page 102 mentions heirs, Randal & Sarah Blackshare.

Tindall, Elizabeth. Dover Hd. Admin. of, to Richard Jefferson. Dec. 8, 1798. Arch. vol. A50, pages 157-160. Reg. of Wills, Liber N, folio 220. Note:—Arch. vol. A50, page 157 mentions heirs, John, Jesse, Isaac & Purnel Tindall, Hannah Short & Lovey Johnson.

Jones, Mary. Admin. of, to Benoni Harris. Dec. 9, 1798. Reg. of Wills, Liber N, folio 221.

Deal [Dale], Elias. Gentleman (yeoman). Will. Made Nov. 16, 1798. Little Creek Hd. Heirs: wife Sarah; son James; dau. Hester; nephew Thomas Deal & niece Sally Deal (children of bro. John Deal); heirs of Moses Barnet, dec'd. Exec'rs, wife Sarah & friend William Harper. Wits., Edward Williams, Jonas Standley, Walter L. Fountain. Prob. Dec. 13, 1798. Arch. vol. A12, pages 174-176 & vol. A13, page 133. Reg. of Wills, Liber N, folio 221.

Fransisco, John. Admin. of, to Elizabeth Fransisco. Dec. 18, 1798. Arch. vol. A18, pages 83-85. Reg. of Wills, Liber N, folio 221. Note:—Arch. vol. A18, page 83 mentions heirs, Charles, Lydia & Esther Fransisco.

Fransisco, Lidia. Will. Made Nov. 7, 1798. Little Creek Neck. Heir: dau. Elizabeth. Exec'x, dau. Elizabeth. Wits., John White, Charles Conner. Prob. Dec. 18, 1798. Arch. vol. A18, pages 86-87. Reg. of Wills, Liber N, folios 221-222.

Shepperd, John. Admin. of, to Mary Shepperd. Dec. 26, 1798. Reg. of Wills, Liber N, folio 222. Note:—Arch. vol. A45, page 231 mentions heirs, Mary & Edward Shepperd; also shows that Mary Shepperd later married Edward Shepperd.

Joy, William. Will. Made May 28, 1798. Heirs: Jane Harper; Elenor Owen; Edward Joy. Exec'r, Edward Joy. Wits., Hugh Megear, Philip Denney. Prob. Dec. 26, 1798. Arch. vol. A28, page 57. Reg. of Wills, Liber N, folio 222.

Snow, Anthony. Farmer. Duck Creek Hd. Admin. of, to James Robinson. Dec. 26, 1798. Arch. vol. A47, pages 232-235. Reg. of Wills, Liber N, folio 222. Note:—Arch. vol. A47, page 232 mentions heirs, Ann & James Snow & Susannah Palmatary.

Smith, Joseph. Minor son of Joseph. Admin. of, to Joseph Nock. Dec. 27, 1798. Arch. vol. A47, pages 103 & 105. Reg. of Wills, Liber N, folio 222. Note:—Arch. vol. A47, page 103 mentions heirs, Benjamin, Sarah, Jane, George & Ann Smith.

Smith, Joseph. Admin. of, to Joseph Nock, D. B. N. Dec. 27, 1798. Arch. vol. A47, page 104. Reg. of Wills, Liber N, folio 222.

Smith, Mary. Admin. of, to Joseph Nock. Dec. 27, 1798. Arch. vol. A47, pages 117-118. Reg. of Wills, Liber N, folio 222. Note:—Arch. vol. A47, page 117 mentions heirs, Ann, Benjamin, George, Jane & Sarah Smith.

Wilds, Joshua. Admin. of, to John Wilds. Dec. 31, 1798. Arch. vol. A55, page 17. Reg. of Wills, Liber N, folio 222.

Morris, Samuel. Admin. of, to Elizabeth Morris. Dec. 31, 1798. Reg. of Wills, Liber N, folio 223.

Foreacres, Sarah. Will. Made Dec. 11, 1798. Duck Creek Hd. Heirs: William, John, Elizabeth, Joseph, Samuel, Sarah, Ann & Henry Foreacres (children of bro. William). Exec'rs, William & John Foreacres. Wits., Elijah Layton, George Cummins. Prob. Jan. 3, 1799. Arch. vol. A18, pages 20-23. Reg. of Wills, Liber N, folio 223.

Dillon, John. Will (copy). Made Jan. 1, 1799. Caroline Co., Md. Heirs: daus. Mary Dillon, Ann Hignutt; sons John, Vinson & Henry. Exec'x, dau. Mary Dillon. Wits., James Harris, Samuel Chaffinch, Massa Chaffinch. Prob. Jan. 8, 1799. Arch. vol. A14, page 137. Reg. of Wills, Liber N, folios 233-234.

Parker, William. Admin. of, to Thomas Parker. Jan. 9, 1799. Arch. vol. A39, pages 58-60. Reg. of Wills, Liber N, folio 223. Note:—Arch. vol. A39, page 58 shows the acct. later settled by William Parker; also mentions heirs, Ann & Thomas Parker.

Polk, Maria. Minor of Daniel Polk. Admin. of, to James L. Clayton. Jan. 14, 1799. Reg. of Wills, Liber N, folio 223.

Jarrell, Robert. Admin. of, to Andrew Naudain. Jan. 15, 1799. Arch. vol. A26, page 167. Reg. of Wills, Liber N, folio 223.

Thompson, Robert. Admin. of, to Mary Thompson, widow. Jan. 16, 1799. Arch. vol. A50, pages 106-109. Reg. of Wills, Liber N, folio 223. Note:—Arch. vol. A50, page 106 mentions heirs, Elizabeth & Robert Thompson; also shows that Polly Thompson later married Lewis Tomlinson.

Butler, Isaac. Admin. of, to Benjamin Butler, of Sussex Co. Jan. 16, 1799. Arch. vol. A7, page 15. Reg. of Wills, Liber N, folio 223.

Longfellow, Thomas. Admin. of, to Margaret Longfellow, widow. Jan. 16, 1799. Arch. vol. A31, pages 74-75. Reg. of Wills, Liber N, folio 223. Note:—Arch. vol. A31, page 74 shows Mary Denny, adm'x, D. B. N., in lieu of Margaret Longfellow.

Mifflin, Warner. Will (unsigned). [N. d.]. Heirs: wife Ann; son Samuel Emlin Mifflin; bro. Daniel Mifflin; Elizabeth Cowgill, Ann Rasin, Warner, Susanna & Sarah Mifflin (children by first wife); another child unnamed; sons-in-law Clayton Cowgill, Warner Rasin. Trustees, bro. Daniel Mifflin, bros.-in-law Jonathan Hunn & Samuel Howell. Exec'rs, [Clayton Cowgill & Warner Mifflin, from admin. acct.]. Wits., Daniel Mifflin, Jonathan Hunn, Samuel Howell. Prob. Jan. 17, 1799. Arch. vol. A35, pages 22-35. Reg. of Wills, Liber N, folios 224-225. Note:—Arch. vol. A35, page 28 mentions an heir, Susannah Cowgill.

Rogers, Joseph. Admin. of, to Mary Rogers. Jan. 17, 1799. Arch. vol. A44, page 127. Reg. of Wills, Liber N, folio 225.

Edmondson, Peter. Admin. of, to Jonathan Alston. Jan. 19, 1799. Reg. of Wills, Liber N, folio 225.

Foreman, Mary. Will. Made Sept. 10, 1791. Heirs: husband John Foreman; James, Edward, Charles & Henry Hendricks (sons of Henry Hendricks). [No exec'rs]. Wits., H. Layton, Ann True. Prob. Jan. 19, 1799. Arch. vol. A18, page 29. Reg. of Wills, Liber N, folio 225.

Milway, James. Will. Made Dec. 26, 1798. Heirs: sons John, James; daus. Deborah & Elizabeth. Exec'x, wife Milly. Wits., Elias Sipple, John Fisher. Prob. Jan. 22, 1799. Arch. vol. A35, pages 136-137. Reg. of Wills, Liber N, folios 225-226. Note:—Arch. vol. A35, page 137 shows Mary Milloway as exec'x; also mentions heirs, John Milloway & Deborah Ward.

Stuart, James. Admin. of, to Jane Stuart, widow. Jan. 23, 1799. Reg. of Wills, Liber N, folio 226.

Dill, Mary. Admin. of, to William Dill, son of Jacob. Jan. 29, 1799. Reg. of Wills, Liber N, folio 226. Note:—Arch. vol. A14, page 107 mentions an heir, Jacob Dill, a minor.

Catts, Thomas. Admin. of, to Mary Catts & Samuel Dewess. Jan. 29, 1799. Arch. vol. A8, pages 98-100. Reg. of Wills, Liber N, folio 226. Note:—Arch. vol. A8, page 99 mentions heirs, James, Amelia, Thomas & Samuel Catts.

Dill, Solomon. Will. Made Jan. 1, 1799. Heirs: wife Sarah; sons Solomon & John; daus. Ledy Clark, Silvaner Cubdg.; grandsons Solomon Greenlee, William Johnson; heirs of Jacob Dill. Exec'rs, wife Sarah & Solomon Dill. Wits., John Buds, William Dill, Christopher Wise. Prob. Jan. 29, 1799. Arch. vol. A14, pages 118-119. Reg. of Wills, Liber N, folio 226.

Scotton, William. Admin. of, to Priscilla Scotton, widow. Feb. 4, 1799. Arch. vol. A45, pages 102-104. Reg. of Wills, Liber N, folio 227. Note:—Arch. vol. A45, page 102 mentions heirs, Amelia, Merritt, Rebeccah, Thomas & William Scotten; page 103 mentions an heir, Minta Vickers.

Shepperd, Benjamin. Admin. of, to Daniel Shepperd, son. Feb. 7, 1799. Arch. vol. A45, page 227. Reg. of Wills, Liber N, folio 227.

Hopkins, Hampton. Admin. of, to McKimmey Smack, D. B. N. Feb. 7, 1799. Arch. vol. A24, pages 247-249. Reg. of Wills, Liber N, folio 227. Note:—Arch. vol. A24, page 247 mentions heirs, Ann & Leah Hopkins.

Jones, James. Admin. of, to John Jones, next of kin. Feb. 11, 1799. Reg. of Wills, Liber N, folio 227.

Baynard, Thomas. Admin. of, to Elizabeth Baynard, widow. Feb. 12, 1799. Arch. vol. A3, pages 87-88. Reg. of Wills, Liber N, folio 227. Note:—Arch. vol. A3, page 88 mentions heirs, Henry, Samuel & Luther Baynard; also shows that Elizabeth Baynard later married Theodore Stradley.

Watkins, Samuel. Admin. of, to George Clow. Feb. 13, 1799. Reg. of Wills, Liber N, folio 227.

Burchinal, Jeremiah. Admin. of, to Thomas Reynolds. Feb. 13, 1799. Arch. vol. A6, pages 193-194. Reg. of Wills, Liber N, folio 227.

Lewis, Thomas, Jr. Admin. of, to Benoni Harris. Feb. 14, 1799. Arch. vol. A30, page 156. Reg. of Wills, Liber N, folio 227.

Taylor, John, Sr. Farmer. Will. Made Jan. 21, 1796. Mispilion Hd. Heirs: sons Peter, William, John, Robert, Major & George; daus. Lida, Chana, Sarah, Stace, Elizabeth; Maryann Kirk. Exec'r, [John Taylor, Jr., from admin. acct.]. Wits., George Graham, Sr., George Graham, Jr., Polly Kirke. Prob. Feb. 14, 1799. Arch. vol. A49, pages 194-200. Reg. of Wills, Liber N, folios 227-228. Note:—Arch. vol. A49, page 195 mentions heirs, Sarah Saterfield, Stacy Murphy & Elizabeth Morgan.

Stant, Zadok. Admin. of, to Elias Jarrell. Feb. 27, 1799. Arch. vol. A48, pages 145-146. Reg. of Wills, Liber N, folio 228. Note:—Arch. vol. A48, page 145 mentions heirs, Thomas & Goldsberry Stant, Elizabeth Bedwell, Katty Parvis & Margaret Rash.

Pleasonton, John. Will. Made Jan. 13, 1799. St. Jones' Hd. Heirs: friend David Pleasonton; sister Elizabeth Lewis, wife of Stephen Lewis; heirs of sister Elizabeth Lewis. Exec'r, David Pleasonton. Wits., Stephen Paradee, Henry Shaw. Prob. Feb. 27, 1799. Arch. vol. A40, page 111. Reg. of Wills, Liber N, folio 228.

Golt, Naomi. Admin. of, to John Golt, eldest son. Feb. 28, 1799. Reg. of Wills, Liber N, folio 228. Note:—Arch. vol. A19, page 127 mentions heirs, Ezekiel, Naomah, Sarah, Rebeccah & John Golt.

Berry, William. Admin. of, to Peter Stout. March 8, 1799. Reg. of Wills, Liber N, folio 229.

Chambers, Frank. Will. Made Oct. 4, 1794. Heirs: son John; Mary Crage, wife of John Crage; Samuel Chambers, son of Jos. Chambers; Mary Crage, dau. of James Crage. Exec'r, son John. Wits., Joseph Alford, Daniel Jackson. Prob. March 8, 1799. Arch. vol. A8, page 140. Reg. of Wills, Liber N, folio 229.

James, Isaiah. Admin. of, to Mary James, widow. March 12, 1799. Arch. vol. A26, pages 87-89. Reg. of Wills, Liber N, folio 229. Note:—Arch. vol. A26, page 87 shows that Mary James later married Nathan Huff; also mentions an heir, Mary James, a minor.

Johnson, Mary. Admin. of, to Gabriel Sneeds. March 16, 1799. Arch. vol. A27, pages 88-89. Reg. of Wills, Liber N, folio 229.

Henry, Matthew. Admin. of, to George Truitt. March 19, 1799. Arch. vol. A23, page 158. Reg. of Wills, Liber N, folio 229.

Quillen, Thomas. Admin. of, to Joseph Quillen, bro. March 23, 1799. Arch. vol. A41, page 244. Reg. of Wills, Liber N, folio 229.

Burrows, Nehemiah. Admin. of, to William Smith. March 27, 1799. Arch. vol. A6, pages 217-218. Reg. of Wills, Liber N, folio 229. Note:—Arch. vol. A6, page 217 mentions heirs, William, Sarah, Rebecca & Elizabeth Burrows & widow Elizabeth Burrows.

Taught, Elizabeth. Admin. of, to Caesar Taught, free Negro. March 29, 1799. Arch. vol. A49, page 173. Reg. of Wills, Liber N, folio 229.

Crippin, James. Admin. of, to John Ralston, Esq. March 29, 1799. Reg. of Wills, Liber N, folio 230.

Saxton, William. Will. Made Jan. 10, 1798. Murderkill Hd. Heirs: wife Catharine; sons Andrew, William & Brincklee; daus. Sarah Rowen (wife of John) & Elizabeth Saxton. Exec'x, wife Catharine. Wits., Abraham Ridgely, Joseph Harper, Benjamin Wells. Prob. March 30, 1799. Arch. vol. A45, pages 49-51. Reg. of Wills, Liber N, folio 233. Note:— Arch. vol. A45, page 50 shows the acct. later settled by Abraham Kimmy & Brincklee Saxton.

Gilder, John. Will (nunc.). Made March 16, 1799. Heirs: bro. Reuben Gilder; John Jenkins (son of Thomas Jenkins). Exec'r, Thomas Jenkins. Wits., Thomas Jenkins, John Gilder. Prob. April 5, 1799. Arch. vol. A19, page 35. Reg. of Wills, Liber N, folio 232.

Soper, Samuel. Admin. of, to Elizabeth Soper, mother. April 15, 1799. Reg. of Wills, Liber N, folio 230.

Farsett, Smith. Will. Made July 15, 1797. Heirs: wife Phebe; nephews Smith & James Farsett; niece Hetty Farsett; children of bro. Robert Farsett (in North Carolina). Exec'rs, Smith & James Farsett. Wits., John Hudson, Luracy Hudson, Daniel Hudson. Prob. April 15, 1799. Arch. vol. A17, pages 42-48. Reg. of Wills, Liber N, folio 230. Note:—Arch. vol. A17, page 47 mentions John & Elizabeth Farsett (children of bro. Robert); also mentions that Hetty Farsett married George Beswick.

Beathards, William G. Admin. of, to Matthew Beathards, son, D. B. N. April 19, 1799. Arch. vol. A3, pages 101-105. Reg. of Wills, Liber N, folio 230. Note:—Arch. vol. A3, page 103 mentions heirs, Matthew, John, Gorman, William, Samuel, Sarah, Dolly & widow Elizabeth Beathards, dec'd.

Beathards, Elizabeth. Will. Made March 13, 1799. Heirs: son Samuel; dau. Doley. Exec'r, [eldest son Matthew Beathards, from admin. acct.]. Wits., William Cullen, Robert Maxwell, Feby Stueard. Prob. April 19, 1799. Arch. vol. A4, page 34 & vol. A3, pages 96-97. Reg. of Wills, Liber N, folios 230-231.

Mitchell, George. Will. Made Sept. 13, 1798. Heirs: wife Susan; son Fenwick Fisher Mitchell; sister Abigail Bell; bros. Nathaniel & William Clayton Mitchell; nephew John Mitchell, son of Wm. Clayton Mitchell; James Evans, son of Sally Evans. Exec'x, wife Susan. Guardian, wife Susan. Wits., William Hale, Risdon Bishop, Abraham Pierce. Codicil, Feb. 3, 1799. Wits., Geo. Kennard, A. Alle, Jr., John Cummins. Prob. April 22, 1799. Arch. vol. A35, pages 172-175. Reg. of Wills, Liber N, folios 231-232 & Liber O, folio 66.

Hindsley, Patience. Admin. of, to Amos Hindsley & John Hindsley. April 29, 1799. Arch. vol. A24, pages 83-87. Reg. of Wills, Liber N, folio 232. Note:—Arch. vol. A24, page 83 mentions heirs, Merrium Scotten, Hannah, John, Amos & Daniel Hindsley; page 85 mentions Patience Bayley, wife of James Bayley.

Brown, Thomas. Admin. of, to Joseph Nock. May 7, 1799. Arch. vol. A6, page 93. Reg. of Wills, Liber N, folio 233.

Leverton, Gary. Admin. of, to Martha Leverton, widow. May 8, 1799. Arch. vol. A30, pages 18-21. Reg. of Wills, Liber N, folio 234. Note:—Arch. vol. A30, page 21 mentions heirs, Moses, Richard & James A. Leverton; page 19 shows that Ephraim Chambers married Martha Messick (late Martha Leverton).

Draper, Isaac. Admin. of, to Martha Leverton, widow. May 8, 1799. Reg. of Wills, Liber N, folio 234.

Truitt, Southern. Admin. of, to David C. Lee. May 10, 1799. Reg. of Wills, Liber N, folio 234.

Clark, Mary. Minor. dau. of Joshua. Admin. of, to Peter Morgan (City of Phila.). May 10, 1799. Arch. vol. A9, pages 65-66. Reg. of Wills, Liber N, folio 234. Note:—Arch. vol. A9, page 65 mentions heirs, Charlotte, Nancy, Penelope & Joshua Clark, Elizabeth Potter, Sarah Morgan & heirs of John Clark.

Wyth, William. Yeoman. Murderkill Hd. Admin. of, to Francis Register. May 15, 1799. Arch. vol. A56, page 188.

Glass, Belitha. Admin. of, to John Pleasonton. May 15, 1799. Arch. vol. A19, pages 64-67. Reg. of Wills, Liber N, folio 234.

Merchant, John. Admin. of, to James Jones. May 16, 1799. Reg. of Wills, Liber N, folio 234. Note:—Arch. vol. A34, page 173 mentions heirs, Samuel, Harriet, Sarah & Charlotty Merchant.

Cox, Edward. Admin. of, to William B. Smith. June 4, 1799. Reg. of Wills, Liber N, folio 234.

Masten, Mathias. Will. Made May 6, 1799. Mispilion Hd. Heirs: wife Hester; sons John, Mathias, Phillip, Stephen & Zachariah; daus. Rachel, Sarah & Ruth Masten, Elizabeth Clampet, Hannah Allen, Mary Wingate. Exec'x, wife Hester. Wits., William Masten, Sr., Thomas Rathel, William Masten, Jr. Prob. June 6, 1799. Arch. vol. A34, pages 44-46. Reg. of Wills, Liber N, folio 235.

Hilliard, Christopher. Will. [N. d.]. Duck Creek Hd. Heirs: wife [Elizabeth, from admin. acct.]; sons Christopher & William; daus. Rebecky Spruance, Saray, Susannah, Rachel, Tamer & Tamsy Hillyard. Exec'x, wife. Wits., John Stewart, James Saxton, John Saxton. Prob. June 10, 1799. Arch. vol. A24, pages 32-34. Reg. of Wills, Liber N, folios 235-236. Note:—Arch. vol. A24, page 33 shows that Elizabeth Hilliard later married Thomas Budd.

Douglass, James. Admin. of, to Mary Douglass & Walter Douglass. June 11, 1799. Arch. vol. A14, pages 205-206. Reg. of Wills, Liber N, folio 236.

Clark, John. Will. Made March 23, 1799. Town of Dover. Heirs: bro. James Clark; friends Dr. James Sykes, John Fisher. Exec'r, Dr. James Sykes. Wits., John Wild, William Pearce. Prob. June 15, 1799. Arch. vol. A9, page 13. Reg. of Wills, Liber N, folio 253.

Amur, John. Admin. of, to Hannah Amur. June 17, 1799. Reg. of Wills, Liber N, folio 236. Note:—Arch. vol. A1, page 136 mentions heirs, Elizabeth Budd, John, Jane, Hannah, Susannah & Margaret Amur.

Hopkins, Robert. Will. Made April 30, 1799. Heirs: wife Dorcus; sons Elias & Hooper; daus. Mary & Mille Hopkins; grandson Robert Gullett. Exec'rs, wife Dorcus & son Hooper. Wits., Richard Fisher, Vincent Dehorty, Zebulen Hopkins. Prob. June 18, 1799. Arch. vol. A25, page 18. Reg. of Wills, Liber N, folios 236-237.

Manlove, George. Will. Made May 30, 1799. Mispillion Hd. Heirs: daus. Sarah Woodmoncey, Emilia & Eunice Manlove; son Alexander; grandson Mathew Manlove. Exec'r, son Jonathan. Wits., John Mason, William Crumpton, William Sorden. Prob. June 18, 1799. Arch. vol. A33, pages 95-98. Reg. of Wills, Liber N, folios 237-238. Note:—Arch. vol. A33, page 96 mentions an Amelia Primrose; also mentions Elizabeth Griffith, formerly Elizabeth Manlove.

Basset, Benjamin. Will. Made April 21, 1799. Old Duck Creek. Heirs: wife Sarah; daus. Ann Burch, Elizabeth West & Temperance Basset. Exec'x, wife Sarah. Wits., Dickinson Webster, Robert Soper, James Henry. Prob. June 22, 1799. Arch. vol. A3, pages 49-50. Reg. of Wills, Liber N, folio 238.

Hudson, John. Farmer. Murderkill Hd. Admin. of, to William Reed. June 24, 1799. Arch. vol. A25, pages 106-108. Reg. of Wills, Liber N, folio 238.

Newsom, Joseph. Admin. of, to Benoni Harris. June 24, 1799. Reg. of Wills, Liber N, folio 238.

Nock, Thomas. Will (unsigned). Made April 6, 1799. Murtherkiln Hd., Heirs: sons Ezekiel, Thomas, Daniel & Oliver; daus. Mary & Phebe. Exec'rs, sons Ezekiel & Thomas. [No wits.]. Prob. July 2, 1799. Arch. vol. A38, pages 36-40. Reg. of Wills, Liber N, folios 245-246. Note:—Arch. vol. A38, page 38 mentions a Pheby Calloway & Thomas Calloway.

Hillyard, Thomas. Admin. of, to Lurana Hillyard. July 30, 1799. Reg. of Wills, Liber N, folio 239. Note:—Arch. vol. A24, page 47 mentions heirs, Anna, Mary, William & Elbourn Hillyard.

Laws, John. Admin. of, to Joseph Barker. July 30, 1799. Arch. vol. A29, pages 156-159. Reg. of Wills, Liber N, folio 239. Note:—Arch. vol. A29, page 156 mentions heirs, Amelia, Polly and Sarah Laws.

Kirkley, George. Admin. of, to Margaret Kirkley. July 30, 1799. Arch. vol. A29, pages 43-44. Reg. of Wills, Liber N, folio 239. Note:—Arch. vol. A29, page 43 mentions an heir, Margaret Kirkley; page 44 shows that Margaret Kirkley, widow, married William Harper, Jr.

Jackson, Thomas. Admin. of, to Ann Jackson. Aug. 1, 1799. Arch. vol. A26, pages 43-44. Reg. of Wills, Liber N, folio 239. Note:—Arch. vol. A26, page 44 mentions heirs, Marriah, Samuel, George & William Jackson & Polly Manning.

Tucker, John. Admin. of, to Moses Clampitt. Aug. 1, 1799. Arch. vol. A51, page 129. Reg. of Wills, Liber N, folio 239.

Seears, William. Admin. of, to Daniel Nowland & Risdon Bishop. Aug. 6, 1799. Reg. of Wills, Liber N, folio 239.

Vanpelt, Joseph. Admin. of, to Elizabeth Vanpelt. Aug. 8, 1799. Arch. vol. A52, pages 11-15. Reg. of Wills, Liber N, folio 239. Note:—Arch. vol. A52, page 11 mentions heirs, James, George, Joseph, Jesse & John Vanpelt; also shows that Elizabeth vanpelt later married Daniel Smith.

Irons, Mary. Admin. of, to Purnal Lofland. Aug. 21, 1799. Arch. vol. A25, page 222.

Stuart, George, Jr. Admin. of, to Daniel Rogers. Aug. 24, 1799. Reg. of Wills, Liber N, folio 239.

Laws, Belitha. Will. Made March 7, 1798. Heirs: wife Nancy; daus. Zipporah Hays (wife of Manlove Hays), Polley, Mattilda & Leah Laws; son Outten. Exec'rs, wife Nancy & bro. Joshua Laws. Wits., Outten Laws, Sarah Laws, Bolitha Anderson. Prob. Aug. 27, 1799. Arch. vol. A29, pages 142-145. Reg. of Wills, Liber N, folio 240. Note:—Arch. vol. A29, page 144 mentions an heir, Sallyann Laws.

Butler, Jonathan. Admin. of, to Jemima Butler. Sept. 2, 1799. Reg. of Wills, Liber N, folio 240.

Bowing, William, Sr. Admin. of, to Elizabeth Bowing, D. B. N. Sept. 6, 1799. Arch. vol. A5, page 36. Note:—Shows that Elizabeth Bowing is adm'x in right of William, Jr., & Susannah Bowing.

Thompson, James. Admin. of, to Thomas Reed. Sept. 17, 1799. Arch. vol. A50, page 87. Reg. of Wills, Liber N folio 240.

Reed, Ebenezer. Admin. of, to James Reed. Sept. 17, 1799. Arch. vol. A42, page 187. Reg. of Wills, Liber N, folios 240-241.

Hendrixson, Henry. Admin. of, to Levi Hatfield. Sept. 18, 1799. Reg. of Wills, Liber N, folio 241.

James, Daniel. Gentleman. Will. Made July 7, 1796. Murderkill Hd. Heirs: nephew Daniel Saunders (son of Samuel Saunders of North Carolina); bros. & sisters of Daniel Saunders; niece Edith (dau. of Samuel Saunders); Daniel & James Jackson (sons of Daniel Jackson); Rebecca Saunders (wife of James Saunders & dau. of half-bro. John Adams & wife of Joseph Saunders); Samuel Freeman; Mary Freeman (dau. of Samuel); Daniel James Reed (son of Samuel Reed); Thomas Purnal; Curtis Marker; Elizabeth Hinmon (dau. of Bailey Hinmon); Bailey Hinmon; Joseph Flood; Rich Heald; Nicholas Ridgely; Elizabeth & Hannah Brooks (daus. of Benjamin Brooks); Alexander Hamilton; Daniel Jackson; Joshua Jones; Thomas Barker; mulatto man Reuben. Exec'rs, friends Andrew Barratt & Joseph Barker. Wits., James Buckmaster, John George, Thomas Buckmaster, Jr. Prob. Oct. 1, 1799. Arch. vol. A26, pages 84-85. Reg. of Wills, Liber N, folios 241-243.

Green, William. Admin. of, to Mary Green. Oct. 12, 1799. Reg. of Wills, Liber N, folio 243.

Johnston, Phebe. Admin. of, to Mary Ann Johnston. Oct. 12, 1799. Arch. vol. A27, pages 96-97. Reg. of Wills, Liber N, folio 243. Note:—Arch. vol. A27, page 96 mentions heirs, Nancy, Priscilla, James, Purnel & Nathan Johnston, Polly Willey, Sarah Brown & Elizabeth Davis; a bro. William Johnston, dec'd, is also mentioned.

Johnston, Nancy. Admin. of, to Mary Ann Johnston. Oct. 12, 1799. Arch. vol. A27, pages 94-95. Reg. of Wills, Liber N, folio 243. Note:—Arch. vol. A27, page 94 mentions heirs, Priscilla, Polly, Sarah, James, Purnel & Nathan Johnston & Elizabeth Davis.

Deweese, David. Will. Made Oct. 12, 1799. Heirs: sons Spencer, David, Jesse; daus. Hessey, Letisia, Nancy. Exec'x, friend Gideon Cullen. Wits., Mary Ann Cullen, Gideon Cullen, Samuel Meredith. Prob. Oct. 21, 1799. Arch. vol. A14, pages 36-39. Reg. of Wills, Liber N, folios 243-244. Note:—Arch. vol. A14, page 38 mentions widow Elizabeth Deweese, dec'd.

Chicken, Rachel. Will. Made Sept. 25, 1794. Little Creek Hd. Heirs: nephew Andrew Naudain; Rebeckah Naudain (wife of Andrew); Catharine Naudain (wife of Arnold, Sr.); Mary Naudain (dau. of Andrew & Rebeckah). Exec'r, Andrew Naudain. Wits., Jacob Stout, Jr., Francis Barber, William Ruth. Prob. Oct. 23, 1799. Arch. vol. A8, pages 169-170. Reg. of Wills, Liber N, folio 244.

Howell, Mary. Admin. of, to Ann Howell. Oct. 23, 1799. Reg. of Wills, Liber N, folio 245. Note:—Arch. vol. A25, page 73 mentions heirs, John Howell & heirs of Nancy Milliss; also shows that Ann Howell married Isaac Grayham.

Polk, Maria. Minor dau. of Daniel. Admin. of, to Samuel White, Esq. Oct. 24, 1799. Arch. vol. A40, pages 167-168. Reg. of Wills, Liber N, folio 245. Note:—Arch. vol. A40, page 167 mentions heirs, Anna, Daniel, Margarett, John & Samuel White Polk & Elizabeth Clayton.

Macey, Daniel. Admin. of, to Thomas Macey. Oct. 24, 1799. Arch. vol. A33, page 45. Reg. of Wills, Liber N, folio 245.

Dewees, Cornelius. Admin. of, to Elizabeth Dewees. Oct. 26, 1799. Arch. vol. A14, pages 32-33. Reg. of Wills, Liber N, folio 246. Note:—Arch. vol. A14, page 32 mentions heirs, Sarah, Mahaly, Cornelius, Nehemiah, Draper & Elizabeth Dewees & Thirzy Bowman (wife of William Bowman).

Colier, Thomas. Admin. of, to Nathan Huff. Oct. 30, 1799. Arch. vol. A10, page 25. Reg. of Wills, Liber N, folio 246.

Cooper, Elizabeth. Admin. of, to John Cooper. Oct. 30, 1799. Reg. of Wills, Liber N, folio 246.

Hopkins, James, Jr. Minor son of James. Admin. of, to William Hopkins. Nov. 8, 1799. Arch. vol. A25, page 9. Reg. of Wills, Liber N, folio 246.

Couch, James. Admin. of, to Jacob Webb. Nov. 9, 1799. Reg. of Wills, Liber N, folio 246.

Ware, William, Sr. Admin. of, to Thomas Pickering, D. B. N. Nov. 11, 1799. Arch. vol. A53, pages 112 & 114-115. Note:— Arch. vol. A53, page 112 mentions heirs, William, John, Nancy, Mary & Elizabeth Ware, Lydia Tygart & Sarah Fulsom.

Coombe, Benjamin. Farmer. Will. Made Dec. 14, 1798. Murtherkill Hd. Heirs: wife Elizabeth; sons Samuel, Benjamin, Nathaniel, Thomas, Joshua & Griffith; dau. Mary Molleston (wife of Henry). Exec'rs, sons Samuel & Benjamin. Wits., Edward Callahan, Asa Willoughby, John Willoughby. Prob. Nov. 11, 1799. Arch. vol. A10, pages 145-148. Reg. of Wills, Liber N, folios 247-248.

George, Samuel. Negro. Admin. of to Jonathan Hunn. Nov. 13, 1799. Reg. of Wills, Liber N, folio 246.

Cain, Thomas. Will. Made Oct. 20, 1799. Mispillion Hd. Heirs: wife Unicey; sons Daniel & John; daus. Rody Cane & Nancy Brown; grandson Tilghman Brown. Exec'rs, wife Unicey Cane & Daniel Cain. Wits., Major Bostic, Nimrod Morris, Hezekiah Masten. Prob. Nov. 15, 1799. Arch. vol. A7, pages 80-82. Reg. of Wills, Liber N, folios 246-247. Note:—Arch. vol. A7, page 81 shows Nancy Brown as wife of John Brown.

Cooper, John. Admin. of, to Elisha Robertson. Nov. 18, 1799. Reg. of Wills, Liber N, folio 247.

Kirkley, Thomas. Admin. of, to Jane Kirkley. Nov. 26, 1799. Reg. of Wills, Liber N, folio 248.

Molleston, William. Admin. of, to John Clayton & George Cummins, D. B. N. Dec. 4, 1799. Arch. vol. A35, pages 223-224.

Millis, Stephen. Admin. of, to James Millis. Dec. 6, 1799. Reg. of Wills, Liber N, folio 248. Note:—Arch. vol. A35, page 126 shows this acct. was later settled by James Sykes.

Carter, Susannah. Admin. of, to Nathan Scott. Dec. 7, 1799. Arch. vol. A8, page 41. Reg. of Wills, Liber N, folio 248.

Crapper, Zadoc. Admin. of, to Mary Crapper. Dec. 9, 1799. Arch. vol. A11, page 213. Reg. of Wills, Liber N, folio 248.

Morris, Elizabeth. Admin. of, to John Rickards. Dec. 14, 1799. Reg. of Wills, Liber N, folio 248.

Morris, Samuel. Admin. of, to John Rickards, D. B. N. Dec. 14, 1799. Arch. vol. A37, page 7. Reg. of Wills, Liber N, folio 248.

Lecompt, Charles. Will (copy). Made Nov. 16, 1799. Caroline Co., Md. Heirs: wife Leah; nephews Charles Lecompt, James Lecompt (son of Anthony), Charles Lary & James Lecompt (son of James); nieces Sarah & Elizabeth Lary, Sarah Lecompt & Rebecca, Elizabeth & Sarah Lecompt (three daus. of Anthony Lecompt); bro. William Lecompt. Exec'rs, wife Leah & Philemon Lary. Wits., Ben. Denny, John C. Laws & Elizabeth Noble. Prob. Dec. 24, 1799. Arch. vol. A29, page 227.

Owen, Ammon. Admin. of, to Charles Pope. Dec. 30, 1799. Reg. of Wills, Liber N, folio 249.

Edenfield, Samuel. Will. Made Oct. 30, 1799. Town of Dover. Heirs: mother Rachel McNatt, wife of Jonathan McNatt; aunt Sarah Edenfield; Elizabeth Wynn, the elder; John Marim. Exec'r, John Marim. Wits., Eliza Wiltbank, Nicholas Ridgely. Prob. Dec. 30, 1799. Arch. vol. A16, pages 27-28. Reg. of Wills, Liber N, folio 249.

INDEX

All names of persons appearing in the text of the probate record abstracts have been alphabetized and included in this section. The original spelling has been retained throughout, except in cases when variations of names that are phonetically the same are grouped. In these cases the names in parentheses indicate the various spellings included in the same name group.

The Arabic numbers following each name in the index indicate the pages on which these names appear. Names of places, such as villages, towns and land tracts, have been excluded from this index.

The absence of a first or given name is indicated by three dots, as . . . .

—A—

Aaron (Aron),
  Cary, 402
  Elizabeth Cary, 402
  Hannah, 402
  James, 283
  Michael Cary, 304, 350
  Michael McCary, 402
  Sarah, 333
  Sarah Cary, 402
  William, 34, 333
Abbott (Abbet, Abbitt),
  Alefair, 376
  Mary, 291
  William, 177, 301
Ackroyd, John, 362
Adams (Addams),
  Ann, 496
  Brinckle, 214, 224
  Eadith, 44
  Henry, 496
  James, 44, 63
  John, 555
  John H., 518
  Joshua, 273
  Levin, 179, 224
  Nathan, 201, 205, 224, 237, 273, 332
  Sarah, 201 332, 334
  Thomas, 47
  William, 52, 205, 441, 463, 489, 534
Adkison, Ann, 297
Aiken (Akin, Ecan), Allen, 219, 223

Akles: see Eckles
Albany (Albenny),
  John, 227, 229
  Joshua, 367
  Rachel, 227
  Thomas, 341, 367
Alberry,
  Benjamin, 144, 174
  Thomas, 203
Alcock (Allcock),
  Burton, 210
  Burtonwood, 268
  John, 362
  Solomon, 362
Aldridge,
  Henry, 115
  Jane, 115
Alee: see Allee
Alexander,
  David, 474
  Francis, 44
  James, 104
  John, 96
  Margaret, 312
  Philip, 430, 474
  Rachel, 474
  Richard, 312
  Susannah, 474
Alford,
  Aaron, 454
  Betsy, 454
  Charity, 355
  Elizabeth, 521

Joseph, 179, 180, 235, 267, 292, 310, 319, 376, 410, 411, 549,
Mary, 140, 180, 195, 310, 381, 411, 468
Moses, 140, 195
Philip Samuel, 355, 380
Thomas, 148, 152, 157, 195, 197, 228
William, 521
Alfree, Paul, 154
Allaband (Alleband, Alliband), Thomas, 486
William, 396, 466, 473, 486, 520
Allbery: see Alberry
Allcock: see Alcock
Alle: see Allee
Alleband: see Allaband
Allee (Alee, Alle, Alley),
A., Jr., 542, 551
Abraham, 36, 60, 190, 207, 223, 235, 253, 260, 278, 299, 307, 329, 330, 416, 531
Abraham, Jr., 221, 235, 320
Abraham, Sr., 175, 253, 307
Abram, 306
Ann, 299, 307, 320, 416
Elizabeth, 36, 50, 299, 307, 320
Gartrude, 50
Hannah, 36
Isaac, 235, 253
Jacob, 36, 50, 70, 139, 146, 185, 223, 235, 253
Jacob, Jr., 199
Jacob, Sr., 183, 185
Johanus (Johanns), 36
John, 36, 43, 50, 149, 199, 253, 260, 278, 320, 339, 353, 389
John, Jr., 223, 240
Jonathan, 223, 237, 253, 299, 307
Mary, 36, 50, 235, 253, 260, 278, 307, 320
Peter, 36, 50, 153, 260, 278
Presley, 260, 278, 320
Rachel, 36, 50, 305, 389
Rebecca, 320, 330
Sarah, 221, 299, 307, 416, 531
Thomas, 320
Allen,
Andrew, 287
Charles, 155
Elizabeth, 286, 287
Francis, 32
Hannah, 552
Henrietta, 287
Hugh, 172
Jacob, 287
James, 40

John, 169, 172, 203, 287, 290
John, Jr., 203
Joseph, 286, 287
Margaret, 287
Nehemiah, 293
Patience, 155
Peter, 109
Rachel, 172
Samson, 16
Sarah, 169, 172, 173
Thomas C., 544
Alley: see Allee
Alliband: see Allaband
Allston: see Alston
Alsop,
Benjamin, 105
Elizabeth, 105
John, 105
William, 105
Alston (Allston, Allstone),
Abner, 190
Andrew, 264
Arthur, 38, 53, 57, 62, 63, 80, 190, 259, 264, 403
Arture, 142
Asbun, 479
Elizabeth, 190, 264, 479
Frances, 80
Hanah, 264, 424
Israel, 112, 190, 283, 318, 479, 485
Jane, 183, 270
Jean, 183
Joab, 190, 485
Job, 190
John, 190
Jonathan, 479, 485, 547
Joshua, 190
Martha, 264
Mary, 283, 479
Rachell, 39
Randall, 112, 190, 218, 264
Sarah, 112, 136, 142, 190, 207, 259, 355, 403, 479, 487, 516
Stephen, 264, 338, 380, 403, 407, 423, 436, 439, 458, 469, 471, 487, 516
Susan, 479
Thomas, 53, 62, 63, 112, 183, 190, 264, 270, 485
Unice, 479
Ambros,
Catherine, 65
Joseph, 65
Rebecca, 332
Amit,
Jane, 104
John, 104

Ammon,
  Ellinor, 532
  Owen, 558
Armor (Amour, Amur),
  Hannah, 347, 553
  Jane, 553
  John, 286, 347, 553
  Margaret, 553
  Susanna, 286, 553
Amos (Amous),
  Catherine, 66
  Elizabeth, 66, 494, 507, 544
  George, 66, 210, 507, 544
  Henry, 66
  James, 494, 507, 544
  Sarah, 66
  Tamer, 66
Amour: see Amor
Amous: see Amos
Amyatt,
  Jane, 104
  John, 104
Anderson,
  Abraham, 145
  Andrew, 356, 374, 457, 472, 485
  Ann, 200, 229, 373, 441
  Anor, 457
  Bolitha, 349, 555
  Clothier, 354, 386
  Curtis, 448
  Daniel, 383, 441
  David, 153, 232, 257, 322
  Edward, 77
  Eli, 441
  Elijah, 200, 248, 275, 383, 441, 481
  Eliza, 469
  Elizabeth, 200, 202, 221, 257, 280, 288, 322, 349, 479, 483, 498
  Esther, 457
  Ezekiel, 200, 286, 289, 349, 437, 441, 469, 506
  Frank, 29
  George, 457
  Gilbert, 448
  Harmon, 448
  Isaac, 145, 441
  Jacob, 145, 458
  James, 32, 142, 177, 178, 183, 200, 221, 255, 286, 288, 289, 324, 441, 448, 457, 479, 498
  James, Jr., 200
  John, 69, 118, 142, 183, 280, 386, 441, 457, 510, 512, 542
  Joseph, 458, 494
  Joyce, 142
  Letitia, 354
  Major, 200, 307, 350, 404, 441, 469, 506
  Mary, 200, 466
  Mary Ann, 512
  Matthias, 448
  Nancy, 538
  Rachel, 356, 374, 457, 485
  Reuben, 448
  Sarah, 275, 383
  Susanna, 481
  Thomas, 302, 383
  William, 200, 248, 272, 273, 287, 448, 457, 512
Anderton,
  Ealce, 271
  Edward, 77
  Hanahretta, 207
  John, 234, 271, 380
  Mary, 77, 105
  Miriam, 271
  Ruth, 271
  Susannah, 271
Andrea, Pheabe, 127
Anguish, Martha, 500
Angus, David, 311
Annand,
  Elizabeth, 29, 35
  William, 21, 24, 28, 29, 30, 35, 44
Annet (Annett),
  Ailse, 188
  Elliner, 144
  Gove, 166
  Penelopy, 166
  Robert, 166
Appleton, Robert, 445
Arderea, Pheabe, 127
Ardess, Robert, 364
Ardis, Joshua, 211
Armitage, Elizabeth, 138, 154, 180
Armstrong, William, 44
Arnett (Arnet),
  Elizabeth, 138
  James, 138
  John, 223, 334
  Rebeccah, 334
  Sarah, 356
  Thomas, 356
Arpin, Ann, 123
Arrington, Sally, 334
Arriskin, John, 18
Arrowsmith,
  Derander, 220
  Edmond, 220
  Henry, 220

Mary, 220
Mirende, 220
Thomas, 220, 287
William, 220
Arthur (Arthurs),
  Ann, 211
  Christian, 474
  Hanah, 211
  John, 378
  Mary, 315
  Robert, 129, 211, 315
  William, 211, 365, 367, 452, 458, 463, 474
Artis, Mary, 315
Asbee,
  Eleanor, 199
  Esther, 199
  Henrietta Mariah, 199
  John, 199
  Sofiah, 199
Asco, Phillis, 64
Ashberry,
  Elenar, 27
  Joseph, 27
Ashburn (Ashborn),
  Catherine, 80
  Martin, 80
  Mary, 224
  Richard, 80
Ashford,
  Catharine, 222
  Elizabeth, 306
  James, 222
  John, 138, 212, 222
  John, Sr., 222
  Martha, 456
  Mary, 138, 212, 222, 372, 505
  Perygran, 222
  William, 222
Ashley, John, 53
Ashton, Joseph, 46
Askins,
  Mary, 435
  William, 435
Atkins,
  Samuel, 18
  Sarah, 380
  Thomas, 380
Attix (Attax),
  Aquilla, 365, 454, 533, 534
  Charles, 454
  Henrietta, 398
  John, 454
  Sarah, 454
  Stephen, 398, 454
  Thomas, 454

Attow, Thomas, 22
Auston, Charles, 33
Aways, Lewis, 34
Axell,
  Samuel, 46, 340
  Sarah, 340
Aydelott,
  Elizabeth, 511
  Joseph, 517, 533
Ayers: see Ayres
Ayler (Aylor),
  Charity, 341
  Elizabeth, 521
  James, 352, 521
  John, 352
  Sarah, 521
  William, 341
Ayres (Ayers),
  Abraham, 346, 384
  James, 384, 462, 489, 490, 491
  Mary, 384, 489, 491
  Shealah, 384
  Simon, 384, 454, 462, 489, 491
  Susannah, 384, 489
  William, 489

—B—

Bacon,
  Ann, 315
  Elizabeth, 63
  Jacob, 315
  Jonathan, 63
Badger,
  Ann, 516
  Edmund, 135, 210
  Eleazor, 210
  Elizabeth, 515
  Jonathan, 515
  Letitia, 210
Bags, Ann, 289
Bahew (Beheu),
  Powell, 100
  Rachel, 100
Bailey (Baily, Baley, Bayly),
  Alice, 420
  Ann, 233
  Edmund, 233, 296, 307, 317, 395, 429, 524
  Edmund, the elder, 524
  Edward, 524
  Elias, 52
  George G., 11, 462
  Isabelle, 420
  James, 420, 551

John, 420
Julea, 404, 433
Mary, 279, 524
Patience, 551
Rachel, 524
Robert, 524
Sarah, 52, 296, 418
Thomas, 279
Baker,
　Elizabeth, 18
　George, 396
　Isaac, 18
　Sarah, 311, 365
　William, 365
　William, Sr., 311
Baldridge,
　Adam, 25
　Elizabeth, 25
Baley: see Bailey
Ball, Samuel, 246
Ballach: see Bellach
Balton, James, 351
Bamton, John, 47
Bane,
　Parey, 355
　Sarah, 355
Banks, John, 29
Bannin, John, 283
Banning,
　Elizabeth, 323, 338, 396, 441, 442, 469, 507
　Esther, 442
　Gartery, 442
　Hester, 95
　James, 536
　John, 251, 270, 283, 297, 335, 338, 355, 396, 439, 441, 469
　Nathaniel, 442
　Phebe, 442
　Phineas, 315, 442
　Priscilla, 315, 442
　Richard, 95, 323, 387, 394, 439, 442, 459
　Sabino, 337
Barber,
　Abraham, 64, 130, 154, 222, 295
　Ann, 130, 222, 295, 436
　Dohertha, 478
　Frances, 330
　Francis, 222, 266, 295, 331, 376, 436, 471, 478, 556
　John, 222, 436, 478
　Jonathan, 295
　Joseph, 222, 295, 317, 331, 471, 478
　Mary, 266, 376

Muselmon, 478
Priscilla, 295
Rachel, 295, 478
Robert, 295
Sarah, 478
Barclay, David, 115
Barcus,
　. . ., 343
　Frances, 534
　James, 415
　Rachel, 343, 415, 463
　William, 412, 534
Bardon,
　. . ., 119
　Mark, 138
Barger,
　Benjamin, 56, 61
　John, 61
　Joseph, 56, 58, 60, 61
　Mary, 61
　Thomas, 61
Barker,
　Abner, 439
　Alifair (Allefare), 472
　Elizabeth, 410
　Esther, 482
　James, 49
　Jane, 180
　Jannat, 119
　Jean, 180, 283
　Joseph, 389, 410, 433, 474, 554, 555
　Mary, 119, 410, 474
　Phebe, 119
　Sarah, 119
　Susannah, 410
　Thomas, 49, 52, 60, 119, 180, 293, 472, 482, 555
　William, 119, 180, 283
Barkhurst,
　George, 305
　Joseph, 305
Barnabey, William, 53
Barnes: see Barns
Barnesley,
　Richard, 54
　Thomas, 54
Barnet (Barnett, Barnat).
　Andrew, 124, 214
　Elizabeth, 165, 214
　Hugh, 124
　Jane, 324
　Jean, 452
　John, 116, 124, 227, 432
　Mary, 227, 324, 539
　Moses, 124, 214, 324, 325, 381, 438, 452, 545

Rachel, 295, 311
Rebeccah, 406
Samuel, 124, 165
Sarah, 214, 302, 324, 325, 381, 452
Solomon, 295, 311, 320, 421, 432
Thomas, 164, 312, 332, 539
Barnhill,
  David, 84, 156
  Margarett, 156
Barns (Barnes),
  . . ., 532
  Ann, 48, 176, 182, 196
  Bridget Charlton, 261
  Catherine, 153, 182
  Charltron, 450
  Eliner, 48
  Ezekiel, 426
  Hannah, 267
  James, 478
  Jane, 182
  John, 18, 41, 48, 84, 153, 167, 176, 181, 182, 188, 198, 225, 253, 272, 312, 406, 450
  John, Jr., 249
  John Letherberry, 261
  John Pryor, 367
  John, Sr., 426
  Mary, 48
  Percilla, 225
  Rachel, 406
  Rebecca, 48
  Sally, 450
  Sarah, 182, 261, 327, 450
  Stephen, 153, 176, 181, 182, 225, 226, 526
  Thomas, 312
  Warner, 450
  William, 84, 153, 176, 182, 225, 236, 367, 373, 408
Barr, Adam, 99
Barratt (Barett, Barrot),
  Andrew, 338, 363, 461, 467, 484, 485, 510, 555
  Benjamin, 145, 187
  Benjamin, Jr., 88, 105
  Caleb, 363
  Elijah, 363, 473, 517, 531
  Dr. Elijah, 543
  Maj. Elijah, 510
  Ezekiel, 477
  George, 76
  Humphrey, 49, 76
  Jane, 293
  John, 76, 263, 305
  Jonathan, 88, 145
  Joseph, 187
  Lydia, 363, 531
  Margret, 447
  Mary, 76, 88
  Mathew, 76
  Miriam, 198, 293, 294, 354, 363, 484, 531
  Moses, 76
  Nancy, 338, 361
  Nathaniel, 363, 531
  Phebe, 49, 76
  Philip, 249, 258, 303, 326, 363, 372, 531
  Roger, 246, 293, 354, 484
  Samuel, 72, 88, 293, 354
  William, 49, 76
Barris, Mary, 152
Barrow,
  Elizabeth, 366
  Gilbert, 366
  Mary, 366
  Samuel, 348
Barry,
  Hannah, 398
  James, 398
  William, 75
Bartlett (Bartlott),
  Ann, 381
  Daniel, 283
  Elijah, 381
  George, 381
  Henerietta, 381
  John, 465
  Jonathan, 170
  Mary, 152
  Nicklos, 13
  Rachael, 170, 193
  Samuel, 170
Barton,
  Joseph, 388
  Mary, 205
Barwick,
  Edward, 389
  Solomon, 332, 389
Basebridge, Tabitha, 95
Basker, Joseph, 64
Basnet, Ralph, 108
Bassett,
  Benjamin, 388, 553
  Richard, 268, 348, 355, 363, 372, 410, 436, 446
  Sarah, 553
  Temperance, 553
Bassill,
  Robert, 149
  Susanna, 149
Batha, Tempest, 11

Batson,
  Catherine, 510
  John W., 510
Batte, Catherine, 369
Battell (Battle),
  Cornelius, 475, 495
  Elizabeth, 148, 336, 459, 475
  French, 148, 336, 345, 395, 459, 475
  James, 475
  John, 459
  John F., 475
  John French, 475
Bauchamp: see Beauchamp
Bawcomb, Peter, 11
Bayard, Susannah, 240
Bayley (Bayly): see Bailey
Baynard,
  Elizabeth, 380, 389, 397, 548
  Henry, 380, 389, 397, 548
  John, 204, 380, 389,, 397, 497
  Luther, 548
  Nancy, 380
  Samuel, 548
  Sarah, 380
  Thomas, 380, 389, 397, 548
  William, 204
Baxter,
  Frances, 152
  Mary, 56
Beachamp: see Beauchamp
Beadwell: see Bedwell
Beady, Phillip, 88
Beakham,
  Francis, 289
  Mary, 289
Bealy, Edmund, 314
Beaman, Edward, 81
Beard,
  Ann, 196
  John, 323
  Mary, 173, 323, 397
  Moses, 173, 196, 397
Beaston,
  John, 267
  Peregrin, 457
  Susanna, 267
Beathards (Bethards),
  Dolly, 551
  Elizabeth, 520, 551
  Gorman, 551
  John, 551
  Matthew, 551
  Samuel, 551
  Sarah, 551
  William, 551
  William G., 520, 551
Beauchamp (Beachamp),
  Caston, 299
  Conston, 299
  David, 257, 332, 351, 385, 400, 404, 405, 487, 540
  Elizabeth, 368
  Esther, 257
  Grace, 257, 294, 332
  Hester, 299
  Isaac, 257, 332, 368, 400, 404, 405, 485
  Jessy, 299
  John, 280, 294, 299, 302, 332, 400, 405, 485
  Joshua, 538
  Levy, 299
  Marcy, 257, 332, 400, 404, 405, 485, 540
  Mary, 280, 353, 368, 388, 400, 405
  Nancy, 400, 405, 512
  Nathaniel, 540
  Newell, 497
  Rachel, 400, 405
  Rachold, 257
  Risdon, 400, 405, 501
  Robert, 299
  Sarah, 388
  Stephen, 299
  William, 257, 332, 368
Beauvett,
  Hannah, 89
  Peter, 89
Beck, Richard, 462, 463, 471, 515
Becket,
  Comfort, 170
  Mary, 170
  Nathan, 170
  Sarah, 170
  William, 170
Beckworth,
  Nancy, 522
  Rhoda, 522
  Sally, 522
  William, 522
Bedlow,
  Ariminta, 374
  George, 374
  Jerusha, 374
  William, 374
Bedshould, Mary, 67
Bedwell (Beadwell),
  Agnes, 386, 453
  Anna, 28
  Caleb, 477
  Deboraugh, 386

Elijah, 261
Elinor, 42
Elizabeth, 386, 503, 549
Ezekiel, 386
George, 477
Henry, 18, 21
James, 123, 256, 477
Jemima, 261, 477
Margaret, 216
Mary, 261
Milicent, 18, 28
Morgan, 42
Preston, 386, 453, 477
Robert, 13, 21, 167, 171, 216, 256
Susannah, 13, 21, 477
Thomas, 14, 19, 20, 21, 22, 25, 27, 28, 29, 33, 261, 477
Beetle, Mary, 480
Beheu: see Bahew
Belch (Beltch),
  Elizabeth, 376, 476
  Joseph, 376, 476
  Nathan, 476
Bell,
  Abigail, 551
  Elizabeth, 332, 389
  Henry, 185, 332, 345, 389, 445
  John, 55, 59, 61, 153, 185, 219, 257, 264, 274, 300, 320, 326, 332, 333, 335, 389, 446, 465, 525
  John Hall, 465
  John, Jr., 106, 330, 367, 372, 402, 419, 516
  John, Sr., 516
  Judith, 171
  Letitia, 247, 257
  Levin, 499
  Lucy, 185, 257
  Margaret, 59, 389
  Mary, 59, 61, 220, 286, 389, 508
  Nancy, 386, 389, 465, 516, 525
  Robert, 173, 185
  Sally, 465
  Sarah, 516, 525
  Thomas, 185, 220, 286
Bellach (Ballach),
  Ann, 126, 473, 499, 500, 536
  Elizabeth, 473, 499, 500
  Hannah, 84, 254
  James, 126, 272, 351, 473, 484, 499, 500
  Jennett, 126
  John, 126, 254, 473, 499, 500, 536
  Mary, 254
  Robert, 113, 126
  Thomas, 366
  Thomas Hanson, 351, 473
Beltch: see Belch

Belveal, A., 205
Beman, Edward, 82
Bendy, Priscilla, 315
Benet: see Bennett
Benn,
  Benjamin, 489
  Elizabeth, 489
  James, 305
  Sarah, 305
Bennett (Benet),
  Andrew, 313
  Angelo, 342, 463
  Benjamin, 383, 463
  Elinor, 167
  John, 209, 219, 264, 313, 383, 463
  Lydia, 433, 518
  Martha, 264
  Rebeccah, 433
  Sarah, 219, 313, 383, 439, 463
  Thomas, 291
  William, 383, 463
Benson (Bensin),
  Christopher, 127
  Daniel, 134, 383
  Dorothy, 127
  Elizabeth, 133
  John, 127, 133
  Jonathan, 205
  Levin, 284, 383, 410
  Mary, 89, 134, 205
  Nancy, 410
  Thomas, 127
  Thomas, Jr., 127
Benston,
  Benjamin, 253
  Daniel, 144, 389
  Elisha, 347
  Elizabeth, 144, 253
  Eunucy, 363
  James, 363
  John, 144
  Levin, 389, 402
  Mary, 144
  Nice, 347
Berchine, Joseph, 386
Bermingham,
  Catherine, 75
  Esther, 75
  John, 75
  Mary, 75
  Richard, 75
  Veronica, 75
Berry (Burry),
  Benjamin, 243, 508
  Charles, 455
  Daniel, 98
  Edward, 47, 62

Elijah, 240, 243, 273, 378, 416
Elijah, Jr., 378
Grace, 378
James, 133, 152, 243, 319, 426, 530
Jemima, 481
John, 243
Joseph, 243, 279
Margaret, 64, 95
Martha, 319
Nancy, 243
Naomy, 15
Peter, 482
Preston, 138, 229
Samuel, 26, 28, 43, 53, 98
Sarah, 53, 98, 141, 202, 331, 468
Susana, 468
Thomas, 54, 62, 64, 106, 461, 475, 481, 511
Unity, 279
William, 11, 12, 13, 15, 133, 141, 243, 331, 378, 455, 482, 508, 517, 549
Berryman, Elizabeth, 483
Bert, Elsberry, 334
Bessex, (Bessix),
  John, 227
  Mary, 157
  Phebe, 157, 227
Best,
  Edward, 171
  Mary, 194
Beswick,
  Curtis, 262
  Eleanor, 142
  George, 150, 262, 551
  Hetty, 551
  John, 150, 262
  Mary, 157, 262
  Nancy, 486
  Phebe, 157, 262
  Polly, 486
  Priscilla, 486
  Robert, 150, 282, 372
  Sarah, 262, 282
  Solomon, 475
  Vincent, 262
  William, 142
Bethards: see Beathards
Betton, Samuel, 344
Betts,
  Ann, 356
  Betsy, 518
  Edward, 19
  Elizabeth, 53, 90, 282, 288, 356
  Isaac, 356, 518
  John, 18, 19, 53
  Mark, 53
  Mark, Jr., 53
  Mary, 19, 30, 33, 34
  Matthew, 53
  Matthew, Jr., 53
  Robert, 30, 40, 48, 53
  Ruth, 86, 90, 182, 214, 356
  Susannah, 356
  William, 53, 90, 243, 282, 349, 356
Bevil, Robert, 54
Bibbin,
  Jane, 198
  Jean, 198, 231
  John, 198, 231
Bickerton, Henry, 159, 178
Bickham,
  Caleb, 460
  Mary, 460
Biddle,
  Augustine, 317
  Jacob, 317, 541
  Perigrin, 459
  Ruth, 317
Biles, John, 28
Bileter (Billiter),
  Daniel, 95, 253, 377, 447
  Elizabeth, 447
  Joab, 95
  Johanna, 95
  John, 95
  Lydia, 447
  Mahala, 447
  Nancy, 447
  Samuel, 447
  Sarah, 89, 95, 447
  Thomas, 95, 119, 120
Billing, John, 457
Biodell, George, 53
Birch: see Burch
Bird,
  Joseph, 334, 381
  Nancy, 334
  Sarah, 108
  William, 108
Birk: see Burke
Birkett, William, 42, 61, 100
Birmingham: see Bermingham
Birum, James, 404
Bisbin, John, 171
Bishop (Biship),
  Benony, 12
  Comfort, 117
  George, 251
  John, 117
  Lucretia, 418, 444
  Reese, 494

Resdon, 312, 438, 448, 452, 490, 494, 551, 554
Risdon, Jr., 433, 448
Risdon, Sr., 448
Samuel, 251
Sarah, 15
Thomas, 22
William, 522
Bivan,
  Mary, 97
  Philip, 97
Black (Blacks),
  Ann, 382
  Betsy, 397
  Catherine, 201
  George, 68, 322
  James, 46
  Jane, 68
  John, 33, 38, 417
  Mary, 340, 394, 419
  Naomy, 393
  Rebecah, 340
  Samuel, 201
  Stephen, 88, 331, 340, 419
  Stephen, Jr., 340
  Thomas, 301, 382
Blackiston,
  Ann, 370
  Benjamin, 311, 370, 462, 463, 514
  Ebenezer, 319, 428, 458, 467, 489
  Ebenezer, Jr., 489
  Elizer, 489
  Frances, 319, 514
  Francis, 370
  George, 319
  Hannah, 370, 402
  John, 319, 370, 494
  Martha, 319
  Nicholas, 370
  Priscilla, 319, 494
  Samuel, 462, 514
  Samuel Spencer, 408
  Sarah, 319,, 370
  Susannah, 489
  William, 103, 175
Blackshare (Blackshear, Blackshere, Blackshiar, Blackshire), ..., 354
  Ann, 225, 234, 264
  Deborah, 263, 377, 433
  Ebe, 169
  Ebenezer, 212, 225
  Eve, 225
  George, 225, 253, 263, 377
  Jane, 196, 225, 264, 316
  Jean, 225, 316
  John, 196, 225, 377
  Meriam, 354, 428, 484
  Morgan, 225, 264, 316, 377, 434, 447
  Norman, 276
  Randal, 136, 169, 428, 434, 475, 544
  Randolph, 420
  Robert, 182, 208, 216, 225, 242, 316, 384, 460
  Sarah, 225, 234, 256, 264, 377, 425, 428, 433, 544
  Susannah, 212
  Thomas, 234, 320, 342, 428
Blackstone,
  George, 530
  John, 530
  Sarah, 530
Bland,
  Ann, 74
  John, 40, 44, 74
Blandon,
  Charles, 424
  George, 424
  Joshua, 424
Bloom,
  Eve, 236
  Mary, 236
  Peter, 236
  Peter, Jr., 236
Bluett,
  Eleanor, 131
  Martha, 131
  Thomas, 131
Blundell,
  James, 248
  Sarah, 248, 476
  Susannah, 248, 295, 476
Blunt, Levy, 148, 176
Blyth, Andrew, 78
Boak,
  Benjamin, 52
  Joan, 52, 53
Boardly,
  Arthur, 469
  Hannah, 469
  Stephen, 469
  Thomas, 469
  William, 468
Boardman,
  Mary, 111
  Robert, 242
Bodaway, Ruth, 513
Boggs (Boogs),
  Benjamin, 505
  David, 262, 286, 405
  Elizabeth, 534
  Esther, 262

Jane, 109
Jennet, 73
John, 81, 143, 219, 262, 273, 286
John, Jr., 219, 273
Joseph, 262, 319, 375, 424, 534
Lewis, 534
Matthew, 155, 219, 229, 273, 286
Miriam, 534
Rachel, 229
Ruth, 375, 381
William, 68, 81, 262, 273
Bohannan (Bohannon),
  Ann, 216
  Lydia, 294
  Mary, 229
  Rachel, 198, 229
  Robert, 134, 216, 229, 294
  Robert, Jr., 229
Boice: see Boyce
Bond,
  Joseph, 332
  Thomas, 254
Bonine, Abel, 325
Boogs: see Boggs
Boon,
  Ann, 495
  Frances, 462
  John, 467
  Lydia, 536
  Perry, 531
  Samuel, 495
  Sarah, 495
  Thomas, 467, 495
Booth,
  Abraham, 264, 432
  Ann, 62, 80
  David, 380
  Eleanor, 80, 131
  Elizabeth, 55
  Frances, 80
  Isaac, 55, 80, 248, 336
  John, 80, 115, 143
  John, Sr., 46, 152
  Joseph, 23, 34, 47, 62, 65, 67, 80, 102, 115, 153
  Leady, 360
  Mary, 62, 67, 80, 94, 143, 152
  Peter, 226, 248
  Sarah, 248
  Tamer, 248
  Thomas, 80, 102, 163
  Waitman, 143, 267, 446
Born, Free, 509
Bostick (Bossick, Bostwick),
  ..., 362
  Abraham, 233
  Ann, 238, 459

  Eleanor, 351
  Elizabeth, 391
  Jacob, 390, 424, 440, 455, 480, 484
  James, 229, 251, 267, 315, 459, 484, 532
  Jean, 484, 532
  John, 142, 247, 440, 459, 462, 484, 532
  Lydia, 484, 532
  Major, 373, 454, 484, 532, 543, 557
  Margaret, 233, 247, 496
  Mary, 229, 440, 459
  Meredith, 533
  Moses, 437
  Noah, 484, 496, 532
  Priscilla, 484, 532
  Rachel, 436, 459
  Robert, 390
  Samuel, 113
  Sarah, 315, 362, 390, 424, 455, 462, 480, 484, 532
  Shadrach, 233, 312
  Thomas, 437
  William, 233, 482, 512, 525
Bouchell, Slayter, 140
Bouden,
  Ezekiel, 115
  William, 115
Bourace, Rachel, 387
Bourke: see Burke
Bourdet,
  Peter, 15, 17, 18, 22
  Stephen, 22
Bowan: see Bowen
Bowcomb,
  Peter, 12
  Ruth, 12
Bowden,
  Ezekiel, 44, 229
  Frances, 44
  Ruth, 229
Bowen (Bowan, Bowin),
  Andrew, 335
  Catherine, 284
  David, 81
  Elizabeth, 452, 497, 536
  Hannah, 116
  James, 284, 449, 452, 497
  Jeremiah B., 536
  Jeremiah Brown, 452
  John, 284, 431, 452, 536
  Joseph, 284, 451, 536
  Mary, 284, 497
  Nathan, 359
  Rachel, 284
  Sarah, 452, 497, 536
  Solomon, 116, 452, 536

Stephen, 359
  Susannah, 284, 497
  William, 210, 284, 497
Bowers,
  John, 33, 39, 42, 61, 109, 221, 359
  Rachel, 221
  Ruth, 221
Bowin: see Bowen
Bowing,
  David, 72
  Elizabeth, 536, 555
  Jeremiah, 536
  John, 536
  Joseph, 536
  Rachel, 289
  Sarah, 291, 536
  Susannah, 555
  William, Jr., 555
  William, Sr., 555
Bowman,
  Ann, 489
  Amelia, 489
  Clear, 480
  Curtis, 442
  Elizabeth, 74, 75, 256, 290
  Henry, 3, 5, 90, 93, 188, 200, 489
  James, 35
  Jane, 56
  Jemima, 256
  John, 25, 35, 68, 274, 489, 497
  Mary, 200, 256, 408, 443, 489, 497
  Miriam, 90, 188
  Nathan, 337, 410, 432, 441, 480, 489
  Nathaniel, 35, 42, 78, 90, 200, 256, 500
  Rachel, 274
  Rebecca, 432, 497
  Sally, 497
  Samuel, 127
  Sarah, 42, 90, 93, 194, 410
  Thirzy, 557
  Thomas, 35, 42, 90, 93, 188, 194, 200, 241, 256, 290, 321, 410, 442, 443, 447
  Thomas, Jr., 121
  Thomas, Sr., 231, 410
  William, 35, 410, 489, 497, 557
Boyce,
  Alexander, 417, 462
  Sarah, 417
Boyd, John, 161, 292, 305
Boyer,
  Ann, 535
  Anthony, 491
  Caleb, 427, 459
  Charles, 427, 439, 536

  Daniel, 91, 324, 406
  Elenor, 91, 535
  Elizabeth, 112, 202, 207
  Francis A. 427
  James, 91, 207, 217, 257, 333, 427, 439, 535
  Littleton, 421
  Margaret, 440
  Mary, 386, 525
  Peggy, 525
  Perrigrine, 535
  Richard, 386
  Ruth, 324
  Sarah, 421
  William, 525
  William K., 450, 465, 500, 510, 525, 535
Boyle,
  Eve, 159
  William, 159
Boyls, William, 135
Bradford,
  Isaac, 453
  Kendal, 453
  Mary, 453
  Pearcy, 453
  Thomas, 453
Bradley (Bradly),
  Benjamin, 326, 405
  Elizabeth, 230, 405
  Henry, 96, 97, 101
  Isaac, 230
  Jesse, 230
  Johanna, 98
  Joseph, 405
  Josiah, 96, 136, 143, 230, 544
  Margaret, 96, 101, 186, 230
  Martha, 493, 524
  Mary, 143, 221, 230, 544
  Nathan, 230, 493, 524
  Rebecca, 498
  Sarah, 449
  William, 136, 186, 230, 442, 544
Bradshaw (Bradsaw),
  John, 15, 16, 24, 25, 32, 35, 36, 62, 109
  John, Sr., 36
  Jonathan, 12
  Sinah, 109
  Thomas, 19
Brady (Bradey),
  Absolom, 145
  Ann, 237, 312, 339
  Benjamin, 26, 29, 405, 422, 503
  Charity, 330
  Daniel, 26
  Eleanor, 145
  John, 298, 317, 513

Jonathan, 310
Margarett, 152
Mary, 29, 91
Mary Ann, 310
Maurice, 440
Philip, 47, 111, 145, 152
Samuel, 91
Salley, 320
Solomon, 111, 250
Susannah, 298

Bragg, Jacob, 63

Brandal (Brandel),
  Charles, 529
  George, 434

Briangan, William, 48

Brannock,
  Ailce, 291
  Elizabeth, 291
  Thomas, 211
  William, 98, 291

Bratcher, Nathan, 380

Bready,
  Absolom, 91
  Elioner, 91
  Philip, 103
  Samuel, 86
  Sarah, 127
  Solomon, 103, 127

Brees, Samuel, 279

Brein: see Bryan

Brian: see Bryan

Briar,
  Alexander, 107
  Mary, 107

Brion: see Bryan

Brice,
  Benedict, 384, 507
  John, 216
  Mary, 384

Brickell, John, 273

Bride, Elizabeth, 32

Briers, Susanna, 369

Bright,
  Elizabeth, 535
  Jonathan, 500
  Rebecca, 449

Brinckle (Brinckloe, Brinckly, Brinky),
  Absbeth, 374
  Amelia, 239, 245
  Ann, 92, 207
  Backstar, 463
  Benjamin, 88, 92, 132, 213, 245, 523
  Betty, 213
  Charity, 74
  Curtis, 47, 54, 99, 132, 157, 177, 178, 214, 215, 227, 282
  Daniel, 88, 92, 99, 127, 130, 132, 149, 150, 157, 255
  Elizabeth, 11, 34, 43, 45, 47, 54, 71, 99, 157, 245, 337, 374, 485, 499
  Elinor, 523
  Emily, 245
  Esther, 157, 164, 209
  Ezekiel, 157, 227
  Hester, 88, 92, 132, 154, 157, 164
  Jemima, 190, 199, 214
  Jesse, 217, 317, 352
  John, 11, 16, 34, 43, 47, 74, 88, 92, 93, 97, 99, 103, 106, 121, 135, 144, 145, 157, 160, 177, 178, 189, 190, 207, 214, 246, 263, 295, 321, 337, 444, 499
  Dr. John, 485
  John, Jr., 92
  John, Sr., 132
  Jonathan, 132, 154
  Joseph, 132, 207, 213, 245, 282, 313
  Kesiah, 157
  Leah, 213
  Margarett, 48
  Mary, 28, 43, 47, 78, 90, 92, 213, 217, 282, 317
  Miriam, 43
  Peter, 43, 47, 48, 54, 99, 127, 157, 207, 213, 217, 227, 425
  Phebe, 246, 328, 403, 479, 496
  Richard, 99, 103, 121, 127, 157, 183, 196, 246, 328, 364, 403, 479
  Ruth, 99, 132
  Sarah, 43, 47, 90, 132, 214, 227
  Sother, 441
  Southby, 245
  Southey, 245
  Susanna, 88, 99, 108, 157
  Tabitha, 108, 183
  Thomas, 88, 92, 154, 157, 164
  William, 22, 28, 35, 43, 47, 99, 127, 157, 207, 213, 217, 227, 245, 282, 313, 486

Brinett,
  Mary, 97
  Paul, 97

Britton,
  Hannah, 510
  Thomas, 510

Broadaway (Broadway),
  Abner, 437
  Ambrose, 396, 417, 437, 516
  Elizabeth, 437
  Isaac, 437, 516

James, 417
Letticia, 521
Mary, 396, 416, 516
Nancy, 352, 437
Patients, 522
Rebecca, 417
Robert, 437, 516, 522
Sally, 515
Samuel, 417, 437, 516, 517
Sarah, 437
William, 416, 437
Brock,
  Abigail, 71
  Richard, 56, 71
Brodie,
  Christian, 429
  Robert, 284, 429
  Thomas, 429
  William, 429
Brooks (Brook, Brookes)
  Abraham, 38
  Ann, 186, 445
  Anna, 72, 156
  Arthur, 36, 52, 69, 73, 110, 253
  Benjamin, 52, 73, 156, 186, 555
  Catherine, 20, 485
  Charity, 186
  Daniel, 156
  Delia, 483
  Edith, 445
  Elinor, 52
  Elizabeth, 555
  Esther, 186
  Granbey, 483
  Hannah, 555
  Isaac, 253
  Isabella, 69, 110
  James, 52, 72, 156
  James, Jr., 52
  Jeane, 73
  Johanah, 253
  John, 92, 156, 186, 423, 445
  John, Jr., 73
  Jonathan, 92, 197
  Linda, 483
  Martha, 186, 197
  Mary, 52, 73, 110, 120, 186
  Matthew, 92
  Moses, 52
  Nicholas, 423, 445
  Rachel, 73, 156, 483
  Rebecca, 186
  Robert, 126
  Samuel, 29, 63
Broom, Grace, 332
Brown (Browne),
  . . ., 393
  Aaron, 317, 342, 408, 413

Agnis, 112
Ann, 76, 176, 194, 263, 269, 320, 499
Benjamin, 51, 184, 202, 238, 246, 302, 317, 320, 388
Benjamin, Sr., 238
Caleb, 291
Catharine, 404
Charles, 320, 428, 521
Christian, 261, 274, 291
Daniel, 18, 25, 47, 76, 104, 133, 209
Darkus, 320
Elizabeth, 29, 47, 76, 104, 130, 133, 194, 205, 246, 249, 284, 291, 320, 329, 406, 410, 428, 446
George, 50, 66, 104, 137, 261, 275, 330
Grace, 110, 112
Hannah, 51, 408
Henny, 514
Hester, 314
Isaac, 342
James, 140, 155, 194, 202, 238, 288, 428
Jane, 187
Jean, 71
John, 15, 29, 71, 76, 104, 106, 125, 130, 160, 176, 191, 202, 212, 238, 241, 243, 274, 284, 291, 317, 329, 395, 409, 410, 432, 433, 439, 498, 499, 542, 557
Jonathan, 238, 380, 388
Joseph, 286, 432
Joshua, 73, 162, 202, 409, 428, 499, 506
Lilley, 514
Lydia, 393, 431, 432
Margaret, 140, 155, 222, 320, 428
Martha, 139, 378
Mary, 104, 130, 238, 314, 380, 499
Matthew, 363, 439
Meriam, 187, 238
Nancy, 251, 274, 363, 439, 492, 505, 557
Nyca, 187
Pemberton, 67, 104, 258
Phillip, 181
Rachel, 112, 130, 141, 187, 238, 317, 499
Ruth, 317
Sally, 468
Samuel, 499
Sarah, 212, 241, 274, 378, 468, 499, 556
Sealy, 238
Severson, 477
Solomon, 291
Stephen, 133, 209, 404
Susan, 380, 388
Susannah, 18, 130, 133, 238

Thomas, 112, 139, 160, 185, 187,
  200, 221, 242, 248, 274, 284, 339,
  378, 388, 435, 468, 533, 535, 551
Tilghman, 557
William, 51, 202, 224, 243, 251,
  274, 275, 291, 315, 317, 320, 363,
  367, 378, 390, 417, 432, 439, 499
Browning,
  Hannah, 533
  Thomas, 368
Broxon,
  John, 461
  John, the younger, 461
Bruce, Susannah, 140
Brudey, Sara, 188
Brumly,
  Samuel, 496, 524
  Sarah, 496
Bryan (Brein, Brian, Brion),
  Daniel, 130
  Elizabeth, 188
  John, 138, 143, 256
  Mathew, 19
  Michael, 475
  Presemene, 138, 143
  Timothy, 320
Bryant, Elizabeth, 488
Bryers,
  Alexander, 92, 134
  Ann, 134
  Elizabeth, 134
  Mary, 89, 134
Buchannon: see Buckannon
Bucher (Butcher),
  Benjamin, 72
  Conselah, 72
  Jacob, 453
  John, 192
  Moses, 72, 135
  Robert, 64, 72, 135
  Sarah, 72, 86, 192
  Selah, 489
  Susanna, 64
  Thomas, 72, 347, 489
Buck,
  Edward, 47
  Elizabeth, 47, 168
  James, 517
  John, 47, 486, 517
Buckannon (Buchannon,
  Buckhannon),
  Andrew, 145
  Betty, 256
  John, 523
  Lydia, 460

Mary, 308
Nancy, 308
Polly, 256
Robert, 144, 161, 170, 294, 308
Sally, 256
Stout, 308
Buckingham,
  Ann, 392, 540
  Barbary, 299, 339
  Elizabeth, 530
  Howell, 160, 291, 299, 392, 540
  Isaac, 299, 392, 530
  Joseph, 275, 285
  Marcy, 160, 221, 265
  Margaret, 299, 392
  Mary, 392
  Sarah, 275, 285
Buckler, Elizabeth, 280
Buckley,
  Ann, 445
  Arnold, 445
  Elizabeth, 445
  James, 209
  Joseph, 445
  Mary, 209
Buckmaster,
  Catherine, 228
  Esther, 114, 236, 268, 380
  George, 380, 518
  Hester, 380
  James, 555
  James Wells, 228
  John Wells, 228
  Katrine, 53
  Mary Wells, 228
  Sarah Wells, 228
  Thomas, 235, 297, 352, 440
  Thomas, Jr., 555
  Unity, 352, 440
  Wilson, 114, 196, 198, 236, 380
Bucknel, Mary, 219
Buckner,
  Aylett, 511
  Thomas, 511
Budd,
  Elizabeth, 553
  John, 548
  Thomas, 553
Buirch: see Burch
Bulger, Peter, 335
Bullen,
  Ann, 330
  Elizabeth, 330
  Hannah, 398
  John, 330, 398

John, Jr., 330
Rachel, 245, 330
Sarah, 330
Bullet,
  Margaret, 237
  Mary, 237
  Peggy, 237
  Polly, 237
Bullock (Bullick),
  Ann, 428
  Dorcus, 311
  Ezekiel, 428
  Isabell, 234
  John, 311
  Mary, 311
  Nancy, 311, 426, 428
  Richard, 311
  Thomas, 311
Bundelyn (Byndelin),
  John Rodulphus, 41, 177
Bunner, Andrew, 416
Bunting, Job, 63
Burbary (Burberry),
  Mary, 19
  Samuel, 12, 19, 34
Burch (Birch, Buirch),
  Ann, 529, 553
  Elizabeth, 204
  George, 511, 529
  Nancy, 511
  Rachel, 364, 400
  Sarah, 428, 529
  Timothy, 444
Burchinal,
  Catharine, 436
  Elizabeth, 386, 477
  Hannah, 477
  Jeremiah, 436, 477, 549
  John, 477
  Joseph, 477
  Nancy, 513, 521
  Rebecca, 477
  Sarah, 477
Burgess, Anne, 33
Burgis, Roger, 29
Burke (Birk, Bourke),
  Charles, 464
  Milliset, 191
  Rachel, 464
  Walter, 269
Burkeloe (Burkeloo, Burkelow),
  Daniel, 111
  Elizabeth, 121
  Harman, 90, 121
  Margaret, 121

Burns,
  Anthony, 261
  Betty, 373
  Darias, 277
  Fanny, 521
  Frances, 261
  Gilbert, 99, 126
  James, 101
  Jane, 521
  Mary, 521
  Rebecca, 277
  William, 521
Burris (Buris),
  John, 191
  Richard, 296
Burrows (Burroughs),
  Abner, 534
  Alice, 139
  Benjamin, 534
  Boaz, 534
  Ebenezer, 370, 400
  Edward, 29, 31, 34, 400
  Elijah, 367, 534
  Elizabeth, 237, 342, 432, 530, 550
  Esther, 342, 366
  Giles, 139
  Isabele, 374
  James, 342, 492, 530
  Jane, 44
  Jesse, 366
  John, 201, 311, 342, 405, 419, 530, 534
  Jonathan, 534
  Lemuel, 237
  Margaret, 242, 530
  Martha, 320
  Mary, 342, 378, 401
  Naomi, 492
  Nehemiah, 432, 550
  Rachel, 337, 534
  Rebecca, 367, 550
  Richard, 239, 342, 530
  Samuel, 194
  Sarah, 34, 335, 342, 405, 550
  Sidney, 534
  Susanah, 419
  Thomas, 237
  William, 44, 201, 237, 239, 337, 342, 368, 370, 401, 492, 501, 530, 534, 550
Burry: see Berry
Burt,
  Elsbury, 407, 417, 420, 471
  Henry, 407
Burton,
  Isabella, 28

John, 28, 31
John, Sr., 16
Josh, 523
Robert, 145
William, 16, 145
Busban, James, 214
Busby,
  James, 214
  Richard, 20
Bush,
  Abraham, 335
  David, 66
  John, 159
Bussee,
  Mary, 137
  Samuel, 137, 222, 433
  Samuel, Jr., 137
  Susanah, 433
Butcher: see Bucher
Butler,
  Andrew, 292, 294, 347
  Benjamin, 547
  Edmond, 126
  Elizabeth, 70, 292, 347, 355, 467
  Esther, 411
  Isaac, 547
  Jane, 408
  Jemima, 555
  John, 70
  Jonathan, 555
  Mary, 126
  Peter, 137
  Richard, 166, 224, 261, 341
Byrem, James, 386
Byrne,
  Anthony, 281
  James, 153

—C—

Cabley, John, 11
Cacey: see Casey
Cadwalader, John, 35, 61
Caffee (Caffey, Caffy),
  Ezekiel, 355
  Mary, 184, 289
  Maryan, 355
  William, 184
Cahall, Elizabeth, 471
Cahoon,
  Charles, 248, 289, 314, 367, 527
  Eleanor, 233
  Elizabeth, 102, 289, 358, 367
  Hannah, 211

  James, 116
  Jane, 314, 367
  Jean, 289, 527
  John, 98, 102, 135, 147, 367, 496, 531
  Lydia, 493, 531
  Mark, 248, 289, 314, 367, 399
  Marmeduke, 102
  Mary, 102, 147, 241, 289, 367, 496
  Mary, Jr., 135
  Nancy, 289
  Rachel, 154, 248, 289
  Samuel, 102, 496
  Sarah, 314, 496, 527
  Thomas, 102, 104, 146, 154, 211, 215, 248, 264, 289, 291, 314, 358, 367, 383, 399
  William, 102, 137, 147, 233, 248, 282, 289, 291, 367, 390, 496
  William, Jr., 243
Cain (Caine, Cane, Kane),
  Ann, 120
  Christian, 465
  Daniel, 120, 213, 255, 359, 522, 557
  Dennes, 120, 213
  Eli, 465
  Elenor, 120, 142
  Francis, 120, 213, 493, 522
  Hastey, 481
  James, 188, 262, 343
  John, 92, 213, 340, 481, 557
  Leah, 255
  Lydia, 481
  Major, 481
  Manasses, 92, 188
  Margaret, 481
  Mary, 292, 465, 493
  Othaniel, 465
  Owen, 92, 188, 343
  Rachel, 188, 522
  Rody, 557
  Ruben, 481
  Sarah, 493, 522
  Susanna, 481
  Thomas, 120, 191, 507, 557
  Tilda, 481
  Triphana, 481
  Unicey, 441, 557
  William, 103
Cairy: see Cary
Calaway: see Callaway
Caldwell (Calwell),
  . . ., 318
  Andrew, 44, 45, 130, 143, 147, 150, 152, 163, 183, 184, 198, 214, 229, 267, 293, 297, 394, 424, 427, 438, 444, 446
  David, 229, 297, 326

Elizabeth, 326, 374
Esther, 332, 394, 444
Hannah, 145, 162, 341, 350
Jabez, 332, 489
James, 95, 145, 239, 251, 255, 262, 332, 341, 350, 394, 428, 446
James, Jr., 255
Jane, 179, 229
Jean, 53
Joannah, 350
John, 180, 332, 347, 384, 385, 394, 427, 428, 433, 444, 446, 473, 544
Jonathan, 184, 196, 332, 384
Joseph, 98, 159, 206, 332, 341, 350, 360, 365
Margaret, 44, 196, 332, 347, 385, 386
Mary, 152, 159, 206, 255, 267, 297, 332, 374, 394, 443, 445, 446
Peggy, 184
Robert, 394, 409, 424, 427, 438, 443, 446
Sarah, 180, 296, 318, 375, 438, 473, 544
Sidney, 489
Timothy, 255, 288, 296, 332, 347, 375, 410, 422, 446, 544
Train, 297, 394, 446, 491
William, 79
Cale,
  John, 54
  Solomon, 54
Calgan: see Colgan
Calhoon,
  James, 218
  Jeremiah, 280
  Mary, 218, 280
Callahan,
  Edward, 236, 352, 451, 517, 522, 557,
  Esther, 451
  Margaret, 451
  Rebeccah, 236
Callaway (Calaway, Calloway),
  Curtis, 425, 488
  Elizabeth, 241, 328, 440
  Esther, 373
  Jacob, 328, 434, 508
  James, 241, 246
  John, 328, 425, 488
  Joseph, 241, 246
  Lammas, 425
  Lammy, 488
  Martha, 440
  Peter, 91, 241, 246, 425, 488
  Phebe, 246, 554
  Ratchel, 241
  Sarah, 241, 425, 488

Selia, 407
Sula, 425, 488
Taner, 488
Theaner, 425
Thomas, 241, 328, 554
William, 425, 488, 511
Calley (Callay),
  Ann, 441
  James, 504
Callowhill, Thomas, 115
Callton, Cornelis, 11
Campbell (Cambel, Campbel, Camel, Cammell),
  Alexander, 336
  Edward, 277
  Elizabeth, 161, 222
  Henry, 155
  Hugh, 78
  James, 198, 222, 345
  Jonathan, 336
  Joseph, 336, 543
  Magdalon, 78
  Margaret, 336
  Mary, 121, 157, 164
  Ruth, 336
  Sarah, 293
  William, 336, 345
Campling, Edward, 67
Candy, (Canday, Candey),
  Cashenna, 271
  Deborah, 115
  Purnel, 499
  Robert, 115
  Sarah, 379
  Sophia, 181, 306, 344, 362, 499
  Susanna, 271
  Thomas, 499
  William, 181, 271, 344, 499
Cane: see Cain
Cannon,
  Ann, 15
  Bridget, 149
  Moses, 15
  Varner (Varier), 14
Cantwell,
  Lydia, 205
  Richard, 205
Capatrick: see Kilpatrick
Cape, Joseph, 91
Capron, Jarrard, 316
Carbine (Carbin, Carben),
  Elizabeth, 356, 360
  James, 90, 116, 164, 167, 188, 217, 356, 360, 415
  Jane, 188, 217

Margret, 217
Mary, 217
Sarah, 217
Cardeen (Carden),
  Daniel, 315, 482, 502
  Deborah, 502, 530
  Elizabeth, 502
  John, 502
  Mariam, 315
  Prudence, 315
  Rachel, 249, 315
  Ruth, 502
  William, 111, 127, 249, 315, 502
Carey (Cairy, Cary, Carry, Carrey, Ceary),
  Ann, 228
  Archibald, 166
  Bowen, 228, 513
  Edward, 201
  Elizabeth, 223, 228
  James, 258
  John, 494
  Molleston, 265
  Mary, 228
  Nehemiah, 369
  Rachel, 494
  Susannah, 201
  Thomas, 228, 376
  Thomas, Jr., 230
  William, 513
Carl, Thomas, 202
Carlisle,
  Elizabeth, 104
  Thomas, 104
Carlton (Carleton),
  Edward, 44
  Margaret, 528
  Richard, 528
Carman (Carmon),
  James, 490
  Joseph, 136, 146, 510
  Joseph, Jr., 207
  Joseph, Sr., 207
  Rachel, 284
Carmean (Curmean),
  Ailce, 270, 426
  Alice, 443
  Elizabeth, 231
  Jacob, 270, 443
Carmichael (Cirmichael),
  Thomas, 228, 236, 257
Carny, Eleanor, 229
Carpenter,
  Ann, 216
  Elizabeth, 156, 244, 361
  Hannah, 247

  James, 361
  Jean, 337
  John, 151, 216, 240, 247, 337
  Mary, 151, 152, 156, 253, 339, 361,
  Richard, 156
  Samuel, 378
  Sarah, 378
  William, 151, 156, 244, 247, 339, 361, 378, 402
  William, Sr., 378
Carr,
  Margaret, 281
  Prudence, 46
  Robert, 46
Carrall, Ambrose, 65
Carrar, John, 155
Carrow,
  Elizabeth, 302, 375
  John, 197, 302
  Timothy, 19
Carson,
  Charles, 407
  Elizabeth, 243
  John, 243
  William, 316
Carter,
  Ann, 11
  Daniel, 477
  Edward, 267, 418, 480
  Edward Broadaway, 418
  Elizabeth, 187
  Eve, 187
  Henry, 457, 464, 476, 517
  Jane, 90, 187, 217
  John, 480
  John Whitacre, 418
  Jonathan, 187
  Joseph, 145
  Leah, 187
  Margarett, 90
  Mary, 128, 418, 422, 480, 505
  Rachel, 187, 418
  Robert, 90
  Ruth, 418, 480
  Samuel, 505
  Sarah, 187, 480
  Susannah, 241, 558
  Thomas, 90
  William, 90, 160, 187, 188, 217, 418, 480
  William, Jr., 128, 187
Carty,
  Ann, 438
  Cornelius, 111
  Darby, 100, 105
  David, 438

Isaac, 157, 193, 200, 250, 255, 306, 365, 370, 438
John, 438
Kesiah, 157
Mary, 111
Samuel, 438
Sarah, 193, 200
Carvil, Isaac, 448
Casey (Casi, Cacey),
  Daniel, 110
  Dinah, 215
  Elijah Foreman, 523
  James, 523
  John, 523
  Mary, 85
  Michael, 121
  Othoniel, 523
  Samuel, 523
  Zebulon, 215
Casson,
  Annaka, 333
  Elizabeth, 326, 338, 355, 397
  Ferdenand, 326, 518
  John, 338, 355, 396
  Miers, 333
Catlin (Cattlin, Catlen),
  John, 467
  Joseph, 409, 444, 467
  Lydia, 409, 467
  Mary, 229, 265, 277, 444, 467, 538
  Polly, 538
  Robert, 265, 277, 467
  Seth, 250
Caton (Caten, Cayton, Katon),
  Agnes, 101
  Benjamin, 101, 174, 243, 280, 508, 530
  Betty, 101
  Elizabeth, 90, 243
  Ester, 101
  James, 243
  Jennett, 101
  John, 101, 121, 154, 155, 191, 207, 224, 225, 229, 231, 236, 241, 243, 439, 508, 529, 530
  John, Jr., 90, 101
  John, Sr., 101
  Margaret, 101, 530
  Mary, 422, 530
  Miriam, 280, 530
  Penelope, 166, 188
  Peter, 508
  Robert, 101, 166, 188
  Sarah, 101
  Susannah, 101
  Thomas, 101
Catrep, Tarrasias, 22

Catron,
  Benjamin, 482
  John, 482
  Peter, 482
Catts (Cats),
  Amelia, 548
  Elizabeth, 292
  James, 270, 385, 505, 548
  John, 239, 287, 385
  Mary, 287, 548
  Penelope, 126, 253, 355
  Prudence, 270, 505
  Samuel, 548
  Stephen, 126
  Thomas, 385, 548
  Vincent, 292, 504
  William, 223, 239, 287, 312
Causey,
  Dianna, 284
  Priscilla, 403
  Sarah, 284
Cavender (Cavendar),
  Jane, 195
  Sarah, 355
  Thomas, 355
  William, 399
Caverly,
  Ann, 463
  Peter, 463
Ceary: see Carey
Ceny, Sarah, 343
Chadick (Chaddack),
  James, 233
  Richard, 398
  Samuel, 233
  Thomas, 233
Chadwick,
  David, 233
  Elizabeth, 253
  Hannah, 232
  James, 233
  Jane, 233
  John, 233
  Jonathan, 233
  Joseph, 223, 233, 253
  Mary, 232, 233
  Susanna, 234
  Thomas, 232
  Winlock, 253
Chaffinch,
  Massa, 546
  Samuel, 546
Chalsant, John, 206
Chambers (Chaimbers),
  Ann, 70
  Ephraim, 552

Esther, 70
Frank, 376, 549
Harry, 159
Henry, 70
James, 70
John, 70, 105, 155, 287, 376, 549
Joseph, 376, 420, 549
Mary, 266, 493, 517
Rachel, 420, 493, 517
Samuel, 549
William, 266

Chamnis,
John, 240
William, 240

Champbell, Sarah, 293

Chance,
Aaron, 493
Alexander, 27, 57, 140, 187, 300
Alexandria, 346, 365
Ann, 66, 493
Caleb, 464
Elija, 298, 300, 346, 365, 370
Elizabeth, 19
Honor, 57
Jemima, 300, 523
Joanna, 27
John, 57, 187
Joseph, 57
Lydia, 242, 300
Mary, 300
Peter, 495
Prudence, 187
Rebecca, 495
William, 57, 150

Chancy, John, 30, 31

Chant,
Elizabeth, 19
John, 13, 19, 20

Chaplin, Jenat, 243

Chapman,
Cornilious, 243
Samuel, 448

Charles,
Levin, 255
Mary, 255

Chase, William, 379

Chattin, James, 291

Cheffins, (Chevins, Chivens, Chiffins),
Abraham, 181
Benjamin, 428, 480
Enoch, 428
James, 319, 428, 448
Margret, 428
Rebecca, 181
Sarah, 428, 448, 449

William, 428, 443

Cherry,
James, 69
Jane, 69
John, 68, 69
Susannah, 69
William, 69

Chevins: see Cheffins

Chew,
Benjamin, 114, 124, 126, 132, 139, 148, 149, 155, 157, 159, 254, 267
John, 375
Mary, 101
Samuel, 61, 101, 114

Chibb, Richard, 76

Chicken (Chickens),
Ann, 157
Daniel, 466, 515
Elinor, 536
John, 60, 83, 91, 263, 338, 346, 466, 515
Judith, 60, 91
Martha, 263
Rachel, 556

Chiffins: see Cheffins

Chiltington,
James, 420
Jane, 420

Chiltman, William, 130

Chipley,
James, 462
Jane, 462

Chipman,
Agnes, 267
Andrew, 414
Benjamin, 258, 267, 299, 321
Elizabeth, 461
Isaac Moore, 414
James, 359, 414
Mary, 258, 267, 308
Peres, 267
Stephen, 267, 359, 461
Susanna, 267
Thomas, 414
Vincent, 414

Chippy, Elizabeth, 520

Chivens: see Cheffins

Chrispin (Chrispen): see Crispin

Christian, Elizabeth, 46

Christopher,
Annsly, 278
Elizabeth, 278
James, 278
John, 278
Ruth, 278, 385

Sarah, 278
Thomas, 278, 385
William, 278

Clammer,
Mary, 490
Nancy, 490

Clampitt (Clampett, Clampet, Clampit),
Allice, 313
Dinah, 295, 404
Ebenezer, 168, 206, 227, 244, 245
Elizabeth, 168, 552
Ezekiel, 168
Govey, 293
Henry, 168, 299
Jane, 227, 244, 245
Jean, 245
John, 47, 52, 168, 208
John, Jr., 206
Jonathan, 288, 353, 416
Judith, 208
Moses, 206, 554
Mary, 293
Nancy, 168
Samuel, 376
William, 168, 208, 313, 379

Clark (Clarke),
Absolam, 300
Alexander, 464
Ann, 93, 233, 258, 338
Benjamin, 161, 175, 210, 218, 233, 237, 263, 474, 505
Betsy, 409
Caleb, 409
Catheren, 68
Charles, 373
Charlotte, 501, 521, 552
Clement, 338
David, 161, 163, 507
Easter, 521
Elenor, 410, 507
Elizabeth, 47, 59, 68, 123, 158, 161, 312, 329, 338, 409, 426, 437, 521, 522
Esther, 409
Ezekiel, 328, 352, 409, 521
Gideon, 519
Hannah, 296
Henrietta, 522
Henry, 409, 437, 522
Hezekiah, 161
Hugh, 409
Isabel, 189, 192
James, 352, 375, 410, 416, 507, 553
James, Jr., 395
Jane, 410, 507
John, 59, 60, 71, 75, 78, 97, 110, 158, 200, 210, 218, 221, 223, 262, 263, 300, 321, 338, 409, 410, 463, 498, 501, 507, 510, 519, 534, 540, 552, 553
John, Jr., 47
Jonathan, 71, 329, 338
Jonathan, the elder, 352
Joseph, 71
Joshua, 161, 321, 349, 501, 552
Katherine, 59, 60
Ledy, 548
Major, 501, 534
Martha, 157
Mary, 75, 352, 410, 416, 501, 507, 552
Maskill (Maskilin), 71, 161, 352, 395, 521
Matthew, 387, 457, 505, 511
Nancy, 501, 552
Nehemiah, 161, 328, 329
Nicholas, 490
Obidienu, 519
Penelope, 501, 552
Priscilla, 409
Race, 161
Rachel, 329, 414, 463
Rebecca, 498, 501, 534
Rhodes, 233, 296
Richard (Miller), 463
Robert, 410, 416, 455, 504, 507, 510
Ruama, 161
Ruth, 199, 237, 269, 474, 505
Sarah, 59, 68, 93, 123, 175, 210, 218, 263, 269, 300, 338, 352, 421, 501, 523, 534
Solomon, 285
Susan, 123
Susannah, 409
Temperance, 71
Thomas, 98, 103, 118, 149, 161, 166, 168, 175, 176, 180, 186, 191, 199, 200, 210, 215, 218, 263, 269, 426, 501, 505
William, 23, 59, 68, 129, 155, 173, 185, 246, 338, 343, 365, 368, 418, 534
Winlock, 123, 338
Zadok Crapper, 522

Clarrothan, Mary Ann, 230

Clary,
Jane, 153
John, 153
Mary, 153
Rebecca, 153

Clay, John, 83

Clayton,
  Charles, 372
  Elizabeth, 341, 372, 411, 513, 556
  Grace, 180
  James, 19, 21, 86, 132, 154, 155, 161, 170, 180, 184, 195, 261, 341, 535
  James, Jr., 106
  James L., 513, 546
  John, 17, 21, 23, 26, 27, 30, 31, 33, 35, 46, 55, 72, 92, 155, 159, 161, 164, 167, 175, 180, 189, 194, 195, 206, 221, 252, 261, 348, 372, 375, 378, 412, 415, 436, 450, 529, 535, 558
  John Edmonds, 412
  John, Jr., 109, 120, 130, 131, 135, 153, 154
  John M., 542
  John, Sr., 180
  Jonathan, 127
  Joshua, 28, 38, 56, 193, 283, 372
  Mary, 12, 21, 221
  Sarah, 193, 224
  Thomas, 372
Cleave, Joseph, 232
Cleaver,
  Hannah, 190
  William, 190
Cleaves, Benjamin, 83
Clefford: see Clifford
Clemens (Clemons, Clemmons),
  Catherine, 491
  Edward, 407, 491, 532
  Elizabeth, 407, 491
  George, 532
  Mary, 491
  Sarah, 226
  Thomas, 226, 491
Clifford,
  Ann, 38, 50, 114
  Daniel, 392, 416, 456
  Elizabeth, 19, 20, 26, 114
  Esther, 114
  George, 19, 20
  Hestor, 120
  John, 20, 22, 26, 50, 114, 380
  Lydia, 456
  Martha, 114
  Mary, 20, 26, 114, 291
  Parnell, 26
  Peter, 114
  Thomas, 20, 22, 26, 50, 55, 114
Clift, Joseph, 447
Clifton,
  Absolom, 87
  Ann, 503
  Benitha, 503
  Clemment, 373
  Daniel, 373, 503
  Ephraim, 87
  Ezekiel, 373
  Isaiah, 373
  James, 503
  John, 87, 503
  Levica, 503
  Levin, 479
  Mahalah, 477
  Margaret, 511
  Mary, 28, 479, 492, 503
  Mathias, 404, 493, 520, 541
  Matthew, 373
  Nathan, 373
  Nathaniel, 503
  Perthenca, 503
  Richard, 373
  Robert, 166
  Sarah, 166, 503
  Seala, 373
  Shadrick, 373
  Thomas, 373, 492, 503
  William, 87
Clinton, Christopher, 77
Clives, Benjamin, 83
Cloak (Cloke),
  Ann, 459
  Ebenezer, 455, 456
  Elizabeth, 421, 456
  John, 459
  Nehemiah, 333, 466
Clothier, (Clother, Cloather),
  John, 152, 441
  Lewis, 147
  Sarah, 441
Cloud (Cloude, Clouds),
  Elizabeth, 471
  James, 471
  John, 471
  John, Sr., 471
  Longpre, 14
  Martha, 471
  Rachel, 471
  Sarah, 471
  William, 471, 515
Clow,
  China, Jr., 398
  George, 534, 548
  Rebecca, 534
Clubb, Richard, 83
Clymer,
  Mary, 451, 490
  Nancy, 451, 490

Coakley,
　James, 369
　Letitia, 324, 528
Coal: see Cole
Coates, Thomas Peachey, 312
Cocker,
　Rachel, 423
　Richard, 423
Cockerel (Cockrel, Cockrill, Cockrell),
　Abraham,, 83
　Elizabeth, 54, 57, 282, 377
　James, 282, 377
Cockran (Cockram, Cockron, Cockrum, Cockrun),
　Agnes, 101, 226
　Christopher, 46, 101, 128
　Daniel, 226
　Jane, 178
　John, 71, 128, 164
　Mary, 245
　Susannah, 46
　Thomas, 98, 245
　William, 350
Cockrell: see Cockerel
Cockrill: see Cockerel
Cockron. (Cockrum, Cockrun): see Cockran
Cocks: see Cox
Codrat: see Coudrat
Codry: see Cordray
Coe,
　Alice, 39
　John, 35, 39
　Mary, 93
　Patience, 35
　Sarah, 35, 39, 132
　Thomas, 35, 39, 132, 147
　William, 35, 39, 56
Coffy, Hugh, 159, 170
Cole,
　Ameli, 177
　Christopher, 262
　Cuthbert, 375, 392, 474
　Edward, 276, 521, 530
　Elizabeth, 28, 108, 474, 538
　Ellinor, 84
　Emilia, 214
　John, 264, 316, 383, 454, 470, 489, 533
　Joseph, 108
　Lemuel, 323
　Margaret, 521
　Mary, 108, 177, 214, 454
　Matilda, 530
　Miriam, 108
　Penelope, 177
　Phebee, 373
　Rebecca, 375, 392, 455, 458, 474
　Richard, 538
　Sarah, 108, 163, 177, 214, 270, 291, 323
　Spencer, 90, 114, 121, 134, 163, 177, 214
　Susannah, 108, 115
　Thomas, 108
　William, 108, 115
Colehale,
　Uphra, 83
　William, 83
Coleman (Colman),
　James, 451
　John, 408
　Sarah, 270, 451, 516
　Thomas, 27
Coleson, William, 40
Coley: see Colley
Colgan (Calgen, Colgun),
　Edward, 311
　Elizabeth, 311
　Isaac, 311
　James, 204
　Jane, 422
　John, 311
　Mary, 311
　Rachael, 311
　Richard, 311
　Sarah, 476
Colley (Collee, Coley),
　Alice, 415
　Daniel, 467
　John Lewee, 97, 133
　Mary Lewee, 133
Collier (Colier, Coller),
　. . ., 505
　Henry, 418
　James, 418
　John Lewis, 133
　Mary, 505
　Thomas, 557
Collinner, Ursilla, 25
Collins (Collings, Collin),
　Alaxander, 302
　Ann, 327
　Benjamin, 327
　Betsay, 302
　Curtes, 302
　Edward, 259, 327
　Elizabeth, 134, 208, 225, 410, 518
　George, 412
　James, 269
　James Staton, 272

John, 249, 533
Johnathan, 302
Mary, 122, 302, 460
Nelly. 269
Rachel, 58, 76, 91, 110
Rebecca, 272, 327
Richard, 134, 302, 327
Sarah, 208
Thomas, 22, 162, 240, 259, 346, 410
Trainy, 339
Uriah, 48
William, 58, 61, 76, 91, 110, 175, 208, 251, 265, 327, 410, 460
Colman: see Coleman
Colt, Deborough, 528
Colter,
  James, 63
  Margory, 63
Colweel, Elizabeth, 301
Comegys,
  Elizabeth, 416
  John, 315
Comerford,
  Peter, 450
  Thomas, 450
Concelio, William, 325
Concelor: see Conselar
Condon, William, 65
Conikin, William, 198
Coningham: see Cunningham
Connell, William, 77
Conner (Connor),
  Abraham, 329, 461
  Anna, 541
  Brian, 371
  Burton, 457
  Catherine, 449
  Cealy, 434
  Charles, 339, 402, 545
  Dennis, 429, 451
  Elizabeth, 335, 461
  Hannah, 354
  John, 351, 354, 377, 403, 429, 461, 541
  Mary, 416
  Minty, 457, 529
  Patrick, 454, 461
  Rachel, 522
  Samuel, 111, 464
  Sarah, 111, 195, 299, 377, 416, 461
  Soloman, 369, 457, 464, 529
  Thomas, 449
  Triphener, 457, 529
  Walter, 522
Connolly (Conolly, Conly),
  Ann, 178
  Henrietta Maria, 27
  Patrick, 413
  Sarah, 208
  Thomas, 178
  William, 208
Connor: see Conner
Conselah (Consela),
  Joanna, 49
  Mary, 86
  Thomas, 49, 86
  William, 86
Conselar (Concelor),
  Elizabeth, 401
  Hannah, 401
  Mary, 170, 401
  Thomas, 401
Consiglio,
  Francis, 231
  Jean, 231
Coodrat: see Coudrat
Cook (Cooke),
  Andrew, 69
  Archaball McK., 57
  Arthur, 39, 40
  Benjamin, 35, 40
  Elizabeth, 39, 414, 421
  Hannah, 49, 89
  James, 384
  John, 35, 37, 39, 40, 89, 123, 327, 378, 394, 399, 400, 412, 421
  Joseph, 35, 40
  Margaret, 35, 123, 498
  Mary, 37, 49, 69, 384
  Michael, 49, 116, 123, 385, 399, 421, 472, 498
  Priscilla, 40
  Robert, 49, 60, 375, 394, 421, 498
  Sally, 516
  Samuel, 338
  Sarah, 35, 40, 61, 76, 421, 488, 493, 516
  Thomas, 40, 61, 76
  William, 73, 247, 250, 260, 414
Coole,
  John, 316
  Rebecca, 455
Cooley, Daniel, 354
Coombe (Coomb, Coombs),
  Benjamin, 332, 338, 357, 450, 517, 544, 557
  Benjamin, Jr., 485
  Elizabeth, 557
  Griffith, 557
  James, 95
  John, 398, 422, 450, 517
  Joshua, 557
  Mary, 450

Nancy, 450
Nathaniel, 557
Samuel, 485, 517, 544, 557
Thomas, 557

Cooper,
Absolum, 469
Catharine, 482
Elizabeth, 469, 484, 516, 557
Frances, 278
George, Jr., 484
George, Sr., 484
John, 484, 557
Lucey, 278
Mark, 414
Mark, Sr., 414
Owen, 260
Richard, 65, 428, 449, 450, 527
William, 414

Copeland, John, 11

Copes,
Robert, 358
Susannah, 358

Copner,
Catherine, 206, 215
Cornelius, 206, 215

Coppage,
John, 356, 362, 390, 412, 440, 424
Martha,, 440
Nancy, 440
Peter, 544
Sarah, 356, 362, 390, 412, 424, 440

Corbet (Corbit),
Isaac, 154
Jacob, 154, 193
Mary, 154
Paty, 413
Rachel, 154
William Fisher, 446
William Strictland, 154, 193

Cordray (Cordry, Cordery, Codery, Coudray),
Deborah, 35
Elizabeth, 365
Hugh, 35
Isaac, 194, 302
Mary, 302, 346
Noble, 346
Thomas, 283, 346, 365, 488

Corey: see Correy

Corker,
Dennis, 173
John, 417
John, Jr., 539
John, Sr., 466
Mary, 173
Rachel, 173, 263

Richard, 466, 539

Corkeran, James, 188

Corkram, Christopher, 40

Cormell, John, 115

Cornelius,
Ann, 420
George, 420
Margaret, 420

Corran, Patrick, 475

Correy (Corey),
Ann, 103, 136
Charles, 103, 136, 354
John, 103, 132
Mary, 103, 132, 136, 354
Molleston, 103, 136, 234, 354
Molleston, Jr., 354
Rachel, 284
Samuel, 103, 104, 136

Corse (Course),
Ann, 375
Benjamin, 375
Elizabeth, 221, 429
George, 356, 378
Hanson, 356, 360, 375
James, 341, 425
John, 356, 360, 375, 378, 425, 429
Rebecca, 406
Susanna, 157, 356, 360, 375, 378
Thomas, 356, 360, 375, 436
William, 200, 211, 228, 341, 356, 360, 375, 378, 392, 406
William, Jr., 364

Cottingham,
Jonathan, 191, 243
Thomas, 243

Cottman,
Joshua, 213
Leah, 213

Couch, James, 557

Coudery: see Cordray

Coudrat (Coudret, Coodrat, Codrat, Cowdratt, Goodrat, Goodratt),
Bardon, 266
Daniel, 119, 120, 138, 213, 266
Elizabeth, 119
Frances, 120, 135
Hillary, 266, 497
John, 120, 173, 268
Joshua, 266
Mark, 119, 138
Martha, 119
Mary, 266, 268
Peter, 61, 80, 85, 100, 114, 120, 268

Coulter,
  Nancy, 490
  William, 490
Course: see Corse
Courtney (Courtne),
  Daniel, 17
  George, 17
  Jean, 33
  John, 17, 100
  Joshean, 17
  Letitia, 78, 85, 100
  Mary, 17, 78, 85, 100
  Nathaniel, 17
  Thomas, 17, 78
  William, 11
Coutts, James, 23
Coverdill,
  Mathew, 480
  Nancy, 480
Coverill, Richard, 374
Covey, Sarah, 435
Covington (Coventon),
  Jeremiah, 46
  Samuel, 82
Cowdratt: see Coudrat
Cowgill (Cowgil, Cowgle),
  Clayton, 193, 214, 215, 334, 436, 469, 547
  Daniel, 312, 460, 462, 469, 484, 500, 526
  Ebenezer, 92, 97
  Elenor, 193
  Ellen, 140
  Elizabeth, 97, 283, 547
  Ezekiel, 136, 140, 148, 193, 278, 351, 359, 398, 460
  Hannah, 116, 150
  Henry, 193, 215, 318, 396, 467
  John, 46, 63, 100, 116, 150, 193, 248, 278, 318, 359, 396, 436
  John, Jr., 334
  Lydia, 150, 334, 392
  Martha, 214, 215
  Mary, 148, 436
  Rachel, 63, 140, 469
  Sarah, 136, 140, 193
  Susannah, 547
  Thomas, 136, 140, 193, 228
Cox (Coxe, Cocks),
  Alice, 470
  Anthony, 411
  Barbara, 266
  Caleb, 411, 501, 518
  Charles, 527
  Daniel, 266, 345, 456, 502, 515
  Daniel Powell, 345
  Edward, 266, 317, 345, 427, 552
  Elizabeth, 480
  Esther, 266
  Gove, 323, 406, 527
  Isaac, 286, 484
  James, 484
  Jarrard, 266
  John, 266, 291, 361, 390
  John, Jr., 470
  John, Sr., 411, 480
  Margaret, 382
  Martha, 411
  Mary, 173, 237, 266, 505
  Matthew, 266, 283, 382, 396, 409, 473, 528, 535
  Nancy, 411
  Nathan, 266
  Nicholas, 345
  Philip, 305
  Powell, 285, 345
  Priscilla, 351
  Rebecca, 406, 527
  Sarah, 345, 473
  Susanna, 318, 351, 484
  Thomas, 142, 237, 266, 291
  Thomas, Jr., 266
  William Clark, 515
Coyle, Patrick, 129
Crabbin, Elizabeth, 384
Crabtree, Samuel, 118
Crafton,
  Joseph, 308
  Mary, 308
Craige (Craigs, Crage),
  Alexander, 86, 87, 134, 217, 234, 257, 297, 315, 440
  Agnes, 87, 223, 264
  Andrew, 144
  Ann, 223, 244, 257, 264, 297
  Annalena, 210, 234, 257, 297
  Barsheba, 515
  Bathshaba, 497
  David, 77
  Ebenezer, 92
  Elizabeth, 77, 83, 86, 87, 150, 223, 419, 474
  Franky, 497
  George, 92
  Henritta, 144
  Henry, 518
  Hugh, 86, 87, 150, 210
  Isabella, 88, 92, 104, 155, 210, 223, 257, 297, 315, 415, 440
  James, 77, 92, 210, 234, 257, 297, 311, 355, 356, 376, 388, 497, 507, 517, 549
  Jane, 92, 155

John, 70, 73, 83, 92, 98, 134, 210,
    223, 234, 243, 244, 257, 276, 315,
    465, 497, 549
Margaret, 86, 87, 98, 134, 223, 285,
    440
Mary, 92, 257, 376, 497, 507, 549
Moses, 86, 87, 210, 234, 257, 297
Leah, 450
Nancy, 232
Nanny, 210, 257, 297
Neiome, 210
Polly, 376
Prudence, 92, 108
Rachel, 465, 474
Samuel, 92, 210, 234, 257, 297, 315,
    388, 419, 493, 497, 507, 541
Sarah, 86, 87, 210, 429
Sophia, 298, 356, 429
Susannah, 315
Thomas, 86, 87, 210, 223, 232
Unity, 440

Crain (Crane),
    Iddy, 253
    Patrick, 267, 276, 288, 295, 371,
        414
    Thomas, 136

Crammer (Crammar, Cramer),
    Catherine, 486
    George, 394, 486, 530, 540
    Jonathan, 394
    Lydia, 394
    Margret, 394
    Mary, 530
    Miriam, 394
    Skidmor, 394
    Thomas, 50, 179, 394, 419, 520
    Susannah, 50
    William, 50

Crane: see Crain

Craner,
    Charles, 348
    Charles, Sr., 348
    Dorcas, 348
    Elizabeth, 348
    Mary, 348
    Moses, 348
    Priscilla, 272
    Samuel, 348
    Thomas, 348

Crankfield (Crankfeald),
    Ann, 259
    John, 502
    Joseph, 502
    Lydia, 502
    Moses, 303, 502
    Nancy, 502
    Rachel, 502

Cranston, Miriam, 381

Crapper,
    Elizabeth, 373
    Levin, 373
    Mary, 174, 296, 558
    Mary, Jr., 298
    Susannah, 321
    Zadok, 174, 242, 270, 296, 298, 558

Crathers, William, 524

Cratis, Ann, 524

Craven, John, 16

Crawford (Crofford),
    David, 221, 245
    Elizabeth, 34, 43, 45
    Evis, 43, 45
    John, 84, 264
    Katharine, 66
    Letitia, 43, 45
    Mary, 43, 45
    Oliver, 244, 288, 241, 356, 374
    Rachel, 288, 356, 374
    Thomas, 30, 41, 42, 43, 45, 56, 59,
        66
    William, 374

Creighton,
    David, 357
    Elizabeth, 357
    John, 357
    Mary, 213, 363
    Matthew, 357
    Robert, 357
    Ruth, 229, 260
    Thomas, 213
    William, 189, 260

Cremean: see Crumean

Crippen (Crippin, Cripen),
    Elizabeth, 42, 301
    James, 442, 550
    John, 42, 442
    Rachel, 442
    Thomas, 42, 58, 82
    William, 197
    William, Jr., 193
    William, Sr., 193

Crispin (Crispen),
    Elizabeth, 88, 212
    Joseph, 88
    Mary, 212
    Sarah, 212
    Silas, 88, 139, 145, 187
    Sylas, 212
    Tabitha, 139, 212, 291, 308

Crockett (Crocket),
    Elinor, 379, 409
    Elizabeth, 252, 379, 409
    Jesse, 317

John, 252, 317, 379, 409
Jonathan, 317, 379, 409, 491
Margarett, 252, 379, 409
Mary, 252, 476
Samuel, 379, 409
Sarah, 491
Crofford: see Crawford
Crompton: see Crumpton
Cromwell, James Oliver, 335
Crooks,
  Ann, 439, 516
  Benjamin, 407, 439, 516
Crosby, Cato, 489
Crosier: see Crozier
Crosley (Crosly), Richard, 36
Cross,
  John, 265, 346, 412
  John, Jr., 346
  William, 133, 265
Crouch, William, 350
Crow, George, 178, 380
Crowy, John, 35
Crozier (Crosier),
  Mary, 282
  Matthew, 259, 282
  Rachel, 259, 282, 314
  Rhoda, 282
  Robert, 282
  Sarah, 282
Crumeen (Cremine, Cremean),
  Elizabeth, 180, 190, 203
  John, 242
  Thomas, 190
Crumpton (Crompton),
  Curtis, 298, 380
  Elizabeth, 211, 542
  James, 542
  Jerimah, 467
  Jennet, 281
  John, 209, 211, 226, 287, 298, 327, 467, 542
  John, the elder, 209
  Mary, 298, 379, 380, 542
  Meriam, 467
  Rachel, 452, 542
  Sarah, 327
  Thomas, 211
  Watkins, 281
  William, 553
Cubbage (Cubbidge),
  Anna, 355, 395
  Deborah, 484
  Elizabeth, 427, 484
  George, 355, 484
  John, 355, 459

Philemon, 314, 355, 395, 404, 427, 484
Rebecca, 314
Silvaner, 548
Thomas, 355
Cuff, Absolam, 29, 33, 34, 43
Culbreath, (Culbreth),
  John, 426, 433
  Jonathan, 388
  Rebecca, 433
  Samuel, 543
  William, 433, 462
Cullen (Cullin),
  Ann, 379, 529
  Charles, 298
  Cornelius, 16
  David, 320
  Elias, 298
  Elizabeth, 524, 529
  George, 298, 529
  Gideon, 556
  Hannah, 296
  Henry, 529
  Hezekiah, 377, 424, 524, 529
  James, 320
  John, 296, 298, 320, 360, 362
  Jonathan, 298
  Mary, 320
  Mary Ann, 377, 529, 556
  Nancy, 298
  Nathan, 320, 524
  Nathaniel, 320
  Pearcy, 378
  Sarah, 320, 378, 529
  Thomas, 320
  William, 320, 378, 551
Cullipher, Benjamin, 410
Cully (Culley),
  Alice, 327
  Arthur, 326, 327
Cummins (Cummings, Cumming, Cuming, Cumings, Cumin, Commings),
  Agnes, 110
  Daniel, 110, 158, 299, 309, 408, 466, 528
  Daniel, Jr., 399
  David, 528
  Delictum, 77, 171, 233
  Elizabeth, 516
  Francis, 528
  George, 309, 399, 410, 421, 435, 441, 450, 468, 502, 528, 532, 542, 546, 558
  Hannah, 110
  James, 273, 300, 436
  John, 528, 551

Leaer, 288
Lumino, 77, 171
Lydia, 436
Mary, 120, 150, 158, 275, 528
Nancy, 528
Patrick, 120, 137, 138, 158, 163
Polly, 516
Rachel, 233
Robert, 42, 53, 54, 74, 77, 111, 117, 137, 163, 171, 317
Sarah, 435
Sibby, 528
Timothy, 106, 110, 528
Violet, 77
Cunningham (Conningham, Coningham, Cunickem),
Andrew, 118
Elizabeth, 351
John, 122, 351
Margrett, 106
Mary, 118
Sarah, 106, 156
Curry (Currey),
Ann, 132
Archibald, 230, 241, 248
Charles, 132
Isaac, 234
James, 215, 387
John, 132
Joseph, 188
Mary, 132, 309
Molleston, 132
William, 309
Curtis (Curtes),
Ann, 11
Caleb, 11, 21, 25
Comfort, 301, 392, 393, 423, 486
Cornelia, 25
Elizabeth, 11, 18, 21, 28, 392, 423, 486
Jehu, 18, 21, 43, 47
John, 11, 18, 21, 22, 43, 88, 122, 392, 486
Mary, 43, 47, 122, 392
Priscilla, 18, 21
Richard, 16, 17, 18, 22, 28
Ruth, 21
Samuel, 18
Sarah, 88, 392, 486
Thomas, 392, 423, 486
William, 122, 392, 423, 486
Winlock, 11, 18
Curwell,
Clayton, 411, 466
Rachel, 411, 466
Cutler,
Sarah, 402
Thomas, 355, 402

Cusins, Sarah, 156

—D—

Dabbs,
Benjamin, 24, 32
Catherine, 32
Easther, 32
Elizabeth, 32
Dagman (Degman),
Peter, 464
Ruth, 385
Dagnell, Ezebell, 213
Dailey (Daily),
Benjamin, 365
William, 413
Dale,
Elias P., 325, 545
Sarah, 325, 381, 452
Dales, Esther, 54
Dallinar (Dellenar, Dillaner),
Charlotta, 287
Richard, 250, 256, 287, 349, 496, 498, 528
Sarah, 287
Danens, Benjamin, 410
Danes, Sarah, 380
Daniel, William, 363
Darbe, Lurania, 191
Darling,
Ann, 151, 179, 262, 296
Daniel, 508
Eleanor, 449, 508
Elizabeth, 179
Esther, 233
Gorden, 179
James, 136, 155, 171, 179, 239, 335, 431, 508
John, 233, 296, 449, 508
Joshua, 398
Lydia, 508
Margret, 156, 179
Mary, 239, 508
Rachel, 449, 508
Richard, 95, 155, 171, 179, 335, 398
Robert, 411
Sarah, 155, 179
William, 134, 155, 158, 171, 179, 239, 272, 296
Darnall, William, 11, 429
Darrach, John, 281, 316, 358, 438, 473
Darson,
Joyce, 73
Richard, 73

Daughtery: see Dehorty
Daus, Neal, 192
Daves: see Davis
David,
  Agness, 110
  Alis, 93
  Ann, 78, 126, 353, 536
  Benjamin, 63, 140
  Catharine, 87, 168
  Charles, 222, 466
  Daniel, 140, 299, 323, 449, 536
  Daniel, Jr., 299, 335, 392, 418, 421, 443
  Daniel, Sr., 449
  Elanore, 140
  Elizabeth, 208, 217, 303, 396
  Evan, 16, 19, 126
  Hannah, 105
  Henry, 536
  Hester, 72
  Isaac, 510
  James, 87, 132, 281, 341, 353, 436, 539
  Jehu, 371
  Jemima, 466
  Jenkins, 79, 87, 93, 103
  John, 71, 72, 81, 87, 90, 98, 103, 105, 110, 149, 169, 281, 353, 385, 466
  Jonathan, 87, 93, 124
  Joseph, 79, 87, 122, 392, 445, 474
  Joseph, Sr., 445
  Joshua, 65, 78, 105, 133, 155, 169, 219, 225, 329
  Katherine, 132
  Lewis, 81, 105, 133, 195, 228, 303
  Lydia, 385, 536
  Margaret, 87, 140
  Mary, 72, 169, 234, 281, 350, 353, 541
  Nancy, 449, 536
  Owen, 93, 234
  Rachel, 81, 139
  Rebecca, 81, 147
  Samuel, 303
  Sarah, 78, 81, 133
  Tabitha, 225
  Thomas, 87
  William, 208, 217, 331
Davis (Daves),
  Abisha, 268
  Ann, 72, 268, 376, 405, 452, 482
  Bowers, 328
  Brinckle, 227, 369
  Caleb, 268, 378, 431
  Comfort, 362
  David, 435
  Eliner, 207
  Elizabeth, 157, 268, 329, 431, 452, 459, 468, 482, 556
  Esther, 272, 411
  Evan, 16
  Ezekial, 431
  Hannah, 483, 521
  Helen, 16
  Isaac, 431, 474, 501, 510, 527
  James, 43, 329, 431, 443, 474, 501
  Jehu, 268, 348, 517
  John, 118, 369, 431, 452, 477, 492, 533
  Joseph, 25, 329
  Joshua, 386, 497
  Leah, 268
  Lewes, 108, 452
  Luke, 272
  Mary, 43, 45, 118, 161, 249, 268, 342, 435, 510
  Matthias, 348, 369, 477, 492
  Mirriam, 328, 376
  Moses, 268
  Nancy, 431
  Nathan, 459, 477, 492
  Nehemiah, 480
  Presilla, 242
  Rachel, 118, 237
  Rebecca, 118, 431
  Rhoda, 529
  Robert, 477, 492
  Sarah, 118, 329, 369, 452
  Solomon, 298
  Susana, 369, 477, 492
  Thomas, 45, 108, 207, 247, 249, 268, 323, 362, 431, 452, 474, 477, 492, 526
  William, 237, 342, 452, 477, 492
Davison,
  James, 254
  Margaret, 175
  Thomas, 175
Dawley, Daniel, 133
Daws,
  Mary, 123
  William, 123, 166
Dawson,
  Ann, 208
  Benjamin, 228, 473
  Catharine, 498
  Daniel, 208, 381, 403
  Deborah, 473
  Elenor, 32
  Elijah, 449, 498
  Elizabeth, 32, 353, 386
  James, 208, 271, 310, 473
  Joanna, 32
  John, 11, 32, 69, 95, 122, 175, 206, 208, 218, 278, 300, 330

Joshua, 208, 260, 271, 418
Margaret, 155
Mary, 69, 310, 418,
Rachel, 300
Richard, 32, 155, 179, 208
Robert, 32, 69, 344
Sarah, 155, 337, 492
Solomon, 473
Thomas, 93, 94, 122, 126, 153, 155, 208, 406
William, 473

Day,
Ariminta, 541
John, 507, 531, 535, 539, 541
Mary, 541
Mathias, 541
Rebecka, 541

Deal (Deel),
Elias, 545
Hester, 545
James, 545
John, 424, 452
Sarah, 545
Thomas, 545

Dean,
Elizabeth, 528
James, 36, 39, 41, 205, 394
Jesse, 394
John, 528
Keziah, 394
Mary, 39, 41, 224
Rebeckah, 394
Ruth, 447
Sarah, 205, 394
Thomas, 224, 325

Deart, William, 79

Deaton,
Elizabeth, 349
Hester, 349

Decoe, Joseph, 145

Deel: see Deal

Degman: see Dagman

Dehorty (Deherty, Doughurty, Daugherty),
Absolam, 490
Benjamin, 275
Charles, 275
Daniel, 512
Elizabeth, 376
John, 275, 475
Mary, 254, 271, 275, 355, 491, 496, 512
Morgan, 275
Prudence, 475
Rebekah, 527
Sarah, 451, 490
Thomas, 501

Vincent, 437, 496, 527, 532, 553

Delabastic, Augustus, 78

Delap,
Agnis, 122
Allen, 76, 96, 153, 154, 206
Ann, 122
Catharine, 408
James, 153
John, 153, 154
Matthew, 153, 154
Peter, 153, 206
Robert, 96
Sarah, 153, 154
William, 153, 206

Dellenar: see Dallinar

Demes, Sarah, 486

Dempsy,
James, 518
Nancy, 518

Denis,
Elenor, 56
Frederick, 56
Thomas, 56

Denman, Frederick, 322

Denney (Denne),
Anne, 102
Benjamin, 475, 558
Christopher, 102, 169, 201, 235, 239, 277, 283, 349
Christopher, Sr., 349
Elizabeth, 223, 282, 410
Evan, 102, 173, 223, 316, 336, 406, 515
Francis, 257, 259, 340
Isabella, 223
Jean, 517
John, 119, 169, 406, 490
Joseph, 169, 223, 394, 406, 414
Margaret, 170
Mary, 252, 410, 547
Philip, 27, 43, 48, 55, 58, 102, 153, 169, 170, 257, 282, 390, 406, 545
Rachel, 48, 324, 390, 453, 483
Sarah, 169, 410
Susanah, 102
Thomas, 517
William, 349, 421, 441

Dennum,
Ann, 322
Arthur, 322
Frederick, 322
John, 322
Michael, 322

Depoister, Elizabeth, 413

[33]

Depray,
  John, 360
  Saley, 360
Derham: see Durham
Derochbrune,
  Charlotte, 367
  Jacob, 367
  Joseph, 367
  Rachel, 367
Derram: see Durham
Derrickson, Jacob, 255
Deshin, William, 475
Devenport, Elizabeth, 221, 265
Devlin, Patrick, 97
Deweese (Dewees, Dewes),
  Cornelius, 193, 368, 441, 540, 557
  Daniel, 193, 386, 390
  David, 441, 556
  Draper, 557
  Elijah, 193
  Elizabeth, 185, 386, 410, 452, 556, 557
  Ezekiel, 185
  Hessey, 556
  Hezekiah, 185
  Isaac, 185, 410
  Jerusha, 390
  Jesse, 556
  John, 193, 386, 452
  Jonathan, 262, 441
  Joseph, 185
  Joshua, 306, 410, 424, 434, 441
  Letisia, 556
  Lewis, 97
  Mahaly, 557
  Mary, 135, 153, 185, 193, 194
  Matthew, 193
  Nancy, 193, 556
  Nehemiah, 557
  Patience, 489
  Rachel, 157, 193, 363, 386, 452
  Samuel, 153, 157, 363, 452, 531, 548
  Sarah, 193, 194, 386, 557
  Spencer, 556
  Suies, 33
  William, 97, 193
Dewnan, Daniel, Sr., 206
Dicheus: see Dicus
Dickerson, William, 232
Dickie, William, 417, 433
Dickinson (Dickenson),
  . . ., 344
  Anne, 232
  Charles, 133
  Deborah 252
  Elizabeth, 187, 232
  Grace, 133, 161
  Henry, 187
  James, 252
  Joanna, 187
  John, 187, 203, 207, 232, 359, 377, 498
  Margaret, 344, 498
  Mary, 187
  Philemon, 187, 207
  Samuel, 40, 187, 240
  Sarah, 147, 232
  Walter, 40, 66, 187, 188, 240
  William, 232
Dickson,
  James, 92
  Richard, 236
  Sarah, 236
Dicus (Dicheus),
  Anna, 518
  Benoni, 518
  Henrity, 278
  John, 216, 278
  Julan, 278
  Mary, 278
  Samuel, 278, 504, 518
  Sarah, 278, 518
  William, 278, 504, 518
Dighton, Richard, 76
Dikens, Nancy, 322
Dill,
  Abner, 415, 452
  Andrew, 452
  Anna, 258, 300, 523
  Benjamin, 255, 247, 410
  Burton, 457
  Eamy, 378
  Edward, 160, 172, 282, 292, 346
  Elijah, 292, 346
  Eliza, 255
  Elizabeth, 346
  Esther, 463
  George, 260
  Hannah, 255
  Hester, 452
  Jacob, 548
  James, 346, 358, 427
  Job, 346
  John, 192, 247, 255, 288, 325, 346, 351, 378, 393, 430, 452, 464
  John, Sr., 392
  Joseph, 346
  Letitia, 452
  Lydia, 255
  Mary, 172, 192, 255, 346, 358, 427, 457, 463, 529, 548
  Nimrod, 346

Philemon, 298, 346
Rachel, 348
Rebecca, 300, 346, 523
Sarah, 346, 457, 459, 529, 548,
Shediru, 314
Solomon, 348, 457, 548
Surepta, 314
Thomas, 464
William, 192, 282, 346, 351, 430, 457, 464, 548
Zepporah, 452

Dillaner: see Dallinor

Dillen (Dillon),
Elizabeth, 489, 538
Henry, 546
James, 538
John, 546
Mary, 546
Nehemiah, 489, 538
Richard, 101
Sarah, 538
Vinson, 546

Dimond, William, 344

Dingeesly, Gartrude, 40

Diskel, Mary, 156

Dithan, Richard, 76

Diton (Ditton),
John, 24
Joshua, 92
Margaret, 92

Diviggins, Joseph, 465

Dixon (Dixson),
Andrew, 488
Ann, 80, 82, 312, 437
Charles, 544
George, 484, 544
Joseph, 524
Robert, 437
Sarah, 295, 304
Thomas, 75, 80, 82, 175
William, 12, 295, 304

Doaney,
Charles, 422, 447
Elizabeth, 422
James, 414
Sarah, 414

Dobson, Edward, 543

Docktree, William, 136

Dodd,
Aron, 340
John, 191
William, 186

Doherty: see Dehorty

Donaldson (Donalson),
Alexander, 46, 78, 85
Charles, 46
Joshan, 100

Donavan (Donafan, Donawan, Dunnavan),
Daniel, 46, 51, 73
Elizabeth, 151
Esther, 73
Johanna, 46, 51
Mary, 46, 51
Randoll, 31, 46, 51
Susannah, 46, 51

Doney,
Charles, 343, 402, 421
Hannah, 153
James, 153, 414
John, 153
Margaret, 171
Peter, 153, 166
Rachel, 166
Stephen, 263

Donn: see Dunn

Donoho (Donneho, Dunahoe),
Ann, 187
Mary, 30
Michael, 21, 30
Somerset, 123

Dorman,
Elizabeth, 505, 522
George, 522

Dorrell,
James, 332, 418
Jane, 418
Mary, 332

Dorson,
Daniel, 381
Richard, 73

Doughurty: see Dehorty

Douglass (Douglas, Dowglass),
Adam, 301
Archibald, 34, 54
James, 553
Mary, 553
Sarah, 378
Walter, 553
William, 300, 378

Dowding,
Elizabeth, 112, 122
John, 105
Joseph, 76, 108, 112, 117, 122
Mary, 105

Dowell, Philip, 131

Dowety,
Rebecca, 406
Vincent, 406

Dowglass: see Douglass

Downam: see Downham

Downey, Thomas, 539
Downham (Downam),
  Agnes, 37
  Ann, 294
  Annis, 179
  Eleanor, 37, 449, 480
  Elizabeth, 280, 383, 480
  Ezekel, 526
  Hanah, 302
  Isaac, 280, 480, 523
  James, 523, 480
  John, 86, 179
  Joseph, 179, 280, 302
  Keziah, 449, 480
  Mary Ann, 179, 192, 480, 526
  Nancy, 480
  Rachel, 280, 411
  Richard, 37, 226, 280, 302, 405, 480
  Ruth, 280, 480
  Sarah, 222, 280, 302, 480, 497
  Susan, 117
  Thomas, 37, 50, 117, 179, 192, 292, 294, 520
Downing,
  Ann, 443
  Benjamin, 240, 340, 431, 511
  Denny, 511
  Elizabeth, 511
  Ezekiel, 240, 324
  Joseph, 240, 340, 443, 511
  Mary, 324, 431, 443, 511
  Nicy, 511
  Perthina, 340
  Roaf, 511
  Susanah, 326
  William, 240, 326
Downs,
  Elizabeth, 360, 499
  Hezekiah, 250
  James, 499
  Levin, 250
  Mitchell, 49, 51
  Nancy, 505
  Patrick, 55, 61
  Rachel, 436
  Stephen, Jr., 388
  William, 118, 131, 250, 436
Doyl, Michal, 244
Doz, Andrew, 164
Draper,
  Alexander, 100
  Ann, 453, 482
  Avary, 287, 368
  Catharine, 453
  Charles, 500
  David, 147
  Digbe, 147
  Eliza, 482
  Elizabeth, 100, 290, 368, 463
  Esther, 100, 368, 441
  Hannah, 147
  Henry, 368
  Isaac, 379, 498, 552
  Jacob Dryer, 147
  James, 147
  John, 368, 453, 482, 525
  Joseph, 100
  Kattran, 482
  Lawrence, 147
  Lemuel, 453, 482
  Mary, 18, 368
  Nancy, 453, 482
  Nehemiah, 144, 453, 482
  Neomy, 100
  Samuel, 453, 482
  Sarah, 144, 290
  Susanah, 525
  Unica, 453, 482
  Whittington, 100, 500
  William, 453, 482
Draughton (Draighton, Drayton),
  Catherine, 169
  Edmond, 292
  John, 146, 147, 169, 171, 218, 292, 376
  John, Jr., 218
  John, Sr., 274
  Robert, 23, 32, 33, 146
  Simon, 147, 376
  William, 376, 407
  Wright, 169
Drew, William, 196, 279, 310, 360, 417
Driskle (Driscal, Driskill),
  Dennis, 118, 158
  Capt. Joseph, 530
  Joseph, 158, 395
  Mary, 158
  Susanna, 158
Drumond,
  James, 99
  Margrett, 99
Dryer, Mary, 21
Dubrois,
  Elizabeth, 30
  John, 16, 18, 30
Dudly, Nickles, 433
Due, Elizabeth, 154, 253
Dugdale, Thomas, 34
Dugerty, Morgan, 306
Duhadway,
  Ann, 291

Catherine, 366, 482, 508, 518
Daniel, 268, 342, 366
Jacob, 95, 291, 436, 482, 518
Jacob, Sr., 268

Dulin, Ann, 454

Dunbar, Samuel, 408

Duncan (Dungan),
  Arthur, 125
  Elizabeth, 300, 325
  John, 300, 331
  Levi, 242
  William, 300, 331

Dunlap,
  Allen, 165
  John, 176
  Matthew, 165
  Peter, 165, 176

Dunn (Dun, Donn),
  John, 22, 23, 24,
  Joseph, 161
  Margaret, 22, 23
  Thomas, 36

Dunnahoe: see Donoho

Dunnavan: see Donavan

Dunning (Duning),
  James, 258
  Jerusha, 258
  John, 189, 202, 228, 258
  Martha, 189, 258, 276
  Mary, 189, 228, 258, 276, 303
  Rachel, 237, 380, 505
  Samuel, 189, 258
  Tamar, 189, 237, 258, 380
  Thomas, 189, 258
  William, 189, 258, 288, 303, 380

Dunwidde,
  James, 350
  John, 350
  Mary, 350
  Nancy, 350
  Samuel, 350

Durborow (Durborough, Durbarow),
  Amy, 525
  Benjamin, 198
  Daniel, 159, 176, 198, 307, 313, 331, 335, 338, 341
  David, 537
  Elis, 132
  Elizabeth, 57, 88, 148, 159, 198, 341
  Hugh, 42, 43, 57, 159, 198, 268, 307, 341, 429, 434, 444, 525
  Hugh, Jr., 56, 64, 66, 75
  John, 148, 537
  Luke, 148
  Lydia, 193, 341
  Mary, 148, 198
  Rachel, 341
  Rebecca, 338, 483
  Sarah, 148, 169, 186, 218, 221, 234
  Stephen, 161, 169, 186, 268
  William, 458

Durham (Derham, Derram, Durrum),
  Benjamin, 384, 528
  Clayton, 401
  Daniel, 384
  Ellenor, 384
  Hester, 384
  Ibba, 528
  Isabella, 528
  Isaiah, 401
  Jemima, 494
  Joanah, 384
  John, 205, 238, 256, 325, 401
  John, Jr., 304
  John, Sr., 304
  Mary, 384, 494, 528
  Rachel, 384
  Rebecca, 401
  Sarah, 384, 494
  Thomas, 384, 494
  Whitington, 373, 401, 474, 494,
  William, 401, 528

Dusha,
  Hester, 502
  John, 502

Dushane,
  Charles, 111
  Garrett, 406
  Jerome, 191
  Mary, 111, 357, 406

Dwoolf,
  Edward, 105
  Sarah, 105

Dwyer (Duyer),
  Harriet, 408
  Joseph, 408
  Judity, 21
  Mary, 20, 21
  Rosamond, 408
  Thomas, 20, 21

Dyal, Michal, 219

Dyer,
  Anne, 30
  Catharine, 436, 443
  Dennish, 22, 30
  Edward, 329
  Elizabeth, 134, 329, 352
  James, 436
  Joab, 436
  John, 134, 436, 443

Martha, 436
Mary, 329, 352
Nancy, 329, 352
Nathaniel, 327
Prudence, 329, 352
Rebecca, 327
Susanah, 450
William, 50, 55

—E—

Eades,
  Daniel, 330
  Mary, 330

Eagle, Thomas, 488, 497, 511

Ebtharp,
  Elizabeth, 229, 257, 307
  Thomas, 229

Ecan: see Aiken

Eckles (Akles, Eccles, Eckels),
  . . ., 437
  Ann, 350, 506
  Anthony, 350, 416, 506, 544
  Benjamin, 505
  Elizabeth, 362, 411, 505
  Esther, 350
  Hannah, 350
  James 505
  Jesse, 350, 506, 544
  John, 235, 350, 362, 411, 416, 505, 506
  Julana, 350, 506
  Lydia, 350, 506, 544
  Richard, 350, 404, 506, 544
  Sarah, 235
  Susannah, 437

Edenfield (Edinfield, Edingfield),
  Ann, 163
  Elinor, 40
  Jane, 176
  John, 23, 40, 181, 261, 389, 437, 487
  Jonas, 40, 117, 176
  Persis, 181, 265
  Rachel, 487
  Rebecca, 40, 51
  Samuel, 558
  Sarah, 395, 558
  Tabitha, 117
  Thomas, 40
  William, 163

Edmonds (Edmunds),
  Alice, 332
  Anne, 28, 29
  Elizabeth, 67, 491
  James, 28, 67, 221, 249
  John, 28, 29, 30, 32, 67, 249
  Joseph, 67
  Margaret, 32
  Mary, 491
  Prisicilla, 18
  Robert, 18, 28, 67, 76, 131
  Sarah, 28, 67
  Susannah 131
  Tabitha, 30, 67
  Thomas, 206

Edmondson,
  Elizabeth, 513
  Emanuel, 391
  Francis, 258, 325, 350
  James, 20
  John, 12, 13, 20, 276, 391, 468, 513, 514, 536
  Joseph, 391
  Joshua, 442
  Lydia, 513, 514
  Margarett, 513
  Mark Greer, 325, 350
  Martha, 442
  Mary, 258, 325, 350
  Peter, 547
  Rachel, 350
  Rebeccah, 350
  Samuel, 20, 325, 350, 536
  Sarah, 20, 350, 471
  Sophia, 468, 514
  Thomas, 20, 391, 468, 471, 514
  William, 20, 325, 350, 468

Edmunds: see Edmonds

Edwards (Edward),
  Andrew, 298
  James, 93, 122, 136, 163, 211, 289, 291
  John, 93, 289, 291, 298, 377, 470
  Joshua, 291, 367, 453
  Penelopy, 328
  Sarah, 377
  William, 93, 328, 392

Egland (Eglin),
  . . ., 248
  Dr. John, 258
  Rachel, 248, 258
  Richard, 258

Eghmont (Edgemont, Egmount),
  Bartholomew, 136
  Christopher, 136
  Cornelius, 136
  Ezekiel, 136
  Laurence, 136

Egnew, James, 180

Ehler, Thomas, 13
Einon: see Eynon
Elbert, Jonathan, 502
Elbourn,
  James, 280
  Rachel, 281
Elder, Thomas, 19
Eldridge,
  Robert, 65
  Thomas, 65
Ellars,
  Benjamin, 365
  Carty, 365
  John, 365
  Mary, 365
Ellingsworth, William, 12
Elliott,
  Edward, 360, 386
  Elizabeth, 279, 314, 360, 367
  Isaac, 342, 360
  John, 25
  Joseph, 527
  Obediah, 279
  Robert, 45
  Ruth, 342, 360, 386
  Susannah, 360
  Thomas, 123, 252
Ellis,
  Ann, 44
  Benjamin, 44
  Eleanor, 407
  James, 107
  Jeffray, 142
  Martha, 142
  Rachel, 37, 39, 55
  Samuel, 407
  Thomas, 37, 156, 407
  Williams, 44, 107
Ellitt (Ellet, Elot),
  Angelico, 32
  Ann, 166
  Edward, 283
  Elinor, 166
  Elizabeth, 53
  Isaac, 33, 39, 283
  Jacob, 283
  Joanna, 33
  John, 32, 33, 39
  Margret, 32
  Martha, 53
  Mary, 33, 283
  Rebecca, 32
  Ruth, 360
  Susannah, 29, 33
  Thomas, 29, 33, 39, 141, 283
  William, 53

Elmer, Jonathan, 254
Elsberry,
  Benjamin, 256
  Elizabeth, 256
  Frederick, 256
  Jacob, 256
  William, 256
Emary: see Emory
Emerson (Emmerson),
  David, 314
  Ellenar, 27
  Emanuel, 114
  Ephraim, 47
  Govey, 162, 166, 202, 220, 248, 250, 278, 359, 361, 476
  Jacob 25, 27, 120, 278, 335, 361, 414
  Jerusa, 126
  John, 27, 110, 148, 162, 278, 361
  Jonathan, 162, 166, 269, 278, 299, 313, 322, 359, 361
  Manlove, 278, 398, 414, 415, 473, 476
  Margret, 25, 24
  Mary, 47
  Michael, 110, 162, 269, 306, 397
  Meriam, 314
  Philemon, 31, 314
  Rachel, 361
  Rebecca, 114
  Ruth, 359, 361
  Sarah, 42, 107, 220, 306, 414
  Unity, 110, 148, 162, 269
  Vincent, 30, 35, 42, 162, 269
  Wilson, 107
Emmett (Emett),
  Jane, 111
  John, 111
Emory (Emary),
  Ann, 344
  Arthur, 15, 414, 484, 543
  Arthur, Jr., 344
  Charles, 297
  Deborah, 414
  Dickenson, 414
  Gideon, 444, 460
  John, 414, 444, 520
  John Wells, 344
  Latilly, 444
  Margaret, 482, 543
  Mary, 397, 460
  Sarah, 444
  Thomas, 397, 414, 444, 484
  Thomas, Jr., 397
  Thomas, Sr., 397, 414
  Tilly, 397, 414
  William, 414

Empson,
  Charles, 148
  Cornelius, 77, 148
  Dorothy, 49, 57
  Hannah, 148, 495
  Margaret, 77, 116
  Mary, 77
  Richard, 48, 49, 54, 55, 57, 77, 116
  Sarah, 148
  Thomas, 57, 62, 77
  William, 148
England,
  Ann, 167
  Daniel, 24
  David, 167, 344
  Ester, 344
  Isaac, 156, 167
  Jacob, 167
  James, 167
  Joseph, 23, 34, 54
  Martha, 167
  Mary, 167
Enloe,
  Elizabeth, 345
  Ridgbal, 345
  Thomas, 174
Ennals,
  Henry, 380
  Joseph, 483
  Mary, 335
Entwesle,
  Edmund, 362
  Elizabeth, 458
  Mary, 362, 458
Erb, Jacob, 340
Erickson (Errickson),
  Johnson, 375
  Mathew, 397
Ervy, William, 325
Esgate,
  Fanny, 281
  Thomas, 41
Espy, James, 78
Esteel,
  Mary, 492
  William, 492
Eubanks (Ewbanks, Hughbanks),
  Benjamin, 190, 327
  Jane, 327
  Sarah, 190
  William, 97
Eustice,
  Charles, 316
  Rachel, 316
Evans (Evan, Evens),
  Alce, 320
  Ann Elizabeth, 452
  Barthulay, 127, 142
  Curtis, 98, 127, 142
  Daniel, 139, 149, 155, 158
  David, 79, 139, 294, 300, 309
  Deborah, 139
  Edmond, 127, 142
  Elizabeth, 139
  Geveullian, 87, 93
  James, 551
  John, 13, 21, 26, 31, 79, 87, 197, 244, 320
  Joshua, 65, 71, 77, 81, 87, 89, 294
  Margaret, 127, 142
  Martha, 31
  Mary, 127
  Philip, 87
  Rees, 452
  Risden, 452
  Sally, 551
  Samuel, 415
  Thomas, 65, 77, 87, 92, 141, 415, 452
  Dr. Thomas, 452
  William, 372
  Zachariah, 139, 252, 423
Everen, Charles, 353
Everett (Everitt),
  Agnes, 24
  George, 24
  Hannah, 402
  James, 402
  Lydia, 17
  Mark, 17
  Thomas, 15
Everson,
  Barnet, 370
  Hannah, 370
Ewbanks: see Eubanks
Ewing (Euin, Euing),
  Elizabeth, 179
  Frances, 179
  James, 129, 179
  Mary, 144, 179
  Maty, 129
  Robert, 144, 179
Ewins, Abraham, 44
Exell (Exall, Excell),
  Samuel, 126, 153, 353
Eynon,
  Catharine, 71, 72, 77
  David, 77, 87
  Elizabeth, 71, 77
  Mary, 71
  Ruth, 340, 470
  Stephen, 340, 470
  William, 77

—F—

Fairess,
  James, 252
  Margaret, 252
Fairfield, Esther, 495
Falconer (Falkner, Faulkner, Folkner),
  Abraham, 153, 354
  Andrew, 383
  Ann, 381
  Burton, 346
  Elizabeth, 136, 153, 182, 383, 495
  Gilbert, 182, 354
  James, 381
  John, 136, 225
  Prisiler, 182
  Samuel, 235
  Sarah, 182, 383
  Sophia, 383
  Thomas, 383
  William, 383, 495
Fall, Hugh, 313
Faral, Robert, 357
Farcett: see Faucett
Fargeson: see Ferguson
Faries,
  Elizabeth, 100, 122, 183, 190
  John, 100, 122, 152
Faris,
  Elenor, 352
  John, 342, 388
  Matthew, 352
Farlow,
  Abigal, 508
  Archibald, 508
  Daniel, 490
  Elijah Lindall, 490
  George, 490, 508
  Jesse, 490
  John, 490, 508
  Leah, 490
  Mary, 508
  Polly, 508
  Samuel, 508
  Sarah, 490
  Turner, 508
  William, 490, 508
Farmer,
  George, 532
  John, 219, 336, 380
Farquhar (Farqueher),
  Alexander, 85
  George, 85, 212
  Hannah, 212
  Isabel, 85
  Isabella, 98
  Mary, 85
  William, 85
Farrow,
  Ann, 381
  Benjamin, 466, 469
  Ebenezer, 522
  Joseph, 324, 381, 481
  Lydia, 324
Farsett: see Faucett
Farson,
  David, 346
  Henry, 119, 130, 132, 136, 137, 152, 155, 182, 200, 231, 346, 412, 418, 537
  Jane, 158, 200
  John, 346, 449, 537
  Margaret, 412
  Mary, 182
  Mary, Jr., 234
  Rebecca, 537
  Susannah, 383, 396
  William, 60, 64, 103, 117, 136, 137, 158, 182, 200, 346, 370, 383, 395
Farsyth, Alexander, 506
Farthing,
  Phebe, 147
  Samuel, 147
Faucett (Farcett, Farsett, Fasset, Fawsitt, Fosett),
  Daniel, 146
  Elizabeth, 551
  Hetty, 551
  James, 551
  John, 551
  Phebe, 262, 551
  Robert, 551
  Sarah, 442
  Smith, 262, 292, 356, 382, 441, 442, 500, 503, 532, 551
Faulkner: see Falconer
Feagins, Mary, 202
Feaston, John, 89
Feddaman: see Fiddeman
Fell,
  Gulielma Maria, 115
  Gulielma Maria Frances, 115
  Mary Margarette, 115
  Robert Edward, 115
Felton,
  Catharine, 310
  John, 310
  Robert, 310
  Sarah, 310
  William, 310
Fenchwait: see Finsthwait

Ferguson (Fargeson, Furguson),
  . . ., 529
  Ann, 529
  Bassett, 529
  Daniel, 511
  Elizabeth, 318
  Francis, 166
  John, 318, 348, 477, 511
  Sarah, 511
Ferrel, Gidion, 540
Few,
  Daniel, 192
  Esther, 192, 233
Fiddeman (Feddaman), Mary, 389, 397
Fiddy, Elizabeth, 391
Fields,
  Abraham, 23, 39, 104, 147
  Ann, 295
  Elizabeth, 39, 154
  James, 309
  John, 295, 362
  Marian, 518
  Mary, 295
  Phillip, 65, 84
  Rachel, 295
  Sarah, 295
  William, 306, 309
Finley (Finlay),
  John, 52
  Joseph, 119
  Nehemiah, 82
Finney,
  Alce, 88
  Ann, 88
  Daniel, 88, 179
  James, 88
  Mary, 179
  Patience, 88
  Robert, 233
  William, 88
Finsthwait (Fenchwait, Finstrait),
  Hannah, 455, 543
  James, 210, 263, 411
  Jonathan, 263, 313, 437, 505
  Martha, 437, 505
  Sarah, 210, 263
  Thomas, 455
Firches: see Furches
Fisher,
  . . ., 340
  Abraham, 406
  Adam, 21, 29, 30, 31, 36, 47, 53, 131, 318
  Alce, 516
  Daniel, 318
  Edward, 256, 283, 287, 304, 313, 314, 447, 540
  Elizabeth, 220, 256, 340
  Ellis, 270
  Esther, 220
  Fenwick, 172, 185, 219, 361, 365, 384, 446, 447
  Fenwick, Jr., 338
  Hannah, 88, 132, 205, 223
  Henry, 311, 413
  Isaac, 47, 62, 110
  Jabez, 447
  James, 270, 443, 446
  John, 47, 60, 131, 205, 235, 255, 483, 510, 520, 536, 539, 542, 547, 553
  Joseph, 47, 60, 62
  Joshua, 389, 415, 425, 446
  Lydia, 516
  Margaret, 256
  Mary, 28, 30, 47, 51, 131, 185, 311, 413
  Miers, 463
  Molleston, 47, 62, 131, 318
  Nicy, 467
  Polly, 467
  Rachel, 335, 516
  Richard, 553
  Ruth, 516
  Sarah, 47, 131, 483, 496
  Susannah, 47, 256, 446
  Thomas, 413, 447
  William, 74, 80, 83, 90, 483, 496
Fitzgerald (Fitzgarrel, Fitz Jarrel, Fitz Jarrold),
  . . ., 286
  Catherine, 31
  Celia, 420
  Edward, 24
  Eleazer, 383, 509
  Elizabeth, 200, 272
  Ezekiel, 420
  George, 359, 420
  Isaac, 420
  James, 21, 31, 32, 52, 272, 383
  John, 52, 383, 420
  Lydia, 286
  Marmaduke, 272
  Martha, 368
  Mary, 272, 383
  Rachel, 272, 359
  Richard, 383
  Robert, 52, 200
  Rowland, 35
  Ruth, 383
  Sarah, 52, 53, 383, 420
  Selah, 344
  Susannah, 52

Fitz Randolph,
  Daniel, 147
  David, 139
Fitzsimons,
  Shockley, 159
  Thomas, 159
Flaharty, John, 84, 89
Fleman,
  George, 58
  Susannah, 58
Fleming,
  Alexander, 156, 230, 253, 349
  Aliss, 156
  Amilia, 349
  Andrew, 349
  Ann, 358
  Archibald, 123, 145, 173, 181, 221, 230, 256, 293, 349
  Archibald, Jr., 349
  Bannia, 358
  Barbary, 349
  Beniah, 459, 519
  Boaz, 358
  Catren, 230
  David, 156
  Elizabeth, 145, 156, 173, 181, 349, 397, 411, 488, 519
  Esther, 181, 349
  George, 156, 177, 181, 221, 349, 393, 411
  Gove, 181
  Hannah, 156
  Hester, 156
  Isaac, 221
  Isabel, 81, 173, 230, 253, 349
  Jacob, 488
  James, 156, 230, 349, 488
  Jehu, 519
  John, 64, 84, 156
  Joseph, 221, 230, 276, 349, 531
  Joseph, Sr., 218
  Lyda, 349
  Mahala, 531
  Margaret, 256, 488
  Martha, 156, 181, 221, 393
  Mary, 84, 358, 531
  Matthew, 230, 349, 358
  Nancy, 488
  Nathan, 349, 358
  Phillis, 156
  Rachel, 276
  Robert, 81, 84, 86, 156, 221, 230, 253, 349, 411, 488, 531
  Robert, Jr., 397
  Samuel, 123, 181, 349, 393, 411, 459, 524, 531
  Sarah, 84, 349
  Thomas, 358
  William, 156, 230, 358
  William, Jr., 177, 221
  William, Sr., 221
Fline, Catron, 23
Flintham,
  Benjamin, 83
Folk, 96
  John, Jr., 64
  William, 69, 83, 87
Flood (Flud),
  Elizabeth, 66, 74
  Joseph, 482, 516, 555
  William, 66, 74
Flowers,
  Elizabeth, 26, 80
  Henry, 22
  John, 21, 26
  Thomas, 21, 80
  William, 422, 429
Floyd,
  Elizabeth, 206
  Gertrude, 190
  Thomas, 206
Flud: see Flood
Flynn,
  Ann, 397, 422
  Edward, 422
  Elizabeth, 422
  John, 397, 422
  Mary, 422
  Rebecca, 422
  Sarah, 422
Folkner: see Falconer
Follis,
  Martha, 422, 456
  Thomas, 422
Folts, Elizabeth, 269
Food, John, 121
Forbes,
  Esther, 462
  Richard, 462
Forbig, George, 13
Forby, James, 14
Forckham, Forcom, Forcum: see Forkum
Ford,
  Ann, 96, 272, 536
  Barshby, 272
  Benjamin, 96
  Daniel, 263, 331, 445, 489
  David, 96
  Edward, 272
  Elizabeth, 96, 500
  Esther, 263
  Frances, 96

Isaac, 272
James, 272
Jemiah, 186
Jeremiah, 451
Jesse, 272, 330
John, 96, 272
Mary, 263, 272, 330, 331
Rachel, 96, 272
Rebecca, 263, 331
Richard, 272
Robart, 272
Susannah, 489
Thomas, 96, 111, 263, 272, 331, 377, 445
William, 96, 263, 272, 449, 536

Foreacre (Foreakers, Fouracres),
Ann, 546
Elizabeth, 445, 546
Henry, 546
Isaac, 429, 506
James, 506
Jane, 521
John, 429, 506, 546
Joseph, 377, 386, 445, 506, 521, 546,
Marcer, 506
Margaret, 542
Robert, 506
Samuel, 539, 542, 546
Sarah, 542, 546
William, 506, 546

Foreman,
Arthur, 356
Dorcas, 523
Henry, 356
John, 547
Mary, 547
Robert, 429

Forker,
Ann, 287
George, 293
Mary, 287
Samuel, 287, 293

Forkum (Forckham, Forcom, Forcum),
Benjamin, 160
Catherine, 152
Elizabeth, 423
Hannah, 192, 239, 278
John, 130, 423, 449
John, Sr., 467
Joseph, 319
Joshua, 449, 458
Mary, 458, 467
Renatus, 239, 278
Renn, 192
Sarah, 130, 171
Wren, 166

Forster: see Foster
Fortescue, William, 38
Fortner,
Ann, 318
James, 318
John, 318
Rebecca, 318
Samuel, 225
Sarah, 318

Fortune, James, 253
Fortus, Tobias, 41
Fosett: see Faucett
Foster (Forster),
Anne, 45
David, 372
Henry, 324
James, 95, 107
Jane, 107
John, 13, 20, 21, 31, 38, 39, 45, 107, 138, 169, 208, 212, 372
Mary, 135, 138, 169, 208, 212, 306, 505
Mathew, 107, 306, 505
Rachel, 324
Rebeccah, 306
Richard, 13
Sidua, 107
Thomas, 107, 169, 252, 372

Foulke, Thomas, 410, 451
Fountain, Walter L., 545
Fouracres: see Foreacre
Fowler (Fowlar),
..., 275
Ann, 343, 463
Archibald, 190
Benjamin, 343, 463
Elizabeth, 343, 463
George, 376
John, 519
Mary, 275, 343, 376, 463
Rachel, 343, 463
Rebecca, 190
Robert, 343
William, 261, 264, 329, 415
William Clark, 343

Fox,
James, 127
Molly, 127
William, 127

Fraizier: see Frazier
Francis,
Ann, 88
Ellis, 253
John, 88
Miles, 145

Francois, Jean, 70
Fransisco (Franciso),
  Charles, 449, 535, 545
  Elizabeth, 86, 535, 545
  Esther, 545
  John, 449, 545
  Lydia, 535, 545
  Patience, 141
  Thomas, 141
Frazier (Frasar, Frashar, Fraizier, Frayzer, Frazar, Freasure),
  Ailse, 268
  Alexander, 201
  Alice, 339
  Andrew, 43, 201
  Cary, 509
  Deborah, 414
  Elizabeth, 70, 133, 161, 201, 226, 339, 395
  George, 339, 453
  Hannah, 43
  James, 70, 339, 414, 418
  John, 247, 339
  Joseph, 104
  Mary, 377, 480, 509
  Rebeccah, 339
  Rhoda, 201
  Sarah, 180, 201, 206, 509
  Susannah, 201
  William, 133, 150, 201, 339, 343, 362, 465, 499, 509, 529
Freame,
  Joseph, 115
  Margaret, 115
  Philadelphia Hannah, 115
Freasure: see Frazier
Freeland,
  Emanuel, 344
  Esther, 23, 26
  Hannah, 55
  Isaac, 22, 65, 66, 87, 115
  James, 55, 125
  Margaret, 344
  William, 23, 26
Freeman,
  Abraham, 286
  Ace, 465
  Alecy, 447, 479
  Ann, 301, 302
  Asa, 526
  Bridget, 253
  Charles, 159, 180, 232, 250
  Daniel, 324, 397
  Elizabeth, 19, 26, 31, 39, 56, 65, 117, 159, 231, 479
  Hannah, 65
  Isaac, 286
  Jacob, 286
  John, 350, 397, 464
  Joseph, 39, 73, 87, 96, 117, 159, 180, 231, 256
  Lydia, 286
  Mary, 31, 39, 65, 96, 293, 555
  Miriam 350
  Moses, 46, 65, 71, 188, 293
  Moses, Jr., 286
  Penelope, 65
  Rachel, 161
  Rebecca, 397
  Samuel, 39, 159, 250, 256, 347, 352, 555
  Sarah, 159
  Thomas, 96, 217, 348
  William, 19, 21, 26, 27, 30, 31, 276, 301, 302, 478
French,
  Alce, 18
  Bable, 323
  Charles, 64, 151
  Christian, 50
  David, 58, 65, 75, 77
  Elizabeth, 50
  George, 312
  Hannah, 233
  Isabel, 72
  John, 22, 23, 26
  Katrain, 50
  Mary, 50, 64
  Robert, 15, 17, 18, 19, 22, 24, 184
  Samuel, 312
  Susannah, 50
  Thomas, 31, 40, 50
Fropp, Abigall, 96
Fryer (Fryar),
  Elizabeth, 131
  William, 130, 131, 203
Fulcian, Cally, 462
Fulcin, Sally, 472
Fullerton,
  Ann, 112, 128
  Catherine, 128
  Elizabeth, 128
  John, 112, 128, 212
  Mary, 128
  Thomas, 128
  William, 128, 219
Fulsom, Sarah, 557
Fultz (Fults), Elizabeth, 269, 476
Furbee (Furbey, Furby),
  Anna, 198, 294, 328, 376
  Benjamin, 70, 207, 217, 296, 353, 398
  Bowers, 207, 328
  Caleb, 130, 207, 217, 225, 303, 328, 376, 433, 507

Elizabeth, 328
Hesther, 408
Jacob, 370, 433, 465, 507
John, 328
Jonathan, 328, 376, 408
Joseph, 435
Margaret, 352, 440
Mary, 207, 217
Michael, 207, 217, 353
Nancy, 217
Sarah, 296, 507
Susannah, 70
Waitman, 328, 376, 440
Furbush,
 Ester, 388
 Richard, 245, 388
Furches (Firches, Furchas),
 Frances, 208, 269
 John, 163, 208, 269, 274, 300, 304, 349
 Mary, 121, 349,
 Mary Ann, 300, 349
 Miriam, 349
 Sarah, 349
 Tobias, 68, 121, 301, 349, 393
Furguson: see Ferguson
Furman, William, 244
Furniss,
 Eleanor, 364
 Robert, 364
Fury, Peter, 382
Fusse, William, 69

—G—

Galloway,
 Daniel, 203
 Elizabeth, 112, 148, 151, 195, 203
 Joseph, 132, 148, 195, 203, 250, 300
 Lydia, 195
 Mary, 132
 Peter, 109, 131, 148, 151
 Richard, 76, 132, 195
 Samuel, 76, 109, 112, 195, 203
 Susannah, 132
Game,
 Elizabeth, 345
 Robert, 345
Gano (Ganoe),
 Ann, 185
 Daniel, 185 .
 John, 427
 Lewis, 185, 377, 427, 447, 463, 512
 Ruth, 377
 Sarah, 512
 Susanna, 165

Gardner,
 Francis, 365
 James, 281, 359, 363, 365, 366
 John, 281
 Mary, 309
 Samuel, 281
Garland,
 Abraham, 367, 375
 Christin, 375
 Ebenezer, 375
 John, 375, 463
 John Chevins, 474
 Rebecca, 375
 Rosamond, 375
 Rose, 365
Garner,
 Rebecca, 450
 Sarah, 450
Garnett (Garnet),
 Elizabeth, 446, 458
 William, 458
Garreld, Robert, 190
Garrell (Garrel),
 Ann, 391
 James, 85, 86, 88, 89, 108, 109, 114, 118
Garrett
 Hannah, 451, 468
 Offee, 29
Garson,
 Henry, 103
 Samuel, 103
Garvey (Garve),
 Elizabeth, 45
 John, 45, 61, 178, 200
 Mary, 45
 Mathew, 45
 Owen, 15, 26, 28, 45, 61, 178, 200
 Sarah, 178, 200
 Silvester, 45
Gascoine (Gascoin, Gasoigne),
 John, 38
 Josiah, 98
 Mary, 202
 Sarah, 38
Gaskins,
 Deborah, 276
 Lear, 72
 Sarah, 320, 450, 478, 518
 William, 320, 381, 450, 478
Gauslin: see Goslin
George,
 Daniel, 411, 412
 Hannah, 411, 412
 James, 411
 John, 410, 411, 412, 478, 555

Margarett, 478
Mary, 411, 478
Newel, 478
Patience, 478
Rachel, 411
Samuel, 557
Susannah, 385
Thomas, 411
Gerrard, William, 335
Gibbon,
  Ann, 13
  Edmond, 13
  Francis, 13
  George, 13
  Martha, 13
Gibbs,
  Ann, 301
  Benjamin, 301
  Edward, 178, 215, 223, 224, 267, 301
  Elizabeth, 301
  John, 135, 301, 358, 423
  Joseph, 301
  Mary, 301
  Nancy, 358, 423
  Thomas, 301
Gibson (Gibbeson),
  James, 507
  John, 430
  Leven, 222, 227, 284, 375
Giffin (Giffing),
  David, 89, 156, 250
  Jonathan, 61, 100, 107
  Phebe, 108
Gifford, John, 417
Gilbert,
  Elizabeth, 167
  John, 167
  Prissila, 42
Gilder,
  Elizabeth, 297
  Eunity, 279, 482, 508
  Henry, 297, 412
  John, 279, 297, 426, 450, 481, 508, 550
  Mary, 412
  Reubin, 297, 550
  Susannah, 412
Gildersleve (Gildersleeve),
  Comfort, 543
  Elizabeth, 121, 207, 313
  George, 422, 492
  John, 313, 411, 517
  Jonathan, 412, 543
  Noah, 146, 207
Giles, James, 167

Gillespie (Gilespy),
  James, 93, 168, 178
Gill, Meriam, 316
Gillow, Alexander, 431
Gilpin, George, 423
Ginings: see Jennings
Ginley, Daniel, 75
Glackan, Patrick, 533
Glanding,
  Rachel, 376
  Thomas, 376
  William, 376
Glann: see Glenn
Glass,
  Belitha, 552
  Mary, 452
Glenn (Glann, Gleen),
  Catherine, 116
  John, 67, 74, 75, 81, 104, 116
  Ketren, 104
  Margaret, 104, 116
  Mary, 99, 104, 116
  Rachel, 42
  Rebecca, 42
  Robert, 99, 116
  Samuel, 42
  Sarah, 116
  Thomas, 104, 116, 292
  William, 105
Glew (Glue),
  Elizabeth, 62
  Rachel, 62, 75
  Rebecca, 62
  Samuel, 31, 62
Glover,
  Alse, 12
  Elizabeth, 31, 36
  John, 12, 36
  Richard, 31, 36
Godfrey, John, 22
Godwin,
  Daniel, 409, 503, 534
  Eleanor, 409, 534
  Ezekiel, 409
  Frances, 454
  Francis, 499
  Henry, 335
  James, 454
  John, 454
  Joseph, 335, 454
  Kimuel, 335
  Mary, 323, 335, 344, 348, 368, 410
  Nahor, 454
  Peter, 454
  Prieston, 335
  Sarah, 467

Susannah, 399
Thomas, 454, 499
William, 335, 454
Goforth (Goeforth),
  Ann, 147
  Elizabeth, 76, 147
  George, 76, 79, 104, 118, 376, 477
  George, Sr., 321
  Hessey, 533
  James, 533
  John, 147, 481, 533
  Jule Ann, 533
  Lydia, 195, 481, 533
  Mary, 147, 189, 533
  Miles, 66, 73, 76
  Nancy, 533
  Peter, 195, 322, 376, 481
  Sarah 148, 209, 322, 376
  Susana, 79
  Tamer, 76
  Thomas, 322, 376
  Zachariah, 28, 33, 79, 130, 132, 147, 149, 209, 247, 322, 376
Gold,
  Sarah, 196
  Thomas, 196, 371
Goldsborrough,
  Charles, 187
  Elizabeth, 187
Goldsmith,
  Elizabeth, 421
  John, 416, 421, 439, 518, 533
  Sarah, 421
  William, 421
Golt,
  Ezekiel, 549
  George, 371
  Isabela, 371
  John, 549
  Naomi, 401, 549
  Rebeccah, 549
  Sarah, 549
  William, 371
Goodfellow,
  Ann, 402
  James, 402
  Joseph, 272
  Margaret, 272, 365
  Sarah, 471
Goodin,
  Daniel, 44
  Elizabeth, 44
  Samuel, 497
Gooding,
  Daniel, 47, 75
  Elizabeth, 47
  Hannah, 75
  John, 85, 113, 175, 176, 190
  Richard, 259
  Sarah, 85, 113, 190, 207
  Susannah, 190
  William, 79, 190
Goodrat: see Coudrat
Goodwin,
  Ann, 425
  Aron, 374, 387
  Benjamin, 237, 277, 278
  Elizabeth, 120, 212
  Jane, 278, 387
  Mary, 266, 387, 462, 470
  Moses, 387, 462
  Samuel, 120, 212, 266, 272
  Sarah, 120
  Susannah, 387
Gordon,
  Coe, 204, 288, 297, 398, 450, 462, 489, 544
  David, 89, 114, 260, 354
  Elizabeth, 69, 95, 204, 361
  George, 74, 87, 89, 128, 130, 177, 196, 331
  Griffith, 89, 107, 114, 204
  Hanah, 450
  James, 32, 41, 54, 87, 89, 95, 179, 207, 260, 304, 330
  James, Jr., 85
  James, Sr., 85
  John, 57, 69, 88, 91, 95, 179, 218, 260, 302, 353, 354, 357, 361, 364, 388, 398, 436, 450
  John, Jr., 350
  Joshua, 89, 114, 333, 352, 354, 485
  Letitia, 89, 114, 204
  Margarett, 95
  Martha, 95
  Mary, 89, 114, 128, 130, 150, 196, 226, 304, 330, 354, 361, 409
  Nanne, 95
  Peggy Caldwell, 312
  Phylis, 179, 218
  Robert, 41, 50, 89, 95, 107, 179, 218, 260
  Ruth, 260
  Samuel, 40, 95, 444, 485, 499
  Sarah, 74, 75, 204, 398, 442, 485, 489, 544
  Seth, 95, 179, 210
  Sidney, 398, 450
  Susannah, 411, 437
Gore,
  Ann, 507
  George, 521
  Hester, 497
  James, 521
  John, 521

Jonathan, 521
Mehala, 521
Rebecca, 521
Richard, 507
Selah 521
Thomas, 521
William, 507
Gorman,
  John, 544
  Sarah, 544
Gormley, James, 71
Gorrell,
  James, 147, 155
  John, 147
  Robert, 147
  Ruth, 147, 155
  Sarah, 147, 155, 159
  William, 147
Gorsuch, John, 213
Goslin (Gauslin),
  Anna, 418
  Mary, 469
  Samuel, 418
  Waitman, 322, 380
Gould,
  Thomas, 196, 219
  William, 531
Gover, Mary, 36
Graden,
  Alexander, 505
  Elizabeth. 505
  James, 505
  Jane, 505
Gragg: see Gregg
Graham (Grayham),
  . . ., 475
  Andrew, 448
  Ann, 511, 556
  George, Jr., 549
  George, Sr., 549
  Isaac, 556
  Janet, 98
  John, 98, 437, 538
  Mary, 475, 538
  Nancy, 466
  Peter, 51, 71, 80
  Racheal, 306
  Robert, 98, 126
  Samuel, 306, 340
  Sarah, 466
  Thomas, 118
  William, 466, 511
Granger,
  Benjamin, 230
  Margaret, 230
Grans, Alexander, 18

Grant, Mary, 135
Gray,
  Allen, 96, 103, 112, 522
  Andrew, 170, 183, 196, 204, 221,
    228, 297, 517
  Anne, 284, 524
  Darcus, 343, 462
  David, 494
  Elizabeth, 170, 243, 352, 484, 516,
    517, 524
  Hannah, 225
  Jacob, 164, 170
  James, 70, 90, 127, 159, 191, 343,
    462, 525
  Jean, 297
  John, 80, 104, 149, 170, 191, 221,
    242, 243, 297, 347, 350, 352, 516,
    517, 524, 525
  Margaret, 127
  Mary, 96, 103, 104, 149, 525
  Peter, 127
  Prudence, 221
  Rachael, 170
  Robert, 96, 112
  Rodah, 170
  Ruth, 225
  Sarah, 80, 204, 221, 223, 225, 231,
    343, 525
  Tabitha, 183
  Thomas, 524, 525
  William, 80, 138, 148, 170, 179, 223,
    228, 249, 276, 297, 484, 505, 517,
    524
  William, Jr., 225
  William, Sr., 225
Graydon (Graden),
  Alexander, 138, 285
  John, 138, 505
  Joseph, 505
  Marrium, 505
  Mary, 102, 138
  Rebecca, 285
  William, 212, 370
Gready, Edmond, 23
Gream, Ann, 45
Green,
  Charles, 149, 195, 196, 221, 265,
    343, 451, 469, 535
  Christopher, 302, 395
  Cuthbert, 176, 226, 248, 299
  Elizabeth, 108, 158, 178, 193, 261
  George, 40, 41, 76, 92, 158
  Hannah, 242
  Henry, 83
  James, 221, 265, 395, 421, 446
  John, 32, 40, 56, 221, 261, 265, 364,
    421, 437, 457, 502, 522
  Jonathan, 421, 504

Lauran, 66, 99
Lucrecia, 515
Mary (Mercy?), 32, 54, 71, 92, 265, 303, 556
Nancy, 522, 529
Penelope, 504
Priscilla, 176, 182, 264
Rachel, 40, 41, 83
Robert, 83
Ruth, 225
Samuel, 515
Sarah, 264, 446, 500, 529
Susannah, 513
Thomas, 32, 40, 48, 54, 61, 72, 73, 76, 80, 83, 99, 106, 108, 116, 142, 149, 158, 189, 221, 265, 294, 500
Thomas, Jr., 364
Thomas, Sr., 221
William, 13, 32, 80, 104, 142, 147, 221, 242, 265, 332, 469, 481, 482, 513, 556

Greenhood,
Joseph, 139
William, 139

Greenlee (Greenley),
Allen, 407
David, 407
Elizabeth, 414
Esther, 407
James, 407, 476
John, 160, 407
Joshua, 414
Michael, 407, 514
Priscilla, 160
Robert, 414
Samuel, 407
Solomon, 548
William, 407, 414

Greenway (Greenaway),
Elizabeth, 48
John, 198, 222
Mary, 222
Nicholas, 41, 48, 57, 62

Greenwood,
Ann, 102
Benjamin, 313
Elizabeth, 49, 313, 535
Fennes, 168
Hannah, 443
James, 535
John, 49, 63, 152, 168, 206, 423
Jonas, 25, 27, 49, 152, 168
Jonathan, 102, 243
Joseph, 102, 241, 243, 266, 273, 311
Margaret, 432
Martha, 311
Mathias, 43
Mary, 49, 297

Mary Ann, 102, 241
Nathan, 458
Phenice, 57, 168
Rachael, 168, 297, 335
Rebecca, 63
Robert, 297
Samuel, 40
Sarah, 168, 273, 290, 297, 312
Susannah, 43
Thomas, 429
William, 102

Greer (Greir): see Grier

Greeves,
Eleanor, 24
Mathew, 24

Gregg (Grigg, Gragg),
Alice, 344, 355
John, 344, 355, 459
Margaret, 166
Mark, 372
Rachel, 372
Rebecca, 372, 426, 433, 462
Samuel, 372
Sarah, 372
Thomas, 372

Gregory (Gregorie),
Jeremiah, 146
Joseph, 64
Mary, 146

Grewell (Grewel, Gruwell),
Abraham, 73
Elizabeth, 122, 515
Jacob, 73, 122, 515, 537, 538
John, 73, 213, 515
John, Sr., 515
Jonathan, 213
Margaret, 537
Mary, 73, 122, 536
Peter, 73, 288
Rachel, 193

Grey: see Gray

Grier (Greer, Greir),
Catherine, 79, 84
David, 78, 79, 84
Elizabeth, 78, 84, 99
George, 51, 78, 85
John, 51, 82, 84, 99, 517
John, Jr., 493
Margaret, 99
Mark, 51, 71, 78, 99, 493, 517
Mary, 51, 78, 84, 517
Rachel, 99
Rebackah, 122
Susannah, 212, 276
William, 69, 81, 122, 212

Griffin (Griffen, Griffing),
  Ann,, 284, 335, 352, 448, 486
  Barthia, 448, 449
  Charles, 448, 449
  Daniel, 66, 284, 448, 449
  David, 284, 418, 427
  Ebenezer, 284, 335, 418
  Elizabeth, 267, 284, 407, 418
  Esther, 458, 486
  Ezekiel, 448, 449
  George, 132, 137, 146, 435
  Henry, 292
  Hillyard, 292
  Isaac, 346, 387, 486
  Jabez, 284, 448, 449
  James, 292
  Jane, 243
  Jean, 292
  Jemima, 396, 427
  John, 140, 292, 537
  Jonathan, 72, 73, 77, 96
  Joseph, 11
  Lydia, 132, 146, 172, 284, 418
  Martha, 240
  Matthew, 119, 284, 418, 449
  Mary, 140, 215, 384, 387, 486
  Nancy, 322, 495
  Nathan, 292
  Owen, 240, 227, 267
  Rebekah, 146
  Samuel, 240, 243, 284, 292, 387, 405, 418, 486
  Sarah, 284, 374
  Solomon, 292
  Susannah, 227, 267
  Thomas, 486
  Timothy, 246
  Unicy, 495
  William, 22, 132, 137, 146, 163, 222, 284, 327, 335, 352, 418, 448, 449

Griffith,
  Abraham, 294
  Daniel, 46, 111
  Edeliah, 430
  Elizabeth, 331, 530, 553
  Eynon, 71
  George, 81
  Hillyard, 285, 401
  Isaac, 240, 285, 331, 401
  James, 285, 401
  Jean, 285, 401
  John, 285, 401
  Lavica, 495
  Margaret, 71, 77, 430
  Martha, 331, 447
  Mathew, 172
  Mary, 111, 242, 285, 401, 494
  Nathan, 285, 401
  Paris, 278
  Rachel, 285
  Samuel, 131, 214, 236, 240, 277, 285, 331
  Soloman, 285, 306, 401

Grigg: see Gregg

Grimes,
  John, 264, 309
  Mary, 152
  Sarah, 264

Griscomb, Tobias, 143

Groenendick, Peter, 24

Groves,
  John, 22
  Joseph, 13
  Thomas, 13, 14

Gruwell: see Grewell

Guessford, Sarah, 482

Gulielma, Christina, 115

Gullett,
  Abraham, 66
  Betty, 384, 527
  Daniel, 527
  Ezekiel, 527
  George, 511, 527
  James, 527
  John, 511, 527
  Joshua, 307
  Lydia, 511
  Samuel, 511
  Solomon, 527
  Rachel, 527
  Robert, 553

Gumly,
  Benjamin, 27, 34, 43
  Edward, 34
  James, 34, 43
  John, 27, 34
  Rachel, 34
  Ruth, 34
  Susanna, 34
  William, 34

Gupton,
  Catherine, 16
  William, 16

Guy,
  Andrew, 227
  Elizabeth, 227
  William, 446, 467, 468, 477

—H—

Hackett,
  Elizabeth, 461
  Thomas, 37, 299

Hackney,
  Cattorn, 165
  John, 165
  Joseph, 165
  Rosener, 165
  Vebey, 165
Hadabough, Abraham, 543
Hadabuck,
  Dolla, 235
  Dorothy, 235
  Jacob, 235
Haggans, Peter, 369
Hagon,
  Elizabeth, 297
  James, 297
Haines (Hanes, Haynes),
  Ann, 253
  Daniel, 143, 213
  Elizabeth, 160
  John, 143
  Joseph Ranaday, 143
  Leah, 253
  Mary, 143
  Rachel, 143, 253
  Rebecka, 398
  Samuel, 143
  Sarah, 253
Hairgrove,
  Ann, 233
  Esther, 368
  George, 69, 233, 268, 371, 427, 459, 516
  Hannah, 69
  Katherine, 233
  Mary, 233
  Sarah, 427
  Stephen, 233, 287, 418
  Thomas, 233
  Unity, 418
Halbert, Thomas, 72
Hale (Hales),
  Ezekiel, 250
  Joseph, 104, 111, 157, 439, 516, 526
  Margett, 250
  Sarah, 277
  Susannah, 111
  William, 551
Haley, William, 370
Hall,
  Absolom, 150
  Alexander, 315, 352
  Allen, 268
  Anna, 32, 42
  Asa, 268
  Clary, 49
  David, 239, 270, 280, 347
  Eleanor, 65, 199, 347
  Elizabeth, 15, 42, 68, 347, 520
  Hannah, 65, 116
  Henry, 40, 41, 49, 106
  Isaac, 32, 189
  Isbil, 347
  Jacob, 32
  James, 347
  Jean, 33
  Jerusha, 224, 247
  John, 32, 39, 40, 42, 52, 58, 60, 65, 84, 86, 113, 126, 189, 212, 247, 266, 347, 443, 457
  John, Jr., 33
  John, Sr., 32, 179, 185
  Jonas, 269
  Jordan, 268
  Letitia, 65, 74, 84
  Lodiwick, 23
  Lucy, 266
  Mary, 32, 49, 106, 203, 239, 270, 347, 443
  Miriam, 347
  Nancy, 443
  Nathan, 268
  Oliver, 266
  Perthena, 268
  Rebecca, 268
  Richard, 307
  Robert, 15, 65, 84, 116, 149, 150, 153, 157, 179, 207, 224, 247, 291, 405, 511
  Rynear, 268
  Salley, 443
  Sarah, 180, 212, 347
  Susanna, 269
  Thomas, 189, 268
  William, 189, 266, 443, 520
  Winlock, 294, 337, 443
Halladay, Joseph, 152
Hallans (Hallands), Jehosaphat, 94, 114
Haller, William, 42
Ham,
  Alexander, 539
  Ann, 539
  Benjamin, 539
  Charles, 539
  Jno., 401
  John, 282, 326, 429, 432, 539
  Dr. John, 539
  John, Jr., 494
  Lurania, 539
  Margaret, 401
  Mary, 539
  Susannah, 401, 539
Hambleton,
  Andrew, 35
  Anna, 525

Betty, 525
James, 35, 525
Major, 525
Nancy, 511
Rhoda, 525
Selathiel, 525

Hamer,
Hannah, 96
John, 291

Hamilton,
Alexander, 259, 412, 493, 513, 555
Andrew, 63, 65, 84
Betty, 525
Hosea, 469
James, 259, 324, 525
John, 130, 172, 173, 176, 197, 217, 220, 287, 500
John, Jr., 220, 458
John, Sr., 458
Jonathan, 500
Mary, 172, 220, 251, 282, 325
Robert, 227, 282, 302
Susanah, 412
Walter, 33, 34

Hammans,
Mary, 160, 177
Susanna, 158, 177, 185
Thomas, 158, 160, 177
William, 91, 104, 158, 160, 177

Hammitt, John, 47, 88

Hammond (Hammon),
Daniel, 94
Elizabeth, 50, 527
Henry, 102
Isaac, 527
John, 94
Lawrence, 386, 391, 438
Mary, 259
Nicholas, 439
William, 334

Hamnitt, John, 59, 90, 177

Hampton,
David, 293
Ruth, 293

Hand, Sarah, 193

Hander,
Cornelius, 233
Jonathan, 233
Mary, 233
Nehemiah, 233
Noumy, 233
William, 233

Handerson,, Sarah, 341

Handley, Elizabeth, 106

Handson: see Hanson

Handy,
Grace, 299, 310
William, 299, 310

Handzor (Handzar, Handzer, Hansor),
Cornelius, 238
Elizabeth, 377
Jemima, 377
Johanah, 377
Naomi, 238
Nehemiah, 170, 377
Rachel, 238
Rhoda, 238
Sarah, 238, 256
Susannah, 528
William, 233, 238

Hane,
Abraham, 451
Sarah, 451

Hanes: see Haines

Hanna (Hannah),
David, 216, 217
Elizabeth, 216
Thomas, 113

Hanner, Archable, 447

Hanson (Handson),
Emelia, 157, 200, 346
Joseph, 346
Lydia, 484
Mary, 157, 339, 351, 444
Samuel, 157, 221, 236, 288, 318, 351, 484
Samuel, Jr., 306
Samuel, Sr., 278
Sarah, 484, 499
Susanah, 67
Thomas, 157, 221, 318, 351, 484
Timothy, 28, 34, 40, 64, 65, 67, 79, 145, 157, 193, 200, 351, 484, 536
Timothy, Jr., 84, 88
Timothy, Sr., 84
William, 60

Hansor: see Handzor

Harbet, Sarah, 413

Harbutt, Thomas, 27, 53

Hardcastle,
Elizabeth, 371, 484, 518, 536
Peter, 371, 484
Philip, 484

Hardesty,
Elizabeth, 322
Thomas, 322
William, 322

Hardin (Harden),
  Ann, 236
  Edmond, 117, 165, 275
  Edmond, Sr., 275
  Hannah, 205, 275
  James, 234
  John, 117, 137, 141, 172, 187, 236, 275
  Leah, 387
  Luke, 272
  Martha, 275
  Martin, 141, 165, 180
  Mary, 367
  Nancy, 386
  Ruth, 275
  Sarah, 137, 165
  Thomas, 165, 172, 203, 204, 205, 239, 275
Harding,
  James, 426
  John, 419, 423
  Leah, 423
  Nancy, 426
Hardis, Joshua, 211
Hare, Lydia, 300
Hargadine, William, 520
Hargrove,
  George, 39, 439
  John, 439
  Sarah, 439
  Stephen, 39, 439
Harminson (Harmanson),
  Ann, 313
  Arman, 379
  Elizabeth, 60, 412
  Harmin, 313
  Isaac, 313
  John, 60, 313, 412
  Sarah, 313
Harmison (Harmson),
  Henry, 58, 61, 234
  John, 61
  Sabrah, 234
Harmon,
  Daniel, 288
  Elizabeth, 289, 463
  Isabella, 328
  Sabrah, 337
  Thomas, 477
Harper,
  Agnes, 232, 370
  Ann, 527
  Caleb, 516
  Christian, 66
  David, 370
  Delilah, 498
  Elizabeth, 99, 373, 527
  Frances, 135
  Hetty, 471
  James, 66, 373, 523
  Jane, 545
  Jean, 515
  John, 66, 69, 135, 232, 253, 370, 373, 515, 516, 543
  Joseph, 425, 471, 475, 479, 495, 498, 516, 526, 527, 550
  Margaret, 399, 554
  Mark, 135, 212
  Mary, 120, 135, 527
  Meriam, 409
  Nancy, 516
  Nathaniel, 515
  Pery, 373
  Peter, 135
  Rebeccah, 516
  Susannah, 66, 516, 527
  Thomas, 66, 99, 527
  Thomas, Sr., 527
  William, 66, 95, 237, 269, 324, 370, 373, 409, 425, 432, 461, 465, 475, 515, 516, 527, 545
  William, Jr., 399, 554
  Zephaniah, 269
Harrad, Thomas, 83
Harrington,
  Aaron, 387, 538
  Abner, 504
  Agnes, 333, 356
  Asa, 504
  Barbara, 504
  Benjamin, 504
  Bersha, 385
  David, 387, 538
  Esther, 203, 263, 353
  Gedion, 309
  Hannah, 504
  Henry, 333, 356
  Isaac, 387, 491, 538
  Jacob, 355, 387, 496, 538
  James, 203, 268, 284, 387, 424, 538
  John, 210, 234, 263, 387, 425, 442, 504, 505, 538
  Jonathan, 387, 538
  Martha, 263, 287, 538
  Mary, 504, 519
  Maryan, 355
  Mathew, 504
  Nancy, 309
  Nathan, 387, 496, 538
  Rebecca, 424
  Samuel, 333, 437, 483, 519
  Sarah, 387, 504, 505
  Susannah, 333, 356
  William, 333, 387, 442, 538
Harriott, Samuel, 45

Harris (Harriss),
  Abraham, 259
  Ann, 282
  Benoni, 413, 499, 508, 523, 545, 549, 554
  Bewly, 523
  Elizabeth, 295, 386, 523
  George, 278, 295, 383, 386, 392
  Hannah, 128, 259
  Henry, 89
  James, 510, 546
  Mary, 89
  Moses, 28
  Samuel, 155
  Sarah, 205,
  Susannah, 355
  William, 20, 128, 259
Harrison,
  John, 44
  Joseph, 536
  Thomas, Jr., 127
Hart,
  Aaron, 130, 217, 362
  Alloner, 130
  Ann, 40, 130
  Edward, 64
  Elijah, 130
  Esther, 191
  George, 24, 32, 86, 119, 130
  George, Sr., 130
  Govey, 321
  Hannah, 182, 322
  Henry, 24, 67, 237
  John, 24, 46, 65, 130, 259, 362
  John, Jr., 128, 340
  Mary, 67, 86, 217, 340
  Naomi, 24
  Sabrough, 128
  Sarah, 130, 259
  Tamer, 237
  Thomas, 130
Hartnell,
  Elizabeth, 16
  Nicholas, 16
  Prudence, 16
  Samuel, 16
Hartshorne (Hartshorn),
  Ann, 500
  Ebenezer, 476
  George, 493
  John, 317, 493
  Mary, 378, 493
Hartup,
  Mary, 509
  Thomas, 509
Harwar,
  Susana, 14
  William, 14

Harwood,
  Elebth, 501
  Elizabeth, 430
  Grace, 430, 501
  Hannah, 62, 63
  James, 520
  Jasper, 26, 430, 455, 501
  John, 345, 417, 430, 501
  Margaret, 430, 501
  Martha, 63, 72
  Mary, 63, 379, 520
  Peter, 345, 541
  Rachel, 63
  Samuel, 379, 520
  Thomas, 63, 189, 430, 435, 455, 501
Hasel: see Hazel
Haskins,
  Govert, 372
  William, 372
Haslet,
  Ann, 309
  Jemima, 214, 309, 310, 337
  John, 214, 227, 228, 256, 262, 298, 309
  Col. John, 310
  Joseph, 309
  Mary, 309
Haslton, William, Sr., 254
Hastings, Isaac, 353
Hatfield,
  Betsy, 526
  Elizabeth, 374
  James, 266, 405
  John, 118, 288, 405, 482, 526
  John, Sr., 289
  Jonathan, 526
  Levi, 526, 555
  Levin, 526
  Levy, 304
  Mary, 304, 474, 526
  Nathan, 526
  Owen, 526
  Sarah, 474, 482, 526
  Thomas, 405
  Wheatly, 526
  William, 482, 526
Hathorne,
  Ann, 149
  Ebenezer, 117, 149, 476
  Elizabeth, 149
  John, 84
  Joseph, 149
  Mary, 149,
  Ruth, 149
  William, 149

Hattabaugh (Hattabough),
  Abraham, 235, 427
  Elizabeth, 260
  Isaac, 235, 427
  Mary, 503
  Warwick, 235, 503
Haughay,
  Levi, 515
  Rebecca, 515
Haul, Robert, 405
Haveloe (Havalow, Havaloe, Heavalo),
  Elizabeth, 538
  Luke, 431
  Sarah, 317
  Zadok, 431, 538
Hawkey,
  Elizabeth, 50
  Hannah, 41
  Martha, 50
  Ruth, 25
  Samuel, 25
  Ursilla, 25
  William, 25, 41, 50
Hawkins (Hawkens),
  Abraham, 129, 177
  Allen, 99, 144
  Ann, 50
  Arnold, 129, 171, 203, 327, 340
  Doraty, 241
  Dorothea, 263
  Eleanor, 99, 144
  Elizabeth, 311, 327
  Grace, 144
  Hannah, 129
  Jacob, 178, 293, 388, 423
  Jacobus, 169
  James, 183
  Jean, 293
  John, 100, 129, 203, 293, 388, 416, 436
  John, Jr., 253
  Mary, 144, 376, 416, 541
  Moses, 311
  Rebecca, 537
  Peter, 376, 423, 501, 502, 542
  Phebe, 311
  Simon, 502
  Susannah, 129, 327
  Thomas, 70, 129, 144, 203, 241, 311, 327, 430, 537
  William, 114, 178, 293, 311, 329, 339, 388, 423, 502, 541
Hayes (Hays, Haze, Heyse),
  Ann, 236
  Benjamin, 236
  Darby, 261
  David, 254

Elizabeth, 38
John, 210, 222, 236, 238, 362
Manlove, 555
Martha, 222, 236, 238
Mary, 254
Robert, 236
Zipporah, 555
Haylor (Haytor),
  David, 67
  William, 67
Haynes: see Haines
Hays, Hayse: see Hayes
Haze: see Hayes
Hazel Hazell, Hazle, Heazel)
  Ann, 354
  Barthia, 234, 395
  Benjamin, 310, 354, 400, 458, 471, 478
  Elizabeth, 272, 400, 540
  Ezekel, 540
  George, 234, 354, 478
  Hugh, 540
  Isaac, 234, 447
  James, 409, 540
  Jonathan, 234
  Martha, 471, 540
  Mathew, 409, 540
  Nancy, 324
  Rachel, 540
  Sarah, 540
  Susannah, 540
  William, 260, 354
Hazeltine,
  . . ., 503
  Elizabeth, 503
Hazzard (Hazard),
  Rachel, 62
  William, 62, 71, 145, 230, 363
Headon, Edward, 444, 535
Heald,
  Joab, 522
  Joseph, 461
  Patients, 522
  Rich, 461, 522, 555
  Synthia, 461, 522
Health,
  Charles, 518
  James Paul, 90
  Martha Ann, 518
  Mary, 64, 74, 135, 141, 374
  Thomas, 64
Heazel: see Hazel
Hedger, William, 64
Heffernan, William, 372
Heirons: see Hirons

Helford, Anna, 151
Hellings,
  Jacob, 247
  Mary, 247
Hemmons,
  John, 106
  Thomas, 106
Henderson,
  Alexander, 108
  Andrew, 182, 187
  John, 187, 541
  Major, 253, 263
  Priscilla, 210, 263
Hendrey: see Hendry
Hendricham (Hendrickam),
  John, 124
  Keitren, 124
  Marget, 124
  Mary, 124
  Moses, 124
Hendricks,
  Charles, 547
  Edward, 547
  Henry, 547
  James, 547
  Sarah, 259
Hendrickson,
  Elenor, 540
  Hendrick, 183
  Henry, 540, 555
  James, 441, 540
  Jecobus, 540
  John, 173, 540
  Samuel, 540
  Sarah, 183
Hendry,
  . . ., 312
  David, 36
  Elizabeth, 263, 337
  Margaret, 312, 337, 350
  Matthew, 279, 337, 346
  Miriam, 337
  Rachel, 337
  Robert, 337, 346
Henry,
  Amely, 460
  Edward, 154, 176
  Elizabeth, 229
  Hugh, 368
  James, 368, 470, 544, 553
  Jane, 217
  John, 152, 217
  Martha, 176, 179
  Matthew, 381, 550
  Rebecca, 152
  Robert, 229, 379
  William, 368

Herbert, Rachel, 38
Hering: see Herring
Herington: see Herrington
Heritage, John, 406
Hermonson, Henry, 166
Herren,
  George, 327
  Mary, 327
Herresle, William, 85
Herrik, Abigale, 540
Herring (Hering),
  Eleanor, 131
  Elizabeth, 358
  George, 358
  James, 131, 358
  John, 358
  Mary, 358
  Riche, 358
  William, 358
Herrington (Herington),
  Aaron, 425, 511, 535
  David, 511
  Elizabeth, 210
  Isaac, 482, 511
  Jacob, 511
  James, 380, 511
  John, 380, 504, 511
  Jonathan, 511
  Margaret, 535
  Martha, 482, 511
  Mary, 535
  Nathan, 511, 535, 541
  Sarah, 504
  William, 511
Herwood,
  Susannah, 254
  Thomas, 254
Hewes: see Hughes
Hewthat,
  Ralph, 18
  Thomas, 18
Heyburn, Henry, 105
Heyse: see Hayes
Hickey,
  Benjamin, 417, 495
  John, 417, 444
  Margaret, 417
  Mary, 417
  Thomas, 417, 495
Hickman,
  Mary, 290
  Noah, 290, 458
Hicks,
  George, 413
  Mary, 413

[57]

Higgins, Francis, 18

Hignutt, Ann, 546

Hiken, Elizabeth, 33

Hilford (Hillford),
  Ann, 215, 254, 294
  Boaz, 437, 505
  David, 177, 210, 215, 254, 255, 258, 294, 437, 505
  Elizabeth, 437, 505
  Ester, 215
  Jane, 215
  Martha, 215, 437, 505
  Mary, 215, 301, 437
  Matthew, 215, 368, 513
  Nancy, 488
  Rachel, 215
  Robert, 437, 488, 505
  Sarah, 294, 476
  Thomas, 215, 294, 312, 437
  Zadock, 437, 505

Hill,
  Arthur, 424
  Crosedill, 502
  Elizabeth, 108, 225, 252, 491, 502
  George, 220, 234
  Hester, 502
  Isaac, 18
  Jacob, 252, 305
  James, 394, 414
  John, 11, 190, 252, 267, 392, 491, 509
  Joseph, 252, 254, 267, 276, 279, 340, 522
  Martha, 220
  Mary, 88
  Naomi, 140
  Nathan, 468
  Perthina, 340
  Phebe, 509, 532
  Rachel, 394, 414
  Rebecca, 481, 495, 502, 515
  Richard, 69
  Robert, 252, 254, 279, 481, 495, 515, 522
  Sally, 486
  Samuel, 18
  Sarah, 468
  Susanna, 220, 252
  Thomas, 113, 157, 225, 252, 254, 267, 276
  William, 220, 390, 502

Hillyard (Hilliard, Hillerd, Hyliard),
  . . ., 248
  Anna, 554
  Benjamin, 48
  Charles, 12, 41, 43, 44, 45, 58, 61, 66, 83, 94, 96, 99, 103, 160, 162, 171, 174, 176, 192, 254, 267, 277, 316, 414, 470
  Charles, Jr., 61
  Charles, Sr., 61
  Charles, the younger, 414
  Christopher, 316, 336, 553
  Easther, 30
  Elbourn, 554
  Eleanor, 192
  Elizabeth, 50, 54, 61, 66, 99, 162, 174, 429, 553
  Hannah, 17
  Jno. , 39
  John, 11, 12, 14, 15, 16, 17, 18, 36, 39, 48, 61, 66, 267, 316, 336, 481
  Joseph, 175, 273
  Lurana, 554
  Martha, 99, 160, 175
  Mary, 12, 93, 94, 96, 99, 103, 134, 491, 554
  Oliver, 12, 48, 104
  Philip, 102, 169, 303, 336
  Rachel, 40, 62, 553
  Rebecca, 137, 169, 316
  Ruth, 267
  Sarah, 248, 336, 553
  Solomon, 48
  Steel, 99, 172, 184
  Susanna, 316, 553
  Tamer, 553
  Tamsy, 553
  Thomas, 12, 14, 48, 102, 137, 316, 336, 554
  Thomas Sipple, 536
  William, 54, 553, 554

Hilman, Majer, 540

Hindley, Daniel, 368

Hinds (Hines),
  Fredrick, 186
  George, 457, 488
  John, 168, 211, 241
  Mary, 168, 241
  William, 168

Hindsley (Hinesly, Hinsley),
  . . ., 119
  Ambrose, 472
  Amos, 472, 502, 551
  Amos, Sr., 502
  Ann, 472
  Daniel, 472, 502, 551
  Elizabeth, 119
  Garrett, 472
  Hannah, 472, 502, 551
  James, 472, 502
  John, 472, 502, 551
  Mary, 472, 481

[58]

Nathan, 472
Patience, 472, 502, 551
Sarah, 513
Solomon, 263, 481

Hine, Fredrick, 170

Hines: see Hinds

Hinesly: see Hindsley

Hinmon (Hineman),
Bailey, 555
Elizabeth, 555
William, 331

Hinsely: see Hindsley

Hinson (Hynson),
Charlott, 484
Hannah, 524
Matthew, 527
Nathaniel, 524
Polly, 527
Sarah, 516

Hirons (Hyrons)
Anne, 318, 381, 411
Charles, 80, 149, 150, 157, 265
Elizabeth, 98, 136, 238
Francis, 28, 33, 90
Grace, 171
Jane, 428
John, 28, 82, 149, 150, 157, 171
Joseph, 428
Keziah, 238
Leah, 428
Letitia, 219
Luke, 96, 238
Margaret, 26, 28
Mark, 96, 157, 195, 241, 428
Mary, 46, 96, 149, 428, 461
Mary Ann, 149, 150
Matthew, 96
Percess, 27, 28, 98
Phebe, 238
Piercey, 26, 113
Rebecca, 96
Robert, 28, 46, 265, 318, 343, 381, 411, 428
Sarah, 52, 241, 244
Simon, 18, 19, 23, 26, 28, 84, 89, 96, 113, 141, 219, 274, 428
Simon, Jr., 21, 326
Simon, Sr., 26, 27, 28
Thomas, 67
Timothy, 136
William, 26, 28, 90, 96, 127, 129, 171, 185, 265, 343, 428

Hitchens,
Josiah, 285
Rebecca, 285

Hobbs,
Solomon, 230
Stephen, 422

Hobkins: see Hopkins

Hobson, Lawrence, 220, 248, 252

Hodge, Henry, 49, 63

Hodgkins, Thomas, 32

Hodgson (Hudgson),
David, 229, 250
Esther, 250
John, 183
Jonathan, 183, 444
Joseph, 183, 250, 363, 404, 444, 477
Mary, 183
Nancey, 250
Robert, 44, 74, 101, 229, 417, 440, 444
Robert, Jr., 183
Robert, Sr., 229
Sarah, 183
Train, 74, 183, 250, 363, 477
William, 229, 250, 363, 444

Hodson, Joseph, 425

Hoff,
Rachel, 156
Richard, 156, 224

Hoffecker (Hoofacre),
Anne, 481
Henry, 461, 481
Sarah, 461

Hogan,
Elizabeth, 319
John, 319

Hogben, Elizabeth, 29

Hogg,
Elizabeth, 64
George, 64
James, 58
Joanna, 58, 64
John, 64
Rebeckah, 64
Susannah, 64

Hogins,
. . ., 342
John, 368
Mary, 342, 530

Holden,
Elizabeth, 391
Frederick, 359
William, 359

Holegeros, Mary, 197

Holland,
Alexander, 167, 178
Bryan, 277

Margaret, 151
Maudlin, 167
Perry, 167
Rebecca, 277
Hollet, Mary, 137
Holliday (Holyday),
Anne, 289
Benjamin, 305, 542
Edward, 225
Elizabeth, 542
Hannah, 305
James, 253, 395
John, 54, 56, 62, 69, 74, 77, 103, 109, 111, 260, 276, 305, 334, 389, 395
Joseph, 158, 334, 389
Mary, 158, 305
Nancy, 174
Rachel, 305
Richard, 157, 158, 174, 206, 289, 370
Robert, 158, 175, 177, 206, 253, 269, 283, 346, 384, 396, 401, 476
Samuel, 489
Susannah, 111
Thomas, 260
William, 305
Holling, Abraham, 226
Hollingsworth,
Elizabeth, 527
John, 527
Margaret, 341
Holloway, Elizabeth, 463
Holly, Sarah, 426
Holmes,
Daniel, 389
John, 322
Holson,
Mary, 344
Purnal, 344
Holston (Hoalston),
Benjamin, 218
Elijah, 218
Esther, 218
John, 533
Lydia, 533
Marcy, 180, 220
Mary, 181, 218, 480
Nancy, 218
Purnal, 181
Thomas, 140
Holyday: see Holliday
Homes,
Daniel, 525
David, 525
Homestead, John, 395

Hones, Rev. John, 85
Hood, Rebecca, 175
Hoofacre: see Hoffecker
Hook,
Margaret, 301
Nancy, 412
Rebecca, 346
Hooker,
Mary, 70
Samuel, 70
Hooper, Richard, 204
Hootten,
Elener, 55
Hannah, 55
Robert, 56
Hopkins (Hoopkins),
Amelia, 456
Ann, 548
Comfort, 456
Dorcus, 553
Edmond, 491
Elias, 553
Elizabeth, 387
Hampton, 506, 548
Henry, 456
Hooper, 553
James, 384, 387, 557
James, Jr., 557
Jean, 164, 384, 456
John, 322, 344, 375, 384, 456
John, Sr., 416
Leah, 548
Mary, 456, 496, 553
Mille, 553
Nancy, 385, 456, 506
Neomi, 387
Ora, 456
Robert, 384, 416, 456, 477, 535, 553
Samuel, 387
Sarah, 387, 456
Waitman, 387
William, 387, 557
Zebulon, 384, 456, 553
Horn,
George, 169, 438
Keziah, 438
Mary, 162
Rebecca, 211
Robert, 214
Sarah, 214
William, 34
Horseman (Horsman),
Mary, 95, 156
Samuel, 95, 151, 156
Thomas, 51, 60, 95, 125
Horsley, James, 97

Horsted, John, 62
Horton, Nicholas, 75
Horyer, Robert, 50
Hosier, Elizabeth, 57, 72
Hoskins,
  Henry, 21, 24
  Rachel, 24
Houldson,
  Abraham, 328
  Elijah, 328
  John, 328
  Mary, 328
  Robert, 328
  William, 328
House,
  Honour, 56
  Thomas, 56
Housman,
  John, 51, 58, 67, 146, 157
  W., 47
Houston (Houstown),
  Benjamin, 272, 290
  Elijah, 272, 290, 362, 411
  Eliza, 411
  Elizabeth, 362, 411, 510
  Esther, 272
  Hannah, 190
  James, 176, 190, 362, 499
  John, 478, 526, 541
  Lydia, 510
  Mary, 272, 362, 499
  Nancy, 272
  Rhoda, 362, 499
  Robert, 510
Howard,
  Ann, 357
  Cornelius, 415
  Elenor, 324, 522
  George, 209
  Jno., 40
  John, 38, 392, 402, 538
  John Gould, 209
  Joseph, 375, 405, 415
  Mary, 40, 357, 392, 405, 415
  Robert, 49
  Samuel, 40, 45
  Sarah, 496, 511, 538
  Stephen, 392
  William, 40
Howell (Howill),
  Ann, 191, 312, 380, 417, 556
  David, 154
  Eleanor, 119, 140
  Elizabeth, 238, 371, 380
  Elizabeth, Jr., 371
  Hannah, 154
  James, 17, 18, 22, 27, 67, 81, 100, 103, 119, 132, 154, 166, 172, 191, 264, 306
  Jas., Jr., 123
  James, Sr., 200
  Jenkins, 122
  John, 20, 100, 312, 380, 556
  Joseph, 145, 154, 166
  Lewis, 62
  Lydia, 119
  Margaret, 122
  Mary, 132, 172, 351, 380, 417, 556
  Morris, 103, 119, 132, 172
  Obedience, 306
  Philip, 132, 172
  Priscilla, 166, 200
  Rhody, 188
  Ruhanna, 312, 371
  Ruth, 154
  Sabrit, 166, 188
  Samuel, 67, 154, 351, 403, 444, 471, 547
  Sarah, 119, 172, 312, 371
  Shadrach, 312
  Susannah, 264, 280, 351
  Thomas, 100, 154, 263
  William, 280, 292, 312, 371, 436, 468
Howren,
  Benjamin, 275
  Mary, 275
Howring,
  Benjamin, 184
  Hester, 517
Hoy (Hoye),
  Phebe, 136, 137, 174, 199
  Rachel, 76, 104
  Richard, 52
  William, 104, 137
Hubbard,
  Charles, 344
  Daniel, 344
  James, 344
  Sarah, 344
Hubbert, Robert, 37
Huddleston, Stephen, 511
Hudgason, Mary, 121
Hudgson: see Hodgson
Hudson,
  Absolem, 54, 345, 363
  Alce, 54
  Alee, 54
  Alexander, 54, 111, 136, 282, 315, 415, 440
  Ann, 54
  Arnold, 54, 103, 287, 290, 326, 345
  Benjamin, 222, 253

Charles, 154
Daniel, 21, 49, 54, 121, 162, 203, 279, 390, 440, 551
Ebenezer, 501
Elenor, 54
Elisha, 121
Elizabeth, 211, 281, 326, 335, 343, 440
Enoch, 282
Isabella, 136, 150
John, 27, 121, 253, 279, 468, 501, 551, 554
Luracy, 551
Lydia, 501
Major, 343
Margaret, 54, 150, 352, 415, 440, 501, 541
Mary, 121, 162, 203, 279, 501
Moses, 359
Nancy, 491
Penelope, 359
Richard, 43
Robert, 121, 364
Ruth, 440
Samuel, 349
Samuel Robinson, 390
Sarah, 54, 220, 279
Senty, 501
Susannah, 54, 364
Thomas, 67
Timothy, 45
William, 145, 211, 349, 358, 373, 388, 390, 440, 501

Huestead, Samuel, 64

Huff,
John, 33
Mary, 550
Nathan, 550, 557

Hughbanks: see Eubanks

Hughes (Huse, Hewes),
David, 90
Isabel, 205
John, 205
Jonathan, 385
Mary, 528
Matthew, 66
Sarah, 205
Thomas, 494

Hughey, William, 241, 249

Hukill, Susan, 539

Hull,
Ann, 223
Daniel, 223
David, 224
James, 224, 354
Mary, 354
Rebecca, 192, 223

Humphries (Humphreys, Humpris),
Alce, 108
Alexander, 38, 72, 108, 277
Alexander, Jr., 108
Elizabeth, 277
George, 456
John, 108, 191, 251,
Margaret, 108
Martha, 298
Mary, 38
Sarah, 108
Susannah, 251, 264
William, 108, 298

Hunn,
Ann, 166, 501
Caleb, 48, 58, 82, 92, 139, 291, 298
David, 139, 291
Ellinor, 35
Ezekiel, 460, 501
Hannah, 92
John, 139, 308, 460
Jonathan, 166, 199, 201, 305, 307, 391, 431, 460, 479, 484, 543, 547, 557
Mary, 90, 92, 108, 166, 201, 245, 291, 317, 460
Nathaniel, 18, 28, 33, 35, 42, 88, 90, 92, 103, 121, 201, 307, 460, 501
Patience, 460
Priscilla, 92, 137
Reynear, 166, 201
Ruth, 82, 92, 137
Sarah, 201
Susannah, 139, 351, 460, 484
Tabitha, 139

Hunt, William, 139

Hunter,
Ann, 145
Elizabeth, 145
Hannah, 145
James, 145, 169, 173
John, 88, 99, 116, 134, 145
Mary, 134, 145, 169, 173, 185, 219, 221, 264
Samuel, 134
William, 145

Hurlock (Hurlick),
Ann, 515
Ebenezer, 515
Elizabeth, 235, 427, 515
Isaac, 158
Jacob, 353, 471, 515
John, 515
Lucrecia, 515
Martha, 515
Mary, 413, 515

Rachel, 515
Samuel, 515
Sarah, 515
William, 427
Hurt, John, 466
Huse: see Hughes
Hussey, James, 202, 246
Huston,
    Alexander, 257, 271, 371
    Ann, 371
    Charles, 390
    John, 371
    Samuel, 371
    Thomas, 510
Hutchins,
    Jno., 541
    John, 417, 433
    Martha, 442, 492
    Thomas, 492
Hutchinson (Hutchenson, Hutchingson),
    Ann, 96
    James, 325, 345, 416, 435
    John, 396, 416
    Margaret, 435
    Mary, 292, 325, 435, 531
    Sarah, 396, 536
    William, 90, 325
Hutchison (Hutcheson, Hutchisson),
    Ann, 359
    James, 310
    John, 322, 353
    Mary, 143, 310, 322
    Matthew, 143, 322
    Nancy, 237
    William, 90, 310, 359
Hutson,
    Alexander, 517
    Ann, 192, 459
    William, 517
Hutt, Hannah, 61
Hutton,
    Eleanor, 111, 152
    John, 45
    Robert, 111
Huzza, Joseph, 479
Hyam, Thomas, 115
Hyatt,
    James, 104, 152
    Mary, 303
Hylands, Meriam, 289
Hyliard: see Hillyard
Hynman, William, 252
Hynson: see Hinson
Hyrons: see Hirons

—I—

Inglis, Charles, 184
Ingram, John, 291
Inloe, Thomas, 213
Ions, Edelia, 270
Irons,
    Anica, 456
    Anne, 318
    Catherine, 87
    Elizabeth, 195, 216, 241, 347
    Hannah, 114, 309
    Henry, 87, 325, 342, 440, 456
    James, 309
    Jane, 422, 532
    Jennet, 366
    John, 82, 87, 129, 261, 309, 325, 440
    John, Jr., 261
    John, Sr., 325
    Joseph, 422
    Leah, 532
    Mark, 445, 488
    Mary, 74, 360, 422, 445, 555
    Naomy, 325
    Owen, 87, 366
    Penelope, 293
    Perce, 274
    Robert, 318
    Sarah, 435, 532
    Simon, 23, 274
    Susannah, 488
    Thomas, 67, 70, 87, 89, 105, 114, 126, 216, 236, 325, 366
    Timothy, 87, 89, 158, 195, 216, 272, 325, 488
    Titus, 289
    William, 216, 392, 435, 532
Ironside (Ironsides),
    John, 258, 394
    Margaret, 394
Isgate, Philip, 173

—J—

Jackson,
    . . ., 280, 493
    Abraham, 87, 120, 170
    Agnis, 493
    Alexander, 354, 383, 412, 449
    Ann, 93, 321, 513, 554

Archibald, 280
Benjamin, 257
Betty, 98
Bredget, 63
Caleb, 123, 299, 444
Christopher, 32, 63
Comfort, 74
Daniel, 323, 549, 555, 568
Eben, 538
Ebenezer, 513
Elizabeth, 35, 93, 98, 102, 169, 244, 284, 304, 319, 368, 412, 413, 493, 497
Esther, 169
Ezekiel, 169, 497
George, 474, 554
Henry, 475
James, 30, 38, 42, 86, 102, 123, 125, 299, 555
Dr. James, 98
Jane, 354
John, 35, 63, 98, 244, 258, 321, 412, 474
Jonathan, 299, 323, 367, 376, 493
Joseph, 123, 284, 299, 304, 389, 412
Kezia, 449
Levi, 367
Lydia, 243
Margaret, 87, 98, 120, 175
Marriah, 554
Mary, 110, 299, 303, 409
Meriam 409
Moses, 169, 175, 439
Nancy, 412
Nimrod, 409
Noah, 412
Polly, 449
Richard, 21, 32, 123, 169, 264, 292
Ruth, 299
Samuel, 409, 554
Susanah, 264, 280, 292, 299, 449
Thomas, 123, 125, 299, 301, 412, 449, 482, 554
William, 98, 100, 120, 123, 125, 130, 232, 299, 554

Jacobs,
  Abraham, 222, 230, 456
  Bozman, 222, 510
  Elizabeth, 149, 230, 270, 328, 510
  James, 510
  Jane, 144
  Jonathan, 510
  Leah, 456
  Mary, 136, 140, 149
  Molton, 510
  Nancy, 510
  Rebecca, 222
  Speakman, 222, 456
  William, 113, 132, 149, 222, 248, 328, 456
Jacquett (Jaquat), Richard, 96, 206
Jadwin, John, 12
Jaffray,
  Henry, 104, 149
  Rebecca, 149
  Sarah, 149
Jakes, Ann, 231
James,
  Caterine, 52
  Celicia, 382
  Daniel, 65, 226, 243, 555
  Elizabeth, 65, 83, 92, 329
  George, 52
  Gwenlian, 92
  Isaiah, 463, 550
  John, 158, 162, 163, 329, 382
  Mary, 550
  Nathaniel, 158, 162, 163
  Richard, 59, 63, 66, 73, 83
  Thomas, 116, 123
Jamison (Jameson, Jemison),
  Alexander, 192, 378
  Andrew, 192, 234, 291, 370, 382, 394, 416
  Janett, 192
  John, 78, 474
  Joseph, 192, 291, 308
  Joshua, 192
  Mary, 308, 378
  Nancy, 416
  Robert, 85, 96, 98, 365, 383, 416, 479, 496
  Dr. Robert, 532
  Sarah, 98
  Thomas, 192, 416
Janney,
  Jacob, 367
  Levi, 367
January, Agnes, 502
Jarold: see Jarrold
Jarrad,
  Mathew, 474, 505
  William, 402
Jarral: see Jarrell
Jarrald: see Jarrold
Jarrard (Jerrard),
  Alice, 339
  Esther, 227, 237
  James, 237, 316, 338

Matthew, 162, 215, 265, 267, 530
Matthew, Jr., 237
Matthew, Sr., 237
William, 338, 339
Wilson, 237, 315

Jarratt: see Jarrett

Jarrell (Jarral, Jarrel, Jarril),
Ann, 529
Comfort, 543
Eleazer, 509
Elias, 523, 526, 529, 549
Elizabeth, 128, 477, 509
Hannah, 529
Hart, 526, 529
Jeremiah, 477, 526, 529
John, 509, 541
Mary, 509, 529
Nancy, 541
Richard, 509
Robert, 509, 543, 546
Ruth, 130, 509, 529
Sarah, 529
Stephen, 301, 381
Susannah Fleming, 509

Jarrett (Jarratt)
Abraham, 32
Easther, 95
Matthew, 95

Jarril: see Jarrell

Jarrold (Jarold, Jarrald, Jarrild),
Anne, 421
Comfort, 449
Elias, 480
James, 393, 426, 431
Jonathan, 393, 431
Lydia, 393, 413, 431
Margaret, 421
Martha, 426
Mary, 393, 413, 421
Morris, 393, 421, 431
Moses, 393, 431
Nancy, 413
Polly, 413
Robert, 422
Sarah, 421
Stephen, 422, 431
Stephen, Jr., 391, 393, 413
Stephen, Sr., 393
Stephen, the elder, 431
Thomas, 449

Jarvis (Jarvice),
Caleb, 457
Daniel, 457
John, 451

Jeans,
Hannah, 530
Isaac, 530

Jefferson, Richard, 535, 545

Jenings: see Jennings

Jenkins (Jenckens),
Andrew, 235, 276, 378
Dolly, 235, 276, 378, 406
Dorothy, 427
Eleanor, 426, 492
Elen, 426
Elizabeth, 157, 450
Ellen, 318
Enoch, 222, 381
Hannah, 158, 280
Jabez, 46, 68, 109, 146, 157, 166, 177, 207, 211, 212, 242, 280, 318, 351, 424, 426, 433, 460, 503, 506
John, 222, 280, 550
Jonathan, 460
Joseph, 157, 280, 284, 351, 359, 391, 424
Mary, 148, 322
Mary Ann, 148
Patience, 460
Rebecca, 146, 212, 280
Samuel, 318, 426, 506
Sarah, 68, 73, 109, 318, 426
Thomas, 50, 280, 351, 391, 424, 450, 468, 471, 477, 503, 550
Timothy, 231, 236, 280, 318, 426

Jenkinson, Emanuel, 20

Jennings (Jenings)
Edward, 45, 57, 63, 77, 79
Elinor, 472
George, 523
John, 523

Jerrard: see Jarrard

Jervis,
Caleb, 437
Daniel, 437
Joseph, 437
Mary 437

Jessop (Jessops, Jesop),
Jacob, 259
Jesper, 16
Mary, 242, 259
Unice, 512
William, 512

Jester,
Abraham, 154
Annice, 178
Arnall, 178
Arthur, 368

Barbara, 154
Catherine, 178
Charles, 304, 385, 495
Charlotte, 373
Daniel, 154, 179, 189
David, 373
Deborah, 464
Delilah, 373
Elenor, 272
Elias, 178, 426
Elijah, 373
Elizabeth, 154, 179, 544
Emanuel, 404, 506
Esther, 333, 368
Ezekiel, 385
Francis, 273, 404
Francis, Jr., 404
Isaac, 154, 350, 495, 497, 511
Jacob, 154
James, 544
Jehu, 273, 404
Jesse, 404, 520
John, 154, 338, 404, 447, 522
Jonathan, 154, 212
Joseph, 106, 154, 333
Joshua, 154, 227, 304, 344, 404
Leah, 432
Lenny, 373
Levi, 544
Lucretia, 338, 348
Lydia, 506, 520
Lyes, 404
Mahaly, 373
Mary, 178, 212, 350, 373, 489, 497, 506
Nance, 272
Rebecca, 360
Richard, 154, 170, 272, 308, 360
Samuel, 464
Sarah, 93, 154, 178, 350, 385, 404, 440, 491, 506, 544
Selia 376
Thomas, 60, 154, 178, 266, 317, 417, 544
William, 170, 272, 373

Jewell,
  Abigail, 463
  William, 463

John,
  Griffith, 77
  Samuel, 151

Johns,
  Elizabeth, 174
  Richard, 137, 139
  Samuel, 132, 148, 159, 174
  Sary, 394

Johnson,
  Abraham, 100
  Agness, 287, 459
  Ann, 87
  Benjamin, 69, 102
  Charlotty, 524
  David, 155, 234
  Elizabeth, 115, 287, 326
  George, 155
  Henry, 463
  James, 115, 155, 182, 287, 362, 459, 463, 468, 519, 523, 524
  James, Sr., 296
  Jean, 287, 290
  Jno., 133
  John, 78, 87, 95, 115, 133, 155, 203, 211, 287, 290, 326, 463, 524, 533
  John, the elder, 290
  Jonathan, 463
  Letitia, 406
  Lovey, 545
  Margaret, 115, 287, 524
  Mary, 102, 114, 153, 155, 182, 287, 296, 459, 463, 533, 550
  Mary Ann, 459
  Nancy, 459, 468
  Nathan, 459, 468
  Priscilla, 459, 468
  Purnel, 459, 468, 524
  Rachel, 115
  Robert, 221, 234, 287, 406
  Samuel, 96, 115, 133, 145, 158, 169, 287, 302, 459, 524
  Sarah, 158, 159, 169, 459
  Susannah, 32, 312
  Thomas, 287, 363, 523
  Walter, 32
  William, 115, 203, 287, 290, 312, 427, 459, 463, 468, 523, 524, 548

Johnston,
  . . ., 483
  Ann, 51
  David, 303
  Elizabeth, 370
  George, 303
  Isaac, 526
  James, 556
  Jean, 69
  John, 526
  Margaret, 526
  Mary Ann, 556
  Nancy, 556
  Nathan, 556
  Pheby, 115, 459, 468, 483, 556
  Polly, 556
  Priscilla, 556
  Purnel, 556
  Rachel, 385
  Robert, 526

Sarah, 556
William, 51, 97, 346, 370, 556

Jois: see Joyce

Jolly, Mary, 188, 216

Jones,
..., 467
Abel, 421, 443
Ann, 478
Anthony, 21
Asa, 513
Barbara, 203, 209
Benjamin, 99, 116, 117, 137, 147, 164, 169, 193, 203, 209, 226, 235, 281, 396, 445, 447, 455
Benjamin, Jr., 209, 276
Bersheba, 416
Brown, 369
Catharine, 94, 101, 210, 298
Charles, 36, 513
Daniel, 17, 370, 429, 503
David, 149, 158, 242, 366, 454, 468, 487
Dolly, 235, 276
Dorothy, 117, 137, 280
Ebenezer, 152, 156, 160
Edelia, 270
Edward, 63, 404
Eleanor, 20, 21, 177, 421, 443, 456, 539
Elizabeth, 18, 25, 41, 73, 242, 369, 447, 455, 518 536
Enoch, 69, 252, 284, 311, 323, 389, 418, 421, 443, 503, 506, 518,
Enoch, Jr., 389
Esther, 456, 462, 539
Evan, 12, 20, 24, 25, 29, 41, 43, 71, 72, 191, 300
Frances, 41, 44
Francis, 11
Gabriel, 32
Griffith, 25, 39, 40, 41, 147, 158
Hannah, 71, 369, 530
Henry, 380
Hezekiah, 369
Isaacs, 94, 235, 369, 513
Isaacs, Sr., 369
Jacob, 149, 264, 281, 295, 311, 478
James, 199, 203, 241, 264, 311, 332, 335, 392, 430, 438, 454, 456, 486, 487, 518, 532, 538, 548, 552
Jane, 40, 72
Jean, 72
Jeanet, 158
Jeremiah, 343
Jerusha, 456, 539
Jesse, 433
John, 22, 32, 58, 69, 72, 81, 101, 132, 149, 158, 172, 207, 311, 369, 456, 457, 470, 513, 548
Jonathan, 503
Joseph, 11, 311, 487
Joshua, 555
Layton, 322, 331, 396, 420, 457, 458
Letitia, 503, 506
Levice, 203
Lewis, 68, 191, 298
Lody, 503
Lydia, 78, 389, 421, 443, 467
Malachi, 145
Manlove, 369
Margaret, 32, 72, 82, 164, 188, 458
Martha, 496
Mary, 17, 116, 143, 150, 172, 199, 226, 281, 331, 369, 396, 421, 443, 454, 458, 538, 543, 545
Mathew, 543
Millesant, 311
Nalce, 462
Nancy, 456
Neley, 539
Nicholas, 203
Peggy, 420, 457
Penelope Holt, 281
Phebe, 101
Philip, 64, 68, 166, 191, 372, 396, 400, 421, 426
Rachel, 295, 311, 436
Robert, 416
Salathiel, 496, 512, 543
Samuel, 101, 311
Sarah, 17, 316, 329, 343, 370
Silas, 396
Stanford, 203, 456
Standford, Jr., 457
Susannah, 470
Thomas, 11, 25, 41, 81, 82, 95, 191, 200, 242, 323
Triphana, 513
Unity, 416
Waitman, 513
Walter, 14, 20
William, 94, 407, 436
Zachariah, 369, 416, 513
Zachariah, Jr., 456

Jordan,
Andrew, 110
Beatrice, 168
Elizabeth, 364, 469
Isabella, 447, 465
Jno., 135
John, 168
Margarett, 110

Rachel, 469, 535
William, 242, 269, 444, 469, 527, 535
Joy,
  Ann, 120, 126
  Edward, 120, 390, 502, 515, 545
  Eleanor, 390
  Jane, 120
  Jean, 390
  John, 119, 120, 126, 340, 390
  Joseph, 126
  Josiah, 120, 126
  William, 545, 390
Joyce (Jois),
  . . ., 529
  Ann, 529
  Henry, 55
  Sally, 524
  Samuel, 191
  Thomas, 480, 524
Jubart,
  Andrew, 191
  Mary, 191
  Peter, 191
  Sarah, 191
Jump,
  Benjamin, 321, 491
  Christopher, 527
  Elijah, 491
  Isaac, 491
  John, 491
  Levin, 465, 488
  Nancy, 488
  Olive, 492, 512, 527
  Samuel, 426
  Sarah, 488, 491
  Solomon, 491
  Sophia, 337
  William, 488, 491
Justice, James, 73

—K—

Kairone, Timothy, 22
Kane: see Cain
Katon: see Caton
Kearle, Thomas, 112
Kearn, Alice, 350
Kearney,
  Dyer, 439
  Euphamia Annabella, 97
  Graham, 97
  Isabella, 97
  Lydia, 413
  Michael, 97
  Morris, 413
  Phillip, 35, 43, 97
  Rebecca, 43
  Rose, 118
  Sarah, 97
  William, 118
Kearsey,
  Daniel, 114
  Elizabeth, 262
  George, 492
  James, 133
  Jemyma, 190, 133
  Mary, 114
  Naomi, 492
Keech,
  Ann, 392
  Jarman, 392
  Nathan, 392
  Rebikah, 392
Keets,
  Mary, 491
  William, 491
Keith (Keeth, Keth),
  Ann, 487, 539
  Elizabeth, 500
  Francis, 98, 129, 135, 151, 152, 173, 324, 370, 500
  Hannah, 173
  James, 151, 173, 216
  Jane, 151, 173, 183, 218
  John, 151, 173, 211, 217, 500
  Miriam, 173
  Sarah, 112, 173, 500
  Thomas, 173, 216, 259, 324, 341, 353, 384, 394, 401, 487
Kelly,
  Anipil, 150
  Elizabeth, 430
  Enock, 212
  Honor, 21
  James, 430, 480
  John, 21, 23, 212
  Margaret, 21, 43
  Mary, 430, 452
  Rebecca, 430
  Rosannah, 472
  Samuel, 150, 269
  Sarah, 23, 24
  Thomas, 430
  William, 38, 204, 472
Kemp,
  Elizabeth, 480
  Henry, 432
  Mary, 432
  Samuel, 313, 315, 480

Kelson,
  George, 401
  Rebekah, 401
Keneam,
  Ambros, 540
  Christian, 540
Kendal (Kendel),
  Benjamin, 326
  Joseph, 326
  William, 182
Kenderdine, John, 174
Kennard (Kenneard),
  George, 551
  Richard, 507
Kent,
  Isaac, 508
  Joseph, 255
  Magdalen, 255
Kernohan,
  Margaret, 498
  Robert, 472, 498, 522
Ketch, James, 130
Keys,
  Ann, 514
  Benjamin, 302
  Derick, Jr., 30
  Elizabeth, 514
  Jno., 469
  Mary, 514
  Pricilla, 514
  Rachel, 469
  Richard, 386
  William, 514
Keyser, Derick, Jr., 30
Killam,
  Catharin, 242
  Isaac, 242
  John, 393
Killen (Killin, Killon),
  Abel, 259, 477, 527
  Adams, 256, 259
  Assenith, 527
  Elizabeth, 223, 527
  Esther, 481
  George, 368
  Henry, 227, 256, 267, 354, 385, 391
  Isaac, 219
  Jacob, 368
  James, 368
  John, 256
  Joseph, 368
  Mark, 250, 256, 367, 437, 481
  Mary, 223, 256, 259, 354, 385
  Nancy, 385
  Polly, 259
  Rebecca, 223
  Robert, 68, 135, 172, 173, 181, 216, 230, 241, 248, 250, 256, 354, 367
  Ruth, 385
  Susanna, 227, 267, 385, 391,
  Thomas, 368
  William, 147, 150, 157, 163, 181, 188, 223, 225, 236, 240, 256, 281, 309, 310, 335, 367, 368, 372, 374, 527
Killingsworth,
  Anderson, 273
  Ann, 273
  Edward, 19, 58
  Elizabeth, 58, 200, 273
  Febe, 273
  George, 58, 133
  John, 58, 60, 273
  Josiah, 225
  Mary, 19, 58, 273
  Nathaniel, 58, 200, 273
  Rachel, 133
  Rebecca, 273, 417
  Sarah, 58, 273, 303
Kilpatrick (Killpatrick, Capatrick),
  Adam, 121, 135
  Alce, 379, 381
  Ealce, 241
  Hannah, 85
  John, 85, 241, 320, 379, 381, 537
  Matilda, 537
Kimmey (Kimme, Kimmy),
  Abraham, 441, 550
  Charles, 284, 290, 498
  Ealender Benson, 284
  Levicy, 307
  Levin, 284, 290
  Mary, 281, 290, 363, 498
  Nancy Addams, 284
  Robert, 284, 307
  Solomon, 284, 290, 307, 498
  Thomas, 284, 290
  William, 284, 307
King,
  Abraham, 462
  Alexander, 326, 393
  Alice, 72
  Anne, 135, 288
  Barbara, 508
  Charles, 64, 69
  Elianer, 276
  Elias, 72
  Elizabeth, 127, 135, 393, 462
  Esther, 326, 393, 411
  Isaac, 88, 90, 97, 135, 245
  Jacob, 135
  James, 135, 208, 274

John, 75, 268, 381, 393, 397, 411, 488, 508
Martha, 245
Mary, 268, 379, 393, 402
Miriam, 208, 274
Nancy, 437
Peter, 135, 142
Richard, 34
Robert, 75, 181, 393, 488
Sarah, 135
Susanna, 135
Valentine, 135, 288
William, 343, 379, 402

Kingham,
  James, 369
  Joshua, 369
  Mary, 369

Kinnamon,
  ..., 465
  Ambros, 540
  Christian, 465, 540
  Samuel, 540
  Thomas, 540

Kirben,
  Elizabeth, 375
  James, 375

Kirk (Kirke),
  Mary Ann, 373, 549
  Polly, 549
  Sarah, 413, 499

Kirklin, Richard, 348

Kirkly (Kirkley),
  Elizabeth, 406
  George, 399, 554
  Jane, 558
  John, 113
  Margaret, 399, 554
  Thomas, 558
  William, 113, 316, 382, 396, 398, 473

Kirk Patrick, David, 144

Kitts, Martha, 204

Knight,
  Betsy, 447
  Caesar, 305
  Daniel, 305
  Darcus, 397, 447
  John, 79, 87, 305, 368
  Joseph, 447
  Mary, 248
  Sarah, 305
  William, 79, 248, 397, 447

Knock,
  Daniel, 469, 537
  Joseph, 469
  Rachel, 537
  Susannah, 469
  Thomas, 278

Knotts (Knott),
  Absalom, 428 538
  Benjamin, 539
  Edward, 200, 223, 273, 348, 351, 428
  Esther, 207, 273
  Ezekial, 428
  Hannah, 351
  Hursley, 428
  Jonathan, 398
  Lurania, 539
  Lydia, 474
  Nancy, 207
  Nathaniel, 398, 517
  Robert, 428
  Sarah, 428, 487
  Thomas, 428
  William, 372, 398, 487, 533, 534

Knox (Nox),
  Daniel, 109
  Ezekiel, 109
  John, 116, 319
  Samuel, 319
  Thomas, 109

Kont, Edmond, 13

—L—

Lackey (Lakey),
  Alexander, 49
  Andrew, 129, 144, 186, 244, 245, 284, 323, 401
  Elizabeth, 58
  Esther, 144
  Gustavus, 58
  Henry, 68
  John, 479
  Katherine, 129
  Mary, 58, 59, 144
  Rachel, 401

Lacompte, Lacount: see Lecompte

Lacy (Lassey),
  James, 215, 230
  Mary, 215, 230
  Nansey, 215
  Rebecca, 215

Ladden,
  John, 161
  Margaret, 161

Ladwell, Elizabeth, 13

Lafferty,
  James 465, 466, 532
  Nancy, 465

Laforge, Ardian, 191
Lain: see Lane
Lakey: see Lackey
Lamb,
  ..., 392
  John, 485
  Margaret, 299, 392
  Rosa, 485
  Susannah, 351
  Thomas, 351, 392, 540
Lambden (Lampden),
  Daniel, 369
  Elizabeth, 369
  George, 369
  John, 369, 441, 519
  Mary, 369
  Matthew, 369
  Nancy, 369
  Sarah, 519
Lambert,
  Henry, 313
  James, 313
  John, 283, 313
  Levi, 313
  Sarah, 313
  Susannah, 283, 313
LaMott, Charles, 41
Lane (Lain),
  Anthony, 373, 520
  Elizabeth, 364
  Gallant, 345
  James, 310, 364
  John, 16, 68, 310, 371
  Joseph, 141
  Lydia, 520
  Margaret, 364
  Maryum, 520
  Mathew, 364
  Priscilla, 364
  Prudy, 364
  Sarah, 371
  Thomas, 364
  Timothy, 364
  William, 345, 397
Lang, James, 138 139
Langrell (Langril, Langrel),
  George, 178
  James, 178
  Rebeckah, 178
  Sally, 467
  William, 178
  William, Sr., 178
Lanthorn,
  Mary, 345
  Sarah, 345
Lardner, Lynford, 94

Larence (Lorrence),
  Margaret, 58
  Rachel, 109
Larkin (Larkins), John, 204
Larwood,
  Elizabeth, 398, 476
  John, 264
  William, 398
Lary,
  Charles, 558
  Elizabeth, 558
  Philemon, 558
  Sarah, 558
Latern,
  Elizabeth, 289
  Joseph, 289
Latcham (Latchamp, Latchem,
    Latchen, Latchum, Lychum),
  Cornelia, 484
  Gabriel, 39
  George, 290, 343
  Esther, 290
  Hester, 343
  Isaiah, 359
  Joseph, 484
  Joshua, 484
  Levin, 544
  Margarett, 488
  Mary, 544
Latham (Leathem, Leathim,
    Lathem),
  Absolem, 69
  Adams, 14, 22, 27, 69
  Ann, 383
  Catharine, 509
  Elizabeth, 383
  James, 383
  James, Jr., 383
  Mary, 69, 383, 448, 509
  Polly, 509
  Rhoady, 509
  Robert, 383, 448, 509
  Thomas, 396
Lattomus, James, 205
Launcelot, James, 16
Lawful,
  Eleanor, 142
  Thomas, 142
Laws,
  Amelia, 554
  Anne, 349
  Bolitha, 218, 270, 290, 349, 555
  Charlote, 349
  Clemon, 510
  Eleshe, 502
  Elijah, 510

Elizabeth, 403
Esther, 349
George, 510
Hesse, 349
John, 349, 403, 554
Dr. John, 539
John C., 558
John M. 502
John May, 510
Joseph, 420
Joshua, 218, 259, 270, 349, 522, 555
Leah, 349, 555
Levicy, 307
Lodowick, 510, 529
Major, 349, 517
Mary, 259
Mattilda, 555
Nancy, 517, 555
Outten, 349, 507, 544, 555
Polly, 554, 555
Rachel, 270, 420
Sarah, 401, 554, 555
Sallyann, 555
Truston, 349
William, 307, 349, 362, 391, 510
Ziporah, 349

Layton,
  Ann, 492
  Elijah, 546
  H., 452, 503, 547
  Mary, 358
  Nicholas, 358
  Sarah, 530
  William, 532

Leach (Leech),
  David, 71, 156, 184
  Mary, 71, 181

Leathem: see Latham

Leatherbury (Leatherberry, Leatherbery),
  Abell, 107
  Ann, 496
  Charles, 107, 283
  Grace, 96
  John, 107
  Jonathan, 96, 107
  Mary, 107, 283, 321
  Sarah, 283, 285
  Thomas, 41, 107, 283, 318, 321
  William, 107, 166, 185, 283, 318, 439

Leavith,
  Mary, 12
  Richard, 12

Leby, Cadrup, 304

Leckey, (Lecky),
  Andrew, 69, 106, 425, 465
  Andrew, the elder, 465
  Esther, 106
  Gustavus, 68
  Henry, 68
  Hugh, 68, 69
  Isaac, 106, 133
  Isabella, 106
  Jane, 106
  John, 68
  Margaret, 68
  Mary, 68, 69, 106
  Robert, 68, 84

Lecompte (Lecompt, Lacount, Lacompte),
  Anthony, 558
  Charles, 528, 558
  Elizabeth, 118, 290, 558
  James, 558
  Leah, 528, 558
  Letitia, 401
  Mary, 339
  Nancy, 528
  Nathan, 339, 498, 528
  Precilla, 528
  Rebecca, 558
  Sarah, 558
  Thomas, 401, 501
  William, 501, 558

Lee,
  David, C., 523, 552
  Elizabeth, 91
  Jeremiah, 316, 343, 525
  Letitia, 206
  Margaret, 468, 471
  Mary, 251
  Richard, 91, 316, 343, 534
  Thomas, 424, 471
  William, 91

Leech: see Leach

Legg,
  George, 341
  James, 122

Leith, Alexander, 121

Lemar,
  Eleanor, 492
  Henry, 492
  John, 501

Lemon, Elizabeth, 249

Lennan, John, 152

Lennard,
  Grace, 196
  John, 195

Lenoir, Isaac, 33

Lenox, James, 483
Lenton,
  Ellinor, 36
  Mary, 36, 51, 52
  Nathaniel, 36
  Rebecca, 36
Lester,
  ..., 39
  Ann, 39
  George, 39, 65, 124
  Joseph, 272
  Mary, 39
  Soden, 361
Letort,
  Ann, 39
  James, 39
Leverton,
  Garey, 483, 552
  James A., 552
  Martha, 552
  Moses, 552
  Richard, 552
  Sarah, 373
Levick (Leyvick),
  Catherine, 231, 260
  Clayton, 61, 105, 140, 195, 205, 221, 231
  Hannah, 55, 61, 205, 231, 260
  Honour, 73
  John, 26, 61, 105, 231, 260, 277, 280
  Lydia, 231, 260
  Margret, 277
  Patience, 75
  Rachel, 120, 343
  Richard, 26, 61, 73, 75
  Richard, Sr., 77
  Robert, 61, 231, 260
  Sarah, 61
  William, 61, 120, 195, 230, 231, 254, 260, 343, 392
Levin, Rees, 93
Lewden, Joseph, 37
Lewis (Lewes, Lues),
  ..., 294
  Abraham, 381
  Amram, 245
  Daniel, 103, 164, 184, 196, 207, 345, 400, 487
  David, 77, 91, 103, 105, 168, 198, 207, 381, 487, 491, 505
  Deborah, 186, 314, 401
  Dorcus, 494
  Elizabeth, 38, 72, 310, 371, 381, 411, 413, 424, 549
  Enoch, 318
  Esther, 443, 444, 445, 446
  Evan, 95, 154, 287, 381
  Evan, Sr., 381
  George, 122
  Hannah, 184
  Henry, 310
  Hester, 534
  Jacob, 487
  James, 77, 103, 245, 253, 293, 318, 324, 424, 440
  Jean, 293, 324
  Joel, 103, 253, 318
  John, 38, 72, 87, 93, 103, 136, 141, 149, 168, 211, 225, 229, 236, 245, 310, 413, 424
  Dr. John, 242
  Joseph, 275, 413, 424, 517
  Kosiah, 72
  Lancelot, 38, 62, 72
  Leah, 528
  Luff, 401
  Lydia, 294, 318, 381
  Margaret, 196
  Mark, 103, 245, 339
  Mary, 103, 121, 184, 242, 244, 245, 310, 413, 444, 494, 505
  Martha, 38
  Peggy, 184, 196
  Phebe, 72, 73
  Phillip, 136, 244, 494, 539
  Rachel, 168, 318, 440
  Rees, 65, 71, 81, 87, 93, 103, 245,
  Richard, 310, 413
  Robert, 375, 381, 424, 438, 444, 446
  Ruhamy, 184
  Ruth, 275
  Sarah, 198, 232, 240, 318, 381, 385, 387, 400, 424, 487, 491
  Stephen, 121, 184, 186, 191, 196, 207, 217, 232, 240, 251, 288, 298, 349, 401, 542, 549
  Stephen, Jr., 400
  Susannah, 105, 110, 207, 217, 298
  Thomas, 95, 242, 310, 413, 424, 505
  Thomas, Jr., 549
  William, 371, 413, 424, 483
Lewkins, Nathaniel, 23
Leyvick: see Levick
Libby, Susanna, 308
Lightly, Mary, 110
Lilly (Lily),
  Elizabeth, 428
  John, 428
  Mary, 308
  Timothy, 308
Linch: see Lynch
Lindsay (Lyndsey),
  David, 133
  John, 45

Linnard, Mary, 332
Linnon,
  Arthur, 189
  Grace, 189
  John, 189
Lisby,
  Jane, 539
  Samuel, 539
Lisenbey, John E., 23
Lisle, Samuel, 237
Lister (Listor),
  Ann, 465, 479
  Elizabeth, 512
  Joseph, 284
  Levi, 465, 479, 493, 512
  Margaret, 458
  Mary, 431, 514
  Peggy, 457
  Peter, 457, 458, 465
  Sorden, 340, 424, 440, 465, 472, 533
  Timothy, 479, 514
  William, 440, 465, 479
Liston (Listen),
  Edmond, 68
  Eve, 225
  Margaret, 23
  Mary, 225, 299, 307
  Rachel, 157
Litman, Edward, 206
Little,
  Ann, 291
  Josiah, 49
  Lazarus, 291
  Mary, 131
  Thomas, 49
Littleton, Thomas, 164
Lloyd,
  Elizabeth, 171, 345
  Robert, 345
  Samuel, 171
Loatman (Lootman),
  Agnis, 109, 195
  Benjamin, 237
  Elizabeth, 347
  Esther, 120
  Jeremiah, 120, 174, 195
  John, 120
Lober: see Lowber
Lock, John, 219
Lockerman: see Loockerman
Lockwood (Loockwood),
  Armwell, 145, 199, 304, 382, 409, 419, 424
  Armwell, Jr., 396, 419, 465, 494
  Armwell, Sr., 494
  Caleb, 382
  Daniel Cummins, 528
  David, 382
  Elizabeth, 382, 396
  Gartery, 494
  Isaac, 494
  Israel Holland, 199
  John, 281, 382, 396, 413, 426, 473, 494, 521, 529
  Levy, 494
  Lucretia, 396
  Margarett, 169, 382, 494
  Mary, 145, 199, 382
  Merium, 382
  Nancy, 382, 409
  Nehemiah, 199
  Rebeckah, 382
  Richard, 162, 169, 275, 304, 363, 382, 396
  Richard Comerford, 396
  Sarah, 382, 409
  Thomas, 396, 449, 450, 494
  Unity, 450, 494
Lodge, Grace, 35
Lofland,
  Purnel, 463, 488, 555
  Solomon, 437
Loftis,
  Barbary, 523
  Burton, 300, 541
  Burton, Sr., 541
  Elizabeth, 541
  Gideon, 520, 541
  John, 300, 392, 523
  John, Sr., 300
  Joseph, 300, 392
  Mary, 541
  Rebecca, 523
  Sarah, 300, 392
  Trace, 520
  William, 541
Lomax, Edward, 225
Long,
  Edward, 50, 79, 264
  Jane, 264
  Jean, 79
  Jennet, 79
  Margarett, 264
  Mary, 209, 211
  Mary Ann, 253
  Samuel, 357
  Sarah, 183
  Susannah, 50
  Timothy, 183
  William, 102, 264

Longfellow,
  Elizabeth, 515
  John, 476, 514
  Margaret, 547
  Rosannah, 476
  Thomas, 547
Longpee, Ruth, 14
Loockerman (Lockerman, Luckerman),
  Elizabeth, 367, 372
  John, 71
  Joseph, 416
  Mary, 430
  Nancy, 257
  Nicholas, 82, 124, 166, 186, 257, 372
  Reuben, 257
  Richard, 257
  Susan H., 541
  Susannah, 257, 372
  Thomas, 71
  Vincent, 150, 156, 179, 204, 257, 262, 309, 430
  Vincent, the elder, 367, 372
  Vincent, Jr., 262, 372
  Vincent, Sr., 281
Loper,
  Elizabeth, 90
  Gartre, 21
  Michael, 21
  Peter, 21
Lord, Henry, 464
Lott,
  Bartholomew, 112
  Cornelius, 136, 186
  Eleanor, 112, 136
  Mary, 136
  Nancy, 136
Loud, Robert, 329
Louder: see Lowder
Love,
  Andrew, 15
  Elizabeth, 15
Lovegrove,
  Gennett, 522
  James, 522
Low,
  Joseph, 28
  Mary, 28
  Samuel, 18, 21, 28
  Sarah, 28
Lowber (Lowbar, Lober),
  Agnes, 356
  Catherine, 371, 444
  Daniel, 351, 482, 483, 503, 508

  Elizabeth, 158, 268
  Gartre, 20
  Grace, 51
  Hannah, 268
  Isaac, 110, 372, 443
  John, 482
  Jonathan, 268, 317
  Letitia, 514
  Margaret, 20
  Mary, 221, 249, 482, 503, 508, 521
  Matthew, 103, 105, 110, 118, 155, 482, 493, 510
  Matthew, Jr., 268
  Matthew, Sr., 268
  Meriam, 268
  Michael, 36, 48, 51, 52, 110, 213, 351
  Peter, 70, 92, 110, 118, 120, 158, 268, 356, 371, 423, 444, 468, 482, 483, 493, 503, 508
  Peter, Jr., 249, 338, 398, 512
  Peter, Sr., 482
  Rachel, 110
  Robert, 129
  Sarah, 317, 514
  Susanna, 268, 514
  Unity, 52
  William, 493, 503, 512, 514
Lowden,
  John, 37
  Josiah, 37
Lowder (Louder),
  Edward, 17
  Ralph, 295
  Sarah, 64
Lowns, Joseph, 85
Lowry,
  Esther, 501
  James, 378
  Jestus, 501
Luckerman: see Loockerman
Lua, Margaret, 514
Lucas,
  Anake, 261
  Mason, 113
  Thomas, 190
Luck,
  Silas, 193
  Silvester, 151, 175, 190, 193, 203
Lucod, Lurana, 64
Lues: see Lewis
Luff,
  Ann, 338
  Caleb, 150, 186, 288, 314, 345, 348, 530

[75]

Deborah, 186, 530
Edward, 447
Elizabeth, 447
Hannah, 33
Hugh, 33
John, 184, 186, 348
Mary, 530
Nathaniel, 33, 42, 58, 89, 90, 93, 102, 134, 150, 160, 184, 186, 307, 330, 348, 401, 431
Nathaniel, Jr., 314, 345, 402, 464, 465
Nathaniel, Sr., 186, 338
Ruth, 530
Sarah, 33

Lukons, James, 251
Lumm, Samuel, 246
Lundergin, James, 391, 400, 441
Lycan, Jacob, 390
Lychum: see Latcham
Lyle, John, 252, 441
Lynch,
  Dr. Cornelius, 106
  Edmund, 435
  Henry, 364
  Joice, 201
  Marten, 67
  Mary, 238, 435
  Nicholas, 238, 384, 435
  Sarah, 339, 342
  Selener, 435
  William, 339, 342, 364, 396
  Winifred, 106
Lyndsey: see Lindsey
Lyson, Theophilus, 155, 185, 220

—Mc—

McAdow,
  Ann, 64
  James, 47, 64
  Jane, 64
  John, 64
  Margaret, 64
  Margery, 64
  Moses, 64
  William, 47, 64
McAlexander, John, 96
McAllister (McCalaster),
  Archibald, 146
  Patrick, 448
McBride,
  Agness, 459
  Ann, 459
  Benjamin, 263, 297, 342
  Elizabeth, 263, 459
  Isabela, 263
  James, 263, 459
  John, 263, 342, 387, 459
  Margaret, 206
  Mary, 428, 521
  Maurice, 166, 459, 488
  Nancy, 521
  Robert, 428, 459, 521
  Roger, 263
  Samuel, 263, 459, 488, 521
  Unity, 521
  William, 206, 263, 521

McCabe (McCeabe),
  Alexander, 104
  James, 104, 156
  Sarah, 104
McCahan (Machan),
  Daniel, 64
  Elenor, 64
  John, 55, 64
McCai, Robert, 281
McCain: see McKean
McCalaster: see McAllister
McCall,
  Alexander, 101
  Clark, 336
  Elizabeth, 380, 537
  George, 229, 252, 289, 330, 354, 428, 446, 471, 537
  Mark, 338, 421, 471
  Samuel, 100, 105, 140, 169, 171, 177, 198, 210, 221, 229, 230, 273, 315, 316, 330, 336
  Dr. Samuel, 252
  Sarah, 229, 336, 380
  Sarah, Jr., 273.
McCally, Samuel, 114
McCannon, Rev. John, 281
McCarady, James 124
McCardell, James, 124
McCarty, Mahale, 433
McCasley, Jacob, 452
McCellen, Thomas, 88
McClain (McClan): see McLane
McClammy, Oney, 136
McClehenny (McCleane),
  John, 110
  Margarett, 110
  Selena, 134
McCleland, Thomas, 91

McClement (McClyment,
    McClements),
  Agness, 194
  Andrew, 194
  Elizabeth, 418
  James, 529
  Robert, 271, 371, 394, 418
  Sarah, 380
  Unity, 418
  William, 354, 384, 462, 478
McClemings,
  Andrew, 210
  Jane, 210
  Robert, 271
  Unity, 271
McClemons (McClemmons),
  James, 242, 330
  Robert, 242
  William, 242
McCludy, James, 93
McClyment: see McClement
McComb (McCombs, McCoomb),
  Bartholemew, 190, 198, 286
  Eleazer, 363, 365, 366, 380
  Eleazer, Jr., 365
  Elizabeth, 307
  Esther, 198, 286, 307, 447, 461,
    465
  Grace, 190
  Isabella, 447
  James, 190
  Jennet, 366
  John, 307, 447, 461, 465
  Jonathan, 307, 513
  Lydia, 366
  Thomas Irons, 366
McCook,
  Archibald, 57
  Lelius, 57
  Gabriel, 58, 59
McCool, James, 58, 59
McCordie, James, 57
McCoy,
  Alexander, 464
  Andrew, 464
  Margaret, 464
McCulloch,
  James, 281
  Mary, 542
  William, 281
McCullogh, James, 252
McCutchen,
  Elizabeth, 149
  Francis, 149
  John, 149, 476

McDaniel (McDanield),
  James, 161, 166, 189
  John, 239
  Mary, 166, 189
McDevett (McDavit, McDavett,
    McDevet),
  Daniel, 152, 177, 180, 182, 183
  James, 177, 185
  Jane, 182, 183
McDonagh, Patrick, 90, 101, 107
McDonagle (McDonougle),
  Margery, 107
McDonald,
  Alexander, 202
  Jno., 540
  Sarah, 202
  Susanna, 540
McDonnel (McDonal),
  Arthur, 80, 105
  James, 80, 202
  John, 80
  Mary, 202
McDowell (McDowel),
  Barsheba, 393
  Daniel, 528
  Hugh, 78, 79, 360, 393
  Hugh, Jr., 360
  James, 44, 78, 528
  Jno., 39
  John, 46, 78
  Robert, 78
McElhenny (Muckelheney),
  Agness, 221, 242
McElroy (McEllroy),
  Allen, 463
  Edward, 259, 320, 421, 463
  Hugh, 173, 192
McElvain, Francis, 223
McEver,
  James, 336
  John, 336, 355, 394
  Mary, 336, 355
  Timothy, 336
McFarland (McFarlen, McFarlin),
  Alexander, 112, 127, 136, 168, 186,
    187
  Eleanor, 112
  Jean, 186
  John, 186, 245
  Mary, 353
  Prudence, 245
  Samuel, 186
  William, 186
McFarsons, Hugh, 426
McGaogey, Phillip, 280

McGarment (McGermant),
. . ., 309
Mary, 309, 357
Robert, 249, 286, 309, 316, 335, 357
McGeah,
Elizabeth, 236
Hugh, 236
Mary, 236
Michael, 236
Sarah, 236
McGear,
John, 283
Martha, 217
Mary, 348
Michael, 217
McGifford,
John, 486
Mary, 486, 540
McGinnely, Daniel, 88
McGinnis (McGinnas),
Catharine, 483
Daniel, 483
James, 378
McGlaughlin, Henry, 397
McGlew, Peter, 183
McGonigal (McGonigel,
McGonagill),
Anna, 501
David, 501
Esther, 501
George, 501
Hessy, 501
Joshua, 501
Rachel, 276
Robert, 348, 406, 467, 501
William, 349
McGoon, James, 58
McGrow, Mary, 89
McGregory, Isabel, 428
McGuyre (McGure),
Elizabeth, 215
Hugh, 215
McHan (Machan, McKaune),
Eneas, 78
John, 57, 249
McHoney, Agnes, 517
McIlhenney,
Agnes, 209
Alexander, 209
McIlvaine,
David, 161
William, 161
McKaune: see McHan
McKay, Catron, 375

McKean (McCain),
Elizabeth, 159, 180
Philip, 159, 180
McKebb, John, 49
McKee (McKey),
Edyth, 333
Elizabeth, 441, 469
George, 139
John, 280
Marjory, 76
Thomas, 76
William, 441
Dr. William, 469
McKell,
Daniel, 84
Elizabeth, 118
McKemmey (McKemmy),
Alexander, 84
John, 198
McKenny (Mackenny),
Alex., 98
Amos, 164, 181
Edmund, 25
Edward, 25, 102
Eleazer, 164, 181
Elizabeth, 25
John, 161, 392
Michal, 20
Patience, 25
William, 84, 483
McKenzie, Alexander, 58
McKinly (Mackinley),
Daniel, 88
Elizabeth, 159
McKinney (Macinnee), Edward, 35
McKinstrey,
Jean, 124
Mary, 305
Richard, 124, 305
McKlehaten, Patrick, 219
McKleway, Francis, 223
McKlue, James, 94
McKracken, Daniel, 75
McKnatt: see McNatt
McKnell, Margaret, 84
McKnit: see McNitt
McKnown, John, 249
McKow, John, 238
McLane (McClain, McClan,
McLeane),
Alexander, 373
Allen, 383, 445, 459, 524
Allen, Jr., 289
Elizabeth, 448

Margaret, 406, 458
Moses, 394, 458
Rebecca, 524
Selena, 134
McLeheney,
  Agnes, 194
  Alexandrew, 194
McManus, James, 339
McMechon, Joseph, 99
McMillan,
  Elizabeth, 76
  James, 61, 62, 67, 69, 71, 74, 76, 91
  Jane, 91
  Jo., 51
  William, 76, 91
McMullen (McMullan, McMulland),
  Francis, 281, 363, 365
  French, 363, 365
  James, 183, 185, 189, 281, 301, 320, 363, 365, 451
  John, 363, 365
  Martha, 363, 365
  Mary, 363, 365
  Nancy, 281
  William Gardner, 281, 366
McMurry,
  John, 180
  William, 180
McNatt (McKnatt, MacNett),
  Ann, 210, 269, 306
  Cathorin, 306
  Elizabeth, 95
  Hanah, 464
  Jean, 306
  John, 35, 95
  Jonathan, 472, 487, 558
  Joseph, 272, 306
  Major, 306, 361, 521
  Mary, 175, 306, 361, 405
  Rachel, 306, 487, 558
  Rebecca, 200, 518
  Richard, 200, 306, 308, 405
  Ruth, 306, 528
  Sarah, 177, 306
  William, 175, 306, 464
McNeal, John, 161
McNitt (McKnitt),
  Cattern, 173
  James, 173, 262, 397
  John, 397
  Joseph, 248
  Magdalene, 262, 397
  Rebecca, 525
  Robert, 397, 401
  Sarah, 248
  William, 397

McPeters (Mackpeters),
  James, 139
  Jane, 139
  John, 139
  Mary, 139
  Sarah, 139
McPherson, Hugh, 440
McQuire, Charles, 457
McSparron (McSparran, McSparren),
  Archibald, 188, 258, 381, 416, 458
  John, 182, 188, 214
  Joseph, 188, 258
  Mary, 223
  Meriam, 256, 467
  Ruth, 182, 214
McVay,
  Denis, 267, 385
  Elizabeth, 319, 432, 458
  James, 319
  John, 385, 432
  Patrick, 156
McWhorty,
  Andrew, 121
  John, 121
McWilliam, Samuel, 359

—M—

Macey (Macy),
  Daniel, 175, 263, 340, 556
  Daniel, Jr., 340
  Elizabeth, 217, 263
  Henry, 340
  Jean, 340
  John, 340, 510
  John, Jr., 352
  Jonathan, 510
  Mary, 153, 340, 352
  Nancy, 509
  Sarah, 263
  Susannah, 340
  Thomas, 153, 217, 263, 340, 509, 556
Machan: see McHan
Macinnee: see McKinney
Mackadow: see McAdow
Mackee: see McKee
Mackey, Patrick, 109
MacKinley: see McKinley
MacKnatt: see McKnatt
Mackpeters: see McPeters
MacNett: see McKnatt

Madden (Maddin),
  Elisha, 449
  Elizabeth, 162
  Lurana, 449
  Patrick, 140, 162
Maddock,
  John, 447, 463
  Meriam, 463
Maddox,
  Alexander, 279
  Jemima, 279
Mafell, Robert, 73
Maffett (Maffet, Maffit)
  Archibald, 386
  Gennit, 386
  James, 172
  Janet, 172
  John, 172, 386, 391, 478
  Martha, 386
  Mary, 386, 391
  Rachael, 172
  Robert, 172, 386, 391
  Sarah, 478
  Susannah, 172
  William, 172, 386, 391, 460, 478
Magair, Mary, 477
Magee, Roger, 182
Maguire, Hugh, 197
Mahanna,
  Benjamin, 165
  Eleanor, 165
  Elizabeth, 165
  John, 165
  Mary, 165
  Sarah, 165
  Sophia, 165
  William, 165
Mahon (Mahan, Mohon, Mohan),
  Alexander, 100
  Daniel, 30, 31
  Dinah, 20
  Else, 45
  Eneas, 100
  John, 19, 20, 51
Mair, Janet, 394, 426
Mairs, Andrew, 347
Males, Margaret, 79
Mallcoon, John, 41
Malone,
  Mary, 193
  Thomas, 193
Malony (Molony),
  James, 52
  Joseph, 173
  Loholen, 52
  Sarah, 173

Malris,
  John, 274
  Sarah, 274
Man: see Mann
Mandrell, Sary, 539
Manering: see Mannering
Manin,
  John, 122
  Patience, 122
Maning: see Manning
Manliff,
  George, 498, 536
  Mary, 536
  Mathew, 498
Manlove,
  . . ., 438
  Abner, 66, 78
  Absolom, 134, 137, 245
  Alce, 16, 17, 161, 188, 194
  Alexander, 553
  Alice, 16, 121
  Ann, 17, 34, 41, 107, 189, 281, 336
  Asa, 270, 296, 516, 529
  David, 516
  Deborah, 186, 314, 438
  Ebenezer, 87, 113, 137, 154, 204,
    207, 218, 242, 256, 270, 279
  Elizabeth, 16, 17, 60, 66, 75, 78,
    97, 125, 193, 194, 211, 277, 314,
    332, 436, 553
  Emanuel, 161, 188
  Emilia, 553
  Ephraim, 66
  Eunice, 137, 553
  George, 16, 17, 34, 53, 97, 211, 218,
    220, 224, 227, 315, 337, 362, 398,
    434, 436, 501, 553
  Gideon, 137
  Hannah, 16, 41, 42, 137, 211
  Hezekiah, 48
  John, 16, 17, 34, 220
  Jonathan, 17, 38, 41, 42, 78, 90, 97,
    123, 161, 186, 188, 250, 256, 314,
    506, 553
  Joseph, 34, 48, 53
  Luke, 17, 34, 41, 48, 53, 59, 60, 68,
    88, 133, 140, 161, 337
  Margaret, 110, 134, 137, 250
  Mark, 14, 16, 17, 25, 28, 30, 34, 38,
    47, 54, 58, 61, 64, 65, 66, 71, 75,
    80, 102, 107, 134, 137, 148, 149,
    162, 164, 170, 189, 190, 192, 281,
    285, 336, 532
  Mary, 16, 34, 38, 41, 81, 97, 125,
    137, 193, 194, 220, 221, 250, 314
  Mary (Lewis), 413

Matthew, 17, 25, 38, 40, 41, 51, 66,
  78, 90, 97, 134, 137, 201, 213,
  220, 227, 250, 285, 314, 315, 553
Mathew, Jr., 51
Miriam, 78
Mott, 315, 436
Nathan, 137, 307
Obediah, 66, 78
Rachel, 17, 34, 47, 62, 134
Rebecca, 17
Robinson, 516
Ruth, 137, 281
Samuel, 16, 62, 75
Sarah, 17, 38, 66, 88, 97, 201, 211,
  270, 296, 314, 315, 332, 349, 398,
  516
Susannah, 34, 40, 48, 78, 90, 97,
  250, 256, 314
Tabitha, 17, 78, 88, 90
Thomas, 270, 363, 378
Tredwell, 220, 532
Vincent, 277
William, 16, 34, 42, 45, 48, 60, 81,
  88, 97, 137, 141, 143, 166, 194,
  199, 211, 260, 282, 297, 332, 507
William Jr., 125, 171

Mann (Man),
  Abigail, 150
  Agness, 150
  Ann, 154
  Annalana, 150
  Samuel, 150
  William, Jr., 184
  William, Sr., 184

Mannering (Manering),
  Isabella, 229
  John, 458
  Peter, 458
  Susannah, 361
  William, 229, 319, 361, 458

Manning (Maning),
  Araminty, 451
  Avis, 321, 325
  James, 210, 321
  John, 93, 341
  Polly, 554
  Rachel, 93

Mannship: see Manship

Mansfield,
  Edward, 482
  Mary, 310, 433
  Thomas, 310, 433

Manship (Mannship),
  George, 273, 285
  Sarah, 273, 285

Manson,
  James, 177, 219

James, Jr., 186
James, Sr., 186
Mary, 239, 244
Sarah, 177
William, 128, 221, 239, 244

Mansur, John, 13

Mant,
  Honour, 165
  Mary, 165

Manwaring,
  Charles, 482
  Comfort, 166
  Elizabeth, 469
  Mary, 166
  Peter, 469
  Priscilla, 166
  Sarah, 166
  Susanah, 482
  Richard, 190, 482, 509
  Thomas, 482
  William, 423

Many (Mannee),
  Francis, 303, 335, 485
  Mary, 303
  Peter, 248

Maram: see Marim

Marce,
  . . , 407
  Lydia, 407

Marcer,
  Margarett, 264
  Stephen, 264

Marcollester, ..., 294

Maree,
  Isaac, 455
  John, 455
  Lydia, 455
  Mary, 455
  Reubin, 455

Marick: see Merrick

Marim (Maram, Mayrom,
  Mearham),
  Charles, 41, 67, 148, 160, 163, 182
    184, 185, 196, 333, 437
  Elizabeth, 160, 163, 185
  Frances, 41
  Hannah, 413
  Henry, 413
  John, 36, 41, 46, 67, 76, 121, 160,
    163, 185, 333, 337, 395, 413, 437,
    473, 558
  Mary, 41, 67, 121, 160, 333
  Meriam, 333, 437
  Ruhamah, 160, 163, 184, 185
  Temmima, 41
  Thomas, 67, 148, 538

Mariner: see Marriner
Maring, Charles, 38
Marker,
  Curtis, 491, 555
  Mary, 311
  Philip, 311
  Sarah, 491
Marley, Abraham, 475
Marratt (Marrett),
  Anne, 281
  Hezekiah, 118
  Isaac, 48, 281
  Jane, 495
  John, 118, 269, 496, 511, 538
  John, Sr., 118
  Joseph, 246, 269, 496
  Mark, 118
  Samuel, 496
  Sarah, 281
  William, 511, 538
  Zachariah, 89, 269
Marriner (Mariner),
  James, 349
  Marteriot, 106
  Mary, 106
  Sophia, 349
  Thomas, 106
  William, 106
Marsh,
  Amelia, 462
  John, 149
  Mary, 406
  William Truax, 406
Marshall,
  Ann, 180
  David, 68, 77, 115, 170
  Edward, 57, 180
  George, 76
  Jane, 55, 59
  Mary, 76
Marston, Nathaniel, 27
Martin (Martain, Marten, Marton),
  Catharine, 298
  Charles, 47
  Elizabeth, 25, 47, 153, 162, 445
  George, 12, 15, 17, 18, 25, 36, 41, 43, 50, 58, 110, 111, 123, 153, 162, 364
  James, 86, 465
  Jane, 47
  Jean, 140
  John, 47, 172, 298
  Josiah, 25, 35, 43, 50, 58
  Mary, 47, 172, 175
  Nancy, 380
  Nathaniel, 47
  Patrick, 163, 175, 194

  Rachel, 49, 58
  Richard, 434
  Sarah, 404, 433
  Ursula, 17, 18, 25
  William, 140
Martindell,
  John, 531
  Meriam, 531
Marvel,
  Eliza, 411
  Nutter, 411
Maryday,
  Francis, 156
  Job, 258
Marydith: see Meredith
Maslin, Thomas, Jr., 485
Mason (Mayson),
  Abraham, 160
  Agness, 438
  Ann, 528
  Caleb, 438
  Carman, 141, 415, 438
  Catharine, 321, 445
  Charles, 141, 337, 378, 442, 534
  Daniel 321
  David, 438
  Deborough, 438
  Elias, 97, 194, 378, 475
  Elizabeth, 217, 257, 475, 528
  Hannah, 438
  Isaac, 77, 97, 102, 160, 321, 454
  Jacob, 97, 378, 454
  Jean, 160
  John, 74, 183, 217, 321, 438, 445, 553
  Joseph, 125, 141, 194, 378, 473, 475
  Joseph, Sr., 378
  Lurania, 141
  Mary, 31, 64, 82, 194, 378
  Mathew, 42
  Michael, 31, 42, 64
  Miles, 39
  Rachel, 64, 337, 534
  Richard, 42, 415, 438, 473
  Richard W., 528
  Samuel, 528
  Sarah, 194, 378, 454, 475
  Thomas, 473
  William, 64, 82, 141, 438, 528
Massey (Massy),
  Elizabeth, 231
  Feby, 483
  Hannah, 497
  John, 231, 245, 510
  Joseph, 176
  Joshua, 483

Nathan, 176, 231
Prudence, 245
Rebecca, 176, 182
Sarah, 176, 231

Masten (Mastin, Maston),
  David, 303
  Eliza, 448
  Gilbert, 477, 530
  Hannah, 47, 530
  Hester, 552
  Hezekiah, 464, 530, 557
  John, 211, 303, 448, 487, 530, 532, 552
  Lyday, 464
  Mary, 487, 530
  Mathias, 285, 502, 530, 532, 552
  Mathias, Jr., 464, 498
  Mathias, Sr., 464, 498
  Philip, 530, 552
  Rachel, 530, 552
  Ruth, 552
  Sarah, 186, 194, 263, 303, 530, 552
  Stephen, 552
  William, 121, 208, 263, 303, 498, 502, 530, 532
  William, Jr., 194, 303, 552
  William, Sr., 552
  Zachariah, 552

Master, William, 113

Mathewson, Andrew, 31

Matthews (Mathews, Mathew),
  Charles, 152
  Claghorn, 151
  Elizabeth, 37, 152
  Griffin, 146
  H., 361
  Hugh, 37, 90
  Isaac, 267
  Jerusha, 267
  John, 298, 300, 381
  Joseph, 302
  Mary, 152
  Mary Anne, 152
  Owen, 221
  Rachel, 186
  Samuel, 24

Maugridge, Joseph, 181

Maxfield (Maxfeald),
  Hannah, 131, 210
  James, 131
  Jean, 131
  Mary, 131
  Samuel, 339
  Sarah, 469
  William, 274

Maxwell,
  Adam, 102
  Alice, 154
  Ann, 157, 164, 347, 485
  Bedwell, 244, 541
  Christini, 334
  David, 244
  Edmonson, 442
  Elce, 102
  Elinor, 139, 161, 174
  Elizabeth, 151, 195, 244, 334, 364, 442
  Esther, 108
  Hannah, 257
  James, 18, 35, 57, 102, 106, 161, 195, 244, 257
  James, Jr., 102, 151
  Jane, 195
  Jean, 195, 244
  Joan, 257
  Joannah, 244
  John, 185, 347
  Lydia, 195
  Maleston, 261
  Marah, 212
  Mark, 102, 238, 327, 380, 382, 388
  Mary, 154, 164, 187, 195, 302
  Mellesent, 244
  Meriam, 238, 388
  Moses, 102
  Naomy, 326
  Nimrod, 157, 164, 174, 187, 209, 288, 442
  Priscilla, 485
  Robert, 75, 102, 108, 119, 144, 151, 212, 244, 551
  S ., 334
  Samuel, 195, 334, 364
  Sarah, 102, 120, 138, 154, 195, 493, 517, 541
  Thomas, 102, 302
  William, 42, 85, 102, 120, 154, 195, 326, 347, 352

May,
  James, 225, 235, 392
  Susanna, 392
  Thomas, Jr., 40

Mayrom: see Marim

Mays,
  Ann, 319
  William, 319

Mearadeth: see Meredith

Mears (Meers, Meres),
  Andrew, 362, 382, 409
  Mary, 382
  Rebecca, 362, 382

Medcalf: see Metcalf

Meeks,
  Ann, 348
  Araminta, 348, 510
  Joseph, 308, 348
  Melkiah, 348
  Robert, 186
  St. Leger, 348
  Sophia, 348
Meekins (Meekings),
  John, 142, 220, 262
  Mary, 142. 220
  Moody, 426
  Thomas, 142
Meers: see Mears
Megear, Hugh, 545
Mellichop (Melechop, Mellochop, Melowchop),
  George, 288
  James, 288, 450
  Sarah, 288, 450
Mellogue,
  Mary, 275
  Samuel, 275
Melowchop: see Mellichop
Melson,
  Elizabeth, 357
  Joseph, 357
Melvill, Allen, 165
Melvin (Melven, Milvin),
  Alifair, 472
  Ann, 146, 216, 259, 266, 528
  Aron, 472
  Bartholomew, 469
  Brummel, 472
  David, 266, 472, 537
  Edmond, 146, 216, 247, 293, 537
  Edward, 216
  Elizabeth, 266
  George, 472
  Hester, 432
  Hilda, 293
  Huldah, 427
  James, 293, 472
  John, 266, 293, 472, 537
  Jonathan, 266, 538
  Joshua, 472, 528
  Margaret, 495
  Mary, 293, 472
  Meriam, 266
  Noble, 472
  Phebe, 180, 247, 259, 266, 472
  Rhoda, 472
  Sarah, 293
  Solomon, 472
Menshall: see Minshall
Meoller, George, 145

Meardith: see Meredith
Mercer,
  Margaret, 432
  Stephen, 375, 432
Merchant,
  Charlotty, 552
  Harriet, 552
  John, 552
  Rachel, 91
  Samuel, 552
  Sarah, 552
  William, 91, 231
Merdith: see Meredith
Meredie,
  Joshua, 142
  Rachel, 142
  Robert, Jr., 142
Meredith (Merydith, Marydith, Meradith, Merdith),
  Abner, 469
  Agness, 243, 517
  Benjamin, 469
  David, 469
  Davis, 469
  Deborah, 503
  Dorcas, 480
  Elizabeth, 240, 331, 337, 348, 356, 387, 464, 502, 503, 516,
  Francis, 156, 387, 423
  Henry, 469
  Hugh, 79
  Jacob, 304, 480, 493, 500
  James, 469
  Job, 126, 199, 231, 356, 436, 469, 540
  Job, Jr., 527
  John, 231, 348
  Jonathan, 489, 504, 538
  Joseph, 240, 486, 490, 500
  Joshua, 118, 302, 517, 540
  Leven, 348
  Levy, 384
  Luff, 302, 339, 368
  Lydia, 469, 480, 493
  Margaret, 533
  Martha, 493, 506
  Mary, 368, 489, 493, 500
  Nathan, 503
  Obedi, 469
  Peter, 469
  Phebe, 525
  Phyllis, 179
  Rachel, 231
  Rebecca, 541
  Richard, 242
  Robert, 56, 126, 331, 237, 337, 541
  Ruth, 302, 339

Samuel, 166, 186, 188, 193, 268,
  294, 304, 500, 503, 506, 556
Sarah, 414, 516
Sophia, 231
Stephen, 469
Susannah, 283, 480
Thomas, 345
Wheelor, 231, 283
William, 179, 218, 229, 244, 288,
  338, 414, 490, 491, 517, 533
William, Jr., 288
William, Sr., 426

Meres: see Mears

Merick: see Merrick

Merine,
  John, 464
  Sarah, 464

Meroney (Merony),
  Elizabeth, 258
  Exsprance, 201
  Isaac, 306
  John, 306
  Mary, 306
  Nathan, 306
  Olanar, 301
  Rachel, 306
  William, 301
  William, Sr., 301

Merrett, Mary, 505

Merrick (Marick, Mireck, Merick),
  Elizabeth, 93, 105
  Isaac, 387
  Israel, 396
  Jane, 421
  Margaret, 387, 409
  Mary, 396

Merydith: see Meredith

Messex (Mezicks), Julien, 295

Messick (Misick),
  Elizabeth, 105
  Martha, 552

Meston, Arthur, 13, 16, 17, 34

Metcalf (Medcalf, Medcalfe, Metcalfe),
  George, 46
  John, 166
  Lascelles, 115
  Mary, 166
  Thomas, 106

Metten,
  James, 358
  William, 358

Meyer, Thomas, 237

Michel: see Mitchell

Middlebrooks, Mary, 413

Middleton,
  Elenor, 95, 151
  George, 95
  John, 95, 245, 270
  Sarah, 414

Mifflin,
  Andesiah, 508, 523
  Ann, 501, 547
  Benjamin, 40
  Daniel, 388, 391, 547
  Daniel, Jr., 438
  Debbe, 424
  Esther, 523
  George, 44
  James, 523
  John, 38, 40
  Martha, 523
  Mary, 523
  Mathew, 508, 523
  Polly, 382
  Samuel, 501
  Samuel Emlin, 547
  Sarah, 438, 523, 547
  Susanna, 547
  Walker, 438
  Warner, 258, 272, 278, 280, 288,
    359, 382, 429, 438, 446, 491, 547

Milborn (Milburn, Milbourn),
  Mary, 535, 538
  Samuel, 404, 535, 538, 541
  Samuel, Jr., 452

Mileham,
  Catherine, 267
  Elizabeth, 267, 363, 483, 486
  Grace, 267
  Hannah, 267, 383
  Harmon, 504
  Margaret, 267
  Mary Ann, 267, 539
  Massey, 267
  Samuel, 267, 363, 387, 486, 504
  Unity, 267
  Walter, 267, 271

Miles, James, 412, 442

Mileway: see Millaway

Millally, Sarah, 152

Millan,
  Abraham, 370
  John, 370
  William, 370

Millard,
  Ann, 317
  Joseph, 317
  Lydia, 317
  Mary, 317
  William, 317

Millaway (Mileway, Milway,
    Milloway),
  Ann, 273
  Deborah, 547
  Elizabeth, 547
  James, 547
  John, 192, 249, 274, 306, 547
  Joseph, 273
  Mary, 547
  Milly, 547
Miller,
  Abraham, 117
  Adam, 141, 204
  Andrew, 117
  Camel, 198
  Chilion, 141, 166, 204, 477
  Conrad, 141, 204, 241, 462, 470
  David, 117
  Dorithy, 141, 204
  Edward, 43, 425, 448, 450, 484, 493,
    499, 510
  Elizabeth, 19, 187, 199, 223, 448
  Enoch, 310
  Hannah, 232
  Henry, 141, 204, 470, 499
  Hester, 232
  James, 34, 448, 499
  John, 81, 117, 141, 144, 150, 157,
    193, 204, 279, 448, 462, 470, 477,
    513, 514
  Dr. John, Jr., 310
  Rev. John, 224
  Joseph, 109, 117, 277, 430, 448, 473,
    484, 499, 542
  Killen, 298, 478
  Lydia, 277
  Margaret, 277
  Martha, 462, 470
  Mary, 30, 193, 298, 477
  Peter, 141, 204, 295, 439, 462
  Peter, Jr, 439, 478
  Peter, Sr., 377
  Rachel, 279, 295
  Rebecca, 232
  Robert, 30, 33, 34, 187
  Samuel, 117, 448
  Sarah, 17, 198, 241, 441, 462, 470
  Stephen, 462, 470
  Susannah, 19, 462, 470
  William, 94, 109, 478
Millis (Milles, Milliss),
  Ann, 380, 407
  Elizabeth, 226
  James, 407, 558
  John, 226, 372
  Nancy, 556
  Stephen, 272, 334, 398, 558
  Thomas, 334

Milloway: see Millaway
Mills,
  George, 50, 138
  John, 22, 107
  Hannah, 107
  Mary, 22, 25, 26, 373
  Nathan, 532
  Prusillah, 532
  Sarah, 138, 202
Miln, John, 97
Milstead, Teresa, 236
Milven: see Melvin
Milway: see Millaway
Minner,
  Elijah, 451, 511
  Elizabeth, 449
  Jesse, 451
  John, 285, 451
  Mary, 451
  Peter, 449
  Sarah, 451
  Stephen, 451
  Thomas, 451, 533
Minors,
  Ann, 486
  Love, 486
  Mary, 200, 486
  Robert, 200, 486
Minshall (Menshall),
  Isaac, 292, 348, 434
  Jane, 353
  Jean, 292
  Samuel, 292
Mireck: see Merrick
Misick: see Messick
Mitchell (Michel, Mitchel),
  Ann, 43, 56, 66
  Charles, 421
  Comfort, 66
  Daniel, 66
  Elizabeth, 505
  Fenwick Fisher, 551
  George, 379, 412, 551
  John, 529, 551
  Mary, 12
  Nathaniel, 551
  Rebecca, 186
  Richard, 12
  Sarah, 529
  Susan, 551
  Thomas, 505
  William Clayton, 551
Mitten (Mittan),
  Cathran, 349
  James, 497
  James, Sr., 497

John, 497
Mary, 497
Miriam, 224
William, 497
Mitter,
  Camel, 198
  Sarah, 198
Moffet,
  Archibald, 377
  John, 377
  Martha, 377
  Mary, 377
  Robert, 377
  Sarah, 377
  William, 377
Moir, James, 31
Mokolls, William, 51
Molan, James, 380
Molleston (Molliston, Moleston, Molestone, Moliston),
  Ailce, 270
  Anne, 30, 81, 89, 337
  Elizabeth, 239, 296, 337
  Elizabeth Ann, 436
  Grace, 30
  Helenor, 33
  Henry, 23, 30, 33, 41, 88, 89, 190, 199, 268, 294, 321, 337, 393, 436, 452, 557
  Henry, Jr., 188
  Jemima, 78, 90, 190
  John, 33, 89, 190, 214, 221, 227,
  Jonathan, 81, 89, 144, 190, 194, 199, 239, 296
  Jonathan, Sr., 239
  Mary, 81, 199, 239, 557
  Sarah, 30, 41, 81, 89, 161, 188, 268, 321, 337
  William, 53, 54, 81, 89, 190, 199, 221, 239, 270, 325, 361, 365, 395, 455, 540, 558
  Dr. William, 258, 436
Molloy, Caleb, 62
Molonix, Easter Ann, 496
Molony: see Malony
Money,
  Ann, 473
  Daniel, 37
  John, 473
Monro (Monroe),
  Betty, 213
  George, 203, 213
Monsie: see Muncey
Montgomery (Montgomerrie),
  Alexander, 94, 203
  Matthew, 302
  William, 415

Moody, Robert, 205
Moore (Moor, More),
  Abraham, 211, 228, 407
  Ann, 277, 303, 321
  Ar., 358
  Arthur, 369
  Breget, 51
  Christiana, 347
  David, 277, 368
  Elizabeth, 146, 211, 277, 305, 310, 337, 368, 453
  George, 345, 492, 494
  Hannah, 198
  Henaritta, 146, 305, 310
  Henry, 62, 146, 247, 368, 407
  Isaac, 414, 533, 534
  James, 28, 71, 104, 116, 122, 163, 193, 198, 242, 276, 277, 407
  Jane, 122, 130, 193
  Jean, 176, 193
  Jerusha, 374
  John, 130, 146, 176, 193, 219, 282, 303, 305, 407, 452, 533
  John, Jr., 220, 321
  Joseph, 277, 339, 347, 407, 542
  Letita, 234
  Lydia, 407, 411
  Margaret, 277, 481
  Martha, 211, 228
  Mary, 62, 117, 130, 163, 176, 277, 282, 356, 492
  Peter, 176, 282
  Rachel, 146
  Rebecka, 50, 62, 219, 220, 310, 417
  Richard, 94
  Robert, 146, 311, 377, 407
  Samuel, 117, 130, 176, 229, 251, 277, 308, 321, 356, 368, 533
  Sarah, 509, 534
  Susannah, 308
  Thomas, 118, 231, 345, 374, 509, 533
  William, 130, 417, 534
Moran (Moron),
  Andrew, 98, 152
  Elizabeth, 152
  Jane, 98
  Margaret, 177, 183
  Mark, 167
  Martha, 151
  Patrick, 183
Morey, Thomas, 131
Morgan,
  . . ., 444
  Abraham, Jr., 20
  Anna, 124
  Arthur, 78, 106, 124

Benitha, 373
Brian, 156
Daniel, 352, 417
David, 15, 49, 76, 80, 100, 101, 117, 180, 460
Elishua, 476
Elizabeth, 20, 48, 51, 52, 106, 117, 125, 161, 189, 244, 252, 476, 549
Esther, 444
Evan, 296, 476
Evan Bradbury, 52
George, 22, 45, 80, 92, 94, 106, 124, 161, 180, 206, 232, 244, 252, 358
Grace, 72, 106, 124, 161
Gwenllyan, 119
Hanna, 161, 378
Hester, 503, 534
Isaiah, 180, 261
Jacob, 161, 245, 252, 301
James, 101, 131, 156, 180, 296, 352, 456, 476
John, 15, 35, 48, 52, 180, 296, 313, 460, 476, 483
John David, 87, 119
John David, Jr., 119
Jonathan, 296,
Joseph, 52
Joshua, 52
Katharine, 80
Marmeduke, 211, 296
Martha, 161, 189, 206, 245, 301, 378
Mary, 94, 100, 161, 179, 296, 373, 378
Matthew, 15, 100
Miriam, 52
Nancy, 358, 476
Patrick, 156
Peter, 552
Phebe, 15, 100, 101, 131
Philip, 20, 41
Rebecca, 425
Richard, 49
Robert, 161, 252, 358
Sarah, 61, 100, 124, 131, 261, 296, 324, 460, 552
Thomas, 296, 364, 476
William, 37, 39, 45, 72, 78, 93, 106, 124, 296, 379, 503

Morman, Abraham, 20

Morphee: see Murphy

Morrett, Sarah, 178

Morris (Maurice, Morice, Morriss), . . ., 517
  Aaron, 248
  Abraham, 47, 48, 51, 53, 71, 100, 105
  Absolem, 215, 434
  Benjamin, 287
  Boas, 296
  Brady, 394
  Brinkley, 373
  Cornelius, 182, 270
  Daniel, 248, 278, 295, 425, 464, 521
  Daniel, Sr., 373
  Deborah, 303
  Edward, 175
  Elijah, 232, 270, 296, 397
  Eliphaz, 270, 307
  Elisha, 159, 235, 267, 270, 272
  Elizabeth, 25, 287, 351, 516, 517, 546, 558
  Emanuel, 394
  Esther, 285, 292, 415
  Fannah, 415
  Febey, 328
  Frederick, 108, 125
  Hannah, 119, 242, 351
  Hezekiah, 464
  James, 49, 50, 77, 91, 109, 116, 129, 147, 156, 169, 171, 175, 176, 180, 183, 184, 208, 292, 346, 384, 400, 401, 407, 415, 416, 466, 473, 542
  James, the elder, 384
  James, Jr., 91, 327, 329, 353, 542
  Jemimah, 406, 496
  Jeremiah, 115, 177, 182, 218, 249, 270, 454
  Jeremiah, Jr., 249
  Jesse, 412
  John, 63, 102, 241, 274, 276, 278, 363, 371, 447, 449, 454, 464, 475
  Joseph, 103, 307
  Joshua, 272, 516
  Jurusha, 413
  Lemuel, 415
  Margaret, 35, 91, 116, 384, 521
  Martha, 351
  Mary, 373, 415, 459, 530
  Masten, 401, 464
  Miriam, 175
  Moses, 353
  Nancy, 521
  Nathaniel, 464
  Nimrod, 557
  Phebe, 116, 129, 307, 425
  Priscilla, 285
  Prudence, 361
  Rachel, 415
  Rebecca, 275
  Richard, 152, 275, 281, 361
  Robert, 373
  Samuel, 154, 351, 415, 546, 558
  Samuel, Jr., 467
  Sarah, 241, 303, 447
  Sealy, 451
  Selah, 415

Solomon, 319
Susannah, 208, 241, 269, 464, 476, 521
Rev. Theophilus, 108
Thomas, 242, 275, 307, 521
William, 45, 47, 63, 119, 126, 197, 251, 270, 285, 307, 328, 431, 447, 462, 468, 475, 521
William, Jr., 169, 419, 434, 468

Morry, James, 39
Mors, Elizabeth, 516
Morton,
Agnes, 252
Catherine, 26
Elizabeth, 252
James, 252
William, 15, 18, 19, 23, 26
Mott,
Adam, 138
Elizabeth, 138
Jerusha, 224
John, 487
Nancy, 294
Richard, 185, 224
Richbell, 138, 146, 174, 201
Samuel, 12, 14
Sarah, 14
Seaman, 487
Stephen, 78
Mucklegeare, William, 38
Muckeleheney: see McElhenny
Mullen (Mullin),
Ann, 138
Daniel, 483
Hanah, 453
Hugh, 483
James, 98
Robert, 138, 151
Thomas, 483
William, 453
Mullet (Mulett),
Elizabeth, 317
Penelope, 213, 242
Thomas, 317
William, 213, 242, 317
Mullin: see Mullen
Mulroney (Mulrony, Mulruny),
Elizabeth, 24, 25
Jane, 25
John, 17, 22, 24, 25
William, 25, 43
Mumford,
Rachel, 275, 399, 433
Solomon, 275, 399

Muncey (Muncy, Munsey, Monsie),
. . ., 350
Abigail, 84, 106
Belliharen, 84
Francis, 84
Garty, 110
Isabella, 304
James, 304, 351
John, 84, 142, 304, 391, 461
Levy, 304
Margaret, 210, 304, 350
Martha, 391
Mary, 84
Nathaniel, 84, 106, 111
Samuel, 84
Sarah, 441
Thomas, 84, 111, 164, 289, 304
Munt,
Abigal, 177
Charity, 177
Elener, 177
Julania, 177
Mariah, 165
Mary, 177, 299
Mary Ann, 177
Robert, 177, 299
Murphy (Murphey, Murfey, Morphee),
. . ., 308
Andrew, 426, 467
Benjamin, 189
Charles, 376, 502
Comfort, 528
Daniel, 528
David, 48, 119, 254
Edward, 30, 31, 177, 289, 327, 345, 411, 505, 528
Hannah, 48
Jean, 262
Jenkins, 502
Johannah, 48, 63
John, 305, 411, 505, 510, 528
Jonathan, 376, 528
Levin, 528
Margaret, 124, 183, 260, 323
Mary, 48, 305, 308, 376, 443, 511
Nicholas, 48
Rachel, 48
Rebecca, 48, 189
Samuel, 48, 510
Sarah, 189, 192, 376, 510
Stancy, 549
Susannah, 249, 254
Thomas, 48, 114, 124, 168, 182, 183, 192, 210, 218, 242, 260, 289, 309, 345, 437, 442, 511
Thomas, Jr., 244
William, 48, 63, 189, 510, 528

Zachariah, 376
Murray,
  Ann, 167, 178
  Bryan, 167
  Elizabeth, 167, 168
  Francis, 150, 168
  Henry, 167
  Jean, 320
  John, 146
  Modlin, 167
  Sarah, 116
  William, 188
Mutton, William, 453
Myers (Miers)
  Mary, 236, 283
  Stephen, 415
  Thomas, 236, 297
  William, 415

—N—

Nabb,
  Charles, 403, 533
  Margaret, 403
Nangisell, Gerthy, 34
Nash,
  Ann, 370
  John, 370
  William, 370
Naudain (Naudine),
  Andrew, 487, 546, 556
  Arnold, Sr., 556
  Catharine, 556
  Mary, 556
  Rebeckah, 556
Naull, Negro man, 302
Neal (Neil, Neill, Neall),
  . . ., 461
  Andrew, 124, 223
  Anne, 394
  Daniel, 394
  David, 124
  Elizabeth, 193, 394
  Francis, 394
  Hannah, 394
  Hugh, 170, 344
  James, 354, 394, 531
  Jonathan, 394, 531
  Martha, 145
  Prudence, 223
  Ruth, 394
  Samuel, 394
  Sarah, 394, 461
  William, 354
  William Charles, 344, 465

Needham,
  Agatha, 344, 375, 469
  Ann, 18
  Benjamin, 334
  Cornelius, 649
  Daniel, 46, 50, 97, 168, 334
  Edmond, 28, 248
  Ezekiel, 14, 239, 281, 295, 334, 384, 425
  Jestinh, 484
  Jonathan, 248, 295, 317, 476, 526
  Phebee, 148, 239
  Ralph, 88, 100, 148
  Sarah, 193
  Susannah, 90, 168
Needles (Nedles, Nedells),
  Andrew, 490
  Anna, 428, 490
  Cubbage, 490
  Elizabeth, 269
  George, 490
  Hannah, 128, 490
  Hursley, 428
  John, 20, 490
  Leucrecia, 428, 483
  Philemon, 490
  Rachel, 463
  Sarah, 355, 428, 451, 490
  Stephen, 428
  Thomas, 259, 341, 451, 490
  Uscelia, 483
  William, 128, 259, 269, 379, 402, 428, 451, 490
Neelson,
  Alexander, 252
  Mary, 252
Neighbours, Jonathan, 313
Neil: see Neal
Nelson,
  Betty, 140
  Elizabeth, 240
  John, 24
  Sarah, 240
New,
  John, 306
  Mary, 211, 225, 226
  Robert, 225, 226
  Sarah, 489
  William, 273
Newcomb,
  John, 438
  Mary, 438
Newell (Newel),
  Elizabeth, 17, 28, 29, 86, 132
  George, 58
  Hannah, 184, 306
  Henry, 184, 214, 249, 306, 394, 405

James, 13
Jno., 132
John, 14, 29, 47, 55, 56, 59, 86, 103, 106, 130, 134, 167, 179, 180, 184, 214
Joseph, 109
Louisa, 132
Lyday, 306
Lydia, 184, 202
Mary, 29, 56, 86, 132
Miriam, 184, 202, 306
Rachel, 132, 214
Samuel, 56
Sarah, 132, 147
Tabitha, 306
Thomas, 86, 103, 132
William, 56, 86, 103, 127, 131, 132, 147, 184, 214, 306

Newgent, Christopher, 44

Newman,
 Daniel Wright, 251
 Delictum, 77
 Edward, 98
 Elizabeth, 329
 John, 211, 223
 Judah, 430
 Lumino, 77, 171
 Margaret, 171
 Mary, 354
 Solothial, 329

Newnam,
 Daniel, 181, 200
 Edward, 98
 James, 375
 Mary, 98, 302
 Richard, 183, 206

Newson,
 Joseph, 554
 Mary, 445

Newton,
 Alace, 71
 Elizabeth, 381
 George, 71
 Henry, 25
 John, 63, 92
 Mary, 25

Nicholas,
 David, 227
 Jane, 155, 227
 John, 227
 Samuel, 155, 227
 Samuel, Jr., 155

Nichols (Nichels, Nicholds, Nickolls, Nicolls, Nicholls),
 Ann, 36, 53
 Comfort, 464
 Edward, 62

Edward, Jr., 209
Edward, Sr., 209
Hannah, 33
Jane, 63
Jeremiah, 20
John, 303
Joseph, 214, 255
Mary, 19, 20, 21, 53, 255
Moses, 139, 170, 314
Robert, 19
Ruth, 314
Samuel, 63, 303
Susanah, 455, 473
Vincent, 455
William, 20, 21, 28, 33, 53

Nicholson,
 Ann, 254
 Elizabeth, 31
 John, 31
 Joshua, 100, 312

Nickerson (Nicoson, Nickeson),
 Abraham, 476
 Elesibeath, 238
 George, 124, 163, 185, 446
 Jeremiah, 36, 46, 60
 John, 163, 185, 333
 Joseph, 36, 46, 60
 Joshua, 46, 60, 124, 128, 163, 182, 238
 Lidey, 46
 Margarett, 146
 Mary, 46, 60
 Nehemiah, 46
 Persella, 46
 Richameg, 46
 Veranica, 124
 William, 476

Nisbet, Eleanor, 78

Niss, John D., 74

Nixon,
 Abraham, 510
 Ann, 324, 362
 Benjamin, 288
 Charles, 324, 354, 362, 372, 400, 417, 420, 430, 431, 510
 Elizabeth, 77, 400, 404, 510, 525
 Joseph, 98, 143
 Nicholas, 27, 28, 77, 324
 Nixon, 324
 Thomas, 56, 77, 101, 143, 167, 179, 196, 232, 275, 321, 324, 325, 462, 470, 499, 528
 William, 510

Noble, Elizabeth, 558

Nock,
 Ann, 46, 137
 Barthia, 137, 157, 395

[91]

Daniel, 46, 73, 119, 131, 137, 284, 351, 468, 514, 554
Ezekial, 46, 137, 166, 280, 284, 351, 554
James, 263, 272, 284
Jane, 532
John, 427
Joseph, 157, 234, 284, 351, 383, 395, 430, 468, 514, 515, 546, 551
Joseph, Jr., 438, 439
Mary, 234, 395, 554
Nathaniel, 309
Oliver, 554
Patience, 46
Phebe, 554
Sarah, 46
Susanna, 383, 514
Thomas, 46, 137, 167, 234, 243, 280, 284, 351, 395, 400, 554
Thomas, Jr., 234
Noel: see Nowell
Norberry, Benjamin, 174
Norrington, Christopher, 63
Norris,
  Elizabeth, 501
  John, 501
  Matthew, 311
Norman, Edward, 125, 136, 145, 173, 190, 205, 217
North,
  Daniel, 329
  John, 329
  Margaret, 359, 407
  Mary, 329
  Rachel, 329, 370
  Richard, 291, 329
  Thomas, 316, 329, 341, 357, 359
  William, 334
Northway, Nicholas, 13
Nowell (Nowells, Noel),
  Edward, 482
  George, 41, 51, 59, 61, 74
  Henry, 403
  Jean, 46
  Jehu, 272
  John, 214
  Margaret, 61
  Sarah, 59, 272, 403
  Sidney, 373, 482
  Stephen, 34
Nowland,
  Daniel, 554
  Louisa, 382
  Mathias, 382, 415
  Sarah, 342, 415
Nox: see Knox
Noxon, Thomas, 84, 105

Noxton, Sarah, 316
Nugent,
  Christopher, 44
  Elizabeth, 44
Numbers,
  Anne, 305
  Barbara, 299, 421
  Benjamin, 435
  Edmund, 435
  Elizabeth, 307
  Jacob, 307
  James, 181, 307, 382, 409, 421, 429
  Jane, 316, 420, 475
  Jean, 316
  John, 229, 238, 257, 299, 301, 307, 418, 421
  Joseph, 307, 382
  Martha, 435
  Mary, 238, 257, 301, 307, 314, 344, 365
  Michael, 305, 307, 316, 384, 420
  Peter, 229, 238, 257, 307
  Rebecca, 181
  Sarah, 238, 307, 339, 414, 429, 491
  Susannah, 238, 307, 418, 420
  Thomas, 307, 435
  William, 257, 307, 379, 387, 421, 491
Nys, Johannis, 74

—O—

Oakford,
  John, 138
  Susannah, 138
Oborn, Mary, 139
Obyle, William, 65
O'Callaghan, Benjamin, 120
Oens: see Owens
Offley (Ofley),
  David, 160
  Elizabeth, 60
  John, 410, 421
  Mercy, 160
  Michael, 91, 258, 346
Ogdon,
  Jonathan, 54
  Nehemiah, 54
Ogle,
  Benjamin, 85
  George, 227, 318, 420, 465
  Sarah, 227, 318
  Thomas, 335, 371

Ohagitha,
  Dennish, 22
  Margaret, 22
O'Heren, Cathern, 54
Ohorrel (O'Horrell, Ohorrill),
  Mary, 31
  Thomas, 26, 31
Oldfield,
  George, 23
  Lydia, 457, 529
Oleger, Mary, 122
Oliver,
  Esther, 290
  Joseph, 368, 442, 452
  Reuben, 290, 304
  Sarah, 368
Olliett, Mary, 132
O'Neal (O'Neil, Oneill),
  Conn, 101
  Constantine, 130
  Elizabeth, 430
  Henry, 533
  Sarah, 60
Onion, David, 104
Opdegrof, Isaac, 51
Orr,
  James, 127
  William, 127
Orry,
  Richard, 104
  William, 104
Osborne (Osburne),
  Charles, 44
  Joseph, 17
Owens (Owins, Owen),
  Amon, 300, 379, 459
  Catherine, 90
  Elenor, 152, 326, 545
  Elizabeth, 236, 244, 326, 380, 532, 533
  Hannah, 206
  Hester, 59
  Ishmael, 206, 503
  James, 69, 133
  John, 505
  Joshua, 443, 503
  Lewis, 23
  Lydia, 300
  Margaret, 170
  Mary, 326
  Matthew, 326
  Owen, 326, 532
  Philemon, 170
  Rachel, 326
  Robert, 379, 459, 532

  Samuel, 505
  Sarah, 505
  Thomas, 133
  William, 236, 244, 326, 379, 380, 505
Owtwell, Ratchel, 248
Oyston,
  John, 370
  Margaret, 370
Ozbun (Ozburn, Ozbeen),
  Elizabeth, 443
  Eunice, 193, 283, 467
  Jonathan, 193, 224, 248, 283
  Susannah, 443
  Tabitha, 283

—P—

Pacely,
  Rachel, 442
  Samuel, 442
Padmore,
  John, 134
  Mary, 134
Pain (Payne, Payn),
  Elizabeth, 43, 48, 63
  Fletcher, 43
  John, 43, 48
  Samuel, 56
  Thomas, 179
  William, 522
Painter,
  George, 258, 283
  Sarah, 256, 258
Palmatary (Palmetree, Palmeterra, Palmater, Palmetory),
  Allen, 129, 183, 293, 451
  Anne, 318
  Eleanor, 15
  Elizabeth, 129
  Grace, 129
  James, 340
  Jean, 340
  Joanna, 15
  John, 15, 129, 270, 533
  Margarett, 270
  Robert, 14, 15, 49, 100, 129, 421, 425
  Sarah, 183, 208
  Susanna, 15, 545
  Tamzy, 425
Palmer,
  Alexander, 274
  John, 274
  Joseph, 317, 318

Pandergrass, Anthony, 112
Paremaine, Henry, 14
Paradee (Parradee, Paudue),
  Benjamin, 53
  Courtney, 189
  David, 128
  Elizabeth, 53, 128
  Hannah, 186, 399
  John, 53, 128, 164, 186, 196, 415
  Lydia, 184
  Margaret, 21, 53
  Mary, 70, 128, 184, 196, 333
  Sarah, 189
  Stephen, 28, 53, 60, 70, 95, 125, 128, 157, 164, 184, 196, 333, 399, 415, 549
  Susannah, 53
  Walter, 67
  William, 379, 409
Paris, Ferd. John, 115
Parke (Park, Parks),
  Alse, 11
  Ann, 84, 223, 228, 237, 457, 546
  Cecilia, 237
  Edward, 11
  Elizabeth, 261, 243
  Frances, 153
  Hugh, 84, 182, 229, 234, 243, 261
  Jane, 457
  John, 55, 252, 335
  Joshua, 457
  Robert, 457
  Samuel, 457
  Sarah, 55, 84
  Susan, 457
  Theodore, 55, 84, 101, 132, 153, 182, 228
  Thomas, 55, 84, 106, 113, 144, 157, 199, 223, 237, 243, 261, 390, 410, 457, 473
Parkason (Parkerson, Parkeson),
  Christopher, 293, 299, 398
  Sarah, 299, 398
  Thomas, 293, 299
Parker,
  Anderson, 140, 526
  Cecilia, 241
  Elizabeth, 213, 233, 542
  Hestear, 64
  James, 326
  Jane, 420
  John, 140, 198, 213, 232, 277, 355, 478
  John, Sr., 140
  Leah, 140, 478
  Margaret, 399
  Mary, 374, 542
  Mathew, 107, 140
  Peter, 399
  Sarah, 140, 198, 239, 277, 399
  Thomas, 107, 140, 149, 233, 266, 277, 347, 399, 411, 420, 546
  Thomas, Jr., 542
  Thomas, Sr., 542
  William, 78, 140, 198, 233, 277, 374, 526, 542, 546
Parkerson: see Parkason
Parmacy,
  Rebecca, 334
  Robert, 334
Parnell (Parnel),
  Abraham, 439
  Edward, 27
Parry (Parray),
  John, 89
  Rachel, 282
  Rowland, 213
  Thomas, 248, 260, 277, 278, 282, 283, 375, 395
  William, 19
Parsons,
  Abraham, 317, 343, 401, 414, 430
  Angelica, 460
  Ann, 437
  Benjamin, 155
  Jean, 311
  Jennet, 311, 358, 369
  John, 109, 301, 306, 334, 377, 381, 480, 499
  John, Jr., 337
  Joseph, 123, 146, 215, 218, 385, 460
  Margaret, 155
  Martha, 343, 432
  Mary, 301, 306, 358, 369, 437, 443
  Michael, 437
  Nancy, 487
  Peggy, 385
  Rachel, 430, 432, 463, 497
  Tomlinson, 443, 487
  William, 45
Parvin, Lydia, 203
Parvis,
  Betty, 86
  Catterine, 12
  Jadwin, 12
  Juda, 12
  Katty, 549
  Lemual, 428
  Richard, 48, 334
  Robert, 12
  Sirelly, 12

William, 12, 86
William, Jr., 448
Paskell, Benjamin, 49
Pasley, Margaret, 127
Paswater, Jonas, 136
Patterson,
  Jean, 324
  John, 240, 456
  Rachel, 240, 331, 456, 464
  Richard, 119
  Robert, 468
Pattison,
  George, 456, 464
  Isaac, 456, 464, 466
  John, 456, 464, 466
  Mary, 464
  Rachel, 456, 464
  Samuel, 387
  Thomas, 456, 464, 466, 542
  William, 456, 464
Patton (Patten, Paten),
  Andrew, 91, 138, 210, 350
  Ann, 390, 433
  Eliner, 84
  Elizabeth, 122, 138
  John, 341, 349, 350, 433, 473, 493, 499, 542
  Major John, 309, 365
  Isabell, 210
  Lydia, 531
  Margaret, 350
  Mary, 210, 350, 409, 448
  Mathew, 531
  Robert, 82, 83, 84, 99, 118, 122, 350
  Thomas, 84
  William, 350, 413
Payne: see Pain
Peal, John, 48
Pearce: see Pierce
Pearson (Pierson),
  Aaron, 219
  Baxter, 425
  Elias, 512
  Elizabeth, 114, 137, 173, 289
  Hannah, 403
  James, 169, 403, 488
  John, 173, 532
  Joseph, 203, 512
  Mary, 37, 201, 271, 462, 472, 490, 511
  Robert, 425
  Sarah, 219, 512
  Rebekah, 271
  William, 114, 137

Peasley,
  John, 196
  Margaret, 196
Pecker, Susannah, 40
Pecue, Febey, 207
Pedrick, Charles, 32
Peers, Elizabeth, 466
Peerson: see Pearson
Pegg,
  Daniel, 18
  John, 295
  Martin, 273
  Valentine, 258, 289
  William, 215
Pell,
  David, 216, 453
  Susanna, 216, 341, 453
Pemberton,
  Israel, 40, 61
  James, 401, 495
  John, 235, 413, 414, 495
  Sarah, 235, 322, 414
Pendegrest (Pendigrist),
  Catharine, 507
  Elizabeth, 507
  Hugh, 507
  Mary, 507
  Patrick, 507
  Rachel, 507
Pender,
  Elenor, 67
  Eve, 67
  Mary Ann, 152
  George 152
Penn,
  Hannah, 115
  John, 115
  Richard, 115
  Springett, 115
  Thomas, 115
  William, 115
Pennell (Penal),
  David, 315
  Elijah, 315
  Elizabeth, 315, 410, 450
  Hannah, 315
  John, 410, 450
  Joseph, 450
  Lydia, 315
  Mary, 315
  Samuel, 315
  Thomas, 450
  William, 315

Pennewell (Pennywell, Pennawell),
  Samuel, 311
  Sarah, 311
  William, 513, 428
Pennington,
  Ann, 321
  Couteler, 146
  Deborah, 50
  Henry, 29
  James, 74
  John, 128
  Martha, 93, 94
  Thomas, 93, 146
  Wheelor, 321, 459
  William, 128, 146
Penny,
  John, 204
  Susannah, 204
Penuel,
  Esther, 461
  William, 315, 356, 461
Pepper, Richard, 39
Perkins,
  Ann, 445
  Elizabeth, 164
  Fran., 20
  Philip, 445
  Thomas, 164, 315, 415, 440, 517
Permain,
  Henry, 27
  Wade, 27
Perry,
  Daniel, 178, 366
  Eleanor, 41, 496
  George, 496
  Hugh, 48
  Mary, 237, 331, 366
  Maudlin, 178
  Rachel, 367
  Thomas, 41
  William, 17
Perrymore, Philip, 173, 176
Person,
  Mary, 136, 149, 194
  Moses, 447
Peterkin,
  David, 209, 393, 432
  David, Jr., 228, 253
  Elizabeth, 228, 258
  John, 301, 393, 414
  Rhoda, 181, 201, 228, 301, 344, 362, 393
  Sarah, 414, 468
  Thomas, 201, 228, 250, 301, 393
Peterson,
  Abraham, 403
  Adam, 205
  Andrew, 49, 154, 193, 327
  Grace, 149
  Henry, 194
  Israel, 193, 327, 410, 451, 468
  Jacob, 149, 347
  James, 527
  John, 428
  Jonas, 264
  Margaret, 421
  Mary, 193, 264, 518
  Peter, 347, 403
  Priscilla, 133, 134
  Sarah, 154, 193
  Thomas, 16, 28
  Veronica, 205
Pettit,
  Edmond, 544
  Rachel, 544
Pettigrew, John, 497, 541
Pheady,
  Mary, 331
  Randolph, 331
Phillips,
  Ann, 135
  Catherine, 80, 135, 150
  Hannah, 62
  John, 55, 59
  Mary, 529
  Thomas, 538
  William, 80, 101, 135
Pickerel (Pickerell, Pickeral),
  Diana, 57, 150
  Littleton, 463
  Mary, 289
  William, 57, 289, 296
  Youell, 296
Pickering (Pickeren, Pickerran),
  James, 180, 214
  Sarah, 179
  Thomas, 400, 486, 557
Pickford,
  Amy, 122
  Mark, 122
Pierce (Pearce, Peirce),
  Abraham, 551
  Elizabeth, 104, 300, 425, 462, 470, 472
  Esther, 243
  Hannah, 381, 455, 543
  Isabella, 223, 306
  Jacob, 342, 487, 543
  Jane, 342, 459, 488
  Jean, 488
  John, 332, 381, 433, 474, 543
  Joseph, 223, 305, 306, 344
  Mary, 543

Nancy, 472
Rachel, 344
Richard, 25
Robert, 104
William, 297, 300, 305, 306, 344, 425, 462, 472, 553
William, Jr., 487
Pierson: see Pearson
Pigott, John, 33
Pindor,
  Alexander, 74
  Elenor, 74, 75
  Elizabeth, 74
  Eve, 74
Pindergrass, Elizabeth, 480
Pines, Ann, 150
Pinkine, Vinson, 484
Piper,
  James, 116, 204
  John, 369
  Ruthy, 339
Pippen, Robert, 482
Pleasonton (Pleasanton, Pleasontine, Plessenton, Plesenton),
  Caleb, 288
  Charles, 154
  David, 124, 129, 154, 186, 251, 288, 401, 434, 489, 549
  Deborah, 186, 288, 403, 493
  Easter, 154
  Edward, 403, 497
  Elizabeth, 129, 251
  George, 154
  John, 43, 80, 154, 175, 201, 251, 288, 401, 467, 489, 549, 552
  John, Jr., 129
  John, Sr., 129
  Jonathan, 124, 129, 154, 288, 295, 298, 386, 440
  Letitia, 251, 434, 489
  Margaret, 402, 403
  Mary, 154, 157, 164, 499
  Nathaniel, 288, 402, 403, 493, 497
  Rachel, 251, 434, 489
  Ruhama, 440
  Sarah, 251, 288 485
  Susannah, 413
Plomstead, Clymon, 40
Plowman,
  Ann, 230
  John, 230
  Josiah, 506
Plummer,
  Annastaticy, 493
  Mary, 202
  Miriam, 493
  Moses, 202

Poillion,
  Hannah, 135
  John, 135
  Sarah, 135
Poition, Ann, 136
Polk,
  Anna, 513, 516, 556
  Daniel, 507, 513, 546, 556
  John, 513, 516, 556
  Lovey, 486
  Margaret, 513, 556
  Margaret Nutter, 488, 507, 516
  Maria, 513, 516, 546, 556
  Peggy, 516
  Samuel, 513, 516
  Samuel White, 556
Pollin (Pollins, Polin),
  Ann, 408
  Merryum, 513
  Susan, 539
  Susannah, 539
Pool, Richard Curry, 364
Poor,
  Fanny, 539
  Henry, 539
  Jane, 539
  Thomas, 539
Pop,
  Agnes, 226
  Joseph, 226
Pope,
  Catherine, 196
  Charles, 196, 281, 319, 370, 453, 460, 525, 534, 558
  Mary, 196, 222
  Rachel, 196
  Sarah, 196
  Susanna, 196
  William, 131, 196
Porter,
  Ann, 331
  Benjamin, 327
  Christian, 540
  Edward, 540
  Elizabeth, 15, 327
  Joseph, 327
  Laurence, 19
  Mary, 25, 327
  Rebecca, 327
  Robert, 15, 19, 22, 25, 26
  Sarah, 296, 327
  Tabitha, 327
  Thomas, 263, 331
  William, 296, 327, 351
Portess,
  Deborah, 27, 28
  John, 27, 28
  Silvanus, 28

Postles,
 Acilia, 524
 Ann, 363
 Elizabeth, 363
 Selah, 524
 Shadrick, 363
 Zadock, 363
Potter,
 Ann, 165
 Benjamin, 374
 Charles, 374
 Dorothy, 137
 Edmond, 374
 Eleanor, 165
 Elizabeth, 271, 552
 Enoch, 259
 Henry, 493
 James, 40, 42, 117, 138, 165, 319, 324, 444
 John, 374, 493
 Mary, 117, 137, 374
 Neomy, 177
 Parismus, 117, 141, 165
 Rachel, 117, 165
 Sarah, 117, 137, 165, 324, 444, 487
 William, 273, 458
Potts,
 John, 514
 Robert, 55
 Stephen, 63
Poulson, William, 255
Poultney, Francis, 115
Pound (Pounds),
 Hannah, 61
 James, 61
 John, 34, 53, 55
 Samuel, 54, 61
Powell (Powel),
 Catharine, 409
 Christian, 38
 Comfort, 187
 Elizabeth, 342
 James, 192
 Jane, 342, 488
 John, 37, 38, 45, 192, 302, 317, 342, 383, 459, 488, 529
 Jonathan, 38
 Joseph, 38, 65, 88, 103, 138, 146, 189, 192, 210, 226, 302
 Martha, 261
 Mary, 189, 200, 342
 Neamiagh, 46
 Nicholas, 62, 145, 170, 200
 Randle, 146
 Rebecca, 145
 Samuel, 38, 453, 479
 Samuel, Jr., 94
 Sarah, 342

 William, 38, 189, 192, 261, 280, 302, 316, 319, 342, 383, 459, 477, 482, 488
 Zodak, 409, 538
Power,
 Abraham, 447
 Hanah, 447
 Margaret, 447
Pratt,
 Ann, 227, 395
 Charity, 423
 Dinah, 150, 194, 227
 Elizabeth, 395
 Esther, 364, 400, 481, 508
 Frederick, 227, 295, 404, 450, 481, 508
 George, 150, 194, 216, 227, 295, 404, 481, 508
 Henry, 508
 Jemima, 450, 481
 John, 508
 Jonathan, 395
 Luke, 227, 295, 328, 334, 369, 404
 Mary, 161, 188, 227, 295, 404, 508
 Nathan, 227, 295, 395, 404
 Polly, 481
 Ruth, 227, 508
 Sarah, 295, 369, 372
 Thomas, 138, 150, 508
 William, 508
Preston,
 John, 456
 William, 40
Prettyman,
 Perry, 514
 Rachel, 514
Prevo,
 Rachel, 259
 Samuel, 259
Price,
 Agnis, 439
 Anna, 15
 Barrow, 366
 Elizabeth, 299, 303
 Hannah, 377
 James, 316
 Jane, 316
 Jean, 316
 John, 14, 15, 37, 110, 377
 Joseph, 110, 303, 526
 Joseph, Jr., 224
 Lanston, 335
 Margret, 299
 Mary, 110, 402
 Neley, 539
 Prudence, 335
 Reece, 67
 Samuel, 366, 526

Susannah, 176
Thomas., 418, 419
William, 224, 303
William, Jr., 402
Prichard (Pritchard),
  Edward, 350
  Margarett, 229
  Robert, 444
  Sarah, 350
Prichett (Pritchett),
  Edward, 350
  Margaret, 444
  Nancy, 527
  Zachariah, 506
Primrose,
  Amelia, 553
  John, 305
  Rebecca, 534
  Sarah, 311
  Thomas, 311, 344, 385, 440, 534
  William, 311
Prittaman: see Prettyman
Proctor, Thomas, 523
Pryor (Prior, Pryer),
  Abraham, 367, 400, 404
  Elizabeth, 367, 404
  Hannah, 87, 117
  Jacob, 114
  John, 37, 87, 179, 256, 309, 330, 355, 367, 372, 400, 404, 412, 417, 525
  John, Jr., 367, 372
  Joseph, 87, 349, 355, 372, 338, 400, 420
Puckim, Eleanor, 401
Pugh,
  Ann, 38
  David, 37, 138
  Gideon, 219
  John, 38
  Judah, 213
  Mary, 219, 250
  Roger, 151, 158, 219, 250, 383
  Sarah, 160, 219, 285
  Susannah, 219
  William, 160, 219, 258
Pulle, Kesiah, 255
Pulling, Richard, 64
Purden (Purdin, Purdon),
  Andrew, 171, 229, 390, 400
  Catherine, 229
  Elizabeth, 400, 450
  James, 255, 304
  Jean (Jane), 229
  John, 199, 229, 390, 400, 408
  Joseph, 229, 450
  Martha, 171

Mary, 199, 229, 304
Prudence, 237, 400, 505
Sarah, 229, 400, 409
William, 507
Purnell (Purnel, Purnal),
  Hinson, 541
  Isaac, 530
  John, 112, 128
  Mary, 541
  Thomas, 555
  Walter, 128
Pursel (Pursele),
  Ann, 270
  Peter, 128
Purtee, Robert Terrell, 210
Purtle, Elinor, 207
Purvis, George, 412
Pusley,
  Daniel, 83
  Thomas, 83
Pusy (Pussey),
  Caleb, 56, 59
  Isabel, 56, 59

—Q—

Quenanault (Quenouault, Quenonall, Quenounault, Quenonaul),
  Paul, 263, 271, 275, 277, 329, 352
  Sarah, 352, 473
  Thomas, 352
Quid-Rale, Peter, 101
Quigley,
  James, 487
  Nancy, 487
Quillen (Quilling, Queling, Queilling),
  Alexander, 93
  Barbary, 42, 93
  Benjamin, 93, 217
  Clement, 204
  Elizabeth, 93, 334, 438
  John, 273, 478, 531
  Joseph, 93, 204, 334, 531, 550
  Lydia, 93
  Martha, 225, 531
  Mary, 204, 209, 478
  Priscilla, 531
  Samuel, 315
  Sarah, 93, 273, 307
  Susanna, 141, 204
  Teague, 93
  Thomas, 93, 315, 550
  Thomas, Jr., 93
Quinley, Ann, 465

Quinlin,
  Ann, 526
  Mary, 526
Quinnolly, Mary, 479

—R—

Rachlege: see Ratledge
Raisin (Raison): see Rasin
Rakes,
  Nicholas, 172
  Weston, 321
Ralph,
  Edward, 239, 240
  Sarah, 239, 240
Ralston (Rolston), John, 305, 349, 358, 373, 384, 393, 456, 467, 468, 477, 550
Raly: see Rawley
Randle (Randoll),
  Elizabeth, 100
  Elizabeth Ann, 99
  Thomas, 99, 100
Rankin, Moses, 98
Rannals (Rannels): see Reynolds
Rash,
  Agnes, 202, 251
  Ambrose, 109, 130
  Andrew, 438
  Ann, 67, 160, 203, 319, 438
  Ansley, 438
  Barbary, 202, 251
  Daniel, 438
  Easter, 438
  Elinor, 67
  Elizabeth, 67, 319
  Grace, 109, 130
  Henry, 160
  James, 192, 239, 259
  John, 67, 74, 109, 130, 160, 192, 251
  John, Sr., 438
  Joseph, 67, 109, 160, 192, 239, 319, 438
  Letitia, 438 439
  Margaret, 549
  Martin, 438
  Mary, 67, 160, 319, 438, 439, 535
  Michey, 239
  Mirim, 251
  Patience, 109, 130, 438
  Samuel, 67, 160, 170, 319
  Sarah, 67, 109, 130, 319
  William, 192, 278, 477

Rasin (Raisin, Raison, Reasin, Reason),
  Ann, 416, 451, 547
  Benjamin, 97, 174, 298, 337
  George, 337, 451
  James, 337
  Joseph, 186, 337, 451
  Kesiah, 174
  Mary, 337, 451
  Philip, 97, 186, 337, 451, 481
  Rachel, 337
  Sarah, 451, 481
  Warner, 547
Rathel, Thomas, 552
Ratledge (Ratlidge, Ratlage, Rachledge, Rattledge),
  Christopher, 216
  Edward, 63
  Elizabeth, 216, 343
  James, 280, 308
  Jemmimah, 280
  John, 41, 280, 343
  Mary, 280
  Moses, 280
  Ruth, 280
  Thomas, 234, 280, 308, 450
  Urselly, 63
  William, 280
Ratcliff, Richard, 12
Rawley (Raly, Releigh, Roley),
  Charity, 345, 375
  Elijah, 345, 375
  Hester, 157
  James, 178, 345, 375
  Philip, 357
Rawlings (Rawlins),
  Anthony, 76, 78, 197, 201, 334
  Cinth., 68
  John, 11, 78
  Mary, 68
  Sarah, 201, 334
Raymond,
  Angelica, 305
  Elizabeth, 208, 262
  Henry, 460
  Jacob, 460
  James, 175, 246, 247, 259, 273, 289, 297, 305, 307, 310, 320, 324, 389, 415, 421, 460, 461, 470, 502, 504, 533
  John, 207, 208, 259, 262, 421, 460, 504
  Jonathan, 76, 79, 84, 95, 113, 207, 259, 421
  Joseph, 460
  Mary, 162, 171, 172, 175, 176, 310, 461
  Presley, 72, 153, 176, 453, 460

Rachel, 207
Sarah, 113, 259, 262
Rea (Reah, Reagh),
  James, 457
  John, 30
  Peter, 457
  Samuel, 60, 299
  William, 308, 457
Read: see Reed
Reading, Charles, 333
Reason: see Rasin
Records, Ann, 495
Reddett, William, 322
Reddick (Redick),
  Benjamin, 197, 268
  Catharine, 198
  Cornelius, 197
  James, 197
  John, 197
  Margaret, 370
  Mary, 197
  Rachel, 197
  Robert, 197
  Robert, Sr., 197
  William, 197, 268, 271
Redeford, Jane, 111
Redgrave,
  Abraham, 429, 483, 489
  Ann, 489
  Susannah, 489
Redin,
  Charles, 376
  William, 376
Redman,
  Esther, 121
  Jane, 58
  Joshua, 121
  Thomas, 23
Reece: see Rees
Reed (Read),
  Abraham, 266
  Ann, 266, 295, 404, 459
  Barbara, 166
  Charles, 333
  Daniel James, 555
  Ebenezer, 459, 501, 555
  Elizabeth, 408
  George, 281, 333, 361, 501, 517
  James, 241, 285, 333, 356, 362, 370, 379, 412, 424, 459, 487, 555
  John, 165, 336, 459, 516
  John, Sr., 459
  Mary, 440
  Mary Ann, 487
  Meriam, 333
  Sarah, 333, 339, 356, 362, 370, 412

  Susanna, 266
  Thomas, 266, 459, 488, 555
  Walter, 220, 266
  William, 342, 440, 459, 554
Rees (Reese, Reec, Reece),
  Abel, 168, 174, 188, 219
  Anne, 229
  Crawford, 137, 243
  Dad, 128, 129
  Daniel, 485
  David, 43, 54, 59, 65, 71, 72, 81, 93, 105, 128, 129, 132, 135, 136, 140, 165, 174, 176, 242, 427, 537
  Edward, 185, 220, 363, 372, 485, 526
  Capt. Edward, 365
  Eleanor, 55, 59, 81
  Elizabeth, 136
  Ephriam, 208
  Esther, 55, 81, 112, 242, 251
  Evan, 54, 55, 59, 77, 81, 111, 185
  Evis, 129, 137
  Hester, 54, 136, 165, 168
  Jane, 251, 363
  Jemima, 427
  Jeremiah, 168, 242, 495
  Jeremiah, Jr., 453
  Jno., 59
  John, 48, 55, 61, 100, 111, 127, 136, 159, 163, 168, 170, 185, 188, 189, 197, 201, 242, 251, 480
  John, Jr., 358
  Jonathan, 136, 165, 216, 249
  Lewes, 105
  Lurania, 159, 170, 201, 221, 265
  Margaret, 136, 165
  Martha, 54, 55, 59, 281, 359, 363, 371
  Mary, 43, 54, 81, 132, 140, 185, 229, 526
  Nathan, 188
  Priscilla, 485
  Rebecca, 219
  Richard, 81, 119, 140
  Robert, 185, 363, 372, 485
  Sarah, 136, 185, 188, 242, 251
  Thomas, 105, 136, 168, 174, 188, 242, 480
  William, 112, 124, 136, 165, 185, 281, 309, 359, 363, 372
Register,
  Elizabeth, 288
  Elijah, 288
  Francis, 288, 518, 524, 539, 552
  Isaac, 288
  Jeremiah, 288
  John, 31, 37, 59, 75, 288, 357
  Robert, 283, 288, 327, 357, 436
  Ruth 357

Sarah, 75, 193
Sophia, 514
William, 31, 37
Rehue,
  Powell, 120
  Rachel, 120
Reily: see Riley
Rench,
  Frances, 530
  James, 530
Renelds (Renolds, Rennolds): see Reynolds
Renshaw,
  Ann, 93
  Martha, 175
  Richard, 93, 94
Revell (Revel),
  Amelia, 245, 441
  Elizabeth, 334, 441
  James, 441
  John, 245, 334, 441
  Josiah, 539
  Margaret, 186
  Mary, 334, 441
  Sabre, 334
  Sarah, 441
  Sarah (Adams), 334
  William, 160, 186, 197, 201, 334, 441
Reyhoe,
  Powell, 120
  Rachel, 120
Reynix, George, 98
Reynolds (Reynalds, Reynills, Renelds, Renolds, Rannals, Runnals, Runneralds, Runnolds),
  Andrew, 297
  Ann, 20, 62, 229, 297
  Catherine, 109, 150, 210, 424, 431, 432, 444
  Daniel, 51, 57, 74, 79, 514, 518, 527, 538
  Eleanor, 308, 431, 425
  Elizabeth, 57, 69, 234, 282
  Ephriam, 191
  Francis, 14, 23
  George, 57, 74, 538
  Grace, 79
  Henry, 191, 291, 308, 380
  James, 365, 425
  Jean, 297
  Joanna, 425
  John, 14, 57, 58, 65, 76, 79, 95, 109, 110 191, 281, 282, 424, 443, 518, 538
  John Christopher, 365
  John, Sr., 57
  Joseph, 14, 451
  Mary, 57, 191
  Michael, 79, 110, 282, 352, 428, 538
  Miriam, 234, 428, 538
  Nancy, 425
  Rachel, 174, 290, 317, 380
  Richard, 118, 191, 266, 278, 308, 331, 367
  Robert, 57, 69, 174, 451, 538
  Ruth, 278, 308, 331, 365
  Samuel, 290
  Sarah, 57, 191, 425
  Stephen, 425
  Susannah, 79, 110
  Thomas, 14, 20, 177, 538, 549
  Waddey, 14
  William, 14, 211, 297, 365, 425, 432
Rhodes (Rhoades, Roads),
  Alice, 80, 93, 112
  Alse, 74
  Anna, 124
  James, 338
  John, 112, 265, 335, 338
  Mary, 335, 338, 339
  Samuel, 339
  William, 100, 112, 265, 312, 316, 332, 335, 338
Rice, Willis, 178
Rich,
  Ann, 323
  Edward, 271, 323, 449
  Mary, 323
  Peter, 323, 475
  Rebecca, 323
  Stephen, 448
  Susanna, 271, 323
  William, 323
Richards,
  Elizabeth, 217, 239
  George, 288
  Henry, 217
  John, 294
  Mary, 287
  Sarah, 189, 191, 288
  William, 239, 287
Richardson (Richeson),
  Ann, 30, 62, 67, 224, 254, 294
  Azariah, 313
  Elizabeth, 313
  Henry, 316
  Izariah, 301
  Jean, 68
  John, 11, 16, 17, 19, 26, 28, 62, 67, 116, 355, 406, 448
  John, Sr., 26

Letitia, 406
Mary, 26, 28, 61
Miriam, 62, 67, 80
Richard, 38, 50, 62, 94, 292
Stephen, 116
Thomas, 68
William, 376
Richee,
  Rebecca, 142
  Samuel, 142
Richman (Richmond),
  Ann, 81, 139
  Evan, 55
  John, 55
  Martha, 81, 86
  Michael, 37, 39, 55, 77, 86, 139
  Temperance, 55
Rickards, John, 402, 558
Ricketts (Rickets, Rickitts),
  Charles, 433
  Elizabeth, 498
  Jonathan, 480
  Nancy, 376
  Rachel, 480
  Thomas, 376, 398
Ridgaway, Zedekiak, 503
Ridge, William, 405
Ridgely (Ridgly),
  Abraham, 375, 550
  Ann, 375, 408
  Ann, the younger, 408
  Charles, 175, 197, 212, 220, 244, 254, 257, 259, 280, 314, 332, 352, 361, 375, 395
  Dr. Charles, 231, 374
  Charles Greenberry, 155, 159
  Charles, Jr., 404
  Elizabeth, 155, 159
  George Wemys, 375, 408
  Henry Moore, 375, 408
  Mary, 159, 197, 220, 375
  Nicholas, 77, 91, 131, 144, 146, 147, 155, 159, 354, 374, 375, 402, 404, 408, 412, 413, 425, 436, 438, 446, 454, 461, 473, 484, 485, 516, 555, 558
  Sarah, 155, 159, 220
  Willimina, 375
Ridley,
  Isaac, 63, 242
  Hannah, 63
  Mansuell, 63
  Mary, 63, 66, 78
  Rachel, 63
  Rebecca, 63
  Samuel, 63
  Sarah, 63

Riggs, Esais, 406, 411
Right: see Wright
Riley (Rieley, Reily, Ryley),
  Elizabeth, 230, 373
  Hugh, 169
  Jean, 289
  Laurence, 230, 373
Ringold (Ringgold),
  John, 286, 370, 454, 456, 464, 483
  Mary, 222, 275
  Thomas, 286
  William, 222, 275
Roach,
  John, 143, 190, 256, 433, 447, 487
  Nanthaniel, 64, 143
  Samuel, 188
  Sarah, 256
Roads: see Rhodes
Roan: see Rowan
Roanny, Peter, 183
Roberson: see Robertson
Robeson, Edward, 458
Roberts (Robearts),
  Annis, 377
  Charles, 48
  Hannah, 115
  Hugh, 335
  John, 209, 410
  Katherine, 75
  Mary, 325, 410
  Thomas, 329, 377, 387
  Timothy, 204
Robertson (Roberson),
  Alexander, 543
  Ann, 525, 542
  Caleb, 525
  Elisha, 557
  Elizabeth, 543
  John, 543
  Mary, 351
  Sarah, 525
  William, 496
Robinson (Robbison, Robison, Robissen),
  Andrew, 180
  Ann, 34, 89, 293
  Asa, 118, 192
  Avis, 137
  Caleb, 525
  Catharine, 89
  Charles, 180, 282, 343, 369
  Daniel, 74, 86, 109, 112, 118, 121, 133, 139, 143, 155, 167, 176, 186, 198, 199, 202, 207, 211, 293, 542
  Daniel, Jr., 192
  Deborah, 342, 542

Elliner, 18, 30
Elizabeth, 121, 156, 167, 455, 542
George, 16, 19, 34, 74, 86, 118, 119, 128, 137, 141, 220, 542
Hannah, 86, 93, 95, 118
James, 72, 291, 455, 542, 545
James, Sr., 501
Jereboam, 86, 167
John, 17, 19, 21, 28, 30, 51, 58, 68, 74, 89, 121, 180, 228, 265, 293, 339, 342, 353, 358, 463, 542
John H., 515
John, Jr., 369
Jonathan, 121, 134
Jordan, 180, 211, 265, 311, 369
Joseph, 211, 228, 291, 293, 542
Lawerence, 74, 86, 89, 128, 182, 238
Lydia, 542
Margaret, 89
Martha, 542
Mary, 30, 74, 78, 84, 121, 134, 141, 220, 265, 282, 291, 339
Miriam, 118
Nancy, 324
Patience, 167, 211
Rachel, 180, 279, 324
Rebecca, 542
Robert, 291
Samuel, 74, 81, 94, 95, 101, 109, 118, 151, 183, 211, 234, 261, 293, 513
Sarah, 25, 86, 121, 134, 156, 180, 228
Septimus, 94
Susannah, 62, 238
Thomas, 89, 293, 369
William, 62, 74, 89, 121, 134, 191, 542

Rochester, Henry, 523

Rock,
Charles, 369
Patrick, 35

Rodney (Rodeney, Rodeny),
Anthony, 29, 38
Caesar, 29, 71, 76, 97, 107, 113, 125, 129, 176, 196, 204, 207, 209, 361, 395
Caesar Augustus, 361, 539
Daniel, 38, 46, 51, 52, 59, 74, 106, 211, 361
Elizabeth, 29, 107, 121
Elizabeth, Jr., 129
George, 29
John, 29
Lavinia, 361
Ledia, 261
Letitia, 361, 395

Margaret, 106, 330
Meriam, 211
Penelop, 42
Rachel, 29
Ruth, 39, 42, 65
Sarah, 28, 29, 33, 361
Thomas, 26, 29, 257, 292, 315, 330, 361, 395, 452, 539
William, 17, 18, 19, 21, 22, 23, 24, 25, 26, 29, 33, 36, 38, 39, 42, 46, 50, 54, 55, 65, 207, 243, 261, 288, 333, 361, 395,
Capt. William, 28

Roe (Rowe),
Ann, 537
Benjamin, 387, 429
Brinkle, 226, 429, 519
Caesar, 225, 226, 387, 429
Elizabeth, 198, 225, 226, 237, 307, 387, 418, 429
Elizabeth, Jr., 307
Hugh, 226, 429
Isabella, 441
James, 198, 225, 226
Jane, 537
Lydia, 429
Maria, 441
Mary, 226, 376, 537
Matilda, 537
Nancy, 441
Naomi, 360
Rebecca, 537
Samuel, 441
Sarah, 537
Thomas, 537
William, 360, 537

Roes: see Rose

Rogers,
Daniel, 555
Edward, 542
Elizabeth, 13
James, 330, 334
John, 13, 204
John E., 542
Joseph, 336, 547
Maria, 542
Mary, 407, 450, 542, 547
Rebeccah, 334
Roger, 204
Sarah, 542
Thomas, 22

Rogerson, Fredelia, 324
Roley: see Rawley
Rolf, Ann, 301
Rolinson, Samuel, 493
Rolph, William, 314
Rolston: see Ralston

Rork,
  Milicent, 190
  William, 190
Rose (Roes),
  Ephriam, 174
  George, 26
  James, 193
  Jude, 26
  Mary, 193
Rositor,
  Elizabeth, 86
  John, 86
  William, 86
Ross,
  Andrew, 202
  Charles, 288
  Elizabeth, 213, 390
  James, 358, 450
  Jane, 216
  John, 124, 213, 390
  Levi, 387, 396
  Margaret, 213
  Mary, 358, 492
  Nathan, 390
  Samuel, 216, 543
  Thomas, 201
  William, 202, 213, 234, 333, 387, 390, 450
Rothwell,
  Henry, 253
  Mary, 253
Rowan (Rowen, Roan),
  Elizabeth, 124, 161, 333, 362
  George, 446
  Hanah, 254
  Henry, 362
  James, 537
  John, 537, 550
  Malachi, 177, 182, 183, 185
  Ruhamath, 446
  Sarah, 537, 550
  William, 91, 124, 161
Rowe: see Roe
Rowland (Roland),
  Ann, 289, 324
  David, 435
  Hugh, 73, 103
  Isaiah, 289, 361, 370
  Isabel, 78, 85
  Jonathan, 335, 350, 368, 382, 429, 434
  Joseph, 489
  Mary, 429
  Polly, 382, 434
  Robert, 71, 78, 84, 85
  Ruth, 361
  Samual, 23
  Thomas, 71

Ruall,
  Elenor, 202
  James, 202
Rue, Mary, 156
Ruley, Michael, 293
Ruluf, Deborah, 54
Runnals (Runnells, Runnels, Runneralds, Runnalds): see Reynolds
Rush,
  Joseph, 45
  Mary, 45, 156, 224
  William, 41, 45
Russ,
  Edward, 327
  Jane, 327
  Robert, 327
Russell (Russel),
  Ebenezer, 75, 102, 186
  Elinor, 496
  Elizabeth, 75, 323
  G., 190
  George, 75, 102
  Grace, 138, 154, 241
  Henry, 241, 442
  Hugh, 245
  John, 241, 242, 245, 267
  Joseph, 154, 241
  Mary, 323, 459
  Tabitha, 184, 186
  Thomas, 183, 219
  Timothy, 245
  William, 138, 241, 323, 443
Russum (Russom),
  Elizabeth, 269
  Peter, 269, 496
  Sarah, 269, 496
  Thomas, 268, 269, 335
  William, 517
Ruth,
  Elizabeth, 489
  John, 230
  Mary, 489
  William, 556
Rutherford (Ruttherford),
  Alexander, 316
  Richard, 151
  William, 228
Rutter,
  Amy, 122
  Jane, 129
  John, 129, 173, 258
  Mary, 258
  Philip, 122
Rutty,
  Daniel, 32, 83
  Elizabeth, 83

Ruwark, Michael, 66
Ryan (Ryon),
  Elizabeth, 305
  John, 143, 229, 231, 234
  Presemene, 143
  Rachel, 496
Ryley: see Riley
Rynet, Elizabeth, 401

—S—

Sackwell, William, 20
Salley, Elizabeth, 203
Sallindine, William, 55
Samples,
  Elias, 103, 174
  Mary, 174
Samuels, John, 58, 60
Sanders,
  James, 94
  Rebecca, 94
Santhers, William, 12
Sapington: see Sappington
Sapp (Sap),
  Amah, 453
  Anne, 98, 197
  Arminta, 486
  Benjamin, 98, 197
  Edward, 98
  Elijah, 481
  Elizabeth, 98, 146, 172, 220, 345
  Esther, 141, 315
  Henry, 98, 197, 214, 265, 271
  Isaac, 141, 146, 172
  Jacob, 453
  James, 98, 246, 424, 486
  John, 98, 345
  Luke, 486
  Lydia, 481
  Peter, 486
  Rachel, 214, 434
  Rebecca, 486
  Sarah, 265, 271
  Unity, 486
  William, 141, 303
Sappington (Sapington),
  Agnes, 195, 224
  William, 175, 195, 224
Sares, William, 448
Satterfield (Saterfield),
  Aaron, 373
  Ann, 533
  Joseph, 373
  Nathaniel, Jr., 373
  Nathaniel, Sr., 373
  Sarah, 549
  William M., 525
Sauls, John, 57
Saulsbury (Saulsbery),
  Eli, 384
  Eliner, 406
  Gove, 406
  Henry, 406
  Marget, 406
  Rebecca, 406
  Thomas, 406, 492
  William, 337, 406
Saunders,
  Abraham, 348
  Clark, 348
  Daniel, 555
  Edith, 555
  Elizabeth, 348
  James, 365, 555
  Joseph, 555
  Paul, 348
  Rebecca, 555
  Robert, 292
  Samuel, 555
  Sarah, 348
  William, 348
Savage, John, 199
Savin,
  Ann, 459
  James, 459
  John, 459
  Joshua, 459
  Mary, 459
  Perigrin, 459
  William, 459, 473
Sawer, Sarah, 252
Saxton,
  ..., 496
  Alexander, 521, 543
  Andrew, 251, 274, 550
  Brinklee, 550
  Catharine, 550
  Eleanor, 496
  Elizabeth, 550
  George, 504
  James, 553
  John, 553
  Nancy, 251, 274
  Prudence, 274, 425
  Rachel, 478
  William, 550
Scales,
  Mariam, 517
  William, 517
Scantlin, William, 182
Schee, James, 526
Scoggins, Nancy, 457

Scott (Scot, Skott),
  Andrew, 242
  Ann Martha, 316
  Elias, 121
  Frances, 159
  James, 159
  John, 31, 38, 316
  Nathan, 558
  Rose, 249
  Samuel, 250
  Thomas, 126
Scotton (Scotten, Scottin),
  Amelia, 548
  Ann, 301
  Araminta, 301
  Eli, 357, 452
  Elizabeth, 301, 540
  James, 301, 376, 421, 454, 466, 540
  John, 301, 404, 421, 433
  Marah, 301
  Mary, 472
  Mealy, 433
  Meriam, 502, 551
  Merritt, 548
  Nathan, 382, 432
  Priscilla, 548
  Rachold, 333, 404
  Rebeccah, 548
  Richard, 452
  Sarah, 404, 433, 452
  Tabitha, 452
  Teeny, 452
  Thomas, 358, 404, 433, 548
  Thomas, Sr., 404
  William, 382, 404, 433, 548
Scronders, James, 442
Scully (Skulley),
  Burton, 300
  John Burton, 300, 457, 529
  Lucretia, 338
  Roger, 338, 506
Scurlog, John, 433
Seaney, Sarah, 368
Searmon, Joseph, 480
Sears (Seears),
  ..., 342
  Elizabeth, 447
  Esther, 342, 530
  William, 474, 554
Seeds,
  Sarah, 167, 184
  William, 167, 184
Seenea,
  Ann, 261
  Bryan, 261
  Elenor, 261
  Elizabeth, 261
  John, 261
  Martha, 261
  Owen, 261
  William, 261
Semans,
  Gilbert, 533
  Jane, 533
  Lambert, 533
  Stephen, 533
  Thomas, 533
  William, 533
Sena, Owen, 109
Seney, John, 310
Servant, William, 102
Severson,
  Ann, 208
  Elizabeth, 291, 529
  James, 208, 270, 353, 529
  John, 143, 208, 385, 529
  Lydia, 385
  Mary, 208
  Mercy, 143
  Rachel, 208
  Robert, 529
  Sarah, 110, 208, 353
  Simon, 208
Sexton,
  George, 227
  James, 336
  Prudence, 363
Seyers, William, 342
Shahan,
  David, 382
  David, Jr., 492
  David, Sr., 492
  Eleanor, 492
  George, 382
  John, 382, 492
  Jonathan, 492
  Joshua, 382, 492
  Louisa, 382
  Susannah, 303
Shane,
  Benjamin, 509, 532
  Edward, 509, 532
  James, 509, 532
  Mary, 509
  Phebe, 509
  Thomas, 509, 532
Shankland, Mary, 397
Shankmire, Peter, 179
Shannon (Shanen),
  Daniel, 149
  Hugh, 157
  Mary, 426
Sharine, Samuel, 471

Sharp,
  Adam, 218
  Edward, 218
  Elizabeth, 22
  George, 23
  John, 218
  Nehemiah, 218
  Rebecca, 419
  Samuel, 345
  Sarah, 63
  Stogdon, 218
  Thomas, 23, 29, 63
Sharpless,
  Joseph, 209
  Mary, 479
Shaver,
  Leven, 369
  Nancy Laws, 505
Shaw,
  . . ., 310
  Agness, 70
  Catherine, 310
  Edward, 335
  Elizabeth, 419
  Ephriam, 70, 150, 162, 210, 234, 255
  Gartery, 304
  Henry, 97, 447, 549
  Hugh, 304, 418
  James, 257, 418, 419, 482, 514, 522
  John, 223, 335
  Joshua, 70, 351, 419
  Leah, 210, 255, 257
  Letitia, 513, 514
  Martha, 70, 236
  Mary, 22, 70, 238
  Naomy, 419
  Prudence, 70
  Richard, 335
  Samuel, 70, 418
  Sarah, 335
  Thomas, 228, 238
  William, 70, 162, 228, 335, 418, 419, 522
Shay, Dennis, 405
Shee (Schea),
  Bertles, 237, 252
  Cecilia, 237, 252
  Dennis, 398
  Elizabeth, 405, 513
Shehorn,
  Cornelius, 346
  David, 382
  David, Sr., 492
  Levicee, 382
  Sarah, 346, 466
  Susanna, 492
Shelley (Shelly),
  John, 246
  Moses, 234, 246

Shelton, Sarah, 438
Shepherd (Shepard, Sheperd),
  Benjamin, 548
  Betsy, 434
  Daniel, 548
  Diana, 215
  Edward, 545
  Esther, 365, 381, 434
  Hester, 434
  John, 15, 33, 545
  Mary, 545
  Nancy, 491
  Rubey, 434
  Samuel, 215
  Sarah, 33
  Thomas, 365, 381, 382, 435
Sheridan (Sheridine),
  Elizabeth, 376
  Jemima, 497
Sheriff (Sherriff),
  Thomas, 225, 266, 296
Sherley: see Shurly
Sherrad,
  Catharine, 145
  Hannah, 193
  William, 193
Sherrard (Sherard),
  Francis, 63
  William, 147
Sherrer,
  Mary, 33
  Robert, 33
  William, 33
Sherry, William, 171
Shervan (Sherven),
  Thomas, 327
  William, 291
Sherwin, William, 125
Sherwood,
  Daniel, 337, 393, 414
  Elizabeth, 206
  Hannah, 206
  High, 337
  James, 76
  Lucretia, 403
  Mary, 206, 393
  Philip, 403
  Sarah, 414
  William, 206
Shields (Sheilds, Shelds),
  Abel, 258, 317
  Elizabeth, 258
  Reubin, 267, 308, 321
Shiner, Mary, 110
Shirley: see Shurly
Shirven, Thomas, 501

Shiver, Mary, 110
Shockley,
  Elias, 442, 480, 490, 510
  Mary, 218
  Sarah, 74, 75
  Thomas, 218, 514
  William, 73, 74
Shoemaker,
  John, 426
  Mary, 426
Short,
  Edward, 527
  Hannah, 545
  Sally, 527
Shuite,
  Elizabeth, 94
  Martha, 94
  Rebecca, 94
Shulcock, Thomas, 454
Shurly (Shirley, Sherley),
  Elizabeth, 17
  John, 17
  Keziah, 174
  Mary, 17
  Naomi, 17
  Richard, 17, 29, 42
  Roger, 17
  William, 90, 121, 163, 174
Shurmer,
  Benjamin, 46, 61, 76, 82
  Sarah, 77, 82, 210, 366
  William, 77, 91, 114, 151, 153, 154, 155, 178, 187, 210
Shusane,
  Penelopy, 328
  Thomas, 328
Shute,
  Elizabeth, 93, 175
  William, 93, 175
Siddin,
  Esther, 200
  William, 200
Sidens, Jane, 327
Silliven (Sylavan),
  William, 130, 131, 144, 167
Silver, Elizabeth, 255
Silvester (Sylvester),
  Benjamin, 247
  Hannah, 247
  Harrington, 422
Silvey, Sipple, 312
Simmons (Simons, Simmonds),
  Cecilea, 224
  Daniel, 333
  Elizabeth, 31, 269
  Fowler, 413
  Henry, 255, 397
  Henry, Jr., 247
  John, 413, 454
  Lewes, 413
  Mary, 31, 333, 413, 447, 465
  Rachel, 111, 334
  Sarah, 30, 31
  Solomon, Jr., 269
  Stephens, 14, 17, 27, 28, 30, 31, 51, 53, 79
  Susannah, 31, 79
  William, 31
Simpkins, Michael, 16
Simpson (Simson, Sympson),
  Benjamin, 437, 496
  Elizabeth, 172
  Jamima, 172
  Jean, 172
  Jennette, 324
  John, 294, 438, 513
  Margarett, 130
  Mary, 218, 294
  Moses, 172, 218
  Robert, 294
  Thomas, 324
  Urcilla, 172
  William, 34, 130, 172
Sims (Sim),
  Elizabeth, 57
  John, 293
  Margaret, 45
Sippen,
  Elizabeth, 30
  Weakman, 30
Sipple,
  Alice, 148
  Ann, 255, 536
  Boaz, 360
  Caleb, 167, 198, 294, 330, 332, 346, 373, 398, 487, 491, 498, 502
  Caleb, Jr., 254
  Catherine, 360
  Christipher, 148, 255
  Elenor, 29
  Eleshe, 502
  Elias, 547
  Elijah, 198, 294, 369, 494
  Elizabeth, 148, 198, 294, 296, 487
  Eliza Tatnall, 536
  Garrett, 198, 267, 278, 294, 338, 357, 374, 487, 536
  Garrett, Jr., 373
  James, 487
  Joanna, 152
  John, 47, 82, 97, 133, 148, 152, 198, 294, 296, 487, 491, 498, 531

Jonathan, 198, 254, 285, 294, 324, 406
Lydia, 108, 267
Martinus, 152, 454, 470
Mary, 148, 198, 294, 321, 337, 369, 509
Nancy, 198, 303, 487
Nathaniel, 152
Priscilla, 148, 531
Prudence, 152
Rachel, 152
Raymond, 148
Rebecca, 470
Ruth, 314, 324, 504
Sarah, 152, 198, 390, 440, 470, 487, 541
Susannah, 51, 333, 356, 498
Sylvia, 148, 390, 440, 541
Thomas, 198, 294, 333, 356, 374, 451, 483, 487, 491, 509, 536
Uriah, 152, 322
Waitman, 60, 101, 106, 108, 143, 162, 198, 294, 394
Waitman, Jr., 92, 249
Waitman, Sr., 67, 267
William, 97, 152, 184, 295, 360
William the younger, 295
Zadock, 498

Sisco,
  Patience, 126
  Sarah, 401
  Thomas, 126

Skewes, James, 480

Skidmore,
  Abraham, 28
  Elizabeth, 50, 81, 89, 112, 258
  Esther, 251
  John, 81, 106, 112, 160, 183, 184, 199
  Joseph, 29
  Mary, 18, 81, 160, 184, 258
  Rebecca, 29
  Sally, 410
  Samuel, 56, 106, 112, 199, 211, 225, 258
  Susannah, 29
  Thomas, 18, 24, 29, 33, 37, 43, 47, 53, 56, 101, 106, 107, 110, 112, 186, 225, 251, 258, 374, 405, 410
  Thomas, Jr., 60, 85, 90, 91
  William, 106, 112

Skillington,
  Ann, 425
  Elijah, 357
  Martha, 359
  Thomas, 210, 280, 357, 359, 371, 378

Skinner (Skiner),
  Betsey, 454
  Daniel, 454
  Elizabeth, 213, 230
  Esther, 177
  John, 454, 539
  Mary, 158
  Meriah, 456
  Nelly, 454
  Rebecca, 454, 482, 503
  Stephen, 454
  Thomas, 454, 456
  William, 86, 177, 230, 454, 482, 515

Sklinton, James, 334

Slater (Slator, Sleighter),
  Agnes, 50, 53
  George, 247
  John, 53
  Jonathan, 430
  Mary, 53
  Rachel, 430
  Thomas, 50, 53, 107, 108, 154, 171

Slaught, John, 240, 328, 354

Slaughter,
  Elizabeth, 360
  John, 181, 360
  Jonathan, 447
  Mary, 26, 181
  Rachel, 447
  Ruth, 463

Slay,
  Edward, 445
  Esther, 445
  George, 445

Sleighter: see Slater

Slocom,
  Benjamin, 294
  Elizabeth, 294
  John, 294
  Joseph, 294
  Mary, 294

Smack,
  Hetty, 517
  Ken., 539
  McKimmey, 472, 517, 548

Small,
  James, 119, 123, 149, 150
  John, 66

Smalley (Smally),
  Elizabeth, 255
  John, 255
  John, Sr., 522

Smedly,
  Mary, 160
  William, 160

Smith (Smyth),
 Abigail, 337
 Abraham, 323
 Agnes, 21
 Alce, 21, 178
 Alice, 406
 Ann, 78, 133, 241, 308, 425, 437, 482, 546
 Barbury, 42
 Benjamin, 162, 271, 302, 347, 366, 408, 437, 458, 541, 546
 Bethia, 21
 Cesar, 425
 Charles, 298, 309, 461
 Daniel, 33, 38, 54, 60, 140, 141, 142, 189, 206, 226, 228, 240, 250, 300, 387, 442, 472, 473, 492, 499, 554
 Daniel, Jr., 482
 Daniel, Sr., 482
 David, 36, 138, 158, 192, 429, 473
 David Melvil, 492
 Denton, 302
 Duncan, 394
 Ebenezer, 406
 Edward, 102, 337, 425
 Eleanor, 539
 Elizabeth, 21, 31, 51, 57, 65, 100, 113, 133, 139, 144, 177, 194, 224, 230, 248, 249, 260, 300, 308, 323, 387, 400, 471, 472, 499, 554
 Ester, 107
 Ewin, 133
 Ezekiel, 492, 532
 Fisher, 408
 George, 400, 408, 422, 428, 443, 546
 George William, 459
 H., 69
 Hadden, 471
 Harrietta, 165, 195, 196, 203, 254, 425
 Henry, 138, 158, 230, 235, 381
 Holiday, 260, 406, 443
 Isaac, 133, 167, 222, 224, 314, 317
 Isabella, 36, 43, 103, 126
 Jacob, 15, 21, 35, 133, 224, 419, 527
 James, 13, 126, 158, 179, 185, 196, 224, 230, 308, 324, 339, 351, 375, 384, 407, 416, 425, 431, 433, 454, 457, 535
 James, Jr., 203, 224, 254
 Jane, 140, 240, 546
 Janet, 350
 Jean, 133, 193, 324
 Jesse, 406
 John, 15, 16, 21, 37, 104, 113, 126, 129, 142, 189, 191, 192, 235, 271, 291, 347, 354, 359, 379, 384, 391, 402, 408, 431, 442, 527
 John Nightingell, 103
 Joseph, 191, 230, 264, 285, 298, 468, 470, 546
 Joseph Nightingell, 103
 Judith, 60
 Katherine, 129
 Leavin, 483
 Levice, 248
 Louisea, 177
 Lydia, 337
 Margaret, 167, 211
 Mark, 49, 51, 64, 75, 78, 82, 120, 133, 139, 144, 152, 155, 161, 194, 224
 Mark, Jr., 222
 Martha, 21, 133, 142, 144, 224, 260, 347, 443, 482
 Mary, 35, 107, 133, 138, 145, 158, 162, 177, 224, 230, 248, 264, 270, 276, 298, 309, 312, 366, 395, 408, 419, 457, 461, 465, 468, 470, 471, 479, 482, 492, 527, 539, 541, 546
 Maurice, Jr., 21
 Maurice, Sr., 21
 Nancy, 249, 431, 471, 511
 Nathaniel, 471
 Nightingal, 103, 191
 Noah, 465, 525
 Olive, 260, 337
 Philip, 375, 377, 411
 Polly, 520
 Rachel, 158, 260, 532
 Ralph, 142, 482
 Rebecca, 113, 167, 177, 200, 235, 238, 248, 351
 Richard, 39, 40, 43, 102, 225, 244, 279, 282, 291, 297, 314, 347, 374, 375, 377, 384, 387, 408, 415, 425, 431, 435
 Robert, 20, 43, 102, 155, 177 200, 211, 248, 270, 420, 425, 435, 438, 479, 514
 Robert, Sr., 406
 Ruth, 297, 408, 539
 Sabrah, 337
 Samuel, 54, 60, 85, 113, 117, 192, 223, 235, 249, 260, 294, 297, 318, 387, 406, 408
 Sarah, 107 129, 189, 191, 192, 260, 291, 354, 375, 379, 391, 402, 425, 431, 442, 446, 471, 525, 546
 Solomon, 21, 100, 443, 506, 515
 Stephen, 425, 532
 Susannah, 129, 277, 407

Thomas, 118, 128, 129, 142, 146, 230, 322, 337, 384, 429, 442, 482, 492, 520, 527
Thomas Murphey, 217
Thomas Peacock, 364
Thomas, Sr., 322
Tishey, 249
Violet, 443
William, 113, 148, 167, 177, 179, 188, 235, 247, 248, 249, 272, 308, 311, 316, 337, 406, 408, 425, 429, 433, 442, 482, 492, 493, 514, 532, 550
William B., 552
William Banning, 337

Smithers,
  David, 388
  Elizabeth, 388
  Esther, 332, 404, 405
  Grace, 388
  John, 190, 388, 393, 540
  Joseph, 388
  Katharine, 543
  Marcy, 487
  Margaret, 538
  Mary, 531
  Nathaniel, 349, 388, 405, 485, 487, 491, 531, 540, 543
  Nathaniel, Jr., 353, 400, 404, 405
  Nathaniel, Sr., 383
  Nimrod, 538
  Patience, 540
  Rachel, 332, 388
  Ruth, 393,
  Sally, 543
  Susannah, 543
  William, 388, 543

Smother, Thomas, 166
Smyth: see Smith
Sneeds, Gabriel, 550
Sneeps, Joseph, 428

Snipe,
  Joseph, 279, 346
  Nancy, 279
  Rachel, 279
  William, 279, 346

Snooke, John, 14

Snow,
  Alice, 131
  Ann, 324, 545
  Anthony, 205, 352, 545
  Benjamin, 205
  Clayton, 461, 455
  David, 83
  Eleanor, 111
  Elizabeth, 147, 148, 327, 461
  Elisha, 59, 63, 83, 102, 147, 205, 327
  Elisha, Jr., 144
  Elisha, Sr., 147
  George, 470
  Hannah, 83
  Isaac, 42, 46, 53, 54, 55, 56, 64, 69, 73, 83, 100, 101, 131, 284, 445, 455
  James, 102, 103, 144, 147, 174, 219, 266, 324, 341, 408, 470, 504, 515, 545
  Dr. James, 460
  Jane, 324
  Jean, 324
  Jesse, 102, 147
  Johana, 142
  John, 83, 102, 111, 142, 170, 193, 220, 284, 341, 401, 457, 470, 504, 515
  Joshua, 102, 219, 227, 279, 290, 324, 346, 428, 431, 470, 479
  Lydia, 284
  Margaret, 220
  Mary, 144, 148, 205, 266, 453, 461
  Nancy, 219
  Phebe, 193, 461, 470
  Rachel, 455
  Rebecca, 495, 515
  Sarah, 87, 170, 214, 219, 284
  Silas, 102, 193, 262, 264, 298, 300, 347, 349, 366, 407, 421, 455, 459, 461, 470
  William, 140, 144, 147, 243
  William, Jr., 300

Soden,
  Amerity, 340
  Dingley Grey, 340
  Elizabeth, 340
  James, 340
  Luramy, 340
  Mary, 340
  Thomas, 340
  Vilater, 340
  William, 340

Somers,
  Rosannah, 143
  Thomas, 143

Soper,
  Elizabeth, 488, 551
  Robert, 488, 553
  Samuel, 551

Sorath, William, 91
Sorden, William, 517, 553

Sorency (Sorinsee),
  Jacob, 99
  Jamima, 299

Souders, Elizabeth, 422
Southard, Benjamin, 60, 235

Southerby, William, 11
Southward, Mary, 408
Soward,
  Eleanor, 303, 304, 500
  George, 303, 304, 492, 500
  Hannah, 513
  Mary, 513
  Rebecca, 303
  Sarah, 303
  Thomas, 303, 304, 424, 500
Sowder,
  Henry, 261
  John, 261
  Margaret, 261
  Mary, 261
  Sarah, 261
Sparks,
  Benjamin, 227, 244, 361
  Deborah, 542
  Jane, 227, 244
  Lambert, 542
Spear (Speer, Sphear),
  Ann, 428
  Elizabeth, 179, 232
  Hugh, 272, 278
  John, 179, 232, 448
  Margaret, 420
  Robert, 428
  Samuel, 420, 448
Spearman, Elizabeth, 469
Spence,
  James, 278, 279
  John, 262, 278, 532
  Martha, 532
  Mary, 262, 279, 532
  Patrick, 532
  Pierce, 532
  Sarah, 532
Spencer,
  Azail, 230, 466
  Benjamin, 189
  Elizabeth, 189, 322
  George, 302
  Henry, 17
  Isaiah, 474
  John, 466, 487
  Joseph, 41
  Lydia, 412
  Mary, 41, 230, 474
  Mary Ann, 525
  Nancy, 487
  Noah, 504
  Persy, 321
  Sally, 525
  Samuel, 41, 71
  Sarah, 41
  William, 101, 322, 353

Spicer, Abraham, 63
Sprague, Paul, 450, 459
Spring,,
  Jesper, 195
  Mary, 128, 195
Spruance,
  Daniel, 396
  Hannah, 257
  Henry, 395, 537
  Jean, 355
  Jemima, 396
  John, 110, 135, 173, 180, 257, 355, 396, 449
  Lydia, 443
  Mary, 110, 396, 443
  Presley, 339, 396, 441
  Presley II, 537
  Rebecca, 537, 553
  William, 396
Spry,
  John, 215
  Joseph, 215
Srowders (Srowder),
  John, 340, 408
  Margaret, 340
Staats, Samuel, 470
Stacie,
  Jane, 19
  Susanna, 19
Stafford,
  Ann, 397
  Elijah, 397, 422
  Elisha, 182
  John, 387
  Joseph, 100
  Mary, 182
  Neomi, 387
  Rachel, 281
  Sarah, 281
Stagge,
  Bedfordberry, 14
  John, 14
  Martha, 14
Standley (Standly),
  . . ., 500
  Elizabeth, 500
  Henrietia, 344
  Jonas, 545
  Joseph, 289
  Nancy, 479
  Richard, 433
  William, 344
Standford, William, 296
Stanley,
  Ann, 370
  Christopher, 15
  John, 15

Stant,
  Charles, 504
  Easter, 477
  Elizabeth, 477
  Goldsberry, 549
  James, 539
  Joseph, 504
  Margaret, 539
  Thomas, 549
  Zadok, 549
Stanton,
  Benson, 323
  Elenor, 75
  Elizabeth, 144, 241
  Jane, 75
  John, 75, 218
  Jonathan, 75, 241
  Mary, 218, 241
  Mathais, 241, 282
  Priscilla, 429
  Sara, 241
  Stephen, 144, 318
  Whittington, 75
  William, 75
Stapleford,
  Bruff, 514
  John, 514
  Robert, 514
  Sarah, 514
  William, 514
Stark,
  Philip, 399, 514
  Susanna, 399, 514
Starker, Andrew, 11
Starkey,
  Ann, 25
  Edward, 23, 25
  Elizabeth, 25
  John, 25
  Mary, 25
  Rebecca, 25
  William, 23, 25, 27
Starling,
  James, 257, 282, 390, 453, 481
  John, 390, 417, 453, 457, 481
  Mary, 453, 481
  Rebecca, 453, 481, 495
Starr,
  Mary, 385, 435
  Samuel, 346, 365, 385, 423
Start,
  Benjamin, 285
  Elijah, 238, 479, 533
  Elisha, 479
  Elizabeth, 479
  Esther, 191, 238
  James, 141, 238, 479, 533
  Jerusha, 238, 479
  Joseph, 238
  Lurania, 141, 238
  Martha, 285
  Mary, 479, 533
Staton (Staten, Stayton),
  Hilla Druman, 495
  Hillard, 460
  Jehu, 235, 272
  Mary, 272
  Nehemiah, 272
Stedham,
  Ann, 491, 507
  Charles, 491, 507
  Emory, 491, 507
  George, 491, 507
  Mary, 507
  Polly, 491
  Thomas, 491, 507, 531
Steel (Steele, Steell),
  ..., 329
  Arthur, 34, 189
  Chen, 69
  Elizabeth, 94
  Esther, 189
  Frances, 30, 34
  Francis, 33
  Hanah, 94
  Henry, 94, 216, 246
  James, 33, 34, 35, 45, 62, 63, 93, 94, 175
  Joseph, 357
  Martha, 93, 96
  Mary, 153, 206, 207, 216, 247, 329, 357
  Matthew, 104, 131
  Nancy, 531
  Rebecca, 72, 93, 94, 175
  Ruth, 45
  Thomas, 64
  William, 30, 33, 34
Steelman,
  John, 295
  Susanah, 209
Steen,
  James, 400, 408, 531
  Rosamond, 408
Stenton, Jonathan, 75
Sterling,
  James, 142, 324
  John, 402
  Mary, 142
  Sarah, 402
Stevens (Stephens, Stevans),
  Ann, 332
  Catherine, 16, 70
  Daniel, 105, 113, 121, 504
  Edmondson, 20
  Elizabeth, 20, 52, 70, 105, 283

Elizabeth Durborow, 429
Francis, 237
George, 185, 305, 309, 511
Hannah, 105
Henry, 16, 100, 105, 195, 231, 239, 260, 331, 332, 413
James, 113, 207, 288
John, 35, 52, 70, 82, 128, 237, 241, 429, 472, 504, 511
Keziah, 52
Letitia, 113, 121
Mary, 105, 113, 226, 429, 504
Mary Ann, 70
Nathan, 332, 338
Polly, 472
Sarah, 309
Susannah, 413
William, 511

Stevenson (Stephenson),
Agnes, 117
Elizabeth, 298
George, 138, 499
Henry, 31
James, 362, 490
Philip May, 373
Robert, 117, 127

Steward (Stuard, Stuerd),
Ann, 172
Catharine, 314
Charles, 297
Feby, 551
Henry, 297
Hugh, 249
James, 318, 517
Jane, 297
John, 172, 215, 248, 297, 349
Mary, 297, 318
Moses, 215
Sarah, 297, 472
Tamer, 248
Thomas, 225, 296, 472

Stewart (see also Stuart),
Ann Wlilam, 401
Catherine, 407
Charles, 85, 378, 401, 480
Jean, 381
James, 275, 318
John, 157, 238, 378, 394, 480, 491, 495, 542, 553
Mary, 189, 324
Moses, 401
Rachel, 275, 401
Ruth, 495
Thomas, 297
William, 480

Stiles (Styles),
John, 42, 148, 153
Martha, 148
Mary, 153

Stinson,
Jane, 180
Jean, 180
John, 320, 366

Stogdell, Elizabeth, 97

Stokely,
Benjamin, 337
Susanah, 337

Stone,
Basil, 16
Catherine, 16, 117
Hugh, 132
James, 117

Stoops,
James, 541
Sarah, 402
Susan H., 541

Story (Storey),
Ann, 346
Francis, 274
James, 144
Marmaduke, 346, 348
Mary, 144
Nancy, 335, 348
Penelope, 213, 241
Peter, 213
Ruth, 274
Thomas Cortly, 335

Stout,
Benjamin, 94, 324, 327, 336, 490, 531, 539
Comfort, 130
Elizabeth, 94
Emanuel, 156, 199
Immanuel, 170, 184, 260, 265, 277, 320, 330
Jacob, 130, 149, 180, 191, 217, 256, 277, 300, 302, 308, 309, 323, 325, 340, 392, 495, 517
Jacob, Jr., 330, 395, 481, 556
Jacob, Sr., 490
James, 539
Margaret, 184, 199, 320, 330, 539
Peter, 146, 156, 212, 281, 549
Rebecca, 146, 212
Thomas, 495, 539

Stow,
John, 354
Sarah, 354

Stradley (Stradly),
Absolum, 484, 515, 538
Absalom, Jr., 459
Anne, 515
Caleb, 515, 538
Darcus, 515
Dill, 314
Dorah, 501

Edward, 232
Elizabeth, 548
Isaiah, 434, 437
John, 230
Lucretia, 403
Margaret, 515, 538
Major, 369
Nanry, 232
Paris, 464
Rebecca, 314, 464
Samuel, 403
Sarah, 267, 434
Theadore, 538, 548
Thomas, 315, 434
Zadock, 434
Zebulon, 515

Stradlin,
  John, 180
  Pearis, 369
Stratton (Stratten),
  Isaac, 293, 323, 417
  Jacob, 214, 293
  Thomas, 13, 14, 214, 534
Straughen (Strawhen),
  David, 15
  El., 15
  Elizabeth, 50
Streep,
  Rachel, 255
  William, 255
Street, Hannah, 482
Strictland (Strictland),
  Catharing, 55
  Katherine, 59
  Rachel, 123, 154, 248
  William, 55, 123, 154
Strong,
  Benjamin, 390
  Samuel, 50, 521
Struthers, Margaret, 408
Stuard: see Steward
Stuart (see also Stewart),
  Alexander, 270
  Andrew, 249
  Ann, 270
  Cartherine, 196, 344
  Charles, 196, 271, 327, 344, 381, 536
  Daniel, 270, 347
  Elener, 270
  Elias, 270, 284
  George, 520
  George, Jr., 555
  Henry, 327
  Hugh, 249
  James, 413, 536, 548
  Jane, 548

Jean, 381
John, 270, 333, 336, 378, 394, 441, 495
Katharine, 271
Magdalen, 499, 520
Mary, 248, 270, 333, 338, 536
Moses, 249, 270
Rachel, 270, 347
Samuel, 344
Sarah, 248, 270, 327, 333
Solomon, 333
Tabitha, 327
Thomas, 333, 381, 536
William, 270

Studers, Marget, 415
Studham, John, 280
Sturgen, Lydia, 166
Sturgis (Sturgess),
  Elizabeth, 42
  John, 53
  Jonathan, 39, 42, 108
  Mary, 149
  Sarah, 343, 392
  Stokley, 73, 108, 129, 149, 150, 173, 184, 205, 254, 343, 392
Styles: see Stiles
Sudrey, John, 164
Suitter, Hugh, 302
Sullivan (Sullyvan),
  Cornelius, 46, 51
  David, 326, 352
  Elizabeth, 326
  Margery, 51
  Mary, 96, 326, 455, 509
  Rachel, 399
  Ruth, 96
  William, 51, 167, 326, 399
Summers (Sumers),
  Bety, 250
  David, 250
  Elizabeth, 99, 313
  James, 250, 315
  John, 135, 233, 250
  Joseph, 135
  Major, 313
  Mary, 233, 250
  Nanney, 250
  Nathan, 250
  Nathaniel, 250, 369, 410, 512
  Nicy, 250
  Polly, 502
  Rachel, 315
  Rosanna, 135, 143
  Sarah, 250
  Sely, 250
  Thomas, 99, 135, 143, 250
  William, 135, 313
  Zael, 502

Sumption, Anthony, 51
Sundergill,
  Ann, 308
  Joshua, 246, 308
  Lambert, 372
  Mary, 308, 372
  Phebe, 308
  Phillip, 246
Sunders, Jacob, 434
Surency, Ann, 276
Sutter (Sutor), Hugh, 214, 297
Sutton (Sutten),
  Ann, 413
  Catherine, 413
  Edward, 413
  Elizabeth, 481
  James, 413, 481
  John, 305
  William, 413
Swails, Elizabeth, 192
Swallow (Swallo),
  Dorothy, 109, 113
  George, 142, 236
  Johana, 142
  John, 142, 263, 380
  Joshua, 113
  Sarah, 380
  Silvanus, 142, 236, 285
Swan,
  Edwd., 523
  Elizabeth, 32
  May, 523
  Priscilla, 523
  Richard, 32
Swancey,
  Barbara, 166
  John, 149
Sweany, Timothy, 428
Swells, Elizabeth, 188
Swift,
  Elizabeth, 97
  Emanuel, 97
  John, 97
  Mary, 97
  Neomy, 97
  Richard, 97
  Sarah, 303
  Thomas, 97
  William, 97
Syddle, James, 135
Sykes,
  Agnes, 257, 325, 454
  Ann, 454
  George, 454
  Harriott, 454

  James, 184, 185, 204, 236, 257, 280, 288, 293, 306, 325, 333, 454, 460, 473, 482, 516, 525, 558
  Dr. James, 434, 447, 553
  James, Esq., 220, 543
  James, Jr., 399
  Lucy Matilda, 454
  Nathaniel, 454
  Stephen, 220, 389, 454
Sylavan: see Silliven
Sylvester: see Silvester

—T—

Tabor, Joseph, 44
Taggart (Taggert, Tagart, Tygart),
  James, 267, 399, 400
  Joseph, 469
  Lydia, 462, 472, 557
  Sarah, 399
  Thomas, 154
Talbert, Elizabeth, 169
Talbot (Talbott, Talbutt),
  Hugh, 175
  Jno., 71
  John, 102, 154
  Sarah, 358, 476
  Susannah, 147
Talfray, Wm., 72
Talley, William, 536
Tanner, Christian, 153
Tanney,
  Jacob, 346
  Lewis, 346
Tarr, Azariah, 439
Tarrant (Tarrent),
  Ann, 84
  Mamlove, 89, 182
  Mary, 89
  Susannah, 55, 89
  Thomas, 55, 70, 71, 81, 84, 89
Tatman, Silvester, 442
Tatnall, Joseph, Jr., 536
Taught,
  Caesar, 550
  Elizabeth, 550
Taylor (Taylar, Tayler),
  Abraham, 30, 470
  Alice, 470
  Amelia, 543
  Ann, 197, 506
  Benjamin, 446, 470, 487
  Caleb, 328
  Chana, 549
  Charles, 470

Elizabeth, 125, 183, 470, 487, 508, 528, 549
Esther, 227, 404, 506
Francis, 43, 281, 282, 508
George, 549
Halburt, 151
Henry, 501
Isaac, 513
James, 59, 125, 272,
Jenifer, 425, 454
John, 118, 151, 298, 355, 388, 470, 487, 549
John, Jr., 151, 549
John, Sr., 151, 549
Joseph, 327, 429, 446, 447, 470
Keziah, 487
Leurenah, 501
Lida, 549
Lydia, 513
Major, 330, 349, 501, 549
Margaret, 373, 470, 501
Mary, 295, 470, 473
Matthew, 125
Nancy, 298, 487, 499
Nathaniel, 543
Peter, 519, 549
Rachel, 151, 519
Richard, 470, 519
Robert, 549
Ruben, 197
Samuel, 470
Sarah, 257, 384, 470, 549
Stace, 549
Susannah, 49
Thomas, 36, 43, 49, 151, 446, 478, 501
William, 118, 151, 388, 447 490, 549

Teague,
  Sarah, 328
  Selby, 336
  Silba, 328

Teat,
  Neoma, 418
  Rhoda, 303
  Robert, 154, 180, 204, 303

Temple (Tempel),
  Anne, 472
  George, 472
  Joshua, 507, 531, 541

Templeman,
  Abigal, 450
  Elizabeth, 356
  Henry, 356

Templin, Isaac, 486

Tennant, Moses, 489

Teppins (Tippen, Tepen),
  Ann, 173
  Elizabeth, 518
  John, 518
  Lidea, 173
  Nancy, 518
  Richard, 173
  Sarah, 173
  Thomas, 173, 518

Tharp,
  Aron, 364
  Daniel, 364, 399
  David, 287, 364, 399
  Isaac, 287, 364, 399
  Isaac, Sr., 364
  James, 364
  Jeremiah, 364
  John, 287, 364
  Joseph, 364
  Nancy, 287, 364
  Peggy, 287
  Precillar, 93
  Rachel, 399
  Ruth, 210
  Sarah, 364
  William, 250, 537

Tharpthorn, Ruth, 263

Thistlewood (Thiselwood),
  Anne, 98
  Garthry, 70
  James, 510
  Magdalon, 52
  Unify, 111
  William, 70

Thomas,
  Agibal, 111
  Anna, 527
  Benjamin, 319, 533
  Daniel, 126, 251, 257, 394, 486, 512, 535
  David, 65
  Deborah, 252
  Edward, 344
  Eleanor, 65, 78, 303
  Elizabeth, 251, 257
  Evan, 395, 442
  George, 232
  Grace, 126
  Griffith, 138
  Hannah, 84, 95, 111
  James, 111, 512
  John, 50, 79, 111, 232, 475, 535
  Jonathan, 319
  Margarett, 265
  Mary, 452
  Mary Ann, 512
  Miriam, 535
  Moses, 533

Philip, 535
Rebecca, 424, 530
Ruth, 111
Sarah, 111, 203, 394, 434, 486
Solomon, 65, 78
Susannah, 535
Thomas, 84, 92, 95, 111, 332
Unity, 535
Wesley, 535
William, 17, 111, 243, 332, 424, 454, 502, 535

Thompson (Thomson, Tompson, Tomson),
. . ., 416
Abraham, 353
Alice, 22
Cary, 431
Celia, 208
Elizabeth, 208, 276, 353, 540, 547
Esther, 208
Ezekial, 99, 127
Hanah, 347
Jacob, 440
James, 94, 109, 274, 295, 353, 540, 555
James, Jr., 353
James, Sr., 353
Jeffery, 15, 175
Jethro, 62, 109, 171, 534
John, 70, 109, 127, 129, 171, 193, 205, 208, 271, 347, 398, 464
Jonathan, 208
Joseph, 109, 144, 175, 229
Liddiah, 431, 432
Martha, 194
Mary, 18, 21, 257, 319, 332, 353, 406, 416, 534, 547
Moses, 194, 293, 459
Moses, Jr., 501
Phebe, 540
Polly, 547
Rachel, 175, 271, 272, 308, 440
Robert, 109, 171, 276, 398, 547
Ruth, 93, 205, 274
Sarah, 320, 360, 540, 541
Sylvester, 132, 184, 208
Susannah, 129, 540
Thomas, 134, 353, 540
Urbanus, 21
Walter, 22
William, 18, 79, 108, 262, 320, 360, 396, 458, 480
William, Jr., 395

Thorel, Mary, 67

Thorne (Thorn),
Betty, 463
Robert, 463
Sydenham, 338, 463

Thornton,
Cathrine, 191
David, 287
Hannah, 287

Thorpe (Thorp),
Hannah, 68
Mark, 68, 123
Samuel, 68

Thorrold (Thorold),
Mary, 28
Timothy, 16, 28

Thrawley, Edward, 451

Throp,
Abigail, 123, 139
Ann, 76, 123
Elizabeth, 123
Hanna, 123
Mark, 123
Samuel, 76, 123, 139

Tibbit,
Mary, 400
Samuel, 400

Tigner, James, 402

Tilghman, Edward, Jr., 267, 361, 410

Tilton,
. . ., 92
Abraham, 416, 531
Ann, 64, 156
Comfort, 130, 139
Elizabeth, 112
James, 253, 265, 281, 307, 365, 366, 385, 416, 450, 470, 531
Dr. James, 416
James, Jr., 490
John, 37, 43, 49, 50, 58, 64, 66, 72, 86, 93, 94, 96, 112, 130, 229, 307
John, Jr., 50, 72, 94, 130
Joseph, 50, 156
Lydia, 416
Mary, 37, 50
Nehemiah, 338, 339, 383, 416
Rachel, 156, 307, 416
Sabrah, 253, 307, 416, 531
Sarah, 156, 224, 307
Thomas, 156, 207, 253, 259, 298, 307, 310, 320, 384, 416, 531

Timmans,
George, 368
Jesse, 368

Tims,
Absolem, 116
Jane, 116

Tinch,
Mary, 326
Samuel, 326, 455

Tindall (Tyndle),
  Elizabeth, 530, 545
  Hannah, 530, 535
  Isaac, 535, 545
  Jesse, 530, 535, 545
  John, 530, 535, 540
  Purnell, 530, 535, 545
  William, 140
Tingle,
  Clowde, 14
  Johana, 14
  John, 14
Tippen: see Teppins
Tippitt, Samuel, 460
Tire,
  James, 38
  Susannah, 66
  Thomas, 66
Toas, Daniel, 38
Tobias,
  Mary, 24, 30
  Tunis, 30
Tobin,
  Cornelius, 176
  Richard, 205
Tolan, Rebecca, 192
Tolly, Mary, 188
Toltwood,
  Elizabeth, 14
  Grace, 14
  Henry, 14
  Jane, 14
  John, 14
Tom,
  Samuel, 161
  William, 161
Tomblin (Tomlin, Tomelin): see Tumblin
Tomlinson (Tomblinson, Tomlenson, Tumlinson),
  Auston, 520
  Betsy, 520
  Cary, 181, 301, 344, 362, 499
  Carry, 306
  Ed., 481
  Elizabeth, 520, 542
  James, 181, 306, 344, 377, 480
  John, 306, 520
  Joseph, 306, 377, 385, 480
  Lewes, 520, 547
  Mary, 306, 344
  Ostend, 542
  Polly, 520, 547
  Rhoda, 181
  Richard, 306, 520
  Sally, 520
  Samuel, 46
  Sarah, 377, 385, 480
  Sophia, 250, 344, 520
  Thomas, 306, 377, 424, 480, 520, 529
  William, 377, 480
Tomson (Tompson): see Thompson
Tong, William, 25
Toogood, James, 204
Tool,
  Charles, 192
  Hannah, 192
Torbert (Torbet),
  Hugh, 166, 187, 405, 448
  Isaac, 448
  Jane, 187, 242, 330
  John, 187, 200, 265, 330, 405
  Margarett, 187
  Peter, 187, 265, 309, 330
  Rachel, 405, 448
  Simon, 187, 265
  Susannah, 187
  William, 330
Town, Elizabeth, 441
Townsend (Townshend, Towsen, Townsin, Tounzend),
  Alce, 437
  Andrew, 178
  Ann, 373, 375, 467
  Ann R., 467
  Ansley, 269
  Brickhus, 472
  Charles, 85, 100, 269, 467, 483
  Ebe, 472
  Eli, 472
  Elias, 280
  Elizabeth, 265, 269, 467, 530
  Epheraim, 269
  Gabriel, 178
  James, 347, 355, 373, 375
  Jeremiah, 472
  John, 31, 59, 79, 85, 100, 105, 328
  Lydia, 59
  Magdalene, 105
  Mary, 85, 87, 100, 269, 364, 542
  Meriam, 269
  Nancy, 472
  Rachel, 269
  Sally, 504
  Sarah, 269, 472
  Stephen, 504, 542
  Solomon, 265, 269, 364, 530
  William, 269, 431, 472, 483
Toy, John, 219
Trail,
  James, 81, 86, 100, 101, 157, 159, 211, 235, 403

Rachel, 100
Train,
  Alice, 235
  Bersheba, 159
  Easter, 159, 234
  Esther, 218, 234
  Hamilton, 81, 159, 211, 235
  Lydia, 403, 532
  Mary, 81, 119, 159
  Rebecca, 157
  Roger, 81
  Sarah, 81
  Timothy, 430
Trapnell, John, 61
Travels, John, 115
Travers,
  Matthew, 475
  Peggy, 475
Treasurers, Richard, 368
Treppet (Treppett): see Trippet
Trewax: see Truax
Trigar (Triger, Trigger),
  Hannah, 212, 287, 293
  James, 287
  Zebedee, 212, 287
Trippet (Trippit, Treppet),
  Alce, 426
  Alice, 297
  Ann, 197
  Caleb, 286
  Daniel, 197
  Elizabeth, 426
  Ellse, 82.
  Gove, 82, 140, 188, 297, 426
  John, 82, 106, 188, 297, 319
  Jonathan, 297
  Mary, 286, 297
  Nancy, 426
  Prinelopey, 82
  Rachael, 297
  Rebeccah, 538
  Ruth, 320
  Sarah, 82, 188
  Waitman, 82, 161, 188, 426
  William, 32, 71, 88, 103, 188, 320, 321, 426
Trood, Henry, 44
Truax (Trewax),
  Benjamin, 399
  Catharine, 399
  Elizabeth, 542
  Henry, 183, 509
  Hennery H., 542
  Isack, 542
  John, 430
  Margaret, 430

Rebecca, 154
Sarah, 183, 542
Susannah, 529
William, 291, 329, 351
Truitt (Truett, Truit),
  Boaz, 413
  Elizabeth, 338
  George, 420, 428, 431, 438, 441, 443, 444, 445, 465, 467, 534, 550
  Henry, 105
  Hezekiah, 215
  Jemima, 343
  John, 343
  Joseph, 463
  Keys, 105
  Martha, 431, 432
  Rebecca, 519
  Susannah, 215
  Southern, 552
  William, 337, 431, 432
  Zadock, 519
Tryall (Trial),
  John, 364
  Mary, 61
Tubman,
  Aninias, 528
  Ann, 528
  Elizabeth, 528
  Jereboam, 528
  John, 528
  Susannah, 528
  Sylvenus, 528
Tucker,
  Barsehba, 366
  Caleb, 268
  Elizabeth, 268
  Jessey, 215
  John, 187, 215, 391, 554
  John, Jr., 163, 164
  Levy, 357
  Zadock, 357
Tufft, Thomas, 219
Tuilly, Robert, 41
Tully, Sarah, 403
Tumbleston, Sarah, 211
Tumblin (Tomblin, Tomlin, Tumlin),
  Alexander, 85, 100
  Anney, 523
  Celah, 288
  Covel, 164, 255, 391
  Elizabeth, 523
  Ephraim, 68
  Hannah, 116
  Isaac, 164
  Jacob, 164

John, 42, 48, 288, 301, 304, 330, 391, 451, 538
Joseph, 116, 204
Judah, 68
Leah, 391
Leare, 523
Levin, 391
Margaret, 164
Martha, 538
Mary, 164, 304, 330, 409, 451
Nathaniel, 61, 164
Neomy, 164
Ruth, 391, 541
Sarah, 391, 523, 526
Saraṯ, 391
Selah, 301, 330
Susannah, 116

Tunissen,
  Mary, 21
  Tobias, 21

Turly (Turley),
  James, 415, 445
  Jerusha, 415, 445
  Mary, 301, 415
  Richard, 342, 415, 445
  Sarah, 342, 415
  William, 131, 415, 445

Turner,
  Beavens, 249
  Benjamin, 467, 519
  Charles, 519
  Elias, 249, 432, 467
  George, 467, 527
  Henry, 249
  Isaac, 131
  Jean Huet, 467
  Jehu, 249, 302, 467, 519
  Jesse, 467, 519
  John, 68, 69, 187, 490
  Joyce, 249
  Lear, 249
  Levicy, 467
  Levin, 467
  Martha, 182
  Martin, 218, 418
  Mary, 218, 432
  Phebe, 131
  Polly, 467
  Rachel, 191, 490
  Reuben, 519
  Richard, 25
  Samuel, 249, 467
  Samuel Bevans, 177, 467
  Sarah, 249
  Tilmon, 519
  Unicy, 519
  William, 519

Turpen, Rachel, 380

Tuthill (Tuthell),
  Charles, 65, 76, 84, 89, 92
  Mary, 84, 92
Twillen, Joshua, 89
Twogood: see Toogood
Tybout,
  . . ., 58
  James, 98, 110, 174
  Rachel, 98, 110, 111, 259
Tygart: see Taggart
Tyler, Mary, 32
Tyndle: see Tindall

—U—

Underhay,
  Heneritha, 186, 216
  Jacob, 186
Underling, Elizabeth, 237
Underwood,
  Abraham, 175, 269
  John, 269
  Joshua, 141, 175, 269, 387
  Mary, 175, 269
  Priscilla, 274
  Richard, 175, 218, 269, 274
  Richard, Jr., 175
  Richard, Sr., 175
  Sarah, 141
Upprithart, Henry, 151
Uptegrove (Updegrove, Upthegrove, Uptigrave, Uptgrove),
  Debarah, 30
  Elizabeth, 166
  Herman, 30
  Isaac, 54, 67
  John, 166, 267
  Joseph, 119, 124
  Mary, 166
  Rachel, 119, 124
  Sarah, 166, 267
  William, 124, 166
Upton,
  Elizabeth, 156
  George, 392
  George, Jr., 300
  Moses, 156
  Sarah, 156, 225
Ussher,
  Arthur, 83, 84, 89
  Rev. Arthur, 84
  Hannah, 182
  John, 182
  Mary, 182

—V—

Van Burkelo (Vanburcaloe),
  Elizabeth, 127
  Herman, 99
  John, 342
  Margaret, 157
  Mary, 445
  Peter, 342, 366
  Samuel, 461
  Sarah, 508
Vanbuskirk,
  John, 115
  Lawrence, 115
Vance,
  Alexander, 85
  Charles, 85
  Elizabeth, 85
  George, 85
  James, 85
  Mary, 85
  Patrick, 85
Vanderford (Vandeford),
  Charles, 226
  Elinor, 116
  Elizabeth, 200, 247
  George, 116
  Jane, 116
  John, 200, 247, 304
  Mary, 116, 203
  Matthew, 271
  Thomas, 116, 226
  Unity, 271
  Vinsant, 239
Vandervour (Vanderver),
  Elinor, 183
  Elizabeth, 393, 512
  Esther, 183
  George, 183
  Grace, 325
  Hollingworth, 183
  John, 183, 393
  Mathew, 183, 271
  Rachel, 183
  Thomas, 417, 512
  Unity, 271
Vandyke (Vandike),
  Andrew, 149
  Ann, 250
  Daniel, 250, 302
  Elizabeth, 250, 324
  James, 250, 290, 293, 302, 306, 341, 407
  John, 149, 407
  John, Jr., 149
  Nancy, 324
  Nicholas, 407, 478
  Rebecca, 407
  Sarah, 290, 401, 407
  Thomas, 250, 407
  William, 369
Vangasco,
  John, 36, 50, 100
  Susannah, 36
Vangaskin (Vangasken),
  John, 163, 229
  John, Jr., 253, 303, 328
  John, Sr., 303, 354
  Sarah, 303, 355
Van Hazel,
  John, 345
  Stacy, 345
Vanhorne, Mary, 97
Vanhoy (Vannoy),
  Abraham, 47, 127, 295, 334, 343
  Abraham, Jr., 402
  Ann, 380
  John, 305, 380, 422
  Sarah, 402
  Susanna, 127
Vanloden,
  John, 456, 461
  Lydia, 461
  Sarah, 461
  Thomas, 461
Vannay, Christian, 40
Vannette (Vennetta, Vanatta),
  Benjamin, 418
  Elenor, 179, 520
  Elizabeth, 168
  James, 168
  Ruth, 419, 423
  Samuel, 180, 520
  Thomas, 418, 423, 442, 520
Vanpelt,
  . . ., 499
  Elizabeth, 387, 472, 499, 544
  George, 387, 472, 554
  James, 554
  Jesse, 554
  John, 554
  Joseph, 368, 377, 387, 472, 554
Vansant,
  Jean, 490
  Margaret, 500
  William, 500
Vanstavern (Vanstavoren),
  Ann, 469
  Cornelius, 437, 469, 535
  Hester, 385
  Nicholas, 469
  Sarah, 324, 460
  Thomas, 469
  William, 324, 460, 469

[123]

Van Winkle,
  Ann, 329
  Benjamin, 329
  Gean, 163
  Jacob, 141, 147, 308, 329
  Jane, 36, 50, 147
  John, 147, 163, 329
  Jonas, 329, 501
  Lurania, 159, 163, 170
  Mary, 265, 278, 308, 329
  Rebecca, 199
  Simon, 36, 50, 142, 159, 147, 163, 170, 199, 329, 381, 467, 469
  Susannah, 147, 329
  William, 329
Vanwye, Jacob, 123
Varnan, Mary, 276
Vaughan (Vaughn),
  Catherine, 35
  Elizabeth, 46
  James, 95
  Joseph, 209
Vaulx,
  Delilah, 373
  William, 373
Veech, John, 178
Venables,
  Catherine, 232
  Elener, 232
  Martha, 232
  Mary, 232
  Purkins, 232
Vennetta: see Vannette
Venoi,
  Abraham, 529
  John, 519
  Rachel, 529
  Sarah, 519
Verden: see Virden
Vessey,
  John, 37
  Robert, 37
  Solomon, 37, 48, 54
Viccory (Vickery),
  Elizabeth, 265, 483, 484, 486
  Ezekiah, 265, 484
  Hezekiah, 384
  John, 265, 483, 484, 486, 504
  Liddia, 265
  Mary, 265, 384, 519
  Solomon, 519
  Thomas, 265, 396, 483, 486, 519
  Waitman, 265, 519
  Walter, 265, 271
Vickers, Minta, 404, 433, 548
Vigor, William, 115

Vincent,
  Barsheba, 495
  Cornelia, 471
  Daniel, 471
  Elizabeth, 538
  Isaac, 471, 495
  James, 495, 497
  Jethro, 538
  Margaret, 471
  Mary, 495
Vining,
  Benjamin, 155, 159, 254, 354, 372, 374
  Elizabeth, 374, 439, 451
  John, 147, 155, 170, 220, 225, 254, 374, 436, 485
  Maria, 510
  Mary, 156, 159, 220, 254, 374
  Nicholas, 155, 159, 254, 343, 374, 396
  Phebe, 220, 254, 374
Vinn, Elizabeth, 520
Vinson,
  Bathsheba, 495
  Eliab, 260, 322, 348, 495, 497
  Elizabeth, 348
  Esther, 208
  Jesse, 208
  Jethro, 544
  Richard, 164
Vinstreet, Hannah, 543
Virden (Verden, Virdin),
  Absolom, 241, 249, 284, 320, 379, 381
  Alexander, 304, 389
  Andrew, 500
  Cynthea, 320, 518
  Daniel, 241, 244, 249, 284, 304, 379, 381, 389, 450
  Ealce, 241
  Eleanor, 241, 304, 381, 389
  Isaac, 241, 379, 381
  John, 141, 241, 365, 379, 381, 427, 450, 500
  John, Sr., 241
  Mary, 450
  Matthew, 450
  Neomah, 304
  Peter, 450, 468
  Prudence, 400, 450
  Samuel, 468
  Sarah, 141, 249, 284, 304, 320, 500
  William, 241, 268, 320, 379, 381, 400, 408, 413, 427, 450
Virgin, John, 498
Volks, Selea, 385

Voshall,
  Augustain, 193
  Daniel, 508
  Elizabeth, 169, 319
  Hannah, 508
  James, 439, 508
  John, 169, 319
  John, Jr., 391
  Joseph, 319
  Levi, 325
  Nancy, 508
  Obediah, 319, 361, 439, 508
  Obediah, Sr., 319
  Owen, 508
  Peter, 68
  Sarah, 391
  Susannah, 68, 73
  Titus, 508
  William, 325

—W—

Wacob: see Wakup
Waddle, Thomas, 16
Wade,
  Elizabeth, 509
  John, 122, 125
  Mary, 125
  Sarah, 98
  William, 509
Wainwright,
  Jane, 322
  Levin, 304, 322
Waite, Capt. Joseph, 127
Wakeman, James, 454
Wakup (Wacob), Sarah, 87
Walker,
  Agnes, 110, 240, 346
  Ailse, 294
  Ann, 12, 141, 208, 268, 271, 381
  Daniel, 28, 493
  Elizabeth, 268
  Isabella, 155
  Jane, 141
  Jean, 141
  John, 12, 17, 23, 25, 28, 30, 74, 112, 117, 131, 141, 208, 222, 260, 268, 294, 312, 436, 443, 461
  Margret, 30
  Mary, 28, 51, 54, 131, 133, 134, 141, 155, 294, 452, 493
  Nancy, 349
  Nancy Ann, 376
  Persilla, 222, 243
  Philip, 127
  Richard, 12, 51
  Robert, 133, 141, 376
  Samuel, 134, 141
  Susanna, 294, 312
  William, 80, 112, 155, 212, 240, 268, 294, 480
Wallace,
  Aramenta, 202, 251, 371
  Barbara, 145, 162
  Barsheba, 202
  Bathsheba, 497
  Benjamin, 145, 162, 207, 234, 262, 341, 519, 537
  Betsey, 456, 464
  Carbine, 537, 543
  Catherine, 213, 231
  David, 145, 202, 251, 323, 366, 403, 426, 458
  Elizabeth, 143, 202, 331, 419, 453, 458, 470
  Frances, 426
  George, 301
  Hannah, 322, 323
  James, 224, 470, 492, 518, 537, 543
  Jenet, 202, 251
  John, 365
  Jonathan, 312, 371, 420
  Joseph, 365, 426
  Joshua, 145, 162, 165, 213, 265
  Josiah, 145, 162, 207, 456, 466
  Josias, 464
  Margaret, 169, 213, 265, 312, 537
  Martha, 331
  Mary, 202, 337, 365, 453
  Matthew, 145, 162, 202, 251
  Rachel, 262, 331
  Reuben, 145, 162, 165, 265, 312, 348
  Rhoda, 145, 162
  Robert, 365
  Ruth, 194
  Samuel, 55, 456, 464
  Sarah, 145, 537
  Sidney, 492
  Solomon, 145, 162, 214, 265, 285, 297, 312, 323, 331, 458
  Thomas, 143, 194, 202, 251, 341, 349, 366, 382, 426
  William, 145, 162, 213, 265, 312, 322, 331, 353, 365, 419, 458
  William, Sr., 212, 231, 323
Waller, John, 123, 131
Wallis, James, 35
Walls,
  Ann, 476
  Henry, 330
  John, Milborn, 535

Walmsley,
  John, 24
  Mary, 24
Walraven, John, 242
Walsh, Lau., 179
Walston,
  John, 419
  Rachel, 522
  Rhoda, 419
  William, 522
Walters,
  Ann, 471
  William, 471
Walton,
  Amy, 378
  Anna, 257, 332, 353, 404, 405, 452
  Bagwell, 353, 393
  Beauchamp, 353, 404
  David, 393, 408, 423, 442
  Elizabeth, 74, 353, 393
  Esther, 353, 404
  George, 74, 112, 125, 209, 353, 378, 393, 423, 486, 493, 536
  Hannah, 150
  Isaac, 353, 404
  John, 17, 74, 150, 353, 393, 404
  Mary, 74
  Mirrium, 393
  Nancy, 408, 442
  Patience, 353, 404, 487
  Rachel, 353, 404, 442
  Ruth, 393
  Sarah, 353
  William, 56, 74, 125, 150, 353, 404
Walvin, John, 50
Wann (Wan), Christopher, 183, 214
Wansey,
  Freegift, 11
  Sherry, 11
Ward,
  Ann, 478, 511
  Deborah, 547
  Eleanor. 151
  Elizabeth, 246
  George, 457, 478, 479, 511
  James, 509
  John, 151, 392, 458, 509, 532
  Mary, 49
  Priscilla, 135
  Thomas, 45, 49
  William, 151, 509
Ware,
  Ann, 222, 330, 331, 436
  Betsy, 472
  David, 330
  Elizabeth, 462, 557
  John, 124, 222, 330, 462, 471, 557
  Mary, 124, 128, 557
  Nancy, 462, 472, 557
  Prescilla, 436
  William, 124, 128, 330, 331, 446, 469, 557
  William, Jr., 446
  William, Sr., 472, 557
  William the younger, 462
Warfield,
  Ann, 155, 159
  Benjamin, 159
  Elisha, 155, 159
  Joshua, 159
  Nicholas, 159
  Rebecca, 159
Warner,
  Edmond, 11
  Ichabod, 142
  Mankin, 410
  William, 417
Warren,
  Benjamin, 92, 131, 202, 212, 266, 518, 536
  Elizabeth, 266, 299
  John, 202, 391, 518, 536
  Mary, 184, 202
  Ruben, 520
  Samuel, 518, 536
  Sarah, 156
  Thomas, 141, 142,
  Zipporah, 518, 536
Warrington,
  Comfort, 283, 368
  Elizabeth, 125, 283, 368
  Esther, 283
  Jacob, 125, 140, 240, 283, 368
  Joseph, 368
  Patience, 283
  Rachel, 283, 368
  Sarah, 283
Waters (Water),
  Ann, 477
  John, 32
  Mary, 62, 67
  Thomas, 336
  William, 477
Watkins (Wattkins),
  Anne, 55, 460
  Christopher, 411, 466
  Elizabeth, 460
  James, 411, 466
  John, 82, 325
  Mary, 290, 460
  Peter, 74, 290, 347
  Rachel, 411, 466
  Robert, 305, 408, 411, 466
  Samuel, 305, 411, 466, 548
  Sarah, 269, 347, 411, 466

Thomas, 305, 411, 460, 466
William, 342, 460

Watson,
Ann, 88
Benoni, 113, 174
Elizabeth, 113
Francis, 113
Jess, 318
John, 72, 397
Margaret, 72, 160
Mary, 223
Maryam, 113
Peter, 88
Priscilla, 309
Pryor, 309
Rebacka, 113
Richard, 72
Solomon, 113
Tabitha, 72
Thomas, 160
William, 113, 167, 223, 325

Watts (Watt),
Ann, 233
James, 191
John, 233, 364
William, 332, 496

Weaver,
Elizabeth, 518
John, 518
Sarah, 518
William, 518

Webb,
Ann, 191
Caleb, 191
Daniel, 191
Elizabeth, 191, 363
Isack, 13
Jacob, 557
John, 191
Mary, 13, 156
Robert, 44
Sarah, 44, 191, 316
Thomas, 316

Webster,
Catherine, 292
Dickinson, 553
John, 292

Wegens, Henry, 336

Welber, John, 382

Welbore,
Sarah, 432
Thomas, 432

Welch (Welsh),
Rebecca, 86
Tamer, 496

Weldon,
Ann, 148
Isaac, 258
John, 258
Joseph, 148

Welley,
James, 12
Mary, 12

Wells,
Agnes, 70
Ann, 65, 375
Arthur, 524
Benjamin, 375, 519, 521, 524, 550
Benjamin, Jr., 524
Daniel, 524
David, 403, 466
Elizabeth, 197, 262
George, 65, 70
Hannah, 524
Henry, 65, 227, 330
Henry, Sr., 262
James, 42, 65, 80, 104, 336, 358, 372, 384
James, Jr., 301
James, Sr., 301, 354
John, 40, 42, 65, 72, 116, 205, 233, 390, 434
Lydia, 390
Maria, 423
Marthew, 466
Mary, 227, 330, 418, 428, 434, 466
Mary, Jr., 466
Nancy, 466
Nathaniel, 156
Patience, 65
Phebe, 116
Phebe Griffin, 100
Rachel, 42, 466, 524
Rebecca, 466, 519
Richard, 129, 156, 157, 159, 184, 195, 197, 210, 228, 403, 466
Dr. Richard, 143
Rody, 466
Sarah, 180, 231, 330, 434
Susannah, 67
Thomas, 42, 65, 228, 231
Thomas, Jr., 67
William, 32, 65, 151, 157, 178, 197, 330, 345, 423, 466, 524

Welsh: see Welch

Wesley, John, 509

West,
Ann, 265, 299
Benjamin, 276, 299, 323
David, 276, 299, 323, 446
David, Jr., 199
Elenor, 91
Elisha, 297, 333

Elizabeth, 333, 386, 424, 498, 553
Ephraim, 333
Hannerata, 323
James, 386
John, 333, 374, 386, 458
John, Jr., 333
Joseph, 276, 299, 323, 389, 446
Mary, 161, 265, 299
Nancy, 525
Rachel, 297
Rebecca, 199
Samuel, 269, 272, 276, 319, 323, 342
Sarah, 224, 265, 323
Susannah, 265
Thomas, 161, 333
William, 155, 224, 323, 386
Westbury (Westbery),
  Mary, 55
  Thomas, 55, 120
  William, 120
Weston, Thomas, 153
Wettswood, Francis, 34
Weyatt (Weyott): see Wyatt
Whaley,
  Amelia, 470
  Daniel, 543
  David, 543
  Elizabeth, 543
  Henrietta Massey, 543
  James, 543
  John, 543
  Levy, 543
  Nancy, 543
  Nathan, 543
  William, 543
Whaling, Phillip, 357, 359
Wharton,
  Ann, 341, 534
  Augustus, 216
  Elizabeth, 337, 463
  Garret, 341, 411, 417
  Grace, 341
  Isaiah, 106, 124, 139, 277, 337, 341, 395, 526
  Mary, 341
  Rixom, 106
  Sarah, 277
  Sipple, 341, 534
  Susannah, 216
  William, 463
Wheatley (Wheatly),
  Arthur, 217, 370
  Mary, 217, 518, 536
  Sarah, 380
Wheeldon,
  John, 385
  Susannah, 466

Wheeler, (Wheelar, Wheelor, Wheler),
  Alice, 344, 355
  Anne, 289
  Bednego, 270
  Elizabeth, 45, 107, 123, 253, 292, 432
  Jesse, 292
  John, 30, 45, 56, 60, 61, 413, 439, 503, 521
  Joseph, 292
  Joshua, 45, 107, 123, 223
  Kesiah, 104, 137
  Lemuel, 440, 449
  Mary, 44, 355
  Mary Ann, 123
  Miriam, 123
  Molleston, 223
  Owen, 181, 289
  Prudence, 270
  Ruth, 299, 440
  Samuel, 123, 223, 204, 253, 299
  Sarah, 123, 204, 223, 253, 355
  William, 44, 95, 158, 203, 230, 292, 344, 355
  Winlock, 123, 253
Wheelton,
  John, 238, 366, 520
  Lurana, 238
Wheler: see Wheeler
Whethered, Mary, 454
Whit, James, 28
Whitaker (Whitacre, Whiteacre),
  Anna, 48, 92
  Elizabeth, 480, 489
  Henry, 198, 480, 538
  Isaac, 300
  James, 467, 480
  Mary, 231, 252
  Mary Ann, 300
  Moses, 48
  William, 231
Whitby, Sarah, 405
White,
  Alexander, 524, 526
  Andrew, 210
  Anna, 479, 482, 488, 498, 511, 516
  Annsley, 273, 274
  Avis, 321, 471
  Baynard, 497
  Benjamin, 30, 33, 34, 51
  Charles, 479, 511
  David, 101, 120, 287, 358
  Deborah, 461
  Edward, 380, 402, 488, 497
  Edward, Jr., 397
  Elizabeth, 95, 210, 282, 339, 361, 420

Esther, 498
Francis, 60
George, 498
Gilbert, 210, 361, 437, 498, 521
Henrietta, 498
Isaac, 379, 402, 526
Isabella, 379, 402, 526
Jacob, 379, 402
James, 59, 67, 141, 160, 182, 210, 215, 250, 270, 282, 339, 361, 398
Jamima, 51
John, 243, 251, 280, 321, 339, 361, 374, 379, 436, 439, 471, 475, 497, 498, 524, 545
Judith, 280
Lydia, 474
Margaret, 133, 144, 224, 361, 488, 521
Martha, 474
Mary, 339, 361, 398, 498, 521, 524
Miriam, 531
Molly, 210
Peggy, 498
Pheby, 498
Rachel, 379
Rebecca, 309, 498,
Richard, 352, 474
Richard, the younger, 309
Robert, 115, 210, 284, 339, 361
Samuel, 111, 452, 488, 497, 510, 513, 516, 543, 556
Samuel, Jr., 488
Sarah, 115, 203, 243, 452, 498
Stephen, 374, 379, 402
Susannah, 339, 361
Thomas, 323, 363, 380, 389, 397, 474, 483, 488, 497
William, 80, 130, 203, 253, 316, 379, 401, 420, 431, 461, 474, 479, 482, 497, 511, 524, 526, 543
William, Sr., 402
Whiteacre: see Whitaker
Whitehall, William, 14
Whitehart (Whitehear, Whithart, Whiteart),
  Allen, 203, 324
  Benjamin, 62
  Elizabeth, 31, 24, 62
  Grace, 68, 201, 203, 319
  Henry, 496
  James, 31, 62, 87, 125
  Jenny, 496
  John, 31, 203
  Mary, 31, 62, 203
  Powell, 125, 200, 203
  Richard, 24, 29, 31, 56, 62, 68
  Samuel, 31, 63, 87, 103, 125, 203, 319, 341, 444
  Sarah, 87, 125, 203
  Solomon, 87, 180, 201, 203, 444
  William, 29
Whitehead,
  Isaiah, 47, 178
  Jacob, 506
  Jaramiah, 415
  Jemimah, 440
  Joseph, 129, 243
  Lemuel, 506
  Sophia, 178
Whiteheart: see Whitehart
Whitel, William, 343, 483
Whitely (Whitely),
  Alexander, 135, 322
  Arthur, 302, 317, 324, 370
  Cetty, 171
  John, 353
  Lucretia, 234
  Sarah, 397
  William, 323, 461, 475, 527
Whiteside,
  Arthur, 119
  John, 93
  Peter, 119
  William, 93
Whitham, Joshua, 56
Whithart: See Whitehart
Whitman,
  Agnes, 347
  Elizabeth, 56, 73
  Jonathan, 56, 73, 347
  Phebe, 56
  Samuel, 56, 73, 224, 347
  Savory, 347
Whittington,
  Elizabeth, 279
  John, 279
Whitwell, Francis, 11
Whyte, James, 32, 33
Wiat (Wiatt): see Wyatt
Wicks, Ebenezar, 77
Wietet, Thomas, 165
Wiggens (Wigens),
  Charles, 542
  Henry, 366
  Robert, 542
Wilcutts (Wilcut, Wilcuts, Wilcot),
  Ann, 182
  Caleb, 399, 452, 485
  Charity, 182
  Comfort, 362
  David, 383, 399, 476
  Elizabeth, 512
  George, 518

Joseph, 182, 364, 383, 399, 514
Josiah, 399, 512, 514
Josias, 182, 383
Levi, 383, 399, 514
Levin, 362, 512
Martha, 182, 383, 399, 514, 528
Mary, 399, 514
Nancy, 383, 399, 485, 514, 528
Polly, 383, 528
Rachel, 364, 383, 399, 476
Reuben, 383
Sally, 383
Sarah, 399, 514
Susannah, 383
William, 383, 399, 514, 536

Wild (Wilds),
Abraham, 359
Elizabeth, 252
Grace, 430
John, 88, 210, 372, 546, 553
Joshua, 88, 421, 430, 546
Mary, 210, 230, 359
Nathaniel, 230, 340, 354
Robert, 86, 213
Ruth, 88
Thomas, 223, 252, 375

Wiles, Nance, 247

Wilkerson,
Adam, 359
Henry, 520
James, 359
Moses, 520

Wilkins,
Mary, 81
Thomas, 360

Wilkinson (Wilkenson, Wilkison),
Aaron, 332
Anthony, 53
Esther, 430
Henry, 261, 332
Isabella, 439
James, 332
Lidia, 332
Moses, 332, 439
Naoma, 332
Rachel, 291, 332, 445
Sarah, 332
Thomas 332, 430
Thomas, Jr., 430
Thomas, Sr., 430
William, 313, 430

Willabaugh: see Willoughby

Willcocks (Willcox),
James, 94
John, 94
Joseph, 23
Mary, 94

Robert, 84, 89, 108, 125, 127, 131, 132, 135, 153, 158, 169, 195

Willey (Wiley),
Ailse, 363
Alce, 242
Gabriel, 242, 363
Levin, 242, 355, 363, 374
John, 242, 281
Polly, 468, 556
Selah, 363
William, 468
Zadock, 242

Williams,
Aaron, 108, 144, 468
Absalom, 314
Alce, 68
Amah, 453
Ann, 25, 30, 421
Aramenta, 371
Benjamin, 453
Caleb, 314
Catherine, 34
Charles, 103
Christopher, 371
David, 525
Deborah, 145, 162, 202, 262, 283
Easter, 436
Edward, 11, 50, 101, 340, 545
Eleanor, 319
Elias, 59
Elizabeth, 59, 108, 165, 191, 241, 315, 503, 541
Ezekiel, 191
George, 63, 503
Grace, 103
Griffeth, 59
Hester, 144
Isaiah, 262, 283
Jacob, 441
James, 60, 181, 227, 314, 315, 453, 482, 502, 503, 519
Jane, 71
Jean, 105
Jerusha, 203, 319
John, 60, 98, 180, 227, 240, 245, 246, 287, 288, 294, 314, 371, 453, 467, 468, 503
John, Jr., 357
John, Sr., 314
Ledey, 60
Levis, 340
Lewis, 103, 140, 340
Margaret, 314, 319, 471
Mary, 34, 41, 58, 59, 66, 99, 103, 181, 227, 246, 348, 371, 423, 453, 486
Miriam, 503
Morgan, 454, 525, 534
Nathan, 171, 423, 486

Owen, 103
Patrick, 165
Penelope, 214, 239, 313, 468
Rachel, 103, 211, 249, 314, 519
Reynear, 30, 34, 89, 90, 103, 108, 144, 163, 174, 177, 201, 214, 239, 245, 270, 287, 313, 369, 468
Richard, 19, 29, 241, 249, 448
Ruth, 340
Samuel, 56, 58
Sarah, 19, 144, 314, 326, 454
Spencer, 468
Susanna, 34, 503
Tabitha, 41, 53, 81, 246
Thomas, 70, 103, 191, 241, 246, 348, 378, 482, 506
Ward, 315, 448
William, 24, 40, 72, 355, 421, 436, 541

Williamson,
  Jacob, 282
  John, 243
  Sampson, 243

Willis,
  Dorithy, 203
  Joshua, 272

Willison, Richard, 29

Willoughby (Willoby, Willabaugh),
  Ann, 414
  Asa, 491, 539, 557
  Eleanor, 412
  Job, 491
  John, 557
  Kitty, 533
  Samuel, 493, 517
  Sarah, 502
  Solomon, 414

Wills,
  Ann, 401, 465
  Hugh, 134, 151
  John, 151
  Mary, 134

Willson: see Wilson

Willy: see Willey

Wilmore (Wilmoore),
  Lambert, 135
  Martha, 135
  Mary, 175
  Thomas, 175

Wilson (Willson),
  Abel, 13, 26
  Abigail, 164
  Agnes, 44, 53
  Alice, 23
  Allen, 323
  Ann, 23, 26, 27, 65, 109, 164, 171, 247, 320, 332, 394, 405

Caesar Rodney, 361, 395
David, 226, 453
Derdin, 166, 184
Ebenezer, 331
Eleanor, 451
Elizabeth, 13, 23, 30, 37, 53, 125, 207, 209, 332, 385, 395, 522
Garteret, 27
George, 73, 93, 109, 127, 164, 166, 195, 211, 249, 363, 364, 389, 394, 395, 400, 405, 406, 410, 446
Gustavus, 394, 401
Hannah, 332
Hosea, 380, 543
Hugh, 23
Israel, 485
Jacob, 164
James, 147, 164, 195, 208, 234, 315, 320, 385
Jean, 369, 453
Jesse, 226
Johanna, 40, 53
John, 19, 23, 42, 51, 52, 59, 60, 65, 76, 135, 141, 164, 207, 226, 304, 325, 332, 361, 386, 394, 407, 451
John, Jr., 66, 127
John, Sr., 125
Jonah, 44
Jonathan, 117, 226, 250, 485
Joseph, 442
Letitia, 45, 332
Lydia, 325, 394
Margaret, 53, 166, 332, 406, 481
Mariam, 332
Martha, 226, 250
Mary, 19, 23, 53, 109, 200, 290, 332, 363, 394, 401, 425, 465, 491, 532
Mary Ann, 138
Mathew, 13, 26, 27
Nancy, 208
Nathan, 332, 481
Patience, 73, 127, 211, 405
Peggy, 405
Peter, 164
Philip, 405
Rachel, 109, 111, 150, 164, 332
Rebeckah, 13
Richard, 13, 16, 18, 23, 30
Robert, 23, 44, 45, 53, 64, 65, 109, 112, 131, 138, 171, 381
Ruth, 164, 332
Samuel, 40, 44, 53, 226, 306, 325, 336, 363, 369, 372, 394, 401
Sarah, 109, 164, 171, 207, 325, 332, 361, 395, 407, 411, 447
Simon W., 336, 341, 382 447
Simon Wilmer, 386, 478
Skidmore, 201, 307, 526

Susannah, 19, 111, 323, 332, 413, 424, 513
Tabithy, 376
Tamsen, 117
Thomas, 69, 70, 76, 80, 125, 188, 203, 207, 226, 248, 263, 290, 325, 394, 395
Thomas, Sr., 27
Thomas Rodney, 478
Thomasin, 117
William, 13, 24, 26, 27, 37, 44, 53, 69, 89, 93, 111, 125, 164, 166, 171, 200, 201, 207, 226, 234, 318, 320, 385, 485. 526
William, Sr., 247
Wiltbank (Wilbank, Willbanks),
Cornelius, 35
Eliza, 558
Elizabeth, 334, 364, 469
Hannah, 291
Isaac, 35
John, 334, 364, 425
Samuel, 35
Windol, (Windul, Windle),
Ann, 355
Elizabeth, 388
Jonathan, 388
Mary, 376
Thomas, 376
William, 355, 376
Windsmore: see Winsmore
Winford,
Alexander, 302, 424
Benjamin, 424
John, 424
Jonathan, 424
Joseph, 424
Margret, 424
Mary, 424
Rebecca, 424
William, 424
Wingate, Mary, 552
Winsmore (Windsmore),
Elias, 496
Elizabeth, 13
Ely, 395
Esther, 154
Mary, 13
Robert, 34, 51, 382
Rosen, 395
Sarah, 395
Susannah, 59
Thomas, 13, 34, 39, 40, 43, 382, 395, 399, 452
Valentine, 395, 399
William, 11, 13, 22, 26, 34, 395
Winterton,
Mary, 109, 125

Nancy, 125
Ralph, 109, 125
Wise (Wize),
Anthony, 204
Christopher, 548
John Fredrick, 479
Mary, 479
With (Wyth, Wythe),
Aner, 539
James, 23
Mary, 524
William, 524, 552
Wodle: see Woodell
Wood,
Aaron, 453
Ann, 257, 407, 453
Catherine, 339
Charles, 271
Elias, 271, 313, 329, 390
Elijah, 241
Elizabeth, 66, 300
Enoch, 271, 429, 456, 464
George, 271
Hannah, 346, 384
James, 22, 453
John, 109, 139, 162, 204, 220, 271, 290, 339, 367, 388, 453, 470, 472, 494
John, Jr., 300
John, Sr., 271
Jonathan, 66
Joseph, 162, 262, 339, 393
Mary, 393
Nicholas, 271
Polly, 388, 520
Rebecca, 109, 429
Richard, 35
Robert, 66, 229, 257, 339, 340
Robert, Jr., 346
Sarah, 220, 271, 290, 434
Stephen, 339
William, 271, 339, 434
Woodcock,
Anthony, 422
Elizabeth, 422
Woodell (Woodal, Woodall, Woodle, Wodle),
David, 83
Elizabeth, 143
John, 137, 532
Joseph, 143
Mary, 143, 532
Rachel, 518
Thomas, 531
Wooderson,
Ann, 140
Richard, 140

Woodle: see Woodell
Woodles, Joseph, 322
Woodley,
 Edward, 133
 Thomas, 389
Woodmoncey, Sarah, 553
Woodrop, Daniel, 457
Woodward, Anthony, 78
Wooters, James, 531
Wootten,
 Eleanor, 125
 Hannah, 59
 Robert, 125
Wonsor, Henry, 109
Word, Patrick, 21
Words, Richard, 475
Worknott,
 Alexander, 460
 Martin, 460
 Mary, 460
Worrall (Worell, Worrel),
 James, 49, 74, 374
 Joseph, 49, 84, 110, 135
 Martha, 49
 Mary, 49, 110, 135
Worth, Jonathan, 419
Worthenton, John, 66
Wrath, William, 106
Wrench,
 Henry, 465
 Nancy, 495
Wright (Right),
 Ambrose, 422
 Fretwell, 163
 George, 544
 Jane, 322
 John, 147, 368
 John Hamer, 291
 Joseph, 322
 Margaret, 169
 Martha, 163
 Mary, 163
 Ruth, 163
 Sarah, 333
 Thomas, 163, 313, 344
 William, 107, 169, 544
Wroten (Wrotten),
 Frances, 492
 Henry, 419, 496
 James, 419, 496
 Sabre, 496
 William, 419
Wyatt (Wiat, Weyatt, Weyott),
 Aaron, 291, 430
 Ann, 329

Boaz, 427
Charlotte, 427
Elizabeth, 427
Furbush, 430
John, 366, 430
Lamuel, 430
Margaret, 481, 496
Mary Ann, 197, 251
Moses, 430
Noah, 451
Sarah, 427
Scinty, 451
Thomas, 197, 329, 430, 457, 481, 486, 496
William, 246, 291, 367, 430, 457, 464
William, Sr., 430
Wynkoop,
 Abraham, 64, 76, 102, 112, 202, 220
 Benjamin, 220, 254
 Esther, 220
 James, 220
 Mary, 220
Wynn,
 Benjamin, 203, 246, 464
 Elizabeth, 246, 360
 Elizabeth, the elder, 558
 Isaac, 246
 John, 246
 Joseph, 246
 Mary, 246
 Simon, 246
Wyth, Wythe: see With

—Y—

Yarnell,
 Martha, 160
 William, 160
Yeats, William, 346
Yester,
 Frances, 350
 Phillis, 350
Yoe,
 Armenta, 327
 Benjamin, 441, 442, 452
York,
 Ann, 518
 Samuel, 422, 428, 494
 Tabitha, 494
 Thomas, 31, 107, 139
Young,
 Ann, 32
 Clear, 480
 David, 385, 395, 456, 480, 481
 Eliza, 513

Elizabeth, 445, 468, 480
Kesiah, 315
Mary, 480
Nancy, 480
Preston, 431
Robert, 468
Thomas, 59
Wells, 315
William, 480

Younger,
  Priscilla, 340
  Thomas, 340

—Z—

Zelefro,
  Elizabeth, 319
  Joseph, 319

www.ingramcontent.com/pod-product-compliance
Lightning Source LLC
Chambersburg PA
CBHW020053020526
44112CB00031B/67